Paul Lauter
Trinity College
General Editor

Richard Yarborough
University of California, Los Angeles
Associate General Editor

Jackson R. Bryer
University of Maryland

King-Kok Cheung
University of California, Los Angeles

Anne Goodwyn Jones
University of Missouri

Wendy Martin
Claremont Graduate University

Quentin Miller
Suffolk University

Charles Molesworth
Queens College, City University
of New York

Raymund Paredes
University of Texas, San Antonio

Ivy T. Schweitzer
Dartmouth College

Andrew O. Wiget
New Mexico State University

Sandra A. Zagarell
Oberlin College

Lois Leveen
Electronic Resources Editor

James Kyung-Jin Lee
The University of California,
Santa Barbara
Associate Editor

Mary Pat Brady
Cornell University
Associate Editor

W9-DIW-654

Instructor's Guide

The Heath Anthology of American Literature

Fifth Edition

Edited by
John Alberti
Northern Kentucky University

Houghton Mifflin Company
Boston   New York

Publisher: Patricia A. Coryell
Executive Editor: Suzanne Phelps Weir
Sponsoring Editor: Michael Gillespie
Development Manager: Sarah Helyar Smith
Associate Editor: Bruce Cantley
Editorial Assistant: Lindsey Gentel
Project Editor: Robin Hogan
Manufacturing Assistant: Karmen Chong
Senior Marketing Manager: Cindy Graff Cohen
Marketing Associate: Wendy Thayer

Printed in the U.S.A.

ISBN: 0-618-54250-7

123456789-MP-09 08 07 06 05

Contents

110   A Sheaf of Seventeenth-Century Anglo-American Poetry

Pedagogical Introduction: Eighteenth Century   113

116   Settlement and Religion

134   A Sheaf of Eighteenth-Century Anglo-American Poetry

137   Voices of Revolution and Nationalism

Pedagogical Introduction: Early Nineteenth Century: 1800–1865   217

458 Critical Visions of Postbellum America

479 Developments in Women's Writing

501 A Sheaf of Poetry by Late-Nineteenth-Century American Women

505 The Making of "Americans"

Pedagogical Introduction: Modern Period: 1910–1945   525

530 Toward the Modern Age

569 Alienation and Literary Experimentation

595 Cluster: Political Poetry in the Modern Period

Pedagogical Introduction: Contemporary Period: 1945 to the Present   723

727   Earlier Generations

903   Cluster: Prison Literature

Pedagogical Introduction

The fifth edition of the Instructor's Guide to *The Heath Anthology of American Literature* features our most extensive effort yet to link text-based and web-based teaching resources. Although the basic format of each Instructor's Guide entry remains the same, with our contributing editors offering a diverse range of suggestions for teaching the materials in *The Heath Anthology*, you will find that many entries feature a new category: "Teaching With Cultural Objects." This new section helps instructors expand the teaching of the texts in *The Heath Anthology* beyond the page into the larger realms of history, society, and culture by pointing to multimedia materials available on the Web and elsewhere that can enrich students' learning experiences and help them explore the complex web of cultural connections informing the words they are reading. Links for "Teaching With Cultural Objects" will also be available on *The Heath Anthology* website.

In addition to new entries for authors and texts added to the 5th edition, the Instructor's Guide also features many updated entries for returning texts as well. In all the entries the central pedagogical belief that has always informed the Instructor's Guide remains the same: the multicultural approach to the teaching of American literature, of which *The Heath Anthology* is a part, represents not just a rethinking of what texts to include on a syllabus or the simple replacement of one group of privileged texts with another but a fundamental reexamination of the purposes and practices of literary study as a whole, of American literature in particular, and of the very meaning of "America" itself.

Overall, the Instructor's Guide is based on three main pedagogical assumptions: (1) that the reading experience of students should be the focus of class discussion and analysis; (2) that classification systems—whether formations of historical periods, cultural movements, or canons of literary value—influence and shape those reading experiences in crucial ways; and (3) that the production, reception, and interpretation of texts is an active process of cultural negotiation, opposition, assimilation and transformation.

This process-oriented approach, stressing the importance of social context in understanding the form and structure of particular acts of writing and reading, should sound familiar to composition teachers and theorists who remind students that in order to figure out what and how to write, a writer needs to ask why and to whom she is writing. Borrowing a term from composition studies, then, we might describe the pedagogical focus of this guide as the study of cultural rhetoric: the analysis of literary texts as complex and purposeful transactions between speaking/writing/reading subjects and the culture that both constitutes that subject and acts as medium and object of that transaction.[1] In Jane Tompkins's words,

> instead of seeing . . . novels as mere entertainment, or as works of art interpretable apart from their context[,] . . . I see them as doing a certain kind of cultural work within a specific historical situation. . . . I see their plots and characters as providing society with a means of thinking about itself, defining certain aspects of a social reality which the authors and their readers shared, dramatizing its conflicts, and recommending solutions. (200)

The pedagogical aim of this approach is to encourage students to consider themselves as just such speaking/writing/reading subjects and to see themselves as active participants in the process of cultural definition and transformation through their interpretation of and response to the texts in *The Heath Anthology* as well as their participation in the institutionalized study of culture—in other words, to see the literature class itself as a kind of cultural work.

In operation, the cultural rhetoric approach is more inductive than deductive, more centrifugal than centripetal. It takes as its pedagogical starting point the variety of American cultural expression and readers' equally various responses to those expressions rather than beginning with predetermined ideas about what "American Literature" is and seeing how well particular texts do or don't fit these criteria. Providing a definition of the *American Renaissance* or *Transcendentalism* before approaching the literature of the 1840s and 1850s does provide students with a means of organizing and understanding that literature, but it also limits both the meaning and scope of the works being considered, moving the focus of the class from the creative activity of reading to the acquisition and preservation of those definitions.

By warning against relying too heavily on reductive historical formulas, however, I am not endorsing a Romantic—or New Critical—belief that we can abandon all such preconceptions and classification systems in order to embrace "the text itself" in some kind of ahistorical purity. Indeed, generalization and classification are central to the learning process, as new information can only be assimilated in terms of preexisting ways of knowing and thinking. In any case, even if instructors could prevent somehow "contaminating" the students' first experience of a text by avoiding sweeping generalizations about historical periods or intellectual trends, students always already bring with them just such large-scale conceptions, generalizations, myths, and beliefs about American cultural history. While *American Renaissance* may only resonate with a small group of students, terms like *slavery, abolition, the Civil War, Manifest*

---

[1] The term *transaction* is borrowed from Louise Rosenblatt's reader-response model of literature pedagogy.

Destiny and *the North and the South* will call forth a wide range of associations, assumptions, and generalizations. These assumptions do not merely influence the reading experience; they are intrinsic to it, and the rhetorical approach to literary study recognizes that it is just as important for students to think about why and how they came to hold these assumptions as it is to question the historical validity of these assumptions. As James Berlin puts it, "In the effort to name experience, different groups [and, I would add, the individuals in and constituted by those groups] constantly vie for supremacy, for ownership and control of terms and their meanings in any discourse situation" (82–83).

In other words, the cultural rhetoric approach in particular and multicultural pedagogy in general are not about replacing "false consciousness" with "true consciousness" or replacing an old-fashioned and rigid classification system with an updated but equally rigid classification system. Instead, the focus on literature as an active strategic cultural process recognizes the pedagogical importance of what Paul Lauter has referred to as "starting points"— the basic frameworks and assumptions readers bring to texts and instructors bring to the class in the form of syllabus design and teaching practices. As a result, many of the pedagogical introductions in the Instructor's Guide suggest that the study of the texts in *The Heath Anthology* begin by exploring the assumptions, biases, and historical consciousnesses that students—and instructors—bring to the classroom. The point of these exercises is not the impossible task of freeing students from the influence of classification systems or preexisting ideas but to study how different assumptions, mindsets, and beliefs affect the reading experience; where these assumptions come from; and, perhaps most important to any rhetorical approach, what and whose interests they serve.

The cultural rhetoric approach implies that a strategic maneuvering for social power, influence, and authority is intrinsic to literary activity, including the reception and discussion of that activity in the classroom. If teaching the new canon means foregrounding discussions about the workings of cultural authority and power, that discussion must also include the classroom and institutional context of instruction as well in order for students to become aware of and reflect critically upon the part they play in arguments about cultural identity and values.

The teaching approaches outlined in this Instructor's Guide do not require completely abandoning the pedagogical techniques that many of us experienced as students and that we use in our own classes. If anything, a cultural rhetoric approach demands an ever closer "close reading," but a close reading that includes the cultural context of the reading experience, a close reading that indeed problematizes the boundary between text and context in order to get at the strategic questions of the kinds of cultural work engaged in by the creators of the texts in *The Heath Anthology*, the students in the classroom, and the teacher in the class.

Course Planning and *The Heath Anthology of American Literature:* Challenges and Strategies

As Paul Lauter notes in his Preface to this 5th edition of *The Heath Anthology of American Literature*, the multicultural movement in American literary and cultural studies has fundamentally changed the experience of teaching and studying what has always problematically been called "American literature." The initial oppositional model, in which a more expansive understanding of cultural and literary history and analysis challenged what seemed a deeply entrenched canon of American literature, has increasingly given way to a situation in which that ongoing challenge has become the norm in the American literature classroom. Jeffrey Insko, for example, points out that for students who entered college in the 1980s and later, their more multiculturally informed literature classrooms did not cause them to "question any deeply held literary values or assumptions, simply because our values (if we had any) were still being formed," and as a result, "one of my first learned American literary values was to question what constitutes American literature. So rather than challenge my views, this notion became, for me, a defining feature of American literature" (345).

To be sure, the multicultural transformation of American literary studies and pedagogy remains very much a work in progress: decentered; uneven; haphazard; always in the process of ongoing debate, definition, and redefinition. Insko's experiences suggest, if anything, the depth and complexity of the challenges that contemporary instructors of American literature and culture now face as we evolve an approach to the study of culture born in opposition and struggle into what AnaLouise Keating calls a "transformational multiculturalism" that "opens space for individual and collective agency that makes change possible (though not inevitable)" (98, 99). As the appearance of a 5th edition of *The Heath Anthology* makes clear, the multicultural transformation of American literary studies is no longer new if no less radical, and the pedagogical challenges and opportunities created by a more diverse and inclusive American literature classroom remain as exciting as they can sometimes be daunting.

One of the key challenges in planning a culturally diverse American literature course is the inevitable and necessary prospect of assigning and teaching texts that an instructor may never have taught before or may be discovering for the first time in *The Heath Anthology*. In fact, one of the goals of *The Heath Anthology* is to encourage instructors to consider using unfamiliar writers and texts as a means of expanding students' conceptions of the possibilities of American cultural history. This is both an epistemological and practical

xix

challenge since the assigning of new texts means not only familiarizing one's self with the text but also finding the time to do so. The introductory material in *The Heath Anthology*, the Instructor's Guide, *The Heath Anthology Newsletter*, and *The Heath Anthology* website provide useful starting points for class development and preparation, but starting points are just that, and the challenges presented by individual texts in *The Heath Anthology* extend to the shaping of the multicultural literature course as a whole.

As described previously, the rhetorical model of multicultural pedagogy, with its focus on how texts operate as part of a field of historical discursive practices, also brings with it the question of integrating such socio-historical information into the classroom. Teaching the literature of slavery, for example, or texts from the 1930s raises the important question of just how much "background" information students and teachers need in order to understand these texts; indeed, they make us rethink the very distinction between "background" and "foreground" and just what we mean by "understanding" a text. The fact that many of the selections in *The Heath Anthology* represent important historical perspectives that have subsequently become marginalized and/or hidden in relation to dominant historical narratives underlines the point that multicultural pedagogy invites us to reexamine critically all our historical and cultural assumptions.

Just as significant as the cultural context of these texts is the diversity of instructional contexts in which *The Heath Anthology* is used: American literature is studied on community college campuses and at major research institutions; in rural, suburban, and inner-city areas; as part of multiterm required survey sequences for majors and in one-term general studies courses. Courses sharing the same name, "Survey of American Literature," can be found in the catalogs of open-admission community colleges with student populations in the thousands and highly selective liberal arts institutions with enrollments in the hundreds. They can exist in one-, two-, and three-term sequences, meaning instructors may approach the teaching of the multicultural literary history of the United States facing anywhere from thirty to ninety-six hours of contact time in the classroom. Add to these facts the crises in funding and working conditions facing the humanities today as more and more survey and other lower-division classes in which *The Heath Anthology* is frequently assigned are being taught by non-tenure-track instructors, graduate students, and adjunct faculty who are given little time, remuneration, or scholarly credit for the kinds of pedagogical and research work called for by a multicultural approach to American literature.

The appearance of *The Heath Anthology of American Literature* itself and the variety of course configurations and pedagogical situations in which it is used present opportunities to extend the investigation of assumptions, mindsets, and beliefs to the structure of courses, curricula, and textbooks. What is the "right number" of texts to read in a course on American literature and culture? Of courses to include in a survey sequence? Of volumes of an American literature anthology? As will be suggested in greater detail in "Beyond the Mastery Model: The Course as Starting Point," the questions of representation and diversity, inclusion and (inevitably) exclusion that the editorial board of *The Heath Anthology* have had to wrestle with are rich materials for class discussion and student engagement

In the following pages and throughout the Instructor's Guide you will find suggestions for turning these challenges into opportunities for rethinking the form and method of the American literature course as well as a description of some of the resources, both print and online, available to adopters of *The Heath Anthology.*

Beyond the Mastery Model: The Course as Starting Point

In *Rhetorics, Poetics, and Cultures: Refiguring College English Studies*, James Berlin called for a literary pedagogy less concerned with "the preservation and maintenance of a sacred canon of literary texts" and one more focused on "the examination and teaching of reading and writing practices" (104–105). This more process-oriented approach toward the teaching of literature suggests a movement away from a "mastery" model of cultural study and a redefinition of what constitutes our professional expertise in the field of American literature. Traditional course titles such as "Survey of American Literature" or "Masterpieces of American Literature" imply that literary study is concerned with a fixed body of knowledge, with questions of literary merit and historical significance as somehow settled and shaped into a broadly held consensus. According to such a model, classroom practice would involve both the transmission and justification of this consensus information. A multicultural pedagogy based in cultural rhetoric, however, sees questions of interpretation, evaluation, and definition as always in process, as anything but fixed and permanent. Such an approach can transform these definitive-sounding course titles from settled destinations into starting points for class investigation, with no guarantees as to where that investigation will lead. This approach brings with it a number of suggestions for a rhetorically focused course design that makes the diversity of instructional contexts into opportunities rather than disadvantages.

Making the Title of the Course a Focus of Critical Concern

Sometimes instructors have great leeway in terms of providing a course title that asks students to question received constructions of American cultural and literary history (some of the section headings in *The Heath Anthology*, for example, would make excellent course titles: "Voices of Revolution and Nationalism" or "Race, Slavery, and the Invention of the 'South'"). Most instructors, however, particularly in lower-division courses, have to make do with traditional course titles. Similarly, instructors also have little choice over whether they have ten, fifteen, or thirty-two weeks to "cover" the range of American literature. The use of *The Heath Anthology*, as a result, may cause instructors to feel that they have either to fit a greater diversity of texts and cultural experiences into the traditional consensus constructions of American literary history implied by those titles or to come up with equally complete alternative stories of their own, and certainly both of these options are open to the instructor. A cultural rhetoric approach, however, offers the additional possibility of focusing class discussion on the question of just what such a revised story would be, or indeed if there would or should be just one story. Such an approach can be a powerful way of considering the functions of narrative forms in both "literary" texts and in the process of constructing history. In this way, texts could be chosen not only on the basis of how well they fit in with other texts or within a given historical narrative, but also on how they may conflict or even oppose other texts in the class. This contrastive approach points to another course design strategy.

Organizing the Class Around Points of Discursive and Rhetorical Conflict

The cultural rhetoric model focuses attention on the ways in which putatively objective-sounding descriptors of historical, cultural, and aesthetic periods—Puritanism, the Romantic era, the Age of Realism, Modernism—are themselves stories, rhetorical constructs, and arguments put forward about the significance and meaning of certain developments in American cultural history. As such, their function is as much prescriptive as descriptive. That is, in the interest of creating a unified way of understanding a given historical and cultural moment, these categories exclude or minimize the importance and influence of some texts as they foreground and highlight others, often in ways that would have been deeply surprising to those alive during those historical periods.

As was mentioned earlier, classification and categorization per se are not bad things; indeed, they are cognitively inevitable. By refusing to fit neatly or easily into these traditional categories, however, many of the texts in *The Heath Anthology* provide the opportunity to open up these categories for discussion, revision, and reformulation. Instead of feeling the need to make sure the texts on the syllabus all cohere with one another, instructors can choose texts that conflict and interfere with one another, particularly those texts explicitly involved in the task of cultural consensus formation. A good example would be the linking of the *Declaration of Independence* with the revisions of that key document offered by both Frederick Douglass ("What to the Slave is the Fourth of July?") and Elizabeth Cady Stanton ("Declaration of Sentiments"). A close comparison and contrast of these texts would reveal complex strategies of protest, cooptation, reinforcement, and radical revision on the parts of Jefferson, Douglass, and Stanton. Stanton's document, for example, both affirms the ideological importance of the original *Declaration* (keeping in mind that the validity of the democratic ideals presented in Jefferson's text was not a settled question in early nineteenth-century America) while pointedly underlining the gendered limitations of that document.

Keating refers to this approach as "relational thinking": understanding that no text, rhetorical strategy, or discourse tradition exists in isolation. She describes her syllabus to her students as

> a series of nonlinear, interlocking dialogues among a variety of different texts and worldviews. I tell students that by requiring them to engage with multiple, interrelated perspectives I hope to encourage their relational thinking skills—their ability to employ analysis, imagination, and self-reflection in conjunction. (106)

These skills can then become an important learning objective of the multicultural literature classroom.

Furthermore, the emphasis on the interaction *between* texts can also point to areas of conflict, contradiction, and negotiation that occur *within* texts. Although many of us were trained to construct literary analyses that ultimately affirmed the unity of the texts we were studying, a more rhetorical approach, by breaking down boundaries between the "inside" and "outside" of texts, between text and context, points to how unity is not a quality a given text has or doesn't have but rather a goal a text may or may not be struggling toward. Thus, the comparison and contrast of the *Declaration of Independence* with the texts by Douglass and Stanton not only points to long-term processes of historical struggle over cultural values and beliefs but also highlights those struggles within the texts themselves, as evidenced, for example, by Jefferson's need to spell out, define, and argue for political rights he claims are "self-evident" or by his inclusion in the version of the *Declaration* he presents in his *Autobiography* of excised material from the draft of the *Declaration*, material relevant to what most of my students have always found to be the most glaring contradiction of the *Declaration*, the insistence on the radical equality of humanity by an aristocratic slave-owner.

This emphasis on process, on discursive confrontation, negotiation, and revision, is one reason for section headings in *The Heath Anthology* such as "Contested Visions, American Voices," "Literature and the 'Woman Question,'" or "Critical Visions of Postbellum America." As the pedagogical introductions to these various sections in the Instructor's Guide will suggest, these groupings can be taken as organizational principles for the development of class syllabi. Unlike traditional "themes," with their suggestion of unanimity and ahistorical relevance, such headings share more in common with what Gregory Jay has called *problematics*. In a way similar to the suggestion of transforming traditional course titles from settled conclusions ("Here is American literature") to open-ended starting points ("What is 'American literature'?"), problematics are more concerned with posing questions than with providing answers, with opening up the processes of rhetorical contestation and negotiation to look at what is at stake in attempts to claim consensus or to insist on cultural definitions. As Jay puts it, "A problematic indicates how and where the struggle for meaning *takes place*" (22, emphases his). As examples of what he means by *problematics*, Jay suggests origins, power, civilization, tradition, assimilation, translation, bodies, literacy, and borders (22). The point is not just to regard these terms as ideas that a given text may be about but as analytical tools to open up questions about how texts participate in ideological processes of cultural definition, a process that includes every course designated by that overall problematic, "American literature."

Involving Students in the Process of Syllabus Formation

This process of questioning assumptions leads directly to issues of context and the site of teaching and learning. One key assumption of cultural rhetoric is that a given text does not mean the same thing to all readers and listeners any time anywhere. Meaning itself is part of the process of historical change and rhetorical conflict. Classes in multicultural American literature must be sensitive to the social, cultural, and historical reality of individual classroom settings, with all the diversity and variability that entails.

This diversity poses a problem not only for instructors but also for the writers and editors of Instructor's Guides such as this one. How can anyone invent teaching strategies applicable to all students everywhere? How can anyone come up with a similarly universal course design? The short answer, of course, is that no one can, but the focus on process indicated previously, on thinking in terms of problematics rather than themes in course design, on looking for points of conflict rather than insisting on consensus, has its classroom component in what Paolo Freire famously labeled a "problem-posing" approach to teaching, one that looks to the students and their own concrete social and cultural experiences to furnish the starting points for the exploration of conflict and consensus, negotiation and protest in cultural history. One means of accomplishing this is simply to involve students in the process of syllabus formation, asking them to choose texts for class reading and to prepare texts for class discussion. If the overall focus of the class has been on the rhetorical interactions among texts, both those included in *The Heath Anthology* and in the larger cultural and historical context, such student involvement need not be overly idiosyncratic or apparently random, although there is always a cultural logic at work in any selection process, whether controlled by students or faculty, that can be usefully explored in class. Indeed, the selection processes used by students are just as relevant to class discussion as the texts eventually chosen.

Redefining Expertise

The question of context also brings us back to the vexing question of how instructors can assimilate and master the wealth of newly highlighted texts found in *The Heath Anthology* along with the rhetorical contexts relevant to those texts, particularly given the increasing constraints on time and resources faced by faculty members at all levels. By emphasizing the importance of historical and social context, moreover, the cultural rhetoric approach in and of itself seems to represent a massive complication of the pedagogical project over the apparently more focused models of close reading favored by traditional New Critical models of literary analysis, models emphasizing the importance of limiting discussion to the "text itself." But as many critics have pointed out, the New Critical model of close reading does not really dispense with the relevance of history and society; it merely assumes the universality of what is in fact a particular and limited historical and cultural understanding. Furthermore, an important impetus behind the multicultural movement in literary studies was the arrival in college classrooms and, later on, the college faculty of people from demographic backgrounds radically different from the small, culturally homogenous group of scholars who developed the New Critical methodology. It was this more diverse group of students and scholars who helped reveal the limitations of the traditional formalist approach.

Given these limitations, what new pedagogical models can instructors follow that do not entail large new investments of time and work that may be hard to come by in today's educational environment? Again, the key here is to follow the emphasis on process, on problem-posing, of structuring the class around questions rather than answers. One way to do this is to redefine our expertise in the classrooms from master knowers to experienced learners. This means defining our authority on the basis of the skills we have developed as researchers and analysts, adept at asking critical questions and finding and evaluating sources of information.

This is not to say, of course, that the lessons we have learned and the knowledge we (and the students) acquire is irrelevant; quite the opposite, in fact, and a key critique put forward by the multicultural movement was how traditional formations of American cultural history have ignored whole areas of scholarly inquiry. This same critique of the inadequacies of these traditional formations, however, extends as well to the notion of a comprehensive or definitive understanding, to claims of having mastered the field. Indeed, the multicultural approach, with its insistence on the tremendous diversity of American cultural history, from the myriad written and oral traditions of the hundreds of precontact indigenous cultures to the truly global origins of the immigrants to the North American continent, both voluntary and involuntary, points out the absurdity of claiming that the study of a small group of writers in English, all mainly from English and Northern European Protestant back-grounds, most of whom lived in the Northeast, however interesting and provocative these writers are, could constitute a comprehensive understanding of American culture.

The growth and interactivity of the World Wide Web has further chal-lenged traditional models of expertise and authority. Digital technology has undermined the material distinctions between the official and the suspect, the professional and the amateur. The opportunities for students have never been greater to explore the wider cultural contexts of their class reading assignments and to engage the discursive struggle over definitions of cultural meaning and significance through the writing and construction of websites that are equally present in cyberspace with those created by more traditionally authorized sources. Rather than gatekeepers of knowledge and expertise, instructors become mentors, advisors, coaches, and even provocateurs, offering strategic advice and posing critical questions while encouraging students to explore, imagine, challenge, and investigate on their own.

A problematic-centered approach, then, to the question of background and research would mean using the resources provided by *The Heath Anthology*, the Instructor's Guide, and *The Heath Anthology* website as starting points rather than destinations for exploration and study. Rather than seeing such research as strictly preparatory and behind the scenes in terms of course con-struction, such exploration can be built into the course itself. The interactive capabilities of *The Heath Anthology* website invite you to share these ques-tions of pedagogy and preparation with your students, using the links within the electronic version of the Instructor's Guide to explore different contrasts and comparisons, to "engage with multiple, interrelated perspectives" as Keating put it. Blurring the distinctions between "preparation" and "instruction" helps open up students' conception of reading beyond the solitary activity of decoding words on a page to an understanding of "reading" as an ongoing, multilinear process of interpretation, negotiation, and revision. In so doing, we broaden the fundamental roles of "student" and "instructor" to recognize our mutual roles in the ongoing transformation of American culture represented by *The Heath Anthology of American Literature.*

Works Cited

Berlin, James. *Rhetorics, Poetics, and Cultures: Refiguring College English Studies.* Urbana: NCTE, 1996.

Insko, Jeffrey. "Generational Canons." *Pedagogy: Critical Approaches to Teaching Literature, Language, Composition, and Culture* 3.3 (2003): 341–58.

Jay, Gregory. "The End of 'American' Literature: Toward a Multicultural Practice." *The Canon in the Classroom: Pedagogical Implications of Canon Revision in American Literature.* Ed. John Alberti. NY: Garland, 1995. 3–28.

Keating, AnaLouise. "'Making Connections': Transformational Multiculturalism in the Classroom." *Pedagogy: Critical Approaches to Teaching Literature, Language, Composition, and Culture* 4.1 (2004): 93–117.

Rosenblatt, Louise. *The Reader, the Text, the Poem: The Transactional Theory of the Literary Work.* Carbondale and Edwardsville: Southern Illinois UP, 1978.

Tompkins, Jane. *Sensational Designs: The Cultural Work of American Fiction: 1790–1860.* New York: Oxford UP, 1985.

As with previous editions of the Instructor's Guide, thanks are due the contributing editors who took seriously not only the preparation of materials for the anthology but also the nuts-and-bolts of class preparation and instruction.

Finally, I'd like to give thanks to Paul Lauter for the continuing opportunity to work on this project, to Lois Leveen for her work on *The Heath Anthology* website, and to Janet Edmonds, Michael Gillespie, and Bruce Cantley at Houghton Mifflin for all of their professionalism and skill in guiding me through this project. As always, I give special thanks to Kristin and Martha for their wisdom, love, and tolerance.

John Alberti
Northern Kentucky University

Using *The Heath Anthology* of *American Literature* Website

When Paul Lauter asked me to write a short piece—"as short as you like"—describing my experience creating a new website for the fourth edition of *The Heath Anthology*, I sent him a haiku:

> *Heath Anthology*
> website: full of resources,
> still not yet perfect.

In the intervening years, I have worked with the other members of the editorial board and with Janet Edmonds at Houghton Mifflin to further refine the site. We've added more resources specific to texts and authors in *The Concise Heath* and in the new fifth edition. John Alberti and I have collaborated to provide greater coherence across the headnotes in *The Heath Anthology*, the print Instructor's Guide, and the electronic resources. As a result, the latest version of the website and the Instructor's Guide reflect the increasing value of online resources to literary studies.

We might all shudder at the student who asks, "I can't find anything for this assignment on the Internet, do you think I should go to the library?" (a direct quotation from one of my classes, I'm afraid). But this question underscores the ease of online research for our students. As instructors, our goal should be to ensure that this ease is coupled with other benefits of the Internet: a breadth of materials accessible to the general user that can serve as a continuously updated archive. The *Heath* site provides students and instructors with especially useful materials related to American literary studies.

Randy Bass introduced the website he designed for the third edition of *The Heath* with this explanation: "It is not merely that new electronic tools are useful to support *The Heath Anthology*, but to support *The Heath*'s project. That is, there is a real, fundamental and logical connection between the tools of electronic textuality and knowledge on the one hand, and new forms of pedagogy, course organizations, and strategies of reading implied by *The Heath Anthology*, on the other."[1] For instructors seeking to situate their students' readings in a sophisticated understanding of the historical and cultural contexts of literary production, the web offers rich possibilities indeed.

---

[1] Randy Bass, "New Canons and New Media: American Literature in the Electronic Age," <http://www.georgetown.edu/faculty/bassr/heath/editorintro.html>.

The value of access to online resources is reflected in the Instructor's Guide for the 5th edition, which includes a category on "Working with Cultural Objects." For teachers whose pedagogical approach is deeply rooted in Cultural Studies and American Studies, this category will reinforce familiar practices; for other instructors, it will suggest new ways to approach literary texts. The cultural objects described may be sound files, photographs or other images, artifacts, or any other relevant item, either directly connected to a writer and/or text or illuminating the cultural context in which the text was produced or which it represents. For example, students might compare the commissioned portrait of Olaudah Equiano with the well-known antislavery image on the "Am I Not a Man and a Brother" medallion created by Josiah Wedgewood to consider issues of representation. How does the portrayal of Equiano in his narrative compare with the visual portrait of him? How do both representations contrast with the generic abolitionist portrayal of enslaved blacks? Such cultural objects enable students to think about individual literary texts as part of larger economies of production and consumption.

Both the print Instructor's Guide and the *Heath* website provide users with numerous addresses for Internet resources that can be incorporated into classroom practices and student assignments. The website makes these resources easy to identify and use by organizing access to online materials through Author Profile pages. If a student is looking for information on an author, she will find a single webpage offering the print edition's headnotes, a list of the author's texts, useful secondary sources, links to a timeline that puts the work into historical context, links to cultural objects that are relevant to the texts, and annotated links to outside Web sources about the author. Instructors visiting the Author Profile page will also find sample approaches and assignments for teaching the author. The instructor preparing a new lecture on Carlos Bulosan or the student trying to write a paper on Phillis Wheatley should be delighted to access these multiple author-related resources from a single webpage.

The website's searchable, three-column timeline situates literary publications in historical and cultural context. The first column indicates the publication of literary works as well as birth and death dates for the authors. The second column lists historical events from the Colonial period to the present. The final column lists major cultural events. Many items in the second and third column link to pop-up explanations and to other relevant resources on the Web. Icons along the timeline connect to cultural objects on the Internet that are useful to readers of particular texts. The timeline can be used inside the classroom or by students working on their own.

The breadth of the anthology has set demanding parameters for the website. Our timeline covers nearly five full centuries (1535–2000), and we are committed to having it be as inclusive as possible. This commitment requires our staff to find sources from different cultural, class, and gender perspectives. It means we have grappled with the ideological implications of listing oral texts by approximate dates of creation and selecting a starting point for the chronology that didn't privilege a European colonialist perspective. The enormous amount of information included in this section of the site is wonderful, although no comprehensive timeline can ever really be complete. Despite my tendency to obsess about possible holes in our chronology, I find myself learning things precisely from the odd juxtapositions the timeline affords. Is it surprising that 1840 saw both the publication of *The Lowell Offering*, a journal of writings by "mill girls," and the first Bachelor of Arts degrees conferred on women in the United States, at Wesleyan College in Macon, Georgia? What should one make of the concurrence in 1831 of *Cherokee Nation v. Georgia*, an appeal to the Supreme Court to preserve tribal lands through recognition of Cherokee national sovereignty; the establishment of the Workingmen's Party in Philadelphia, Boston, and New York City; the first Convention of People of Color in Philadelphia; the inaugural publication of William Lloyd Garrison's *The Liberator*; and Nat Turner's insurrection in Virginia? The implications suggested by such proximate entries provide new ways for instructors and students to think about the social and political forces that shaped the creation and reception of literary texts.

While I hope the resources available on our site encourage instructors to adopt *The Heath Anthology*, the editorial board and Houghton Mifflin have always conceived of the site as an integral part of what an adopting instructor and her students "get," not merely as an ancillary advertisement for or addendum to the print edition. The Author Profile pages, Timeline, Cultural Objects, and other resources enable the current generation of *Heath* users to explore American literature in rich new ways.

Whatever the functions of our website, however, there are two things it cannot do. It cannot teach, and it cannot learn. It is a tool to facilitate contextually rich, multimedia pedagogy. It is a resource students can use on their own or in conjunction with specific assignments. Similarly, this Instructor's Guide is designed to support instructors as they teach an even greater range and diversity of selections from *The Heath Anthology*. Together, these resources promise ways to enhance any American literature course.

To return to my haiku: the final line, "still not yet perfect," continues to ring true. That "still" underscores that the value of the website will continue to grow, based not only on my work and the input of the editorial board and Instructor's Guide contributors but also on the use of the site by the very people for whom it was created, adopters of *The Heath Anthology*. Just as each text in the print anthology might be taught in innumerable ways, each resource included in the Instructor's Guide and on the website can be put to myriad uses by teachers and students as they explore the bounty of American literature.

Lois Leveen
Portland, OR

Pedagogical Introduction

Colonial Period
to 1700

Native American Oral Literatures
Cluster: America in the European Imagination
New Spain
Cluster: Cultural Encounters: A Critical Survey
New France
Chesapeake
New England
A Sheaf of Seventeenth-Century Anglo-American Poetry

The first day of my American literature survey course begins with a simple assignment: "Tell the story of America in one paragraph. You have five minutes." Declining all requests from students to elaborate further, I ask them to work in groups and prepare to share what they come up with. When they are done (or when I call time), each group reads its story aloud. As students share their stories, two results become quickly apparent. First, no two stories are ever exactly alike, and second, in the midst of this variety definite patterns and genres begin to emerge. Some begin with Columbus, some with the Revolutionary War, some with the indigenous peoples of the Americas, and occasionally even the Big Bang makes an appearance. Some stories feature a theme—the Rise of Freedom, for example—while others move grimly from war to war. Some are heroic in tone, some cynical, and some are mini-jeremiads decrying the gap between ideals of freedom and democracy and a history of greed and exploitation.

I begin my course this way to make several points about the study of something called "American Literature," not the least of which is questioning the idea of "beginnings" itself. By asking students to write a story, I also want to focus our attention as a class on how narrative habits and discursive traditions influence the ways we understand the past. Who are the protagonists and antagonists of our stories? Is there a central conflict? And what would happen if we worked in a storytelling tradition other than the Aristotelian model so central to European cultures?

The focus on historical and cultural specificity in organizing the texts in the Colonial Period to 1800 section of *The Heath Anthology* helps alert students to the contingency of history, to an awareness that any unified or coherent narrative of "American" origins is a retrospective construct. You could say that *The Heath Anthology* actually begins several times in several cultural traditions, complicating the idea of any single "beginning." Indeed, the new "Cluster: America in the European Imagination" stresses that "America" is precisely an imaginative construct, and that both native peoples and European

3

explorers/invaders made sense of their encounters in relation to the stories and mythologies provided by their own cultures.

The section headings in *The Heath Anthology* represent a continued focus on place and cultural specificity as key determinants in analyzing and interpreting the multicultural texts of the Americas. Whereas the opening sections on Native American oral traditions ask students to consider large global patterns of difference between "European" and "Native" worldviews, between Christian and non-Christian cultures, subsequent divisions complicate these initial distinctions by recognizing that "culture" does not refer to a homogeneous, static structure of social meaning. Instead, any given cultural structure is itself a dynamic, volatile field of divisions and alliances, fissures and reformulations. From an examination of the cultural contact, collision, and invasion following Columbus, *The Heath Anthology* explores cultural divisions both large and small, both those between indigenous and European peoples and those within each group, especially given that neat distinctions between the wholly "Native" and wholly "European" began to dissolve upon the first interactions between these groups.

While Andrew Wiget's excellent introductions to the sections on "Native American Oral Narrative" and "Native American Oral Poetry" stress crucial commonalties among native peoples in relation to European cultural practices, the anthology also locates each selection of indigenous texts within specific tribal cultures and contexts. Similarly, contact between European and native peoples is organized according to major European "tribal" groups—Spanish, French, and English—posing the pedagogical question of how terms like "Native American" and "European" both organize but also inevitably limit our understanding of culture contacts. Further, the division of the English colonies on the basis of geography (Chesapeake and New England) adds another intracultural variable, while the inclusion of texts such as Richard Frethorne's complaint about his exploitation as an indentured servant and Nathaniel Bacon's revolutionary manifesto point to deep divisions of social class that divided the various colonial enterprises, divisions that led into the development of the American systems of racial definition and oppression.

Thus, as students read Cabeza de Vaca's captivity narrative, they can consider not only the various rhetorical purposes served by Cabeza's descriptions of the indigenous societies he encountered but also the internal conflicts among the Spanish explorers/invaders based on social rank and ethnocentric hubris that fractured and doomed the expedition. A consistent foregrounding of the relationships among language, culture, power, and privilege help problematize in useful ways the question of with whom in these historical texts we as contemporary readers might identify as "our" ancestors.

The "Cluster: Cultural Encounters: A Critical Survey" connects these historical examples of cultural rhetoric with our own modern-day efforts to understand and revise history. The inclusion of important contemporary scholarly work on the meaning of these early encounters helps students to understand their own roles as cultural critics in the making, reading, and studying of literature as part of a process of imagining their own stories of America.

Native American Oral Literatures

Contributing Editor: Andrew Wiget

Classroom Issues

Teachers face a number of difficulties in bringing before their students something as unfamiliar as Native American oral literatures. The problems will vary, of course, from situation to situation. Jeanne Holland's article in the Bibliography on page 17 outlines some of the difficulties she faced in using the first edition of this anthology, some of which we have tried to remedy in later editions, others of which I addressed in an issue of *The Heath Anthology of American Literature Newsletter* (see Bibliography).

In the absence of real knowledge about other cultures or other periods in time, most students tend to project their own sense of appropriate human behavior onto all other peoples and call it "universal human nature." The principal problem teachers will have, not only with their students but also with their own experience, is the recognition that people in other cultures understand the world and human behavior in significantly different ways. This means, in literary terms, that we may not be able to apprehend the motivation of characters nor the significance of their actions without supplying a good deal of cultural information. To address this problem, instructors should avail themselves of the notes that are supplied with the texts, perhaps even going over this material explicitly in class, coupled with the additional information provided in the headnotes and the introductions. There are also a number of resources readily available that an instructor can consult. Wiget's *Native American Literature* and Ruoff's *American Indian Literatures* constitute a very valuable core of essential reference works. Instructors should also consult the Smithsonian's multivolume *Handbook of North American Indians* for its many articles on the history and culture of specific tribes and its extensive bibliographies, and Murray (1990) for a thorough discussion of how the dynamics of the translation/transcription situation shape the text we read.

Many students will come to class with assumptions about how American Indians lived, their historical relations with the United States, and their contemporary situation. Many of these stereotypes—that Indians were in

perfect harmony with nature; that they were communalists and shared everything; that they did not believe in any form of individualism; and most fright-
eningly, that there are no more real Indians today—will need to be addressed
in class as a preface to the discussion of any kind of Native American literature. Concerning stereotypes, I find it best to begin any discussion of Native
American literature with an exploration of what students in fact think they
know about Native Americans, and I provide some basic background in terms of
the population of Native Americans as of the latest census, cultural information about modes of living and adaptation to particular environments, and
historical information. I also make it a point to emphasize that every society
has evolved a useful and fitting adaptation to its social and physical environment. That adaptation is called *culture*. Culture is a system of beliefs and
values through which a group of people structure their experience of the world.
By working with this definition of culture, which is very close to the way
current criticism understands the impact of ideology upon literature, we can
begin to pluralize our notion of the world and understand that other peoples can
organize their experience in different ways and dramatize their experience of
the world through different symbolic forms. If time is available, I would
highly recommend that the class view "Winds of Change," a PBS documentary
that dramatizes the adaptability of contemporary Indian cultures and goes a
long way toward restoring the visible presence of Indian diversity.

Many forms of Native American literature also employ different kinds of
artistic devices that are unfamiliar or even antithetical to conventional Anglo-
American notions of aesthetic response, such as acute brevity, much repetition,
or cataloging. None of these literary conventions appeal to the experience of
contemporary readers. To address this problem, I illustrate how cultural
conventions that students assume as essential characteristics of literary experience, in fact, have changed over time. This is very easy to do. A classic example
is to point out how conventional notions of what constitutes good poetry have
changed significantly from the Renaissance through the early nineteenth
century and up to the present day, and that we recognize contemporary poetry
as being marked by the absence of some features that used to be valued as significant in poetry. This will show the changeableness of literary forms and
undermine the students' assumptions that the way things look today is the
basis for all judgments about what constitutes good art. I might also indicate
the important influences of American Indian literature on American literature,
and that some of these Native forms and conventions and themes were borrowed
by Anglo-American writers from Cooper through the Imagists and up to the
present.

Classroom Strategies

Anthologies present the possibility of successfully developing several teaching strategies. There is enough material in the entire anthology, for instance, to develop a semester-long course just on American Indian literatures. Most teachers, however, will be teaching American Indian traditions in the context of other American literatures. I will suggest three basic strategies.

I think the most important teaching strategy for Native American literature is to single out one text for extensive in-class treatment and to embed it richly in its cultural and historical context. Work through a text with constant reference to notes. Also offer startling images for the class's contemplation, inviting them to reflect upon a range of possible meanings, before suggesting how this imagery or symbol might have meaning in its original cultural context. It's also very helpful to use films because they provide visual connections to the cultural environment. I would particularly recommend for a general southwestern Native American worldview, *Hopi: Songs of the Fourth World*, a film by Pat Ferreiro.

A second strategy uses culturally related materials, or even materials from the same tribe, and teaches them back to back, mixing the genres, in order to let the context that you develop for one enrich the other. There is enough Iroquoian and Zuni material here, for example, to do just that. An especially good unit would include showing the film, teaching the Zuni "Talk Concerning the First Beginning," contrasting it with Genesis, then moving on to teach "Sayatasha's Night Chant" under the Native American Oral Poetry section. This way the cultural context that you have built up (by understanding fundamental symbols like corn and rain and how they emerge from the people's experience with the land) can serve more than one work.

A third strategy I have used successfully involved what I have called elsewhere "reading against the grain." Many Native American texts invite comparison with canonical texts from the Euro-American literatures. I always teach the Zuni creation story with readings from the Bible. Genesis 1 through 11 offers two versions of the creation of the world and a flood story as well as opportunities to discuss social order in chapters 4, 5, and 10. Genesis 27, which gives the story of Jacob and Esau, provides a biblical trickster figure in the person of Jacob. And finally the book of Judges, with its stories of Samson and Gideon, provides good examples of culture heroes, as do other classics such as the *Aeneid*, the *Odyssey*, and the various national epics. These classical works are also good counterparts to the Navajo story of Changing Woman's children, the hero twins, who are also on a quest to transform the world by ridding it of monsters, which, like Grendel or the Cyclops, are readily understood as projections of our fears and anxieties as well as interesting narrative agents. The Yuchi story of "The Creation of the Whites" and Handsome Lake's version of "How America Was Discovered," together with the Hopi version of the Pueblo

Revolt, are powerful antidotes to the European mythopoeticizing of the invasion of North America. This is a point I emphasize in my article on "Origin Stories," which reads the Zuni emergence story against Villagrá's epic poem on the history of New Mexico and Bradford's *Of Plymouth Plantation*, both of which are excerpted in this anthology. Finally, the Iroquoian description of the confederacy is usefully compared with colonial political documents that envision various social orders, including the Declaration of Independence, the Constitution, and the Federalist papers.

Native American Oral Narrative

Contributing Editor: Andrew Wiget

Major Themes, Historical Perspectives, Personal Issues

Some very important themes evolve from this literature. Native American views of the world as represented in these mythologies contrast strongly with Euro-American perspectives. Recognizing this is absolutely essential for later discussion of the differences between Anglo-Americans and Native Americans over questions of land, social organization, religion, and so on. In other words, if one can identify these fundamental differences through the literature very early on, then later it becomes easier to explain the differences in outlook between Native American peoples and Anglo-American peoples that often lead to tragic consequences.

If culture is a system of beliefs and values by which people organize their experience of the world, then it follows that forms of expressive culture such as these myths should embody the basic beliefs and values of the people who create them. These beliefs and values can be roughly organized in three areas: (1) beliefs about the nature of the physical world, (2) beliefs about social order and appropriate behavior, and (3) beliefs about human nature and the problem of good and evil.

The Zuni "Talk Concerning the First Beginning" speaks directly to the nature of the physical world. If we look closely at the Zuni "Talk," the story imagines the earth as hollow, with people coming out from deep within the womb of the earth. The earth is mother and feminine, and people are created not just of the stuff of the earth, but also from the earth. They are born into a particular place and into a particular environment. In the course of this long history, imagined as a search for the center (a point of balance and perfection), they undergo significant changes in their physical appearance, in their social behavior, in their social organization, and in their sense of themselves. By the time they have arrived at Zuni, which they call the center of the world, they have become pretty much like their present selves. It is especially important to follow the notes here with this selection and with the Navajo selection. Both of these stories talk about transformations in the physical world. The world is populated by beings who are also persons like humans; all of the world is animated, and there are different nations of beings who can communicate with each other, who are intelligent and volitional creatures.

Both the Zuni story and the Iroquoian story of the origins of the confederacy also talk about how society should be organized, about the importance of kinship and families, about how society divides its many functions in order to provide for healing, for food, for decision making, and so on. The Iroquoian confederacy was a model of Federalism for the drafters of the Constitution, who were much impressed by the way in which the confederacy managed to preserve the autonomy of its individual member tribes while being able to manage effective concerted actions, as the colonists to their dismay too often found out. The Navajo story of Changing Woman and the Lakota story of White Buffalo Calf Pipe Woman are important illustrations not only of the role of women as culture heroes, but also of every people's necessity to evolve structures such as the Pipe Ceremony or the Navajo healing rituals to restore and maintain order in the world.

The Raven and Hare narratives are stories about a Trickster figure. Tricksters are the opposite of culture heroes. Culture heroes exist in mythology to dramatize prototypical events and behaviors; they show us how to do what is right and how we became the people who we are. Tricksters, on the other hand, provide for disorder and change; they enable us to see the seamy underside of life and remind us that culture, finally, is artificial, that there is no necessary reason why things must be the way they are. If there is sufficient motivation to change things, Trickster provides for the possibility of such change, most often by showing us the danger of believing too sincerely that this arbitrary arrangement we call culture is the way things really are. The Bungling Host story, widespread throughout Native America, humorously illustrates the perils of overreaching the limits of one's identity while trying to ingratiate one's self.

Significant Form, Style, or Artistic Conventions

Perhaps the most important thing that needs to be done is to challenge students' notions of myth. When students hear the word *myth*, they succumb to the popular belief that mythology is necessarily something that is false. This is a good place to start a discussion about truth, inviting students to consider that there are other kinds of truth besides scientific truth (which is what gave a bad name to mythology in the first place). Consider this definition of myth: "The dramatic representation of culturally important truths in narrative form."

Such a definition highlights the fact that myths represent or dramatize shared visions of the world for the people who hold them. Myths articulate the fundamental truths about the shape of the universe and the nature of humanity.

It is also important to look at important issues of form such as repetition. Repetition strikes many students as boring. Repetition, however, is an aesthetic device that can be used to create expectation. Consider the number three and how several aspects of our Euro-American experience are organized in terms of three: the start of a race ("on your mark, get set, go"); three sizes (small, medium, and large); the three colors of a traffic signal; and, of course, three little pigs. These are all commonplace examples, so commonplace, in fact, that initially most students don't think much of them. But there is no reason why we should begin things by counting to three. We could count to four or five or seven, as respectively the Zunis, the Chinooks, and the Hebrews did. In other words, these repetitions have an aesthetic function: they create a sense of expectation, and when one arrives at the full number of repetitions, a sense of completeness, satisfaction, and fulfillment.

Original Audience

The question of audience is crucial for Native American literature, in that the original audience for the literature understands the world through its own experience much differently than most of our students do. As a result, it's important to reconstruct as much of that cultural and historical context as possible for students, especially when it has a direct bearing upon the literature. So, for instance, students need to know in discussing Zuni material that the Zunis, Hopis, and Navajos are agricultural people and that corn and moccasins figure prominently as symbols of life. Rain, moisture, and human beings are imagined in terms of corn, and life is understood as an organic process that resembles a plant growing from a seed in the ground, being raised up, harvested, and so forth. Historically, it's important to realize too that visions of one's community and its history differ from culture to culture. So, for instance, the Hopi story of the Pueblo revolt imagines the revolt as a response to a life-threatening drought that is caused by the suppression of the native religion by the Franciscan priest. This way of understanding history is very different from the way most of our students understand history today. Its very notion of cause and effect, involving as it does supernatural means, is much more closely related to a vision of history shared by Christian reconstructionists, seventeenth-century Puritans, and ancient Hebrews.

At the same time, students should be cautioned about the presumption that somehow we can enter entirely into another cultural vision, whether it be that of the Lakota during the Ghost Dance period of the 1880s or the Puritan Separatists three centuries earlier. This is not only a matter of translation and transcription. As both Murray and Clifford point out, what is sometimes blithely called "the need to understand" or "the search for knowledge" is not a neutral quest, but one determined in great measure by the often unarticulated aims and attitudes of the dominant society that structures fields of inquiry and creates the need for certain kinds of information. Although most contemporary students often assume that all differences can be overcome, the facticity of difference will remain.

Questions for Reading, Discussion, and Writing

1. The number of works addressed in this section is so great and the material so varied that particular questions would not be useful. A good lead-in to all of these works, however, would focus on motivation of characters or significance of action. I would want students to identify some action in the narrative that puzzles them, and would encourage them to try to explain the role of this action in the narrative and what might motivate it. They will not necessarily be successful at answering that question, but the activity of trying to answer that question will compel them to seek for meaning ultimately in some kind of cultural context. There is, in other words, a certain kind of appropriate aesthetic frustration here, which should not necessarily be discouraged because it prepares the student to let go of the notion that human behavior is everywhere intelligible in universal terms.
2. I usually have students write comparative papers. I ask them to identify a theme: for example, the relationship between human beings and animals, attitudes toward death, the role of women, or other similar topics, and to write comparatively using Native American texts and a Euro-American text that they find to be comparable.

Native American Oral Poetry

Contributing Editor: Andrew Wiget

Classroom Strategies

The Inuit and Aztec poetry requires the introduction of cultural background in order to understand some of its themes and imagery, but it is much more accessible than "Sayatasha's Night Chant." Because it is expressive of individual emotional states, it is much closer to the Western lyric poetry tradition and therefore more readily apprehended by students than the long Zuni chant.

"Sayatasha's Night Chant," on the other hand, is very difficult for students for a number of reasons, which, if properly addressed, make it a rich aesthetic experience.

First of all, it is absolutely essential to refer students to the notes that supply important, culture-specific, contextual information that is necessary for understanding the poems. This is less urgent in the more accessible poetry of the Aztecs and the Inuit, but it is required for the other very brief song texts and especially for "Sayatasha's Night Chant," which I think will pose the most problems for students. One can enrich the cultural context of the "Chant" by teaching it in conjunction with the Zuni "Talk Concerning the First Beginning." This origin story establishes some of the fundamental symbols that are expressive of the Zuni worldview and some of the fundamental themes so that if the students read "Sayatasha's Night Chant" following the emergence story, they can carry forward some of the cultural information acquired from reading the origin story to support their reading of "Sayatasha's Night Chant."

Major Themes, Historical Perspectives, Personal Issues

The Inuit and Aztec poetry is relatively accessible to students, who recognize in it some fundamental human emotions that have literary expression in Euro-American traditions as well. The Inuit poetry is remarkable for its juxtaposition of human beings against the natural world. Nature is viewed as an enormous arena that dwarfs human beings, who are continually struggling to secure their existence. Much of the Inuit view of nature corresponds rather well to the notions of the Romantic sublime. This is a Nature that the Inuit face with a combination of awe, terror, and humility, as reflected in the Copper Eskimo "Song" and Uvavnuk's "Moved." On the other hand, the "Improvised Greeting" suggests that in the presence of such an overwhelming Nature, which isolated people, the experience of social contact was a cause for tremendous joy. And yet, as the "Widow's Song" suggests, alienation from one's community left one isolated and trapped in one's self. (Inuit poetry can be very reflective.) Orpingalik's song speaks to a loss of competence and power experienced in one's old age that undermines the sense of accomplishment and identity. A good poem to read to workaholics, whose identity usually rests in their work!

Aztecs, it seems, are familiar to everyone. Their popular reputation rests on a series of images—the offering of human hearts to the sun, cruel and violent warfare, a powerful militaristic empire—many of which were true. Thus it comes as a surprise, having set up this cultural and historical context, to discover a poetry whose central theme is the fragility of life, the transience of beauty, and the elusiveness of truth. At the height of their power, the Aztecs experienced life, beauty, and truth as inexorably slipping away. They expressed this theme in their poetry through three images or vehicles, the most important of which are images associated with flowers. Flowers in their fragile beauty represented for the Aztecs the very essence of life. In the poem "Like Flowers Continually Perishing," the poet imagines that we are like flowers slowly dying in the midst of and despite our beauty. Flowers throughout literature are symbols of fragility as well as great beauty. A second cluster of images has to do with feathers. Feathers in Aztec culture represented things of great value and preciousness because many of them had to be imported from the jungles of Central America. They were also objects of great delicacy, and, like flowers, became symbols of the fragility, beauty, and preciousness of life. The third and most important image was poetry itself. Aztecs wrote poetry to achieve immortality. Because they experienced life as transient, they looked to create an ideal world through the images articulated in their poetry. In this they felt they were imitating their principal deity, Omeoteotl, the creator of the universe, also called the Lord of the Close and the Near. Omeoteotl achieved immortality through creativity, and the Aztec poets sought to do the same.

"Sayatasha's Night Chant" is more accessible to students if one can view it as a quest, in which a human being, representing the Zuni people, is sent on a journey from the village to the Zuni "heaven," Kothluwalawa. The purpose of this journey is to obtain the seeds and power needed to regenerate life for a new year. "Sayatasha's Night Chant" is a poem recited in the context of a world renewal ritual. In narrative form, it describes how a man has been appointed in the beginning of the poem (line 106) to represent the Zuni people. His mission, which takes the better part of a year to accomplish, is undertaken because the world is in need of renewal (line 67). His appointment takes place in January, and throughout the next nine or ten months this person is busy visiting many shrines at Zuni to plant prayer sticks (physical representations of the basic elements of life in this world) as offerings to the deities (lines 120–33). Later, forty-nine days before the Shalako ceremony in early December, the man who will impersonate Sayatasha is formally invested with the symbols and the costume of his role (see notes 8 and 9). Now having been transformed into a being who represents the spirit world of the rain-bringing ancestors, the Sayatasha impersonator returns to the village bearing the seeds of new life. Before he reaches the village, however, he visits twenty-nine separate springs around Zuni, each of which represent the different places where the Zuni people stopped on their way to the Center of the World, the village of Zuni. In reenacting this migration, the Sayatasha impersonator recovers the force, energy, and potency of that first creation to reenergize life in the village. The poem ends as the Sayatasha impersonator, on the eighth night of Shalako, confers upon the entire village the blessings of life and fertility that he had been sent to gain for them.

Significant Form, Style, or Artistic Conventions

Students need some initial help in understanding the meaning of prevalent images, like flowers in Aztec poetry. They might also need assistance in seeing some potent juxtapositions that occur in the Inuit poetry. For example, the despairing woman in the "Widow's Song" holds an amulet (a token of religious faith) in her hands while she stares angrily at the northern lights that taunt her with their beauty and promise.

In the case of "Sayatasha's Night Chant," there is much ritual language, and students will need help in working through the characters and understanding the ritual actions that are a key to the poem. Ritual poetry is very formulaic and repetitive. Students are frequently frustrated by repetition and aggravated by the apparent lack of spontaneity and the stiltedness of the language. Point out to them that in serious religious settings, spontaneity is not valued, not only in Zuni settings but also in ritual contexts throughout the world, including Euro-American cultures. It's also good to develop in them some understanding of the key symbols, like water and corn as symbols of life. Water, in particular, is something that they ought to be able to relate to. Notes 1, 3, and 8 should help students understand ritual poetry.

All of these songs were sung in different ways, which affects the way in which they were experienced. The "Night Chant" is just that, a narrative chant in which the words are uttered on a sustained tone with a falling tone at the end of each line. The short songs were sung to more complex melodies, sometimes by the individual alone, sometimes with an audience chorus response. Short songs were often repeated many times in order to deepen the emotional experience stimulated by the song.

Original Audience

I make it a point to try to reconstruct the cultural context of the poems' origins in order to recover for the students the aesthetic force that these poems must have had for their original listeners. I remind them of the terrible and frightening confrontation that human beings have with the physical environment in the Arctic and how people cling to each other under such circumstances. Understanding the relationship between the physical and the social worlds in Inuit life is a necessary precondition for understanding the poetry. The same thing is true of the Aztecs. One juxtaposes the poetry against the cultural and historical context from which it emerged.

In all cases, I also stress the unique context in which these songs were first performed. The Eskimo, for instance, had song festivals in which these very intense and private songs were sung in public. The Inuit, in other words, had created a socially sanctioned forum for the expression of one's most private joys and griefs. This suggests a new way of thinking about the function of poetry and the relationship between an individual and his social context. Among the Aztecs, poetry was composed principally by the nobility, most of whom had also earned great fame and success as warriors. It is effective to point out to students that the poetry most sensitive to the fragile beauty of life was created by the noble warrior class. In terms of the Zuni poem, it is useful to remind students that ritual poetry is recited publicly in the context of a variety of significant and meaningful religious actions, and that these actions are as much a part of the total experience as the recitation of the poetry. Consider also Jane Green's "Divorce Dance Song" as a kind of publication. The notion that poetry is coupled with action and so comes closer to approximating the condition of drama than any other Western form is initially unfamiliar to students. They may need some help in realizing that poetry, even in the Western tradition, emerged from the recitation of hymns in dramatic settings in ancient Israel and Greece.

Comparisons, Contrasts, Connections

The Aztec and Inuit poetry compares well in theme and form to British and American Romantic lyric poetry. Certainly the Aztec poetry compares well with Western poetry in the elegiac tradition. The Inuit and Aztec poems also offer opportunities for comparing and contrasting the role of poetry as a vehicle for self-expression and for the creation of individual identity, another important Romantic theme. One can contrast "Sayatasha's Night Chant," in which the individual identity of the speaker of the poem is totally submerged in his ritual role or persona, with the Inuit and Aztec poetry in which the "I" reflects the personal identity of the poet/subject. "Sayatasha's Night Chant" can also be effectively contrasted with British and American poetry whose subject is the power of Nature. Reading "Sayatasha's Night Chant" against Bryant's "Thanatopsis," Emerson's "Nature," or Thoreau's *Walden* will lead students to consider Native American views of Nature as something very different from the Anglo-American Romantic understanding of Nature. Such contrasts are especially instructive because they enable students to understand why Native Americans and Anglo-Americans might hold different attitudes toward the land and activities involving the natural world.

Discussion Strategies

Begin the discussion of Eskimo and Aztec poetry by inviting students to consider, in the case of the Eskimo, the physical environment in which the Inuit people live and the need for powerful social bonds in the face of the overwhelming power and intimidating scale of the natural world of the Arctic. By the same token, begin the discussion of Aztec poetry with a presentation of the scale and scope of the Aztec military, political, economic, and social achievements. In both cases the poetry stands against this powerful cultural context and effectively discloses its key themes sometimes by contrast to one's expectations (as in the case of the Aztecs) and sometimes by conforming to one's expectations (as in the case of Inuit poetry). With "Sayatasha's Night Chant," I usually begin by insisting that most cultures have rituals, such as first fruit feasts (like our Thanksgiving) or foundational feasts (like our Fourth of July or New Year's), which are designed to commemorate the forces of life and order that structure and animate our world. I talk about the role of ritual in people's lives, and I disassociate ritual from its popular definition of something routine. This discussion of ritual and the role of the sacred in culture is an enormously valuable preface to approaching this particular poem.

Questions for Reading, Discussion, and Writing

1. I would draw students' attention in the Eskimo poetry to the place of human beings in the physical universe and the relationship of the individual to society; and in the Aztec poetry, to the images of flowers and to the function of poetry. In "Sayatasha's Night Chant," I would focus on important images such as cornmeal and invite students to make connections between symbols that they discover in "Sayatasha's Night Chant" and their antecedents in the Zuni origin myth, "Talk Concerning the First Beginning."
2. Aside from obvious thematic papers focused around topics such as nature, death, ritual, and so on, I would invite students to write on broader topics such as the role of poetry in these societies and to compare how poetry functions in them with how it has functioned in the Western tradition.

Bibliography

Babcock-Abrahams, Barbara. "'A Tolerated Margin of Mess': The Trickster and His Tales Reconsidered." *Journal of the Folklore Institute* 9 (1975): 147–86.

Bunzel, Ruth. "Zuni Ritual Poetry." *47th Annual Report of the Bureau of American Ethnology* (1930): 611–835.

Clements, William N. *Native American Verbal Art: Texts and Contexts.* Tucson: U of Arizona P, 1996.

Fenton, William. "This Island, the World on Turtle's Back." *Journal of American Folklore* 75 (1962): 283–300.

Finnegan, Ruth. *Oral Poetry: Its Nature, Significance and Social Context.* Cambridge: Cambridge UP, 1977.

Geertz, Clifford. "Religion as a Cultural System." *The Interpretation of Cultures.* New York: Basic Books, 1973.

Holland, Jeanne. "Teaching Native American Literature from *The Heath Anthology of American Literature.*" *CEA Critic* 55 (1993): 1–21.

Hymes, Dell. *"In Vain I Tried to Tell You": Essays in Native American Ethnopoetics.* Philadelphia: U of Pennsylvania P, 1981.

Krupat, Arnold. *Ethnocriticism: Ethnography, History, Literature.* Berkeley: U of California P, 1992.

Leon-Portilla, Miguel. *Pre-Columbian Literatures of Mexico.* Norman: U of Oklahoma P, 1969.

Lowenstein, Tom, trans. "Introduction." *Eskimo Poems from Canada and Greenland.* Pittsburgh: U of Pittsburgh P, 1973.

Murray, David. *Forked Tongues: Speech, Writing, and Representation in North American Indian Texts.* Bloomington: Indiana UP, 1990.

Radin, Paul. *The Trickster.* New York: Schocken, 1972.

Richard, Gladys. "Literary Types and the Dissemination of Myths." *Journal of American Folklore* 34 (1914): 269–307.

Ruoff, A. LaVonne Brown. *American Indian Literatures: An Introduction, Bibliographic Review, and Selected Bibliography.* New York: MLA, 1990.

Sturtevant, William, ed. *Handbook of North American Indians,* 15 vols. Washington, DC: Smithsonian Institution Press.

Swann, Brian, ed. *Smoothing the Ground: Essays on Native American Oral Literature.* Berkeley: U of California P, 1987.

——— and Arnold Krupat, eds. *Recovering the Word: Essays on Native American Literature.* Berkeley: U of California P, 1987.

Tedlock, Dennis. *The Spoken Word and the Work of Interpretation.* Philadelphia: U of Pennsylvania P, 1983.

Toelken, J. Barre. "The 'Pretty Language' of Yellowman: Genre, Mode, and Texture in Navajo Coyote Narratives." *Genre* 2 (1969): 21–235.

Wheeler-Voegelin, Erminie, and R. W. Moore. "The Emergence Myth in Native America." *Indiana University Publications in Folklore 9* (1957): 66–91.

Wiget, Andrew. "Aztec Lyrics: Poetry in a World of Continually Perishing Flowers." *Latin American Indian Literatures* 4 (1980): 1–11.

————. "Native American Oral Literature: A Critical Introduction." In *Dictionary of Native American Literature*. Ed. Andrew Wiget. New York: Garland, 1994, 3–18.

————. "Oral Narrative." Chapter 1. *Native American Literature*. Boston: Twayne, 1985.

————. "Oratory and Oral Poetry." *Native American Literature*. Boston: Twayne, 1985.

————. "Reading Against the Grain: Origin Stories and American Literary History." *American Literary History* 2 (1991): 209–31.

————. "Sayatasha's Night Chant: A Literary Textual Analysis of a Zuni Ritual Poem." *American Indian Culture and Research Journal* 4 (1980): 99–140.

————. "A Talk Concerning First Beginnings: Teaching Native American Oral Literatures." *The Heath Anthology of American Literature Newsletter* IX (Spring 1993): 4–7.

————. "Telling the Tale: A Performance Analysis of a Hopi Coyote Story." *Recovering the Word: Essays on the Native American Literature*. Ed. Brian Swann and Arnold Krupat. n.p., n.d.: 297–336.

Cluster: America in the European Imagination

Contributing Editor: Ivy Schweitzer

Classroom Issues and Strategies

The purpose of this cluster is to give students a sense of the preconceptions Europeans brought to their thinking about the various reports of New World exploration. It implicitly argues that Europeans had cultural and psychological "lenses" through which they saw and interpreted the information at first trickling into and then flooding Europe about "America" after its "discovery" at the end of the fifteenth century. The cluster is unique in *The Heath Anthology* offerings because none of these commentators actually visited the New World but instead based their representations of it on reports, hearsay, and, we argue, fantasies and desires for an idealized or demonized other. Thus, these texts provide revealing information about how leading thinkers across Europe imagined America, the "New" World, the Other. Studies of "proto-colonialist" discourse suggest that explorers, conquistadors, and settlers brought very definite preconceived notions with them to the New World, based on imagery circulating in Europe about other exotic and sometimes mythic places—the Far East, the Golden Age, the Earthly Paradise. These notions often persisted despite concrete and material evidence to the contrary. For example, New World exploration was quite expensive, requiring ships, supplies, knowledgeable mariners, and paid sailors. The champions and leaders of these expeditions were often under enormous pressure to prove the profitability of their endeavors; frequently the number of mineralogists and lapidaries on these journeys far exceeded the number of missionaries. In addition, many reporters claim to have seen or heard of gold, or the golden city of Cibola, or mistook indigenous grasses for the valuable "silk grasse," though the two looked nothing alike. This cluster also allows students to compare and contrast different European fantasies and desires and the literary figures in which they were expressed. Students can think about the ways in which the image or fantasy of the New World was employed by these writers for purposes other than merely informing the eager readers of exploration narrative about "discoveries."

Major Themes, Historical Perspectives, Personal Issues

This cluster is primary dedicated to providing historical perspectives on the early exploration and encounter narratives in the first section of *The Heath Anthology*. Each writer and artist included here has a complicated argument that uses one culture to mirror the other. Students can consider the role of the ancient writers in these arguments, the ongoing debate about what makes a perfect society. Students can also consider the roles of religion and gender in these representations and the role of difference. Do cultural differences in the European mind always imply inferiority, barbarity, and savagery? Can people be equal and different? What is the function of knowledge in the power politics depicted in these representations? Can one know another without or outside a politics of power? And how do these questions influence our own present struggles with differences, inclusion, discrimination, and the construction of democratic communities?

Both Donne's poem and Galle's engraving are especially suited for close analysis of images and details, and their cultural and political import. Discussions of these texts can be used to practice analytical skills by looking closely at the figurative language of Donne's poem, its allusions, and the power dynamics set up and then unsettled in its paradoxes. The imagery in van der Straet's drawing contains details that are highly allegorical—the relative positions and state of (un)dress of the two major figures. One could ask students to consider the function of heterosexuality and heteroerotic relations in reference to the adventure of conquest and exploration.

Significant Form, Style, or Artistic Conventions

The excerpts in this cluster encompass a wide variety of forms and styles which would be helpful to mention and which students will meet again in their readings in this period. Many of them are characteristic of European humanism, the movement away from Medieval scholasticism and an absolutist worldview, and contain a fresh look at and use of the ancient "pagan" thinkers of Greece and Rome.

More's *Utopia* helped to define the genre of the utopian narrative, the story of finding a perfect society, wedded to the travel account and philosophical satire. He uses wit, paradox, and self-contradiction to mount a critique of European society and mores.

Montaigne developed the genre of the personal essay to record his voluminous reading, but it quickly became a means of disclosing and exploring individual consciousness.

Van der Straet was born in the Netherlands, trained in Antwerp, but spent his entire career in Italy, where he was a protégé of Varsari, worked in Florence for the Medici family and assisted in frescos, but was mainly a tapestry designer. He used a Mannerist style characterized by grace, poise, facility, and sophistication.

Donne is considered the founder of the Metaphysical school of poetry, which is known for its pervasive use of paradox, novelty, incongruity, strong rhythms that give the powerful effect of a specific speaker, and the use of *conceits*, comparisons in which the tenor and vehicle of the metaphor are ingeniously related. "Elegy XIX" illustrates this style, especially the central conceit of seduction used to express the "discovery" of the New World by the likes of Walter Raleigh, his court rival.

Bacon wrote in a philosophical style that expresses his belief in the rational soul and the importance of natural inquiry as a cooperative undertaking. Like More, he combines the travel narrative with satire to offer another version of an ideal society, this one based on scientific research and a belief in community, which inspired later scientific undertakings.

Original Audience

All of these excerpts were aimed at a fairly educated reading and viewing audience interested in and, in many cases, hungry for accounts of the New World. These readers, largely male and elite, would have been familiar with classical writings from the works of Erasmus, such as Plato, Aristotle, Cicero, and others. They would know Plato's description of the ideal republic, Aristotle's views in the *Politics*, and Cicero's account of the Roman republic. They would have been familiar with some of the early accounts of New World exploration by Columbus and Amerigo Vespucci. Donne's poem can be read specifically in terms of the court intrigues and coterie literary productions of the 1590s, but this information is not necessary to an understanding of the poem's use of America as a figure for an eroticized otherness.

Comparisons, Contrasts, Connections

Students can compare the entry on Columbus, which contains reports about his voyages that disclose the cultural biases he brought to his encounter with the native inhabitants, his habit of describing the New World in terms of the Old, and his rhetoric of wonder, with the political satire of the English writer Thomas More and the cultural critique of European ethnocentrism of the French intellectual Michel de Montaigne excerpted here. Or students can compare the eyewitness reports by any of the Spanish explorers or Harriot's "A Briefe and True Report" with the satires and utopias described here to think about the notions of the "noble" as well as "ignoble savage" and what these myths have in common. Students can compare Montaigne's use of the Indians as a mirror to Baron de Lahontan's writing a century later. Instructors can also ask students to do some imaginative reversals in relation to these accounts, as in the Sample Assignment for this cluster. That is, imagine the encounter from the perspective of indigenous peoples in ways that account for the perceptions of the explorers but point to different epistemological structures. For example, in the excerpt from "The Coming of the Spanish and the Pueblo Revolt," the Hopi reporter talks about the people's initial fear of the Spanish priest but notes that "later they decided he was really the Bahana, the savior, and let him build a mission at Shung-opovi." The Aztecs in Mexico had a similar reaction to the approach of Cortez.

Working with Cultural Objects

In the Sample Assignment for this Cluster, I suggest students look at the Orozco murals at Dartmouth College for a modern Mexican visual imagination of pre-Columbian Mexican culture and myths surrounding the advent of the Europeans. The mural and supporting materials such as information on Orozco and the tradition of mural painting and an interpretation of "The Epic of American Civilization" can be found at <http://www.dartmouth.edu/~library/Orozco>.

For a document from the early seventeenth century founding of Hampton, New Hampshire that invokes the principle of *vacuum domicilium*, see <http://www.hampton.lib.nh.us/hampton/documents/statepapers1.htm>.

It is also instructive to compare van der Straet's influential depiction of the "discovery" of America with images taken from drawings made by eyewitnesses. Students can view the copper plate engravings published by Theodore De Bry and his sons beginning in 1590, which were widely copied and circulated in Europe in the seventeenth and eighteenth centuries. The initial offering contained engravings based on watercolor sketches by John White, who accompanied Thomas Harriot on one of the first English voyages to Virginia: <http://www.library.upenn.edu/exhibits/rbm/kislak/viewers/debryengravings.html> or <http://www.csulb.edu/projects/ais/woodcuts>.

Questions for Reading, Discussion, and Writing

1. How does More's attitude about the profitable use of "ground void and vacant" help to justify the European land grab in America? What does it say about his perception of native farming techniques and thus European conceptions of their level of "civilization"? How does it reflect on Europeans' ability to accept cultural differences?

2. How does Montaigne reverse the usual values that anchor European identity, and to what end? In what way can European society of the time, especially Catholic France, which was waging internal war against its Protestant population, the Huguenots, be considered symbolically anthropophagic, or self-consuming?

3. What is the relation of the Adam and Eve story of creation to the scenarios in Donne and van der Straet? The function of nakedness and dress? Why are the cannibals in the engraving female, and what message does this representation send?

4. How does the elevation of rationality and the scientific method, as in Bacon, bear on the experience of newness and otherness? What is the intellectual "position" of the scientific observer, or one who posits "objectivity," and what kind of power relation does this construct with what or who is observed? How do these assumptions bear on encounters with the "others" of the "New" World?

Sample Assignment

Ask students to imagine one of the famous "encounters" between Europeans and indigenous people from the point of view of the natives and what preconceived notions they may have harbored about strangers, white people, and bearded and armed men arriving in tall ships. This could involve asking students to do research on pre-Columbian materials such as oral histories, codexes, petroglyphs, or works like the Mayan *Chilan Balam* or the *Popol Vuh*. At Dartmouth, I encourage students to go into our Reserve Corridor and study Jose Orozco's mural, "The Epic of American Civilization," in which a modern-day Mexican artist (early 1930s) visually imagines pre-Columbian Mexican culture and the impact of the coming of Europeans on the north-south relationship. This mural and supporting materials can be found at <http://www.dartmouth .edu/~library/Orozco>. Students can also look at Nahuatl accounts of the coming of Cortez, which help to contextualize native reactions to the conquistadors. Or students can read the final pages of Michael Dorris's children's book *Morning Girl* (1992), a story that concludes with a description of the landing of Columbus's party on the shores of Hispaniola from the point of view of a young, imaginative Taino girl. Ask them to outline how Dorris, himself Native American, imagines a native response to Europeans as others. Students can also consult Native American materials such as "Creation of the Whites" or "The Coming of the Spanish and the Pueblo Revolt" (also in *The Heath Anthology*). Why does Dorris choose a young girl as his protagonist? How does her reaction explain or account for the interpretations of the Spaniards (i.e., mistaking native generosity for ignorance of what is "valuable"), and, more importantly, how does her commentary turn the tables to provide a very different reaction to otherness and cultural differences? The point of the assignment is to get students to work with pre-Columbian and Native American materials and to think about the relativity of cultural values. Also, it encourages them to examine the sources of our almost reflexive responses to others and newness and the implications of those responses, and to ask whether differences always imply a politics of power. How are selves already constituted by others, identity by difference?

Bibliography

Arber, Edward, ed. *The First Three English Books on America: 1511–1555* by Richard Eden. 1895. New York: Kraus, 1971.

Bucher, Bernadette. *Icon and Conquest: A Structural Analysis of the Illustrations of de Bry's "Great Voyages."* Trans. Basia Miller Gulati. Chicago: U of Chicago P, 1981.

Certeau, Michel de. *Heterologies: Discourse on the Other*. Trans. Brian Massumi. Minneapolis: U of Minnesota P, 1986.

Greene, Roland. *Unrequited Conquests: Love and Empire in the Colonial Americas*. Chicago: U of Chicago P, 1999.

Honour, Hugh. *The New Golden Land: European Images of America from the Discoveries to the Present Time*. London: Allen Lane, 1976.

Hulme, Peter. *Colonial Encounters: Europe and the Native Caribbean, 1492–1797*. London: Methuen, 1986.

Greenblatt, Stephen, ed. *New World Encounters*. Berkeley: U of California P, 1993.

Moffitt, John F., and Santiago Sebastián. *O Brave New People: The European Invention of the American Indian*. Albuquerque: U of New Mexico P, 1996.

Pagden, Anthony. *The Fall of Natural Man: The American Indian and the Origins of Comparative Ethnology*. Rev. ed. Cambridge, UK: Cambridge UP, 1986.

Scanlan, Thomas. *Colonial Writing and the New World, 1583–1671*. Cambridge, UK: Cambridge UP, 1999.

Shakespeare, William. *The Tempest*.

Todorov, Tzvetan. *The Conquest of America: The Question of the Other*. Trans. Richard Howard. New York: Harper, 1984.

New Spain

Requerimiento, ca. 1512
Aristotle
Christopher Columbus (1451–1506)
Fray Marcos de Niza (1495?–1542)
Pedro de Casteñeda (1510?–1570?)
Gaspar Pérez de Villagrá (1555–1620)
History of the Miraculous Apparition of the
Virgin of Guadalupe in 1531
Sor Juana Inés de la Cruz (1648–1695)
Don Antonio de Otermín (fl. 1680)
The Coming of the Spanish and the Pueblo Revolt (Hopi)
Don Diego de Vargas (?–1704)

Contributing Editors: Juan Bruce-Novoa and Ivy Schweitzer

Classroom Issues and Strategies

Students' lack of general historical knowledge is compounded by the usual disinformation they learn about U.S. history as taught in this country. To address this problem, I give the students a list of historical facts as they probably have learned them (i.e., dates of Jamestown, Plymouth, etc.), and we discuss this traditional way of teaching U.S. history. I sometimes ask them to draw a map representing U.S. history in movement. Then I give them a second list with the Spanish and French settlements included and discuss how this new context changes the way we conceive of U.S. history. Next, I take time to explain the European backgrounds of the fifteenth and sixteenth centuries in which Spain, the first national state, was a dominant power and England a marginal and even second-rate power. Third, I emphasize the economic reality of colonization. Students must understand that none of the Europeans viewed the Native Americans as equals. The destruction of the Acoma people is just the start of a long U.S. tradition of subjugating conquered peoples and should not be read as a Spanish aberration. Cabeza de Vaca's experience is important in prefiguring not only captivity literature but also migrant literature of the nineteenth and twentieth centuries: he and his comrades had to assimilate and acculturate to survive, working at whatever jobs they could get among a majority culture that did not necessarily need or want them around.

Students often ask why these texts are important and how they relate to more conventional U.S. literature. You might suggest that they consider changing their traditional concept of the United States as an English-based country and entertain the paradigm of a land from the start where several language groups and distinct origins contended. Students should be taught that this situation remains the same, in spite of the assumption that English won out. The forces present in the early period are still contending for a place in U.S. territory. Perhaps the oldest tradition in the United States is the struggle among different groups for the recognition of the right to participate fully in determining the future of this land.

The central issue raised by these selections documenting the origins of the Virgin of Guadalupe story and the history of the Pueblo revolt revolves around the opposing forces of colonialism and native resistance to it. In my experience students tend to side with the Native Americans against the Spanish, focusing on the Hopi text and its act of direct and simple rejection through violence. The protests against the Columbus quintcentennial celebrations provided added impetus to this anti-Spanish sentiment, especially among the U.S. Latino population. Students should be encouraged to engage in a discussion of the legal and moral rights of conquest, but care should be taken to avoid focusing solely on the Spanish. Certainly by the seventeenth century, the other major powers in the Americas, the English and the French, were dealing with similar resistance in very similar ways. No European colonial power willingly gave up possession of American territory to its native inhabitants; the U.S. government followed suit in later centuries.

"The History of the Miraculous Apparition of the Virgin of Guadalupe" is an important text because of its appearance everywhere Mexicans have settled in the United States. The hybrid character of the figure of the Virgin of Guadalupe suggests an alternate image of American identity, one of a cultural and biological fusion of Old and New World peoples.

Major Themes, Historical Perspectives, Personal Issues

The headnotes specify two major themes: the newness of the experience and the need to relate it in European terms. Columbus initiated the dialogue between American reality and the European codes of signification.

Another theme is the strategies utilized to convince powerful readers of the benefits of the New World. Again, Columbus marks the beginning. These authors are constantly selling the unknown to potential investors and visitors. Here begins the tradition of hawking new property developments beyond the urban blight of the reader's familiar surroundings and promoting fantasies of ideal realms or cities of untold wealth.

Cabeza de Vaca introduces the familiar theme of wandering the back roads of the country—a sixteenth-century Kerouac. It is the theme of finding oneself through the difficult pilgrimage into the wilderness—a Carlos Castaneda *avant la lettre*. Cabeza de Vaca is transformed through suffering, perseverance, and the ability to acculturate.

Another theme is the sincerity of the religious motivation of the explorers and settlers of New Spain in light of the contradicting evidence of economic ambitions. Cabeza de Vaca's account calls into question Spain's justification of its imperial designs and strong-arm methods. This conflict between philanthropic ideals and exploitative motivation still underlies U.S. foreign policy.

This theme emerges as well in the history of resistance efforts such as the Hopi revolt or the Virgin of Guadalupe. Two contradictory themes dialogue throughout these texts: the Native Americans' determination to defend their culture to the death, and the colonizers' determination to hold conquered territory with equal zeal. Both feel bound by their specific and divergent cultural codes of behavior to resist the efforts of the other and neither seems willing to compromise. The Virgin of Guadalupe, however, represents a possible point of mediation. Her tale raises the theme of miscegenation, one that has been treated very differently in Latin America and the United States.

Students lack the historical training to contextualize these tales. The headnotes, as well as references to studies of the period, provide a good introduction. It is important to keep in mind that these texts reflect the ongoing efforts of the Spanish empire to perpetuate itself by maintaining order and control over its territory and inhabitants.

Significant Form, Style, or Artistic Conventions

First, the form of much of the texts from New Spain is the epistolary chronicle: a subjective report on the events of exploration and conquest without the limitations of supposedly objective historical science. It is a personal account like a memoir, but it is also a letter to a powerful reader, not to the general public. It has no literary pretensions, but the circumstances demanded rhetorical skill.

Second, the period is one of transition from the Middle Ages to the Renaissance, so there will be mixtures of characteristics from the two, the Medieval chronicle alongside the Renaissance epic of Villagrá or the satires of Sor Juana Inés.

Style is also hybrid. While most of these authors were educated well above the average commoner of the period, most of the early explorers were not trained in letters. Thus their writing is mostly unpretentious and direct. Again, Villagrá and Sor Juana Inés are the exceptions.

Most of these texts record personal experiences in the New World and New Spain and thus have a ring of realism and direct contact with the land and native people. Students should be encouraged to look for the European filter through which these experiences are recorded, in terms of voice, imagery, comparison, and attitudes. Students can also look for an emerging "American" voice and set of concerns, specifically in Cabeza de Vaca. Villagrá, by contrast, uses classical forms and epic conventions to render the conquest of New Mexico heroic. Toward the end of the century, Sor Juana Inés challenges the reigning gender conventions in colonial New Spain in her use of poetry, the most elite of forms, for her satires, meditations, and religious dramas.

The differences in the formal character of Native and European texts reflect the conflicting issues mentioned previously. While Spanish officials use the written word, with the full authority of a document within a legalistic political order, the anonymous Hopi resistance text began as oral tales and preserves a kinship with folklore and clandestine communications. The Guadalupe text is, like the image of the Virgin herself, a hybrid of elite and popular styles. The governmental texts obey the conventions of bureaucratic communiqués, employing the rhetoric of political justification that underlies hegemonic regulations; the other texts counter this rhetoric through an appeal to a sense of common justice for the oppressed at the margins of that same order.

Original Audience

The audience for the exploration narratives of New Spain were specifically the powerful kings and queens of Spain, including their advisers and ministers and perhaps members of the court and potential investors and backers, although some of these narratives were translated and read across Europe as part of the general populace's fascination with accounts of the New World. They can be compared to U.S. military reports on Vietnam or propaganda films on World War II, like *Victory at Sea,* to get a sense of the rhetoric of nationalistic justification. Sor Juana Inés, whose concerns are spiritual and philosophical as well as social, was writing for a growing class of Creole settlers in Mexico as well as for an elite, educated class of Spaniards.

The Guadalupe text was intended for the Native Americans of central Mexico; a proselytizing text for people of non-European cultures, it was originally published in Náhuatl and thus not directed at a Spanish readership. However, one must consider that the great majority of Native Americans could not read in any language, so the text could have well been intended for trained clerics to use in evangelizing.

The Hopi text was originally an oral story repeated by and for members of this and other tribes. It is still found among the oral tradition tales in the Southwest.

Comparisons, Contrasts, Connections

Many of the writers in this section can be compared and contrasted with each other, and with similar exploratory accounts from New France, the Chesapeake, and New England. Students might consider how the attitude toward and treatment of Indians differ among the three major imperial powers. Comparisons with the early accounts of the Jamestown and Massachusetts Bay Colonies as well as of the Jesuits in New France would allow students to compare the sense of newness, the use of divine right to justify imperial projects, and the determination to hold and civilize what was considered wilderness. Students can also compare and contrast the competing narratives of origin that emerge from these three imperial projects, as well as issues of millennialism, the role of poetry in the formation of the nation-state, America as an adopted "homeland," and the sex-gender systems imposed by the colonial regimes. Captivity narratives provide a fruitful comparison: Cabeza de Vaca with Mary Rowlandson, John Williams, or Father Isaac Jogues. Sor Juana Inés can be compared with Anne Bradstreet or Sarah Kemble Knight to illustrate differences in the experiences of colonial women in Catholic and Protestant traditions.

The Otermín and Vargas texts can be read with Villagrá's account of the resistance at Acoma a century earlier; stylistic differences arise from the roles the authors played within the imperial system. Villagrá chronicled his experience in the epic verse common to his time, free to fictionalize the events and characters, while Otermín and Vargas wrote in the governmental form that they were expected to use to report facts without embellishments.

Students can compare these texts with Thomas Morton's account of the massacre of the Wessaguscus by the Plymouth colonists. Also, they could consider the difference between the positive image of miscegenation in the Virgin of Guadalupe and the negative image of that possibility in Mary Rowlandson's captivity.

Questions for Reading, Discussion, and Writing

1. Ask students to review what they learned about this period in previous classes: who, what, where, when, why. Have them formulate a brief summary on the period according to this training. Have them compare it with the list of places and events you gave them at first, and then consider what the second list implies.
2. General assignments: Write about how this information changes their view of U.S. history. Write on the imagery used by the authors to characterize the New World.

3. Consider the role of violence in the colonization of the Americas.

   Specific possibilities: On Cabeza de Vaca: Compare his experience with Robinson Crusoe's. On Villagrá: Compare his version with the Native American one in the anthology selections.
4. Ask students to consider the moral and political issues surrounding the Hopi revolt in a contemporary setting. The particular locality and region in which your institution is located should fit the purpose, since it is difficult to find any place in the United States that did not experience a similar frontier situation at some point. Have them ponder what it would mean for them and their families to be forced to relinquish their property and return to their ancestors' homeland. What would they expect of their elected official, the court, the police, and the military?
5. Have students think of the Virgin of Guadalupe metaphorically as a figure of cultural confluence designed to ameliorate conflict among ethnic and racial groups. Ask them to consider if such figures could be useful now in the United States and if they have existed in our history. Is the model of hybridism (cultural and racial) viable in the United States?

Álvar Núñez Cabeza de Vaca (1490?–1556?)

Contributing Editor: Katherine E. Ledford

Classroom Issues and Strategies

The necessarily fragmentary nature of the excerpted sections from *La Relación* can frustrate students, causing them to feel lost themselves. Requiring students to read the author headnote with its outline of the "who/what/where" of the expedition provides a helpful structure for them to refer to as they travel with Cabeza de Vaca. While the particulars of Cabeza de Vaca's route are a subject of debate, bringing a map of the Gulf Coast, the Southwest, and Mexico into the classroom can drive home the point of the scope of this journey. Likewise, situating the expedition in the history of colonial exploitation of the New World via a discussion of Spanish economic and military dominance during the time places the issues Cabeza de Vaca raises, particularly in the Proem, in an international rather than Spanish national context. For some students, studying a "Spanish" text in an American literature course is perplexing. Redefining "America" away from a traditional Anglocentric focus by pointing out the impact of Spanish, French, *and* English exploration and settlement in all of North America will help students reconceptualize both America and American literature.

Major Themes, Historical Perspectives, Personal Issues

A major theme of *La Relación* is the reduction of Cabeza de Vaca, a well-born, powerful conquistador, to a desperate state—naked, cold, starving, alone, and near death—and his redemption from such circumstances by the power of religious faith, human perseverance, and the kindness of strangers. Reinventing himself as a healer and trader, Cabeza de Vaca adapts to the cultural and material facts of his new world, an alteration symbolic of the changes required of all immigrants and emblematic of the new American self emerging from contact between Europeans and Native Americans. The hybridization of Cabeza de Vaca, a Spaniard who "goes native" to such an extent that his fellow countrymen, when they stumble upon, him do not recognize him as European, speaks to the power of the American landscape, both physical and cultural, to effect the creation of a new American self. Cabeza de Vaca's total reliance on Native Americans for the necessities to sustain his life and his subsequent recognition of their humanity is a powerful personal alteration. The development of that change is interesting to trace and promotes a close, careful reading of the text.

Another major theme is the translation of novel landscapes, peoples, and cultural circumstances into a European system of signification. The Proem tackles this task most clearly with its translation of Cabeza de Vaca's "discoveries" into a unit of currency for colonial barter. Cabeza de Vaca does not return to the colonial capital with the traditional offering of gold, but presents information about the New World as an equal, if not more valuable, commodity. The amalgamation of his experiences in the wilderness, while effecting a personal transformation thematically linked with Christ's ordeal in the wilderness, for example, operates beyond him in a colonial system that privileges the collection of knowledge for economic exploitation's sake.

Perhaps the most prominent theme, at least the one cited most often by Cabeza de Vaca himself, is the breakdown of the casually religious individual preoccupied with worldly concerns and the gradual reconstruction of that person into a pious, religiously centered follower of Christ and worshipper of God. Many students find this transformation appealing and inspiring. Gingerly probing the utility of this central theme and examining its archetypal nature, while respecting the apparent sincerity of Cabeza de Vaca's turn toward the spiritual, allows students a multilayered view of authorial purpose.

Significant Form, Style, or Artistic Conventions

La Relación incorporates several elements of literary forms common to European texts written about New World exploration and conquest. Most prominent is the chronicle or report linked with the epistolary form. *La Relación* is both a personal account, or memoir, and a governmental document, a report of a civil servant's activity on behalf of the crown. Cabeza de Vaca was not a literary artist employing language and imagery for artistic purposes; however, his text displays sharp rhetorical skills and an attention to the well-formed, powerful sentence. An especially delicate issue to tease out of classroom discussions is the reliability of a text that purports to record personal experiences. Some students hesitate to question the text, comfortable in regarding the work as Cabeza de Vaca's lived experience and therefore "truthful," and need to be pushed to consider the issues that colored his reportage and shaped his story.

Original Audience

As was typical of the period, *La Relación* identifies the King of Spain as its intended audience through the Proem, an introductory letter addressed to him. Conventions of the time dictated that the king be the focal point of the public presentation of the text, but Cabeza de Vaca expected the king's advisers and ministers to read the document along with other interested members of the court and individuals who had, or wished to have, an economic interest in the exploration of the New World. The text also circulated across Europe, read by a more general audience interested in information about the New World. Attention to audience provides a neat entry point in classroom discussions to the role outside forces played in shaping the text.

Comparisons, Contrasts, Connections

La Relación compares nicely with other writings about New Spain collected in *The Heath Anthology*, especially the account by Christopher Columbus. Exploratory accounts from New France, the Chesapeake, and New England shed light on common European reactions to the physical space of the New World and its inhabitants. Tracing differing attitudes toward and treatment of Native Americans by the imperial powers places *La Relación* in a tradition of complex cultural encounter, one that forms the bedrock of the American experience. English accounts from Jamestown and the Massachusetts Bay Colonies along with narratives by Jesuits in New France offer the opportunity to explore the role religious conviction and the concept of divine right played in the conquest and exploitation of the New World. Comparing Cabeza de Vaca's account with the captivity narratives of Mary Rowlandson, John Williams, and Father Isaac Jogues provides an opportunity to examine the impact of larger governmental policies on individuals and to study systems of cultural identification and their centrality to the individual's identity.

Another intriguing source for comparison is the 1991 film *Cabeza de Vaca*, by Nicolás Echevarría, based on Cabeza de Vaca's journey. Echevarría creates several Native American characters and scenes not in *La Relación*, so it is a good idea to have students read the text before viewing the film. The film is not an exact rendering of *La Relación* and cannot substitute for the text. (A warning to students on this point might be appropriate.) It does, however, remain faithful to the themes and issues raised in *La Relación,* and its dramatization can interest students ambivalent to or put off by the sixteenth-century literary style of Cabeza de Vaca's text. The film is a powerful interpretation of the ordeal's effect upon one man and his European compatriots and a poignant statement about what contact heralded for Native Americans.

Working with Cultural Objects

Cabeza de Vaca's world of exploration, first contact, and wilderness may feel so foreign to students that they may have trouble engaging with the subjects of discussion through a reading of *La Relación* alone, especially given the text's sixteenth-century literary style. A gallery of images collected by the Cabeza de Vaca *Relación* Digitization and Access Project at Texas State University–San Marcos (see <http://www.library.txstate.edu/swwc/cdv/about/slideshow.html>) is valuable for stimulating conversations, especially among students inclined toward visual learning. The 1905 painting by Frederic Remington called *Cabeza de Vaca in the Desert* (<http://www.library.txstate.edu/swwc/cdv/about/remingtoncabeza.html>) is especially provocative because it takes some time to identify Cabeza de Vaca among his Native American companions. Comparing Remington's interpretation of Cabeza de Vaca with the more contemporary, traditional image of a well-born, Spanish emissary (<http://www.library.txstate.edu/swwc/cdv/about/cabeza.html>) drives home the hybridization of the man who resulted from this ordeal.

Controversy surrounds reconstructions of Cabeza de Vaca's route. A discussion of this issue, with links to scholarly articles outlining possible routes, is available at <http://www.library.txstate.edu/swwc/cdv/the_route/index.html>. Direct students to a map at <http://www.library.txstate.edu/swwc/cdv/the_route/whitehead.html> that superimposes three possible routes. Discuss the significance of the changes between the traditional routes in blue and black and the most recent, interdisciplinary reconstruction in red. The latest reconstruction has Cabeza de Vaca and his companions traveling much farther and much more extensively in what is now Mexico. You can use this map as a teaching tool to raise the issue of what is America and what is American literature. Does this reduction of the amount of time he spent in what would become Texas impact his standing as an "American" writer?

Questions for Reading, Discussion, and Writing

1. Consider the ways in which audience shapes the text. How might Cabeza de Vaca's account have differed if he were telling it to the king of another nation, a friend, or a native person in America?
2. Consider the circumstances of the text's composition. It was written after, not during, the eight-year ordeal. How might this have impacted the story Cabeza de Vaca tells? How does this fact make you regard detail in the narrative?
3. How does Cabeza de Vaca translate new landscapes, new peoples, and new experiences for a European reader? What types of imagery and symbolism does he use?
4. Does the inclusion of Cabeza de Vaca's account in an American literature course alter your concept of America and/or literature? In what ways is *La Relación* an American tale? Consider issues of immigration, exploitation, captivity, and transformation.
5. As a tale of religious awakening, *La Relación* focuses on Cabeza de Vaca's personal development. In what way, if any, does his transformation impact the people around him, specifically the Native Americans?

Bibliography

Adorno, Rolena, and Patrick Charles Pautz. *Alvar Núñez Cabeza de Vaca: His Account, His Life, and the Expedition of Pánfilo de Narváez.* Lincoln: U of Nebraska P, 1999.

Branch, Michael P. *Reading the Roots: American Nature Writing Before Walden.* Athens: U of Georgia P, 2004.

Howard, David. *A Conquistador in Chains: Cabeza de Vaca and the Indians of the Americas.* Tuscaloosa: U of Alabama P, 1997.

Krieger, Alex D., and Margery H. Krieger, eds. *We Came Naked and Barefoot: The Journey of Cabeza de Vaca across North America.* Austin: U of Texas P, 2002.

Wild, Peter. *Alvar Núñez Cabeza de Vaca.* Boise, MT: Boise State UP, 1991.

Wild, Peter. *The Opal Desert: Explorations of Fantasy and Reality in the American Southwest.* Austin: U of Texas P, 1999.

Williams, Jerry M., and Robert Earl Lewis, eds. *Early Images of the Americas: Transfer and Invention.* Tucson: U of Arizona P, 1993.

Wood, Michael. *Conquistadors.* Berkeley: U of California P, 2000.

Web Links

A comprehensive site collecting documents about Cabeza de Vaca and his journey, including an online text of *La Relación*: <http://www.library .txstate.edu/swwc/cdv>

Historical, biographical, cultural, and scientific information pertinent to Cabeza de Vaca's journey: <http://www.english.swt.edu/CSS/Vacaindex .HTML>

A segment of the PBS television program *Conquistadors* devoted to Cabeza de Vaca: <http://www.pbs.org/conquistadors/devaca/devaca_flat.html>

The website of an organization dedicated to scholarly research about Estevan-ico, an African enslaved by the Spanish and Portuguese and one of the four survivors of the expedition: <http://www.estevanico.org>

Information about the 1991 film *Cabeza de Vaca,* including synopsis, scene analyses, reviews, sound clips, and images: <http://www.lehigh.edu/~ ineng/pag2/pag2-title.html>

Information about Cabeza de Vaca's act of planting a cross near the present-day town of Ojinaga, Mexico, and the town's commemoration of that event: <http://www.ojinaga.com/cabeza/index.html>

Cluster: Cultural Encounters: A Critical Survey

Contributing Editor: Danielle Hinrichs

Classroom Issues and Strategies

This cluster encourages students to explore and imagine the many types of cultural encounters that took place in early America and to investigate how explanatory paradigms of encounter have shaped the formation of American literature by emphasizing certain types of stories. Students will likely be somewhat familiar with the idea of the frontier and will be able to contrast this explanation of encounter with others that emphasize North-South interactions, international cultural identities, and historically sporadic encounters in the same geographical region.

Major Themes, Historical Perspectives, Personal Issues

Turner's description of frontier is both binary and linear, suggesting only two groups of people in Early America: European, technologically advanced settlers and Native Americans, whose displacement, for Turner, represented the birth of American identity. Consider assignments and discussions that emphasize the multiplicity of Native American tribes and traditions and the diversity of settling groups. Spanish, French, English, and Dutch settlers all approached Native American tribes with different goals and strategies, and all were influenced differently by their interactions. Similarly, Cherokees, Iroquois, and Ho Chunk all had very different ways of approaching and responding to European settlers.

Disproportionate power relationships are central to understanding the dynamics of encounter. Encourage students to consider the types of power held by European colonists, by Native Americans, and by African slaves. How was the power structure unequal, and how did those with less power use cultural encounters to leverage what power they could achieve?

Significant Form, Style, or Artistic Conventions

Most of the excerpts in this section are from contemporary scholarly texts and contain some challenging terms and language. Encourage your students to look up difficult words in a dictionary and to read the passages more than once. Ask them to keep a list of important terms that recur throughout several of the excerpts and that demonstrate dialogue within an academic discourse community.

You might also remind your students that Frederick Jackson Turner's essay was presented as a speech before it was published. Have a student read the excerpt aloud. Do they recognize rhetorical strategies specific to Turner's oral context?

Original Audience

Frederick Jackson Turner announced the "closing" of the American frontier in an address to visitors of the 1893 World's Columbian Exposition in Chicago. The address received little immediate attention, but its influence grew quickly and continues to reach popular and scholarly audiences. Turner's original audience was fascinated with the notions of technological progress showcased in many of the fair's exhibits, and students might want to consider how the idea of progress in Turner's work is shaped by or reinforces other images of progress at the fair.

Comparisons, Contrasts, Connections

Many of the selections in *The Heath Anthology* could be read as literature of cultural encounter. Olaudah Equiano would be particularly relevant to Gilroy's ideas of transcontinental and interracial influence.

William Bradford's *Of Plymouth Plantation* represents a New England–centered encounter. Students might read this selection and discuss both the power and the limitations of this focus. Bradford's work also lends itself to an interesting discussion about the role of wilderness in encounter narratives and in Turner's description of the frontier.

Working with Cultural Objects

Looking at visual representations of the frontier encourages students to recognize the popular, lasting appeal of Turner's vision of the frontier and to begin asking questions about the reasons for this popularity. Distribute copies of John Gast's painting of *American Progress* (see <http://www.csubak.edu/~gsantos /img0061.html>) or have students find additional images that draw on or reinforce the assumptions of Turner's writings.

The University of Washington Library has an online collection that includes images of the frontier in history and in popular culture. Students might investigate these sources at <http://www.lib.washington.edu/exhibits /FRONTIER/Image/>.

Questions for Reading, Discussion, and Writing

1. At the end of the excerpt from "The Significance of the Frontier in American History," Turner says that to "study this advance, the men who grew up under these conditions, and the political, economic, and social results of it, is to study the really American part of our history." Who does Turner mean when he refers to "the men who grew up under these conditions"? Does he mean European men, Native American men, or both? Who is he including in his address when he refers to "our history"?

2. What is the role of Native American communities in Turner's description of the frontier? To what extent does Turner recognize more than one Native American community?

3. Turner suggests that the "wilderness masters the colonist" and then that the colonist "transforms the wilderness." What is the role of wilderness in the formation of American identity, and how is it related to notions of progress?

4. How does Wiget's description of Pueblo-based encounters between the Spanish and Native Americans complicate or question Turner's description of the frontier?

5. Describe the differences and similarities between encounters based on the goal of conquest and those based on intentions to convert. How would a conversion goal affect the way that two cultures approach and understand each other?

6. Kolodny wants to "eschew the myth of origins." What is the *myth of origins*? Which American origin stories are you familiar with, and why might Kolodny want to dismantle or discredit these narratives?

7. How is Mary Louise Pratt's "contact zone" different from or similar to Frederick Jackson Turner's version of "frontier"?

8. How does the phrase "cultural encounter" obscure or complicate racial categories? In what way are terms like *creolisation* or *hybridity* "more difficult" than *black* and *white*? In what ways are *creolisation* or *hybridity* "unsatisfactory"?

9. How does encounter create "cultural mutation" and "restless (dis)continuity"?

10. How is the concept of "trans-American imaginary" different from or similar to Pratt's notion of the "contact zone"?

11. How has the frontier paradigm lead to a focus on England and New England and excluded literatures "not written in English, literatures written in unofficial vernaculars, literatures that look South and West instead of North and East"?

New France

René Goulaine de Laudonnière (fl. 1562–1582)
Samuel de Champlain (1570?–1635)
The Jesuit Relations: The Account of
Father Isaac Jogues, 1647

Contributing Editors: John Pollack and Ivy Schweitzer

Classroom Issues and Strategies

Like the texts from New Spain, these texts will be unfamiliar to U.S. students of literature and history, as will be the prominence of France in the early colonization of North America. Students will probably know less about New France than about New Spain since there is no major contemporary movement in the United States to revise the history of French exploration and settlement in the Americas. But these texts can provide another opportunity for students to reconsider the monocultural and monolinguistic origins of U.S. culture. One could ask students to think about political, linguistic, and cultural issues in Canada, the largest nation in North America, and how Canadian policies on the issues of bilingualism, native (or first peoples') rights, and assimilationism differ from U.S. policies. How do U.S. relations with and attitudes about Canada differ from relations with and attitudes about Mexico in the South?

Major Themes, Historical Perspectives, Personal Issues

One might begin with a brief overview of the history of French exploration and settlement in the New World (consult the introduction, "Colonial Period to 1700") and the history of the conflicts between France and Spain over Florida, and later between France and England in northern North America. Particularly important is a clarification of the religious issues and their impact on imperial projects in the New World. Spain's colonial emissaries were Roman Catholic, and their missionaries came from the Dominican, Jesuit, and Franciscan orders. English colonialism was carried out largely by Protestant groups who demonized Catholics and regarded their missionizing as satanic seduction. France's Catholic kings had a more ambivalent relationship with Rome and saw themselves as head of a national church. Like England, France experienced a Protestant Reformation in the mid-sixteenth century; its adherents were called Huguenots, who suffered persecution and suppression. Several groups of Huguenots, like the English Pilgrims and Puritans in New England, attempted to establish colonies in French-claimed regions of the New World but were defeated and ejected by the Spanish. The spread of Protestantism caused a Counter-Reformation across Europe, out of which emerged the Jesuits in Spain, a group of Catholic priests with an active, rather than a contemplative, mission to spread Christianity to as wide an area as possible, from neglected regions in rural and urban Europe to India, China, Japan, and the Americas. Jesuit methods included open-air preaching and the use of catechisms in order to instruct children. In Europe, the Jesuits enjoyed remarkable success, but in Canada the results were more mixed. Jesuits sought to induce nomadic Native groups to settle in villages near the French in order to minister to them more regularly, but few Native groups accommodated them. The missionaries also attempted to impose monogamy and a European-style sexual division of labor upon Natives; Native women seem to have been particularly resistant to this tactic.

Significant Form, Style, or Artistic Conventions

The three selections in this section represent three different kinds of writing. Laudonnière was a Huguenot nobleman who served under Jean Ribault and helped establish, first, the colony at Port Royal, South Carolina, and when this failed, Fort Carolina in Florida. After his defeat by the Spanish, Laudonnière, who had been wounded in the fight, escaped to France and wrote a history of the colony that remained unpublished for twenty years. Like other early colonial writers, his account is a personal memoir inflected by political motives, specifically a critique of Huguenot activities and actions. Champlain acquired a reputation as a navigator from expeditions to the West Indies and Central America, so he was invited to go to North America in 1603, where he retraced Jacques Cartier's earlier trip up the St. Lawrence in 1534–1535. When his report was published, it sparked interest in further exploration and settlement, especially when an English colonial expedition spent a winter in Kennebec (now Maine) in southern Acadia in 1607. A commoner given an honorary title by Henry IV, Champlain would have had a basic education; his reports (seven in all) are factual narratives interested in landscape and the resources for settlement. He was instrumental in allying with the Algonquina and Montagnais against the Iroquois, and so was also interested in native culture to the extent that it impacted on his colonization efforts. Father Isaac Jogues was a Jesuit on a mission to the Huron Indians. His account was compiled by his superior, Jerome Lalement, with the particular intent of all the Jesuit *Relations*: to justify the missions in the New World and glorify the sacrifice of the missionaries.

Original Audience

Laudonnière and Champlain were writing for an educated French audience, people at court with the money and influence to enhance France's colonial efforts. Laudonnière's account, as a religious adventure, attracted a wide audience in Protestant Europe. Champlain's books were read by elite audiences fascinated with accounts of the New World. Jogues's account is only a short excerpt from a remarkable output of Jesuit documents that runs to seventy-three volumes covering two centuries in the standard modern edition (ed. Thwaites). In seventeenth-century France, the *Relations* were bestsellers, circulating widely among the royalty and elite, as perhaps among the marginally literate as well, as part of the Counter-Reformation movement in France.

Comparisons, Contrasts, Connections

Laudonnière can be compared with other colonists who observed native customs, such as Champlain, Columbus, Cabeza de Vaca, and John Smith. Champlain's accounts express the European's response to the expanse and wildness of the New World, and can be compared with the extravagant rhetoric of Fray Marcos de Niza and the failed expeditions of Coronado, as recorded by Pedro de Casteñeda, as well as the ideologically motivated descriptions of the land by Thomas Morton, William Bradford, and Samuel Sewall.

   The relation of Father Jogues raises several points of comparison. One is the central political and economic role assigned to the Jesuits in New France by Cardinal Richelieu, contrasted with the marginal position of John Eliot and Puritan missionaries in New England, and the almost complete lack of English missionary efforts in Virginia. (A group of English Jesuits spent only a brief time in Maryland during the 1630s.) Like missionaries in New Spain, the Jesuits were central figures in the colonial regime; however, they enjoyed far less military support than their Spanish counterparts. It is interesting to compare missionary methods among the French, Spanish, and English, and the attitudes they had about each other. Roger Williams and John Williams are scathing in their condemnation of Jesuit methods of conversion. Students also have to come to terms with the remarkable strength of the Jesuit religious conviction. They can think about Father Jogues's *Relation* as a captivity narrative and consider how it contrasts rather sharply with what we have come to regard as the originary "American" captivities of Cabeza de Vaca and Mary Rowlandson. Jogues never doubts himself or his faith and appears entirely prepared to submit to kidnapping and torture in the fulfillment of his mission. The strength of the Hurons' faith is equally remarkable, although both can be read as textual "creations" by Jesuit editors who, seeking to gather support for their cause among French readers, shaped their *Relation* to privilege a particular religious interpretation of events in which Jogues and the Huron converts are martyrs suffering intense earthly pains but winning eternal glory for their cause.

Jogues's *Relation* can also be compared with English and Spanish texts in terms of the way the narrative voice spiritualizes the landscape, and the comfort it feels in this alien place. The graphic nature of this account serves to remind us of the violence and bloodshed endemic in colonial North America, often glossed over in other accounts. The narrative also illustrates the interrelationships among competing colonial groups (a map is of great benefit here): in a few pages, Jogues passes from Quebec, to the Huron country, to Mohawk villages, and to the Dutch settlement at Fort Orange. Finally, students can compare the way this narrative represents native people, their customs, and their thinking about captives and missionaries with the representations by Laudonnière, Champlain, Columbus, Casteñeda, Roger Williams, and Cotton Mather. To what extent does Jogues engage in the construction of "good" and "bad" Indians, from his very interested point of view?

Questions for Reading, Discussion, and Writing

1. As with the selections from New Spain, you can ask students to consider the role of violence in the colonization of the Americas.
2. Students can compare/contrast the representation each of these texts gives of the New World, the native populations, and the possibilities for colonization and think about the differences in terms of the audience and intentions of the texts.
3. In the twentieth century, Jesuit accounts have been used by anthropologists, linguists, folklorists, historians, and literary critics seeking information about French and Native cultures in the seventeenth and eighteenth centuries. But what is the value of these texts as historical "evidence"? To what extent do we "hear" Native voices in an account such as Jogues's? What can and can't we learn about the Jesuits, the Hurons, or the Mohawks from this piece?

Chesapeake

Thomas Harriot (1560–1621)

Contributing Editor: Thomas Scanlan

Classroom Issues and Strategies

It was not until 1585, almost a full century after Christopher Columbus had claimed vast portions of the New World for Spain, that an English expedition, led by Sir Richard Grenville, established a colony on Roanoke Island in what is today part of North Carolina's Outer Banks. Sponsored by Sir Walter Raleigh, Grenville's expedition followed the voyage to Roanoke led by Arthur Barlowe and Philip Amadas in the previous year. Thomas Harriot's *A Briefe and True Report of the New Found Land of Virginia* renders an account of what he and the other members of Grenville's expedition team found in their voyage. Accompanying Harriot and the others on that expedition was John White who, having sailed with Martin Frobisher in 1577 in his exploration of Greenland and Baffin Island, was already a veteran explorer by the time he joined Grenville in 1585. White would of course become better known as the governor of the ill-fated second Roanoke colony. The members of this so-called "lost" colony set sail from England in May of 1587. While White himself returned to England for supplies shortly after he arrived in Virginia, those who stayed behind at the Roanoke colony had vanished by the time White reached the area again in 1590 with the needed supplies. Although the mysterious disappearance of the Roanoke colonists significantly dampened English enthusiasm for colonial adventure, Thomas Harriot's pamphlet was published at a moment when the English were feeling very optimistic about their affairs both at home and abroad. Fifteen-hundred-and-eighty-eight, the year Harriot's *Briefe and True Report* was published, was also the year that the English defeated the Spanish Armada. Moreover, Harriot's readers would not yet have known of the fate of the second Roanoke colony.

Comparisons, Contrasts, Connections

There are basically two ways to approach Harriot's *A Briefe and True Report*: either from a comparative perspective or from an Anglo-American one. In the comparative frame, Harriot works well when read alongside other narratives of early European contact with America and its native people. Instructors, therefore, might wish to pair Harriot with one or more of the following authors: Columbus, Cabeza de Vaca, or Champlain. Students could be asked to compare the attitudes of these writers toward the notion of colonial undertaking, generally speaking: Do they seem to have the same goals in embarking on colonial voyages? Do they write their accounts for the same reasons? Are they taken aback by anything they see or do? More specifically, students could be asked to compare the attitudes of the various writers toward the native people they encounter: What sorts of details do they choose to give us? Do they seem to view the native people as a resource to exploit or as potential neighbors? Do they seem to admire the native inhabitants?

Read as one of the earliest chapters in the English colonization of America, Harriot might be paired with Thomas Morton, William Bradford, Roger Williams, or Mary Rowlandson. Each of these writers offers students a different version of the English colonial mindset. Students could be asked to find similarities as well as differences among the five, and then they could be asked to account for what they find. For example, can one see an evolution of a colonial ideology from Harriot to Rowlandson? Does English colonial writing appear to be monolithic or heterogeneous? Is there anything in Harriot's text that seems to anticipate the negative views toward the Indians in the writings of Bradford and Rowlandson? Finally, can Harriot be useful as background for reading nineteenth-century texts that portray Native Americans—for example, Sedgwick and Cooper?

Working with Cultural Objects

Whether one reads Harriot comparatively or not, one will want to be sure to consider introducing students to the spectacular images that accompanied the second edition (1590) of Harriot's text. These copperplate engravings by Theodor DeBry were based on the watercolor drawings of John White, who accompanied Harriot to the New World in 1585. Influenced both by the accounts of explorers returning from the New World and by the prevailing artistic conventions of the day, DeBry's stunning engravings can complete a picture that Harriot's text seems only to gesture at. By examining these images, students will see the extent to which early settlers felt genuine admiration for the native people they encountered. But they will also see the extent to which Europeans tended to infantilize the natives, often treating them as nothing more than wild children desperately in need of European civilization. DeBry's images have been widely reproduced and are available online at <http://www.docsouth.unc.edu/nc/hariot/hariot/html>.

Edward Maria Wingfield (1560?–1613?)

Contributing Editor: Liahna Babener

Classroom Issues and Strategies

Despite its centrality in the colonization of America, there is very little particular data and few firsthand accounts of the Jamestown enterprise. A comparison with other eyewitness accounts (John Smith, Richard Frethorne) helps clarify and balance Wingfield's point of view. Presentation of background on the settlement history of Jamestown is also useful, as is a review of the political, religious, and social issues that shaped colonization experiences in various regions of America, particularly New England, the Middle Colonies, and the South.

Students are most interested in the problems of maintaining discipline, managing provisions, and fostering cooperation. They like to explore the contrasts between settlements undergirded by strong religious ideology and those driven by economic ambitions (often reluctantly concluding that the former are more "successful" if also more regimented communities). Students also debate whether Wingfield is too timorous, whether he pads his case, and whether he manipulates their sympathies.

Major Themes, Historical Perspectives, Personal Issues

1. The problem of leadership and political authority in early colonial government. Class, economic, and political conflicts among constituencies of colonists. The impact of these issues on the evolution of colonial democracy. Relations between New World and mother country.
2. Wingfield's personal strengths and failings as a colonial administrator. The conflicts between the drive toward anarchy and the pressure for authoritarian government, in which Wingfield is poised precariously between the two.
3. Conditions of life at Jamestown, including class stresses, daily life and its deprivations, illness and calamity, the absence of women, etc.
4. Can we begin to discern an image of America (as a culture in its own right, as distinct from its English occupants) in this document?
5. In what ways does the Jamestown experience, as Wingfield tells it, reflect the fact that it was an all-male society?

Significant Form, Style, or Artistic Conventions

We may view this document as a political treatise, apologia, manifesto, historical chronicle, and memoir. A consideration of the conventions of each genre and a comparison with other examples of each from the colonial period is illuminating. We may use it to discern the ethos of a male English gentleman and explore the collision between his worldview and the realities of life in Virginia under the devastating stresses of colonization.

Original Audience

Because the document is a self-defense, it is useful to determine whom Wingfield meant to address and how his particular argument might appeal to his implicit audience. Would investors in the Virginia Company respond differently from fellow colonists? Would upper-class readers respond differently from the working class? Which groups might be alienated by his self-portrait and vision of leadership?

Comparisons, Contrasts, Connections

Compare accounts of the Jamestown settlement and issues of colonial governance by John Smith (*A True Relation of Occurrences and Accidents in Virginia*, 1608, and *General History of Va.*, 1624) and Richard Frethorne ("Letters to His Parents"). Other documents that explore the pressures facing colonial executives and the crises of colonization and community include Bradford's *Of Plymouth Plantation* and Morton's *The New English Canaan*. Especially suitable for its parallel case of deposed leadership and its differing vision of government is John Winthrop's "Speech to the General Court" included in his *Journal*. What differences between religiously and economically motivated settlements can be seen?

Questions for Reading, Discussion, and Writing

1. (a) Discern the underlying worldview of Wingfield, taking into account his background as an upper-middle-class male Englishman and perhaps a Catholic.
   (b) Identify his various strategies of self-justification. Are you sympathetic? Why or why not? Do you think his audience is won over? Explain.

    (c)   Which issues seem more imperative: political struggles over power or economic struggles for provisions? What about military concerns about the colony's safety from Indians?

2. (a)   Compare Wingfield's style of leadership with Bradford's, Morton's, Winthrop's, John Smith's.

    (b)   Re-create a vivid picture of daily life at Jamestown.

    (c)   How might the situation have been different if women had been present in the colony from the outset? If Wingfield had been an artisan or worker?

    (d)   What were the particular obstacles to effective governance at Jamestown?

Bibliography

There is surprisingly little particularized history of Jamestown. Wingfield appears as a footnote or brief entry in most textbooks or historical accounts of the Jamestown colony. In John C. Miller's chapter "The Founding of Virginia" in *This New Man, The American: The Beginnings of the American People* (1974) there is a substantive and articulate account of the colony's story. Richard Morton's treatment of the same material in the first two chapters of Vol. 1 of *Colonial Virginia* (1960) is also useful and very detailed, though, again, it does not contain much express material on Wingfield.

John Smith (1580–1631)

Contributing Editor: Amy E. Winans

Major Themes, Historical Perspectives, Personal Issues

Since the time of their writing, Smith's works have evoked wildly divergent responses from readers: Smith has been viewed both as a self-aggrandizing and inaccurate historian and as the savior of the Virginia colony and friend to Native Americans. For example, one historian, Karen Ordahl Kupperman, has suggested that Smith's writing was most self-consciously literary—and therefore most historically suspect—in those passages that recount his interchanges with Powhatan. Interestingly, she and others also contend that Smith offered his readers a fairly reliable ethnographic account of Native American life. Students might usefully examine the process of Smith's self-fashioning that has evoked this variety of responses. Such an examination could also provide the basis for a discussion of the opposition between the New England and Virginian models of colonization as well as strategies of self-representation.

Comparisons, Contrasts, Connections

Smith's individualized portrait of Powhatan is unique among early writers, who often referred to Native Americans in much more generic terms, typically invoking a Manichean allegory. Still, these selections can usefully be compared with the selections from Roger Williams, Thomas Morton, and William Bradford. Consider, for example, the differences between Smith's account of Powhatan and Bradford's accounts of Samoset, Squanto, and the Pequot War. As background for this discussion, review differences between the Jamestown settlement and the Massachusetts settlements. Smith should also be examined in the context of the other Jamestown writers included in the anthology: Richard Frethorne and Edward Wingfield.

Working with Cultural Objects

I have found it helpful to broaden students' understanding of colonial discourse, storytelling, and history writing by examining a brief excerpt from the conclusion of Disney's film *Pocahontas* after we have discussed Smith's writing. Consider similarities and differences between the rhetorical strategies of the colonial text and the contemporary film.

Bibliography

Greene, Jack P. *Pursuits of Happiness: The Social Development of Early Modern British Colonies and the Formation of American Culture.* Chapel Hill: U of North Carolina P, 1988. See Chapter 1 for a useful comparative social history of Virginia and New England.

Kupperman, Karen Ordahl. *Indians and English: Facing Off in Early America.* Ithaca: Cornell UP, 2000.

Tilton, Robert S. *Pocahontas: The Evolution of an American Narrative.* New York: Cambridge UP, 1994.

Richard Frethorne (fl. 1623)

Contributing Editors: Liahna Babener and Ivy Schweitzer

Classroom Issues and Strategies

Virtually no historical data about Frethorne is available, but we can place him in the context of the Jamestown colony since he settled near that village. He also draws a revealing picture of the deteriorating relations between the English settlers and the Indians that is consistent with the history of Jamestown in the period between the two attacks on the colony by the Powhatan chief Openchancanough. The first, which Frethorne refers to, occurred in 1622 and the second in 1641. Both attacks were in retaliation for specific incidents of murder and depredation on the part of the English, but were responses, more generally, to English expansion into native lands and the resulting erosion of native lifeways.

The writer's candor about his own experience is compelling. He used vivid details to describe his discontent, deprivation, and discomfort. The small specifics of daily life (quantities and kinds of food, items of clothing, catalogs of implements) and the data of survival and death (lists of deceased colonists, trade and barter statistics, numerical estimates of enemy Indians and their military strength, itemized accounts of provisions, and rations records) lend credibility to Frethorne's dilemma and enable students to empathize with his distress.

Students respond to reading Frethorne with questions like these:

What happened to Frethorne?

Did he remain in the New World, return home, or die?

Did he receive provisions from his parents?

Why is there no other historical record of his life or his fate?

Why was there so much rancor over provisions, and why couldn't the English authorities address the scarcity?

Major Themes, Historical Perspectives, Personal Issues

Invite students to imaginatively re-create, through the details in the text, the world Frethorne inhabited, gleaning his worldview as a white, Christian, European (English), and presumably working-class man. What assumptions does he make about the mission of settlement, the character of the New World, the nature of the native peoples, the relationships between colonists? What does he expect in terms of comfort and satisfaction? What class attitudes does he reveal? Compare his implicit vision of the New World with the region he actually encounters. What religious, social, political, and ethical beliefs does he bring to his account, and how do they shape his view of his experience? What can be inferred about the constraints upon indentured servants—and the lives they led—from Frethorne's record?

Significant Form, Style, or Artistic Conventions

1. Consider the "letter" as a literary genre, exploring issues of format, voice, reliability and self-consciousness of speaker, assumed audience, etc.
2. Discuss the letter as a social history document as well as a personal record and literary construct.
3. Discuss the strategies of persuasion and justification employed by the speaker. How does he win over his parents' support and pity through rhetorical tactics as well as emotional expression?
4. Consider the literary precedents and background of biblical allusion related to Frethorne's letter.

Comparisons, Contrasts, Connections

1. Use other letters and firsthand accounts from colonists in the New World: cf. letter from "Pond," a young Massachusetts settler, to his parents in Suffolk, England (repr. in Demos, John, ed., *Remarkable Providences, 1600–1760*. New York: Braziller, 1972, p. 73).
2. Use Pond to compare New England and Jamestown experiences.
3. Use chronicles by Bradford, Smith, and Wingfield—recording both personal and communal life in the colonies—to discover the diversity of such experiences and the impact of his background and ethos upon Frethorne's viewpoint in these letters. Use women's accounts to identify gender issues.
4. Compare Frethorne's account of his indenture to James Revel's account of his experience as a transported felon a half a century later. Has the life of an indentured servant changed much with the economic expansion of the colony?

Questions for Reading, Discussion, and Writing

1. (a) Invite students to itemize the basic assumptions (worldview components) that Frethorne brings to his experience—these then become the

basis for class discussion (as we discern them from evidence in the document).

(b) Ask students to try to determine what aspects of Frethorne's appeal have been calculated to move his parents to aid him. How does he use persuasive and manipulative techniques (or does he?) to affect them?

2. (a) Write out responses to (a) and (b) above.

(b) Using other primary sources, imaginatively re-create the world of Jamestown by inventing your own letter or diary entry or newspaper story or other fabricated "document" that conveys a vivid sense of colonial life.

(c) Write an imagined reply from Frethorne's parents.

Bibliography

A good description of the events at Jamestown from the native as well as the English perspective is Frederic W. Gleach, *Powhatan's World and Colonial Virginia: A Conflict of Cultures* (Lincoln: U of Nebraska P), 1997.

Nathaniel Bacon (1647–1677)

Contributing Editor: Jim Egan

Classroom Issues and Strategies

Students are often interested in the circumstances surrounding Bacon's writing. How did it circulate if not through publication, and who were its readers? A discussion of the circumstances of its production can lead to an investigation of a variety of early modern cultural attitudes and presuppositions. For instance, you might have students examine the different notions of the purposes and goals of publication, the different ways in which communities were organized prior to the market-driven conceptions that modern students tend to bring to the classroom, and the different notions of authorship that dominated the early modern period. Such a discussion might also profitably lead into a consideration of the notions regarding rank and status on which the manifesto and declaration—and the rebellion itself—rely.

Major Themes, Historical Perspectives, and Personal Issues

Any number of themes emerge in these documents. Some major ones include

1. The racial classification of not only the Native American population but also the English colonists
2. The battle over who can claim legitimate authority in the colonial environment
3. The nature of rebellion
4. The relationship of the "people" to their "rulers"

Significant Form, Styles, or Artistic Conventions

A reading of the manifesto and declaration provides the occasion for a discussion of what constitutes literature. In other words, you might want to ask your students why such seemingly nonliterary works are included in an anthology of American literature, and what this inclusion tells us about the period under study as well as the period in which we now live. Indeed, such questions can sometimes lead students to interrogate the very goals of literary studies. What is to be gained, they might ask, from studying this text in a literature class? Alternatively, what gets lost in the attention to such "nonliterary" forms?

Original Audience

Bacon's manifesto and declaration first circulated in manuscript form in Virginia during the rebellion. Within a year it had made its way across the Atlantic to England, and when it did, it became part of various—and sometimes conflicting—published accounts of the rebellion produced, in the first place, to influence English public opinion regarding the rebellion. The document became part of continuing efforts by those in England to sway public sentiment not only for or against colonization schemes in the first place but also for or against various ways of governing those colonies.

Comparisons, Contrasts, and Connections

Since many historians have used Bacon's Rebellion as a pivotal point in the transformation of racial and political attitudes, the manifesto and declaration can be read in relation to earlier works concerning the Native Americans as well in comparison with later works by writers such as Paine and Jefferson.

Working with Cultural Objects

Most websites devoted to a comprehensive guide to American history contain references to and often detailed narratives of the events and characters of Bacon's Rebellion. To help your students see the rebellion from a more material-ist perspective, you might have students visit <http://www.vahistorical .org/sva2003/bacon.htm>. This site contains an image of a manuscript copy of "Bacon's Epitaph," a very brief poem eulogizing the leader of the rebellion. They can get a better sense of the material objects used during the war by going to <http://www.apva.org/apva/bacons_castle_rebellion.php>, which has pictures of a house and artifacts purportedly used by Bacon's group as shelter during the rebellion.

Questions for Reading, Discussion, and Writing

Bacon's work raises questions about the nature of authority in colonial Virginia. The following are some possible topics for discussion.

1. On what basis does Bacon seek to establish his authority with his readers? What kinds of terms does he invoke, in other words, to convince his readers that he, rather than the governor, should be believed?
2. How does Bacon defend his treatment of the Indians in the rebellion? What kinds of terms does he use to differentiate his own treatment of Native Americans from that of the governor's party? Is there any way that these two conflicting portraits of Native Americans inform the way Bacon wants us to understand the colonists themselves?

Bibliography

Allen, Theodore. *The Invention of the White Race*. Vol. 2. London: Verso, 1997.

Brown, Kathleen M. *Good Wives, Nasty Wenches, and Anxious Patriarchs: Gender, Race, and Power in Colonial Virginia*. Chapel Hill: U of North Carolina P, 1996.

Morgan, Edmund S. *American Slavery—American Freedom: The Ordeal of Colonial Virginia*. New York: Norton, 1975.

Webb, Stephen. *1676: The End of Independence*. New York: Knopf, 1985.

James Revel (after 1640s–?)

Contributing Editor: Jim Egan

Classroom Issues and Strategies

The poem lends itself to a consideration of popular cultural forms circulating during the period. It can be used to stimulate discussion on the different kinds of literature available to readers at the time, and it can be used to help students see the didactic nature of much of that material. As such, it can also serve as a stimulus for students to consider the various purposes to which literature has been and is put. It can be used, in other words, to discuss the kind of work literature might be said to perform in a culture. Indeed, since the author and date of the poem are in dispute, the very importance of attributing a poem to a particular person can be interrogated. In addition, the poem raises historical questions for many students. Were such scenarios common, they might ask, for instance, and how accurate is this portrayal? Once the question of historical veracity or lack thereof has been addressed, the work such poetry did in creating a vision of the colonies—however accurate—in England can be investigated.

Major Themes, Historical Perspectives, and Personal Issues

The following are some of the principal themes that emerge in this poem, but this brief list hardly exhausts the poem's thematic potential.

1. The colonies as a source for personal and spiritual rejuvenation
2. The relationship between labor and identity
3. The relationship between racial and national identity in the figure of the slaves working side by side with the narrator
4. The figure of the transported felon as a type in literature relating to the colonies

Significant Form, Styles, or Artistic Conventions

The poem combines musical with poetic forms. Given its status as an object meant to be consumed by as broad a public as possible, the work lends itself to a consideration of the styles that contemporaries considered accessible to such a reading public. It relies on generic conventions, in other words, that differ from many "canonical" poems of the period in its simplicity of form and style and, as such, asks us to consider how the style tells us something about how a culture at large is imagined.

Original Audience

Given that the date of the poem has yet to be established, the original audience is itself a matter for debate. The earliest known printed version appeared in the eighteenth century as a chapbook, a form that was usually undated and often anonymous. These works were generally cheaply produced and sold at relatively inexpensive prices in the hopes of drawing an extensive audience of literate but not elite consumers.

Comparisons, Contrasts, and Connections

Revel's poem makes a wonderful comparison with works by the New England Puritan poets such as Bradstreet, Wigglesworth, and Taylor in that this work can help students see more precisely what those poets were trying to accomplish and the underlying assumptions about the relationship between literature and reading that animate these very different poems. It allows one to help students understand, in other words, the differing outlooks on colonization and community operating in the different colonial regions. The poem also lends itself to some very productive contrasts with many other works of the period that seek to show the relationship between the colonies and England.

Working with Cultural Objects

Students can get a better sense of just what a broadside looked like by visiting either of two sites, <http://www.nls.uk/broadsides/broadside.cfm/id/15166> and/or <http://www.docsouth.unc.edu/southlit/revel/menu.html>. Each of these sites contains images of editions of Revel's poem as well as background information on, in the first case, the broadside tradition and, in the second, the literature of the American South.

Questions for Reading, Discussion, and Writing

1. How does this poem cast the social settings that the narrator inhabits? What, in other words, are the defining features of English society, according to this poem, and what are the defining features of colonial Virginia society? Does the poem suggest any relation between the two?
2. The narrator begins and ends the poem in England. What function or functions, then, does the image of America serve in this poem?
3. Discuss the image of the family in this poem. How does it compare with the use of the family in other works relating to colonial British America?

Bibliography

Preston, Cathy L., and Michael Preston, eds. *The Other Print Tradition: Essays on Chapbooks, Broadsides, and Related Ephemera.* New York: Garland, 1995.

Shields, David. *Civil Tongues and Polite Letters in British America.* Chapel Hill: U of North Carolina P, 1997.

——. "Literature of the Colonial South." *Resources for American Literary Study* 19 (1993): 174–222.

Spufford, Margaret. *Small Books and Pleasant Histories: Popular Fiction and Its Readership in Seventeenth-Century England.* Athens: U of Georgia P, 1982.

New England

Thomas Morton (1579?–1647?)

Contributing Editor: Kenneth Alan Hovey

Original Audience

Most students have some knowledge of Puritans and their role in the settlement of New England, but very few are familiar with pioneering Cavaliers like Morton. His values, therefore, and their relation to the more familiar swash-buckling Cavaliers of Europe need to be carefully explained. According to his own self-description, Morton was the university-educated son of a soldier, devoted to the British crown and old English ways, and a staunch supporter of the Church of England, its liturgy, and its holy days.

His portrait of the Indians is an attempt to show how, despite their uncivilized state, they share many values with the traditional Englishmen whom he takes to be his audience. The Indians' personal modesty, hospitality to strangers, respect for authority, and even religious views mirror those of England, and their contentment surpasses that of the English because of their greater closeness to nature. They are swashbucklers without the trappings of Europe, indulging in pleasures because they are natural and upholding author-ity because it allows indulgence. By contrast, the Pilgrims appear to be ill-educated rabble-rousers who despise all tradition and authority. Devoid even of common humanity, they serve their own self-glorifying appetites and deny the bounty that nature has left open to all.

Comparisons, Contrasts, Connections

Morton is best read beside Bradford to bring out the full contrast between their views of Cavaliers, Indians, and Pilgrims. Morton also provides an interesting contrast in style to Bradford. Both works are highly rhetorical, but where Bradford uses his rhetoric to magnify God and humbly to minimize his poor persecuted people, Morton uses his to satirize those same people and to flaunt the superiority of his own wit and learning. All students should be able to pick out the clear cases of Morton's fictionalizing, especially in the account of Standish's response to Morton's escape, and some may see how he used *Don Quixote* and medieval romance to shape his own mock-romance.

The contrast between Morton and Bradford can serve not only to establish the relative credibility of the two authors and the nature of their rhetoric, but to raise important moral questions about the whole colonial endeavor, especially with respect to the Indians. Were the Pilgrims, for instance, inhumane in denying the Indians firearms? Did Morton display true humanity in encouraging the Indians, male and female, to party with him and his men? To what extent could both groups be called hypocritical? Did British culture corrupt natural Indian ways, or did Indian ways corrupt in different ways both the industrious Pilgrims and the pleasure-loving Cavaliers? Can the meeting of two such different cultures ever bring out the best in both, especially when each is itself divided into tribes or factions? Such questions rise naturally from much of colonial literature but perhaps most glaringly from Morton's work.

In addition to the contrast afforded by reading Morton and Bradford together, instructors can also consider pairing Morton with Thomas Harriot, Roger Williams, or Mary Rowlandson. All of these writers wrote about their contacts with Indians. Students might be asked whether religion seems to influence the authors' views of the Indians. (Williams and Rowlandson were Puritans while Harriot and Morton were not.) Students might also be asked whether they perceive any sort of progression or evolution in the English attitudes toward the Indians from the early contacts to the late seventeenth century. Finally, students should be asked to file away their impressions of these early writings so that they might revisit them later on when they read such writers as James Fenimore Cooper, Catharine Maria Sedgwick, and William Cullen Bryant.

John Winthrop (1588–1649)

Contributing Editor: Nicholas D. Rombes Jr.

Classroom Issues and Strategies

The sweeping nature of the *Journal* encompasses social, political, economic, and "daily survival" issues. Thus, it might be wise to focus on an area, or areas, at least to begin with. When looking at cultural or historical implications, consult supplemental information. That is, although Winthrop's writings illuminate his biases and assumptions, they "shape" the history of the period as well as record it.

Students are generally shocked by the rigidity of Winthrop's view of the world. Their shock may be addressed by consulting outside sources (e.g., on the Hutchinson affair) and making them aware of Winthrop's assumptions concerning power, patriarchy, etc., as well as the position and voice of women in the Puritan community. However, it might be wise to note, as well, how our twentieth-century notions of what is fair and unfair can sometimes impose themselves upon the cultural environment Winthrop was operating within. Winthrop and the Puritans should be approached not only as philosophical, political, and religious figures but also as real people who struggled daily against nature, hunger, and disease.

Students are often curious about the distinctions among the Covenant of Works, the Covenant of Grace, and the Elect. You might explore the notion of community and social structures and the role of the individual in these structures, or you could discuss the Bible as a typological model for the Puritans, as well as Puritan conceptions of original depravity, limited atonement, grace, and predestination.

Major Themes, Historical Perspectives, Personal Issues

Certainly, based on the selections in this anthology, it would be fruitful to focus on the Hutchinson controversy and its implications for the Puritan oligarchy. Examine the early Puritans' conception of liberty and its inextricable connections with their obligation to God. Likewise, the notion of a "city upon a hill" and the Puritans' link between America and the "new Israel" is important. You could discuss as well the providential interpretation of events and the nature of hierarchy in the Puritan community.

Significant Form, Style, or Artistic Conventions

Winthrop had training as a lawyer; the style and form of *A Modell of Christian Charity* reflect this. Likewise, the entire self-reflexive nature of the *Journal* lends itself to examination: Who was Winthrop's audience? Where does the *Journal* belong in the convention of the personal narrative or spiritual autobiography? What was his purpose for writing?

Original Audience

Recent examinations of *A Modell of Christian Charity* suggest that the sermon was not only intended for those who would soon be settling in America but also for those who were growing weary (and by implication becoming disruptive) during the long voyage aboard the *Arbella*. In what ways was Winthrop's audience (especially in the *Journal*) himself?

Comparisons, Contrasts, Connections

Perhaps compare Winthrop's sermons with those of Jonathan Edwards (who was writing a century later). Note how the style changed, as did the emphasis on religious experience (the experience becomes more sensory and less restrained). Compare Winthrop's vision of God's grace with Roger Williams's vision.

Questions for Reading, Discussion, and Writing

1. (a) What motivated the Puritans to flee England?
   (b) Did the Puritans have a "blueprint" for organizing their new communities, or did the social structure evolve slowly?
   (c) From what type of social, cultural, religious, and economic background did Winthrop emerge?
2. (a) Examine Winthrop's 1645 speech in which he responds to charges that he exceeded his authority as governor. Is this speech a fruition (or expression) of the Puritan ambiguity between the value of religion and the value of individual liberty?
   (b) How did the Hutchinson controversy potentially threaten the Puritan oligarchy?
   (c) Explore the "spiritual autobiography" and its characteristics. What philosophical purposes did it serve? What pragmatic purposes?
   (d) In *Modell*, have students trace image patterns Winthrop uses, that is, allusions to biblical passages, discursive form of sermon, etc.

William Bradford (1590–1657)

Contributing Editor: Phillip Gould

Classroom Issues and Strategies

Bradford's history at once perpetuates and demystifies the mythic status that mainstream American culture has bestowed upon the "Pilgrims" of New England. This might be a useful place to start: the ways in which Bradford's narrative mythologizes first-generation heroism and yet exposes the all-too-human squabbling, selfishness, and greed of the Plymouth settlers.

The tension between Bradford's desire to construct a place for Plymouth in a divine historical plan, and his eventual, implicit recognition of the diminution of Plymouth's status, lends itself to discussion of the nature of history-writing in general. This tension, which involves Bradford's painful negotiation of correctly reading providential design, shows students how the supposedly objective genre of "history," like all forms of narrative, is a construction of prevailing ideologies.

As in Winthrop's *Journal, Of Plymouth Plantation*'s account of the quotidian realities of a frontier society dismantles the quasi-Victorian stereotypes that students bring to the concept of the "Puritan" (or, in this case, the Separatist). As a text composed, for all intents and purposes, on the frontier, students might consider how this historical reality also shapes Bradford's treatment of Amerindians.

The issue of Bradford's composition of his history may raise issues about the coherence of the text. Do students see distinctive subjects, thematic motifs, or narrative tones in each of the two parts?

Major Themes, Historical Perspectives, Personal Issues

The concept of community pervades the entire text of Bradford. The history demonstrates the problematic maintenance of the national covenant—the community's collective dedication to live by the purity of God's ordinances—as a parallel to the covenant of grace, by which each individual "saint" was redeemed (through Christ) by belief itself. Ironically enough, the logical extension of a "covenanted" people was a communitarian enterprise that at first simulated a kind of socialism, one which soon proved to be untenable. In Bradford's account of this minor crisis lies (as in a well-crafted novel) a foreshadowing of the eventual dispersal and fragmentation that later beset the colony. In this context, *Of Plymouth Plantation* recounts both the internal (material greed, "wickedness") and external (Thomas Morton, the Pequod—so far as Bradford perceives them) threats that constantly besieged the community.

The relationship between sacred and secular history, if theologically reconcilable, poses another thematic tension in the text. Bradford's insistence upon the "special providences" of God (those reserved for the elect in times of crisis) exists in counterpoise with the detailed catalogs of human negotiations, contrivances, and machinations that describe daily life in England and America.

Some scholars believe that Bradford's wife committed suicide while awaiting disembarkment from the *Mayflower*. This personal tragedy, along with the cycles of disappointment and success that Bradford underwent, and the constant struggle to maintain the communitarian ideal, all raise the issue of his narrative tone. The text modulates tenors of resolve, sadness, and humility.

The final section of Bradford's annals for 1642 concerns the indictment and execution of Thomas Granger for buggery. Considered a worse offense then either premarital heterosexual sex or adultery, bestiality ranked with sodomy as "things fearful to name." In considering Bradford's tortured response to the outbreak of "wickedness" in Plymouth, students can be asked how sanctioned and proscribed modes of sociality and sexuality define communal identity. Fellowship "between men," to use Eve Kosofky Sedgwick's formulation, was integral to the social structure of Plymouth Colony. But what made Plymouth novel was the inclusion of women, children, and servants—of families—in the venture of colonizing North America. One way to approach the Thomas Granger section is to discuss the tension between a communal ideal of society as a juridical commonwealth founded on a sacred bond between men and one where issues of procreation and reproduction have become more important. Jonathan Goldberg's chapter on Bradford in *Sodometries* (1992) is suggestive for this type of discussion. Granger's class status, a servant, also is relevant to issues of social reproduction. Bradford laments the necessity of bringing in outsiders to labor for the colony and further that these may reproduce and dilute the core constituents of the original covenant. Thus bestiality, a profane intermixing of different species, evinces once again the strain of Plymouth's dual missions, one religious and the other secular.

Significant Form, Style, or Artistic Conventions

Of Plymouth Plantation exemplifies, perhaps as well as any colonial New England text, the aesthetic virtues of the "plain style." The simplicity of its syntactic rhythms and the concreteness of its imagery and tropes demonstrate the rhetorical power of understatement. The plain style theoretically reflected the need to erase the self (which Bradford also achieves in referring to himself as "the governor") in the very act of creation, by having one's words stylistically approach the biblical Word of God. Bradford's history, however, shows students how the theological rigors of Puritan thought nonetheless allowed for distinctive "voices" to emerge, in this case, Bradford's uniquely compassionate, humble, and sometimes embittered one.

The issue of Puritan typology—which reads the Old Testament not only as a prefiguring of the New Testament, but of contemporary history as well—is also somewhat problematic in Bradford's history. The correlation, in other words, between the Old Testament Hebrews and the Plymouth "saints" is not a stable one. For example, when Bradford alludes to Mount Pisgah in chapter IX, he, in effect, suggests a distinction between the Israelites' Promised Land and the wild terrors of New England.

Original Audience

The private nature of Bradford's history and its delayed publication in the nineteenth century complicate the issue of the text's reception. A close reading, however, suggests that Bradford appeared to have envisioned multiple audiences for the text. As certain scholars have noted, the narrative seems to be addressed to lukewarm Anglicans at home, the remaining Scrooby Congregation, members of the larger Massachusetts Bay colony, and, perhaps most visibly, to members of the second generation who had strayed from the founders' original vision.

Moreover, students might be reminded that, despite its delayed publication, the manuscript significantly influenced a number of later New England historians such as Nathaniel Morton, Cotton Mather, and Thomas Prince.

Comparisons, Contrasts, Connections

Although the latter sections of Winthrop's *Journal* were written retrospectively, *Of Plymouth Plantation* provides a useful distinction between a retrospective narrative and an ongoing chronicle of historical events.

Bradford's relatively austere prose style, as well as his problematic moments in interpreting providence—and thus the meaning of New England—contrasts strikingly with the productions of Cotton Mather. These distinctions help to prevent students' tendencies to see "Puritanism" as a monolith. There are parallels, however, between Bradford's mythologizing of first-generation founders like Brewster and John Robinson and the kind of biography Cotton Mather conducts in the *Magnalia*.

Bradford's history is an early instance of themes prevalent in American immigration and frontier literatures. The cycles of struggle, survival, and declension characterize, for example, a much later writer—such as Willa Cather, who was far removed from Puritan New England. The instability of community in these genres make for a line of thematic continuity between

Bradford and writers of frontier romance such as Catharine Maria Sedgwick and James Fenimore Cooper.

Bibliography

Cressy, David. *Coming Over: Migration and Communication Between England and New England in the Seventeenth Century.* Cambridge, UK: Cambridge UP, 1987.

Daly, Robert. "William Bradford's Vision of History." *American Literature* 44 (1973): 557–69.

Goldberg, Jonathan. "Bradford's 'Ancient Members' & 'A Case of Buggery Amongst Them.'" *Sodometries: Renaissance Texts, Modern Sexualities.* Palo Alto, CA: Stanford UP, 1992, 223–46.

Howard, Alan B. "Art and History in Bradford's Of Plymouth Plantation." *William and Mary Quarterly* 3rd ser. 28 (1971): 237–66.

Levin, David. "William Bradford: The Value of Puritan Historiography." *Major Writers of Early American Literature.* Ed. Everett Emerson. Madison: U of Wisconsin P, 1972. 11–31.

Martin, John Frederick. *Profits in the Wilderness: Entrepreneurship and the Founding of New England Towns in the Seventeenth Century.* Chapel Hill: U of North Carolina P, 1991.

Read, David. "Silent Partners: Historical Representation in William Bradford's *Of Plymouth Plantation.*" *Early American Literature* 33:3 (1998): 291–314.

Wenska, Walter P. "Bradford's Two Histories." *Early American Literature* 8 (1978): 151–64.

Roger Williams (1603?–1683)

Contributing Editors: Raymond F. Dolle and Renée L. Bergland

Classroom Issues and Strategies

Most of the selections included here are drawn from Roger Williams's only published book, *A Key into the Language of America*. It is important to present *A Key* as a utilitarian travel guide; white readers could have carried it with them in Narragansett country (and many did). But the work is also a socio-linguistic treatise and an extended sermon. Williams is very explicit in stating that his book is written on many levels: he writes that "a little *Key* may open a *Box*, where lies a *bunch of Keys*." Students may find these multiple layers of meaning difficult, but many of them will enjoy Williams's puns and paradoxes.

One of the most striking features of *A Key into the Language of America* is that Williams embeds a detailed critique of white, Christian New England into his portrait of Narragansett New England. Williams never explicitly criticizes Christianity or Christian values, but he does repeatedly assert that few Christians live up to Christian ideals. It isn't that Narragansett culture is *more* virtuous than European or Euro-American culture, but that all cultural groups are equally far from Williams's Puritan ideals.

Another distinctive feature of *A Key into the Language of America* is its form. In a sense, this book is a dictionary; but it is a dictionary in dialogue form. Rather than word lists and grammar paradigms, Williams presents short dialogues that imply specific situational contexts. In this aspect, the book resembles current-day Berlitz language handbooks. But *A Key* goes much beyond Berlitz. Each chapter includes a few dialogues, followed by "Observations" that explain an ethnographic context for each dialogue, and then by a "Generall Observation" that shifts the focus from the Narragansett context to the human condition. Finally, each chapter concludes with a "More particular" observation, an emblematic poem that shows readers the point of the chapter. These "More particular" observations function like the final couplets of Shakespearean sonnets—they provide the zingers.

Williams's use of dialogue is important. Even Williams's more well-known but difficult tract, *The Bloody Tenent*, is written as a dialogue. This tract lays out Williams's central notions of the separation of church and state and the importance of the freedom of conscience. It was a response to John Cotton's defense of the theocracy of Massachusetts Bay that exiled Williams for his "unorthodox" views. You may want to ask students to consider the effect of dialogue and why Williams returned to this form over and over.

Students admire Williams's rebellion against authority and his argument for individual liberty of conscience. Although they may not understand his religious beliefs, they respect his courage and determination to stand up for what he believed and for the right of others to follow their beliefs.

Parallels between the Indians' religious beliefs and Christian concepts often surprise students and stimulate discussion of the nature of religion.

Williams's apparent toleration of personal religious differences often confuses students because it seems to contradict his radical and extreme Puritanism. Students must be reminded that although he accepted sects such as the Quakers into Providence plantation, he did not think that their beliefs were acceptable. Rather, he believed that the free search for Truth and the liberty to argue one's beliefs would lead the elect to God.

Major Themes, Historical Perspectives, Personal Issues

Roger Williams was sheltered by the Narragansetts after he had been banished from the Puritan colonies. In order to understand the conflict between Williams and the Puritan leaders that led to his banishment, we need to understand the three extreme positions he expounded:

1. Civil magistrates should have no jurisdiction over religious matters, and Christian churches should be absolutely divorced from worldly concerns (i.e., separation of church and state)—a position destructive to the prevailing theocracy of Massachusetts Bay and Plymouth. The elect had to be free to seek God according to their beliefs. His letter "To the Town of Providence" refutes the *reductio ad absurdum* charge that this position leads ultimately to political anarchy if individuals can claim liberty of conscience to refuse civil obedience.
2. The Puritans should all become Separatists because the Church of England was associated too closely with political authority—a position that jeopardized the charter and the relative freedom it granted.
3. The Massachusetts Bay Company charter should be invalidated since Christian kings have no right to dispose of Indian lands—a position again based on separation of spiritual and material prerogatives. Williams was a friend of the Narragansett Indians, a defender of their legal property rights, and an admirer of their natural virtue. He devoted much of his life to understanding their language and culture so that he could teach them about Christ. Many Christian missionaries believed the "savages" had to be civilized before they could be Christianized, but the colonization of the Indian lands often had tragic effects. The importance of bringing knowledge of Christ to the Indians, despite this dilemma, created one of the central conflicts in Williams's life.

The banishment of Williams from the colony reflects basic conflicts and concerns in the patriarchal Puritan society of colonial New England. The community leaders felt an urgent need to maintain authority and orthodoxy in order to preserve the "city on a hill" they had founded. Any challenge to their authority undermined the Puritan mission and threatened the New Canaan they had built with such suffering and at such great costs. However, the zeal and pure devotion needed to continue the efforts of the founding fathers were too much for most colonists; the congregational social structure began to fracture almost before it was fully established. Not only did secular attractions, worldly concerns, and material opportunities distract immigrants, but the strict requirements for church membership denied many full status in the community. Like Anne Hutchinson, the figure at the center of the Antinomian controversy, Williams advocated attractive individualistic principles that threatened the prevailing system. The colony banished him from Christ's kingdom in America in an attempt to hold their community of saints together.

Williams's sympathetic treatment of the Narragansett stands in sharp contrast to his satiric descriptions of European hypocrisies. This makes sense when *A Key* is read in the context of Williams's own story of being banished from the colonies and sheltered by the Narragansetts.

Significant Form, Style, or Artistic Conventions

The introduction to *A Key* (in fact, the title itself) invites attention to Williams's figurative language, as in the proverb, "A little key may open a box, where lies a bunch of keys." The meaning and implications of such statements are fruitful points for class discussion. Other good examples are the ship metaphor in the letter to Providence and the emblematic poems at the end of the chapters in *A Key*.

Throughout *A Key*, especially in the General Observations, the satiric contrast between true natural virtue and false Christianity creates a tension that invigorates the text and makes it a unique example of the promotional tract tradition.

The "stories" of intercultural contact that emerge in the dialogic vocabulary lists are worth attention.

Original Audience

Although Williams usually wrote with particular readers in mind, his themes and subjects have universal relevance and can still reward readers today.

Williams tells us that he intended *A Key* "specially for my friends residing in those parts." In other words, he wants to instruct fellow missionaries and traders how to interact with his other friends, the Indians. He is determined to dispel the stereotypes and false conceptions of them as subhuman savages current in the early colonies. Images of the Indians in writings from Williams's contemporaries and earlier explorers should provide students with a clear sense of the audience, their assumptions, and their needs. Williams has much to say about interracial understanding, respect, and harmony.

The audience for the letter to Providence is again quite specific, readers with a particular misconception and need. Williams writes to settle a controversy over freedom of conscience and civil obedience. Again, this controversy is still alive, and we can consider Williams's statement in light of the writings on the subject by such people as Thoreau and Martin Luther King Jr.

Comparisons, Contrasts, Connections

Williams's descriptions of the Indians can be compared to descriptions in many other texts, ranging from the orthodox Puritan attitudes toward the satanic savages, as in Mary Rowlandson's captivity narrative, to eighteenth- and nineteenth-century Romantic tributes to the Noble Savage. It is also fruitful to compare Williams's attitudes with those of the Spanish and French explorers and traders and missionaries like the French Jesuit, Father Isaac Jogues.

Williams is often seen as a forerunner of Jefferson and Jackson, but we must remember that he did not advocate liberty as an end in itself for political reasons but rather as a means to seek God.

Questions for Reading, Discussion, and Writing

1. (a) What can we infer about Williams's intentions from the fact that he chose to compose *A Key into the Language of America* as an "implicit dialogue" rather than as a dictionary?
    (b) Characterize the persona of the first-person narrator in *A Key*. What kind of person does Williams present himself as?
    (c) How is Williams's book like a key?
    (d) How do the various sections of each chapter in *A Key* relate to one another and to the whole work?
    (e) What lessons can a Christian learn from the Indians?
    (f) Why might Williams once have objected to Europe and the rest of the West being referred to as "Christendom"?
    (g) In what ways was a colony in the New World like a ship at sea?
    (h) What did Williams gain from his treaty with the Indians besides legal ownership of some land?

2. Here are some alternative writing assignments:
   (a) Personal Response Paper: Ask the students to compare one or more of Williams's observations to their own experiences and observations.
   (b) Creative Response Paper: Ask the students to write a letter back to Williams, written by a spokesperson for the town of Providence, refuting Williams's argument and defending the right to act as one believes one's religious beliefs demand.
   (c) Creative Research Paper: Assign supplemental readings from Winslow's biography of Williams (or other sources) related to his trial and banishment. Then ask the students to compose a transcript of the trial proceedings or a speech by Williams defending himself.

Bibliography

Brotherston, Gordon. "A Controversial Guide to the Language of America, 1643." *Literature and Power in the Seventeenth Century.* Ed. Francis Barker et al. Essex, UK: U of Essex, 1981. 84–100.

Felker, Christopher D. "Roger Williams's Uses of Legal Discourse: Testing Authority in Early New England." *New England Quarterly* 63 (1990): 624–48.

Grumet, Robert S. *Northeastern Indian Lives, 1632–1816.* Amherst: U of Massachusetts P, 1996.

Guggisberg, Hans R. "Religious Freedom and the History of the Christian World in Roger Williams' Thought." *Early American Literature* 12.1 (1977): 36–48.

Kaufmann, Michael W. *Institutional Individualism: Conversion, Exile, and Nostalgia in Puritan New England.* Hanover, NH: Wesleyan UP, 1998.

Keary, Anne. "Retelling the History of the Settlement of Providence: Speech, Writing, and Cultural Interaction on Narragansett Bay." *New England Quarterly* 69.2 (1996): 250–86.

LaFantasie, Glenn W. "Roger Williams: The Inner and Outer Man." *Canadian Review of American Studies* 16 (1985): 375–94.

Lovejoy, David S. "Roger Williams and George Fox: The Arrogance of Self-Righteousness." *New England Quarterly* 66.2 (1993): 199–225.

Murray, David. "Using Roger Williams' Key into America." *Symbiosis* (1997): 237–53.

Peace, Nancy E. "Roger Williams—A Historiographical Essay." *Rhode Island History* 35 (1976): 103–13.

Schweitzer, Ivy. *The Work of Self-Representation: Lyric Poetry in Colonial New England*. Chapel Hill: U of North Carolina P, 1991.

Skaggs, Donald. *Roger Williams' Dream for America*. New York: Peter Lang, 1993.

Teunissen, John J., and Evelyn J. Hinz. "Anti-Colonial Satire in Roger Williams' *A Key into the Language of America*." *Ariel* 7.3 (1976): 5–26.

———. "Roger Williams, Thomas More, and the Narragansett Utopia." *Early American Literature* 3 (Winter 1976–1977): 281–95.

Wertheimer, Eric. "'To Spell Out Each Other': Roger Williams, Perry Miller, and the Indian." *Arizona Quarterly* 50.2 (1994): 1–18.

Thomas Shepard (1605–1649)

Contributing Editor: Gregory S. Jackson

Classroom Issues and Strategies

Shepard's autobiography provides a wide-ranging interdisciplinary portrait of transatlantic Anglo-America, spanning a number of important historical, cultural, and ideological divides. As a transitional document with roots deeply embedded in British ecclesiastical and political canons, colonial ideology, and continental philosophical and literary traditions, the autobiography can thus play a key role not only in a unit on the American Puritans but also in broader American, British, and postcolonial surveys. For students who too often view "America" as a nation that rose *sui generis,* whose social customs and cultural traditions began and evolved in hermetic isolation from European influences, Shepard's autobiography provides a powerful corrective. No single text in the early colonial American tradition paints a more comprehensive picture of the origin of the cross-cultural dialogue between America and Great Britain that began in the seventeenth century and remains vital even today.

Major Themes, Historical Perspectives, Personal Issues

Since the groundbreaking works of V. L. Parrington and Perry Miller, scholars have recognized the connection between nineteenth- and twentieth-century narratives of American exceptionalism and seventeenth-century New England millennialism, the belief in a progressive history that sees the culmination of time in a golden age of Messianic reign. Less noticed in early American scholarship, however, is the way in which this progressive historical narrative fostered the spread of Humanism, the increasingly secular belief in the perfectibility of the human being. Taken together with a millennial sense of destiny, Puritan Humanism was to work all kinds of mischief upon and within the more restrictive, less democratic political system of a constitutional monarchy.

Shepard's life story presents a poignant contradiction between the Puritans' own exile in the name of religious tolerance and their often brutal persecution of the Quakers and Anabaptists. Doctrinal differences were cruelly suppressed, and perceived heretics—like Roger Williams, Anne Hutchinson, and John Wheelwright—were, after being tarred with the broad brush of Arminianism, banished from the Massachusetts Bay Colony. As students become more sophisticated in their understanding of historical causality, they often translate this contradiction into a myth of national origin, viewing the nation's revolutionary emphasis upon individual liberties as a safeguard mounted in opposition to "Puritanical" social control.

Such a myth predisposes even advanced students to a thinly fleshed understanding of the rich intellectual and religious heterodoxy within New England Puritanism. It disguises the important Puritan influences on early U.S. nationalism, and students come to view the political origins of the nation as wholly distinct from Puritan culture. Reading out of historical context, students often assume, for instance, that the constitutional safeguard separating church and state was intended to circumscribe the authority of the post-Revolution church in order to protect the democratic sovereignty of national government. They fail to see this safeguard as mutually protective, originally designed, in fact, to preserve the autonomy of the colonial Puritan Church from the coercive authority of the state-sponsored Anglican Church, which had a political sovereign as its head.

Thus, the American literature survey provides an important venue to begin complicating this conventional narrative. Students should first be reminded of the liberal tradition that descends from Puritanism. Shepard's focus on Puritan education at Cambridge University and what would become Harvard College, his emphasis on the new science, and his repeated allusions to Hebrew and Classical Greek and Roman languages, law, and arts place his autobiography on the cusp of the cultural shift from Medieval Scholasticism to the Early Modern metaphysics, even as these interests reveal the Puritan debt to Humanism. Certainly one can see the emphasis the Puritans placed on "liberty of conscience" and human volition—what Milton describes as man's having been created "sufficient to stand but free to fall." Their stress upon the individual's role in the "completion" of sacred, preordained history is written large in the credo of the American Revolution, and redacted broadly through the various nineteenth-century manifestoes of universal suffrage, from the abolition of slavery and African-American civil rights to women's political enfranchisement and child-labor laws.

Our students' impressions about Puritan culture are not altogether wrong. The humanist impulse passed down from the Puritans to nineteenth-century liberal reformers never lost its double edge. The egocentrism fostered by a divine plot of election and reprobation, in league with a solipsistic individualism encouraged by the doctrine of free will, often led to movements that simply peddled social bigotry under the guise of progressive reform. If Puritan Humanism, through its emphasis on volition and the individuated conscience, would advance such noble nineteenth-century reforms as abolitionism, temperance, women's suffrage, transcendental utopianism, and Bellamistic Nationalism, to name but a few, its perverse emphasis on selective regeneration and strict adherence to a belief in providential history would help to justify social policies as lurid as the postbellum eugenics movement and as horrific as racial and social supremacy and Native American genocide.

Finally, students are often surprised to learn of the political traditions that this country inherited from Puritanism, not only in law and social custom but also in forms of government and constitutional philosophy. Shepard's emphasis on the Puritans' struggle to balance the doctrine of free will—the individual's right to will or nil as he saw fit—with a Covenant theology that sought to unify New England's social order powerfully registers the Puritans' place in the larger seventeenth-century discourse on social contract. It places the New England Puritans in company with such important seventeenth-century Contractualists as Thomas Hooker, Thomas Hobbes, John Locke, and James Harrington, all of whom were brought up under Calvinist discipline. As "contract" implies, the Puritans, like their eminent contemporaries, proffered "consent" as the trigger for social contract. Thus, contractualism as a political and social arrangement evolves out of the Protestant emphasis on individual volition. But whereas Locke and Harrington saw rational self-interest as the motivation for the individual's consenting to mutual alliance, and Hobbes saw the fear of human nature as the fundamental impetus behind man's allegiance to state, the Puritans viewed the soul's desire for grace as the basis for social contract, in the form of a covenant between the visible church and God. Shepard's focus on human volition in his autobiography—exhibited on the macrolevel in his depiction of the tensions between Anglican coercion and Puritan consent, and on the microlevel in the citizen-subject's internal struggle to balance allegiance to state (or king) with "liberty of conscience"—poignantly demonstrates, however, the perpetual rub between consent and social contract. In this tension, we see the cornerstone of a modern democracy built from the enduring conflict between the civil liberty of the citizen, on the one hand, and the sovereignty of the state, on the other.

Thus, Shepard's autobiography provides a portrait in miniature of the contradictory legacy of Puritanism on American culture. In truth, if the Puritan emphasis on the unmediated relationship between the individual and God tended to increase the consciousness of the self as a spiritual entity, inspiring an egocentrism that did not suffer difference gladly, that same nascent individualism also tended to a kind of democratization of moral and social outlook. And if the Puritan emphasis on "liberty of conscience" was for a time pressed into the service of a theocracy that denied that same liberty to others, it was also this crucial liberty that would empower the American colonists to break their imperial bonds. Although Puritan theology could not ultimately survive its structural contradictions that pitted the need for social controls against the individual's spiritual autonomy, its theological imperatives spurred on the American Enlightenment, and its Protestant insistence upon free will provided the foundation of a century that was to give birth to human civil liberties. Perhaps Puritanism's most surprising legacy, however, was the blueprint it provided for American federalism. Puritan covenant ("Foederal") theology and its organization of the Church into self-directing congregations democratically united through representation to a larger religious coalition established a pattern for American republicanism.

Significant Form, Style, or Artistic Convention

An analysis of genre and other literary conventions in relation to Shepard's autobiography helps students not only to situate the Puritan writers in a broader context of Anglo-American literary tradition but also to understand the complex ways in which generic form and linguistic style were often a vital part of social ritual and cultural values long before they were prized as aesthetic conventions. Understanding the complex interplay between form and function in early American discursive/oral practices—such as sermons, confessionals, captivity narratives, political jeremiads, and devotional poetry—will enrich students' understanding of later American authors and their works. For example, the use of first-person narration by a broad range of nineteenth-century authors—including Ralph Waldo Emerson, Lydia Maria Child, Harriet Beecher Stowe, Frederick Douglass, Walt Whitman, and Henry Adams—was as much a celebration of regional memory and cultural atavism as it was an index of nineteenth-century literary vogue.

One useful way to approach Shepard's work is by reading from our present literary perspective backward through time. As the rootstock of American life writing, Shepard's narrative is the literary forebear of several genres in the American autobiographical tradition. From this Puritan tradition of the devotional confession evolved such disparate cultural forms of self-expression as the Puritan conversion narrative, the early American captivity narrative, the African-American slave narrative, the rogue journal, the modern memoir, and the first-person narration of American fiction, in the vein of Charles Brockden Brown, Edgar Allan Poe, and Mark Twain.

The American tradition of life writing is a product of the Protestant Reformation. Because Protestantism rejected clerical mediation between the individual and God, it placed new emphasis on spiritual independence, essentially requiring individuals to monitor their own moral behavior and to evaluate their own spiritual progress. The idea of religious self-scrutiny as the primary duty of the individual is not an innovation of Protestantism. Since at least Augustine, introspection has been an essential feature of Christian spirituality and its conversion morphology. John Calvin, however, elevated introspection as the essential mechanism of the Protestant conversion process, bequeathing to the Anglo-American Puritans of Shepard's generation a belief in the necessity of scrutinizing the "inner man" for evidence of his or her place in the divine plan of election and reprobation.

This shift from mediated salvation to a self-directed relationship with the divine resulted in what scholars of Early Modern subjectivity refer to as an "internalization of conscience." In effect, an increased awareness of the individual's inner impulses and immoral compulsions—and the continuous self-scrutiny required to expose them—tended to deepen the sense of human interiority, marking a break between early modern psychology and its scholastic and classical precursors. Both the internalization of conscience and the need to track spiritual progress required a method of self-inventory that could be plotted over time. Not surprisingly, the Puritans turned to life writing as the most effective means of graphing their spiritual progress, thus registering and regulating their moral conduct. As Perry Miller and Thomas H. Johnson have pointed out, almost every literate Puritan kept some kind of journal with daily entries. These journals logged spiritual progress, cataloged sins, traced isolated thoughts and actions for larger patterns, accounted for personal frailty, decried moral backsliding, and praised spiritual victories, functioning all the while as a kind of internal dialogue between the supplicant and God. In this way, the autobiographer transformed his life into narrative as an elaborate explanation of how his moral choices and actions revealed his place in God's providential scheme.

Located in Shepard's autobiography are the inchoate conventions that would become "indigenous" New England literary forms. Shepard's agonistic internal monologues and spiritual doubt look forward to the pietistic self-abnegation of later Puritan diarists, from the pathetic lamentations of Michael Wigglesworth to the obsessive self-doubting of Maria Sedgwick, Amos Bronson

Alcott, Theodore Parker, Henry Ward Beecher, Herman Melville, and Margaret Fuller. In Shepard's account of his youthful, preconversion depravity—an Augustinian conceit—we see a foreshadowing of Benjamin Franklin's cosmopolitan trope of vaunted libertinism, itself a near contemporary of the great secular confessions of the Calvinist-reared Samuel Pepys and Jean-Jacques Rousseau. And in Shepard's obsession with the visible signs of God's saving grace, we see the model for Puritan-born Franklin's American myth of the self-made man, where the rags-to-riches plot bespeaks social, rather than spiritual, election. Thus, Shepard's fierce Protestant self-reliance and moral self-fashioning are the psychological and generic precursors to later autobiographical traditions. The increasingly self-conscious, modern identity construction of latter-day autobiographers—Franklin, Emerson, Henry David Thoreau, Frederick Douglass, Elizabeth Cady Stanton, Henry Adams, and Walt Whitman, to name but a few—announces the sea change from the deep sacramentalism of New England's feudal origins to the democratization of the young nation's moral and social outlook.

In his practice of "reading" the external world as a system of signs, Shepard foregrounds the alienated self-detachment and inner isolation present in Puritan captivity narratives such as Mary Rowlandson's. As both Shepard's and Rowlandson's narratives remind us, however, Puritan life writing participated in the seventeenth-century shift to an empirical epistemology equally suited to a wide array of disciplines and genres. In secular form, the self-detached gaze and ideology of the good Puritan as "outside" chronicler of world action—a kind of primitive anthropology—is the antecedent to the "objective," empirical studies of the American Enlightenment, best exemplified in the scientific writings of Cotton Mather, Jonathan Edwards, Jared Eliot, Franklin, William Bartram, and Thomas Jefferson, and in the journals of Meriwether Lewis and William Clark. And this new epistemology predicated on John Locke's sensual psychology would inspire a new genre—one that was both a symptom and a purveyor of modernity. As Ian Watt has taught us, the individual identity particularized by continued self-examination contained the narrative seeds of modern realism that would transform the Puritan allegory into the novel: two genres still intermingled in the works of the nation's earliest novelists, from Charles Brockden Brown, Rebecca Rush, and Susanna Rowson to Catharine Sedgwick, Hannah Webster Foster, and Tabitha Gilman Tenney. Finally, more recently, critics have described the Puritan concept of earthly stewardship—manifested in Shepard's representation of the dignity of manual labor and cultivation of both earth and soul—as the forerunner of the developing canons of literary ecology, precociously present in the nature writing of Jefferson, Edward Everett, Emerson, and Thoreau and showcased in the sublime grandeur of the Hudson River School's romantic landscapes.

Original Audience

Shepard's autobiography differs strikingly from the life writing of most first-generation New England Puritans—such as William Bradford, John Winthrop, and Anne Bradstreet—in that it was intended for a public audience. Few of the New England clergy went to the trouble to revise their journals and diaries into a formal and cohesive life story. That Shepard did so bespeaks a different set of priorities from the customary purposes of Puritan introspection. By shaping the daily record of his life into a coherent narrative, Shepard sets out to create a history, to unfold the place of the Puritans in God's larger providential design. The narrative's implication is that when readers consider the evidence that Shepard lays before them, they cannot but fail to see the mark of salvation in the miracles wrought in the lives of Shepard's company.

As Shepard saw it, every detail of his narrative had a larger, providential significance. Thus, his education at Cambridge, the Anglican persecutions that gave to Puritan conviction a martyr's resolve, the perils at sea that forged the bonds of a covenant, and even the sudden remove of Thomas Hooker and his congregation to Connecticut—leaving empty houses and a vacant church to be filled by the new immigrants—were all events portending the arrival of Shepard's company, not merely to a physical location in the New World but to a spiritual place in the New Jerusalem. For Shepard takes the design of his providential narrative from biblical typology, subtly re-creating the Old Testament tribulations of God's chosen people in their journey from bondage to salvation. In this typological structure, the Puritans play the role of God's captive children in Egypt to the Anglican bishopric's Pharaoh. The plot of the autobiography thus turns with the biblical trope: like the Hebrew exodus from Egypt across the Red Sea, the Puritans take flight in ships upon the ocean, a diaspora that would leave their descendants on three separate continents. Like the children of Israel wandering in the Sinai desert, the Puritans suffer trials and tribulations in the wasteland of the Atlantic. Finally, like Israelites entering the Land of Canaan, the Puritans arrive at the promised land, a tried and worthier people. Such typology offers a plausible explanation for the Puritan animosity toward Native American cultures, for both biblical Canaan and America, as the "New Canaan," were inhabited by what their respective invaders deemed an "unclean" people.

Thus Shepard renders the process of determining an individual's state of grace—his or her knowledge of election—as a pilgrimage in which the spiritual trials of doubt, despair, greed, sloth, and other sins, or "the rulers of darkness" and "the spiritual wickedness in high places," are made manifest in the flesh as physical contests to be won. If Shepard's autobiography begins to resemble Christian's journey in John Bunyan's *Pilgrim's Progress,* or Red Crosse Knight's crusade in Edmund Spenser's *The Faerie Queene,* it does so for good reason, for religious allegory and spiritual autobiography in the Augustinian tradition are closely related. Shepard's insistence upon rendering each personal experience as a moral lesson cast in terms of biblical typology—as a mark of God's favor or the sting of his chastising rod, or as Satan's temptation—eradicates the particular, effacing the individual circumstances and the temporal index that cooperate to create historical specificity. He even abstracts the unique and privileged position of the autobiographer: that is, typological tropes transform the "I" of the first-person narrative into a communal plurality of Shepard's audience. Shepard essentially becomes an "Everyman," a position in his allegory that the Puritan readers assumed, as they recast their own experience in the template of Shepard's typology. Thus, unlike autobiographies in the memoir tradition of today, spiritual autobiographies were interactive. They evoked the reader to respond. Such narratives were not only offered to Christians—particularly young readers—as models of how to wage the "good fight," but they also provided a kind of heuristic—a typological template—by which the young reader could plot his or her own spiritual journey upon the communal path of regeneration. Shepard's autobiography as allegory instilled a particular community hermeneutic practice—or way of interpreting the external world as a sign system of divine meaning.

Anne Bradstreet (1612?–1672)

Contributing Editor: Pattie Cowell

Classroom Issues and Strategies

There are many ways to approach Bradstreet: as a "first" (given that she is the first North American to publish a book of poems), as a Puritan, and as a woman. I have found an interplay of all three approaches useful for piquing student interest. Those who are skeptical of my feminist readings may be caught by historical and cultural perspectives. Those who think they want nothing to do with Puritanism may be intrigued by Bradstreet's more personal writings.

Beginning students are generally unfamiliar with the historical and theological contexts in which she wrote. Many close off their reading of Bradstreet and other Puritan writers because they disapprove of what they think they know about Puritan theology. Brief background materials make that context more accessible and less narrowly theological.

Again for reasons of accessibility, I usually begin with the more personal poems from the second edition. The poignancy of Bradstreet's elegies, the simplicity of her love poems, the stark reality of her poem on childbirth, the wit of "The Author to Her Book"—all travel across the centuries with relative ease, even for less skilled readers. When these immediately readable poems are placed in the context of women's lives in the seventeenth century and in the North American colonies, most students find a point of entry.

Major Themes, Historical Perspectives, Personal Issues

Thematically, Bradstreet's body of work is both extensive and varied. Teachers will find much that can be linked with other materials in a given course. Bradstreet wrote on culture and nature, on spirituality and theology, on the tension between faith and doubt, on family, on death, on history. I like to suggest the range of her subject matter for students and then concentrate on a single thematic thread (though the thread I choose varies with my interests of the moment). It is a strategy that helps students follow their own interests of the moment at the same time that it allows us (by close reading) to see the skills Bradstreet had developed. "In Honour of . . . Queen Elizabeth" is a fine poem for tracing both thematic threads and poetic technique, though its length and complexity present problems for beginning students. "The Prologue" is more manageable in a single class session, short enough to allow multiple readings to develop but complex enough to tantalize. Many of the other short personal pieces—well represented in *The Heath Anthology* selections—work effectively with this approach too.

The remarkable nature of Bradstreet's accomplishment is highlighted when students learn the historical conditions women poets struggled with. Women who wrote stepped outside their appropriate sphere, and those who published their work frequently faced social censure. The Reverend Thomas Parker, a minister in Newbury, Massachusetts, gives a succinct statement of cultural attitudes in an open letter to his sister, Elizabeth Avery, in England: "Your printing of a book, beyond the custom of your sex, doth rankly smell" (1650). Compounding this social pressure, many women faced crushing workloads and struggled with lack of leisure for writing. Others suffered from unequal access to education. Some internalized the sense of intellectual inferiority offered to them from nearly every authoritative voice.

Bradstreet's personal situation gave her the means to cope with some of these obstacles. Before she came to North America, she received an extensive education; she had access as a child to private tutors and the Earl of Lincoln's large library. She was part of an influential, well-to-do family that encouraged her writing and circulated it in manuscript with pride. Her brother-in-law, John Woodbridge, took the manuscript collection to London for publication. Such private support did much to counteract the possibility of public disapproval.

Significant Form, Style, or Artistic Conventions

Bradstreet's attention to form and technique is usefully studied in the context of two quite different aesthetics, both of which influence her: Puritanism's so-called plain style (marked by didactic intent, artful simplicity, accessibility, and an absence of rhetorical ornamentation) and seventeenth-century versions of classicism (which stressed poetry as imitation, exalted the genres of tragedy and epic, and worked toward unity of action, place, and time).

Original Audience

Discussions of seventeenth-century English and New English audiences allow room for fruitful digressions on colonial literacy, manuscript culture, print culture, publishing, and book distribution. I frequently challenge beginning students to develop a description of Bradstreet's original readers by exercising their historical imaginations. Those who haven't read much history keep running into the barriers I set for them, but the exercise is useful nonetheless. They begin to "see" the circumstances of literate and literary culture in an environment that is sparsely populated, with only a fledgling publishing and book distribution establishment, without libraries, with books as relatively expensive luxuries.

Having imagined how Bradstreet's poems might have fared with her original audience, I ask students to compare themselves with those readers. How well do her themes and strategies travel across time? What elements seem to connect to contemporary concerns? What fails to relate? Why?

Comparisons, Contrasts, Connections

Bradstreet can usefully be read in relation to

- other Puritan writers, especially the poet Edward Taylor.
- contemporary British women writers, such as Katherine Philips.
- the Mexican nun Sor Juana Inés de la Cruz (Bradstreet's contemporary, also heralded as "the tenth muse").
- Phillis Wheatley. Because Wheatley wrote more than a century later, from a black perspective and in a neoclassical tradition, she provides points of sharp contrast. But on certain themes (humility, the importance of spirituality), their voices merge.

Bibliography

Caldwell, Patricia. "Why Our First Poet Was a Woman: Bradstreet and the Birth of an American Poetic Voice." *Prospects* 13 (1988): 1–35.

Cowell, Pattie, and Ann Stanford, eds. *Critical Essays on Anne Bradstreet.* Boston: Hall, 1983.

Dolle, Raymond F. *Anne Bradstreet: A Reference Guide.* Boston: Hall, 1990.

Eberwein, Jane Donahue. "'Art and Nature's Ape': The Challenge to the American Poet." *Poetic is in the Poem: Critical Essays on American Self-Reflexive Poetry.* Ed. Dorothy Z. Baker. New York: Lang, 1997.

———. "'No Ret'ric We Expect': Argumentation in Bradstreet's 'The Prologue.'" *Critical Essays on Anne Bradstreet.* Eds. Pattie Cowell and Ann Stanford. Boston: Hall, 1983. 218–25.

Hammond, Jeffrey A. *The American Puritan Elegy: A Literary and Cultural Study.* New York: Cambridge UP, 2000.

Kopacz, Paula. "'Men can doe best, and women know it well': Anne Bradstreet and Feminist Aesthetics." *Kentucky Philological Review* 2 (1987): 21–29.

Richardson, Robert D., Jr. "The Puritan Poetry of Anne Bradstreet." *Critical Essays on Anne Bradstreet.* Eds. Pattie Cowell and Ann Stanford. Boston: Hall, 1983. 101–15.

Schweitzer, Ivy. "Anne Bradstreet Wrestles with the Renaissance." *Early American Literature* 23 (1988): 291–312.

Stanford, Ann. "Anne Bradstreet: Dogmatist and Rebel." *Critical Essays on Anne Bradstreet.* Eds. Pattie Cowell and Ann Stanford, Boston: Hall, 1983. 76–88.

White, Elizabeth Wade. "The Tenth Muse—A Tercentenary Appraisal of Anne Bradstreet." *Critical Essays on Anne Bradstreet,* Eds. Pattie Cowell and Ann Stanford. Boston: Hall, 1983. 55–75.

Michael Wigglesworth (1631–1705)

Contributing Editor: Danielle Hinrichs

Classroom Issues and Strategies

For students, and for many literary scholars, Puritan ideology and Puritan poetry often seem distressingly at odds with modern aesthetics. This is a particularly vexing issue for Wigglesworth's modern readers because the poet-minister fully embraced Puritan theology and a literary aesthetic based on didacticism and biblical exemplum. Critics have long suggested that Wigglesworth's intense faith precluded true artistic expression. As recent scholars like Jeffrey A. Hammond and Ronald A. Bosco have argued, however, an appreciation of Michael Wigglesworth's poetic depends upon an acceptance of Wigglesworth on his own terms and upon an understanding of Puritan literary expectations, which often "did not distinguish between aesthetic and spiritual response" (Hammond 8). Puritans believed that poetry should move readers' spirits, drawing them closer to God. Students will gain more from reading Wigglesworth's diary and poetry if they are asked to enter Wigglesworth's world as fully as possible and to try to glean from his writings a sense of Wigglesworth's personal and literary objectives. Although students will discover very different purposes in Wigglesworth's diary and his published poems, they will also find similarities that may lead them to an understanding of the confluence of Wigglesworth's private and public goals. He often wrote poetry about issues in his own life, and he gained authority by telling readers that direct experience informed his public writing. In his diary, he sought to move himself closer to God, and in his poems he urged others toward the divine.

Major Themes, Historical Perspectives, Personal Issues

Throughout Wigglesworth's writings, he attempts to counter what he perceived as the waning spiritualism of mid-seventeenth-century New England. As Bosco points out, by the 1660s the New England Puritans seemed to be moving steadily away from the firm religious ideals of the original settlers. Wigglesworth's sometimes fiery style and didacticism should be seen as a part of this attempt to right the course of Puritanism in an era marked by declining attention to Puritan standards and discipline. The evidence of God's displeasure with this wayward trend seemed everywhere apparent to Puritan leaders. Puritans constantly searched the material world for spiritual meaning; "Believing that God spoke to his people through events, believing that God's will or disposition toward his people was discernible in everything from the weather to the state of New England's economy, New England's orthodox leaders put their symbolic imaginations to work" (Bosco xx). Wigglesworth took his place among these leaders and preached about the signs of God's disapprobation in his sermons and in his poetry. In one of the diary excerpts included in this anthology, Wigglesworth interprets a fire, a very common event in seventeenth-century New England, as an incident invoked by God to punish sinners.

Wigglesworth's intense anxiety about his sexuality has contributed to his reputation as a conventionally grim and dark-hearted Puritan. Students should resist reading Wigglesworth's sexuality in terms of contemporary ideas and norms and attempt instead to explore the ways in which ideas about sexuality and definitions of masculinity and femininity are fluid and particular to a historical context. Alan Bray's article, listed in the bibliography that follows, provides a valuable historical lens through which to view Wigglesworth's candid and anguished comments about sexuality and masculinity. Bray suggests that Wigglesworth's obsessive guilt does not arise from the dreams themselves: in Wigglesworth's day, dreams were believed to unfold beyond the rationality and will of the individual, and thus, they could not implicate the dreamer in a sinful act. Wigglesworth feels guilt, then, Bray argues, not because he dreams and ejaculates during sleep, but because Wigglesworth believes that his dreams evince a weakness caused by venereal disease (207). His fears about masculinity exist within this specific context of seventeenth-century Puritan society. According to Bray, Wigglesworth's struggle against feminization has less to do with his desire for his students (all male) than with his inability to control his sexual thoughts. The Puritan man becomes feminized through lack of restraint: "What these avowedly unmasculine figures share, drunkard, glutton, fornicator, and sodomite alike, is a ruinously unrestrained appetite without 'masculine' restraint; and the sodomite's improper sexual appetite is but one expression of this" (209). As Bray points out, Puritan culture and definitions of Puritan manhood seem entirely out of place in our current consumer economy, an economy that prizes lack of restraint. Raising these issues with students will help them look more carefully at how Wigglesworth defines sexuality, masculinity, and guilt and how these terms bear on Wigglesworth's other themes. As Walter Hughes suggests, "It is perhaps a mistake to try to distinguish between overtly erotic uses of these [sexualized] words and figurative ones. Sometimes these words relate directly to Wigglesworth's quite real desire for his students or to his frequent nocturnal emissions and 'vile dreams'; but other times they are applied to moments of inattention in church, concern for his economic welfare, or overinvolvement in his studies" (110). Wigglesworth's constant attempts to divert his thoughts from his students often become a part of his larger goal to rid himself of all powerful attachments to worldly things (Verdun 226).

Reading Wigglesworth's diary excerpts and poem together may allow students to explore Wigglesworth's struggle to disengage himself from the material world and fully embrace the spiritual realm, a major theme in both selections. In "Vanity of Vanities," Wigglesworth warns his readers that the more one derives from the world, the more one desires, and no matter how much one achieves, the things in the world are, in the end, not enough: "Most wretched man, that fixed hath his love/Upon this world, that surely will deceive him." Death comes for everyone, rich, poor, powerful, and weak alike, and only devotion to God remains. Wigglesworth's catalog of past heroes, marked by strength and riches, demonstrates the limits of all human achievements, no matter how grand.

Significant Form, Style, or Artistic Conventions

Wigglesworth's readers would have easily identified his references, biblical and otherwise. His poetry is characterized by a plain style, accessible language, and persuasive tone that sometimes bears the tenor of a fervent warning and sometimes assumes the voice of a sympathetic teacher. Bosco explains that Wigglesworth "related his personal experience or advice through homely language and commonplace events; he alluded to accessible biblical figures and stories for authority higher than his own to underscore both the universality of his experience and the valor of such advice as he might offer" (xxv). Wigglesworth wrote much of his poetry in the form called fourteeners, a jogging, easily memorized verse that readers often read or recited out loud.

Original Audience

Wigglesworth directed his poetry toward a broad audience, seeking to convince Puritans of the significance of their own salvation. In the preface to *The Day of Doom*, Wigglesworth calls upon his muses: *"Oh! Guide me by thy sacred Sprite/So to indite, and so to write,/That I thine Holy Name may praise,/And teach the Sons of Men thy wayes."* Through poetry, he strove to praise God and to instruct his readers about God's ways. In this sense, it is useful to discuss Wigglesworth's biography and to ask students to consider how Wigglesworth used poetry to reach a larger congregation than he could address as minister at Malden. Wigglesworth's *Diary* assumes a very different tone from that of his poetry in part because of his intended audience. Not meant for publication, Wigglesworth's introspective diary existed for only one reader: Wigglesworth himself. If Wigglesworth crafted his dairy in any sense for an outside audience, he crafted it for God, to whom Wigglesworth occasionally speaks directly in the pages of his diary. Wigglesworth also used a shorthand code for some entries, often those expressing his worries about sexuality and his fondness for his students; these coded passages further emphasize the very private nature of this writing. Although the diary and poem share common themes, Wigglesworth conveys the themes differently for his distinct audiences.

Comparisons, Contrasts, Connections

Scholars frequently compare Wigglesworth's poetry with the poetry of Anne Bradstreet and Edward Taylor, often with unfavorable results for Wigglesworth. Nevertheless, reading Wigglesworth's work in the context of these other Puritan poets helps the reader to understand both a contextual confluence of Puritan aesthetic ideas and a striking variety of Puritan viewpoints and approaches. Wigglesworth's works might also be read effectively alongside Puritan sermons and compared to other diaries and journals, such as William Byrd's *Secret History*.

Questions for Reading, Discussion, and Writing

1. Wigglesworth refers to biblical passages throughout his poetry and his diary. His Puritan readers would have immediately recognized these biblical references. Consider the complete biblical passages and discuss how these allusions function in Wigglesworth's writing.
2. Describe the relationship between the individual and the community in Wigglesworth's *Diary* and/or in his poem.
3. Wigglesworth expressed concern for seventeenth-century New England's waning spirituality. How does Wigglesworth address this growing secularism and God's response?
4. Choose a theme common to both Wigglesworth's diary and his poem and discuss the similarities and/or differences in how that theme is conveyed in the two different genres. How does the intended audience of each work affect the presentation of your theme?
5. Discuss gender in Wigglesworth's diary in terms of any or all of the following: Wigglesworth's masculinity, his sexuality, and his relationship with his wife.

Bibliography

Bosco, Ronald A. "Introduction." *The Poems of Michael Wigglesworth*. Ed. Ronald A. Bosco. Maryland: UP of America, 1989. ix–xliii.

Bray, Alan. "The Curious Case of Michael Wigglesworth." *A Queer World*. Ed. Martin Duberman. New York: New York UP, 1997. 205–15.

Crowder, Richard. "'The Day of Doom' as Chronomorph." *Journal of Popular Culture* 9 (1976): 948–59.

Hammond, Jeffrey A. *Sinful Self, Saintly Self: The Puritan Experience of Poetry.* Athens: U of Georgia P, 1993.

Hughes, Walter. "'Meat out of the Eater': Panic and Desire in American Puritan Poetry." *Engendering Men.* Ed. Joseph Boone. New York: Routledge, 1990. 102–21.

Pope, Alan H. "Petrus Ramus and Michael Wigglesworth: The Logic of Poetic Structure." *Puritan Poets and Poetics: Seventeenth-Century American Poetry in Theory and Practice.* Ed. Peter White. University Park: Pennsylvania State UP, 1985.

Verdun, Kathleen. "'Our Cursed Natures': Sexuality and the Puritan Conscience." *New England Quarterly* 56.2 (1983): 220–37.

The Bay Psalm Book (1640)

The New England Primer (1683?)

Contributing Editor: Jean Ferguson Carr

Classroom Issues and Strategies

Readers may assume that both of these texts are simply functional transmissions of doctrine and discipline, representing a narrow and dogmatic religious culture of merely antiquarian interest. Readers should be encouraged to question their prejudgments both about Puritan culture and about religious/educational texts, particularly texts that have many parts and that are written not by a single author but by a group representing broader cultural interests and values. They need to see these texts as an emergent culture's effort to formulate values that can be taught and maintained.

For example, in reading the psalms, it is useful to compare the *Bay Psalm Book* version with those of the King James translation or others, noting the choices made and the interpretation those choices represent. Also, in reading the *Primer,* consider what those lessons suggest about not only what the culture authorized teachers to enforce but also what the culture feared or had difficulty controlling.

Students are often unnerved by the old-style spelling, but with a little practice they can read the material smoothly. Once they are comfortable with these external issues, they are often surprised and impressed by the frankness with which such topics as death, sin, and governmental punishment are treated.

Major Themes, Historical Perspectives, Personal Issues

The *Psalm Book* reflects a concern about making worship contemporary, particular to their time and place and special circumstances as pilgrims to a new land. The book's design and production stress the belief that faith must be attended to on a daily basis by each individual. The small books, written in English and in contemporary verse forms, could be carried into the home and the place of work, their lessons repeated to ward off the dangers and temptations of life in a "wilderness." The *Primer* recognizes the difficulties of remaining faithful and obedient, and it values learning as a way to preserve from one generation to another "that part,/which shall never decay," the cultural and religious values of the community which cannot be silenced by the state or death.

Significant Form, Style, or Artistic Conventions

John Cotton's preface is a fascinating document about translation, advocating use of the vernacular and defending "modern" poetry. The psalms are "contested" versions, retranslated to mark a cultural and religious difference from those versions widely used in Europe and England, as well as to distinguish the Massachusetts Bay Colony Puritans from the Plymouth Pilgrims, who used the Sternhold-Hopkins Psalter of 1562.

Original Audience

The *Psalm Book,* written and printed by the Puritans of Massachusetts Bay Colony in 1640, was designed to allow a whole congregation to sing psalms together in church and at home. Neither Cotton's essay nor the poems have been attended to by modern critics: the psalter has been generally treated as a simple "text" of antiquarian interest only. The *Primer* was the chief educational text of the New England colonies for over a hundred years, from its first printing in 1683.

Comparisons, Contrasts, Connections

Melville's call for American readers to "boldly contemn all imitation, though it comes to us graceful and fragrant as the morning; and foster all originality, though, at first, it be crabbed and ugly as our own pine knots" ("Hawthorne and his Mosses," 1850) suggests how the psalms and Cotton's preface might usefully be reread. The *Bay Psalm Book* can be compared with the literary credos of Emerson and Whitman, which prefer originality over literary polish or imitative technical perfection. The *Primer* could be used to frame discussions about attitudes toward learning and childhood, toward the propagation of cultural values through books. It serves as a useful anthology of cultural concerns to compare with such later textbooks as McGuffey's *Eclectic Readers* or Webster's *American Speller*.

Questions for Reading, Discussion, and Writing

1. (a) Compare two versions of a psalm (perhaps King James, Isaac Watts, Bay Psalm, or a modern version). What do the changes suggest about what is valued by the translator? What do they suggest about how the translator understands the difficulties or possibilities of faith?

    (b) What does John Cotton's preface propose as the important considerations for poetry and religious song? What established values is he thus opposing?

    (c) What seem to be the daily conditions of life for the readers of the primer, as exemplified in the lessons' details? What did they have to fear or to overcome?

    (d) How does the *Primer* envision the relationship of parent to child? Of state to citizen? Of God to person?

    (e) How do the lessons demark proper social relations? How do they suggest the community's ability to contain crime or misbehavior?

    (f) How does the primer propose to shape (control?) speech and writing?

2. (a) Compare the claims about poetry and national literature in Cotton's preface to one of the following texts: Emerson's "The Poet," Whitman's "Preface" to *Leaves of Grass*, Rebecca Harding Davis's *Life in the Iron Mills*, Melville's "Hawthorne and His Mosses."

    (b) Discuss how *The New England Primer* represents both the importance and difficulty of learning cultural values and behavior.

    (c) Compare *The New England Primer* as a cultural artifact with a contemporary textbook for children. What seem to be the fears each text guards against? What does each text presuppose about childhood and children? How do they represent the relationship of school to children, of parents to children? What do they propose as the proper subjects for children?

Mary White Rowlandson (Talcott) (1637?–1711)

Contributing Editor: Paula Uruburu

Classroom Issues and Strategies

The narrative is best approached from several perspectives, including literary (what makes it a work of literature?), historical (where does fact mix with fiction?), and psychological (what factors may be affecting Rowlandson's interpretation of her experience?).

Students respond well to the personal diary-like quality of the narrative and the trials Rowlandson undergoes. Although most side with her, some also recognize the hardships the Indians have experienced at the hands of the colonists.

Major Themes, Historical Perspectives, Personal Issues

It is important for the students to get the straight historical facts about King Phillip's War, during which Rowlandson was taken captive. This allows them to see both sides of the issues that caused the "war" and to better understand the Indians' plight as well as Rowlandson's reaction to her eleven-week captivity.

Significant Form, Style, or Artistic Conventions

Discussion of the Indian captivity narrative as a genre is essential. Also, a background on Puritan sermons and their reliance upon the Word in the Bible is important since the movement/structure of the narrative juxtaposes real events with biblical comparisons or equivalents.

Original Audience

We discuss how the Puritans would have responded to the narrative and why Rowlandson wrote it. I ask students for their own reaction (with whom does their sympathy lie—the settlers or the Indians?). We then look at Benjamin Franklin's essay "Some Remarks Concerning the Savages of North America" for an ironic comparison/contrast and then discuss the changes in perception from his time until now.

Feminist perspective: In what ways does this narrative lend itself to a greater understanding of the woman's place in Puritan history? How does being a woman affect Rowlandson's point of view?

Comparisons, Contrasts, Connections

Using Bradstreet's poetry (especially "Some Verses Upon the Burning of our House") and Winthrop's sermon, give two different views of the details and effects of covenant theology on ordinary people's lives and how they were expected to respond to traumatic or trying events and circumstances.

Questions for Reading, Discussion, and Writing

1. How does the *Narrative* demonstrate Puritan theology and thinking at work?
2. In what ways does Rowlandson use her experience to reaffirm Puritan beliefs? How does she view herself and her fellow Christians? How does she see the Indians? What do her dehumanizing descriptions of the Indians accomplish?
3. Are there any instances when she seems to waver in her faith?
4. Why does Rowlandson distrust the "praying Indians"?
5. How does she use the Bible and varied scriptural allusions in her analysis of her captivity and restoration?
6. Does her worldview change at all during her eleven weeks of captivity? Why or why not?
7. How does the *Narrative* combine/demonstrate/refute what William Bradford in *Of Plymouth Plantation* and John Winthrop in *A Modell of Christian Charity* had to say about the Puritan's mission in the New World?

After addressing any number of the previous questions, aimed at a basic analysis of the *Narrative*, an instructor can then continue with a discussion of the possible motives Rowlandson had for writing it. This aspect appeals to students who are most interested in trying to understand the human being behind the prose.

1. Compare and contrast the Indian captivity narrative with the slave narrative genre. What elements and conventions do they share? How do they differ?
2. Explain how Rowlandson's narrative reinforces her worldview. Where (if at all) does her covenant theology fail her or seem insufficient to explain actions and events?

Edward Taylor (1642?–1729)

Contributing Editor: Karen E. Rowe

Classroom Issues and Strategies

Students may recoil from Taylor's overly didactic, seemingly aesthetically rough or unpolished poetry, in part because he seems too preoccupied with issues of sin and salvation, which they find alien. The fundamental need is to familiarize students with basic Puritan concepts, biblical sources and allusions, and the meditative tradition. This background allows students and teachers to move beyond the easy post-Romantic definition of the poetry as "lyric," which locks the class into a quick survey of only the occasional poems. Taylor may also seem both too easy ("doesn't he tell it all?") and too complicated because of arcane word choices, the curious compounding of images, and the plethora of biblical images.

The organization of selections in *The Heath Anthology* permits one for the first time to trace Taylor's chronological development as a poet and also emphasizes a more personalized Taylor. By clustering selections from the *Meditations* and engaging students in playing with the multiple meanings of curious words, the poetry comes alive as an intricate orchestration of recurrent themes and interconnected images. The point is to capture Taylor's imaginative flexibility as much as his tortured angst while at the same time seeing all of his poetry as part of an overriding concern with personal preparation for heaven and with how Taylor as poet can best serve God—and in what language.

Students respond initially to the personal anguish and graphic degradations to which Taylor submits himself, yet they are also quick to recognize the pattern of self-abasement followed by Christ's intervention and reelevation of humankind. Through class discussion, they revise their thinking about both the seeming lack of sophistication in Taylor's poetry and the dismissal of Puritan poets.

Major Themes, Historical Perspectives, Personal Issues

Probably completed in 1680, *Gods Determinations* usefully introduces students to Taylor's major dilemmas as preacher and individual saint—how to ascertain *and* sustain the belief in one's place among God's Elect and what standards of admission to uphold for Church membership. In its historical context, *Gods Determinations* reflects Taylor's local need to found a frontier Church for the true Elect (1679). His battles were against both the wilderness and the Indians without and Satan within. This minisequence from among the total of thirty-five poems allows one to talk about the difficult progress from conversion to justification and sanctification in two ways. A narrative reading opens with the magnificent evocation of God's creation, then the "Souls Groan" for salvation and "Christs Reply" as a lover or mother to a lost child counseling the soul to accept Christ's purifying grace to ensure the final triumphant entry into "Church Fellowship rightly attended," whether on earth or in heaven. Hence, the poem becomes a narrative of a spiritual journey. Taylor's position is as narrator and as voice of the saint.

One can also read the poems as a "debate," emphasizing various oppositions—between God and fallen man, the unworthy Elect soul and grace-giving Christ, the doubting soul and Satan the tempter, between Christ and Satan, hence between lowly earthly things and God's grandeur, being outside the covenant community of Elect saints and being within (the coach), between doubt and assurance, sin and salvation. Thus, *Gods Determinations* captures the dynamic *psychomachia* of both providential history and the individual soul that arches dramatically from the perfect promise of Creation, through the sinful downfall and soul's constant battle against Satan's renewed temptations, to the final joyful envisioning of "The Joy of Church Fellowship rightfully attended."

The Occasional Poems, which include eight numbered poems, were probably begun in the early 1680s, just as Taylor had completed *Gods Determinations* and was initiating the early *Preparatory Meditations.* Because these poems are the most "lyrical," they are more accessible to modern students. But what motivates Taylor is a desire to meditate upon natural "occurants" in order to extract allegorical or spiritual meanings.

Taylor's fondness for extended metaphors is apparent in his famous "Huswifery," which leads to discussion of Taylor's frequent use of spinning and weaving terms, frequently in relationship to poetic language or the need for the "Wedden garment" of righteousness that robes mankind for the Lord's Supper and union with Christ. "Upon Wedlock, & Death of Children" reveals Taylor at his most personal because the death of infants severely tested Taylor's faithful submission, as a loving father and husband, to God's divine plan, yet also strengthened the "True-Love Knot" binding him to both wife and Deity. It usefully links with other poems from *Edward Taylor's Minor Poetry*, which trace his domestic relationship with Elizabeth Fitch from his courtship (1674) to her death (1689).

"A Valediction to all the World preparatory for Death" permits comparisons among different versions, showing Taylor's substantial revision of late poems even during a time of severe illness. Although only one of the total eight canticles is included in *The Heath Anthology*, it nevertheless displays Taylor in the process of shedding worldliness, particularly all things that appeal to the senses and sensualities of the flesh. His "farewell" to the world, the flesh, and the devil is renunciatory and poignant, a meditation on "vanity of vanities, all is vanity" (Ecclesiastes 12:6–8) that evokes the very fondness for created nature that he appears to abjure.

"A Fig for thee Oh! Death" expresses Taylor's defiance of death, and it is a *memento mori* meditation that should be placed side by side with his later Canticles poems, in which he envisions the beauties of heaven. His anticipation of the final judgment and reunion of body and soul gives rise to an ecstatic affirmation of faith in the divine promise of eternal life.

As a complete sequence, the poems selected here, together with those from the *Preparatory Meditations*, trace Taylor's preoccupations over a lifetime:

- from the early focus on creation to the later renunciation of earthly vanities
- from his earliest attempt to map the soul's conflicts with Satan to his later celebration of Church fellowship, the Lord's Supper, and Christ as the divine host
- from his domestic espousal to his spiritual union with Christ as the eternal Bridegroom
- from his questioning of poetic status to his desire to be another David or Solomon, singing hymns for all eternity
- from his entrance into the minister's life to his death—the end of a long preparation recorded in a virtual poetic autobiography

Significant Form, Style, or Artistic Conventions

Taylor's verse experiments range from the varied stanza and metrical forms in *Gods Determinations* and the Occasional Poems to the heroic couplets of "A Valediction to all the World preparatory for Death" and "A Fig for thee Oh! Death." Variety also appears in Taylor's choice of forms, including a debate or narrative sequence of lyrics in *Gods Determinations*, elegies, love poems, a valediction and reflection on worldly vanities, and *memento mori*—all of which were commonplace among his English predecessors such as John Donne, George Herbert, and Henry Vaughan. For a more in-depth study of form, students might be urged to read and compare Taylor's elegies on public figures with those on personal losses, such as "Upon Wedlock, & Death of Children" and "A Funerall Poem upon . . . Mrs. Elizabeth Taylor," all in *Edward Taylor's Minor Poetry*.

Taylor's form and style sometimes seem too predictable because of the unchanging six-line, iambic pentameter, ababcc stanza of the *Preparatory Meditations*. Discussion should relate his use of a disciplined, even caged and controlled, verse form to his concept of poetry as ritualistic praise, as a rational framework within which to explore (and contain) irrational impulses of the rebellious soul, as a stimulus to imaginative imagistic variations, and as a habitual exercise of spiritual preparation. These poems are meditative self-examinations, illustrating the Puritan requirement to prepare the heart and soul before entering the Church or partaking of (and administering) the Lord's Supper. They also mediate between Taylor's composition and delivery of his Sacrament sermon.

As Louis Martz has argued in his "Foreword" to *The Poems of Edward Taylor* (1960), treatises, such as Richard Baxter's *The Saints Everlasting Rest* (1650), articulated a process that utilized the soul's three faculties: the Memory draws forth scriptural doctrines that the Judgment (or understanding) considers, thereby rousing the soul to feel the affections of the Will, particularly love and desire that lead to hope and joy. Taylor's meditations seem both to recapitulate reasoned doctrinal analysis and to elicit emotionally affecting responses or, as he declares, they "force my Will, and Reason to thee [God] so," that "my Soule, rid of their Sophistry/In rapid flames of Love to thee may fly" (2.36.27, 29–30). Each meditation disciplines the mind by formally squeezing theological complexities into an inflexible stanza and rhyme scheme, yet each also releases spiritual affections through cumulative floods of ingenious images and metaphors. Thus, the *Preparatory Meditations* raise useful critical questions about changing artistic tastes and conventions since the reasoned didacticism that in Taylor's meditations seems too dominant—a remnant of analysis of a biblical text or a tortured theological exegesis—fulfilled a seventeenth-century model of religious poetry that emphasized instruction more than pleasurable entertainment or romantic diversion. On the other hand, the boldly imaginative and highly evocative conceits seem to modern consciousnesses more the "stuff" of poetry that stems from personal confession and lyrical introspection, like that to be found much later in Emily Dickinson's similarly angst-ridden poems of doubt and faith. In Taylor's poetic art, both strands interweave, spiritual yearnings and effusions rising up naturally from reasoned scriptural analysis.

Taylor's imagistic variations in the *Preparatory Meditations* permit one to teach him in different combinations and ways. Structurally, the poems reflect differing manipulations of image patterns such as the focus on a single metaphor ("Prologue," 1.6, 1.8, 2.50); figural images and interpretations (1.8, 2.1, 2.26, 2.50); allegorical panoramas of salvation history (1.8, 2.50); associational tumblings of images (2.26, 2.115); magnifications and diminutions ("Prologue"); and allegorical love poems that anatomize the Bridegroom's and Spouse's beauties (2.115).

Thematically, poems cluster around recurrent ideas such as Christ's nature and life (1.8, 2.115); man's nature and estate (1.6, 1.8, 2.1, 2.26, 2.50); Old Testament types (persons, events, ceremonies) that foreshadow New Testament fulfillments in Christ (2.1, 2.26, 2.50); the Lord's Supper as sacramental feast

(1.8); the marriage of Christ to his Bride, signifying the Church and individual soul (2.115); and the necessity of poetic praise ("Prologue").

As a study of Puritan preparationism and aesthetics, the *Meditations* also reveal Taylor's yearnings to celebrate the Lord's Supper with a cleansed soul, robed for the feast in the wedding garment of righteousness (2.26, 2.115), and to create poetry as a medium for spiritual purging and preparation ("Prologue"). Wracked by despair over his diseased, leprous condition as an inheritor of Adam's original sin (2.26), Taylor nonetheless seeks through Christ a "cure" that will heal his soul and assure him of his divine election. Washed clean in a "Chrystall Crimson Fountain" by partaking of Christ's body (1.8) and blood celebrated in the Lord's Supper, Taylor can momentarily anticipate the eschatological redemption that secures his place in eternity, where he will be robed in wedding finery to unite with Christ the Bridegroom (2.115) at the marriage feast.

Chronologically, the *Meditations* open with the first series' dichotomy between mankind (a "Crumb," yet imprinted with the divine "Image, and Inscription") and the perfect Christ of the Incarnation ("Heavens Sugar Cake"). In keeping with a reorientation in Taylor's preaching, the second series begins anew with the Old Testament typology (2.1, 2.26). He then shifts to a focus on the Christology of the New Testament in poems (2.50) that correspond with the *Christographia* sermons, then to Meditations on God's providential deliverance of Israel (2.58–61) and on the Lord's Supper (2.102–111), and finally to the Canticles (2.115), Taylor's most sensual love poems, which anticipate the heavenly union beyond death (as also in the "Valediction").

Finally, the poems can be organized to reflect the context and progress of mankind's existence, beginning with the magnificence of the creation in the "Preface" to *Gods Determinations* and the providential schema mapped out in Meditation 2.50. Man's fallen nature (2.1, 2.26) yet divine aspirations (1.6) necessitate Christ's intervention and redemptive grace, brought about through His incarnation (1.8, 2.1), shedding of blood on the cross, and His eternal Godhead. Mankind's spiritual pilgrimage, like Taylor's, concludes with the anticipation of the espousal between Elect souls and Christ (2.115) and of the heavenly feast, which the Lord's Supper commemorates and foreshadows (1.8, "Valediction").

Original Audience

Taylor never published his poetry, although he carefully transcribed many poems in the manuscript "Poetical Works." A consideration of audience must, therefore, take account of the fact that the elegies and perhaps *Gods Determinations* were written in a more public mode, but that the majority of his Occasional Poems, the *Preparatory Meditations*, and the later "Valediction" and "A Fig for thee Oh! Death" are intensely personal, written it would seem for an audience of God or Christ alone, or as meditative self-examinations of Taylor's soul. As readers, we eavesdrop on Taylor, but we are not easily invited into the poems, except insofar as we identify with the Elect soul in its struggles or with Taylor as a representative pilgrim in his journey toward salvation.

Comparisons, Contrasts, Connections

Fruitful comparisons can be drawn both intratextually and extratextually. For the *Preparatory Meditations,* corresponding sermons are extant from *Upon the Types of the Old Testament* (Meditations 2.1, 2.26) and from the *Christographia* (Meditation 2.50). Edward Taylor's *Treatise Concerning the Lord's Supper,* notably Sermon 4, yields excellent excerpts on the need to prepare for the Lord's Supper and the wearing of the "wedden garment" for the feast. Because Taylor habitually clusters poems on the same biblical text, providing students, for example, with all three Meditations (1.8–10) on John 6: 51, 55, "I am the Living Bread" and "My Blood is Drink indeed," contextualizes a reading of Meditation 1.8 and of the Lord's Supper. Similarly, a short typological series, such as 2.58–61, permits a study of Taylor's fascination with the Exodus of Israel from Egypt and with the various types that foreshadow man's spiritual journey to salvation under the New Testament, as well as a more specific contextualizing of Meditation 2.60B on the "Rock of Horeb." Meditations 2.102–111 combine a theological defense with a festal celebration of the Lord's Supper, and the Canticles series that opens with Meditation 2.115 yields many examples of Taylor's interpretation of sensual imagery.

Comparisons with George Herbert's *The Temple,* particularly poems on the types, with John Donne's sonnets on the Ascension, death, and Christ as Spouse, and of Meditations 2.24 and 2.50 with contemporary Christmas poems on the Incarnation by Herbert, Southwell, and Milton enable students to identify different poetic styles and to place Taylor in a broader seventeenth-century meditative tradition.

One might also compare Anne Bradstreet's "The Prologue" and "Author to her Book" with Taylor's meditations on poetic craft in "Were but my Muse an Huswife Good," the "Prologue" to the *Preparatory Meditations,* and Meditation 2.43. Bradstreet's "Vanity of all Worldly Things" and "The Flesh and the Spirit" complement Taylor's "Valediction," and her poems "In Reference to Her Children 23 June 1659" and "Before the Birth of One of her Children" work in tandem with Taylor's "Upon Wedlock, & Death of Children," as do Bradstreet's several elegies on various grandchildren ("In Memory of my Dear Grandchild Elizabeth Bradstreet" and "On my Dear Grandchild Simon Bradstreet"). Selections from the prose meditations of Bradstreet also provide an intriguing counterpoint to Taylor's poetic meditations.

Taylor's Puritan belief in the transcendent perfection of God's divine Word and his preoccupation with his own linguistic inadequacy usefully herald issues of self-consciousness about language, words, poetry, and human fallibility versus divine incomparability that take us in an arc through Emerson to Dickinson and beyond. In frequent allusions to pens, quills, ink, letters, melodies, and tunes, and even in minitreatises on language (refer students to Meditation 2.43), Taylor foregrounds his concerns about "Speeches Bloomery" and the aesthetics of earthly hymns. Original sin, he bemoans, infects his very language since "words are befould, Thoughts filthy fumes" like "Will-a-Wisps that rise/From Quagmires, run ore bogs where frogs do Croake" (2.43.19, 20–21). Although he acknowledges that for mankind "Words" are the "finest twine of reason," they are nonetheless "Too Course a web for Deity to ware," so he must beg God's pardon that "I have no finer Stuff" (2.43.11, 12, 26). But Taylor's denigration of his poetic skill gives rise to an equally compelling countermovement to define himself as a "singer," modeled after the psalmist David or a lyric poet, such as Solomon, so that he too can "sing together fore his blessed face/Our Weddin Songs with Angells mild*****/In ravishing notes throughout Eternity" (2.133.44–46). Extracting the phrases, allusions, and metaphors that circle around writing not only enables students to generate a theory of Puritan esthetics that Taylor espouses, but it also sets up discussions that inevitably come forward with later poets, Whitman included as well as the later moderns, about poetry, voice, words as signifiers and signs, and language as constructed and elusively imperfect.

Presentational and Strategic Approaches

It proves particularly helpful to provide students with background information about key Puritan concepts, some of which are detailed in the headnote for the Edward Taylor selections. Many of these should also be discussed in relationship to other Puritan texts. But one can also prepare handouts on typology by listing Taylor's sermons and poems on the types (see *Saint and Singer*); a diagram of Israel's tabernacle and temple and its furnishings, together with a synopsis of the role of the High Priest and of the significant ceremonies; excerpts from a good Bible dictionary on major biblical figures or events; or predistributed excerpts from key biblical passages related to a poem's imagery. Visual arts only approximate the verbal, but Vaughan's emblem of the stony heart from *Silex Scintillans* for "The Ebb & Flow" or Renaissance paintings of death's heads ("A Fig"), worldly vanities and the heavenly Paradise ("Valediction"), Christ, and the Lord's Supper instructively guide textual analysis. A diagram labeling parts of the spinning wheel and spinning process illustrate Taylor's love of using weaving, looms, and webs as metaphors for poetry and for the construction of the self in "Huswifery." Comparing metaphysical with typological conceits stimulates discussion about poetic technique (e.g., Meditations 2.50 on Old Testament types and New Testament fulfillments and 2.26 on Christ's blood as the sacrificial purification of mankind's sin). Finally, reading poems aloud in class captures the surprisingly personal voice and intensity of many poems.

Questions for Reading, Discussion, and Writing

1. Specific questions can be generated easily for most poems, but it helps students (not only with Taylor but also with the study of other Puritan literature) to ask them to research key terms, using Donald Stanford's glossary, a well-annotated Bible with a concordance such as the *New Oxford Annotated Bible with the Apocrypha*, an ecumenical study Bible, the New Scofield Reference edition, Johnson's *The Poetical Works of Edward Taylor*, or the *Milton Encyclopedia.* Terms might include *Elect/election, covenant, baptism, Lord's Supper, preparation, law, grace, typology, providential history, apostasy, marriage, the Dove, the Rock, first fruits, offerings/sacrifices, Adam and Eve, the Garden of Eden, the Fall, Passover, the Exodus, Christ's incarnation, the crucifixion and resurrection, the Bride and Bridegroom, New Jerusalem,* and the *Second Coming.* One can assign students to look up the Bible verses mentioned in the footnotes or to read selections from Genesis, Exodus, Psalms, Canticles, the Gospels, Hebrews, and Revelation. Because of Taylor's playfulness with different meanings of a single image, students might be asked to look up in the *Oxford English Dictionary* the complete history of "fillet," "squitchen," "screw" and "pins," "knot," "kenning," "huswifery," "cocks," or "escutcheon" (one word each, perhaps). They might research the construction of the spinning wheel, thumbscrews and rack, tenon and mortise carpentry, the tabernacle and temple, a mint, and an alembic. Such preparation frequently alerts students to Taylor's multiple strands of imagery, his tricky punning, even humorous use of language, and the variety of areas from which he draws images and metaphors (architecture, horticulture, heraldry, carpentry, clothing, book-binding, warfare, alchemy, music, classical mythology, history, printing, domestic chores).

2. Obvious paper assignments involve interpretive readings of poems not otherwise studied in class. Advanced students can be encouraged to compare Genesis as the principal creation story with the "Preface" to *Gods Determinations*, Meditation 2.50, and his "Valediction to all the World preparatory for Death." Analysis of different strands of imagery that cut across several poems allows students to see Taylor's recurrent methods and themes, as with the water, blood, and wine associated with

Christ and the Lord's Supper. Similar assignments might be made around the concepts of the feast, marriage, the garden, reciprocal relationships (master and servant, Bridegroom/Beloved and Bride/Spouse, God and the elect), or around broad areas of imagery such as purification by fire, water, and blood ("Christ's Reply," 2.1, 2.26), and writing/ imprinting ("Prologue," 1.6, 2.50, "Valediction").

3. Creative writing assignments also immerse students in the complexities of Taylor's artistry while challenging them to write poetry that captures his fundamental theological concepts and the Puritan vision of mankind's history and life in relationship to Christ. Students can be asked to choose a biblical verse (perhaps one of Taylor's own), a dominant image, or an Old Testament type in order to create a preparatory meditation imitative of Taylor's metrical form and imagistic techniques; to write a lyric on a natural "occurant" or domestic event; to imagine a valediction or *memento mori* poem reflecting the vanity of this world and joys of the heavenly paradise; to use Canticles as a model for a love poem either written to Elizabeth Fitch, Taylor's wife, or as a celebration of the anticipated nuptials between Taylor and Christ as Bride and Bridegroom; or to generate a debate (in allegorical form perhaps) between Christ and Satan over man's soul. Students may also choose to create two poems on the same subject that reflect the different style and poetic forms preferred by Anne Bradstreet and Edward Taylor.

Teaching Issues and Interpretation

Placing Taylor in the context of other Puritan literature becomes illuminating in two ways because it responds to the question of what is poetry supposed to be and do. First, Taylor's work shows how the Puritan emphasis on spiritual examination of the individual soul can take the form of meditative and autobiographical poetry. Poetry for Taylor is both an immediate preparation for his ministerial administering of the Lord's Supper *and* a lifelong preparation for eternal life. Students often stumble with Taylor's poetry because they do not understand how intensely Taylor renounces this world in favor of a spiritual life within and a heavenly life yet to come. But they can identify with the human psychology of doubt, fear, loss, and a need for some form of consoling grace, comfort, or higher being to give meaning to the innately corrupt heart.

Second, because Taylor is the most prolific poet of America's first two hundred years (the anomaly of a "poet in the wilderness"), his meditations open up the question of a supposed Puritan disdain for poetry. Taylor's own puzzling over the proper uses of poetic language appears in "Were but my Muse an Huswife Good," the "Prologue" to the *Preparatory Meditations*, Meditation 2.43, and "A Valediction to all the World." By setting Taylor in a seventeenth-century tradition of paraphrases of Psalms, Job, and Canticles and, thus, the sanctioned acceptance of biblical poetry, and of a respect for *Sola Scriptura* as the model of language to be imitated, students can begin to appreciate the roots of an American tradition of poetry. The association of Taylor with David and Solomon as biblical models of poets becomes a useful end point for discussion because it points to Taylor's hope for his role in heaven, validates poetry as a medium of spiritual expression acceptable to God, sets the standards for "a transcendent style," and defines poetry as a ritual (meditative) offering of praise and worship.

Bibliography

Selections from the *Preparatory Meditations* and *Gods Determinations* have been published by permission of Donald E. Stanford, ed., *The Poems of Edward Taylor* (New Haven: Yale UP, 1960) and the "Occasional Poems," "A Valediction . . . ," and "A Fig for thee Oh! Death" by permission of Thomas M. and Virginia L. Davis, eds., *Edward Taylor's Minor Poetry* (Boston: Twayne, 1981).

Aside from sources already mentioned in the headnote's bibliography and the footnotes, the introductions to Taylor's published works by Donald Stanford, Norman Grabo, Thomas and Virginia Davis, and Charles Mignon always prove helpful. The most succinct biographical sketch is Donald Stanford's "Edward Taylor" in the *Dictionary of Literary Biography*. Michael Schuldiner has edited the most recent collection of essays in *The Tayloring Shop: Essays in Honor of Thomas M. and Virginia L. Davis* (1997). Key chapters on Taylor are found in Sacvan Bercovitch's *Typology and Early American Literature*, Michael Colacurcio's *Doctrine and Difference*, Albert Gelpi's *The Tenth Muse*, Barbara Lewalski's *Protestant Poetics and the Seventeenth-Century Religious Lyric*, Mason Lowance's *The Language of Canaan*, Earl Miner's *Literary Uses of Typology*, Peter White's *Puritan Poets and Poetics*, Ivy Schweitzer's *The Work of Self-Representation*, and Jeffrey Hammond's *Sinful Self, Saintly Self*.

Samuel Sewall (1652–1730)

Contributing Editor: Susan Clair Imbarrato

Classroom Issues and Strategies

Samuel Sewall's extensive, fifty-six-year diary, kept from 1674 to 1729, with details on family, politics, religion, social events, weather, and trade, provides students with a unique, eyewitness perspective of colonial Boston. It is helpful to remind students that the seventeenth-century diary was a "semipublic" document intended as a family record rather than a private, confessional one. As a Puritan, Sewall also used the diary as a tool for self-examination. This self-scrutiny demonstrates the Doctrine of Preparation and illustrates the rigors of living as an "elect" and a model Puritan. Even his uncharitable remarks or observations about lapsed behavior are used to emphasize a point about community and religious norms.

Sewall's recantation of his participation as a judge in the Salem witch trials and his entries on courtship draw attention for his willingness to admit failings. His distress over the deaths and illnesses of family members surprises students who imagine that a belief in the Doctrine of Predestination would preclude expressions of personal sorrow. Students might be surprised by the 1700 publication date for *The Selling of Joseph*, the "earliest work against slavery printed in Massachusetts," and yet be puzzled by its lack of moral outrage for the institution itself.

Major Themes, Historical Perspectives, Personal Issues

The Doctrines of Preparation and Predestination inform Sewall's *Diary* with its constant self-scrutiny and self-examination. This is evidenced in Sewall's examination of his role as a judge during the witchcraft trials and later in his public recantation of this role. Sewall also examines the impact of the witchcraft trials on the Puritan community.

The Selling of Joseph argues against the slave trade along religious and ethical terms and undermines its economic justifications. These points will become central to the slave narratives of Olaudah Equiano and Frederick Douglass and to the abolitionist movement.

Significant Form, Style, Artistic Conventions, and Original Audience

The episodic structure of Sewall's *Diary* focuses on the details of everyday life and provides rich social history and a valuable historical document. Sewall's *Diary* offers an excellent example of how a Puritan employed the Doctrine of Preparation ad the practice of self-examination.

The Selling of Joseph combines the sermon with the political tract. *The Selling of Joseph: a Memorial* was originally printed in Boston by Bartholomew Green and John Allen on June 24, 1700. The pamphlet was widely printed and read aloud.

Comparisons, Contrast, Connections

The *Diary* can be compared with John Winthrop's diary; Samuel Pepys's *Diary*, William Bradford's *Of Plymouth Plantation*; Mary Rowlandson's *Narrative of the Captivity*, and Sarah Kemble Knight's *Journal*.

The *Selling of Joseph* can be compared with John Woolman's *Journal*, Cotton Mather's *Wonders of the Invisible World*, and Benjamin Franklin's *An Address to the Public: From the Pennsylvania Society for Promoting the Abolition of Slavery*.

Working with Cultural Objects

The following websites can provide useful materials:

- "Chapter 1: Early American Literature to 1700—Samuel Sewall (1652–1730)." *PAL: Perspectives in American Literature: A Research and Reference Guide, An Ongoing Online Project*. Copyright © Paul P. Reuben: <http://www.csustan.edu/english/reuben/pal/chap1/sewall .html>
- Scott Atkins. *The American Sense of "Puritan."* Capitol Project, from the American Studies group at the University of Virginia: <http://www. xroads.virginia.edu/~CAP/puritan/purmain.html>
- William S. Reese. *The First Hundred Years of Printing in British North America: Printers and Collectors*. Copyright © 1990 by American Antiquarian Society: <http://www.reeseco.com/papers/first100.htm>

Salem Witchcraft Websites:

- Salem Witch Museum: <http://www.salemwitchmuseum.com>
- Salem Chronology: <http://www.salemweb.com/memorial/default.htm>

Questions for Reading and Discussions/Approaches to Writing

1. What does Sewall's *Diary* reveal about his Boston Puritan community's character and concerns?
2. Discuss Sewall's personal reactions to the illnesses and deaths in his immediate family. How do these reactions counter stereotypes about Puritans?
3. How does Sewall's depiction of his courtship of Madame Winthrop compare with contemporary concerns about marriage and prenuptial contracts?
4. What are the main arguments in Sewall's *The Selling of Joseph*? Which arguments are the most convincing? Discuss slavery, doctrinal law, labor, and economics.

Bibliography

a. Archives

The Samuel Sewall Papers are housed at the Massachusetts Historical Society.

b. Biographical Information

Amacher, Richard E. "Samuel Sewall." *Dictionary of Literary Biography: American Colonial Writers, 1606-1734.* Ed. Emory Elliott. Vol. 24. Detroit: Gale, 1984. 278–83.

Elliott, Emory. "New England Puritan Literature." *The Cambridge History of American Literature, 1590–182.* Ed. Sacvan Bercovitch. Vol. I. New York: Cambridge UP, 1994. 171–306.

Winslow, Ola E. *Samuel Sewall of Boston.* New York: Macmillan, 1964.

Wish, Harvey. "Introduction." *The Diary of Samuel Sewall.* Ed. Harvey Wish. New York: Putnam's, 1967.

c. Historical Contexts

Brown, Richard D. *Knowledge Is Power: The Diffusion of Information in Early America, 1700–1865.* New York: Oxford UP, 1989.

Cohen, Charles L. *God's Caress: The Psychology of Puritan Religious Experience.* New York: Oxford UP, 1986.

Delbanco, Andrew. *The Puritan Ordeal.* Cambridge, MA: Harvard UP, 1989.

Hall, David D. *Worlds of Wonder, Days of Judgment: Popular Belief in Early New England.* Cambridge, MA: Harvard UP, 1989.

Kagel, Steven E. *American Diary Literature, 1620–1799.* Boston: Hall, 1979.

Lovejoy, David S. "Between Hell and Plum Island: Samuel Sewall and the Legacy of the Witches, 1692–97." *New England Quarterly* 70 (1997): 355–68.

Towner, L. W. "The Sewall-Saffin Dialogue on Slavery," *William and Mary Quarterly* 21 (1964): 40–52.

Wall, Helena M. *Fierce Communion*. Cambridge, MA: Harvard UP, 1990.

Cotton Mather (1663–1728)

Contributing Editors: Kenneth Alan Hovey and Gregory S. Jackson

Classroom Issues and Strategies

The challenge in teaching Mather is to humanize him without sacrificing the complexity that makes him so fascinating. One strategy might be to stress his burdens as an eminent figure in a prominent Puritan family at a time of radical change.

Students might identify with Mather's strenuous attempts to live up to his perfectionist father, Increase Mather, who in his prime dominated the Bay Colony's intellectual and political life. Cotton's fragile constitution, particularly as a child, suggests how fierce the struggle sometimes was; and there often seems to have been a contest in his life between optimistic self-assertion and an equally potent despair. Prodigious works like the *Magnalia Christi Americana* show Mather responding to cultural shocks in the same way he confronted personal ones—by attempting to situate them within ever larger and more dramatic Old Testament typological narratives. Instructors may then explore the tools with which he does so: both the typological figures that convey Mather's optimism and the ambiguities and contradictions that confess his despair.

Major Themes, Historical Perspectives, Personal Issues

As New England became increasingly secular and commercial, and as the semblance of orthodoxy gave way to religious diversity, Mather strove, both ideologically and personally, to adapt to the change, though this struggle often introduced visible theological contradictions into the very system that he dedicated his life to shoring up. Although a guardian of Puritan tradition, he was nevertheless an avid naturalist, a member of the British Royal Society, a leader in the revolt against Governor Edmund Andros—appointed by the king— and, through his interest in evangelical piety, a religious progressive. His numerous biographies of first-generation Puritans assert the continued vigor of

New England's millennial role: Mather repeatedly relies upon elaborate figures to link the colony with both ancient Israel and the Apocalypse. Underlying his interest in witchcraft, for example, is the millennial conviction that great troubles would mount as the last days approached, while his portrait of Hannah Dustin suggests an American biblical heroine smiting the enemy and loosening the bonds of captive Israel. Thus, Mather's writing often reveals the tensions in his hard-won position. His marking off of witches, Native Americans, and the disorderly suggests not only a constant need to police his ideology but also an acknowledgment of its increasingly rapid erosion.

This erosion was hastened by a shift in the New England worldview, a split between a more cosmopolitan group of Puritan merchants, who studied Descartes at Harvard and read widely in the works of Isaac Newton and John Locke, and an older, more conservative group of Puritan ministers and colonists. While many of the former party bitterly condemned the Salem witch trials at the time, many of the latter viewed them as an offensive strike against the forces of evil. Thus the witch trials accentuated two competing worldviews: the one an ebbing Platonic view of a corresponding universe in which the moral battles fought in this world were part of the larger cosmic struggle between good and evil, and the other a modern materialist view predicated upon scientific empiricism and the exaltation of instrumental reason and human rationality. Students can often better understand this epistemological shift if the instructor compares and contrasts the deeply pietistic Mather with Benjamin Franklin, Mather's deistic younger contemporary who was also born into a Boston Puritan family. Even in their passion for science the two are quite different. Whereas Franklin, like Locke, seems to pursue science in the Baconian tradition of secular Humanism, Mather, like Isaac Newton and Jonathan Edwards, continually presses scientific discovery into the service of theological validation.

Like his father's *Essay for the Recording of Remarkable Providences* (1684), Cotton Mather's *Wonders of the Invisible World* (1693), his defense of the Salem court in the aftermath of the trials, epitomizes the ebbing worldview of a corresponding universe. By cataloging a series of prodigies and omens, Mather supported the Salem court's finding that witches were indeed conspiring with Satan to corrupt the New England Church. Those who saw the witch hunt as a reckless indulgence of superstition, however, immediately lampooned this treatise on the supernatural. In essence, the Salem witch trials would become a contest between two radically opposing points of view. Nowhere is this difference in epistemology better expressed than in the transatlantic controversy over what constituted legitimate "evidence" in the Salem witch trials.

The court convicted the accused for a capital offense almost exclusively on what was termed "spectral evidence," a witness's testimony that he or she saw a spectral image of the accused performing a preternatural feat. For the most part, the controversy over "spectral evidence" did not hinge upon the veracity of the preternatural feat itself—few doubted the manifestations of demonic forces—rather, it hung upon a finer point. Whereas for the court, ocular evidence of a preternatural act—such as the appearance of a neighbor as a demonic specter—was proof positive of the alleged witches' compact with Satan, for others, like Increase Mather, such "spectral evidence" begged a question that undermined its validity as a litmus test of witchcraft: If Satan could take the form of animals, why could he not assume the appearance of any person, thus implicating an innocent in his ruinous plot? Still others, such as Robert Calef and Thomas Brattle, rejected outright the accusations of witchery as simple-minded superstition. As Mather well knew when he wrote *Wonders* in defense of the Salem executions, the stakes were enormous: what had been a trial to determine the course of individual lives had become a trial to determine the course of an entire culture; and what had been adjudicated in the zeal of religious devotion in a provincial court would forever after be tried in a spirit of secular rationalism in the court of public opinion. It was a wager Mather lost to history. His homiletic report of the trials would become the "bible" of Washington Irving's Ichabod Crane and would make Mather's name a symbol of Puritan superstition in spite of his contributions to early American rational and scientific thought. Although Mather would continue to find momentous importance in common incidents, never again would he do so with such abandon.

Significant Form, Style, or Artistic Conventions

Mather's distinguishing literary characteristic is the degree to which he merges history and autobiography. Certain elements of Mather's approach to church history, for example, can be found in the numerous models that he used, among them William Bradford. But whereas Bradford's *Of Plymouth Plantation* is narrated in the modest, self-effacing manner one associates with Puritan saints, Mather constantly intervenes, forcing his own voice upon the reader. Such obtrusiveness makes sense if one realizes that Mather's real interest lies not only in conveying the facts of men's lives but also in turning lives into instructive "examples"—examples that allow him, in turn, to extend his own sense of the Puritan errand. In this regard, it may be useful to compare Mather's self-presentation with that of Mary Rowlandson, whose wilderness ordeal also spoke to New England's providential fortunes.

Mather's treatment of cultural "others" also bears notice. His treatment of Native Americans, for example, has neither the sympathy of William Byrd's nor the almost clinical detail of Rowlandson's portraits. What it does, rather, is expose the ideological uses to which Mather put Native Americans, as figures in New England's cosmic drama. Conversely, although his plea, in *The Negro Christianized*, for justice to African-American "servants" stopped short of calling for emancipation, it nevertheless insisted that God is colorblind. Converting slaves contributed to the rising glory of Christian America, as Mather found by ministering to his own slave, Onesimus, the slave he acquired in the same year he published *The Negro Christianized*. Relatively speaking, Mather was apparently a humane, liberal, but suspicious slave owner, teaching Onesimus to read and write and allowing him outside income, but keeping him under strict surveillance.

Finally, Mather has been profitably compared with much later figures such as Henry Adams, whose cultural inheritance left them unprepared for change.

Questions for Reading, Discussion, and Writing

1. Compare the court records of *Wonders of the Invisible World* to Mather's account of the Goodwin children in book VI of the *Magnalia*. What kinds of concerns does Mather bring to these more personal encounters?
2. Compare Mather's benevolent project in *Bonifacius* with those described in Franklin's *Autobiography*. What impulses unite the two endeavors? How are they different?
3. Sample other sections of the *Magnalia*. If Mather intends for New England, whether it "Live any where else or no," to "Live in [his] History," what cultural aspects does he choose to preserve, and how successful is his project?
4. How does Mather's history differ from Thomas Shepard's earlier history of New England, from Shepard's *Autobiography*? What rhetorical strategies do they have in common? And in what important ways do these two different historical accounts differ in their vision of the Puritans' "errand into the wilderness"?
5. Compare Mather's *The Negro Christianized* to Samuel Sewall's *The Selling of Joseph*. How does the possibility of miscegenation and the confusion of racial identities serve both to limit and clarify the Puritan sense of self?

Bibliography

Instructors will find a number of primary works on the witch trials not only accessible to students but also provocative in the classroom: Deodat Lawson, *A Brief and True Narrative of Some Remarkable Passages* and "Christ's Fidelity the only Shield"; Cotton Mather, "A Brand Pluck'd out of the Burning"; and Robert Calef, *More Wonders of the Invisible World*. In addition to the secondary works mentioned in the anthology, instructors might consult David Levin,

Cotton Mather: The Young Life of the Lord's Remembrancer (Cambridge, MA: Harvard UP, 1978); Richard Lovelace, *The American Pietism of Cotton Mather* (Grand Rapids, MI: Christian UP, 1979); Mason Lowance, *The Language of Canaan* (Cambridge, MA: Harvard UP, 1980); and Michael Winship, *Seers of God* (Baltimore: The Johns Hopkins UP, 1996).

John Williams (1664–1729)

Contributing Editors: Rosalie Murphy Baum and Elizabeth Dillon

Classroom Issues and Strategies

The popularity of the captivity narrative during the Puritan period is being repeated today among students who vicariously enjoy the narrators' experiences and realize the effect such narratives have had on popular frontier and Wild West adventure stories. To many students already familiar with Mary Rowlandson's 1682 *Narrative,* John Williams's 1707 narrative is especially welcome—not simply because it offers a male version of captivity but also because it describes captivity both by the Indians (for eight weeks) and by the French (for two years). The primary difficulty students have in reading the narrative lies in their lack of knowledge of the French and Indian War and of the differences between Roman Catholicism and Puritanism.

Background information about the relationship between the French and English in North America can eliminate this difficulty and give students a more accurate idea of colonial history. To be stressed first is the fact that the hostilities between the French and the English in North America began as early as 1613 and that the period between 1613 and the Peace of Paris in 1763 was one in which some six extended conflicts, or "wars," resulted in captives, usually women and children, being taken from New England to Canada.

Students also need to be reminded of the theological and ritualistic differences that distinguished the Puritans from the Established Church of England. Roman Catholicism represented a structure and theology even more pernicious to Puritans than the structure and theology of the Church of England. In such a context, Williams's strong reaction to the Indians' taking him "to a popish country" (Québec) and to the efforts of the French Jesuits to convert him to Roman Catholicism becomes clear.

Major Themes, Historical Perspectives, Personal Issues

The Redeemed Captive is, then, an excellent work to dramatize for students what the French and Indian Wars were about and to clarify the antagonism between Catholics and Puritans during this period. It is also a form of the jeremiad more readable and interesting to modern students than most of the Puritan sermons, histories, or personal narratives.

In addition, it illustrates "the significant mythic experience of the early white-Indian relationship" (Louise K. Barnett, *The Ignoble Savage*) and the "Puritan myth of 'America,'" "the first coherent myth-literature developed in America for American audiences" (Richard Slotkin, *Regeneration Through Violence*). Students can see in both Williams's and Rowlandson's narratives the way in which such accounts typically open with an Indian raid in which white settlers are brutally massacred and then proceed to describe the inhuman hardships Indians inflict upon their captives. The concept of the Indian is that of satanic beast. No attempt is made in these narratives to indicate that the Indian aggression is a part of the hostilities of decades and may have been provoked or equaled by white aggression. Little note is made of the decency or kindnesses of the Indians: such good fortune as the captive may experience is never attributed to the customs or virtue of the Indians but to God. Living conditions that are everyday parts of the Indian life or result from the normal state of travel at that time are regarded by captives as horrendous personal injuries being deliberately and cruelly inflicted upon them by the Indians. Clearly no cognizance is taken of the inherent difficulties that arise when two such disparate cultures come together under conditions of warfare.

Williams's narrative also demonstrates that anxieties about encountering alien cultures extended to the French (as Catholics) as much as to the Indians; he shows equal concern over the threat of Catholicism as over Indian "savagery." His narrative thus indicates that in this early period, the *racial* distinction between white Europeans and Native Americans was not the sole boundary between civilized and savage for Williams. Rather, religious and cultural differences were keenly felt in relation to Indians *and* Europeans. This may prove a useful point of discussion for students, enabling them to consider changing understandings of race over the course of American history, and relations between racial and cultural difference.

A final significant aspect of Williams's narrative is his concern for his daughter Eunice, who does not return to New England even when later offered the chance to do so. The threat of "going native" is often at stake in captivity narratives, particularly with respect to women and children. John Demos's *The Unredeemed Captive* gives a full account of Eunice Williams's fascinating history, including her marriage to a Mohawk man, the many years of attempts by her family and authorities to have her returned to New England, and her visits to her brother in Longmeadow, Massachusetts, in her old age.

Significant Form, Style, or Artistic Conventions

Of particular interest to many students will be the subject of the captivity narrative as a genre particularly American in its subject matter years before American writers—like Freneau, Bryant, Irving, Cooper, Hawthorne, and James—became concerned about the question of an inherently *American* literature. This genre was clearly, in its early stages, a religious statement, emphasizing redemptive suffering, with the captivity being either a test that God had set for his people or a punishment to guide them from their evil ways. Williams's narrative was such an excellent example of the type that Sunday School versions appeared as late as the 1830s and 1840s (e.g., Titus Strong's *The Deerfield Captive: an Indian Story, being a Narrative of Facts for the Instruction of the Young*).

Original Audience

Students should be reminded too, of course, that Williams is writing for a Puritan audience. Thus, for a people familiar with the jeremiad, he emphasizes God's wrath against his people for their shortcomings, but also rejoices in God's mercy and goodness toward his people. (See Sacvan Bercovitch, *The American Jeremiad*, for a study of the negative and positive sides of the jeremiad.) He assumes the satanic nature of the Indians, particularly fearsome creatures by which God tests his people or punishes them. And he stresses the diabolical nature of the Jesuits, who, in their zeal to convert him to Roman Catholicism, make him attend a Latin Mass, urge him to pray to the Virgin Mary, and try to force him to kiss a crucifix.

Questions for Reading, Discussion, and Writing

For their writing assignments, some students may wish to read other captivity narratives either to compare narratives of redemptive suffering or to trace the changes in the genre emerging during the propaganda and fictionalized thriller stages. Wilcomb E. Washburn's *Narratives of North American Indian Captivities* offers facsimile reprints of 311 such narratives dating from the late seventeenth century to the late nineteenth century.

But even without such additional reading, the possibilities for essays based upon Williams's narrative are considerable. Students may wish to discuss Williams's *The Redeemed Captive* as a jeremiad, comparing it to jeremiads they have read in other genres. They may wish to examine Williams's narrative techniques, especially with a view to the contribution the genre has made to the horror story or thriller. Students interested in women's studies or feminist criticism may wish to consider conceptual and stylistic differences between the narratives of Rowlandson and Williams. Students interested in Indian studies can compare attitudes toward the Indians in Williams and other authors studied (e.g., in Bradford, Roger Williams, Cotton Mather, Rowlandson, or, moving into a later period, Franklin, Freneau, Bryant, Cooper, or Melville). Students familiar with Joseph Campbell's *The Hero With a Thousand Faces* can consider the archetypal nature of *The Redeemed Captive*, perhaps in the light of other works they have read. Students may also wish to consider more contemporary versions or analogues of the captivity narrative, such as the 1956 John Wayne film, *The Searchers*, or the Iranian hostage crisis of 1979–1981.

Specific discussion questions concerning Williams's narrative might include the following: What is Williams's purpose in writing the narrative? Why was the captivity narrative such a popular American genre, both in the eighteenth century and in subsequent periods? Why might women and/or children be more likely to remain with Indian tribes? Why are Catholicism and Native American culture such significant threats to John Williams and to Puritan New England? To what extent is Williams concerned about the following issues: racial difference, cultural difference, religious difference?

Bibliography

Of particular value as background reading for teaching *The Redeemed Captive* is Wilcomb E. Washburn's "Introduction" to *Narratives of North American Indian Captivity: A Selective Bibliography* (1983), xi–lvv; and Edward W. Clark's "Introduction" to *The Redeemed Captive* by John Williams (1976), 1–25.

A number of secondary sources on the captivity narrative explore the relations among cultural boundaries, gender, and the captivity genre in American culture, including Michelle Burnham's *Captivity and Sentiment: Cultural Exchange in American Literature 1682–1861*; Gary Ebersole's *Captured by Texts: Puritan to Postmodern Images of Indian Captivity*; and Christopher Castiglia's *Bound and Determined: Captivity, Culture-crossing, and White Womanhood for Mary Rowlandson to Patty Hearst*.

A Sheaf of Seventeenth-Century Anglo-American Poetry

Contributing Editors: Jeffrey A. Hammond and Ivy Schweitzer

Classroom Issues and Strategies

While students are pleasantly surprised at the diversity of poets and poetic themes in early America, they are often disappointed with the poems themselves. This disappointment is a good starting point for discussion since it highlights the differences between seventeenth-century and contemporary expectations and responses regarding poetry. When students articulate what disappoints them about much of the verse—the generalized speakers, the religious themes, the artificial language, the high level of allusion—they begin to understand that art and its cultural functions are subject to historical change. Good questions to begin discussion of particular poems in this selection include: Why was the poem written? What reading response does the text seem to foster? What is the relationship between the poem and the values of the culture that produced it? What view of poetic language does the poem seem to demonstrate?

Major Themes, Historical Perspectives, Personal Issues

These poems also become more interesting for students when they are asked to identify the blend (or opposition) of Old World and New World features—formal as well as thematic—within the texts. Another issue concerns the expected functions of verse in the seventeenth century. Once students realize that poets were more interested in voicing communal values, commemorating important events, and seeking coherence in their world than in expressing "original" ideas, the poems begin to make better sense. Students may not agree with the literary conventions they encounter, but they will gain a better contextual understanding of them. This in turn may help them see that modern reading expectations also exist in a particular historical and cultural framework.

Significant Form, Style, or Artistic Conventions

For most students these poems are quite difficult. The syntax is sometimes cramped into a rigid meter (Wilson and Alsop), the allusions often seem remote and excessive (Saffin), the speakers seem remote and impersonal, and, for many, the poem's ideology seems trite or alien (Goodhue). A discussion of "metaphysical" wit often helps students understand—if not enjoy—the seemingly strained effects in many of the poems. The Renaissance view of poetry as a frankly artificial discourse is also helpful. The poet is usually not trying to replicate "natural" speech in texts that were written, in one sense or another, for the ages.

Original Audience

The selections here reflect a wide range of intended readers. Students might try to determine the nature of those readers (their social class, education, reading expectations) as a means of humanizing the texts. This will also underscore the contrasts between the literary culture that these poems embody and the students' own literary culture, including its microcosm in the English classroom.

Comparisons, Contrasts, Connections

Students familiar with the English cavaliers and metaphysical poets will bring a great deal to the discussion of these poems, especially in matters of form and style. It is also useful to compare the poems with other treatments of similar themes: Saffin with Shakespeare's sonnets, French with later slave narratives, Steere with later Romantic depictions of nature, Goodhue with Bradstreet, Alsop with promotional tracts, and Ebenezer Cook, Wilson, and Hayden with Milton's *Lycidas*. In addition, any of the poems could be profitably compared with works by Bradstreet, Wigglesworth, or Taylor.

Questions for Reading, Discussion, and Writing

1. What do the poems suggest about the cultural functions of poetry in the seventeenth century?
2. What do they suggest about the relation between individual identity and culture or ideology?
3. What do they suggest about seventeenth-century distinctions between "poetic" discourse and everyday speech?
4. What implied readership is suggested in their diction and allusions?
5. In what sense(s), thematic or formal, are the poems "American"?
6. In what sense(s), thematic or formal, are the poems "British"?
7. What expressions of the cultural diversity characteristic of a later America seem already present in these poems?
8. Do thematic or formal differences emerge in the work of the female and male poets collected here?

Bibliography

Cowell, Pattie. "Introduction" and Headnotes. *Women Poets in Pre-Revolutionary America.* Woodbridge, CT: Hall, 1981.

Meserole, Harrison T. "Introduction" and Headnotes. *American Poetry of the Seventeenth Century.* New York: Norton, 1985.

Scheick, William J. "The Poetry of Colonial America." *Columbia Literary History of the United States.* Ed. Emory Elliott. New York: Columbia UP, 1988.

—— and Joella Doggett. *Seventeenth-Century American Poetry: A Reference Guide.* Woodbridge, CT: Hall, 1977.

—— and Catherine Rainwater. "Seventeenth-Century American Poetry: A Reference Guide Updated." *Resources for American Literary Study* 10 (1980): 121–45.

Silverman, Kenneth. "Introduction" and Headnotes. *Colonial American Poetry.* New York: Hafner Press, 1968.

White, Peter, ed. *Puritan Poets and Poetics: Seventeenth-Century American Poetry in Theory and Practice.* University Park: Pennsylvania State UP, 1985.

Pedagogical Introduction

Eighteenth Century

Settlement and Religion
Cluster: On Nature and Nature's God
A Sheaf of Eighteenth-Century Anglo-American Poetry
Voices of Revolution and Nationalism
Cluster: On the Discourse of Liberty
Patriot and Loyalist Songs and Ballads
Contested Visions, American Voices

Although affected by work in multicultural U.S. history, the dominant popular conception of the American eighteenth century remains a consensus model focused on the triumph of a united band of Patriot revolutionaries against the forces of British imperialism, a view reinforced by the continued popularity of the culture industry devoted to retelling stories of the so-called "Founding Fathers." The categories used in *The Heath Anthology*, however, work to restore a sense of the flux, dynamism, and contingency of that period, a social, political, and rhetorical struggle captured in the phrase "Contested Visions." These contests took place both within Anglo-American communities and across the wide, diverse range of American society. "Voices of Revolution and Nationalism" as well as the section on "Patriot and Loyalist Songs and Ballads" challenge the common belief that Anglo-Americans were of one mind about the revolution. Texts by women writers, by adherents of different religious communities, and by members of different social classes show that whatever Thomas Jefferson may have claimed about the truths he articulated in *The Declaration of Independence*, they were anything but "self-evident" at the time. Indeed, by placing the founders in their cultural contexts, we can read a text like the *Declaration* not simply as an enumeration of timeless truths but also as an argument designed to achieve specific and complex political and social ends. Similarly, the new "Cluster: On Nature and Nature's God" and "Cluster: On the Discourse of Liberty" provide thumbnail overviews of the ferment and debate over the "new" concepts of "Nature" and "Liberty" within the dominant Anglo-American tradition. Such a view in the classroom provides a sense of the very real stakes involved in "literary" questions of form, style, and structure.

Just as important, the inclusion of other revolutionary voices, from Handsome Lake to Toussaint L'Ouverture, raises questions about the complexity and diversity of the revolutionary energies at play in eighteenth-century America. The idea of the "Founding Fathers" as national myth is further complicated by Fray Francisco Palou's biography of Junipero Serra, an example of mythmaking involving a different "Founding Father." For students who have never done so, considering "American" cultural history from the perspective of the Spanish

115

colonial experience can open discussion about the meaning of the cultural and historical center and margins, of frontier and wilderness, and about the traditional view of American history as a movement to the West from the East Coast.

Settlement and Religion

Sarah Kemble Knight (1666–1727)

Contributing Editor: Kathryn Zabelle Derounian-Stodola

Classroom Issues and Strategies

Because Knight uses humor and fiction in her journal, students find it more accessible than many other early American texts. They respond positively to the journal as travelogue and can relate to Knight's role as a savvy observer and recorder of cultural norms. Moreover, they are fascinated that this is an early woman's text that does not show stereotypical female qualities of victimization and passivity and that contradicts the still-prevalent notion of Puritans as dour and doom-laden. However, teachers should encourage students to analyze Knight's self-fashioning and go beyond her endearing surface qualities as author and subject to find evidence of more negative qualities, including rampant racism and classism. The *Journal* is not a politically naive text.

Major Themes, Historical Perspectives, Personal Issues

1. Gender issues: the position of women—especially women writers—in late seventeenth- and early eighteenth-century New England. In theory, Puritans used the topological significance of Eve's creation from Adam's rib to emphasize women's dependence and domesticity. Women were expected to marry and to serve God, their father (while unmarried), and their husband. Sermons, for example, frequently stressed the ideal female qualities of modesty, piety, humility, patience, charity, and so on. But in practice, of course, women were often far from this ideal (Knight certainly seems to revel in her independence), and in a frontier society they sometimes had to take on men's work. Thus, evidence shows that women became printers, stationers, and innkeepers, for example—usually on the death of their father or spouse. Sarah Kemble Knight is a case in point,

and instructors might ask students to find textual evidence of Knight's refusal to play the stereotypically passive female role Puritan culture assigned to her. Moreover, compared to the contemporaneously published works of such other well-known Puritan women writers as Anne Bradstreet and Mary Rowlandson, Knight's unpublished (until 1825) narrative is more private and secular in nature.

2. Views of the frontier and the wilderness. This text makes a particularly useful contrast to Mary Rowlandson's captivity narrative in terms of the authors' presentation of the frontier. Whereas Rowlandson sees her enforced journey as taking her into what she calls "the vast and howling Wilderness," Knight voluntarily undertakes her journey and overcomes the natural obstacles in her way (bad weather, swamps, high rivers, and so on) despite unconvincing protestations that she is only a feeble woman.

3. Class, race, regional, and cultural issues: particularly Knight's views of blacks, American Indians, and white settlers at all social levels in Massachusetts and in the other colonies she travels through from Boston to New York. In this regard, I particularly commend Julia Stern's article "To Relish and to Spew: Disgust as Cultural Critique in the *Journal of Madam Knight*," *Legacy* 14 (1997): 1–12, which extends the argument of Scott Michaelsen's earlier article, "Narrative and Class in a Culture of Consumption: The Significance of Stories in Sarah Kemble Knight's *Journal*," *College Literature* 21 (1994): 33–46. Stern points out that the journal "provides an extraordinary anatomy of early eighteenth-century America as a multi-racial, multi-cultural body" and that it functions as a "meditation on the complexity of class" (1). This is effected by Knight's emphasis on, and judgment of, things oral, specifically, what people say and eat and how they speak and eat. Students and instructors alike cannot miss the many textual references to bad food and bad manners. While Knight often presents her disapproval and disgust humorously, in fact they indicate that she is "a fervent believer in hierarchy" (Stern 6). Knight's determination to maintain social distinctions makes her a snob and a racist. Although Knight is, perhaps, the most scathing about whites who allow their slaves to eat at the table with them, her scorn also descends on others who do not keep their allotted social position.

Significant Form, Style, or Artistic Conventions

Discuss the traditions of various life writings including diaries, journals, and spiritual and secular autobiographies and also explain how the *Journal* fits the fictional genre of the picaresque (look up a definition in any literary handbook). Also, don't overlook the fact that the journal contains quite a few poems written by Knight, some of them no more than doggerel (as in the wonderful "I ask thy Aid, O Potent Rum!"), but other more lyrical and accomplished pieces as well. Compare the popular, colloquial quality of this work with more academic texts to understand its place in early American literary activity and to help students understand generic distinctions as well as generic interrelationships. While instructors should be flexible about enforcing overly rigid generic divisions, it is helpful to define some of the following differences for students and then invite them to consider texts they have read that might be placed in certain categories:

- Personal letter: relatively short; writer may deliberately fashion an epistolary self and voice; reader is clearly designated; function is probably private; and the text is not likely to have been revised. Examples include Richard Frethorne's three letters home.
- Diary: focuses on externals or on highly personal internal matters; tends to be unrevised, immediate, and fragmentary; may extend for many years; and usually has no audience beyond the writer (indeed, some writers— such as William Byrd in his coded diaries—went to great lengths to stop others from being able to read their private diaries). Examples include William Byrd and Samuel Sewall.
- Journal: may focus more on internal, though not necessarily highly personal, matters; may be somewhat revised; may be written shortly after the fact and thus may reinterpret and reflect on events; may extend over a relatively short and designated time period and may memorialize a specific event such as a journey or a courtship; appears to be relatively coherent; and may have been written for a specific small audience of family and friends, though not usually with an eye to publication. Knight's journal fits this definition well.
- Autobiography and spiritual autobiography: often considered the most "literary" of the genres because they are more carefully structured and composed. The autobiography, of course, charts an individual's personal and sometimes public life (Franklin's *Autobiography* is a prime example); the spiritual autobiography charts an individual's spiritual development and is often written for publication to encourage backsliders or attract converts. Rowlandson's narrative is a good example of a Puritan spiritual autobiography and those by Elizabeth Ashbridge and John Woolman are excellent examples of Quaker spiritual autobiographies (the latter two texts published posthumously).

Original Audience

Knight's work was not written with publication in mind, and indeed although composed during her journey from Boston to New York in 1704–1705, it was not published until 1825. Certainly the journal seems to have had therapeutic value in allowing Knight to vent her spleen over various difficulties in her trip (usually bad food and bad accommodations). But she probably took such care to record details so she could read it to family and friends or circulate it among them. When first published, the journal was thought to be fictional, but doubts about its authenticity have long since vanished.

In his edition of the *Journal* in *Journeys in New Worlds* (Madison: U of Wisconsin P, 1990), Sargent Bush also discusses the circumstances that led to its publication in 1825. It was published, and perhaps edited, by Theodore Dwight Jr., of New York, son of Theodore Dwight Sr. (who was one of the so-called Connecticut Wits intent on producing a native American literature after the Revolution). In recovering and publishing Knight's document, Dwight Jr., was providing one more example "of this growing sense of the validity of American expression" (Bush 79) as opposed to outmoded European models. The 1820s also saw the publication of such American texts as "Rip Van Winkle" and "The Legend of Sleepy Hollow" and early works by James Fenimore Cooper and William Cullen Bryant.

Questions for Reading, Discussion, and Writing

1. Knight as heroine or picara (the protagonist in a female picaresque).
2. Presentations of the wilderness. Indeed, this would be a good early American text for applying eco-critical approaches.
3. The document as a secular manifestation of Puritanism.
4. Knight's classism and racism.
5. Knight's middle-class consumer values and her desire for upward mobility.
6. Knight as a storyteller, as a spinner of yarns (note that there are many stories within stories in the *Journal*).

Louis Armand de Lom d'Arce, Baron de Lahontan
(1666–1715)

Contributing Editor: Susan Castillo

Classroom Issues and Strategies

In these excerpts from Lahontan's New Voyages to *North America*, what most students will find of interest is the complex nature of Lahontan's attitudes toward Native Americans. In the first excerpt, "A Discourse of the Interest of the French, and of the English, in North America," Lahontan comes across as a hard-headed pragmatist whose main concern is the bottom line of financial profit. Students can analyze his proposed economic strategy and its underlying assumption that it is desirable to "reduce them [Native Americans] to one half of the power they are now possessed of." It would be useful to discuss the nature of ethnocentrism and the sort of attitude that would lead Lahontan to believe that he had the right to do so. In the first excerpt from Volume II, "Giving an Account of the Customs, Commerce, Religion and Strange Opinions of the Savages of that Country," students could discuss Lahontan's characterizations of the ways in which Indians are presented in the histories of Canada written by the Jesuits and the Recollects. What conclusions do these cause him to reach about the nature of historiography? How does his own experience of Native Americans contradict the descriptions of the Jesuit and Recollect friars? One of the most fascinating aspects of Lahontan's text is the way in which he uses his discussion of Native culture to criticize French society. In the excerpt from "A Short View of the Humors and Customs of the Savages," what conclusions does he draw about Native concepts of property ownership and attitudes toward the aged? In the excerpt from "An Account of the Amours and Marriages of the Savages," how does Lahontan describe gender roles, courtship customs, sexuality, and attitudes toward romantic love among Native Americans?

Major Themes, Historical Perspectives, Personal Issues

Major themes in Lahontan include the contrasts between Native and French society, strategies of colonization, and the alienating effects of European religion. Students may wish to look into the ways in which Lahontan is an inheritor of Renaissance iconoclasts like Montaigne and a precursor of Enlightenment thinkers like Jean-Jacques Rousseau and their concepts of the Noble Savage.

Significant Form, Style, or Artistic Conventions

Lahontan was an enthusiastic reader of the satirical *Dialogues* of Lucian. In the classroom, it would be interesting to discuss the nature of satire and to cite instances of satirical reference in Lahontan's prose. How does he use the conventions of satire to critique not Native American customs but rather those of his own mother country?

Original Audience

Lahontan's *New Voyages to North-America* was a runaway bestseller, with translations into English, German, Dutch, and Italian. It would be interesting to discuss with students the reasons for this success—among which might be cited his fluid and ironic prose, his racy descriptions of Native sexual mores, and his vivid descriptions of Native life.

Comparisons, Contrasts, Connections

Students might enjoy comparing and contrasting Lahontan's view of the Indians with that presented in the Jesuit Relations, online at <http://www.puffin.creighton.edu/jesuit/relations>.

Working with Cultural Objects

There is a "Musée virtuel de la Nouvelle-France," which can be translated into English and features descriptions of Lahontan's voyages, maps of the route, the original title page for his "Memoires," and images from that work at <http://www.civilization.ca/vmnf/explor/laho_f2.html>.

William Byrd II (1674–1744)

Contributing Editor: Susan Scott Parrish

Classroom Issues and Strategies

Byrd offers students a number of things: an antidote to the deep gravity and eschatological passion of Puritan texts, a representation of the wilderness and of Native Americans they could productively compare with Mary Rowlandson's, Cabeza de Vaca's, and those in other works, the opportunity to read his two histories comparatively and think about the different rhetorical devices Byrd used for a familiar versus a public audience, and an example of an Augustan colonial's competing allegiances to both wit and science.

In a 1736 letter to the London naturalist Peter Collinson that accompanied a copy of his longhand journal of the dividing line expedition, Byrd apologized: "This is only the skeleton and ground-work of what I intend, which may some time or other come to be filled up with vessels, and flesh, & have a decent skin drawn over all to keep things tight in their places, and prevent their looking frightful." A year later, Byrd wrote again: "It was as you may easily see, compos'd in the rough woods, and partakes of the place that gave it birth." These remarks raise a number of questions: What was "frightful" during Byrd's expedition, the scandalous acts of rape, theft, and aggression that took place on the line, or merely his uncouth assimilation to the wild? Which parts of his two *Histories* represent the "vessels and flesh" and which parts the "decent skin"? Does Byrd see language as a source of creation or containment or dissimulation? How does a place give birth to a text? How do Byrd's transatlantic allegiances affect his representation of the "rough woods"? Is this text regional or transatlantic?

Major Themes, Historical Perspectives, Personal Issues

Along these lines, Douglas Anderson, in "Plotting William Byrd" (*William and Mary Quarterly*, 3rd Series, LVI, 1999: 701–22), performs an excellent reading of the abiding narrative paradigm Byrd developed through both his diaries and his *Histories*, namely a constant alternation—rather than division—between plots, voices, and meanings. He argues that Byrd, "drawing upon the fertility and mutability of language," shows "how boundaries can frequently cloud distinctions that they pretend to clarify" (702–03). Distinctions, for example, between secrecy and disclosure, containment and resistance, principle and appetite are established only to be jumbled up, crossed, shifted, or entangled much as different meats are jumbled in the expedition's stewpot, felled trees are crossed in the Dismal Swamp, borders of land shift with the tides, and briars entangle the trailblazers as they attempt to hack a straight westward line. In particular, the temporal and moral containment implicit in the late seventeenth-century journal form, the preponderance of didactic Christian texts in the Westover library, the confluence of Lent with the spring portion of the expedition, and Byrd's frequent allusion to the Israelites in the Wilderness evince Byrd's strong tendency toward a Judeo-Christian discipline and interpretive frame. Yet Byrd constantly reveals how events (and men's passions) disorder such a management of experience, making the *Histories* complex polyphonic records of life in a colonial border territory.

Kenneth Lockridge, in *The Diary, and Life, of William Byrd II of Virginia, 1674–1744* (1987), especially 127–43, offers us help with the *Histories* through his analysis of Byrd's literary processes of colonial self-fashioning. He argues that Byrd's early life, characterized by exile from his place of birth and his family (especially the example of a present father) and by isolation from the wealthy English he lived among, forced Byrd to construct an image of the English gentleman wholly from conduct books; this early textual borrowing of Englishness encouraged Byrd's translation of his own life into a compulsively kept text—the ongoing diaries—in which he daily reviewed for himself his performance (or slips in performance) of the various offices of patriarchal gentility, namely, classical learning, physical discipline, mastery of "his people," and of his passions. Byrd's colonial insecurity, also manifested in highly conventional prose attempts (love letters, character portraits, satires), gave way, after his final return home to Virginia, his acceptance of the social burden and opportunities of his elite colonial status, and the running of the line in 1728, to a maturity of outlook and of prose. Byrd recognized that the "humble" form of the journal, one that he had long been practicing, was the most suitable genre to narrate his country's struggle toward civilization.

Roderick Nash, in chapter three of *Wilderness and the American Mind* (1982), provides an environmentalist background to Byrd. Nash records the translation of a European appreciation for wilderness, begun by naturalists like John Ray and William Durham in the late seventeenth century and continued by Deists and promoters of "the Sublime" in the eighteenth, to the colonies. Nash cites Byrd and John Bartram as somewhat lonely colonial exemplars of an early "Romantic primitivism." Rather than viewing the wilderness as a reviled place of trial that the Christian passes through to earn heavenly salvation as many Puritans had, or as a dark chaotic void that needed to be "vanquished," or, in gentler language, "improved" into a pastoral or agrarian state as many pioneers did through the nineteenth century, Byrd, at least in part, saw wilderness as a "natural laboratory" where the mind of the observer could be improved by discovering God's playfully hidden secrets.

Significant Form, Style, or Artistic Conventions

The "secret history" was a popular genre in Byrd's time and one that was well-represented in Byrd's library with titles like *Royal Mistresses of France: Or, the Secret History of the Amours of the French King.* An insider's account of scandal, it was usually associated with court intrigue and was meant to produce smirks and titillation through its public exposure and even social critique of the private dealings of powerful people. That Byrd employed such a genre for a wilderness expedition suggests that he wanted to show his readers his knowledge of both settings (court and woods) and his witty ability to translate each world to the other. To be funny but not seditious, the language of the genre's curiosity needed to imply more than it said. In Byrd's *Secret History*, he favored the double-entendre, for it could simultaneously suggest scandal while ameliorating its tangible ugliness by a retreat into linguistic play. For example, when Byrd uses the words *curiosity* and *examined*, and the phrase "ranging over her sweet person" in describing an instance when a number of the commissioners are sexually assaulting a female servant, he turns this tawdry scene into a palimpsest of lechery, medical and scientific inquiry, and territorial exploration.

His *History* belonged to the genre of the New Scientific travel narrative. Typical of this genre was a catalog and description of natural rarities and aboriginal peoples, leavened at times by the author's relation of his own physical peril. Thus, when composing his *History*, Byrd needed to improve the linear plodding of the longhand journal with intriguing excursions of action and information and needed to retreat from the *Secret History*'s concept of curiosity as lechery: As a once quite active member of the Royal Society and a reader of its manifestoes, Byrd knew that the New Science defined curiosity as a learned, disinterested, and gentlemanly attribute, and that it eschewed rhetorical figures like the double-entendre in its pursuit of referential purity. To show that he could see and know the world in this authoritative way, Byrd included numerous references drawn from his extensive library, particularly to other histories and travel narratives such as those of Herodotus and John Smith. While Mary Rowlandson sustained herself with biblical passages on her further "removes" from the English habitations, Byrd made sense of the Virginia backwoods through comparative ethnography and historiography.

In the end though, Byrd was too much of a "wit" to drain all satirical undercurrents out of his narrative as he "drew a tight skin over" the disturbing scenes of the journey. Thus what Byrd does carry over from the *Secret History* and what amounts to his major innovation to the British natural history travel genre is his exhibition of language's referential waywardness. Byrd questions the ability of both imperial words and of his expedition's system of signs to refer naturally to the land they seek to describe. In the opening pages, for example, Byrd shows the decomposition of the title and place "Virginia" as he relates how later colonies were cut, hacked, and dismembered from the original New World English territory. Not only the temporal but also the geographical "place of beginning" is likewise fraught by disputes about language: no one can agree on what point of land "the North Shore of Corautck Inlet" signifies. Byrd's *History* sets in relief, in a number of crucial moments, the unnatural or discursively constructed nature of the commission's work of binding signs to places. Though his *Histories* are about settlement—about settling a controversy so that British colonials could settle in a frontier territory, Byrd *unsettles* royal assumptions about linguistic acts of possession, and he *unsettles* the New Scientific assumptions about the purity of language in its reference to nature. In this sense, Byrd's texts are both possessive and dispossessive.

Comparisons, Contrasts, Connections

Out of these various analytical frames, we can generate some ideas for placing Byrd in tension with other authors in the anthology and some useful questions for the classroom. One could teach Byrd within a unit on the wilderness with authors such as Rowlandson, Cabeza de Vaca, Jefferson, Hawthorne, and

Thoreau. What is Byrd's attitude toward the wilderness: Does he appreciate it, want to vanquish or improve it, see it topologically or for its material details, or all of the above? One could place Byrd alongside other colonial satirists like Morton, Cook, and Sarah Knight, and focus on the tensions between the metropolis and the provinces: Is Byrd promoting his newfound Eden or strengthening his metropolitan allegiances by making fun of the "backward" frontier? One could teach him with Franklin: How are their confessions of moral slippings and stagings of exemplary selves similar? In general, one could ask: What divisions does Byrd set up in these texts, and do these divisions hold?

Jonathan Edwards (1703–1758)

Contributing Editor: Carol M. Bensick

Classroom Issues and Strategies

Assuming that most users of *The Heath Anthology* will be instructors of the American Literature survey course, the teacher of these selections will probably have a week on Edwards. By the time you reach Edwards, the students will be accustomed to reading nonfiction "as literature."

The two "Narratives" probably will be found the most entertaining. Start with "A Faithful Narrative," the simpler and more direct of the two. A brief description of the work itself and an explanation of the occasion for its composition (noting that Benjamin Colman is a minister of a rival branch of post-Puritanism, one skeptical of evangelicalism) is enough to permit the students to follow the story with interest on their own. Inevitably, the "Personal Narrative," a more private piece of writing, is harder for a student reader to follow. There are some options, however. Having taught "A Faithful Narrative," the instructor can portray Edwards as spurred by the events chronicled in that text, including his own part in hearing the validity of the would-be new church members' narratives to try to recall his own exemplary experience, hoping to guide himself thereby in the assessment of the applicants' testimonies and to stimulate empathy with what they are undergoing. Here the teacher might draw a parallel with Edward Taylor's "Preparatory Meditations," in which a pastor similarly performs on himself the same activity he intends to perform publicly on his congregation—namely, evangelical preaching—in order to produce the same effect of activated piety. Such activities might be compared with the self-analysis conducted in modern days by classical Freudian psychotherapists, or with the imaginable activities of scientists who perform physical experiments on themselves (particularly William James's experimentation with nitrous oxide).

With "Sinners," the requirement for the intelligibility that is the pre-requisite for enjoyment is conversance with the Bible. Looking up the individual citations is more likely to distract and antagonize the biblically illiterate, and I suggest advising the students to skip or skim the citations and attempt to read the sermon "for the story." Beginning with the title, the teacher can ask the following questions: Who is the protagonist with whom the reader identifies? (the sinner); Who, from his point of view, is the antagonist? (God); What is the situation? (God is holding you up, but any minute now, God will drop you into hell). With this much established, the teacher could challenge the students to make these abstractions real to themselves. The idea would be to get them to see that Edwards is interpreting the natural fact of the occurrence of sudden deaths as a providential sign, which he then goes on to use as an argument to motivate a certain class of the individuals in the audience to adopt a certain behavior.

The class should understand that in "Sinners," a minister is trying to get new members to join his particular sect's churches. The teacher might invoke a parallel with a salesman; what Edwards is selling is church membership. They should be able to see from "A Faithful Narrative" that the "terror" ceases with the cessation of God's "anger." Once inside the church, the convert will enjoy good times. (Here the teacher might suggest a comparison with Taylor's "Gods Determinations.") By the end of the class, students minimally ought to be able to tell you that this sermon will only be scary to a subgroup of the audience and that the members of that subgroup have it (as far as the sermon lets on) entirely within their own power to exempt themselves from the terror.

The instructor should remind students of how long young Edwards himself went before conversion, how scared he was at the threat of sudden death in his fit of illness, and how delighted he was to get onto God's right side. Students should understand that Edwards's God is not always angry and not angry at everyone, and that such fits of anger have a cause. Under original sin, you can explain, no single human being deserves being spared from hell; Christ has promised that an unknown parcel of humans nevertheless shall enjoy just this reprieve; all they have to do is join the churches; and a group of individuals are actually hesitating to take advantage of this limited-time-only, never-to-be-repeated offer! What's a God to do?

Finally, one would like the students to surmount, as definitely as possible, certain historical solecisms and biographical stereotypes that older anthologies have long inculcated. Whatever they think, the students should be embarrassed to be caught ever again saying that Edwards is "a Puritan" (have them compute how long after the *Mayflower* Edwards was born); gloomy (have them tally up the forms of the words "pleasure," "sweet," "joy," "delight" in "A

Personal Narrative"); or sadistic. On the latter point, referring back to "Sinners," you can show them that the path of cruelty for Edwards, who has the power to admit you to the fellowship of salvation, would have been to leave you in your unconverted state until you suddenly dropped dead.

Elizabeth Ashbridge (1713–1755)

Contributing Editor: Liahna Babener

Classroom Issues and Strategies

Most students are unfamiliar with the doctrinal differences between the Anglican and Quaker faiths, upon which Ashbridge's *Account* hinges. They tend to be uncomfortable with early Quaker preaching practices, doctrinal assumptions, and social customs. This discomfort sometimes alienates students or prevents them from empathizing with Ashbridge's dilemma. Such anxieties, however, are almost always overcome by the power and poignancy of the text itself.

Providing background about religious and doctrinal tensions in the Great Awakening and gender patterns in colonial America is crucial, and the adoption of a feminist strategy of reading is particularly important. Comparing other accounts of those who have been impelled by spiritual conviction to act against convention and law is illuminating, as is reading personal narratives of women of the period who use the autobiographical text as a private means of self-vindication in a patriarchal culture.

Students enjoy discussing whether Ashbridge is heroic or perverse. They often identify with her independent spirit and even her proto-feminist rebellion, but they lament her increasingly dour tone and her failed marriage. Some wonder whether she gave up too much for conscience's sake. Some students see the husband as abusive or imperious but cannot help sympathizing with his distress over losing a mirthful wife. Students also wonder if Quakers courted their social estrangement, contributing to their own victimization, and ask whether Quakers should be blamed or censured for their martyrdom.

Major Themes, Historical Perspectives, Personal Issues

1. The expressly female dilemma of having to choose between conscience and husband, as well as the social stresses upon a woman who defies traditional and prescribed sex roles, thereby threatening the stability of the patriarchal order

2. The doctrinal and social conflicts between Anglicans and Quakers in early America; more broadly, the pressures from a predominantly Anglican, increasingly secularized culture to tame or compartmentalize religious fervor
3. Ways in which women autobiographers use personal narrative for self-vindicating purposes, or for private rebellion against patriarchal norms
4. The degree to which autobiography may be read as factual truth as opposed to an invention or reconstruction of reality; the reliability of the personal narrator as witness to and interpreter of events; the fictional elements of the genre
5. Making a living (as a woman) in colonial America
6. Marriage, husbands' prerogatives, men's and women's ways of coping with marital estrangement
7. The nature of religious conviction; Quaker doctrine, patterns of worship, and social customs

Significant Form, Style, or Artistic Conventions

Study the document as an example of the genre of spiritual autobiography, of personal narrative, of female and feminist assertion, of social history, of eighteenth-century rationalism, and at the same time of revivalist ardor. Explore to what degree the document is confessional and to what degree it may be understood as contrivance or fiction. How is the author "inventing" herself as she writes? How does she turn her experience into a didactic instrument for the edification of her readers?

Original Audience

Social, historical, religious, and political contexts are primary issues. The composition and publication history of the text—penned just before Ashbridge's death—are also illuminating, especially considering that no version of the document in Ashbridge's own hand survives, and scholars are not in consensus about which extant version of the autobiography may be considered authoritative or closest to the original. Consider the Great Awakening audience who may have read this account of religious conversion. Does the document create a sense of feminine solidarity? Can one theorize about the kind of audience to whom Ashbridge directed the *Account*?

Comparisons, Contrasts, Connections

Compare this work with other Great Awakening spiritual autobiographies such as Jonathan Edwards's "Personal Narrative." Puritan introspective literature and conversion stories, particularly by women, are instructive (such as those by Elizabeth Mixer and Elizabeth White); chronicles of Quaker experience or persecution in colonial America (such as Jane Hoskin's Quaker autobiography or Hawthorne's tale, "The Gentle Boy") are revealing. Diaries, journals, and letters of early American women documenting romantic, religious, and social experiences (compare Sarah Kemble Knight, Jarena Lee, Sarah Osborne, Abigail Adams, and so forth) are useful. Franklin's more cunning and more secular *Autobiography* makes an apt parallel.

Questions for Reading, Discussion, and Writing

1. (a) Characterize Ashbridge's spiritual struggles and marital dilemmas. Does she resolve the former at the expense of the latter?
   (b) In what ways do you empathize with Ashbridge in her conflict with her husband? Why or why not? How might you act differently from either or both of them in this situation?
   (c) Does the community treat Ashbridge fairly following her conversion?
   (d) What implicit moral and spiritual advice does the piece contain?
2. How does Ashbridge structure the narrative and construct herself as a character in her own story to win sympathy and intellectual support from readers? Is she successful?
3. (a) Write a counterpart narrative (or defense) from the husband's point of view.
   (b) Write an Anglican's critique of or commentary upon Ashbridge's behavior.
   (c) Invent an imaginative dialogue between Ashbridge and Jonathan Edwards (or any of the following) concerning religious or gender issues: Anne Hutchinson, Mary Rowlandson, Anne Bradstreet, Samuel Sewall, Sarah Kemble Knight, Benjamin Franklin, Abigail Adams, and so forth.

Bibliography

The most significant published source is Daniel Shea's edition of Ashbridge's *Some Account of the Fore Part of the Life of Elizabeth Ashbridge*, available with his detailed introduction and textual notes, in *Journeys in New Worlds: Early American Narratives*, ed. William L. Andrews et al. (Madison: U of Wisconsin P, 1990), from which this excerpt is drawn. Christine Levenduski's dissertation, "Elizabeth Ashbridge's 'Remarkable Experiences': Creating the Self in a Quaker Personal Narrative" (University of Minnesota, 1989), is an invaluable book-length discussion of the text and its author. Carol Edkins's "Quest for Community: Spiritual Autobiographies of Eighteenth-Century Quaker and Puritan Women in America," in *Women's Autobiography: Essays in Criticism*, ed. Estelle C. Jelinek (Bloomington: Indiana UP, 1980), pp. 39–52, also discusses Ashbridge substantively. Shea and Levenduski contain useful bibliographies of further materials providing background to Ashbridge's life and narrative.

John Woolman (1720–1772)

Contributing Editor: James A. Levernier

Classroom Issues and Strategies

Students often have a difficult time reading eighteenth-century nonfiction prose. The issues it reveals seem dated and unexciting to them. A writer like Woolman comes across as a moral "antique" to students who would much prefer to skip over the entire period and move on to Melville, Hawthorne, and Poe in the next century.

I try to point out to students that Woolman is, in many ways, very contemporary. He almost single-handedly defied many of the conventional views of his day and was willing to stand up and take the heat for things that he believed in. I also point out that the principles that Woolman uses to deal with the evils he perceives in society are by no means dated. Many of the issues he brings up still exist today but in different, more subtle forms, and it is our responsibility to deal with those issues. Social injustices, bigotry, and poverty are, unfortunately, still very much with us today. Woolman offers us an example and guidance in such matters.

Students are often quite interested in Quakers and their culture. Most of them have heard something about Quakers, but they don't really understand them. They are usually quite moved by the conviction behind Woolman's writings and can identify with it. They want to know if he was typical of Quaker thinking and why they haven't been taught more about the effect of Quaker ideas on American culture.

Major Themes, Historical Perspectives, Personal Issues

Woolman writes about many themes that should be emphasized:

1. Slavery as a historical issue
2. Racism and prejudice as issues that are still very much alive today
3. The responsibility of the individual for social injustices
4. The need for conviction and passion in our moral and social lives
5. The potential of any one person for bringing about true reform

Significant Form, Style, or Artistic Conventions

In discussing Woolman, one needs to discuss the practice of keeping journals among Quakers and early Americans generally. Why did Quakers keep journals? Why did they publish them? An analysis of Woolman's simple and direct style is very useful for seeing the "art" in the *Journal* since his style of writing very effectively underscores and enhances the power of his convictions. I also draw connections between journals written by Quakers and journals written by Puritans to the north. Quaker journals have an inner peace that Puritan journals often lack.

Original Audience

Woolman wrote the *Journal* and his *Plea for the Poor* for future generations. He certainly knew that the *Journal* at least would not be published in his lifetime. There is a rhetorical strategy behind the *Journal* that revisions within the work reveal. Clearly, Woolman wanted us to see the effects of the workings of the "Inner Light" in his own life so that we could perhaps begin to cultivate with equal effect the "Inner Light" he felt was within each of us. *Considerations* (I and II) were more immediate in their audience concerns; they are persuasive tracts, meant to bring about immediate action through a direct appeal to the consciences of those who read them.

Comparisons, Contrasts, Connections

Woolman can be tied to nineteenth-century American autobiographers, especially Henry David Thoreau and Henry Adams. The Quaker influence can also be connected to John Greenleaf Whittier, Emerson, and Whitman. The connections between the Quaker "Inner Light" and the type of transcendentalism expressed in Emerson's works, particularly in *Nature*, should be emphasized. Woolman also should be compared and contrasted with the journal writers and autobiographers of seventeenth- and eighteenth-century New England. John Winthrop, for instance, kept a journal for far different reasons and with far different results than did Woolman.

Questions for Reading, Discussion, and Writing

1. (a) Would Woolman feel that his life and ministry made a difference to the world of today?
    (b) How would he feel about today's world? About social injustice in third-world countries? About our response as individuals and as Americans to poverty and social injustice in other lands?
2. Comparison/contrast papers are very useful ways to develop insights into Woolman. He can be compared, for example, with Bradford, with Emerson, with Adams, and with Whitman. Sometimes I ask students to envision three or more writers together in a room today discussing an issue. What would each writer say about the issue? About feminism, for example, or the atomic bomb? This device often helps students to enter the writer's world and better understand the imaginative process.

Francisco Palou (1723–1789)

Contributing Editor: Juan Bruce-Novoa

Classroom Issues and Strategies

Students may think that the text is an anachronism, coming late in history. While the East Coast is in the midst of its independence struggle, Serra and Palou are still founding missions. Students have been taught to think of Spain as finished internationally after the Great Armada.

The eighteenth century was one of expansion and renewed vitality for Spain. Its missionaries and soldiers were moving on all fronts, founding new cities in Texas and northern New Mexico, moving into the Mississippi and Ohio valleys, solidifying their position in the Caribbean basin, and spreading north along the Pacific Coast to counter the southern movement of the Russians from Alaska. Missionaries were the Spanish equivalent of frontiersmen, but they prove how much better organized the Spanish expansion system was. Also, students should be told that the treaty between France and England in 1763 acknowledged Spain's traditional claim to the Mississippi Valley, which was disputed by the French.

Students often question the purpose of the missionary project. It has become fashionable to denounce Serra as an exploiter of Native Americans, so instructors may find it necessary to prepare for a discussion of the moral issues involved in the activities of Christian missionaries anywhere in the world. More useful, however, is to turn the discussion toward a consideration of how models are always ideologically based and serve the purpose of social indoctrination.

Major Themes, Historical Perspectives, Personal Issues

Consider the following: the theme of personal sacrifice and determination in the face of great odds; the theme of the traditional moving of borders farther into the territory of the non-Christian that comes from Spain's reconquest of their own territory from the Moors (700–1492).

There is also the literary motif of creating models of cultural behavior in texts that will be used to teach the young.

Significant Form, Style, or Artistic Conventions

The form is biography. Students should consider the task of depicting the life of another, the choices made to emphasize certain traits, the strategies used to convince the reader of the author's objectivity and reliability.

There is also the similarity to the writing on the lives of the saints. Students might consider which virtues are held up for imitation in different settings and times.

Original Audience

Readers then were much closer to the ideals expressed by Palou, probably coming from the novices of religious orders. They were much more willing to believe in the values reflected in the life of Serra. Now there is little sense of divine mission in life nor of the virtue of extreme sacrifice for the common good. Students must be urged to comprehend the energy of societies in expansion.

Comparisons, Contrasts, Connections

Compare this writer with Cotton Mather, as the headnote mentions. Both writers attempt to create models for new generations who have forgotten their founding fathers. One could also pick a favorite section from John F. Kennedy's *Profiles in Courage* to compare with Serra.

Questions for Reading, Discussion, and Writing

Pose the question of role models in society in different periods. Ask students to consider where the models come from and what purpose they fulfill. How do they differ then and now? They can be asked to write an essay about someone they would want to be the role model for their generation.

A Sheaf of Eighteenth-Century Anglo-American Poetry

Contributing Editors: Pattie Cowell and Ivy Schweitzer

Classroom Issues and Strategies

Beginning students struggle with these materials, partly because they arise from a time and aesthetic unfamiliar to them and partly because poetry as a genre seems more difficult to many of them. I find it most effective to try two contradictory strategies simultaneously: I ask students to stretch their historical imaginations with a bit of time-travel ("Dr. Who" comes to mind), and I try to highlight the ways in which the themes and concerns of these poets are still with us.

Though the time-travel is more fun at first for me than for the students, most of them get the idea soon enough. I take them back to a time when there was no United States, when poetry was the primary literary genre (and changes were in store), when midwives outnumbered physicians, when western Pennsylvania seemed like the outer edge of white civilization, when manuscript culture flourished alongside a fledgling printing industry, when individualism was not a cultural value (or even a part of the English language), when periodicals were a new phenomenon, when literacy rates were changing dramatically. The more concrete the context becomes, the more accessible the poetry. Some of this can be structured around a fairly accessible piece—Turell's "Lines on Childbirth," for example—if we try to reassemble as much as one can of Turell's world as we read: her literary aesthetic, her educational opportunities, health care, family life, and so forth.

Finding issues relevant to contemporary concerns in these poems is deceptively easy. While it is important not to construct eighteenth-century poets in our own image, they wrote about many of the things that concern us still: the stresses of war, the joys and struggles of family life, health and its absence, nature and human nature, travels, gender roles, religion, race and racism, the human comedy.

Major Themes, Historical Perspectives, Personal Issues

The eighteenth-century poets represented here concern themselves with issues of class, race, and gender. Ebenezer Cook's "Sot-weed Factor," for example, is a freewheeling satire that takes class consciousness as a given for commenting on the conditions of life in colonial Maryland. Much of the humor derives from the pitiful way colonial subjects—farmers, yeomen, businesspeople, laborers—measure up to their English counterparts. Sarah Morton's "The African Chief " is a prominent example of colonial concern over slavery. The anonymous "Lady's Complaint" attacks gender-based inequalities. And many other examples in this selection touch these issues as well.

From a historical perspective, eighteenth-century poets struggled with the cultural devaluation of poetry as a genre. As prose became more popular and socially influential, poetry lost much of its audience. Poets wrote implicit defenses of poetry, perhaps as counterweights to the shared cultural assumptions that produced de Tocqueville's (later) disparaging comment: "I readily admit that the Americans have no poets; I cannot allow that they have no poetic ideas." Thus poetry itself becomes an important theme.

In addition, the perennial question of geography may be significant here. Is this poetry English or American? Is the tradition that produced it a continuation of Old World traditions or evidence of New World exceptionalism? Or both? Poets continued to invent the New World, and in the later part of the century, the New Republic. What shape did these inventions take? How did they change over time? How did expectations clash with reality? How did authority mediate experience?

Significant Form, Style, or Artistic Conventions

The selections here vary tremendously in form, but students will find a background in neoclassical aesthetics useful for most of them.

Original Audience

The original audience for eighteenth-century American poetry depended on the vehicle for distribution. Of course, it was restricted to the literate, making it a mostly white audience. But beyond that given, audiences would vary. Periodical poetry would have wide regional circulation, especially in urban areas. Books and chapbooks might circulate in both England and the colonies.

Manuscript verse would circulate largely among family and friends of the writer, perhaps in a club or salon setting, groups more frequently found among well-to-do readers.

Comparisons, Contrasts, Connections

Comparisons with contemporary English poets can be instructive. Geographical or regional contrasts among the colonial selections illustrate the lack of a national voice until very late in the century.

Bibliography

Cowell, Pattie. *Women Poets in Pre-Revolutionary America.* Troy, NY: Whitston, 1981. Entries grouped by individual poets, so access to relevant material is relatively easy.

Davis, Richard Beale. *Intellectual Life in the Colonial South.* Vol. III. Knoxville: U of Tennessee P, 1978. On William Dawson.

Individual entries in *American Writers Before 1800.* Ed. James A. Levernier and Douglas R. Wilmes. Westport, CT: Greenwood, 1983.

Lemay, J. A. Leo. "Ebenezer Cooke." *Men of Letters in Colonial Maryland.* Knoxville: U of Tennessee P, 1972. 77–110.

———. "Richard Lewis and Augustan American Poetry." *PMLA* 83 (March 1968): 80–101.

Silverman, Kenneth, ed. *Colonial American Poetry.* New York: Hafner, 1976. Anthology.

Watts, Emily Stipes. *The Poetry of American Women from 1632 to 1945.* Austin: U of Texas P, 1977. 9–61.

Voices of Revolution and Nationalism

Handsome Lake (Seneca) (1735–1815)

Contributing Editor: John Alberti

Classroom Issues and Strategies

It is important to provide students with the historical context for the creation and reception of Handsome Lake's mythic allegory. Discussing both how this story represents an expression of Handsome Lake's mystical vision and how it functioned as part of an emerging nativist protest against European colonization can help students understand the political qualities of "How America Was Discovered" in particular and the formation or mythic stories in general. That the story survived as part of an oral tradition until Arthur C. Parker made this transcript in 1923 attests to its enduring value and usefulness in Native American culture. Students can be encouraged to speculate about why this story proved to be an effective expression of cultural resistance for two centuries.

"How America Was Discovered" is not only a significant document in the history of Native American resistance but also an important example of cultural syncretism and synthesis. Some students may view the issue of cultural resistance in either/or terms: either native peoples maintain an "authentic" cultural tradition unchanged by colonial pressures, or they succumb to total assimilation into the dominant culture. Indeed this binary view has marked the logic of much U.S. government policy toward Native Americans. Instead, Handsome Lake's story represents both the result of what was, at the time, three hundred years of interaction between Europeans and Native Americans and his strategic rhetorical intervention into that history in the name of building political solidarity.

Have students make charts listing what they see as the "native" and "European" elements of the story. Remind them that this is less an empirical exercise than a lesson in interpretation. Ask, for example, why students made the choices they did in preparing their charts, and what other ways the same story elements could be understood. Although "How America Was Discovered" stands as a rejection and condemnation of the European cultural values and the spiritual pollution Handsome Lake sees as the result of European conquest, it also demonstrates his deep understanding of European religious mythology, a mythology that proves useful to Handsome Lake in providing an opponent against which native solidarity can be defined.

Comparisons, Contrasts, Connections

"How America Was Discovered" works well in several different groupings of texts. It can be read with Christopher Columbus's journals and the Yuchi story, "The Creation of the White," as examples of different and differing creation stories about America. As an example of strategic mythmaking for the purposes of cultural definition, it can be compared with William Bradford's account of the history and meaning of the Plymouth settlement and J. Hector St. John de Crèvecoeur's *Letters from an American Farmer*.

"How America Was Discovered" can be studied along with the story of the Virgin of Guadalupe as an example of cultural syncretism that combines assimilation and resistance. And of course, Handsome Lake's rhetorical strategy of criticizing the dominant Christian society on the basis of religious hypocrisy is an important tradition in both the literatures of Native American resistance and of the anti-slavery and civil rights movements.

Benjamin Franklin (1706–1790)

Contributing Editor: Etta Madden

Classroom Issues and Strategies

Man of Myth and Multiple Personae: The most significant issue to discuss when teaching Franklin's writing is the mythic figure that surrounds his name in American culture. If you have reminded students of the literary concept of *persona* and introduced Franklin as a writer adept at creating such characters, lectures and discussions may then center upon the literary techniques of each work assigned and the types of personalities presented rather than on the biographical details of Franklin's life (a subject many will have discussed in American history courses). With this distinction between life and work underscored, students may consider with each work assigned how the persona created and represented in it fosters or undermines an ideal in America.

Major Themes, Historical Perspectives, Personal Issues

American Ideals: Franklin's writings provide an excellent lens through which shifting American ideals may be examined. As an eighteenth-century writer, Franklin should be associated with the empiricism and rationalism of "new science" in the Enlightenment as well as with the formation of the new nation.

As an Enlightenment thinker, for example, Franklin questions his culture's attitudes toward religion, women's roles, and slavery. In so doing, he presents himself as a rebellious and radical reformer and an advocate for religious freedom, female education, and abolition of the slave trade.

Such advocacy and even the topics remain significant in American culture today. Likewise, the entrepreneurship and work ethic he celebrates in the autobiography and in the pithy sayings of the *Almanac* continue to be valued in our society. Yet they may be seen as an extension of seventeenth-century Puritan culture, in which outward behavior often was read as a sign of internal righteousness and election. Certainly, Franklin's concern with economic success and such topics as debt and paper currency have contributed to our national ideals, but material exchange and monetary solvency were significant to earlier colonists on the East Coast as well as in Spanish America.

Additionally, Franklin's drive to be successful in the earthly realm reflects an assertive egotism to which students often respond strongly—both negatively and positively. In the *Autobiography*, for example, Franklin's friends, acquaintances, and even his wife may be seen as steppingstones assisting the eager entrepreneur to higher planes in his career. Although Franklin uses humor to discuss openly his vanity and lack of humility, class discussion should point to the ways in which his self-assertion, associated with American manhood and nationalism and often celebrated, is achieved at a cost to others.

Significant Form, Style, or Artistic Conventions

Satire and Humor: Most students find Franklin's humorous tone and his prose style a relief after reading seventeenth- and early eighteenth-century materials. They should be reminded that the style is not simply emblematic of Franklin's personality as a man who rejected the spiritual concerns of his ancestors but also reflects shifts within the larger culture: ornate prose popular among seventeenth-century writers gave way in the eighteenth century to more direct syntax, and the types of texts printed and circulated in the colonies became increasingly more diverse, reflecting the developing variety and interests of readers.

Life-writing: The *Autobiography* employs commonplaces of life-writing that have existed since Augustine's *Confessions* and that appeared frequently in spiritual narratives of the seventeenth century. Since Franklin refers within the autobiography to his admiration of John Bunyan's *Pilgrim's Progress* and Daniel DeFoe's fiction, the narrative influences of these works upon Franklin's should be considered. Franklin included and excluded events as he chose, shaping those he included so that they engaged and affected readers as he wished. As the hero of his narrative, he is not unlike that of a picaresque novel or a *bildungsroman* of the eighteenth century.

Original Audience

Each of Franklin's works was written for a specific audience. The information provided in *The Heath Anthology*, such as the appearance of the "Witch Trial at Mount Holly" in the *New England Courant* and the "Speech of Polly Baker" in the *Gentleman's Magazine*, and the popularity of *Poor Richard's Almanac* may be used to begin discussion about literacy and print culture in colonial America. These works reflect the literary diversity within the colonies as well as within eighteenth-century periodicals. Likewise, the pseudonymously published works should elicit discussion of the political factions of the revolutionary era and the debates about the shape of new nation.

Overall, consideration of Franklin's audiences contributes to our understanding of his adeptness at crafting language to appeal to diverse readers. This rhetorical skill culminates in the *Autobiography*, written for his son, for himself (to satisfy his own vanity, he explains), and for posterity so that others might know how to achieve success. The latter-stated purpose is extremely problematic since his modeling implicitly excluded females and since his son, at midlife when the work was written, had already passed through the formative period of youth and adulthood in which the work's ideals would be adopted most easily.

Comparisons, Contrasts, Connections

The shorter pieces by Franklin provide contrasts with many other pieces within *The Heath Anthology*, often illuminating their eighteenth-century context. "Witch Trial at Mount Holly," for example, pairs nicely with Cotton Mather's "Wonders of the Invisible World," especially since Mather considered himself a rationalist yet wrote of the witches in Massachusetts and adamantly proclaimed his unbiased, direct style at recording the courtroom testimonies. Likewise, the humorous voice of Polly Baker parallels Sarah Kemble Knight's confident record of her travels while it reminds readers of the punishment for sexual sin in William Bradford's *Of Plymouth Plantation* and Ann Hutchinson's banishment from Boston because of her behavior and testimony. Reading "Remarks on the Slave Trade," students may see that Franklin was not the first to write on slavery but that he addresses a topic considered by Mather ("Negro Christianized") as well as by John Woolman ("Considerations on the Keeping of Negroes") in the eighteenth century.

When reading the *Autobiography*, students may more fully compare Franklin's idealized identity and his writing style with that of seventeenth-century predecessors and eighteenth-century contemporaries. Michael Wigglesworth's journal and Jonathan Edwards's spiritual narrative provide masculine examples of Puritan self-examination and human depravity, foreshadowing Franklin's secular system of moral perfection and the sovereignty of his reason. Elizabeth Ashbridge's *Account*, while providing a female perspective of life-writing and sensational narrative, also raises issues of personal authority and agency, partially vexed by gender.

The *Autobiography* may be used quite successfully as a precursor to works that follow in *The Heath Anthology*. Franklin's proclaimed agency and autonomy prove flawed when the model for those enslaved, such as Olaudah Equiano and Frederick Douglass. Although Equiano and Douglass, like Franklin, uphold reason and literacy as crucial to their liberation, each adds a realistic wrinkle to Franklin's model. Equiano, for example, makes obvious through his manumission that his liberation is not of himself, and Douglass fights physically to prove his worth as a man. Even nineteenth-century fictional works such as Irving's "Rip Van Winkle" and Hawthorne's "My Kinsman, Major Molineaux" may be read as satires of the model of manhood Franklin's autobiography provides.

Working with Cultural Objects

The stereotypes of Franklin in American culture emerge not only from his autobiography but also from the numerous portraits in which he appears as a man of science and a statesman. Examining a cluster of portraits, noting such details as their composition dates, Franklin's posture and clothing, and the backgrounds helps students understand the way in which material self-presentation contributes to these stereotypes. Many of the portraits may be downloaded from the sites listed on the Benjamin Franklin author profile page: <http://college. hmco.com/english/lauter/heath/5e/students/author_pages/contemporary/fr anklin_be.html>.

For those who appreciate visual learning and would like more biographical information than the headnote provides, a brief two-part movie is available at <http://www.earlyamerica.com/ben-movie.htm>.

Franklin's scientific work is of interest to many. A fine overview of his place among men of science and his contributions to the field are available in David Ferro's illustrated essay at <http://www.earlyamerica.com/review/ summer97/science.html>.

Questions for Reading, Discussion, and Writing

The following topics may be used either to direct students as they read or as essay questions to synthesize class lectures. In the former case, after assigning a topic or individual questions, instructors may begin class discussion with students' responses to them. As each topic is rather broad, it is imperative that students be reminded that they need to bring in a list of specific passages that illustrate their answers to the questions. In the latter use, instructors would need to have provided for each topic the concrete examples from which the conclusions might be drawn. The Website Pedagogy section presents a version of question 2a (on food and drink) along with specific examples.

1. Rags to Riches
   a. To which events in Franklin's early life does he attribute his success?
   b. To which people?
   c. For what reasons might his successes and their contributing factors be unavailable to others in America?
2. Mind, Body, and Spirit
   a. How do Franklin's attitudes toward food and drink reinforce or reform attitudes presented in seventeenth-century texts?
   b. How do his attitudes toward physical labor and recreation reinforce or reform attitudes presented in seventeenth-century texts?
   c. How do his attitudes toward literacy and education reinforce or reform attitudes presented in seventeenth-century texts?
   d. How do Franklin's attitudes toward religion reinforce or reform attitudes presented in seventeenth-century texts?
3. Gender Roles
   a. Make note of Franklin's mention of females in the autobiography.
   b. How would you describe his view of women?
   c. How does Franklin reinforce or reform the views presented in other works by men in the eighteenth-century?
   d. How does Franklin's life story differ from the first-person account of Elizabeth Ashbridge, Sarah Kemble Knight, or Mary Rowlandson?
4. National Ideals
   a. As a "Founding Father" of the new nation, Franklin advocated through his writings several ideals. Describe his view of an ideal citizen, referring to specific passages within the works.
   b. Describe Franklin's view of an ideal nation, referring to specific passages within the works.

Bibliography

The following works provide information about the topics discussed previously. Many are accessible to advanced undergraduate students.

Baker, Jennifer J. "Franklin's Autobiography and the Credibility of Personality." *Early American Literature* 35.3 (2000): 274–93.

Chaves, Joseph. "'A Most Exquisite Mechanic': Labor and Leisure, Printing and Authorship in the Periodical Essays of Benjamin Franklin." *Papers of the Bibliographical Society of America* 96.4 (Dec. 2002): 521–30.

Ferro, David L. "Promoting Science Through America's Colonial Press: How Ben Franklin Used His Newspaper—*The Pennsylvania Gazette*—to 'Popularize' an Evolving Science." <http://www.earlyamerica.com/review/summer97/science.html>.

Fichtelberg, Joseph. "The Complex Image: Text and Reader in the Autobiography of Benjamin Franklin." *Early American Literature* 23.2 (1988): 202–16.

Fortune, Brandon B., with Deborah J. Warner. *Franklin and His Friends: Portraying the Man of Science in Eighteenth-Century America*. Washington, DC: Smithsonian, 1999.

Kullman, Colby H. "Benjamin Franklin's Humor and the American Revolution: An Explosion of Popular Culture Satirical Techniques." *George Washington in and as Culture*. Ed. Kevin L. Cope and William S. Pederson. New York: AMS, 2001. 269–77.

Larson, David M. "Benjamin Franklin's Youth, His Biographers, and the Autobiography." *Pennsylvania Magazine of History and Biography* 119.3 (1995): 203–23.

Lemay, J. A. Leo and P. M. Zall, eds. *The Autobiography of Benjamin Franklin: A Genetic Text*. Knoxville: U of Tennessee P, 1981.

Lemay, J. A. Leo. *Benjamin Franklin: A Documentary History*. 1997 <http://www.english.udel.edu/lemay/franklin/>.

Mulford, Carla. "Figuring Benjamin Franklin in American Cultural Memory." *New England Quarterly* 72.3 (1999): 415–43.

Palmeri, Frank. "History, Nation, and the Satiric Almanac, 1660–1760." *Criticism: A Quarterly for Literature and the Arts* 40.3 (1998): 377–408.

Shurr, William H. "'Now, Gods, Stand Up for Bastards': Reinterpreting Benjamin Franklin's Autobiography." *American Literature* 64:3 (1992): 435–51.

Van Gastel, Ada. "Franklin and Freud: Love in the Autobiography." *Early American Literature* 25.2 (1990): 168–82.

Mercy Otis Warren (1728–1814)

Contributing Editor: Ivy Schweitzer

Classroom Issues and Strategies

Mercy Otis Warren is one of only two women writers included in the selections on Revolutionary and nationalist writing. The other is Abigail Adams who, like Warren, was a voluminous correspondent but did not write polemical works for publication. Both women moved in the highest circles of patriotic activity and observed developments firsthand, and both made claims for the inclusion of women's perspectives in the fight for freedom and in the new nation being formed. Both had educations far inferior to those of the men around them. Only because Warren's older brother decided not to prepare for college was she allowed to take his place and study with her brother James. When James, an idealist and gifted rhetorician, suffered severe injuries from a beating at the hands of angry Tories, Warren was asked by the men in her circle to step in and use her "God given gifts" in the service of the great cause of freedom. She went on to write some of the most potent and widely read propaganda of the Revolution, as well as a multivolume history of the period, a wide range of poetry, and historical plays that explore on a more philosophical level the role of women in revolutionary societies. One strategy to pursue in the classroom is to look at the circumstances under which earlier women wrote: Did they have fathers or husbands who encouraged them? Did they have access to education and books? Look also at the genres in which they wrote (religious poetry, love lyrics, translations, captivity narratives, didactic works) and compare these to Warren's circumstances and the various genres in which she chose to write. Important, also, is to elucidate the attitudes during this period toward women who spoke and acted publicly. You can ask students to think about the relationship of gender and genre, and how periods of crisis like the American Revolution momentarily relaxed those conventions to allow women and other subordinated groups access to the literary territory of the dominant groups.

Major Themes, Historical Perspectives, Personal Issues

The selections represent a wide range of writing from Warren's canon, including poetry, satiric and propagandistic drama, excerpts from her historical plays, and prose passages from her *History*. Some major themes include

1. The political and moral argument for separation from England

2. The connection between reason and passion in personal relationships and public issues; the centrality of "virtue" in the pantheon of the republican values
3. The importance of liberty to "domestic" happiness in the several senses of that word, and the role of both men and women in achieving and maintaining it
4. The obligations of public intellectuals and civic leaders; their relationship to authority, power, and ambition
5. The circumstances surrounding the "Boston Tea Party," which inspired Warren's satiric drama *The Group,* her scathing representation of Tories, American-born loyalists who betrayed the country of their birth, and the mandamus council installed after the Boston protest. The corruption of the powerful due to greed and personal ambition are important themes in her satires and dramas

Significant Form, Style, or Artistic Conventions

A reading of *The Group* provides the occasion for a discussion of literary forms prominent during this period, the role of propaganda, the status of drama in the colonial period, when it was illegal to stage plays in public in Puritan Boston, and the function of satire. Why does Warren choose satire as the vehicle for her critique, and why does she choose not to portray patriots or debates between Whigs and Tories in her drama? What is the effect of giving the entire drama over to the villains, as it were? The power of this satire comes across best when you discuss who these characters were, how they were related to Warren or her circle, and how their actions and speeches contribute to the picture Warren paints of their greed and corruption. A discussion of Warren's choice of inflated idiom and allusions to ancient Greece and Rome will also help students understand her critique. These plays were not meant to be staged, but were printed in newspapers and pamphlets. How does that contribute to their effect?

Original Audience

In her satiric dramas, Warren aimed for a wide and diverse audience of readers—Americans and patriots; working, middle, and upper classes—and she strove for a particular effect. Her poetry and her historical dramas use historical situations analogous to the crisis in America to raise the controversial issue of women, and specifically mothers, as leaders and revolutionaries, and were aimed at a more select audience, a circle of literate and educated readers in a position to shape cultural norms. Warren's *History* of the Revolution was written for the younger generations who, Warren felt, needed to know about the momentous events that created the republic in order to honor and preserve it.

Comparisons, Contrasts, and Connections

Warren can be read in the company of her contemporary patriotic writers like John Adams, a close friend; Tom Paine, and Thomas Jefferson. She can be compared with other women writers in *The Heath Anthology* to measure how far women had come by 1776 in their struggle to emerge from the anonymity of the domestic realm. Her poetry can be read in relation to other women writing poetry in her day: Annis Boudinot Stockton, Elizabeth Graeme, and Sarah Wentworth Morton, whose husband was also a Boston patriot. Her politics can be compared with those of other women writers like Judith Sargent Murray, who championed women's rights to equal education. Warren was the first American woman to write drama, and *The Group* can be compared with early plays and satires like Royall Tyler's *The Contrast* or Susanna Rowson's *Slaves in Algiers*. Finally, Warren can be considered as a historian, a conventionally masculine preserve. What did it mean for her to describe not only the characters of the principal actors but also battles, military strategy, social theory, and political intrigue during the new nation's most critical period? How does her extraordinary contribution to colonial letters counter her contemporaries' disdain of the capabilities and rights of women?

Bibliography

Anthony, Susan. *First Lady of the Revolution: The Life of Mercy Otis Warren.* Garden City, NY: Doubleday, 1958.

Baym, Nina. "Between Enlightenment and Victorian: Towards a Narrative of American Women Writing History." *Critical Inquiry* 18.1 (1991): 22–41.

Oreovicz, Cherly. "Heroic Drama for [an] Uncertain Age: The Plays of Mercy Otis Warren." *Early American Literature and Culture: Essays Honoring Harrison T. Meserole.* Ed. Kathryn Zabelle Derounian-Stodola. Newark: University of Delaware, 1992. 192–210.

Richards, Jeffrey. *Mercy Otis Warren.* New York: Twayne, 1995.

J. Hector St. John de Crèvecoeur (1735–1813)

Contributing Editor: Doreen Alvarez Saar

Classroom Issues and Strategies

Letters is a very accessible text; the greatest difficulty in teaching it is establishing the cultural context that makes structural sense of the whole. Generally, students read the text as the simple story of a farmer and as "truth" rather than as fiction. The teaching challenge is to get students to see how political ideas structure the text. One way into the text is to have students read Letter II and count the references, both direct and indirect, to the way society should be organized. In the opening section of the letter, James compares his situation to the state of other farmers in other nations. Later in Letter II, note now the supposedly neutral descriptions of animals are used to talk about the conduct of humans in society.

Students are also generally intrigued by the idea that members of the colonies were actually against the Revolution.

Major Themes, Historical Perspectives, Personal Issues

In the course of *Letters*, through the character of James, Crèvecoeur describes how social principles laid out by the new American society operate in the life of an individual American. There are many interesting themes that can be pointed out in the text: the nature of the American character; the work ethic, the responsibility of the individual, anti-intellectualism; the farmer as a prototype of the American character; the treatment of slaves; the view of new immigrants and their ethnicity; literary resonances such as the escape from civilization in Letter XII and stereotypical American characters. One theme that is frequently overlooked is James's desire not to participate in the Revolution. Students believe that all colonists accepted the righteousness of the Revolutionary cause. A discussion of James's feelings helps students recognize the constancy of division in society and is useful for later discussions of the social and literary reactions to the Civil War and the Vietnam War.

Significant Form, Style, or Artistic Conventions

Eighteenth-century Americans did not share our modern idea that politics and art must be kept separate. Thus, some forms of eighteenth-century writing do not conform to common notions about genres and form. For an interesting discussion of the social form of the American novel, see Jane Tompkins's discussion of

Charles Brockden Brown's novels in *Sensational Designs*. Further, the form of *Letters* is related to other less common genres like the philosophical travel book, which was often epistolary in form (Montesquieu's *Persian Letters* is a good example).

Original Audience

When students read *Letters*, they find its substance very familiar because much of this material has become part of the mythology of America. Students need to be reminded that *Letters* was one of the first works describing the character of the average American. Also, its American readers were a society of colonials who had just overturned centuries of tradition and were attempting to define themselves as something new in order to distinguish themselves from those who were exactly like them but born under monarchical governments in Europe. European readers were trying to make sense of this "new man."

Comparisons, Contrasts, Connections

Letters is a good literary expression of the political principles in the Declaration of Independence and Paine's *Common Sense*. It is very useful to read *Letters* in tandem with Book II of Timothy Dwight's *Greenfield Hill*, which is another imaginative creation of the "ideal" average American.

Bibliography

For a quick introduction to the political rhetoric of the period, instructors might read: pp. 82–86 in *A Cultural History of the American Revolution* by Kenneth Silverman (excerpted in *Early American Literature*, edited by Michael Gilmore); chapters 1 and 2 of Gordon S. Wood's *The Creation of the American Republic*; and Doreen Alvarez Saar's "Crèvecoeur's 'Thoughts on Slavery': Letters from an American Farmer and the Rhetoric of Whig Thought" in *Early American Literature* (Fall 1987): 192–203.

Thomas Paine (1737–1809)

Contributing Editor: Martin Roth

Major Themes, Historical Perspectives, Personal Issues

Nature and Reason are not abstract principles for Paine. They are not categories through which it is useful to think about things but rather dynamic principles that Paine almost literally sees at work in the world. Reason in *Common Sense* is masculine, a most concrete actor pleading with us to separate from England or forbidding us to have faith in our enemies. Nature is feminine; "she" weeps, and she is unforgiving as part of her deepest nature. Should these agencies be regarded as philosophical principles? As deities? Are they coherent characters? Can they be identified by collecting all their behaviors and their metaphoric qualifications?

How do we think about Paine as an author, a writing "I"? One of his works is presented as having been written by an embodied principle of "common sense," and another piece, *The Age of Reason,* a work on the general truth of religion, opens in an extremely private, confessional mode. But he writes in this way to prove that he could have no private motives for misleading others. What kind of stakes are being waged by writing a work on religious truth just before you die? Is there any distinction for Paine between the private and the public I, the private and the public life? Notice how many statements fold back upon the self: "it is necessary to the happiness of man that he be mentally faithful to himself " and "my own mind is my own church."

Paine evokes the splendor of the visible world to close a unit opened by the notion of a privileged book, a "revealed" book, a Bible. How are the book and the world opposed to each other? One of these ways is as writing and speech; although, actually, the world transcends the distinction between writing and speech: it "speaketh a universal language" which "every man can read." Could Paine's distrust and rejection of the Bible be applied to those other "revealed" and "privileged" pieces of writing, literary "masterpieces"? Much of Paine can be read as an attack on the book, a motif that connects him with Mark Twain at the end of the next century.

In *The Rights of Man,* Paine assumes that the right to engage in revolution is inalienable. How does he understand this? Can time and complexity alter this characteristic of the nature of things? What is a government for Paine? The metaphors that he uses should again remind us of Twain, images of stealth and deceit, images of theatricality used for purposes of fraud.

Family is crucial here, too, as Paine examines the absurdity of hereditary aristocracy. In this as in almost everything he does, the later writer that Paine most evokes is Mark Twain, here the Mark Twain of *A Connecticut Yankee* and

The American Claimant. Among the resemblances to Twain that should not be overlooked is a vein of extremely cunning black humor in much of *The Age of Reason.*

John Adams (1735–1826)
Abigail Adams (1744–1818)

Contributing Editors: Albert Furtwangler and Frank Shuffelton

Classroom Issues and Strategies

The formality and elevated decorum of John Adams's language challenge many students, but the opening anecdotes and the witty exchanges between John and Abigail encourage readers to see the personalities behind the mannered language. John Adams (and to a lesser extent Abigail as well) is also somewhat difficult because he has been mythicized as a Founding Father, a figure of national piety who no longer commands a ready allegiance. Additionally, the interests of the Adamses in politics and morality do not strike all students as "literature." On the other hand, the questions raised in this material about the political relationships between men and women and by the exchange between Adams and Jefferson over the meaning and impact of "talent" continue to be crucial in our own time. The formal language, the learned references, if brought into play in discussions about the contemporary power of the issues debated by the Adamses and their friends, can set limits on the tendency toward "presentism," and the urge to see the significance of the past only in terms of present meanings. The Adamses talk about questions we care about, but their language, their style, remind us that they did not necessarily see these questions as we do.

Major Themes, Historical Perspectives, Personal Issues

Major themes in the writing of the Adamses and their friends relate to the discourse of republicanism that dominated the political and social thinking of enlightened people in the eighteenth century. Adams and many others of his time feared the corruption that he thought inevitably followed upon the increasing sophistication of a developing civilization. His letter to his friend Mercy Otis Warren offers a synopsis of this attitude, including the fear of social laxity that will unleash self-indulgent passion, the unnatural tastes fostered by a burgeoning commercial society, and the disruption by faction of the social harmony needed to sustain a republic. Abigail's desire to return to her farm, described at the end of her journal entry on her return from Europe, links this republican attitude with the pastoralism found in the work of writers like Crèvecoeur, Jefferson, and James Fenimore Cooper, perhaps even with Huckleberry Finn's famous "lighting out."

Abigail Adams's prodding of her husband to "Remember the Ladies" has become a classic benchmark of an emerging feminism, but she is surely no feminist. Nonetheless, she figures as a splendid example of that new sort of woman that Linda Kerber has referred to as the "republican mother" (*Women of the Republic*, 1980). Women like Adams and Mercy Otis Warren took a direct interest in the outcome of the American Revolution, and they spoke their thoughts in private and public, opening the way, perhaps, for more forthright arguments on the behalf of women, such as those by Judith Sargeant Murray and, in a later period, Margaret Fuller.

After the ratification of the Constitution and the creation of the federal government, Adams feared anarchic excesses, encouraged by the French Revolution, among the ill-educated and easily misled populace. Jefferson and the leaders of the emerging Republican party castigated Adams and the Federalists as "monocrats" who wished to seat political power in the hands of a few men of property and family. Adams's belief in a government of laws, however, as well as his suspicion of power that was exerted only by privileged groups, earned him the distrust of Hamilton and the more extreme Federalists. The controversies among these people were not merely over a share of political power, but over the much more crucial question of whether the nation could continue to exist as such. The genuine fear of disorder and social collapse that motivated Adams appears in a different guise in the fiction of Charles Brockden Brown. Jefferson's comments regarding his trust in the good sense of the common people reveal an attitude different from that of Adams, but even he, especially at the end of his life, expressed his fear for the survival of the American experiment. In his correspondence with Jefferson, however, Adams seems rather to have enjoyed playing the cynical foil to his friend's optimism.

Significant Form, Style, or Artistic Conventions

All of the Adams materials included here are drawn from the personal, private genres of the journal and letters. They were intended to be read by trusted family and friends, but they were also expected to be shared among a circle of such readers. Jefferson expected that Abigail Adams would read his letters to John, and similarly John Adams would have expected Mercy Otis Warren to have shared her letter with her husband, James, a political leader in Massachusetts. Such correspondence was one aspect of the eighteenth-century republic of letters, the public sphere of discussion about social, political, and learned questions that occurred independently of the narrow limits of the family as well as of the overview of the state. Considered in this way, the letters between John and Abigail, for instance, are both the intimate exchange of husband and wife and the communication between a constituent and her delegate to the revolutionary Congress of 1776.

Comparisons, Contrasts, Connections

These selections make a lively contrast to the impersonal rationality of the Federalist essays or the *Declaration of Independence*. The journal selections can be used in the context of earlier and later traditions of journal-keeping in New England and are interesting for their moral introspection and regulation as well as for their attention to the way human beings live in the world. They take an interesting position among Winthrop, Sewall, Sarah Kemble Knight, and Emerson and Thoreau. Similarly, Adams's concern for a virtuous republic can be framed against Winthrop's discussion of the city on a hill and Thoreau's "Resistance to Civil Government."

Bibliography

Adams's grandson, Charles Francis Adams, edited his *Works* (1850–1856) in ten volumes, still a useful source for those who wish to read more. Albert Furtwangler discusses Adams's newspaper debate with a loyalist in *American Silhouettes* (1987); this book also contains a discussion of Adams and Jefferson. Peter Shaw's *The Character of John Adams* (1976) is a significant discussion, as is Joseph J. Ellis, *Passionate Sage: John Adams and America's Original Intentions* (1993). Edith Gelles, *Portia: The World of Abigail Adams* (1992), is particularly illuminating on the role of letters in Abigail Adams's life.

Thomas Jefferson (1743–1826)

Contributing Editor: Katherine E. Ledford

Classroom Issues and Strategies

Most students' previous encounters with Jefferson have come in history courses or, more generally, through common knowledge of him as a "Founding Father." His presence in a literature classroom is a surprise to many and may provoke gentle skepticism, if not outright concern that he is in the "wrong" place. Given that Jefferson's work is usually read early in survey courses, these selections can be used to open a discussion about what constitutes literature, and, perhaps, interdisciplinary studies, a fruitful one for courses that incorporate other selections from *The Heath Anthology* formerly considered outside the bounds of literature, such as oral narratives and poetry, narratives of exploration and travel, captivity narratives, religious tracts, and letters. Students readily grant poetry, fiction, and drama a place at the literary table, but they are unsure about the inclusion of political documents, scientific books, and letters such as Jefferson's. The copyedit of the *Declaration* from Jefferson's autobiography can be used to point out the crafted, audience-centered, even artistic nature of Jefferson's texts. A focus on word choice and shades of meaning reveals Jefferson, and his contemporaries, as being acutely aware of the power of words, whether in public documents or in private correspondence.

The major issue students want to discuss today is Jefferson's relationship with Sally Hemings, his slave, and its impact on his credibility. Given the topic's recent appearance in the popular press, many students have already formed opinions about the validity of the Hemings's family claim of Jefferson ancestry, the DNA evidence that most scholars find persuasive, and the impact such a relationship has on Jefferson's legacy. (See *The Heath Anthology* Web resources for documents outlining the merits of claims about a Jefferson/Hemings relationship.) Some students want to brand Jefferson a hypocrite—citing his proclamation that all men are created equal while owning, and most likely fathering, slaves—and leave it at that. Discussing the problems with applying today's standards of racial enlightenment to the eighteenth-century mindset while also acknowledging the trauma racist attitudes and actions caused can be a productive way to begin. The selections from *The Heath Anthology* offer ample opportunity to explore the contradictory nature of Jefferson's attitudes toward African Americans. Contrast his gracious letters to Benjamin Banneker and the Marquis de Condorcet with his "scientific" observations about blacks in *Notes on the State of Virginia*. Note his attempt to censure the slave trade in the *Declaration*, his scheme for phasing out slavery in Query XIV of *Notes*, his trepidations about such a change in his letter to Peter Carr, and the personal anxiety the peculiar institution caused him as he contemplated the future of the republic he had helped found. As most classroom discussion will reflect, Jefferson's relationship with slavery, on several levels, is problematic—for him and for us, today.

Major Themes, Historical Perspectives, Personal Issues

Other major themes in this selection of texts include the character of Native Americans and their incorporation into the nation. Jefferson's plan for settling Native Americans into small towns and onto individually owned farms reflects his belief in the ideal of the yeoman farmer as central to national stability and connects with larger issues of national expansion and Indian removal emergent in the first decades of the nineteenth century, themes shared by writers such as James Fenimore Cooper and exercised in the governmental policies of Andrew Jackson.

The shape and role of government is another prominent theme, especially as it relates to individual responsibility in citizenship, a concern manifest in the state versus federal positions of Alexander Hamilton, John Jay, and James Madison. Jefferson's championing of the common sense of the common citizen as the bedrock of republican success marks him as philosophically advanced in light of the historical extension of enfranchisement to all citizens. His blindness to the equality of the black, Native, and female citizen with the white male citizen, however, tempers this progressive strain and reminds us that Jefferson, however gifted, remained a man of his times.

Finally, this selection of texts shows Jefferson's commitment to scientific and philosophical thinking. He engages with some of the most important debates of his time, including the Count de Buffon's theory of North American degeneracy and differences among the races. Couched firmly in the Enlightenment, Jefferson believed scientific investigation could explain many of the mysteries surrounding him. In the spirit of the times, Jefferson was an accomplished botanist, gardener, architect, musician, mapmaker, inventor, scholar, writer, and politician, although, ironically, he was never a good public speaker.

Significant Form, Style, or Artistic Conventions

Jefferson operates within the forms of political debate, scientific and philosophical investigation, and correspondence, all of which impose their own stylistic conventions. Students may be most surprised by the style of eighteenth- and early nineteenth-century correspondence, especially the elevated diction, formality, and lofty subject matter that marked letters among Jefferson's class. Likewise, *Notes*, Jefferson's only book, follows a particular form of scientific and philosophical debates, that of "query" and essay-length answer.

Original Audience

Although some of Jefferson's writing was clearly intended for public consumption, such as the *Declaration*, some of it also operated in a more limited space. Jefferson treated much of his correspondence as only semi-private, aware that his ideas, and sometimes his actual letters, might be shared with the recipients' family and friends. His desire for maintaining a record of his correspondence and of the ideas therein led him to invent a device that, through the linkage of a second pen to the one he wielded, copied his text, an indication of the seriousness with which he approached his voluminous correspondence. Likewise, *Notes* began as a document to be circulated among friends and associates. Faced with unauthorized publication, of his book, Jefferson chose to release the text publicly. Jefferson's relationship with an audience was sometimes bold, sometimes intimate, and sometimes reluctant.

Comparisons, Contrasts, Connections

Reading Jefferson's letters alongside those of John Adams and Abigail Adams provides space for comparing and contrasting style and intellectual content, especially the letters to and from Jefferson and Adams in the Adams section. Jefferson's work and Crèvecoeur's *Letters from an American Farmer* can be constructively paired in a couple of ways. First, contrast the literary device of correspondence in *Letters* with Jefferson's actual letters—a nice way to point out the limitations and freedoms the form offers in different settings. *Notes* compares and contrasts well with *Letters* as texts attempting to define America geographically, economically, socially, and politically. Jefferson's careful consideration of the ideal education for a young man can be contrasted with his surprise at being consulted on the topic of female education. The differences between his recommendations for young men and those for young women offer insights into gender expectations of the time. The eloquence and intelligence of texts by African Americans such as Briton Hammon, Prince Hall, and Olaudah Equiano speak volumes when contrasted with the image of black people Jefferson paints in *Notes* and in his letters. Likewise, selections by Native Americans, especially Elias Boudinot, provide comparisons and contrasts to the plan Jefferson laid out for their settlement and incorporation, questioning the authority of government and the boundaries of nation. More generally, complex discussions can emerge from comparing and contrasting our notions of order in the natural world with those of Jefferson and his contemporaries, revealing how those differences impact attitudes toward race and gender, for example.

Bibliography

Bernstein, Richard B. *Thomas Jefferson*. New York. Oxford UP, 2003.

Ellis, Joseph J. *American Sphinx: The Character of Thomas Jefferson*. New York: Knopf, 1997.

Gilreath, James, ed. *Thomas Jefferson and the Education of a Citizen*. Washington, DC: Library of Congress, 1999.

Gordon-Reed, Annette. *Thomas Jefferson and Sally Hemings: An American Controversy*. Charlottesville: UP of Virginia, 1997.

Kennedy, Roger G. *Mr. Jefferson's Lost Cause: Land, Farmers, Slaves, and the Louisiana Purchase*. New York: Oxford UP, 2003.

Lewis, Jan E. and Peter S. Onuf, eds. *Sally Hemings and Thomas Jefferson: History, Memory, and Civic Culture*. Charlottesville: UP of Virginia, 1999.

Onuf, Peter, ed. *Jeffersonian Legacies*. Charlottesville: UP of Virginia, 1993.

Wallace, Anthony F. C. *Jefferson and the Indians: The Tragic Fate of the First Americans*. Cambridge, MA: Harvard UP, 1999.

Federalist and Anti-Federalist Contentions

Contributing Editor: Nicholas D. Rombes

Classroom Issues and Strategies

Students generally respond with more enthusiasm to the Federalist/Anti-Federalist debate once they realize that the issues raised by the debate were very real. It often helps, initially, to have students think of "current event" issues of contention today, such as the "pro-life"/"pro-choice" abortion debates. This helps students to see that debates over the Constitution were not merely abstract exercises in rhetorical showmanship but were real debates about issues that mattered.

Students also seem to identify with one of the three "voices" of *The Federalist Papers*, as well. Some students, for instance, wish that Jay had contributed more essays, finding his voice more democratic and populist than Hamilton's or Madison's. This can lead to fruitful discussions about the rhetorical strategies employed by all three authors as well as the audience they were addressing.

Major Themes, Historical Perspectives, Personal Issues

Many students assume that once the Revolutionary War was over, the country was solidified and unified. Therefore, it is helpful to review certain key issues such as states' rights, fear of a standing army, and fear of factions. Anti-Federalists argued again and again that a national government was merely a prelude to the establishment of an aristocratic class. Indeed, many Anti-Federalists drew upon the rhetoric of the Revolution to argue against a strong national government.

The Federalist conception of human nature as essentially selfish and depraved is also important to note since Federalists relied on such conceptions to justify their call for a mildly interventionist national government. Students are often shocked to learn that the word *democracy* was not held in high regard as it is today, and are interested in the distinctions among democracy, monarchy, and republicanism.

For years, many scholars have contended that the Federalists were basically conservative upper-class supporters of the status quo and that the Anti-Federalists were more "populist." Scholars such as Herbert J. Storing have recently suggested, however, that, if anything, Anti-Federalists were more conservative than their Federalist counterparts, as evidenced in the fact that many Anti-Federalists feared the very idea of change and experimentation that would result from the new form of government proposed by the Federalists.

It is also helpful to introduce students to some of the basic ideas of writers such as Hobbes, Locke, and Montesquieu, all of whose writings influenced the Constitution to varying degrees.

Significant Form, Style, or Artistic Conventions

Students are interested in the different "voices" of Hamilton, Madison, and Jay. Note also how the authors of *The Federalist Papers* allude to classical regimes and civilizations not only to help their arguments but also to show their learning. Finally, note how many of the letters begin with references to "objections" to the proposed Constitution—instructors may want to use this to show that these debates were very real.

Original Audience

The Federalist Papers originally appeared as a series of essays in New York newspapers between October 1786 and August 1787. Based on the language and tone of the essays, ask students to try to construct an audience for them; would this audience be literate? Educated? What economic class might constitute the majority of the audience? What race? Gender?

Questions for Reading, Discussion, and Writing

1. Ask students to perform a rhetorical analysis of *The Federalist Papers*, paying special attention to how the authors construct their arguments (logos), how they bolster their authority and credibility (ethos), and how they use the beliefs, fears, and assumptions of their audience (pathos) to help their arguments.
2. Ask students to try to reconstruct the Federalist conception of the relationship between "the people" and government. From where does authority ultimately derive? If students have spent time studying the Puritans, ask them to consider the ultimate sources of authority in Puritan writings as compared with Federalist and Anti-Federalist writings. Has the source of authority shifted from God to humans and civil institutions?

Bibliography

Cary, George W. *The Federalist: Design for a Constitutional Republic*. Urbana: U of Illinois P, 1989.

Epstein, David F. *The Political Theory of The Federalist*. Chicago: U of Chicago P, 1984.

Furtwangler, Albert. *The Authority of Publius: A Reading of the Federalist Papers*. Ithaca, NY: Cornell UP, 1984.

Main, Jackson Turner. *The Anti-Federalists: Critics of the Constitution, 1781–1788*. New York: Norton, 1961.

Toussaint L'Ouverture (1744?–1803)

Contributing Editor: Danielle Hinrichs

Classroom Issues and Strategies

Teaching Toussaint L'Ouverture within the context of an American Literature survey course will necessitate some delving into the history of Saint Domingue (now Haiti) and colonization. What will certainly be unfamiliar intellectual terrain for many students, however, will raise thought-provoking questions that have a bearing on many other readings in *The Heath Anthology*. Toussaint's work presents an opportunity to discuss processes of colonization and practices of slavery in an America that clearly extends beyond the present U.S. borders. When discussing the historical context of Toussaint's writings, connections can be made between the maroon colonies that formed the impetus and power of the slave revolt in Saint Domingue and communities of escaped slaves in other parts of the Americas. The maroon revolt might also be discussed in the context of other forms of slave resistance, including more subtle forms of resistance, evident in American fiction and nonfiction. Toussaint and Saint Domingue served as a tremendous example of the efficacy of slave resistance for the entire world. As George F. Tyson explains, "The creation of a 'Black Republic' generated shock waves of alarm throughout the plantation sphere, raising the possibility of other successful uprisings of the oppressed black masses and an end to white supremacy in the hemisphere" (1). Toussaint's writings convey the political maneuvering of imperial interests, making Saint Domingue an apt demonstration of the competing cultures that battled for power throughout the Americas. The revolution in Saint Domingue is also complexly intertwined with the historical events of the French revolution, and Toussaint's writings can raise interesting questions relevant to political revolution throughout the Old World and the New. Students will gain more from reading Toussaint L'Ouverture if they are introduced to Saint Domingue's historical context and relevant issues before they read Toussaint's writings. It would also be very helpful to read Toussaint's proclamations and letter after other works on colonization or slavery, works by Prince Hall or Lemuel Haynes, for example, so that students have been introduced to these major themes and issues before they encounter the sometimes complex historical references of Toussaint's writings.

Major Themes, Historical Perspectives, Personal Issues

Saint Domingue was a prized and valuable colony in the eighteenth century. Its sugar and coffee industries generated immense profits, but its enormous plantations depended on a slave economy that instituted brutally violent practices in order to produce more abundant crops. Several imperial interests attempted to control the island's wealth, including England, Spain, and France. Toussaint was born on the western portion of the island, controlled by the French, but he also served the Spanish when he believed that they might abolish slavery on the island, and he fought against England in order to garner support from the other colonial powers. The French revolution further complicated these alliances. Toussaint first sided with the Royalists, believing that only a king could abolish slavery, but he shifted his allegiance when the French Republic declared slavery illegal. Toussaint not only had to negotiate between these competing imperial powers but also had to mediate between competing class and race factions at home. Students in the United States are often accustomed to thinking of race and power in binary terms. It will be important, therefore, to establish the complex hierarchical structure of the island in which the *Grand Blancs* (white plantation owners and French officials) asserted power over the *Petit Blancs* (white overseers, artisans, shopkeepers, and soldiers), who asserted power over free blacks (mainly mulattoes), who had more power and privileges than slaves. All of these groups were trying to maintain or gain power in the community. Toussaint's background as a slave meant that his goals and initiatives often collided with those of the mulattoes, who not only struggled to increase their power in society but also continually fought to maintain the privileges they already enjoyed. Toussaint's writing must be considered at this nexus of competing powers and factions. Understanding the stakes and complexities of the social climate will allow students to more easily recognize Toussaint's often simultaneous attempts to defend himself, attack his enemies, and unify the population of Saint Domingue.

Toussaint's personal history also helps to demonstrate some important themes in his writing. His life as a slave was unusual in Saint Domingue in that he received liberal treatment from his master, he read widely, and he gained a very deep sense of religion from his godfather, a priest. When Toussaint achieved power in Saint Domingue, he made Catholicism the state religion. One of the most important and interesting themes to consider, then, is how Toussaint uses religious language to put forth political objectives.

Significant Form, Style, or Artistic Conventions

Toussaint's letters and proclamations are characterized by careful and convincing logic and persuasive and eloquent language. He often uses questions and exclamatory statements to create a stirring and rousing tone that attacks his enemies and calls his audience to action. His letters and proclamations are, in essence, public addresses to large political bodies, and Toussaint continually defines himself on a public stage.

Original Audience

Both genre and historical context contribute to making the question of audience crucial and potentially fruitful for students reading the work of Toussaint L'Ouverture. On a fundamental level, students should think about the generic qualities of letters and political declarations, their audiences and functions. Toussaint's proclamations are formal political declarations meant to be heard or read by the entire population of Saint Domingue, their goal as large and encompassing as their intended audience. Through these proclamations, Toussaint attempts to gain widespread public support for his goals and to defend himself on the political stage. The language is thus persuasive, inclusive, and powerful, attempting to unite his public behind a certain cause. Toussaint's

"Letter to the Directory" specifically addresses a governing body in France. The uniqueness of the epistolary genre lies in its exchange between a clearly defined reader and a writer and in its expectation of reply. Toussaint's letter, however, is an unusual epistolary example in that it addresses a political body and thus is exceedingly public and political. Because a member of the directory had recently made disparaging remarks against Toussaint, he approaches his audience as a somewhat hostile one and vigorously defends his political reputation. His tone is argumentative, and his evidence is detailed. In the very complex cultural climate of Saint Domingue, one in which alliances and allegiances were continually in flux, the intended audience of a document has an enormous influence over its language and content.

Comparisons, Contrasts, Connections

A comparison of Prince Hall and Toussaint L'Ouverture is very effective because Hall refers to the Saint Domingue revolution, underscoring the significance of this movement throughout the Americas, and because the two politically active authors take up similar themes and confront similar audiences. Both write directly to political bodies, and both employ extensive references to religion and the language of equality. Both are also persuasive and eloquent writers who seek to rouse their audiences to political action. Lemuel Haynes provides a very interesting counterpart to Toussaint in terms of exploring revolution and the use of enlightenment thinking throughout the Americas. Haynes uses the language of the American revolution to argue against slavery and to defend the rights of freedom for all. All three writers, Hall, Toussaint, and Haynes, make religion an important part of their persuasive writings.

Questions for Reading, Discussion, and Writing

1. Consider the relationship between politics and religion in Toussaint's writing. How does Toussaint employ religious language for political purposes in his proclamations and/or in his letter?
2. Discuss the differences and similarities between Toussaint's proclamations and his letter. Does the intended audience change the tone of his writing and the content of his argument? Which techniques and allusions are similar in his proclamations and his letter? How are his goals similar, and how are they different?
3. The French imperialists both enabled and obstructed Toussaint's rise to power in Saint Domingue. Toussaint existed, therefore, in a politically unstable position and sought to both rally the island behind his own cause and woo the support of the powerful French government. How does Toussaint portray his relationship with the French government?

4. In which contexts and for what purposes does Toussaint invoke the language of the French revolution?

5. Throughout Toussaint's political maneuverings, he sought a permanent end to slavery. How does Toussaint convey this goal in the excerpted writings? Pay particular attention to the language and tone of his discussions of slavery.

6. What is the rhetorical effect of Toussaint's frequent use of questions and exclamatory statements? Examine moments in the texts when he includes questions and exclamations and discuss the purpose of these strategies within the context of his argument.

7. Toussaint's writings address large public audiences and serve to place and define Toussaint L'Ouverture within the political realm. How does Toussaint define himself for his audience? How does Toussaint strive to shape public perception of himself and his political goals?

Bibliography

James, C. L. R. *Black Jacobins.* New York: Vintage Books, 1963.

Langley, Lester D. "The Haitian Revolution." *The Americas in the Age of Revolution, 1750–1850.* New Haven: Yale UP, 1996, 122–144.

Ros, Martin. *Night of Fire: The Black Napoleon and the Battle for Haiti.* New York: Sarpedon, 1994.

Stein, Robert L. *Leger Felicite Sonthonax: The Lost Sentinel of the Republic.* Cranbury, NJ: Associated UP, 1985.

Tyson, George F., Jr. "Introduction." *Toussaint L'Ouverture.* Englewood Cliffs, NJ: Prentice, 1973. 1–22.

Patriot and Loyalist Songs and Ballads

Contributing Editor: Rosalie Murphy Baum

Classroom Issues and Strategies

Most students enjoy Patriot songs and ballads but approach Loyalist works with shyness and curiosity. Their studies in elementary, middle, and high school have led them to think of the Revolutionary War as a completely justified and glorious chapter in American history; they tend not to be aware of the Loyalist (Tory) view of the conflict. At the same time, however, their consciousness of recent American history and international events (e.g., the Vietnam War, the Persian Gulf War, the Israeli-Palestinian struggles, the wars in Iraq and Afghanistan) have made them increasingly aware of the complexity of historical events and of the need to understand both sides of issues. The fact that the songs and ballads reflect and articulate two conflicting *American* views about a momentous period can be of great interest to students once they overcome their qualms about literature that questions or criticizes national decisions and actions.

Major Themes, Historical Perspectives, Personal Issues

Reading the Patriot and Loyalist songs and ballads provides a glimpse of the popular sentiments being expressed in newspapers, periodicals, ballad-sheets, and broadsides during the Revolutionary period. The selections in the text represent various forms: the song and the ballad, the selection addressed to the public at large and the selection addressed to the child, the work expressing the Patriot or Loyalist position, and the work commemorating the life of a particular hero. The usual themes of the Patriot and the Loyalist writers are summarized in the introduction to the selections.

A good glossary of literary terms can offer students information about the usual form and conventions of the song and ballad. Students should anticipate uneven work in popular songs and ballads, written in haste and for immediate practical purposes. At the same time, however, they may wish to examine what in these works accounted for their great popularity during the period and their survival through the years. Of particular interest might be an imaginative reconstruction of the response of both Patriot and Loyalist to either a Patriot or a Loyalist song.

Probably the most important facts students need to consider before reading Patriot and Loyalist songs and ballads are (a) at the time of the Revolutionary War, the Loyalists were Americans just as much as were the Patriots (Rebels or Whigs); (b) the Loyalist group included some of the leading figures in the country at the time (e.g., Chief Justice William Allen, the Rev. Mather Byles, Samuel Curwen, Joseph Galloway, Governor Thomas Hutchinson, the Rev. Jonathan Odell, Chief Justice Peter Oliver, the Rev. Samuel Seabury, Attorney General Jonathan Sewall), figures whom students tend not to recognize because of the usual emphasis in the classroom upon only Patriot figures; (c) whatever knowledge the students have of Loyalists probably comes from the remarks and writings of Patriots and thus is heavily slanted. The classroom emphasis on Patriot leaders and Patriot arguments, of course, distorts the political complexion of the time and does not help the student to appreciate the complex issues and emotional turmoil of a period in which it is believed that about one-third of the people were Patriots, one-third Loyalists, and one-third neutrals, with Loyalists being especially strong in Delaware, Maryland, New Jersey, New York, and Pennsylvania.

Comparisons, Contrasts, Connections

The sentiments of these works, both Patriot and Loyalist, can be compared very successfully with the ideas expressed by prose writers like John Adams, Benjamin Franklin, Thomas Jefferson, and Thomas Paine, Patriots who are frequently anthologized. Students, however, may also be interested in reading a few of the Loyalist prose writers such as the Rev. Samuel Seabury ("A View of the Controversy Between Great Britain and Her Colonies") and Joseph Galloway ("Plan of a Proposed Union Between Great Britain and the Colonies" or "A Candid Examination of the Mutual Claims of Great Britain and the Colonies"). Students interested in popular culture may wish to pursue the difficult question of what characteristics distinguish popular literature, like these songs and ballads, from serious literature, like the poems of William Cullen Bryant, Walt Whitman, or Emily Dickinson. There could be considerable controversy about where the poetry of Philip Freneau should fit in such a comparison.

Approaches to Writing

Some students may simply wish to report on additional Patriot and Loyalist songs and ballads and can consult Frank Moore's *Songs and Ballads of the American Revolution* (1855, 1964) for the most complete collection. Other students may wish to consider the degree to which the Revolutionary War was very much a civil war. They might compare such a struggle to the conflict between the disparate cultures of the whites and Indians reflected in Puritan literature, or draw parallels between the civil conflict in America and similar hostilities in countries throughout the world today.

Bibliography

Two kinds of information can be particularly useful for students or instructors in studying the Patriot and Loyalist songs and ballads. The introductions to *Prose and Poetry of the Revolution* (1925, 1969), edited by Frederick C. Prescott and John H. Nelson, and to *The World Turned Upside Down* (1975), ed. James H. Pickering, give excellent, brief overviews of the period and of the literature.

William H. Nelson's *The American Tory* (1961) offers an excellent discussion of Loyalist views.

Wallace Brown's *The King's Friends* (1965) attempts to identify who the Loyalists were and to determine their motives for remaining loyal to the king.

Contested Visions, American Voices

Jupiter Hammon (1711–1806?)

Contributing Editors: William H. Robinson and Phillip M. Richards

Classroom Issues and Strategies

African-American literature emerges at an auspicious time in the settlement of North America. The number of blacks entering the colonies increased markedly at the middle of the eighteenth century. Settled blacks in the New World may have acquired a new self-consciousness as they encountered large numbers of newly arrived Africans. Their consciousness as a separate group was defined by laws restricting racial intermarriage, by racist portrayals in the press, and by their increased involvement in the evangelical religion that emerged in the aftermath of the Great Awakening.

Jupiter Hammon, whose life roughly covers the span of the eighteenth century, was in an excellent position to see these trends. His writing reflects his efforts to evangelize his black brethren at a time when most African Americans were not Christians. He is a traditional Calvinist. He is aware of Africa and the experience of the middle passage. Not surprisingly, his use of traditional evangelical rhetoric is deeply suggestive of the political implications that this discourse might have in the work of future writers.

Students should be aware that we read Hammon as we might read any American Calvinist writing in the last half of the eighteenth century. We look for the rhetoric that underlies his evangelical strategies; we try to establish the speaker's relationship to his white and black audiences; and we assess the way in which the religious language of his discourse begins to acquire a political resonance, particularly in its use of words such as *king, nation, salvation,* and *victory.*

Major Themes, Historical Perspectives, Personal Issues

Psalms is the most quoted biblical book in the poem addressed to Phillis Wheatley. Why would Psalms be such an important book to a black preacher-poet such as Hammon? What importance do you think the broad sweep of Old Testament history might have had to Hammon? What importance did this history have to evangelicals and political revolutionaries in late eighteenth-century New England? At what points do you think that Hammon and his white evangelical peers' understanding of scripture might have diverged?

What poem by Phillis Wheatley has Hammon obviously read? Why do you think that he seized upon this verse in his own longer poem? What stance does the speaker of this poem assume toward his ostensible reader, Wheatley? Does this stance resemble the speaker's stance in Hammon's other work?

Significant Form, Style, or Artistic Conventions

Examine the formal impact of the literary structure of the Psalms on Hammon's poems. What literary influence do hymn stanza form and sermon form have on his writing? In what social context do hymns and sermons occur? Why would Hammon be attempting to evoke that context in his writing?

Comparisons, Contrasts, Connections

In what way does the rhetoric of Christian salvation, both personal and national, imply a historical construct? Compare Hammon's and Wheatley's use of that construct. Why would such a construct be important to early American black writers?

Think of other early American writers who treat the subject of salvation in radically different ways. Would Jonathan Edwards and Benjamin Franklin respond to Hammon in the same ways? How would the two white writers differ, if they differed at all?

Questions for Reading, Discussion, and Writing

Describe the way in which Christian thought and rhetoric structured Hammon's racial consciousness. Why is it significant that America's first black writers are Puritans? In what sense could a shared religious belief be important for racial relations in the late eighteenth and early nineteenth century?

James Grainger (1721?–1766)

Contributing Editor: Thomas W. Krise

Classroom Issues and Strategies

James Grainger's *The Sugar Cane* (1764) offers one of the best descriptions of a staple crop plantation in the eighteenth century, as well as a good example of the adaptation of classical forms to the American experience. The fourth and final book of the poem offered in *The Heath Anthology* presents Grainger's advice to the planter on how to manage the slave population.

Students will require some orientation to classical poetics, both in their original Greek and Roman patterns and in their English varieties in the eighteenth century. Grainger's georgic (from the Greek for "farmer") poem varies from the standard georgic in that the poet is advising not a hands-on farmer but rather a manager of a large-scale plantation and factory system. It also replaces the standard closing paean to the ideal farm with an uncomfortable (both for us and the poet) vade mecum to the purchase and management of slaves. Descriptions of slavery are also likely to draw most students' attention.

Considerations of the tradition of neoclassical poetry and *The Sugar Cane*'s place in both American and British literature will help broaden students' appreciation of this poem.

Major Themes, Historical Perspectives, Personal Issues

Students will need some orientation to the British West Indies, which, before the American Revolution severed them from their fellow colonists on the North American continent, were part of the same unitary "British Empire in America." It is important to emphasize that the West Indies were the destination of many more enslaved Africans than North America was. More than three times as many were transported to the sugar plantations of Barbados, Jamaica, the Leeward Islands (including Grainger's St. Christopher), and others. By the 1770s, the wealth generated by these relatively small island colonies exceeded the combined wealth of all thirteen continental colonies.

Tropical diseases (Grainger's medical specialty), extreme weather, and hard conditions resulted in a much higher death rate for the enslaved populations in the islands than for those on the continent. As a result, the vast majority of the slaves working on sugar plantations were African-born, hence Grainger's heavy emphasis on the choice and "seasoning" of new slaves rather than on the management of native-born or long-accustomed slaves.

It is also important to note that Grainger writes at the moment of Britain's stupendous victory over France in the Seven Years War (America's French and Indian War). Besides conquering Canada, much of India, and other posts throughout the world, Britain added more than a dozen valuable Caribbean sugar islands to its empire. Within a dozen years, London's high-handedness in dealing with its newly expanded empire would lead to the American Revolution, but in the early 1760s, the future looked bright and peaceful. As Virgil's *Georgics* celebrates the peace brought by Augustus's victories, Grainger's poem celebrates the happy conclusion of decades of Anglo-French warfare.

Significant Form, Style, or Artistic Conventions

Perhaps better than any other eighteenth-century English poem in the neoclassical vein, *The Sugar Cane* marries the dream of social order represented by the steady march of iambic pentameter within the formal conventions of the Augustan poetic heritage with the anxious need to maintain social order within a violent and volatile slave society by all means necessary. Grainger is innovative in introducing many new places, terms, flora, and fauna to English poetry. He also tries to dignify the slave owner by conflating him with the noble farmers to whom georgics are addressed from Hesiod and Virgil onward. Grainger's planter shares in the glories of labor without performing any of the ennobling work.

Original Audience

Samuel Johnson wrote a review of *The Sugar Cane* as soon as it was published in London, describing it as the best poem to arise to date from British America. James Boswell discusses Grainger and his georgic in *The Life of Johnson*, reporting that the poem was read in manuscript to a group of wits at the house of Sir Joshua Reynolds, a friend of Grainger's. Clearly, then, Grainger's chief literary audience was intellectual London. The fact, however, that Grainger addresses his fellow colonists and that several West Indian editions of the poem were published suggest an interest in an American audience.

Grainger's poem inspired at least three other works: John Singleton's *A General Description of the West Indies* (1767), the anonymous *Jamaica, A Poem, In Three Parts* (1777), and portions of John Gabriel Stedman's *Narrative* of the Surinam slave revolt (1796).

Comparisons, Contrasts, Connections

Descriptions of slavery by opponents of the system, especially those written by slaves themselves, can help balance and contextualize the presentation of *The Sugar Cane.* Olaudah Equiano's autobiography is by far the most sophisticated and influential. Other useful sources include Stedman's *Narrative,* Vincent Carretta's *Unchained Voices* anthology, and *Caribbeana: An Anthology of English Literature of the West Indies, 1657–1777.*

As a georgic, *The Sugar Cane* is indebted especially to Virgil's *Georgics* and James Thomson's *Seasons* (1726–1730). Its digressions on Caribbean plants and animals echo the many prose and verse descriptions of the natural history of the region from 1492 onward, especially Edmund Hickeringill's *Jamaica Viewed* (1661), Richard Ligon's *A True and Exact History of Barbados* (1657), and Sir Hans Sloane's *A Voyage to the Islands* (1707–1725). Its topographical, imperial, and commercial aspects continue the tradition of Sir John Denham's "Cooper's Hill" (1642) and Alexander Pope's "Windsor Forest" (1713).

The Sugar Cane's most direct imitation can be found in John Singleton's *A General Description of the West Indies* (1767), which shifts the emphasis from georgic to topographical poem, providing more detailed descriptions of the islands, people, and customs of the West Indies. The anonymous author of another long topographical poem, *Jamaica, A Poem, In Three Parts* (1777), takes issue with Grainger's poetical support for the inhumanity of slavery. In his *Narrative* (1796), Stedman follows the *Jamaica* poet in lamenting Grainger's attempt to dignify the system.

Questions for Reading, Discussion, and Writing

1. How does the poem's form (georgic in blank verse) relate to its didactic purpose (teaching the management of a slave plantation)? How would other forms and genres change the character of Grainger's message?
2. What effect do Grainger's learned footnotes have on the experience of reading the poem? Do the scientific digressions enhance or detract from the poem?
3. How does Grainger represent the living conditions of plantation slaves? How does he justify British involvement in slavery?
4. How does the narrator handle the apparent conflict between his aim of teaching planters how to grow sugar cane using slave labor and his dismay over the "heart debasing" nature of slavery?
5. Which aspects of the poem are distinctly American? Which British?
6. How does *The Sugar Cane* relate to other American poems of the eighteenth century?

Bibliography

In his study of commercial and imperial poetry, David S. Shields provides the most extensive discussion of *The Sugar Cane* published to date.

Olaudah Equiano's narrative offers the best description of slavery in the eighteenth century from the point of view of a former slave. Vincent Carretta's anthology includes a number of accounts of West Indian and North American slavery written by Africans.

Addison, Joseph. "Essay on the Georgic." 1697.

Anonymous. *Jamaica, a poem, in three parts. Written in that Island, in the Year MDCCLXXVI. To which is annexed, A Poetical Epistle From the Author in that Island to a Friend in England.* London, 1777.

Boswell, James. *The Life of Samuel Johnson, LL.D.* Ed. G. B. Hill. Rev. ed. Ed. L. F. Powell. 6 vols. Oxford: Oxford UP, 1934–1964.

Carretta, Vincent, ed. *Unchained Voices: An Anthology of Black Authors in the English-Speaking World of the 18th Century.* Lexington: UP of Kentucky, 1996.

Equiano, Olaudah. *The Interesting Narrative of the Life of Olaudah Equiano, or Gustavus Vassa, the African. Written by Himself.* London, 1789. Ed. Vincent Carretta. New ed. New York: Penguin USA, 1995.

Johnson, Samuel. Review of Grainger's *The Sugar Cane. Critical Review* (October 1764): 170.

Krise, Thomas W. *Caribbeana: An Anthology of English Literature of the West Indies, 1657–1777.* Chicago: U of Chicago P, 1999.

Shields, David S. *Oracles of Empire: Poetry, Politics, and Commerce in British America, 1690–1750.* Chicago: U of Chicago P, 1990.

Singleton, John. *A General Description of the West-Indian Islands, As far as relates to the British, Dutch, and Danish Governments, From Barbados to Saint Croix. Attempted in Blank Verse.* Barbados, 1767.

Stedman, John Gabriel. *Narrative, of a five years expedition, against the revolted Negroes of Surinam.* London, 1796. New ed. of 1790 manuscript. Ed. Richard Price and Sally Price. Baltimore: Johns Hopkins UP, 1988.

Samson Occom (Mohegan) (1723–1792)

Contributing Editor: A. LaVonne Brown Ruoff

Classroom Issues and Strategies

"A Short Narrative of My Life" (dated September 17, 1768) is one of the earliest life histories written by an American Indian. Shortly after he returned from England in the spring of 1768, Occom began his "Short, Plain, and Honest Account of my Self " in order to refute false reports that he was a Mohawk, that Wheelock received large sums for his support, and that he had been converted just before the English tour in order to become a special exhibit (Blodgett 27). An important topic both in his narrative and sermon, as well as in the selection from Apess and Copway, is religious conversion. Students, who generally cannot understand why Indians became devout Christian converts, need to know that for Indians and for slaves, Christianity offered the possibility of being regarded by whites as equals under God. Indian authors, like slave narrators, frequently contrasted whites' professed Christianity with their mistreatment of minorities. Students also need to understand that until at least the late nineteenth century, most Indian education was conducted under the auspices of religious organizations. In the twentieth century, many reservation schools were still run by churches; even the Indian schools controlled by the government had a strong religious orientation.

Occom's narrative offers the opportunity to follow the stages of his movement from traditional Mohegan life to conversion and acculturation, his methods of teaching his Indian students and conducting church services, and resentment of being paid far less than white preachers because he was Indian.

In discussing "A Sermon Preached by Samson Occom," students should be given information about the structure and general content of execution sermons. All this is included in the text headnote and in the following section.

There are a number of issues that can help them see the significance of this sermon. I have had good discussions of why execution sermons were so popular during this period. I often relate these sermons and the confessions they contain to modern-day confessional talk shows.

Another issue is the delicate political task Occom faced in addressing both a white and Indian audience. See the discussion of style that follows.

Major Themes, Historical Perspectives, Personal Issues

1. Identify the Mohegans as a tribe and give some sense of their background. A member of the Algonkian language family, the Mohegans originally were the northernmost branch of the Pequots, the fiercest of the New

England tribes. During the 1637 war with the English, the Pequots were massacred near what is now Stonington, Connecticut. Led by their chief Uncas, the Mohegans, who sided with the English in the war, joined in the massacre. After the war, they remained at peace with the English but resumed hostilities with their old enemies, the Narragansetts. For a brief period, the Mohegans, then numbering 2,000, greatly expanded their territory. However, this had shrunk drastically by the end of the seventeenth century. English settlers, who regarded the nomadic Mohegans as idle thieves, issued orders to remove them from the towns. Uncas and his sons further decreased Mohegan territory by making large land transfers to the whites. By the end of the century, the Mohegans were no longer independent. The first successful attempt to gather them into Indian villages was made in 1717. Eight years later, the Mohegans numbered only 351 and were split into two opposing camps, located one-half mile apart on the west side of the Mohegan river between New London and Norwich, Connecticut.

2. "A Short Narrative of My Life." Issues for discussion include the status of New England Indians in 1768, the relationship of the document to the spiritual confessions so popular in this period, and Occom's concept of self as expressed in his narrative.

3. "A Sermon Preached by Samson Occom."
   a. Why were execution sermons so popular in this period? (See the following section.)
   b. Structure and general content of the execution sermons.
   All this is included in the text headnote and in the following section.

Significant Form, Style, or Artistic Conventions

In "A Short Narrative of My Life," which was not written for publication, Occom uses a much more conversational style than he does in "A Sermon." Why?

The latter is a typical example of the popular genre of the execution sermon. The first publication in New England to combine the offender's "True Confession" with the "Dying Warning" was Increase Mather's *The Wicked mans Portion* [sic] (1675). His *A Sermon Occasioned by the Execution of a Man found Guilty of Murder* [sic] (1686) expanded the literary form by including the murderer's complete confession as allegedly taken down in shorthand. The 1687 second edition added a discourse between the prisoner and minister, designed to introduce realism. Lawrence Towner argues that the genre demonstrated that New Englanders committed crimes and were led to contrition. Because the listeners to the sermons and readers of the "True Confessions" and "Dying Warnings" were at worst minor sinners, it was necessary to trace the criminal's career back to its origins and to generalize about the nature of crime. As criminals increasingly became outsiders (blacks, Indians, Irishmen, or foreign pirates), the tone of the True Confessions and Dying Warnings changed from moral suasion to titillation. So popular became the genre that in 1773, the year after the publication of Occom's sermon, eleven separate publications dealing with the condemned prisoner Levi Ames were printed. Wayne C. Minnick suggests that the authors of execution sermons ranked among the "best educated, most influential men of their society" (78).

A particularly important issue is the rhetorical strategies Occom uses to appeal to the church fathers, a generally white audience, Moses Paul, and Indian listeners. Having students pick out the phrases and comments that Occom makes to each person or group will help them see how skillful he was. Students need to realize what a politically delicate position Occom was in—he needed to educate his white audience without alienating them and to balance his presentations to the three groups that constituted the total audience. Another point to discuss is how Occom presents himself in the sermon.

Original Audience

It is important to get students to understand the religious milieu of the period, which responded to execution sermons as a form of spiritual confession. This can be compared with the confessions of contemporary born-again fundamentalists. The sermon was sometimes delivered in church on the Sunday or Thursday before the execution, but most frequently just before the time appointed for the hanging. Audiences numbered between 550 and 850.

Comparisons, Contrasts, Connections

"A Short Narrative"—The descriptions of Indian life can be compared with those by George Copway. Comparisons can also be made to the accounts of Indians in the "Colonial Period to 1700" section, the accounts of Indian relations in selections by John Smith and Thomas Morton, and the descriptions of Indian life in the captivity narratives of Mary Rowlandson and John Williams.

Increase and Cotton Mather and Jonathan Edwards—the structure and general themes of their execution and other sermons—can be compared. These preachers emphasized dramatic conversion, which Edwards described as a three-stage process: (1) Fear, anxiety, and distress at one's sinfulness; (2) absolute dependence on the "sovereign mercy of God in Jesus Christ"; and (3) relief from distress under conviction of sin and joy at being accepted by God (Goen 14). This process, reflected in Occom's sermon, became the norm in the Great Awakening and in subsequent revivalism. Evangelists also used emotional extravagance in their sermons.

Questions for Reading, Discussion, and Writing

"A Sermon." Call attention to the structure and the concept of redemption through confession of sin. I do not assign a paper on this work. If I did, two possible topics would be Occom's use of distinct rhetorical strategies to appeal to the various groups in his audience and to Moses Paul; and the extent to which Occom follows the standard structure and basic content for such sermons (see text headnote).

Bibliography

Conkey, Laura E., Ethel Bolissevain, and Ives Goddard. "Indians of Southern New England and Long Island: Late Period." *The Northeast*. Ed. Bruce G. Trigger. *Handbook of North American Indians*. Vol. 15. Washington, DC: Smithsonian, 1978. 177–89. Valuable introduction to these tribes.

Goen, C. C. *Revivalism and Separatism in New England, 1740–1800: Strict Congregationalists and Separate Baptists in the Great Awakening*. New Haven: Yale UP, 1962.

Heimert, Alan. *Religion and the American Mind: From the Great Awakening to the Revolution*. Cambridge, MA: Harvard UP, 1966.

Jennings, Francis. *The Invasion of America: Indians, Colonialism, and the Cant of Conquest*. New York: Norton, 1976. Standard work on the subject, with lengthy bibliography.

Minnick, Wayne C. "The New England Execution Sermon, 1639–1800." *Speech Monographs* 35 (1968): 77–89.

Salwen, Bert. "Indians of Southern New England and Long Island: Early Period." *The Northeast*. Ed. Bruce G. Trigger. *Handbook of North American Indians*, vol. 15. Washington, DC: Smithsonian, 1978. 160–76. Informative introduction to these tribes.

Sturtevant, William C., ed. *Handbook of North American Indians*. Vol. 13. Washington, DC: Smithsonian, 1978.

Towner, Lawrence L. "True Confessions and Dying Warnings in Colonial New England." *Sibley's Heir. A Volume in Memory of Clifford Kenyon Shipton*. Boston: Colonial Society of Massachusetts and UP of Virginia, 1982. 523–39. The articles on the execution sermon by Minnick and Towner are especially good.

Trigger, Bruce G., ed. *Handbook of North American Indians: Northeast.* Ed. William C. Sturtevant. Vol. 15. Washington, DC: Smithsonian, 1978.

Washburn, Wilcomb E. "Seventeenth-Century Indian Wars." *The Northeast.* Ed. Bruce G. Trigger. *Handbook of North American Indians.* Vol. 15. Washington, DC: Smithsonian, 1978. 89–100. Good overview of these wars.

Briton Hammon (fl. 1760)

Contributing Editors: John Alberti and Amy E. Winans

Classroom Issues and Strategies

Students will understand Hammon's narrative better if they are aware of its connections to the traditions of the captivity narrative, slave narrative, and eighteenth-century autobiography. They might also consider how the status of Hammon's text as the first African-American prose text published in North America may have influenced Hammon as a writer and literary pioneer and how our own cultural/historical position affects our expectations of and reactions to this landmark text.

Major Themes, Historical Perspectives, Personal Issues

Nothing is known about Hammon other than what is contained in his narrative, but the text does raise issues about the relation of social class to slave status in early eighteenth-century America (Hammon's lack of specificity about his employment status, the common use of the term *master* by slaves and hired servants alike) as well as the complex relations among British and Spanish colonials, native peoples, and African Americans. Students might discuss how they make sense of Hammon's description of Indians attacking English colonists while negotiating and bartering with the Spanish and then later of his attempts to "escape" from Spanish captivity to England. Students may also wonder why Hammon makes no explicit reference to his racial identity.

Significant Form, Style, or Artistic Conventions

The style and form of the captivity narrative is particularly relevant to
Hammon's text, especially in terms of its narrative structure. Drawing in part
from narratives of Christian spiritual salvation, captivity narratives typically tell of a fall from an Eden of unappreciated security and safety, a trial by
"devilish" savages, and an eventual redemption marked by a return to
"civilization." That most of Hammon's captivity is spent among the Spanish
complicates the basic "civilized/savage" dichotomy that structures the
conventional captivity narrative. John Williams's *The Redeemed Captive
Returning to Zion*, describing his own captivity by French Catholics in Canada,
is a good reference on this point.

Comparisons, Contrasts, Connections

In addition to Williams's narrative, Hammon's text can be compared with
other captivity narratives, most famously that of Mary Rowlandson. Olaudah
Equiano's *Interesting Narrative* provides an example of a strategic inversion of
the Euro-American captivity narrative by casting Europeans in the role of
"savage" captors; it is a key document in the emerging literature of abolition
and an early exploration of the complex questions of identity in African-American culture. By comparing Hammon's text with Equiano's and those of other
eighteenth-century African-American writers, such as Phillis Wheatley,
Prince Hall, and Jupiter Hammon, students can explore the question of the
rhetorical construction of racial identity as a way of thinking about how race
functions in our understanding of Hammon's text.

Bibliography

Andrews, William L. *To Tell a Free Story: The First Century of Afro-American
Autobiography, 1760–1865.* Urbana: U of Illinois P, 1986.

Winans, Amy E. "Diversity and Difference in African American Writings."
Teaching the Literatures of Early America. Ed. Carla J. Mulford. New
York: MLA, 1999. 27–47.

Prince Hall (1735?–1807)

Contributing Editor: William H. Robinson

Classroom Issues and Strategies

I have encountered no insurmountable problems in teaching Hall except to point out to students the differences (which may well have been "diplomatic") between Hall's almost illiterate manuscripts that were designed to be published and several of his other more acceptably normal manuscripts.

Although Hall wrote and published correspondence and wrote and co-signed almost a dozen petitions, I include him among examples of early American oratory. (*Note:* Hall's petition "To the Honorable Council" can be found in the "Cluster: On the Discourse of Liberty.")

Frequently asked student questions: In the two known Masonic "charges" that Hall published (1792 and 1797), where did he find the courage to be so outspoken? Could he find a presumably white Boston printer to publish the pieces?

Major Themes, Historical Perspectives, Personal Issues

Hall was concerned with many aspects of racial uplift for black America and wrote about them all.

Significant Form, Style, or Artistic Conventions

As mentioned previously, in class I note how Hall's nearly illiterate petitions, requiring an editor's "corrective" attention, may have been deliberately deferential. Hall was aware that not many white printers or publishers would readily publish manuscripts written by obviously literate blacks.

Original Audience

I point out the real differences in tone and general deference between Hall's petitions designed for white Boston legislators and other prominent whites, and the tone and racial outspokenness of his "charges," formal annual addresses to his fellow black Masons.

Comparisons, Contrasts, Connections

Although no black writer contemporary with Hall was so widely concerned with racial uplift, his work might be compared with Phillis Wheatley's letters, which are also concerned with black uplift and even "proper" Bostonian antislavery protest.

Questions for Reading, Discussion, and Writing

I have asked students to compare the differences in tone and understanding of biblical injunctions between Jupiter Hammon and Prince Hall.

Bibliography

Crawford, Charles. *Prince Hall and His Followers.* New York: The Crisis, 1914. 33.

Kaplan, Sidney. *The Black Presence in the Era of the American Revolution.* Washington, DC: Smithsonian, 1973. 181–92.

Walker, Joseph. *Black Squares and Compass.* Richmond: Macon, 1979. *passim.*

Olaudah Equiano (1745–1797)

Contributing Editor: Angelo Costanzo

Classroom Issues and Strategies

I use Equiano as an introduction to American slave narrative literature and demonstrate the important influence of autobiographical form and style on the whole range of African-American literature up to the present day, including its impact on such writers as Richard Wright, Ralph Ellison, Alice Walker, and Toni Morrison.

Students are particularly interested in the way the whites conducted the slave trade in Africa by using the Africans themselves to kidnap their enemies and sell them into slavery. Equiano was sold this way. Also their interest is aroused by Equiano's fascinating descriptions of Africa as a self-sufficient culture and society before the incursions of the whites. Students are moved by the graphic scenes of slavery, the Middle Passage experience described by

Equiano, and his persistent desire for freedom. Most of all, they enjoy reading the first-person account of a well-educated and resourceful former slave whose life story is filled with remarkable adventures and great achievements.

Since students have no prior knowledge of Equiano's life and work, I give background information on the history and commerce of the eighteenth-century slave trade, placing in this context Equiano's life story—his kidnapping, Middle Passage journey, slavery in the Western world, education, religion, and seafaring adventures. I also describe his abolitionist efforts in Great Britain, and I say something about his use of neoclassical prose in the autobiography.

Major Themes, Historical Perspectives, Personal Issues

The students need to know about the slave trade and the condition of slavery on the Caribbean islands. As for the literary aspect of Equiano's work, the students should be instructed about the genre of spiritual autobiography, its structure, methods, and styles. In particular, information should be given on how spiritual autobiography was used in the formation of the new genre of slave narrative literature, mainly the three-part structure of slavery, escape, and freedom that corresponds to the spiritual autobiography's three parts that describe the life of sin, conversion, and spiritual rebirth.

Equiano's great autobiography illustrates influences from several popular schools of personal writing current in the eighteenth-century Western world. Among these are the spiritual autobiographical writings of St. Augustine and John Bunyan, the descriptive travel literary works of Daniel Defoe and Jonathan Swift, and the secular stories that display a hardworking youth's rise from rags to riches in the commercial world. The latter pattern can be seen quite well in Benjamin Franklin's *Autobiography*, a work that shares some interesting parallels with Equiano's narrative. Equiano, like Franklin, is an enterprising young man rising up in life and playing numerous roles that help to develop his character in a free world of possibility. Both Equiano and Franklin use self-ironic humor to depict their adventures, and frequently they see themselves acting the role of the picaro figure—a stratagem used many times for survival purposes.

Another eighteenth-century mode of writing observed in Equiano's work is the primitivistic style that is related to the noble savage ideal. Equiano was aware of this type of writing, especially in the books on Africa by Anthony Benezet, the Quaker antislavery writer; when Equiano recalled his early days in Africa, he relied heavily on his reading in the primitivistic literature. However, Equiano's autobiography is remarkable in the account he gives of his African days because his recreation is a mix of primitivistic idealism and realistic detail, in which he never expresses shame or inferiority regarding his African heritage. Africa is an Eden where its inhabitants follow their own cultural traditions, religious practices, and pastoral pursuits. But although Africa is a happy childhood land for Equiano, he is not blind to the evil events that lately have befallen his people.

The Europeans have entered to plunder, enslave, and introduce the despicable inventions of modern technological warfare. Equiano himself is a victim of that situation when he is kidnapped and sold into slavery. His early experiences in the American colonies are re-created with a sense of awe and wonder as the young picaro slave observes the Western world's marvels. He is saved from a life of plantation slavery, but his seafaring service gives him the opportunity to witness firsthand the brutal practices of slavery in several areas of the world. Equiano's life story is a journey of education in which he goes from innocence in the African Eden to the cruel experience of slavery in the West.

Significant Form, Style, or Artistic Conventions

I always discuss Equiano's work in conjunction with the whole genre of spiritual autobiography. I show how Equiano adapted the autobiographical form to his invention of the slave narrative. I also explain the primitivistic elements in his work and say something about the eighteenth-century neoclassical style of writing.

In accordance with the pattern of spiritual autobiography, Equiano's narrative follows the three-part structure of spiritual and physical enslavement, conversion and escape from slavery, and subsequent rebirth in a life of spiritual and physical freedom. Not until he gains his physical liberty is Equiano able to build his character along personal, religious, and humanitarian lines of development. This is the reason he places his manumission paper in the center of his narrative and records his jubilation on attaining his freedom. From that point on in the autobiography, Equiano uses a confident, exuberant, and crusading tone and style as he relates his immersion in the honorable aspects of Western society while he denounces the West's inhumane practices of slavery.

Original Audience

I emphasize the fact that Equiano's reading audience was mostly composed of American and European abolitionists. His immediate purpose was to influence the British political leaders who were debating the slave trade issue in Parliament in the late 1780s. However, Equiano's work was read and discussed by numerous religious and humanitarian readers on both sides of the Atlantic. His work went through many editions and was translated into several languages. It appeared in print well into the middle of the nineteenth century, and its influence on the whole range of slave narrative literature was strong.

Comparisons, Contrasts, Connections

The best comparison is with Frederick Douglass's *Narrative* (1845), which follows the three-part pattern of spiritual and slave autobiographical work. Douglass's work depicts the same search for identity involving the attainment of manhood, education, especially the ability to read, and the securing of physical and spiritual liberations. Other connections concentrating on the spiritual conversion account in chapter 10 of Equiano's work may be made with the *Narrative of the Captivity and Restauration of Mrs. Mary Rowlandson* and Jonathan Edwards's *Personal Narrative*.

Questions for Reading, Discussion, and Writing

1. Questions may deal with definitions of primitivism, form of autobiography (spiritual and secular), history of slave trade and slavery, and eighteenth-century writing styles.
2. (a) Why does Equiano stress that the Africans are "a nation of dancers, musicians, and poets"?
   (b) Chapter 1 contains a mix of borrowed information and personal recollections by Equiano on traditions, familial practices, and religious observances of the Africans. Do you find this technique assists Equiano's aim to erase Western readers' misconceptions about Africa?
3. (a) Describe the primitivistic elements in Equiano's description of his stay in Tinmah.
   (b) What kind of picture does Equiano paint of his African slave experiences as opposed to his later encounters with slavery in the Western world?
   (c) What signs of European influence does Equiano observe during his slave journey to the coast?
   (d) Discuss the reversal situation of the cannibalistic theme demonstrated by Equiano's initial meeting with the white slave traders on the African coast.
   (e) What are some of the white world's magical arts Equiano observes with a sense of awe and wonder?
   (f) Equiano's account of the talking book is a commonly described experience in early slave works. What significant traits of the young enslaved person does the story reveal?
4. How does Equiano's conversion account compare with the spiritual narratives by Jonathan Edwards and Mary Rowlandson?

Bibliography

Andrews, William L. *To Tell a Free Story: The First Century of Afro-American Autobiography, 1760–1865.* Urbana: U of Illinois P, 1986. (See especially chapter 2.)

Costanzo, Angelo. *Surprizing Narrative: Olaudah Equiano and the Beginnings of Black Autobiography.* Westport, CT: Greenwood Press, 1987. (See especially chapter 4.)

Davis, Charles T. and Henry Louis Gates Jr., eds. *The Slave's Narrative.* New York: Oxford UP, 1985. (See Paul Edwards's essay, "Three West African Writers of the 1780's.")

Equiano, Olaudah. *The Interesting Narrative of the Life of Olaudah Equiano, or Gustavus Vassa, the African. Written by Himself.* London, 1789. Ed. Angelo Costanzo. Peterborough, Can.: Broadview Press, 2000.

Gates, Henry Louis, Jr., and William L. Andrews, ed. *Pioneers of the Black Atlantic: Five Slave Narratives from the Enlightenment, 1772–1815.* Washington, DC: Counterpoint Press, 1998.

Judith Sargent Murray (1751–1820)

Contributing Editor: Amy M. Yerkes

Classroom Issues and Strategies

The central issue that emerges in a first reading of Murray's writings is the apparent contradiction between her conservative Federalist agenda and her more liberal platform for feminist reform. Murray maintained that society must be based on a strict adherence to order—political, social, family, and personal order—while promoting a change of women's place within that order. This hierarchical Federalist platform is also in conflict with Murray's Universalist religious beliefs, which argue for each individual's ability to establish a direct link with God. By placing her writings within their historical framework, however, some of this tension can be resolved.

An awareness of the central debates of the early Republic—debates on the structure and role of government, on the role of women in the new Republic, on the proper education for the new citizenry—will allow students to appreciate why Murray's responses to these debates were so complex. Reading the selections from The Federalist and Anti-Federalist Papers, as well as the writings of John Adams, Thomas Paine, and Thomas Jefferson (all included in the anthology) will help students to understand the historical framework for Murray's work.

Major Themes, Historical Perspectives, Personal Issues

In addition to those themes just outlined, Murray was engaged in a struggle to define and create a truly "American" literature. Students might therefore examine her choice of subject matter in the essays, her epilogue to Tyler's play *The Contrast*, and her novel *The Story of Margaretta*. While the latter work has not been included in the anthology, it is available both on microfilm in the Evans series and in Nina Baym's edition of *The Gleaner* (Union College Press, 1992). Murray's novel continues her exploration of the role and education of women in the new nation.

Murray was also engaged in a reevaluation of history and subscribed to the belief that history was fundamentally progressive. By her own commitment to bettering the education of women and by reevaluating past women's history, Murray hoped to usher in a "new era in female history."

As with many of her contemporaries, Murray drew heavily from the Enlightenment philosophy of such writers as John Locke and Jean-Jacques Rousseau. Her emphasis on reason as the central governing principle of human beings and her educational beliefs might be fruitfully compared to those of her European predecessors.

Significant Form, Style, or Artistic Conventions

Murray's most successful literary work is her *Gleaner* essay series; while the topics of these essays are progressive, the form is rather conventional, following such famous prototypes as the essays of Addison and Steele. The development of Murray's persona, Mr. Vigillius, however, is more innovative; his interaction with the audience, his reporting style, and his personality allow for interesting discussion.

Other considerations of interest are those of poetic style and her voice as an essayist. While students may find Murray's poetry and essays stylistically constrained, she herself insisted that she was primarily interested in developing a new content for American literature rather than establishing new literary forms.

Original Audience

Since much of Murray's work was originally printed in journals, any consideration of audience should address the readers of these periodicals and the serial nature of the presentation. Furthermore, she was appealing to a very diverse audience: readers who would adhere to her conservative Federalist agenda as well as those liberals who were interested in women's issues. Certainly this wide audience consideration brings with it beliefs about how to appeal to "male" versus "female" readers (as defined in the late eighteenth century). The ways in which Murray was trying to subvert the traditional assumptions that linked masculinity with reason and femininity with passion (the less desirable of the two traits) would allow for an interesting consideration of audience.

Comparisons, Contrasts, Connections

Murray's writings beg comparison with many of her better-known contemporaries, and it is astonishing to realize that she preceded many of these contemporaries in addressing certain issues. For example, her essay *On the Equality of the Sexes* offers an argument very similar to that found in Mary Wollstonecraft's *A Vindication of the Rights of Woman*. Discussion might also focus on a comparison between Murray's feminist essays and those of her nineteenth-century American counterparts Sarah M. Grimké and Elizabeth Cady Stanton.

Fruitful comparisons can be made between *The Story of Margaretta* and contemporary sentimental novels such as Hannah Webster Foster's *The Coquette* and Susanna Rowson's *Charlotte Temple*. Murray's two plays (included in her 1798 collected edition of *The Gleaner*) exhibit an interest in rendering the American experience—an interest shared by her contemporary Royall Tyler, whose play, *The Contrast*, also appears in the anthology.

Questions for Reading, Discussion, and Writing

1. Of particular interest in Murray's essays on the equality and education of women are the strategies she adopts to prove this equality. Students might be asked to analyze these strategies and to speculate on why she adopted them, given the time when Murray was writing and her Federalist/Universalist beliefs.
2. Students could explore Murray's guidelines for developing and promoting American literature (in this case, drama) by focusing on the prologues and epilogues she wrote for well-known American plays.

Note: The questions mentioned previously would also serve as helpful writing assignments and research paper topics.

Bibliography

Until recently, the only biography of Murray was *Constantia: A Study of the Life and Works of Judith Sargent Murray, 1751–1820,* by Vena Bernadette Field (Orono, ME: University Press, 1931). A more recent overview of her life and work can be found in Sheila Skemp's *Judith Sargent Murray: A Brief Biography with Documents* (1998).

A brief but helpful critical evaluation of Murray's essay series is by Bruce Granger in *American Essay Serials from Franklin to Irving,* chapter VIII (1978). Mary Beth Norton's *Liberty's Daughters: The Revolutionary Experience of American Women 1750–1800* (1980) and Cathy Davidson's *Revolution and the Word: The Rise of the Novel in America* (1986) include insightful analysis of Murray's work. Pattie Cowell offers an insightful overview of Murray's poems in *Women Poets in Revolutionary America 1650–1775* (1981). Two recent editions provide additional analysis of Murray's work, especially her essays: Nina Baym, *The Gleaner* (Union College Press, 1992), and Sharon Harris, *Selected Writings of Judith Sargent Murray.*

Ann Eliza Bleecker (1752–1783)

Contributing Editor: Allison Giffen

Classroom Issues and Strategies

The History of Maria Kittle is one of the earliest fictionalized captivity narratives, and Bleecker writes in the mannered and hyperbolic language of feeling typical of late eighteenth- and early nineteenth-century novels. Because the text illustrates an interesting transition between two distinct genres, an action story of Indian attack and captivity and the more introspective novel of sensibility, I like to begin discussion by having students think about the text specifically in terms of literary history. A productive line of inquiry is to have students begin by looking at the differences between Bleecker's narrative and Mary Rowlandson's. Since the excerpt focuses on the last third of Bleecker's text, a particularly useful angle is to have students consider the different ways in which redemption plays out in both texts. What happened to religion in Bleecker's text, and what qualities does she value in her heroine? What role does maternal loss play in the two texts? How might these differences relate to the different historical moment of each writer? Such questions can lead students to think about the ways in which genres change and develop in relation to a writer's particular historical and cultural concerns.

Major Themes, Historical Perspectives, Personal Issues

There are a number of interesting tensions in this text. Along with the tensions between competing genres, there are some interesting tensions related to Bleecker's treatment of race and gender. Building on the issue of redemption, I like to have students think about who are the heroes and who is doing the redeeming in Bleecker's narrative. There are no white men acting as saviors to the women, and the text emphasizes the redemptive effects of female friendship. Yet at what cost? Who are the women being saved from, and how does Bleecker represent the Native Americans? Such questions can lead into some interesting discussion of some of the underlying racist structures of the Indian captivity narrative. It is also useful for later discussion of nineteenth-century debates about race and "the woman question."

Significant Form, Style, or Artistic Conventions

Another useful strategy is to have students compare and contrast Bleecker's "Retreat from Burgoyne," an autobiographical poem which describes the death of her daughter Abella, with *The History of Maria Kittle*. The two texts share some striking similarities in content, including a concern with grief and maternal loss. Study of these similarities can lead to interesting discussion about the uses (and abuses) of biography in literary criticism. While treating similar subject matter, these texts are, of course, quite different genres, and focusing on their distinctions permits students to think about the differences between poetry and prose.

Original Audience

Bleecker never published in her lifetime. Instead, she created her own private audience by including her poems and narratives inside letters sent to a close community of female friends and family members. As a young woman, Bleecker moved from her home in New York City to a small town north of Albany, where she felt cut off from family and friends. Consequently, letters were important to her, and she relied on a strong and supportive community of sympathetic women friends to whom she wrote regularly. The significance of both the letter form and female friendship is evident in *The History of Maria Kittle*, which not only thematizes female friendship in its plot line but is also shaped as a letter to her half-sister Susan Ten Eyck. This work, then, offers students a wonderful opportunity to think about the relationship between gender and genre and the role of female friendship for Early American women writers.

Comparisons, Contrasts, Connections

As noted above, it is useful to compare Bleecker's narrative to other Indian captivity narratives, especially Mary Rowlandson's. Another interesting angle is to compare *The History of Maria Kittle* to the work of both Hannah Webster Foster and Susannah Rowson. The work of all three writers has a similar didactic intent, and together, they contribute to a tradition of women writers writing to women readers.

Bibliography

Christopher Castiglia's *Bound and Determined: Captivity, Culture-Crossing, and White Womanhood from Mary Rowlandson to Patty Hearst* (1996) is very helpful for teaching *The History of Maria Kittle*, especially chapter 4, "The Wilderness of Fiction: From Captivity Narrative to Captivity Romance." For a perceptive discussion of the role of sentiment in the construction of national identity, see Michelle Burnham, *Captivity and Sentiment: Cultural Exchange in American Literature, 1682–1861* (1997).

Philip Freneau (1752–1832)

Contributing Editor: David S. Shields

Classroom Issues and Strategies

Some of Philip Freneau's poems require an explanation of the changing political context of the 1770s through 1790s so that their arguments may be understood. Freneau's religious poetry, with its striking absence of scriptural allusion and Christian doctrine, may prove rather alien to students of traditional Christian background.

Discriminations between the beliefs of Patriots and Loyalists, Whigs and Tories, must be supplied for the poems of the 1770s. Discussion of the split of the American revolutionaries into Federalist and Jeffersonian factions during the 1790s is also helpful. "To Sir Toby" is an excellent poem with which to examine the legal justifications of slavery employed during the late 1700s.

I find that early American political cartoons provide a useful way of introducing students to the context of Freneau's politics. (Michael Wynn Jones's *The Cartoon History of the American Revolution* is a good source.) Sometimes I get a reproduction of one of the newspapers in which a Freneau poem first appeared to show how closely his worldview was tied to the journalism of the era.

Major Themes, Historical Perspectives, Personal Issues

Freneau was a radical advocate of political democracy. As the chief literary spokesman for the Jeffersonian program, he is an original expositor of certain powerful American political myths: of universal liberty, of the reasonability of the common man, of the superior morality of the life of the farmer to that of the commercial enterpriser. These myths still inform political discourse.

As a nature poet, Freneau presents little difficulty to the student, for his arguments are simple and his language straightforward.

Significant Form, Style, or Artistic Conventions

Freneau cultivated a variety of styles, most of which were suited to the newspaper readership of common Americans he envisioned as his audience. As a political poet, he employed the usual neoclassical devices of parody, burlesque, and mock confession in his satires; in his political admonitions he practiced "Whig sentimentalism" in his anti-slavery verse and the "progress piece" in his historical ruminations. In general, Freneau was an eighteenth-century neoclassicist in his political verse. His nature studies and theological speculations, however, looked forward to Romanticism, particularly in its representation of a natural world suffused with divine vitality.

Original Audience

Revolutionary and post-Revolutionary Americans were immersed in political rhetoric. The common reader knew a surprising amount of political theory. An interesting exercise is to isolate the imagery in the poems connected with various political systems—monarchy, aristocracy, republicanism, democracy—and construct the mental picture that Freneau projected for his readers.

Comparisons, Contrasts, Connections

Freneau's nature poems work well with those of William Cullen Bryant. The closest analogue to his political poetry is found in Francis Hopkinson (not frequently anthologized) and Joel Barlow.

Questions for Reading, Discussion, and Writing

1. I usually suggest that a student pay particular attention to the adjectives Freneau employs.
2. I take a poem from a Federalist Connecticut wit (Richard Alsop, Timothy Dwight, or Lemuel Hopkins) and ask the students to contrast the ideals of government, citizenship, and policy found in it with those expressed in a political poem by Freneau.

Timothy Dwight (1752–1817)

Contributing Editor: Susan Clair Imbarrato

Classroom Issues and Strategies

- Discuss how Dwight's *Greenfield Hill* offers a utopian vision of America.
- Explain the terms *pastoral* and *prospect poem*.
- Explain how Dwight's didactic style reflects Augustan models such as the writing of Pope and Dryden.

Major Themes, Historical Perspectives, Personal Issues

- Federalist views of the New Republic
- Millennial view of America
- The Connecticut Wits and literature as social criticism
- Enlightenment idealism, creating the perfect world

Significant Form, Style, or Artistic Conventions

- Dwight's adoption of the pastoral to evoke an idyllic America
- Application of Greek and Roman myth to the founding of America
- Didactic poetry of the eighteenth century; use of heroic couplets for epic poems

Original Audience

Greenfield Hill was printed in New York by Childs and Swaine in 1794.

Comparisons, Contrast, Connections

John Denham's *Cooper's Hill* (1642), Alexander Pope's *Windsor Forest* (1713), James Thomson's *The Seasons* (1726–1730), Oliver Goldsmith's *The Deserted Village* (1770)

Working with Cultural Objects

- Timothy Dwight. *The Conquest of Canaan; A Poem in Eleven Books.* Hartford: Elisha Babcock, 1785. Harris Collection of American Poetry and Plays, Brown University. Copyright © 2001 by Brown University Library. All rights reserved. <http://www.brown.edu/Facilities/University_Library/exhibits/leaves/harrearly.html>.
- PAL: Perspectives in American Literature: A Research and Reference Guide: An Ongoing Online Project © Paul P. Reuben: Chapter 2: Early American Literature 1700–1800—The Connecticut Wits: <http://www.csustan.edu/english/reuben/pal/chap2/connwits.html>.
- The Library of Congress: Religion in Eighteenth-Century America: <http://www.lcweb.loc.gov/exhibits/religion/rel02.html>.

Questions for Reading and Discussions/Approaches to Writing

1. Discuss the structure and plan of *Greenfield Hill*. Is there an overall, coherent portrait, or are there contradictions, and if so, are they resolved?
2. Compare *Greenfield Hill* with Dwight's collaboration with *The Anarchiad*.
3. Examine the speaker's attitudes toward Native Americans as presented in Book Four. Compare these attitudes to those expressed in the writings of Christopher Columbus, Bartolomé de las Casas, Cabeza de Vaca, Benjamin Franklin, Samson Occom, or Crèvecoeur.

Bibliography

a. Archives

The Dwight Family Papers are housed at the Yale University Library.

b. Biographical Information

Cunningham, Charles E. *Timothy Dwight, 1752–1817*. New York: Macmillan, 1942.

Fitzmier, John R. *New England's Moral Legislator: A Life of Timothy Dwight, 1752–1817*. Bloomington: Indiana UP, 1999.

Freimarck, Vincent. "Timothy Dwight." *Dictionary of Literary Biography: American Writers of the Early Republic*. Ed. Emory Elliott. Vol. 37. Detroit: Gale, 1985. 127–46.

Howard, Leon. *The Connecticut Wits*. Chicago: U of Chicago P, 1943.

Silverman, Kenneth. *Timothy Dwight*. New York: Twayne, 1969.

c. Historical and Critical Contexts

Briggs, Peter M. "Timothy Dwight 'Composes' a Landscape for New England." *American Quarterly* 40 (1988): 359–77.

Dowling, William C. *Poetry and Ideology in Revolutionary Connecticut*. Athens: U of Georgia P, 1990.

Elliott, Emory. *Revolutionary Writers: Literature and Authority in the New Republic 1725–1810*. New York: Oxford UP, 1982.

Grasso, Christopher. *A Speaking Aristocracy: Transforming Public Discourse in Eighteenth-Century Connecticut*. Chapel Hill: University of North Carolina P, 1999. Published for the Omohundro Institute of Early American History and Culture.

Hatch, Nathan O. *The Sacred Cause of Liberty: Republican Thought and the Millennium in Revolutionary New England*. New Haven: Yale UP, 1977.

Kafer, Peter K. "The Making of Timothy Dwight: A Connecticut Morality Tale." *William and Mary Quarterly* 47 (1990): 189–210.

Kamensky, Jane. "'In These Contrasted Climes, How Chang'd the Scene': Progress, Declension, and Balance in the Landscapes of Timothy Dwight." *New England Quarterly* 63 (1990): 80–109.

Shields, David S. "British-American Belles Lettres." *The Cambridge History of American Literature, 1590–1820.* Ed. Sacvan Bercovitch. Vol. 1. Cambridge, UK: Cambridge UP, 1994. 307–43.

Wells, Colin. *The Devil and Doctor Dwight: Satire and Theology in the Early American Republic.* Chapel Hill: U of North Carolina P, 2002.

Phillis Wheatley (1753–1784)

Contributing Editor: William H. Robinson

Classroom Issues and Strategies

One of the difficulties in teaching Wheatley comes in trying to illustrate that she certainly was much more racially aware, and anti-slavery, in her letters (which were intended to be private) than in her more widely known verses (written for a general white public).

I show how, in spite of her fame and the special indulgence of the Wheatley family who owned her, Phillis was necessarily aware of her blackness; for example, in racially segregated church pews, in the widespread menial work (street sweeping and the like) that blacks were forced to do, and in the general lack of educational facilities for Boston blacks.

Students (and even scholars) are sometimes wary of the authenticity of Phillis Wheatley's poetic abilities and, accordingly, ask germane questions. Such students and scholars are disabused of their doubts when confronted with copies of extant manuscripts of verses and letters written when Phillis was known to have not been in the company of whites.

Major Themes, Historical Perspectives, Personal Issues

It is important to note that Phillis was very much aware of herself as a *rara avis,* who worked hard to show that, given the training and opportunity, blacks could write verse as well as any comparably educated and advantaged Bostonian.

Significant Form, Style, or Artistic Conventions

Familiar with rhetorical devices of classical prosody (especially as practiced by the English masters, Alexander Pope, John Milton, and so on), Phillis preferred a predominant usage of the Neoclassical couplet, which, on occasion, constrained her seemingly natural tendencies toward Romanticism.

Original Audience

Most of her verse was written for prominent white figures of her day—e.g., General Washington, several prominent Boston divines—but in several of her elegies and her "Nature pieces" she wrote some lines that have continuing value to audiences of today. Her work was published largely at the behest of the whites for whom she wrote.

Comparisons, Contrasts, Connections

No other colonial black versifier wrote with Phillis's obviously superior sophistication, and comparison of her work with that of black contemporaries is usually done at the expense of the other writers.

Questions for Reading, Discussion, and Writing

I have asked students to examine Phillis's verse and letters for instances of her acquired Boston gentility and of her racial awareness and of herself as "the Colonial Boston poet laureate."

Bibliography

Mason, Julian. *Poems of Phillis Wheatley, Revised and Enlarged.* Chapel Hill: U of North Carolina P, 1989. 1–39.

Robinson, William H. *Critical Essays on Phillis Wheatley.* Boston: Hall, 1982. passim.

———. *Phillis Wheatley and Her Writings.* New York and London: Garland, 1984. 3–69, 87–126.

Lemuel Haynes (1753–1833)

Contributing Editor: Phillip M. Richards

Classroom Issues and Strategies

Lemuel Haynes represents the most complicated African-American response to the strands of evangelical culture and Revolutionary politics of the late eighteenth century and the early nineteenth century. In many respects his work should be read in the context of theological writers such as Jonathan Edwards and political thinkers such as Thomas Jefferson. If America was, at this time, defining itself as a Christian Republican nation, then how did such a definition affect a figure such as Haynes?

Haynes, like Equiano, is a committed Calvinist. He firmly rejects theological innovations, such as Universalism, that were part of the liberalization of Protestant thought in the nineteenth century. What might such a radical Calvinism mean in the hands of a black thinker in the late eighteenth century? How might Revolutionary conceptions of liberty in the period have been informed by Calvinist notions of spiritual liberty?

Haynes's political writing significantly comes before his longer theological efforts. His tract on Revolutionary politics was written before his entrance into the ministry. How might the political ideologies of the Revolution have affected Haynes's later development as a minister?

Major Themes, Historical Perspectives, Personal Issues

We tend to think of the late eighteenth century as an age of politicization and secularization embodied in a figure such as Benjamin Franklin. Religion and theological formulations, however, remained very important for literate blacks such as Phillis Wheatley, Jupiter Hammon, and Haynes. Why is this so? What does their intensely religious emphasis mean for these writers' larger relationship with an emerging American culture?

Significant Form, Style, or Artistic Conventions

Discuss the importance of the sermon form to Haynes. What was the social, political, and even economic function of the sermon during the Great Awakening and Revolutionary periods? How does Haynes draw upon these functions in his own work?

Original Audience

For whom is Haynes's work written? How do his discourse, his language, his themes, and his ideas reflect his chosen audience? What advantages does the sermon form give to a black addressing this audience?

Comparisons, Contrasts, Connections

Haynes grew up in a literary context similar to Wheatley's and Hammon's. Haynes's literary development was shaped by the presence of evangelical groups, patrons, revivalist religion, and Revolutionary politics. All of these themes inscribe themselves in his writing. One might compare Haynes's consciousness of the conditions of his work with that of Wheatley or Hammon.

Bibliography

The best introduction to Haynes is *Black Preacher to White America: The Collected Writings of Lemuel Haynes, 1774–1883.* Ed. Richard Newman. Brooklyn: Carlson, 1990.

Joel Barlow (1754–1812)

Contributing Editor: Susan Clair Imbarrato

Classroom Issues and Strategies

- Discussion of poetry as a commemorative genre in the Homeric tradition of epic poetry provides a helpful context for Barlow's "The Prospect of Peace," *Vision of Columbus,* or *The Columbiad.*
- Other general themes include Barlow's millennial vision of a national genius rising up from American culture and its connection to the federalism of the New Republic.
- Explain the mock-heroic form to introduce Barlow's "The Hasty Pudding."
- Discuss the tone and subject matter of "Advice to a Raven." Students may be surprised by Barlow's range of tone and subject matter as exemplified in these two poems.

Major Themes, Historical Perspectives, Personal Issues

- America as the site of the New Millennium
- Reason, faith, and sciences coexist harmoniously in "The Prospect of Peace" and represent an Enlightenment ideal
- Celebration of the domestic, rural life of Barlow's Connecticut childhood

Significant Form, Style, or Artistic Conventions

- Barlow combines the narrative poem with the heroic couplet to elevate tone and meaning.
- The poet incorporates classical allusions, biblical imagery, and American figures.
- Barlow adopts the classical styles of the epic and the mock heroic to American topics, and frequently uses the heroic couplet, rhyming iambic pentameter, to underscore an elevated meter and style.

Original Audience

The Hasty-Pudding: a poem, in three cantos. Imprint: [Fairhaven, VT]: Printed and sold [by J. P. Spooner] at the printing office in Fairhaven, [1796]. Advertised in the *Farmer's library,* Nov. 23, 1796. Ascribed to the press of J. P. Spooner by McCorison.

Comparisons, Contrasts, Connections

Alexander Pope's "Elegy to the Memory of an Unfortunate Lady" (1717); Pope's *The Rape of the Lock* (1712); Timothy Dwight's *Greenfield Hill* (1794); William Cullen Bryant's "The Prairies" (1832); Walt Whitman's *Leaves of Grass* (1855).

Working with Cultural Objects

- *The Vision of Columbus; a poem in nine books.* By Joel Barlow, Esq. Hartford: Printed by Hudson and Goodwin, for the author, 1787. Harris Collection of American Poetry and Plays, Brown University. Copyright © 2001, Brown University Library. All rights reserved. <http://www.brown.edu/Facilities/University_Library/exhibits/leaves/harrearly.html>.
- *The Columbiad: a poem.* By Joel Barlow. Philadelphia: Printed by Fry and Kammerer for C. and A. Conrad, Philadelphia; Conrad, Lucas, and

Co., Baltimore, 1807. Bookplate of John Allan. Harris Collection of American Poetry and Plays, Brown University. Copyright © 2001, Brown University Library. All rights reserved. <http://www.brown.edu/Facilities/University_Library/exhibits/leaves/harrearly.html>.
- "Chapter 2: Early American Literature 1700–1800—The Connecticut Wits." *PAL: Perspectives in American Literature: A Research and Reference Guide: An Ongoing Online Project.* Copyright © Paul P. Reuben. <http://www.csustan.edu/english/reuben/pal/chap2/connwits.html>.
- The History Place: Prelude to Revolution, 1763 to 1775: <http://www.historyplace.com/unitedstates/revolution/rev-prel.htm>.

Questions for Reading and Discussions, Approaches to Writing

1. Analyze nature's role in "The Prospect of Peace." How is this representation an eighteenth-century construct? How do form and content together emphasize Barlow's poetic meaning?
2. Discuss Science's role in "The Prospect of Peace." Why is Franklin evoked?
3. How does corn pudding function as a metaphor or unifying symbol in "Hasty Pudding"? How does this multicultural symbolism contrast with a European culture of privilege?
4. Barlow composed this nostalgic poem while running for public office in France. How does this context influence the poem?
5. Research Barlow's political career and his shift from conservative Federalist to supporter of the French revolution and friend of Jefferson.

Bibliography

a. Archives

The Joel Barlow papers are housed at the Houghton Library, Harvard College Library, Harvard University.

b. Biographical Information

Elliott, Emory. *Revolutionary Writers: Literature and Authority in the New Republic 1725–1810.* New York: Oxford UP, 1982.

Miller, Victor C. Joel Barlow: *Revolutionist, London, 1791–1792.* Hamburg: de Gruyer, 1932.

Tichi, Cecelia." Joel Barlow." *Dictionary of Literary Biography: American Writers of the Early Republic.* Ed. Emory Elliott. Vol. 37. Detroit: Gale, 1985. 18–30.

Woodress, James. *A Yankee's Odyssey: The Life of Joel Barlow.* Philadelphia: Lippincott, 1958.

c. Historical and Critical Contexts

Arner, Robert. "The Smooth and Emblematic Song: Joel Barlow's *The Hasty Pudding.*" *Early American Literature* 7 (1972): 76–91.

Dowling, William C. *Poetry and Ideology in Revolutionary Connecticut.* Athens: U of Georgia P, 1990.

Howard, Leon. *The Connecticut Wit.* Chicago: U of Chicago P, 1943.

Lemay, J. A. Leo. "The Contexts and Themes of 'The Hasty-Pudding,'" *Early American Literature* 31 (1982): 3–23.

Mulford, Carla, "Joel Barlow's Radicalism in *The Conspiracy of Kings.*" *Deism, Masonry, and the Enlightenment: Essays Honoring Alfred Owen Aldridge.* Ed. J. A. Leo Lemay. Newark: U of Delaware P, 1987. 137–57.

Steele, Timothy. *All the Fun's in How You Say a Thing: An Explanation of Meter and Versification.* Athens: Ohio UP, 1999.

Royall Tyler (1757–1826)

Contributing Editor: Susan Clair Imbarrato

Classroom Issues and Strategies

- Define and explain the characteristics of the sentimental drama or comedy of errors.
- Students might find the dialogue a bit contrived. Explain the style as being representative of the genre and the early National period.
- Explain and identify stock characters: the rake, the coquette, the rustic, the fop, the gentleman, and the lady.

- A brief synopsis of Richard Sheridan's *The School for Scandal* is also helpful in setting the context for the plot and pivotal screen scene.
- Students might enjoy reading *The Contrast* aloud and hearing the language to catch the humor more easily.

Major Themes, Historical Perspectives, Personal Issues

- The Restoration comedy and critique of social class
- The notion that high culture can not only be taught but that it is desired, even though unattainable materially. Discuss the ways that Tyler represents these differences through language and material acquisition
- The relationships expressed between culture and gender; how gender is defined through dress, speech, reading materials, and mannerisms
- The adaptation of British styles to an American context, and how this adaptation is used to underscore the contrast between British-European decadence and American virtue
- Introduction of American types: the Yankee, the rustic, the gentleman, the coquette
- The various contrasts as represented by characters and their relationships.
- The significance of the wedding between Manly and Maria

Significant Form, Style, or Artistic Conventions

- Tyler's adaptations of British comedy to American subject matter
- The contrast lies not only in class issues but also in distinctive sensibilities between the British and American character as Tyler portrays them.
- These contrasts were particularly delightful to his New Republic audience.

Original Audience

The Contrast was well received from its first performance in New York on April 16, 1787. It appeared again in New York on April 18, May 2, and May 12, and in Baltimore on August 12, 1787. It was published in 1790 to good success: *The Contrast: A Comedy; in Five Acts*: "written by a citizen of the United States; performed with applause at the theatres in New-York, Philadelphia, and Maryland; and published (under an assignment of the copy-right) by Thomas Wignell; Philadelphia: From the press of Prichard & Hall, in Market Street, between Second and Front Streets., M.DCC.XC [1790]," American Antiquarian Society.

Comparisons, Contrast, Connections

Dr. Alexander Hamilton's *The Itinerarium* (1744); Richard Sheridan's *The School for Scandal* (1777); Hannah Webster Foster's *The Coquette* (1797); Susanna Rowson's *Charlotte Temple* (1791); Hugh Breckenridge's *Modern Chivalry* (1792)

Working with Cultural Objects

- Early American Theatre: <http://www.lib.virginia.edu/speccol/exhibits/theatre/early.html>.
- "Chapter 2: Early American Literature: 1700-1800—Royall Tyler (1757–1826)." *PAL: Perspectives in American Literature: A Research and Reference Guide: An Ongoing Online Project.* Copyright © Paul P. Reuben: <http://www.csustan.edu/english/reuben/pal/chap2/tyler.html>.

Questions for Reading and Discussions, Approaches to Writing

1. Identify the central "contrasts" in this play. What do they reveal about Tyler's view of American culture?
2. Discuss how romantic love is favored over marriage of convenience. How is this perspective supported? Which characters are sympathetic? Why?
3. Discuss the popularity of this play and its appeal to Tyler's contemporary audience.
4. Research contemporary reactions, different theatrical performances, and the play's longevity.
5. Analyze Judith Sargent Murray's comments on the play.

Bibliography

a. Archives

The bulk of the Royall Tyler Papers are housed at the Vermont Historical Society, Montpelier, Vermont.

b. Biographical Information

Tanselle, Thomas G. *Royall Tyler.* Cambridge, MA: Harvard UP, 1967.

Carson, Ada L., and Herbert L. Carson. *Royall Tyler.* Boston: Twayne, 1979.

Gatson, James C. "Royall Tyler." *Dictionary of Literary Biography: American Writers of the Early Republic*. Ed. E. Elliott. Vol. 37. Detroit: Gale, 1985. 279–89.

c. Historical and Critical Contexts

Bushman, Richard L. *The Refinement of America: Persons, Houses, Cities*. New York: Knopf, 1992.

Evelev, John. "The Contrast: The Problem of Theatricality and Political and Social Crisis in Post-Revolutionary America," *Early American Literature* 31 (1996): 74–98.

Richards, Jeffrey H. *Theatre Enough: American Culture and the Metaphor of the World Stage, 1607–1789*. Durham: Duke UP, 1991.

Shields, David S. "British-American Belles Lettres." *The Cambridge History of American Literature, 1590–1820*. Ed. Sacvan Bercovitch. Vol. 1. Cambridge: Cambridge UP, 1994. 307–43.

Hendrick Aupaumut (Mahican) (1757–1830)

Contributing Editor: Daniel F. Littlefield, Jr.

Classroom Issues and Strategies

Some students may be concerned about the deviations from "standards" in matters of syntax and grammar, so you might ask them to examine these deviations in such writers as Sarah Kemble Knight. Have them consider the Southwestern humorists of the nineteenth century, for example, as models of the ways writers play on the deviations for literary effect. Suggest to students that Aupaumut's style may be seen as an example of "authentic" English dialect of an American Indian. Have them compare the Fus Fixico letter by Alexander Posey for a literary use of an Indian's English dialect.

Students are amazed at how little the questions of race/political power, race/social bias, and race/fear have changed in two hundred years. And expect to hear this question: "Could Indians actually write back then?"

Major Themes, Historical Perspectives, Personal Issues

1. Indian identity, racial self-consciousness. (Aupaumut is painfully aware that he is an Indian writing about Indians. He is also aware of his odd position in defending the United States when the Indians have ample reason to doubt it. Note the *I—they* posture he takes.)
2. Ethnic identity in the emerging new nation.
3. Indian-white relations, colonial period to period of Indian removal

Original Audience

An Indian, having visited tribes in the old Northwest, is making recommendations concerning the posture the United States should take toward those tribes. His report indicates that he advised the tribes how they should act. Also, the piece is a defense of himself against accusations that he betrayed his trust. While his audience was mainly public policy makers, the piece speaks with pointed relevance today about the American Indians' (reasonable) distrust of federal policy makers. (Some things have not changed in the past two hundred years.)

Comparisons, Contrasts, Connections

The "assimilated" Indian, since the "Praying Indians" of the Puritan period, has been in an anomalous position. Aupaumut is caught between the expectations of two societies. Compare this position with those of Copway, Apess, and Boudinot. For texts related to the Indians' distrust of the Europeans, see relevant sections of Smith, Bradford (more relevant to Aupaumut), Franklin, and the Pueblo Revolt texts. Compare also Jefferson's letters to Benjamin Hawkins and to Handsome Lake, as well as Handsome Lake's own view of white civilization.

Bibliography

Ronda, Jeanne, and James P. Ronda. "'As They Were Faithful': Chief Hendrick Aupaumut and the Struggle for Stockbridge Survival, 1757–1830." *American Indian Culture and Research Journal* 3.3 (1979): 43–55.

Hannah Webster Foster (1758–1840)

Contributing Editor: Lucy M. Freibert

Classroom Issues and Strategies

Teaching Hannah Foster's *The Coquette* raises three issues: (1) the lack of name recognition of both author and work; (2) the question of quality, given previous exclusion of *The Coquette* from the canon; and (3) the effort required on the student's part to extract the narrative from the epistolary structure.

Strategies for dealing with these issues include the following: (1) Explain the lack of recognition by pointing out that in the latter part of the nineteenth century, publishers, influenced by academics and critics, discontinued the publication of works by women, who had been extremely popular in the earlier part of the century. (2) To circumvent the assumption that previous exclusion from the canon indicates a lack of literary excellence, select several interactive letters from *The Coquette* and ask some imaginative students to present them to the class in a "readers' theater" format. For the same class session, ask the other students to do a close reading of the letters in order to determine how Foster makes the characters believable and interesting to twenty-first-century readers by delineating sex roles and including customs, manners, and conventions. This combination of approaches will enable the student to recognize Foster's artistry. In a subsequent class, point out how Foster's use of distinctive voices representing various perspectives eliminates didacticism and sharpens her feminist focus. Especially helpful in this regard is Sharon M. Harris's "Hannah Webster Foster's *The Coquette*: Critiquing Franklin's America" in *Redefining the Political Novel: American Women Writers, 1797–1901* (Knoxville: The U of Tennessee P, 1995). Small group discussions enable students to clarify questions about the plot structure.

The plot element students bring up most frequently is the dependence of men in these novels on the money they acquire by marriage to women of means. The question asked by both male and female students is: Why didn't Sanford expect to have a regular job? A question frequently asked by young men is: Why didn't Eliza want to marry? Young women want to know: Why didn't Eliza get a job?

Major Themes, Historical Perspectives, Personal Issues

Teaching Hannah Foster's *The Coquette* (1797) within the context of the National Period offers students opportunities to acquire historical, cultural, and literary insights. As Walter P. Wenska Jr. points out in "*The Coquette* and the American Dream of Freedom" (*Early American Literature* 12.3 [Winter 1977–78]: 2434–55), *The Coquette* raises "the question of freedom, its meaning and its limits, in a new land newly dedicated to births of new freedoms," a theme treated subsequently by many American writers. Wenska sees Eliza Wharton as a rebel who seeks a freedom not typically allotted to her sex, and he shows how she consistently rejects the advice of friends who encourage her to settle into the "modest freedom" of marriage.

Like Wenska, Cathy N. Davidson in *Revolution and the Word: The Rise of the Novel in America* (New York: Oxford UP, 1986) recognizes *The Coquette* as much more than "simply an allegory of seduction." Davidson reads it as "less a story of the wages of sin than a study of the wages of marriage" and as "a dialogical discourse in which the reader was also invited to participate if only vicariously." Davidson's analysis of *The Coquette* is indispensable reading for anyone who would teach the novel thoroughly, as are Carroll Smith-Rosenberg's "Domesticating 'Virtue': Coquettes and Revolutionaries in Young America" in *Literature and the Body* (Baltimore: The Johns Hopkins UP, 1988); Kristie Hamilton's "An Assault on the Will: Republican Virtue and the City in Hannah Webster Foster's *The Coquette*" (*Early American Literature* 14, 1989); and Sharon M. Harris's "Hannah Webster Foster's *The Coquette*: Critiquing Franklin's America," cited previously. Harris argues cogently that Foster imagines alternative lifestyles for women, challenges "the 'truth' of patriarchal structures established to guide—and to control—women's lives, by satirizing the Franklinesque use of maxims . . . , [and] illuminates the political ideology of excluding women from citizenship and systems of power that is fostered in the social milieu."

Space limitations prevented the inclusion of excerpts illustrating the discrepancy between the freedom boasted by the Republic and the social and political restrictions placed on women (see Letter XXIII, for example). The instructor can deepen the students' understanding of the novel's significance by reading some of the political discussions and pointing out how popular iconography showed Young America as a woman pitted against the worldly European male.

Significant Form, Style, or Artistic Conventions

The American novel had its origin in the seduction novel appropriated from the British sentimental tradition of Samuel Richardson and his followers. To make the sensational story of the "ruin" of an innocent girl palatable to readers steeped in Puritan thought, early novelists emphasized the factual and educative nature of their works. Alexander Cowie in *The Rise of the American Novel* (1948) says that didacticism was, in fact, a "*sine qua non* of the early novel."

Although the novel as genre had come into its own by the time Foster wrote *The Coquette*, authors continued to claim basis in fact in order to justify the publication of risqué materials. The preceptress in Foster's *The Boarding School* explains the prevailing objections: "Novels, are the favorite and the most dangerous kind of reading, now adopted by the generality of young ladies. . . . Their romantic pictures of love, beauty, and magnificence, fill the imagination with ideas which lead to impure desires, a vanity of exterior charms, and a fondness for show and dissipation, by no means consistent with that simplicity, modesty, and chastity, which should be the constant inmates of the female breast."

While voicing opposition to the novel in general, Foster and other novelists characterized the reading of their own works, which were "founded on fact," as warnings, to keep young women from peril. As Lucy Sumner's last letter in *The Coquette* (LXIII) states, "From the melancholy story of Eliza Wharton, let the American fair learn to reject with disdain every insinuation derogatory to their true dignity and honor." In *The Boarding School*, a former student justifies reading Samuel Richardson's novels by claiming "so multifarious are his excellencies, that his faults appear but specks, which serve as foils to display his beauties to better advantage."

Original Audience

A very effective way of handling student inquiries about who read *The Coquette* is to read to the class a passage from Elias Nason's biography of Susanna Rowson. Writing in 1870, Nason describes the readership of Rowson's best-selling novel, *Charlotte Temple*, with which *The Coquette* competed during the National Period, as follows:

> It has stolen its way alike into the study of the divine and into the workshop of the mechanic, into the parlor of the accomplished lady and the bed-chamber of her waiting maid, into the log-hut on the extreme border of modern civilization and into the forecastle of the whale ship on the lonely ocean. It has been read by the grey bearded professor after his "divine Plato"; by the beardless clerk after balancing his accounts at night, by the traveler waiting for the next conveyance at the village inn; by the school girl stealthfully in her seat at school.

Insofar as this description applies to *Charlotte Temple*, it likely also applies to *The Coquette*.

Comparisons, Contrasts, Connections

Novels that invite comparison and contrast with *The Coquette* are William Hill Brown's *The Power of Sympathy* (1789) and Susanna Rowson's *Charlotte Temple* (1794), with which it competed for favor through the early decades of the nineteenth century. Frank L. Mott discusses the popularity of these novels in *Golden Multitudes: The Story of Best Sellers in the United States* (New York: Macmillan, 1947).

All three works treat the seduction theme and claim to be based on fact. The British title of *Charlotte Temple* was *Charlotte, A Tale of Truth* (1791); the seduction possibly involved Colonel John Montrésor, a cousin of the author (Richard S. Birdsall, "Susanna Haswell Rowson," *Notable American Women* 3 [Cambridge: Harvard UP, 1971]). *The Power of Sympathy* drew on the seduction of Frances Theodora Apthorp by her sister's husband, Perez Morton (William S. Kable, "Editor's Introduction," *The Power of Sympathy* [Columbus: Ohio State UP, 1969]); and *The Coquette,* on the seduction of Elizabeth Whitman of Hartford, Connecticut, by a person of disputed identity (Aaron Burr and Pierrepont Edwards, son of Jonathan Edwards, being among the "accused"). Extensive, yet inconclusive, discussion of the Elizabeth Whitman story appears in Jane E. Locke's "Historical Preface" to the 1855 edition of *The Coquette* (Boston: William P. Fetridge and Co., 1855), Caroline Dall's *The Romance of the Association: or, One Last Glimpse of Charlotte Temple and Eliza Wharton* (Cambridge: Press of John Wilson and Son, 1875), and Charles Knowles Bolton's *The Elizabeth Whitman Mystery* (Peabody, MA: Peabody Historical Society, 1912).

Significant differences separate *The Coquette* from *The Power of Sympathy* and *Charlotte Temple.* Characters in *Charlotte Temple* follow relatively stock patterns. Only the villainous Mademoiselle La Rue and Belcour display individuality. Charlotte, generally passive, succumbs easily to La Rue's temptations and threats, Montraville's persuasion, and Belcour's deceit. The characters in Brown's novel have interesting potential. Harriot, for example, displays strong powers of observation, and Ophelia speaks forcefully. But they employ the same voice as Rowson's narrator—the voice and style of the sentimental novel.

Questions for Reading, Discussion, and Writing

1. Students should be asked to consult the *Oxford English Dictionary* for the meanings of *coquette* and *rake*, paying special attention to the changes in meaning through time. They might also be asked to investigate the concept of *dowry,* noting what brought about the end of the practice of providing a dowry. Ask them to find out whether the epistolary form is used in novels today.

2. Paper topics may include the following:

    argumentative—Eliza Wharton and Peter Sanford are/are not equally responsible for Eliza's death, or Eliza Wharton's fall was entirely her own fault.

    analytic—a character study of Eliza Wharton using her letters alone, or a character study using only the letters of others.

    research paper—compare *The Coquette* to a British epistolary seduction novel, focusing particularly on social issues.

    research paper (nonliterary)—a study of property rights of men and women in eighteenth-century America.

Bibliography

Helpful sources have been provided previously. Both students and teachers might find quick access to the beginnings of the American novel in the introduction, didactic, melodrama, and satire/humor sections of *Hidden Hands: An Anthology of American Women Writers, 1790–1870*. Ed. Lucy M. Freibert and Barbara A. White (New Brunswick, NJ: Rutgers UP, 1994). See also Linda Kerber's *Women of the Republic: Intellect and Ideology in Revolutionary America* (Chapel Hill: U of North Carolina P, 1989).

Websites to explore include

Origins: The Female Form as Allegory (Text Drawing) <http://xroads. virginia.edu/~CAP/LIBERTY/lady_frm.html>.

Keep Within Compass (Drawing) <http://www.library.csi.cuny.edu/ dept/americanstudies/lavender/graphics/compass.jpg>.

(Plus page of text): <http://www.library.csi.cuny.edu/dept/american studies/lavender/quesorig.html>.

Susanna Haswell Rowson (1762–1824)

Contributing Editor: Laraine Fergenson

Classroom Issues and Strategies

Susanna Haswell Rowson's *Charlotte Temple*, one of the most popular American novels of the late eighteenth and nineteenth centuries, contains timeless themes of seduction and abandonment, loss of innocence, and betrayal of trust—

themes that resonate with modern readers despite the book's quaint and heavily didactic style. Where Rowson's language may not be clear to modern readers (e.g., where she uses "eagerly" for "anxiously"), a note is provided in the text. But apart from the issue of clarity, some students may be put off by Rowson's rather heavy moralizing and by her eighteenth-century style, for example, in such melodramatic lines as "I am snatched by a miracle from destruction!" or "It is not too late to recede from the brink of a precipice, from which I can only behold the dark abyss of ruin, shame, and remorse!"

One approach to discussing this type of language is to ask students to consider the author's audience and her purpose in writing. As Susanna Rowson saw it, she was arming young women for survival in a perilous world inhabited by seducers, hypocrites, and false friends. The society that forms the background of the novel was dominated by a rigid moral code, and violations of it were dealt with very harshly. Keeping in mind that Rowson intended to reach "the young and thoughtless of the fair sex" (see her "Author's Preface"), and, if possible, to protect these vulnerable young women from the pain of social rejection, the modern reader can better understand the author's emphatic moralism and melodramatic language.

An interesting point to discuss in the classroom is the influence of Mademoiselle La Rue and Belcour in Charlotte's seduction. It is clear that in the "Conflict of Love and Duty," the defeat of the latter is due almost as much to La Rue's manipulations as to Charlotte's feelings for Montraville. Charlotte makes her fateful decision to elope after both La Rue and Belcour have "seconded the entreaties of Montraville," and later, when Charlotte regrets her decision, it is La Rue who pressures her into going to meet with Montraville, knowing that the self-delusive Charlotte will not be able to keep her resolve to bid him good-bye and return to the school. Since peer pressure of all sorts is an issue with which modern students are familiar, it might interest them to discuss its application to an eighteenth-century novel.

Major Themes, Historical Perspectives, Personal Issues

The theme of seduction and betrayal that dominates *Charlotte Temple* is easily recognizable to modern students. They may see it as rooted in the traditional view of woman as a helpless victim, who must have the support of either her parents or a lawful husband. Ellen Brandt discusses the novel's "Clarissa theme," derived from the works of Samuel Richardson, to whom Rowson was indebted. Inevitably, the young woman who abandons the wisdom of her parents for the false promises of a lover is doomed to an early death. An instructor might wish to bring into the discussion the famous song from Oliver Goldsmith's *The Vicar of Wakefield* (1766):

When lovely woman stoops to folly,
    And finds too late that men betray,
What charm can sooth her melancholy,
    What art can wash her guilt away?

The only art her guilt to cover,
    To hide her shame from every eye,
To give repentance to her lover,
    And wring his bosom—is to die.

Students may want to discuss other works that contain elements of or variations on this theme, such as Theodore Dreiser's *An American Tragedy* (see below).

Rowson's place in American literary history is an intriguing topic. Despite the formidable reputation she enjoyed in the Federalist period, her importance as the first best-selling American author, and the enduring popularity of *Charlotte Temple*, Rowson, by the middle of the twentieth century, was virtually ignored in anthologies of American literature. Ellen Brandt says she became "a 'forgotten' woman in the archives of our cultural history." A discussion of possible reasons for Rowson's eclipse and the recent revival of interest in her is a good way to begin or conclude the class work on this author.

The historical background of *Charlotte Temple* and the importance of Rowson as a major literary figure during the nation's infancy should be emphasized. In the preface to her insightful work on Rowson, Patricia Parker states the following:

> Rowson lived during a crucial period in our nation's history, as it turned from provincial colony to preindustrial nation. She herself strongly identified with the political objectives of the new republic and came to consider herself American despite her British birth, as she lived most of her life in this country. Her writings reflect an increasing concern with freedom and democratic principles, both politically and sexually. To study her song lyrics and theatrical compositions during the 1790s is to understand the popular taste of the American public who were trying to decide how to live with their newly acquired independence. (Preface i)

Some of Rowson's song lyrics have been excerpted in the works of Parker and Brandt, and an interesting discussion might grow from reading them to the class. Further, Rowson's role in the early American theater and her association with the prominent theater company of Thomas Wignell could be explored. Instructors interested in Rowson's theatrical career should consult Amelia Howe Kritzer's article entitled "Playing with Republican Motherhood: Self-Representation in Plays by Susanna Haswell Rowson and Judith Sargent Murray."

The American Revolution had a great impact on Rowson's life and work. She was one of the first writers to use it as the background for a novel. Montraville and Belcour are both British soldiers being sent to America to fight against the rebels. Charlotte, wondering about La Rue's desertion of Belcour, reflects that she thought only true love had made La Rue follow her man to the "seat of war." Montraville, seducing Charlotte, says, "I thought that you would for my sake have braved the dangers of the ocean, that you would by your affection and smiles, have softened the hardships of war."

Significant Form, Style, or Artistic Conventions

An instructor presenting selections of *Charlotte Temple* would do well to read the entire novel in order to appreciate fully its structure and the sophistication of its characterization. By explaining the motivations of the characters at length, Rowson makes their actions believable and, in doing so, invalidates the charge that she was merely a writer of melodrama. Her portrayal of Charlotte is masterful. The girl's naive and ingenuous character is rendered convincingly. Rowson details the progress of her seduction with sympathy and keen psychological insight.

Rowson devotes considerable space in this short novel to describing Charlotte's parents, and with good effect. Lucy Eldridge (later Temple) and her father had been driven to a debtor's prison by the machinations of an unscrupulous man with designs on Lucy. Her refusal to submit to the kind of arrangement Charlotte enters with Montraville brings disaster upon the household, but the Eldridges and Temple never doubt that she has done the right thing. It is thus doubly poignant that Lucy's daughter, Charlotte, should yield as she does. It is ironic and also perfectly understandable that a couple so idealistic, so perfectly loving, and so trusting could produce a child as dangerously naive as their Charlotte.

Montraville, too, is carefully drawn. Although he plays an evil role in the story, he, like Clyde Griffiths in *An American Tragedy*, is no villain. Attracted to Charlotte and unable to resist seducing her, though he knows that her lack of fortune will make marriage impossible, he abandons her because, misled by his deceitful friend Belcour, he doubts her fidelity, and because he cannot resist the charms of Julia Franklin, his new love, who is conveniently wealthy and therefore a good marriage prospect. Although Montraville causes great harm to Charlotte, he, like her, is not so much evil as weak, and he suffers intense pangs of conscience—and eventually an early death—for what he has done. By making Montraville a sympathetic human being rather than a stock figure of evil, Rowson lends plausibility to her story, and she accomplishes her goal, which is to show that yes, such things can really happen—even to the most well-meaning people.

Original Audience

Charlotte Temple was originally published in England, but when Rowson saw it republished in America, she was no doubt aware that its subtitle was particularly appropriate for her American audience. Influenced by their Puritan heritage, the hardworking inhabitants of a new and growing country might look askance at reading novels, but might be more receptive to "a Tale of Truth," only disguised by a "slight veil of fiction" and written to preserve the "happiness of that sex whose morals and conduct have so powerful an influence on mankind in general."

The most striking aspect of the audience of this book is that it was quite clearly intended to be female. In her "Preface" Rowson explicitly states that she is writing to "the fair sex," specifically to the "young and thoughtless" among them, and in the asides in which she comments on the story, she addresses her readers as "my dear girls." In one aside, interestingly, Rowson addresses herself specifically to the "sober matron" who might be reading the book before she trusts it "to the eye of a darling daughter." But even though she may depart from her view of the audience as exclusively young, it is apparent that this is a book written by a woman for other women, and throughout the nineteenth century and into the twentieth, the book's readership was largely female, a point that was not lost upon its detractors. For example, *Charlotte Temple* was described disparagingly by Carl Van Doren as appealing to an audience of "housemaids and shopgirls" (*The American Novel*, 1921). A class discussion might center on the reasons for the book's appeal to such an audience. Instructors might raise the issue of the vulnerability of women of lower socioeconomic status and hence their identification with Charlotte.

Comparisons, Contrasts, Connections

As noted earlier, Rowson has often been compared with Samuel Richardson, the British author of *Pamela, or Virtue Rewarded* (1740) and *Clarissa, or, the History of a Young Lady* (1747–1748). The similarities between Rowson and Richardson are obvious, both in theme and style. Richardson is known for the epistolary form, and in *Charlotte Temple*, letters (often ones that do not get delivered) play an important role.

Another comparison mentioned earlier is with Oliver Goldsmith's *The Vicar of Wakefield* (1766), a novel dealing with seduction and the economic oppression of a family by a rake with designs on a virtuous daughter—a situation strikingly similar to one of Rowson's subplots, the story of Charlotte's parents. In her *Women and the Rise of the Novel, 1405–1726*, Josephine Donovan discusses the relationship between chastity and economic security in a rigidly moralistic world in which a woman who loses her virginity "loses her market value as well as her honor, and she must die" (120).

This theme can lead us to a comparison between *Charlotte Temple* and Theodore Dreiser's *An American Tragedy* (1925). The plots have many similarities: in both novels a self-indulgent young man of little personal wealth, but with wealthy connections, seduces a poor girl and then falls in love with another woman, who offers not only superior attractiveness but money as well. In both stories, the young man, seeing the first girl as an obstacle to his material and romantic happiness with the second, regrets his rashness in seducing the first, who is pregnant and dependent on him. In both novels the seduced women die. Montraville does not plot to kill his mistress, as Clyde plans to and in effect does, but Charlotte dies as a result of her lover's neglect.

Both Dreiser and Rowson depicted, to quote Charlotte, "a very bad world"—but their analyses were different. Rowson's solution to the evil was not to change that world, but to help develop in women the strength, wisdom, and common sense they would need to deal with it as it was. Where Dreiser saw Roberta and Clyde as victims of social and economic inequality, Rowson saw Charlotte and Montraville as victims of individual failings. Whereas Dreiser's novel is a sweeping indictment of the class system in America, Rowson's is an indictment of personal evil and weakness.

Even if Rowson seems to have focused on individual failings rather than the failings of society, it is helpful to analyze *Charlotte Temple* by placing it within the socioeconomic context of the American nation. In tandem with the theme of economic inequality is the view of Charlotte as a hopeful immigrant to the new world, an immigrant for whom the grand promises of America, like the promises of her seducer, prove false. In her introduction to the Penguin Classic edition, which includes both *Charlotte Temple* and *Lucy Temple*, Ann Douglas asserts that Charlotte, like Susanna Rowson herself, is an immigrant seeking success in the New World. Although Charlotte agrees to accompany Montraville because she loves him and is not—at least consciously—seeking to wed for money, she expects to marry him and take up "a new and more exciting life" (xxii) as his wife once they disembark in America. For Douglas, Montraville's violation of this promise and his eventual abandonment of Charlotte represent the idea that "If America is a land of promise, it is also an academy in promises deferred, broken and betrayed" (xxiii).

Questions for Reading, Discussion, and Writing

1. Look up information about Rowson's life and show how her biography and the historical period in which the novel is set influence the work.
2. Prepare a critical evaluation of the novel. Consider the author's development of the characters, the plotting of the novel, and the novel's impact on the reader.

3. Write a paper comparing and contrasting *Charlotte Temple* and *An American Tragedy*. (This assignment might be suitable for a term paper or special individual project.)

Bibliography

Brandt, Ellen B. *Susanna Haswell Rowson, America's First Best-Selling Novelist*. Chicago: Serba Press, 1975.

Davidson, Cathy N. Introduction. *Charlotte Temple*. New York: Oxford UP, 1986.

———. *Revolution and the Word: The Rise of the Novel in America*. New York: Oxford UP, 1986.

Derounian-Stodola, Kathryn Zabelle. "The Gendering of American Fiction: Susanna Rowson to Catharine Sedgwick." *Making America/Making American Literature: Franklin to Cooper*. Eds. A. Robert Lee and W. M. Verhoeven. Amsterdam and Atlanta: Rodopi, 1996. 165–181.

Charles Brockden Brown (1771–1810)

Contributing Editor: Susan Clair Imbarrato

Classroom Issues and Strategies

- Discuss Brown's use of the gothic as a criticism of reason as the guiding force in human actions.
- Discuss the narrator's compelling style.
- "Somnambulism. A Fragment" will likely remind students of Poe, who was three years old when Brown died. Compare the styles of the two writers.

Major Themes, Historical Perspectives, Personal Issues

- The gothic mode and psychological themes
- The landscape, specifically the woods, as a setting for terror and fear
- The gothic as a critique of New Republic values and assumptions of human rationality
- Brown's dedication to a literary life and its effect on his subject matter and experimentation

Significant Form, Style, or Artistic Conventions

- Brown's adaptation of the gothic to an American setting; using the gothic to critique Enlightenment ideals
- The use of an unreliable narrator and its psychological implications, as in the notion of the "double"

Original Audience

- Brown was critically acclaimed on both sides of the Atlantic and enjoyed an international reputation as one of the first professional American authors.
- "Somnambulism. A Fragment" was published anonymously in 1805 in *The Literary Magazine and American Register*, a journal that Brown founded and edited from 1803 to 1806.

Comparisons, Contrast, Connections

Ann Radcliffe's *The Mysteries of Udolpho* (1794) and *The Italian* (1797); Matthew G. Lewis's *The Monk* (1796); Mary Shelley's *Frankenstein* (1818)

Working with Cultural Objects

- "Chapter 2: Early American Literature: 1700-1800—Charles Brockden Brown." *PAL: Perspectives in American Literature: A Research and Reference Guide: An Ongoing Online Project.* Copyright © Paul P. Reuben. <http://www.csustan.edu/english/reuben/pal/chap2/brown.html>.
- *Timeline: The Russian Campaign and Napoleon's Defeat, The Napoleonic Satires.* Housed in the Anne S. K. Brown Military collection of the John Hay Library, Brown University: <http://dl.lib.brown.edu/napoleon/time6.html>.

Questions for Reading and Discussions, Approaches to Writing

1. Discuss the psychological themes in one of Brown's works. How do a character's irrational or subconscious actions express doubts about human rationality? How does fear function as a character in the story?
2. Examine the duality or double nature of the narrator. What is Althorpe's connection to Nick Handyside?
3. Discuss Brown's impact as an editor and his contributions to the literary community.

4. Contrast Brown's works with a contemporary sentimental novel to emphasize the difference in intentions, style, and mood.
5. Compare Brown's works with those of Poe or Hawthorne.
6. Discuss the subversive qualities of the gothic as a challenge to Enlightenment principles.

Bibliography

a) Archives

The Charles Brockden Brown papers are housed the Bowdoin College Library, Brunswick, Maine.

b) Biographical Information

Clark, David L. *Charles Brockden Brown: Pioneer Voice of America.* Durham: Duke UP, 1952.

Gilmore, Michael T. "The Literature of the Early Revolutionary and Early National Periods." *The Cambridge History of American Literature, 1590–1820.* Ed. Sacvan Bercovitch. Vol. I. New York: Cambridge. UP, 1994. 541–693.

Ringe, Donald A. *Charles Brockden Brown.* New York: Twayne, 1966.

Rosenthal, Bernard. "Charles Brockden Brown," *Dictionary of Literary Biography: American Writers of the Early Republic.* Ed. E. Elliott. Vol. 37. Detroit: Gale, 1985. 69–80.

Warfel, Harry R. *Charles Brockden Brown: An American Gothic Novelist.* Gainesville: U of Florida P, 1949.

c) Historical and Critical Contexts

Axelrod, Alan. *Charles Brockden Brown: An American Tale.* Austin: U of Texas P, 1983.

Barnard, Philip, Mark L. Kamrath, and Stephen Shapiro, eds. *Revising Charles Brockden Brown: Culture, Politics, and Sexuality in the Early Republic.* Knoxville: U of Tennessee P, 2004.

Barnes, Elizabeth. *States of Sympathy: Seduction and Democracy in The American Novel.* New York: Columbia UP, 1997.

Christophersen, Bill. *The Apparition in the Glass: Charles Brockden Brown's American Gothic.* Athens: U of Georgia P, 1993.

Cody, Michael. *Charles Brockden Brown and The Literary Magazine: Cultural Journalism in the Early American Republic.* Jefferson, NC: McFarland, 2004.

Crain, Caleb. *American Sympathy: Men, Friendship, and Literature in the New Nation.* New Haven: Yale UP, 2001.

Davidson, Cathy. *Revolution and the Word: The Rise of the Novel in America.* New York: Oxford UP, 1986.

Elliott, Emory. *Revolutionary Writers: Literature and Authority in the New Republic 1725–1810.* Oxford: Oxford UP, 1982.

Grabo, Norman S. *The Coincidental Art of Charles Brockden Brown.* Chapel Hill: U of North Carolina P, 1981.

Hinds, Elizabeth J. W. *Private Property: Brockden Brown's Gendered Economics of Virtue.* Newark: U of Delaware P, 1997.

Peter Kafer, *Charles Brockden Brown's Revolution and the Birth of American Gothic.* Philadelphia: U of Pennsylvania P, 2004.

Lewis, Paul. "Charles Brockden Brown and the Gendered Canon of Early American Fiction." *Early American Literature* 31 (1996): 167–89.

Samuels, Shirley. *Romances of the Republic: Women, the Family, and Violence in the Literature of the Early American Nation.* New York: Oxford UP, 1996.

Stern, Julia A. *The Plight of Feeling: Sympathy and Dissent in the Early American Novel.* Chicago: U of Chicago P, 1997.

Watts, Steven. *The Romance of Real Life: Charles Brockden Brown and the Origins of American Culture.* Baltimore: The Johns Hopkins UP, 1994.

Pedagogical Introduction

Early Nineteenth Century
1800–1865

Native America
Spanish America
Narratives from the Mexican and Early American Southwest
The Cultures of New England
Race, Slavery, and the Invention of the "South"
Literature and the "Woman Question"
The Development of Narrative
Cluster: Humor of the Old Southwest
The Emergence of American Poetic Voices

Most anthologies of literature published over the last fifty years have relied on criteria derived from traditional New Critical models of literary analysis. Those models valued what was taken to be the inherent formal complexity of individual texts, a complexity seen as separate and separable from the historical and cultural circumstances of the production of the text. As a result, many pedagogical arguments over the canon have centered on whether certain texts were "complicated" enough to sustain extended classroom discussion or analysis and thus merit inclusion in an anthology or a course syllabus. The implication was that some texts were somehow self-evident in their meaning and intent, and therefore "simple," while other, seemingly more complicated texts, demanded and therefore deserved close scrutiny; for example, what can you say about a novel as supposedly straightforward and uncomplicated as *Uncle Tom's Cabin*? But the ambiguous, self-referential *Benito Cereno* provides plenty of material for class discussion.

As many instructors will testify, however, classroom experience often tells a different story, where few if any nineteenth-century texts, no matter how supposedly "simple" or "straightforward," are experienced as self-evident by first-time readers in the class. There are at least two other pedagogical problems stemming from an emphasis on "formal complexity" as well: the circularity of the argument—very often definitions of formal complexity were based on the same texts they were supposed to define—and, even more important to literary studies, such a critical model failed to account for a large number of texts considered significant by nineteenth-century readers, and thus prevented a richer understanding of cultural history.

The grouping of texts in this section of the anthology according to regional cultures, ethnic identities, and social conflicts addresses these concerns in the classroom by recognizing that literary and linguistic complexity resides not apart from but within the historical, cultural, and geographic context of a text. Such an approach emphasizes texts as rhetorical performances, performances as complex as the rhetorical demands and contingencies to which they respond:

219

A Christian Indian appealing to a dominant culture audience responsible for both his religious faith and the subjugation of his people (Elias Boudinot); a Northern single mother writing satirical denunciations of male dominance for a popular press dominated by male editors and publishers (Fanny Fern); an ex-slave demanding both racial justice and gender equality before an audience of white women (Sojourner Truth). The title alone of Angelina Grimké's "Appeal to the Christian Women of the South" suggests the complexity of the rhetorical situation she faced (and hence makes a good starting place for class discussion), balancing issues of gender, race, religion, region, and class in arguing for the abolition of slavery. The inclusion of "The Invention of the South" in the title of the section on race and slavery makes the point that none of these terms represent a settled or fixed concept, but like the idea of America itself, they have evolved as part of a dynamic process of cultural conflict and self-definition.

By challenging the notion of "background" material, the interrelationship of text and context in this rhetorical approach has important pedagogical implications for the question of how much historical information students need to understand any text, whether its author is Ralph Waldo Emerson or Sojourner Truth; Abraham Lincoln or Mariano Guadalupe Vallejo. Students can be encouraged to explore the historical context *through* the text by raising questions of rhetorical strategy. Beginning with the ideas and assumptions about slavery and abolition, the struggle for women's rights, the Indian experience, or the history of the West that students bring with them, the class can then explore how a particular text confirms, resists, or otherwise complicates those ideas and assumptions. Exploring the students' reading experiences of the texts can lead to questions about why writers use a certain vocabulary, set of references, or variety of rhetorical strategies, and these questions in turn involve thinking about who the contemporary audience(s) for that text were and what expectations and values they held. Elaine Sargent Apthorp's teaching guide for John Greenleaf Whittier, for example, contains excellent examples of assignments designed to focus students' attention on the complexity of Whittier's performance as a public poet dedicated to political activism.

The Development of Narrative

The organizational logic of *The Heath Anthology* invites students to regard texts not as static set pieces but as complex rhetorical performances embedded in cultural debates over race, gender, political legitimacy, and economics. While this "cultural rhetoric" approach seems especially suited for the consideration of "noncanonical" material that doesn't fit neatly into the traditional genre categories of poetry, drama, and fiction (for example, newspaper columns, personal letters, memoirs, political speeches), it represents not a special technique to use with "unusual" materials but rather a means of seeing all texts—and all acts of reading—as performative. Instead of regarding the textual performances in the sections on narrative and poetry as standing apart from earlier, less "literary" selections, instructors can use a cultural rhetoric approach to raise questions about the differences in motive, impact, and strategy in such works on race and slavery as Frederick Douglass's autobiography, Harriet Beecher Stowe's openly polemical novel *Uncle Tom's Cabin*, and Herman Melville's elusive *Benito Cereno*. The class might, for example, analyze Nathaniel Hawthorne's allegorical meditations on gender, aesthetics, obsession, and domination in such stories as "Rappaccini's Daughter" and "The Birth-mark" in the light of the arguments regarding the political and social status of women in the nineteenth century raised by Margaret Fuller and Elizabeth Cady Stanton.

Depending on the background and training of individual instructors, the names found in "The Development of Narrative" will represent a mix of the intensely familiar with the radically new, the canonical with the noncanonical. This mix will also be true for some students; for others, however, "familiarity" may indicate little more than name recognition and carry few if any implications of "greatness" or "classic" status. For the instructor unsure of how to approach the new, and for the students to whom almost every nineteenth-century text is strange and remote, the first step may be the question of the canon itself, and specifically an expansion of the question Judith Fetterley reports her students asking in regard to Caroline Kirkland: Why haven't we heard of these writers before? (For other writers the question would be the reverse: Why *have* we heard so much about them?) As the class reads through these selections, they can classify or reclassify the writers in terms of technique, subject matter, or audience appeal. Such discussions can provide the foreground for considerations of how canons have been constructed historically (it can often be illuminating to look at copies of tables of contents from anthologies from the nineteenth century to the present).

The Emergence of American Poetic Voices

If many students come into class with the assumption that "poetry" is necessarily distant and obscure, the section on "Songs and Ballads" asks us to think about both our definitions of poetry and where these definitions come from. This in turn can involve discussions about the different kinds of cultural work poems do, from self-expression to the ritual building of a sense of communal solidarity, from self-examination to social protest. Equally important is the inclusion of song lyrics, for they remind students that not only is poetry still an active part of contemporary cultural life in general, but it is also part of many students' lives in particular. If anything, the contemporary rise of hip-hop culture, rap music, and poetry slams demonstrates the same ongoing vitality and cultural relevance of the experiments in language represented by the songs and ballads as well as avant gardists such as Whitman and Dickinson.

If the texts in the previous sections provide cultural context for these poems, then the inclusion of poetry and fiction in the sections themselves gives students practice in discussing issues of genre and style from different perspectives. How would we read Whitman differently, for example, if he were included in the section on abolitionist literature? If Emily Dickinson or Frances Sargent Locke Osgood were included in the section on the "Woman Question"? What other possibilities are there and what do they reveal?

Native America

Teaching the Texts in "Native America"

Contributing Editor: Maureen A. Konkle

Classroom Issues and Strategies

Native writing generally requires a lot of historical background in order for students to understand its significance. My experience is that if students know little or nothing about Native history in the United States, they have had plenty of experience with representations of Indians, so I begin by asking them about the kinds of representations with which they're familiar, to provide a kind of baseline. This approach has elicited some surprising responses—for example, the sitcom *Saved by the Bell* had an Indian character, and *The X-Files* had a series of story lines connecting Indians with aliens. I've asked students to go to the mall, the supermarket, or the local chain bookstore and look for images of Indians. I also regularly ask students what they did in elementary school to celebrate Thanksgiving. Though they tend to talk about the predictable friendship theme, the most consistent practice seems to have been making my-hand-is-a-turkey refrigerator art, which makes me wonder whether there's increasing discomfort with the conventional Thanksgiving narrative.

There's also the matter of Indian sports mascots, which always brings up the sentiment that these particular stereotypes are "positive"; therefore, it doesn't make sense for Native people or anyone else to be offended by them. My purpose in having students talk about all of this is to introduce the problem of misrepresentation for Native people and also to demonstrate that the misrepresentation of Native people is embedded in U.S. culture. It doesn't matter whether some people, non-Native or even Native, think Chief Illiniwek is a "positive" representation of Indians; it's still misrepresentation with a distinct history that is inextricable from the political oppression of Native people in the United States. Continuing to use these images only further obscures that history.

Misrepresentation is a major theme in Native writing of this era, as it obviously is for African Americans, elite white women, the working classes, and other groups of people excluded from political authority. (That's also one way of connecting Native writing with writing by other groups of people in the United States.) I want students to be self-conscious about misrepresentation so that when they read, they can begin to be critical about their initial responses to the writing. This process is streamlined by the fact that the ideas about Indians today are not that much different from the ideas about Indians in the early nineteenth century. Then when I talk about the writing, I point out how the writers address the misrepresentation of themselves and what they offer in place of it.

Major Themes, Historical Perspectives, Personal Issues

Here I want to present an overview of the Euro-American thinking about Indians and Native analysis of that thinking, including the political and historical context for the representation of Indians, major themes in the representation of Indians, the political position of Native peoples in the United States, and early Native writers' critiques of misrepresentation.

Political and Historical Context

The three areas most relevant to understanding the historical and political context of the representation of Indians in North America are (1) the theory of property as a justification for colonization, (2) the emergence of theories of racial difference in the late eighteenth century and their naturalization in the early nineteenth century, and (3) the history and consequences of treaty making with Native peoples in the United States.

(1) Property. It's commonly reiterated in U.S historiography that Europeans justified colonization in North America by arguing that ownership of property in land does not occur until that property is "improved" through commercial agriculture. Although John Locke articulated this theory of property in his *Second Treatise of Government* in the late seventeenth century, scholars have noted that that justification predates Locke; in fact, Puritans in New England justified their acquisition of land in this way. They have also pointed out that this theory of property—which became widely accepted, and was used to

justify colonization around the world—also enshrined a certain form of English (as opposed to Dutch or French) colonialism and colonial agriculture as the norm. Locke, who famously wrote the *Fundamental Constitutions of Carolina* in 1669 and was involved in the administration of that colony and in other colonial ventures, provided a justification for appropriating Native land without the dwellers' consent. His theory of property also provides a framework for understanding some of the essential elements of the representation of Indians in North America.

In keeping with European thought on the inhabitants of the Western Hemisphere, Locke positions Indians as man in the state of nature, the earliest form of human society. Native people in North America, then, are something like walking theoretical abstractions. This view has two significant consequences: first, in the state of nature, Indians have not yet formed political societies, which occurs when societies require laws to protect property as Locke defines it; and second, as members of the earliest form of human society, it's still possible for Indians to be raised up, as it were, to civilization and *inclusion* in political societies, which are necessarily European. Historically, Locke's theory of property denies that Native peoples existed in political societies at the moment when English settlers were making all kinds of agreements with Native political societies in North America because they had to. Thus, the theory of property justifies the acquisition of Native land without the Natives' consent by denying the incontrovertible fact that English settlers were forced to recognize the existence of Native political societies that controlled land. In addition, it justifies this by positioning of Native people—Indians—as abstractions, inhabitants of the earliest form of human society, people who may, some day, hypothetically, become civilized, but who need to be worked on. Specifically, Indians needed to acquire the two principal requirements of political society in European theory: commercial agriculture and Christianity.

(2) Racial Difference. The late-seventeenth and early eighteenth-century justifications for colonization and emerging ideas about Native peoples' relation to Europeans in North America exemplified by Locke's theory of property remain a part of the thinking about Indians but are overlaid (so to speak) by later thinking about racial difference. From the late eighteenth and into the mid-nineteenth century, ideas about the inherent difference of "races" become systematized and naturalized. These center on the assertions that, in this case, Indians do not have the moral or intellectual capacity to form political societies and, more importantly, that because they are Indians, they never will. The familiar stereotypes of Indians from this era have to be understood within the larger framework. They are not just "negative"; they are part of a larger system of knowledge about human societies in European and Euro-American thought in which, in world-historical narrative, Indians form the earliest and most primitive human society and Euro-Americans form the most advanced. For example, the vengeful Indian stereotype has to be understood within the larger set of ideas about Indians' inherent incapacity to form political societies. That is, the vengefulness of Indians demonstrates that they do not have reason; therefore, driven only by their savage emotions, they cannot form political societies. The misrepresentation of Indians is always ultimately about denying that Native political societies exist since the fact that they formed political societies was their principal threat to Euro-American authority.

(3) Treaties. In back of these theories about both property and racial difference lies the historical problem for Europeans in North America of having made treaties with Indian nations. From the beginnings of settlement, Europeans made a range of agreements with tribes, which became commonly known as "Indian nations" in legal discourse by the mid-eighteenth century, not just for the sale of land but also for military alliances and other relationships. Such agreements were necessary principally because English colonization in North America consisted of settlements that were exposed militarily and economically and that therefore needed to make alliances with Indian nations. Despite the widespread acceptance of the theory of property Locke articulated, imperial governments in North America, British and colonial, established themselves as the sole authority for dealing with Indian nations and recognized those Indian nations as autonomous political entities. By the Proclamation of 1763, the British Crown formally positioned itself as the only authority for making agreements with Indian nations. The U.S. government, in both the implications of the Constitution's Commerce Clause and in a series of Trade and Intercourse Acts beginning in the 1790s, followed suit, recognizing Indian nations as nations proper, meaning that Europeans had no authority over the internal affairs of Indian nations and that Indian nations' consent to treaties was necessary for those treaties to be legitimate. Particularly with the rise of the new United States, the legitimate control of land, gained through the consent of Indians and the rule of law, is a fundamentally important idea, especially among the political elite. Jefferson in *Notes on the State of Virginia* insists that all the land in Virginia was legally obtained through legitimate treaties with Indian nations. Benjamin Franklin, who served as a Pennsylvania commissioner at a number of mid-eighteenth century treaties and then published them for public consumption, made the same kinds of arguments as well.

The Lockean justification for appropriating Native land without obtaining the inhabitants' consent coexists—uneasily—with the political and ideological necessity of making treaties with Indian nations in the period. Indeed, the theory of property exists *because* of the problems represented by recognizing the existence of Native political societies. The inescapable fact of having to make treaties in order to establish the legitimacy of the new government's claim on territory leads to some serious contradictions, which find their way into the thinking about Native peoples. A treaty is a contract; a contract requires the free consent of the parties to it. Likewise, those who are somehow mentally deficient cannot make legitimate contracts. If theories of racial difference maintain that Indians are morally and intellectually incapable of forming political societies, how can one then explain the fact of treaties having been made with Indians? How can Indians in the state of nature form political societies that the United States must recognize as sovereign nations? The predominant answer to these questions was that Indian nations were an earlier form of political society—if one had to admit that they formed anything like a political society—and that Indians were going to disappear anyway, posthaste; they just hadn't quite done so yet. The death of Indians is the solution to the contradictions of Euro-American relations with Native peoples.

The problem with all of this working smoothly, if paradoxically, is Native people themselves. Although having treaties didn't save them from violence and oppression, treaties did serve as a political mechanism through which they could resist imperial expansion and also served as a rallying point, a means of articulating a different vision for the political landscape of North America, one in which they could coexist with Euro-Americans, who obviously weren't going anywhere else. Native efforts to use the treaties reached a high point in the antebellum era in the Cherokee Nation cases, *Cherokee Nation v. Georgia* (1831) and *Worcester v. Georgia* (1832). In these cases, the Cherokee Nation argued that because the United States had made treaties with the Cherokees, the state of Georgia's actions abrogating the authority of the Cherokee government were unconstitutional because treaties are made between nations, and the state of Georgia must be subject to the authority of the federal government. The Supreme Court agreed, holding in *Cherokee Nation* that Indian nations were nations in that they were autonomous to the United States, and that the United States had no authority over their internal affairs, nor did the state of Georgia. At the same time, however, the Court relied on the theory of racial difference to assert that because they were *Indian* nations, they must necessarily be inferior to the U.S. government and, indeed, not long for the world because being savage nations, they could not withstand the contact with civilization and would necessarily, along with Native peoples themselves, disappear soon enough. Indian nations were therefore in a state of "pupilage" in relation to the United States until such time as they naturally disappeared. This is the doctrine of domestic dependent nations, which is often cited as the principal holding of the case.

In *Worcester*, Marshall held that the long history of treaty making and the Proclamation of 1763 established that Indians did form political societies recognized as such from the beginning of the European presence in North America, that those political societies could not be controlled by Euro-Americans, and that any transfer of land had to be accomplished through a legitimate treaty between an Indian nation and the U.S. government. The reason why treaties with Indian nations continued to be made was to establish the legitimate authority of the United States for·land, in keeping with the rule of law and the principle of consent. The actual making of treaties, then, involved on the one hand, an ideology that required at least the appearance of Native peoples' consent and on the other, all the means of coercion, force, and under- handed machinations that interested parties could come up with. It's impor- tant to note, however, lest the ubiquitous sentimental rhetoric of "broken treaties" be mistakenly assumed—and it's a rhetoric that invokes Indians' inevitable doom—that while Native people lost much more than they gained in the nineteenth century, in the twentieth, treaties became a main means through which Indian nations asserted political autonomy and the redress of grievances. Indeed, the Cherokee Nation cases, particularly, are often cited as the foundation of contemporary Indian law.

Major Themes in the Representation of Indians

Instead of cataloging the different kinds of Indian stereotypes, I think it's more useful to consider the representations in terms of two overarching themes that describe how Euro-Americans thought about Indians: savagery versus civiliza- tion, and sympathy.

(1) Savagery Versus Civilization. From the beginnings of European writing about the Western Hemisphere, its Native peoples were figured as embodi- ments of the earliest form of human societies, the Garden of Eden or, later, as in Locke's theory of property, the state of nature. At least as Locke describes this in the late seventeenth century, the state of nature and civilization could coexist, although the one would eventually have to give way to the other. This view allows for a persistent strain of thought maintaining that Indians can be "improved" and civilized, and ostensibly made part of [European] political society. Throughout the eighteenth century and certainly by the first quarter of the nineteenth, however, the idea that the state of nature and civilization can coexist without a definite endpoint to that coexistence shifts so that the state of nature must and will give way—soon—to civilization. Civilization was often represented as sweeping across the North American continent, literally engulfing Indians in their state of nature along the way. By the first quarter of the nineteenth century, it was settled knowledge that Indians *must* disappear; God's will, the history of human civilization, and the logic of expansion (one and the same) demanded it. U.S. expansion was represented in grand abstract terms: the ongoing violent conflict between Native peoples and Euro-Americans was always explained as an abstract and inevitable conflict between savage and civilized. This perception has the obvious effect of eliding and otherwise avoiding the explicitly political conflict over land and treaties. At the same time, the providential death of Indians would solve the problem of treaties being necessary to legitimate U.S. control of territory.

The fact that Indians must die, as well as the persistent idea that they might hypothetically become citizens if only they could be Christianized and turned into farmers, differentiates nineteenth-century thinking about Indians from the thinking about African Americans, who were represented as beasts permanently unfit for Euro-American political society. Still, like other groups of racially differentiated people, Indians in the United States are represented as being without history and without a future, but especially without the capacity to form political societies. Therefore, Indians' councils consist of absurd harangues, they make no sense in negotiations, and they don't deserve the status of nations. When threatened, they are mere savages run amok.

(2) **Sentiment.** Although literary critics have asserted that middle-class white women were especially prone to sympathize with Indians, to represent them as noble and doomed savages, and that this somehow demonstrated that middle-class white women were taking a radical political stand with respect to Indians, it is not the case that women were more sympathetic toward Indians than men of the time were. In elite discourse during the first half of the nineteenth century, and indeed, throughout the century, it was the norm for both male and female writers to mourn the passing of the Indian and even to condemn the bad behavior of Euro-Americans. John Marshall himself begins his majority opinion in *Cherokee Nation v. Georgia* with an utterly conventional lament for the doomed savage. As with the abstractions of the savage versus the civilized framework, sympathy for Indians couches the messy and violent political conflicts between Native peoples and expansionist Euro-Americans in streamlined and palatable abstractions. Furthermore, writers—including Cooper, Irving, Sedgwick, Emerson, Thoreau, Fuller, and many others—both commonly depict unrepentant savages and sympathize with doomed Indians. This habit is not a contradiction: the first is an element of the narrative of the inevitable conflict between savagery and civilization, and the second demonstrates the proper middle-class response to this large issue of the age. No one ever feels sorry for an Indian who survives; only dead Indians get white middle-class sympathy.

(3) **Incorporation.** While the notion that Indians are savages in the state of nature and that they can somehow be acted upon to take up Christianity and commercial agriculture and therefore become civilized—that is, U.S. citizens—remains operative throughout the nineteenth century, the theory of racial difference at the same time insists that Indians cannot possibly change, really, because they are inherently different. These two strains of thought remain locked together throughout the nineteenth century, with the second usually canceling out the first. Considered together, however, the two reveal what's actually at stake for Native peoples politically in the United States To return to Locke's philosophy as a paradigm for justifying colonization, the theory of property rests on the denial that Native people form political societies, but it

also extends the idea of incorporation into European political societies to Indians since they are in the state of nature and can be hypothetically improved. But if Indians are hypothetically incorporated into Euro-American political society, they no longer have control of their own territory; they no longer form separate political societies. Those who advocated the "civilizing" of Indians through Christianity and commercial agriculture are both following the imperial logic set out in the late seventeenth century and continuing to occlude its political effects. The fact remains that when Indians were hypothetically "civilized," at least as Euro-Americans understood the term, they would therefore hypothetically give up their political autonomy and control of their land, which is the entire object of European and U.S. imperialism in North America.

It's common in the scholarship to take the sympathy directed at Indians in white discourse at face value and to assert that whites weren't racist toward Indians, that they meant well even though they were obviously ethnocentric. This argument or theme, which is common in U.S. historiography, misses the point because it assumes that citizenship in the United States is a good thing for Indians. The idea is that it's all right for white "friends of the Indian" to have been ethnocentric because ultimately they were offering Indians "inclusion" in the United States, and that in the end would be a great benefit to them. The problem with this view is that it is counter to virtually everything written by Native people almost up to the end of the nineteenth century, when some elite Native leaders began to advocate citizenship in the United States as a last resort, the only means left of their being treated with equal humanity. And certainly those elite leaders are a minority among Native people. It doesn't matter whether or not white reformers meant well when they advocated that Indians become Christians and agricultural producers; they were nevertheless following the logic of imperialism, and all of them understood that by "civilizing" Native people in that way, they would be necessarily destroying Native peoples as Native peoples, which would be accomplished by destroying their governments as much as by outlawing their cultural practices. Quite a few of the later-nineteenth-century advocates of Indian assimilation admitted that such assimilation would be the end of Native people, politically and culturally, if not biologically. Becoming U.S. citizens was the last thing that Native people wanted in the nineteenth century; they already had their own political societies, and for the most part they argued to be left alone to exist in them. The idea that citizenship in the United States would be a great benefit to Native people was itself a product of the processes of European imperialism in North America.

(4) Native Criticism. To properly contextualize Native writing, especially in the nineteenth century, this entire history has to be taken into account. The difficulty is that so much of what's written about Native peoples and Native writing still retains elements, and sometimes entire arguments, of this essentially imperialist history. For example, it's common for literary critics to insist that Indians thought of nations as cultural, as opposed to political entities, an argument that goes straight back to the denial that Native political societies existed (even as settlers had extensive relations with them and even depended on them in various ways) in the seventeenth-century justifications for English colonialism in North America. Most Native writers in the nineteenth century were overwhelmingly involved in the political efforts of their tribes; someone like George Copway, who wasn't, is the exception rather than the rule. They argued for their autonomy from Euro-American rule; they did not, as some critics have claimed, petition to become citizens of the United States.

In the nineteenth century, Native writers write about political autonomy, the history of Native political societies, and the recognition of Native humanity. Because the representation of Indians positions them as outside time and change, as embodied abstractions representing the earliest moment of human society—and, as always, going to die off in the very near future—Native writers of the period often write historically to demonstrate the continuity of Native peoples from the time before Europeans to the present moment. They often describe assaults on Native political societies, and the reformation of those societies, and they often make use of the doomed Indian motif not as an accurate representation of what will happen because it must, but rather to depict what has happened because white people made it happen. With few exceptions, Native writers insist on the validity of oral or traditional knowledge, and even its superiority to European knowledge. Whereas Euro-American writing describes the imperial conflict in North America in the abstract terms of the conflict between savagery and civilization, Native writers write about specific histories and specific actions by whites, arguing that the disappearance of Native peoples is not inevitable, but rather the result of ignorance and political oppression.

When these writers write about Native peoples in the process of being civilized—though many insist that Indians already are civilized without the help of white people—they describe a process of becoming *modern* in terms of accepting the technological, political, and religious advances of Euro-American society. However, they don't consider being incorporated politically into the United States as the goal of efforts to "civilize" Indians. In fact, they argue that becoming civilized will guarantee their continued political autonomy. When these writers write about being "civilized" then, they contest the logic of imperialism by insisting on the autonomy of Indian nations, and on their desire to *coexist* politically with the United States, rather than be subsumed by it. Thus, these writers violate the occluded terms of imperial discourse even when they might appear to be engaging those terms. The key is that they are almost always writing about the political autonomy of Indian nations, which fundamentally violates imperial discourse, however else these writers might position themselves with respect to Christianity, commercial agriculture, patriarchal social relations, and the like.

Native writers also struggle to make themselves heard by audiences that they are well aware are not especially capable of hearing what they have to say. Early Native writers, to a remarkable degree, often point to the political effects of misrepresentation, arguing that misrepresentations of Indians allow whites to oppress Native peoples. Like African-American writers on their relations with whites, they are often quite specific about the psychological effects of those misrepresentations on both Native and white people. The keen knowledge of the discrepancy between their own lives and the expectations of white audiences often provokes some very pointed verbal play. A favorite is to reverse savage and civilized; another is to invoke the idea that Native peoples are more naturally Christian than the Christians who oppress them. They will often use the figure of the doomed Indian rhetorically to set up a consideration of how exactly so many Native peoples died, and the answer is never because of God's will but rather because of the willful actions of white men.

It's also important to note the rapidity with which racial difference became naturalized in the first half of the nineteenth century. Historians have argued that race and especially color became a naturalized category by the 1830s. William Apess's "Indian's Looking-Glass for the White Man," for example, responds to color as a new and dominant marker of inherent racial difference in the mid-1830s. Before and up to this era, Native writers and speakers, particularly the Cherokees, could expect a more varied response to their arguments on the part of white audiences. While many whites were prepared to see only fantasy Indians, the highly visible political struggles of the Cherokees made the idea of a modern Indian person conceivable, at least for a portion of the white public, for a period of time. After the 1830s, however, even tenuous ideas about the capacity of Native peoples to adapt to change and live in the modern world as Indians in Indian nations had very much faded from white society as ideas about inherent racial difference became dominant. In this setting, white audiences expected Indians to look the part, to perform their piece. Native writers had to decide for themselves how to deal with what really was a condition of their existence in white society. Copway, for example, performed in what he advertised as a "chief's costume," although he certainly wasn't the political leader of any Ojibwe band. Ely Parker, a Seneca who provided information to Lewis Henry Morgan for his *Notes on the Iroquois*, also gave lectures on Iroquois history and tradition to various white organizations in the 1850s, at which he refused to appear in costume. He did, however, often wear the Red Jacket medal, which George Washington gave to the Seneca leader Red Jacket, who was well known for his rejection of Euro-American society and his insistence on the autonomy of tribal governments. Parker and other Native writers of the time were fond of sly manipulations of whites' inane ideas about Indians, very much in the manner of contemporary Native writing. The stark difference, from the perspective of Native writers, between their reality and the white fantasies with which they had to deal certainly made irony, but often also sarcasm, thinly veiled and otherwise, characteristic of their public writing in these years.

Traditional knowledge occupies the most complex position in early Native writing. Most of the writers were professing Christians, if not missionaries of one kind or another. They are almost always talking to white audiences and having to argue for the humanity of Native peoples in the face of violence, oppression, and misrepresentation. Furthermore, the dichotomy between savage and civilized was the inescapable frame within which they had to argue, a situation which, in effect, forced them to accept the definition of "civilization" or to redefine it in whole or in part. There were a range of opinions on the matter. Euro-American thought represented Native traditional knowledge as the opposite of civilization and civilized thinking, as mere superstition—quaint, maybe picturesque, but certainly not real knowledge, which was scientific, verifiable, and accurate. The representation of Native traditional knowledge always confirmed what Euro-Americans thought about Indians in the first place. When Native writers of this era represented traditional knowledge, it was often incomplete in a way. Their main political object, to argue for the humanity of Native people (and all the rights that accrue from that humanity), put traditional knowledge in a secondary position, where the contradictions inherent in attempting to reconcile traditional knowledge with modernity were not necessarily worked out completely. There are two persistent strategies that Native writers employ with regard to traditional knowledge, however. The first was that they historicized traditional knowledge, representing that knowledge as an earlier point in the development of Native people from the state of nature to civilization, following from the argument that Native people can be raised up to civilization and be as modern as Euro-Americans (if they accept the superiority of Euro-American civilization). The second strategy was that most writers argued that traditional knowledge was not quaint superstition but rather valid knowledge and, in fact, superior in its account of Native people than Euro-American knowledge. Very few Native writers—Elias Boudinot being the primary example—reject the validity of traditional knowledge out of hand. But again, these writers don't spend that much time, comparatively, talking about traditional knowledge when their primary purpose was to present political and humanitarian arguments to the white public. One can probably also say that the place of traditional knowledge in the modern world was too complex a topic to be dealt with, too difficult to resolve, when Native peoples were in such desperate straits.

Bibliography

Historical Background:

Mills, Charles W. *The Racial Contract*. Ithaca: Cornell UP, 1997.

Stewart, James B. "Modernizing 'Difference': The Political Meaning of Color in the Free States, 1776–1840." *Journal of the Early Republic* 19.4 (1999): 691–713.

Tully, James. "Rediscovering America: The Two Treatises and Aboriginal Rights." *An Approach to Political Philosophy: Locke in Contexts*. London: Cambridge UP, 1993.

Native History:

Wilkins, David E. *American Indian Politics and the American Political System*. Lanham, MD: Rowman, 2002.

Representations of Indians:

Deloria, Philip J. *Playing Indian*. New Haven: Yale UP, 1998.

Jane Johnston Schoolcraft (Ojibwa) (1800–1841)

Contributing Editor: James W. Parins

Classroom Issues and Strategies

Establishing a framework for discussion helps in teaching Schoolcraft. The instructor needs to address the prehistoric nature of the original oral tales and aspects of the oral tradition itself and, in addition, explain how the tales were enhanced stylistically and rhetorically once they were written down. The dual audiences (of the original tales and the written versions) need to be addressed as well.

As a helpful teaching strategy, draw parallels with other oral tales, for example, Njal's *Saga, Beowulf,* and the *Iliad*. All these existed first in the oral tradition and were later written down. All included super- or preternatural elements.

Students usually have questions on the differences in social values between the American Indian and "mainstream" cultures.

Major Themes, Historical Perspectives, Personal Issues

Of particular importance are creation myths or stories that explain how things came to be.

Significant Form, Style, or Artistic Conventions

Students can compare the author with others writing in the "standard" style of the time, Hawthorne and Irving, for example, particularly in their self-conscious use of terms like *legend*.

Original Audience

Teachers need to address the preliterate society for which the tales were originally composed as well as the non-Indian audience Schoolcraft was writing for. Points to be made include the following: The style was embellished for the non-Indian audience; students should be directed to find examples. Schoolcraft's Romantic style differs from some other narratives, including slave narratives.

Comparisons, Contrasts, Connections

Oral texts from other traditions can be compared and contrasted. Cusick's work is especially helpful for comparison within the American Indian context.

Major George Lowrey (Cherokee) (c. 1770–1852)

Contributing Editor: Maureen A. Konkle

Classroom Issues and Strategies

Please see the material on "Teaching the Texts of 'Native America'" for background on the representation of Indians and Native writing in this era. I also think it's important to situate this piece in the history of Cherokee removal and with regard to the complex role that Sequoyah plays in Cherokee politics and culture—at the time and to the present day.

Major Themes, Historical Perspectives, Personal Issues

There are two aspects of background that I'd like to emphasize in relation to Lowrey's account of Sequoyah: the concept of "civilization" in relation to the Cherokees, and the Treaty of New Echota and the Cherokee removal, which is the setting for Lowrey's reading of his biography and his production of Sequoyah as an important—really iconic—Cherokee figure.

The Cherokees and "Civilization." John Ross and the other Cherokee leaders mounted a sophisticated political campaign to make the Cherokees' arguments heard in Congress and by the public at large. In public appearances and lectures, memorials to Congress, pamphlets, and newspaper articles, they argued, as they did before the Supreme Court, that the U.S. government, and before it, the British government, had recognized the autonomy of the Cherokee Nation as such in numerous treaties which had been duly ratified by the Senate and that the United States could not declare supremacy over the Cherokee Nation or force the Cherokee Nation into any actions without compromising its founding principles. This argument was widely discussed in the 1820s and into the 1830s in periodicals, newspapers, and public meetings. The Cherokees were for a time relatively widely supported by whites who argued that if the United States disregarded its treaties with sovereign nations, it compromised its core principles, and to do so was a grave ethical and moral transgression. A particular theme in this writing was the use of force: many commentators observed that if the American revolutionaries righteously threw off the tyrannical power of the British King, it did not look good for the U.S. government some years later to use tyrannical power to destroy the Cherokees and other Indian nations.

As a part of their efforts to establish that the U.S. and European governments had already recognized their nation's political autonomy, the Cherokee elites argued that they were the most "civilized" of the Indian nations, moving ever forward in the number of Christians, the children in school, the land under agricultural cultivation, the "improvements" made. This was a politically astute argument to make. From the beginning, European writers had figured the inhabitants of the Western Hemisphere first as inhabitants of a Garden of Eden and later as inhabitants of the state of nature and therefore in both cases representative of the earliest form of human society. In this thinking, Europeans positioned Native peoples in the Western Hemisphere as theoretical abstractions, and in that capacity, Europeans believed that Native peoples in North America could hypothetically be "improved" and civilized. The catch in that line of thought, however, is that the only way for Indians to demonstrate their "civilization" is to first, become like Euro-Americans—that is, become Christians and labor in commercial agriculture—and second, become incorporated into Euro-American political society—that is, hypothetically, to become citizens of the United States. Again, according to European thought, to be civilized and to form a political society is to be Christian and to practice commercial agriculture (the two principal requirements). As they were—unchanged—Indians were held to be incapable of forming political societies. The important underlying factor in this line of thinking was that, hypothetically, once Indians became civilized and citizens of the United States, they would necessarily give up their claims to land and political autonomy. That is the object of U.S. imperialism in North America.

The Cherokee elites made an important distinction in this thinking about who was civilized and who was not. They argued that their rapid acquisition of Euro-American practices and beliefs only *strengthened* their case that they formed a nation whose territory and autonomy the U.S. and European governments had historically recognized and that neither the United States nor any of its constituent states could legitimately violate. The Cherokees and other Native writers who argued for the "civilization" of Native peoples were talking about a different trajectory, one in which Native political autonomy remained intact, and Native people *coexisted* with the Euro-American government rather than became incorporated into it or subordinated to it. For Native writers of this era, to become "civilized" was to adapt to Euro-American society and take up its practices, but at the same time not to give up political autonomy. In fact, many Native writers of the era argued that adaptation to Euro-American practices was their only hope of remaining sovereign Indian nations. Furthermore, Native writers held a wide range of opinions about the nature and extent of the adaptations they would have to make, and the people in the Cherokee Nation were no exception to this general rule. So while some writers like Elias Boudinot denigrated traditional practices and beliefs, seeking to erase them and replace them with Euro-American practices and beliefs, many others described a range of accommodations to change that retained a belief in the validity and often in the superiority of traditional culture. George Lowrey himself might serve as an example of this kind of complexity of thought about being Native and Cherokee in the modern world.

Sequoyah's syllabary and Payne's projected history of the Cherokees can also be viewed in this light. The Cherokee elites used the syllabary to strengthen their arguments that they were civilized, and the syllabary perfectly demonstrates the distinctions that they made with regard to Euro-American thought on the topic. That is, the syllabary demonstrated, they argued, that the Cherokees were rapidly catching up with Euro-Americans, and more importantly, that they were doing it on their own terms. They were adapting to modern society, but they were still Cherokees, which is not just a cultural distinction, as it is usually understood, but is, more importantly, a political distinction. The Cherokees are often described in the scholarship as "separatist," the implication of which seems to be that their rejection of political incorporation into the United States even while they advocated Christianity and commercial agriculture was an unfortunate, even bad, thing.

The elite Cherokees and their spokesmen insisted, however, that the Cherokee Nation as an autonomous political society could exist in the modern world—not eventually disappear because it was "savage"—and that Cherokees themselves could define their own identity and history. Their efforts were not "separatist" but rather anti-imperial.

Payne's projected history can also be seen as an effort on the part of Cherokees—at John Ross's instigation—to define themselves in the modern world. Many Native writers and leaders of the time wrote or spoke of writing histories of their tribes; most famously, the Tuscarora David Cusick published his *Sketches of Ancient History of the Six Nations* in 1826. But William Apess at least talked about writing a history of the Pequots, and the Seneca leader Cornplanter summoned an interpreter to take down his history of the tribe in the 1820s, which his friends apparently convinced him to destroy. Despite the ongoing crisis in the Cherokee Nation in the 1830s, or maybe because of it, Ross supported Payne's idea of a Cherokee history and publicly endorsed him. In a letter to be read to Cherokee elders, Ross vouched for Payne's sincerity, asked them to tell Payne what they knew about Cherokee history and traditions, and told them that once Payne finished the book, he would call a council of elders together so that they could review and vet the book before it was published. At the very least, this puts Ross's supposed rejection of Cherokee tradition in a different light and adds to what can be understood about the complexity of Native peoples' thinking about traditional knowledge in the early nineteenth century. This is certainly an area for further research. At present, I think you can say that you can't assume to know what Native people thought about traditional knowledge, no matter how "acculturated" they might appear to have been, if there is no record to go on and that you can assume that they meant to decide for themselves what they thought about their identity and history in the context of the wrenching changes that they endured.

Treaty of New Echota. In December 1835, the Cherokee crisis came to a head. After his defeat in October, Schermerhorn let it be known that the Cherokees were expected at another conference in December so that a removal treaty could be signed and that those who didn't attend would be counted as being in favor. The majority of the Cherokees refused to go, counting on the fact that treaties had to have the consent of the nation—or at least the appearance of the consent of the nation—before they could be construed as legitimate. The so-called Treaty Party of Cherokees, a minority led by Major Ridge and John Ridge, the father of John Rollin Ridge; Elias Boudinot; and Boudinot's brother, Stand Watie, signed the Treaty of New Echota, which was immediately widely recognized as having been coerced. After some controversy, the Senate nevertheless ratified it. Ross led the fight against removal for several more years; he employed Payne to help draft correspondence and other official statements. By the summer of 1838, the U.S. Army was rounding up Cherokees and confining them to what, in the 1930s, the historian Grant Foreman called "concentration camps" throughout Cherokee territory—first in Georgia, North Carolina, Tennessee, and Alabama, and then in larger groups in fewer camps in Tennessee and Alabama. A drought prevented them from moving west in the summer of 1838. Ross managed to convince the U.S. government to let the Cherokees move themselves west rather than be moved under military supervision, but he didn't receive permission until the fall of 1838. See the National Trail of Tears Association website at <http://www.nationaltota.org/the-story> for an overview. This is an excellent summary of the Trail of Tears that presents historical details (like the system of camps) that are frequently lost in accounts that put this story within the frame of narratives of Indians' doom.

In 1839, Elias Boudinot, John Ridge, and Major Ridge (the cousin, father, and grandfather of John Rollin Ridge) were assassinated for violating Cherokee law by signing the Treaty of New Echota, which was only one event in the ongoing factional conflicts in the Cherokee Nation throughout the 1830s and 1840s in Indian Territory. Stand Watie, Boudinot's brother, escaped. In 1840, John Payne stayed several weeks with Ross at his new home, meeting Sequoyah and attending a murder trial at the Cherokee court at the capital, Tahlequah, which he wrote about in several long newspaper dispatches, later published as *Indian Justice: A Cherokee Murder Trial in 1840* (Norman: U of Oklahoma P, 2002). In this he sought to show how, despite what they had suffered, the Cherokees were working to reorganize their government and move forward.

Significant Form, Style, or Artistic Conventions

The piece presents some problems in that it is Payne's transcription of Lowrey's written account, translated for Payne as Lowrey read it, by someone unnamed. In terms of Payne's style of writing, it's important to remember that he was a sometime literary journalist in the 1830s and 1840s. In fact, Payne had a habit of publishing literary magazines throughout his life. In 1804, he and a friend who was learning to be a printer published *The Fly*; in 1805, at fourteen, he published *The Thespian Mirror*, which was dedicated to reviews of the current theater. In 1827, he published another literary paper in London called *The Opera Glass*. His idea for a literary magazine that sent him eventually to the Cherokee Nation was therefore an old habit. When he returned to New York City in 1836, he began contributing to *The Ladies' Companion*, a monthly; he was editing it by August of that year. He published at least one account of the non-Native aspects of his trip south: a visit to the Louisville, Kentucky, home of George Keats, brother of John; he also included unpublished poems by John Keats that were in the possession of his brother. The owner of the paper, W. W. Snowdon, dismissed Payne in November 1836, replacing him with Ann Stephens. Snowdon wrote in the October 1837 issue of the magazine: "Mr. Payne never held the slightest control over the pages of this work, notwithstanding assertions that have been circulated to the contrary, much to the detriment of the magazine."

Payne's style might be compared with that of the material from Fanny Fern in the anthology. Payne demonstrates in this manuscript some of the characteristic features of literary journalism of the time, especially the picturesque nature of it. He has a light touch. He represents these Cherokees as a jovial group joining in with the story about a remarkable comrade—who is nevertheless human himself, spending perhaps a little too much time chasing after girls as a young man, drinking too much, and so on. It works in this case to humanize the Cherokees by representing them in a fashion similar to the depiction of whites.

Original Audience

This piece wasn't published until 1970, in the *Journal of Cherokee Studies*; it's taken from Payne's manuscript collection at the Newberry Library. I think it can be read as a draft of what Payne might have written in this history and also in terms of his background as a literary journalist. You could speculate on whether the Cherokees' story could be told in the context of the literary journalism of the era—sentimental, picturesque, domestic, and so on—that is, on whether it would serve the Cherokees politically to have their story told in that way. There is also, of course, the scene that Payne describes and the moment in which Lowrey read his account of Sequoyah. One can imagine that the story of Sequoyah was meant to shore up the Cherokees' belief in their ability to adapt to new circumstances and even thrive in them at a time when whites relentlessly sought to destroy them, literally, in so many ways. There is Lowrey himself, a man who dressed traditionally but was a Presbyterian and a government official—and possibly also a slave owner, like a minority of other Cherokees, many of them of the educated, Christian elite. The complexities of the scene can be brought out in class. At the same time, Sequoyah is one of many Native leaders who were widely recognized in both Euro-American and Native societies—including King Philip, Handsome Lake, Black Hawk and many others—although for different reasons. For example, in Euro-American representations, Red Jacket was a popular figure of the noble savage who tragically defended his people in the face of inevitable doom. For Iroquois and other Native writers of the time, however, he was a figure of political and cultural resistance, principally because he defended Seneca and Iroquois political autonomy from the United States.

Comparisons, Contrasts, Connections

- Among the Native writers, this piece would compare especially on the style to the excerpts from George Copway; certainly to Boudinot and the Cherokee memorials historically, and especially in terms of how Boudinot represents Sequoyah as contrasted with how Lowrey and Payne represent him.

- Anthologies of American Literature inevitably begin with a set of translated Native American oral traditions, the sources of which may or may not be identified. It's a structure that reinforces the notion that Indians are the "first Americans" and therefore it's morally right that they be politically incorporated into the United States as long as we appreciate their cultures. Lowrey's story of Sequoyah might be compared and contrasted with the "oral traditions" opening this anthology in a number of different ways—for example, on the meanings of orality versus writing in Euro-American thought and for Native people, on the definition of *oral tradition* (is the story of Sequoyah oral tradition?), and so on.

- To go back to Payne's style, this piece might be compared with examples in the anthology from the same time frame regarding its features of narrative and characterization.

- The story of Sequoyah might also be understood in relation to other mythic and mythologized figures in the early nineteenth century: Sojourner Truth, for example, among African Americans, who, like Sequoyah, learned to publicize herself; or among Euro-Americans any number of people, including Puritan figures, Revolutionary figures, and frontier types like Daniel Boone, who were mythologized by a range of writers from Parson Weems to Washington Irving and Henry Wadsworth Longfellow.

Working with Cultural Objects

- Sequoyah Research Center/American Native Press Archives: <http://www.anpa.ualr.edu>. Includes Chronicle of the Trail of Tears and other features.

- Trail of Tears Association: <http://www.nationaltota.org>. Provides a historical overview of the Trail of Tears and outlines current efforts to commemorate it.

- Cherokee Nation in Oklahoma (official site): <http://www.cherokee.org>. Both this website and the Eastern Band of Cherokees website can be looked at for information on how Sequoyah and his syllabary are a continued part of Cherokee life in the twenty-first century.

- Eastern Band of Cherokees (official site): <http://www.cherokee-nc.com>.

Questions for Reading, Discussion, and Writing

1. How do Lowrey and Payne represent Sequoyah? What kind of a person is he? How does this view contrast with stereotypical ideas about Indians of the time?
2. What's the effect of Payne's description of the group's participation in and reaction to the story? How does he depict contemporary Cherokees, about whom the white public was quite curious?

Bibliography

Bender, Margaret. *Signs of Cherokee Culture: Sequoyah's Syllabary in Eastern Cherokee Life.* Chapel Hill: U of North Carolina P, 2002.

Monteith, Carmeleta. "Literacy Among the Cherokee in the Early 19th Century." *Journal of Cherokee Studies* 9.2 (1984): 56–75.

Payne, John Howard. "The Cherokee Cause." *Journal of Cherokee Studies* 1.1 (1976): 17–22.

Perdue, Theda. "The Sequoyah Syllabary and Cultural Revitalization." *Perspectives on the Southeast: Linguistics, Archeology and Ethnohistory.* Ed. Patricia Kwachka. Athens: U of Georgia, 1994. 116–25.

Stearns, Bertha-Monica. "John Howard Payne as Editor." *American Literature* 5.3 (1933): 215–28.

Elias Boudinot (Cherokee) (c. 1802–1839)

Contributing Editor: James W. Parins

Classroom Issues and Strategies

Boudinot seeks to and succeeds in breaking the stereotype of the Indian established by Irving's "Traits of Indian Character" and other writing that established the Indian as uneducated and shirtless. Two major issues that interest students are cultural discontinuity and the position of minorities in American culture.

Major Themes, Historical Perspectives, Personal Issues

Major themes include the perceptions of minorities by the dominant society, the role of the government in protecting the minorities against the majority, and the social responsibilities of the majority toward minorities.

Significant Form, Style, or Artistic Conventions

In many ways, Boudinot is using "standard" methods of persuasive discourse in use at the time. Students should examine his oratorical and rhetorical devices, including diction and structure.

Original Audience

It is important to stress that Boudinot was trying to persuade his white audience to take a particular course of action.

Comparisons, Contrasts, Connections

Boudinot was writing in the oratorical mode used by mainstream writers at the time. Compare with works by Ralph Waldo Emerson, Frederick Douglass, and Chief Seattle.

Questions for Reading, Discussion, and Writing

Students should explore the historical situation in which the address was written, should do comparative studies, and should examine rhetorical and oratorical devices.

John Ross et al. (Cherokee)

Teaching material for John Ross is available on *The Heath Anthology of American Literature* website. (To access the site, please go to the Houghton Mifflin college homepage at <http://www.college.hmco.com>. Select *English*; then select *The Heath Anthology* textbook site.)

William Apess (Pequot) (1798–?)

Contributing Editor: A. LaVonne Brown Ruoff

Classroom Issues and Strategies

Apess was a powerful orator and the first American Indian protest writer. At a time when whites presumed Indians were dying out or being moved west of the Mississippi, Apess attacks whites' treatment of Indians using forceful language and rhetorical skill. He contrasts the abject degradation of Indians with their natural ingenuity.

The instructor should address attitudes toward the Indians and explain problems faced by Indians in the early nineteenth century. Consider presenting historical material on what had happened to East Coast Indians. The Pequot history (Apess's tribe) is briefly outlined in the section of the headnote on teaching strategy.

Students often ask why Indians turned to Christianity and used it as an appeal to their white audiences. See comments on the Occom selections.

Major Themes, Historical Perspectives, Personal Issues

1. Indian-white relations—especially the impact of the Indian Removal Bill. Apess is clearly reacting to the whites' attitudes reflected in the bill to remove Indians from east of the Mississippi River and to the stereotypes of Indians present in Indian captivity narratives.
2. Emphasis by American Indian authors and slave narrators on achieving equality through Christianity.

Significant Form, Style, or Artistic Conventions

1. Use of persuasive oratorical style and appeal to emotions of audience. Note how Apess compares non-Indians' professed Christianity with their unchristian treatment of Indians and blacks.
2. Use of a series of rhetorical questions to his audience about what Indians have suffered.
3. Use of biblical quotations to support position.

Original Audience

1. Religious orientation of audience, which would have expected appeals to biblical authority.
2. Prejudice toward Indians of early-nineteenth-century audiences.

Comparisons, Contrasts, Connections

Compare with speeches by Indians, Copway's autobiography—sections on worth of Indian and picture of Indian family life, which buttress Apess's arguments for treating Indians as human beings.

Compare with slave narratives, which also argue for essential humanity of people of all races.

Questions for Reading, Discussion, and Writing

1. Relationship between publication of this document and debate over passage of Indian Removal Bill. Also relationship to miscegenation bill in Massachusetts passed around this time.
2. (a) Compare/contrast the oratorical styles used by Apess and Douglass and their treatment of Indian-white relations.
   (b) Compare and contrast the oratorical style used by Apess and American Indian orators such as Logan and Seattle.
   (c) Discuss Apess's and the slave narrators' criticisms of the treatment of Indians and slaves by white Christians.
   (d) Discuss the influence of Christianity and its concept of the essential equality of all men under God as expressed by Apess and Copway and by slave narrators such as Douglass.

John Wannuaucon Quinney (Mahican) (1797–1855)

Contributing Editor: Maureen A. Konkle

Classroom Issues and Strategies

Please see the material on "Teaching the Texts of 'Native America'" for background on the representation of Indians and Native writing in this era.

Significant Form, Style, or Artistic Conventions

Although Quinney himself is obscure today and his speech even more so, the speech itself demonstrates many of the key arguments, themes, and conventions of Native writing in English in the nineteenth century. He begins his speech with a declaration of his Indianness, then disputes the account of Native peoples given by whites. Like William Apess, he reads Euro-American writing on Native people against the grain. He incorporates the doomed Indian motif as a point of departure for criticism of whites; he insists on the superiority of oral tradition to written records; he argues that whites have consciously misrepresented Native people; he rejects the idea that Indians' supposed disappearance is God's will; he deploys the Indians are more Christian than actual Christians trope. Furthermore, like many Native writers at the time, Quinney describes the government and political relations of the Mahican and later Stockbridge people: he emphasizes the existence of a political society when Euro-Americans insist that Native peoples are not capable of forming them. He comments on being an object of white curiosity, then reverses the terms to evoke how Native peoples might have felt on first seeing Europeans. He describes in detail the subterfuge in which whites engaged to get Stockbridge land, a practice on the part of tribal leaders that are present in the records of treaty councils going back to the seventeenth century.

Original Audience

This speech was first printed in the *Albany Freeholder* on July 12, 1854, with an introduction appealing to the editors of other newspapers to copy and circulate the speech. The introduction states that an audience of two thousand people heard the speech and that Quinney was preceded by local dignitaries. It also recommends the speech as an example of "the peculiarities of Indian elo-quence." But the introduction also notes that the speech "contains several hard hits" and that the last half of it "is a bold, stern, and manly protest against the uniform and persistent injustice which has been meted out to the Indian race." I think it can be surmised, since Quinney introduces himself as the "Last of the Mohicans," that it was in that capacity that he was invited to give the speech. I think it can also be surmised that his audience was probably not expecting to be excoriated for a history of violence, and in fact, that they probably didn't even hear that argument in Quinney's oration. To return to the discrepancy between Indian reality and white fantasy, the sentimental mindset, the idea that the proper response to Indians is to express sympathy for them, makes the absorption of very pointed critique quite easy. Quinney might mean to use "Last of the Mohicans" as a rebuke to his audience, but they would be ever-ready to muffle that rebuke in the abstractions of the conflict between savage and civilized and doomed tragic Indians. Quinney could be heard and co-opted as the "Last of the Mohicans," lamented, but not regarded as speaking about anything on which action could or should be taken. There are many accounts of Native speakers undercutting their white audience's expectations in this way, whether the audiences understood what was going on or not.

Comparisons, Contrasts, Connections

There are many comparisons and connections to be made with this particular text:

- **Native Writing.** Quinney can be compared with Elias Boudinot on "civilization," with William Apess on the politics of misrepresentation, and with Copway on the validity of traditional knowledge. One might look at Seattle's speech of questionable provenance and compare it with Quinney's. His account of the political struggles of the Stockbridges can be compared with the Cherokee memorials on their own struggle. For tribal and regional context, he can be compared with Aupaumut, his fellow Mahican; with Samson Occom; and with Handsome Lake, whom Stockbridge leaders perceived as a threat.
- **Representation of Indians.** Quinney's account of Native life might be contrasted with any of the antebellum writing on Indians by Freneau, Sigourney, Sedgwick, Cooper, Osgood, and Whitman.
- **Representation of Indians from Beginnings.** Quinney can be compared or contrasted with the trajectory of Euro-American thinking about Native peoples—from Las Casas, Winthrop, Morton, John Williams, Benjamin Thompson, Lahontan, Franklin, Crèvecoeur, Jefferson (Declaration, *Notes on the State of Virginia*, and Indian addresses), and Timothy Dwight.
- **Relations to African-American Writing.** Obvious comparison can be made with Frederick Douglass's fifth of July speech, "What to a Slave is the Fourth of July?" but also with David Walker's *Appeal* and the works of Olaudah Equiano and Frances E. W. Harper.

Working with Cultural Objects

At about the time Quinney gave his speech, there were two well-known collections of Indian portraits: the McKenney-Hall Portrait Gallery, which was first published in 1838, and George Catlin's Indian portraits, which he began painting in the 1830s and with which he toured Eastern cities and Europe. Catlin painted Quinney's portrait in the early 1830s at Green Bay. Quinney's portrait from 1842 by Charles Bird King was the last portrait included in the McKenney-Hall Portrait Gallery and pictures him with the 1842 memorial of the Stockbridge Nation rolled up in his hand. Background and images of Catlin's

Indian portraits and the McKenney-Hall Portrait Gallery (neither of them including Quinney's portrait, however) can be found at the following two websites:

- Digital Archive of the McKenney-Hall Portrait Gallery at the University of Washington Libraries Website: <http://www.content.lib.washington.edu//mckenneyhallweb/index.html>
- Online Exhibition at the Smithsonian American Art Museum: <http://www.americanart.si.edu/collections/exhibits/catlin/highlights.html>

These two websites can be used to foster discussion as to how Euro-Americans represented Indians in contrast with how they represented themselves.

Questions for Reading, Discussion, and Writing

1. How would you describe Quinney's perspective on being the "Last of the Mohicans"?
2. What are some of the implications that Quinney discusses concerning the violation of the kindness and hospitality that Native peoples first showed Euro-Americans?

Bibliography

Brasser, Ted J. *Riding on Frontier's Crest: Mahican Indian Culture and Culture Change.* Ethnology Division Paper No. 13. Ottawa: National Museums of Canada, 1974.

Konkapot, Levi. "The Last of the Mohicans." *Collections of the State Historical Society of Wisconsin* 4 (1859): 303–07.

Marsh, The Rev. Cutting. "The Stockbridges." *Collections of the State Historical Society of Wisconsin* 4 (1859): 299–301.

Memorial of the Stockbridge Nation of Indians in Wisconsin. Senate Doc. No. 189, 27th Congress, 2nd Session, 10 February 1842. Washington, DC: Thomas Allen, 1842.

Quinney, John W. *Memorial of John W. Quinney.* 1852. *Collections of the State Historical Society of Wisconsin* 4 (1859): 321–33.

Stockbridge Indian, A. "Death of John W. Quinney." *Collections of the State Historical Society of Wisconsin* 4 (1859): 309–11.

Seattle (Duwamish) (1786–1866)

Contributing Editor: John Alberti

Classroom Issues and Strategies

While many of the other Native American texts included in *The Heath Anthology* will be new to most students, many readers will probably be familiar with some version of Chief Seattle's speech. This popularity is directly tied in with the vexed question of the translation and recording of Native oral performances. The headnote in *The Heath Anthology* details the history of the dissemination of Seattle's speech, from Henry A. Smith's original translation to Ted Perry's recent revision, a text that forms the basis for the popular children's book (which may be its most familiar form for many students) and even bumper stickers.

One place for class discussion to start, then, is the question of why this text has proven so popular, both among Native and Euro-Americans. Why would non-Native Americans be so drawn to a text that draws such a critical portrait of European Christian culture? This discussion can lead to issues of the construction of Indian identity and history within larger nationalist American histories and ideologies, ranging from the *topoi* of the noble but vanishing Indian so important to the novels of James Fenimore Cooper to the more recent construction of the Indian as ecological scold. Such cultural formations suggest that many Euro-American readers have looked and look to Seattle's speech less out of curiosity about Duwamish culture and history and more out of concerns rooted in the dominant society, particularly the consequences of unlimited growth and development and the destruction of the environment, but also ambivalence and guilt about the destruction of Native peoples and cultures.

These questions can then lead back to the difficulties Native speakers face in making their perspectives heard within larger national discourses (Seattle's text, for example, repeatedly calls attention to the fact that the U.S. government is under no compulsion to pay attention to his remarks), a rhetorical challenge faced by any speaker or writer in a position of lesser power vis-à-vis a dominant culture and discourse system. In this way Seattle's speech can be compared to the writings of nineteenth-century African-American writers like Frederick Douglass and Harriet Jacobs, both strong and powerful writers who nevertheless wrestled with the challenge of having their voices co-opted by white abolitionists who, though sympathetic and working in solidarity with Douglass and Jacobs, still often expressed attitudes toward slavery that had as much to do with concern over the consequences of slavery for the soul of white America as with the political oppression of the slaves themselves. While both Douglass and Jacobs were at least able to produce the written texts they offered to the national debate over slavery (although both faced skepticism over their abilities to do so and had to include prefaces from white writers vouching for their abilities), the cultural co-optation from the beginning of Seattle's voice is marked everywhere in Smith's text by the use of phrases (such as "the great— and I presume—good White Chief ") that clearly sound like a nineteenth-century Euro-American man of letters. As a result, the class can consider to what extent an appreciation among non-Native readers for what is thought to be Seattle's views represents a substantive change in behavior and attitude or a means of assuaging guilt (and these need not be mutually exclusive reactions, of course). What seems positive about the popularity and popularizing of Seattle? What is disturbing or destructive?

George Copway (Kah-ge-ga-gah-bowh; Ojibwa) (1818–1869)

Contributing Editor: A. LaVonne Brown Ruoff

Classroom Issues and Strategies

Students need information about the Ojibwas as a group. They also need to understand the relationship between Copway's autobiography, the Indian Removal Bill, and the attempts to move the Ojibwa out of Minnesota. They need as well an understanding of how Native American autobiography differs from that of non-Indians. See discussion below.

Students respond much more enthusiastically to Copway's description of traditional life than to his references to Christianity. (For Indians' attitudes toward conversion to Christianity, see the comments on Occom and Apess.)

Major Themes, Historical Perspectives, Personal Issues

The Ojibwa or Chippewa are numerically the largest tribe in the United States and Canada. A member of the Algonkian language family, they are spread out around the western Northern Great Lakes region, extending from the northern shore of Lake Huron as far west as Montana, southward well into Wisconsin and Minnesota, and northward to Lake Manitoba. In early historic times, the Ojibwa lived in numerous, widely scattered, small, autonomous bands.

Families hunted individually during the winter but gathered together as groups during the summer. Thus, the term *tribe* is appropriate in terms of a common language and culture but not in terms of an overall political authority.

In the seventeenth century, they were mainly located in present-day Ontario. Their hereditary enemies were the Hurons and Iroquois on the east and the Fox and Sioux on the west.

Copway's autobiography, his plan for a separate state for Indians, and his history of the Ojibwas were undoubtedly responses to efforts of the Lake Superior Ojibwa to resist removal from 1847 through 1849. In 1850 President Zachary Taylor authorized immediate and complete removal of the Ojibwas from the lands ceded in 1842 (Kobel 174–82).

One important issue is the fact that Copway presents himself as a "noble-but-literate and Christianized" savage, an example of what Indians can become if whites educate and Christianize, rather than eradicate, them. By describing the achievements of his father and ancestors, he emphasizes the nobility of his lineage and thus legitimizes his narrative. (Emphasizing one's heritage was a technique also used by slave narrators.) Related to this is the issue of his difficult task of creating audience sympathy for the Ojibwa people and their beliefs while showing the necessity of Christianizing Indians.

Another issue is the techniques he uses to describe the Ojibwas and their traditions to convince readers that Indians were human. Copway emphasizes the basic humanity and generosity of the Ojibwas toward one another, values that non-Indian Christians would recognize as similar to their own. He also humanizes his people by citing examples of how his parents cared for and loved their children. These examples counteract the stereotype of the bloodthirsty Indian ever ready to violate a fair maiden or dash out the brains of an innocent baby, depictions all too common in the captivity narratives popular well into the 1830s.

Significant Form, Style, or Artistic Conventions

Copway's *Life, Letters and Speeches* is the first book-length autobiography written by an Indian who was raised in a traditional Native American family. The pattern of including oral tradition, history, and personal experience is one that characterizes most later Indian autobiographies. This mixed form, which differs from the more linear, personal confession or life history of non-Indian autobiographies, was congenial to Indian narrators accustomed to viewing their lives within the history of their tribe or band, clan, and family.

Copway uses a romantic style designed to appeal to the popular taste of the period. His emotional appeals and oratorical style capture his audience's attention. He also uses literary allusions to demonstrate his literacy—the reference to viewing his life "like the mariner on the wide ocean" making "his way amidst surging seas" is undoubtedly meant to remind his audiences of Byron's *Childe Harold's Pilgrimage*. The lines of poetry, probably written by his wife, Elizabeth Howell, also add to this image of Copway as an educated and accomplished man. His romantic tone·and language, like that of Robert Burns and other authors before him, allow Copway to cast himself in the image of a person of humble beginnings who has become a writer. Giving students some understanding of the backgrounds of English and American Romantic attitudes toward idealizing humbler life and using representatives of the lower class as the subject of literature, particularly in the late eighteenth century, will help students understand why Copway creates himself as he does.

Original Audience

Copway's primary audience was non-Indian. A powerful platform speaker dressed in full Ojibwa regalia, he aroused considerable public enthusiasm for his lectures on traditional Indian life during his tour of the eastern United States and later during his tour of Great Britain, where the second edition of his autobiography was published.

Comparisons, Contrasts, Connections

Copway's description of traditional Ojibwa life and mores can be compared with those incorporated into the stories by Jane Schoolcraft (Ojibwa). The selection can also be compared with Occom's "Short Narrative of My Life." The issues Copway raises with regard to Indian-white relations can be compared with those raised by Occom and Apess. Copway's description of Ojibwa world-views and his stress on the importance of oral traditions can be compared with those expressed in the selections of Native American oral narratives and poetry.

Questions for Reading, Discussion, and Writing

An important question for both reading and writing is how Copway presents or creates himself to show the Indians' essential humanity and their potential for being assimilated into the dominant culture. Discuss Indian worldviews and the importance of oral traditions as reflected in Copway's autobiography and selections from Native American oral literature. An additional topic would be Copway's use of Romantic language and tone. Students might compare his style with that of other early nineteenth-century American writers. Students might also compare Copway's description of Native American people and their lives with captivity narratives by John Williams and Mary Rowlandson.

Bibliography

Boatman, John. *My Elders Taught Me: Aspects of Western Great Lakes American Indian Philosophy.* Lanham: UP of America, 1992.

Densmore, Frances. *Chippewa Customs. Bulletin of the Bureau of American Ethnology.* No. 86. Washington, DC, 1929. Minneapolis: Ross, 1976. Essential work.

Landes, Ruth. *Ojibway Religion and the Midewiwin.* Madison: U of Wisconsin P, 1968. Basic work on the subject.

Ritzenthaler, Robert E. "Southeastern Ojibwa." *The Northeast.* Ed. Bruce G. Trigger. *Handbook of North American Indians.* Vol. 15. Washington, DC: Smithsonian, 1978. 743–59.

Robers, E. S. "Southwestern Chippewa." *The Northeast.* Ed. Bruce G. Trigger. *Handbook of North American Indians.* Vol. 15. Washington, DC: Smithsonian, 1978. 760–71.

Tanner, Helen H. *The Ojibwas: A Critical Bibliography.* Bloomington: Indiana UP, 1976.

Trigger, Bruce G., ed. *The Northeast. Handbook of North American Indians.* Ed. William Sturtevant. Vol. 15. Washington, DC: Smithsonian, 1978.

Vizenor, Gerald (Ojibwa). *The People Named the Chippewa. Narrative Histories.* Minneapolis: U of Minnesota P, 1984.

Warren, William W. (Ojibwa). *History of the Ojibways, Based on Traditions and Oral Statements.* Collections of the Minnesota Historical Society. No. 5. 1885. Rpt. Intro. by W. Roger Buffalohead. Minneapolis: Ross, 1957. Minneapolis: Minnesota Hist. Soc., 1984.

John Rollin Ridge (Cherokee) (1827–1867)

Contributing Editor: James W. Parins

Classroom Issues and Strategies

The question of assimilation of a minority figure into white society should be raised. The historical context needs to be firmly established and the implication of assimilation should be addressed, especially as it relates to the loss of culture. The introduction should be consulted carefully as it will help in this regard.

Major Themes, Historical Perspectives, Personal Issues

The major themes include Ridge's views on progress and how it comes about, the tensions between the dominant society and minorities, and the Romantic aspects of his poetry.

Significant Form, Style, or Artistic Conventions

In his poetry, Ridge follows many of the Romantic conventions common in American and British literature of the period. His prose reflects a vigorous editorial style that spilled over from his journalism into his other prose literary efforts.

Original Audience

Ridge was writing for a white, educated audience. His work is relevant now in terms of the majority-minority relations and is valuable in a historical context.

Comparisons, Contrasts, Connections

Any of the contemporary poets can be fruitfully compared. Contemporary prose writers include Mark Twain, Joaquin Miller, and Bret Hart.

Questions for Reading, Discussion, and Writing

Topics include the Romantic elements in his work, the idea of progress in nineteenth-century society, and his attitudes toward the American Indians. The latter subject is interesting because of Ridge's ambiguity toward this topic.

Spanish America

Tales from the Hispanic Southwest

Contributing Editor: Genaro M. Padilla

Classroom Issues and Strategies

Students may need to be reminded that these tales are usually performed orally, so instructors should help students recreate the oral tradition out of which they emerge. I often read these tales aloud and try to actually reconstruct the performative features of the tale.

Significant Form, Style, or Artistic Conventions

Again, the cultural value attached to oral tradition and collective audience should be borne in mind.

Original Audience

The best/ideal audience is youngsters who are still shaping their social and ethical beliefs.

Comparisons, Contrasts, Connections

Other folk tale types should be useful, especially those sustained by other immigrant groups—Italians, Greeks, and so on.

Questions for Reading, Discussion, and Writing

1. (a) What are our common ideas about death? Why do we avoid discussing death?

(b) How do stories entertain us into ethical behavior?
2. (a) Students might compare these tales with others they have heard or read.
(b) They might consider the "usefulness" of the moral tales in a largely secular world.

Lorenzo de Zavala (1788–1836)

Contributing Editor: John-Michael Rivera

Classroom Issues and Strategies

Teaching students early Mexican and Texas cultural and political history is essential for understanding Zavala. Students need to be aware that Mexico was founded as a nation in 1821 and that Zavala was key in writing its constitution, which he modeled after the U.S. constitution. Reading Zavala will help students understand that Enlightenment ideals such as a liberal democracy and citizenship were not solely located within the borders of the United States but rather also emerged in Mexico and parts of Latin America. It is important to teach students general concepts of democracy and relate that in the nineteenth century, this form of political organization was still very new to Americans and Mexicans. As such, works like Zavala's travel narrative were not only surveys of the land and customs of the American people but were also studies of the very fabric of democracy itself.

Major Themes, Historical Perspectives, Personal Issues

Zavala is an incredibly complicated and important literary figure. He lived under Spanish Colonial rule as a Mexican Creole, helped lead the Mexican independence movement from 1810 to 1821, wrote a significant portion of the Mexican Constitution, and, after leaving Mexico as a political exile, helped write the Texas Constitution. As such, Zavala's own national and ethnic subject position is complicated. Zavala spent most of his life as a Mexican citizen, but after the political environment in Mexico became unstable for him, he left and became a supporter of Texas's independence, becoming the republic's first vice president in 1836. Because of his political work in Texas, Mexico viewed Zavala as a traitor for decades. It is important to point out, however, that Zavala wrote his travel narrative in order to represent a story of both American and Mexican nationhood that he hoped would help foster a liberal identity for the Mexican people. Zavala's book stands as one of the first texts to investigate the early relationship between not only the political constitutions of Mexico and the United States but also of the two peoples themselves. Standing as a cultural mediator between the two countries, Zavala was fostering comprehension of the foundations of Mexican and American democratic peoplehood during the years that lead up to the United States–Mexico War of 1846–1848. In this way, Zavala renders a complicated portrait of United States/Mexico relations and the colonial contact between the two states that began between 1821 and 1824—the monumental period when the colonized people of Mexico broke away from Spanish despotism and created a national, democratic constitution under the United States's imperial gaze at Mexican lands to the west. In the end, Zavala's *Journey to the US* stands as a representative cultural text of this early and dynamic period in American and Mexican history and renders a more complete and complicated portrait of the contradictory but interconnected making of the Mexican national, the United States–Anglo, and the people who are now defined as Mexican Americans.

Significant Form, Style, or Artistic Conventions

Zavala's work should be located within and against the travel narrative genre and the writing of American enlightenment thinkers.

Original Audience

Although it was published in limited numbers in Paris while he was a political exile from Mexico, Zavala wrote his book for Mexicans. It was not widely read by Mexicans, however, until Mexico posthumously published it in 1846, ironically, the year that would begin the United States–Mexico War (1846–1848).

Comparisons, Contrasts, Connections

Comparisons should be made with Alexis de Tocqueville. One could also make interesting parallels between Zavala and Olaudah Equiano.

Questions for Reading, Discussion, and Writing

1. What role does travel play in the formation of the subject and the nation?
2. How does Zavala negotiate among political, environmental, and cultural description?

Narratives from the Mexican and Early American Southwest

Pio Pico (1801–1894)

Teaching material for Pio Pico is available on *The Heath Anthology* website. (To access the site, please go to the Houghton Mifflin college home page at <http://www.college.hmco.com>. Select *English*; then select *The Heath Anthology* textbook site.)

Mariano Guadalupe Vallejo (1808–1890)

Contributing Editor: Genaro Padilla

Classroom Issues and Strategies

Students' lack of historical knowledge about the United States–Mexican War (1846–1848), especially events in California, can be a problem. Some historical background needs to be given; Vallejo should be read as a colonized subject. His historical personal narrative gives the Mexican version of events.

Students often wonder why Vallejo seems politically contradictory. They ask whether he wrote other material and are curious about his social position.

Major Themes, Historical Perspectives, Personal Issues

Vallejo's sense of betrayal comprises an important and intriguing theme. From the selection one can surmise that he actually favored American annexation of California but was summarily imprisoned by a group of Americans he refers to as "thieves."

Mariano Vallejo was born into a prominent family in Monterey, California. Vallejo early decided to pursue a career in both politics and the military and by age twenty-one had been elected to the territorial legislature and had distinguished himself in various campaigns against the Indians. Vallejo supported the American presence in his region, hoping that the *yanquis* would bring both prosperity and stability. Accordingly, Vallejo became one of the most prominent *California* supporters of the American annexation of California.

The movement toward American control of California accelerated with the Bear Flag Revolt of 1846. Vallejo was inexplicably taken prisoner by the troops of John C. Frémont and held for two months, an experience that should have raised doubt in Vallejo's mind about his pro-American sympathies. But Vallejo persisted in his allegiance and eventually served in the state's first senate. In the early 1850s he filed for validation of his Mexican land-grants, only to lose much of his property in a ruling by the United States Supreme Court. By the 1860s, his fortune and influence had declined considerably, and a wiser Vallejo sat down to compose a "true history" of his territory, free of myths and lies. After a series of mishaps and distractions, he completed his five-volume chronicle and donated it to H. H. Bancroft, the celebrated California historian. Vallejo lived quietly thereafter, tending to the 280 acres of land he had left of his once-vast empire. He looked back on his support of American expansion with great bitterness.

In "Six Dollars an Ounce," Vallejo writes of an economic revolution that changed California as decisively as San Jacinto changed the course of Texas history. He recounts how the Gold Rush of 1849 threw California into a frenzy. Previously reasonable men gave up respectable trades and careers to pursue the yellow metal. As Vallejo tells it, the Gold Rush unleashed the meanest of human qualities—distrust, avarice, and violence among them—and accelerated the destruction of traditional *California* culture. In the Americanization of California, Vallejo notes that he witnessed change but not progress.

(Biographical and historical information contributed by Raymund Paredes.)

Significant Form, Style, or Artistic Conventions

The Vallejo selection should be thought of as autobiographical historiography.

Original Audience

It was written as a revisionist version of historical events that Vallejo wished Americans would hear.

Comparisons, Contrasts, Connections

Comparison might be made with Native American orations on tribal displacement, uncertainty, and subjugation.

Questions for Reading, Discussion, and Writing

1. What is the standard version of the Bear Flag Revolt in California in 1846?
2. How does the Vallejo version humanize the Mexican populace?

Bibliography

Padilla, Genaro M. "The Recovery of Chicano Nineteenth-Century Autobiography." *American Quarterly* 40.3 (1981).

Pitt, Leonard. *The Decline of the Californios.* Los Angeles: U of California P, 1969. A good background history of events during the period.

Richard Henry Dana Jr. (1815–1882)

Teaching material for Richard Henry Dana Jr. is available on *The Heath Anthology* website. (To access the site, please go to the Houghton Mifflin college homepage at <http://www.college.hmco.com>. Select *English*; then select *The Heath Anthology* textbook site.)

Alfred Robinson (1806–1895)

Teaching material for Alfred Robinson is available on *The Heath Anthology* website. (To access the site, please go to the Houghton Mifflin college home page at <http://www.college.hmco.com>. Select *English*; then select *The Heath Anthology* textbook site.)

Josiah Gregg (1806–1850)

Teaching material for Josiah Gregg is available on *The Heath Anthology* website. (To access the site, please go to the Houghton Mifflin college home page at <http://www.college.hmco.com>. Select *English*; then select *The Heath Anthology* textbook site.)

Frederick Law Olmsted (1822–1903)

Contributing Editor: John Alberti

Classroom Issues and Strategies

As Raymund Paredes notes in his introduction to the section on narratives of the American Southwest, writers like Frederick Law Olmsted "were primary creators of enduring images of peoples and cultures in the Southwest and other places." This idea—that Olmsted writes as part of a larger communal process of creating images and stereotypes of the Southwest informed by his own political beliefs and cultural biases—can function as the central learning objective in discussing the excerpt from *A Journey Through Texas*. Rather than reading Olmsted's text as an objective report of what life was like in San Antonio in the 1850s, students can read *A Journey* as part of the process of national identity formation, a process that, of course, continues to the present day.

The specific direction of class discussion about Olmsted's work of geography and ethnography depends on the geography and demography of your particular classroom. Even today, reaction to Olmsted's descriptions and commentary will differ according to whether the Southwest represents a far-off part of the United States or the world immediately outside the classroom door. In some areas of the country, the dominant Catholic culture of Mexican-American Texas will seem as exotic as it did to the northeastern and Protestant Olmsted; in others, Olmsted's discussion of what Mexicans are like will more readily strike students as reductive.

One focal point of the cultural work that Olmsted is engaged in and a useful starting place for classroom discussion is his discussion of relations between "Americans" and "Mexicans." Instead of thinking of them as settled categories, students can be encouraged to see these groups as cultural formations in process as the Southwest was annexed by the United States. Students can then carry this process forward into the present day by collecting contemporary examples of image making in relation to the Southwest: photographs, advertising, marketing strategies, the changing demographics of the United States. How much do the images endorsed by Olmsted endure today? In what ways do modern discussions of Southwestern identity represent a continuation of or reaction against texts such as Olmsted's?

The Cultures of New England

Lydia Howard Huntley Sigourney (1791–1865)

Contributing Editor: Sandra A. Zagarell

Classroom Issues and Strategies

Among the biggest hurdles contemporary readers face when encountering much antebellum poetry is this poetry's appeal to a general readership and its conventionality. I'd begin by discussing the often sentimental and religious character of antebellum public poetry and its accessibility, in form and content, to a broad readership. I'd invite students to think about the cultural functions of such poetry as well as the personal effects it could have had on readers who lived in a society in which mortality rates were high, personal hardships frequent, and social inequities sharp. I'd also point out the great antebellum popularity of religious literature and stress similarities between some of Sigourney's poetry and religious meditative essays or tracts. If students are familiar with hymns, they might compare voice, emotions, and language in some of the poems to those in hymns. Finally, I'd encourage students to recognize the social critiques embedded in much of Sigourney's writing—of gender constraints and patriarchy ("The Suttee," "To a Shred of Linen," "The Father"), of the genocide of Native Americans ("The Indian's Welcome to the Pilgrim Fathers," "Indian Names").

Major Themes, Historical Perspectives, Personal Issues

Sigourney was an educator, a historian, and a devout Christian, and much of her work was, in Nina Baym's phrase, "activist and interventionist." She capitalized on her role as a writer for the general public, producing writing that was often moral and didactic. Her work approached public subjects like social cohesion, social responsibility, nature, and history and encouraged readers' emotional responses to these subjects. Many of her poems, such as "The Suttee" and "The Indian's Welcome to the Pilgrim Fathers," cultivate her readers' sympathy with people from other nations or cultures; often, as in these poems, they also seek to mobilize readers' sympathies on behalf of social betterment (the condition of [all] women in "The Suttee," the nation's treatment of Native Americans in "The Indian's Welcome to the Pilgrim Fathers"). Even in many of her elegies she evokes the experience of death and loss common to all of her readers: "Death of an Infant" is an excellent example.

Significant Form, Style, or Artistic Conventions

Sigourney was a prolific and varied writer. I would draw attention to the adroitness with which her work exhibits the stylistic versatility of public verse. Among the forms her poems take are the ode, the nonsubjective lyric, elegy, and narrative and descriptive verse. She wrote in a variety of meters and verse patterns. Her poetry is situated in a sentimental tradition that contrasts with the Romantic one more familiar to, and more highly valued by, readers in the academy. The striking absence of the subjective consciousness of an organizing persona is a feature I would stress. As Annie Finch has observed, Sigourney's poetry gives religious, moral, and emotional truths to what seems an independent or nonpersonal voice, or appears to represent nature or natural states without a mediating subjectivity.

I would also emphasize the poetry's focus on sentiments that are communally accepted (or should be, in Sigourney's eyes), and the ways in which it solicits readers' sense of connection with the subjects represented. Her poems often generalize a highly emotional situation in an objective mode that retains emotional coloration, as in "Death of an Infant," or describes natural phenomena in profoundly felt religious terms, as in "Niagara." She also uses the nonsubjective descriptive poem to represent the history or circumstances of members of racial or national groups different from those of her readers in order to invoke readers' sympathies, and frequently portrays constraints within gender with great feeling. Thus, without direct authorial comment, "The Father" dramatizes the extraordinary possessiveness of the lawyer-father and the dehumanizing inability to feel, and to grieve, to which the individualistic masculinity he embraces condemns him. The tears he finally sheds convert him to a selfless ethos, and arguably a communal one, which is similar to that of many of the poems. The implicit critique of antebellum masculinity in "The Father" also compares significantly with the much more direct exposé of patriarchy in a foreign country in "The Suttee."

I also call attention to the wit Sigourney's poems can display: "To a Shred of Linen" elicits an earlier agrarian New England while reflecting wryly on continuing societal ambivalence about women's creativity in a sphere other than the domestic.

Original Audience

Sigourney was antebellum America's most popular woman poet. She wrote for a Northern (and, increasingly, a western) general readership. She published her work in newspapers and religious magazines, in anthologies and annuals, and in book form. She wrote using a variety of popular forms, including educational books, histories, and advice manuals as well as poetry, sketches, and autobiography. Her work helped create a community of readers in antebellum America, and much of it can be read as a conscious contribution to the establishment of America as a cohesive, humane, and Christian nation.

Comparisons, Contrasts, Connections

Many connections suggest themselves. The egolessness of Sigourney's highly public poetry can be contrasted interestingly with the subjectivity of Dickinson's very private poetry, just as Sigourney's conventionality contrasts with Dickinson's unconventionality. Similarities between the two can also be explored—their concerns with nature, with religion, and with women's circumstances—as can the use to which both put religious verse forms. Sigourney's work can also be compared fruitfully with that of contemporary male public poets. For instance, the presence of a perceiving persona in the poems of Bryant and the absence of such a persona in hers illuminates the permissible stances of male and female poets while the use to which each puts these conventions can also be discussed. Additionally, the sympathy she elicits for Native Americans contrasts interestingly with the perspective of his "The Prairies," whereas a comparison of the relative reticence of the religious sentiment of her "Niagara" with the more consistent religious didacticism of his "To a Waterfowl" can show that gendered poetic stances did not absolutely determine the tone or approach writers took.

"The Father" can be taught very successfully with Poe's "Ligeia." Both are gothic short stories, written in the first person, that involve a man's possessive, and obsessive, love for a woman. Poe's stress on psychology contrasts nicely with Sigourney's emphasis on gender.

Questions for Reading, Discussion, and Writing

1. How do we read these poems? What reading strategies are effective? (Such strategies might include exploring the trajectory of students' emotional responses to particular poems, discussing the ways in which certain poems elicit connections to students' personal experience, talking about the religious sentiment or the urge toward "humanitarian" connection, which some students may find compelling and others offensive.)

2. What is the effect of the generalized emotion, not tied to a particular speaker or persona, in many of the poems? Does it increase the poems' accessibility? Contribute to their didacticism?

3. How does "The Father" dramatize the self-serving nature of the narrator's fatherhood without overtly commenting on it? (Consider the effects of features such as the prominent "I," the sentence structure, the absence of characters' names, the kinds of analogies the narrator makes.) Why does his friends' concern allow him to cry? What sorts of changes does this expression of grief precipitate in him?

Ralph Waldo Emerson (1803–1882)

Contributing Editor: Jean Ferguson Carr

Classroom Issues and Strategies

Given the difficulty students often have with Emerson's style and allusions, it seems very important to address Emerson not as the proponent of a unified philosophy or movement (e.g., Transcendentalism or Romanticism), but as a writer concerned with his audience and his peers, and constructing himself as an American scholar/poet/seer. This might lead to, for example, focusing on what specific definitions or categories Emerson faces (categories such as what is "literary" and what is "poetic," what authorizes a scholar as "learned"). And it leads to paying attention to how Emerson characterizes his audience or reading public, how he addresses their difficulties and expectations, and how he represents his "times." Working from Emerson's journals can be extremely useful in this context; students can see a writer proposing and reflecting and revising his own articulations. Emerson's vocabulary and references can be investigated not simply as a given style but as material being tested, often being critiqued as it is being used. His method of writing can be investigated as a self-reflective experimentation, in which Emerson proposes situations or claims, explores their implications, and often returns to restate or resituate the issue.

It can be particularly useful to have students read some of Emerson's college journals, which show his uncertainty about how to become an "American scholar" or "poet." The journals, like "The American Scholar," show Emerson teaching himself how to read differently from the ways advocated by past cultures and educational institutions. They show him sorting through the conflicting array of resources and texts available to a young man in his circumstances and times.

Students can also situate Emerson in a range of cultural relationships by using Kenneth W. Cameron's fascinating source books that reprint contemporary materials, such as *Emerson Among His Contemporaries* (Hartford: Transcendental, 1967), or *Ralph Waldo Emerson's Reading* (Hartford: Transcendental, 1962), or *Emerson the Essayist* (Raleigh: Thistle, 1945).

Major Themes, Historical Perspectives, Personal Issues

Emerson's concern with proposing the active power of language—both spoken and written—in constructing an emergent culture that will be different from the cultures of Europe is a central interest. His attention to what it means to make something "new," and his concern about the influence of the past, of books and monuments, mark him as an important figure in the production of a "national" literature. Emerson's investigation of reading as creative action, his efforts to examine the authority and effects of religious and educational institutions, help frame discussions about literature and education for subsequent generations. As a member of the Boston cultural and religious elite of the early nineteenth century, Emerson reflects both the immersion in and allegiance to English culture and the struggles of that American generation to become something more than a patronized younger cousin. Emerson's tumultuous personal life—his resignation from the ministry; the deaths of his young wife, son, and brothers; his own ill health—tested his persistence and seemingly unflappable energy and make his advocacy of "practical power" neither an abstract nor a distanced issue.

Significant Form, Style, or Artistic Conventions

Emerson challenges and investigates formal traditions of philosophic and religious writing, insisting on the interpenetration of the ideal and the real, of the spiritual and material. His speculations about self-reliance move between cultural critique and personal experience as he uses his own life as a "book" in which to test his assumptions and proposals. The essays often propose counter-cultural positions, some of which are spoken by imaginary bards or oracles, delivered in the form of fables or extended metaphors. Emerson's essays enact the dramatic exchanges in such arguments, suggesting the authority and limitations of what is spoken in the world as "a notion," as what "practical men" hold, or as what a "bard" might suggest. Emerson's journals show him rethinking the uses of a commonplace book, examining his own past thoughts and reactions as "evidence" of cultural changes and problems. Emerson argues for a "new" mode of poetry, one that emulates the "awful thunder" of the ancient bards rather than the measured lines of cultured verse.

Original Audience

Many of Emerson's essays were initially delivered as lectures, both in Boston and on his lecture tours around the country. His book *Nature*, the volumes of *Essays*, and his poems were reprinted both in Boston and in England. Several of his essays ("Love," "Friendship," "Illusions") were bound in attractive small editions and marketed as "gift books." His poems and excerpts from his essays were often reprinted in literary collections and school anthologies of the nineteenth century. Emerson represents the audiences for his work in challenging ways, often imagining them as sleeping or resistant, as needing to be awakened and encouraged. He discusses their preoccupation with business and labor, with practical politics and economy; their grief over the death of a child. He uses local and natural images familiar to the New Englanders at the same time that he introduces his American audiences to names and references from a wide intellectual range (from Persian poets to sixth-century Welsh bards to Arabic medical texts to contemporary engineering reports). He has been a figure of considerable importance in modern American literary criticism and rhetoric (his discussions about language and speech, in particular), in American philosophy (influencing William James, Dewey, and more recently William Gass), and in discussions about education and literacy.

Comparisons, Contrasts, Connections

Emerson has been particularly significant as a "founding father," a literary figure that younger writers both emulated and had to challenge, that American critics and readers have used to mark the formation of a national literature. He is usually aligned with the group of writers living in or near Concord, Massachusetts, and with the Boston educational and literary elite (e.g., Bronson Alcott, Nathaniel Hawthorne, Margaret Fuller, and Henry David Thoreau). He also is usefully connected with English writers such as Carlyle, Wordsworth, and Arnold. Whitman proclaimed a link with Emerson (and capitalized on Emerson's letter greeting *Leaves of Grass*); Melville proclaimed an opposition to Emerson (and represented him in his satire *The Confidence-Man*). It is useful to consider Emerson's effect on younger writers and to consider how he is used (e.g., by such writers as T. S. Eliot) to represent the authority of the literary establishment and the values of the "past."

The following women writers make intriguing comments about Emerson in their efforts to establish their own positions: Elizabeth Stuart Phelps, Louisa May Alcott, Rebecca Harding Davis, Lucy Larcom (also the delightful mention of reading Emerson in Kate Chopin's *The Awakening*). Many writers "quote" Emersonian positions or claims, both to suggest an alliance and to test Emerson's authority (see, for example, Douglass's concern about "self-reliance" in his *Narrative*, Hawthorne's portrait of the young reformer Holgrave in *The House of Seven Gables* or of the reformers in *The Blithedale Romance*, Davis's challenging portrait of the artist in "Life in the Iron Mills").

Questions for Reading, Discussion, and Writing

1. (a) How does Emerson characterize his age? How does he characterize its relations to the past?
    (b) What does Emerson see as the realm or purpose of art? What notions of art or poetry is he critiquing?

(c) How does Emerson represent himself as a reader? What does he claim as the values and risks of reading? What does he propose as a useful way of reading?

2. (a) Emerson's writings are full of bold claims, of passages that read like self-confident epigrams ("Life only avails, not the having lived"; "Power ceases in the instant of repose"; "What I must do is all that concerns me, not what the people think"; "Travelling is a fool's paradise"). Yet such claims are not as self-evident as they may appear when lifted out of context as quotations. Often they are asserted to be challenged, or tested, or opposed. Often they propose a position that Emerson struggled hard to maintain in his own practice, about which he had considerable doubts or resistance. Select one such claim and discuss what work Emerson had to do to examine its implications and complexities.

(b) Emerson's essays are deliberately provocative—they push, urge, outrage, or jolt readers to react. What kinds of critiques of his age is Emerson attempting? And how? And with what sense of his audience's resistance? How do these function as self-critiques as well?

(c) Test one of Emerson's problematic questions or assertions against the particular practice of Emerson, or of another writer (e.g., Whitman, Hawthorne in *The Blithedale Romance*, Rebecca Harding Davis, Frederick Douglass). Examine how the issue or claim gets questioned or challenged, how it holds up under the pressure of experience. (Some examples of passages to consider: "The world of any moment is the merest appearance"; "The poet turns the world to glass, and shows us all things in their right series and procession"; "Every mind is a new classification.")

Bibliography

Buell, Lawrence. "Ralph Waldo Emerson." *The American Renaissance in New England*. Ed. Joel Myerson. *Dictionary of Literary Biography*. Vol. 1. Detroit: Gale, 1978. 48–60.

Levin, David, ed. *Emerson: Prophecy, Metamorphosis, and Influence*. Papers of the English Institute. New York: Columbia UP, 1975.

Matthiessen, F. O. *American Renaissance: Art and Expression in the Age of Emerson and Whitman*. New York: Oxford UP, 1941.

Myerson, Joel, ed. *Emerson Centenary Essays*. Carbondale: Southern Illinois UP, 1982.

Packer, Barbara. "Uriel's Cloud: Emerson's Rhetoric." *Emerson's Fall.* New York: Continuum, 1982. 1–21.

Porte, Joel, ed. *Emerson: Prospect and Retrospect.* Cambridge, MA: Harvard UP, 1982.

Sealts, Merton M., Jr., and Alfred R. Ferguson, eds. *Emerson's "Nature"—Origin, Growth, Meaning.* 2nd ed. Carbondale: Southern Illinois UP, 1979.

Yoder, Ralph A. "Toward the 'Titmouse Dimension': The Development of Emerson's Poetic Style." *PMLA* 87 (1972): 255–70.

John Greenleaf Whittier (1807–1892)

Contributing Editor: Elaine Sargent Apthorp

Classroom Issues and Strategies

Students may be put off by various features of the poetry, such as the regularity of meter (which can impress the twenty-first-century ear as tedious—generally we don't "hear" ballads well anymore unless they are set to music), conventional phrasing and alliteration, place-names in "Massachusetts to Virginia," and the effect of stereotyping from a clumsy effort to render black dialect in "At Port Royal."

I think we can take clues from such responses and turn the questions around, asking why, in what context, and for what audience such poetry would be successful. Consider reasons why one might want to give his verses such regular meter, such round and musically comfortable phrasing; consider the message of the verses, the political protest the poet is making—and the mass action he is trying to stimulate through his poetry. This could lead to a discussion of topical poetry, the poetry of political agitation/protest, as a genre—and of Whittier's work as a contribution to that tradition.

Some activities that can bring this home to the students include (1) having students commit a few stanzas to memory and give a dramatic recitation of them to the class (when one has fallen out of one's chair shouting defiantly, "No fetters on the Bay State! No slave upon our land!" one knows in one's own body why declamatory poetry is composed as it is), and (2) comparing samples of topical poetry and song by other authors (e.g., poetry of the Harlem Renaissance; the evolutions of "John Brown's Body," "The Battle Hymn of the Republic," and "Solidarity Forever"; union ballads ["The Internationale"] and protest songs of the Great Depression [Woody Guthrie's "Deportees," for example], and contemporary popular songs of protest such as Bruce Springsteen's "Forty-one Shots.")

One can use the same general strategy in discussing other thorny elements in the students' experience of the poetry, that is, asking why a person working from Whittier's assumptions and toward his objectives would choose to compose as he did..What might the effect of all those place-names be on an audience of folk who came from all of those places? How do we respond to a song that mentions our home town? Which praises it for producing us? Which associates us, as representatives of our town, with other towns and their worthy representatives? Assuming that the poet did not mean to convey disrespect to the speakers of the dialect he sought to represent in "At Port Royal," we could ask why he would try to represent the dialect of the enslaved. (Even without recourse to evidence of Whittier's views on African Americans, this is easy enough to demonstrate: summon up some Paul Lawrence Dunbar or Robert Burns or Mark Twain and consider briefly the difficulties writers face in trying to represent on paper the elements of speech that are uniquely oral—inflexion, accent, and so on.)

When you talk in class about these poems as instruments in abolition agitation, students may want to know how blacks responded to Whittier's poetry (Frederick Douglass applauded Whittier as "the slave's poet"), whether Whittier read aloud to audiences, or whether readers committed the poetry to memory and passed it on to others (including nonliterate others) by recitation.

Major Themes, Historical Perspectives, Personal Issues

Naturally one would have to speak about the abolition movement, as these poems were written to express and to further that cause.

Specific to understanding Whittier as an abolitionist, it would be good to point out that the first abolition society was founded by Quakers (a few words about John Woolman and about the Quaker beliefs that led so many of them to labor against slavery—inward light, reverence for all souls, and so on.).

Specific to understanding some of the appeals Whittier makes in "Massachusetts to Virginia," one should remind the student of the Revolutionary and democratic heritage of Massachusetts—the state's role in the Revolutionary War, its founding by religious dissenters, its tradition of the town meeting, and so forth.

Significant Form, Style, or Artistic Conventions

Aside from the issue of topical poetry, it would be appropriate to talk a little bit about the "fireside poetry" that was popular throughout the century in the United States—the characteristics of poetry of sentiment, the kind of audience to which it appealed, and the expectations of that audience. In a way this was the most democratic poetry the nation has produced, in that it was both effectively popular and written expressly to appeal to and communicate with a wide audience. To speak of it as popular rather than elite culture might be useful if one is scrupulous to define these as terms indicating the work's objectives and function rather than its aesthetic "quality" or absolute "value." The artists worked from different assumptions about the function of poetry than those that informed the modernist and postmodern poets of the twentieth century. The audience for poetry in America was as literate as primary education in "blab" schools and drilling in recitation from McGuffey's readers could make it. Good poetry was something you could memorize and recite for pleasure when the book was not in hand, and it was something that stimulated your emotions in the act of reading/reciting, recalling to a harried and overworked people the things they did not see much in their day's labor and the values and feelings an increasingly commercial and competitive society obscured.

Original Audience

It would also be useful to point out that the audience Whittier sought to cultivate were northern whites who had no firsthand experience of conditions in slave states, whose attitude toward blacks was typically shaped more by what they had been told than by personal encounters with black Americans, free or slave. To get such an audience to commit itself to agitation on behalf of American blacks—when that entailed conflict with southern whites and might imperil free white labor in the North (if masses of freed blacks migrated to northern cities to compete for wage-labor)—was a task and a half. He would have to draw his audience to this banner by identifying his cause with that audience's deepest beliefs and values (such as their Christian faith, their concern for their families and for the sanctity of the family bond, their democratic principles and reverence for the rights of man, their Revolutionary heritage, and so on).

Comparisons, Contrasts, Connections

These poems work well in tandem with other topical/protest poetry and songs and/or with another abolition piece. One could compare the effects of Whittier's poetry with the effects of a speech or essay by Frederick Douglass,

Wendell Phillips, Henry Highland Garnet, Theodore Weld, the Grimké sisters, William Lloyd Garrison, and others.

Questions for Reading, Discussion, and Writing

1. I would alert the class in advance to the function these poems were designed to fulfill, that is, to stir northern listeners and readers—many of them white—to outrage on behalf of slaves and to action defying slave-holding states. How do you get an audience to care for people who are not related to them, not outwardly "like" them (skin color, dialect, experiences, and so on), nor a source of profit by association or alliance? How do you persuade strangers to risk life, prosperity, and the cooperation of other powerful Americans whose products they depend upon, to liberate what Southerners defined as property— perhaps violating the Constitution in doing so?

   It might be fruitful to ask that they compare Whittier's topical/protest poetry with the work of a poet like Dickinson—asking that they bracket for the moment questions of which they prefer to read and why, in order to focus instead on the different relationship established between poet and audience. How does Dickinson seem to perceive her calling/duty as a poet? To what extent does Dickinson challenge/disrupt the expectations and the shared assumptions of her culture? For what purpose? Toward what effect? Does Whittier engage in this or not? Why (given his objectives)?

2. This is a very challenging assignment, but it really stimulates an appreciation of Whittier's achievement and is a hands-on introduction to topical poetry—to the effort to employ the aesthetic as a tool for persuasion and political action.

   Have students compose a short poem designed (1) to awaken an audience to concern for an issue or for the plight of a neglected, abused, disenfranchised, or otherwise suffering group, and (2) to stimulate assent in the broadest possible audience—agitating as many as possible while offending as few as possible. Then have the students report on the experience: What problems did they have in composing? How did they opt to solve those problems? Why did they choose the approach and the language they chose? Compare their solutions to Whittier's. At stake would be the quality of the students' analyses of their own creative processes, not so much the instructor's or class's opinion of the poem's effectiveness (though such reader response might form part of the "material" the students would consider as they analyzed and evaluated the task of composing this kind of poetry).

Bibliography

Instructors in search of materials on the poet may start with Karl Keller's bibliographical essay on Whittier studies in *Fifteen American Authors Before 1900* (Ed. Robert Rees. Madison: U of Wisconsin P, 1984), which can direct instructors to studies that explore a variety of questions about the poet's life and work.

Two studies I have found useful for their emphasis on Whittier as abolitionist poet/political activist are (1) Albert Mordell's *Quaker Militant, John Greenleaf Whittier* (Boston: Houghton, 1933) and (2) Edward Charles Wagenknecht's *John Greenleaf Whittier: A Portrait in Paradox* (New York: Oxford UP, 1967). In Wagenknecht I would refer the reader to the chapters "A Side to Face the World With" and "Power and Love."

John Pickard's introduction to Whittier, *John Greenleaf Whittier: An Introduction and Interpretation* (New York: Barnes, 1961) provides a good tight chapter on Whittier's abolition activities (ch. 3).

Sarah Margaret Fuller (1810–1850)

Contributing Editor: Joel Myerson

Classroom Issues and Strategies

Students have problems with Fuller's organization of her material and with nineteenth-century prose style in general. The best exercise I have found is for them to rewrite Fuller's work in their own words. My most successful exercises involve rewriting parts of *Woman in the Nineteenth Century*. Students are amazed at the roles given to women in the nineteenth century and wonder how these women endured what was expected of them.

I ask students to reorganize the argument of Fuller's work as they think best makes its points. This process forces them to grapple with her ideas as they attempt to recast them.

Major Themes, Historical Perspectives, Personal Issues

Transcendentalism, women's rights, critical theory, gender roles, and profession of authorship, are all important themes in Fuller's writing.

Original Audience

I give a background lecture on the legal and social history of women during the period so students can see what existing institutions and laws Fuller was arguing against.

Comparisons, Contrasts, Connections

Woman in the Nineteenth Century: Emerson's "Self-Reliance" and Thoreau's *Walden* for the emphasis on individual thought in the face of a society that demands conformity; Lydia Maria Child's novels for depictions of gender roles; Sarah Grimké's *Letters on the Equality of the Sexes;* Frederick Douglass's *Narrative* for the way in which another outsider speaks to a mass audience.

Questions for Reading, Discussion, and Writing

1. Compare "Self-Reliance" or *Walden* with *Woman in the Nineteenth Century* as regards the responsibilities of the individual within a conformist society.
2. Discuss whether Zenobia in Hawthorne's *The Blithedale Romance* is a portrayal of Fuller, as some critics suggest.
3. Compare or contrast Fuller's ideas on critical theory with Poe's.
4. Compare Fuller's solution to the assignment of gender roles to Kate Chopin's in *The Awakening* or Theodore Dreiser's in *Sister Carrie.*
5. Compare the ways in which Fuller and Douglass attempt to create a voice or authority for themselves in their narratives.

Bibliography

Read Robert N. Hudspeth's chapter on Fuller in *The Transcendentalists: A Review of Research and Criticism.* (Ed. Joel Myerson. New York: MLA, 1984) and see Myerson's bibliographies of writings by and about Fuller; also read in Hudspeth's edition of Fuller's letters.

Henry David Thoreau (1817–1862)

Contributing Editor: Wendell P. Glick

Classroom Issues and Strategies

In my experience, an understanding of Thoreau rarely follows the initial exposure to his writings. The appreciation of the profundity and subtlety of his
thought comes only after serious study, and only a few of the most committed
students are willing to expend the necessary effort. Many, upon first reading
him, will conclude that he was a churlish, negative, antisocial malcontent; or
that he advocated that all of us should reject society and go live in the woods;
or that each person has complete license to do as he/she pleases, without
consideration for the rights of others; or that he is unconscionably doctrinaire.
His difficult, allusive prose, moreover, requires too much effort. All such
judgments are at best simplistic and at worst, wrong.

If an instructor is to succeed with Thoreau, strategies to meet these responses will need to be devised. The best, in my opinion, is to spend the time
explicating to students key sentences and paragraphs in class and responding to
questions. Above all, students must be given a knowledge of the premises of
Romanticism that constitute Thoreau's worldview.

Major Themes, Historical Perspectives, Personal Issues

What are Thoreau's premises, the hypotheses from which he reasons? Even
the most recalcitrant reader should be willing to acknowledge that the question
of most concern to Thoreau is a fundamental one: "How, since life is short and
one's years are numbered, can one live most abundantly?" In other words, what
values should one live by? "Where I Lived, and What I Lived For," from
Walden, was Thoreau's personal answer, but he insists that he has no wish to
prescribe for "strong natures" who have formulated their own value systems.
All persons should live "deliberately," having separated the ends of life from
the means, he argued; and the instructor should aid students to identify those
ends. Accepting without examination current social norms, most persons give no
thought, Thoreau charged, to the question of the values by which they live.

Thoreau's absorption with physical nature will be apparent to all students. Stressing the linkage of all living things, he was one of the first American ecologists. But the instructor should point out that for Thoreau nature was
not an end in itself but a metaphor for ethical and spiritual truth. A walk in
the woods therefore was a search for spiritual enlightenment, not merely a
sensory pleasure. One should look "through" nature, as Thoreau phrased it, not

merely "at" her. Honest seekers would find the same truths. Belief in the existence of a Moral Law had had by Thoreau's day a venerable history. Jefferson, for example, opened the *Declaration of Independence* with an appeal to the "self-evident" truths of the Moral Law. Thoreau's political allegiance was first to the Moral Law, and second to the Constitution, which condoned black slavery.

Significant Form, Style, or Artistic Conventions

Thoreau's angle of vision is patently that of American Romanticism, deeply influenced by the insights of Kant and Coleridge and Carlyle. But Thoreau's style differs markedly from that of Emerson, whose natural expression is through abstraction. Thoreau presents experience through concrete images; he "thinks in images," as Francis Matthiessen once observed, and employs many of the resources of poetry to give strength and compressed energy to his prose. Widely read himself, he is very allusive, particularly to classical literature, and is one of America's most inveterate punsters.

Original Audience

The recognition that Thoreau was one of America's greatest writers, like the recognition of Melville and Poe, was a twentieth-century phenomenon. Emerson recognized Thoreau's importance when the younger man died in 1862, detailing both the dimensions of his genius and his personal eccentricities in an extended obituary. James Russell Lowell, shortly after Thoreau's death, accused him of having been a "skulker" who neglected his social responsibilities. But a few nineteenth-century friends like H. G. O. Blake, William Ellery Channing, and Emerson kept Thoreau's reputation alive until Norman Foerster, F. O. Matthiessen, and an expanded group of later twentieth-century critics became convinced of the qualities of mind and art that have elevated Thoreau into the first rank of American prose writers. *The Recognition of Henry David Thoreau* (Michigan, 1969) traces the vicissitudes of Thoreau's reputation from the publication of his first book, *A Week on the Concord and Merrimack Rivers* (1849), to his present eminence in the literary canon.

Comparisons, Contrasts, Connections

Walden is *sui generis* though there are contemporary writers, for example, Wendell Berry and E. B. White, who have clearly been influenced by this book in both style and thought. N. C. Wyeth, the American painter, confessed to being "an enthusiastic student of Thoreau." Of major twentieth-century writers,

Robert Frost was probably most indebted to Thoreau. Martin Luther King's philosophy of passive resistance to the state is clearly borrowed from Thoreau's "Resistance to Civil Government." Some Thoreau scholars have discerned Thoreau's influence in Yeats, Tolstoy, and Gandhi.

Questions for Reading, Discussion, and Writing

Though Thoreau's life was short, it was fully lived. Conscientiously, he recorded his thoughts in a journal that extends to many volumes over more than twenty years. Consequently, he has something to say about many of the issues that concerned people in his own time and that still concern us today. I have found it profitable to ask students to write papers taking issue with him on some position he has argued, making certain that they fully understand what his position is. Thoreau is an economist, political theorist, philosopher, literary critic, poet, sociologist, naturalist, ecologist, botanist, surveyor, pencil maker, teacher, writer—even jack of manual trades, so that whatever a student's primary interest may be, the probability is that Thoreau had something to say about it.

The issues of bigotry and racism that so concerned Thoreau will always provide topics for student papers.

Bibliography

Research now extant on Thoreau would fill a fair-sized library. Particularly useful in getting a sense of its scope and variety is *The New Thoreau Handbook,* ed. Walter Harding and Michael Meyer (New York, 1980). This should be supplemented with the section on Thoreau in the annually published *American Literary Scholarship* (Duke) and the running bibliography in the *Thoreau Society Quarterly.* Very useful also are the many articles on Thoreau in the annual *Studies in the American Renaissance,* ed. Joel Myerson. Collections of critical essays on Thoreau have been edited by Sherman Paul, John Hicks, Wendell Glick, and Joel Myerson. The standard biography is still *The Days of Henry Thoreau* by Walter Harding (New York, 1965).

Race, Slavery, and the Invention of the "South"

David Walker (1785–1830)

Contributing Editor: Paul Lauter

Classroom Issues and Strategies

The first problem with teaching this author is the militance of Walker's *Appeal.* Some students (especially whites) are troubled by the vehemence with which he attacks whites. *They,* after all, don't defend slavery, so why should *all* whites be condemned? Some (especially students of color) prefer not to get into open discussion where their sympathies with Walker's views will necessarily emerge. Some also don't like his criticism of his fellow blacks. Some of the material included in this selection suggests that Walker viewed at least some whites as potential allies and was concerned not to alienate all white people but rather to win them over to his view.

A second problem is the rhetoric of the *Appeal.* It uses techniques drawn from sermons (note especially the biblical references) and from the political platforms of the day. Most students are unfamiliar with religious or political rhetoric of our time, much less that of 150 years ago.

One way of beginning to address these problems is to ask students whether they think Georgia officials were "correct" in putting a price on Walker's head and in trying to get his *Appeal* banned from the mails. This can be put in the form of "trying" the text, with arguments for prosecution and defense, and so on. Is Walker guilty of sedition, of trying to foment insurrection?

Another approach can be to use a more recent expression of black militance, for example, Stokely Carmichael on black power: "When you talk of black power, you talk of building a movement that will smash everything Western civilization has created." How do students feel about that? Would Walker approve? Sometimes an effective way to begin class discussion is by reading aloud brief *anonymous* student responses.

Major Themes, Historical Perspectives, Personal Issues

It's critical for students to understand the difference between "colonization" schemes for ending slavery (which would gradually send blacks back to Africa) and Walker's commitment to immediate and unconditional emancipation.

If they have read earlier (eighteenth-century) expressions of black protest (e.g., Prince Hall, Olaudah Equiano), it's important and useful to see how Walker departs from these in tone as well as in audience and purpose.

Ultimately, the question is what does Walker want to happen? Blacks to unite, to kill or be killed, if it comes to that?

Significant Form, Style, or Artistic Conventions

To some extent the rhetorical questions, the multiple exclamation points, the quoting of biblical passages, and the heated terminology are features of the period. It can be useful to ask students to rewrite a paragraph using the comparable rhetorical devices of our day. Or, vice versa, to use Walker's style to deal with a current political issue like the level of unemployment and homelessness among blacks.

Original Audience

This is a central issue: the *Appeal* is clearly directed to black people, Walker's "brethren." But since most black slaves were not literate, doesn't that blunt the impact? Or were there ways around that problem?

Why isn't Walker writing to whites since they seem to have a monopoly of power? Or is he, really? Does he seem to be speaking to two differing audiences, even while seeming to address one?

Comparisons, Contrasts, Connections

The Walker text is placed with a number of others concerned with the issue of slavery in order to facilitate such comparisons. While some share the religious rhetoric (e.g., Grimké), others the disdain of colonization (e.g., Garrison), others the appeal to black pride (e.g., Garnet), others the valorization of a black revolutionary (e.g., Higginson), all differently compose such elements. What links (values, style) and separates them?

Questions for Reading, Discussion, and Writing

1. How does Walker's outlook on slavery (on whites, on blacks) differ from X (X being any one of a number of previous writers—Franklin, Jefferson, Equiano, Wheatley)?

    Why would the government of Georgia put a price on Walker's head?

2. I like the idea of asking students to try adapting Walker's style (and that of other writers in this section) to contemporary events. It helps get them "inside" the rhetoric.

William Lloyd Garrison (1805–1879)

Contributing Editor: Paul Lauter

Classroom Issues and Strategies

Students often don't see why Garrison seemed so outrageous to his contemporaries. Of course slavery was wrong; of course it had to be abolished. There seems to be a contradiction between the intensity of his rhetoric and the self-evident rightness (to us) of his views.

He may also strike them as obnoxious—self-righteous, self-important, arrogant. That's a useful reaction, when one gets it. Even more than Thoreau, who students "know" is important, Garrison may be seen (and be presented in history texts) as a fringy radical. He tends to focus questions of effectiveness, or historical significance, and of "radicalism" generally.

It can be useful to ask whether Garrison is an "extremist" and, if so, whether that's good or bad. (Some may recollect Barry Goldwater on the subject of "extremism.") Garrison was committed to nonviolence, but wasn't his rhetoric extremely violent? Are his principles contradicted by his prose?

Particularly effective presentational strategies include asking these questions:

- Would you like to work with/for Garrison? Explain your reasons.
- What would Garrison write about X (an event expressing prejudice/discrimination on campus or in the community)?

Students often ask the following questions:

- Why was Garrison important? *Was* he important?
- Why was he involved in so many reforms?
- Didn't his many commitments dilute his impact?
- Wasn't he just a nay-sayer, opposed to everything conventional?

Major Themes, Historical Perspectives, Personal Issues

Students are not generally familiar with the difference between colonization as an approach to ending slavery and Garrison's doctrine of immediate and unconditional emancipation.

They are even less familiar with the implications of evangelical Christianity, as interpreted by people like Garrison. They have seldom been exposed to concepts like "perfectionism," "nonresistance," and "millennialism." The period introduction sketches such issues.

It can be important to link Garrison's commitment to abolitionism with his commitments to women's rights, temperance, and pacifism. If students can see how these were connected for Garrison and others, they will have a significant hold on antebellum evangelical thinking.

The issue raised by Tolstoy (see headnote) is also significant: What human interactions are, or are not, coercive? How is political activity, like voting, coercive? What alternatives are there? Tolstoy's comments also foreground the issue of human rationality, and they suggest the importance of Garrison's thought and practice to nineteenth-century reformers.

Significant Form, Style, or Artistic Conventions

Students can find it interesting to analyze a typical passage of Garrisonian rhetoric—for example, "I am aware, that many object to the severity of my language. . . . Tell a man whose house is on fire, to give a moderate alarm." One finds in that paragraph the whole range of his rhetorical techniques.

How does he compare with an Old Testament prophet like Jeremiah?

Original Audience

Since the work included in the text is the lead editorial for the *Liberator*, the question of audience (or audiences) is crucial. In the passage noted above, Garrison is arguing *against* a set of unstated positions—those who claim to be "moderates," the apathetic. Indeed, through the editorial, he addresses a whole range of people, most of whom—when one looks closely—he assumes disagree with him. In a way, the editorial can be used to construct the variety of opposed viewpoints, and if students can do that, they may also be able to discuss why Garrison takes his opponents on in just the ways he does.

Comparisons, Contrasts, Connections

The Garrison text is placed with a number of others concerned with the issue of slavery in order to facilitate such comparisons. While some share the passionate rhetoric (e.g., Walker), others the disdain of colonization, others the sense of commitment and the view that people can achieve change (e.g., Grimké), all differently compose such elements. What links (values, style) and separates them?

He is particularly interested in comparison with Grimké and Thoreau on the issue of civil disobedience, which doesn't come to the surface in this editorial, but is implicit in it. In particular, Garrison does focus on the idea that "What I have to do is to see, at any rate, that I do not lend myself to the wrong which I condemn" (to quote Thoreau). His emphasis on satisfying his own conscience is important, but is that a sufficient criterion for action? Is this editorial what Thoreau means by "clogging with your whole weight"?

Questions for Reading, Discussion, and Writing

1. (a) What is Garrison arguing against?
   (b) How has he changed his own position regarding the abolition of slavery?
   (c) Is it sufficient to "satisfy" one's own conscience? What does that mean?
2. (a) One can easily find quotations suggesting that Garrison was an ineffective windbag. How do students respond to such accusations?
   (b) Do you think his approach would be effective today regarding racism in American society?
   (c) Are Garrison's objectives and his style at war with one another?

Bibliography

The four volumes edited by Garrison's children, *William Lloyd Garrison, 1805–1879; the Story of His Life Told by His Children,* provide a rich source not only of Garrison's writing but also of the contexts in which he wrote. They are especially useful for any students interested in doing papers on any aspect of Garrison's life or work.

Lydia Maria Child (1802–1880)

Contributing Editor: Jean Fagan Yellin

Classroom Issues and Strategies

To some, Child's writings appear all too commonplace, not radically different from writings that twenty-first-century readers associate with lady-like nineteenth-century writers. Yet Child is radical, although it is sometimes difficult for today's students to understand this. They often ask about her relationship to the feminist movement.

She wrote about the most controversial issues of her time, and she published her writings in the public sphere—in the political arena which, in her generation, was restricted to men. Today's readers need to read Child carefully to think about what she is saying, not merely to be lulled by how she is saying it. Then they need to think about the tensions between her conventional forms and her highly unconventional content.

Focus on problematic passages. What do you do with the first sentence of her Preface to the *Appeal*? It reads like the beginning of a novel—like a private, emotional appeal to readers, not like an appeal to their intellects and not like a public political appeal. Yet it is public and it is political. How does Child's narrator present herself ? How does she define her audience? What are the consequences of this strategy for today's reader? What do you think were the consequences of this strategy for the reader in Child's day?

Major Themes, Historical Perspectives, Personal Issues

Major themes: Chattel slavery and white racism; women's rights; life in the cities; problems of class in America; social change and "Progress."

Historical and personal issues: Garrisonian abolitionism; the movement for women's rights; the development of the Transcendental critique of American society; women's role in American journalism; the discovery of urban poverty in America; the invention of the Tragic Mulatto in American fiction.

Significant Form, Style, or Artistic Conventions

Child characteristically uses a conventional style and appears to be writing from a posture relegated to women novelists and to commonsense male news analysts. But she is saying things that are quite different from other nineteenth-century American writers of fiction *in re:* attitudes about race and gender, just as she is saying things that are quite different from other nine-teenth-century American journalists *in re:* attitudes about class and race, and slavery and women's rights. Look at her language and her syntax. Then try to locate the places in her text where she does not say the expected, but instead says the unexpected.

Original Audience

With Child, this seems easy because—as her style suggests—she appears to be appealing to the common man and the common woman; she is not writing for a "special" audience of "advanced thinkers."

Comparisons, Contrasts, Connections

Perhaps it would be interesting to contrast Child's newspaper rhetoric with that of Garrison—or even to contrast her *Appeal* with Angelina Grimké's *Appeal* and with Sarah Grimké's *Letters* in terms of language and syntax and logic—and of course in terms of audience. Like Jacobs and the Grimkés, Child is an American woman who condemns chattel slavery and white racism and attempts to assert women's rights. In what ways does she approach these issues differently from Jacobs and the Grimkés? And it would be interesting to read Child in relation to Emerson and Thoreau, who, like Child, were developing critiques of American capitalist culture. In what ways is Child's critique similar to Emerson's? To Thoreau's? In what ways is it different? Furthermore, it would be interesting to read Child's fiction in relation to American mytholo-gists. Irving and Cooper presented types of Dutch America and of the West. What mythic types does Child present?

Questions for Reading, Discussion, and Writing

I try to stress the exceptional: Why was Child's membership in the Boston Atheneum revoked when she published the *Appeal*? What is so terribly outra-geous about this book? Why might she have omitted Letter 33 from the edition of *Letters*? How could this letter have affected the sale of the book? It is hard, today, to see Child as a threat. Why did she appear a threat in her own time? Why doesn't she appear a threat today?

Angelina Grimké (1805–1879)
Sarah Moore Grimké (1792–1873)

Contributing Editor: Jean Fagan Yellin

Classroom Issues and Strategies

Angelina Grimké's *Appeal to the Christian Women of the South* is filled with biblical quotations and allusions; it is written as an evangelical appeal, as the appeal of a Christian woman to other Christian women to act to end chattel slavery. Not only is the language that of evangelical abolitionism, but the logic is as tightly constructed as a Christian sermon. In short, it is difficult to read. In like manner, the language in Sarah M. Grimké's *Letters on the Equality* is Latinate, stiff, and formal. Her language, too, makes slow going for the modern reader.

Try teaching Angelina Grimké's *Appeal to the Christian Women of the South* as a religious argument. The informing notion here is that slavery is sin, and that immediate abolition of slavery means immediate abolition of sin, perhaps immediate salvation. Grimké's tactic is to legitimize—using biblical references—the unprecedented involvement of American women in the public controversy over chattel slavery. She is arguing that slavery is sin and must be ended immediately; and she is arguing that women not only can end it but that they are duty-bound as Christians to do so.

Read Angelina Grimké's *Letters to Catharine Beecher* as a completely different version of the same argument. Where *Appeal* was couched in religious rhetoric and theological argument, *Letters* is written from a political perspective. It is useful to compare/contrast these, to see Grimké moving, both intellectually and formally, toward a secular stance and toward a straightforward assertion of women's political rights.

Consider the following approach with Sarah Grimké's *Letters on the Equality of the Sexes and the Condition of Woman, Addressed to Mary S. Parker, President of the Boston Female Anti-Slavery Society:* Help students discover that the title suggests the letter's central ideas, first, concerning the equality of the sexes, which, Grimké argues, was created by God, and second, concerning the condition of woman, which, she argues, is oppressive and which was imposed not by God but by man. The full title concludes with the phrase *Addressed to Mary S. Parker, President of the Boston Female Anti-Slavery Society.* This points toward Grimké's suggestion that the way to rectify the current sinful situation is by women uniting, organizing, and acting, as in the Boston FASS under the leadership of Parker. The title spells out the argument of the *Letters;* it is basically a theological argument for women's rights.

Major Themes, Historical Perspectives, Personal Issues

In a letter she had impulsively written to the abolitionist William Lloyd Garrison, Angelina Grimké had aligned herself with the abolitionists. Garrison published the letter without her consent, and she was condemned by her meeting (she had become a Quaker [Orthodox]) and even by her sister, her main emotional support. She stuck by her guns. However, although she refused to recant, she was for a time unable to decide what action she should next take. Writing the *Appeal to the Christian Women of the South* was the first public abolitionist document that Angelina Grimké wrote *as* a public document, to be printed with her name on it. Here she commits herself, as a Southern woman of the slave-holding class, to abolitionism—and to an investigation of women's activism in the anti-slavery cause.

A. E. Grimké wrote the *Letters to Catharine Beecher* for the weekly press during the summer of 1837, while she was traveling and lecturing as an "agent" of the American Anti-Slavery Society. She wrote them to answer Catharine Beecher's attack on her lecturing that had been published as *An Essay on Slavery and Abolitionism, with Reference to the Duty of American Females, Addressed to A. E. Grimké.* Beecher, a leading educator, developed the notion of the moral superiority of females and, asserting the importance of the home, argued that women should oppose slavery within the domestic circle but should not enter the public political sphere—as Angelina Grimké was doing. In her *Letters*, Angelina Grimké defends her almost unprecedented behavior by arguing for women's political rights. The *Letters* should also be read in relation to the abolitionists' petitions—to local, state, and national legislative bodies—to end slavery and to outlaw various racist practices. These petitions were circulated by men and, as Grimké urges here, by women as well. Historians have traced the later petition campaigns of the feminists to these anti-slavery petition campaigns.

In *Letters*, Sarah Grimké raises a whole range of feminist issues—the value of housework, wage differentials between men and women, women's education, fashion, and the demand that women be allowed to preach. (She was bitter that she had not been permitted to do so.) Furthermore, she discusses the special oppression of black women and of women held in slavery.

Significant Form, Style, or Artistic Conventions

Angelina Grimké's *Letters* should be read and contrasted with her *Appeal*, then with other writings by nineteenth-century feminists, both black and white.

Similarly, Sarah Grimké's *Letters* should be read and contrasted with pre-1848 feminists like Margaret Fuller, then with Stanton et al. This text marks a beginning. American feminist discourse emerges from this root.

Original Audience

Angelina Grimké's *Appeal*: Audience is stated as the Christian women of the South; by this Grimké means the free white women—many of them slaveholders, as she herself had been—who profess Christianity. It is worthwhile examining the ways in which she defines these women, and exploring the similarities and differences between her approach to them and the patriarchal definition of true womanhood generally endorsed at the time. The patriarchy was projecting "true womanhood" as piety, purity, domesticity, and obedience. Angelina Grimké urges her readers to break the law if the law is immoral—to be obedient not to fathers, husbands, and human laws, but to a Higher Law that condemns slavery. And she urges them to act not only within the "domestic sphere" allocated to women but also within the "public sphere" that was exclusively male territory.

Angelina Grimké's *Letters:* Written directly to Catharine Beecher, these were published weekly in the abolitionist press, then compiled into a pamphlet that became an abolitionist staple and stands as an early expression of the notions that would inform the feminist movement in 1848.

Sarah Grimké's *Letters on the Equality*, like Angelina's *Letters to Catharine Beecher*, were published in the weekly press, then collected and published as a pamphlet.

Comparisons, Contrasts, Connections

Compare Angelina Grimké's *Appeal* with Lydia Maria Child's *Appeal in Favor of that Class of Americans Called Africans*. Compare both with African-American anti-slavery writings by Walker, Garnet, Truth, Harper, Jacobs, Douglass, and Brown. As suggested above, Angelina Grimké's *Appeal* and her *Letters to Catharine Beecher* present an interesting comparison. Both might be read in connection with the writings on women by Fuller, Child, Stanton, and Fern, as well as in connection with the responses to chattel slavery by white women like the Southerner Chesnut and Northerners like Child and Stowe, as well as by African-American women like Truth, Jacobs, and Harper.

Sarah Grimké's *Letters* should be read in relation to the writings of other nineteenth-century feminists like Stanton and in relation to anti-feminist polemics, as well as in relation to depictions of women in nineteenth-century literature by writers such as Hawthorne, Stowe, Cary, and Stoddard.

Questions for Reading, Discussion, and Writing

Direct students' attention to the epigraph to Angelina Grimké's *Appeal*. Why Queen Esther? In what ways do Grimké's *Letters* differ from her *Appeal*? How is the argument different? How is the style different? What are the consequences of these differences? In what ways do Sarah Grimké's *Letters* differ from her sister's writings? Why did the later feminists designate Sarah Grimké's *Letters on the Equality* an important precursor?

Henry Highland Garnet (1815–1882)

Contributing Editor: Allison Heisch

Classroom Issues and Strategies

Ideas that seem radical in one era often become common sense in another and thus may appear obvious to the point of being uninteresting. Furthermore, out of its historical context, Garnet's "Address to the Slaves of the United States" may be hard for students to distinguish from other, more moderate abolitionist appeals.

Garnet's diction is primarily that of a highly literate nineteenth-century black man who has had a white education in theology. Students will understand what he's saying, but unless they can *hear* his voice, they'll have trouble feeling what he means.

To teach Garnet effectively, his work should be presented in the context of the wider (and, of course, two-sided) debate on abolition. Second, it's important to pay attention to the form of this address and to its actual audience: Garnet is speaking before the National Negro Convention (1843). Is he speaking to that audience, or is he trying to communicate with American slaves? The former, obviously. Ideally, some of this should be read aloud.

Despite his radicalism, Garnet fits comfortably into a tradition of "learned" nineteenth-century religious/political orators. As such, Garnet is a fine representative of the abolitionists who made the argument against slavery in part by demonstrating their intellectual equality with whites. But there is another strain of American abolitionists—perhaps best represented by Sojourner Truth—who made the same argument on personal and emotional grounds, and whose appeal belongs to another great American tradition, one that is in some sense almost anti-intellectual in its emphasis on the value of common sense and folk wisdom. Particularly since those two traditions are alive and well in contemporary America, it is useful to place them side by side.

Major Themes, Historical Perspectives, Personal Issues

It may be useful to point out that Garnet's appeal failed (by a single vote) to be adopted by the Convention. Why might this have happened? Garnet's speech is steeped in Christianity, but he seems to advocate violence in the name of Christianity. When is the use of force legitimate? Useful? How is his position different from those taken by contemporaries such as Frederick Douglass? Garnet's audience is implicitly exclusively male. How can one be so opposed to slavery and yet so unconcerned about women's rights?

Significant Form, Style, or Artistic Conventions

Although this speech was eventually printed (1865), it was obviously written for oral delivery. Nevertheless, Garnet's pretext is that he is writing a letter; could his pretended audience of slaves have actually received such a letter? Certainly not. What is the rhetorical purpose of pretending to address one audience while actually addressing another? Could Garnet's "Address" be regarded as a sermon? If so, can a sermon also be a call to arms? It is useful to approach the "Address" as a piece of argumentation, to see how Garnet makes his case, and to show how it builds itself through repetition (e.g., the repeated address to "Brethren") and through the chronological deployment of names of famous men and famous deeds to his conclusion, which is a call for armed resistance.

Original Audience

The simplest way to evoke a discussion of audience is to ask a set of fairly obvious questions: What is the stated audience? What is the "real" audience? How large an audience would that have been in the 1840s?

Comparisons, Contrasts, Connections

First, and most obvious, Garnet can be contrasted with Martin Luther King Jr. to discuss theories of resistance and passive resistance. (Consider especially the "Letter from Birmingham Jail" with its "real" and "implied" audiences.) It is also useful to have students read the "Address" against Lincoln's Gettysburg Address or the Second Inaugural (to compare form and content). Garnet may be read against David Walker (to show similarities and differences, the evolution of the radical position) and against Frederick Douglass (to discuss styles of persuasion).

Questions for Reading, Discussion, and Writing

Questions *before* reading: Who or what is Garnet's real audience? Why does he pretend to be writing a letter?

Bibliography

Bremer, William. "Henry Highland Garnet." *Blacks in White America Before 1865*. Ed. Robert Haynes. New York: n.p., 1972.

Quarles, Benjamin. *Black Abolitionists*. New York: n.p., 1969.

Schor, Joel. *Henry Highland Garnet*. Westport, CT: Greenwood, 1977.

Frederick Douglass (1818–1895)

Contributing Editor: James A. Miller

Classroom Issues and Strategies

Readers tend to read Douglass's *Narrative* sympathetically but casually. Although they readily grasp Douglass's critiques of slavery in broad and general terms, they tend to be less attentive to *how* the narrative is structured, to Douglass's choices of language and incident, and to the ideological/aesthetic underpinnings of these choices.

I find it useful to locate Douglass historically within the context of his relationship to the Garrisonian wing of the abolitionist movement. This requires students to pay more attention to the prefatory material by Wendell Phillips and William Lloyd Garrison then they normally do. I also try to focus their attention on the rhetoric and narrative point of view that Douglass establishes in the first chapter of his *Narrative.*

Questions students often ask include the following:

- How does Frederick Douglass escape?
- How does he learn to write so well?
- Is Douglass "typical" or "exceptional"?
- Why does Anna Murray appear so suddenly at the end of the narrative?
- Where is she earlier?
- What happens to Douglass after the narrative ends?

Major Themes, Historical Perspectives, Personal Issues

Paying careful attention to the unfolding of Douglass's consciousness within the context of slavery draws attention to the intersection of personal and historical issues in the *Narrative*. The movement from slavery to "freedom" is obviously important, as is the particular means by which Douglass achieves his freedom—the role literacy plays in his struggle.

Significant Form, Style, or Artistic Conventions

Douglass's command of the formal principles of oratory and rhetoric should be emphasized, as well as his use of the conventions of both sentimental literature and the rhetoric and symbolism of evangelical Christianity. In short, it is important to note how Douglass appropriated the dominant literary styles of mid-nineteenth-century American life to articulate his claims on behalf of African-American humanity.

Original Audience

Through a careful examination of Douglass's rhetorical appeals, we try to imagine and re-create Douglass's mid-nineteenth-century audience. We try to contrast that audience to the various audiences, black and white, that constitute the reading public in the late twentieth century.

Comparisons, Contrasts, Connections

Jacobs's *Incidents in the Life of a Slave Girl*—for a contrasting view of slavery through a woman's eyes and experiences. Thoreau's *Walden*—for a view from one of Douglass's contemporaries. Franklin's *Autobiography*—for another prototype of American autobiography.

Questions for Reading, Discussion, and Writing

1. What is the function of the prefatory material? Why does Douglass add an appendix?
2. What is the relationship of literacy to Douglass's quest for freedom? Of violence?
3. What idea of God animates Douglass?
4. How does Douglass attempt to engage the sympathies of his audience?

Bibliography

Gibson, Donald B. "Christianity and Individualism: (Re-)Creation in Frederick Douglass's Representation of Self." *African American Review* 26 (1992): 591–603.

Kibbey, Ann. "Language in Slavery: Frederick Douglass's *Narrative.*" *Prospects: An Annual of American Cultural Studies* 8 (1985): 163–82.

O'Meally, Robert G. "Frederick Douglass's 1845 *Narrative:* The Text Was Meant to Be Preached." *Afro-American Literature: The Reconstruction of Instruction.* Ed. Robert B. Stepto and Dexter Fisher. New York: MLA, 1978.

Sekora, John. "Comprehending Slavery: Language and Personal History in Douglass' Narrative of 1845." *College Language Association Journal* 29 (1985): 157–70.

Smith, Stephanie A. "Heart Attack: Frederick Douglass's Strategic Sentimentality." *Criticism* 34 (1992): 193–216.

Stepto, Robert B. "Narration, Authentication and Authorial Control in Frederick Douglass's *Narrative* of 1845." *Afro-American Literature: The Reconstruction of Instruction.* Ed. Robert B. Stepto and Dexter Fisher. New York: MLA, 1978.

Stone, Albert C. "Identity and Art in Frederick Douglass' *Narrative.*" *College Language Association Journal* 17 (1973): 192–213.

Sundquist, Eric J. "Slavery, Revolution and the American Renaissance." *The American Renaissance Reconsidered.* Ed. W. B. Michaels and Donald E. Pease. Baltimore: Johns Hopkins UP, 1985.

Nancy Gardner Prince (1799–1859?)

Contributing Editor: Cheryl J. Fish

Classroom Issues and Strategies

Students and instructors may find Nancy Prince's writing style somewhat cryptic and hard to follow, and they may find it frustrating that she leaves out seemingly vital information or skips ahead without transitions. Thinking about the ways in which Prince's style itself suggests a discourse of mobility full of movement and sharp juxtapositions might be a fruitful way to approach the text. It is also important to place Prince's narrative within the context of the influence of the African-American oral tradition, the black church, and scripture and to realize that her formal education was most probably limited. Instructors might guide students in groups to examine the rhetorical strategies Prince employs to gain authority and critique various policies in the United States and abroad and to consider how she represents her encounters with various native Jamaicans, missionaries, teachers, Maroons, and colonial administrators. What was her stated purpose in traveling to Jamaica, and what else is implied? How does she handle the danger and contradictions she finds?

Major Themes, Historical Perspectives, Personal Issues

In historicizing Nancy Prince's narratives, it is important to examine how they document a mobility away from home and traditional domestic obligations. Yet Prince's travels were not undertaken solely for the sake of adventure or education, like the popular "Grand Tour" of the era. Rather, Prince mentions her desire to seek a "field of usefulness" as a worker in benevolent causes at home and abroad, where she would take care of others and engage in practical communal projects. However, her presence in the context of emancipation and political upheaval meant she had to carefully negotiate a balance between the expectations evoked by her place outside a traditional "woman's sphere" with the anger and passion of her corrective vision.

In terms of the themes and personal issues evoked in Prince's narrative, it would be fruitful to compare and contrast her travels with those of the African Olaudah Equiano, as well as with the slave narratives written by Frederick Douglass and Harriet Jacobs, to see the important differences in writing by free blacks and by former slaves. In terms of the gender and racial issues raised by Prince's narrative, the Grimké sisters and Sojourner Truth, contemporaries of Prince who received more public attention than she, provide important contextual grounding.

Significantly, travel enabled Prince to make comparisons and interventions across national boundaries, using the example of the freed Jamaicans and their industriousness to argue for the end of slavery in the United States and to point to the corruption of colonial and post-colonial policies. While Prince was in Jamaica in 1841, a number of the old Maroons (fugitives who had hidden in the hills from British and Spanish masters), who had been banished from the island and removed in 1795 to Nova Scotia and then to Sierra Leone, returned. Prince's discussion of the Maroons raises the question of who has the right to citizenship and rule, which connects to her black readers' anxieties about their status as American citizens.

Original Audience

Nancy Prince was a member of the Garrisonian-influenced Boston Female Anti-Slavery Society, and she sold copies of her works at the offices of the *Liberator* and at the New England Anti-Slavery Convention. There were also small notices in the pages of Garrison's paper advertising her services as a tailoress and publicizing a talk she was to give based on her travels to Russia. Her primary audience would have been Northern black and white abolitionists and their friends, and those interested in the lives of former slaves after emancipation in Jamaica. Prince was also a member of Boston's First African Baptist Church under the leadership of Thomas Paul. Prince was writing to help earn a living as she struggled financially and refused help from charity; buying her book, published in three slightly different editions, would have been a way for friends and brethren to show their support.

Questions for Reading, Discussion, and Writing

1. How does Nancy Prince's narrative engage with the popular African-American theme of "uplifting" or helping the race? How does her desire to travel and see the results of emancipation for herself push it to another dimension?

2. How does Prince represent herself in relation to those she meets in Jamaica? Give examples from the text to compare and contrast her various encounters and responses to those she meets in Jamaica.

3. In what condition does Nancy Prince find the freed slaves? What was most surprising for Prince in what she discovers, and what was most surprising for you? How do you think her narrative was received back in New England?

4. Why are the Maroons especially intriguing to Prince? How is their historical situation of relevance to the issues and questions raised by Prince's narrative and other writing by African Americans in the antebellum period?

5. Nancy Prince narrates a harrowing journey home—what themes reoccur while she is in transit, and what is their significance? How do her religious convictions enable her to respond to attacks and dangers posed by being a free black whose boat docks in Southern states, where she could be beaten or enslaved? What kind of help does Prince seek during her travels?

6. Write an account of a journey you have taken to a foreign country. What aspects of that culture and its people were most striking, delightful, or threatening to you? Did you ever feel at risk personally? How would you write about that risk? Discuss how Prince's narrative can be instructive in

thinking about a travelogue as a political document or as a narrative of struggle and resistance for a particular readership.

Bibliography

Fish, Cheryl J. "Journeys and Warnings: Nancy Prince's Resistant Truth Telling in New England, Russia, and Jamaica." *Black and White Women's Travel Narratives: Antebellum Explorations.* Gainesville: UP of Florida, 2004.

Gunning, Sandra. "Nancy Prince and the Politics of Mobility, Home and Diasporic (Mis)Identification." *American Quarterly* 53.1 (2001): 32–69.

Peterson, Carla L. *Doers of the Word: African-American Women Speakers and Writers in the North.* New York: Oxford UP, 1995. Contains a chapter on Nancy Prince.

Caroline Lee Hentz (1800–1856)

Contributing Editor: Anne Jones

Classroom Issues and Strategies

Most students will find it easy to dismiss the arguments, the rhetoric, and the writing in this tendentious chapter. What can make things initially more interesting is a careful analysis of the tactics Hentz is so obviously—or maybe not so obviously—using on her readers. What's the point of the setting, in a small village, on a Saturday night? What is she appealing to with her description of the landlord as an "Indian" looking man? What about those "delineators of the sable character"? The dying young woman's function can't be missed, but what about the Northern gentleman who accompanies Moreland as he carries her bundle?

Analysis of certain passages invites at least some debate, opening the issues beyond the question of slavery and encouraging students to make argumentative distinctions. What about Grimby's self-contradictory claims (a free country where all must conform, a loss of distinction that means loss of difference); does Hentz have a viable point here? And what about the domestic care versus public welfare point? Are these issues necessarily tied to a defense of slavery?

It could be useful, too, to have students rewrite the story from the point of view of another character. Is Albert having private thoughts of a different sort? Could a sentence like "I wish I may find everybody as well off as I am" be interpreted as double-voiced discourse? What is motivating the landlord? How does the young woman feel about the men's charity? What do such imaginative efforts show us when we look again at Hentz's point of view strategies?

These discussions raise the question of how we can understand— instead of demonize—people who actively supported slavery, who unashamedly proclaimed black racial inferiority, and who believed, like Moreland, in a clearly hierarchical, authoritarian society. Or *should* we try to understand such positions? Students may discover in thinking about Hentz that their opposition to slavery and racism has never really been thought through. This chapter will give them a chance to do that.

I might start with Bertram Wyatt-Brown's words from *Southern Honor*: "It is hard for us to believe that Southerners ever meant what they said of themselves. How could they so glibly reconcile slaveholding with pretensions to virtue? . . . [Yet] apart from a few lonely dissenters, Southern whites believed (*as most people do* [emphasis added]) that they conducted their lives by the highest ethical standards" (3). What standards does Hentz invoke? Which do you accept? Which do you reject, and why?

Major Themes, Historical Perspectives, Personal Issues

These are fairly self-evident, I think, particularly when read in the context of abolitionist writing in the anthology. The chapter may be unsettling to students who come to proslavery writing with moral certainties in place. Reading proslavery arguments together with abolitionist arguments, however, can help them clarify their own positions not only on slavery but also on how to think about the problems of poverty and racism that, unlike slavery, remain unresolved today. I have found students to be very responsive to the early chapters in Lillian Smith's *Killers of the Dream* (New York: 1962), where she eloquently dramatizes the complexity and personal pain of ideological conflict for children and young people, in this case white Southern girls who are torn between family and personal values. Faulkner's "Barn Burning" can be read in similar ways.

Significant Form, Style, or Artistic Conventions

Clearly Hentz is working within conventions—clichés—of writing that she feels will work rhetorically to persuade and soften her readers. Students might find it fun to identify what they see as clichéd language, predictable plotting (what do you suppose will happen to that not-dead twenty-year-old whose memory preoccupies Moreland?). Could there be canny reasons for such a lack of originality?

Original Audience

Try asking students who they think the intended audience is. They will probably guess white Northerners. How did they know this? This will take them back to the experience of reading the text to see how the words worked on them. Note, for instance, that Hentz carefully explains "Mars" and the relationship of insult to class (in Southern honor, one could not be insulted by—hence one did not respond to—an inferior). These details suggest she is not preaching to the choir. Are there audiences she would not address? If not, why not? Try asking students to rewrite this for a contemporary audience, with contemporary cultural issues in mind. Or ask them to debate the issue of slavery orally (pro and con). If they resist, ask them to discuss their resistance. If they do not resist, ask them to discuss their lack of resistance.

Comparisons, Contrasts, Connections

First compare Fitzhugh's very male-focused defense of slavery with Caroline Hentz's. Is hers markedly "womanly"? From comparing these texts, what can we learn about the nineteenth-century cultural gender differences that each author assumes and exploits? Is Fitzhugh turning for support to nineteenth-century women's culture when he argues for the superiority of "domestic" slavery over slavery to capital? Is Hentz doing the same when she compares the public institutions of the North with domestic ones in the South? Next compare these writers' arguments with abolitionists' arguments. How do abolitionists deal with Southern claims about the "hireling's" misery and the slave's relative comfort? About the variety of treatment slaves received? About the emotional relations with slaves? Slave narratives make an excellent comparison also; see Harriet Jacobs, in particular.

George Fitzhugh (1804–1881)

Contributing Editor: Anne Jones

Classroom Issues and Strategies

The most pressing issue will most likely be simple incredulity on the part of students. Not only does Fitzhugh defend a system (slavery) whose evil is a modern given, but he believes abolition "will soon be considered a mad infatuation," England will return to slave-holding, and Southern thought will lead the Western world.

An interesting starting point then could be the question of tone. Is this guy serious? How can we be sure that sentences like "This, of itself, would put the South at the lead of modern civilization" or "How fortunate for the South that she has this inferior race" are not dripping with sarcasm? Is irony contextual? In what context do these seem ironic statements?

Of course, they are perfectly "straight" in the context of Fitzhugh's essay and audience, which raises the more profound question for the class to deliberate: How can we understand (if, indeed, we should try to understand) and not criticize people who supported slavery and who adhered to the notion of black racial inferiority? Fitzhugh's essay from *Southern Thought* may help students discover that their opposition to slavery and racism has never really been understood.

Start with Bertram Wyatt-Brown's words from *Southern Honor:* "It is hard for us to believe that Southerners ever meant what they said of themselves. How could they so glibly reconcile slave-holding with pretensions to virtue? . . . [Yet] apart from a few lonely dissenters, Southern whites believed (*as most people do* [emphasis added]) that they conducted their lives by the highest ethical standards" (3). What standards does Fitzhugh invoke? Which do you accept? Which do you reject, and why?

Major Themes, Historical Perspectives, Personal Issues

The vexed relation to socialism evident in Fitzhugh's text might come as a surprise. A connection between socialism and Southern thought is evident again in the modern period, when the Southern Agrarians find themselves sympathetic, like Fitzhugh, to this "other" critique of industrial capitalism and bourgeois individualism. How does Fitzhugh separate his views from those of socialists?

Fitzhugh clearly has an ideological project in mind here; he even locates the most practical venues for indoctrinating the South (and next, the world!) in "Southern Thought." What do students think about such a project? How different is it from contemporary advertising and marketing strategies? More advanced students might compare it to Gramsci's notions of counter-hegemonic discourse to be developed by organic intellectuals.

Fitzhugh's racism, which he separates so carefully from his defense of slavery as an institution, is of course egregious. It should, however, be understood (which is not to say condoned) in the context of widespread contemporary beliefs in scientific racism. See, for instance, "Race" by Kwame Appiah in Frank Lentricchia and Thomas McLaughlin, eds., *Critical Terms for Literary Study* (1990). Can we separate his argument for enslavement of blacks from his argument for black difference? What are some modern arguments for black difference and separation? How do they differ from Fitzhugh's? Are they legitimate? Why or why not?

Such questions may be unsettling to students who come to proslavery writing with moral certainties in place. As noted in the previous section, reading proslavery arguments together with abolitionist arguments, however, can help them clarify their own positions not only on slavery but also on how to think about the problems of poverty and racism that, unlike slavery, remain unresolved today. I have found students to be very responsive to the early chapters in Lillian Smith's *Killers of the Dream* (1962), where she eloquently dramatizes the complexity and personal pain of ideological conflict for children and young people, in this case white Southern girls who are torn between family and personal values. Faulkner's "Barn Burning" can be read in similar ways.

Significant Form, Style, or Artistic Conventions

Fitzhugh's allusions (e.g., to abolitionists by name and to European history) may be obscure. Try assigning one name/reference to each student for a collective information pool.

Original Audience

Try asking students who they think the intended audience is. They will probably guess other literate white Southerners, and they will be right (like much proslavery argument, it appeared in a Southern publication). But how did they know this? This will take them back to the experience of reading the text to see how the words worked on them. How might Fitzhugh have addressed another audience—the British middle class, free/enslaved Southern blacks, for instance? Are there audiences he would not address? If not, why not? Try asking students to rewrite this for a contemporary audience or to debate the issue of slavery orally (pro and con). If they resist, ask them to discuss their resistance. If they do not resist, ask them to discuss their lack of resistance.

Comparisons, Contrasts, Connections

First, compare Fitzhugh's very male-focused defense with Caroline Hentz's defense of slavery. Is hers markedly "womanly"? From comparing these texts, what can we learn about the nineteenth-century cultural gender differences that each author assumes and exploits? Is Fitzhugh turning for support to nineteenth-century women's culture when he argues for the superiority of "domestic" slavery over slavery to capital? Next, compare these writers' arguments with abolitionists' arguments. A particularly interesting comparison would be with Angelina Grimké, who in "Appeal to the Christian Women of the South" wrote to a similar audience and thus constructed her rhetoric based on presumably similar understandings of what might work with Southerners. How do abolitionists deal with Southern claims about "slavery to capital"?

Frances Ellen Watkins Harper (1825–1911)

Contributing Editor: Elizabeth Ammons

See later entry in "Critical Visions of Postbellum America."

Thomas Wentworth Higginson (1823–1911)

Contributing Editor: Paul Lauter

Classroom Issues and Strategies

It's almost impossible for students to connect the apostle of Nat Turner with the "mentor" of Emily Dickinson; a Christian minister; a colonel of a black Civil War regiment; an active feminist; an important nineteenth-century editor. All these roles were filled by Thomas Wentworth Higginson, yet only the first two aspects are represented by the texts. So the real issue is whether or not he is significant. And if he is, why?

If students know Higginson at all, they will probably know him as the man who, in putting Dickinson poems into print, disgracefully smoothed them out, changing her words, her punctuation, even her meanings. Why read such a fellow? Why in the world did Dickinson write to him?

At the same time, he doesn't smooth out Nat Turner. Yet, like any historical writer, he "constructs" Nat Turner in a particular way. The nature of that "construction" is not easy to define.

Sometimes it's useful to begin from an example of what Higginson (and Todd) did to a Dickinson poem. Their choices say something about Dickinson, about nineteenth-century sensibilities, and—with Higginson's and Dickinson's letters—about their unique relationship. The revised Dickinson also raises the question of why one might want to include Higginson in this anthology.

At one point in the 1960s, students had heard about William Styron's "Confessions" of Nat Turner. It may still be useful to bring up some of the summary accounts in magazines like *Newsweek* of Styron's version and the controversy that surrounded it. Higginson's picture is, of course, quite different, yet both can be understood, among other ways, as serving certain historical needs in their audience.

Major Themes, Historical Perspectives, Personal Issues

Is there any unity at all to Higginson's life as minister, military man, activist, writer, editor, mentor? More than most, Higginson's extraordinarily varied career expresses a nineteenth-century commitment by a well-to-do white man to racial, gender, and class equality—in politics, in social relations, and in culture. His sensitivity—and his limitations—say a great deal about the power as well as the constraints upon that kind of progressive politics, and about the forms of culture it inspired. To see why Dickinson sought him out and yet would not be limited by him reveals a great deal about the cultural revolution her writing represents, as well as about the strengths of what Higginson can be taken to illustrate.

The essay on Nat Turner also is very useful in relation to the other abolitionist writers, especially Walker and Garrison. Though Nat Turner's rebellion came after Walker's *Appeal* and the beginning of *The Liberator*, there are ways in which it was taken, literally and symbolically (as Higginson implies), as an outgrowth of such writings.

Significant Form, Style, or Artistic Conventions

Higginson commands a fine and varied prose style, and it can be very rewarding for students to examine certain of his paragraphs—like the initial one on the files of the Richmond newspaper, the early one on the participants in the rebellion, the one on the lives of slaves not being "individualized," and the final one of the essay.

Original Audience

The essay and the letter can be usefully compared on this ground. They are not very distant in time yet quite distinctly conceived because of audience.

The essay was written before the Civil War began, yet was published only after. What does that say about the limits of "acceptable" discourse? What does the essay imply about the readership of the *Atlantic*, in which it was published?

Comparisons, Contrasts, Connections

Higginson's construction of Nat Turner can usefully be compared with Phillips's portrait of Toussaint, with Frederick Douglass's self-portrait (as well as with his picture of Madison Washington), and with the black characters of Melville's "Benito Cereno." All these texts involve the issue of the "heroic slave"—what constitutes, "heroism" in a slave. Underlying that is the issue of what constitutes "humanity," since for many Americans, black people were not fully human.

Working with Cultural Objects

Charles Burnett's documentary, *Nat Turner: A Troublesome Property*, traces how the meaning of Nat Turner and his rebellion has been contested from Higginson's time to today. Information about the film is available at <http://www.pbs.org/independentlens/natturner/index.html> and at California Newsreel, <http://www.newsreel.org>.

Questions for Reading, Discussion, and Writing

How does Higginson account for Nat Turner's motivations and actions?

Why did the essay on Nat Turner remain unpublished until after the Civil War began?

Why, given Higginson's letter about Emily Dickinson and her letters to him, did she wish to write to him?

What does Higginson's relationship to Dickinson (and the way he helped publish her poems) tell you about the kind of culture he represents?

What are the predominant features in Higginson's portrait of Nat Turner? What are the alternative views of Nat Turner between which he is choosing? Is Higginson's Nat Turner a hero or a terrorist?

Bibliography

Henry Irving Tragle's *The Southampton Slave Revolt of 1831* and Herbert Aptheker's *Nat Turner's Slave Rebellion* contain useful brief materials on Nat Turner, including the text of his "confessions," as compiled by Thomas Gray. The view of Nat Turner in that and other texts usefully contrasts with Higginson's.

If one is interested in the problem of how writers construct historical accounts (an issue quite relevant to Melville's "Benito Cereno," for example), such materials provide a useful case in point.

Harriet Ann Jacobs (1813–1897)

Contributing Editor: Jean Fagan Yellin

Classroom Issues and Strategies

Primary problems that arise in teaching Jacobs include:

1. The question of authorship: Could a woman who had been held in slavery have written such a literary book?
2. The question of her expressions of conflict about her sexual experiences.
3. The question of veracity: How could she have stayed hidden all those years?

To address these questions, point to Jacobs's life: she learned to read at six years. She spent her seven years in hiding sewing and reading (doubtless reading the Bible, but also reading some newspapers, according to her account). And in 1849, at Rochester, she spent ten months working in the Anti-Slavery Reading Room, reading her way through the abolitionists' library.

Discuss sexual roles assigned white women and black women in nineteenth-century America: free white women were told that they must adhere to the "cult of domesticity" and were rewarded for piety, purity, domesticity, and obedience. Black slave women were (like male slaves) denied literacy and the possibility of reading the Bible; as Jacobs points out, in North Carolina after the Nat Turner rebellion, slaves were forbidden to meet together in their own churches. Their only chance at "piety" was to attend the church of their masters. They were denied "purity"—if by "purity" is meant sex only within marriage—because they were denied legal marriage. The "Notes" to the standard edition of *Incidents* read: "The entire system worked against the protection of slave women from sexual assault and violence, as Jacobs asserts. The rape of a slave was not a crime but a trespass upon her master's property" (fn 2, p. 265). Denied marriage to a man who might own a home and denied the right to hold property and own her own home, the female slave was, of course, denied "domesticity." Her "obedience," however, was insisted upon: not obedience to her father, husband, or brother, but obedience to her owner. Slave women were excluded from patriarchal definitions of true womanhood; the white patriarchy instead formally defined them as producers and as reproducers of a new generation of slaves, and, informally, as sexual objects. Jacobs is writing her narrative within a society that insists that white women conform to one set of sexual practices and that black women conform to a completely contradictory set. Her awareness of this contradiction enables her to present a powerful critique, but it does not exclude her from being sensitive to a sexual ideology that condemns her.

Concerning the accuracy of this autobiography, refer to the exhaustive identification of people, places, and events in the standard edition as well as the recent biography of Jacobs. Concerning the period in hiding, point out that the date of Jacobs's escape has been documented by her master's "wanted" ad of June 1835, and the date of her Philadelphia arrival has been documented by June 1842 correspondence; both are reproduced in the standard edition. Discuss the history of Anne Frank—and of others who hid for long periods to avoid persecution (e.g., men "dodging" the draft during World War II and the Vietnam War, etc.).

Major Themes, Historical Perspectives, Personal Issues

Themes: The struggle for freedom; the centrality of the family and the attempt to achieve security for the family; the individual and communal efforts to achieve these goals; the relationships among women (among generations of black women; between black slave women and slave-holding white women, between black slave women and non-slave-holding white women); the problem of white racism; the problem of the institution of chattel slavery; the issue of woman's appropriate response to chattel slavery and to tyranny: Should she passively accept victimization? Should she fight against it? How should she struggle—within the "domestic sphere" (where the patriarchy assigned women) or within both the domestic and the "public sphere" (which the patriarchy assigned to men)? How can a woman tell her story if she is not a "heroine" who has lived a "blameless" life? How can a woman create her own identity? What about the limits of literary genre? What about the limits imposed on women's discussion of their sexual experiences?

Historical Issues: These involve both the antebellum struggle against white racism and against slavery, and the struggle against sexism. Jacobs's story raises questions about the institution of chattel slavery; patriarchal control of free women in the antebellum period; the struggle against slavery (black abolitionists, white abolitionists, within the white community, within the free black community, within the slave community); the historic struggle against white racism (in the antebellum North); the historic effort of the anti-slavery feminists, among the Garrisonian abolitionists, who attempted to enter the public sphere and to debate issues of racism and slavery (women like Sarah and Angelina Grimké, like Amy Post, who suggested to Jacobs that she write her life story, and like Lydia Maria Child, who edited it); the Nat Turner revolt; the 1850 Fugitive Slave Law; the publication of *Uncle Tom's Cabin*; the firing on Fort Sumter.

Personal Issues: The narrator constructs a self who narrates the book. This narrator expresses conflict over some of her history, especially her sexual history (see above). She is rejected by her grandmother, then later accepted (but perhaps not fully); near the end of her book, she wins her daughter's full acceptance. All of this speaks to the importance of intergenerational connections among the women in this book. Near the conclusion, the narrator expresses her deep distress at having her freedom bought by her employer, a woman who is her friend: she feels that she has been robbed of her "victory," that in being purchased she has violated the purity of her freedom struggle. Writing the book, she gains that victory by asserting control over her own life.

Significant Form, Style, or Artistic Conventions

Incidents appears to be influenced by (1) the novel of seduction and (2) the slave narrative. It presents a powerful, original transformation of the conventions of both of these genres. What is new here is that—in contrast to the type of the seduction novel—the female protagonist asserts her responsibility for her sexual behavior instead of presenting herself as a powerless victim. This is a new kind of "fallen woman," who problematizes the whole concept of "fallen womanhood." In contrast to the type of the slave narrative, *Incidents* presents not a single male figure struggling for his freedom against an entire repressive society, but a female figure struggling for freedom for her children and herself with the aid of both her family and of much of a black community united in opposition to the white slavocracy. Even from within that slavocracy, some women assert their sisterhood to help. The language in *Incidents* suggests both the seduction novel and the slave narrative. The passages concerning Brent's sexual history are written in elevated language and are full of evasions and silences; the passages concerning her struggle for freedom are written in simpler English and are direct and to the point—or they are hortatory, in the style of Garrisonian abolitionism.

Original Audience

I have touched on this above, in discussing history. Jacobs's Linda Brent writes that she is trying to move the women of the North to act against slavery: these, I take it, were free white women who were not (yet) committed to abolitionism and who were not (yet) engaged in debate in the "public sphere." In class, we talk about the ways in which Jacobs's Linda Brent addresses her audience in Chapter 10, and the ways in which, as a writer reflecting on her long-ago girlhood, she makes mature judgments about her life.

Comparisons, Contrasts, Connections

Incidents can fruitfully be compared/contrasted with the classic male slave narrative, Frederick Douglass's 1845 *Narrative*. It can also be read in connection with *Uncle Tom's Cabin*, *The Scarlet Letter*, and with "women's" fiction, much of which ostensibly centers on a woman's sexual choices and possibilities, and on women's intergenerational relationships.

Questions for Reading, Discussion, and Writing

Study questions: Find a troubling passage. What is troubling? Why? What does this suggest? Why do you think that *Incidents* was believed the production of a white woman, not of a former slave? Why do you think that *Incidents* was thought to be a novel, not an autobiography?

Mary Boykin Chesnut (1823–1886)

Contributing Editor: Minrose C. Gwin

Classroom Issues and Strategies

It is important to consider Mary Chesnut and her work in context. Chesnut is well known for her criticism of slavery and patriarchy. Yet she is also very much a member of the wealthy planter class in her views on race. In addition, this is a massive work—close to 900 pages. It is, therefore, difficult to find "representative" sections that capture the breadth and sweep of the work as a whole.

In teaching Chesnut consider these strategies:

1. Provide historical context with attention to the intersections of race, class, and gender in Southern culture. Consider especially the relative positions of white women and African-American women in a patriarchal slave society. Students also need to understand the rise and fall of the Confederacy.
2. Require students to read and report on diverse sections of the work.

Students often ask questions related to Chesnut's "feminism" and her attitude toward race. For example, why does she blame African-American women for being sexual victims of white men? How implicated is she in the patriarchal order?

Major Themes, Historical Perspectives, Personal Issues

1. This is an important *social* history of the Civil War era in the South.
2. At the same time, it is interesting both as a woman's autobiography—a *personal* history of struggle and hardship—and as a remarkable story of the trauma experienced by both white and black women in the Civil War South.

Significant Form, Style, or Artistic Conventions

This autobiography is a combination of a journal written on the spot and reminiscences of the Civil War period. (See *The Private Mary Chesnut* for the former.) There is, therefore, a fascinating *combination* of the personal and the public in Woodward's edition.

Original Audience

Hundreds of war reminiscences were published in the forty to fifty years after the Civil War. Poorly edited versions, both called *A Diary from Dixie*, were published in 1905 and 1949. Installments of the first edition were published in *The Saturday Evening Post*. Readers then were more interested in the actual events of the war years so vividly portrayed by Chesnut.

Comparisons, Contrasts, Connections

I would suggest a contrast/comparison to an African-American woman's slave narrative, perhaps Harriet Ann Jacobs's *Incidents in the Life of a Slave Girl*, which also decries white men's sexual misuse of female slaves—from the point of view of the victim. (Also see *Uncle Tom's Cabin* for similar themes.)

Questions for Reading, Discussion, and Writing

1. (a) Describe how Chesnut created this massive volume.
   (b) Describe the life of an upper-class white woman in the Old South.
   (c) Describe the editorial history of this volume.
2. (a) Compare with slave narrative, abolitionist or pro-slavery fiction, realistic or plantation fiction, or modern woman's autobiography.
   (b) Discuss Chesnut's relationships and attitudes toward black women, her own husband and father-in-law, female friends (e.g., Varina Davis), or her own slaves.
   (c) Describe how fictional techniques bring life to the diary format.

Bibliography

Fox-Genovese, Elizabeth. *Within the Plantation Household: Black and White Women of the Old South.* U of North Carolina P, 1988.

Gwin, Minrose. *Black and White Women of the Old South: The Peculiar Sisterhood in American Literature.* U of Tennessee P, 1985. Chapter 2.

Jones, Anne Goodwyn. "Southern Literary Women, and Chronicles of Southern Life." *Sex, Race, and the Role of Women in the South.* Ed. Joanne V. Hawks and Sheila L. Skemp. UP of Mississippi, 1983.

Junker, Clara. "Writing Herstory: Mary Chesnut's Civil War." *Southern Studies* 26 (1987): 18–27.

Muhlenfeld, Elisabeth. *Mary Boykin Chesnut: A Biography.* Louisiana State UP, 1981.

Woodward, C. Vann. *Mary Chesnut's Civil War.* Yale UP, 1981. Introduction.

———— and Elisabeth Muhlenfeld. *The Private Mary Chesnut.* N.p.: Oxford UP, 1985. Introduction.

Wendell Phillips (1811–1884)

Contributing Editor: Allison Heisch

Classroom Issues and Strategies

Students tend not to know enough history (or, for that matter, geography) to understand the setting for *Toussaint L'Ouverture.* In addition, Phillips's view of race and racial difference will strike some students as condescending: He sets out to "prove" that Toussaint is "okay" and seems to imply that his sterling example proves that some blacks are "okay" too. This is not the sort of argumentation that we like nowadays, for we've understood this as tokenism.

A quick history/geography lesson here (including Napoleon and the French Revolution) is in order. Also, review the attitudes toward race generally taken in this period. I've given background reading in Stephen J. Gould's *The Mismeasure of Man* as a way of grounding that discussion. It is equally useful to pair Phillips with a figure such as Louis Agassiz to show what style of thought the "scientific" view of race could produce. Yet students can and do understand that styles of argument get dated very readily, and this can be demonstrated for them with various NAACP sorts of examples.

Students often ask, "Is this a true story?" (Answer: Sort of.)

Major Themes, Historical Perspectives, Personal Issues

Phillips's emphasis on the dignity of the individual. The idea of the hero (and the rather self-conscious way he develops it—that is, in his emphasis on Toussaint's "pure blood" and his deliberate contrast of Toussaint with Napoleon). It's useful to show Toussaint as Phillips's version of "the noble savage" (an eighteenth-century British idea still current in nineteenth-century America).

As the headnote points out, the immediate occasion of Phillips's speech was the issue of whether blacks should serve in the military. Since the issue of military service—that is, of women and homosexuals in the military—has been a vexed one in the recent past, it may be useful to point to this historical context for the speech and to the relationship between its rhetoric and content and its functions in its time. This may also raise the question of the symbolic significance of military prowess in general.

Significant Form, Style, or Artistic Conventions

This piece needs to be placed in the broader context of circuit-speaking and in the specific context of abolitionist public speaking. It should also be located in the debate over slavery.

Original Audience

Phillips's assumptions about his audience are very clear: there is little doubt that he addresses an audience of white folks with the plain intent of persuading them to adopt his position, or at least to give it a fair hearing. Students may very well say that Phillips *has* no contemporary audience, and that is probably true. It's useful, however, to point out that long after Phillips's death black students memorized this piece and recited it on occasions such as school graduations. Thus, while the people who first heard this piece were certainly very much like Phillips, his second (and more enduring) audience was an audience of black people—largely students—who probably knew and cared nothing about Phillips but embraced Toussaint L'Ouverture as their hero. That phenomenon—the half-life of polemic—is very interesting.

Comparisons, Contrasts, Connections

It is useful (and easy) to present Phillips with other white abolitionists (such as Garrison and Thoreau) or to read Phillips against black orators (F. Douglass, H. H. Garnet, David Walker). Another tack is to put him in a wider spectrum of white antislavery writing: read him with John Greenleaf Whittier or even Harriet Beecher Stowe. One approach to take is to compare his oratorical style with that of Garnet or Douglass. Another is to show the breadth of antislavery writing, particularly with reference to the particular genres involved. If the students don't notice this, it's important to point out that this is an antislavery piece by implication: Phillips does not address the subject directly.

Questions for Reading, Discussion, and Writing

1. I like to have students identify the intended audience for me: How do they know to whom Phillips is speaking?
2. From Phillips's vantage, what are the traits of this ideal black hero? (Part of the point here is to get them to understand Phillips's emphasis on Toussaint's appreciation for white people and to see what kinds of fears he implicitly addresses.)
3. In what ways is this effective (or ineffective) as a piece of argumentation?
4. Is this piece propaganda? And, if so, what *is* propaganda? What are the differences (in terms of content and specifics) between Phillips's argument and one that might be made in a contemporary civil rights speech?
5. A good topic for getting at the heart of the matter (a very good paper topic) is a comparison of Toussaint L'Ouverture and Uncle Tom.

Bibliography

Bartlett, Irving. *Wendell Phillips, Brahmin Radical*. Boston: Greenwood, 1973.

Bode, Carl. *The American Lyceum: Town Meetings of the Mind*. New York: Southern Illinois UP, 1968.

Korngold, Ralph. *Two Friends of Man: The Story of William Lloyd Garrison and Wendell Phillips and Their Relationship with Abraham Lincoln*. Boston: n.p., 1950.

Stewart, James Brewer. *Wendell Phillips, Liberty's Hero*. Baton Rouge and London: Louisiana State UP, 1986.

Abraham Lincoln (1809–1865)

Contributing Editor: Elaine Sargent Apthorp

Classroom Issues and Strategies

Lincoln's words are familiar to students, who have received those words, or the echo of them, by a hundred indirect sources, and who sometimes conflate the Gettysburg Address with the Pledge of Allegiance—and not by accident. (Similarly, the man himself has been rendered unreal by his status as a culture hero and icon; part of the reconstruction process entails restoring personhood to this historical figure—reconstructing his statesmanship and character by describing the context in which he grew and worked, the forces he had to contend with as a politician and as President, etc.) A problem is how to make the words live in their original context—so that by stripping them temporarily of their canonization in the store of U.S. holy scriptures, we can see why they were so appropriated—what it was about these words that moved Americans in the aftermath of the war. And what about Lincoln's construction of these statements has made them so emblematic of cultural ideals we still cherish (however vague their application)?

To give the meanings back to the words, we need to (1) restore vividly the historical context in which these speeches were composed and to which they were addressed, and (2) read slowly and explicate together as we go. What precedents and values is he calling to his listeners' minds? What does he ask them to focus on? What doesn't he choose to talk about, refer to, or insinuate?

Major Themes, Historical Perspectives, Personal Issues

I've tried to canvass these in the headnote. It's important that the students know, for example, that the battle of Gettysburg was in many respects the turning point in the Civil War. It was the farthest advance the Confederate forces were to make. In addition, it was the bloodiest and most costly battle (in sheer number of lives lost on both sides) in what was a devastatingly bloody war (over 600,000 battle casualties over four years, with another million and more dead from disease via infected wounds, malnutrition, and inadequate medical attention).

Students should know something of how Lincoln was perceived in the North and South during his presidency, the polarized forces with which he had to contend even among the nonseceding members of the Union, his concern for maintaining the loyalty of slave-holding border states and holding out hope for reunion with the Confederate states, in tension with the pressure he felt from the radical Republicans who urged the emancipation of slaves by executive proclamation, and so forth. This kind of information helps us to interpret both of the Lincoln documents in our selection.

Significant Form, Style, or Artistic Conventions

Again, see the headnote on style—biblical allusions and cadence, lawyer's cutting and distinguishing, simplified syntax and diction. In a discussion of oratory as it was practiced in this period, point out ways in which Lincoln participated in and departed from the practice of oratory that was considered eloquent in that day (e.g., Edward Everett who preceded Lincoln on the podium at Gettysburg).

Original Audience

1. The audience could tolerate, and indeed expected, long, florid, syntactically complex speeches. They were, at the same time, both more literate and more aural than we are (we're more visual, attending to images rather than words or sounds).
2. The audience were Christians. War had bitterly divided North from South; politicians debated while many people experienced death at rebel or Yankee hands. Lincoln had to consider how to appease the vindictive rage/triumph/urge-to-plunder of the conquering Union supporters while establishing foundation for political and economic reconstruction and rebuilding. He had to rally maximum support (reminding North and South of their common faith; characterizing the war as a war for the Union's democratic survival, not as a war to free slaves or alter the economic order of society—using Union and Constitution, obscuring states' rights).
3. Consider our own time, and our longing for the rock of humane statesmanship that Lincoln has represented in the popular mind. Consider the motives behind his canonization after assassination, when he had been so unpopular while alive in office. Consider the uses Lincoln has been put to, by politicians, etc. Consider the evolutions in public perception of Nixon, Kennedy, etc.

Comparisons, Contrasts, Connections

1. A bit of Everett's speech at Gettysburg for comparison with Lincoln's little Gettysburg Address.
2. Samples of biblical prose for comparison with Lincoln's.

3. Elements of debates with Stephen Douglas in 1858, again for comparison.
4. Dr. Martin Luther King Jr.'s "Letter from Birmingham Jail," "I Have a Dream," and other works, to discover the uses of Lincoln for other politically active people/groups.

Bibliography

Studies on Lincoln's life and career exist in flourishing and staggering abundance, and most of them examine the language of his speeches and other public and private documents to help develop their interpretations of Lincoln's character, attitudes, and policies as they evolved.

Steven B. Oates's *With Malice Toward None* offers what is finally a sympathetic and admiring account of Lincoln, but it is tempered and qualified by a scrupulous confrontation with inconvenient evidence and careful consideration of the poles of controversy in Lincoln studies between which he means to place his own interpretation.

There are also a number of essays that explore Lincoln's writings as works of literature, which trace one or more of the several strands of law, rural imagery, backwoods humor, Shakespeare, and the Bible, which inform Lincoln's rhetoric. Entire books have been devoted to establishing the historical contexts in which Lincoln developed the Gettysburg Address or the Emancipation Proclamation, but for the instructors on the go nothing beats Jacques Barzun's *Lincoln the Literary Genius* (Evanston, IL: Evanston, 1960). It's short but covers much ground and offers perceptive close analysis of Lincoln's rhetorical techniques and style—both identifying these elements and suggesting their effects and implications.

One more recent study that employs analysis of Lincoln's speeches is Charles B. Strozier's psychoanalytic study of Lincoln, *Lincoln's Quest for Union: Public and Private Meanings* (Urbana and Chicago: U of Illinois P, 1987; Basic, 1982), chapters 6–9 but especially chapter 7, "The Domestication of Political Rhetoric."

Literature and the "Woman Question"

Sarah Moore Grimké (1792–1873)

See material under "Angelina Grimké" and "Sarah Moore Grimké" earlier in this guide.

Sojourner Truth (c. 1797–1883)

Contributing Editor: Allison Heisch

Classroom Issues and Strategies

One reason why Sojourner Truth has not appeared in conventional American literature anthologies until now is that the texts are stenographic transcriptions of spontaneous speeches. Thus, even the orthography is "made-up." Students may tend to dismiss this as nonliterature. Also, the interior structure of the speeches does not follow expected expository modes (i.e., there's no "beginning," "middle," and "end"), so they are vulnerable to rigidly "logical" analysis.

Sojourner Truth offers a wonderful opportunity to raise large questions: What is literature? And what is American literature? Are speeches literature? Is it literature if you don't write it down yourself? What is the purpose of literature? It is useful to set these speeches for the students in the context of antislavery meetings, to describe where and how they were held, and also who participated. Students may have difficulty with these texts; old-fashioned close reading in class will help.

I like to talk about "unpopular ideas": Sojourner Truth has several of these! It is also useful to place her in the tradition of oral literature.

Responses to Truth vary widely, depending on the class. Some students may make the argument that she is hostile to men. Generally discussion goes in the direction of contemporary issues involving women.

Major Themes, Historical Perspectives, Personal Issues

Why did racial equality take precedence over equality of the sexes? How can we explain the conflict between racial and gender equality? What is the difference between Sojourner Truth's argument and the contemporary argument for "comparable worth"?

Significant Form, Style, or Artistic Conventions

Ordinarily, we are able to separate a writer from her work. In this case, we have not only oral presentation but also a style of presentation in which the speaker presents herself as the major character in the work. In some sense, therefore, she is the subject of her work. To what literary and quasi-literary categories could you assign these speeches (fiction, autobiography, prophecy)? How do they "violate" traditional genre boundaries? Where does oratory end and drama begin? These speeches provide a splendid opportunity to demonstrate to what extent our literary categories are a construct, one that not only defines and makes rules, but one that also excludes.

Original Audience

Because Sojourner Truth's speeches were transcribed and preserved by her admirers, it is by no means clear how her original audiences really responded. We have the laudatory side only. Just the same, it is apparent that to many of her contemporary listeners, she was a figure of mythic proportion. To get at the issue of audience, it's useful, first, to have the students identify the issues of continuing importance that she raises. Second, it is helpful to show them a contemporary parallel (such as Barbara Jordan's "We the People" speech) as a means of generating discussion.

Comparisons, Contrasts, Connections

Frederick Douglass ("What to the Slave Is the Fourth of July?") and Henry Highland Garnet ("An Address to the Slaves of the United States") show the tendency of abolitionist literature to regard slavery as a phenomenon affecting black men and, coincidentally, to consider the abuse of black women largely as an affront to their husbands and fathers. Truth's views can usefully be contrasted with those of some writers, black and white, who believed that women could best exercise power by influencing their husbands.

Questions for Reading, Discussion, and Writing

1. What issues does Sojourner Truth raise that you consider to be of contemporary importance?
2. Compare the positions on civil rights taken by Frederick Douglass and Sojourner Truth.

Bibliography

Lerner, Gerda. "While the water is stirring I will step into the pool." *Black Women in White America: A Documentary History*. New York: n.p., 1973.

Stanton, Elizabeth Cady, et al. "Sojourner Truth." *History of Woman's Suffrage*. 3 vols. 1881–1886. New York: n.p., 1970.

Fanny Fern (Sara Willis Parton) (1811–1872)

Contributing Editor: Barbara A. White

Classroom Issues and Strategies

I have found Fern most accessible to students when presented as primarily a humorist and satirist, rather than a "sentimentalist," and a journalist rather than a novelist. However, I try to avoid setting her up as an exception, as Nathaniel Hawthorne did, a writer "better" than the typical "scribbling woman." Ann Douglas Wood sets Fern apart for her refusal to disguise her literary ambition and conform to prevailing rationales for women writing, and Joyce W. Warren tries to rescue her from classification as a sentimentalist instead of a satirist; Warren includes no "sentimental" pieces in her selection from Fern's work. One might argue, however, that Fern should be recognized as the author of "Thanksgiving Story" as well as "Critics," and that while she was more outspoken than most of her sister authors, she also resembles them in many ways.

Major Themes, Historical Perspectives, Personal Issues

The rights of women and the problems and status of female authors are obvious Fern themes. I believe it is also important to emphasize Fern's treatment of class since she is unusual for her time in portraying domestic servants and factory workers as well as middle-class women.

Students have been responsive to approaching Fern through the issue of names and their symbolism. When I was in graduate school studying nineteenth-century American literature, female writers other than Emily Dickinson were mentioned only to be ridiculed as having three names. To use more than two names, like Harriet Beecher Stowe, or two initials, like E. D. E. N. Southworth, was to be *ipso facto* a poor writer, and it was just as bad to adopt an alliterative pseudonym like Grace Greenwood or Millie Mayfield. I don't recall the professors ever referring to Grata Payson Sara Willis Eldredge Farrington Parton, "Fanny Fern."

The "Grata Payson" was supplied by the writer's father, who named her after the mother of a minister he admired; the rest of the family objected to "Grata," and in the first of a series of symbolic name changes, she became "Sara," discarding the influence of the father and his orthodox religion. Later in life Fern explained her pen name as inspired by happy childhood memories of her mother picking sweet fern leaves. In a further repudiation of patriarchal tradition Fern, although she is often referred to in literary histories as Sara

Parton, did not use that name; she preferred her pseudonym, extending it to her personal life and becoming "Fanny" even to family and friends.

Ann Douglas Wood (see headnote) views the *nom de plume* "Fanny Fern" as an emblem of Fern's "artistic schizophrenia." She points out that "Fern" is a woodsy, flowery name typical of "sentimental" writers while "Fanny" suggests the rebel (Fern, who was given the nickname "Sal Volatile" at the Beecher school, once remarked, "I never saw a 'Fanny' yet that wasn't as mischievous as Satan"). Wood, noting the two different types of sketches Fern wrote, concludes that she possessed "two selves, two voices, one strident and aggressive, the other conventional and sentimental." Mary Kelley, in *Private Woman, Public Stage* (Oxford, 1984), also stresses Fern's "dual identity" in arguing the thesis that female authors of the nineteenth century experienced a split between their private selves and public identities. (Teachers who plan to assign *Ruth Hall* should also see Linda Huf's comments on this issue in her chapter on the novel in *A Portrait of the Artist as a Young Woman* [Ungar, 1983].)

Although the "split personality" approach interests students and helps illuminate the cultural context in which women wrote, it can be overdone. Early in her career Fern was obviously searching for a voice, trying out the more conventional approach in pieces like "Thanksgiving Story" and expressing herself more daringly in "Soliloquy of a Housemaid." But it could be argued that once she established herself, she successfully united the Fanny and the Fern in her writing—and in her life shed the identity given her by men and became the person she herself created. In any case, it is typical of Fern, who possessed the unusual ability to mock herself, to create a final irony by making fun of her pen name. She advised budding authors in search of a pseudonym to "bear in mind that nothing goes down, now-a-days, but *alliteration*. For instance, Delia Daisy, Fanny Foxglove, Harriet Honeysuckle, Lily Laburnum. . . ."

Significant Form, Style, or Artistic Conventions

Fern's writing is especially useful for getting students to think about style and tone, and the discussion can be related both to the split personality issue raised above and the question of literary worth. Although some students have considered Fern's style human and spontaneous, probably accounting in large measure for her popularity, others have criticized it as too loud ("noisy," "braying"). They tend to view the italics, capital letters, and exclamation points with suspicion ("unprofessional," "feminine," "schoolgirl"). One student claimed that a writer who employs expressions like "Heigho!" and "H-u-m-p-h!" cannot be "taken seriously." He could not explain why, any more than most students (or critics) have been able to explain very successfully what "sentimental" means and why it's bad to be so.

Original Audience

The question of literary value can easily be related to that of audience. Fern's "Thanksgiving Story" lends itself to discussion of these issues. The question of whether "Thanksgiving Story" is "worse" than the other selections by Fern, and how so, can be used to provoke discussion of the standards by which literature is judged (and who does the judging) and of the differences between nineteenth- and twentieth-century readers.

Comparisons, Contrasts, Connections

Fern's work can easily be compared and contrasted with that of just about any woman of her time. She can also be paired with male writers, such as Walt Whitman (*Fern Leaves* and *Leaves of Grass*) and Ik Marvel (Donald Grant Mitchell), the essayist, who gained fame at about the same time as Fern. Or she can be treated along with other nineteenth-century humorists.

If Fern's relationship with Walt Whitman is to be emphasized, see J. F. McDermott, "Whitman and the Partons" (*American Literature* 29 [1957]: 316–19) and William White, "Fanny Fern to Walt Whitman: An Unpublished Letter" (*American Book Collector* 11 [1961]: 8–9). In "Fern Leaves and Leaves of Grass" (*New York Times Book Review*, April 22, 1945) it is suggested that Whitman imitated *Fern Leaves* in choosing both his title and his binding, particularly the floral designs on the cover. Fern's review of *Leaves of Grass* is reprinted in Warren, pp. 274–77.

In a course that includes Harriet Jacobs's *Incidents in the Life of a Slave Girl* (1861), students will enjoy knowing that the "Mr. Bruce" for whom Jacobs works as a nursemaid was N. P. Willis, Fern's brother; Fern satirizes her social-climbing brother in "Apollo Hyacinth." Jacobs kept her writing of *Incidents* secret from Willis, she wrote her friend Amy Post, because "Mr. W is too proslavery he would tell me that it was very wrong and that I was trying to do harm or perhaps he was sorry for me to undertake it while I was in his family" (*Incidents,* ed. Jean Fagan Yellin, 1987, p. 232). Harriet Jacobs and Fanny Fern were friendly; for an account of their relationship, see Joyce W. Warren, *Fanny Fern* (see headnote).

If the students read "The Declaration of Sentiments," they may want to see Elizabeth Cady Stanton's review of *Ruth Hall* in *Una* (February 1855), pp. 29–30. Stanton's defense of Fern is discussed in Linda Grasso's "Anger in the House: Fanny Fern's *Ruth Hall* and the Redrawing of Emotional Boundaries in Mid-Nineteenth-Century America," in *Studies in the American Renaissance* (1995), pp. 251–61.

Questions for Reading, Discussion, and Writing

1. I prefer to have students read her without any initial intervention.
2. For the intrepid—have students try to imitate Fern's style. This demonstrates that it's not "natural," that is, easy, but you may not be forgiven for this assignment. It is also illuminating to compare the original version of "Soliloquy of a Housemaid" (in Warren) and the collected version in this anthology—so that students can see how Fern revised her seemingly slapdash work.

Bibliography

Joyce W. Warren's *Fanny Fern: An Independent Woman* (1992) has become the standard biography. An overview of Fern's writings is available in Nancy A. Walker's *Fanny Fern* (Twayne, 1993).

Elizabeth Cady Stanton (1815–1902)

Contributing Editor: Judith Wellman

Classroom Issues and Strategies

Stanton's autobiography reads well, in a fresh, personal, and modern style. Students do, however, benefit from some introduction to the Seneca Falls Declaration of Sentiments.

I usually ask students to analyze the Declaration of Sentiments in two ways:

1. How is it like/unlike the *Declaration of Independence*? It is almost identical to the *Declaration of Independence* in the preamble, except for the assertion that "all men and women are created equal." It is also divided into three main parts, as is the *Declaration of Independence*. Instead of grievances against King George, however, the Declaration of Sentiments lists grievances of women against the patriarchal establishment. Supposedly, the women tried to use the same number of items in 1848 as the Second Continental Congress incorporated in 1776, but the 1848 document actually contains one or two fewer.
2. How many grievances of 1848 are still issues for feminists today?

3. Teachers might ask students to imagine they were present at the Seneca Falls convention. Would they have signed this document? Why or why not?

4. Students might also imagine they were Elizabeth Cady Stanton in 1848. What was her state of mind? Does this document reflect her personal life or only her political ideals?

5. Ask students (individually or in groups) to select the one or two grievances from 1848 that they would consider important issues today and to defend their choices in writing or in class discussion. Or ask them to choose one or two contemporary issues that did not appear in the Declaration of Sentiments and to consider why they are important today but were not stated publicly then.

6. Students are often amazed that women were citizens without citizenship rights. They are also amazed at how many issues from 1848 are still unresolved. They have no trouble agreeing that "all men and women are created equal," but they do not always agree on what that means.

   They ask about how well this Declaration was received (widely reported, mixed reception), and they are curious about the relationship between Elizabeth and Henry. While Henry voted to admit women as delegates to the 1840 World Anti-Slavery Convention in London, he refused to attend the Seneca Falls convention, ostensibly because he did not agree with Elizabeth's demand for women's right to vote.

Major Themes, Historical Perspectives, Personal Issues

1. What was the political and legal position of women in the early Republic? Were women, for example, citizens? What did citizenship mean for women?

2. What alternative vision did the women and men who signed the Seneca Falls Declaration of Sentiments propose for women?

3. To what extend did the Declaration of Sentiments reflect issues in Stanton's personal life as well as in her political ideals?

Significant Form, Style, or Artistic Conventions

Contrast between the Declaration of Sentiments, with its attempt to reflect revolutionary writing and therefore revolutionary, egalitarian ideals, and Stanton's own account of her life, designed to emphasize her own experiences, which results in a more direct and personal style.

Original Audience

Professors might emphasize the universal character of the Declaration of Sentiments. It was not designed to appeal to some Americans only but to all Americans.

Comparisons, Contrasts, Connections

Comparison with the *Declaration of Independence* is useful.

Bibliography

Burns, Ken, and Paul Barnes. *The Story of Elizabeth Cady Stanton and Susan B. Anthony: Not for Ourselves Alone.* Video. Walpole, NH: Florentine Films, 1999.

DuBois, Ellen C. *The Elizabeth Cady Stanton–Susan B. Anthony Reader.* Rev. ed. Boston: Northeastern UP, 1992.

Gordon, Ann D., ed. *The Selected Papers of Elizabeth Cady Stanton and Susan B. Anthony: In the School of Anti-Slavery, 1840–1866.* Vol. I. New Brunswick, NJ: Rutgers UP, 1997.

Griffiths, Elisabeth. *In Her Own Right: The Life of Elizabeth Cady Stanton.* New York: Oxford UP, 1984.

Waggenspack, Beth Marie. *The Search for Self-Sovereignty: The Oratory of Elizabeth Cady Stanton.* New York: Greenwood, 1989.

Ward, Geoffrey. *Not for Ourselves Alone: The Story of Elizabeth Cady Stanton and Susan B. Anthony, An Illustrated History.* New York: Knopf, 1999.

Wellman, Judith. "The Seneca Falls Women's Rights Convention: A Study in Social Networks." *Journal of Women's History* 3 (1991): 9–37.

The Development of Narrative

Cluster: Humor of the Old Southwest

Davy Crockett (1786–1836)
Mike Fink (1770?–1823?)
Augustus Baldwin Longstreet (1790–1870)
George Washington Harris (1814–1869)

Contributing Editor: Anne G. Jones

Classroom Issues and Strategies

The most crucial problem is getting them read at all. These writers are typically included in anthologies but excluded in syllabi—*vide* the syllabi in *Reconstructing American Literature.* Secondly, the dialect and spelling are forbidding. And finally, this work comes with its set of literary critical stereotypes: it has been a favorite of many of the more conservative literary historians, who tend to see it mainly as grist for Twain and Faulkner mills. Finding new ways to think about the material could be a problem.

Thinking about these writings in the light of gender, race, and class makes them accessible and interesting to students. Indeed, the selections have been chosen with gender issues especially in mind. Having students prepare to read them aloud as a performance should help make the dialect more accessible. And suggesting innovative pairings—with Marietta Holley, with rap lyrics, with "Legend of Sleepy Hollow," for example—should enliven the reading further.

Major Themes, Historical Perspectives, Personal Issues

The construction of gender on the frontier seems a major project of this writing. The texts can be analyzed closely to see how they construct both manhood and womanhood, and how those constructions differ from mainstream American engendering of the period. The strong and sexual woman in particular appears anomalous; these texts both present and demonstrate some ambivalence about such figures. Class issues are crucial too, particularly in the relation between the voices in the texts: the controlling, omniscient, standard English voice and the disruptive, "carnival" voice in the "Dedicatory" set up the most familiar opposition, one that takes various forms in the selections.

Significant Form, Style, or Artistic Conventions

Much of this material is transcribed from or inspired by anonymous oral sources. And if students have performed selections, the question of the relation between oral and written texts can be foregrounded. The use of language in these selections is a second major stylistic concern; the vigor and power of this writing are attractive and invite students to look closely at specific linguistic strategies—metaphors and similes, concrete versus abstract diction, etc. And the stories by Harris and Longstreet offer two ways of rendering plot, the one loose and almost episodic, and the other tightly controlled.

Original Audience

The audience for this work most likely consisted of educated white men, "gentlemen of some means with a leisurely interest in masculine pursuits," as Cohen and Dillingham put it. They were likely, too, to be Southerners and proslavery Whigs. The audience's relation to the texts, then, was at least a step removed from the primary characters; these tales and stories seem to enable identification with the "masculinity" of the Crocketts and Finks and even Suts, and at the same time allow an "educated distance" from that identification. What happens now, when the audience has vastly changed? How many different ways can these texts be read? How does audience determine a text's meaning?

Comparisons, Contrasts, Connections

Washington Irving ("Legend" inspired much Southwest humor); Hannah Foster and Susanna Rowson (see Cohen and Dillingham: gender issues); Harriet Jacobs and Frederick Douglass (struggle with voices); Marietta Holley (women's versus men's humor); Mark Twain and William Faulkner (do they revise the tradition? how? what do they retain?).

Questions for Reading, Discussion, and Writing

1. (a) Do the women in these selections surprise you? Think about how and why. To what uses is this "strong woman" put in the selections? What do you think has happened to this figure of woman? Does she survive anywhere in our literature?
   (b) What can you say about the structure of each selection?
   (c) How many voices can you hear in these selections?

(d) What type of manhood is constructed in these pieces? How does "The Death of Mike Fink" fit in?

(e) What does Sut want from the quilting party? Why does he do what he does?

2. (a) Consider "Mrs. Yardley's Quilting Party" in the light of Elaine Hedges's book on quilting, *Hearts and Hands*.

(b) Consider some implications of the various types of narration.

(c) How do language and subject converge in the "Dedicatory" and another text of your choice?

(d) How is the "strong woman" used in these selections?

Bibliography

Cohen, Hennig and William B. Dillingham, eds. *Humor of the Old Southwest.* Athens: U of Georgia P, 1975, xiii–xxviii. The introduction is useful for information, but also as a representative of a particular critical position on the material. The remarks on gender are particularly provocative.

Curry, Jane. "The Ring-Tailed Roarers Rarely Sang Soprano." *Frontiers* II: 3 (1977): 129–40.

Washington Irving (1783–1859)

Contributing Editor: William Hedges

Classroom Issues and Strategies

Students generally know the two short stories ("Rip" and "Sleepy Hollow"). With the selections from *History*, it is wise to avoid tipping off students in advance to Irving's attitude toward the treatment of Native Americans by European-Americans; see if they can penetrate through the technically sophisticated irony to Irving's scathing condemnation; some may be tempted to read the passage as approving the harsh treatment. (Note that, strictly speaking, the passage is concerned with Latin America, not America as a whole. But students can be asked whether it has relevance to North American policies relating to Indians.)

Emphasize Irving's humor before getting too serious. Give students a chance to talk about what they find entertaining in the selections and why. Also, try comparing responses of male and female students to "Rip Van Winkle." How sympathetic are each to Rip? Look at the story as the first in a long line of texts by male American writers in which a male protagonist forsakes civilized community life for the wilderness (or the sea) on a quest of sorts and perhaps joins forces with a male companion(s). Consider the psychological or cultural significance of such narratives, as well as the role of and attitude toward women they portray.

Major Themes, Historical Perspectives, Personal Issues

History: Racism, its guises and rationalizations; what it means to be truly civilized—or savage.

"Rip Van Winkle": Loss (and discovery?) of identity; a challenge to American values, the work ethic. Does Rip himself represent anything positive? George III vs. George Washington (is the story antirepublican?); is the story sexist?

"Sleepy Hollow": Artificiality vs. naturalness; Puritan-Yankee intellectual pretentiousness, hypocrisy, greed, and commercialism as threats to an American dream of rural abundance and simple contentedness; the uses of imagination.

Significant Form, Style, or Artistic Conventions

With the *History* selection, questions of burlesque irony, the reliability of the narrator: Is Irving's persona, the peculiar Diedrich Knickerbocker, a party to the irony? Is he being deliberately ironic himself (saying just the opposite of what he believes about treatment of Native Americans), or does he seem duped by the defenses of brutal mistreatment that he offers? Does it matter which? Could it be either one—or both? Is the reader being played with?

The two stories were written ten years after the *Knickerbocker History*. *The Sketch Book,* from which the two stories come, is generally taken to be the beginning of Irving's transformation into a romantic writer of sorts. What romantic elements can be seen in "Rip" and "Sleepy Hollow"?

These two stories are also, arguably, the beginning of a new genre, the short story. If so, what makes these narratives short stories as opposed to earlier kinds of tales?

Original Audience

Relate Irving's commercial success beginning with *The Sketch Book* to the burgeoning of American popular culture in the early nineteenth century. Discuss *The Sketch Book* as context of "Rip" and "Sleepy Hollow" and the huge vogue for "sketch" books, literary annuals, and gift books that follows.

Comparisons, Contrasts, Connections

Compare the selection from *History* with Franklin's Swiftian satires, "The Sale of the Hessians," "An Edict by the King of Prussia"—or Swift's "A Modest Proposal" itself.

Compare and contrast the rural felicity of the inhabitants of Sleepy Hollow with Crèvecoeur's idealization of American rural life in the *American Farmer* or Jefferson's famous agrarian pronouncements in query XIX of *Notes on Virginia*.

What distinguishes Irving as a short story writer from Hawthorne or Poe?

Questions for Reading, Discussion, and Writing

1. The humor of the *Knickerbocker History*—have students read sections of it.
2. Political satire and opinion in the *History*—consider specifically the anti-Jeffersonianism of the section on Governor Kieft. Prepare a personal interpretation of one of the two stories.
3. Papers on varying or contrasting approaches to "Rip" or "Sleepy Hollow," consulting some of the interpretations listed in the bibliography. Discuss the humor in either story.

Bibliography

Fetterly, Judith. Chapter on "Rip Van Winkle." *The Resisting Reader*. N.p.: n.p., 1978. A feminist interpretation.

Hedges, William L. Article on the *History*. *The Old and New World Romanticism of Washington Irving*. Ed. Stanley Brodwin. N.p.: n.p., 1986. *Knickerbocker*'s politics and Irving's disorienting humor.

Hoffman, Daniel. Chapter on "Sleepy Hollow." *Form and Fable in American Fiction*. N.p.: n.p., 1961. Folkloristic interpretation, Native American humor.

Martin, Terence. "Rip, Ichabod, and the American Imagination." *American Literature* 31 (1959): 137–49.

Ringe, Donald A. "New York and New England: Irving's Criticism of American Society." *American Literature* 21 (1967): 455–67. Irving's pro-Dutch, anti-Yankee posture.

Roth, Martin. Chapters on *Knickerbocker* and on the two stories. *Comedy in America: The Lost World of Washington Irving.* N.p.: n.p., n.d. Very original criticism, mythic and cultural.

Seelye, John. "Root and Branch: Washington Irving and American Humor." *Nineteenth-Century Fiction* 38 (1984): 415–25. Very solid, well-balanced approach.

Young, Philip. "Fallen from Time: The Mythic Rip Van Winkle." *Kenyon Review* 22 (1960): 547–73. Jungian, the motif of the long sleep in world literature.

Zlogar, Richard J. "Accessories That Covertly Explain: Irving's Use of Dutch Genre Painting in 'Rip Van Winkle.'" *American Literature* 54 (1982): 44–62. Argues story is critical of Rip.

James Fenimore Cooper (1789–1851)

Contributing Editor: Geoffrey Rans

Classroom Issues and Strategies

I have found it better not to insist on Cooper's formal powers at the outset, nor even on his obvious importance as an innovator and initiator in American fiction. Rather, it is effective to invite the students to discuss the substantive issues that arise in a reading of Cooper. Their importance and typicality in the American literary experience remain alive to students in various historical transformations, and Cooper presents them in unresolved and problematic formations.

While the passages selected in *The Heath Anthology* raise obvious and important issues—of empire, of political theory, of nature versus civilization, law, conservation, religion, race, family, American history—one Leather-Stocking novel should be studied in its entirety. Depending on where the instructor places most emphasis, *The Pioneers*, *The Last of the Mohicans*, and *The Deerslayer* are the most accessible. In any case, any study of even the selected passages requires some "story-telling" by the instructor.

The discussion of *The Pioneers* or other novels can become, as well, a discussion of the competing claims on the student's attention to form and content: whether form is always possible or desirable; whether the unresolved issues in history are in any sense "resolved" in works of art; how the desire for narrative or didactic closure competes with the recognition of an incomplete and problematic history and political theory. Approach questions of empire, race, progress, civilization, family, law, and power, and lead back from them to the literary issues.

Major Themes, Historical Perspectives, Personal Issues

1. Historical myth and ideology. How do they differ? How do they interact?
2. Nature/civilization
3. Law
4. Power and property
5. The land
6. Violence
7. Race
8. Gender and family
9. Cooper's contradictory impulses: see Parrington (10)
10. Hope/disappointment
11. The environment

Significant Form, Style, or Artistic Conventions

1. Didacticism, resolved and unresolved
2. Romance—the Scott tradition: see Orlans (10)
3. Myth
4. Romanticism
5. Conventions of description and dialogue, epic and romantic
6. Epic
7. For advanced students: the question of the order of composition, and the literary effect on the reader of anachronism

Original Audience

I stress how the issues that were urgent to Cooper and his readers (they are evident in the novels, but see also Parrington) are alive today. Some attention should be given to the demand for a national literature, and the expectations of the American Romance (see Orlans).

Indispensable reading for this period is Nina Baym's *Novelists, Readers and Reviewers* (Ithaca: Cornell UP, 1984).

Comparisons, Contrasts, Connections

Here are some pursuable issues:

1. Crèvecoeur: slavery, Indians, the agrarian ideology and its betrayal
2. Relate to other writings on the encounter of white and red—see Smith, Winthrop, Williams, Crèvecoeur, Franklin, Jefferson
3. Stowe—on race, slavery, Christianity and its betrayal, didacticism— Twain, Frederick Douglass
4. The nonfiction writers of the Revolution and the New Republic: Jefferson, the Federalists
5. Faulkner: race, history. Carolyn Porter's chapters on Faulkner (see 10) might seem relevant to Cooper to some instructors.
6. Catharine Sedgwick's *Hope Leslie*

Questions for Reading, Discussion, and Writing

1. Before starting Cooper, an assembly of the issues raised in the course about form, the canon, and the literature of Colonial, Revolutionary, and New Republican times should be given by the instructor.
2. I have found the following areas particularly fruitful for student essays on Cooper:
   (a) Confusion, contradiction, and resolution
   (b) Myth versus reality
   (c) Race
   (d) Law and justice
   (e) Power in all its forms: class, race, military, political, and property
   (f) Attitudes toward nature and the environment

Bibliography

The chapters on Cooper in the following books (subtitles omitted):

Bewley, Marius. *The Eccentric Design.* New York: Columbia UP, 1961.

Fisher, Philip. *Hard Facts.* New York: Oxford UP, 1985.

Marx, Leo. *The Machine in the Garden.* New York: Oxford UP, 1964.

Orlans, G. Harrison. "The Romance Ferment after *Waverly.*" *American Literature* 3 (1932): 408–31.

Parrington, Vernon L. *Main Currents in American Thought.* Vol. 2. New York: Harcourt, 1927.

Porter, Carolyn. *Seeing and Being.* Middletown: Wesleyan UP, 1981. The chapters on Faulkner.

Rans, Geoffrey. "Inaudible Man: The Indian in the Theory and Practice of White Fiction." *Canadian Review of American Studies* VII (1977): 104–15.

Smith, Henry N. *Virgin Land.* New York: Vintage, 1950.

Tompkins, Jane. "Indians: Textualism, Morality, and the Problem of History." *Critical Inquiry* 13 (1986): 101–19.

———. *Sensational Designs.* New York: Oxford UP, 1985.

Catharine Maria Sedgwick (1789–1867)

Contributing Editors: Barbara A. Bardes and Suzanne Gossett

Classroom Issues and Strategies

There may be some difficulty in helping students compare early nineteenth-century attitudes toward Indians, who are here referred to as savages, to Sedgwick's treatment of Native Americans, which is so different from that of her contemporaries. Be sure students know the legend of Pocahontas. The tradition of sympathy for Native American culture should be traced back to the period of Spanish arrival and to the literature of the early Puritan colonies. The selections from Cabeza de Vaca and Roger Williams are helpful in this context. It may also be useful to discuss conflicting attitudes toward the primitive: as dangerous savage and as nature's noble soul. The capture of Faith Leslie (and her eventual marriage to Oneco) should be compared with Mary Rowlandson's "Narrative of the Captivity and Restauration." Mention that according to legend, one of Sedgwick's female ancestors experienced a similar abduction.

Students need to understand Sedgwick's complex attitude toward the early Puritan colonies, which combines patriotism with objections to Puritan oppressiveness. At this point they will need some biographical and historical background, first on Sedgwick and then on the Puritans. They may be referred to the writings of John Winthrop, who appears in the novel. It is also important to note the place of women in the early American republic as teachers of the political culture yet subordinate within the home. Emphasize that Sedgwick occupied an unusual position as an important woman writer, and discuss why she shows so much sympathy for those without power in the society. Some thought should be given to the "ventriloquization" of Native American culture as a way for Sedgwick to express questions about women's culture.

Major Themes, Historical Perspectives, Personal Issues

1. Sedgwick's picture of solidarity between women (Hope and Magawisca).
2. Sedgwick's sympathy for the Indians who are being destroyed by the English settlers. The Indian massacre repeats an English one; students can be asked to read the "Speech of Chief Seattle" and to compare its rhetoric with the speech of Mononotto in the first selection from *Hope Leslie*. Sedgwick's sympathy is also shown in the discussion of the marriage of Faith Leslie to an Indian.
3. The political significance of Hope and Magawisca's defiance of the Puritan magistrates: the way in which both Indians and women are excluded from the political system. The emphasis throughout on the political and personal need for liberty and independence. Contrast Magawisca's defiance of the English with the historical Pocahontas's marriage to an Englishman. Discuss the conflicting ideas of natural law and patriarchal law that underlie Magawisca's and Winthrop's positions.
4. The place of the family in the political order and the place of women within the family. The family is seen as the primary unit in politics and each family is represented by its male adult members. The interests of wives and children (who have no public voice in political decisions) are represented by the men.
5. "To my dying mother thou didst promise kindness to her children. In her name I demand of thee death or liberty." If time permits, discuss the nineteenth century "cult of the mother" and its manifestations in this novel.

Significant Form, Style, or Artistic Conventions

Sedgwick is important for her participation in the creation of a national literature. Both the extensive descriptions of nature and the subject matter of the novel are specifically American. *Hope Leslie* shows formal development from earlier American women's novels, though it includes, characteristically, a heroine who is to some extent deprived of parental support and creates her own success before marriage. It avoids, however, the "seduced and abandoned" plot found in *The Coquette* and *Charlotte Temple*, as well as excessive sentiment.

Sedgwick allows her heroine to defy female norms conventional both in life and literature. She also deploys the power of public oratory within a novelistic context, and has more "public" scenes than would be expected in a "woman's" novel.

Original Audience

The blend of historical fact and adventure made *Hope Leslie* acceptable reading for young women. The novel was very popular, partly because it fit into a tradition that was established by Sir Walter Scott.

Comparisons, Contrasts, Connections

The novel should be compared with *The Last of the Mohicans*, published one year earlier. Sedgwick even refers to Cooper's novel in the text. But she countenances marriage between an Indian and a white woman, and she shows sympathy for the motives of the Indian attack on the white settlers. In addition, Sedgwick does not make women merely the means of alliance between men, but she puts them at the center of her novel rather than on the margins.

Questions for Reading, Discussion, and Writing

1. (a) Compare the representation of the Indian massacre in *Hope Leslie* with the massacre that occurs in *The Last of the Mohicans*.
    (b) Consider how Sedgwick equates her two heroines, Magawisca and Hope Leslie. In what ways is the scene at the mothers' graves a defining moment in the relationship of the two women?
    (c) What is the basis for Magawisca's refusal of Puritan authority? Is it defensible?
2. (a) Consider the political implications of the parallel judgment scenes in *Hope Leslie*, when Everell is "tried" by the Indians and Magawisca is tried by the Puritans. Do Governor Winthrop and Mononotto operate out of the same principles?
    (b) Compare Cooper's and Sedgwick's attitudes toward relations between the Indians and the white settlers.
    (c) Compare the sympathy for the Indians' vanishing culture in *Hope Leslie* with the narrator's sympathy for undisturbed village life in Washington Irving's "The Legend of Sleepy Hollow." What forces might motivate these two writers to come up with similar attitudes toward vanishing American cultures?

3. Consider Sedgwick's female characters in this novel: In what ways do they fit female stereotypes of the early nineteenth century, and in what ways do they express Sedgwick's own vision of women in the republic?

Caroline Kirkland (1801–1864)

Contributing Editor: Judith Fetterley

Classroom Issues and Strategies

Most of the students I have taught love Caroline Kirkland. They find her eminently contemporary. Her prose style is accessible, she is funny, and she deals with a subject familiar to nearly all Americans—the frontier. Some students are put off by her middle-class bias and perspective; they find her attitudes toward the locals patronizing, and they object to the fact that (unlike Jewett) Kirkland provides very little space for the stories of any of these people as told by themselves.

Kirkland's letters sound like they were written yesterday to the students reading the letter. One obvious way of breaking open the text and inviting discussion is to ask students to pick one of her "natives" and have them write what they imagine that person would say about their new neighbor, Caroline Kirkland, if they wrote a letter to one of their friends who has moved farther west.

Students often wonder why they have never heard of Kirkland before. They want to know what else she wrote. They wonder why she is so concerned with the issue of manners and ask what happened when she published her book.

Major Themes, Historical Perspectives, Personal Issues

Kirkland is accessible in part because she is writing about a subject that has been made central to the study of American culture—the frontier, the movement west of white settlers. Kirkland is important because she is dealing with this phenomenon from the point of view of the woman who was required, often not of her own will, to follow the man to his new home. She writes specifically of the cost to women of the male model of "upward mobility"—the pattern of constantly moving on under the guise of improving one's position. This theory of "improvement" of course takes no account of the woman's position, which is usually worsened as a result. Thus the most important feature of Kirkland for the survey course is the fact that she inserts the woman's perspective into this male cultural pattern. Kirkland's work thus provides the context for discussing the commitment of the mid-century women writers to values of home, domesticity, and so on.

Kirkland is equally important as an example of a relatively early American woman writer who successfully established a voice. The instructor should be familiar with Kirkland's essay "Literary Women," collected in *A Book of the Home Circle* (1853), and included in the volume of Kirkland's work from the Rutgers Press American Women Writers series. Kirkland was well aware of the prejudices against women writers and of the strictures governing what they were and were not supposed to write. Her decision to lace her text with literary references may in part have stemmed from her desire to define herself clearly as a literary woman and to defy the strictures and the stereotypes. In a context where there was so much harassment of women writers, her voice is remarkably clear and confident. She writes with a sense of authority and conviction that is not modulated through any other agency. She writes because she likes to write, not because she is trying to save the world or support her children. She is a rare example of an early American woman writer who wrote carefully and published only what she felt was well written.

Significant Form, Style, or Artistic Conventions

First, Kirkland defines herself as a realist. Since American literary history has been based, until very recently, on a study of the works of male American writers, the governing generalization insists that realism in American literature is a post–Civil War phenomenon. However, American women writers were experimenting with realism in the decades before the Civil War, and Caroline Kirkland was among the first, the most explicit, and the most articulate. Clearly defining herself against the romantic views of the West provided by contemporary male writers, Kirkland claims to write the truth about Michigan, which means that she intends to include the difficulties that face women who try to put together three meals a day in the wilderness, the state of the Michigan roads with their enormous pot holes, and the general slovenliness of the "natives." So certainly any discussion of Kirkland needs to address her conception of realism and the general contours of American literary history that emerge from including women writers in the map of the territory.

Second, Kirkland identifies herself as participating in a tradition set by women writers. She ends her preface to *A New Home* with a reference to "Miss Mitford's charming sketches of village life" and with a "humble curtsey." It is important to explore the degree to which Kirkland establishes throughout her text her connection to a tradition of women writers presenting a woman's point of view. As is clear from the preface, Kirkland embraces an iconography that clearly identifies her as a woman writer (men don't curtsey), and she wishes to remind her readers that they are reading a work written by a woman. In the process of so doing, she is also attempting to explore the nature of a woman's aesthetics. Implicitly, and on occasion explicitly, she is asking, what kind of book does a woman write, given the nature of woman's experience and perspective?

One can also raise here the question of genre—to what extent is Kirkland's voice, her authority, tied to her use of a relatively unconvention-ridden genre, namely the letter home? Is she freed to do her best because she is not trying to be a great writer but is trying only to write interesting letters to the folks back home? Students might be encouraged to look into the use of the letter as a form for published writing by both men and women in the nineteenth century.

Original Audience

As I have said earlier, Kirkland is useful for raising the larger question of the relation of the nineteenth-century American women writers to their audience. Nineteenth-century white middle-class American male writers had problems establishing an audience, a sense of who they were writing to. A new view could and should question these assumptions. Hawthorne's preface to *The Scarlet Letter*, the chapter on the Custom-House, can serve perhaps as a paradigm for the male situation. Here Hawthorne reveals his fear that he is speaking to no one except himself. Kirkland, on the other hand, has a very clear sense of the "you" at the other end of her letter. One can certainly raise with students the question as to why it is that Kirkland might have such a clear sense of audience. To what degree does it have to do with the world she describes women as inhabiting—a world in which loved ones are left behind, a world in which the letter (and think of the implications of this fact—here we look forward to *The Color Purple*) was left in the hands of women, a world in which there was a clear sense of community and of someone who would want to know what was happening to their daughters who had gone west?

It seems fairly obvious that Kirkland assumed her readers would be of the same social class as herself. Whether or not she assumed her readers would be primarily women is a more complex question. My own sense of Kirkland leads me to believe that she assumed a readership made up of men as well as women, that she was not of that group of women writers who were writing essentially to women even though they knew and hoped that men might read their books and thus overhear their conversation. But I also think Kirkland took her women readers seriously and wrote at least in part to educate them.

Comparisons, Contrasts, Connections

I have already suggested many points of comparison. I will just reiterate them here. Kirkland can be compared with many male writers in terms of her presentation of the frontier and the experience of westward and "upward" mobility. She can also be compared with many male writers in terms of her attitudes toward and handling of the issue of class. A writer like Hawthorne is so completely class-bound that class is never even an issue in his work. In many of the classes I have taught on Kirkland, I have been able to use students' anger at Kirkland's classism to raise the issue of class prejudice in writers like Hawthorne. Many students have come to realize that writers like Hawthorne protect themselves, albeit unconsciously, against charges of classism by simply never raising class as an issue. Kirkland is at least aware that American society is profoundly affected by the issue of class. Kirkland can also be compared to male writers in terms of the question of audience, as discussed above.

Kirkland can be fruitfully compared with other nineteenth-century American women writers in terms of the issue of voice. Students can compare the authority with which Kirkland speaks to the less secure voice of certain other women writers. She can also be compared with other women writers in terms of her commitment to realism and in terms of her commitment to presenting the woman's story.

Bibliography

I refer the instructor to the discussion of Kirkland in Annette Kolodny's *The Land Before Her* and in my own *Provisions*.

There is also a Twayne series book on Kirkland that is useful for an overview but does not provide much in the way of criticism and would not be of much use in the classroom.

Nathaniel Hawthorne (1804–1864)

Contributing Editor: Rita K. Gollin

Classroom Issues and Strategies

Some students find Hawthorne too gloomy, too dense, and too complex. And few understand Puritan beliefs about self, sin, and America's moral mission as they evolved into the antithetical beliefs of transcendentalism. Even fewer recognize how persistently Hawthorne involves the reader in his own efforts to probe such antitheses.

To address these problems, try approaching Hawthorne as a riddler and wry joker who challenged all authority including his own. Students enjoy recognizing Hawthorne's self-mockery and his various forms of ironic self-presentation. Though self-mockery is most overt in Hawthorne's letters and prefaces (the introduction to "Rappaccini's Daughter," for example), students can quickly discern the skepticism underlying Hawthorne's uses of laughter, his assessments of America's Puritan past and quotidian present, and his anatomization of his major characters. Introduce recurrent patterns of character, theme, image, and so forth, then invite students to identify variations on those patterns within Hawthorne's works.

Comment on Hawthorne's attempts to mediate between Puritan beliefs and Emerson's, then encourage students to locate how each of his fictions incorporates, accepts, or rejects particular beliefs. Alert them to Hawthorne's assumptions about what human wholeness and happiness require—including the interrelationship of the mind, heart, spirit, will, imagination, and accommodation, though not indulgence, of bodily needs.

One useful strategy is to ask students what a story is "about," then what it is also "about." They soon realize that informed attention yields expanded meaning.

Current debates about canon formation and absolute literary value provide a useful context for discussing Hawthorne's reputation. Briefly sketch how criteria for judgment have changed over time (e.g., after publication of *The Scarlet Letter*, after Hawthorne's death, during the centenary celebrations of his birth, and during the heyday of New Criticism), and provide some comments about current critical approaches to Hawthorne, including those of feminists and new historicists. Then invite discussion of why Hawthorne has been considered a major writer from the 1830s to the present.

Major Themes, Historical Perspectives, Personal Issues

Hawthorne's major themes and thematic patterns include self-trust versus accommodation to authority; conventional versus unconventional gender roles; obsessiveness versus open-mindedness; hypocrisy versus candor; presumed guilt or innocence; forms of nurturance and destructiveness; the penalties of isolation; crimes against the human heart; patriarchal power; belief in fate or free will; belief in progress (including scientific, technological, social, and political progress) as opposed to nostalgia for the past; the truths available to the mind during dream and reverie; and the impossibility of earthly perfection.

Historical issues include marketplace facts—for example, where Hawthorne's short stories first appeared (unsigned and low-paid) and which stories he chose to collect in *Twice-Told Tales* and in later anthologies. Related issues include how each book was advertised, how well it sold, how much money Hawthorne earned for it, and how it was reviewed. Students should also know something about the whys and wherefores of Hawthorne's career options during and after college, of his undertaking literary hackwork and children's books, of his interlude at Brook Farm, of his appointments to the Boston Custom House, the Salem Custom House, and the Liverpool consulate, and of his efforts to win reinstatement at the Salem Custom House. Additional historical issues include Puritan versus Whig ideas about the self and the historical past; the political practices and social climate of Jacksonian democracy; and genteel assumptions about women's roles. Still other historical issues concern the particular place and period in which Hawthorne set each story.

Personal issues include the various ways Hawthorne's family history and specific events in his life informed his writings—most obviously the introduction to "Rappaccini's Daughter" and his letters and journals. Students can easily recognize how "Young Goodman Brown" incorporates facts about his Puritan ancestors, and they are interested in asking such questions as whether the concern with female purity in "Rappaccini's Daughter" and "The Birth-mark" may reflect Hawthorne's anxieties in the aftermath of his marriage, and how Hawthorne's anxieties about his role as an artist are expressed in "The Birth-mark" and the Custom House introduction to *The Scarlet Letter*. Students might also speculate about how Hawthorne's experiences of intimacy and deprivation in the aftermath of his father's death inform his fiction (e.g., Robin's nostalgia for a home that excludes him). Other personal issues that interest students include Hawthorne's relationship to the Mannings' mercantile values, his antipathy to Salem, his experiences at Bowdoin College (including his nonconformity and his friendships with Bridge, Pierce, and Longfellow), his lifelong strivings to develop his talents and support himself by his pen (during his self-defined "twelve lonely years," during his political appointments, and so forth), his secret engagement, and his identity as doting but fallible husband and father.

Significant Form, Style, or Artistic Conventions

1. Sketch versus tale and short story.
2. Romance versus novel.
3. Characters: recurrent "types" and interrelationships; authorial intrusion or objective display; heroism, villainy, and what Hawthorne seems to condemn, admire, or sadly accept.
4. Image clusters and patterns (for example, dark versus light, natural versus unnatural, sunshine and firelight versus moonlight and reflections, labyrinths).

5. Subjective vision (including fantasies, reveries, dreams, and narrator's questions about objective "reality").
6. Narrative antecedents, including biblical parable, Spenserian romance, allegory (Dante, Bunyan, and others), gothic horror tales, sentimental love stories, old wives' tales, fairy tales, and so on.
7. Reworking of notebook entries into fiction, and the relationship between earlier works and later ones.
8. Hawthorne's open-ended endings.
9. The relation of prefaces and expository introductions to Hawthorne's plots.
10. Narrator's options to the reader (e.g., saying, "Be it so, if you will" after asking if Goodman Brown had only dreamed about a witch-meeting).

Original Audience

For the tales and sketches: students should know something about the gift books and periodicals that published Hawthorne's early work (including the practice of anonymous publication, payment, and other material published in a volume where Hawthorne appeared), and reasons for Hawthorne's difficulty in publishing a collection.

For the collections: Hawthorne's 1837 letter to Longfellow; Hawthorne's selections and sequence for a particular volume; his publishers; reviews and advertisements.

For the novels: Hawthorne's aims as expressed in letters, journals, and prefaces and through his narrators; marketing, sales, and reviews; James T. Fields as publisher, editor, banker, and friend—and securer of English copyrights.

For all the fiction: Hawthorne's challenges to period assumptions about gender roles, parent-child relationships, social and scientific progress, the trustworthiness of sense data ("seeing is believing"), and the importance of the inner life.

Comparisons, Contrasts, Connections

- Irving: Use of America's past including folktales, popular myths, picturesque and sublime settings
- Poe: Use of gothic settings, themes, and characters; interest in dreams and other threshold states, and in sensitive individuals' propensities to madness
- Melville: Plumbing of the dark depths of the human mind, antipathy to authority, celebration of individual striving and sympathetic nurturing

- Emerson: Celebration of striving toward self-fulfillment, criticism of hereditary privilege, egalitarian vision
- Stowe and the "damned mob of scribbling women": Celebration of women's capacities for dignity and heroism, religious piety
- James: Sensitive hero/narrator; psychological scrutiny; unresolved questions
- Conrad: Journeys to the heart of darkness; parallel of outer and inner experience
- Jewett: Minute attention to nature and to unheroic characters
- Welty: Comic irony, ambivalence, anti-authoritarianism, densely detailed landscapes
- Flannery O'Connor, Updike, Borges: Queries into the mystifying complexities of human behavior, dark comedy

Questions for Reading, Discussion, and Writing

Provide some information about books that helped shape Hawthorne's imagination (including historical and scientific writings and the popular literature of his day). Students can better appreciate "Rappaccini's Daughter" after learning about Hawthorne's uses of Milton, Spenser, Dante, and the Bible; his variations on the courtship plot in popular magazines; and his skepticism about contemporary scientific experiments (as well as scientific controversy in Renaissance Padua).

Students enjoy connecting particular works with subsequent ones— most obviously, tracing connections of "Mrs. Hutchinson," "Young Goodman Brown," "My Kinsman, Major Molineux," "The Minister's Black Veil," Hawthorne's letters to Fields, and *The Scarlet Letter*.

"Cultural" questions that students enjoy addressing include attitudes toward art in general and fiction in particular in nineteenth-century America. (Here they need definitions of such terms as *picturesque* and *sublime*.)

Formal questions that students can ask of each story include a comparison of the first and last views of a particular character; Hawthorne's ambivalent treatment of women, writers, and artists, but also father figures; the questions the narrator raises but leaves unanswered; Hawthorne's use of "preternatural ambiguity"—offering alternative naturalistic explanations for what seems to be supernatural; exposition versus dramatized scene; parallels between inner and outer landscapes; and a story's formal design (symmetries, contrasts, repetitions, suspense, climax, and so forth).

Bibliography

In addition to the secondary works mentioned in the anthology, I would recommend recent books on Hawthorne and his period by Nina Baym, Michael Davitt Bell, Sacvan Bercovitch, Gillian Brown, Laurence Buell, and Philip Fisher, but also books written decades ago by Richard Harter Fogle, Roy R. Male, Leo Marx, and F. O. Matthiessen.

Edgar Allan Poe (1809–1849)

Contributing Editor: William Goldhurst

Classroom Issues and Strategies

Students confuse Poe's narrator with the author, so that in stories involving drug addiction and murders, students often say "Poe this" and "Poe that" when they mean the narrator of the tale. Poe's reputation for alcohol abuse, drug abuse, poverty, and bizarre personal habits—all exaggerated—often comes up in classroom discussion and should be relegated to the irrelevant. Students ask: "Was he an alcoholic?" "Was he a drug addict?" "Was he insane?" I quickly try to divert attention from such gossip to the themes of Jacksonian America, asking them to ponder the nature and value of Poe's vision.

I have a slide lecture, largely biographical, which always is well received. Lacking such materials, I would recommend a line-by-line reading of the major poems, with explanations as you go along. Particularly, "The Raven" and "Ulalume" are understandable by this method. I would also prepare students for effects late in "Ligeia," then have them read aloud the last few pages of this tale. I always prepare the class for the Poe segment with a quick review of President Andrew Jackson's policies and what is meant by "Jacksonian Democracy." I believe this to be essential for a study of Poe.

Major Themes, Historical Perspectives, Personal Issues

Stress Poe's affinities with mainstream America. He was culturally informed, rather than isolated, reclusive, and warped. I have spent years studying his ties to Jacksonian popular culture. It is unrealistic to ask all teachers to be informed to this extent; but the point should be made, and repeatedly.

Significant Form, Style, or Artistic Conventions

Poe's fictional architecture is unparalleled. Stories such as "The Purloined Letter" and "Ligeia" have definite form and symmetry. On another level, while most critics align Poe with the gothic tradition, I emphasize his links with the sentimental writers of his time and earlier.

The "cycle" form practiced by many painters of his time is reflected in poems such as "The Raven."

Original Audience

It is important to establish the fact that death literature was common in Poe's day, owing to the high mortality rate among the young and middle-class citizens. In some ways Poe participated in the "consolation" movement of this time, by which he attempted to comfort the bereaved.

Comparisons, Contrasts, Connections

Poe compares with James Fenimore Cooper, Washington Irving, Charles Brockden Brown, William Gilmore Simms, Donald G. Mitchell—in fact, he relates in revealing ways to most of his contemporaries.

Questions for Reading, Discussion, and Writing

1. I always ask students to express their concept of Poe the man and Poe the author before we begin our studies. Later, I hope they have changed their image from the stereotype to something closer to reality. I also ask the students to mention more recent figures who compare to Poe. If they say Stephen King, I argue the point. I try to introduce them to Rod Serling and Alfred Hitchcock.
2. Explain the steps involved in the "Initiation Ritual," and then ask the students to trace the initiation pattern in Poe stories. It works out very well for all concerned.

Bibliography

Editions of Poe:

The standard edition is the *Collected Works of Edgar Allan Poe*, ed. T. O. Mabbott et al. 3 vols. Cambridge, MA: Harvard UP, 1969. Volume 1 of this edition is the best edition of Poe's poems.

Poe's critical and aesthetic works are collected in *Edgar Allan Poe: Essays and Reviews*. New York: Library of America, 1984.

Imaginary Voyages contains texts and elaborate notes for Poe's *Hans Pfaall, Pym,* and *Julius Rodman,* ed. Burton Pollin. Boston: Twayne, 1981. "Eureka" is included in the Penguin Edition of *The Science Fiction of Edgar Allan Poe,* edited by Harold Beaver.

The best student edition is *The Short Fiction of Edgar Allan Poe,* ed. Stuart Levine and Susan Levine. Urbana: U of Illinois P, 1976, 1990.

Biographies:

Of Primary Importance: "Annals" in T. O. Mabbott's Vol. 1 of the *Collected Works of Edgar Allan Poe.* A year-by-year summary of Poe's activities, reliably documented.

The Poe Log, ed. Dwight Thomas and David Jackson. Boston: Hall, 1987. The most complete documentary of Poe's professional and personal history.

Edgar Allan Poe: A Critical Biography by Arthur Hobson Quinn. Appleton, 1941; reissued New York: Cooper Square, 1969. Still the best Poe biography by a conscientious scholar.

Poe's letters have been brilliantly collected and edited in two volumes: *The Letters of Edgar Allen Poe.* 2 vols. Ed. John Ward Ostrum. New York: Gordian, 1966.

Two recent biographies contain some of the old patronizing and sensational features of nineteenth-century commentary and should be approached very skeptically:

Edgar Allan Poe: Mournful and Never-ending Remembrance by Kenneth Silverman. New York: HarperCollins, 1991.

Edgar Allan Poe: His Life and Legacy by Jeffrey Meyers. New York: Scribner's, 1992.

Criticism:

Reviews and essays about Poe during his lifetime are collected in *Edgar Allan Poe: The Critical Heritage,* ed. I. M. Walker. London: Routledge, 1986.

More recent criticism is collected in *The Recognition of Edgar Allan Poe*, ed. Eric Carlson. Ann Arbor: U of Michigan P, 1966.

Poe Studies: Dark Romanticism, a periodical published at Washington State University in Pullman, WA, publishes up-to-the-moment bibliographies listing critical articles on varied aspects of Poe.

The best and most complete critical book ever published on Poe is the recent release *Companion to Poe Studies*, ed. Eric Carlson, Greenwood, 1996, which has twenty-five chapters by Poe scholars on different aspects of Poe's fiction and poetry, including his influence overseas, and many interpretive essays, all on a relatively high professional level. For Poe overseas, supplement the *Companion* with Carl Anderson's excellent *Poe in North-Light*. Durham: Duke UP, 1973.

An extraordinary collection of Poe photographic portraits and daguerreotypes has been assembled in *The Portraits and Daguerreotypes of Edgar Allan Poe*, collected by Michael J. Deas, U of Virginia P, 1989.

Much attention has been given recent psychoanalytic and deconstructive Poe criticism. Central arguments in these areas are collected in *The Purloined Poe*, ed. John Muller and William Richardson. Baltimore: Johns Hopkins UP, 1988.

Concentrated criticism of Poe's one novel is collected in *Poe's Pym: Critical Explorations*, ed. Richard Kopley. Durham: Duke UP, 1992.

Myths and Reality: Thy Mysterious Mr. Poe, ed. Benjamin Franklin Fisher IV. Poe Society of Baltimore, 1987. Contains thoughtful essays on the tales and the life.

The Rationale of Deception, by David Ketterer. Baton Rouge: Louisiana State UP, 1979. Contains some insightful commentary on the tales.

Poe's Fiction: Romantic Irony in the Gothic Tales, by G. R. Thompson. Madison: U of Wisconsin P, 1973. Reads most of Poe's effects as humorous satires or hoaxes.

A delightful review of Poe correspondence, clippings, and early criticism is found in *John Henry Ingram's Poe Collection at the University of Virginia*, ed. John Carl Miller. Charlottesville: UP of Virginia, 1960.

The standard bibliography, but active only to 1967, is *Edgar Allan Poe: A Bibliography of Criticism,* ed. J. Lasley Dameron and Irby Cauthen Jr. Charlottesville: UP of Virginia, 1974. As mentioned earlier, recent criticism is regularly listed in *Poe Studies: Dark Romanticism.*

Harriet Beecher Stowe (1811–1896)

Contributing Editor: Desirée Henderson

Classroom Issues and Strategies

Like many of her contemporaries, Harriet Beecher Stowe believed that writers had a responsibility to use the power of literature to intervene in political debates, inspire moral improvement, and relieve the suffering of the unfortunate. This belief helps explain the divided (and sometimes divisive) nature of Stowe's work as she sought to combine entertainment with social reform. In other words, Stowe challenged many dominant nineteenth-century beliefs and practices, but she did so by appealing to the widest possible reading audience, a contradiction that may serve as a starting point for class discussion. Stowe's goals will be evident to students when they read *Uncle Tom's Cabin,* as she depicts Uncle Tom as an intelligent and gentle Christian in order to undercut racist ideas about ignorant, violent, and heathen slaves; they will also perceive that the consequence is that Tom is unbelievably perfect and disturbingly submissive. Beginning with broad questions about the role of literature in shaping society (why can fiction be a powerful political tool? does it still have that function today?) allows students to appreciate Stowe's intentions. This provides a basis for an examination of Stowe's use of race and gender stereotypes; ask students to consider if stereotypes ever have a positive purpose. Students will want to discuss how the meaning of the term *Uncle Tom* has evolved since the nineteenth century and what this indicates about the state of race relations today. Demonstrating the longevity of *Uncle Tom's Cabin* in American culture, film, and advertisements (still evident on certain brands of rice or cream of wheat) will communicate Stowe's continuing influence on popular images of slavery.

Major Themes, Historical Perspective, Personal Issues

The idea of power through powerlessness, submission, or victimization is evident in most of Stowe's work. Stowe is interested in exploring how those most disempowered (slaves, women, children, and so on) gain a measure of control even in moments of their worst suffering. When Uncle Tom chooses to die at the hand of Legree ("I know, Mas'r; but I can't tell anything. *I can die!*") or when Mrs. Marvyn accepts Candace's consolation during her paroxysm of grief ("Jes' come right down to whar poor ole black Candace has to stay allers,—it's a good place, darlin'!"), these characters are empowered by accepting or even choosing their submission. Literary critics have argued that these representations preserve rather than reform social divisions of power and powerlessness, implicitly valorizing and even eroticizing suffering for its own sake. But the popularity of Stowe's martyr characters suggests that nineteenth-century Americans found the idea of salvation through suffering a compelling one. Ask students how Stowe's model of behavior may have reflected or influenced the social movements of the time, including the abolitionist and women's rights movements. Stowe may be seen as advocating a middle-ground between radical arguments for social change and a conservative embrace of the status-quo, but does this equivocation render her position ineffectual?

Significant Form, Style, or Artistic Conventions

Stowe's writing exemplifies two important styles of early American fiction, sentimental and regional, and often seeks to combine the two. Sentimental fiction, also known as domestic fiction, is typically thought of as literature for women, dealing with domestic concerns or romantic drama, but it is aesthetically defined by its emphasis upon emotion (sentiment, sensibility). Sentimental literature seeks not only to dramatize the experience of emotion but to provoke an emotional response in the reader, resulting in the "sentimental equation," or an equivalency between audience and text. Key to the political use of sentimentality is the belief that impacting the reader's emotions will necessarily result in a change in action, whether it be thought or behavior. Students can be asked to consider what techniques Stowe uses to draw upon the reader's emotions, such as establishing similarities between readers and characters, placing characters in extreme physical or moral danger, dramatizing battles between good versus evil, and so on. Ask students what Stowe intends for her readers to *do* as a result of these emotional provocations? What role models does Stowe provide to demonstrate appropriate social or political behavior? Discuss the contradiction in the concluding scene of *Uncle Tom's Cabin*, in which young George Shelby refuses to assist Legree's slaves in one breath and swears to do *"what one man can"* to end slavery in the next, in order to examine the efficacy of sentimental politics.

Stowe's exploration of regionalism is evident in her depiction of vernacular speech. Students will correctly notice that Stowe employs vernacular most often when depicting African Americans. However, if they compare the speech of the slave trader Haley and that of the escaped slave George Harris in *Uncle Tom's Cabin*, they will see that vernacular is often a marker of class status or intelligence, as well as race. Ask students whether Stowe's use of vernacular speech has the effect of rendering her characters stereotypical or authentic. It can also be useful to consider how Stowe's writing evolves from sentimentalism towards realism. Is there a difference between her use of vernacular in *Uncle Tom's Cabin* and in *The Minister's Wooing*?

Original Audience

In many ways, Stowe helped to create a new reading audience. She began writing during the early decades of the popular literature phenomenon and it is important to contextualize her work within this historical moment. The rise of popular literature was the result of technological advances in printing and shipping that made it possible to mass produce and quickly distribute books, making fiction cheap and accessible to a wide reading audience. No longer earmarked for upper- or middle-class readers, popular literature proliferated and created a body of fiction that students will recognize through the terms *dime novel* and *penny press*, as well as more contemporary terms like *pulp fiction*, *trash fiction*, or *airport reading*. It is worthwhile to have students examine what differentiates popular literature from serious or high literature, and why Stowe chose to write in the former. This can also be a point at which to discuss canon reformation and to ask students whether popular fiction deserves to be studied in college classrooms.

Stowe benefited immensely from the popular literature phenomenon and would commonly publish her work in multiple forms—first in a serialized form in magazines and then as complete novels. *Uncle Tom's Cabin* was first serialized in *The National Era* before it was published as a novel in 1852. In explaining how this novel established the concept of the bestseller, emphasize that *Uncle Tom's Cabin* went beyond the number of books sold, to include the widespread marketing of related materials and adaptations that is common today. Ask students whether the novel's popularity would have assisted or detracted from its political impact; ask them to reflect on Stephen Hirsh's statement that Uncle Tom was "the most frequently sold slave in American history."

Although *Uncle Tom's Cabin*'s popularity cut across class, Stowe's intended audience was primarily white Northerners; Stowe repeatedly addresses her readers as observers of slavery rather than participants. However, the publication statistics tell us that the novel was read by individuals across the nation, who had divergent reactions. Have students explore how the South responded by examining selections of "anti-Tom" literature. Equally important are the reactions of African-American authors and political figures of the time; it may be interesting to have students who have read Frederick Douglass' *Narrative of the Life* speculate on why he endorsed Stowe's novel.

Comparisons, Contrasts, Connections

Uncle Tom's Cabin should be central to discussions of nineteenth-century anti-slavery literature. Stowe's fictional representation of slavery can be compared with slave narratives by Frederick Douglass and Harriet Jacobs, among others. Stowe's influence on African-American writers can be seen in Frances Harper's poetry. One provocative point of contrast is between the character of Uncle Tom in Stowe's novel and Babo in Herman Melville's "Benito Cereno." Ask students to analyze the two authors' use of racial stereotypes. In addition to her contributions to antislavery literature, Stowe is clearly participating in the ongoing conversation about women's rights; her justification of Eliza and Rachel Halliday's antislavery acts can be readily compared with Angelina Grimké's advice in her *Appeal to the Christian Women of the South*. But Stowe's idealistic portrait of the Quaker homestead can also be juxtaposed with Fanny Fern's satire of domestic life, "Hints to Young Wives."

Stowe's *The Minister's Wooing* is clearly in dialogue with the Calvinist doctrine of Jonathan Edwards. Posing Candace's evangelical argument against Edwards's "Sinners in the Hands of Angry God" can instruct students in the evolution of American religious traditions. Also, Stowe's depiction of Sojourner Truth contributes to discussions of Truth's distinctive oratorical voice; students can explore how Truth serves as a model for the character of Candace.

Working with Cultural Objects

In order to convey to students the popularity and significance of Stowe' *Uncle Tom's Cabin*, direct students to the invaluable website, *Uncle Tom's Cabin and American Culture* at <http://www.iath.virginia.edu/utc>. The editor, Stephen Railton, has compiled an extensive collection of Uncle Tom memorabilia—commonly known as "Uncle Tomitudes"—spanning the nineteenth and twentieth centuries. Students may find particularly interesting the silent film versions and animated adaptations of the novel from the 1920s and 1930s. Ask students what this visual archive tells us about why the novel has had such a long-lasting place in American culture.

This site also contains numerous Southern "anti-Tom" texts which capture an alternative response to the novel. Of particular note is *Aunt Phillis' Cabin, or Southern Life as It Is* (1852) by Mary Henderson Eastman at <http://www.iath.virginia.edu/utc/proslav/eastmanhp.html>. One of the best-known "anti-Tom" novels, it can provide students with a glimpse into the Southern perspective on the validity and sanctity of the institution of slavery. Direct students toward chapter 3, which describes a slave owner's generous treatment of his slaves, Uncle Bacchus and Aunt Phillis, or chapter 4, which depicts how abolitionists exploit rather than assist an escaped slave named Susan.

Discussion Questions

1. What is the purpose of the parallel story lines in *Uncle Tom's Cabin* in which Tom moves south, deeper and deeper into slavery, and Eliza's family moves north towards freedom?
2. Why does Stowe choose to omit the details of Tom's beating and death? Does this make her critique of slavery more or less effective?
3. Why does Stowe use the black character Candace as the mouthpiece for her critique of Calvinist doctrine in *The Minister's Wooing*?
4. Why does Stowe compare Sojourner Truth to the Libyan Sibyl? Does the comparison work to elevate Truth or render her static and ineffective?

Bibliography

A extensive bibliography of primary and secondary materials by and about Harriet Beecher Stowe has been complied by Martha L. Henning and Susan Goodwin. It is available at <http://www.digital.library.upenn.edu/women/stowe/stowbib.html>.

William Wells Brown (1815–1884)

Contributing Editor: Arlene Elder

Classroom Issues and Strategies

It would be extremely useful to recount briefly Brown's own history and to emphasize that he was self-taught after his escape from slavery and, therefore, influenced strongly both by his reading and by the popular ideas current during his time, for instance, common concepts of male and female beauty. Reading the class a short historical description of a slave auction and some commentary about the sale of persons of mixed blood, since even one drop of "Negro blood" marked one legally as black, hence appropriately enslaved, would also provide a context for the chapters from *Clotelle*.

One might provoke a lively discussion by quoting some of the negative comments on writers like Brown present in "The myth of a 'negro literature'" by LeRoi Jones (Amiri Baraka) in *Home Social Essays* (New York: Morrow, 1966) or Addison Gayle Jr.'s designation of Brown as "the conscious or unconscious propagator of assimilationism" (*The Way of the New World, The Black Novel in America*, 11. New York: Anchor, 1976). Any denigration of functional or committed art by critics with New Critical persuasions should provoke thought about the novel's place in the black canon as well as raise current theoretical issues about the political role of art and the artist.

Students are interested in the verification of the sale of "white" slaves: the historical basis for Clotelle as the alleged daughter of Thomas Jefferson; questions of nineteenth-century popular characterization as a source for Brown's handling of his protagonists; the whole genre of the slave narrative; and theoretical issues such as art versus propaganda.

Major Themes, Historical Perspectives, Personal Issues

1. Brown's own personal experience as an aide to a slave trader.
2. The sexual exploitation of both female slaves and white wives by slave owners. Harriet Jacobs's *Incidents in the Life of a Slave Girl* provides an actual situation of sexual exploitation. Since selections from *Incidents* appear in *The Heath Anthology*, it might be useful to teach *Clotelle* in conjunction with this slave narrative.
3. The historical role of Christianity as both an advocate of slavery and, for the slaves, a source of escapism from their situation.
4. The presence of rebellious slaves who refused to accept their dehumanization.

Significant Form, Style, or Artistic Conventions

One needs to place *Clotelle* within the dual contexts of the black literary traditions of slave narrative and folk orature and the mainstream genre of popular nineteenth-century drama and fiction. This dual influence accounts for what appears to be the incongruous description of Jerome, for instance, who could be seen, in his manly rebellion against an unfair beating, as a fictional Frederick Douglass but also is described in a totally unrealistic way both to appeal to racist standards of beauty and to correspond to images of heroes in popular white novels.

Original Audience

Of equal influence on Brown's composition of *Clotelle* are his two very different audiences, the white middle class and the black "talented-tenth," with very different, sometimes conflicting, expectations, histories, aesthetics, education, and incomes, to whom Brown and other nineteenth-century black novelists had to appeal. Interestingly, there is still no homogeneous audience for black writing, *Clotelle* included, because American society is still not equal. Therefore, it should not surprise an instructor if the selections arouse extremely different responses from various class members.

Comparisons, Contrasts, Connections

Brown's intertwined aesthetic and political complexities are echoed not only in the writing by other nineteenth-century African-American novelists but also in the work of all ethnic American writers, especially those of the present day, for whom issues of constituency and audience are extremely complicated. It is for this reason that *Clotelle* is extremely useful to demonstrate not only common subjects and themes with the slave narratives but, just as interesting, the influence of society upon artistic choices and the paradoxical position of the ethnic artist vis-à-vis African- and Euro-American literary heritages and his or her mixed constituency.

Questions for Reading, Discussion, and Writing

1. Chapter II:
    (a) How is the idea as well as the historical reality of slaves being treated as dehumanized property expressed in Brown's language and imagery?
    (b) How does the auction process reveal the complete dichotomy between the interests of the slaves and those of their traders and owners?
    (c) What is the intended effect of Brown's description of Isabella on the auction block?
    (d) Why does Brown link the image of the auction block with that of the church spires in this chapter?
2. Chapter X:
    (a) What is the symbolic/thematic effect of Brown's description of Isabella's garden?
    (b) What does this chapter reveal about the sexual exploitation of both female slaves and the wives of the white masters? What contradiction does it suggest about the possibly comforting concept of a "good master"?
    (c) Have we been given enough information to explain Linwood's behavior? How do we account for Isabella's continued kindness toward him?
3. Chapter XI:
    (a) Why doesn't Linwood accept Isabella's offer to release him from his promise to her?

   (b) Do you think a nineteenth-century reader might react differently
       from a modern one to the unbelievability of Linwood's mutterings in
       his sleep? If so, why?
   (c) What is the function of religion for Isabella?
4. Chapter XVIII:
   (a) How do you explain Brown's incongruous physical description of
       Jerome?
   (b) Who are George Combe and Fowler, and why are they alluded to
       here?
   (c) What do the allusions to certain well-known lovers reveal about
       Brown's reading?
5. (a) Comparison with details of slave life, especially female concubinage
       found in Harriet A. Jacobs, *Incidents in the Life of a Slave Girl, Writ-
       ten by Herself*.
   (b) Discussion of Isabella and Clotelle as representatives of the popular
       "tragic octoroon" stereotype.
   (c) Comparison of *Clotelle* with another nineteenth-century African-
       American novel about a female slave and her liberation, Frances E.
       W. Harper's *Iola Leroy*.
   (d) Discussion of Jerome as a "counterstereotype" intended to refute nega-
       tive popular images of blacks. A look at Frederick Douglass's *Narra-
       tive of the Life of Frederick Douglass* as well as Thomas Dixon Jr.'s
       The Clansman would provide polar contexts for this subject.

Bibliography

Dearborn, Mary. *Pochahantas' Daughters: Gender and Ethnicity in American
     Culture.*

Gates, Henry Louis Jr. "Race," *Writing and Difference.*

Kinney, James. *Amalgamation: Race, Sex, and Rhetoric in the Nineteenth-
     Century American Novel.*

Takaki, Ronald T. *Violence in the Black Imagination* (especially Part III on
     Brown and *Clotelle*).

Herman Melville (1819–1891)

Contributing Editor: Carolyn L. Karcher

Classroom Issues and Strategies

The primary problems I have encountered in teaching Melville are the difficulty of the language and the complexity of the narrative point of view. This is particularly true of "Benito Cereno," but *Billy Budd* and "The Paradise of Bachelors and the Tartarus of Maids" also present problems for students unaccustomed to allusive and circuitous language and a complex narrative stance. Students usually find "Bartleby" and "The Encantadas" much more accessible. "Hawthorne and His Mosses" is daunting to students because of its allusiveness. It also needs to be set in the context of debate over how nineteenth-century American writers should go about producing an authentic national literature.

Each of the Melville selections demands a somewhat different strategy. What works best for me is not to teach Melville's writings together in a separate unit, but to group individual Melville pieces with texts by other authors on similar themes. For example, "Hawthorne and His Mosses" would make most sense to students in a unit on debates over literary nationalism and aesthetic theory, which could include Emerson's "The American Scholar," Poe's "The Philosophy of Composition" and review of Hawthorne's *Twice-Told Tales*, Fuller's "A Short Essay on Critics," and Whitman's 1855 Preface to *Leaves of Grass* and *Democratic Vistas*. A unit on the Transcendentalists (Emerson, Thoreau, and Fuller) can be used to introduce such themes as individualism versus social responsibility (Emerson's "Self-Reliance" and Thoreau's "Resistance to Civil Government"); alienation and the critique of industrial capitalism (Thoreau's *Walden*); the critique of patriarchy and marriage as an institution, the parallels between the oppression of women and the enslavement of blacks, and the deconstruction of "true womanhood" and "woman's sphere" as ideological concepts (Fuller's *Woman in the Nineteenth Century*). In a follow-up unit of fiction illustrating these themes, "Bartleby" and "Billy Budd" would fit nicely with the Thoreau selections while "The Paradise of Bachelors and the Tartarus of Maids" would work well after Fuller, along with Elizabeth Stoddard's "Lemorne *Versus* Huell," Alice Cary's "Uncle Christopher's," and Caroline Kirkland's *A New Home*. In my own current syllabus, I introduce the issue of women's rights by teaching Sarah Grimké's *Letters on the Equality of the Sexes, and the Condition of Woman* (#8); selections from Fuller's *Woman in the Nineteenth Century*; Stanton's "Declaration of Sentiments"; Fanny Fern's "Hints to Young Wives," "Soliloquy of a Housemaid," and "Working-Girls of New York"; and Sojourner Truth's "A'n't I a Woman?" I then devote several sessions to varieties of narrative and representations of women, in which I group "The Paradise of Bachelors and the Tartarus of Maids" together with Poe's "Ligeia" and "The Oval Portrait," Hawthorne's "The Birth-mark" and "Rappaccini's Daughter," Kirkland's *A New Home*, Cary's "Uncle Christopher's," and Stoddard's "Lemorne *Versus* Huell." "Benito Cereno" obviously cries out to be assigned with other texts on slavery. Any of the following would work well: David Walker's *Appeal*, Henry Highland Garnet's 1843 "Address to the Slaves of the U.S.A.," Thomas Wentworth Higginson's "Nat Turner's Insurrection," Wendell Phillips's "Toussaint L'Ouverture," Douglass's *Narrative*, Jacobs's *Incidents in the Life of a Slave Girl*, Lydia Maria Child's "Slavery's Pleasant Homes," and selections from her *Appeal*, and Stowe's *Uncle Tom's Cabin*. Olaudah Equiano's *Interesting Narrative* also helps illuminate "Benito Cereno," though it is probably best to teach it with eighteenth-century selections.

I generally try not to overwhelm students with long analyses of style and point of view, but some brief treatment of these matters is indispensable, especially in the case of "Benito Cereno." I often begin by reading key passages aloud to the students and having them analyze the tone of Melville's rhetoric. When they actually hear the tone, they can usually pick up the undercurrent of satire in "The Paradise of Bachelors," the smug insensitivity of Bartleby's employer, and the sense that both Delano and the reader are being subtly mocked.

The question of tone leads easily into the issues of narrative point of view and audience. It is, of course, essential for students to realize that Bartleby's story is narrated by his boss and that "Benito Cereno," though in the third person, is narrated primarily from Delano's point of view, except for the Deposition, which represents Benito Cereno's point of view. After establishing these facts, I ask the students to consider why Melville did not choose instead to narrate his stories from the viewpoints of Bartleby, Babo, and the factory operatives in "Tartarus of Maids."

It is extremely effective to emphasize the continuing applicability of Melville's insights to our own times. Some of the issues his fiction raises are more relevant than ever. Many students (and their parents) work at jobs as meaningless and dead-end as Bartleby's and identify strongly with him. One student described the law copyists as "living xerox machines." Other students have drawn parallels between Bartleby and the homeless. The disparities between rich and poor are even more glaring now than at the time Melville wrote "The Paradise of Bachelors and the Tartarus of Maids" and the phenomenon called the "feminization of poverty" adds another relevant twist to those disparities. In the 1960s, "Benito Cereno" evoked Malcolm X and the Black Panthers; in the 1990s, the struggle in South Africa. *Billy Budd* has perhaps never been more relevant than in our own era, with its wholesale glorification of militarism and its rollback of democratic rights in the name of national security.

The most persistent questions my students raise are why Melville chose to address issues of such vital importance through literary strategies so oblique and circuitous, and whether these strategies were at all effective in subverting his readers' ideological assumptions, let alone transforming their political consciousness.

Major Themes, Historical Perspectives, Personal Issues

A major source of Melville's continuing power is the prescient insight he displays into the central problems of our culture: alienation; violence against women and the repression of the "feminine in man" that usually accompanies it; the widening gap between a decadent ruling class and the workers it immiserates; racism and an ever-more-brutal assault against the world's peoples of color; an unbridled militarism that threatens our very existence while demanding that we resign our civil liberties and human rights in the name of national security. Thus the most effective way of teaching Melville is to encourage students to draw contemporary lessons from the historical predicaments he dramatizes so compellingly.

Each story, of course, centers around a different theme. In teaching "Bartleby" and "The Paradise of Bachelors and the Tartarus of Maids," I emphasize Melville's critique of capitalism and the alienation it produces. "The Communist Manifesto" and Marx's essays "Estranged Labor," "The Meaning of Human Requirements," and "The Power of Money in Bourgeois Society" from *The Economic and Philosophic Manuscripts of 1844* are extraordinarily relevant to these two stories and illuminate them in startling ways. However, I find it preferable to let Marx indirectly inform the approach one takes to the stories, rather than to get sidetracked into a discussion of Marx. A secondary theme in "Bartleby" is the Christian ethic of Matthew 25, which Melville counterpoises against the capitalist ethic of Wall Street (see Bibliography for useful articles on this subject).

"The Paradise of Bachelors and the Tartarus of Maids" naturally invites a feminist as well as a Marxist approach. Margaret Fuller's *Woman in the Nineteenth Century*, Sarah Grimké's *Letters on the Equality of the Sexes, and the Condition of Woman*, and Lydia Maria Child's *Letters from New York* #34 (Women's Rights) provide a ready-made framework for a feminist analysis of that story. Though "Benito Cereno" and *Billy Budd* do not focus on women, a feminist approach can enrich the students' understanding of key episodes and subthemes.

In "Benito Cereno," for example, Delano's racist stereotypes not only prevent him from recognizing that a slave revolt has occurred on board the *San Dominick*, but also distort his perception of the African women's role in that revolt. Just as Babo protects his fellow rebels from discovery by catering to

Delano's stereotypes about blacks as faithful slaves, so the African woman Delano ogles does so by catering to his stereotypes about African women as sexual objects and primitive children of nature. By reading between the lines of the Deposition from a feminist perspective, we see that the African women have probably been sexually victimized by both their master and Don Benito and that they have played an active role in the revolt. Melville's references to the "inflaming" songs and dances they sing while their men are fighting indicate his possible familiarity with such sources as Equiano's narrative, which speaks of African women's participation in warfare.

Similarly, in *Billy Budd*, Melville connects his critique of militarism and the dehumanization it generates with a critique of Western culture's polarization of masculine and feminine. The feminine imagery Melville uses to describe Billy suggests that he represents what Vere later calls the "feminine in man," instructing his drumhead court that "she must be ruled out" of their deliberations. It also suggests that one of the roots of Claggart's and Vere's homosexual attraction to Billy is his embodiment of the "feminine in man" that they have repressed in themselves and must continue to repress by killing Billy. Here again, Margaret Fuller's analysis of the ways in which patriarchy victimizes men as well as women is relevant.

"Benito Cereno" obviously needs above all to be set in the contexts of the antebellum slavery controversy and of the prior historical events to which the story refers (summarized in the footnotes): the Spanish Inquisition; the introduction of African slavery into the Americas under Charles V; the African slave trade and its relationship to the activities of sixteenth- and seventeenth-century English buccaneers; the Santo Domingo slave uprising of 1797–1804; the slave revolt on board the Spanish ship *Tryal* that the real Captain Delano had helped suppress; and the uncannily similar slave revolt that occurred on board the Spanish slave-trading schooner *Amistad* in 1839 (for useful articles on these aspects of the story, see the Bibliography below). As mentioned under "Classroom Issues and Strategies" above, the easiest means of teaching "Benito Cereno" in historical context is to assign it in conjunction with other texts on slavery.

Billy Budd reverberates with implications for the nuclear age and its strategy of Mutually Assured Destruction (MAD). Readers will also find Melville's exploration of Vere's and Claggart's repressed homosexuality highly pertinent to debates over ending the ban against gays in the military. Teachers should not be afraid to exploit the story's contemporary relevance, but they should also set the story in its twin historical contexts—1797, the date of the action, and 1886–1891, the period of composition. See H. Bruce Franklin's "From Empire to Empire," cited below, for an invaluable discussion of these historical contexts.

Teachers might point out that "Bartleby" draws on Melville's experiences of working as a clerk for a brief period and also reflects attitudes he must have associated with his brother Allan, a lawyer; that Elizabeth Shaw Melville's debilitating pregnancies, as well as an actual visit to a paper mill, helped generate the feminist insights Melville displays in "The Paradise of Bachelors and the Tartarus of Maids"; that Judge Lemuel Shaw's conservative views on slavery and controversial role as the first Northern judge to send a fugitive slave back to his master may explain the circuitous form Melville adopts in "Benito Cereno"; and that the suicide of Melville's son Malcolm in 1867 may have some bearing on *Billy Budd.*

Significant Form, Style, or Artistic Conventions

The traditional grouping of Melville with Hawthorne and Poe obscures not only the social vision but also the concept of art differentiating Melville from such canonical figures. Unlike them, Melville persistently rejects "the symmetry of form attainable in pure fiction," holding instead to the principle that "Truth uncompromisingly told will always have its ragged edges." Teachers should point out the way in which Melville deliberately subverts formalist conventions in "Benito Cereno" and *Billy Budd* by appending the Deposition and the three chapters of sequel that force readers to determine the truth for themselves. It might also be useful to point out that the concept of art Melville articulates at the end of *Billy Budd* directly opposes Vere's doctrine of "measured forms" (see Edgar A. Dryden, cited below). In contextualizing Melville with writers like Olaudah Equiano, David Walker, Henry Highland Garnet, Thomas Wentworth Higginson, Frederick Douglass, Lydia Maria Child, Margaret Fuller, Alice Cary, Fanny Fern, and Harriet Beecher Stowe, among others, teachers might suggest comparisons between their aesthetic of "Art for Truth's Sake" (as Elizabeth Stuart Phelps called it) and Melville's concept of literature as "the great Art of Telling the Truth" (delineated in his review "Hawthorne and His Mosses"). Although Melville's short fiction is much less accessible and more oblique than the protest writings of these other authors, it is important to remember that four out of his first five books were autobiographical accounts of his life as a sailor—a genre not very different from the slave narrative. All five are filled with explicit and passionate social protest, culminating in *White-Jacket*'s powerful appeal for the abolition of flogging in the navy, another parallel with the slave narrative.

Stylistically, I like to emphasize Melville's use of irony and grim humor. If one adopts Babo's point of view in reading "Benito Cereno," one is struck again and again by the humor of the story. The shaving scene is one of the best examples, and I like to go over it at length, beginning with the way in which Babo responds to Don Benito's slip of the tongue about Cape Horn by suggesting that Don Benito and Delano continue the conversation while he shaves his master.

"Bartleby," too, presents many examples of Melville's incisive irony and grim humor. See, for instance, the scene in which Bartleby announces that he will "do no more writing" and asks the narrator, "Do you not see the reason for yourself?"—to which the narrator, who does not see, responds by postulating that Bartleby's vision has become "temporarily impaired."

Original Audience

I generally let the subject of audience come up spontaneously, which it nearly always does. The students often infer—correctly—that Melville was writing for an audience linked by sympathies of class and race to the lawyer in "Bartleby," the bachelors in "Paradise," and Captain Delano in "Benito Cereno." I then talk a little about Melville's social milieu and the readership of *Harper's* and *Putnam's*. (The latter was moderately antislavery, and distinctly more progressive than *Harper's*, which Lydia Maria Child characterized as proslavery; nevertheless, its readers shared some of the racial and class attitudes Delano exemplifies.)

The question of audience is related to the literary strategy Melville adopted. In discussing Melville's rhetoric and the discomfort it provokes in a reader who has an obscure sense of being made fun of, we speculate about whether Melville hoped to jolt readers into thinking about the implications of their attitudes.

Comparisons, Contrasts, Connections

See suggestions above under "Classroom Issues and Strategies." Bartleby has often been seen by critics as a Thoreau-like figure in his passive resistance, but Thoreau's perspective on industrialization, capitalism, and alienation actually contrasts with Melville's, which is closer to Marx's.

Both Rebecca Harding Davis's "Life in the Iron Mills" and Alice Cary's "Uncle Christopher's" can be paired effectively with "The Paradise of Bachelors and the Tartarus of Maids." Davis's narrator, like Melville's, is an outsider complicit by her class position in the oppression of the workers with whom she sympathizes, and Davis, like Melville, projects herself into workers of the opposite sex. Issues of creativity, class, and gender also intersect in "Iron Mills" and "Paradise and Tartarus." Cary's "Uncle Christopher's," like "Paradise and Tartarus," reveals the world of the patriarchs to be as sterile and perverted as the world of the patriarchs' victims. Both "Uncle Christopher's" and "Tartarus" are pervaded by images of freezing cold and make metaphorical use of an icy landscape. The seven girls winding seven skeins of blue yarn and knitting seven blue stockings in Cary's story recall the "blank-looking" factory girls "blankly folding blank paper" in Melville's; in both cases the women are silent and only the noise of their work is heard. While Melville's story comments on how women factory operatives are deprived of a home life and turned into machines, Cary's story shows how the home itself is turned into a factory, whose "boss" is not an "old bachelor" but the patriarchal father.

The reasons for grouping "Benito Cereno" with other works about slavery are obvious, but teachers can help students make specific connections between the slaves on board the *San Dominick* and Douglass's battle with Covey, between the African women among them and Equiano's reminiscences of women's participation in battle, between the *San Dominick*'s "true character" as a slave ship and Equiano's description of the slave ship that transported him across the Atlantic, between Melville's use of the Deposition (and of the three appended chapters in *Billy Budd*) and Child's use of newspaper accounts at the end of "Slavery's Pleasant Homes."

At the same time, one can contrast Melville's rhetorical strategy with the more direct strategy of appeal for the reader's sympathy that other anti-slavery writers adopt. One can further contrast the male and female writers' perspectives on slavery. For Melville and Douglass, the slave's attempt to reclaim his "manhood" by fighting back and risking his life for freedom is central, while the female slave's attempt to defend her children and to resist the violation of her humanity through rape is peripheral. For Stowe and Jacobs the reverse is true; Child balances the two perspectives in "Slavery's Pleasant Homes."

Billy Budd invites comparison with Thoreau's essay on civil disobedience, which casts an ironic light on the arguments Vere uses to have Billy sentenced to hanging. If teachers decide to group *Billy Budd* with the writings on slavery rather than with those on industrialism and the oppression of women, they can underscore the parallels Melville suggests between the condition of sailors and that of slaves (a theme he develops at great length in *White-Jacket*). The Black Handsome Sailor who appears in the opening pages of *Billy Budd* and incarnates the ideal of the Handsome Sailor more perfectly than Billy also provides a strong, positive counterimage of blacks, offsetting the seemingly negative stereotypes presented in "Benito Cereno." Formally as well, the two stories have much in common and invite comparison with "Slavery's Pleasant Homes."

Questions for Reading, Discussion, and Writing

I do not like to use study questions because I find them too directive. I prefer to train students to become attentive readers through more indirect strategies. My principal strategy (borrowed from H. Bruce Franklin) is to give students a quiz requiring them to analyze several key passages in the text, prior to class discussion. (The lawyer's description of the place he assigns Bartleby in his office would be a good choice. So would the passage about the "odd instance" Delano observes of "the African love of bright colors and fine shows.")

I can, however, supply some questions I regularly ask in the course of class discussion.

Questions for Class Discussion of "Bartleby"

1. What does the subtitle of "Bartleby" suggest? What is the significance of Wall Street and the walls in the story?
2. What is the significance of the information that the narrator provides about himself and his employees at the beginning of the story? How does it prepare us to understand Bartleby and the narrator's attitude toward him?
3. Why does Melville tell the story from the point of view of the employer rather than of the office staff or of Bartleby himself? What effect does this narrative strategy have on the reader?
4. How reliable is the narrator? Are there any indications that he might be obtuse or unreliable? Give examples.
5. What incident unleashes Bartleby's passive resistance? What escalates it at each point?
6. What assumptions govern the question that the narrator asks Bartleby: "What earthly right have you to stay here? Do you pay any rent? Do you pay my taxes? Or is this property yours?"
7. What ethic does Melville implicitly oppose to the ethic of Wall Street? (This question leads into a discussion of the New Testament echoes running through the story.)
8. Why does the narrator conclude that Bartleby "was the victim of an innate and incurable disorder"? How does it affect our responses to the story if we accept this conclusion?
9. What is the significance of the postscript the narrator appends to the story? What psychological (or ideological) purpose does it serve for the narrator? What symbolic purpose does it serve for Melville?
10. How much has the encounter with Bartleby changed the narrator by the end of the story? Is the narrator "saved"?

Questions for Class Discussion of "Paradise and Tartarus"

1. What contrast does the opening of "Paradise" draw between the bachelors' haven and the outside world? How does Melville develop the implications of the opening passage in the rest of the sketch?

2. How might the fate of the medieval Knights Templars be relevant to the nineteenth-century Templars?

3. Read out loud the paragraphs about the survival of Templars in modern London and ask: What effect does this imagery have? What attitude does it create toward the Templars?

4. Read out loud the description of the Templars' banquet and ask: What is the significance of this imagery? What associations does it suggest to you? (The teacher might amplify the discussion by pointing out the parody of Plato's *Symposium* suggested by dubbing the field-marshall/waiter "Socrates.") What bearing does this description have on the second sketch of the pair?

5. What role does the narrator play in each of the two sketches? How would we situate him vis-à-vis the bachelors of the first sketch and the factory owner and the workers of the second sketch?

6. What business takes the narrator to the paper mill? What might his "seedsman's business" symbolize?

7. Why does Melville link these two sketches as a pair? What devices does he use to cement the links? What connections does he invite readers to make between the bachelors and the maids, between Temple Bar and the New England paper factory? How is the contrast between the bachelors of the first sketch and maids of the second sketch continued within the second sketch?

8. Read out loud the passage describing the landscape of Devil's Dungeon and ask what its imagery suggests.

9. What is the significance of the imagery Melville uses to describe the factory? (Read aloud passages drawing the students' attention to the girls' dehumanization and the machine's preemption of their reproductive functions.)

10. What is Melville critiquing in this pair of sketches? Why does he link the economic to the sexual, production to reproduction?

11. Depending on the order in which assignments are made, teachers can also ask questions about:
    — the continuities linking "Bartleby" with "Paradise and Tartarus."
    — the similarities and differences between Melville's and Alice Cary's critiques of patriarchy.
    — the similarities and differences between the perspectives that Melville and Fanny Fern offer on working women.

— the insights that emerge from reading "Paradise and Tartarus" in the light of Sarah Grimké's *Letters on the Equality of the Sexes*, Lydia Maria Child's "Letter from New York" #50 on Women's Rights, and Margaret Fuller's *Woman in the Nineteenth Century.*

Questions for Class Discussion of "Benito Cereno"

1. Through whose eyes do we view the events in the story? Where in the text does Melville shift into Delano's point of view? Whose point of view does the Deposition represent? (N.B.: I have found again and again that students confuse third-person narrative with omniscient point of view and confuse a character's subjective point of view with first-person narrative. Unless instructors take special care, students will end up referring to Delano as the narrator in their papers and exams.)

2. Why doesn't Melville choose to write the story from Babo's point of view? What might his purpose be in confining us to Delano's and later Benito Cereno's point of view? What limitations does this narrative strategy impose on us as readers?

3. How reliable are Delano's perceptions of reality? What tendencies in particular make him an unreliable interpreter of the behavior he sees manifested on board the *San Dominick*? (Draw the students' attention to the racial assumptions embedded in his perceptions of the oakum-pickers and hatchet-polishers; in his endorsement of the "contrast in dress, denoting their relative positions," that distinguishes Don Benito from Babo; in his ogling of a naked African woman and his failure to realize the terrible irony of the possibility that she might be one of "the very women Mungo Park saw in Africa, and gave such a noble account of"; in his belief that the blacks are "too stupid" to be staging a masquerade and that no white would be "so far a renegade as to apostatize from his very species almost, by leaguing in against it with negroes"; in his ludicrous misinterpretation of Babo's intent in using the flag of Spain as a bib. Obviously there will not be time to discuss all these passages, but one or two should be singled out for discussion.)

4. The best example of how Delano's racism keeps him from recognizing that the blacks have staged a revolt is the episode in which he sees Babo use the flag of Spain as a bib for Don Benito, but misinterprets it as an "odd instance of the African love of bright colors and fine shows." How does that episode originate? (Draw the students' attention to Don Benito's slip of the tongue and Babo's quick invention of the shave as a ruse to prevent further inopportune slips. Use an analysis of the episode to show how brilliantly Babo manipulates Delano's prejudices.)

5. What attitude toward slavery does Delano exhibit? How does his attitude differ from Benito Cereno's? (Point out passages showing Delano's

envy of Don Benito, even as he feels the Yankee's superiority to the decadent slave-holding aristocrat; most crucial is Delano's insistence on pursuing and capturing the *San Dominick* with its cargo of slaves "worth more than a thousand doubloons.")

6. Most of the confusion in interpreting "Benito Cereno" arises from the latter part of the story. It is easy to see that Delano's view of blacks as stupid is wrong, but does Melville present Benito Cereno's view of blacks as a corrective to stereotype, or merely as another stereotype? Does the Deposition represent the "truth"?

7. How does the language of the Deposition differ from the language Melville uses elsewhere in the text? What makes us take it for the "truth"?

8. What is Benito Cereno's interpretation of events, as opposed to Delano's initial interpretation? How does he explain the slaves' revolt?

9. Does the Deposition indirectly provide any alternative explanations of why the blacks may have revolted? What does it tell us about the blacks' actual aims? How do they try to achieve those aims? (If necessary, point out the hints that the slave women have been sexually abused by Aranda and Cereno; also consider the conversation between Cereno and Babo during the revolt, when Babo asks Cereno to transport the blacks back to Senegal and promises that they will abide by the rationing of water and food necessary to effect such a long voyage.)

10. Does Melville provide any clues to an interpretation of the story that transcends the racist stereotypes of Delano and Cereno? (Point out the allusions to the ancient African civilizations of Egypt and Nubia; the allusion to Ezekiel's Valley of Dry Bones; the symbolism of the *San Dominick*'s "shield-like stern-piece" and the way in which the identities of the masked figures get reversed at the end of the story.)

11. What is the narrative point of view of the few pages following the Deposition? How do you interpret the dialogue between the two captains? Does it indicate that either Delano or Cereno has undergone any change in consciousness or achieved a new understanding of slavery as a result of his ordeal?

12. What seems to be the message of the scene with which the story ends? What do you think Melville was trying to convey through the story? How does the story continue to be relevant or prophetic?

13. How would you compare "Benito Cereno" to David Walker's *Appeal*? Henry Highland Garnet's 1843 "Address to the Slaves of the U.S.A."? Thomas Wentworth Higginson's "Nat Turner's Insurrection"? Wendell Phillips's "Toussaint L'Ouverture"? Douglass's *Narrative*? Lydia Maria Child's "Slavery's Pleasant Homes"? Stowe's *Uncle Tom's Cabin* (or any other assigned readings on slavery)?

Questions for Class Discussion of *Billy Budd*

1. Why does Melville begin the story with a description of the Handsome Sailor? What does this figure seem to represent? What is the significance of the fact that the first example Melville cites of the Handsome Sailor is "a native African of the unadulterate blood of Ham"? What characteristics does Billy share with the black Handsome Sailor? What is the purpose of the analogies Melville suggests between the "barbarians" of pre-Christian Europe, Africa, and the South Seas? In what respects does Billy fail to conform fully to the Handsome Sailor archetype?

2. What are the historical contexts of the story? What is the purpose of the historical background Melville supplies on the Nore and Spithead mutinies? (Note that the story takes place only a few years after the American War of Independence against Britain and that it begins with an impressment, recalling the frequent impressment of American sailors by the British—one of the grievances that led to the War of 1812. See H. Bruce Franklin's "From Empire to Empire" for a full discussion of the story's historical contexts.)

3. What is the significance of Billy's being impressed from the *Rights-of-Man* to the *Bellipotent*?

4. What relationship does Melville set up among Billy, Claggart, and Vere? What qualities does each represent? Why are Claggart and Vere attracted to Billy? In what ways is he a threat to them?

5. How do you interpret Melville's definition of "Natural Depravity"? To whom does it most obviously apply in the story? To whom else might it also apply? (A number of critics have pointed out the applicability of the passage to Vere as well as Claggart.)

6. How does the tragedy occur? How might it have been avoided?

7. How does Melville invite the reader to judge Vere's behavior and decision to hang Billy? What passages, dialogues, and scenes must we taken into account?

8. What tactics and arguments does Vere use to sway his officers? What are the political consequences (in real life as well as in the story) of accepting Vere's arguments? Do you see any contradictions in Vere's arguments, or do you find them rational and persuasive? Is Melville's description of "Natural Depravity" at all relevant to an evaluation of Vere's conduct at the trial ("Toward the accomplishment of an aim which in wantonness of atrocity would seem to partake of the insane, he will direct a cool judgment sagacious and sound")?

9. How do you interpret the many biblical allusions in the story? In what ways do they redefine or amplify the meaning of the story? What relationship(s) do you see between the religious and political interpretation

the story invites? How does Melville characterize the role of the chaplain?

10. After the hanging, Vere forestalls possible disturbances by ordering the drums to muster the men to quarters earlier than usual. He then justifies his action by explaining how he views art and the purpose it serves: "'With mankind . . . forms, measured forms, are everything; and that is the import couched in the story of Orpheus spellbinding the wild denizens of the wood.'" Does Melville endorse this concept of art in *Billy Budd*? How does the form of the story jibe (or conflict) with Vere's ideal of "measured forms"? How does the glorification of the Handsome Sailor, and the imagery used to describe him, jibe (or conflict) with Vere's view of "the wild denizens of the wood"?

11. What is the effect of the three sequels Melville appends to the story? What further light do they shed on Vere and on the political interests governing his decision? To whom does the story give the last word?

12. Depending on the order of assignments, teachers can invite students to draw connections among:
    — the status of slaves, sailors, and factory workers.
    — the legal arguments Vere uses in his role as prosecuting attorney at Billy's trial and the portrayal of lawyers and the law in "Bartleby" and "Paradise and Tartarus."
    — Thoreau's essay on civil disobedience and Vere's defense of martial law and the Articles of War.
    — Vere's insistence that "the heart, sometimes the feminine in man, be ruled out" and Fuller's critique of the rigid sexual stereotypes that patriarchal ideology imposes on men and women.

Questions for Class Discussion of "Hawthorne and His Mosses"

1. How would you compare "Hawthorne and His Mosses" with Emerson's "The American Scholar," Poe's "The Philosophy of Composition" and review of Hawthorne's *Twice-Told Tales*, and Whitman's 1855 Preface of *Leaves of Grass*?

2. To what extent (or in what ways) do you find this essay helpful for understanding Hawthorne's fiction?

3. To what extent (or in what ways) do you find it helpful to illuminating Melville's own artistic aims and practices?

4. Of the Hawthorne stories Melville praises, which ones continue to be highly regarded today? Does Melville omit mention of any stories in *Mosses from an Old Manse* that regularly appear in present-day anthologies? What do you make of the differences in aesthetic taste or judgment that this might suggest?

5. What does Melville value most in Hawthorne's fiction? What does he mean by "blackness"?
6. Why does Melville argue against idolizing Shakespeare? How would you sum up his opinion of Shakespeare?
7. What are the implications of Melville's view that Americans should give their own authors "priority of appreciation" before acknowledging the great writers of other lands? How might this view apply to other nations or groups attempting to create a literary tradition of their own?
8. What do you make of Melville's list of the significant American writers among his contemporaries? Which ones are still considered major American writers? Whom does Melville omit from his list?
9. Why does Melville disparage Irving? What does he reveal in the process about his own literary aims and values?

Since I group readings together, I also try to formulate paper topics that involve comparisons and contrasts of several readings. Most of the following topics are thematic. Instructors who would prefer formalist topics that focus exclusively on Melville's stories might adapt some from the questions for class discussion listed above.

Choose two or three works from the following list, and compare and contrast their literary styles, narrative techniques, and handling of point of view: Hawthorne's "The Birth-mark" or "Rappaccini's Daughter"; Poe's "Ligeia" or another Poe story of your choice; Kirkland's *A New Home— Who'll Follow?*; Cary's "Uncle Christopher's"; Stoddard's "Lemorne *Versus* Huell"; Melville's "Bartleby" or "The Paradise of Bachelors and the Tartarus of Maids" or "Benito Cereno" or *Billy Budd*.

Compare and contrast the aesthetic theories and views of literary nationalism reflected in several of the following: Emerson's "The American Scholar," Poe's "The Philosophy of Composition," Melville's "Hawthorne and His Mosses," and Whitman's Preface to the 1855 edition of *Leaves of Grass* or *Democratic Vistas*.

Choose some issue explored in the assigned readings and compare and contrast several works that provide different perspectives on it:

1. Use Thoreau's discussion of alienation in *Walden* as a framework for analyzing "Bartleby." In the process, compare and contrast the two authors' political perspectives.
2. Use Thoreau's "Resistance to Civil Government" as a framework for analyzing Bartleby's interaction with his employer. You may wish to consider the forms of "resistance" the other office workers engage in as well.
3. Use Thoreau's "Resistance to Civil Government" as a framework for analyzing *Billy Budd* and the issues it raises.

4. Compare and contrast Thoreau's and Melville's critiques of industrialism and capitalism in *Walden* and "The Paradise of Bachelors and the Tartarus of Maids."

5. Compare and contrast Melville's "The Paradise of Bachelors and the Tartarus of Maids" and Cary's "Uncle Christopher's," focusing on some of the following points: the perspectives each provides on the effects of patriarchal (and/or capitalist) ideology; the causes to which each story attributes the dehumanization and sterility it depicts; the kinds of contrasts each story sets up between oppressor and oppressed; the narrative point of view; the role of landscape and setting; the use of symbolism and metaphor. Instructors can suggest similar comparisons with Rebecca Harding Davis's "Life in the Iron Mills."

6. Apply Sarah Grimké's, Lydia Maria Child's, and/or Margaret Fuller's analysis of "the woman question" to one or more of the following:
   —Hawthorne's "The Birth-mark" and/or "Rappaccini's Daughter"
   —Poe's "Ligeia"
   —Melville's "The Paradise of Bachelors and the Tartarus of Maids"
   —Elizabeth Stoddard's "Lemorne *Versus* Huell"
   —Caroline Kirkland's *A New Home—Who'll Follow?*
   —Alice Cary's "Uncle Christopher's"
   —Harriet Jacobs's *Incidents in the Life of a Slave Girl*
   —Emily Dickinson's poems (selections of your choice)

7. Apply one or more of the following works to an analysis of Melville's "Benito Cereno":
   —David Walker's *Appeal*
   —Douglass's *Narrative*
   —Henry Highland Garnet's "Address to the Slaves of the U.S.A."
   —Wendell Phillips's "Toussaint L'Ouverture"
   —Thomas Wentworth Higginson's "Nat Turner's Insurrection"

Choose some aspect of slavery explored in the assigned readings, and compare and contrast the perspectives these various works provide on it.

1. The issue of slave resistance and rebellion (can include violent and nonviolent, individual and collective resistance).

2. The issue of Higher Law versus the law of the land.

3. The contrast between the masters' and the slaves' viewpoints and values (e.g., Douglass and Jacobs and their fellow slaves versus their masters; Uncle Tom, Chloe, Cassy, etc., versus the Shelbys, St. Clares, and Legree; Babo versus Cereno and Delano).

4. Religion and slavery, or religion and militarism (can include the indictment of the church's hypocrisy, the use of the Bible to support or condemn slavery, the theme of apocalyptic judgment, the use of typology and religious rhetoric and symbolism).

5. Comparative analysis of the rhetorical techniques, purposes, and intended audiences of three writers among those assigned, or of the metaphors each writer uses to describe slavery and structure his/her narrative.
6. The use of irony in the antislavery argument (can analyze the different types of irony found in slave songs, Douglass's and Jacobs's narratives, Child's antislavery writings, *Uncle Tom's Cabin*, and "Benito Cereno").
7. The image of Africa and the portrayal of the slave trade in Equiano's narrative and "Benito Cereno."
8. Double meanings and the theme of appearance versus reality in any of the assigned readings.
9. The theme "Slavery proved as injurious to her as it did to me" (a quotation from Douglass's *Narrative* as applied to the individuals who people the assigned works, or to the North and the South, blacks and whites, oppressed and oppressing classes, the American nation in general).
10. The picture of slave life and the slave community that emerges from any three of the assigned works (preferably three representing different racial, regional, or gender perspectives).
11. The theme "Slavery is terrible for men, but it is far more terrible for women," as dramatized in several of the assigned readings.

Bibliography

For a broader intellectual context, teachers who have time to read "The Communist Manifesto" and perhaps Marx's essays "Estranged Labor," "The Meaning of Human Requirements," and "The Power of Money in Bourgeois Society," from *The Economic and Philosophic Manuscripts of 1844* will find them extremely relevant to both "The Paradise of Bachelors and the Tartarus of Maids" and "Bartleby." In particular, Marx discusses workers' reduction to commodities, their enslavement to machines, and their resulting alienation.

For a complete bibliography, covering all of Melville's short fiction except *Billy Budd* and including overviews of the stories' reception, see Lea Bertani Vozar Newman's *A Reader's Guide to the Short Stories of Herman Melville* (Boston: Hall, 1986). See also Brian Higgins's *Herman Melville: A Reference Guide, 1931–1960* (Boston: Hall, 1987), covering all Melville criticism published since 1930. For an excellent reconstruction of the stories' chronology, circumstances of composition and publication, and contemporary reception, see Merton M. Sealts's Historical Note in the Northwestern-Newberry edition of *The Piazza Tales and Other Prose Pieces, 1839–1860* (Evanston and Chicago: 1987, 457–533). The volume also reprints the chapter of Delano's *Narrative* that Melville used as a source.

For biographical studies that situate Melville and his family in the context of contemporary politics, see Michael Paul Rogin, *Subversive Genealogy: The Politics and Art of Herman Melville* (New York: Knopf, 1983), especially chapters 6 and 9; Laurie Robertson-Lorant, *Melville: A Biography* (New York: Clarkson Potter, 1996); and Hershel Parker, *Herman Melville: A Biography* (Baltimore: Johns Hopkins UP, Vol. 1, 1996; Vol. 2, 2002).

The following new essay collections contain articles on one or more of the anthologized stories: Myra Jehlen, ed., *Herman Melville: A Collection of Critical Essays* (Englewood Cliffs, NJ: Prentice, 1994), especially Arnold Rampersad's "Melville and Race," Eric J. Sundquist's "'Benito Cereno' and New World Slavery," Robyn Wiegman's "Melville's Geography of Gender," Eve Kosofsky Sedgwick's *"Billy Budd:* After the Homosexual," and Barbara Johnson's "Melville's Fist: The Execution of *Billy Budd*"; John Bryant and Robert Milder, eds., *Melville's Evermoving Dawn: Centennial Essays* (Kent, OH: Kent State UP, 1997), especially Bryant's "Introduction," Arnold Rampersad's "Shadow and Veil: Melville and Black Consciousness," Wai Chee Dimock's "Reading the Incomplete," and H. Bruce Franklin's "Past, Present, and Future Seemed One"; and Robert S. Levine, ed., *The Cambridge Companion to Herman Melville* (Cambridge, UK: Cambridge UP, 1998), especially Sterling Stuckey's "The Tambourine in Glory: African Culture and Melville's Art," Robert K. Martin's "Melville and Sexuality," and Cindy Weinstein's "Melville, Labor, and the Discourses of Reception."

For feminist criticism portraying Melville as hostile to women, see Joyce W. Warren, *The American Narcissus: Individualism and Women in Nineteenth-Century American Fiction* (New Brunswick, NJ: Rutgers UP, 1984), chapter 5; and Elizabeth Renker, *Strike through the Mask: Herman Melville and the Scene of Writing* (Baltimore: Johns Hopkins UP, 1996). For more sympathetic or nuanced feminist perspectives on Melville, see Kristin Herzog, *Women, Ethnics, and Exotics: Images of Power in Mid-Nineteenth-Century American Fiction* (Knoxville: U of Tennessee P, 1983), chapter 2; the essays on "Women in Melville's Art" and "Women on Melville" in the February 1986 and September 1994 issues of *Melville Society Extracts;* Laurie Robertson-Lorant, "Melville's Embrace of the Invisible Woman," *Centennial Review* 34 (Summer 1990): 401–11, as well as her *Melville: A Biography,* cited above; and Judith Hiltner, "Disquieting Encounters: Male Intrusions/Female Realms in Melville," *ESQ* 40 (2nd Quarter 1994): 91–111.

Listed below are the critical studies I have found most useful for illuminating the Melville selections in this anthology, and for developing approaches toward teaching them.

For books containing relevant discussions of more than one story, see Rogin, cited above; Marvin Fisher, *Going Under: Melville's Short Fiction and the American 1850s* (Baton Rouge: Louisiana State UP, 1977), especially the chapters on "Bartleby" and "The Paradise of Bachelors and the Tartarus of Maids";

and H. Bruce Franklin's chapter on Melville in *The Victim as Criminal and Artist: Literature from the American Prison* (New York: Oxford UP, 1978), as well as his earlier sections on "Bartleby" in *The Wake of the Gods: Melville's Mythology* (Palo Alto: Stanford UP, 1963); Joyce Sparer Adler, *War in Melville's Imagination* (New York: New York UP, 1981), especially the chapter on *Billy Budd*; and Robert K. Martin, *Hero, Captain, and Stranger: Male Friendship, Social Critique, and Literary Form in the Sea Novels of Herman Melville* (Chapel Hill: U of North Carolina P, 1986), especially the chapter on *Billy Budd* and pp. 105–06 on "The Paradise of Bachelors."

On "Bartleby," in addition to the books cited above see Stephen Zelnick, "Melville's Bartleby, The Scrivener: A Study in History, Ideology, and Literature," *Marxist Perspectives* 2 (Winter 1979/80): 74–92; and Donald M. Fiene, "Bartleby the Christ," in Raymona E. Hull, ed., *Studies in the Minor and Later Works of Melville* (Hartford: Transcendental, 1970), 18–23; David Kuebrich, "Melville's Doctrine of Assumptions: The Hidden Ideology of Capitalist Production in 'Bartleby,'" *New England Quarterly* 69 (Sept. 1996): 318–405; Richard R. John, "The Lost World of Bartleby, the Ex-Officeholder: Variations on a Venerable Literary Form," *New England Quarterly* 70 (Dec. 1997): 631–41; and Barbara Foley, "From Wall Street to Astor Place: Historicizing Melville's 'Bartleby,'" *American Literature* 72 (Mar. 2000): 87–116.

On "The Paradise of Bachelors and the Tartarus of Maids," in addition to the works cited above see Beryl Rowland, "Melville's Bachelors and Maids: Interpretation Through Symbol and Metaphor," *American Literature* 41 (Nov. 1969): 389–405; Philip Young, "The Machine in Tartarus: Melville's Inferno," *American Literature* 63 (June 1991): 208–24; Michael Newberry, *Figuring Authorship in Antebellum America* (Palo Alto: Stanford UP, 1997), chapter 1; and Sandra Harbert Petrulionis, "Re-Reading 'Bachelors and Maids': Melville as Feminist?" *Melville Society Extracts* 110 (Sept. 1997): 1, 5–10.

Four books situate Melville in the slavery controversy: Carolyn L. Karcher, *Shadow over the Promised Land: Slavery, Race, and Violence in Melville's America* (Louisiana State UP, 1980), especially chapters 1 and 5; Rogin, *Subversive Genealogy*, cited above; Eric J. Sundquist, *To Wake the Nations: Race in the Making of American Literature* (Cambridge, MA: Belknap Press of Harvard UP, 1993), chapter 2; and Maggie Montesinos Sale, *The Slumbering Volcano: American Slave Ship Revolts and the Production of Rebellious Masculinity* (Durham: Duke UP, 1997), chapter 4. Robert E. Burkholder's splendid collection, *Critical Essays on Herman Melville's "Benito Cereno"* (Boston: Hall; New York: Macmillan, 1992), includes a number of recent articles, along with some earlier criticism of the story. All the essays are illuminating, but see especially Brook Thomas's "The Legal Fictions of Herman Melville and Lemuel Shaw," Sandra A. Zagarell's "Reenvisioning America," Eric J. Sundquist's "*Benito Cereno* and New World Slavery," Sterling Stuckey's "'Follow Your Leader': The Theme of Cannibalism in Melville's *Benito*

Cereno," Carolyn L. Karcher's "The Riddle of the Sphinx: Melville's 'Benito Cereno' and the *Amistad* Case," and H. Bruce Franklin's "Past, Present, and Future Seemed One." On the relevance of the Spanish Inquisition to "Benito Cereno," see John Bernstein, "'Benito Cereno' and the Spanish Inquisition," *Nineteenth-Century Fiction* 16 (March 1962): 345–50. For black perspectives on the story's dramatization of slavery and racism, see Charles E. Nnolim, *Melville's "Benito Cereno": A Study in the Meaning of Name Symbolism* (New York: New Voices, 1974); Gloria Horsley-Meacham, "Bull of the Nile: Symbol, History, and Racial Myth in 'Benito Cereno,'" *New England Quarterly* 64 (June 1991): 225–42; and Joshua Leslie and Sterling Stuckey, "The Death of Benito Cereno: A Reading of Herman Melville on Slavery," *Journal of Negro History* 67 (Dec. 1982): 287–301. The latter argues convincingly that Melville shows an understanding of African culture based on reading Mungo Park. See also the essays by Horsley-Meachan and Stuckey in Burkholder, ed. On Delano's "enactment of white manhood," see Dana D. Nelson, *National Manhood: Capitalist Citizenship and the Imagined Fraternity of White Men* (Durham: Duke UP, 1998), 1–4, 197–203. For an approach that examines editorial policy and periodical readership as well as "authorial choices," see Sarah Robbins, "Gendering the History of the Antislavery Narrative: Juxtaposing *Uncle Tom's Cabin* and *Benito Cereno, Beloved* and "*Middle Passage*," *American Quarterly* 49 (Sept. 1997): 531–73. On teaching "Benito Cereno," see Robert S. Levine, "Teaching in the Multicultural Classroom: Reconsidering 'Benito Cereno,'" in *Teaching What You're Not: Identity Politics in Higher Education*, ed. Katherine J. Mayberry (New York: New York UP, 1996), 241–58.

Study of *Billy Budd* should begin with the indispensable notes provided by Harrison Hayford and Merton M. Sealts in their 1962 edition (U of Chicago P). Besides pointing out innumerable parallels between *Billy Budd* and Melville's other works, of which *White-Jacket* and *Israel Potter* are the most relevant, Hayford and Sealts sum up previous criticism. Among recent critics, Milton R. Stern formulates the most persuasive version of the pro-Vere interpretation in his 1975 Bobbs-Merrill edition of the story. Offering the strongest rebuttals and the most satisfying readings of the story are Adler (cited above) and H. Bruce Franklin, "From Empire to Empire: *Billy Budd, Sailor*," in A. Robert Lee, ed., *Herman Melville: Reassessments* (London: Vision, 1984). Containing pertinent historical information, despite a strained thesis, is Stanton Garner, "Fraud and Fact in Herman Melville's *Billy Budd*," *San Jose Studies* 4 (May 1978): 82–105. Edgar A. Dryden, *Melville's Thematics of Form: The Great Art of Telling the Truth* (Baltimore: Johns Hopkins UP, 1968) 209–16, analyzes the way in which the form of *Billy Budd* subverts Vere's doctrine of "measured form." For a valuable analysis of the critical controversies *Billy Budd* has generated, see Geraldine Murphy, "The Politics of Reading *Billy Budd*," *American Literary History* 1 (Summer 1989): 361–82. For new perspectives on "Billy Budd," see Brook J. Thomas, *Cross-examinations of Law and Literature:*

Cooper, Hawthorne, Stowe, and Melville (Cambridge, UK: Cambridge UP, 1987), chapters 9–10; Eve Kosofsky Sedgwick, *Epistemology of the Closet* (Berkeley: U of California P, 1990), chapter 2; Hershel Parker, *Reading "Billy Budd"* (Evanston: Northwestern UP, 1990); Kathy J. Phillips, "*Billy Budd* as Anti-Homophobic Text," *College English* 56 (Dec. 1994): 896–910; H. Bruce Franklin, "*Billy Budd* and Capital Punishment: A Tale of Three Centuries," *American Literature* 69 (June 1997): 337–59; Susan Mizruchi, *The Science of Sacrifice: American Social Theory* (Princeton: Princeton UP, 1998), 89–188; Jeff Westover, "The Impressments of Billy Budd," *Massachusetts Review* 39 (Autumn 1998): 361–84; Robert K. Martin, "Melville and Sexuality," in Levine, ed., cited above; and Cynthia J. Davis, "Nation's Nature: 'Billy Budd, Sailor,' Anglo-Saxonism, and the Canon," *Race and the Production of Modern American Nationalism*, ed. Reynolds J. Scott-Childress (New York: Garland, 1999), 43–65.

On "Hawthorne and His Mosses," see Parker, *Herman Melville*, 752–81, cited above; and Ellen Weinauer, "Plagiarism and the Proprietary Self: Policing the Boundaries of Authorship in Herman Melville's 'Hawthorne and His Mosses,'" *American Literature* 69 (Dec. 1997): 697–717. For a broader cultural context, see Lawrence W. Levine, *Highbrow/Lowbrow: The Emergence of Cultural Hierarchy in America* (Cambridge, MA: Harvard UP, 1988), chapter 1.

Alice Cary (1820–1871)

Contributing Editor: Judith Fetterley

Classroom Issues and Strategies

Students are turned off by what they perceive as her didacticism, the morals attached to the ends of the stories. They also have trouble with what they perceive as her Christian dogma or perspective. And occasionally they perceive her stories as sentimental.

These problems are endemic to the reading of texts by nineteenth-century American women writers. They are useful and interesting problems to encounter in the classroom because they raise quite clearly the issue of aesthetic value and how the context for determining what is good art changes over time. The instructor needs to be aware of how contemporary critics have addressed this issue. The single best book for the teacher to have and use is Jane Tompkins's *Sensational Designs*. The instructor might wish to assign the last chapter of this book, "But Is It Any Good?" to the class since this chapter raises directly the questions most of them have about nineteenth-century women's texts.

Compared with other nineteenth-century American women writers, Cary is minimally didactic, Christian, or "sentimental." So, in teaching her, my approach consists of comparing her work with that of writers who are much more didactic, Christian, and "sentimental" and asking how it is that she avoids these patterns. What fictional techniques has she developed to tell the story she has to tell without in fact resorting to didacticism, etc.? This usually leads into a discussion of the form of the short fictional piece, and more specifically into a discussion of regionalism. (See the *Norton Anthology of American Women Regional Writers*, edited by Fetterley and Pryse.)

Students respond to the issue of storytelling—how women tell stories and the relation between their telling of stories and their context of domestic work. They are also interested in the issue of landscape—how Cary manages to create a mood through her description of the landscape and how she manages to convey the open-ended nature of her stories. Their lack of plot in the conventional sense is worthy of discussion as is the fact that Cary tells stories about women's lives and experience from the point of view of a female narrator.

Major Themes, Historical Perspectives, Personal Issues

It is important to emphasize that Cary was essentially a self-made writer. She had little formal education, little support from family or extended personal contacts; yet she made herself into a poet whose name was known throughout the country. Her decision to move to New York in 1850 represented an extraordinary act of self-assertion for a woman at the time. She determined that she needed to get out of the "provinces" in order to have the literary career she wished, and she did it. She set up a household in New York that included two of her sisters, and she supported this household by her own work. She is an example of the way in which nineteenth-century American women writers were able to set up supportive networks that were based on connections with other women. She is also an example of a nineteenth-century American woman writer who was genuinely financially independent of men. She ran her house, earned the money for it, and handled her money herself.

In terms of literary themes, it is important to emphasize the fact that Cary began to write seriously about her Ohio neighborhood after she left it for New York. She saw herself as trying to present a realistic picture of this neighborhood and to create a place in literature for the region, but she was able to do this only after she had left it for New York.

Significant Form, Style, or Artistic Conventions

It is important to point out that Cary thought of herself primarily as a poet. Her reputation during her lifetime and thereafter was based on her poetry. The conventions that governed poetry by women in the nineteenth century by and large produced a body of poetry that is not of interest to the late twentieth-century reader. The novel was also a highly determined form. Women were expected to write certain kinds of novels, to produce "women's fiction" with the appropriately feminine perspective and set of values. The short fictional sketch, however, was a relatively undetermined territory. It was not taken as seriously as were the novel and poetry, and no theory existed as to what kind of fictional sketch a woman should or should not write in order to demonstrate that she was in fact a woman. As a result, in writing her Clovernook sketches Cary was on her own, so to speak. She was able to write organically, to let the shape of the fiction emerge from the nature of the story she wished to tell. As a result, her short fiction holds interest for the contemporary reader; it seems fresh, new, not written to fulfill convention or previously determined script, but deriving from some deep personal place that produces a uniquely marked and signed prose. Thus any discussion of Alice Cary needs to address the role that the form of the fictional sketch plays in creating fiction that interests us. In other words, the issue of form is central to the discussion of Alice Cary. Specific features of this form include the freedom this form gives to focus on character and setting as opposed to plot; the lack of closure in many of Cary's sketches; the intermingling of realism and surrealism. For a fuller discussion of these and other issues relative to the form of the sketch in relation to Alice Cary, I refer the instructor to my "Introduction" to the Rutgers Press edition of the short fiction of Alice Cary, *Clovernook Sketches and Other Stories.*

It is also important to discuss the issue of realism in relation to Cary. Since American literary history, until very recently, has been based on a study of male writers, the predominant view is that realism began in America after the Civil War. However, women writers were experimenting with realism in the decades before the Civil War. Cary's "Preface" to the first volume of Clovernook sketches, published in 1852, lays out her theory of realism. She sees herself as participating in the effort to write about American subjects, and she sees herself as doing something "new" in choosing to write about these subjects as "they really are." In making this choice she is in effect following the lead of writers like Caroline Kirkland and participating in the development of realism as a mode suited to the needs and interests of women writers in the nineteenth century. Alice Cary thus provides the instructor with the opportunity to at once raise the issue of the bias in literary history and the issue of the development of realism as an American mode.

Original Audience

As I have indicated above, Cary's primary audience during her lifetime was for her poetry. Her short fiction was not a big popular success and was not reprinted. But the nineteenth century, as I said before, did not take the genre of short fiction as seriously as it did that of poetry and the novel. So in a way this does not tell us much about how well her short fiction was received by her readers. Her short fiction, much of which was initially published in periodicals, may well have been as popular as that of any other contemporary writer, male or female. The point is that the genre itself was not as popular. Interestingly enough, however, Cary's greatest critical successes came from her short fiction. Once again, though, this may simply indicate that the genre itself was not taken very seriously.

Comparisons, Contrasts, Connections

Cary can be fruitfully compared with a number of different writers in a number of different contexts. She can be compared with writers like Poe and Hawthorne in the use of fiction as dream work and projection. She creates the same kind of uncanny, eerie, dreamlike atmosphere that they do. She can also be compared with them in terms of her use of the first-person narrator and the complexities of that narrator's relation to the story she tells and the characters she creates. She can also be compared with them in terms of her use of setting.

She can be compared with nineteenth-century women writers like Caroline Kirkland for her use of realism and for her commitment to telling the woman's side of the story. She can also be compared with other nineteenth-century women writers for her ability to avoid some of their didacticism, Christian moralizing, and "sentimentality."

She can be most interestingly compared with Emily Dickinson in her ability to place herself and her imagination at the center of her work. Very few nineteenth-century American women writers were able to overcome the dicta that required of women self-effacement in literature as in life. Dickinson overcame it by virtue of not publishing. Cary overcame it through her use of the nonconventional form of short fiction. Her work is remarkable for the sustained development of first-person narration. Her collections of Clovernook sketches are as much about the narrator as they are about anything else. She creates a remarkable I/eye for her work.

Bibliography

I refer the instructor to the discussion of Alice Cary in *Provisions* and to the "Introduction" to the Rutgers Press volume of Cary's short fiction, *Clovernook Sketches and Other Stories*. Also see Annette Kolodny, *The Land Before Her*.

Elizabeth Stoddard (1823–1902)

Contributing Editors: Sybil Weir and Sandra A. Zagarell

Classroom Issues and Strategies

Stoddard's terse narrative style; the limitation of point of view to the indirect, ironic woman narrator; and the oblique portrayal of the major act on which the plot turns may make it difficult for students to follow "Lemorne *Versus* Huell." Also, students unfamiliar with conventions of gothic fiction and midcentury history may miss much of the social commentary. It may therefore be useful to ask students to review the plot. It may also be useful to give background on sentimental fiction's featuring of courtship plots and frequent endorsement of female self-sacrifice and male paternalism (as in *The Wide, Wide World*) so that students get a sense of Stoddard's critique of such conventions.

Major Themes, Historical Perspectives, Personal Issues

Although Stoddard's major subjects, like those of many antebellum women writers, include her protagonists' urges toward selfhood and the sociocultural conventions that thwart or channel those urges, she is at once far more ironic about conventions—including literary conventions—and far more sympathetic to women's personal ambition, her own as well as her protagonists', than a Susan Warner or a Maria Cummins. In "Lemorne" she calls attention to the limitations that gender and class impose on her protagonist and to the limitations of the feminine strategies of irony and passive aggressiveness with which Margaret both adapts to and resists her circumstances. She also emphasizes romantic love as a convention that facilitates the bartering of women and portrays marriage and family as institutionalizing the possession of women who are without power. These aspects of "Lemorne" exhibit the intense critique of bourgeois Victorian American gender arrangements to be found in much of Stoddard's fiction. At the same time, "Lemorne" is unquestioning of other dimensions of antebellum America. It uses slavery and the Fugitive Slave Law as vehicles to suggest the need for more liberal circumstances for white women while remaining silent about the circumstances of the enslaved population of the United States. In converting slavery to a metaphor for the condition of white women, Stoddard participates in a construction of white femininity that relies on a racially polarized society and is prevalent throughout the nineteenth century and well into the twentieth—as Hazel Carby demonstrates in *Reconstructing Womanhood*.

Significant Form, Style, or Artistic Conventions

Primary questions have to do with Stoddard's use of the literary traditions of her day—traditions of sentimental fiction and gothic romance. She undercuts the standard courtship plot with her ironizing of the hero as rescuer, yet sustains a degree of erotic intensity rare in fiction by antebellum women writers and much influenced by Charlotte and Emily Brontë, whom she esteemed highly. I'd also emphasize Stoddard's interweaving of the Fugitive Slave motif and references to European literature, and her satirization of Newport society.

I would also stress Stoddard's humor and her importance "as an experimenter in narrative method. She anticipates modern fiction in using a severely limited mode with minimal narrative clues" (Buell and Zagarell, "Biographical and Critical Introduction," p. xxiii).

Original Audience

"Lemorne *Versus* Huell" was first published in *Harper's New Monthly Magazine,* suggesting that Stoddard's fiction was directed to a middle-class, educated audience. In fact, neither her short fiction nor her novels were ever popular or recognized beyond a small circle of intellectuals and writers. Presumably, the audience of her own day was put off by her elliptical style and by her often satiric questioning of prevalent assumptions about female virtue, self-abnegation, and religious piety, as they may also have been by what James Russell Lowell termed her "coarseness."

Comparisons, Contrasts, Connections

I would compare Stoddard's fiction with that of Stowe and Spofford. For example, in what ways does her characterization depart from Stowe's emphasis on religious piety? How do her use of an unusual situation and her intensity compare with those of Spofford? How, and under what circumstances, do all three writers emphasize their heroines' self-reliance (or the perils of self-abnegation)? Other appropriate comparisons and contrasts have to do with point of view (emphasizing Stoddard's rather unusual use of first-person narration) and with gender commentary. An interesting comparison can be made with the journalistic essays of Fanny Fern, which also take up the marriage contract, the condition of women, and women's work, though in a very different mode, and which also use humor, though of a much broader kind.

Questions for Reading, Discussion, and Writing

1. What is the effect of the first-person narrative?
2. In what ways is distance from the narrator achieved?
3. What do you make of the ending? Is it unexpected? How does it affect your assessment of Margaret's passivity? Of her marriage?

Rebecca Harding Davis (1831–1910)

Contributing Editor: Judith Roman-Royer

Classroom Issues and Strategies

Problems in teaching Davis include dialect, allusions, confusing dialogue, hard-to-identify speakers, vague frame story, religious solutions, and the juxtaposition of sentimental language with religiosity and realism. To address these problems consider the following:

1. Explain the dialect (see the footnotes).
2. Try to ignore the allusions; most are not important to the heart of meaning.
3. The names of characters, their jobs, the speakers, and their roles need to be clarified:

    Kirby, son of Kirby the mill owner—He is aware of the problems of the workers but sees them as insoluble; he takes the attitude of Pontius Pilate.

    Dr. May, a town physician—He is idealistic, sympathetic to the workers, but naive about reality and thus unintentionally cruel to Hugh.

    "Captain"—The reporter for the city paper.

    Mitchell, Kirby's intellectual brother-in-law, visitor to the South—He is cold, cynically socialistic.

4. Discuss the frame story. Careful readers will find inconsistencies in the frame narratives that explain the narrator's perspective. Early in the

story, the narrator "happens" to be in the house, apparently a visitor, but at the end of the story, the house and statue of the korl woman seem to belong to her. The story of the Wolfe family is said to be set thirty years in the past, so how did the narrator come to know it in such intimate detail? One of my students suggested that the narrator may be Janey, who has somehow risen above her environment and become a writer, a solution that is provocative and unsubstantiated by the text.

5. Show how Davis is ambiguous about a religious solution. She espouses it, but her realistic picture of the problem is so vivid that it seems impossible to the reader that just Quaker kindness will solve the problems.

6. The swing between romanticism and realism is at the heart of this author.

Some students find this work depressing, but some like it. They can be asked to compare it with the situation of the poor today, especially the homeless and today's immigrants. Students can also be interested in a discussion of religion's role in comforting and/or silencing the poor.

Major Themes, Historical Perspectives, Personal Issues

"Life in the Iron-Mills" is an accessible text that can be assigned and discussed in a single class meeting. Many students reject the "naturalistic" view inherent in the story that the characters could do little to help themselves. Contemporary students, educated to believe in the Alger myth, are eager to protest that Hugh could have lifted himself out of his poverty or moved to the city to become an artist.

Perhaps a greater problem may be students' unwillingness to see the feminist subtext of the story discovered by Tillie Olsen. The story deals quite openly with the life of an iron-worker; how, then, do we find in it the story of a thwarted "spinster" fiction writer? To make this reading credible, students will need to know something of Davis's life story (see headnote); the position of unmarried women in society (their dependence on their families, the lack of socially acceptable ways for a woman to earn a living, and the impossibility of living alone); and the incredible isolation of writers who lived anywhere in America outside of Boston and perhaps New York at this period. In the context of a traditional American literature survey, Davis's frustration could be related to that of writers like Cooper and Irving and the sense of the United States as an artistic wilderness that prevailed early in the century.

Significant Form, Style, or Artistic Conventions

As far as style, many would have found the work oppressively realistic and unpleasant. The Hawthornes used words like "gloomy" and even "mouldy" to describe Davis's writing.

Original Audience

The work was written for an upper-middle-class and upper-class audience, the readers of the *Atlantic*, who were the elite of the country at the time. Many had familiarity with languages and the literary allusions in the work as well as intimate knowledge of the New Testament. Most were "liberal" Christians and although some were social reformers, virtually all believed the individual Christian had a responsibility to people like Hugh and Deb. The audience was highly receptive to Davis's message.

The difference in the audience now is that college students come from a broader spectrum of society. This has two effects: First, some of them may have worked in factories or come from blue-collar families and have experience closer to that of Hugh and Deb; second, the language of the text is apt to be more difficult for them. The excess of punctuation is an impediment. The sentimental exclamations probably differ little from some kinds of contemporary popular literature that students may have encountered.

Comparisons, Contrasts, Connections

Davis can be compared with

1. Hawthorne, who had an influence on Davis, especially *House of the Seven Gables*; American Romantic literature.
2. Dickens—sentimental realism.
3. Popular literature of today.
4. Novels of social criticism, such as *Uncle Tom's Cabin*; even later muckraking novels, such as *The Jungle*.

Questions for Reading, Discussion, and Writing

1. What is the purpose of the rhetorical questions posed by the author/narrator at various points in the story? Do they refer simply to the prospect of salvation for a man convicted of stealing, or do they imply the naturalistic view that Hugh's theft is excused by his unfortunate environment and heredity? Some students may recognize what is probably

religious rhetoric in the questions: perhaps the teacher can simply encourage students to seek additional possibilities.

2. They could write a paper discussing the story as a transitional work between Romanticism and realism, using traits outlined in Richard Chase's *American Novel and Its Tradition*.

Bibliography

Tillie Olsen's essay in the Feminist Press edition is probably the most accessible place to go for additional information. It is highly personal but helpful.

The Emergence of American Poetic Voices

Songs and Ballads

Contributing Editor: Paul Lauter

Classroom Issues and Strategies

Students immediately ask, "Is it literature?" The songs raise all of the issues about "popular culture," including their "quality" as literary texts, their changeableness from version to version, their audience, their relationship to music. Can they be, should they be, studied in a literature classroom rather than in a music classroom?

It is useful to play versions of the songs and ballads—especially the spirituals. Surprisingly few students have ever actually heard such a song, and they often find them powerful. But this can be overdone—after all, the musical vocabulary is, on the whole, even more remote from student culture than are the texts. A less inhibited or more skilled instructor may wish to involve students in the singing; indeed, some may be able to lead a class, and that experience can pay off significantly when one gets to the question of audience.

It can be important to confront directly the question of what constitutes the domain of "literature." Who decides what is included there? And on what basis? If these texts are, as some are, extraordinarily simple, does that remove them from what we think of as significant literature? Are there questions of audience and function involved? What are—and have been—the functions of such songs? Who sings them, and when, and why? Are these significant literary questions?

Another issue best confronted directly is the question of the mutability of such songs. Is it a good thing or a bad thing that people change them?

Major Themes, Historical Perspectives, Personal Issues

Obviously, the spirituals draw deeply on the Bible, especially the Old Testament. Many are built on a fundamental analogy between black slaves and the Hebrews. They can also be read ethnographically, for they express a good deal about the character and functions of religion and other forms of culture in the slave period.

Both the songs of black and white communities interestingly focus on everyday experiences of work, courting, religion (as well as on eschatological visions).

Significant Form, Style, or Artistic Conventions

The headnote points to a number of formal features, like refrains and repetitions, qualities of language, characteristic patterns of imagery, the ways in which songs are taken up, reframed, renewed. It can be useful to discuss how these songs are similar to and different from more "formal" poetry and also from one another.

Original Audience

The most interesting issue may be how, in the origins of such songs, the distinction between creator/singer and audience did not, on the whole, exist. The end of the Introduction to the period considers that issue. Raising this problem allows a class to explore the difference between culture as a commodity produced by persons other than oneself, and culture as an integral part of human life, serving a variety of functions, including discharging grief, inspiring hope, and offering opportunities, in the *singing*, for physical and psychological expression. The song, Bernice Reagon has pointed out, is only the vehicle or perhaps excuse for the singing.

Comparisons, Contrasts, Connections

This unit is designed to allow, indeed, encourage, comparisons among varieties of poetic texts from very different cultures.

Questions for Reading, Discussion, and Writing

1. (a) How are these songs similar to/different from more formal kinds of poetry?
   (b) What patterns of imagery, features of language, do you notice?
   (c) What are the structural features common to some or all of these songs?
2. (a) Make up an additional verse to . . . (Useful since it helps students see the formal features of a text, and also to overcome their wariness of "poetry.")
   (b) Should such songs (or other forms of popular culture) be taught in literature courses?

Bibliography

The first chapter of Lawrence Levine's *Black Culture and Black Consciousness* offers important insights about the functions and structure of spirituals.

William Cullen Bryant (1794–1878)

Contributing Editor: Allison Heisch

Classroom Issues and Strategies

Most of the Bryant selections in the anthology are ruminative poems about the nature of life and the nature of nature. Some students really like this sort of thing, but substantial numbers are allergic to it.

The most effective strategy I have found is to provide visual backup in the form of a Hudson River School slide show. A fancy version would parallel English Romantic poets (especially Gray, Cowper, and Wordsworth) and painters (e.g., Constable and Turner).

Bryant is a fine example of a writer who was not only popular but also famous in his day. He can be used to open a discussion of the social and histori- cal implications of such popularity (why it comes and why it goes), the essen- tially political character of anthologies (yes, even this one), and the idea of "fame" in connections with contemporary poets and poetry.

For students (and they are many) who do not naturally respond to Bryant, the questions generally run to "Why are we reading this?" Or, more decorously, "Why was he so popular?" Yet they do respond to him as an example of how the American high culture invented itself. In an altogether different vein, the personal philosophy expressed in "Thanatopsis" has some enduring appeal.

Major Themes, Historical Perspectives, Personal Issues

Bryant is very useful as a means of demonstrating the imitative mode through which New Englanders of an intellectual bent sought to establish an acceptable American literary voice. This is easily demonstrated by pairing his poems with comparable English productions. He can also be linked to the Transcendentalists—though with great caution, since much more is going on.

Significant Form, Style, or Artistic Conventions

Again, he should be shown in connection with his English models. It's useful to point out the self-conscious regularity of these poems both in connection with their particularly derivative subject matter and in contrast with the form and subjects of those contemporary poems and songs (well represented in this anthology) that were not informed by the dominant English literary culture.

Original Audience

I have usually talked about Bryant's audience in connection with the expansion of publishing in nineteenth-century America—especially magazines and newspapers. Ordinarily, students have no idea what a nineteenth-century newspaper would have looked like or contained. They never expect them to contain poetry. To demonstrate the probably contemporary audience, I have found it useful to collect and read commercially produced greeting cards.

Comparisons, Contrasts, Connections

Freneau's "The House of Night" may be read with "Thanatopsis" to demonstrate both the imitation of dominant English poetic forms and transatlantic lag-time in creating them for American audiences. Obviously, Bryant may be read with Emerson and Thoreau as a pre- or proto-Transcendentalist. It is interesting to contrast Bryant's earnest view of nature with Emily Dickinson's ironic one. Bryant's poem on Abraham Lincoln against Whitman's ("When Lilacs Last . . . Bloom'd") makes a memorable contrast between Anglophile American poetry and poetry with a genuine American accent.

Questions for Reading, Discussion, and Writing

1. (a) Based upon what you can glean from these poems, what sort of religious and philosophical outlook does this writer have?

(b) Compare the view of nature in poems such as "To a Waterfowl" and "The Yellow Violet" with that in "The Prairies."

2. Bryant's "Thanatopsis" is often read as a proto-Transcendentalist poem; yet it was discovered and rushed to publication by Bryant's father, who by all accounts was a Calvinist. Some options:

(a) Provide a Calvinist "reading" of "Thanatopsis."

(b) Locate, compare, and explain potentially "Transcendental" and "Calvinist" elements in the poem.

(c) Argue that it's one or the other (very artificial, but effective).

Bibliography

Brown, Charles H. *William Cullen Bryant.* New York: Scribners, 1971.

Henry Wadsworth Longfellow (1807–1882)

Contributing Editor: Allison Heisch

Classroom Issues and Strategies

If students have encountered Longfellow before taking a college course, the poems they know are not in this anthology: *Evangeline, The Song of Hiawatha, The Courtship of Miles Standish.* The Longfellow of this anthology is our turn of the twenty-first-century "revisionist" Longfellow, and except in poems such as "A Psalm of Life," he is almost unrecognizable as a writer who might have written those famous poems. If students have not actually read Longfellow, but merely heard of him (the typical case), they want to know why he's so famous.

Longfellow *is* accessible, and the fact is that in almost any class there will be students who adore "A Psalm of Life" and students who cannot stand it. Such a division, of course, presents the teacher with an ideal point of departure.

Although Longfellow is now very unfashionable, he is nevertheless an excellent vehicle for teaching about poetry either to the unlimited or the turned-off. Oddly enough, students in general respond to the story of his life almost more readily than to his poetry. That, therefore, is a good place to begin. They often ask about his fame. Some respond very positively to his sentimentalism, which can be tricky.

Major Themes, Historical Perspectives, Personal Issues

Longfellow's themes in the poems in this collection are nearly indistinguishable from those of his contemporaries in England. It's useful to show him, therefore, as an example of the branch of American literature that created itself in admiring imitation of English literature. He is also that rare thing, a genuine celebrity of a poet, whose fame has subsided and whose stature has shrunk accordingly. Many of the poems we now admire most are from his later years and conform better to modern taste than the poems for which he was famous in his lifetime. Thus, he can be used as a good example of the ways in which changing literary taste alter literary reputations.

Significant Form, Style, or Artistic Conventions

Longfellow's poems are not only accessible in their meaning, but they are also highly regular in their form. It is very simple to teach metrics with Longfellow because he provides easy and memorable examples of so many metrical schemes. These can be presented in connection with Longfellow's personal history, for he is of course an academic poet, and as such a poet writing often self-consciously from a learned perspective. Thus, nothing with him seems wholly spontaneous or accidental.

Original Audience

Two points are easy and convenient where audience is concerned: First, the fact that Longfellow was in his time as popular as a rock singer might be in ours. Second, the fact that while he was writing for an audience descended from transplanted Englishmen, he was nevertheless trying to create for them an American poetry crafted from "native" materials, thereby making chauvinist myth. Admittedly, it's hard to get to that point from the selections in the present anthology, but since "The Jewish Cemetery at Newport" was originally part of *The Courtship of Miles Standish,* a way *can* be found.

Comparisons, Contrasts, Connections

There are many directions to travel here: First, locate Longfellow in New England with Emerson and the Transcendentalists; second, locate him as a (necessary?) predecessor to Whitman, and then compare their views of America; third, set his view of life and nature against that of native poets.

Questions for Reading, Discussion, and Writing

1. (a) To whom is he writing? What is his message?
   (b) Translate "A Psalm of Life" *literally* and say whether you agree or disagree.
   (c) What are Longfellow's favorite words?
2. How has Longfellow changed or maintained his essential view of life between "A Psalm of Life" and "Aftermath"?

Bibliography

Because his poetry is more impressive taken together than individually analyzed, Longfellow has commanded whole books more often than single articles.

Wagenknecht, Edward. *Henry Wadsworth Longfellow.* New York: Ungar, 1986.

Frances Sargent Locke Osgood (1811–1850)

Contributing Editor: Joanne Dobson

Classroom Issues and Strategies

Students generally find Osgood appealing. Her apparently self-contradictory take on the position of women can be addressed through discussion of "A Reply," in which Osgood speaks of the necessity for women in a repressive society to express themselves obliquely rather than directly.

Major Themes, Historical Perspectives, Personal Issues

Osgood is generally a sentimental poet; that is to say, she is concerned primarily with affectional issues. My essay on literary sentimentalism in *American Literature* (1997) might help an instructor define the broader contours of sentimental literary practice. In addition, her focus on gender politics—on the inequitable balance of power between the sexes in a patriarchal society—could be looked at in light of the women's rights movement of the 1840s. Students will inevitably be interested in Osgood's relationship with Poe, so a knowledge of his life would help; however, I would advise against allowing romantic speculation to dominate discussion. Osgood's apparently unhappy marriage to a husband who traveled extensively and her residency at the Astor Hotel could be discussed in light of contemporary expectations for domestic life, and her arch and flirtatious self-presentation could be explored from the perspective of cultural expectations for female behavior. Class issues and the international nature of Osgood's experience could also be usefully considered.

Significant Form, Style, or Artistic Conventions

Osgood's versification is skillful, even brilliant, and provides material for aesthetic discussion. Instructors might find it useful to research the poetic tradition of the *blason* before approaching "The Maiden's Mistake," a witty deconstruction of a misogynist tradition. My essay on Osgood's poetry in *American Literature* (1993) offers further "salon" verses. See also my essay on sentimental literary practice, noted above.

Original Audience

Osgood had at least two primary contemporary audiences: a wide-ranging public audience, to whom she catered and who seemingly adored her, and an elite private audience of her sophisticated New York City peers, for whom she wrote a number of poems to be read aloud at salon gatherings.

Comparisons, Contrasts, Connections

A comparison of Osgood's private poetry with that of her small-town New England contemporary Emily Dickinson could elicit some lively discussion. Her connection with Poe is a natural for discussion.

Questions for Reading, Discussion, and Writing

Look at other poets in Griswold's *Female Poets* for comparison of themes and realizations.

Consider "A Reply" in the context of Griswold's assumptions about female authorship as revealed in his introduction.

Read "Lines on . . . a Bill for the Protection of the Property of Married Women" (1848) in light of the Seneca Falls "Sentiments."

Compare "To a Slandered Poetess" and Emily Dickinson's "I'm Nobody!" (J288).

Compare Osgood's "Alone" and Edgar Allan Poe's "Alone."

Bibliography

Along with the material listed in the text, it would be useful to look at Rufus Griswold's *The Female Poets of America* (1848), both the general introduction and the introduction to Osgood's work. Other helpful contemporaneous publications are *The Memorial: Written by Friends of the Late Mrs. Osgood*, edited by Mary E. Hewitt in 1851, and Poe's considerations of Osgood in *Godey's Lady's Book*, March and September of 1846. Poe biography is generally biased against Osgood, but Kenneth Silverman's *Edgar A. Poe: Mournful and Never-ending Remembrance* (1991) gives a fairly objective account.

Walt Whitman (1819–1892)

Contributing Editor: Betsy Erkkila

Classroom Issues and Strategies

I use the 1855 versions of "Song of Myself" and "The Sleepers" because I think these poems represent Whitman at his unrevised best. I begin with a biographical introduction, stressing Whitman's active engagement as radical Democrat and party journalist in the major political conflicts of pre–Civil War America. The inscription poem "One's-Self I Sing" and his vision of the poet balanced between pride and sympathy in the 1855 Preface serve as a good introduction to "Song of Myself." I usually begin by asking the students to talk about Whitman's free verse technique. What ordering devices does he use in the opening lines to achieve his poetic design: these include repetition, biblical parallelism, rhythmic recurrence, assonance, and consonance.

Section 15 is a good illustration of the ways Whitman's catalog technique serves as a democratizing device, inscribing the pattern of many and one. By basing his verse in the single, end-stopped line at the same time that he fuses this line—through various linking devices—with the larger structure of the whole, Whitman weaves an overall pattern of unity in diversity. This pattern of many and one—the *e pluribus unum* that was the revolutionary seal of the American republic—is the overarching figure of *Leaves of Grass*.

I present "Song of Myself" as a drama of democratic identity in which the poet seeks to balance and reconcile major conflicts in the body politic of America: the conflict between "separate person" and "en masse," individualism and equality, liberty and union, the South and the North, the farm and the city, labor and capital, black and white, female and male, religion and science. One can discuss any of the individual sections of the poem in relation to this conflict. Moments of particular conflict and crisis occur in sections 28 and 38. I ask the students to discuss the specific nature of the crisis in each of these sections. Both involve a loss of balance.

In section 28, the protagonist loses bodily balance as he is swept away by an erotic, masturbatory urge. Ask the students to think about why a masturbation fantasy occurs in a poem about democracy. Ask them to think about why the masturbatory fit is represented in the language of political insurrection. These questions lead to interesting observations about the relation between political power and power over the body. Masturbation is, in effect, the political ground on which Whitman tests the theory of democracy. Within the democratic economy of his poem, the turbulence of the body, like the turbulence of the masses, is part of a natural regenerative order.

If section 28 involves a loss of bodily balance, section 38 involves a loss of self in empathetic identification with others. In discussing the crisis in section 38, ask the students what Whitman means by the lines: "I find myself on the verge of a usual mistake." This will usually lead back to the end of section 3, where the poet begins identifying with scenes of suffering, carnage, and death. Some of these scenes are linked with the nation's history: the hounded slave, the Texas war, the American Revolution. The poet appears to be on the verge of losing faith in the divine potency of the individual and the regenerative pattern of the whole. He resolves the crisis by remembering the divinity of Christ as a living power existing within rather than outside of every individual.

The resolution of this crisis leads to the emergence of the divinely empowered poet who presides over the final passages of the poem, declaring his ultimate faith in the "form, union, plan" of the universe. Here you might want to discuss the relation between this poetic affirmation of democratic faith and union and the fact of an American Union that was in the throes of dissolution.

Since Whitman's poetic development corresponds with stages in his own and the nation's history, a chronological presentation works well in the classroom. After discussing "Song of Myself," you might want to discuss other 1855 poems such as "The Sleepers" and "There Was a Child Went Forth." "The Sleepers," which was toned down in later versions, represents in both its form and its content the half-formed, erotically charged, and anxiety-ridden fantasies of the dream state. The poem anticipates Freud's "unconscious" and the literary experiments of the surrealists. But the poem is revolutionary not only in its psychosexual dimension. The poet also descends into a kind of political unconscious of the nation, dredging up images of regeneration through violence associated with Washington and the battle for American independence, the slave as black Lucifer, and the Indian squaw.

If you have time to do later work by Whitman, the 1860 poems might be grouped together since they correspond with a period of both personal and national crisis. Within the context of *Leaves of Grass*, "Out of the Cradle Endlessly Rocking" appears to respond to this crisis. Ask the students to comment on the differences between the "amative" poems of *Children of Adam* and the "adhesive" poems of *Calamus*. This will lead to a discussion of Whitman's sexual politics.

Women students have particularly strong and mixed reactions to "A Woman Waits for Me": they are attracted by Whitman's celebration of an erotically charged female body, yet are repelled by the fact that she seems rhetorically prone. The students will usually note that Whitman's poems to men seem more immediate and personal than the poems of *Children of Adam*. "In Paths Untrodden" reflects Whitman's split at this time between the public culture of democracy and his desire to tell secrets, to "come out" poetically by naming his hitherto unspeakable passion for men. You might want to remind the students that the term "homosexual" did not yet exist, and thus Whitman was breaking the path toward a language of male love. His invention is particularly evident in "When I Heard at the Close of the Day," where the power and tenderness of his feelings for his lover are linked with the rhythms of a completely natural order. The "confessional" note in the poems anticipates the later work of Allen Ginsberg, Robert Lowell, and Sylvia Plath. Ask the students to reflect on why it was the poems of *Children of Adam* and not *Calamus* that most shocked the literary establishment. It was really not until Allen Ginsberg wrote his comic tribute to Whitman, "In a Supermarket in California," that Whitman, the homosexual poet, came fully out of the closet—at least in America.

I usually begin discussion of the war poems by asking how the experience of fratricidal war might affect Whitman as the poet of national union. This will lead to reflections on the tragedy of the Civil War. The poems of *Drum-Taps*—which proceed from militant exultation, to the actual experience of war, to demobilization and reconciliation—might be read as an attempt to place the butchery of the war within a poetic and ultimately regenerative design. Ask the students to compare Whitman's war poems with his earlier poems. They are at once more formally controlled and more realistic—stylistic changes that are linked with the war context. "A March in the Ranks Hard-Prest, and the Road Unknown" and "The Artilleryman's Vision" are proto-modern poems in which the individual appears as an actor in a drama of history he no longer understands or controls. Whitman's ambivalence about black emancipation is evident in "Ethiopia Saluting the Colors." "Vigil Strange I Kept on the Field One Night" and "As I Lay with My Head in Your Lap Camerado" are particularly effective in suggesting the ways the wartime context of male bonding and comradeship gave Whitman a legitimate language and social frame within which to express his love for men.

In discussing Whitman's famous elegy on the death of President Lincoln, it is interesting to begin by asking what remains unsaid in the poem. For one thing,

Lincoln is never named as the subject within the context of the poem; his death becomes representative of all the war dead. By placing Lincoln's death within a timeless regenerative order of nature, Whitman's "Lilacs" also "covers over" the fact of Lincoln's unnatural and violent assassination. Although the vision of battle in section 15 is often passed over in critical considerations of the poem, this bloody sight of "battle-corpses" and the "debris" of war is, I believe, the unspeakable horror and real subject of the poem.

Democratic Vistas (1871) might be read either as an introduction to or a conclusion to the study of Whitman. In the essay, he struggles with the central tensions and paradoxes of American, New World experience. These conflicts intensify and are more urgently addressed in the post–Civil War period as the unleashed force of market capitalism and the dynamic of modern civilization appear to spin out of control. "Who bridles Leviathan?" Whitman asked in Democratic Vistas. It is a fitting question with which to conclude the study of Whitman and to begin the story of the modern world.

Emily Dickinson (1830–1886)

Contributing Editors: Peggy McIntosh and Ellen Louis Hart

Classroom Issues and Strategies

Students may have problems with the appearance of the poems—with the fact that they are without titles; that they are often short and compact, compressed; that the dash is so often used in the place of traditional punctuation. Some students will be put off by the grammatical elisions and ellipses, and some by the fact that the poems often do not quickly display a central, controlling metaphor or an easily identifiable narrative theme. Students who are already intimidated by poetry may find the poems difficult and unyielding. Some, however, may find Dickinson's brevity and conciseness startling and enjoyable. Those who have false notions that everything in poetry means or symbolizes something else, and that the reader must crack the code and come up with a "solution" to each poem's meaning, will be frustrated by Dickinson or will read the poems with atrocious insensitivity. Dickinson's work requires intense concentration, imagination, and unusually high tolerance for ambiguity.

Some students may want to dismiss Dickinson as an "old maid" or as a woman who "missed out on life" by not marrying. One student asked, "Why didn't she just move to Boston and get a job?" Students want to know about Dickinson's life and loves, her personal relationships with both men and women; they are curious about why she chose not to publish; they are interested in her religious/spiritual life, her faith, and her belief in immortality. They want to know what the dilemmas of her life were, as they manifested themselves in her writing: What her psychic states were, what tormented her, what she mourned, what drove her close to madness, why she was fascinated with death and dying. Addressing these questions allows the opportunity to discuss the oversimplifying and stereotyping that result from ignorance of social history as well as insistence of heterosexism.

Students should be prepared for the poems by being encouraged to speculate. An instructor can invite students to explore each poem as an experiment, and to ease into the poetry, understanding that Dickinson was a poet who truly "questioned authority" and whose work defies authoritative readings. All of her difficulties as listed above can be seen as connected with her radically original imagination.

Students can be directed toward approaching these poems with "lexicon" in hand, as Dickinson wrote them. Here is the perfect opportunity for an exercise with the *OED*. Students can be asked to make a list as they read of words that begin to seem to them particularly Dickinsonian; "Circumference," for example. They can also list characteristic phrases or images. The selection of poems can be parceled out in certain groupings in which linked images, emotions, or descriptions of natural phenomena are easily recognizable.

Students can be assigned to write journals in which they record their first impressions and discoveries, as well as later commentary on poems and further stages of interpretation. Asking people to read poems out loud will help them to learn to hear the poet's voice and to tune their ears to her rhymes, rhythms, and syntax. Above all, the instructor should not pretend assurance about Dickinson's meanings and intentions.

It works well to have students make a selection of poems on a theme or image cluster, and then work in groups with the selected poems, afterwards presenting their readings. Such group work can create flexibility while giving students confidence in their own perceptions.

Another presentation that is very useful is the kind of demonstration Susan Howe gives and which some other teachers now use. Make a copy of a Thomas Johnson version of a poem and then make a typed transcription of the same poem using Franklin's *Manuscript Books.* This can lead to interesting discussions of editing questions involved with Dickinson: how to represent the line breaks and the punctuation; how to render these unpublished poems in print.

Major Themes, Historical Perspectives, Personal Issues

Students need to know something about Dickinson's life, her schooling, religious upbringing and subsequent rebellion, her family members, and the close friends who became the audience for her poems. (Much of this is outlined in the headnote.) They will be helped by having some historical sense of women and men in nineteenth-century New England. They need information on women's habits of reading and writing, on friendships among women, religious revivalism, and life in a small college town like Amherst. Awareness of class, class consciousness, and social customs for families like the Dickinsons and their circle of friends will help prevent questions like the one cited above on why Dickinson didn't just move and "go for it" in a city. Students should be discouraged from discussing the poems as "feminine" or as demonstrating "the woman's point of view."

A discussion of homophobia is necessary. Here the headnote should be helpful. The love poems are not exclusively heterosexual. Students should be encouraged to examine the erotics of this poetry without being limited to conventional notions of gender. Dickinson uses a variety of voices in these poems, writing as a child (often a boy), a wife-to-be, a woman rejected, and as a voice of authority which we often associate with maleness. These voices or roles or "poses," as they are sometimes called, need to be identified and examined. Here are the multiplicities of self. Do we need to reconcile these voices? What happens when we don't? Students may reflect on or write about multiplicities of experience, perspective, and voice in themselves.

Significant Form, Style, or Artistic Conventions

Information should be provided about other American and British writers publishing at this time, those whom Dickinson read, those especially popular at the time but not as well known, as well as those still recognized: Emerson, Longfellow, Stowe, Helen Hunt Jackson, Elizabeth Barrett Browning, George Eliot, Dickens.

Dickinson's poetry is very dissimilar to poetry being published at the same time. Attention needs to be drawn to this fact and to the originality, the intentional and consistent innovativeness, of her style. Questions of style can also lead to observations concerning the thin line between poetry and prose in Dickinson's letters, and about the complex and integral relationships between the two genres throughout her writing. Students can be invited to read letters as poems and to read poems as letters, exploring the ways in which Dickinson's work challenges traditional notions of the boundaries of genre.

Students need to know about the publishing and editing history of the poems, to understand how Dickinson worked—collecting poems into packets, identifying words for revision, sending poems to various recipients, and apparently avoiding publication during her lifetime. There is also the question of the editing: What did a given poem look like when early editors published it, and when Thomas Johnson published the same poem in the variorum edition? Students should be made familiar with Thomas Johnson's variorum as well as R. W. Franklin's *Manuscript Books of Emily Dickinson*. What did the variorum edition of the poems bring to Dickinson scholarship? What was available before? What has R. W. Franklin's publication of the manuscript books meant? And what about Susan Howe's argument that Dickinson's original line breaks must be honored? Some students may wish to take up the question of how to represent in type Dickinson's marks of punctuation.

For two poems in our selection we include in footnotes all the "variants," or alternate word choices Dickinson noted for each poem. Using Franklin's *Manuscript Books,* students can observe in detail the poet's system for marking possible changes and listing variants. Furthermore, study of the facsimiles in the Franklin edition will give students an opportunity to observe the artistic conventions in Dickinson's manuscripts—lineation and punctuation as well as her handwriting, or calligraphy, and her use of space between letters, words, and at the end of a line. Investigation of the manuscripts will give students the opportunity to discuss what has been lost in her visual art in the print transcriptions of the poems. In addition, reading the poems in the manuscript volumes encourages students to test out the theories of some critics that these volumes are artistic units with narrative and thematic cohesion.

It is important to point out that the number that appears at the head of each poem in our selection is not a part of the space of the poem, and that these numbers were never used by the poet. They were established by Thomas Johnson in his attempt to arrange the complete poems chronologically. Since so few of Dickinson's manuscripts can be dated, the Johnson numbers are most often speculative. Their standard use has been as a system of reference, and as convenient as this system may be, a less artificial way of referring to a poem is to use the first line.

Original Audience

Students should look at Franklin (or photocopies of pages from Franklin) to see how the "packets" or "fascicles" looked. Reading poems sent in letters or with letters is a way of considering audiences, both Dickinson's immediate audience and her writing for posterity. The variorum edition identifies poems sent in letters; the three volumes of *Letters* list many enclosed poems.

Comparisons, Contrasts, Connections

Dickinson can be read with her contemporaries, the American and British writers of her time. She may also be read in the context of twentieth-century New England writers, Robert Frost and Robert Lowell, for example, or with current New England women writers, May Sarton and Maxine Kumin, for example. A regional sense is a strong thread in Dickinson's writing. She may be read in the context of experiments in modernism, in relation to e. e. cummings, for example. Dickinson also fits within a continuum of American women poets from Anne Bradstreet and Phillis Wheatley through Amy Lowell, Gertrude Stein, Edna St. Vincent Millay, H.D., Marianne Moore, Sylvia Plath, Anne Sexton, Adrienne Rich, Audre Lorde, and Judy Grahn. (This, of course, is only one selection, which represents many of the best-known American writers. There are other such lists.)

Questions for Reading, Discussion, and Writing

Cumbersome term papers "arguing" a single thesis on Dickinson are usually quite out of tune with her own multifaceted sensibility and intelligence. Reading a poem as a statement of a creed, that is, as a "proof" that Dickinson believed this or that, is usually fatal to common sense. We suggest that the following fifteen writing assignments on Dickinson will suit a variety of students with a variety of learning styles.

1. All her life, Emily Dickinson seems to have felt she was encumbered by structures that did not fit her, whether structures of religion, belief, value, language, thought, manners, or institutions. If you share her feeling, give some examples of her sense of the problem and then some examples of your own sense of it, in your life.
2. The year 1862, during which Dickinson wrote more than 300 poems, seems to have been a year of great emotional intensity for her. Drawing on poems from 1862 given in this anthology, trace some recurrent themes or designs in the poems of that year.
3. Kathleen Raine has written: "For the poet when he begins to write there is no poem, in the sense of a construction of words; and the concentration of the mind is upon something else, that precedes words, and by which the words, as they are written, must constantly be checked and rectified."

    If this quotation rings true for you, choose one or more poems and discuss the "something else" and the process by which Dickinson apparently revised toward it, using Johnson's three-volume edition, which shows all known revisions.
4. You are Emily Dickinson. An acquaintance who does not know you very well has just suggested that the time you spend alone must feel somewhat empty. Write a fragment of a letter or a poem in which you respond as you think she might.
5. Many of Dickinson's poems are not so much about ideas or themes as about the process of seeing or coming to see, or guess, or know. Trace the *elements of process* in one or more poems; then imitate the sense of process in a passage of poetry or prose of your own.
6. What do you appreciate about Emily Dickinson, and what do you think she hoped readers would appreciate about her?

7. Read Jay Leyda's collection of documents about Emily Dickinson's year of college in *The Years and Hours of Emily Dickinson,* and read Dickinson's letters from her year away. Compare your own college experience with hers. Considering both the pressures on you and the pleasures you experience, how do you differ from or resemble her?

8. Dickinson's poems have both authority and obliqueness, as suggested in her line "Tell all the Truth but tell it slant." Discuss examples of Dickinson's techniques of slantwise style and some of their effects on you as reader.

9. Reading Dickinson is a personal matter, and readers' perceptions of her change continually. On each of three different days, begin an essay entitled "On Reading Emily Dickinson." Do not work for consistency, but rather for a fresh account of your perception on each day.

10. For many English and American poets, moments of "seeing" accurately have often been moments of affirmation. For Dickinson, they were often moments of pain. Discuss any aspects of the poems on pain that interest you, shedding light, if possible, on her words "A nearness to Tremendousness/An Agony Procures. . . ."

11. Richard Wilbur wrote:

    "At some point Emily Dickinson sent her whole Calvinist vocabulary into exile, telling it not to come back until it would subserve her own sense of things. . . . Of course, that is not a true story, but it is a way of saying what I find most remarkable in Emily Dickinson. She inherited a great and overbearing vocabulary which, had she used it submissively, would have forced her to express an established theology and psychology. But she would not let that vocabulary write her poems for her."

    Analyze some of the religious poems that seem to you unorthodox or surprising, and write a short piece of your own, in poetry or prose, in which you use the vocabulary of a religious tradition in an unusual way that "subserves your own sense of things."

12. Write four alternative first paragraphs to a paper entitled "Emily Dickinson."

13. Imagine a conversation between Emily Dickinson and any one of the other women writers read for this course. What might they have to talk about? Add a third woman (perhaps yourself) to the conversation if you like. Draw on all the sources of evidence that you have.

14. Dickinson used traditional hymn meter, but her poems are not like traditional hymns. Choose the words to any hymn you know and rewrite them until they sound as much like Dickinson as possible. You may virtually have to abandon the original hymn.

15. Emily Dickinson's first editors thought they were doing her a favor by changing certain words, repunctuating her poetry, and standardizing the line breaks. Using the three-volume Johnson edition and the Franklin

manuscript books, judge for yourself, in the case of two or three poems in which changes were made.

Bibliography

Eberwein, Jane Donahue, ed. *An Emily Dickinson Encyclopedia.* Westport, CT: Greenwood, 1998.

Farr, Judith. *The Passion of Emily Dickinson.* Cambridge, MA: Harvard UP, 1992.

Grabher, Gudrun, Roland Hagenbuchle, and Cristanne Miller, eds., *The Emily Dickinson Handbook.* Boston: U of Massachusetts P, 1998.

Howe, Susan. *The Birth-mark: Unsettling the Wilderness in American Literary History.* Middletown, CT: Wesleyan Press, 1993.

———. *My Emily Dickinson.* Berkeley: N Atlantic Books, 1985.

Murray, Aife. "Miss Margaret's Emily Dickinson," *Signs: Journal of Women in Culture and Society.* Spring 1999.

Sewall, Richard B. *The Life of Emily Dickinson,* 2 vols. New York: Farrar, 1974.

Smith, Martha N. *Rowing in Eden: Rereading Emily Dickinson.* Austin: U of Texas P, 1992.

Wolosky, Shira. *Emily Dickinson: A Voice of War.* New Haven: Yale UP, 1984.

Pedagogical Introduction

Late Nineteenth Century
1865–1910

Nations, Regions, Borders
Cluster: Literacy, Literature, and Democracy in Postbellum America
Critical Visions of Postbellum America
Developments in Women's Writing
A Sheaf of Poetry by Late-Nineteenth-Century American Women
The Making of "Americans"

The conjunction/contradiction of the terms *nation, regions,* and *borders,* along with the focus on gender indicated by *women's* writing, suggest both a turn away from a deductive approach to literary categorization and analysis based on assumptions concerning what is universal or central about the human—and more specifically the national—experience and a move toward an inductive approach that recognizes the value of regarding the specificity of cultural context in understanding how a text works. Rather than *a priori* assuming certain texts or cultural experiences to be marginal because they foreground issues of region and gender, thereby asserting the centrality of other texts supposedly free of such "ancillary" considerations, we can instead expand the possibilities for classroom discussion and pedagogical practice by regarding all human experience and cultural expression as profoundly "regional," as intimately concerned with questions of geography and gender, as well as race, social class, and other crucial processes of social definition. To group together, either in the anthology or on a syllabus, Henry James and Charles Chesnutt, African-American folktales and the works of Samuel Clemens, is not to argue for the "equivalency" of these texts according to some external standard of literary evaluation but to invite a consideration and comparison of their regionalness—the unique cultural contexts of their productions—as well as the dialogue, debate, and competition going on among them. Instead of using a set methodology for the reading of all texts, the conjunction of the texts in these sections asks students and teachers to consider how different texts signal different audience expectations, how they indicate or counterindicate a desired audience, how they speak to a variety of audiences and audience expectations at once—how "regions," whether regions of gender or geography, race or class communicate with each other across borders of race, culture, gender, and class.

If we regard all texts as regional, from the perspective of pedagogy the primary region for class investigation is the classroom itself, where the particularity and "regionality" of each student's response to the literature occurs. As a preparation for a discussion of terms like *central* and *regional, major* and *minor, representative* and *marginal,* students can explore their own responses to see what they find familiar and foreign in these texts, which borders these texts ask them to cross. Here again the inductive approach works well, for while such reactions will obviously vary from student to student, and from class to class, they provide us with a region-specific context for the consideration of the reception history of these works. Following Judith Fetterley's lead in *The Resisting Reader*, both women and men in the class can explore the traditional experience of reading texts that assume the centrality of male experience; similarly, all students can consider the difference represented by texts that assume the definitiveness and centrality of female experience. Students from outside the Northeast can discuss what it's like reading texts that take the geography, climate, and culture of New England as a norm or that figure the West as someplace wild, exotic, and mysterious. Clearly, this approach allows for a variety of cultural configurations and can be adapted to the specific demographics of the individual classroom.

Late-nineteenth-century women's writing, because it was long dismissed as merely "regionalist" writing, is in many ways now central to this regional approach to pedagogy. In her essay "'Distilling Essences': Regionalism and 'Women's Culture,'" Marjorie Pryse suggests that the women writers traditionally classified as "regionalists" (writers like Mary E. Wilkins Freeman and Sarah Orne Jewett) used the idea of regional rhetorically as a means of demonstrating that supposedly universal terms like *mother, home, black,* and *white* are in fact socially constructed while at the same time negotiating a cultural space to make such demonstrations. These texts thus raise the question of how to get to center stage from the margins. Such a question functions as both a means of interpreting a story like Alcott's "My Contraband" and of understanding Alcott's position as a writer. Such a manipulation of center and margin can be applied equally to Paul Laurence Dunbar or Charles Chesnutt, who write of the African-American experience in the language of formal European literary traditions (Henry Louis Gates Jr.'s work on the African-American cultural tradition of "signifyin[g]"—of both appropriating and ironically transforming forms and values from the dominant culture as part of an originally African rhetorical tradition—is especially applicable here as well as suggestive of rhetorical strategies used by any marginalized group) and to Samuel Clemens, who uses dialect and satire to write about a middle-class white world he both despised and aspired to.

One initial point of departure for classes using *The Heath Anthology* is the question of what difference the Civil War makes, both in general historical terms and in relation to these particular issues. Many institutions still structure their survey classes using 1865 as the "border" between old and new, the past and the modern, and this division reflects and reinforces widespread, if often conflicting and loosely defined, beliefs about the Civil War as the seminal event in American history. Again, the versions of this general historical sense the students bring to class can create the context for the reading and discussion of these post–Civil War texts, beginning with considerations of how different interpretations and representations of the Civil War serve different social, political, and cultural purposes.

The issue of race and the struggles of African Americans in post–Civil War America find representation here in the work of Frances Ellen Watkins Harper, while the majority of the texts in this section focus more on the evolution of the women's movement and the efforts of both Native American and Latino cultures to survive the continuing expansion of the U.S. empire. Again, the idea of cultural rhetoric can serve as a pedagogical entry into these texts by asking how these writers positioned themselves amidst various and often conflicting cultural identities related to gender, ethnicity, social class, religion, and region.

The question of empire—political, economic, and cultural—one particularly important to the historical study of post–Civil War America and of increasing relevance at the beginning of the twenty-first century—can provide entry to these texts as well. Henry Adams's famous, and now canonical, use of the image of the Virgin and the dynamo to signify the cultural difference of modernity can be paired with Upton Sinclair's metaphor of "the jungle," along with his harrowing depictions of the meat-packing industry, as contrasting yet not necessarily contradictory visions of the impact of the expanding capitalist economy. In both cases, asking students to consider the perspectives from which these accounts are written (that of a member of one of America's elite families versus that of a crusading socialist journalist) can lead to discussions that integrate issues of political philosophy, rhetorical purpose, audience, tone, diction, and structure.

For example, Adams's scholarly allusions and ornate prose style, which are often alienating for students, can be studied as strategies meant to register with different members of the reading public in specific ways so that questions about the difficulty of his style can lead to questions both about the audience he wants to reach and the audience he doesn't, and about why a writer would deliberately aim for a narrow readership while making claims for the universality of his analysis. The students can then examine where they feel they stand in relation to Adams's intended audience. The same questions, of course, can be posed in relation to Sinclair. In his case, the strategy is to reach a wide readership and incite moral outrage. Such questions of audience and rhetorical purpose lead to questions of canonicity, questions of which styles and strategies come to be considered "literary," which styles merely instrumental. Seeing and reading Adams in terms of his particular cultural and social position extends this discussion of canonicity to considerations involving the supposed universality of certain texts and the equally supposed limited appeal of others. Why, for example, has the skillfully rendered mid-life crisis of an upper-class New England intellectual been seen as universal in significance while the carefully constructed portrayal of the social practices leading to the nervous breakdown of a middle-class woman (Charlotte Perkins Gilman's "The Yellow Wall-

Paper") has until recently been ignored or thought of as interesting only to a limited group of readers? Just as important, why have attitudes changed regarding "The Yellow Wall-Paper"? The purpose of such questions is not to insist that students adhere to a new version of the canon or simply to discredit an older version, but to understand that all considerations of literary merit and cultural significance take place in the context of changing social and cultural values and as part of ongoing debates about those values, debates that include college students as both observers and participants.

The new "Cluster: Literacy, Literature, and Democracy in Postbellum America" not only provides an important context for thinking about the political and cultural dimensions of the stylistic choices made by turn-of-the-twentieth-century writers like Adams and Sinclair but also situates contemporary college students and instructors as part of that same context. Contemporary higher education, and particularly its populist expansion through the creation of land grant universities, has its foundation in the postbellum period, and the discussions about the importance of literacy and "literary" culture to a democratic society still resonate today in the legacy of classes in literary study designed for an increasingly broad spectrum of the population. Something as mundane as a general studies literature requirement stands as the contemporary manifestation of the arguments and ideas found in this cluster.

The Making of "Americans"

While earlier in American history, writers like Benjamin Franklin, Hector St. John de Crèvecoeur, Ralph Waldo Emerson, and Frederick Douglass can be seen to have engaged in a highly self-conscious process of creating models for a national identity, the texts in this section can be read as attempts to assimilate, negotiate, and restructure established myths of national identity, especially in the context of late-nineteenth-/early-twentieth-century patterns of immigration from Eastern Europe and Asia. Students can prepare for reading these texts by exploring their own received versions of these myths and by discussing various myths of immigration and assimilation, including the implications, desirability, and undesirability of the "melting pot" and other metaphors.

Beyond this examination of cultural mythology, the class can ground their discussions by compiling their own individual and family immigration histories. This project can include oral histories and research into various immigrant experiences. These immigration histories, along with the texts in this section, can then be approached in terms of how they do or don't fit into stereotypical models of the American self and the immigrant experience; more specifically, students can discuss the strategies these writers—as well as students and their ancestors—used in confronting these models. Rather than simply reacting to a cultural situation, these texts attempt in various ways to alter and revise that situation. How did the large influx of Russian and Eastern European Jewish immigrants, for example, adapt to and transform the American cultural landscape? Finally, Gertrude Bonnin's text continues the tradition among Native American writers of turning the immigrant myth inside out by addressing the question of how members of indigenous cultures deal with the experience of finding themselves strangers in their own land.

Bibliography

Fetterley, Judith. *The Resisting Reader: A Feminist Approach to American Fiction.* Bloomington: Indiana UP, 1978.

Gates, Henry Louis, Jr. *The Signifying Monkey: A Theory of African-American Literary Criticism.* New York: Oxford UP, 1988.

Pryse, Marjorie. "'Distilling Essences': Regionalism and 'Women's Culture.'" *American Literary Realism* 25 (1993): 1–15.

Nations, Regions, Borders

African-American Folktales

Contributing Editor: Susan L. Blake

Classroom Issues and Strategies

Some of the questions I would anticipate from students are: The tales are so simple—are they really art? If they didn't actually contribute to the abolition of slavery, how are they subversive? Both African-American students and others may be made uncomfortable by stereotypical characterizations and dialect. What's the point of perpetuating images of slavery today? Answering these questions is not easy; I've tried to address them in the material that follows.

Major Themes, Historical Perspectives, Personal Issues

Folktales interpret the experience of tellers and audience. While motifs endure from century to century and culture to culture, details and emphases vary with group experience and individual talent. Indeed, the art of the tale is to adapt the traditional motif to particular circumstances. Most African-American tales are about power relations, but as power relations are contextual, so are interpretations of the tales. Students familiar with slavery and willing to take metaphoric leaps will be able to read the John and Old Marster tales and the animal stories as critiques of slavery and, more generally, a racist society. But it is important, too, to think of the range of meanings the tales might hold for tellers and listeners in various social positions at various historical moments.

The ongoing conflict between John and Old Marster dramatizes the contradiction between humanity and slavery. The John tales turn on the paradox that John is a man and yet a slave, Old Marster's colleague/ confidant and yet his chattel. John keeps trying to close the gap between his status and that of Old Marster. When he succeeds—in, for example, claiming a right to the chickens he's raised—he in effect achieves freedom. Even when John fails or appears foolish, the tale still skewers slavery by its use of metaphor. There is little evidence, however, that these tales were told during slavery, and the slave-master relationship they depict, between two individual men, for all its metaphoric power, is narrow and relatively genial. Another way to think of the tales would be as an interpretation of race relations under "freedom" as slavery.

Unlike the John tales, the animal tales, which were told during slavery, do not distinguish neatly between unjust and justified antagonists. They can, however, be seen as a pointed refutation of the romantic myth of the old plantation that developed in the 1830s and may be most popularly represented in *Gone with the Wind*. On the plantation of myth, status is based on virtue, and human relations are governed by honor, pride, justice, and benevolence. In the recognizably human society of the animal tales, status is based on power, honor is absent, pride is a liability, justice is anything you can get away with, and benevolence is stupidity. Animal characters provide not only camouflage for social criticism but the essential metaphor of society as jungle.

The two conjure tales collected by Zora Neale Hurston, in which the rivals for the power represented by conjure are not master and slave but male and female, provide an interesting counterpoint to the John tales and animal stories. These tales draw attention to the absence of women in the other tales and raise a host of questions: Are they about gender conflict? Is there a specifically woman's point of view missing from the body of African-American tales? Is it significant that these tales were collected and published by one of the few female folktale collectors? Would these tales be read the same way in the 1930s and the 1990s?

Significant Form, Style, or Artistic Conventions

Folktales might be said to have three audiences, all of them in some sense "original": The people who hear and help create the oral tales; folklorists who persuade storytellers to perform their tales for publication; and readers of the published collections. It can be difficult for students to grasp that the tales were not "written" by a single "author" but are the product of a historically and politically mediated collaboration. Some of the stylistic features of the tales are conventional—the reproduction of animal sounds in dialogue, for example, and the retort that concludes the tales of John "stealing" Old Marster's livestock. At the same time, the tales bear the stamp of an individual performer's style and emphasis—E. L. Smith tells a snappy tale, John Blackamore a highly developed one; Mrs. Josie Jordan's "Malitis" concludes with a comment on slavery, J. D. Suggs's "Who Ate Up the Butter?" with a comment on the present. The tales also show the fingerprints of the collectors: the introductions to the two tales of the Flying Africans from *Drums and Shadows*, the distanced narration of Zora Neale Hurston's two conjure tales, the gratuitous misspellings ("lide" for "lied," "rode" for "road") in W. A. Eddins's "How Sandy Got His Meat." It would be useful for students to look for evidence of both the performers and the collectors in the published texts. For example, what are the characteristics of John Blackamore's or J. D. Suggs's style? Which tales seem most nearly quoted from the performer, which most edited by the collector, and why? What can you tell from the texts about the collectors' attitudes toward the tellers or the interaction between collectors and tellers? How might the conditions of collecting—the historical moment, the collectors' race (Hurston is black; the other collectors represented here are white), and the recording technology—affect the collecting event and the published text?

Comparisons, Contrasts, Connections

Comparison between any of the tales and a European, African, or other American variant (Dorson, *American Negro Folktales*, provides comparative references) highlights both the political analysis and the art of the African-American tale. Comparison between the told-for-true story "Malitis" and any of the food-stealing stories in the John cycle reveals the conventions of folk fiction. Comparisons might also be drawn with contemporary African-American humor, rap lyrics, the tales of the Southwestern humor tradition, and the fiction of Langston Hughes, whose Simple stories update the John tales, and Toni Morrison, whose *Song of Solomon* is based on the tale of the flying Africans. A comparison between Zora Neale Hurston's fiction and the folktales she published might illuminate her strategies in folktale editing as well as fiction.

Questions for Reading, Discussion, and Writing

Topics for discussion, in addition to those suggested above, include the following: The function of violence in the animal stories, John as loser and fool, the way retorts work, kinds of racial experience not reflected in the tales, narrative strategies of indirection, whether and in what contexts the stories could be considered subversive.

The repetition of plot elements in a number of short texts makes folktales good subjects for analytic papers. Students might also write their own folktales following a traditional pattern. The terms of a creative assignment, which might be worked out by the class in discussion, should be quite specific so that writing their own tale helps students see the structure, implications, and limitations of the traditional form. Such an assignment might be the following: Write a John tale in which John transgresses against slavery in some way not represented in the tales we've read (learns to read, dances with Old Marster's daughter), or the slave is not John but Johnetta, or the two protagonists are not slave and master but representatives of some other relationship of unequal power (student-teacher, worker-boss). In any case, establish at the beginning that the dominant character trusts and depends on the subordinate and conclude the tale with a retort that undermines the principle of the unequal power relationship that has been transgressed.

Samuel Langhorne Clemens (Mark Twain)
(1835–1910)

Contributing Editor: Susan K. Harris

Classroom Issues and Strategies

Mark Twain's works can be approached from a number of directions, depending on the pedagogical situation and the preferences of the instructor. Major areas tend to be his use of the English language, including his mastery of various American dialects; his status as a regionalist writer, especially as regards the Mississippi Valley region and the Nevada/California gold-mining regions; and his interventions into the racial debates of the late nineteenth and early twentieth centuries. *The Heath Anthology* selections, especially "Buck Fanshawe's Funeral," "A True Story," "The Celebrated Jumping Frog of Calavaras County," and the excerpt from Twain's *Autobiography*, have been chosen to help illustrate these areas. Additionally, as the "Questions for Reading, Discussion, and Writing" suggest, Twain was always deeply concerned about the human capacity for moral action, both on personal and communal levels (as in "Hadleyburg") and on national ones (as in "The War Prayer" and "As Regards Patriotism"). Depending on the selections chosen, a useful classroom strategy might be to ask students to think through the writing in light of contemporary events, including the lingering trauma of the Civil War and the postwar explosion of capitalist expansion (remembering that Twain and Charles Dudley Warner provided the name for the period that came to be called the "Gilded Age").

Significant Form, Style, or Artistic Conventions

Like Walt Whitman, Twain works the poetic elements of the English language. Repetition, both of phrases and of syntax, is one of his stylistic highlights. A useful "close reading" exercise could be created from examining sections of the extract from the *Autobiography* or from "A True Story" to see how Twain manipulates the language for poetic or emotional effect.

Dialect, including variants of standard middle-class white dialect, is another area in which Twain excels. "Buck Fanshawe's Funeral" and "A True Story" both show how Twain delighted in projecting particular points of view through regional dialect. Social class is an issue as well here; students may enjoy trying to sort out ways that Americans classify each other in terms of race, class, and region.

The "framed story," in which a Standard-English-speaking narrator introduces characters and then sits back while they take over the story's narration, was a standard convention in nineteenth-century American storytelling, especially in the regionalist stories produced during the antebellum period. Twain used this convention in stories such as "Jumping Frog," "Buck Fanshawe's Funeral," and "A True Story." A discussion of the relationship between the framing narrator and the audience, on the one hand, and the framing narrator and the dialect characters, on the other, can help students understand some of the "literary politics" of establishing the legitimacy of dialect voices for a readership for whom Standard English was the only linguistic variant considered to carry authority.

Original Audience

In the early days—during the time when he wrote "The Celebrated Jumping Frog of Calavaras County"—Twain's audience was the readers of local newspapers in Nevada Territory and California. By the 1870s, he was established in the East and publishing in well-known venues such as the *Atlantic Monthly*. By the late 1880s, his audience was worldwide. One area of discussion might concern how his various readerships might have received his work. Remembering that in the early 1890s Twain went on a lecture tour around the English-speaking world (which included India and South Africa), this exercise might be extremely interesting in a classroom with a sizeable proportion of students who are recent immigrants. Who read Twain outside of U.S. boundaries, and how did they respond to his writings? How do contemporary readers outside U.S. borders respond to Twain?

Comparisons, Contrasts, Connections

Mark Twain is always cited as one of the artists responsible for creating a uniquely American form of the English language. Linguistically, he can be compared with writers such as Walt Whitman, whose experiments with words, syntax, rhythms, and voice are similar. His short stories are heavily dependent on forms created by earlier regionalist writers, including the dialect stories in the African-American tradition, so it is useful to examine his stories along with those by Augustus Longstreet, George Washington Harris, and Charles Chesnutt as well as African-American folktales. Both for comparisons and contrasts, the spectrum of late-nineteenth-century depictions of American characters can be seen by comparing and contrasting the regionalists who were being published in the *Atlantic Monthly* in the late nineteenth century: Twain, Mary E. Wilkins Freeman, Bret Harte, George Washington Cable, Paul Lawrence Dunbar, and others. And for contrasts, it's always interesting to contemplate the fact that William Dean Howells was close friends with both Mark Twain and Henry James.

On a different note, in the early twentieth century Twain, Howells, and William James were all members of the Anti-Imperialist League. Teachers interested in working with world events might want to create a unit in which issues of national concern (questions of the color line, for instance) are considered in tandem with international issues (the Spanish-American War, the Boer War, the Boxer Rebellion). Twain wrote occasional pieces on all these events, one sign that this writer, like several of his friends, was ready to begin assessing America's standing in a global context.

Working with Cultural Objects

Mark Twain House and Museum, Hartford, CT: <http://www.marktwainhouse.org>

Mark Twain Boyhood Home and Museum: <http://www.marktwainmuseum.org>

Elmira Center for Mark Twain Studies: <http://www.elmira.edu/academics/ar_marktwain.shtml>

Mark Twain (website for PBS film by Ken Burns): <http://www.pbs.org/marktwain>

Questions for Reading, Discussion, and Writing

1. In 1865, Clemens wrote to his brother Orion that although he had once hoped to be a "preacher of the gospel," he had "renounced" that ambition in favor of another "call"—"to literature, of a low order—i.e.[,] humorous. It is nothing to be proud of, but it is my strongest suit, and if I were to listen to that maxim of stern *duty* which says that to do right you *must* multiply the one or the two or the three talents which the Almighty entrusts to your keeping, I would long ago have ceased to meddle with things for which I was by nature unfitted and turned my attention to seriously scribbling to excite the *laughter* of God's creatures."[1] Despite his renunciation, most readers have detected a moral impulse running through much of Twain's work, a way of using humor to mask a stringent critique of human nature. What are some of the themes on which Mark Twain preaches? What contemporary issues trigger his need to instruct his contemporaries?
2. How does Twain experiment with voice and point of view? For instance, in "Buck Fanshawe's Funeral," he juxtaposes the voices—manifested both as dialect and as worldview—of a young seminary student from the East and a Western rough. How does he build humor from a situation in which the two parties are trying to arrange a funeral?
3. "The War Prayer" and "As Regards Patriotism" were both written in response to the Spanish-American War, the United States' first imperialist venture. What was Twain trying to accomplish with these pieces? In your opinion, are these two works only relevant to the events that provoked them, or are they still relevant today?

Bibliography

Camfield, Gregg. *The Oxford Companion to Mark Twain.* New York: Oxford UP, 2003.

Fishkin, Shelley F. ed. *A Historical Guide to Mark Twain.* New York: Oxford UP, 2002.

---

[1] Mark Twain, *Mark Twain's Notebooks and Journals,* ed. Frederick Anderson, Michael B. Frank, and Kenneth Sanderson, vol. 1, (1855–1873) 92, Twain's emphasis.

Kaplan, Fred. *The Singular Mark Twain: A Biography.* New York: Doubleday, 2003.

LeMaster, J. R., and James D. Wilson, eds. *The Mark Twain Encyclopedia.* New York: Garland, 1993.

Zwick, Jim, ed. *Mark Twain's Weapons of Satire: Anti-Imperialist Writings on the Philippine-American War.* Syracuse: Syracuse UP, 1992.

Additional Web Resources:

The Mark Twain Papers and Project (the major collection of Mark Twain books and manuscripts in the world): <http://www.bancroft.berkeley.edu/MTP>

TwainWeb (Web service of the Mark Twain Forum: <http://www.yorku.ca/twainweb>.

Mark Twain (informational faculty page on Mark Twain): <http://www.guweb2.gonzaga.edu/faculty/campbell/enl311/twain.htm>

Mark Twain Circle of America (provides links to archives and related Mark Twain topics): <http://www.citadel.edu/faculty/leonard/mtcircular.htm>

Multimedia Resources:

Adventures of Huckleberry Finn. CD-ROM Electronic Book. Contains texts, critical articles, timelines, and guides to historical contexts. Available from Buffalo and Erie County Public Library, 1 Lafayette Square, Buffalo, NY 14203 Phone: 716-858-8900.

"Interview with Hal Holbrook" (informative interview with the reigning Mark Twain impersonator). *NOW with Bill Moyers.* PBS. 19 March, 2004. PBS Home Video.

Joel Chandler Harris (1848–1908)

Contributing Editor: George Friedman

Classroom Issues and Strategies

Get ready to meet some resistance to Harris, particularly to the Tar-Baby story, because the dialect is initially so daunting. It might be useful to tell students (particularly those from north of the Potomac River) that the dialect becomes easier to read as the story progresses; if you have the time at the end of the class preceding the Harris assignment, you might want to go over some of the more common words such as "sezee," "kaze," "gwine." I have on occasion been asked (by students who never saw "Song of the South") just what a Tar-Baby looked like; I use the analogy of a snowman.

As for "Free Joe," I find it useful to ask students to look for signs that this story was the creation of a *white* man. Your most perceptive students will have no trouble zeroing in on such lines as "The slaves laughed loudly day to day, but Free Joe rarely laughed. The slaves sang at their work and danced at their frolics, but no one ever heard Free Joe sing or saw him dance." Students should also notice and question Harris's assertion that no slave could possibly envy Joe's freedom.

In many instances, discussion of these lines generates a lively debate over the nature of slavery and harshness of life on an antebellum plantation. That slaves sang in the course of their daily labor is not to be denied, but it is useful to point out the lyrics of these songs, particularly the more religious ones, with their strong emphasis on the book of Exodus and eventual emancipation.

Students should also be encouraged to debate Harris's principal message in "Free Joe," and in particular the overall impression he wants to convey of Joe himself. Is it fair to dismiss Joe as an "Uncle Tom," passively taking whatever meanness that Spite Calderwood doles out? Students who characterize him as such will be challenged by others, who will point out that in the world of central Georgia in the middle of the nineteenth century, there wasn't much Joe could do to resist Calderwood. Nonetheless, other students will say that he doesn't seem to need to suppress rage because he doesn't seem to feel any rage to begin with. A related question then arises: Is Harris's principal point in this story that no one should have such boundless power over the life of someone else, or is he saying that an African American is unable to function without a white guardian? Let your class discuss this at some length, but don't expect a consensus.

Major Themes, Historical Perspectives, Personal Issues

As the preceding section suggests, "Free Joe" opens up a host of questions about the nature of slavery in the antebellum South and the extent to which a "Free Negro" was really free. You might want to tell your students that historical accounts of Southern slavery have varied drastically in their characterizations of it, with some historians likening plantations to "vocational training schools" and others declaring Southern slavery the cruelest in western history, principally because it did not face organized opposition from the church, and masters were rarely encouraged, by the clergy or anyone else, to emancipate their slaves or even to think of them as human beings.

It is useful to point out that Harris's treatment of slavery is much closer to the first of these two characterizations, and to put both "Free Joe" and the Tar-Baby story in the context of an age that sentimentalized the antebellum South—to point out that in story after story in the closing decades of the nineteenth century, the antebellum South was depicted as a land where races lived in harmony and both master and mistress considered their slaves part of the family, as did the slaves themselves. Point out that this idealized version of the antebellum South survived well into this century and reached its apogee in *Gone with the Wind.*

Original Audience

Harris's original audience, particularly for the Uncle Remus stories, was heavily Northern. The stories originally appeared in his Atlanta *Constitution,* but they were quickly syndicated, and appeared in many Northern newspapers. He also put out an *Uncle Remus Magazine* at the turn of the century, and it had a brisk sale nationwide. Letters to Harris, reprinted by his daughter Julia, suggest that some of his most admiring readers considered themselves sincere champions of the rights of African Americans.

It is very important to stress that at the turn of the century there were a great many writers and politicians eager to roll back the Thirteenth, Fourteenth, and Fifteenth Amendments, and that these people railed against African Americans in extremely shrill and vicious terms, to very wide and very gullible audiences. It might be useful to quote from Thomas Dixon's *The Leopard's Spots,* which sold over a million copies in 1902, or read from Senator "Pitchfork Ben" Tillman's (a Democrat from South Carolina) famous speech on the floor of the Senate in defense of lynching. Harris's condescension toward African Americans might look a bit less defamatory when placed alongside such savage and widely accepted views of the race.

Comparisons, Contrasts, Connections

In addition to the comparisons and contrasts cited above, Charles W. Chesnutt's Uncle Julius stories offer the most logical point of contrast—to both the Uncle Remus stories and "Free Joe." It is useful to point out that Uncle Remus's only apparent motive in telling his stories is to entertain a little white boy whereas Chesnutt's Uncle Julius is a far craftier character; he always has an underlying motive rooted in his own self-interest. Regardless of the Chesnutt story you use, it will depict the institution of slavery itself in terms far more bleak than what is found in Harris's stories—no one sings in Chesnutt's stories and no one frolics, either.

Other African-American writers of the age suggest themselves: certainly Dunbar's poem "We Wear the Mask" could be cited since the mask Dunbar describes in this poem appears to have fooled Harris himself. Booker T. Washington's own memories of slavery would form a useful comparison, as would the more critical observations of W. E. B. Du Bois, in "The Sorrow Songs."

Questions for Reading, Discussion, and Writing

I've already suggested the most fruitful questions: For the Tar-Baby story, you might ask why these stories would have held so much appeal for the slaves themselves. See if your students can discern for themselves the connections between the weak but wily rabbit and the slave, and between the strong but oafish fox or bear and the master.

For "Free Joe," ask them to look for signs that the work was written by a white man and see how many pick up on Harris's emphasis on the slaves' singing and dancing and his certainty that no slave would ever envy Joe's freedom.

One final point for discussion in "Free Joe" would be Harris's attitude toward poor whites, as represented by the Staleys. For one whose origins were themselves so humble, Harris seemed to have very little sympathy for poor whites; the Staleys are insensitive and superstitious. They nevertheless open the only doors in the story for Joe; does Harris want us to think of them in a positive light?

Bibliography

For "Free Joe," try R. Bruce Bickley, *Joel Chandler Harris* (1987), pp. 113–16, and Catherine Starke, *Black Portraiture in American Fiction* (1971), pp. 53–54.

Just about everything written about the Tar-Baby Story concentrates on Harris's use of dialect. The best of such studies is probably Lee Pederson's "Language in the Uncle Remus Tales," *Modern Philology* 82 (1985): 292–98.

A useful source for Harris is the *Atlantic Historical Journal* 30 (1986–1987): iii–iv. The entire issue is devoted to articles on the man and his work.

Charles Waddell Chesnutt (1858–1932)

Contributing Editor: William L. Andrews

Classroom Issues and Strategies

Classroom issues include: How critical or satirical of blacks is Chesnutt in his portrayal of them? Does he treat them with sympathy, even when they behave foolishly? Is Chesnutt's satire biting and distant or self-involving and tolerant?

There's rarely one source of authority in a Chesnutt story. Different points of view compete for authority. Get the students to identify the different points of view and play them against each other.

Stress that Chesnutt's conjure stories were written in such a way as not to identify their author as an African American. How effective is Chesnutt in this effort?

Students want to know what Chesnutt's social purposes were in writing his conjure stories. How could stories about slavery have any bearing on the situation of blacks and on race relations at the turn of the century—when Chesnutt wrote—and today?

Major Themes, Historical Perspectives, Personal Issues

Major themes include the following: Chesnutt's attitude toward the Old South; the myth of the plantation and the happy darkey; the mixed-blood person (monster or natural and even an evolutionary improvement?); and miscegenation as a natural process, not something to be shocked by.

Significant Form, Style, or Artistic Conventions

Chesnutt wrote during the era of literary realism. What is his relationship to realism, its standards, its themes, and its ideas about appropriateness of subject matter and tone?

Original Audience

I stress that Chesnutt wrote for genteel magazine readers much less critical and aware of their racism than we. How does he both appeal to and gently undermine that audience's assumptions?

Comparisons, Contrasts, Connections

Chesnutt wrote to counter the stories of Thomas Nelson Page and Joel Chandler Harris. Chesnutt might also be compared to Paul Laurence Dunbar and Frederick Douglass as depicters of blacks on the plantation before the Civil War.

Bibliography

Read the chapter on the dialect fiction in William L. Andrews, *The Literary Career of Charles W. Chesnutt* (Baton Rouge: Louisiana State UP, 1980).

Cluster: Literacy, Literature, and Democracy in Postbellum America

Contributing Editor: Sandra Zagarell

Classroom Issues and Strategies

This cluster suggests paths for thinking about the roles writing and reading in English, as well as culture in general, played in the postbellum nation. Instructors might find the questions raised and themes identified useful in teaching American literature in other periods as well. Literacy, kinds of literacy, and relationships between forms of literacy and cultural-political belonging are ongoing issues in American literature and are important as well in American history. Similarly, dialogue and debate over what "literature," or writing, is and should be and over the relationship between writing/literature and the nation's acknowledged populace, its social structures, its political institutions, its policies, and its future occur throughout American history.

The overview essay refers to numerous selections that can be taught in conjunction with selections in the cluster. Related foci and other selections also suggest themselves. The African-American folktales, Cable's "'Tite Poulette," Oskison's "The Problem of Old Harjo," the *Corridos*, the selection from Maria

Ruiz de Burton's *The Squatter and the Don*, and the two selections by Sui Sin Far lend themselves to expanded discussion of literacy. The folktales and *corridos* give a sense of some of the intricate oral cultures that continued to flourish in postbellum America; in different ways, they also reflect on the difficulties of translating oral expression into print. These selections further exemplify the existence of diverse cultures and languages within the country; the last six also shed light on relations between those for whom languages and cultures other than English were native and the nation, which American English represented. Discussion of these how these languages and cultures, along with vernaculars celebrated as American, contributed to American literature in English could also be augmented by reading such selections as Chesnutt's "Goophered Grapevine," poems by Paul Laurence Dunbar, Twain's "Jim Smiley and His Jumping Frog," Posey's "Fus Fixico's Letter Number 44," and the selection from Cahan's *Yekel*.

For those who want to consider the different forms realism took, the commentary in the overview essay and the writing within the cluster could frame discussion of virtually any of the fiction in Volume C. Consideration of realism/realisms might well take up the implications of debates over realism, over what was "real" and "realistic," and over what qualified as acceptable "realistic" form, style, and appeal to readers.

Significant Form, Style, or Artistic Conventions

Another related topic, one that might serve as a unit in a course on the era or one on nineteenth-century American literature, is poetry. The dialect poetry so popular in the postbellum period can clearly be discussed in conjunction with the cluster's themes; so, too, could the "plain" poetry of Stephen Crane and the poems Alexander Lawrence Posey wrote for his newspaper. Poems included in the "Sheaf" by women poets might be considered in this context as well. The cluster's themes connect directly to some of those; others raise questions about such matters as women poets' access to print, the diverse voices in which they wrote, and their range of subject matter—all of which reflect, indirectly if not directly, on what a democratic culture might be expected to encompass.

The cluster may thus also be useful as an entrée to consideration of the many forms in which postbellum Americans wrote, including the essay as well as poetry, and of the expanding appetite for reviews, literary criticism, and cultural and political commentary. These interests might be connected to many of the circumstances that make this period so compelling. The presence of many traditions, cultures, and languages within the nation; the expansion of higher education; the emergence of professions; an intensifying sense of cosmopolitanism as privileged Americans traveled—and worked—abroad in increasing numbers; the commodification of culture: these are only a few of the era's earmarks with which literacy, literature, and democracy are interwoven.

Paul Laurence Dunbar (1872–1906)

Contributing Editor: Kenny J. Williams

Classroom Issues and Strategies

Although Paul Laurence Dunbar also produced novels, short stories, and a large number of poems written in conventional English, he is best known for his adoption in verse of what was presented as the language (or "dialect") of the black Southern folk. Indeed, he has been viewed by some commentators as an artist who used negative stereotypes of his own people to satisfy a white audience, and there are still those who suggest that his work lacks substance.

In his lifetime, however, Dunbar was generally considered to be a symbol of African-American literary artistry and an apt representative of his race. Yet close reading of his poetry reveals him to be far more than an unimaginative purveyor of antiblack images. Moreover, few modern readers are aware of the essays on American race relations and other contemporaneous issues that Dunbar published at the height of his popularity. It is perhaps no wonder that from shortly after his death through the mid-twentieth century, his name was associated with numerous respected institutions in the African-American community. Practically gone now are the various Paul Laurence Dunbar Literary Societies that flourished throughout the country, but the schools and housing projects bearing his name still exist in many cities.

In order for students to appreciate the enduring literary achievement represented by Dunbar's best work, they should be given some sense of the daunting obstacles arrayed against black authors at that time and, accordingly, of the complex constraints placed upon them by white editors and readers alike. To put it another way, students should be encouraged to consider not just *what* Dunbar wrote but *why* he wrote as he did.

Significant Form, Style, or Artistic Conventions

One cannot overemphasize the fact that Dunbar lived during a period when the access allowed blacks to major white publications was extremely limited. Although there were a number of important African-American periodicals in existence as well, for the ambitious black author eager to make his or her mark on the mainstream literary landscape, publication in magazines such as *Century* and the *Atlantic Monthly* constituted the height of success. All too often, however, editors of these and similar periodicals expected African-American writers dealing with black material to follow the conventions of what has been termed the Plantation Tradition, which dominated the literary representation of black life and culture in the late nineteenth century. When coupled with the popularity of dialect verse of all kinds at the time, these conventions (perhaps best embodied in the fiction of Joel Chandler Harris and Thomas Nelson Page) exerted tremendous pressure upon aspiring African-American authors. As a result, one should urge students not to search Dunbar's work for outright protest and direct rejection of the dominant racial stereotypes of the day but rather to attend to the subtle use of irony and the often veiled allusions to the dilemmas of race that mark much of his writing.

It is also important to recall that Dunbar wrote at a time when American poetry was in a state of transition. Authors such as Henry Wadsworth Longfellow and James Whitcomb Riley were seen as "true" poets, and such sentimental pieces as Eugene Field's "Little Boy Blue" and Will Carleton's "Over the Hills to the Poorhouse" were celebrated as the epitome of poetic genius. Although Emily Dickinson had died in 1886, her work was virtually unknown until the 1930s, and scant serious attention was paid to Ralph Waldo Emerson's poetic theory or Walt Whitman's free verse innovations. The invigorating literary experiments of the modernist period were still several years off.

The state of American poetry at the turn of the century explains, to some extent, the diverse, occasionally conflicting formal strains in Dunbar's work. If, on the one hand, his dialect poems reflect his adoption of stylistic strategies of both James Whitcomb Riley and also the Plantation Tradition writers, on the other hand, he modeled his conventional English poetry after the popular sentimental magazine verse of his day. Ultimately, neither approach was conducive to a realistic rendering of either the psychology or the vernacular expressions of African Americans. (One should also keep in mind that Dunbar was born and raised in the post–Civil War North and thus had little firsthand knowledge of Southern life generally and none of slavery.)

Original Audience

Dunbar was read widely in both the black and the white communities, with the extraordinary sales of his books making him one of the most successful American writers of his time, regardless of race. Some attention should be given in the classroom to the possible consequences for Dunbar's art of this dual audience, especially given that most white readers were not just unaware of the complexities of African-American life and culture but possessed of attitudes toward blacks shaped primarily by the racist images disseminated in the popular press, on the minstrel stage, and by post-Reconstruction Southern politicians.

Comparisons, Contrasts, Connections

Despite the creative and personal tensions that plagued his tragically brief career, Dunbar was, without question, the single most influential African-American poet before Langston Hughes, even if many of the writers of the generation that followed his rejected aspects of his work. Extremely useful comparisons can and should be drawn between Dunbar's poetry and that of the New Negro Renaissance.

Questions for Reading, Discussion, and Writing

For "Mr. Cornelius Johnson, Office-Seeker":

1. What did the Reconstruction Amendments to the U.S. Constitution (1865–1870) accomplish? What did they fail to do?
2. Johnson is both a believing fool and a sad figure of a man who is not only a victim but also a victimizer. His hope for a political future in payment for his support, and his lack of understanding of the political process are told with an admirable economy of language—as in the ironic use of "Mr." in the title. Given the method of character presentation, do you—as the reader—sympathize with Cornelius Johnson? Do you find any weaknesses in him that might tend to explain his predicament?

For Dunbar's poetry:

1. By "scanning" Dunbar's poetry, does a reader learn anything about Dunbar's poetic technique?
2. Analyze Dunbar's representation of black Southern life in "When Malindy Sings" and "An Ante-Bellum Sermon." In particular, consider the tactics he utilizes in attempting to undermine the stereotypes that his characterizations appear on the surface to endorse. How successful are these tactics? Examine the role of religion and the use of irony in both poems.
3. From your knowledge of Frederick Douglass, does Dunbar's poem entitled "Frederick Douglass" transmit important information about the nineteenth-century leader? The poem, demonstrating none of the technical innovation of which Dunbar was capable, might seem so pedestrian today that readers will overlook the force of its emotion.
4. The complexity of "We Wear the Mask" is perhaps obscured by the simplicity of the poem's language. Central to an understanding of the work are the opening lines: "We wear the mask that grins and lies,/It hides our cheeks and shades our eyes." The fact that the "mask" is lying

rather than the wearer of the mask suggests something of the irony of the poem. If one assigns an active role to the mask, a reader can legitimately ask: Is the mask lying to the wearer, or is it lying to the observer? Composed of three variant-length stanzas with an unusual consistency of rhyme, this early poem illustrates Dunbar's ability to operate within the constraints of linguistic control. In "Sympathy," he demonstrates emotional control. The repetition of "I know why the caged bird sings" may have been directly related to his own daily experience in an elevator cage; however, the poem transcends the personal and rises toward the universality of enduring literature.

Bibliography

Gayle, Addison, Jr. *Oak and Ivy: A Biography of Paul Laurence Dunbar.* Garden City: Anchor-Doubleday, 1971.

Martin, Jay, ed. *A Singer in the Dawn: Reinterpretations of Paul Laurence Dunbar.* New York: Dodd, 1975.

Revell, Peter. *Paul Laurence Dunbar.* Boston: Twayne, 1979.

Williams, Kenny. *They Also Spoke.* Nashville: Townsend, 1970.

George Washington Cable (1844–1925)

Contributing Editor: James Robert Payne

Classroom Issues and Strategies

Students need to have some knowledge of southern American history as distinct from the historical emphasis on the Northeast that generally prevails in American history and literature courses. They should have a sense of the historical pluralism of Southern American society, understanding that it includes American Indians, blacks, Hispanic Americans, and exploited poor whites as well as the conservative white elite, which tends to be the object of most attention. Cable's perception of multicultural southern America is central to his fiction.

Students need to be reminded that not all southerners supported slavery before the Civil War nor did all support segregation after the Civil War. For example, George Washington Cable, a middle-class white native of Louisiana, actively supported civil rights through his writings and through ordinary political work.

To break up tendencies to stereotype the South, students may be reminded that many Southern cities voted against secession from the Union before the Civil War, and the voting was by white males only. Cable's fiction is expressive of pluralism in Southern life and values.

With specific reference to "'Tite Poulette": Discuss Cable's portrayal of the limits that confront Creole women as well as the possibilities for those women to achieve some kind of autonomy. For Zalli and 'Tite Poulette, the double standard of sexual morality is further complicated by their racial identity while their class status as free people of color limits their professional opportunities. Consider how Cable's evocation of New Orleans history as one of repeated conquest and rebellion lends additional significance to his narrative of "two poor children."

Major Themes, Historical Perspectives, Personal Issues

1. A central theme of Cable's fiction is the impact of the complex history of the American South on modern Southern life. In his sense of the profound influence of history on the present, Cable anticipates the later master southern fictionist, William Faulkner.

2. An issue that might be regarded as more personal concerns Cable's relation to New Orleans Creoles (in New Orleans, people of French or Spanish ancestry who preserved elements of their European culture). Creoles felt that their fellow New Orleanian betrayed them by what they saw as Cable's excessively biting satire and critique of the Creole community in his fiction.

Significant Form, Style, or Artistic Conventions

Cable needs to be taught as a Southern American realist author (at least insofar as his early, most vital fiction is concerned) who combines tendencies of critical realism (in his critique of Southern social injustice and hypocrisy) and local color realism (in his evocation of old New Orleans and plantation Louisiana in all their exoticism).

Yet unlike the work of his fellow realists of the North, such as William Dean Howells and Henry James, Cable's greatest works, *Old Creole Days*, *The Grandissimes*, and *Madame Delphine*, are historical "period" fictions.

Original Audience

In Cable's day, many Southerners objected to what they saw as his unjust and disloyal criticism of Southern social injustice. More specifically, some of Cable's New Orleans Creole readers expressed offense at what they regarded as Cable's sharp satire (amounting to caricature, as they saw it) on the Creole community. Cable found his readership by publishing his fiction in *Scribner's Monthly*. It was a readership much like that of his fellow authors William Dean Howells and Henry James, essentially middle class, "genteel," and mostly outside the South. Cable's audience today admires his work as giving the best depiction of old New Orleans and of Louisiana as well.

Comparisons, Contrasts, Connections

1. *Mark Twain*—The greatest of all southern writers of Cable's day, Mark Twain, is comparable to Cable in certain important ways. Both were essentially liberal Southerners whose writings effectively criticized problems in Southern life. Both Mark Twain and Cable also convey their love and understanding of their region through their endeavors to convey its varied dialects, complex social relationships, and dramatic history.
2. *Kate Chopin*—Cable shares with his fellow Louisiana writer Kate Chopin a strong interest in the Louisiana French-American community and the tensions between the French and Anglo communities, as well as a concern for the situation of women in the South of their day.

Questions for Reading, Discussion, and Writing

1. (a) Consider how the critical realist Cable undercuts romantic myths of the "noble aristocracy" of the "Old South."
2. (a) In an essay, discuss the significance of Cable's method of representing American language in relation to his themes. Hint: Remember that American language does not always mean English. Consider his representation of communication in French and, depending on which of Cable's works are being studied, other languages.
    (b) Consider residual romantic tendencies in the fiction of the Southern realist George Washington Cable.
    (c) In an essay, discuss and demonstrate—with specific references to passages of Cable's fiction—how Cable undercuts ethnic stereotyping in his work.
3. (a) In an essay, examine the many ways in which Cable implies throughout "'Tite Poulette" that women are treated as a form of property to be owned or exchanged. With reference to specific exam-

ples, discuss this issue in light of Cable's general focus on different kinds of possession and trade.

(b) Kristian Koppig's delirious cry that 'Tite Poulette is "jet white" exemplifies the illogic of legal and social codes governing interactions between members of different racial groups. Using the characters from the story as examples, consider how institutions such as the legal system, the church, or capitalism impact the construction of individual identity. What are the risks of violating such authority?

4. (a) The geographical setting of this story is bounded by the swamp. Consider the ways that the image of the swamp works within the contexts of American westward expansion and the mythology of Southern culture.

Bibliography

Butcher, Philip. *George W. Cable.* New York: Twayne, 1962. Short, highly readable, solid book-length study of Cable and his work.

Clark, William Bedford. "Cable and the Theme of Miscegenation in *Old Creole Days* and *The Grandissimes.*" *Mississippi Quarterly* 30 (Fall 1977): 597–609.

Eaton, Richard Bozman. "George W. Cable and the Historical Romance." *Southern Literary Journal* 8 (Fall 1975): 84–94.

Hubbell, Jay B. *The South in American Literature: 1607–1900.* Durham: Duke UP, 1954. Section on Cable.

Payne, James R. "George Washington Cable's 'My Politics': Context and Revision of a Southern Memoir." *Multicultural Autobiography: American Lives.* Ed. James Robert Payne. Knoxville: U of Tennessee P, 1992. 94–113.

Petry, Alice H. *A Genius in His Way: The Art of Cable's Old Creole Days.* Rutherford, NJ: Fairleigh Dickinson UP, 1988. Short, readable, stimulating new study of Cable's best short fiction.

———. "Universal and Particular: The Local-Color Phenomenon Reconsidered." *American Literary Realism: 1870–1910* 12 (Spring 1979): 111–26.

Pugh, Griffith T. "George Washington Cable." *Mississippi Quarterly* 20 (Spring 1967): 69–76.

Turner, Arlin, ed. *Critical Essays on George W. Cable.* Boston: Hall, 1980.

————. *George W. Cable: A Biography.* Baton Rouge: Louisiana State UP, 1966. The best single source on Cable by far.

Grace King (1852–1932)

Contributing Editor: Anne Jones

Classroom Issues and Strategies

"The Little Convent Girl," a small jewel of a story, should be accessible and immediately interesting to most student audiences since it represents its issues so starkly and since those issues (for example, cultural repression and its internalization, the awakening of desire and identity, the loss and discovery of parents, and the impact of religion, racism, and gender) are concerns of many undergraduates. Happily, the story also provides the opportunity for some remarkable conjunctions of teaching strategies: its taut, understated, suggestive style invites careful close readings, its allusions and issues invite intertextual and contextual readings, and the political questions it raises, concerning the intersections of race and gender, invite readings through contemporary theory, such as Judith Butler's essay on Nella Larsen's *Passing* (in *Bodies That Matter* [New York: n.p., 1993]).

Students might be drawn into these discussions through the highlighting of key words, images, and phrases (see below, "Significant Form"), historical allusions (see below, "Major Themes"), or intertextual connections (see below, "Comparisons"). Or, for something a bit different, they might "enter" the story by focusing not on text but on the white space that intrudes into it immediately after the first utterance of the word *Colored!* What happens in the month between that utterance and the girl's death—in the white space? If students are invited to invent and compare their own narratives to fill in this absence, many of the story's central ambiguities may surface as well.

Major Themes, Historical Perspectives, Personal Issues

Grace King has frequently been seen as a woman of letters whose major projects, both literary and personal, had to do with defending the conservative South. It is certainly possible to read "The Little Convent Girl" in such a vein, as the story of the terrible consequences of miscegenation, for example: after all, her parents' cross-racial relationship ends in the girl's death. But the story's position on race is complicated by its connection with gender. Blackness—from the bodies of laborers to the curl of the girl's hair—represents a vitality and desire whose "management" becomes a repeated question in the story; the fact that the girl's vitality and desire are "managed" by a repressive churched femininity suggests an alliance between racial and sexual problematics frequently thought to be more characteristic of Northern than Southern discourses. Cincinnati was, of course, a major center for slaves seeking freedom. The story appeared in 1893, three years before Plessy *v.* Ferguson authorized segregation, and in the thick of the proliferation of Jim Crow laws and practices in the South. King even uses the phrase "Jim Crow"—but how? In what ways does the story comment on its historical context?

Significant Form, Style, or Artistic Conventions

This story seems to be looking toward modernism, with its understatement, its absences, its unobtrusive symbolism, and its economy of language. "Unpacking" passages can be a fruitful enterprise. The first paragraph, for example, suggests several continuing themes: the question of the significance of "good-bys," the connection between the girl's passivity and the bolted door, and the journey down river, away from the historical site of freedom for slaves. Other image patterns worth tracing with care include mouths and lips; sound and noise; needlework; pleasure and constraint (*ad libitum* literally means "at pleasure"); the doubled rivers and mothers; and, of course, whiteness and darkness.

The point of view from which the story is narrated is critical, for it never allows readers to "enter" the girl's thoughts and—since she doesn't speak— keeps her subjectivity opaque. How precisely can we describe the point of view? And how does the narration achieve its power?

Original Audience

"The Little Convent Girl" appeared in Grace King's collection *Balcony Stories* (New York: Century, 1893) and in *Century Magazine* XLVI (August 1893): 547– 51. In both forms it reached a wide national audience of men and women who were most likely white and middle class. *Balcony Stories* remained in print a remarkably long time; new editions were published in 1914 and 1925.

Comparisons, Contrasts, Connections

Robert Bush suggests comparing "The Little Convent Girl" as a "mixed blood" story with Sherwood Bonner's "A Volcanic Interlude" and George W. Cable's

"'Tite Poulette" and "Madame Delphine." One might add Kate Chopin's "Désirée's Baby" and Charles Chesnutt's "The Wife of His Youth" to that list, among others. Mark Twain's *Adventures of Huckleberry Finn* tells a very different story of a slow boat down the Mississippi and a problematic arrival, but one whose differences might help to highlight the conjunctions between race and gender that seem so crucial to King. Kate Chopin's sketch "Emancipation" plays on some of the same liberation keys; *The Awakening* introduces what King's story avoids, female desire expressed as explicit sexuality, but its thematics of mothering and its relation to female desire (Adele Ratignolle's "mothering" of Edna on the beach, for instance, and its effects on Edna's voice) are worthy of comparison. Frances E. W. Harper treats "passing" from the point of view of the woman who "knows" she is black, in *Iola Leroy*; and Anna Julia Cooper, in *A Voice from the South*, in a sense gives speech to the silent convent girl. The life of an octoroon woman in New Orleans is imagined by Quentin Compson and his roommate in *Absalom, Absalom!* by William Faulkner.

Alice Dunbar-Nelson (1875–1935)

Contributing Editor: Akasha (Gloria) Hull

Classroom Issues and Strategies

The state of African-American literature when "Sister Josepha" was published (1899–1900) was the transition period between post-slavery Reconstruction and the flowering of black literature in the nineteen-teens (1915 into the Harlem Renaissance)—before Booker T. Washington's *Up From Slavery* (1901) and W. E. B. Du Bois's *The Souls of Black Folk* (1903) had articulated the terms of a racial debate that highlighted the difference between old and new ways of conceptualizing and presenting (politically and artistically) black American culture. There was continuing richness of folk literature, but it still did not represent an extensive scribal tradition. Two black men-of-letters had achieved national recognition—Paul Laurence Dunbar for his dialect poetry (which, despite its original genius, still used familiar minstrel and plantation motifs) and Charles Chesnutt, author of *The Conjure Woman* and *The Wife of His Youth* (1899), stories that featured a tale-telling trickster figure and the "color line," respectively. Clearly, Dunbar-Nelson is helping to define a nascent modern tradition, and doing so in ways that avoided limitations and stereotypes but also skirted race.

One must remember, too, the context of nineteenth-century popular fiction with its penchant for narrative modes and devices we now eschew—romance, melodrama, moralizing, and so on. Of particular relevance is the flourishing of the local color tradition, in which women writers excelled. The South and Louisiana had its representatives, and Dunbar-Nelson wrote and was read in the light of George Washington Cable and Kate Chopin. In an early letter to her, Paul Laurence Dunbar said:

> Your determination to contest Cable for his laurels is a commendable one. Why shouldn't you tell those pretty Creole stories as well as he? You have the force, the fire and the artistic touch that is so delicate and yet so strong.
> Do you know that New Orleans—in fact all of Louisiana—seems to me to be a kind of romance land. . . . No wonder you have Grace King and Geo. W. Cable, no wonder you will have Alice R.[uth] M.[oore] [Dunbar-Nelson's pre-marriage name].

Major Themes, Historical Perspectives, Personal Issues

Race and racism within the United States is a contextual given. One of the specific results/manifestations that is relevant is *intra*-racial color prejudice, especially the prejudice against darker-skinned black people and the hierarchy of color. So is the phenomenon of "passing" (usually economically motivated). Dunbar-Nelson herself casually passed on occasion—to see a theatrical performance, to have a swim at a bathing spa, to travel comfortably.

The ambiguous racial status of the Louisiana Creoles is an even further refinement on the race-racism theme. Their admixture of French-Spanish-Indian-black-white blood, their often free status, their closed/distinct society/culture, and so on, set them apart. Readers did not (do not?) tend to see these Creole characters as black/African Americans, but as some kind of non-white exotics.

Significant Form, Style, or Artistic Conventions

Race and the African-American writer. There has always been feeling and discussion on the black writer's proper role/stance with regard to her/his racial roots and the use of this material. This has been complicated by the pseudo-argument of whether one wants to be a "black writer" or a "writer" (recall the shibboleth of being "universal").

Original Audience

Answering questions like this was also affected by questions of audience and readership since the authors had to write for predominantly white or mixed audiences. Furthermore, whites controlled the mass markets. Black newspapers and journals furnished independent outlets, but these were comparatively few and small. Clearly, Dunbar-Nelson was writing for a larger, mostly white readership. She had also learned from experience that this audience did not accept controversial treatments of blacks or black-white relations.

Comparisons, Contrasts, Connections

Dunbar-Nelson has usually been taught—if at all—as a very minor female poet of the Harlem Renaissance, partly because of that period's notoriety and also because only a few of her poems have been available. Literary historians knew/know of her "Creole stories," but they have not been easy to access. It radically alters our view of her to see that poetry was the least significant genre for her and short fiction the most important. After *Violets* and *St. Rocque,* she wrote two other collections that were never published (though a few individual stories were): *Women and Men,* more nature and original Creole and non-Creole materials, and *The Annals of 'Steenth Street,* tales of Irish tenement youth set in New York City. She also wrote various other types of stories until she died.

Bibliography

Possible further reading: Two other Dunbar-Nelson stories: "The Goodness of St. Rocque," which typifies, perhaps, her mode in these works; and "The Stones of the Village," an even more overt and tragic handling of race, passing, and the black Creole; plus "Brass Ankles Speaks," an autobiographical essay about growing up in New Orleans as a "light nigger," which Dunbar-Nelson wrote pseudonymously toward the end of her life.

Secondary criticism: The biographical-literary chapter devoted to Dunbar-Nelson in Gloria T. Hull, *Color, Sex, and Poetry: Three Women Writers of the Harlem Renaissance* (Bloomington: Indiana UP, 1987), and the Introduction to *The Works of Alice Dunbar-Nelson.*

Ghost Dance Songs

Please refer to the headnote in the text for complete information.

Alexander Lawrence Posey (Creek) (1873–1908)

Contributing Editor: Bethany Ridgway Schneider

Classroom Issues and Strategies

Present the "Ode" in the context of American poetry of the nineteenth century; it consciously follows in the tradition of Bryant and Longfellow and should be taught as such. The Hotgun poem and Fus Fixico letter will be more complicated for students, who may struggle with the dialect. Negotiate the question of dialect writing as you would with other dialect writers of the time: for example, Clemens, Harris, Chesnutt, Dunbar, and Chopin. Point out that Posey admired such writers but held them up to very high standards of accuracy, scorning writers of "Indian" dialects who relied on stereotype rather than the particularities of regional speech.

Students are interested in Posey's political involvement, particularly his efforts to form the Indian state of Sequoyah. They are fascinated by the "Americanization" of Indians like Posey—his classical education and early romantic lyrics—and the effects that "Americanization" has on Indian nationalisms (e.g., Posey's refusal to publish the Fus Fixico Letters outside of Indian Territory).

Major Themes, Historical Perspectives, Personal Issues

1. The seeming inconsistencies in Posey's notion of Indian potential, for example, the extent to which Posey and other Indian writers embraced the notion of the "vanishing Indian" and the extent to which they resisted it.
2. Indian humor—students are often surprised to find humor in pieces by Indian writers and are much more comfortable with uncomplicated "tragic" voices.
3. The tension between "traditional" ways and modern or "Americanized" ways, particularly surrounding the problem of materialism. The problem of a simultaneous nostalgia for a perceived "simple" traditional past and the perceived need to "progress" into modernity.

4. The role of the "editorial," and the way in which the Fus Fixico letter can be seen as political intervention.

Significant Form, Style, or Artistic Conventions

The same questions that apply to any lyrical poetry, dialect poetry, and dialect prose apply to Posey's writing in these genres. His dialect writings fit perfectly into the local color movement and should be seen in conversation with writers like Harte, Cable, Chopin, Garland, and Harris. The implication—that Indian Territory can be seen as a region just like the West or the South—is fascinating.

Original Audience

Posey published most of his poems and letters in Indian Territory publications, even explicitly refusing to publish some of his work in "white" magazines. Because of the U.S. policy of assimilation and explicit attempts to destroy Indian cultures, languages, and practices, Posey witnessed, across his lifetime, a radical decrease in Indian culture. His work attempts to document that passing and thus anticipates the work of Indian writers of the late twentieth century and early twenty-first, whose writing focuses largely on rediscovering lost cultural practices.

John Milton Oskison (Cherokee) (1874–1947)

Contributing Editor: Bethany Ridgway Schneider

Classroom Issues and Strategies

Students are interested in the broad question of Indian-white relations at this time, especially the efforts to make Indians conform to the expectations of white society, as opposed to the exclusion of blacks during the same period. Students are also very interested in the specific question of Cherokee-white relations, particularly Cherokee gender constructions, and the history of the Cherokee nation in Oklahoma, and they are intrigued by the problems of nationhood raised by the idea of "Indian Country" vis-à-vis the United States. The question of the role of religion in the battle over cultural sovereignty is also fascinating to students, who are often very willing to debate the relationship of religion to cultural survival and integrity.

Major Themes, Historical Perspective, Personal Issues

1. The battle over ideology, and the imposition of one ideology over another
2. Historical and cultural background resulting in different worldviews
3. Conflicting gender roles and differing expectations of womanhood
4. Religious zeal and the destruction of culture

Significant Form, Style, or Artistic Conventions

The story sits firmly within the short story form and should be treated as such. It draws from the local color and regionalist traditions of the late nineteenth and early twentieth centuries.

Original Audience

This piece was written for a broad audience of both white and Indian readers at the time that federal Indian policy was attempting to mainstream Indians and to consciously destroy cultural and religious difference—to "kill the Indian and save the man."

Comparisons, Contrasts, Connections

Oskison's story reads very well alongside the works of Posey ("Fus Fixico Letter") and Eastman ("The Great Mystery"). It also reads well alongside "Ghost Dance Songs," which records Western Indians' anti-assimilationist response and attempt to negotiate the imperatives of both traditional religion and Christianity. Chesnutt and other contemporary black writers provide a fascinating comparison. Following on the questions of religious conflict, Bonnin's "Why I Am a Pagan" makes a perfect pair with this story.

Corridos

Contributing Editor: Raymund Paredes

Major Themes, Historical Perspectives, Personal Issues

In this group of *corridos*, it's important to note that American cowboy culture derives largely from Mexican culture: the *corrido* "Kiansis I" lauds the superiority of Mexican cowboys over their Anglo counterparts. The point is that

Mexican Americans have resented the appropriation of their culture without due recognition. "Gregorio Cortez" and "Jacinto Treviño" are epic ballads that deal with Mexican/Mexican-American responses to "American" injustice and bigotry. They are also of great interest because they make no distinction between a Mexican citizen and resident like Treviño and a resident of the United States like Cortez. Both are simply "mexicanos" who fight for their community's rights and dignity.

Corridos not only treat epic historical issues like cultural conflict along the south Texas border but also focus on more intimate matters that reflect and preserve traditional family values. "El Hijo Desobediente," one of the best-known and best-loved of *corridos,* emphasizes the need for sons to respect their fathers. In this ballad, the son Felipe is agitated to the point of threatening his father, an action that seals his tragic fate.

A final point about *corridos* to be made here is that this musical tradition is still vigorous and still exists primarily in Spanish. "Recordando al Presidente" fondly recalls John F. Kennedy, whose Catholicism endeared him to "mexicanos" and other Latinos. The "Corrido de César Chávez," of still more recent origin, recounts the victory of Chávez and the United Farm Workers over grape growers as a result of a brilliantly executed boycott.

María Amparo Ruiz de Burton (1832–1895)

Contributing Editor: Jesse Alemán

Classroom Issues and Strategies

I often begin teaching Ruiz de Burton's work by offering a brief account of her life because it reflects the cultural contradictions that shape Mexican-American history and identity. Her marriage to Henry S. Burton and her East Coast experiences situate her within Anglo America. Her land troubles and eventual dispossession position her in Mexican-American history, and her two novels place her within and against American and Mexican-American literary traditions. Students often find her biography fascinating, and the collusion of race, class, gender, and nation in her life extends to an analysis of her work. *The Squatter and the Don* in particular invites students to consider the relationships among class status, racial identity, and the formation of stereotypes. I've found it effective to compare and contrast the representation of each character to unpack how Ruiz de Burton counters prevailing stereotypes of Mexicans, draws class distinctions between sympathetic and unsympathetic Yankees, and maintains a racial distinction between Californios and Indians. The reference to the Don's daughters by the younger generation of American settlers also introduces the notion of romance as a resolution to national conflict, an idea that can be connected to Ruiz de Burton's biography as well as the history of Anglo-Mexican marriages in nineteenth-century California. Students may see no difference between Anglo-American racism and Ruiz de Burton's sense of class privilege and whiteness, and they may be right, but it's also important to emphasize the way Ruiz de Burton uses race, class, and romance to position Mexican Americans within the United States's imaginary citizenry.

Major Themes, Historical Perspectives, Personal Issues

The selection provides an opportunity for students to research the 1846–48 Mexican War and the 1848 Treaty of Guadalupe Hidalgo. The war years marked the nadir of the United States's "Manifest Destiny," doubled the nation in size, and in effect created a Mexican-American population that became foreigners in their native land. Especially in California, the 1851 Land Law displaced Mexican landowners, and the rapid changes in California's economy (from agricultural to industrial) further pauperized the state's Mexican gentry. Ruiz de Burton's narrative is an alternative history of the Southwest, one that doesn't celebrate the settling of the West but critiques it as rampant Yankee squatterism. At the same time, the class should discuss the cultural contradictions of Ruiz de Burton's critique—that Californios were themselves a Mexican colonial elite that displaced California's Indian population and were quite willing to profit from Manifest Destiny, as the Don's plan demonstrates. Mexican-American historical background also contextualizes the novel's themes. The don's plan, for instance, reverses the usual "tradition versus progress" theme. Although he's a vestige of California's Old World, the Don proposes a progressive future for San Diego that the squatters reject. Legality is also a central theme in the selection as Ruiz de Burton critiques the supposed objectivity of laws and reveals a gap between the letter of the Land Law and the natural law of the land.

Significant Form, Style, or Artistic Conventions

The Squatter and the Don is essentially a historical romance that uses cross-cultural marriages to resolve the national conflict between Anglo and Mexican Americans, but the narrative is also novelistic as it incorporates multiple discourses: literary, historical, romantic, legal, and national (Spanish, English, and nonstandard English). The text thus hybridizes the traditional form of the historical romance with the modern style of the novel. It also combines romance with realism, resembles an American jeremiad that calls for the country to live up to its lost ideals, and predates the political critiques of the Muckraking movement.

Original Audience

It's most likely that Ruiz de Burton was writing to an Anglo-American audience, especially considering the novel's cultural critique, its counterconstruction of California whiteness, and its publication in English. Ruiz de Burton's "C. Loyal" pseudonym and the incorporation of Spanish in the text, however, suggest that Californios may be the novel's shadow audience. Indeed, the novel's narrator functions as the representative voice of the Californios, speaking for them rather than to them.

Comparisons, Contrasts, Connections

Students should read Ruiz de Burton alongside José Martí, a selection of *corridos*, and works by William Dean Howells, Frank Norris, Edith Maud Eaton (Sui-Sin Far), Mary Austin, and Gertrude Bonnin (Zitkala-Sa). Ruiz de Burton's critique of American colonialism echoes Martí's, but while Martí foregrounds *mestizaje*, Ruiz de Burton erases it. Her narrative also challenges the status often accorded to *corridos* as the representative literary form of Mexican Americans. If *corridos* represent a proto-Chicano, working-class identity that resists American assimilation, Ruiz de Burton's novels are high-brow modes of literary production that speak for an entirely different class of Mexican Americans. Students may see strains of Howell's realism and Norris's naturalism in Ruiz de Burton's style, and Eaton, Austin, and Bonnin offer contrasting views on the relationship between gender, national identity, and racial assimilation that is at the center of Ruiz de Burton's work.

The Squatter and the Don might also be used to encourage students to think about the complexity and contradictory space the term *Mexican American* embodies. While *corridos* precede the Ruiz de Burton entry in *The Heath Anthology*, Howells and James follow it, and Ruiz de Burton's place in-between is telling, for while *The Squatter and the Don* echoes the protest politics that characterize *corridos*, her romance narrative carries traces of historical realism (such as the dispossession of Mexican Americans), and her representation of American squatters prefigures James's dyspeptic Americans in Europe.

Working with Cultural Objects

The Treaty of Guadalupe Hidalgo website at the Library of Congress at <http://www.loc.gov/exhibits/ghtreaty> is a crucial site for any study of nineteenth-century American or Mexican-American literature. It offers the entire text of the treaty, including Article X, the so-called "citizenship" article that promised Mexican Americans equal rights but was later expunged from the

Treaty. The site also offers maps of the disputed treaty area and invites students to navigate further the online archives of the Library of Congress.

Another useful collection of online maps is available at the Society of California Pioneers website at <http://www.californiapioneers.org/Terr Amb1.html>. These maps offer several visions of nineteenth-century California that prove helpful for establishing the geography of *The Squatter and the Don,* especially in relation to the gold and railroad industries that figure heavily in the novel.

Finally, *The Journal of San Diego History* at <http://www.sandiego history.org/journal/84summer/burton.htm> contains a historical article on María Amparo Ruiz de Burton that is useful for its biographical information, its images of Ruiz de Burton's family (husband, daughter, and son), and its history of Rancho Jamul, the land grant that is most likely fictionalized in *The Squatter and the Don.*

Questions for Reading, Discussion, and Writing

1. What's wrong with the Land Law and No Fence policy, and how does Ruiz de Burton critique them? Is her critique relevant to contemporary laws?
2. Why is it important that Ruiz de Burton emphasizes the "whiteness" of the Californios? What kinds of historical and social "politics" are involved with such a claim?
3. How would you characterize the narrator of the selection? You might consider the narrator's tone and references to literature and law.

Bibliography

Aleman, Jesse. "Historical Amnesia and the Vanishing *Mestiza*: The Problem of Race in *The Squatter and the Don* and *Ramona.*" *Aztlan* 271 (2002): 41–59. A comparison of two nineteenth-century novels that considers their use of race in relation to Mexican and Native Americans.

Montes, Amelia Mana de la Luz, and Anne Elizabeth Goldman, eds. *María Amparo Ruiz de Burton: Critical and Pedagogical Perspectives.* Lincoln: U of Nebraska P, 2004. Collection of Essays, teaching resources, and bibliography on Ruiz de Burton's life and writings.

Sanchez, Rosaura, and Beatrice Pita, eds. *Conflicts of Interest: The Letters of María Ambaro Ruiz de Burton.* Houston: Arte Publico, 2001. Collection of Ruiz de Burton's letters and writings in English and Spanish, with editorial commentary and illustrations of the author and her family.

William Dean Howells (1837–1920)

Contributing Editor: Gary Scharnhorst

Classroom Issues and Strategies

The leading American novelist of the late nineteenth century (Mark Twain was considered too vulgar, and Henry James too foreign), Howells is largely unknown to students nowadays. His modern critical reputation too often centers on his (in)famous assertion in *Criticism and Fiction* (1891) that "the smiling aspects of life" are the "more truly American." In his Nobel Prize acceptance speech in Stockholm in 1930, for example, Sinclair Lewis excoriated Howells: he was "one of the gentlest, sweetest, and most honest of men, but he had the code of a pious old maid whose greatest delight was to have tea at the vicarage."

Yet Howells was scarcely the timid or prudish writer his modern reputation would suggest. In fact, he was a staunch defender of unpopular, progressive, even radical causes, and in the mid-1880s, under the influence of Tolstoy, he became a socialist. Howells's vehement protest of the "civic murder" of the Haymarket Square anarchists in 1887 epitomizes his willingness to risk his popular reputation for political and social principle; it also set a precedent for subsequent protests over the fates of such celebrated defendants as Sacco and Vanzetti and the Scottsboro boys. He was an outspoken critic of military imperialism, and he was a founding member of the NAACP. He also treated issues of sexuality without apology, as in "Editha." As James Tuttleton remarks, "Howells's contemporaries hardly thought him a spokesman for conservative gentility, and he was no stranger to controversy in his own time."

Still, Howells occupies at best an ambiguous position in the contemporary literary canon. His reputation has been in slow eclipse since early in this century. As he wrote Henry James in 1915, "I am comparatively a dead cult with my statues cast down and the grass growing over them in the pale moonlight." His critical stock has slowly risen over the past half-century, however. Several of his novels, including *A Hazard of New Fortunes*, *The Rise of Silas Lapham*, and *A Modern Instance*, are available in classroom editions; a definitive edition of his writings, including six volumes of his letters, has been issued; and the W. D. Howells Society sponsors sessions at the annual conventions of the American Literature Association. Howells's decanonization early in the twentieth century and his modest postwar revival may prompt a class discussion of the process of canon formation.

Major Themes, Historical Perspectives, Personal Issues

Like other realists such as Mark Twain, Stephen Crane, Theodore Dreiser, and Willa Cather, Howells began his professional career as a journalist. That is, he was by training a skilled observer of human behavior. His narrators, as in "Editha," portray characters with subtle nuances, often in an ironic voice. How complicit is Editha in the death of George Gearson, for example? How is she changed, if at all, by the experience?

I usually teach "Editha" in conjunction with Mark Twain's "The War Prayer." Both texts betray their authors' condemnation of imperialism and protest the mindless patriotism that celebrated the Spanish-American War.

Howells's radicalism is nowhere more apparent than in the letters—one published, the other unsent—he addressed to the editor of the *New York Tribune* to protest the pending executions of the Haymarket anarchists. I would emphasize the risks Howells incurred in his public protest—he was, after all, dependent upon public goodwill for his livelihood—and I would speculate on his apparent reticence to publish the second, longer, angrier letter.

Significant Form, Style, or Artistic Conventions

Howells was both the leading American theorist and practitioner of literary realism, a brand of fiction that insisted upon "a truthful treatment of materials." Realism was fundamentally democratic insofar as it presumed a broad and informed readership, and it was socially critical insofar as it indicted naive sentimentality, urban squalor, racism, oppressive marriage, or small-town parochialism. Though the strategy of realism seemed to valorize normal and commonplace events, and though it has been disparaged and dismissed by poststructural theorists, Howells obviously believed realism represented an evolutionary leap forward from literary romanticism: "It remained for realism to assert that fidelity to experience and probability of motive are essential conditions of a great imaginative literature," as he argued in 1891.

Ever respectful of his literary ancestors, however, Howells readily acknowledged Hawthorne's influence on his own work. As Robert Emmet Long explains, "Howells's assimilation of Hawthorne's romance into his realism coincided with James's assimilation of Hawthorne during the same period." Like Hawthorne's romances, Howells's fiction often questioned but rarely criticized conventional moral standards. Note the allusion to Hawthorne's *The Blithedale Romance* in the excerpt from *Suburban Sketches*.

The so-called Dean of American Letters toward the end of his long career, Howells was a prominent Gilded Age liberal intellectual. As James W. Tuttleton has noted, his "literary interests" were "catholic and wide-ranging" and his sympathies were "perceptive and generous." Not surprisingly, then, he also welcomed new voices in American literature. There was "a solidity, an honest observation, in the work" of such women writers as Rose Terry Cook, Mary E. Wilkins, and Sarah Orne Jewett, "which often leaves little to be desired," he wrote in *Criticism and Fiction* (1891). He hailed the work of such African-American writers as Charles Chesnutt and Paul Laurence Dunbar, though he was not entirely free of racial stereotyping.

Original Audience

As one of the characters in Howells's novel *A Hazard of New Fortunes* (1890) remarks, "women form three fourths of the reading public in this country." The United States was "a nation of women readers," as he later remarked. As astute judge of the literary market, Howells took care to pitch his fiction to women readers, or at the very least not to offend them. As John W. Crowley contends, despite Howells's "life-long ambivalence toward women," some of his fiction merits a place in the feminist canon.

Comparisons, Contrasts, Connections

As editor of the *Atlantic Monthly* from 1871 to 1881 and later as a prolific reviewer, Howells helped promote both the "local colorists" and regionalist on the one hand (e.g., Mark Twain, Mary Wilkins Freeman, Charles Chesnutt, Sarah Orne Jewett, Paul Laurence Dunbar), and the "psychological realists" on the other (e.g., Henry James and Charlotte Perkins Gilman). That is, he may be conveniently (and conventionally) situated between Mark Twain and James, an intermediary figure in the literary history of the period. His patronage of such black writers as Chesnutt and Paul Laurence Dunbar, however, was not entirely free of bias: while acknowledging his help, for example, Dunbar complained that he thought Howells had caused him "irrevocable harm" by urging him to specialize in dialect verse. Late in his career, Howells also promoted the writings of an emerging school of American literary naturalists, including Frank Norris, Theodore Dreiser, and Stephen Crane.

Bibliography

The best recent overviews of Howells criticism are John Crowley's "Howells in the Seventies" and "Howells in the Eighties" in *ESQ: A Journal of the American Renaissance* (1979, 1986–1987). Also, Chapel Petty-Schmidt has compiled a checklist of Howells scholarship, "Criticism of W. D. Howells: A Selected Checklist," *American Literary Realism* (1988). The research annual *American Literary Scholarship* also contains yearly updates of Howells criticism.

The standard biographies of Howells are Edwin H. Cady's *The Road to Realism* (1956) and *The Realist at War* (1958); and John W. Crowley's *The Black Heart's Truth: The Early Career of W. D. Howells* (1985) and *The Dean of American Letters: The Late Career of W. D. Howells* (1999).

Henry James (1843–1916)

Contributing Editor: Alfred Habegger

Classroom Issues and Strategies

In "The Art of Fiction," many of James's literary references will be unfamiliar to the students. In addition, the debate about the status and artistry of the novel that James enters will also be new terrain for the students. Provide them with the context of the debate by having them summarize the opening paragraphs of the essay. Ask them to locate James's central criticisms of Besant's theory of fiction. Then have them find James's own claims about the ideal aims and techniques of the novel.

In "Daisy Miller," students may well miss the important social nuances of the language used by the characters and the narrator. Most of us take for granted certain usages—"ever so many," "it seems as if," "I guess," "quaint"— that are indications of the Millers' lack of cultivation. Also, there are some genteelisms in their speech—Mrs. Miller's "the principal ones." Then there's the narrator's somewhat inflated diction—"imbibed," "much disposed towards."

Distribute ahead of time a short list of usages, divided according to categories and ask the students to add some usages from their own reading of "Daisy Miller."

Another problem that should be mentioned is point of view. Tell the students ahead of time that "Daisy" uses the technical device of restricting the reader's perspective to what one character sees and knows. Ask them to decide what character this is. Give examples; find exceptions in which the narrator speaks out.

"Daisy Miller": Some students inevitably despise Daisy for her occasional social crudity and inexperience. A good tactic to deal with this attitude is to emphasize such matters right at the start, trusting to other students to feel that they must speak up and defend Daisy's naturalness and boldness. I also recommend getting the obvious fact that the Millers represent vulgar new money out in the open from the start; otherwise, some rather slow readers will triumphantly announce this fact later on in order to simplify the heroine's character.

Students will appreciate some facts about Rome. The story takes place before the floor of the Colosseum was excavated and before the cause of malaria was discovered. The 1883 Baedeker guide reminded tourists of the traditional danger of malaria: "In summer when the fever-laden *aria cattive* [bad air] prevails, all the inhabitants who can afford it make a point of leaving the city." Some students will have no experience of Giovanelli's type— the public dandy and lounger.

Students consistently enjoy analyzing and judging (with great ferocity) the various characters. I am often surprised at the harsh judgments passed on Daisy's flirtatiousness and game playing.

Major Themes, Historical Perspectives, Personal Issues

In "Art," emphasize the importance of this essay within the context of James's significant body of criticism and American letter, more generally. This will help them grasp the prescient nature of this essay as well as the breadth of complexity of James's artistic endeavor.

In "Daisy Miller" students will probably need a detailed explanation of the Colosseum scene, where Winterbourne finally makes up his mind about Daisy, not only deciding that she isn't respectable but showing her by his behavior that he scorns her as beyond the pale. He learns the truth about her (and his own feelings for her) too late, of course.

Significant Form, Style, or Artistic Conventions

"The Art of Fiction" lays the foundation of James's realist approach. At the same time, the essay itself, in its leisurely pace, witty yet informal tone, and seemingly circuitous structure, serves as a good example of late-nineteenth-century essayist writing.

"Daisy Miller" may be presented as a classic instance of nineteenth-century realism in presenting "a study" of a modern character-type. Simultaneously, since the story follows Winterbourne's point of view, James's subject becomes a double one and also concerns the male character's process of vision and understanding. In this sense, the story is about Winterbourne's "studying."

Original Audience

For "Art," ask the students to deduce James's intended audience by examining his literary references as well as his generalizations about the novel's readership.

In "Daisy Miller" students will need help in grasping the leisure-class European social code: the importance of restraint, public decorum, the drawing of lines. When Daisy looks at Winterbourne and boasts of having had "a great deal of gentleman's society," she doesn't know (though Winterbourne and James do) that she is coming on precisely as a courtesan would.

Comparisons, Contrasts, Connections

When teaching "The Art of Fiction," have the students apply James's theories of realism and the importance of the writer's donnee to "Daisy" or "The Jolly Corner." Ask them to evaluate these works of fiction using his criteria.

Questions for Reading, Discussion, and Writing

1. Ask students to pay attention to those situations in "Daisy Miller" in which one character tries to gauge or classify another. They may notice that Winterbourne's social judgment is much shakier than at first appears. Not only does he misread Daisy (in the Colosseum), but he is also wrong in pronouncing Giovanelli "not a gentleman." Giovanelli turns out to be a respectable lawyer.
2. I like to ask students to compare and contrast the scene in the Colosseum in which Winterbourne decides Daisy is a reprobate and laughs in her face to the scene in *Huckleberry Finn* in which Huck decides to go to hell out of friendship with Jim. One character gives way to a rigid social exclusion; the other defies it.

Bibliography

The preface that James wrote for "Daisy Miller" in the New York edition is illuminating but must be used with care. The preface was written about thirty years after the story, and James's attitudes had changed somewhat. Now he was much more uneasy about the vulgarity of speech and manners of American women, and he decided he had been too easy on the Daisy Miller type. Hence he labeled this story "pure poetry"—a way of calling it romance rather than realism.

Two helpful and somewhat contrasting studies are Wayne Booth's discussion of "Daisy Miller" in *The Rhetoric of Fiction* and Louise K. Barnett, "Jamesian Feminism: Women in 'Daisy Miller,'" *Studies in Short Fiction* 16:4 (Fall 1979): 281–87.

It's difficult to know whether Daisy Miller is a historically accurate type. Upper-class single women did not apparently go out alone in the evening in New York of the 1870s, but they did not require a duenna when accompanied by a man.

Kate Chopin (1851–1904)

Contributing Editors: Kate McCullough and Peggy Skaggs

Classroom Issues and Strategies

Chopin's irony is too subtle for many students, who may see her female characters as cold, unloving, unfeeling women. Edna Pontellier, in particular, they often read as a selfish and "bad" mother as well. In other words, students today still hold many of the notions about women that inspired Chopin's best irony and satire. Placing Chopin's work in the context of late-nineteenth-century legal, economic, and social constraints on women can help students to understand better the conditions that Chopin was critiquing. Class discussions that focus on detailed close readings of the text can help illuminate how irony works to make that critique.

Since Chopin wrote everything she produced during the last decade of the nineteenth century but was not critically celebrated until the last quarter of the twentieth century, she offers a fine vehicle for exploring the intellectual and aesthetic tides of U.S. thinking and U.S. literature. In many ways she is emblematic of the nineteenth century, with her works' mixture of romanticism, realism, and naturalism. Yet in other ways her work augers the late-twentieth-century interest in feminism and existentialism. Thus she works well as a bridge between the two centuries and can also serve to introduce a conversation about the ways that literature raises different issues for different generations of readers and critics. Moreover, her works' mixture of radical and conservative representations of womanhood can help complicate students' assessments of not just her work but of literature in general. That is, an examination of the ways in which her radical sexual politics coexist with her conservative racial politics can help students understand both that literature reflects the complexities of its historical period and that literary texts are (for the most part) not easily reducible to a single theme or position.

Major Themes

Chopin's representation of regionally specific womanhood via heroines who are class, ethnically, and racially marked allows for both a discussion of the roles of women in her stories and a discussion of how these stories are participating in the broader post-Reconstruction U.S. discussion on American identity. Southern womanhood as a theme can lead both to a focus on Chopin's representation of the female erotic and maternal and to a discussion of the ways in which these representations participate in regionalism as a literary form.

Significant Form, Style, or Artistic Conventions

Since Chopin's work contains clear elements of romanticism, transcendentalism, realism, naturalism, existentialism, and feminism, her stories can help students understand these literary modes and the directions in which U.S. literature has developed during the last century and a half. Chopin's style offers opportunities to discuss the uses and effects of conciseness; strong, clear imagery; symbolism; understatement; humor; and irony.

One can also focus on Chopin as a writer of regional literature. A class might trace (in her stories in particular but also in *The Awakening*) the representation of a local community via the use of dialect, the attention to the specifics of place, and the emphasis on detail. This formal approach can work well to illustrate the connections in literature between form and content since a focus on the regional can be used to demonstrate that the regional setting makes possible Chopin's representations of a female erotic and maternal while her representations of a female erotic and maternal are vehicles for her articulation of regional identities.

Original Audience

I contextualize Chopin's work within the broader national uses of regional literature in the post-Reconstruction period as a tool of national reconciliation. I discuss the Northern control of the publishing industry, and the use of Southern literature specifically to depict the South as a "quaint," "backward," or even "exotic" region rather than a hostile or threatening one. I position Chopin as cannily drawing on these conventions while simultaneously undermining them by offering a complex representation of Southern women. I often read excerpts from contemporary reviews of Chopin's short story collections (available as primary sources but also helpfully covered in the Toth biography) to illustrate how critics positioned her as a chronicler of "quaint" and "primitive" "folk."

I also use reviews to contextualize *The Awakening*. Citing the vitriolic responses to Edna Pontellier helps make clear to students how radical Chopin's representation of female agency and desire was to her contemporaries.

Comparisons, Contrast, Connections

Chopin was widely read in French literature and particularly admired Maupassant's stories, translating a number of them into English. Many critics have noted his strong influence, especially apparent in the sharp, ironic conclusions Chopin produced in many stories ("The Story of an Hour" and "Désirée's Baby," for example). The influence of Hawthorne, Whitman, and Henry James has been noted as well.

This unit might be productively paired with readings of other Southern writers of the period—George Washington Cable, Grace King, or Alice Dunbar-Nelson, for instance—to raise the issue of literature's cultural work of reconciliation in the late nineteenth-century period. Alternately, Chopin works well as part of a unit on nineteenth-century women writers, a unit that might include varying forms and writers from Harriet Ann Jacobs to Louisa May Alcott to Rebecca Harding Davis to Maria Amparo Ruiz de Burton (to name just a few).

Working with Cultural Objects

Many students are unaware of the vast changes in U.S. women's position in the last century and a half. To give them some sense of the legal, economic, and social constraints on women as well as some sense of the ways in which women were positioned differentially according to both race and class, the class might be asked to read through the timeline of the legal history of women in the United States found at <http://www.legacy98.org/timeline.html>. The class might then compare the status of women in their own day and in Edna Pontellier's day and in Désirée's day.

To aid in a discussion of regionalism in *The Awakening*, the class might consult a history of French Creoles of Louisiana at <http://www.yale.edu/ynhti/curriculum/units/1992/2/92.02.02.x.html>. For general interest, see excerpts from interviews conducted for the PBS production *Kate Chopin: A Re-Awakening* at <http://www.pbs.org/katechopin/interviews.html>. This includes an interview with her grandson, David Chopin.

Questions for Reading, Discussion, and Writing

In class discussion we look at specific instances of irony in order to help students recognize it more easily.

1. Trace the literal and figurative manifestations of Edna Pontellier's understanding of herself and her predicament in patriarchal society. How do her extramarital romances and her artistic ambitions coincide or conflict?
2. Evaluate *The Awakening*'s ending. What is the symbolic significance of Edna's drowning in the sea? How does this ending function as a critique of aristocratic Creole society at the turn of the century?
3. Consider the role of class in Edna's positioning. I sometimes use Richard Brodhead's discussion of the rise of travel/leisure/vacation (in his *Cultures of Letters*) here as well as the notion that women by this period

were assigned the role of conspicuous consumption for the family, a role that demonstrated class privilege through leisure activity and spending.

4. Compare the treatment of Désirée and La Blanche in "Désirée's Baby." What might this comparison tell us about the way in which race recast the meaning of motherhood under slavery?

Bibliography

Approaches to Teaching Chopin's "The Awakening," ed. Bernard Koloski (New York: MLA, 1988), offers background, biographical information, discussion of critical studies, a bibliography, and aids for teaching both *The Awakening* and Chopin's stories.

Michele A. Birnbaum's "'Alien Hands': Kate Chopin and the Colonization of Race." *Subjects and Citizens: Nation, Race, and Gender from Oroonoko to Anita Hill*, ed. Michael Moon and Cathy Davidson (Durham: Duke UP, 1995), 319–41, provides an acute and illuminating reading of the role of race in *The Awakening*.

Anna Shannon Elfenbein's *Women on the Color Line: Evolving Stereotypes and the Writings of George Washington Cable, Grace King, and Kate Chopin* (Charlottesville: UP of Virginia, 1989) contains a nuanced reading of "Désirée's Baby."

My *Regions of Identity: The Construction of America in Women's Fiction 1885-1914* (Palo Alto: Stanford UP, 1999) locates Chopin's short fiction within the context of the politics of U.S. regionalism.

Peggy Skaggs' *Kate Chopin* (Boston: Twayne, 1985) offers helpful biographical material and readings of both *The Awakening* and Chopin's stories.

Helen Taylor's *Gender, Race and Region in the Writings of Grace King, Ruth McEnery Stuart and Kate Chopin* (Baton Rouge: Louisiana State UP, 1989), like Elfenbein's book, provides a useful comparative reading of Chopin's work.

Biographical information is readily available, but the definitive biography is Emily Toth's *Kate Chopin: The Life of the Author of "The Awakening"* (New York: Morrow, 1990), an invaluable resource in any teaching of Chopin.

Ambrose Bierce (1842–1914?)

Contributing Editor: Cathy N. Davidson

Classroom Issues and Strategies

Two primary issues present themselves in teaching "Chickamauga." First, the details are grotesque. The procession of bloody, dying men and the macabre humor of the small child mounting one as he would a pony (or his father's slaves "playing horsey") often disturbs students very much. This, of course, is exactly Bierce's intention. Second, the ending seems like a gratuitous trick. Is it necessary that the child be deaf and dumb? Realistically, this is necessary since the child does not hear the great battle—we are told so explicitly. But it's also important symbolically: the temptation to war is so great in male culture that even this small child learns it, even though there is so much he does not understand.

To address these issues, first I read some conventional war accounts and war stories—or even the lyrics to war songs. I then read aloud the most grotesque parts of Bierce. I next ask my students which is, in its consequence, the more violent. We then discuss protest literature and Bierce's disgust that the several prominent generals of the Civil War were rewriting the incomparably brutal history of that war. Second, we go through the story isolating how the child learns, what he knows and doesn't. The picture book lesson at the beginning makes the point that a child is already learning values at the earliest age, prelinguistically. These are *powerful* messages, calls to violence.

Try reading some definitions from the *Devil's Dictionary*. "*War*, n. A by-product of the arts of peace. War loves to come like a thief in the night; professions of eternal amity provide the night." "*Peace*, n. In international affairs, a period of cheating between two periods of fighting."

I usually give a full biographical lecture on Bierce because he was such a character and such a successful muckraker. Students are always fascinated by his disappearance—no skeleton was ever found. (Several expeditions were mounted and, since he was over six feet tall and had a full head of pure white hair, the rumors of his every move were rampant: but there has never been confirmation of his death.) Brigid Brophy insists he did not die but merely came back again when the world was more ready for his wild, stylistic experiments. According to Brophy, he now writes under the nom de plume of "Jorge Luis Borges." (Actually, since Borges died recently, I suppose that must mean Bierce finally did, too.)

Major Themes, Historical Perspectives, Personal Issues

War, the tendency toward violence, the idea that we fear what we do not know but perhaps should most fear what we know (i.e., ourselves, our fellow humans, those people we love who nonetheless perpetuate the values of violence). The child sees nothing wrong with war until it literally comes home—the burned house, the dead and probably raped body of the mother. Note, too, the rampant animal imagery throughout the story. Early critics called it an "allegory," and it is.

Significant Form, Style, or Artistic Conventions

Unlike most so-called naturalists, Bierce blamed humans, not Fate, for determining the course of human existence. However, he was a naturalist in his use of macabre and even lurid details that force the reader to see the full implications of war. Stylistically, he brilliantly mimics the actions of the boy (as well as his perceptions, devoid of sound and often sense, since, as a small child, he lacks the experience to know what is harmful, what not: bears are cute in the picture books; so is war) and of the dying soldiers. The famous passage of the ground in motion and the creek relies in repetition to heighten the sense of relentless violence. Allegory is another important genre to discuss and elucidate here.

Original Audience

I always discuss the memoirs of the Civil War veterans as well as the beginning of America's full-fledged attempt at imperialism in Latin America, the Spanish-American War. Bierce, in his other capacity as a journalist, vociferously denounced the war that William Randolph Hearst bragged he started (saying people buy newspapers during wars). Bierce was fired from that job but went on to other newspapers, where he was equally adamant in his opposition to the war. He died (or rather disappeared) sometime in 1914, over seventy years old, when he went to Mexico to see Pancho Villa firsthand. Carlos Fuentes's *The Old Gringo* is a retelling of Bierce's journey into Mexico, where peasants still insist Bierce wanders the Sierra Madres.

Comparisons, Contrasts, Connections

Stephen Crane learned his craft from Bierce. Hemingway later borrowed some of his techniques. Bierce is highly regarded by postmodernists such as Fuentes as well as Jorge Luis Borges and Julio Cortázar. He is said to be similar to Guy de Maupassant or O. Henry. But while both of those authors use trick endings, most of Bierce's "tricks" have some larger metaphysical purpose.

Questions for Reading, Discussion, and Writing

1. I let students be surprised by the ending and horrified by the language. I try not to give anything away before they get to the story.
2. I sometimes have them do historical research on the Spanish-American War.

Bibliography

I have a long section on "Chickamauga" in my *Experimental Fictions of Ambrose Bierce*.

Hamlin Garland (1860–1940)

Contributing Editor: James Robert Payne

Classroom Issues and Strategies

Discussion and explanation of Garland's populist values and political activities definitely enhance an appreciation of his fiction, as does some consideration, however brief, of his interest in Henry George's economic theories. Relate the populist movement of late nineteenth-century America to present-day grievances and problems of American farmers. More generally, compare social and political tensions between Southern, Midwestern, and Western American regions on the one hand, and the Northeastern region on the other in Garland's day and today.

Garland's profound empathy for the life situation of the rural and small-town Midwestern farm woman requires discussion and may be productively studied in relation to Garland's biography. If feasible (depending on student interest), compare Garland's "single-tax" notions (derived from Henry George, 1839–1897) with present-day tax reform schemes. What would be the social impact of such schemes, then and now?

Students express interest in Garland's representation of the impact on rural society of national economic policies and laws. They are also interested in comparing the role of women in rural America as given in Garland's writing with what they perceive as the role of women in rural areas today. Students will also compare the impact of land speculators and monopoly industries on society today with the impact of such forces as represented in Garland's writings.

Major Themes, Historical Perspectives, Personal Issues

1. Central to much of Garland's best fiction and autobiography is an attempt to contrast actual conditions of American farm families with nineteenth-century (and earlier) idealizations of farm life.
2. As we see in his story "Up the Coulé" and elsewhere, Garland was very interested in the drama inherent in relations between farm families and their urbanized children.
3. Garland's theme of white America's injustice to Indians, apparent in his novel *The Captain of the Gray-Horse Troop* and his collection the *Book of the American Indian*, is very important though neglected in teaching and writing about Garland.

Significant Form, Style, or Artistic Conventions

1. If the instructor is interested in such conventions as "realism" and "naturalism," Garland may be taught as a transitional figure between the relatively genteel realism of William Dean Howells and the harsher naturalism we associate with Stephen Crane (as in *Maggie*, 1893) and Theodore Dreiser (as in *Sister Carrie*, 1900).
2. Consider represented speech in Garland's fiction, including suggestions of German language, as we see in "Up the Coulé," as indicative of Garland's efforts toward realism.

Original Audience

Although Garland's early fiction, such as that collected in *Main-Travelled Roads* (which includes "Up the Coulé"), shocked many with its frank portrayal of the harshness of actual farm life as Garland perceived that life, by the end of his career, particularly through such works as *A Son of the Middle Border*, Garland was a recognized, even beloved, chronicler of the opening up and settlement of the American Midwest and West. In Garland's day, many rural midwesterners read *A Son of the Middle Border* as their region's analogue to Benjamin Franklin's *Autobiography*. Readers today value Garland's work as giving a most authentic dramatization of post–Civil War Midwestern rural life.

Comparisons, Contrasts, Connections

Emile Zola (1840–1902)—French naturalist author who endeavored to convey an accurate picture of the poor and marginalized of France in his day. Compare and contrast with Garland's drama of the harsh life on nineteenth-century American farms.

Willa Cather (1873–1947)—Compare Cather's presentation of rural Midwestern life with Garland's. Is the picture that Cather gives us more balanced, varied, and perhaps more positive than Garland's generally bleak views?

John Steinbeck (1902–1947)—With particular reference to Steinbeck's *The Grapes of Wrath* (1939), compare the unrest of farmers in 1930s (Steinbeck) with that in the late nineteenth century (Garland).

Questions for Reading, Discussion, and Writing

1. Items that follow refer specifically to Garland's story "Up the Coulé":
   (a) As you read, recall a time when you returned to your parental home after a considerable period of absence during which you achieved, perhaps, a new sophistication. Compare your experience, feelings, and family tension with the family tensions and feelings represented in "Up the Coulé."
   (b) Compare Garland's portrayal of farm life with your experience of farm life.
2. Discuss Garland's fiction against the background of the populist movement of late-nineteenth-century America.
   (a) Research Garland's autobiographies, especially *A Son of the Middle Border* and *A Daughter of the Middle Border*, and trace autobiographical tendencies in Garland's fiction.
   (b) Research Henry George's "single-tax" theories (see George's *Progress and Poverty*, 1879) and compare George's ideas and themes with ideas implicit in Garland's *Main-Travelled Roads* stories.
   (c) Compare and contrast themes and values of Garland's *A Son of the Middle Border* with Franklin's *Autobiography*.

Bibliography

Ahnebrink, Lars. *The Beginnings of Naturalism in American Fiction.* Cambridge: Harvard UP, 1950, 63–89. European influences on Garland.

Bledsoe, Thomas. "Introduction." *Main-Travelled Roads.* New York: Rinehart, 1954.

Folsom, James K. *The American Western Novel.* New Haven: College and UP, 1966. 149–55, 180–84. On Garland's writings about Indians.

Gish, Robert. *Hamlin Garland: The Far West.* Boise State University Western Writers Ser. 24. Boise: Boise State UP, 1976.

McCullough, Joseph B. *Hamlin Garland.* Boston: Twayne, 1978. Short, readable, solid introductory book.

Pizer, Donald. "Hamlin Garland's *A Son of the Middle Border:* Autobiography as Art." *Essays in American and English Literature Presented to B. R. McElderry, Jr.* Ed. Max L. Schultz. Athens: Ohio UP, 1967. 76–107.

———. *Hamlin Garland's Early Work and Career.* Berkeley: U of California P, 1960. Best treatment of Garland's most vital years as fictionist.

———. "Herbert Spencer and the Genesis of Hamlin Garland's Critical System." *Tulane Studies in English* 7 (1957): 153–68.

Taylor, Walter F. *The Economic Novel in America.* Chapel Hill: U of North Carolina P, 1942, 148–83. On Garland's social and economic views.

Walcutt, Charles C. *American Literary Naturalism, A Divided Stream.* Minneapolis: U of Minnesota P, 1956. 53–63.

Stephen Crane (1871–1900)

Contributing Editor: Donald Vanouse

Classroom Issues and Strategies

Stephen Crane's works present sudden shifts in tone and point of view, and frequently the works end without establishing either certainty about characters or resolution of thematic issues. Crane's imagery is vivid, but the works seldom provide final interpretations (e.g., the empty bucket in "A Mystery of Heroism"). These qualities contribute to Crane's multilayered irony.

The instructor should attempt to shift the focus from *resolving* issues of plot or character (e.g., "Is Collins a hero?") to showing the students that Crane seems to encourage the reader to *enrich* and *reevaluate* ideas about patterns of action and thought. Crane asks questions rather than providing answers.

Consider using the poems to introduce some of his major themes. Crane seems to have valued the poems quite highly as expressions of his sense of the world. In like manner, the pace and drama of "A Mystery of Heroism" and "The Bride Comes to Yellow Sky" make them easier as doorways to Crane than the more stately and ambitious reflectiveness of "The Open Boat."

Like other scholars, students in class often are concerned with Crane's attitude toward God. It is useful—if complex—to invite them to look at "God Lay Dead in Heaven," "A Man Said to the Universe," "Do Not Weep, Maiden, For War Is Kind," "Chant You Loud of Punishments," and "When a People Reach the Top of a Hill." These poems, along with the "prayer" in "The Open Boat," indicate the *variety* of religious experiences in Crane.

Major Themes, Historical Perspectives, Personal Issues

Crane writes about extreme experiences that are confronted by ordinary people. His characters are not larger-than-life, but they touch the mysterious edges of their capacities for perception, action, and understanding. In his themes and styles, Crane is an avant-garde writer.

The New York City sketch, "A Detail," was reprinted in 1898 with "The Open Boat," and the two works express parallel naturalistic themes. In both, individuals are shown to struggle for communication while being buffeted by tumultuous forces. "A Detail" is about an old woman looking for work in New York City.

Significant Form, Style, or Artistic Conventions

Crane's works reflect many of the major artistic concerns at the end of the nineteenth century, especially realism, naturalism, impressionism, and symbolism.

His works insist that we live in a universe of vast and indifferent natural forces, not in a world of divine providence or a certain moral order. "A Man Said to the Universe" is useful in identifying this aspect of Crane. But Crane's vivid and explosive prose styles distinguish his works from those by many other writers who are labeled naturalists.

Many readers (including Hamlin Garland and Joseph Conrad, who were personal friends of Crane) have used the term *impressionist* to describe Crane's vivid renderings of moments of visual beauty and uncertainty. Even Crane's "discontinuous" rendering of action has been identified as impressionist. Such structures parallel the decenterings in Impressionist paintings.

In "The Open Boat," Crane has been seen as a symbolist narrative. Perhaps it is most appropriate to see the story as a skeptical balancing of concern with vast archetypes such as the sea with an equal concern with the psychology of individual perception.

Original Audience

Crane had a popular audience as well as a cultivated, literary audience during his lifetime.

Crane was a "star" journalist, and he published many of his best fictional works in the popular press. Nonetheless, his comment in his poem that a newspaper is a "collection of half-injustices" indicates his skepticism about that medium of communication.

Comparisons, Contrasts, Connections

Crane's relationship to naturalism links him to such writers as Frank Norris, Theodore Dreiser, and John Dos Passos.

Crane's brief free-verse poems invite comparison with those of Emily Dickinson (Howells read them to him) and with a number of twentieth-century poets, particularly those influenced by imagism (Carl Sandburg, Amy Lowell, Ezra Pound, William Carlos Williams, for example). In brevity and in the author's desire to escape conventional poetic rhetoric, these poems are comparable to Crane's. There are, of course, some vast differences in subject. Crane's poems "The Impact of a Dollar" and "A Newspaper" are early instances of pop art in literary subject matter that connects to William Carlos Williams, Alan Ginsberg, and Amiri Baraka (Leroi Jones).

Questions for Reading, Discussion, and Writing

1. Why does Crane use the term *Mystery* in the title of his war story? What is the mystery? Or do you find more than one?
2. In "The Bride," Crane seems interested in the role of women. Does the story show a shift of power from male violence?
3. In "The Open Boat," Crane seems very interested in what the correspondent learns. What does he learn about nature? Or about seeing nature? Or his relationship to other human beings?
4. How useful is "A Man Said to the Universe" in understanding the correspondent's experience?
5. "There Was a Man with Tongue of Wood" and "Chant You Loud of Punishments" are poems about poetry. What do these poems say about Crane's ambition or purpose as a poet?
6. Crane's vivid prose makes him particularly valuable in developing student skills in discussing literary style. Also, his spare and startling structures (especially "endings") provide useful occasions for assignments on literary structure.

7. Crane's relationship to naturalism provokes questions about the possibilities of individual freedom and responsibility.

Bibliography

The facts of Crane's life were blurred by the 1923 biography by Thomas Beer. *The Crane Log: A Documentary Life of Stephen Crane* by Stanley Wertheim and Paul Sorrentino is an essential source for Crane biography.

Jack London (1876–1916)

Contributing Editor: Joan D. Hedrick

Classroom Issues and Strategies

I explore the way in which the class divisions of society, demarcated by "The Slot," create divisions in an individual's consciousness. This opens up a way to discuss "South of the Slot," particularly if students have themselves experienced a self divided between two (or more) cultures. I have found that foreign students and working-class students have very strong, positive responses to London's stories of the hazards of cultural mobility.

Major Themes, Historical Perspectives, Personal Issues

The double is a familiar theme in American literature, but London gives it a new twist by exploring it in class as well as psychological terms. London's politics were shaped in the 1890s by the depression, labor disputes, and the Socialist Labor Party. During the same period he also determined that he would become a writer, motivated in part by his fear of slipping into the underclass, which he called "the Social Pit." London struggled to reconcile his radical, working-class identity with that of his middle-class, literary self. His satirical portrait of Freddie Drummond distances him from a self he might have become. Exploring with considerable wit the contrasting social types of the university professor and the working-class labor leader, "South of the Slot" displays London's lifelong quest for a humanity that the class divisions of his society rendered difficult.

Significant Form, Style, or Artistic Conventions

In general, naturalism is the literary movement that provides the best context for Jack London. Naturalism has been understood as a dialectic between free will and determinism (Charles Child Walcutt, *American Literary Naturalism, a Divided Stream* [Minneapolis: U of Minnesota P, 1956]), but it is probably most intelligible through social history. The appeal of naturalistic tales is often escape. The urban problems of unemployment, labor wars, and poverty are left behind for a spare scenario in which an individual can be tested. A stock naturalistic device involves taking an "over-civilized" man from the upper classes into a primitive environment where he must live by muscle and wit. Frank Norris uses this device in *Moran of the Lady Letty,* as does London in *The Sea-Wolf. The Call of the Wild* also fits this pattern, although here the hero is a dog. Buck, a dog of northern ancestry who has been raised in southern California, is kidnapped and taken to Alaska, where he must adapt to snow and the rule of the club.

In another common naturalistic pattern, the hero who stays in the city either becomes an ineffectual dandy or degenerates into a lower-class brute. Frank Norris's *Vandover and the Brute,* set in San Francisco, traces the downward arc of Vandover's career from a Harvard education through the urban horrors of drink, dissipation, and aimless drifting to his ultimate reward: he literally becomes a primitive brute when he falls victim to lycanthropy and finds himself barking like a wolf. London treats these materials more realistically, yet employs the same pattern whereby the city is associated with degeneration and the open country with rebirth. Both *Burning Daylight* and *The Valley of the Moon* contrast the vitality of the heroes in the country with the dissipation and bad luck they encounter in the city. "South of the Slot" departs from this pattern by portraying the city as the setting for a working-class victory.

Original Audience

London's goal was to write radical stories and publish them in mainstream, middle-class journals. "South of the Slot" was published in 1909 in *The Saturday Evening Post,* George Lorimer's highly successful magazine for upwardly aspiring self-made Americans.

Comparisons, Contrasts, Connections

As a story about a double, "South of the Slot" may be compared with Poe's "William Wilson" or with Hawthorne's stories of allegorically paired characters, such as Arthur Dimmesdale and Roger Chillingworth in *The Scarlet*

Letter. Treated as a story of social types, it may also be compared with Stowe's portraits of class, race, and regional types in *Uncle Tom's Cabin.*

Questions for Reading, Discussion, and Writing

I begin discussions of London by putting up on the board a paired series of contrasts between working-class and middle-class stereotypes. In "South of the Slot" this contrast is embodied in Big Bill Totts and Freddie Drummond. Then I ask, where do these notions come from? Why is the lower class associated with, for example, muscle and a free expression of sexuality? What are the psychosocial implications of this division of human characteristics along class lines?

Critical Visions of Postbellum America

Standing Bear (Machunazha Ponca) (1829–1908)

Contributing Editor: R. D. Theisz

Classroom Issues and Strategies

In order to assist students in achieving a meaningful response to this text, we must provide some ethnographic contextualization for them in order to familiarize them with the historical framework of this text. Post–Civil War America reveled in the notion of *Manifest Destiny,* a crusading colonization of United States lands west of the Mississippi with total disregard for the rights of their indigenous owners. The hunger for "free land," as it was perceived in non-Indian America, led to a dispossession and exploitation of the original owners, the residual consequences of which cry out for moral and material recompense to this day.

In addition, the nature of orality and its entextualization, of capturing oral performance in alphabet (print) form require some examination. The nature of Native American oratory, in this case the common exchange between the Native spokesmen (almost all were men) and U.S. federal officials, military representatives, or outside non-Indian representatives reflects the increasingly disparate power relationship between the Native spokesmen and European/American representatives. This may be exemplified in one simple illustration. In the sixteenth and seventeenth centuries, Native practice commonly addressed non-Indian representatives confidently as "Brothers," but by the late nineteenth century, relationships had shifted so significantly in favor of the non-Indian that "Father" and "Grandfather" became common forms of address employed by Native spokesmen, "his Indian children." Positions of strength have thus yielded to a Native recognition of cultural and political subordination and the subsequent appeals to human morality, law, and fairness.

Major Themes, Historical Perspectives, Personal Issues

Several major themes may be explored, such as the reasons for America's frequent and cyclical interest in Native American cultural and political issues. When do mainstream Americans pursue a need to purge themselves of guilt or engage in a search for more "primitive" and thus more authentic indigenous experiences? Another theme, of course, is the nineteenth-century tide of *Manifest Destiny* sweeping all other considerations before it in its dispossession of Native owners. Modern readers seem to be fascinated by the drama of the ultimately faceless and immoral American bureaucracy, buttressed by the ideology of progress, which is confronted by the heroic but doomed action of the tribal individual or group.

Yet another theme to be considered is the alternative manner of viewing and expressing human experience in public discourse. Lineal Western thinking, critical analysis, classical explication, or whatever the modes of discourse may be, encounter a divergent manner of presenting ideas in cyclical patterns, frequent metaphors, loosely associated clusters of ideas, or seemingly disconnected or even digressive trains of thought that pay witness to the individual Native orator.

Significant Form, Style, or Artistic Conventions

The nature and principles of Native American oratory need to be introduced. The works cited at the end of the headnote can provide a beginning. Native American speechmaking can be divided into a ceremonial and secular tradition (see Ruoff). An additional short speech by Standing Bear, "My hand is not the color of yours," before Judge Dundy will deepen students' responses to this text (*From the Heart*, ed. Lee Miller, 225).

Comparisons, Contrasts, Connections

Other Native speakers—and eventually writers—in the late nineteenth century and early twentieth century echo Standing Bear's view of his relationship to the creator, the relationship of Native people to United States federal policy, and to the course of the historical fate of their cultures (see Nabakov).

Postmodern concern with various marginalized and exploited peoples—especially those of color—broadens the perspective presented by Standing Bear.

Charles Alexander Eastman (Sioux) (1858–1939)

Contributing Editor: Douglas Sackman

Classroom Issues and Strategies

Consider Eastman's status as an intercultural figure whose life and work mediated between white and Indian culture and society. There may be a tendency to privilege Eastman's writing as both authentic and ultimately representative of the "Native American view." Students may too easily come to the conclusion that Eastman gives *voice* to the Other. Such a conclusion can be problematic because, first, it equates the individual author with the group, reinscribing the idea that the other is a collective while only members of the dominant culture can be creative individuals, and second, voice can suggest that which is unmediated and even biological, reinforcing the essentialist idea that Native Americans are natural beings.

The notion of positionality may have advantages over voice. Discussing how his position as a representative of Native Americans was constructed may be surprising since students might imagine that it was simply a birthright. You may explore how in the text Eastman positions himself as an authority, and how that position relates to the poles of Indian and white identity. Where does his authority as a spokesperson come from? As an authentic "other," or because he has received a "white" education? Having students see how his authority comes in part from both elements should begin to reveal the complexity of his identity. It also can be useful to discuss the antimodernism of turn-of-twentieth-century America and how its desire for the authentic, the natural, and the spiritual prepared an eager audience for Eastman's writing. Though Eastman valorizes traditional ways, he was not simply a "traditional" Indian thrust into a "modern" nation. Eastman was as modern as any of his contemporaries, perhaps never more so than when he was talking about traditional Indian life.

In Eastman's day and in our own time, representatives of the Other have often been limited to two roles: witnesses or informants. It can be productive to organize the discussion of the two pieces around these two admittedly constraining roles. For the first selection, "The Great Mystery," consider Eastman's position as a native informant on Indian spirituality. As is suggested in the headnote, the piece does more than simply explain a truth about native culture as it fashions a pan-Indian spirituality that is then used to legitimize native culture and indict white spiritual declension or hypocrisy. For "The Ghost Dance War," consider Eastman's role as a witness. What is a witness? How does Eastman balance his identity as at once an Indian, a representative of the U.S. Government, and a scientifically trained physician? Have students consider what kind of distance there might have been between Eastman and the Sioux people of Pine Ridge when he arrived, fresh from his schooling in the East, as the "white doctor" in 1890. Why would he feel the need to keep "composure" when his Indian companions were "crying aloud"? What is his view on the Ghost Dance religion? It is worth discussing whether Eastman seems to have completely bought into white culture at the time of his arrival and then has that faith in its progressive nature shaken by the events of Wounded Knee, or if he seems more skeptical from the outset. How does the fact that his account was published twenty-six years after the event itself shape how we might answer that question? The role of the witness can be incorporated into larger discussions of the status of autobiography, especially in how the telling of a personal life can have profound political implications.

Major Themes, Historical Perspectives, Personal Issues

The larger historical context includes the military, economic, and cultural dispossession of the Sioux and other Native Americans during the nineteenth century. The Santee Sioux uprising of 1862 and the military conflict with the U.S. government was one event in that larger history of dispossession. The conflict separated Eastman from his father and from other whites, but the ironic aspect of this is that the elder Eastman converted to Christianity and then sent the younger Eastman in a direction in which he would have close contact with whites. The millenarianism of the Ghost Dancers also needs to be understood in the context of dispossession and cross-cultural conflict.

In addressing the identity Eastman creates, issues surrounding assimilation and nationalism should be considered. In 1879, Joseph Henry Pratt, whose motto was "Kill the Indian and save the man," founded the Indian Industrial School at Carlisle, Pennsylvania. We might now label this approach to education and reform "cultural genocide." At the time, reformers held a variety of views on the value of native culture. Though some did not share Pratt's view that native culture was an absolute obstacle to survival in modern America, most white reformers believed that white culture was superior. But as the notion of a ladder of civilization from the savage to the civilized partially gave way to cultural relativism in the early twentieth century (especially under the influence of anthropologist Franz Boas and his students), more room was created to assert the value of Native American culture. Eastman used his authority and skills gained by successfully completing an education that did not value Native American culture in order to reclaim and legitimate that culture. One can view this as ironic, and it is certainly a confirmation that those who negotiated between cultures faced a predicament that could not be resolved with absolute purity. While historical perspectives can inform our reading of the texts, the texts themselves offer interesting perspectives on history. To what extent does Eastman's account of the Ghost Dance War question the triumphalist master-narrative of Manifest Destiny? To what extent does Eastman's portrait of native religion before the intrusion of whites create an idyllic past in which everything was perfect and nothing changed? This view contradicts the view of many Christian missionaries and academics in the late nineteenth century, who felt that Indians had lived from time immemorial in spiritual and technological darkness. But Eastman's version of precontact history also parallels the views of whites since it presents Indian society as immune to change and development.

Significant Form, Style, or Artistic Conventions

It should be noted that the first selection is from a set of essays on native religion while the second is from Eastman's autobiography *From Deep Woods to Civilization*. The first essay seems a hybrid of argumentative essay, insider ethnography, and philosophy of religion. For the second piece, readers should pay attention to how Eastman moves from journalistic reporting to revelation of his own emotions and thoughts to a larger agenda of social criticism based on the events that he witnessed. The role of a white editor is less pronounced in Eastman's account of his life than it is for other Native Americans (e.g., Black Elk or Sarah Winnemucca). While his wife collaborated in the writing, to a large extent Eastman avoided the issue of having an outside editor reshape his life by translating from oral testimony into written work.

Comparisons, Contrasts, Connections

Eastman's texts can be compared with the writings of other Native Americans (such as Winnemucca, Oskison, Standing Bear, or Zitkala-Sa). It has been argued that the modernist form of autobiography, with its need to explore and reveal the interior self, has been resisted by Native Americans since, among other things, they tend to view the community as more important and meaning-ful than the self. Comparison with other autobiographical writing might yield insights on this issue. It could also be interesting to read his works alongside those of other Americans who were marginalized from the national community, particularly African Americans. W. E. B. Du Bois's notion of "double conscious-ness," which he developed in *The Souls of Black Folks*, can be compared to

Eastman's exposition of native culture and spirituality as developed in *The Soul of an Indian*. Eastman's discussion of religion might also be read in relation to the tradition of the American Jeremiad. He certainly indicts contemporary Christianity as a fallen form of religion and urges a renewal through a revitalization of root Christian values. In his version of Puritan self-critique, though, he contributes a significant twist, arguing that Native American spirituality embodied a pure form of Christianity. You might also explore how his understanding of religion compares with transcendentalism.

Sarah Winnemucca (Thocmetony) (c. 1844–1891)

Contributing Editor: Karen L. Kilcup

Classroom Issues and Strategies

It is important to emphasize that this selection represents a part of a varied and much longer narrative. Moreover, like many nineteenth-century Indian texts, it encodes a negotiation between an Indian author and a white editor. Winnemucca was fortunate to obtain a sympathetic, reform-minded editor in Mary Mann (sister of social activist Elizabeth Palmer Peabody and Sophia Peabody Hawthorne, Nathaniel Hawthorne's wife), but students should be invited to consider the ways in which editors (the writers' contemporaries as well as present-day) can and do shape texts.

One way to initiate this investigation of the selection process is to ask students to spend a brief time, in or out of class, writing their own autobiographies, then exchanging with a partner who selects for presentation to the class the most "representative" or "interesting" paragraphs, also editing them for style. What gets left in and what is taken out? What is emphasized? Why? How do considerations of audience influence the selection process? How does the identity of the editor potentially affect this process? An alternative to this student writing assignment is to assemble small groups of students who are required to take another autobiography in *The Heath Anthology* and reduce it by half, asking the same questions.

Another issue that is productive for discussion is the matter of students' emotional responses to Winnemucca's narrative. White students, in particular, may feel guilt or responsibility for the destruction of Paiute culture, especially given the kindness, trust, and idealism of Chief Truckee. Ask students to think about the author's goals: Does she want to provoke (paralyzing) guilt or action? How does she accomplish her purposes—what textual features stand out in this context? What emotions does the narrator project (anger, frustration, courage)?

This discussion can open out into productive consideration of readers' emotional responses to texts more generally and of the means by which authors engage with or distance from affective matters.

Major Themes, Historical Perspectives, Personal Issues

In addition to the obvious matters of Paiute dislocation, the transformation of a way of life, and the loss of traditional resources, an important issue for students to understand is the continuing prejudice in mainstream culture against women speaking in public. Because of this prejudice, Winnemucca's reputation was constantly assailed; hence, her editor, Mary Mann, thought it prudent to include an appendix of character references for the author in *Life Among the Piutes*. Reading aloud or photocopying some of these references will provide students with a sense of the gendered social environment in which Winnemucca worked.

These character attacks were also part of the racism endured by Native Americans. A related issue is the assumption of the sexual availability of Indian women to white men, a matter Winnemucca exposes quite plainly. Students should know about the cross-racial nature of this sexual appropriation, and comparing Winnemucca's account to others by African-American writers (like Harriet Jacobs) is extremely productive.

Another important feature of Winnemucca's narrative is the internal division among the Paiutes, with some favoring the principle of hospitality initiated by Chief Truckee and others favoring the more cautious approach of her father. This kind of split, which sometimes reflected a conscious white strategy of "divide and conquer," occurred from the beginning of white-Indian relations; another example is the fragmentation of the Iroquois Confederacy during the Revolution, when some member tribes aligned them-selves with the British and others with the revolutionaries.

Winnemucca's courage in the face of the fragmentation and dislocation of her people is an important subtext of the narrative, especially when contrasted with the cowardice of white soldiers and settlers whom she describes in later chapters. In addition, she overturns the "bring in the cavalry" myth that has permeated American popular culture, depicting the U.S. military as an ally that frequently intervened to protect the Indians from the depredations of white settlers. On the other hand, we see the corruption of government agents and the government itself, which is in sharp contrast to their putative "Christian" principles.

Significant Form, Style, or Artistic Conventions

Genre and the "mixing" of genres (according to Western standards) feature prominently in *Life Among the Piutes*. The selection in *The Heath Anthology* incorporates a range of Indian and Western traditions. Emphasizing oral narrative in Chief Truckee's retelling of the Paiute myth, the opening chapter also included elements of tribal history, coup tale, autobiography, vindication story, dramatic narrative, sentimental drama, and sensation story. Winnemucca's individual voice comes through vividly and confidently, reflecting her success as a platform performer; at the same time, her story represents the collective experiences of her people, conserving Paiute history and culture.

Original Audience

Aimed at educating a white audience about what the subtitle indicates— "Their Wrongs and Claims"—Winnemucca's narrative purpose is clearly stated by Mary Mann: "Mrs. Hopkins came to the East from the Pacific coast with the courageous purpose of telling in detail to the mass of our people, 'extenuating nothing and setting down naught in malice,' the story of her people's trials." A useful exercise is to highlight the purpose of the volume as Mann outlines it and to compare this purpose to the text itself.

Comparisons, Contrasts, Connections

The autobiographies and political writing of William Apess, Charles Eastman, and Zitkala-Sa offer extremely useful links. In addition to the writers' depictions of tensions among the Indians themselves, consider the situation of the writer in relation to his/her tribe (as "insider" or "outsider" or both), the use of a plural or individual voice, and the "political" and/or "personal" nature of this autobiography. It is also useful to juxtapose Winnemucca's narrative to other life writings by immigrant and nonwhite writers such as Anzia Yezierska, Younghill Kang, and Sui Sin Far; to captivity narratives such as Mary Rowlandson's; and to "mainstream" autobiographies like Benjamin Franklin's.

Questions for Reading, Discussion, and Writing

1. Discussion of how racism affects men and women differently.
2. Discussion of film/media images of Native Americans, both in the past and today. The stereotype of the noble savage as well as the howling savage.

3. How does oral tradition influence Winnemucca's narrative? What textual features help indicate its oral resonances and roots?
4. What are today's attitudes toward women's public roles? How do those attitudes vary in different regional, ethnic, and religious communities?

Bibliography

Bataille, Gretchen M., and Kathleen M. Sands. *American Indian Women, Telling Their Lives.* Lincoln: U of Nebraska P, 1984.

Brumble, H. David, III. *American Indian Autobiography.* Berkeley: U of California P, 1988.

Canfield, Gae W. *Sarah Winnemucca of the Northern Paiutes.* Norman: U of Oklahoma P, 1983.

Georgi-Findlay, Brigitte. "The Frontiers of Native American Women's Writing: Sarah Winnemucca's *Life Among the Piutes.*" *New Voices in Native American Literary Criticism.* Ed. Arnold Krupat. Washington, DC: Smithsonian, 1993. 222–52.

Ruoff, A. LaVonne B. "Early Native American Women Authors: Jane Johnston Schoolcraft, Sarah Winnemucca, S. Alice Callahan, E. Pauline Johnson, and Zitakala-Sa." *Nineteenth-Century American Women Writers: A Critical Reader.* Ed. Karen L. Kilcup. Oxford and Cambridge, UK: Blackwell, 1998.

———. "Three Nineteenth-Century American Indian Autobiographers." *Redefining American Literary History.* Ed. A. LaVonne B. Ruoff and Jerry W. Ward. New York: MLA, 1990. 251–69.

Sands, Kathleen M. "Indian Women's Personal Narrative: Voices Past and Present." *American Women's Autobiography: Fea(s)ts of Memory.* Ed. Margo Culley. Madison: U of Wisconsin P, 1992. 268–94.

Strange, William C. "Story, Take Me Home: Instances of Resonance in Sarah Winnemucca Hopkins' *Life Among the Piutes.*" *Entering the 90s: The North American Experience: Proceedings from the Native American Studies Conference at Lake Superior University.* Ed. Thomas E. Schirer. Sault Ste. Marie: Lake Superior UP, 1991. 184–94.

Frances Ellen Watkins Harper (1825–1911)

Contributing Editor: Elizabeth Ammons

Classroom Issues and Strategies

Two primary issues in teaching Harper are (1) the high-culture aesthetic in which students have been trained makes it hard for them to appreciate Harper and find ways to talk about her; (2) most students' ignorance of nineteenth-century African-American history deprives them of a strong and meaningful historical context in which to locate Harper's work.

To address the first issue, I ask students to think about the questions and methods of analysis that they may bring to the study of literature in the classroom. What do we look for in "good" literature? Their answers are many but usually involve the following: it should be "interesting" and deal with "important" ideas, themes, topics. It should be intellectually challenging. The style should be sophisticated—by which they mean economical, restrained, and learned without being pretentious. It should need analysis—that is, have many hidden points and many "levels" of meaning that readers (students) do not see until they get to class. Then we talk about these criteria: "Interesting" and "important" by whose standards? Theirs? *All* of theirs? Whose, then? *Why* is intellectually hard literature judged better than "easy" literature? Why is lean, restrained, educated style "better" than fulsome, emotional, colloquial, or vernacular style (except for keeping professors employed)?

The point here is to talk about the aesthetic students have been taught in school to value and to ask these questions: Where does it come from? Whose interests does it serve (in terms of class, race, ethnic group, and gender—both now and in the past)? What values does it reflect, morally and spiritually (intellect is superior to feelings, transmitting tradition is a primary goal of high-culture literature, etc.)? Thinking about our own aesthetic assumptions and expectations in these ways proves a good way of getting us to see that what we probably accept unquestioningly as "good art" (whether we "like" such art or not) is just one definition of "good art." We can now ask: What aesthetic is Harper writing out of? Is hers the aesthetic we have just described, and is she simply not very good at it, or—at best—only half-way good at it? Or is she speaking and writing out of a different aesthetic—perhaps a mix of what we are familiar with plus other things that many or all of us are not familiar with?

To address the second problem, the historical ignorance that can hamper students' understanding of Harper, one useful strategy is to assign a few short reports for students to present in class. The topics will depend on what selections by Harper one is teaching and what resources are available, but might include such things as racist stereotypes of black people in newspaper cartoons in the nineteenth century, women's resources against wife-abuse in the nineteenth century, the formation of the WCTU (Women's Christian Temperance Union), the division between white feminists and black people created by the fight for the Fifteenth Amendment, or the founding of the National Association of Colored Women. Such reports can give a sense of the intense climate of controversy out of which Harper wrote and can involve the students in the process of creating a historical context for Harper. Also, having students prepare these reports in pairs or small groups is a good way of spreading the work around, counteracting problems of nervousness about making presentations, and having them work corporately rather than individually—which is particularly appropriate for Harper.

Harper, like many other nineteenth-century writers, wrote to be heard, not just read. Therefore, a good strategy is to have students prepare some of her work outside of class to deliver in class.

Major Themes, Historical Perspectives, Personal Issues

Two major themes I emphasize in Harper are, first, her commitment not to individual psychology, ethics, development, and fulfillment but to the *group*. Harper, like Emerson, is ever the teacher and preacher, but the philosophy that she comes out of and lives is not, like his, individualistic—not focused on the self or Self. It is group-centered. I think that this is one of the most important points to make about Harper. Therefore, I ask my students to think about this question: Is the classic dominant-culture American schoolroom theme of the Individual versus Society relevant to Harper? If so, where and how? If not (and often it is not), what question(s) about America does Harper place at the center? If we use her, a black woman, as "the American"—that is, if we follow her lead and place her at the center rather than at the margin—what does "America" mean? What dominant theme(s) define Harper's America?

Second, I emphasize that Harper is a political writer and a propagandist. Art and politics are not alienated for her but inseparably dependent: art is not above politics; it is the tool of politics. I ask the class to think about our customary high-culture disdain for art in the "service" of politics, our disdain for art as propaganda. Why do we have that disdain? What art is not political?

Significant Form, Style, or Artistic Conventions

Often Harper writes and speaks in popular forms. I ask the class to identify the forms and think about how they work. The sermon, the political stump-speech, melodrama, the ballad, African-American storytelling, and vernacular verse are among the forms Harper draws on. How do these forms work? What devices do they rely on (e.g., accessibility rather than abstruseness, repetition of the familiar, audience response/recall/participation, deliberate emotion-stirring, etc.)? We talk about the appropriateness of these characteristics of form, style, and artistry to Harper's mission of reaching and affecting large numbers of people, including people not often written for or about with respect by white writers.

Original Audience

The questions of Harper's current audience inevitably comes up in the discussion of aesthetics. Because we have been taught not to value the kind of literature she created or to know much about or take seriously the issues she addressed (group justice as opposed to individual development, wife abuse and alcoholism in the nineteenth century; voter fraud and corruption, lynching, divisions between black feminists and white feminists, employment barriers to middle-class blacks in the nineteenth century, black women as the definers of women's issues), most of us have not been exposed to Frances Ellen Harper. Clearly, this will continue to change as the authority of identifying what is good, valuable, and important expands to include people traditionally excluded from the profession of professor (white women, people of color). Or will it? I ask how many students in the class plan to be teachers and scholars.

In her own time Harper was very popular and widely acclaimed, especially among black people. She was the best-known black poet between Phillis Wheatley and Paul Laurence Dunbar. "The Two Offers" is probably the first short story published in the United States by any black author. For many years *Iola Leroy* was considered the first novel written by a black American woman. Harper's public speaking was uniformly praised as brilliant. In light of the gap between Harper's reputation in her own day and the widespread ignorance about her today, audience as a social construct—as something that doesn't just "happen" but is constructed by identifiable social forces (economics; the composition of the teaching profession in terms of race, gender, and class)—and the issue of why we teach the authors we teach are central to discussion of Harper.

Comparisons, Contrasts, Connections

Many other writers compare well with Harper, but especially other black women writers in *The Heath Anthology*. Harriet Jacobs, Sojourner Truth, Alice Dunbar-Nelson, and Pauline Hopkins. Comparing these writers can give a glimpse of the range of black women writers' work in the nineteenth century, which was broad. It is very important to teach more than one or two black women writers before 1900 and to make comparisons. Otherwise, there is a tendency to generalize one author's work and point of view into "the black woman's" perspective, of which there was not one but were many. That point—the existence of great difference and variety as well as common ground—should be stressed.

Questions for Reading, Discussion, and Writing

1. Preparing an oral delivery, as suggested above, is an excellent way to get "inside" a work. Also, a good exercise is to ask the class to choose one piece and extrapolate from it the aesthetic principles governing it. Before class they should try to arrive at a statement of what a particular poem or speech or piece of fiction does—the effect it is designed to have on the reader/listener—and how it accomplishes that end. Then have them form small groups and work together to make up and write down "A Brief Writer's Guide for Young Writers by Frances Ellen Watkins Harper" to discuss in class.

2. A good assignment for Harper is to ask students to think about her as a black woman writer. What did each of these three terms mean to her? How do the three terms clash? How do they cooperate?

Bibliography

Useful discussion can be found in Elizabeth Ammons, *Conflicting Stories: American Women Writers at the Turn into the Twentieth Century* (1991); Hazel V. Carby, *Reconstructing Womanhood: The Emergence of the Afro-American Woman Novelist* (1987); Claudia Tate, *Domestic Allegories of Political Desire* (1992); Frances Smith Foster, *Written by Herself: Literary Production by African American Women, 1746–1892* (1993); and Carla L. Peterson, *"Doers of the Word": African-American Women Speakers and Writers in the North (1803–1880)* (1995).

Charlotte Perkins Gilman (1860–1935)

Contributing Editor: Elaine Hedges

Classroom Issues and Strategies

Students like "The Yellow Wall-Paper" and don't have serious difficulty understanding it, and they enjoy discussing the meanings of the wallpaper. They may, however, oversimplify the story, reading the ending either as the heroine's victory over her circumstances, or her defeat. Have students choose and defend one or the other of these positions for a classroom debate (with the aim of showing that there is no easy resolution). Students might also want to debate (attack or defend) the role of the husband in the story.

Background information on medical treatment of women, and specifically white, middle-class women, in the nineteenth century, especially Dr. S. Weir Mitchell's "rest cure" (mentioned in the headnote) is useful.

Naive students sometimes wonder why the woman in the story can't just leave; they need to understand the situation of white, middle-class married women in the nineteenth century: the censure against divorce and their limited opportunities in the paid labor force.

"Turned," like "The Yellow Wall-Paper," deals with the situation of women inside marriage, but it offers a wife who takes matters into her own hands and re-creates her life. The two stories can thus be profitably compared and contrasted. Significant differences, of course, include the greater freedom (she is childless) and professional training (she can support herself) of the wife, Mrs. Marroner, in "Turned." Gilman, in her major sociological work, *Women and Economics*, argued that only economic independence would release women from their subordination within marriage, and Mrs. Marroner is an example of this thesis. One might note the changes in her attitude toward Gerta, from a class-biased one to one of female bonding. "Turned" is also note-worthy as a frank treatment of an issue—an employer's sexual abuse of a female domestic—that wasn't openly discussed in fiction at the time.

Major Themes, Historical Perspectives, Personal Issues

Consider both stories as critiques of male power, including sexual power, and of marriage. Students can be asked how relevant these critiques are today: whether similar or comparable situations still exist.

Significant Form, Style, or Artistic Conventions

In "The Yellow Wall-Paper," less sophisticated students may identify the narrator with Gilman since the story is based on an episode in her life. Discussion of the literary convention of the first-person point of view and of differences between an author and her persona are useful. The dramatic immediacy of the first-person point of view (versus the use of the third person in "Turned") can be demonstrated.

Although Gilman's intention in both stories was didactic (she wrote "The Yellow Wall-Paper," she said, to warn readers against Dr. Mitchell's treatment), discussions of form and style can suggest how a text can transcend its author's intention or any narrow didactic purpose. In what ways is "Turned" more clearly didactic than "The Yellow Wall-Paper"?

"The Yellow Wall-Paper" is, of course, highly appropriate for a discussion of symbolism: how it emerges and operates within a text. Students enjoy discussing the symbolism of the wallpaper and of the room to which the narrator is confined.

Original Audience

I discuss Gilman's difficulty in getting "The Yellow Wall-Paper" published and ask students to consider why it might have disturbed her contemporaries. (It was rejected by the editor of the *Atlantic Monthly* on the grounds that it would make readers too miserable.) Gilman received letters of praise for the story from readers who read it as an accurate clinical description of incipient madness. In 1899, a few reviewers read it as a critique of marriage and of medical treatment of women.

Readers in Gilman's time would have been familiar with Poe's stories. Might "The Yellow Wall-Paper" have been perceived as similar to a Poe story? In what significant ways is it different from Poe's stories?

"Turned" is one of about two hundred short stories Gilman wrote and published in her magazine, *The Forerunner.* They were intended to dramatize the ideas she expounded in her nonfiction about women's roles and status in society, and to suggest reforms. *The Forerunner* never had a circulation of more than a thousand copies. Today, however, more and more of these stories by Gilman are being reprinted. For others, see Barbara H. Solomon, ed., *HERLAND and Selected Short Stories of Charlotte Perkins Gilman* (New York: Penguin USA, 1992), and Robert Shulman, ed., *"The Yellow Wall-Paper" and Other Stories* (New York: Oxford, 1995).

Comparisons, Contrasts, Connections

In the same section of the anthology, other texts dealing with marriage and with male-female power relations include Elizabeth Stuart Phelps's, some of Kate Chopin's, and Mary Wilkins Freeman's.

Two of Emily Dickinson's poems provide useful contexts for "The Yellow Wall-Paper": "Much madness is divinest sense" and "She rose to his requirement."

Bibliography

Elaine Hedges, Afterword, *The Yellow Wall-Paper* (Feminist, 1973) has an analysis of the story and a brief biography of Gilman.

Catherine Golden, ed., *The Captive Imagination: A Casebook on "The Yellow Wallpaper"* (Feminist, 1991) reprints a good selection of both nineteenth-century materials relevant to the story and contemporary critical treatments of it.

Ann Lane, ed., *The Charlotte Perkins Gilman Reader* (Pantheon, 1980) includes a selection of Gilman's stories and excerpts from her longer fictions, including the utopia, *Herland*. See also Denise D. Knight, ed., *"The Yellow Wall-Paper" and Selected Stories of Charlotte Perkins Gilman* (Newark: U of Delaware P, 1994).

Finley Peter Dunne (1867–1936)

Contributing Editor: Charles Fanning

Classroom Issues and Strategies

There are two kinds of pieces here: vignettes of daily life and national commentary. Discuss the aims of each kind and Dunne's ways of achieving them. The vignettes are like short stories; the commentaries are closer to the traditional newspaper column.

The issue of dialectical writing should be raised. What are the risks entailed? What are the benefits?

Major Themes, Historical Perspectives, Personal Issues

Immigrant/ethnic voices in the 1890s. Consider Dunne as presenting "Irish-American" perspectives: Ireland as a colonized country, the perspective on imperialism, reactions against American Anglophilia. The rise to respectability in the new world of Irish immigrants.

Dunne switched gears in 1900, moving to New York and national commentary, leaving the community-based Chicago perspective behind. What did he gain and what did he lose by this shift?

Significant Form, Style, or Artistic Conventions

Consider the limits of the weekly newspaper column. How did Dunne work within them and expand the possibilities? Look again at the issue of dialect writing and what the quality of these pieces tells us about the level of literacy (very high) assumed in the newspaper audience from the 1890s to World War I.

Original Audience

Newspaper readers, at first in Chicago and then all across the country in the syndicated post-1900, pieces were Dunne's original audience. In fact, he was the most famous columnist in America from 1900 to 1914. Why was this so?

Comparisons, Contrasts, Connections

Useful comparisons can be made with contemporary columnists familiar to the college-age audience such as Dave Barry or Maureen Dowd.

Compare also the ethnic perspective of other writers of the eighteen-nineties and subsequently. Dunne's pieces add the Irish-American voice to this chorus.

Compare other nineteenth-century humorists, from Mark Twain to the lesser figures—Artemus Ward, Petroleum V. Nasby, James Russell Lowell in the "Big'low Papers." A comparable twentieth-century figure to Mr. Dooley is Harlem's Jesse B. Semple, or "Simple," the creation of Langston Hughes.

Questions for Reading, Discussion, and Writing

Students may try their hands at writing a short, short story with some of the punch of Dunne's best work, such as "The Wanderers," or writing a column of commentary on national policy comparable to "Immigration," which again in our time is a big issue. Such an exercise should illustrate the genius of the original pieces, which looks so effortless upon first reading.

Bibliography

The most accessible paperback collection of Dunne's Chicago pieces is Charles Fanning, ed. *Mr. Dooley and the Chicago Irish: The Autobiography of a Nineteenth-Century Ethnic Group* (Washington: Catholic U of America P, 1987). The most accessible paperback collection of Dunne's national pieces is Robert Hutchinson, ed. *Mr. Dooley on Ivrything and Ivrybody* (New York: Dover). A recent assessment of Dunne can be found in J. C. Furnas, "The True American Sage," *American Scholar* 60 (Autumn 1991): 570–74.

Upton Sinclair (1878–1968)

Contributing Editor: James C. Wilson

Classroom Issues and Strategies

Students generally respond to Sinclair's portrait of the unsanitary conditions in the meat-packing industry. They tend to be interested in the history of *The Jungle*—how it was written, the federal legislation that was passed because of the public reaction to it, etc. The most difficult problem in teaching *The Jungle* is how to approach a text in which literary qualities are subordinated to political purpose. *The Jungle* does not lend itself to the kinds of literary discussions that most of us are accustomed to.

A cultural studies approach works well with *The Jungle*. Students can contextualize the novel using resources and historical materials readily available on the Internet. *The Jungle* can also be approached as a political novel. Compare *The Jungle* to other political novels the students might have read. Discuss the criteria by which we evaluate—or should evaluate—a political novel. Should our criteria include social and/or political considerations? (It might be useful here to draw a parallel between a political novel and a postmodern novel, for example, in which ideas overshadow the other ingredients of the fiction.)

Major Themes, Historical Perspectives, Personal Issues

Any discussion of *The Jungle* should mention the unsanitary conditions in the Chicago meat-packing industry at the turn of the century and the federal legislation that Congress passed as a result of the national furor that Sinclair's muckraking novel created. However, it is equally important to emphasize that *The Jungle* was—and is—primarily an indictment of wage slavery. Sinclair's purpose in writing the novel was to document the inhumane treatment of working men and women in industrial capitalism and to argue that socialism provided the only solution to the problem.

Significant Form, Style, or Artistic Conventions

Questions of style and form often seem irrelevant to *The Jungle.* However, it is possible to discuss the primitive, at times brutal, prose of the novel as an appropriate vehicle to convey the quality of human life that Sinclair found in the stockyards of Chicago.

Comparisons, Contrasts, Connections

The Jungle should be considered in the context of three separate but related literary movements in America. First, the novel comes out of the muckraking era. The Muckrakers—so named by Theodore Roosevelt because they, like the Man with the Muckrake in *Pilgrim's Progress,* looked down at the filth and ignored the celestial crown—exposed and attempted to correct graft and corruption in both government and business. The most famous of the Muckrakers, in addition to Sinclair, were Lincoln Steffens and Ida Tarbell, whose major works, *The Shame of the Cities* and *History of the Standard Oil Company,* respectively, appeared in 1901.

The Jungle also has its roots in American naturalism, with its first twenty-one chapters conforming, in both form and content, to the typical naturalistic novel of that period. For example, both style and psychological complexity are subordinated to the necessary machinations of the plot—the inevitable movement toward chaos and disintegration. Jurgis and his family, like the heroines of Stephen Crane's *Maggie,* Frank Norris's *McTeague,* and Theodore Dreiser's *Sister Carrie,* are victims of hereditary, environmental, social, and economic forces beyond their control—forces that shape their lives in an impersonal, mechanistic way.

Of course, what distinguishes *The Jungle* from these other examples of American naturalism is the turn toward socialism in the last four chapters, which allows Sinclair to end his novel on an optimistic note. The fact that Sinclair was a socialist, and that he used his writing as a vehicle to express his socialism, identifies him with the group of radical writers and artists that was centered in Greenwich Village (where the radical socialist magazine *The Masses* was published) and that included Floyd Dell, Randolph Bourne, Lincoln Steffens, Max Eastman, and John Reed. Sinclair, like these other socialist writers of the progressive era, understood that journalism and fiction could be used as political tools. Sinclair's critique of American capitalism has much in common with his fellow socialists in the pre–World War I period.

Questions for Reading, Discussion, and Writing

1. (a) Discuss *The Jungle* as an indictment of wage slavery and compare it to other works of literature that attack antebellum slavery (e.g., Harriet Beecher Stowe's *Uncle Tom's Cabin*).

    (b) Discuss Sinclair's portrait of industrial capitalism in *The Jungle*. Look at the connection between the meat-packing industry and the other institutions represented in the novel. Look at the function of money and the false sense of security it promises. Look at Jurgis's response to hardship: "I will work harder."

    (c) Discuss Sinclair's portrait of European immigrants in *The Jungle*. Discuss his portrait of the American city at the beginning of the twentieth century and compare it with other treatments of the American city in similar novels.

2. (a) Examine one or more of the major works of other American writers referred to as Muckrakers (especially Lincoln Steffens's *The Shame of the Cities* and Ida Tarbell's *History of the Standard Oil Company*). Compare these works with *The Jungle*. What common values and assumptions do all of these works share?

    (b) Explore Sinclair's connection with the radical writers who wrote for *The Masses* (1911–1917). Read Sinclair's novel *King Coal* (1917) and compare its treatment of the Colorado mine wars of 1913–1914 with Max Eastman's in "Class War in Colorado" (*The Masses*, June 1914) and John Reed's treatment of the famous Patterson, New Jersey, textile strike in "War in Patterson" (*The Masses*, June 1913).

Bibliography

Especially helpful are the chapters on *The Jungle* in the following critical works:

Harris, Leon. *Upton Sinclair: American Rebel.* New York: Crowell, 1975.

Herms, Dieter, ed. *Upton Sinclair: Literature and Social Reform.* Frankfurt: Peter Lang, 1990.

Mookerjee, R. N. *Art for Social Justice: The Major Novels of Upton Sinclair.* Metuchen, NJ: Scarecrow, 1988.

Scott, Ivan. *Upton Sinclair, The Forgotten Socialist.* Lewiston, NY: Mellen, 1997.

Henry Adams (1838–1918)

Contributing Editor: Earl N. Harbert

Classroom Issues and Strategies

Explain Henry Adams's point of view as an outsider even when he writes about his own life. Note also his allusive, old-fashioned prose style, which is so different from that of (for example) Hemingway. Discuss Adams's lack of dependence on the economic rewards that his writings might bring and his unusual authorial attitudes. Also important is an extended exploration of the meaning and usefulness of his key symbols.

In teaching Henry Adams, especially the entries included in *The Heath Anthology*, I emphasize the following five themes:

1. Although born into a tradition of elite political, social, and intellectual leadership, Henry Adams remained essentially an observer rather than a participant in the robust American life of the 1860–1912 period. Writing in all literary forms, his point of view is that of an outsider—even when he tells about his own life (as the third-person narration in the *Education* demonstrates).

2. A writer by choice, tradition, and careful training, Adams's economic independence allowed him always to do the work of his choice: namely, to pursue a broadly cultural and historical study of the past and present (represented in the selections from *Chartres* and the *Education*).

3. As a pioneer in intellectual history as well as an interested student of science, Henry Adams sought to measure the European twelfth century against the American late nineteenth and early twentieth century. His method concentrated on the vital principles that characterized both eras. Thus, the medieval virgin (religion) appears first in *Chartres* and later is compared and contrasted with the modern dynamo (the force of electric power), when the conjunction becomes explicit in Chapter 25 of the *Education*. Adams uses the same symbolic progression to suggest the path of his personal intellectual voyage to increased understanding.

4. Adams's poem defines this intellectual journey in a more personal and perhaps a more compelling form. In particular, it reveals the deference (or even skepticism) that prevents the author from accepting simplistic judgments on history, religion, and other topics that he discusses.

5. At its best, the thought and writing of Henry Adams resist what he finds to be the narrow parochialism of American experience. Building on this belief, Adams attempts to move his readers toward some larger understanding—even at some artistic cost in didacticism and possible misinterpretation.

As a practical minimum preparation for any instructor, and as the next step for any interested student, I recommend a careful reading of the entire *The Education of Henry Adams*, edited by Ernest Samuels.

Major Themes, Historical Perspectives, Personal Issues

1. Henry Adams's life of privilege, born into a family that had achieved three generations of elite political and intellectual leadership
2. Henry Adams's displacement from that role in the United States from 1860 to 1918
3. Henry Adams's lifelong concern with finding in history (human experience) some key to understanding and useful application
4. Henry Adams's reclusive, "anti-confessional" pose as author (versus moderns and postmodern)

Significant Form, Style, or Artistic Conventions

Consider the definitions of *autobiography* and *biography* as matters of traditional literary form, but modified significantly in Henry Adams's work.

Original Audience

I raise the question of the initial audience for Adams's private printings of both works. Thus, questions of interpretation become relative to considerations of audience.

Developments in Women's Writing

Julia A. J. Foote (1823–1900)

Contributing Editor: William L. Andrews

Classroom Issues and Strategies

Julia Foote's intensely religious view of life often contrasts with the secularism of today's students. Students often wonder whether she was self-deceived in thinking herself authorized by the Holy Spirit to assert her will over those of the general mass of people in her church. It is important, therefore, to emphasize the relationship of Foote's religious worldview to her feminism. She supports her feminism by citing biblical precedent.

Major Themes, Historical Perspectives, Personal Issues

Major themes include Foote's search for her authentic self and the black woman's search for power and voice in male-dominated religious institutions.

Significant Form, Style, or Artistic Conventions

How does Foote turn a straightforward narrative of her life into an argument for Christianity, feminism, and holiness?

Original Audience

I stress to the students that Foote is addressing someone in particular—ask them how they can identify who this is.

Comparisons, Contrasts, Connections

Interesting comparisons can be made with slave narrators like Frederick Douglass since Foote and Douglass are both concerned with affirming their sense of a spirit within that owes its allegiance only to transcendent ideals.

Bibliography

Andrews, William L., ed. *Sisters of the Spirit: Three Black Women's Autobiographies of the Nineteenth Century.* Bloomington: Indiana UP, 1986. Discusses and annotates Foote's entire autobiography.

Louisa May Alcott (1832–1888)

Contributing Editor: Cynthia Butos

Classroom Issues and Strategies

Students' understanding of the story may benefit from a review of the relevant material found in *The Heath Anthology* in the introduction to "Early Nineteenth Century: 1800–1865." Sections on "The Debates over Racism and Slavery" and "The Debate over Women's 'Sphere'" are particularly helpful.

Depending upon students' experience with reading nineteenth-century Civil War fiction, they may not be aware of the more radical undercurrents found in Alcott's racial stereotyping and in Faith's explicit sexual attraction to Robert in the beginning of the story. A number of critics have pointed to Alcott's characterization of Robert both as a (white) man and a (black) slave. When Faith sees him as a white man, she is attracted to him. But when Robert reminds her that he was a slave, either by addressing her as his mistress or by his melancholy and vengeful moods, her reaction to him varies from a nurse/maternal figure to a mistress who tells him what to do.

The ending of the story may also pose a problem for students who are not accustomed to nineteenth-century sentimental fiction. The utopian conclusion is especially jarring in light of the more gothic elements in the story, and some readers are put off by it. Students should understand that although the Civil War allowed greater freedom for women writers to deal with radical subjects such as interracial attraction (especially a white woman's attraction to a black man) and incestuous relationships, limits existed. By not having Robert kill his brother, even in battle, and by having Robert die as a result of bravery in battle, Alcott ultimately ends the tale within the boundaries for abolitionist fiction.

Major Themes, Historical Perspectives, Personal Issues

As an abolitionist story, the message is clear: slavery is wrong. But like other writers before her (Thomas Jefferson in *Notes on the State of Virginia* and Harriet Beecher Stowe in *Uncle Tom's Cabin*), Alcott emphasizes that slavery harmed not only those enslaved but also those who enslaved.

A feminist message also underpins the story. Faith renames "Bob" Robert, and Robert ultimately takes *Dane* as his surname, reversing the conventional gender role. The issue of Faith's control over the brothers' situation is also noteworthy. Faith is able to intercede in the brothers' quarrel by using her "woman's voice," a predominant theme in mid-nineteenth-century women's fiction. When Robert is poised to strangle his unconscious brother, Alcott boldly claims her woman's voice: "one weapon I possessed,—a tongue,—often a woman's best defence; and sympathy, stronger than fear, gave me power to use it." In fact, Faith's "voice," her power of reasoning tempered with sympathy, persuades Robert to allow his brother to live. As with other Alcott characters, notably Jo March in *Little Women,* Robert must learn to control his baser passions, to rise above what slavery has taught him. He must learn what women know: That through the goodness of "heart," of spirit, he can earn redemption and ultimately be reunited with Lucy.

Significant Form, Style, or Artistic Conventions

This story moves between conventions of sentimental and gothic fiction. Following the sentimental genre, "My Contraband" encourages the reader "to feel right" when Faith comforts Robert about Lucy and convinces him not to kill his brother and when Alcott concludes with a description of Robert's heroic actions that earn him a place in heaven with Lucy and God. In the gothic tradition, however, Alcott includes the forbidden sexual undertones in Faith's attraction to Robert, shocks the reader when Robert throws off his shirt to show Faith his lash marks, and builds suspense around the brothers' incestuous relationship.

Original Audience

Over Alcott's objections, the story was originally published as "The Brothers" at the insistence of James Field, editor of the *Atlantic Monthly.* Alcott later titled it "My Contraband; or the Brothers," her preferred title, when it was reprinted in 1869. The two titles obviously highlight different aspects of the story: "The Brothers" immediately focuses attention on the relationship between Robert and Ned while "My Contraband" emphasizes the first-person narrative of Faith and her role in the brothers' relationship. Alcott's insistence on highlighting Faith's importance is in keeping with her underlying feminist theme.

Audience expectations and forbearance quickly evolved during the Civil War. Alcott's story "M.L." was rejected for publication in the *Atlantic* in 1860 because, Alcott wrote in her journal, "it is anti-slavery and the dear South must not be offended." What Alcott doesn't mention is that "M.L." was probably the first abolitionist tale to allow a white woman to marry an ex-slave even after learning of his racial background. However, only three years later, in 1863, shortly after the publication of "My Contraband," the *Atlantic Monthly* published the controversial "M.L."

Comparisons, Contrasts, and Conventions

Alcott's abolitionist stories follow many of the conventions used by other writers of the time. Alcott admired Harriet Beecher Stowe's work, and the two writers' work share themes about family, "heart," and a woman's ability to enact change by helping others to act morally. Since slavery was clearly an immoral practice to Alcott, she could enter the political dialogue, like Stowe before her, while writing about women's concerns of morality.

Robert's story also contains many of the elements found in slave narratives: incestuous relationships, horrific treatment of slaves, and separation of slave families.

Harriet Prescott Spofford (1835–1921)

Contributing Editor: Thelma Shinn Richard

Classroom Issues and Strategies

Students need to develop an appreciation for "domestic imagery"—symbols and images drawn from female experience but used to represent universal values. In addition, they also should become aware of the transitional elements from romance to realism evident in the writings of Spofford and her contemporaries.

To address these issues, show contemporary appreciation of Spofford in better-known authors (such as Dickinson and Whittier). Help students discern the *patterns* of imagery so that they do not dismiss individual images as "popular" or "sentimental." Point out the metaphorical implications of the setting which, while realistic (with its historical roots in Spofford's family), is also part of the romantic tradition.

Major Themes, Historical Perspectives, Personal Issues

Major themes include:

> The female artist
> Humanity as animal versus spirit
> Music/art as communication
> Romance versus realism (particularly in defining *naturalism*)
> The forest in American literature
> Importance of popular culture (well-known songs)
> Preservation of family history (true incident)

By basing "Circumstance" on an incident in the life of her maternal great-grandmother, Spofford shifts time and place to enter Hawthorne's "neutral territory, . . . where the Actual and the Imaginary may meet." While Hawthorne turns back two centuries to the suggestion of a historical event in *The Scarlet Letter*, however, Spofford chooses a closer time and a specific personal/historical moment. In doing so, she reflects the female consciousness that personal events—events recorded orally and handed down from mother to daughter—define human history perhaps more accurately than official records. In these records she finds a circumstance that can embody female and human experience in finite and infinite terms.

Although *circumstance* refers to essential and environmental conditions in which we find ourselves, the singular form specifically refers, according to *Webster's New Collegiate Dictionary*, to "a piece of evidence that indicates the probability or improbability of an event." While the existence of God cannot be proved, Spofford can present a "circumstance" that indicates for her its probability. And so she has in this story. The religious theme is all the more powerful because it is couched in the "Actual" and discovered by a woman not given to the "Imaginary." Spofford reveals Hawthorne's "neutral territory" to be the world in which we live, and it is in her journey through this world that the narrator must find evidence of the omnipresence of God.

Significant Form, Style, or Artistic Conventions

Spofford anticipates the styles and themes of the realists, even of the naturalists who will surround her later writing career. Already in this 1860 story, her narrator must abandon her romantic notions of nature ("If all the silent powers of the forest did not conspire to help her!") and face that "the dark, hollow night rose indifferently over her." At the same time, she has recognized the naturalistic corollary to nature's indifference in humanity's animal antecedents. Impending death by a "living lump of appetites" forces her to acknowledge the self-loathing as the beast "known by the strength of our lower natures let loose." The primitive cannibalism of humanity seems to be reflected in her fear of becoming a part of the beast again: "the base, cursed thing howls with us forever through the forest." Such pessimistic reflections indeed bring misery, as they will to later writers. "The Open Boat" finds Stephen Crane's correspondent (also reflecting a true incident in Crane's own life) similarly trapped in nature and discovering its indifference to him.

Original Audience

Consider the following:

1. The time period during which the story was written and the New England setting
2. The fact that the story was first published in a periodical
3. The Puritan background of Spofford's contemporary audience
4. The familiarity of the audience with the popular music mentioned

Comparisons, Contrasts, Connections

Useful comparisons may be made with the following works:

> Emily Dickinson, "Twas like a maelstrom"
> Nathaniel Hawthorne, "Young Goodman Brown"
> Stephen Crane, "The Open Boat"

Questions for Reading, Discussion, and Writing

1. What songs do *you* know that she might be singing in each category? Where did you learn these songs? From whom?
2. (a) Find parallels in your experience to the story, its themes and particulars (consider sharing family stories).
   (b) Examine the roots of a genre (e.g., oral roots of fiction).
   (c) Interpret one art through another (art and music here).
   (d) Also try traditional thematic and stylistic approaches and comparisons with other stories.

Bibliography

Fetterley, Judith. *Provisions.* Bloomington: Indiana UP, 1985.

Halbeisen, Elizabeth K. *Harriet Prescott Spofford: A Romantic Survival.* Philadelphia: U of Pennsylvania P, 1935.

Marshall, Ian. "Literary and Metaphoric Harmony with Nature: Ecofeminism in Harriet Prescott Spofford's 'Circumstance.'" *Modern Literary Studies,* 23:2 (Spring 1993): 48ff.

Solomon, Barbara H., ed. *Rediscoveries: American Short Stories by Women, 1832–1916.* New York: Penguin, 1994.

Constance Fenimore Woolson (1840–1894)

Contributing Editor: Sharon L. Dean

Classroom Issues and Strategies

Students new to literary study sometimes have difficulty hearing the voice of the narrator in "'Miss Grief.'" To help them with this, I read the first few paragraphs aloud and ask how reliable this first-person narrator is. I then ask them to find places in the text where he shows sympathy for Miss Grief or where he helps her with her career and to assess whether or not he has done enough. I point out that his voice postdates his marriage to Ethelind Abercrombie and ask what that marriage tells us about his character.

Students are also split on whether or not Miss Grief is a good writer. Some recall their own experiences in writing classes and ask if she is someone who refuses to listen to constructive criticism. Putting this question in the context of the narrator's inability to revise the physician out of Miss Grief's story enables them to see that, the quality of Miss Grief's writing aside, Woolson is raising questions about what it means to write in a different voice. When Woolson references this physician as an "especial figure in the carpet" who cannot be taken out "unless you unravel the whole," she is using a phrase that Henry James later picks up as the title for his 1896 short story, "The Figure in the Carpet."

Major Themes, Historical Perspective, Personal Issues

Because Woolson's manuscripts have been lost, no composition dates exist for her stories, but both "'Miss Grief'" and the story she published just before it, "The South Devil" (*Atlantic Monthly*, February 1880), were likely written just after the death of her mother in February 1879. This would explain the sense of loneliness and rootlessness embedded in these stories and the sense that one way of combating these feelings is to focus on creating art. Other avenues for understanding the story would be in light of Woolson's own habits of travel, of the rising tendency of American artists to live abroad, and of what a few scholars believe is Woolson's lesbian theme.

Cheryl Torsney has read "'Miss Grief'" in the light of Woolson's own difficulty with her publishers James Osgood and the Appletons, who at this point in her career were failing to market her books and to follow through with tacit publishing agreements and even with payment. Other scholars, such as Leon Edel, have seen in the story Woolson's fear that Henry James might reject her writing the way the narrator rejects Miss Grief's. We should remember, however, that Woolson wrote this story before she met James and that she had, as Torsney has shown, other literary father figures in people like poet E. C. Stedman, novelist and critic William Dean Howells, and even in her great-uncle James Fenimore Cooper, whose middle name she shared and conspicuously displayed as a way of marketing her work. Stedman helped her in her negotiations with her publishers and James supported her both by valuing their literary friendship and by including her in his profiles of writers collected in *Partial Portraits* (1887). But to have one's work promoted and to be treated fairly by publishers and critics is also to be placed under an obligation to them. Cheryl Torsney has shown that Woolson felt pressured by this sense of obligation to her last publisher, Harper and Brothers. In the light of this sense of obligation that she developed later in her career, one could read "'Miss Grief'" as a commentary on her own fears that success might bring so much pressure that she could, like the narrator, sell her integrity for fame.

Significant Form, Style, or Artistic Conventions

One of the most striking things about "'Miss Grief'" in relation to Woolson's other stories is its lack of physical setting. Because she published it in May 1880, just six months after she sailed for Europe, we can explain this absence in terms of her lack of familiarity with the European landscape. The story is also one of the few she wrote from a first-person male point of view. On the other hand, it possesses the rich allusiveness that Woolson drew on in all her work. Literary, biblical, and mythological references abound. Pointing out the footnote references to these and having students discuss their significance should give them further insight into the complexities and ambiguities of the text.

Original Audience

When Woolson published "'Miss Grief'" in 1880, she had been publishing successfully for a decade in such literary magazines as *Lippincott's, Harper's New Monthly Magazine, Harper's Bazar, Appleton's Journal,* and the premier magazine of the day, the *Atlantic Monthly.* At this period in her career, she also began to publish novels, first in serial form and then in book form. One measure of her popularity is that her first novel, *Anne* (1883), sold over 50,000 copies. Although her later novels did not replicate this success, throughout her lifetime she remained a popular writer and gained increasing respect from critics and reviewers of her day.

Comparisons, Contrasts, Connections

Students can draw connections between "'Miss Grief'" and any work they may have encountered that addresses issues about artists or the nature of art or about women's roles. Possibilities include James's "The Real Thing" and "The Aspern Papers," Gilman's "The Yellow Wall-paper," and Wharton's "The Touchstone." They could also pursue James's possible response to his relationship with Woolson in "The Beast in the Jungle."

Questions for Reading, Discussion, and Writing

1. I have used a number of questions to open discussion of "'Miss Grief'":
    (a) Why is Miss Grief so persistent? How does the narrator feel about this? How do we feel?
    (b) What is Miss Grief's position in life?
    (c) What is Serena's role? How do you explain the name change? (A student once pointed out to me that *Serena* was a generic name for a servant, such as *the Irish Biddy*.)
    (d) What does this story suggest about the nature of art? About women who strive to become artists?
    (e) What does the narrator learn/fail to learn from Miss Grief? Could Miss Grief be a figment of his imagination? If so, what would she represent?
2. The range of Woolson's writing offers numerous avenues for study. Students who want to look at "'Miss Grief'" in relation to other work by Woolson will find comparisons in "The Street of the Hyacinth," "At the Château of Corinne," and "In Sloane Street." Those wishing to look at other stories by Woolson in relationship to other writers could do valuable studies of "The Lady of Little Fishing" and Harte's "The Luck of Roaring Camp," "Castle Nowhere," and Cooper's *The Deerslayer* or Hawthorne's "Rappacinni's Daughter," "Sister St. Luke" and Freeman's "A New England Nun," "The Front Yard" and Wharton's "Mrs. Manstey's View," or "A Transplanted Boy" and James's "The Pupil." A less academic writing assignment might ask students to chronicle their own struggles with being accepted as artists or writers.

Bibliography

Useful background on nineteenth-century travel can be found in William W. Stowe, *Going Abroad: European Travel in Nineteenth-Century American Culture* (Princeton: Princeton UP, 1994). Two articles on Woolson and other writers are Caroline Gebhard's "Constance Fenimore Woolson Rewrites Bret

Harte: The Sexual Politics of Intertextuality," *Critical Essays on Constance Fenimore Woolson*, ed. Cheryl B. Torsney; and Linda Grasso's "'Thwarted Life, Mighty Hunger, Unfinished Work': The Legacy of Nineteenth-Century Women Writing in America," *American Transcendental Quarterly* 8 (June 1994): 97–118 (on Woolson and Mary Wilkins Freeman).

Fred Kaplan's James biography *Henry James: The Imagination of Genius* (New York: Morrow, 1992) and Lyndall Gordon's *A Private Life of Henry James* (New York: Norton, 1998) both present a more sympathetic view of Woolson than does Leon Edel's biography of James. The *Dictionary of Literary Biography* (1982) includes an entry on Woolson and another in its volume titled *American Women Prose Writers 1870–1920* (2000). The Constance Fenimore Woolson Society has a full bibliography on its website at <www.gvsu.edu/woolson/>.

For a nonacademic view, see Joan Weimer's use of Woolson in her memoir of recovering from back surgery, *Back Talk: Teaching Lost Selves to Speak* (New York: Random, 1994).

Sarah Orne Jewett (1849–1909)

Contributing Editor: Elizabeth Ammons

Classroom Issues and Strategies

I've encountered some problems teaching Jewett's *Country of the Pointed Firs* because at first it seems dull to students, but they love "A White Heron" (hereafter WH), and I'm confident that they will also respond enthusiastically to "Martha's Lady." (There is, by the way, a film of WH that many people find excellent.)

Students often don't like the ending of WH (the author's intrusion) and are baffled by it; they wonder about Sylvia's mother—what's Jewett saying about her?—and about why the girl's grandmother sides with the man. Also they wonder why the bird is male.

Major Themes, Historical Perspectives, Personal Issues

Both of these stories are characteristic of Jewett, not only in focusing on women but also in focusing on women-centered or women-dominated space, geographic and psychic. The existence and meaning of such space probably identify the most basic theme in Jewett. Female-defined reality is threatened but then reaffirmed, at least for the present, in WH, in which the intrusion of a man from the city into the grandmother/cow/girl-controlled rural space upsets the daily harmony, and potentially the life-balance itself, of nature.

Historically these stories explore the strength and depth of female bonding at a time when same-sex relationships between women in western culture were being redefined by sexologists such as Freud and Havelock Ellis as pathological and deviant. Jewett recognizes in WH the threat posed to same-sex female bonding by the allure of heterosexuality in the person of the hunter, who is sexy and deals in violence and death: If Sylvia falls for him, she will be participating, symbolically, in her own death (the killing and stuffing of the heron).

Sororal, filial, maternal, erotic: Bonds between women in Jewett's work no doubt reflect her own feelings and those of women close to her. While she numbered men among her friends and associates, her closest, most intimate friends were women. Debate about whether to call Jewett a lesbian writer exists because the term was not one Jewett would have used; our highly sexualized twentieth-century view of same-sex romantic and erotic attachment may very well not be a historically accurate way to describe Jewett's world, fictive or biographical, so labels need to be carefully thought about. Whatever terminology is used, though, the central, deep, recurrent theme in Jewett's work is love between women.

Also, race is an important topic in these two stories, even though—or especially because—it is not explicitly acknowledged. In WH, the overdetermination of whiteness—the bird, the cow's milk, the emphatically pale skin of Sylvie—in combination with the tale's rejection of city/industrial life points to Jewett's creating a tale about protecting and preserving whiteness itself (the bird) from threatened attack (the hunter).

Some good questions to consider in teaching both of these stories are: How do these fictions inscribe whiteness as a racial category? How are they about white culture? White people? White anxieties? White dominance?

Significant Form, Style, or Artistic Conventions

Certainly WH plays with masculine form, reproducing in its structure the build to a high climax (literally the tippy-top of a tree) that both traditional, white, Western dramatic structure (exposition/conflict/complication/climax/resolution) and, it can be argued, male-dominated heterosexual relations inscribe. Then, at the end of WH, Jewett disrupts and undoes this tight, linear pattern with a flossy, chatty final paragraph so exaggeratedly "feminine" in character as to call attention to itself. One question often asked by students is: Why does the narrative voice switch like this in the end? One answer is that, just as Sylvia's decision thwarts the hunter, the narrative switch at the end deliberately deconstructs the traditional inherited masculine narrative pattern of climax-oriented fiction grounded in aggression and conflict that has preceded.

Original Audience

Jewett was widely read and admired in the late nineteenth century, but until recently she has been dismissed in the academy as minor, regional, slight. Her recent revival reflects in large part the increasing numbers and strength of women in the profession of professor and scholar. Not of interest (threatening?) to a predominantly white, male, heterosexual group of critics and scholars, Jewett is now finding an increasingly large audience as women gain power within the system of higher education. That is, Jewett is the beneficiary of a new group of people being able to define what is "interesting" and "important." Thus Jewett, when we ponder the question of audience, vividly raises highly political issues: Who defines what is "good" and worth studying? How do the politics of gender and sexual orientation shape the politics of the classroom without their ever even being acknowledged? What writers and kinds of writers are currently being excluded or denigrated because of the composition of the profession of professor?

Comparisons, Contrasts, Connections

Jewett is often compared quite productively with Mary Wilkins Freeman, a fellow New England writer. Jewett admired Harriet Beecher Stowe's New England writing and therefore is fruitfully thought of in conjunction with Stowe. Since Willa Cather was encouraged by Jewett to write full time and, particularly, on the topic of women's relationships with each other, Cather's work is very interesting to compare and contrast with Jewett's. As a regionalist—a writer engaged in trying to capture in detail and with great accuracy and sensitivity life as it was experienced in a particular region rather than attempting to fill in a huge and more diffuse canvas, Jewett compares illuminatingly with other regionalists, especially across regions: Kate Chopin and Alice Dunbar-Nelson focusing on New Orleans; Hamlin Garland picturing the northern Midwest; Abraham Cahan on the Lower East Side in New York.

Questions for Reading, Discussion, and Writing

1. WH: Who/what does the heron symbolize? Why is the cow in the story? Why does it matter that Sylvia is nine years old? Why is the heron *white*?

2. These two stories together and individually lend themselves well to traditional kinds of textual analysis of symbols, imagery, characterization, authorial point of view, and so forth: for example, animal imagery and symbolism in either or both; nature as a character in either or both; comparing the portraits of old women in the two stories.

Bibliography

Two sources for essays are *Critical Essays on Sarah Orne Jewett* (Boston: Hall, 1984) and *The Colby Library Quarterly: Special Issue on Jewett* (March 1986). The two stories included in the *Heath Anthology* are discussed from various points of view in a number of excellent essays in these two volumes. An important book-length study is Marilyn Sanders Mobley's *Folk Roots and Mythic Wings in Sarah Orne Jewett and Toni Morrison* (1991). Also *New Essays on The Country of the Pointed Firs,* ed. June Howard, contains valuable essays that can be applied to these two stories.

Mary E. Wilkins Freeman (1852–1930)

Contributing Editors: Leah Blatt Glasser and Sandra A. Zagarell

Classroom Issues and Strategies

The best strategy in approaching Mary Wilkins Freeman's work is to provide a full context for both her life and period and to select particularly paradoxical passages for class discussion. Discuss the endings of her stories, which sometimes disappoint or surprise students. Have students consider possible revisions of these endings and then discuss why Freeman might have chosen to conclude as she did.

Students may wish to consider the title of "The Revolt of 'Mother'" and its implications. What is the nature of Sarah's "revolt"? Why does Freeman put *mother* in quotation marks?

Focus on Sarah Penn's determination to have the art of her domestic work recognized and valued. Sarah watches her husband build a new barn for the animals in place of a promised and much needed new home. Study closely the passages that capture the pleasure Sarah takes in claiming the barn as a space for her ingenuity and artistic vision. Ask students to consider what light Freeman sheds here on the domestic realm, both its limitations and its possibilities.

Students appreciate discussion of the relationship between Sarah's construction of a decent work environment in the form of a fine kitchen and Freeman's construction of the story. Just as Sarah struggles to be heard, Freeman fought to be taken seriously as a writer. To what extent does Sarah's rebellion mirror Freeman's reconstruction of the domestic arena in her fiction? Converting the home into a battlefield for Sarah's assertion of her needs, Freeman redefines *bravery* in women's terms. Focus on Sarah's articulation of her hardships and demands for recognition when she attempts to "talk plain" to her husband. Students will enjoy reading this scene out loud. A close study of Freeman's language will help students recognize her insightful analysis of communication in the context of gender. When Sarah turns her "talk" into action, her husband must finally hear and understand the meaning of her words.

The ambiguous ending of the story is important to analyze. Has Sarah gained power within the marital realm, and if so, what sort of power is this, and what are its implications and limitations?

The energy of Sarah's rebellion reflects the pleasure Freeman took in transforming her own mother's subservience into revolt and creating the home her mother never had. Students may be interested to know that Freeman's father, Warren Wilkins, gave up his plan of building the house Eleanor, Freeman's mother, had hoped for. Instead, the family moved in 1877 into the home in which Eleanor was to serve as hired housekeeper. Freeman's mother was thus "deprived of the very things which made a woman proud, her own kitchen, furniture, family china; and she had lost the one place in which it was acceptable for her to be powerful: her home" (Clark 177).

Freeman's critique of "Revolt of 'Mother'" in the *Saturday Evening Post* in 1917, long after the publication of the story, fuels lively discussion. In the following excerpt, Freeman disparages her story for its lack of realism:

> In the first place all fiction ought to be true and "The Revolt of 'Mother'" is not true. . . . There never was in New England a woman like Mother. If there had been she certainly would have lacked the nerve. She would also have lacked the imagination. New England women of that period coincided with their husbands in thinking that the sources of wealth should be better housed than the consumers.

What does Freeman's comment suggest about her understanding of the effects of nineteenth-century female ideology?

"A New England Nun" provides an excellent instance of Freeman's ambiguity. Ask students to identify the tone and implications of the story's early, almost literal framing of Louisa Ellis at her sewing, seated in her sitting-room window, within the context of the end of the day's work for the laborers in the fields outside and the "general stir arising over everything for the mere sake of subsistence—a premonition of rest and hush and night." Focus on passages that depict Louisa's domestic activities and her attitudes toward them with an eye toward teasing out both the potential divergences between the narrator's perspective on Louisa's life and her own and the narrator's sympathetic conveying of Louisa's attitudes toward her domestic life and her ambivalence about marriage. Students are generally enthusiastic about discussing the implication of Caesar, the once-ferocious dog Louisa has kept chained up for fourteen years, which Joe Daggart threatens to free, and of the pet bird upset by Joe's masculine presence. A challenge in such discussions is to get students to acknowledge the obvious psychological connotations of these animals' presence yet resist pegging Louisa's edginess about an intimate relationship with Joe as a global judgment of her. Much of the artistry of "A New England Nun" lies in its complicated representation of Louisa's "path" as "narrow" yet also fulfilling, and its acknowledgment of Louisa's physical and emotional discomfort with Joe can be seen as representing a response that is viable on her part. Moreover, it's important to get students to view her discomfort in the context of the narrative's emphasis on the many aspects of her autonomy, which Louisa would have to relinquish in marrying Joe. Close attention to the story's final sentences will help keep before students the irresolvable irreconcilability of the choices Louisa is faced with, the gains and losses of the one she makes, and the doubleness of the story's projected attitude toward all of this.

Once students see the extraordinary complexity of the narrative, it would be fruitful to invite them to consider it in the context of its initial appearance in Harper's *Bazar*, a magazine addressed to urban or urban-identified women of the middle classes; its banner proclaimed its commitment to "fashion, pleasure, and instruction." The 7 May 1887 issue—in which "A New England Nun" appeared—followed the magazine's typical format, featuring engravings of young women in the height of fashion on the cover and containing patterns for such consumables as lace as well as fiction, essays, and artwork treating contemporary subjects and a back section devoted to advertisements for skin creams, corsets, cocoa, and other consumer goods—even for personal shoppers. The world the *Bazar* reflects, in other words, is contemporary and cosmopolitan and emphatically consumerist. The rural New England life Freeman's story depicts appears to offer a stark contrast to it. What, students might consider, would the appeal of Freeman's story have been to the *Bazar's* readers? If you have access to numbers of the *Bazar* from the era, students will find it fascinating to pursue such questions by looking at the magazine carefully, paying special attention to the range of attitudes toward women it exhibits.

Freeman's unhappy marriage to Dr. Charles Freeman is interesting to consider in relation to her depictions of the struggles for female autonomy both within and outside marriage. In a letter to a newly married friend, Harriet Randolph Hyatt Mayor, she had written, "I shall find the old you. It will never be lost. I know how you feel . . . I am to be married myself before long. . . .

If *you* don't see the old *me*, I shall run *until I find her*" (Kendrick 205). Unfortunately, Freeman was forced to confine the "old me" until her husband's alcoholism and abusive behavior finally ended in his being committed to the New Jersey State Hospital and her separation from him.

Major Themes, Historical Perspectives, Personal Issues

The major themes of Freeman's work illuminate aspects of her life. Mary Wilkins Freeman's words to describe the feeling of receiving her first acceptance and check for a short story provide an interesting context: "I felt my wings spring from my shoulders, capable of flight, and I flew home" (*New York Times*, April 1926). Her statement characterizes the dilemma this remarkable turn-of-the-century New England writer faced, the paradox that she expressed in almost all of her work. Feeling "capable of flight" because of the power of her capacity as a writer, Freeman nevertheless could only fly "home." Most striking in her life and work is the haunting echo of two inner voices: one voice that cries out for rebellious flight, another voice that clings to the safety of home. The heroines of Freeman's short stories, even as they rebel, struggle with this conflict. Students may compare the heroines of "A New England Nun" and "The Revolt of 'Mother,'" listening for the ways in which Freeman invests the women with power and yet simultaneously limits their power, bringing their rebellious "flights" to what Freeman considered "home"—the realities of nineteenth-century New England. What do these heroines suggest about the options of marriage and "spinsterhood" in the nineteenth century?

It is important to explore her depiction of relationships between women, her focus on the role of work in women's lives, the way in which she explores the psychology of rebellion as characters rebel, submit, or face the consequences of their rebellion. Of particular interest in offering a biographical context is the intensity of Freeman's relationship with Mary Wales, with whom she lived for twenty-five years. Her stories reflect a great understanding of female friendships.

Significant Form, Style, or Artistic Conventions

Freeman has often been categorized as a local colorist, a New England writer of the post–Civil War period whose primary talent lay in depicting the peculiarities of her region. She offers a vivid sense of New England life; at the same time, her work has an intensely psychological focus and is especially illuminating about women's conflicts during her era. Her use of dialect may be compared with Mark Twain's as she manages to bring us the voices she knew with fine precision.

Original Audience

Freeman published in magazines for women readers such as Harper's *Bazar* and the family magazine *Harper's Monthly*. She was influenced at times by her editors' emphasis on propriety and their attention to codes governing women's conduct, and endings like that of "The Revolt of 'Mother'" couch rebellious content in acceptable domestic scenes. Many stories, including "A New England Nun," reflect on the complicated relationship between the rural life her fiction portrayed and the metropolitanism of the venues in which her work appeared.

Comparisons, Contrasts, Connections

It is fruitful to compare Freeman with male peers such as Mark Twain, Henry James, and William Dean Howells. Her capacity for psychological portrait compares well with James, and many of her heroines may be compared with the heroines in James's short fiction. She participated in a project with James and Howells, a collaborative novel entitled *The Whole Family: A Novel by Twelve Authors* (Harper, 1908). Her chapter in this novel should be compared with the chapters by James and Howells. Freeman enraged her male counterparts when she transformed the figure of "the old maid" as conceived by Howells in his first chapter into a boldly sensual and liberated single woman in her chapter entitled "The Old Maid Aunt." Twain's use of dialogue and humor may also be explored in relation to Freeman's. Finally, she should be compared with other American women writers at the turn of the century (particularly Sarah Orne Jewett, Charlotte Perkins Gilman, Edith Wharton, Willa Cather).

Questions for Reading, Discussion, and Writing

1. (a) Study the role of work in each story in relation to the development of Freeman's heroines.
   (b) Analyze the conclusions of "A New England Nun" and "The Revolt of 'Mother.'" What seems paradoxical or unexpected? How do these conclusions relate to earlier stages of revolt in each story?
   (c) Analyze unmarried and married life in "A New England Nun" and "The Revolt of 'Mother.'" To what extent to these heroines both rebel and conform to the strictures of nineteenth-century expectations for women?
2. Students enjoy focusing on the development of Freeman's heroines, their contradictions and strengths. Consider a paper on the attitudes toward women the story suggests and its influence on the heroine's actions. Ask students to study a particular scene or set of images (Sarah Penn's work in her house: "She was an artist"; Louisa's domestic pursuits in "A New

England Nun." Does Freeman's work suggest anything about her sense of the artist?).

Bibliography

The most recent literary biography on Freeman is *In a Closet Hidden: The Life and Work of Mary E. Wilkins Freeman* by Leah B. Glasser (Amherst: U of Massachusetts P, 1996), a feminist study that demonstrates the way in which Freeman's life and fiction are interwoven and suggests her lifelong struggle between autonomy and rebellion.

The most recently published selection of Freeman's stories is *Mary Wilkins Freeman Reader*, ed. Mary R. Reichardt (Lincoln: U of Nebraska P, 1997).

A useful and brief discussion of Freeman's life and work is "Profile: Mary E. Wilkins Freeman" by Leah B. Glasser in *Legacy: A Journal of Nineteenth Century American Women Writers* 4 (Spring 1987).

Useful biographical material can also be gleaned from *The Infant Sphinx: Collected Letters of Mary E. Wilkins Freeman*, intelligently edited and introduced by Brent L. Kendrick. Her letters, though cautious and unrevealing on the surface, hint at the intensity of her relationship with her childhood friend Mary Wales. Freeman lived with Wales for over twenty years, and it is likely that much of her focus on friendships between women was drawn from this relationship. The difficulties of her marriage are also apparent in many of her letters written during that trying period of her life. The numerous letters she wrote to her editors reveal Freeman's seriousness about her career.

The two earlier biographies on Freeman are useful, although somewhat outdated: Foster's *Mary E. Wilkins Freeman* and Westbrook's *Mary Wilkins Freeman*.

Interpretive studies of her work can be found in Clark's Afterword to *The Revolt of Mother and Other Stories*, Marjorie Pryse's Introduction and Afterword to *Selected Stories of Mary E. Wilkins Freeman*, and Leah B. Glasser's essays "Discovering Mary E. Wilkins Freeman" in *Between Women* and "The Stranger in the Mirror" in the *Massachusetts Review* (Summer 1984).

Pauline Elizabeth Hopkins (1859–1930)

Contributing Editor: Jane Campbell

Classroom Issues and Strategies

It is essential that students grasp the obstacles facing an African-American woman of Hopkins's day. Her ability to surmount cultural, racial, and gender barriers in order to write and publish fiction is extraordinary. Because most students will not have read *Contending Forces*, the instructor will need to review the novel, including its plot. The headnote and the contextual material at the beginning of each excerpt should augment understanding.

I recommend journal writing to give students an opportunity to consider how Hopkins does and does not seem relevant to our times or to their lives. Journals can also lead to fruitful comparisons with other works read so far in the course.

Students might work in small groups or pairs to raise questions about any barriers to understanding these excerpts. Some male students need coaxing to identify with the material. Such problems as students might raise may then be tackled by the class as a whole.

Major Themes, Historical Perspectives, Personal Issues

I emphasize lynching and Ku Klux Klan activities and stress that the Klan is still active all over the United States. I also discuss interracial bloodlines, voting disenfranchisement, job discrimination against African Americans, and color prejudice both during Hopkins's day and in contemporary times. Students who are not African American may be shocked or surprised by the historical particulars and contemporary examples of racism, Klan activities, and discrimination, but they also express gratitude about learning of these realities. Students of color, usually painfully cognizant of such issues, may be open to sharing their experiences, citing specific examples of racism in their community or on campus. The instructor also should stress Hopkins's emphasis on feminist issues such as rape, female bonding and empowerment, and women's collective political action.

It is essential that students grasp the obstacles facing an African-American woman of Hopkins's day. Hopkins's ability to transcend cultural, racial, and gender barriers in order to write fiction is extraordinary. I would also make sure that students understand that Hopkins is one of a handful of black women novelists who managed to surmount these obstacles but that scholars are still seeking to identify other undiscovered writers.

Significant Form, Style, or Artistic Conventions

Fitting Hopkins into the tradition of African-American writers involves discussion of the cultural/literary conventions of the time, e.g., the tragic mulatta and educated diction.

I also detail the primary conventions of women's romance, including a beautiful, talented, strong heroine, usually an orphan, who overcomes numerous obstacles and serves as a model for her audience; an emphasis on the pleasures of homemaking, love, and motherhood; villains seeking to compromise the heroine's virtue; and marriage as a joyous conclusion to the narrative. Hopkins, like her female contemporaries, chose the romance as an appropriate vehicle for appealing to a wide audience. By pointing out parallels between Hopkins's work and contemporary romance novels, such as Harlequins, and mainstream films, the instructor may show how Hopkins profitably mined this genre, interweaving politics and entertainment, thus raising the consciousness of a large audience.

Original Audience

Hopkins wrote to a mixed audience of African Americans and Caucasians. Her use of romance conventions demonstrates that most of her readers were women. Clearly, *Contending Forces* fosters positive images of African Americans while instructing the audience about the historical particulars of racism.

Comparisons, Contrasts, Connections

If students have read well-known contemporary African-American novels such as Alice Walker's *The Color Purple*, Toni Morrison's *Beloved*, or Maya Angelou's *I Know Why the Caged Bird Sings*, they will discover parallels. Pearl Cleage's *What Looks Like Crazy on an Ordinary Day* offers a contemporary version of the Clubwomen Movement. Novels such as Susanna Rowson's *Charlotte Temple* and Harriet Jacobs's *Incidents in the Life of a Slave Girl* might link Hopkins with earlier white and black authors concerned with similar issues and using the same literary mode to present them.

Working with Cultural Objects

Historically, light-skinned African Americans resulted primarily from the masters' legal right to rape their female slaves. Even among African Americans, prejudice toward light complexions has continued to exist since slavery, a legacy of the dominant white culture's preference for fair-skinned people.

Although admittedly diminishing within the black community in recent years, color prejudice remains pronounced among whites. Bleaching creams are products designed to lighten skin, and though more prevalent in Hopkins's time, they are still sold today. Photographs of advertisements promoting these products can be found at <http://www.prmuseum.com/kendrix/beauty.html #top>.

"The Sewing Circle" depicts a gathering of African-American women sewing garments for a church fair. An American folk art practiced in many communities, quilting has a particular history among African-American women. Examples of quilts can be found at <http://www.womenfolk.com/ historyofquilts/afam.htm>.

Questions for Reading, Discussion, and Writing

1. What did you learn from "The Sewing Circle" about African Americans during Hopkins's day? Are there any contemporary groups that correspond to such a gathering among women? What do women gain from such "female only" spaces?
2. What political issues emerge from "Luke Sawyer Speaks to the League"? How are these issues gendered?
3. Is either of these selections "dated"? How might the stories offered in these chapters be different if they were written today? What similar stories are still being told?
4. How does Hopkins fictionalize positive images of African Americans in these two selections?
5. How do you account for Hopkins's cultural references, such as her mention of Paderewski? Can you recall similar kinds of references in any other literature during her day?
6. What connections can you find between the two selections?
7. What expectations did you have when reading the titles for these two chapters? How were these expectations altered as you read the selections?
8. How do you interpret Mrs. Willis's assertion that "there is no such thing as an unmixed black on the American continent"? Why does she introduce this topic?
9. Define the terms *mulatto* and *quadroon*. Are questions of skin color still alive today, both within and beyond the African-American community? What are their origins?
10. How do you account for the resurgence of interest in early African-American women writers? Did these selections inspire you to read the entire novel? Explain why or why not.

Bibliography

Allen, Carol. *Black Women Intellectuals: Strategies of Nation, Family, and Neighborhood in the Works of Pauline Hopkins, Jessie Fauset, and Marita Bonner.* New York: Garland, 1998.

Campbell, Jane. "Female Paradigms in Frances Harper's *Iola Leroy* and Pauline Hopkins's *Contending Forces.*" *Mythic Black Fiction: The Transformation of History.* Knoxville: U of Tennessee P, 1986; rpt. 2003.

Carby, Hazel V. *Reconstructing Womanhood: The Emergence of the Afro-American Woman Novelist.* New York: Oxford UP, 1987.

Somerville, Siobhan B. "Inverting the Tragic Mulatta Tradition: Race and Homosexuality in Pauline Hopkins's Fiction." *Queering the Color Line: Race and the Invention of Homosexuality in American Culture.* Durham: Duke UP, 2000.

A Sheaf of Poetry by Late-Nineteenth-Century American Women

Contributing Editor: Paula Bennett

Classroom Issues and Strategies

With the exception of Emily Dickinson and, less dependably, Phillis Wheatley, undergraduate students are likely to know nothing about pre-twentieth-century American women poets. Their heads are filled, however, with a great many notions about nineteenth-century women generally: they were sexually and politically repressed, they were excessively "genteel," they put pantaloons around piano legs, and so forth. If students have read *Huckleberry Finn* somewhere along the way, they may also believe that the poetry these women wrote was sentimental, morbid, clichéd, and eminently not worth reading—unless one wanted a good laugh. When they encounter strong examples of nineteenth-century American women's writing, their first response is, therefore, surprise and their second (very often) anger. They want to know who these women were, what else they wrote, and why their poetry was erased. Male students are often embarrassed by the obvious sexism that went into this erasure, so it helps to note that excepting Whitman, male nineteenth-century poets have not fared much better. On the positive side, because this poetry is utterly new to them, students are very curious about it and open to a wide variety of thematic, formal, historical, theoretical, and biographical approaches. Teachers are probably best advised to take the approach or approaches most useful and comfortable for them and that best fit their overall course plans and objectives.

Major Themes, Historical Perspectives, Personal Issues

By the end of the nineteenth century, American women had experienced massive changes in subjectivity, freeing many of them, particularly those from the middle class, to enter the public domain as writers, doctors, ministers, journalists, artists, and politicians. Liberated, partially at least, from the restrictions (and pieties) of domesticity, these women wrote poetry that was extraordinarily varied and thematically rich, especially in its contestation of domestic ideology. Thus, for example, Sarah M. B. Piatt's speaker uses her poetry to interrogate "true womanhood," the joys of domesticity, and the value of tears. Comparing herself in "Shapes of a Soul" to a snake on the one hand and a tiger on the other, she dismisses out of hand the idealized versions of womanhood within which society (represented in the poem by an implied male interlocutor) seeks to constrain her. As made by the most subtle and broadest ranging of these poets, Piatt's attack on domesticity cannot be separated from her uniquely alienated position as a Southerner who moved north in 1861 and refused to blind herself to the social inequities that were constitutive of *both* geopolitical locations. As she demonstrates in poems such as "Giving Back the Flower," "The Palace-Burner," and "His Mother's Way," "domesticated" women, no less than "worldly" men, were ultimately responsible for the miseries (from war to starvation) that the defense of slavery and the runaway growth of laissez-faire capitalism created between them. She deconstructs the binaries of gender even as she deconstructs the difference between North and South.

Along with attacking domestic ideology, these poets take on other controversial issues as well. Alice Dunbar-Nelson ("You! Inez!") and Sophie Jewett (all three selections) write passionate love poetry to women. In the tradition of nineteenth-century women's poetry from Lydia Howard Huntley Sigourney on down, these poets also write pervasively on social issues, as, for example, Ella Wheeler Wilcox does in "Goddess of Liberty, Answer" (a bitterly sardonic response to Emma Lazarus's far better known, but far less honest, "The New Colossus"), Elaine Goodale Eastman does in "The Wood-Chopper to His Ax" and "The Cross and the Pagan," and Alice Dunbar-Nelson does in "The Proletariat Speaks." Conversely, in the final decades of the century, a number of poets such as Sophie Jewett show a protomodernist tendency to turn away from the social in order to thematize their own subjectivity or (most strikingly in Reese) their relation to their art. These poets are as much harbingers of "high" modernist poetry as the more socially oriented poets are continuators of a tradition that would produce in the twentieth century the social protest poetry of writers such as Langston Hughes.

Significant Form, Style, or Artistic Conventions

If late-nineteenth-century women's poetry is thematically rich, it is also formally varied. Indeed, for students who have been taught to believe that only Whitman and Dickinson experimented stylistically in the century, this sheaf can help them establish a new and much more flexible set of parameters by which stylistic "experimentation" can be measured. As the metrically innovative work of Piatt and the poets of the nineties suggest, free verse is not the only test of a radical poetics or a poetics of change. While free verse is represented here in the work of Dunbar-Nelson, what is most striking about these poets is the degree of freedom they achieved when using traditional forms, especially in their handling of cadence. Theirs is not the voice of the metronome but of subtle writers who learned to bring speech rhythms to fixed traditional meters well before Frost.

Equally interesting—and possibly more exciting for some students to trace—is the way one can see a modernist linguistic stance emerge in this poetry. Read for their handling of imagery, late-nineteenth-century women poets can clearly be seen moving toward the precise language and vivid images associated with writers such as Amy Lowell, Ezra Pound, and H.D. Indeed, their use of imagery can achieve the kind of indeterminacy generally associated only with modernist poetry. Clearly for these poets, art's didactic function—its *raison d'être* for so much of the nineteenth century—no longer holds. Demonstrating such stylistic shifts helps students understand the complexity of artistic fashion, even as it demystifies the contribution of "major" writers such as Pound and H.D.

Original Audience

Like most poets of the nineteenth century, the poets collected in this sheaf not only published widely in newspapers and magazines but also produced books. Not counting juvenilia, Piatt published over four hundred poems in newspapers and periodicals, among them thirty-four poems in the *Atlantic Monthly* alone. Other poets also published heavily in these venues. Their audience was, therefore, national, reasonably well-educated, and largely middle-class. (This was true for writers of color as well as for white authors.) Indeed, this audience was probably largely composed of women (and men) much like themselves. They are not poets writing "high art" for an elite few, nor did they intend their art to become (as, say, T. S. Eliot's arguably did) "canonical."

Comparisons, Contrasts, Connections

The most important comparison, contrast, and connection to be made is to their contemporary Emily Dickinson. Other useful comparisons would be to such "modernist" poets as Pound and H.D. on the one hand and the political poets in "Cluster: Political Poetry in the Modern Period." Cary Nelson's recovery work, like that represented by this "sheaf" of poets, raises important questions about canonization as well as the evolution of poetic style and the "radical" possibilities latent in traditional forms, which students may find interesting to ponder.

Questions for Reading, Discussion, and Writing

A number of these poets/poems beg for comparison/contrast approaches, for example, Eastman and Johnson present two contrasting writers (one white, one Native American) dealing with Native American survival; Piatt and Dunbar-Nelson treat women in relation to war. Then there are deliberately controversial questions one can ask: Is Jewett writing "lesbian" poetry, and if so, how does one define it? When a poet like Piatt relies so heavily on dialogue and invented speakers (Dickinson's "supposed person"), what happens to the notion of "voice"? Is "political" poetry (such as Wilcox's "Goddess of Liberty, Speak" and Eastman's "The Cross and the Pagan") "poetry"?

Bibliography

Biographical and critical material for most of these authors is very scanty and frequently inaccurate. The most useful general study is Emily Stipes Watts, *The Poetry of American Women from 1632–1945*, Austin and London: U of Texas P, 1977. In *Repression and Recovery: Modern American Poetry and the Politics of Cultural Memory* (Madison: U of Wisconsin P, 1989) Cary Nelson treats the theoretical issues involved in the recovery of lost poets of the 1910–1940 period, and much of what he says can be applied to the earlier poets as well.

The Making of "Americans"

Abraham Cahan (1860–1951)

Contributing Editor: Daniel Walden

Classroom Issues and Strategies

Students need to understand the following: (1) the Eastern European Jewish culture out of which Cahan came, (2) New York City as a fast-changing urban and technologized environment in the late nineteenth and early twentieth century, and (3) the nature of ethnicity in the context of the forces of Americanization.

To address these topics, I require I. Howe and E. Greenberg, Introduction to *Treasury of Yiddish Stories* (for the European culture), and Moses Rischin, *The Promised City: New York's Jews 1880–1920,* for the culture of New York City. For an introduction to Cahan as a realist, see Jules Chametzky, *From the Ghetto,* and Sanford Marovitz, *Abraham Cahan.*

Students tend to identify with Cahan's attempts to find himself, a newcomer, a Jewish immigrant, in urban New York. They are surprised that this man, as an editor and novelist, was such a big influence in the 1900–1940 era. They tend to ask about the Eastern European culture, what New York was *really* like in the 1910s and 1920s, and why and how people struggled for identity in the face of overt oppression, poverty, and discrimination.

Major Themes, Historical Perspectives, Personal Issues

Help students understand the parallel themes of ethnicity/identity and assimilation/Americanization. In *Yekl,* Cahan begins to address these themes; in *The Rise of David Levinsky* (1917) he was able to develop character and relationships in the context of the turn-of-the-century culture.

Significant Form, Style, or Artistic Conventions

Cahan was a realist who had mastered English. His style bore the impress of his Russian literary and cultural background as well as his having come out of an Eastern European Jewish culture.

Original Audience

It is necessary to prepare a word list or glossary of those few Yiddish words that are used. A contemporary American audience has to learn to tune in the late-nineteenth- and early-twentieth-century Russian and Jewish cultures from which Cahan came.

Comparisons, Contrasts, Connections

The classic Russian authors, like Tolstoy, Dostoyevsky, and Turgenev, should be mentioned and briefly explained. W. D. Howells and his circle were also an influence on Cahan. Lastly, Yiddish authors like Mendele and Sholom Aleichem should be referred to. All were influences on Cahan, who absorbed their work even as he reflected the culture of New York City in the 1890–1913 era.

Working with Cultural Objects

I use the following films:

1. *The Inheritance* (a documentary made by Amalgamated, 1964).
2. *The Distorted Image* (a set of slides on stereotyping by B'nai B'rith, Anti-Defamation League).
3. *The Chosen* (film of Chaim Potok's novel).
4. *Hester Street* (film of Cahan's novel *Yekl*).
5. *The Pawnbroker* (film of Wallant's novel).

Questions for Reading, Discussion, and Writing

1. (a) Explain the religio-cultural ethos of nineteenth-century Eastern European Jewry.
   (b) What was the literary culture of nineteenth-century Russia?
2. Abraham Cahan: Russian Jewish Realist.
   Abraham Cahan: Yiddishist, Reformer, Novelist.
   Abraham Cahan: Editor and Mediating Influence.
   Abraham Cahan: American Democratic Pragmatic Socialist.

Edith Maud Eaton (Sui-Sin Far) (1865–1914)

Contributing Editors: Amy Ling, King-Kok Cheung, Dominika Ferens

Major Themes, Historical Perspectives, Personal Issues

If students are to appreciate the work of Edith Eaton fully, they must be given its historical and social context, namely the reception of Chinese by dominant Americans before and during her period. Students should know that though the Chinese were never enslaved in this country, as were Africans, they were brought here in large numbers as indentured laborers or coolies. The Chinese Exclusion Act was only repealed in 1943, and naturalized citizenship for Asians was permitted in 1954, long after African Americans and Native Americans were recognized as American citizens. Initially attracted to California by the discovery of gold in the mid-nineteenth century, by the 1860s thousands of Chinese laborers were enticed here to construct the mountainous western section of the transcontinental railroad. Almost from the beginning, prejudice against them was strong. They were regarded as an alien race with peculiar customs and habits that made them unassimilable in a nation that wanted to remain white; their hard-working, frugal ways and their willingness to work for lower wages than whites rendered them an economic threat and thus targets of racial violence.

Into this environment, Edith Eaton came as a small child from England, living first in Hudson City, New York, and later settling in Montreal. Though her writing career began on the Montreal newspaper, *The Star*, she was to make her mark in the United States (she lived most of her adult life in Boston, Seattle, and San Francisco), writing articles and short stories using the Chinese pseudonym Sui-Sin Far.

Edith Eaton's autobiographical essay and her stories, of which "In the Land of the Free" is an example, show what it was to be a Chinese woman in the white man's world. Though Eaton herself was only one-half Chinese (and one-half English), she was devoted to her mother and to the cause of counteracting the hatred and prejudice against her mother's people that was so pervasive during her own formative years. She took the Chinese name of a flower popular among the Chinese (*Sui-Sin Far* means Chinese narcissus) and courageously asserted her Chinese heritage.

In "Leaves" she describes through personal anecdotes her growing awareness of her own ethnic identity, her sensitivity to the curiosity and hostility of others, the difficulty of the Eurasian's position, and the development of her racial pride. The other theme apparent in "Leaves," and in many of her short stories, is Eaton's defense of the independent woman. The biographical fact that Eaton herself never married and the intimate details of her journal entries would indicate that she is telling her own story, but she refrained from identifying herself out of a delicate sense of modesty.

"In the Land of the Free" is typical of Edith Eaton's short fiction. Her themes are of utmost importance: racial insensitivity, the human costs of bureaucratic and discriminatory laws, the humanity of the Chinese. The creation of rounded characters is a secondary concern. Lae Choo is little more than maternity personified, maternity victimized by racial prejudice. But the very portrayal of a Chinese woman in the maternal role—loving, anxious, frantic, self-sacrificing—was itself a novelty and a contribution, for the popular conception of the Chinese woman, whose numbers were few in nineteenth-century America, was that of a sing-song girl, prostitute, or inmate of an opium den. In Lae Choo, Eaton gives the reading public a naive, trusting woman whose entire life is devoted to the small child that the law of "this land of the free" manages to keep away from her for nearly one year. By the end of the story, the irony of the title becomes forcefully apparent.

Onoto Watanna (Winnifred Eaton) (1875–1954)

Contributing Editor: Dominika Ferens

Classroom Issues and Strategies

It is challenging to teach the work of Onoto Watanna because students who have not previously worked with popular fiction tend to dismiss "A Half-Caste" as melodramatic pulp fiction. However, you may help students to reconstruct the historical and literary context of the story and explain why a strictly formalist approach is counterproductive in the case of popular fiction. Onoto Watanna was, after all, a highly successful author of middlebrow fiction, not a failed highbrow author. You could ask why her works sold so well. Might the reasons for her success be the same reasons why she received so little critical attention from ethnic studies scholars until the 1990s? If her work initially seems straightforward and didactic, point out its ambivalences.

Onoto Watanna's controversial public persona presents a second challenge. Whereas her literary sister Edith Eaton/Sui-Sin Far claimed Chinese identity and tried to make herself useful to the Chinese immigrant communities in North America, Onoto Watanna felt accountable to no one except her editors and readers, ignored the limitations of authentic racial identity when it suited her, yet exploited her readers' faith in racial authenticity when she passed for Japanese. Consequently, while Sui-Sin Far's position at the head of the Asian-American literary canon is secure, Onoto Watanna is often discussed not as a writer in her own right but instead as a foil for her politically engaged sister.

Questioning the notion of authenticity is a good place to begin. Onoto Watanna exchanged her Chinese identity for a less stigmatized Japanese one. Why did she not pass permanently for white, as did many of her siblings? (She often passed for white for the sake of convenience.) Brian Spooner, in his essay "Weavers and Dealers: The Authenticity of an Oriental Carpet" (1989), has pointed out that authenticity has less to do with the material attributes of an artifact than with our desire to see it as genuine. People in the West have a profound interest in the authenticity of the exotic because they imagine the modern West as lacking in authenticity, flooded with mass-produced goods, and alienated from the "natural state." Need first-hand experience of a place, the fact of having actually been there, be the prerequisite for writing fiction about it? Why did Onoto Watanna's strategy of passing for Japanese discredit her in the eyes of some late-twentieth-century readers?

On the other hand, because ethnic minority writers are few, whatever they publish is viewed by both mainstream and minority readers as representative of the group. What is problematic about the fact that Onoto Watanna, Maxine Hong Kingston, and Amy Tan became popular American novelists by writing about Asia without having been there? Why do books about the everyday lives of Asian Americans in contemporary urban settings not sell as well? The fact that, whether they choose to or not, Asian-American writers carry the burden of representation could be a useful point of departure for a discussion.

Major Themes, Historical Perspectives, Personal Issues

Onoto Watanna worked patiently and deliberately to erode the common belief that culture is racially determined around the time when the anthropologist Franz Boas first began to put forward similar notions in American academia. She transplanted Japanese characters to the United States and had Japanese families raise white children, showing successful experiments in cross-cultural assimilation. By using biracial figures she questioned the easy assumptions about appropriate racial and cultural identity. But traces of essentialism do appear in her fiction: for instance, the character Kiku in "A Half Caste" suggests she is bold and rebellious because she is half-white. Rather than invalidate Onoto Watanna's contribution to the understanding that race is culturally constructed, those moments of slippage should help us to understand how difficult it was to sustain an oppositional discourse of race when the official discourse was overwhelmingly essentialist.

Since the 1990s, the idea that racial, gender, and sexual identities are performed has inspired many interesting studies in the humanities. Onoto Watanna's work lends itself to such investigations. Performance (or nonperformance) is the central theme of "A Half Caste." It was also one of the major problems in the author's life: how to build credibility in the eyes of her readers, how to assert a marketable difference, how to maintain a consistent authorial persona, and eventually, how to disentangle herself from that persona when it began to stifle her literary ambitions.

Critic Jean Lee Cole (2002) has pointed out that a major theme in Onoto Watanna's work—one that has been passed over because critics focus on the orientalist aspect of her work—is the contemporary debate concerning the "woman of genius." To a large segment of the American public, this concept was an oxymoron, yet with the emancipation and greater participation of women in the public sphere, writers like Mary Austin, Theodore Dreiser, Willa Cather, and many others began to question the belief that genius is a male attribute. Many of Onoto Watanna's women characters, including Kiku, express their originality and creativity through dance, song, and writing literature.

Significant Form, Style, or Artistic Convention

Onoto Watanna made her name as a writer of middlebrow fiction for popular women's magazines such as *Ladies' Home Journal, Current Literature*, and *Harper's Weekly*. She clearly felt at home within the rigid conventions of romantic fiction. Under the cover of highly contrived, melodramatic plots; Japanese settings; and ethnically marked speech, she smuggled fairly outrageous ideas into the homes of her enchanted late-Victorian readers. (Consider the fact that "A Half Caste" is about sex-tourism, miscegenation, and incest.) Though it is clear from the early reviews that readers often missed the critical message of Onoto Watanna's fiction, it did help to change widely accepted views about race, culture, and the "Orient."

Never having set foot in Japan, Onoto Watanna learned about Japanese culture and aesthetics from scholarly works, guide books, and travel narratives. Traces of these genres can be found in her "Japanese" romances that delighted readers across the United States.

Bound in silk and stamped with floral designs that matched the names of the heroines, several of her books had print runs of well over ten thousand copies. Her imitations of the Japanese aesthetic were clearly convincing. "This type is new," wrote an enthusiastic reviewer, "the ethical quality is foreign, and the artistic form a thing by itself. There is beauty and a spirit of fine breeding in this curious love story, as well as in the pictures which are Japanese in detail and delicacy of line" (*Critic*, Aug. 1904).

Original Audience

Because Onoto Watanna was an avid collector of reviews of her own work, we have access to hundreds of reader responses, which she neatly pasted into scrapbooks. Virtually every American newspaper and glossy magazine paid tribute to her talent. An Australian reviewer claimed that Onoto Watanna's work "gives a deeper insight into Japanese life than exhaustive tomes of erudite scholars" (*Sydney Herald*, 30 Jul. 1904). Others wrote about the intoxicating and addictive effect of her poetic prose. Even William Dean Howells, the dominant literary critic of the era, commended Onoto Watanna on her "very choice English" and raved about the "indescribable freshness in the art of [*A Japanese Nightingale*] . . . which is like no other art except in the simplicity which is native to the best art everywhere" (*North American Review*, Dec. 1901). Publishers pressed Onoto Watanna for more works in the same vein. When she wrote a novel set in the United States and narrated by a working-class Irish character, Doubleday insisted on publishing it under her Japanese pen name. Eventually, to make a break with Japonica, she published two autobiographical novels, *Me: A Book of Remembrance* (1915) and *Marion* (1916), anonymously.

Comparisons, Contrasts, Connections

Onoto Watanna is often passed over or deprecated in Asian-American literature courses that prominently feature the work of her sister Sui-Sin Far. Yet the sisters shared many thematic interests. Sui-Sin Far's autobiographical essay "Leaves from the Mental Portfolio of an Eurasian" and Onoto Watanna's "A Half Caste" can be compared in terms of various responses to being the object of the orientalist gaze, the theme of ethnic performance, and the experience of biraciality as a source of inner conflict.

Scholars have shown that Onoto Watanna can be usefully studied alongside the major American writers of middlebrow fiction such as Edna Ferber, Zona Gale, Anita Loos, or Anzia Yezierska. Her naturalistic novel *Cattle* makes for interesting comparisons with Willa Cather's prairie fiction.

"A Half Caste" and many other stories by Onoto Watanna are also part of the American literature of passing and are worth studying alongside the fiction of Charles Chesnutt, James Weldon Johnson, Jessie Fauset, and Nella Larsen.

Maxine Hong Kingston, Amy Tan, and David Henry Hwang stand as interesting late-twentieth-century analogies to Watanna.

Working with Cultural Objects

Consider opening the class by playing an excerpt from Giaccomo Puccini's opera *Madama Butterfly* and helping students to summarize the libretto (most will know the rough outline of the plot from pop-cultural references). You could also ask students to talk about recent Hollywood reincarnations of Madame Butterfly.

First editions of many of Onoto Watanna's novels are still available in university and public libraries. It is worth bringing a copy into class to let students see the richness of the bindings, the gilt-edged pages, and the illustrations based on nineteenth-century Japanese prints.

Students also learn a great deal by seeing Onoto Watanna's short stories in their original glossy magazine context. New meanings emerge when they see them offset by other—racially marked and unmarked—stories, advertisements influenced by the Japanese aesthetic, cooking recipes, and advice columns.

Questions for Reading, Discussion, and Writing

1. In what ways does "A Half Caste" question racial and cultural "authenticity"?
2. Consider "A Half Caste" as a story of racial passing. Compare it with other narratives of passing, such as those included in Charles Chesnutt's *The Wife of His Youth* or James Weldon Johnson's *Autobiography of an Ex-Colored Man.*
3. What made Edith Eaton/Sui-Sin Far a more acceptable forerunner of Asian-American literature than Winifred Eaton/Onoto Watanna?
4. Consider Onoto Watanna's protagonists in light of theories of identity as performance.
5. What made Onoto Watanna a best-selling author by early-twentieth-century standards? Can some of the same reasons for her popularity be used to explain the popularity of Maxine Hong Kingston and Amy Tan today?

Bibliography

Researching the fiction of Onoto Watanna has recently been made easier by the fact that three of her novels were reprinted by academic presses (*Heart of Hyacinth, A Japanese Nightingale,* and *Me: A Book of Remembrance*). Thirteen short stories and six essays are now available in a collection titled *"A Half Caste" and Other Writings,* edited by Linda Trinh Moser and Elizabeth Rooney. Additional stories, recently discovered by Jean Lee Cole, are accessible on the Web at <http://www.etext.lib.virginia.edu/modeng/modengW.browse.html>. There is also a meticulously researched biography by Diana Birchall.

Mary Austin (1868–1934)

Contributing Editor: Vera Norwood

Classroom Issues and Strategies

Students have difficulty responding to Austin's strident individualism and her vacillation between ardent feminist and male-identified writer. The best approach is to provide contextual background that reveals that Austin was not alone in her struggles to write from both inside and outside her culture.

Once we have addressed some of the difficulties of voice in this autobiography, I have the best luck with teaching what I think Austin as a writer was best at evoking. Her strength was in describing and evaluating the interior domestic spaces of her house and the natural and built environments of the Midwest and Far West, thus raising questions about the sort of material world women valued and created. Teaching sections of the auto-biography in conjunction with *The Land of Little Rain* and *Lost Borders* encourages literature students to think about various ways in which women have created appropriate spaces and changed the places they settled, both indoors as craftswomen and outdoors as gardeners and preservationists.

The main question Austin's autobiography engenders is how accurate a reflection she provides of late-nineteenth-century women's lives. Not that this is an issue with the particular selection made for the anthology, but Austin's depiction of the American Indian and Hispanic populations of the Southwest raises more questions and issues than the gender-related material. Teachers who branch out into other of her regional works will need to be prepared for these questions.

Major Themes, Historical Perspectives, Personal Issues

Austin was a Progressive Era writer, deeply involved in supporting regional diversity, multicultural perspectives, and environmental preservation. Students understand her authorial voice better when they know something about her work in these areas. Austin belonged to a generation of creative women struggling to shift from nineteenth-century lives as private, housebound, husband-and-father dominated people to twentieth-century roles of modern, independent individuals influencing social and political trends. Students should also know something of her private circumstances: the long separation and eventual divorce from her husband, the birth of a retarded daughter, the necessity that she write a great deal to earn her living—each played a part in producing the sometimes contradictory voice appearing in her work.

Significant Form, Style, or Artistic Conventions

Obviously, some familiarity with autobiographical conventions is useful. Gender is an important variable when reading any autobiography. We discuss male and female voices, stressing that women began to write after men had established the basic form, so their works often combined male traditions with female experimentation. In Austin's case, the experiment is in her use of different voices for the visionary, individualistic persona and for the traditional, good daughter.

Original Audience

Austin's audience in her time was more male than it is currently. Her reputation as a political activist and writer was with regionalists and environmentalists, among whom the leading lights were men. In many ways, her autobiography was written with an eye to setting herself off from the "ordinary" woman of her generation, of claiming a specialness that would put her in the male leagues while also encouraging other women to break free from gender-role proscriptions. In the process of this somewhat divisive attempt, however, she created a persona with a strong feminist character. In our time, it is that visionary woman who speaks to a much larger audience of women readers. For this audience, Austin is less interesting for what she did in the public sphere of environmentalist politics than for her scathing critique, and frustrated rejection, of the nineteenth-century gender-role model offered her by her mother.

Comparisons, Contrasts, Connections

I teach Austin with Sarah Orne Jewett and Charlotte Perkins Gilman. All three worked in approximately the same time period and struggled with the same gender-role restrictions. Jewett and Gilman are particularly useful in tempering some of the negative reactions students have to Austin's voice. Also useful are Benjamin Franklin's and Frederick Douglass's autobiographies. Teaching these with Austin provides students with a better understanding of the genre in which Austin worked.

Questions for Reading, Discussion, and Writing

1. The main introduction I make to any autobiography is to suggest that students think about what sort of people have written their life story. Generally, such authors are engaged in an act of self-creation, which assumes that there is something unique to their life. I ask students to look

at strategies the author uses to present herself as, in some way, remarkable. With autobiographies by women this becomes a particularly useful question to begin the study of how gender comes into play in issues of genre.

2. Selecting comparative/contrastive passages from the writers mentioned above and having students look for similarities/ differences has been successful. With Austin, Jewett's story "The White Heron" provides a good starting point for looking at landscape values as they are impacted by gender. Also, "The Basket Maker" chapter in *The Land of Little Rain* offers an opportunity for students to analyze how material from the autobiography matches Austin's more "fictional" work. This is a good exercise for demonstrating how much Austin created her autobiographical persona out of her earlier writing.

Bibliography

Really the best additional reading a teacher could seek is more Austin. Mary Austin was a prolific, wide-ranging writer, and one should be aware of the work on which her reputation is based. I would advise reading some of the stories in *Lost Borders* and a few chapters of *Land of Little Rain* as the best preparation for teaching Austin.

Gertrude Bonnin (Zitkala-Sa) (Sioux) (1876–1938)

Contributing Editor: Kristin Herzog

Classroom Issues and Strategies

Without a knowledge of Zitkala-Sa's life and considering the near impossibility for an American Indian woman of her time to publish independently, students will wonder where these stories fit in. It is important to point out the extreme difficulties of a writer trying to preserve a tribal heritage and yet also trying to communicate to a white audience.

Besides dealing with matters of biography, history, and style, I think approaching these early American Indian authors from the religious perspective (Native American spirituality versus enforced assimilation to Christian beliefs) is effective in helping students to sense the very basic dilemma of a writer, a problem of cultural and spiritual identity that goes deeper than mere issues of civil rights, important as they are.

Students easily identify with the aspect of social criticism or rebellion, but may not find the style particularly attractive because they do not know the historical and biographical background and the tastes of the literary market at this time.

Major Themes, Historical Perspectives, Personal Issues

Zitkala-Sa is a transitional writer whose life and work express deep conflicts between tradition and assimilation, literature and politics, Native American religion and Christianity. If we focus on the tension between her artistic and her political commitments, she can be seen in the middle between Susette LaFlesche, whose fiction was almost submerged by her political speaking and writing, and Leslie Marmon Silko, who is able to create a blend of traditional and modern fiction that organically incorporates a political stance.

Nor by far are all of her political activities reflected in her writings; in her editorials for the *American Indian Magazine*, for example, she discussed controversial issues like the enfranchisement of American Indians, Indian contributions to military service during World War I, corruption in the Bureau of Indian Affairs, and allotment of tribal lands. The selections reprinted here from *American Indian Stories* are neither essays of cultural criticism nor strictly autobiographical accounts. They are an attempt at turning personal experience as well as social criticism into creative "stories."

One aspect of Zitkala-Sa's imbalanced, but path-breaking, attempt to merge cultural criticism and aesthetic form is her struggle with religion. In Parts IV and V of "School Days," she vividly describes the little girl's night-mares of the palefaces' devil and the bitterness she felt when a schoolmate died with an open Bible on her bed, listening to the "superstitious ideas" of the paleface woman taking care of her. While Charles Eastman in *Indian Boyhood* (published in 1902, two years after "School Days") uses the word *superstition* for some of his Sioux traditions, Zitkala-Sa turns the matter around: Christianity to her is superstitious.

Similarly, "Why I Am a Pagan" is an unusual statement in her time. Its sentimentality and self-consciously "poetic" language can partly be ascribed to the popular journal style of the time. There is daring in her point of view. Interestingly, she does not satirize a white preacher but rather one of her own kin whom she sees as tragically duped by the Christian "superstition." Even though we learn from other sources that she and her husband denounced the Peyote religion and therefore to some extent hampered the fight for American Indian freedom of religion, the fact remains that she asserted the dignity of Indian religion and put her finger on two blind spots of Christianity that are being overcome only in our time: the disregard for nature and the disrespect for other cultures. What Christian theology is learning today from ecology and anthropology as well as from some of its own forgotten roots, Native American writers learned from their ancient tribal traditions.

Significant Form, Style, or Artistic Conventions

The selections from "The School Days of an Indian Girl" expose the blatant injustice of stripping a child of language, culture, religion, and familiar surroundings. At the same time they express the irony that the maltreated student is extremely unhappy upon returning home and finally feels the urge to return to the place of her earlier sufferings. While the style is sometimes stilted or sentimental, it is at other times direct and powerful, as, for example, in the passage on the hair cutting. In learning about American Indian customs and beliefs ("short hair was worn by mourners, and shingled hair by cowards"), we are made to experience the trauma of the child. In hearing the mother's desperate cry for help from the spirits of her departed warrior brothers, we can sense the tragic family divisions caused by forced assimilation.

Comparisons, Contrasts, Connections

The many years of literary silence in Zitkala-Sa's life seem to indicate a serious break between artistic endeavors on the one hand and relentless activism on behalf of American Indian health, education, legal representation, and voting rights on the other. However, in her few publications she actually anticipated the concerns of contemporary writers. In blending autobiography with creative narrative, elements of tribal traditions, and social criticism, she helped to pave the way for those recent writers who have focused more clearly and more comprehensively on their own traditions.

Questions for Reading, Discussion, and Writing

1. (a) What is your knowledge of American life around 1900 in terms of what you have "absorbed" over the years? In terms of consulting recent scholarly works?
   (b) What do you suppose were the difficulties of a Native American woman writer in writing for a white audience around 1900?
2. (a) How are literary art and protest merged in Zitkala-Sa's work?
   (b) How did Zitkala-Sa pave the way for contemporary American Indian writers like Leslie Marmon Silko, Paula Gunn Allen, or Louise Erdrich (in case contemporary American Indian women authors have been read in the class)?

Bibliography

Allen, Paula Gunn. *The Sacred Hoop: Recovering the Feminine in American Indian Traditions.* Boston: Beacon, 1986. 82.

Dockstader, Frederick J. *Great North American Indians: Profiles in Life and Leadership.* New York: Von Nostrand, 1977. 40f.

Eastman, Charles A. *Indian Boyhood.* New York: McClure: 1902. 172, 177. Christianity and superstitions. See also Hertzberg, *The Search for an American Indian Identity*, especially 256ff. and 262.

Fisher, Alice P. "The Transformation of Tradition: A Study of Zitkala-Sa and Mourning Dove, Two Transitional Writers." Diss., City U of New York, 1979. 36. On the quality of the passage on hair cutting.

Fisher, Dexter. "Zitkala-Sa: The Evolution of a Writer." *American Indian Quarterly* 5 (Aug. 1979): 229–38.

Hertzberg, Hazel W. *The Search for an American Indian Identity: Modern Pan-Indian Movements.* Syracuse: Syracuse UP, 1971. Describes her political activities.

Littlefield, Daniel F., Jr., and James W. Parins. *A Biobibliography of Native American Writers, 1772–1924.* Metuchen, NJ: Scarecrow, 1981. 17f. For a list of writings by Zitkala-Sa. See also the Supplement to this volume (1985), p. 16.

Olsen, Tillie. *Silences.* New York: Delta/Seymour Lawrence, 1978. Helpful in explaining to students the many reasons for a break in creativity, especially as it pertains to women and members of minorities.

Schöler, Bo. Introduction to *Coyote Was Here*, p. 10.

Stout, Mary. "Zitkala-Sa: The Literature of Politics." *Coyote Was Here: Essays on Contemporary Native American Literary and Political Mobilization.* Ed. Bo Schöler. Aarhus, Den.: Dept. of English, U of Aarhus, 1984. 74.

Young, Mary E. "Bonnin, Gertrude Simmons." *Notable American Women, 1607–1950: A Biographical Dictionary.* Vol. I.

Mary Antin (1881–1949)

Contributing Editor: Richard Tuerk

Classroom Issues and Strategies

Students are often unfamiliar with the time period treated in *The Promised Land*, especially so with aspects of the Great Migration and of immigrant settlement in America in the late nineteenth and early twentieth centuries. Especially important is conveying to them the kinds of conditions the newly arrived immigrants encountered in large Eastern cities. Students are also unfamiliar with the kinds of conditions the immigrants lived in in the Old World.

Most of the questions I hear from students concern life in the Old World; however, most material treating Old World life has been omitted from the anthology. Other questions involve the urban environment of the newly arrived immigrant. Strangely enough, few of my students question Antin's idea that total assimilation is desirable.

Major Themes, Historical Perspectives, Personal Issues

Loosely structured around the Book of Exodus, from which Antin gets her title, *The Promised Land* tells of her being born anew as an American and of her realization that as one of "the youngest of America's children," she is in an ideal position to appreciate and understand her new country. In recent years, critics are beginning to view the book as being more ambiguous than was previously thought, finding indications in it that Antin is not wholly negative toward the Old World and not wholly positive toward the New World, although she undeniably extols the virtues of total assimilation and holds herself up as a model for all immigrants to follow. Still, the book stands as one of the classic American immigrant autobiographies and, unlike Michael Gold's *Jews without Money* and Ludwig Lewisohn's autobiographical volumes, as one of the foremost works extolling the virtues of America and Americanization for immigrants and their children.

Antin's emphasis on Americanization and total assimilation deserves careful scrutiny. I try to discuss the values of an ethic of assimilation as well as the problems it presents. I usually contrast Antin with at least one author— usually Ludwig Lewisohn, although Leslie Marmon Silko would do as well— who questions the ethic of assimilation. Particularly apt books for contrast are Lewisohn's *Up Stream* and Silko's *Ceremony*. I also discuss the related theme of initiation in Antin's book.

The work may be treated in terms of its sociological content, that is, in terms of what it reveals about the expectations and possibilities of an immigrant girl in America around the turn of the century. It also may be treated in terms of the role of the public schools in helping (perhaps forcing) the immigrant to come to terms with American culture and society. However, the work may also be treated as a piece of literature.

Significant Form, Style, or Artistic Conventions

As I see it, *The Promised Land* is a tale of initiation, even of rebirth. Antin's being reborn as an American provides her with her principal form in terms of her contrasting Old World and New and in terms of her growth in the New World. The book is, among other things, a study in radical discontinuity in terms of the relations of Antin's Old World life to her New World life and of continuous growth in terms of her New World life.

Original Audience

Antin says that she is writing for all Americans, and her statement seems correct. I mention the tremendous popularity of her work and its use, either in whole or in part, in classrooms in public schools throughout America. Chapters from it became parts of textbooks used from coast to coast.

Comparisons, Contrasts, Connections

Other works of initiation are especially useful for comparison, particularly those dealing with initiation into American society. Ethnic tales of initiation make instructive objects of comparison, works like Leslie Marmon Silko's *Ceremony*, Ludwig Lewisohn's *Up Stream*, O. E. Rolvaag's *Giants in the Earth*, and Richard Wright's *Black Boy*.

Even more helpful, however, is comparing Antin's book with Mark Twain's *Adventures of Huckleberry Finn*. These works are in many ways very similar yet at the same time radically different, especially in terms of their evaluations of American society. Whereas Antin desires assimilation above all, Huck learns to loathe the idea of being assimilated into American society.

Working with Cultural Objects

I use photographs by people like Jacob Riis (see http://www.masters-of-photography.com/R/riis/riis.html>) to try to give the students a feeling for life in the immigrant quarters. I also use books containing photographs by people like Roman Vishniak to give them a feeling for Old World Orthodox Jewish life. Frankly, I find that photographs have a stronger impact on my students than simple descriptions and statistics do.

Questions for Reading, Discussion, and Writing

1. In what ways is Antin's experience in the New World unique? In what ways is it typical?

   In what ways is she unique? In what ways is she typical? As you read the selection, it might help to bear in mind that she insists that she is representative of all young immigrants.

   What is her attitude toward public schools?

   How realistic is her evaluation of America?

2. Compare Antin's attitude toward public schools with your own attitude; what incidents in her life and in yours are responsible for the similarities and differences in those attitudes? Trace the steps by which Antin shows herself becoming Americanized.

José Martí (1853–1895)

Contributing Editor: Enrique Sacerio-Garí

Classroom Issues and Strategies

Students face a difficult task as they read Martí within an *American* anthology. Even as part of a diverse group, with some knowledge of the role of the United States in Latin America and an awareness of issues of identity in our hardly homogeneous society, your strategy must recognize the exciting difficulties of reconciling differences in Martí's text as well as in your own classroom. What is *your* America? I would ask the students. A good day may bring many voices that speak about communities, regions, neighborhoods, nations, ethnicity, race, and class. Are we empowered or disempowered by our most intimate America? In "Our America," does Martí empower a nation, a people, a whole continent, with his voice? The obstacles to integrating the different views may then be discussed, leading (perhaps) to Martí's call for understanding by means of direct knowledge and respect of others and by self-esteem through self-knowledge. Stylistic issues of images and themes that surface and resurface (see below) could be related to the sociopolitical experiences of nations and groups.

Is *Nuestra América,* a text published in New York and Mexico City in 1891, representative of the literature of the United States at the end of the nineteenth century? At the beginning of the second millennium, is *Nuestra América* now more within the United States or excluded from the United States? Discuss the following statement by LeAlan Jones:

Where we live is a second America, where the laws of the land don't apply and the laws of the street do. You must learn *Our America* as we must learn your America, so that maybe, someday, we can become one.

LeAlan Jones and Lloyd Newman with David Isay, *Our America: Life and Death on the South Side of Chicago.* New York: Washington Square P, 1998.

Major Themes, Historical Perspectives, Personal Issues

A discussion of Martí's emphasis on the racial composition of America, and his vision aligned with the indigenous groups, should contrast civilization and barbarism, false erudition and direct knowledge, imported colonizer culture and indigenous culture. Here, one could ask where the indigenous groups are now and how Martí's treatment of transcultural and transracial issues contrasts with current views. Another important topic is the psychology of the colonial situation, which could reconsider the polemics between Mannoni and Fanon. Martí's text could help promote thoughts on the hybrid nature of Latin America, where the metaphors of Ariel and Caliban are reconciled as an empowered *mestizo* culture.

As you explore our America as distinct realities, you could probe the class as to basic knowledge of geography and history of various regions and the culture of different Native American peoples. Considering the historical background offered in the introduction to "Our America," you might ask the class to research topics such as the name *America*, Pan-Americanism in the late nineteenth century and free trade in the early twenty-first century, writing in exile, immigrant voices in New York journals, ethnic and racial issues then and now, and how to "do the right thing." An interesting comparison could be made with Jacob Riis (1849–1914), another famous New York City nocturnal walker, who immigrated from Denmark in 1870. As a reporter and photographer for the *New York Tribune,* he conducted a crusade against the dire conditions of the slums around "the Bend" of Mulberry Street. He was a close friend and biographer of Theodore Roosevelt.

Significant Form, Style, or Artistic Conventions

Read the first two paragraphs in class. A thorough discussion of this passage should be sufficient to acquaint the students with Martí's *modernista* style, which he initiated in Latin America. If further work with *modernista* poetics is desired, exposure to the ideals of Parnassian poets and the musicality of symbolist writers should be considered. This close reading will facilitate intra-textual understanding of subsequent elaborations as, for example, "[l]et the world be grafted onto our republics, but the trunk must be our own." An examination of resurgent images associated with greed, war, ignorance, and violence, contrasted with an informed resistance and knowledgeable (natural) defenses, may lead to a good discussion of how a reader produces meaning within Martí's text. Footnotes 4, 9, and 14 to Martí's essay offer suggestions on reading other passages.

Comparisons, Contrasts, Connections

Of significance to an American poet in New York in the latter half of the nineteenth century was Ralph Waldo Emerson and Walt Whitman. In one of the notebooks he left with his literary executor, Martí describes a future project, "My Book: *The Rebel Poets*," in which he planned to study Walt Whitman. Indeed, a backward glance over Martí's works reveals many references to Whitman, including a historic essay "El poeta Walt Whitman," published in Mexico and Argentina in 1887. In a necrological note, published in Caracas in 1882, Martí describes Emerson as "a man who found himself alive, shook from his shoulders and his eyes all the mantles and all the blindfolds that past times place over men, and lived face to face with nature, as if all earth was his home." With candor, "flooded with his immediate age," as Whitman advised American poets of all nations, Martí wrote poetry and prose distilled from his experiences as a human, political, transcultural being. Martí strove to remove all the layers of the unexamined, taxing culture of Europe as false erudition, and demanded that Americans stand face to face with *nature*, that is, the hybrid *cultures* significant of our real lands. By knowing each other's poets, mythologies, and noblest expectations, without reverting to hatred and racism, Martí expected the new Americans to rise.

Most significant to new American readers would be an acquaintance with the works of Latin American poets who follow Martí and Whitman. You might consider using Nicaraguan poet Rubén Darío's "To Roosevelt," written after the United States invasion of Panama, or "The Heights of Macchu Picchu" by Chile's Pablo Neruda. Martí's own *Simple Verses* could be suggested as part of your supplemental readings.

Pedagogical Introduction

Modern Period
1910–1945

Toward the Modern Age
Alienation and Literary Experimentation
Cluster: Political Poetry in the Modern Period
The New Negro Renaissance
Issues and Visions in Modern America

A good place to begin class discussion of this section of *The Heath Anthology* is the meaning of the term *modern* itself. Trying to define this word can lead to questions about where to locate the border between the past and present—a question implied by the phrase "*Toward* the Modern Age"—and hence to questions about the uses of literary, historical, and cultural classification systems. For example, how does the adjective *modern* affect our reading of a particular text? What difference does it make to read W. E. B. Du Bois, James Weldon Johnson, and Booker T. Washington as precursors of modern African-American literature instead of reading them as descendants of and respondents to Frederick Douglass, Harriet Jacobs, or Phillis Wheatley? Or as contemporaries of Edith Wharton and Willa Cather? Groups of students could be asked to read writers collected in just these different configurations to compare the various perspectives that emerge.

These exercises suggest further experiments in classification and reclassification. In the *Instructor's Guide* entry for "Cluster: Political Poetry in the Modern Era," Cary Nelson asks what difference the label "political" makes in reading these poems—and by extension what difference the same label would make to other texts, or what different labels would mean to the texts in that same section. What if the poems of T. S. Eliot, Ezra Pound, or Amy Lowell were labeled as primarily "political" rather than "experimental" or "personal"? What is the effect of encountering Langston Hughes in both the section on political poetry and the section on "The New Negro Renaissance"? Such questions also involve the instructor in the process of critical re-evaluation and reclassification, for as instructors we carry the biases and perspectives of our own academic training and reading histories. For many of us, the definition of the word *modern* in terms of literary history almost automatically suggests the term *modernism*. While for many students all of the writers in these sections will be new, for others, as for most instructors, certain names will leap out, but perhaps in unusual or nontraditional places. If, as an instructor, you find it curious to see Ezra Pound and T. S. Eliot so separated in the table of contents, or to see Pound next to Amy Lowell and Eliot following e. e. cummings, such a reaction can be brought into class discussion. The addition of the "Cluster: Modernism, Lyric Poetry, Facts" in the main text reinforces the idea of "modernism" as an imaginative construct, a set of lenses through which to read a group of writers. Thus, Hughes is classified as a modernist, a political poet,

527

and as a member of the "New Negro Renaissance." Each angle of vision towards Hughes produces new insights, no one of which is exhaustive.

These reactions are one way of situating the instructor's reading history and academic training in terms of the particular course, or providing a context in which to evaluate and understand the instructor's expertise, and also to illustrate the benefits offered by unsettling and reexamining traditional patterns of thought.

These questions of how classification systems of literary and cultural evaluation are formed return us to the use of "regionalism" as a definitive concept in multicultural pedagogy; the understanding that all classification systems, methods of reading, and historical narratives are social constructions connected to particular historical contexts and serving various but equally particular social, cultural, political, and psychological purposes. While the idea of replacing the universal with the regional—or asserting the universality of being regional—may seem new, it's a move comparable to the project of modernism as traditionally understood: the effort to make "Alienation and Literary Experimentation," terms suggestive of the marginality of the artist as social outsider, into what Eliot regarded as the mainstream of literary tradition—what we refer to today as the "canon." This paradoxical idea of the centrality of alienation often holds an added irony for many students reading these now-canonical high modernist texts for the first time in terms of their own sense of alienation from these self-consciously difficult texts.

Rather than assuming the centrality of a certain definition of *modernism*, regarding each text as regional turns student frustration and puzzlement—essential parts of the learning process, after all—into material for discussion rather than barriers to be overcome. Instead of guessing ahead of time which writers certain students will find difficult and which accessible, interesting, and boring, the various reading experiences students bring into class, perhaps expressed in the form of a reading log, can lead to questions of audience and purpose. "Alienation" can begin with questions about how writers—all writers, both in the anthology and in the chairs of the classroom—either consciously or unconsciously invite and/or discourage various groups of readers. These questions lead to others about the writer's purpose and strategies, an approach especially though not exclusively useful for the most self-consciously experimental and difficult texts.

Among these purposes and strategies are claims to universality. By beginning with the assumption that all writers are regionalists, we move beyond the idea that while certain groups of writers write for everyone, others represent a special or local case. The writers of "The New Negro Renaissance," for example, are typical, not exceptional, in their attention to the specific contours of particular cultural experiences: the place of African Americans in U.S. society; the role of the intellectual in the African- American community; the experience of being members of a literary and cultural movement. From this perspective,

T. S. Eliot and Ezra Pound, William Carlos Williams and Wallace Stevens are also regionalists, writing from particular cultural positions to particular audiences. If the traditional high modernists claim universality and cultural transcendence as part of their strategy, these claims are just that—strategies— and thus comparable with the strategies and claims for universality of Kay Boyle, Langston Hughes, Theodore Dreiser, or Edna St. Vincent Millay. Issues of race, gender, and class affect these strategies in terms of the traditional assumptions they carry about centrality, marginality, and importance: Gertrude Stein and Ezra Pound are both gendered writers; T. S. Eliot and Zora Neale Hurston are both writers who deal with issues of race as well as with what constitutes a literary tradition.

Finally, questions of canonicity raise questions of influence; how later writers and readers are affected by the poetic strategies and cultural theories of earlier writers and the implications for reading implicit in those strategies, issues that Eliot himself foregrounded as part of his artistic project. If some students bring to class assumptions about the inherent difficulty and obscurity of poetry, about the need to "interpret" poetry, or even about what constitutes poetry, the consideration of these writers as making various claims about what literature is, who should write it and read it, and what its cultural purposes are, can help students construct a genealogy of their own ideas about literature and reading and/or the ideas they have encountered in previous English classes.

Issues and Visions in Modern America

The texts in this section continue to address the questions of assimilation, confrontation, and transformation of the evolving myth of "Americanness" raised in "The Making of Americans,'" focusing particularly on the experiences of Native Americans, Asian Americans, and Southerners. This seemingly incongruous grouping highlights important issues related to that myth: both how that myth is profoundly regional in definition within the borders of the United States (where does the "All American" live? What are the images associated with the idea of a "typical" American town?) and how various immigrants' experiences became conflated within that myth into a single archetypal immigrant's story, usually centered on the arrival of European immigrants in New York. The poetry of anonymous Chinese immigrants not only allows for an exploration of the experience and challenges faced by Asian immigrants arriving in the American West, traveling east to a new land against the traditional European myth of west-ward expansion, but points out again the importance of recognizing the classroom as region—whether it is located in the South, the West, the Midwest, or the East; and paying attention to and making a subject of class discussion the specific immigration histories the students bring with them as part of their identities.

In addition to the continuing exploration of cultural assimilation and resistance, the other major issue addressed in these selections is the Great Depression, the collapse of the U.S. economic system that intensified patterns of internal migration (from East to West and from South to North) that continue to this day. As with immigration, class discussion can start by investigating the images of the depression in the historical consciousnesses of the class and asking students to explore their own relevant family histories. Such explorations will inevitably raise questions of social class and work, particularly as they relate to various educational institutions (community colleges, regional public universities, research institutions), including questions about the relation of a modern college education to the demands of the marketplace. Thus, reading the work of Meridel LeSueur, Clifford Odets, or Pietro Di Donato highlights not only questions about the role of the artist and the purpose of art, but also the purpose of the college literature course for students facing an increasingly competitive and uncertain economic future. Such a discussion provides an important perspective for considerations of canonicity in terms not just of creating demographically representative curricula in an abstract sense but of classes that address the concerns and ambitions of students by choosing groups of texts that in their action and interaction reflect, amplify, complicate, and clarify these concerns. Reading proletarian literature from the thirties in conjunction with T. S. Eliot, for example, broadens the implications of both types of texts and opens the paths of access to them as well.

Toward the Modern Age

Booker Taliaferro Washington (1856–1915)

Contributing Editor: William L. Andrews

Classroom Issues and Strategies

Students typically ask questions like these: Why was Washington such an accommodationist? Why did he seem so ready to accept the values of the dominant culture and political system? Why was he always so restrained and unwilling to say anything to upset the white supremacy status quo? I point out Washington's training at Hampton Institute, where he learned very early what white people wanted and how little could be accomplished without pleasing them. Also note that Washington is trying to build a source of black power in the South and cannot do so unless he makes his work seem apolitical (when it isn't).

Consider also these questions: What is the best way for a minority group to advance its own cause when faced with either outright hostility or fear and mistrust? Is Washington's tactic the most effective? What are its costs and advantages?

Major Themes, Historical Perspectives, Personal Issues

What is Washington's relationship to Douglass, the leader whose mantle he adopted? What kind of realism is Washington advocating, and how does it accord with literary realism? How does Washington fit into the tradition of the Franklinesque self-made man?

Significant Form, Style, or Artistic Conventions

What sort of slave narrative is Washington writing, in contrast to Douglass? Compare the first two chapters of both men's autobiographies to see where they resemble each other and where they differ. Generally Washington poses as a man of facts, not feelings, but does he sometimes betray strong feelings?

Original Audience

Stress the willingness of turn-of-the-century readers to believe a black man who is full of optimism about progress. How might such a message be received today—with how much suspicion?

Comparisons, Contrasts, Connections

Compare to Douglass and Chesnutt, especially in their depiction of slavery. Why would Washington play down the horrors of slavery?

Bibliography

I recommend the chapter entitled "Lost in a Cause" in Robert Stepto's *From Behind the Veil*. Urbana: Illinois UP, 1979.

W. E. B. Du Bois (1868–1963)

Contributing Editor: Frederick Woodard

Questions for Reading, Discussion, and Writing

"The Song of the Smoke" is a poem of celebration of blackness. It was written during a period of great social and political weakness of black people. List the attributes of blackness celebrated in the poem and suggest how each attribute contributes to a positive image. Consider why Du Bois may have felt it necessary to write of blackness in such exalted terms.

Ask students to characterize the effect of verbal repetition, rhythm, and variation of line length in the poem. How do these characteristics relate to the central metaphor, "smoke"?

Select an edition of the volume *The Souls of Black Folk* and peruse the beginning of each chapter. Find lines of poetry and a musical score. Consider the possible significance of these two art forms to the major theme of the book. Note that "Of the Sorrow Songs" contains comments on the music and names the songs.

The "veil" is one of Du Bois's most famous symbols. Consider possible meanings for it in "Of Our Spiritual Strivings," particularly at the beginning of the essay, where he boasts of living "above the veil."

Relate the section in "Of Our Spiritual Strivings" out of which the famous Du Bois passage on twoness comes (beginning with "After the Egyptian and the Indian, the Greek and Roman" and ending with "Shout, O Children!/Shout, you're free!/For God has bought your liberty!") to a reading of "The Unhappy Consciousness," a chapter in Hegel's *Phenomenology of Mind*. Then develop a list of supporting evidence to justify the probable influences of the Hegelian argument on Du Bois's thinking in his essay. Additional reading in Hans-Georg Gadamer, *Hegel's Dialectic: Five Hermeneutical Studies*, translated by P. Christopher Smith (New Haven: Yale UP, 1976) should provide excellent analysis of Hegel's ideas and method. See particularly Chapters 2 and 3.

Note throughout the essays collected here that Du Bois uses the terms *Negro, black,* and *African American* almost interchangeably. On closer examination, you may discern a specific context that differentiates the use of each term. Develop a rationale for use of each term in a specific context.

"Of the Sorrow Songs" is considered one of Du Bois's most enduring statements on African-American folk art. Using the content of the essay, trace the evolution of the African song to a unique American folk expression.

James Weldon Johnson (1871–1938)

Contributing Editor: Arthenia J. Bates Millican

Classroom Issues and Strategies

Next to James Weldon Johnson's name and date of birth in a biosketch is the familiar catalog of his accomplishments as educator, journalist, lawyer, composer, librettist, poet, novelist, editor, social historian, literary critic, diplomat, fighter for the rights of his people and the rights of all. Yet he is remembered today, almost exclusively, as the author of "Lift Every Voice and Sing"; and to some degree as the author of the "Creation," the first sermon in *God's Trombones.*

One mythic error is still in vogue for the less ardent student, and that is the indictment leveled against the author who "talks black" but who was never really given to the black ethos. This accusation comes as an error of identification. Some students assume that Johnson himself is the protagonist of the novel *The Autobiography of an Ex-colored Man.* Actually, the author's friend, "D_____," Douglas Wetmore, is the model for the protagonist. Thus, one encounters the problem of coping with an author with name popularity, but who is not known despite his myriad contributions to American and African-American literary culture.

The writer can best be made accessible to students, first, by introducing *Along This Way,* his authentic life story, as well as the history of the Harlem Renaissance and the rise of Marxist ideology. In the index, the entry "Johnson, James Weldon" is a reference guide in chronological order that gives the chance to examine items of choice.

Johnson may stand in clearer relief by using an "exchange" pattern of image-making. For example, discuss W. E. B. Du Bois as a "politician" who engaged in "political" actions at times.

An indirect form of transformation of real life act to art can be traced in an evolutionary process that produced *Trombones.* First, Johnson visited a Jacksonville church during his childhood days where he saw the African shout. Second, he visited "Little Africa." Third, he listened to his father as a gospel preacher. And finally, he heard gospel preachers when he was field secretary for the NAACP. The Kansas City sermon spurred these recollections and brought on a feeling that gave him import to black soul, the African communal spirit.

Students usually respond to the following issues:

1. The failure of the "Talented Tenth" to understand the economic imperatives that would involve all Americans.

2. The failure of the Johnson legacy to maintain itself with the onset of Marxism and the rise of proletarian literature.
3. The failure of Fisk and Atlanta universities to play a significant role in building a Johnson file of note.
4. The reason so little is known about J. Rosamond, Johnson's coeditor and collaborator.
5. In a quiet way, Johnson is receiving scholarly interest. Will it be potent enough to continue into the twenty-first century?

Major Themes, Historical Perspectives, Personal Issues

Exemplary themes of major import in the Johnson canon begin with "Lift Every Voice" and "Bards." They relate to the black presence in America via the "peculiar institution," slavery, but maintain relevance to the American Dream, "holy hope," and self-realization. Typical themes of historical significance are freedom and authority, liberty and responsibility, the artist in America, and society and the individual. On the personal level, in terms of the author's race and his innate concerns, the theme of historical references is stressed in order to give credence to and assess values that originated in Africa. Other themes in the "personal" category are men's ways with God; the mystical aura of the creative imagination; the power, beauty, and "essential rhythm" of indigenous black folk poetry; justice, liberation, and peace.

Significant Form, Style, or Artistic Conventions

Johnson's reputation as a writer rests on his novel and *God's Trombones*. His idea that prose should state facts enables him to write a realistic novel. He treats themes such as namelessness, racial self-hatred, the black mother's ambiguous role, and the white patron/white liberal who appears in the modern novel by blacks.

As a poet, he went through a long evolutionary stage of development. His first poems, *Jingles and Croons,* are written in the "Dunbar" tradition of accommodation, imitation, and limitation in terms of the two emotions allowed: pathos and humor. The plantation and the minstrel stage are background sources.

When Johnson wrote "Lift Every Voice" in 1900, he had become imbued with the Victorian conventions of English verse. Rudyard Kipling, the poet laureate (the court poet), wrote many occasional poems, including "Recessional," which served as a model for the black national anthem in form and structure.

Walt Whitman, the poet who gave birth to a new American poetry, wrote in free verse. *Song of Myself* set the stage for the freedom, individual experimentation, and the new theme of egalitarianism that appear in one aspect of Johnson's poem "Brothers." He used free verse in *Trombones.*

The coming of the New Negro to New York in the post–World War I period, "thoughtwise" and "boywise," combined to form Harlem as the New Jerusalem for blacks. This city became the place for conscious black artists who revered their African past and their southern roots. *Trombones* is grounded in this tradition. It makes use of African rhythms; it employs intonations of Southern folk idioms, thus enforcing the power of black speech devoid of the artificial "cant of literary dialect." Therefore, Johnson set the stage for future poets who desired to honor the oral tradition in their conscious literary works.

Original Audience

Black literature written in the nineteenth century and in the first four decades of the twentieth century was written basically for a white reading audience. At that time there were few if any student audiences on any level who studied works by blacks. In black schools, great racial personalities were presented to the students during Negro History Week. Now there is Black History Month.

Black literature in class is a phenomenon of the 1960s. Black studies programs became a part of the school curriculum in America. Therefore, the audience in class is a rather new phenomenon.

The class audiences that began as "black" or "white" at first might be one now of new minority constitution: women, handicapped people, elderly citizens, third-world students, and/or others. For the black work to be valid, then, it must have appeal to other ethnic groups since the world is now a global village.

For the new class, forums, debates, and formal and informal class reports by individual students may enhance interpersonal communication. For the dissemination of facts, the wonders effected by technology are countless. Students may have access to films, recordings, videotapes, and audiotapes for reviewing material introduced earlier in formal class lectures by the professor.

Comparisons, Contrasts, Connections

Fellow novelists of the Harlem Renaissance who honored the theme of "passing" (Johnson claimed authorship for *The Ex-colored Man* in 1927), such as Walter White in "Flight" (1926), Jessie Fauset in "Plum Bun" (1928), and Nella Larsen in *Passing* (1929), promoted the aesthetic indigenous to African literature: art for life's sake. The "for-life's-sake" element is now dated because these authors were intent on presenting the "better elements" in black life to squelch the ardor of the *Nigger Heaven* (1926) vogue fathered by Carl Van Vechten and adhered to even by Claude McKay in *Home to Harlem* (1928).

Stephen Henderson, author of *Understanding the New Black Poetry* (1973), has indicated that black speech, black song, black music (if one can make such distinctions) are imbued with "experiential energy." On this premise, Johnson, the poet who cultivated his black ethos, is best compared with Langston Hughes (1902–1967).

Questions for Reading, Discussion, and Writing

1. Does Johnson's high degree of Euro-American acculturation deflect from his African-American altruism?
2. Is he rightfully classed as a Victorian in terms of middle-class prudery and respectability?
3. Do you agree with George Kent's view that "his cosmopolitanism always extends his reach and his grasp" (*In Blackness and the Adventure of Western Culture*, 1972, p. 30)?
4. The editors of *The Conscious Voice* (1965) suggest that the poem is the rendering of experience—which also suggests "the intricacy of the poet's involvement in the world." Does Johnson use a suitable aesthetic distance from his subject matter in the poems "Lift Every Voice" (1900), "Fifty Years" (1853–1913), and "Saint Peter Relates An Incident" (1930)? (Refer to outside sources for the latter two poems.)
5. How can one justify the author's use of the compensatory Christian ethic in "Lift Every Voice," "Bards," "Listen Lord"—a prayer—and the sermons in *Trombones* when he himself is an agnostic? (Refer to outside sources for the latter two poems.)
6. Three reigning poets influenced Johnson's development as the second outstanding African-American poet: Rudyard Kipling, English; Walt Whitman, American; Paul Laurence Dunbar, African American. How?
7. Racial violence in the poem "Brothers" (1916) is attended with a plea for brotherhood. What is its advantage over literary dialect?
8. How does the longevity of the oral tradition substantiate its worth in the use of black idiomatic expression in African-American literature?

Suggested paper topics:

Period and Genre: The Color-line Novel

1. Before Johnson (1912)
2. During the Awakening (1915–1920)

3. During the Harlem Renaissance (1920–1930)
4. During the 1960s in Louisiana (Ernest Gaines)

Period:

1. The Influence of the Harlem Renaissance on West African Poets
2. Influence of the African Poets, like Leopold Senghor, on African-American Poets during the 1960s

Genre:

1. Poetry by "White" Black Authors
2. Protest Poetry
3. The "Coon Song" on Broadway
4. The Folk Sermon as Literary Genre

Bibliography

Copeland, George E. "James Weldon Johnson—a Bibliography." Master's thesis. School of Library Science at Pratt Institute, Brooklyn, NY, 1951.

Davis, Thadious. "Southern Standard-Bearers in the New Negro Renaissance." *History of Southern Literature* 2 (1985): 291–313.

Fleming, Robert. "Contemporary Themes in Johnson's *Autobiography of an Ex-colored Man*." *Negro American Literature Forum* 5 (1970): 120–24.

Johnson, J. W. "The first and second book of American Negro Spirituals, 1925." *God's Trombones*. New York: Penguin, 1927.

Levy, Eugene. *James Weldon Johnson: Black Leader, Black Voice*. Chicago: U of Chicago P, 1973. The J. W. Johnson "Prefaces" offer rich critical insight about his work *The Book of American Negro Poetry*, 1922, 1931.

Mcghee, Nancy B. "The Folk Sermon." *College Language Association Journal* 1 (1969): 51–61.

Millican, Arthenia B. "James Weldon Johnson: In Quest of an Afro-centric Tradition for Black American Literature." Diss. Louisiana State U, 1972. Chapters 6, 7, and 10 detail facts on the form and structure of dated poems.

Edwin Arlington Robinson (1869–1935)

Contributing Editor: Nancy Carol Joyner

Classroom Issues and Strategies

Robert Stevick has said that "Robinson's poetry deserves the attention it does not contrive to attract" (Barnard, *Centenary Essays,* 66). To introduce Robinson's subtlety, read the poems out loud and more than once. Robinson once told a reader who confessed to being confused about his poetry that he should read the poems one word at a time. Robinson was very sensitive to the sound of words and complained of not liking his name because it sounded like a tin can being kicked down the stairs. He also said that poetry must be music. This musical quality is best perceived by reading his poetry aloud.

Major Themes, Historical Perspectives, Personal Issues

Robinson is a "people poet," writing almost exclusively about individuals or individual relationships rather than on more common themes of the nineteenth century. He exhibits a curious mixture of irony and compassion toward his subjects—most of whom are failures—that allows him to be called a romantic existentialist. He is a true precursor to the modernist movement in poetry, publishing his first volume in 1896, a decade notable from the point of view of poetry in America only because of one other publication: the first, posthumous, volume of poems by Emily Dickinson. As the introduction emphasizes, many of Robinson's poems are more autobiographical than their seeming objectivity indicates immediately.

Significant Form, Style, or Artistic Conventions

Although Robinson's subject matter and philosophical stance differ markedly from that of his predecessors,' his form is unremittingly traditional. He considered movies, prohibition, and free verse "a triumvirate from hell," and said that if free verse were as easy to write as it was difficult to read, he was not surprised there was so much of it. In his early work Robinson experimented with difficult French forms, like the villanelle and rondeau, but his longer work is written almost exclusively in blank verse. Robinson is one of America's greatest practitioners of the sonnet and the dramatic monologue.

Original Audience

For the first twenty years of Robinson's writing career, he had difficulty in getting published and attracting an audience. He published his first two volumes privately, and the publication of the third was secretly guaranteed by friends. He did receive positive reviews from the beginning, however, and with the publication of *The Man Against the Sky* in 1916 his reputation was secure. For the rest of his life he was widely regarded as "America's foremost poet," as William Stanley Braithwaite put it. Both academics and the general public held him in high esteem, as attested by the fact of his winning three Pulitzer Prizes for poetry for volumes published in 1921, 1924, and 1927, when his *Tristram* became a national bestseller.

Comparisons, Contrasts, Connections

Critics have pointed out that Robinson is a descendant of Anne Bradstreet, and in their deceptively plain style and solitary careers they make an interesting comparison. Sometimes Robinson and Edgar Lee Masters have been confused, with people mistakenly assuming that Masters had an influence on Robinson, when the reverse must be true.

The most obvious and fruitful writer for comparison/contrast is Robert Frost, only five years younger than Robinson but nearly twenty years behind him in publication. They share a New England background, contemporaneity, and allegiance to formal writing, but they were decidedly different in lifestyle, in personality, and finally in their poetry, with Robinson's being the most honest. (Biographers of both poets report that Frost was extremely jealous of Robinson but that the reverse was not true.)

A comparison in the presentation of women in "Aunt Imogen" and Frost's "A Servant to Servant" or "Home Burial" is instructive in showing differing attitudes the poets hold toward women. Unlike many of Frost's poems, Robinson's sympathetic portrayal of his characters seems genderless.

Questions for Reading, Discussion, and Writing

1. Discussions of point of view, tone, and especially individual diction choices are useful in class. How does the word *alnage* work in "The Clerks," for instance, or what meanings can be placed on "feminine paradox" in "Aunt Imogen"? Robinson is spare in his allusions, but such reticence gives greater force to them when they appear. Discuss the ironic context of "Momus," Apollo in "The Tree in Pamela's Garden," and Roland in "Mr. Flood's Party."

2. Possible paper topics are contrasts between Robinson's poems from a woman's point of view and similar poems by contemporaneous authors, such as Robert Frost and T. S. Eliot; comparisons of characters in Robinson's poems, such as Pamela and Aunt Imogen; and imagery in "Mr. Flood's Party" and "Eros Turnannos." Numerous close readings have been published on the last two poems mentioned. Reviews of criticism along with an original interpretation of either would be an accessible research topic.

Bibliography

Coxe, Louise O. *Edwin Arlington Robinson: The Life of Poetry.* New York: Pegasus, 1969.

Joyner, Nancy C. "Edwin Arlington Robinson." *Dictionary of Literary Biography.* Vol. 54. 366–88.

Squires, Radcliffe. "Tilbury Town Today." *Edwin Arlington Robinson: Centenary Essays.* Ed. Ellsworth Barnard. Athens: U of Georgia P, 1969, 175–84.

Ellen Glasgow (1873–1945)

Contributing Editor: Linda Pannill

Classroom Issues and Strategies

Glasgow fails to make the New Woman convincing. The philosopher Judith Campbell takes her iconoclastic new book from a muff and presents it ("my little gift") to the lover for whom she is willing to sacrifice a career. She does not perceive his jealousy of her own job offer. In dialogue she repeats his words back to him. That Judith Campbell seems more like a Southern belle than a philosopher speaks to the power over heroine and perhaps author of an old-fashioned ideal of womanhood and to the difficulty for writers of Glasgow's generation who are working to create new characters and plots.

When teaching Glasgow's work, symbolism is a good place to start. Estbridge's idealism and his ruthlessness are seen in fire images: the portrait of Savonarola over a fireplace; the "flame" of love; "burned his boats"; burning his papers; the reference to the Grand Inquisitor. Other symbols include Judith's veils, the storm, Estbridge's name (East? China?), the Christmas setting (connected with his feeling "born anew" and her initials), and the doctor's garden. Judith is compared to a cypress, presumably like the one that did not survive. The remaining tree is a tough ailanthus, common though originally from China. Estbridge feels Judith is the "temptation" to disobey society's rules, but after all he will stay in his fallen garden with his sick wife. (That the younger colleague is named Adamson reinforces the Edenic motif, a favorite of the author's.)

The burden on a woman of trying to live up to a man's ideal, a theme throughout Glasgow's work, is interesting to the students. Yet they find Glasgow herself old-fashioned in her preoccupation with romantic love and with the goodness and beauty of her heroines. Along with the dire plots and the reappearances of weak male characters, this calls for an explanation that students will seek first in the author's life. They should be encouraged to look beyond.

Major Themes, Historical Perspectives, Personal Issues

Because of wide reading on the subject, Glasgow considered herself something of a philosopher. Like Judith Campbell, she wrote, and like her, she had an affair in New York with a married man, by some accounts also a doctor. In *The Woman Within*, the author depicts a conflict in her own life between woman and artist roles, love and ambition. Neither choice seems right.

Significant Form, Style, or Artistic Conventions

Irony underlines John Estbridge's self-centeredness and Judith Campbell's self-sacrifice, traits Glasgow found typical of men and women. Judith gives up an appointment at Hartwell College, previously her heart's desire, to run off with Estbridge. He misses the appointment with Judith to accept a faculty appointment. His is the "Professional Instinct," here the "instinct to yield." A too-obvious irony is the timing of the traffic accident that gives Estbridge the opportunity to betray Judith (or the author the opportunity to rescue her).

Original Audience

Both Raper (in *The Sunken Garden*) and Godbold point to a letter from Pearce Baily, a prominent New York neurologist, advising Glasgow on the story. "The Professional Instinct" deals, of course, with a doctor who has helped a writer in her work. Ellen Glasgow decided not to publish the short story and seems not to have finished revising.

Comparisons, Contrasts, Connections

Mary Hunter Austin and Willa Cather, like Glasgow, were long considered regional writers, though not all their work is set in the desert Southwest or Nebraska, as not all Glasgow's is set in Virginia. Recent feminist scholarship emphasizes these authors' concern with sex roles and their problematic self-concepts as women writers.

Questions for Reading, Discussion, and Writing

1. (a) Explain the allusion to Savonarola.
    (b) Why is the point of view effective?
    (c) Consider Tilly Estbridge and Judith Campbell as foil characters.
    (d) What seems to be the target of Glasgow's satire?
    (e) To what extent is the reader prepared for the ending?
    (f) To what extent is Glasgow the literary realist she considers herself?
2. (a) Why might Glasgow have chosen not to publish the story?
    (b) To what extent are both Judith Campbell and John Estbridge autobiographical characters?
    (c) Ellen Glasgow considered herself a feminist. How is the feminism of her period (not our own) reflected in the story?
    (d) In Glasgow's version of society, what kinds of power, if any, do women have?
    (e) How might the influence of Darwinism and Social Darwinism be seen in Glasgow's depiction of the relationship between the sexes?

Bibliography

Glasgow, Ellen. *The Woman Within.* New York: Harcourt, 1954. Chapters 1, 8–9.

Wagner, Linda. *Ellen Glasgow: Beyond Convention.* Austin: U of Texas P, 1982. Chapter 1.

Edith Wharton (1862–1937)

Contributing Editor: Elizabeth Ammons

Classroom Issues and Strategies

In my experience, students divide sharply on Wharton. Some love her work, responding particularly to the elegance and precision of her prose and the sharpness of her wit; others don't like her at all, finding it hard to "get into" her fiction because she seems so cold, the prose seems so detailed and self-conscious, and the subject matter is so elite.

Mainly I try to get the two groups talking/arguing with each other. The result usually is that each can appreciate the point of view of the other, and we can start there: with a view of Wharton in which she is both marvelously accomplished as a stylist within a particular aesthetic and—in some ways on the very same grounds—limited as a writer by class and temperament.

One issue students are very interested in is sexuality in Wharton's fiction, ranging from what birth control was available at the time and in the class she wrote about to what her own attitudes toward sex were. Another question is Why care about all these rich privileged people in Wharton's fiction? Who cares? (One response I give to this is that the top of the pyramid gives a very good sense of what the whole culture aspires to since those are the people that everyone envies and wishes to be—or is supposed to envy and wish to be. Wharton's fictive world tells us a lot about how the whole culture works and what it values and is supposed to value.) Finally, a question that often gets asked is "What other works by Wharton would you recommend reading?" A good sign.

Major Themes, Historical Perspectives, Personal Issues

Major themes in Wharton's work include the effects of class on both behavior and consciousness (divorce, for example, often horrifies the established upper class as much for its offense against taste as for its violation of moral standards); the American belief in progress as actual and good (many "advances" Wharton welcomed; others she was contemptuous of); the contrast between European and American customs, morality, and sensibility; the confinement of marriage, especially for women; women's desire for and right to freedom in general, and particularly sexual and economic freedom, and the reality that, usually, the desire and right are thwarted; the preference of powerful, white, usually upper-class men for childish, dependent women; the complexity and pain of relationships between women within patriarchal culture, including (and especially) rivalry and animosity among women.

Historically, Wharton was both the product and the beneficiary of a highly developed, even if recent, high-culture tradition of brilliant, educated women able to write and publish fiction for a living. Before Wharton, in France and England George Sand, Madame de Staël, Jane Austen, George Eliot, Mrs. Gaskell, and the Brontës had used fiction to examine many of the issues that engaged Wharton: marriage, the restraints of class, the repression of "respectable" women's sexual desire, the structure of patriarchal power, and the desire of middle-class white women for respectable, paid work. In the United States, in addition to popular women novelists in the nineteenth century, artistically ambitious women writers such as Elizabeth Stuart Phelps and Sarah Orne Jewett preceded Wharton. Contemporary with Wharton was a whole group of accomplished women fiction writers—Chopin, Austin, Hopkins, Dunbar-Nelson, Cather, Stein. The point is that Wharton's work, historically, is rooted not only in the tradition of social and psychological realism commonly associated with Howells and James (writers she admired), but also in the realism and social criticism of women writers publishing before and contemporary with her who were concerned with many of the same issues that engaged Wharton, particularly issues centered on women's experiences and problems.

Personally, Wharton treated many of the issues of her own life in her fiction: her estrangement from and anger at her mother; her frustration with the limitations placed on women, and especially women of the upper class; her miserable marriage and the stigma against divorce, again particularly in her class but also generally; her fear of the ways in which cautiousness and selfishness can corrupt one's soul; her knowledge that female sexuality, despite society's repression of it, was a potent source of creativity.

Significant Form, Style, or Artistic Conventions

"The Valley of Childish Things" is a parable, but the other selections here are classic conventional modern short stories in terms of form and effect. Wharton can be used to show perfect mastery of conventional form. Her taut, elegant prose and expert command of dramatic structure beautifully manipulate the conventional Western short story pattern of exposition/conflict/complication/climax/resolution. Typically, the climax appears almost at the very end of a Wharton story, creating a very long, strong buildup of anticipation and then a swift, deft finish. You can practically teach the standard modern Western short story—at its best—from a Wharton story.

Original Audience

Wharton was a best-selling author at the turn of the century and into the 1920s; she was also highly acclaimed by critics. After the 1920s, she was taught less and less in schools and universities until before and following World War II she was virtually untaught. She was viewed as a disciple of Henry James and he, but not she, was taught. In the late 1960s and then on through the 1990s, Wharton has steadily and dramatically regained both an academic audience and a general readership, clearly as a result of the most recent wave in the women's movement. In other words, her work attracts attention now for the very reasons it was generally dismissed in the middle of the twentieth century: its focus on women and women's experiences and its emphasis on social context, customs, pressures, and manners as human variables rooted in time, class, gender, nationality, and culture.

Comparisons, Contrasts, Connections

Useful contrasts could include authors such as Harriet Beecher Stowe or Frances Ellen Watkins Harper, who wrote fiction for explicit and avowedly political ends; Mark Twain, who was interested in communicating an almost felt sense of a very different America, the rural Midwest and the white South; Upton Sinclair (whose politics Wharton did not like but whose right to say what he wanted she vigorously defended), who identified with the working class and the poor and wrote muckrakers; or Jack London, who celebrated much of the same white masculine power ethic that Wharton disliked. Another good contrast is Henry James; though often cited as Wharton's mentor (he was one), James is also quite different from Wharton: he is much wordier, more intrusive and self-indulgent authorially, and inclined to Victorian notions of self-sacrifice and self-immolation.

Questions for Reading, Discussion, and Writing

1. When I use study questions for Wharton, I use standards closely keyed to the piece at hand: e.g., for "Roman Fever": Where does the hatred between the two women come from? What is its source? What is the source of the source? For "The Other Two" I might ask: Where do Wharton's sympathies lie in this story? On what do you base your opinion?
2. In addition to standard analytical/critical papers that ask students to work out an interpretative position by arguing closely from the text (which works very well for Wharton), I have found that Wharton is a good author to use for creative-writing paper assignments, which I do in "straight" English courses on the theory that one excellent way of getting

inside poetry or fiction is to try to create some yourself. For Wharton, I might ask students to reread "The Valley of Childish Things" and then write their own gender parable for the late twentieth century of about the same length and structural strategy. For "Roman Fever," I might ask them to write a short story about the two middle-aged women from Barbara's point of view. I spin off Wharton either formally or specifically in subject matter; also I give a rather directed assignment since one of my goals is to get students to think more about a particular piece by Wharton, how it works or what it says. I have learned that if the creative assignment is too loose, it can let them wander so far from the Wharton text that they discover no more about it than they knew before writing.

Bibliography

See Barbara A. White, *Edith Wharton: A Study of the Short Fiction* (1991). Relatively little Wharton criticism focuses on the short stories, so often it is necessary to adapt general criticism on her. Three provocative books are Elizabeth Ammons, *Edith Wharton's Argument with America* (1980); Cynthia Griffin Woolf, *A Feast of Words: The Triumph of Edith Wharton* (1977); and Candace Waid, *Edith Wharton's Letters from the Underworld* (1991).

Good articles can be found in Harold Bloom, ed., *Edith Wharton* (1986); and *Critical Essays on Edith Wharton* (1998).

Edgar Lee Masters (1869–1950)

Contributing Editor: Ronald Primeau

Classroom Issues and Strategies

Some students expect—even demand—that poetry be very "difficult" to be deemed worthwhile. When Masters is relatively simple in form and message, that throws them. To address this issue, talk about popular arts, the oral tradition, the enormous popularity of *Spoon River*, and the fact that all poetry need not be academic.

Masters provides a good chance to talk with students about what they think poetry is or ought to be and how the literary establishment can or cannot control popular opinion. Use some multimedia presentations, reading out loud. Bring in some actors from university theater.

Students are interested in events from the poet's life and factors that led him to write this kind of poetry. They wonder how any book of poems could have been *that* popular. No TV back then, they suspect.

Major Themes, Historical Perspectives, Personal Issues

Consider what it means to live in small-town America, how it is attractive to try to sum up a lifetime on a gravestone, the importance of peer pressure and what others think. Think about Masters's life as a lawyer and how that affected his poetry.

Significant Form, Style, or Artistic Conventions

It is important to discuss basic elements of form and meter in order to see how Masters alluded to, and modified, existing conventions. It is crucial to see that he was outside developing critical norms and how that has clearly limited his inclusion in the critical canons.

Original Audience

Spoon River reached a mass audience when it was written and still sells better than most poetry. Today, however, the audience is largely academic and concerns are more in the direction of scholarship and how to teach the works rather than popularity and whether they speak to an age. Discuss with students questions of popular taste and the split between mass art and high art.

Comparisons, Contrasts, Connections

Compare with Thornton Wilder's *Our Town*. Perhaps even show a video if there's time. There are recordings of *Spoon River*—and a musical. Read Masters alongside Whitman. Talk about how he hid copies of Shelley and Goethe behind law books when people thought he was supposed to be working.

Questions for Reading, Discussion, and Writing

1. (a) Who are these speakers?
   (b) To whom are they speaking?
   (c) What is our role as readers?
   (d) What have you underlined or written in the margin and why?

    (e) Which of these characters would you like to know better and why? What was Spoon River like as a place?

2. (a) Discuss the conflicts between standards for "high" art and "mass" art. Who sets criteria and how?

    (b) Compose your own gravestone biography and message to the world—à la *Spoon River*.

    (c) Write a portrait of your home town—à la *Spoon River*.

Bibliography

Flanagan, John T. *The Spoon River Poet and His Critics.* Metuchen, NJ: Scarecrow, 1974. A very useful reference guide.

Primeau, Ronald. *Beyond Spoon River: The Legacy of Edgar Lee Masters.* Austin: U of Texas P, 1981. Reevaluates Master's place in the American tradition; see chapters 1–2 for useful background on Masters.

Willa Cather (1873–1947)

Contributing Editor: Margaret Anne O'Connor

Classroom Issues and Strategies

The headnote to this Cather story stresses biographical information, which should prompt questions that will stimulate classroom discussion. Philip Gerber's bare-bones chronology in his Twayne volume on Cather is an accurate outline and an excellent choice for a chronology to supply to students. Sharon O'Brien's more detailed and topic-oriented chronology (in her edition of five of Cather's book-length prose publications for the Library of America in 1986, pp. 1296–1318) would be an excellent biographical summary for instructors to have at their disposal.

Comparisons, Contrasts, Connections

Compare Cather with Sarah Orne Jewett. Cather knew Jewett and admired her work. She even wrote an appreciative preface to a two-volume edition of Jewett's stories in 1925. An expanded version of the preface appears in the essay "Miss Jewett" in *Not Under Forty* (1936), an essay that makes it clear that

Cather saw herself as aspiring to achieve many of the strengths as a writer that she found in Jewett's work.

Questions for Reading, Discussion, and Writing

1. In your reading of the story, who is the most important character? In your reading, who is the most reliable narrator? Who is the "hero"? Who is the most sympathetically presented character?
2. One writing assignment I would suggest is in the form of a reading "quiz." Before discussing the work in class on the day it is the assigned reading, ask students to write a one-sentence summary of the story. Ask everyone to exchange papers and have students read aloud sentences that described a different central issue than the one each of them selected as at the heart of the story.

Bibliography

For the most part, the biographies by O'Brien, Woodress, and Lee, and book-length critical studies such as those by David Stouck and Susan Rosowski present the most sensitive readings of Cather's life and work.

One particularly fine "older" source is *Willa Cather: A Pictorial Memoir* (Lincoln: U of Nebraska P, 1974), with photographs by Lucia Wood and text by Bernice Slote. It's an excellent brief introduction to the world of Willa Cather.

Susan Glaspell (1876–1948)

Contributing Editor: Arthur Waterman

Classroom Issues and Strategies

It's important to show how the details of the play "Trifles" transcend local color and address universal concerns. Students should come to see that the precise setting and time lead to a universal and timeless experience.

Ask students to envision what the play would be like if it were three acts and the background and main characters were fully presented. Point out how the very restrictions of the one-act play enhance the tensions and meaning. The play has been popular since it was first produced and has been seen (1987, 1988) on PBS television, which indicates that it appeals to diverse audiences.

Susan Glaspell is an interesting example of the late-nineteenth-century woman writer, raised in the local color tradition, who radically altered her life and art after her marriage and moved east. She "came of age" about the same time American writing moved from regionalism to modernism, and she helped found the modern movement in American drama. Once her experimental period was over, she returned to fiction and to her earlier themes—much more maturely presented. Whether her retreat back to regionalism was because her husband died or because she felt more secure in the older tradition, no one can say.

Major Themes, Historical Perspectives, Personal Issues

1. Regional: The play conveys the brutal experience of being a farm wife in Iowa during the latter half of the nineteenth century.
2. Sexual: In this play women are pitted against men—Minnie against her husband, the two women against their husbands and the other men. The men are logical, arrogant, stupid; the women are sympathetic and drawn to empathize with Minnie and forgive her her crime.
3. Mythic: The setting—a lonely, bleak, cold landscape; the main characters are never seen on stage and assume a shadowy, almost archetypal presence; the struggle between them is echoed by the antagonisms between the two women and three men on stage; the result is that a brutal murder is forgiven because of the more terrible tragedy beneath it.

Significant Form, Style, or Artistic Conventions

This play presents most of the qualities of local color writing: exact detail, local speech and customs, a strong sense of place. It avoids some of the excesses of that genre: idealization of character, emphasis on the unique and colorful aspects of the locale, and sentimentality. The demands of the one-act drama— its compression, single set, limited characters, tight plot, single mood—all protect the play from the excesses of its convention and enhance its virtues.

We should also note that the play carefully distinguishes between the affairs of men and the concerns of women. The men intrude on the woman's world, dirtying her towels, scoffing at her knitting and preserves. As we move into the kitchen, the men are left out and the awful details of Minnie's life are revealed to Mrs. Peters and Mrs. Hale so that when the men return, we see how blind they are and we, the audience, accept their decision not to reveal Minnie's motive.

Original Audience

We know the play was based on an actual trial Susan Glaspell covered as a reporter in Des Moines. In this sense, the play was written for a Midwestern audience to dramatize the terrible life of a farm wife, isolated and dependent on her husband for her physical and emotional needs, with the occasional tragic consequences the play depicts. But the play was written after Susan Glaspell had left the Midwest, after she had lived abroad, married, and moved to Provincetown. She had time to ponder the implications of the event and see the tragedy in larger terms, so she was able to transform a journalistic story into a universal drama.

Comparisons, Contrasts, Connections

Zona Gale's "Miss Lulu Bett" (1920) is about a Wisconsin spinster who revolts against Midwestern prudishness to seek her own fulfillment. The play has many local color attributes and treats ironically some of the themes in "Trifles."

A better comparison is to be found with John M. Synge's "Riders to the Sea," a one-act tragedy about the lives of fishermen in the Aran Islands. Both plays transcend local color detail to reach mythic concerns, both use a piece of irregular sewing to reveal information, and both present an essential conflict between the men who go out to battle nature while the women remain to nurture beauty and sustain life.

Questions for Reading, Discussion, and Writing

1. If students have been reading someone like Bret Harte, I'd suggest they think about the advantages and disadvantages of local-color writing. Also, I would suggest they examine the one-act play form to see what can and cannot be done with it.
2. I would center on short questions about technique: How does the physical location of the characters help develop the theme? Who are more fully developed, the two women or the three men? Indicate several ways Susan Glaspell conditions the audience to accept the final decision.

Bibliography

See the primary and secondary works listed with the headnote.

Robinson Jeffers (1887–1962)

Contributing Editor: Arthur B. Coffin

Classroom Issues and Strategies

Many readers/critics feel that Jeffers's most readable poetry is in his lyric poems; others feel that his most powerful verse is in his long narrative poems, which, of course, cannot be anthologized. It is useful—perhaps necessary—therefore to provide students a sense of the larger context in which the lyrics stand and to describe the evolution of Jeffers's personal philosophy, which he called "Inhumanism." Even students who respond readily to Jeffers's reverence for a distant God made manifest in the "beauty of things" (i.e., nature)—and many of them embrace these views instantly—will ask, "Where's this guy coming from?" Consider some of the following suggestions.

One may assign individual students or groups of students narrative poems to read and report on to the class, but, with the exception of "Roan Stallion," this process is long and sometimes laborious. And it is time-consuming in the classroom. The traditional approach of lecturing to provide the necessary context is the most efficient one. (As the bibliography indicates, there is a large body of scholarly work to draw on for this purpose.)

Students respond to Jeffers's concern for the beauty of nature and the divinity he finds there. Often they are receptive to the theme of the destructive nature of human beings, especially to human pollution of the earth. Many students are drawn to what they identify as Jeffers's isolationism, his fiercely held individualism. In addition to questions about Jeffers's religious views and his varied intellectual background, they often ask about the poet himself, biographical data which, in this instance, do not take one far from the texts.

Major Themes, Historical Perspectives, Personal Issues

With the publication of the long narrative "Tamar" (1924), Jeffers declared his literary independence and attempted to write poetry appropriate to the times as he saw them. In "Self-Criticism in February," which reviews this effort, he wrote, "[this] is not a pastoral time, but [one] founded/On violence, pointed for more massive violence." Like T. S. Eliot and others, Jeffers searched myth and literature for a "usable past," but he employed these materials more radically than his peers, who, he thought, were fading out in effete aestheticism. Generally, Jeffers saw Euripides's tragic vision as more akin to his own than those of Aeschylus and Sophocles; in the Roman poet Lucretius (*On the Nature of Things*, which embodies the materialism of Epicurus), Jeffers found support for his view of nature and divinity; classical mythology and tragedy helped him to structure his personal vision and poems. American capitalism was morally bankrupt and defacing the landscape; both American politics and international affairs were threatened by "Caesarism"—ruthless leaders and timid followers. The advent of nuclear war seemed to assure the imminent destruction of human beings—but, for Jeffers, not of the world itself—which change, the poet believed, would allow the beauty of the world (the manifest God) to start over again, without the contaminating presence of mankind. His doctrine of Inhumanism—"a shifting of emphasis from man to not-man; the rejection of human solipsism and recognition of the transhuman magnificence"—encourages humans to become "uncentered" from themselves. "This manner of thought and feeling," he wrote, "is neither misanthropic nor pessimistic. . . . it has objective truth and human value."

Significant Form, Style, or Artistic Conventions

Jeffers's early verses are late-Victorian in manner, reflecting the influences of Dante Gabriel Rossetti, Algernon Swinburne, and George Moore, but prior to writing "Tamar" he decided to break with modernism, which he saw typified by Mallarmé and his followers. These modernists had forsaken content, Jeffers believed, in favor of aesthetics, which weakened their verse. His narrative poems are heavily laden with statement and action, and their lines are long and supple after classical models. "Apology for Bad Dreams" and "Self-Criticism in February" tell us nearly all there is to hear about Jeffers's poetic. Despite Jeffers's disclaimer (and the views of critics who agree with him on this point), I see him as a modernist sharing much with other modernists such as Robert Lowell, T. S. Eliot, Wallace Stevens, and Theodore Roethke, who also tried to reorder a fragmented world and to find adequate structures for the task. It may be useful to compare Jeffers's views of religion, order, fictive constructs, and reality with the more sophisticated ones of Wallace Stevens (cf. Stevens's "Sunday Morning," "The Idea of Order at Key West," "The Snow Man," and others).

Original Audience

In several places, Jeffers said that he wrote for all time, not for the moment (even though many of his lyrics of the 1940s are very topical, like carping letters to the editor that criticize world leaders indiscriminately), because he believed poetry should bespeak permanence. His work was very popular during the late 1920s and the 1930s (he appeared on the cover of *Time* magazine), but his audience left him during WWII, when his individualism and their patriotism diverged in a wood. During the 1960s and 1970s, his work was widely translated in Europe, where he gained an enthusiastic readership in the Slavic countries. On this continent, he has been adopted by members of the ecology movement, disaffected members of traditional institutional religions, and academic scholars, who together have revived his reputation. Although Jeffers had been severely slighted in the academic texts of recent decades, he is one of the few poets, I find, that the general student is most apt to have read *before* taking an American literature or poetry course.

Jeffers's disinterest in a particular audience—his writing for all time—simplifies the audience problem in class and permits a wide range of responses.

Comparisons, Contrasts, Connections

Compare Jeffers's themes to Euripides's, whose tragedies he used and "adapted" as in Jeffers's Broadway hit *Medea*. He follows the Greek closely, but the differences are arresting.

Consider also Lucretius, whose version of Epicurus' materialism attracted Jeffers, who fused it with his pantheistic view of nature.

For another interesting comparison, look at Shelley, whose view of Prometheus and the poet as legislator are reflected in Jeffers. Jeffers's incest theme has been traced to Shelley.

Nietzsche's philosophy appears to have attracted but not to have held Jeffers. Nietzsche's *Thus Spake Zarathustra, Beyond Good and Evil,* and *The Birth of Tragedy* would be the main texts of interest.

Wallace Stevens's interest in the imagination, reality, and fictive constructs provides bases for comparison/contrast.

T. S. Eliot's use of mythic materials and the literary tradition to construct an authentic religious outlook suggests some interesting similarities and dissimilarities.

Eugene O'Neill was similarly preoccupied with Greek tragedy.

Theodore Roethke's mystical view of nature and of the spirit that resides in nature offers fertile possibilities for comparison/ contrast.

W. B. Yeats's interest in towers, in social unrest versus change, and in the cycles of nature compare with those of Jeffers.

Ansel Adams's photographs of "Jeffers country" offer opportunities for discerning comparisons/contrasts between visual and literary texts.

Working with Cultural Objects

An appealing approach from the students' perspective is to introduce Jeffers's *Not Man Apart* (ed. David Brower, San Francisco: Sierra Club, 1965; Ballantine Books: New York, 1969), which, taking its title from a Jeffers line, is a collection of magnificent Ansel Adams photographs of the Big Sur landscape (accompanied by quotations from Jeffers), which has a central role in this poetry.

Hearing these poems is very important, and, whether or not the instructor is a competent reader of these verses, he or she might consider obtaining recordings of William Everson's superb reading of them. One (formerly available from Gould Media, 44 Parkway West, Mount Vernon, NY 10552-1194; Tape #826) was titled *The Poetry of Robinson Jeffers*. Two others are still available from Big Sur Tapes, P.O. Box 4WB, Tiburon, CA 94920: Tape #06103 (*Poetry of the Earth* by William Everson) and Tape #06101 (*A Dramatic Presentation of Robinson Jeffers* by William Everson and Gordon Newell) at <http://www.bigsurtapes.com>.

Questions for Reading, Discussion, and Writing

1. After reading the Jeffers poems included in the text (and any others of his you wish to look at), write two or three pages of response to them. In your brief paper, assume that you are a developer (real estate or commercial, for example), or an environmentalist (perhaps a member of the Sierra Club or other similar group), or a TV evangelist, or some other role of your choice. You should imagine how you think the person you choose to be in your paper would most likely respond to Jeffers's work.

2. You have just been reading Jeffers, and your roommate or brother or sister or parent comes and says, "Reading Jeffers? What does he have to say? Should I read his poems?" Assuming that you and your interrogator are on good terms, write a compact essay summarizing what Jeffers says and include in your response to the last question why you make the recommendation you give. Saying simply "yes" or "no" or "you're too young (or old)" to the last question is to evade its point; develop a reasoned reply. Be specific.

Bibliography

For the instructor in survey courses, the handiest and most comprehensive source is Robert Brophy, *Robinson Jeffers* (Boise: Western Writers Series, 1973); James Karman, *Robinson Jeffers: Poet of California* (1987) is excellent for biographical information. *Jeffers Studies*, which replaced the *Robinson Jeffers Newsletter*, continues to keep one abreast of current Jeffers scholarship. The Robinson Jeffers Association website is an invaluable resource: <http://www.jeffers.org>.

Robert Frost (1874–1963)

Contributing Editor: James Guimond

Classroom Issues and Strategies

Students generally respond well to the basic emotional or psychological experiences expressed in Frost's poems. Some of them—for example, ones who have had a philosophy course or two—may raise questions about the implications of poems like "Design." Students often have difficulty appreciating (a) the skill and subtlety with which Frost uses traditional poetic devices such as rhyme and meter; (b) the sparse pleasures he discovers in some of his rural and natural subjects; (c) the bleakness and/or ambiguity of his more "philosophical" poems. Sometimes they also have difficulty understanding that the values he presented in his poems were derived from a type of community or society that was very different from their own: one that was rural, fearful of change, distrustful of technology, proud of craftsmanship, and deeply committed to privacy and self-reliance.

Regarding the formal devices and ambiguity, there is no substitute for traditional "close reading." (Quotations from Frost's essays "The Constant Symbol" and "The Figure a Poem Makes" can be helpful in this regard.) The sparse pleasures can be seen in a poem like "The Pasture," and the bleakness can be discerned in the endings of "Once by the Pacific" and "Desert Places." The social values can be seen in a dramatic poem like "The Ax-Helve," as well as in "Mending Wall."

When teaching the dramatic poems, it is helpful to discuss their plots and characters with students because Frost sometimes presents these elements in an oblique way.

Major Themes, Historical Perspectives, Personal Issues

Major themes would include

1. The limitations and isolation of the individual in either a social or natural environment, plus the related theme of how difficult it is for the self to understand existence.
2. The ambiguity of nature when it is considered as a source of wisdom.
3. Frost's sensitivity to the theme of entropy, doom, and extinction.

Frost usually deals with personal issues so covertly in his poetry that it is not very fruitful to discuss those topics in detail. If the teacher wishes to do so, however, he or she should consult Thompson's biography. For historical issues, the Cowley and O'Donnell essays in James Cox's *Robert Frost: A Collection of Critical Essays* are helpful.

Significant Form, Style, or Artistic Conventions

Special emphasis should be placed on

1. His skill in synthesizing traditional formal devices with vernacular speech patterns and language.
2. His ability to develop metaphors.
3. How relatively "unmodern" or traditional he was in relation to some of his contemporaries.

Original Audience

I emphasize that during the 1920s, 1930s, and 1940s Frost had a strong appeal for a conservative readership who did not understand or appreciate modernism very well. Since such readers could be quite influential in academic, editing, and Pulitzer-Prize–judging circles, some of Frost's popularity should be considered in this context.

Comparisons, Contrasts, Connections

Contrasts with Wallace Stevens, William Carlos Williams, Ezra Pound, and T. S. Eliot are appropriate; and comparisons with Henry Wadsworth Longfellow, William Cullen Bryant, Edward Arlington Robinson, and the British Romantics and Georgians (e.g., Edward Thomas) can be helpful.

Questions for Reading, Discussion, and Writing

1. (a) What would it be like to live on an isolated farm in 1900?
   (b) Find the rhymes in specific poems and discuss why Frost emphasized these words.
   (c) What are the emotional connotations of the images in certain poems?
   (d) Who is the speaker of the poem, and why is he or she speaking?
   (e) How does Frost develop a metaphor in an assigned poem?
2. (a) Comparison-contrast topics work well if they are focused on specific issues like free verse versus traditional meters.

(b) What is Frost's persona, and how does he develop it in a variety of poems?

(c) How does Frost create conflict or tension in his poems, and how does he resolve it?

(d) How closely does Frost follow his own poetic "rules" as he states them in "The Figure a Poem Makes"?

(e) Compare the "philosophy of life" which is expressed in a poem like "Directive," "Design," or "Desert Places" with the ideas in an essay by Ralph Waldo Emerson, such as "Nature."

Bibliography

The books by Richard Poirier and Frank Lentricchia are particularly useful, and there are good essays in the critical anthologies edited by Cox, Gerber, Bloom, and Cady and Budd.

Sherwood Anderson (1876–1941)

Contributing Editor: Martha Curry

Classroom Issues and Strategies

Teachers should avoid three erroneous approaches to Sherwood Anderson's writings: regarding him primarily as a novelist, as a regional writer, or as author of only one important book, *Winesburg, Ohio.*

Regarding the first error: even in his best novel, *Poor White,* Anderson has difficulty sustaining plot and characterization. Anderson succeeds best in the smaller narrative form of the short story. "Hands" and "Death in the Woods" exemplify many of the characteristics of the masterpieces of Anderson's storytelling art: direct authorial address to the reader; a circular, not linear, narrative structure; plot subordinated to characterization; simple style and vocabulary; and images drawn from elemental aspects of nature.

Regarding the second error: Although Anderson is one of the many regional writers who chronicle the changes that took place in the Midwest at the turn of the century as a result of industrialization, primary emphasis should be placed on his role as a storyteller.

Regarding the third error: Neither *Winesburg, Ohio,* from which "Hands" is taken, nor *Death in the Woods,* with its title story, is a collection of isolated stories but, rather, short story cycles; that is, collections of stories with common themes, imagery, and tone, and often with common setting and characters. An understanding of the short story cycle, from Homer's *Odyssey* to Chaucer's *Canterbury Tales* to Joyce's *Dubliners* will help in understanding Anderson's work.

Students are amazed at how contemporary Anderson is. He speaks to their concerns regarding loneliness, fragmentation, and the search for beauty and wholeness. They also are intrigued by the artistry that a small work like a short story can achieve.

Major Themes, Historical Perspectives, Personal Issues

After they study "Hands," students can read the whole of *Winesburg*. Reading the story of Wing Biddlebaum will prepare students to explore two themes discernible in "Hands" and carried forward in the rest of *Winesburg*. First, explain the theme introduced in *Winesburg*'s first section, "The Book of the Grotesque," the theme of the misunderstood inhabitants of Winesburg trapped in their loneliness by one "truth" that has turned into a falsehood. Second, explain the theme of the gnarled apples explicated most fully in the second story of the collection, "Paper Pills." In the orchards of Winesburg are gnarled, twisted apples, rejected by the apple pickers but savored by the narrator and his readers, that is, by the few who can recognize their sweetness. Wing Biddlebaum in "Hands" and Ma Grimes in "Death in the Woods" are two of Anderson's grotesques, people trapped in their own in-ability to find the "truth" of their lives and thus unable to grow to maturity, but possessing their own sweetness and beauty.

Regarding historical issues: When *Winesburg* was published in 1919, it was considered scandalous because of its direct treatment of sex. "Hands," with its sympathetic portrayal of homosexuality, was one of the stories often cited. We know from many of Anderson's reminiscences, however, that he had a particular fondness for "Hands." In his *Memoirs* (ed. Ray Lewis White, Chapel Hill: U of North Carolina P, 1969, p. 237) he calls the story "my first authentic tale" and claims that he "completed it cleanly at one sitting." On page 352, he also claims it was written "in one sitting. No word of it ever changed." The manuscript of *Winesburg* with the Sherwood Anderson Papers at the Newberry Library in Chicago, however, contains extensive revisions. Nonetheless, the statements just quoted from his *Memoirs,* although false if taken literally, are substantially correct. By temperament Anderson was disinclined to rework, correct, fill in details. Instead, as we know by the many versions of the same story in his unpublished work at the Newberry Library, he often rewrote and rewrote whole stories.

A historical perspective to bring to "Death in the Woods" is the fact that Anderson tried to write this story to his satisfaction. As we know from a note attached to a holograph housed with the Anderson Papers in the Newberry

Library, Anderson's first attempt to write this story is a short sketch called "Death in the Forest." Chapter XII of *Tar: A Midwestern Childhood* (Cleveland: P of Case Western Reserve U, 1969, pp. 129–41) also tells the story of an old woman's death in the woods on a snowy night. A slightly expanded version of this episode, told by a first-person narrator, appeared in *American Mercury* (IX, 7–13), in September of the same year, that is, 1926. Since the 1933 title story in the collection *Death in the Woods* is practically identical with the version of the story that appeared in *American Mercury,* we can assume that Anderson worked on "Death in the Woods" from the mid-1910s, the time he was writing the *Winesburg* stories, until 1926.

When we consider this background concerning the composition of "Hands" and "Death in the Woods," we can see that both stories exemplify Anderson's usual method of storytelling. Anderson writes and rewrites his stories until he is satisfied with them, just as his narrators try again and again to tell the "real" story hidden beneath surface events.

Significant Form, Style, or Artistic Conventions

Attention should always be drawn to the importance of the narrator in Anderson's stories. Although "Hands" is told in the third person, the narrator speaks directly to the reader in the tradition of oral storytellers, thus bringing the reader into the creation of the story. Twice in the story the narrator says that both the teller of the tale and the listener, in this case, the reader, have to become poets. The reader is urged to accept the narrator's invitation to "look briefly into the story of the hands. Perhaps our talk of them will arouse the poet who will tell the hidden wonder." Earlier in the story the narrator assures the reader that "Sympathetically set forth"—as Anderson surely does—Wing's story "would tap many strange, beautiful qualities in obscure men. It is a job for a poet."

In "Death in the Woods" the central character is not Ma Grimes but the mature narrator who looks back on earlier experiences: the sight of an old, oppressed woman trudging from her farm into town in order to obtain the necessary food for her men and animals; the time he worked for a German farmer who hired a "bound girl"; the moonlit winter night he saw half-wild dogs almost revert to wolves in the presence of the near-death of a human.

The teacher must stress the role of the mature narrator as he struggles to weld his diverse experiences and images into a whole that will bring order out of their diffuseness and beauty out of their ugliness. All of her days Ma Grimes "fed animal life." Only at the end of the story does the reader realize that the most important life Ma Grimes fed was the creative life of the narrator. Thus, the story as a whole demonstrates, as Anderson explains in its final sentence, "why I have been impelled to try to tell the simple story over again." The reader feels, as the story comes to a close, that now, after perhaps ten or twelve years, Anderson has been able to create a beautifully unified work of art.

Comparisons, Contrasts, Connections

Since much of Anderson's fiction relies heavily on his own experiences, the best background materials for teaching "Hands" and "Death in the Woods" are primary, not secondary, sources, although excellent critical articles on both stories can easily be found by means of the standard indexes. Nonetheless, the best background information still remains Anderson's own words. Anderson's three autobiographies, *Tar, A Story Teller's Story,* and *Memoirs,* all available in critical texts edited by Ray Lewis White, have excellent indexes that will lead the reader to the appropriate sections.

Questions for Reading, Discussion, and Writing

1. In regard to "Hands," call the students' attention to
   (a) Society's attitudes toward homosexuality at the time Anderson was writing the story and now. Explore the students' own attitudes, and compare them to Anderson's treatment of Wing Biddlebaum.
   (b) The role played by George Willard, especially the role played by his absence in this story. Explain that George Willard's growth to maturity, through his interaction with all the characters in the stories, is actually the central story of *Winesburg.* Let the students sense the relation between George and Wing, and, again, make them enter the story.
   (c) The moment with which the story opens and closes: "the half decayed veranda of a small frame house" on the edge of town. This moment becomes the center around which the rest of the story circles. Explain Anderson's development of this nonlinear plotting and his influence on later short story writers.
   (d) The many images in the story. A few examples are the importance of dreaming, the allusion to Socrates, the "breaking wings of an imprisoned bird," and, of course, Wing's hands themselves.
2. In regard to "Death in the Woods," call the students' attention to
   (a) The various levels of the story: story of Ma Grimes, her relationship to the men and animals in the story, her role as "feeder" of life.
   (b) The function played by the dogs, both literal and symbolic.
   (c) Growth of the narrator from a young boy to a mature artist.
   (d) The difficulty the narrator has in telling the story.
   (e) The many images in the story, both from nature and from art.

3. I have had great success in having students write a short story or character sketch about one of the "grotesques" they meet in everyday life,
someone they see on the bus or subway, in the supermarket or on the street,
at home or in school. They must approach this character with great
respect and love, as Anderson does, and try to imagine and then tell the
character's story of isolation, fear, and, ultimately, of beauty.

Bibliography

Read: *Winesburg, Ohio*, a very short book. Several other stories in Maxwell
Geismar's *Sherwood Anderson: Short Stories*.

If there is time, read: Chapter XII of *Tar*. "Death in the Forest," edited by
William Miller and printed as an appendix to Ray Lewis White's critical
edition of *Tar*, pp. 231–36. Selections from White's critical edition of Sherwood
Anderson's *Memoirs*.

Chapter I of *Representative Short Story Cycles of the Twentieth Century*
by Forest L. Ingram (The Hague: Mouton) for Ingram's theory of the short-story
cycle.

The Chicago Renaissance in American Letters: A Critical History by
Bernard Duffey (Westport, CT: Greenwood, 1954), chapter 10, "Three Voices of
the Liberation," about Francis Hackett, Harriet Monroe, and Margaret Anderson and the little magazines they founded; and chapter 11, "The Struggle for
Affirmation—Anderson, Sandburg, Lindsay."

Theodore Dreiser (1871–1945)

Contributing Editor: John Alberti

Classroom Issues and Strategies

In many ways, students may be struck by the modernity of "The Second Choice."
Dreiser describes life in a lower-middle-class suburb where a young unmarried
woman commutes between her retail sales job and her parents' modest home.
Seemingly content, she is awakened to romantic dreams and ambitions by a
young man with big dreams of his own. After he leaves her, the young woman is
left with the prospect of settling for her "second choice," her long-time suitor
who holds out the promise of a life little different from that of the other
women in her neighborhood. Similarly, Dreiser's modernity manifests itself in
his open acknowledgment of sexual desire and his frank critique of the myths of

romantic love and personal transcendence, all the while displaying sympathy for their powerful attraction.

On the other hand, Dreiser presents a subtle yet nonetheless devastating depiction of the constraints imposed by gender in his own time. Even before she is left behind by Arthur, Shirley is unable to imagine any future for herself that does not depend on a relationship with a man. Along these lines, discussion might begin by asking students to list what they find most and least contemporary about Shirley's situation. An obvious example immediately relevant to the classroom is the question of education. Women today of a comparable class background to Shirley would most likely find themselves in college, and the prospect that such a young woman in the twenty-first century might aspire to an independent career at least the equal of Barton's or Arthur's might initially make some students reluctant to fully sympathize with Shirley's dilemma in the story. Such a discussion can provide an important context for students' reactions to the decisions Shirley makes and the attitudes she expresses. Rather than judging her by modern standards, the class can consider what structural conditions limit her desires and imagination.

Of course, the myth of romantic love and the cultural tradition of designating heterosexual marriage as the most desirable outcome for any woman's life is still very much with us, and Dreiser's story raises the question of how much Shirley's disappointment is related to actual qualities possessed by Arthur and Barton and how much to the socially constructed image of female desire presented by her culture. Dreiser also attends with an almost sociological rigor to the specific contours and limitations of social class. Shirley, for example, envies the "girls" who were "so much more fortunate. They had fine clothes, fine homes, a world of pleasure and opportunity in which to move." Shirley's class resentment raises the idea and ideal of "a world of pleasure and opportunity," a utopian vision that in the end proves unattainable and therefore more a source of despair than of hope.

In the end, Dreiser resists providing the reader with a narrative twist or surprise either for the tragic or the comic. Barton reacts to Shirley's halfhearted efforts at reconciliation exactly as she predicts, and nothing about the conclusion suggests that her life will be other than that of the other married women on Bethune Street. The story can thus be read as an exemplar of Dreiser's tragic determinism, of human beings fruitlessly hoping to escape the resistless forces of natural desire and the class system.

Given their experiences with the conventions of short fiction and stories about romantic love, students can be asked whether the ending surprises, disappoints, or satisfies them and why. Dreiser is often called pessimistic. Does the class agree? How do we define a term like *pessimism* in relation to a term like *realism*?

Comparisons, Contrasts, Connections

Raymond Carver's "What We Talk About When We Talk About Love" provides an interesting, more contemporary examination of the idea of romantic love. Carver's minimalism derives in part from Dreiser's style in its lack of authorial intrusion and resistance to elaborate prose style.

Bibliography

Gerber, Philip. "Theodore Dreiser." *Dictionary of Literary Biography.* Vol. 9. Detroit: Gale, 1981. Biographical sketch.

Griffin, Joseph. *The Small Canvas: An Introduction to Dreiser's Short Stories.* Fairleigh Dickinson, 1985.

Edna St. Vincent Millay (1892–1950)

Contributing Editor: John J. Patton

Classroom Issues and Strategies

Students have few problems reading Millay's poetry because the poet is forthright in expressing her emotions, ideas, and experiences. Obviously such references as those to Euclid and Endymion require explanation. Occasionally the diction needs some explication because of Millay's fondness for archaic and Latinate words.

Not much more is required than the teacher's ability to clarify some allusions and an occasional word or phrase. Any teacher of modern American literature should also have no problems with the references to city life and to issues of the times, which are generously sprinkled throughout Millay's work. As for accessibility, some benefit will come from placing Millay in the context of the poetry of the 1920s and 1930s as one of those like, for instance, Robert Frost, Archibald MacLeish, and Edward Arlington Robinson, who carried forward the more traditional verse form and techniques in the face of the experimentalism of T. S. Eliot, Ezra Pound, Wallace Stevens, and William Carlos Williams. Millay also wrote on subjects that have a long history in English verse—the natural scene, romantic love, impermanence and death, and even poetry itself and the poet. Some students may therefore possibly view her as "old-fashioned" in contrast to the more experimental poets of her time. What must be emphasized is that Millay and other technically conservative poets flourished alongside the "New Poets," the modernists, and similar poets and that they produced poetry with less emphasis on intellectualization and more on overt feeling. It is characterized by forthrightness of expression, clarity of diction, and avoidance of ambiguity and of the esoteric and erudite as a source for figurative language.

Millay is one poet in particular whose work benefits from being read aloud in order to do justice to its melodic qualities. In her own recording of some of her poems, Millay emphasizes the songlike nature of much of her verse. Teachers should play this recording for students or, of course, have them read the poems aloud themselves.

Students often raise gender issues. For example, they ask whether it makes any difference that the poet is a woman. Does gender show itself in any apparent way, allowing for those instances where the poet deliberately displays it as in the speaking voice used or the pronoun gender? How is Millay's stance as a "liberated" woman shown in her poetry, if at all? Another issue is relevance. In what ways are Millay's poems relevant to today's lives? Are her concerns significant to present-day readers? Is it readily apparent that her poetry dates largely from the 1920s and 1930s?

Major Themes, Historical Perspectives, Personal Issues

Millay's interest in heterosexual relationships is a major theme in her poetry, whether between husband and wife, as in "An Ancient Gesture," or between disaffected lovers, as in "The Spring and the Fall." Few American poets in this century have written on this subject with the combined artistry and diversity of Millay. "Love is not all" and "Oh, sleep forever in the latmian cave" are from *Fatal Interview,* a fifty-two sonnet sequence that deals with the course of a love affair from beginning to end.

Millay should not, however, be associated exclusively with this kind of poetry. Another major theme is the integrity of the individual, which Millay valued highly for herself as well as for others. "The Return" describes a man who has apparently "sold out" in order to escape into the illusory "comfort" of nature. In "Here lies, and none to mourn him" Millay is describing a humankind that has fatally compromised itself by, perhaps, a reliance on technology (others see it as a comment on war).

A related theme, the integrity of the artist, is touched on in "On Thought in Harness." Millay also had a high degree of social consciousness. She spoke out against the execution in 1926 of the anarchists Sacco and Vanzetti, she wrote about the wars in Spain and China, and she devoted a volume of verse, *Make Bright the Arrows,* to concern about World War II. "Here lies, and none to mourn him" is one of an eighteen-sonnet sequence in this volume.

Significant Form, Style, or Artistic Conventions

Millay's relationship to the poetry of her time should be discussed, as well as her antecedents in verse and her achievements in the sonnet and the lyric. Her immediate contemporaries include notably e. e. cummings, T. S. Eliot, Robert Frost, Amy Lowell, Marianne Moore, Ezra Pound, and Edward Arlington Robinson. Millay, like Frost and Robinson, was a conservative in verse form and technique, a "traditionalist." Although highly aware of the work of her contemporaries, she steered clear of all "schools," such as imagists, modernists, objectivists, and so on. Some critics place her in a line of descent from such late-nineteenth-century English poets as Robert Browning and Algernon Swinburne.

A widely read person, Millay absorbed influences from sixteenth- and seventeenth-century English poets, hence her devotion to the sonnet form, in which she has no peer in all of American literature. The sonnet "His stalk the dark delphinium" is noteworthy because Millay used tetrameter verse rather than the more common pentameter. Millay's lyrics display a wide variety of form. Students may gauge her breadth in lyric poetry by contrasting the mixed verse feet and line lengths in "Spring" and its abrupt turns of phrase with the melodic flow of "The Spring and the Fall" and its regularity of form.

Original Audience

Millay continues to appeal to a large audience, as shown by the publication in the fall of 1987 of a new edition of her sonnets, a volume of critical essays, and an annotated bibliography of secondary sources. A very large audience of readers in her own time admired her frequent outspokenness, her freshness of attitude, her liberated views as a woman, and the reflection in her poetry of an intensely contemporary sensibility. She is quintessentially modern in her attitude and viewpoint even if her language is often redolent of earlier poets. Although it is true that Millay's poetry has great appeal to women readers, she must not be either presented or viewed as writing solely for women because of the evident limitations it would place on appreciation of her accomplishment.

Comparisons, Contrasts, Connections

To illustrate Millay's mastery of the sonnet, a comparison should be made with Keats as her nearest equivalent. Both display the same ease and control in the form. The sonnets of Sir Philip Sidney, for one, may be used to show Millay's historical connection with the great sonneteering tradition in English. Direct comparison with Shakespeare would be useful only to illustrate her range of achievement—181 sonnets in the latest edition.

Millay's lyric poetry can be compared with that of several late-nineteenth-century English lyricists, such as Dowson, D. G. Rossetti, and Housman (Browning and Swinburne have already been mentioned).

Her relationship to older American poets is less clear. She seems to have been little interested in them. Commentators have related her work in ways to that of Emerson and Holmes and perhaps some of Whittier and Longfellow, but not at all to Whitman and Dickinson. As noted above, Millay stands apart from the experiments and innovations in verse in her own time. She should be more meaningfully compared with Robinson, MacLeish, Frost, and Masters, among others, who, while employing conservative prosodic techniques, expressed a contemporary point of view.

Questions for Reading, Discussion, and Writing

1. "Spring": What is suggested about life by images of the empty cup and uncarpeted flight of stairs?

   "The Return": Why is Earth not able to comfort the despairing Man?

   "Here lies, and none to mourn him": What seems to have "cut down" Man (the human race)?

   "Love is not all": Although love is not "all," would the poet easily give it up?

   "On Thought in Harness": Explain the significance of the title with reference to the poem.

   "Oh, sleep forever": Restate the last two lines in your own words.

   "His stalk the dark delphinium": Explain why "all will be easier" when the mind grows its own "iron cortex."

2. The student who selects Millay could read more of her work and then write about a major theme in the work.

   Another possibility is that a student might read further in her sonnets; read sonnets by others, e.g., Sidney, Donne, and Keats; and then write an analytical paper on differences and/or similarities in form, predominant subject matter, diction, and so on.

   Another assignment would be to read other American women poets of the time (Crapsey, Teasdale, H.D., Wiley, Amy Lowell) to show any similarities based on their sex.

Bibliography

Allen, Albert. "Millay and Modernism." *Critical Essays on Edna St. Vincent Millay.* Ed. William B. Thesig. Boston: Hall, 1993. 266–72. Millay's "stylistic uncertainties" and social consciousness poems place her outside the High Modernism movement.

Douglas, George H. "Edna St. Vincent." *Women of the 20s.* Dallas: Saybrook, 1986. 104–47. A view of Millay as one who "exhibits the temper of the times."

Fried, Debra. "Andromeda Unbound: Gender and Genre in Millay's Sonnets." *Twentieth Century Literature* 32 (Spring 1986): 1–22. A valuable study of Millay as a major sonneteer.

Gray, James. *Edna St. Vincent Millay.* Minneapolis: U of Minnesota P, 1967. Forty-six small pages provide a thoughtful overview of Millay's life and career.

Klemans, Patricia. "Being Born a Woman: A New Look at Edna St. Vincent Millay." *Colby Library Quarterly* 15 (March 1979): 7–18. Millay is seen as a liberated woman who introduced the personality of the "passionate woman" into love poetry.

Rovit, Earl. "Our Lady Poets of the Twenties." *Southern Review* 16 (January 1980): 65–85. Rovit offers an informative context, showing the challenges faced by women poets during Millay's early years.

Sprague, Rosemary. "Edna St. Vincent Millay." *Imaginary Gardens: A Study of Five American Poets.* Philadelphia: Chilton, 1969. 135–82. Millay's poetry is related to her life and times.

Stanbrough, Jane. "Edna St. Vincent Millay and the Language of Vulnerability." *Shakespeare's Sisters: Feminist Essays on Women Poets.* Ed. Sandra M. Gilbert and Susan Gubar. Bloomington: Indiana UP, 1979, 183–99. A sense of vulnerability, victimization, and constriction appears in some of Millay's poems.

Wilson, Edmund. "Epilogue 1952: Edna St. Vincent Millay." *The Shores of Light.* New York: Farrar, 1952. 144–93. An authoritative personal and critical view of Millay by a major critic who knew her all her adult life.

Alienation and Literary Experimentation

Ezra Pound (1885–1972)

Contributing Editor: Betsy Erkkila

Classroom Issues and Strategies

Pound's announcement of the principles of imagism in "A Retrospect" provides an excellent introduction to the poetics of literary modernism. Like Hemingway in prose, Pound turns away from the "emotional slither" and abstract rhetoric of romantic and Victorian writers toward an emphasis on precision and concision in language and imagery. The poem "In a Station of the Metro" puts Pound's imagist theory into practice. Pound was struck by the beauty of a crowd of faces he observed in the Metro at La Concorde in Paris; he tried to represent the experience first in a thirty-line poem; then through a Kandinsky-like splash of color; finally, he says, he found the best form for the experience in the model of Japanese *haiku* poetry. The poem interweaves subjective impression with objective expression, presenting in miniature the controlling myth of Pound's work: the discovery of light amid darkness, fertility amid waste, figured in the myth of Persephone in the Underworld.

In teaching "Hugh Selwyn Mauberley" and *The Cantos,* you might want to prepare a handout explicating some of the allusions in the poem. You can use Ruthven's *Guide to Personae,* Brooker's *Student's Guide to the Selected Poems of Ezra Pound,* and Kearns's *Guide to Ezra Pound's Selected Cantos.* Begin by asking students to think about the overall import of "Hugh Selwyn Mauberley." On the broadest level, the poem is a compelling critique of the modern age; more specifically, it is about the plight of the artist, and of Pound in particular, in the modern world. Look at the ways the opening section on "E.P." works formally. The poem moves not by linear progression but by the juxtaposition of images as emotional and intellectual complexes; meaning develops not through direct authorial statement but by engaging the reader in a continual process of interpretation.

Major Themes, Historical Perspectives, Personal Issues

While Pound buries the aesthete figure of his early period in the opening section of "Hugh Selwyn Mauberley," he does not renounce the value of artistic creation as a source of personal and social renewal; he represents and asserts the enduring value of beauty and song in "Envoi," which is modeled on the poem "Go, Lovely Rose" by the seventeenth-century English poet Edmund Waller.

The postwar context of the poem should be emphasized; sections IV and V contain one of the most negative and moving chants against war in modern literature.

Significant Form, Style, or Artistic Conventions

If Pound is the first or only modern writer you are discussing, you might want to begin by discussing the relation between an increasingly complex and allusive form and content among modern writers and the increasing isolation and alienation of the artist in the modern world. Pound went abroad both physically and mentally in his early period, seeking models and masks in past literatures, including Greek (Homer), Latin (Virgil, Ovid, Catullus), Italian (Dante, Arnaut Daniel, Guido Calvalcanti), French Provençal (Bertran de Born), and Chinese (Li Po, Confucius). During the war years, as he began to turn his attention toward the contemporary world, he also turned backward toward the native tradition of Walt Whitman. This turn is evident in the raw and comic exuberance of "A Pact," in which Pound seeks to come to terms with Walt Whitman.

Comparisons, Contrasts, Connections

Pound's evocation of war might be compared with Eliot's *The Waste Land*, Hemingway's *A Farewell to Arms*, and "The Walls Do Not Fall" in H.D.'s *Trilogy*.

After "Hugh Selwyn Mauberley," Pound turned his main attention to his epic *Cantos*, which he worked on for the remainder of his life. In a letter to W. B. Yeats, he said he intended to write one hundred cantos, modeled on a Bach fugue: "There will be no plot, no chronicle of events, no logic of discourse, but two themes, the Descent into Hades from Homer, a Metamorphosis from Ovid, and mixed with these, medieval or modern historical characters." As Pound's comment suggests, the poem has three analogues: an Odyssean journey, modeled on Homer's *Odyssey*; an ascent through Inferno and Purgatory toward the light of Paradiso, modeled on Dante's *Divine Comedy*; and from Ovid's *Metamorphosis* a series of "magic moments" in which divine energies are revealed in the physical world.

Pound speaks in a personal voice that anticipates the confessional strain in the poems of Allen Ginsberg, Robert Lowell, and Sylvia Plath.

Questions for Reading, Discussion, and Writing

Ask students to note how Canto XLV examines the relationship between politics and poetry. Normally, the students respond positively to this poem as a chant against the commercialization of the modern age; in fact, the poem might be compared with Ginsberg's chant against Moloch in section II of *Howl*. Ask the students if there is any problem with the term *usury*, which Pound defined as "A charge for the use of purchasing power, levied without regard to production; often without regard to the possibilities of production." Discuss the ways the charging of interest became—through Christian prohibition—associated with the Jewish people. Is Pound's chant against usury also a chant against the Jews; and insofar as it is, how does this affect our reading and evaluation of the poem?

This discussion should raise some of the same questions about the relationship between politics and poetry, fascism and modernism, that were at the center of the debate about Pound receiving the Bollingen Award for the *Pisan Cantos* in 1949. The same questions, it might be pointed out, are at the center of the reconstruction of American literature. The "Pound Problem" is a telling instance, not only of the ways poetry is political, but also of what happens when the poem's politics are "out of tune" with the politics of the dominant culture. One might ask how Pound's anti-Semitism differed in kind and degree from the racism and anti-Semitism that one finds in other major American writers. And why was Pound singled out for persecution at this time?

The "pull down thy vanity" section of Canto LXXXI in the *Pisan Cantos* reveals a new attitude of *humilitas* and *humanitas*; Pound speaks in a personal voice that anticipates the confessional strain in the poems of Allen Ginsberg, Robert Lowell, and Sylvia Plath. The *Cantos* are incomplete and inconclusive: they end with two fragments, including Canto CXX, which are, like the *Cantos* themselves, a figure of the fragmentation and incompleteness of the modern world. Pound's final words are at once an apology and an admission of failure: "Let those I love forgive/what I have made." Ask the students if they agree with Pound's final assessment of his epic. Is there, ultimately, any value in his work?

Amy Lowell (1874–1925)

Contributing Editor: Lillian Faderman

Classroom Issues and Strategies

I generally use Amy Lowell's work to explore two major issues: the imagist movement as it was imported into the United States and the treatment of lesbian material by a lesbian poet who felt the need to be more closeted in her writing than in her life. While the subject of Lowell's imagism is easy to introduce, the subject of homosexuality in her life and writing has been more difficult because students are sometimes uncomfortable with the topic, and they are ignorant of the history of censorship and homophobia in the United States. The study of Lowell's life and work presents a good opportunity to open these important subjects to discussion.

Lowell's lesbianism and the ways in which it is manifested in her writing generally stimulate some of the liveliest discussions of the course. For example, some students question, as did the critics who dampened her popularity in the years immediately after her death, whether a writer who is homosexual can have anything significant to say to the heterosexual majority. My approach is to draw an analogy (or, with any luck, to have students in the class draw the analogy) to the profound impact on white readers of works by writers of color. "Differentness" becomes the theme of the discussion.

This preliminary discussion of ethnic and racial difference and its impact on writing and reading leads to a discussion of sexual difference and its parallel impact. Either members of the class or I will bring up other writers with whom most of the class may be familiar and whose work they considered no less effective because those writers were gay or lesbian (e.g., Walt Whitman, Carson McCullers, Tennessee Williams, Elizabeth Bishop). The focus of the discussion then turns to the value of borrowing the spectacles of one who is different in order to glance at the world. The session is useful for all students but especially important for homosexual students, whose lives are seldom recognized or affirmed in classroom discussion.

Major Themes, Historical Perspectives, Personal Issues

In a discussion of Lowell's life and work, I introduce two kinds of history—literary and social—and I show the ways in which they mesh. I first focus on the history of the imagist movement that I began when the class read Pound and H.D.; then I explore what attention Lowell garnered for imagism in the United States, why and how she succeeded, and how she modified imagism in her work. I also look at her creation of the dramatic monologue and discuss the historical background of public literary performance.

I am equally concerned with raising the issue of self-censorship and encoding in Lowell's poetry, especially in those poems in which she does not create a literary persona but rather speaks in what appears to be her own voice. To this end I talk about the shifting notion of "standards of decency" and censorship laws. I talk at some length about Lowell's own erotic and affectional relationships with women, and the discrepancy between her brash self-presentation in public and her subdued self-presentation in her autobiographical writing, such as the 1919 series "Two Speak Together," from which many of the Lowell selections in *The Heath Anthology* are taken. Lowell's self-censorship motives are revealed to the class through a letter she wrote to D. H. Lawrence, whose patron she was, scolding him for endangering his literary reputation by trying to publish material such as the lesbian scene in his novel *The Rainbow*, which got him into trouble with the censors:

> I know there is no use in counselling you to make any concessions to public opinions in your books and, although I regret sincerely that you cut yourself off from being published by an outspokenness which the English public does not understand, I regret it not in itself . . . but simply because it keeps the world from knowing what a great novelist you are. I think you could top them all if you would be a little more reticent on this one subject [explicit sexuality]. You need not change your attitude a particle, you can simply use the india rubber in certain places, and then you can come into your own as it ought to be. . . . When one is surrounded by prejudice and blindness, it seems to me that the only thing to do is to get over in spite of it and not constantly run foul of these same prejudices which, after all, hurts oneself and the spreading of one's work, and does not do a thing to right the prejudice.

The class then explores the ways in which Lowell appears to have taken her own advice. If the beloved in the "Two Speak Together" series is Ada Russell, as Lowell admitted to John Livingston Lowes, Lowell herself may be presumed to be the speaker. I introduce the topic of encoding and its ubiquitousness in homosexual literature of earlier eras. How does Lowell disguise the fact of her gender and thus the lesbian content in these poems? How does she use her "india rubber"? What in terms of her sexual identification is hidden and what is overt in her poem about women writers, "The Sisters"?

Finally, I look with my class at the treatment of heterosexuality in Lowell's poetry. Students are often surprised when they realize that "Patterns," a poem that speaks quite explicitly about a woman's heterosexual desires, was published only a decade and a half after the end of Victorianism. Many students praise Lowell's courage in her use of this material. Others suggest that her heterosexual erotic images lack originality and mimic the stuff of cheap romance novels. (One student compared them to the clichés of Harlequin romances of our era: pink and silver women surrendering their soft and willing bodies to heavy-booted men in dashing uniforms.) In general, my students come to prefer the short lyric poems whose material seems fresher and more deeply felt than her dramatic monologues such as "Patterns," which, for decades, remained the only of Lowell's poems to be frequently anthologized.

Significant Form, Style, or Artistic Conventions

With regard to her style and form, I spend most of the Lowell sessions considering her as an imagist or an "Amygist." We discuss her interest in orientalism, which predated her Pound years. If I have not already done so, I introduce the class to the haiku and tanka forms. I also bring in some examples of "imagist" poems Lowell wrote even before she learned of the existence of the imagist movement.

We also discuss Lowell's other poetic innovations, such as her polyphonic prose (prose poetry) and her interest in some of her poetry in the folk materials of non-Euro-Americans. This emphasis leads to a further consideration of how writers who are different often develop a literary interest in other forms of differentness. Finally, we discuss the dramatic monologue form and the use Lowell makes of it in "Patterns" and other poems.

Comparisons, Contrasts, Connections

Lowell's imagism should, of course, be compared with that of Pound and H.D. Her dramatic monologues should be compared with Pound's *personae* and with the Victorian British author Robert Browning's *dramatis personae*. The class will also find a comparative discussion of Lowell and Gertrude Stein interesting. Both saw themselves (and were) movers and shakers in the business of literature. Both were extremely interested in experimental literary techniques and had a coterie of young writers around them whom they helped and influenced. Both were approximately the same height and weight. Both had women lovers who served them as muses, secretaries, critics, housekeepers, and guards against an intrusive public. Astrology buffs in the class will be amused to learn that Lowell and Stein were both born in 1874, in the eastern United States, less than a week apart. On a more serious note, the ways in which Lowell encodes her lesbian material should be compared with Stein's lesbian encoding and with H.D.'s treatment of her own bisexuality in her writing.

Questions for Reading, Discussion, and Writing

1. My study questions emphasize the form and content of her work as well as the particular challenges she faced as one who wrote poetry that was often erotic while she felt constrained to conceal the lesbian source of her eroticism. I encourage students to pay attention to how Lowell's imagist techniques are manifested in many of her long poems as well as in her shorter, more tanka-like poems. My questions also draw attention to the feminist message in Lowell's work (while I point out that, paradoxically, she rejected an affiliation with the feminist movement of her day, insisting—as did Gertrude Stein—that such concerns had little to do with her). Finally, my questions address the subject of encodement in literature and the ways in which Lowell, in particular, encodes.

2. I allow my students who wish to write on Lowell a choice of approaches. Several students who have elected to write analyses of her longer poems have been interested in exposing Lowell as a feminist writer, focusing on "Patterns" (an expression of a woman's right to sexual desire, a complaint against the ways in which women are constrained) and "The Sisters" (how women writers "think-back"—to use Virginia Woolf's phrase—through their female predecessors).

My students have also been interested in writing comparisons between Lowell and H.D., or Lowell and Pound as imagists.

Lowell's work often inspires students to ask if they can do a creative writing assignment in which they try their hand at the haiku, the tanka, and then Western imagism.

Some of the most successful assignments have been those that explore gender encoding in Lowell's short poems: for example, how do we know (or do we know?) that the speaker (who is the lover) in the "Two Speak Together" series is a woman?

Bibliography

From the years immediately following her death until the 1970s, Lowell was largely neglected by critics. Students will be interested in exploring the grounds on which she was dismissed after having been so successful during her lifetime. Therefore, the following works will be of historical interest: Clement Wood, *Amy Lowell*. New York: Vinal, 1926; Hervey Allen, "Amy Lowell as a Poet." *Saturday Review of Literature* 3:28 (5 Feb. 1927): 557–58; Winfield Townley Scott, "Amy Lowell Ten Years After." *New England Quarterly* 8 (June 1935): 320–30.

Gertrude Stein (1874–1946)

Contributing Editor: Cynthia Secor

Classroom Issues and Strategies

Many students will have heard that Stein is "difficult," so they come to her work expecting not to understand. They expect "style" and "experimental strategies," but not content. There exists no cottage industry "explicating" her difficulty, so one does not have easy sources of data such as a *Readers' Guide to Gertrude Stein* to which to refer students. In addition, her lesbianism and feminism put off some readers, if they get far enough into the text to see it.

One needs to begin by saying that these texts are the creation of an extremely well-educated woman—an American, a Jew, the child of immigrant parents, a lesbian, and a feminist—whose life experience and literary production bridge the Victorian and modern eras.

Her two enduring concerns are to portray the experience of woman and to explore what it means to present the fact or act of perception—which can be described as how we organize what we see.

How Gertrude Stein organizes what she sees and how she presents "seeing": this is probably enough metaphysics for a beginning.

When students see that the texts are about something, something very serious and important to the author, they relax and "read" the text.

The texts included here allow you to trace the evolution of Stein's style from realistic and naturalistic through abstract and cubist to simple and straightforward. You can also compare and contrast her representation over the years of women, femininity, and culturally determined depictions of women. Bridgman (p. 104) notes this preference in subject matter. Why and how she chose to depict women adds a new dimension to American literary history. My students have enjoyed "opening up" the style only to discover that it really is about "something."

Consider asking your students to write about a subject matter of their own choice in each of the styles represented in the anthology. Ask them to choose something from their own experience that they think will "fit" with that style. Have them comment on what they have learned from the exercise. Does the style determine a range of appropriate experiences? Can you truly use her style with your experience? How does the "fit" fit? When does it not? Did you learn something new about your experience by "seeing" it as Stein would have at the time she used that style? The underlying point here is that her "style" literally changes from text to text. The style is specific to the matter at hand.

Students become engaged with Stein's ideas, values, and experience as a woman. Her response to war interests them. They are interested in her ideas about democracy, race, geniuses; about why ordinary people are worth so much serious attention. They like the children's stories, when we get into what it means to write for children. Detective story buffs get into her ideas about the detecting mind.

My experience has been that once students believe she is serious, they give her serious attention and are fascinated by how she chooses to present the fabric of her life. Hers is a powerful mind, and they respond to it. How she turns marginality into centrality is of interest to most of us.

Even so, their question continues to be "Why is she so hard?"

Major Themes, Historical Perspectives, Personal Issues

Gertrude Stein is interested in

- what it is to be an American
- what it is to be a woman
- how people see things
- how people tell stories

She describes her own ordinary experience.

She writes about ordinary, commonplace people in such a manner that the absolute uniqueness of each is captured. This is her contribution to the American tradition of democracy and individualism.

She writes extensively about her life, and her growth into her life, as a major American writer of the twentieth century. She comments on culture, art, politics, and sexuality.

Significant Form, Style, or Artistic Conventions

Begin by showing how her work grows out of the American tradition of realism and naturalism.

Then show how she, in a typically twentieth-century fashion, becomes concerned with how we see what we see. As an American, a first-generation child of European Jewish parents, a woman, a lesbian, a feminist, and an artist, she is fully aware of marginality and centrality and ponders the process by which we organize experience and assign centrality, value, and worth. Remember that she was educated at Harvard University in philosophy and at the Johns Hopkins University in medicine.

She is fully aware that what she is has not historically been treated as fully human, fully civilized. Her literary strategies of a lifetime can be seen to be attempts to portray each life, each point of view, as fully real, absolutely present, and of equal value.

Original Audience

I focus on the willingness to continue writing serious and challenging texts without benefit of a wide contemporary audience. She says she writes for herself and strangers.

Serious writers, common readers, the audiences of her operas, and readers of her autobiographies and essays are variously able to articulate what attracts them and compels their attention. She tries very hard not to be influenced by "audiences."

Comparisons, Contrasts, Connections

Stein is so self-consciously American and so well read that it is fruitful to take her poetry and prose and set it beside such writers as Dickinson, Whitman, James, Wharton, Norris, and Dreiser and see what she does with related subject matter—her forms are radical critiques of the relation between content and form in American naturalism, romanticism, and realism.

Flaubert and Mann are interesting set beside her early prose works. Similarly, Hemingway's early short stories are profitably set beside hers. One can see how she evolves a prose style in which the subject matter and the mode of narrative are about equal in weight. It helps to see that she is looking steadily at the "real" world as she evolves her prose and poetic (and hybrid) conventions.

Cluster T. S. Eliot, Joyce, Pound, and Stein. Often these male contemporaries are on her mind as she does something different. She does not share their interest in the past. She evolves a presentation of female persons independent of patriarchal myth.

Questions for Reading, Discussion, and Writing

1. I ask them to recall what was happening politically, socially, and artistically from 1874 to 1946. What events, achievements, personalities, movements, and concepts associated with those years have a bearing on how we perceive women, Americans, immigrants, Jews, lesbians, and geniuses? This lets us look at who "we" are, what we "see," and how it provides for us a context for understanding what Stein is doing with her writing.
2. (a) Characterize Stein's "modernist" strategies. T. S. Eliot and James Joyce add layers of meaning and mythic reference; she seems bent on stripping meaning away and living in a literal present represented as fully as possible. Is this a strategy for writing beyond patriarchy rather than shoring it up or representing fully its complexity?

(b) Stein's impulse to describe, speculate, and pontificate places her firmly in the tradition of Emerson and others. She writes about herself as a Jew, a lesbian, a Westerner, an American, an expatriate, and a bourgeois Victorian lady of limited but comfortable means. How does she expand our definition of American individualism?

(c) How does one integrate her comparatively large body of erotic poetry into the American literary tradition? What does it mean that a major American woman writer born in 1874 writes extensively about sex, and that her partner is a woman? How does it enlarge our concept of female sexuality and of female experience?

(d) It is useful to talk about the tradition of female biography, autobiography, letters, and memoirs, and how this differs from the male tradition. Stein both writes directly about her experience (*Everybody's Autobiography, Paris France*) and incorporates it into fiction (*The Making of Americans*, "Ada"). How does she extend our understanding of this mode?

(e) A number of Stein's works, including *The Mother of Us All*, have been set to music or produced for the stage. What critical language is appropriate for discussing prose and poetry that experiment with generic conventions and concepts normally applied to scene design, ballet, opera, or piano compositions?

(f) What does it mean that fifty years after her death, we still do not have major editions of her letters; her notebooks; scholarly editions of her works; adequate representation in teaching anthologies; study guides that would make her obscurity as clear as we find that of T. S. Eliot, James Joyce, and Ezra Pound?

(g) What did Stein gain and lose by living in a foreign country, where the daily language was other than the language of her childhood, her art, and her domestic life? Hemingway, Wharton, and Baldwin also lived abroad. Why? What other American writers chose to live abroad for long periods of time? Why?

(h) What does it mean that over half of her work was published posthumously and that most of her serious work, when published in her lifetime, was not widely read or understood? What comparison can be made with Emily Dickinson's accomplishment, limitations, and reputation?

Bibliography

Bassoff, Bruce. "Gertrude Stein's 'Composition as Explanation.'" *Gertrude Stein Issue*. Spec. issue of *Twentieth Century Literature* 24.1 (Spring 1978): 76–80.

Benstock, Shari. *Women of the Left Bank: Paris, 1900–1940.* Austin: U of Texas P, 1986. Chapter 5.

Dubnick, Randa. *The Structure of Obscurity: Gertrude Stein, Language, and Cubism.* Urbana and Chicago: U of Illinois P, 1984. Chapters 2 and 5.

Katz, Leon. "Weininger and *The Making of Americans.*" *Gertrude Stein Issue.* Spec. issue of *Twentieth Century Literature:* 24.1 (Spring 1978): 8–26.

Kostelanetz, Richard. *The Yale Gertrude Stein.* New Haven and London: Yale UP, 1980. Introduction.

Secor, Cynthia. "Gertrude Stein: The Complex Force of Her Femininity." *Women, the Arts, and the 1920s in Paris and New York.* Ed. Kenneth W. Wheeler and Virginia L. Lussier. New Brunswick: Transaction, 1982. 27–35.

———. "*Ida*, A Great American Novel." *Gertrude Stein Issue.* Spec. issue of *Twentieth Century Literature:* 24.1 (Spring 1978): 96–107.

Sutherland, Donald. *Gertrude Stein: A Biography of Her Work.* New Haven: Yale UP, 1951. Chapter 4.

William Carlos Williams (1883–1963)

Contributing Editor: Theodora R. Graham

Classroom Issues and Strategies

Students' assumption that what appears simple is simplistic can be a problem with teaching Williams's poetry. Some students feel the need to sketch in the house, barn, and fields behind the wheelbarrow and white chickens. For others, lack of experience with innovative line breaks and visual effects causes initial confusion. Many do not at first listen for the voice(s). They do not pay attention to speakers and therefore miss the tonal shadings, irony, humor, and other effects, including the sometimes clinical objectivity of poems related to visual art.

I recommend that students read poems aloud from the beginning. I read a poem aloud myself in class as a "possible interpretation" and have students comment on or revise the reading. I also use transparencies of shorter poems, occasionally changing the line breaks in an "edited version" to call attention to Williams's technique of fragmentation (not breaking necessarily with a syntactic unit).

Students often ask if Williams is usually the speaker in the poem. They wonder how autobiographical his work is and whether his work as a doctor really influenced the way he wrote and what he wrote about. Those interested in form ask whether a single sentence, broken up on the page, can be a legitimate poem.

Major Themes, Historical Perspectives, Personal Issues

Williams champions the American idiom and the "local"—either the urban landscape or one's immediate environment. He pays close attention to ordinary scenes (some purely descriptive; others as compositions as in visual art), the working class, and the poor. Williams's work often demonstrates the artist's need to destroy or deconstruct what has become outworn and to reassemble or recreate with fresh vision and language. His own "hybrid" background is, in his view, particularly American. He uses his experience as a doctor, married man and father, son and friend, in some of the poems, fiction, and plays. In addition, he demonstrates the need to discover rather than impose order or reality.

Significant Form, Style, or Artistic Conventions

It is important to be familiar with imagist principles and the serious thrust of Williams's "no ideas but in things," as well as with his sometime view of the poem as "a machine made out of words." Students should be aware of inductive process and attempt to relate this to Williams's emphasis on particulars, perhaps comparing it with Frost's statement that a poem does not begin with an idea. But whereas Frost embraced and adapted traditional forms, around 1915, Williams began experimenting in shorter poems with innovative line breaks, speaking voices, and a kind of stripped-down language (as he said of Moore, washing words with acid). Readers of Williams should also be familiar with the Armory Show (1913) and how cubist fragmentation and photography became sources for new ideas in the arts through Alfred Stieglitz's Gallery "291" and magazine *Camera Work*, through gatherings at the home/"gallery" of Walter Arensberg in New York City. Since Williams lived a short train ride from the city, he was able to frequent these shows, gatherings, and even studios, like that of Marsden Hartley, with Demuth, a good friend.

That the young Williams was at first influenced primarily by Whitman and Keats and began by writing conventional verse makes his departure from tradition all the more radical.

Original Audience

Point out through a dateline the birth dates of Frost, Stevens, Williams, Pound, Moore, and Eliot—and include on the same dateline how old each poet was in 1912 (the date of what is sometimes referred to as the beginning of a poetic renaissance: the start of *Poetry* magazine). Audience was created by editors of little magazines (as new audiences for art were stimulated by opening of small galleries in New York), some—like Williams (see *Contact* I and II)—poets or fiction writers. *Poetry, Others,* the *Egoist, Criterion* (see *Little Magazines,* ed. F. Hoffman), and other magazines published on both sides of the Atlantic gave poets a place to present their work without considering the strictures of conventional larger-circulation magazines. The *Dial,* edited in the twenties by Marianne Moore, offered a coveted prize, which Williams was awarded.

The audience was not mainstream, not large; but it was generally sophisticated and knowledgeable about new developments in the arts and music. It could also be educated by the writers to be responsive to new work.

Now, of course, the modernists are all anthologized and acknowledged, both in their own rights and as influences for poets of following generations. That does not make them, however, easy to read. And the poems anthologized for secondary-level students often do not present their most controversial, and perhaps most interesting, writing.

Comparisons, Contrasts, Connections

Students may be asked to discuss how poems begin, or to compare two or more poets' process of revision. They may be asked to compare/contrast the speakers' dilemmas in Frost's "Design" or other "dark" poems and Williams's "These." They could look as well at the forms each poet has chosen and discuss the possible reasons for what Frost would consider the "playing tennis with the net down" of Williams's verse. One could also discuss Williams's relationship to Pound and the latter's influence on early Williams, as well as Williams's negative views of Eliot's expatriation and verse.

Working with Cultural Objects

I sometimes use art slides that relate to specific poems (Demuth's "I Saw the Figure 5 in Gold"; "Tuberoses"; Picasso's "Girl with a Hoop"; Sheeler's "Classic Landscape"). Images of Sheeler's "Classic Landscape" and the text of Williams's "Classic Scene" and Demuth's "I Saw the Figure 5 in Gold," along with Williams's "The Great Figure," are available online at <http://www.emory.edu/ENGLISH/Paintings&Poems/ClassicScene.html> and at <http://www.emory.edu/ENGLISH/Paintings&Poems/GreatFigure.html>.

Questions for Reading, Discussion, and Writing

1. Students generally have a set of strategies for reading that include giving attention to speaker, setting (time of year, time of day, description), various devices, audience, and so on, that they have adapted to their own use as they become more sophisticated readers. I try not to reduce each writer to a set of questions but do suggest that with Williams they read aloud and look carefully at how Williams develops a speaker, how words—used sparingly—can "tell" more because of juxtaposition or because of their place in a visual composition.

2. Students are particularly interested in interrelations among the arts, in particular with Williams of poetry and visual art. Williams's favorite painter among the cubists was Juan Gris. Some of his work, because it includes what Williams called "the recognizable object" in a new relation to its context, can be interesting to compare with carefully selected Williams poems (and they can see *Spring and All* for Williams's comments on Gris). Also, Williams's work in relation to that of Charles Demuth, Charles Sheeler, and Alfred Stieglitz provides stimulating possibilities. Can a linear art such as poetry come close to resembling a spatial art such as painting or photography?

Bibliography

The secondary bibliography on Williams is very long. An instructor might consult Paul Mariani's edition of the secondary sources, arranged according to periods in Williams's writing, chronologically (published by the American Library Association). And then select more recent articles from this book's lists.

James Breslin's study of *WCW* and Thomas Whitaker's shorter introduction in the Twayne series remain useful.

Specialized studies of Williams and the arts by Bram Dijkstra, Dickran Tashjian, Peter Schmidt, and Christopher MacGowan provide helpful background.

Williams's *Autobiography* and *I Want to Write a Poem* (ed. Edith Heal) offer insights, not always totally reliable, in the poet's own words.

The *William Carlos Williams Review*, published since 1975, prints articles, reviews, biographical information, unpublished letters, and other manuscripts.

Eugene O'Neill (1888–1953)

Contributing Editor: James A. Robinson

Classroom Issues and Strategies

Problems with teaching O'Neill include (1) students' lack of acquaintance with drama as a genre, which leads to problems of point of view, etc.; (2) for *Hairy Ape*, fragmentation of the action and styles—its antirealism bewilders some; I often scan the final scenes in discussion in explaining the expressionism of earlier scenes; (3) difficulty with identifying tone: students don't know whether the work is tragedy, comedy, or satire; whether to identify with the hero or laugh at him.

To address these issues, (1) emphasize the absence of point of view as an opportunity, not a problem, and use the central conflict to generate theme—in what ways do Yank and Mildred contrast? What do these contrasts represent (socially, sexually, psychologically)? (2) Relate the fragmentation of setting to that found (or made possible) by film as medium; compare other fragmentations to poetry (T. S. Eliot's *The Waste Land*) and fiction (Faulkner) contemporary with the play. (3) Define Yank as both hero and antihero (using Esther Jackson's definition in *The Broken World of Tennessee Williams*); identify targets of satire (distorted characters, for example) and ask how they relate to Yank's tragic journey toward awareness and toward death.

Consider approaching this play as an existential text (as Doris Falk does in her book on O'Neill) in which Yank is guilty of "bad faith" in his early identification with something outside of himself—steel—leaving him no place to turn when that identification collapses. Finally, consider a Freudian approach for some scenes, like scene 3 with its blatant phallic and vaginal symbolism; you could also see Yank as "id" struggling toward "ego" in some ways, as animal striving to become a human individual.

Major Themes, Historical Perspectives, Personal Issues

Personal Issues: O'Neill's relationship to women, particularly his blaming of his mother for his "fall" from innocence; O'Neill's lapsed faith in the Catholic God, leading to a philosophical search similar to Yank's; O'Neill's love of death.

Historical Issues: modern industrial capitalism as destructive of harmony (Paddy versus Yank) but O'Neill's lack of faith in social solutions (repudiation of Long).

Themes: alienation as major theme, not "belonging"—dramatized in dialogue, setting, sound effects, and character distortions as well as in action, a quintessential modern theme.

Significant Form, Style, or Artistic Conventions

The primary question is the theatrical mode of expressionism, and why O'Neill chose a style employing distortion and fragmentation for themes of industrialism and alienation.

A related issue is how this expresses the experimental spirit of the 1920s and the questioning of American bourgeois culture spearheaded by Mencken and others—particularly the recognition of class divisions apparent in other works, like *Gatsby*.

Original Audience

The Broadway audience of the 1920s accepted O'Neill's experimentation, partially because he was promoted by influential critics; but the reviews of *Ape* were mixed. You could cite reviews from leftist journals about the criticism of capitalism in the play to ignite discussion as to whether this is a central theme. Recently, Joel Pfister has argued along New Historicist lines that O'Neill's Broadway audiences were dominated by members of an emerging professional-managerial class that would empathize with the play's presentation of Yank's *angst* as philosophical and universal rather than class-based and historically determined.

Comparisons, Contrasts, Connections

As indicated above, the play invites comparison with *The Waste Land* (fragmentation) and *The Great Gatsby* (social criticism) as well as with figures like Stephen Crane and Theodore Dreiser and Jack London (the latter influenced O'Neill, in fact), whose American naturalism emphasized the animal, instinctual behavior of man. Darwinism, the struggle toward evolution (note Yank's emergence from the sea onto land in scene 5) clearly informs the assumptions of the play.

Questions for Reading, Discussion, and Writing

For "genre": the key is central conflict (here, Yank versus Mildred) and how this generates the themes of the play.

For expressionistic aesthetic: point out parallels to/influence of cinema, especially *The Cabinet of Dr. Caligari* and *Metropolis*.

Bibliography

Read the *Ape* chapter in Doris Falk, *Eugene O'Neill and the Tragic Tension*; Doris Alexander, "Eugene O'Neill as Social Critic," *American Quarterly* (Winter 1954; rpt. in Oscar Cargill et al., *O'Neill and His Plays*—which is also useful for O'Neill's extra-dramatic utterances, several of which are in *Ape*); the chapter on *Ape* in Timo Tuisanen, *O'Neill's Scenic Images*; the chapter on *Ape* in Travis Bogard, *Contour in Time: The Plays of EO*; my article, "O'Neill's Distorted Dances," in *Modern Drama* 19 (1976); Jean Chothia, "Theatre Language: Word and Image in *The Hairy Ape*," in *Eugene O'Neill and the Emergence of American Drama*, ed. Marc Maufort; and the section on *Ape* in Joel Pfister, *Staging Depth: Eugene O'Neill and the Politics of Psychological Discourse*.

Djuna Barnes (1892–1982)

Contributing Editor: Catharine R. Stimpson

Classroom Issues and Strategies

Problems with teaching Barnes are also opportunities. They include (1) her life and complicated childhood—for example, a suffragist grandmother, a lecherous father; (2) her Bohemian adulthood—she lived and worked in avant-garde circles in New York and Europe and was also bisexual; (3) her comic wit and anguished vision; and (4) the range of her writing. Because she was a professional writer, with no other income for the most part, she took on a gamut of styles (journalism, plays, poems, stories, burlesques). She often parodies older forms; for example, *Ryder,* the bildungsroman, and picaresque novel. If students don't know the original, they miss her great wit.

Her biography is still emerging, but tell the story of her life. Let students see her courage, adventurousness, and harsher characteristics; for example, she traveled in hard-drinking circles. Critics/readers are rediscovering and recovering Barnes, seeing afresh how much she did, who she was, what her circles were, how much it mattered that she was a woman writer, and how destructive that ghastly childhood was. Make the class part of the process of rediscovering and recovery, part of the adventure. Show students, too, what she was parodying, what part of literary history she was utilizing.

Help students with her dualistic vision, her sense of contradiction and irony. We are born, but born to die. The womb is a tomb. We are corrupt, but we love and desire. We descend in order to ascend.

Major Themes, Historical Perspectives, Personal Issues

Trace the travails of a young, beautiful, really bright, ironic, bisexual woman making her way in a tough world. Culturally, look at what it means to be modern; to be avant-garde; to go for the new, vital, disorderly, outlawed, carnivalesque. Barnes knew almost everyone, so she is a way into modern culture; for example, she interviewed James Joyce. Historically, she is twentieth century. She lived through two world wars, in a world where God had disappeared, though she yearned for faith; in which the corrupt and vile seemed to dominate history.

Significant Form, Style, or Artistic Conventions

Barnes mastered several genres. Use her journalism to show the mass media, especially the mass newspaper. Use her short stories to show a combination of flat realism and the grotesque, the weird; use *Ladies Almanack*, for one, to show both satire and inside jokes (Barnes was spoofing women's circles in Paris in the 1920s). Use *Nightwood* to show the modern novel, its suspicion of a straight, linear narrative; its interest in consciousness and language and clashing points of view; the darkness of vision, life as a nightwood; its wild humor; its blurring of sexual identities; its sense of history as a fall. Like a surrealist, Barnes explores the unconscious. Like a symbolist, she incarnates the invisible in a sensible thing.

Original Audience

Barnes was very conscious of writing for specific audiences. She also cared, despite her bohemianism, for the approval of male cultural authorities, especially T. S. Eliot, who endorsed *Nightwood*. Toward the end of her life, Barnes wrote very little, but certain people kept her reputation alive because they loved her despite her bitter, often destructive, wit and the difficulty of her work. After her death, feminist critics have helped to reevaluate her. Another biographer, Andrew Field (1983)—who also writes about Vladimir Nabokov—likes quirky, elusive, brilliant, cosmopolitan figures.

Comparisons, Contrasts, Connections

Try teaching her stories with Sherwood Anderson, *Winesburg, Ohio* (1919), for the meticulous observation of despair; *Ladies Almanack* with Gertrude Stein, *The Autobiography of Alice B. Toklas* (1933), for Parisian adventures; *Nightwood* with *Ulysses* for the experimental modern novel; and, for very hard work, the play *Antiphon* with T. S. Eliot's *The Cocktail Party* (1950), for the use of older dramatic forms for metaphysical and psychological exploration.

Questions for Reading, Discussion, and Writing

1. I prefer to have students keep journals rather than ask study questions because the journal picks up students' immediate reactions, no matter how hostile they are. If the class is too large, you might ask them to write out their own study questions. If a study question is a necessity, try to get at Barnes's sense of family, which is bleak but convinced of the family's necessity; or her sense of differences: how different people can be, perhaps, from "ordinary" life. Though students might not adore this, ask about futility, and, among the deluded, about failure.
2. Barnes was also a good artist. A student might write about her use of pictures, her visual skills, either through her own illustrations or through her vivid, metaphoric, visual language.

Bibliography

Phillip Herring, *Djuna: The Life and Work of Djuna Barnes* (New York: Viking, 1995), is the most recent biography.

Silence and Power, ed. Mary Lynn Broe (Carbondale: Southern Illinois UP, 1991) uses the lens of feminist criticism.

Douglas Messerli's *Djuna Barnes: A Bibliography* (1975) is an excellent survey of criticism up to the mid-1970s.

Elizabeth Madox Roberts (1881–1941)

Contributing Editor: Sheila Hurst Donnelly

Classroom Issues and Strategies

Discuss point of view with emphasis on the use of a central consciousness; provide information about the development and social implications of regionalism; instruct students about the use of symbolism and other figurative devices; prepare them for a complicated story structure. Such a general introduction will help readers appreciate Elizabeth Madox Roberts.

Until recently students have not been exposed to Roberts's work. Because her short stories are unavailable, my students are familiar with her best novels, *The Time of Man* and *The Great Meadow.* Some students find her complex structure and style of "symbolism working through poetic realism" difficult. Most enjoy the challenge; the characters many times face the perennial problems of youth. More experienced "city kids" have trouble empathizing with the rural mentality—social reality, sense of community—until the basics are explored: love, sex, birth, death—the equalizers.

Major Themes, Historical Perspectives, Personal Issues

Roberts is concerned with the universal, the "Everyman" theme, as it grows out of her Pigeon River Community. She is preoccupied with the intimate connection between the past and the present. This connection is often reflected in her innovative stylistic techniques. Oftentimes she bounces between past and present with little warning. Many of her works develop initiation themes through penetrating dramatization of psychological crises.

Roberts's writing was influential to early modern American literature because of her introspective and poetic style, her sense of Southern rural community, her concern for the individual, and her emphasis upon the indomitable human spirit. Her works are primarily concerned with the way individuals apprehend reality. Here again innovative technique comes into play.

In contrast to the novels, her stories are highly concentrated: limited in time and space and rendered in swift, artful strokes. But, like her best novels *The Time of Man* and *The Great Meadow,* her stories derive their substance from the characters. Their points of view convey the stories, which oftentimes are variations on the initiation theme. Her best stories in this vein are "On the Mountainside," "The Scarecrow," "The Sacrifice of the Maidens," "Swing Low Sweet Chariot," and "Death at Bearwallow."

Significant Form, Style, or Artistic Conventions

A thorough discussion of regionalism is helpful in introducing Roberts and solidifying her important place and influence in Southern Renaissance literature. While a discussion of her admiration for Berkeleian philosophy may be a point of interest and investigation for advanced students, it is not necessary for the enjoyment of her work.

Original Audience

Roberts can be discussed against the backdrop of the Lost Generation (*The Time of Man* was published in 1926, the same year as Hemingway's *The Sun Also Rises*) as well as the movement toward an agrarian revival of the 1920s and 1930s (*I'll Take My Stand: The South and the Agrarian Tradition*). Today, a discussion of her Kentucky women provokes some high-powered and thoughtful commentary on women then and now. Many of her works lend themselves well to feminist and New Historical criticism.

Comparisons, Contrasts, Connections

Comparisons can be made with Ellen Glasgow, Willa Cather, Jesse Stuart, William Faulkner, and Robert Penn Warren, to name a few. She can also be compared with the many more modern female writers such as Kate Chopin, Zora Neale Hurston, Carson McCullers, and Toni Morrison. She can be contrasted with any of the Lost Generation authors. Bases for comparison and contrast lie in personal background, fictional style, theme, region, and current meaningfulness. Mainly, fruitful comparison and contrast are gained from her novels, as her characters are more complex and profoundly developed than those in her short stories. Her works can be contrasted with more short-sighted regional stories in that they represent "small self-contained centres of life" (Allen Tate) which root in a specific geographical region, adapt to the land, create a pattern of life, and then in turn become aesthetic, taking on universal and archetypical dimensions.

In all her works, Roberts masterfully blends poetry and realism. She, like William Faulkner, is never far from the sweat and agony of the human spirit and, like Faulkner too, she believes that humanity will not only endure, but will prevail.

Questions for Reading, Discussion, and Writing

1. How do events in your past affect moments, decisions, relationships, and so on, in your present? future?
2. What sentiments do you attach to sense stimuli: smells, places, particular events, garments, and so on—the stuff of symbolism?
3. I have had special success with two types of papers:
   (a) Position papers in which students take issue with the characters' responses to particular events. They engage in hypothetical arguments and bring to bear their individual beliefs. These papers tend to generate a more penetrating discussion of all that shapes a character while encouraging students to trust their own analytical skills.
   (b) Explication of the text using a quotation from the author about her work, which forces students to grapple with an understanding of the author's artistic credo in conjunction with her works. For example, Roberts would say, "Life is from within, and thus the noise outside is a wind blowing in a mirror." This riddling line can be applied to many of her stories and novels, including "Death of Bearwallow."

      Comparison/contrast papers with instructor's guidance are also a favorite of mine.

Bibliography

The *Southern Review* 29.4 (1984) has several essays as well as personal reminiscences.

Read Campbell and Foster's study, *Elizabeth Madox Roberts: American Novelist* (1956).

H.D. (Hilda Doolittle) (1886–1961)

Contributing Editor: Susan Stanford Friedman

Classroom Issues and Strategies

Like much modernist poetry (e.g., Pound's, Eliot's), H.D.'s poetry is "difficult" for students. Mythological and biblical allusions are common in her poetry. Her imagist poetry is "impersonal" (like Eliot's)—that is, its relationship to human emotion is often deeply encoded. Her epic poetry is vast and complex in scope; its linguistic, religious, and psychological dimensions are sophisticated and multilayered. Her perspective as a woman is quite different from that of the modernist male poets with whom she shares a great deal.

I have found students very responsive to H.D. when I have used the following strategies. Contextualize H.D.'s work in relationship to (1) modernism (students often expect a male poet to be "difficult," but resist having to work hard to read a woman poet); (2) women's poetry and feminist theory— especially feminist concepts of revision of patriarchal myths and traditions; (3) the mythological allusions (get students to relax and see that without footnotes, H.D. provides all the information they need); (4) the musical and syntactic structures of her poetic language. Her imagist poems can be read as poems about the (female) self resisting stereotypical femininity (they are not "nature" poems). I have had great success in teaching *Trilogy* as a poem about war from a pacifist perspective akin to Virginia Woolf's in *Three Guineas*.

Students are intrigued by the following: (1) Gender. They are fascinated by H.D. as a window into the problems and achievements of women's creativity. They love, for example, to read her famous "sea garden" poems (e.g., "Sea Rose") as encoded statements of female vulnerability and rejection of a suffocating femininity. (2) War and peace. Students are very interested and moved by her response to war. They are intrigued by the goddesses and matriarchal religions. (3) Initially, students are afraid of H.D.—real "poetry anxiety." They think they won't be able to understand it because it has so many allusions. But when they are given a framework for thinking about poetry, they are very responsive.

Major Themes, Historical Perspectives, Personal Issues

The headnote summarizes the major themes. To summarize, I think H.D. should be taught with emphasis on the following themes:

1. her attempt to understand the roots of cataclysmic violence and propose a revision of renewal and peace
2. the intersection of the historical and the personal in her stance as a woman
3. her characteristically modernist sense of quest in a shattered and war-torn world
4. her sense of the sacred, manifested in both female and male forms
5. her exploration of language—its magic (as logos), its music, its power as something women can claim to reconstitute gender and a vision of the cosmos

Significant Form, Style, or Artistic Conventions

H.D. is best taught as a modernist and a woman writer. The selections give you the opportunity to show her development from an imagist poet in the teens to an epic poet of the 1940s and 1950s. Her imagist poetry—represented here by two poems from *Sea Garden* ("Sea Rose" and "The Helmsman") and her most frequently anthologized poem, "Oread" (often discussed as the "perfect" imagist poem)—was highly innovative in its form and a central influence on modern poetry. Imagism, however, became a craft in the service of larger visions after 1917. "Helen," published in the 1920s, is characteristic of a large number of revisionist myth poems that she began writing in her postimagist phase and that have had a strong influence on contemporary women's poetry. In writing epics (some critics prefer the term *long poem*), H.D. went against the engrained masculine conventions of the genre to forge a woman's epic form. The selections from *The Walls Do Not Fall* and *Tribute to the Angels* (the first two volumes from *Trilogy*) emphasize the poet's placement in history (literally, in London, during the nightly bombing raids of World War II) and the syncretist mythmaking of the modernist poet-prophet. These sequences can be taught in the context of religious poetry, but students should be encouraged to compare her female-centered vision with those traditions that she transforms. In teaching any of H.D.'s poetry, its strong musical quality can be emphasized. Within the *vers libre* tradition, she nonetheless established complex patterns of sound based on assonance, dissonance, occasional rhyme (including internal and off rhymes), rhythmic and syntactic patterns, and repetition.

Original Audience

H.D.'s work should always be grounded in its historical period. H.D.'s imagist verse was written in the exhilarating prewar world of the avant-garde and then during the devastating Great War. Her epic poetry was written in the forties and fifties after another great war. Her audience during these years was in effect primarily the avant-garde that was "making news" in all the arts. She was not a "popular" poet, but she has often been known as a "poet's poet." Since the second wave of feminism, she has been widely read by women and men who are interested in women's writing.

Comparisons, Contrasts, Connections

1. Male modernists: Ezra Pound, T. S. Eliot, William Carlos Williams, Wallace Stevens, Robert Hughes, W. B. Yeats, and D. H. Lawrence. Like these men, she experimented with poetic language. Like them, she increasingly wrote quest poetry in which the poet figures as a central

mythmaking figure creating new meanings in a world whose symbolic systems have been shattered.

2. Female modernist writers: Marianne Moore, Virginia Woolf, Gertrude Stein, Mina Loy, and Djuna Barnes are modernist women writers with whom H.D.'s reconstructions of gender share a great deal—thematically and linguistically.

3. Fruitful comparisons can also be made with William Blake, Emily Dickinson, Dante, and Homer.

Questions for Reading, Discussion, and Writing

Explication assignments work well with H.D.'s imagist poems. But the best papers I have received from undergraduates ask the students to examine how H.D. engages in a gender-inflected revisionist mythmaking in her poems. The students trace the conventional myth H.D. invokes and then examine thematically and linguistically how she uses and transforms the tradition.

Bibliography

Collecott, Diana. *H.D. and Sapphic Modernism.* Cambridge, UK: Cambridge UP, 1999.

DuPlessis, Rachel Blau. *H.D.: The Career of That Struggle.* Brighton: Harvester, 1986.

Edmonds, Susan. *History, Psychoanalysis, and Montage in H.D.'s Long Poems.* Palo Alto: Stanford UP, 1994.

Friedman, Susan S. *Psyche Reborn: The Emergence of H.D.* Bloomington: Indiana UP, 1981. See especially pp. 56–59 and chapters 7 and 8.

————. *Penelope's Web: Gender, Modernity, H.D.'s Fiction.* Cambridge, UK: Cambridge UP, 1990. Introduction and chapter 1.

Friedman, Susan S., and Rachel B. DuPlessis, eds. *Signets: Reading H.D.* Madison: U of Wisconsin P, 1990. See especially essays by Morris, Pondrom, Gregory, Laity, Gubar, Gelpi, and Ostriker.

Gregory, Eileen. *H.D. and Hellenism: Classic Lines.* Cambridge, UK: Cambridge UP, 1997.

Laity, Cassandra. *H.D. and the Victorian Fin de Siècle: Gender, Modernism, Decadence.* Cambridge, UK: Cambridge UP, 1996.

Rich, Adrienne. "When We Dead Awaken: Writing as Re-Vision." *On Lies, Secrets, and Silences: Prose.* New York: Norton, 1979. 33–49.

Cluster: Political Poetry in the Modern Period

Contributing Editor: Cary Nelson

Classroom Issues and Strategies

Instructors who have followed the efforts to expand the canon will have read poems like the ones in this section before. Many students, however, may not have. My own experience is that most undergraduates find this poetry quite exciting and are eager to talk about it. The only exception may be those English majors who have been persuaded by other instructors that good poems are never political. An open debate on these issues is the best way to handle the problem. Certainly the clichés about political poetry being rapidly dated and stylistically flat and uninteresting should not survive reading this section. Among the things that students may find surprising are efforts by white poets like Boyle and Taggard to address the problem of race in America. A number of these poems will benefit from detailed close readings; they can also be grouped together in a variety of ways for more general discussions.

Major Themes, Historical Perspectives, Personal Issues

This section offers both an opportunity to study several poets (Hughes, Rolfe, and Taggard) in detail and a chance to reflect on the wide visibility of political poetry in the modern period. Political poetry was influential not only in the 1930s but also throughout a thirty-year period beginning about 1915. After students have read through this section, they may want to ask what justifies the category "political poetry." What holds this section together and differentiates it from other twentieth-century poetry? Are Langston Hughes's poems here "political" in a way some of his poems elsewhere in *The Heath Anthology*, including "The Negro Speaks of Rivers" and "The Weary Blues," are not? Are Taggard's poems political in a way, say, poems like Amy Lowell's "Venus

Transiens" and "Madonna of the Evening Flowers" are not? Is Edwin Rolfe political in a way that Robert Frost and Wallace Stevens are not?

As a descriptive category, political poetry has been around for some time. Our sense of what poems belong in that category, however, continues to change. For some readers, political poetry is either poetry written about major, public historical conflicts, like wars, or poetry supporting some political cause, party, or set of beliefs. Of course, those beliefs have to be set aside culturally and marked as "political" rather than "natural." If, on the other hand, we define politics more broadly as a concern with all of the hierarchical structures that shape social life, that empower some people and disempower others, that elevate some values and concerns and trivialize or demonize others, then clearly "politics" is a much larger subject than some of us have thought. In that sense, all modern poems dealing with race, gender, and economic equality are deeply political. One effect of studying this section and thinking about that issue may be to begin making connections with other poems in *The Heath Anthology* and making politics in this broader sense central to modern literary history. Certainly from my perspective the poems in the anthology by Muriel Rukeyser, Countee Cullen, Claude McKay, and Langston Hughes, among others, along with the section of anonymous poems by early Chinese immigrants, should be considered honorary members of this cluster.

As the introduction to the cluster suggests, one important issue here is the relevance such purportedly "topical" poems have to us many years later. As these poems suggest, the topics many political poems take up—injustice, prejudice, inequality—unfortunately have a long and continuing life. Kalar's abandoned papermill is hardly unfamiliar in the industrial workplace of the 1990s. The working environment in Olsen's "I Want You Women Up North to Know" can be found replicated throughout contemporary America. Fearing's critique of the culture of consumption, commodification, and greed in "Dirge" (located in the "Cluster: Modernism, Lyric Poetry, Facts") is, if anything, more pertinent now than it was when the poem was written. Hughes's attack on religious hypocrisy in "Goodbye Christ" speaks to problems with institutionalized religion that are unique neither to that decade nor to this century.

Yet just as we need to highlight the continuing relevance of these poems, we also need to recognize the special historical conditions to which they speak. Two things instructors may want to do are to supply additional information about the poems' historical contexts and to encourage students to do further background reading on their own. Some (necessarily condensed) examples of that kind of information follow.

"Papermill" (Kalar), "Dirge" (Fearing), "In a Coffee Pot" (Hayes), "Season of Death" (Rolfe), and "Up State—Depression Summer" (Taggard): These poems all deal with the experience of the Great Depression. Kalar was a worker-poet who worked in the timber industry in Minnesota prior to the widespread unemployment of the 1930s. Rolfe grew up in New York City and worked in a number of jobs before becoming a journalist and poet; he was periodically unemployed in the Depression. "Season of Death" and "In a Coffee Pot" both depict New York settings, but they are also typical of other Depression-era cities. A "coffee pot," by the way, is a small coffee shop. A background lecture on the economic, social, and political effects of the Depression might be helpful. It is also useful to make students aware that journals, newspapers, and anthologies publishing poems like these helped make Depression poetry something of a collective project. Hundreds of poems like these made the protest poetry of the Depression part of a mass movement. For more detailed information on "Dirge," see Fearing's *Collected Poems* (1993).

"A Communication to Nancy Cunard" (Boyle) is based, as the note to the poem points out, on the famous Scottsboro case of the 1930s. The nine young black men (aged thirteen to twenty-one) were arrested in March of 1931 and quickly tried and convicted—without adequate representation and on the basis of unconvincing evidence. All but one were sentenced to death. The radical legal-action group International Labor Defense took up their case and helped publicize it both here and abroad. Widespread protests combined with the ILD's legal actions won a new trial in 1933, just before which Ruby Bates repudiated her rape charge. Nevertheless, an all-white jury convicted them again. That trial was then overturned, and two years later the U.S. Supreme Court ruled that defendants' rights were violated by the exclusion of blacks from juries. A 1936 trial failed again to get them released. After that, a plea bargain won freedom for four of the men while five remained in prison. The last was released in 1950. Also see Countee Cullen's poem "Scottsboro, Too, Is Worth Its Song."

"Goodbye Christ" (Hughes) and "Stone Face" (Ridge) were both reprinted in unique broadsides that gave those poems special meaning and distinctive social uses. Hughes's poem was reprinted on hate sheets several times in the early and late 1940s as part of national right-wing smear campaigns against Hughes. Ridge's poem was published as a very large and quite striking broadside as part of the effort to free Mooney from prison. (For reproductions of both broadsides see Nelson, "Modern Poems We Have Wanted to Forget," *Cultural Studies*, 1992.) Mooney was imprisoned from 1916 to 1939. With perjured testimony, he was convicted of murder, despite the fact that he was nowhere near the scene when the bomb was planted. A federal commission later found that Mooney was indicted only because he was an effective labor organizer whom conservatives wanted to eliminate. The judge and jury publicly admitted the verdict was an error. Under the circumstances, President Woodrow Wilson made a plea for mercy, and Mooney's death sentence was commuted to life, but he remained in jail. It may be interesting to compare "Stone Face" with Boyle's "A Communication to Nancy Cunard" and with Edna St. Vincent Millay's "Justice Denied in Massachusetts" since all mount left critiques of American justice.

"First Love" and "Elegia" were both written some years after Rolfe returned home from service in the Abraham Lincoln Battalion in the Spanish Civil War. The introduction to Rolfe's *Collected Poems* (1993) includes detailed analyses of both these poems, and the notes to the poems at the back of that book are considerably expanded from what it was possible to present here. Instructors may find it interesting to compare these poems with the earlier poems Rolfe wrote while he was in Spain from 1937 to 1938. It is important to be aware that "Elegia" was written in Los Angeles in 1948, after the Hollywood blacklist was in place and the long postwar purge of the Left had begun. Its sense of mourning for an antifascist alliance politics is thus relevant not only to Spain but also to the United States.

"Proud Day" (Taggard) commemorates a concert that Marian Anderson presented on the steps of the Lincoln Memorial in Washington, DC, after her request to present an Easter Sunday concert at Constitution Hall, the largest Washington auditorium, was turned down by the Hall's manager and by its owners, the Daughters of the American Revolution. The D.A.R. maintained a "white artists only" policy for Constitution Hall, and Marian Anderson was black; thus neither that date nor any other was acceptable to them. In protest against the D.A.R.'s action, Eleanor Roosevelt, then First Lady, resigned from the organization and helped arrange the alternative concert at the memorial. It should be noted that Washington was a rigidly segregated city during the 1930s.

Significant Form, Style, or Artistic Conventions

Among the most important things to note about this group of poems is its rhetorical, formal, and stylistic diversity. A number of the poems employ experimental modernist devices for social commentary and political advocacy, offering convincing evidence against the uninformed but common claim that political poets rejected modernism. On the other hand, there are many opportunities here to compare and contrast different styles—lyrical, reportorial, satiric, elegiac, hortatory, reflective. There are long and short poems, traditional and mixed forms. Opportunities for comparison and contrast with more canonical modern poets abound. One may also question what it was possible to accomplish in different genres by comparing these poems with some of the socially conscious prose in *The Heath Anthology*.

Original Audience

This is at once a very difficult question and an important one. Our interest, first of all, should not only be in the original audience for a poem but in all the significant audiences that are part of its reception and use. Several of these poems have immensely complex and interesting histories of dissemination in different contexts. Their "original" audience may in fact be partly accidental, an historical effect not part of the poet's intentions. But the whole history of reception and interpretation by different audiences often helps explain a poem's present status. Again, I cannot present that history for all eighteen poems, but I can give a few instructive examples.

Olsen's poem was first published in *Partisan* in 1934. *Partisan* was the magazine of the John Reed Club in Hollywood, California. It featured the work of young revolutionary writers who regularly met together to comment on one another's work. There were John Reed Clubs in a number of U.S. cities in the early 1930s. Olsen's first immediate audience was thus the growing constituency of radicalized writers and those who followed their work. It would be another matter entirely for her poem actually to reach the bourgeois "women up north" whom the poem addresses. Getting that message across would thus be a task for the readers of *Partisan*.

Langston Hughes's "Goodbye Christ" was written in the Soviet Union and first published in *The Negro Worker*, probably without Hughes's permission, in 1932. That appearance was, however, a good deal less important than its subsequent redistribution in a prolonged racist and anticommunist campaign against Hughes, which included its republication in the *Saturday Evening Post* in 1940, its quotation in a J. Edgar Hoover speech in 1947 (read by one of Hoover's deputies), and its being read into the U.S. Senate Record in 1948. See Rampersad's *The Life of Langston Hughes* (1986, 1988) for further details.

Edwin Rolfe's "Elegia," written in 1948, was rejected for publication by the journal *Masses and Mainstream*, in part because the editors objected to the religious references. It was translated into Spanish by the scholar and Spanish exile José Rubia Barcia. Barcia sent the Spanish version to the filmmaker Luis Buñuel in Mexico, who in turn gave it to the poet and Spanish exile Manual Altolaguirre. Altolaguirre printed it as a pamphlet in Mexico City in 1949, and the poem was subsequently read aloud in groups of Spanish exiles throughout Latin America. The original English-language version was not published until 1951.

Questions for Reading, Discussion, and Writing

With seventeen poems by nine different poets, the number of questions one might ask about this cluster of poems is considerable. Let me offer a few examples:

1. Taggard's "Up State—Depression Summer" and Fearing's "Dirge" deal respectively with rural and urban settings and are written in very different styles. Do they share any explicit or implicit values?

2. One might argue that Kalar's "Papermill," Hayes's "In a Coffee Pot," Hughes's "Air Raid Over Harlem," and Rolfe's "Season of Death" all deal with devastated human landscapes. How do they compare with Eliot's *The Waste Land*, a poem written a decade earlier and with a different political understanding of what may be related social realities?
3. What kind of impact does Olsen's "I Want You Women Up North to Know" have on the audience addressed in the title?
4. What is the relationship between the more lyrical and the more polemical language in Rolfe's "Elegia"? What role does romantic love play in his "First Love"? How does he transform the ballad stanza in "Asbestos"?
5. What role does wit play in Hughes's "Goodbye Christ" and Fearing's "Dirge"?
6. How does Ridge complicate our sense of the public use of individual suffering in "Stone Face"?
7. What different and similar kinds of cultural work might these poems do in their own time and ours?

Questions like these can serve either for class discussions or for paper topics. For term papers, however, I like to encourage students to read further in a poet's work. One interesting question not answerable without further reading is what happened to these poets after the 1940s. Some did not survive the decade; others stopped writing poetry. But Boyle, Hughes, and Rolfe continued to write powerful political poems after World War II and into the 1950s. Students could write about that later work or make it the subject of in-class reports.

Bibliography

Students interested in reading widely in Depression-era political poetry face some difficulty, since much of the work is out of print. The work of several of these poets, however, is readily available. *Collected Poems* were published for both Fearing and Rolfe in 1993, and both books have critical introductions and detailed textual notes explaining historical references that may now be obscure. Boyle's *Collected Poems* (1991) remains in print. Students should be warned that Langston Hughes's most widely distributed book, his *Selected Poems* (1959), excludes his more aggressively political poems; for that work students should consult the *second* edition of *Good Morning Revolution* (1993) and *The Panther and the Lash* (1967). Although Taggard's books are all out of print, they will be available in most research libraries. The two volumes that include most of her political poems are *Calling Western Union* (1936) and *Long View* (1942). In addition to the general critical books listed in the introduction to this cluster of poems, students or faculty interested in some of the specific historical issues addressed might consult the following: Dan Carter, *Scottsboro: A Tragedy of the American South* (1984); Richard Frost, *The Mooney Case* (1968); Robert McElvaine, *The Great Depression* (1984); Robert Rosenstone, *Crusade of the Left* (on the Americans in Spain, 1969); Hugh Thomas, *The Spanish Civil War* (1977).

e. e. cummings (1894–1962)

Contributing Editor: Richard S. Kennedy

Classroom Issues and Strategies

Sometimes students are not aware that the *visual* presentation of a poem is part of its overall statement. In addition, they are sometimes puzzled by cummings's unusual linguistic usage: the use of nouns as verbs, other locutions of nouns, and so on (e.g., the world is made of "roses & hello," "of so longs and ashes").

When I call students' attention to ways that words or presentations on the page actually function, this most often brings home an effect that may have been missed. Sometimes I simply ask students for their individual responses and find that they really can *feel* the significance of an unusual expression.

I have sometimes begun class by asking, "How does cummings indicate in his poems that he is a painter as well as a poet?" Another simple approach is to ask, "How does cummings seem different from any other poet whose work you have read?" I have also asked students at some point in a discussion, "Why are these linguistic presentations that cummings makes classified as poems?" (This last, of course, is not asked about his sonnets or rhymed stanzaic verses.)

Students vary in their responses, but most of them react deeply to his outlook on life—his valuing of love, nature, human uniqueness. Fewer students appreciate his play with form. Almost all enjoy his humor and satire. Nearly every student joins him in his antiwar stance.

Major Themes, Historical Perspectives, Personal Issues

cummings is, in his general outlook on life, an unabashed romantic. He affirms life wholeheartedly in all its multiplicity, but especially in whatever is simple, natural, loving, individual, unique. Above all, he emphasizes feeling and emotion rather than thought or analysis. He rejects those social forces in life that hinder the unique and individual expression of each person's essential being. He is particularly hostile to forces that promote conformity, group behavior, imitation, artificiality. He regards technology and the complexities of civilization as dehumanizing. Above all, he abominates war, which he looks upon as the ultimate negation of human values.

Although cummings maintains the same general views throughout his life, he is more affirmatively exuberant in his early career and more light-heartedly iconoclastic. In his later career, he is more serene in his response to the basic good things of life and to the beauties of the natural world, but more harshly satiric in his denunciation of what he opposes.

cummings's play with language, punctuation, and capitalization and his visually directive placement of words on the page are congruent with the new movement in the arts that began in the 1900s in European painting—the movement toward "break up and restructuring" that was part of the revolt against realism in modern art.

Original Audience

cummings does not address a particular audience, although he assumes that his readers are generally educated in literature and the arts.

Comparisons, Contrasts, Connections

cummings's work may be associated with the experiments in language and form that are found in the writings of T. S. Eliot, Ezra Pound, Gertrude Stein, and John Dos Passos. He may be contrasted with writers in the realistic or naturalistic vein, such as Theodore Dreiser, Sherwood Anderson, Edward Arlington Robinson, Robert Frost, and Ernest Hemingway.

Questions for Reading, Discussion, and Writing

1. I have sometimes lectured on his characteristic ideas and attitudes and then asked students to point out which poems illustrate these best. Or I have lectured on his special techniques and expressive devices in order to alert the students to ways of reading and understanding his work.
2. I have sometimes asked students to compare a cummings sonnet with a conventional one, or to compare a cummings lyric with one by Frost.

   I have also asked students to point out the likenesses and differences between a specific cummings work and one by Eliot or Pound.

Bibliography

Richard S. Kennedy's introduction to the typescript edition of *Tulips & Chimneys* by cummings (Liveright, 1976) summarizes his view of life and his poetic techniques.

Norman Friedman's *e. e. cummings: The Art of His Poetry* (Johns Hopkins UP, 1960), chapters 3 and 4, deal clearly with his attitudes and his poetic devices.

Richard S. Kennedy, *Dreams in the Mirror: A Biography of e. e. cummings* (Liveright, 1980) is the definitive biography.

Richard Kostelanetz, *Another e. e. cummings* (Liveright, 1998), emphasizes the more experimental work of cummings.

T. S. Eliot (1888–1965)

Contributing Editor: Sam S. Baskett

Classroom Issues and Strategies

For the uninitiated reader, Eliot's poems present a number of difficulties: erudite allusions, lines in a number of foreign languages, lack of narrative structure compounded by startling juxtapositions, a sense of aloofness from the ordinary sensory universe of day-to-day living. For the more sophisticated, Eliot's "modernism," his quest for "reality," may seem dated, even "romantic"; the vision of the waste land, stultifying and bleak; the orthodoxy of "The Dry Salvages" a retreat from the cutting edge of late twentieth-century thought and poetic expression.

To address these problems, explain the most difficult and essential passages, providing some framework and background, without attempting a line-by-line gloss of all the references and their ramifications. The poems, especially *The Waste Land*, should not be treated as puzzles to be solved, but rather, the early poems at least, as typical "modernism" which Eliot "invented" in *The Waste Land* and "Prufrock," a product of symbolism, images, and aggregation. Emphasize that this is all the expression of a personal, intense, even romantic effort by Eliot to get things "right" for himself in his search for order in his life, a validation of his existence, in a word, for "salvation." Emphasize continuing themes, continuing and changing techniques as Eliot attempts to translate, as he said of Shakespeare, his own private agony into something rich, strange, and impersonal.

Students often ask why Eliot is so intentionally, even perversely, difficult. Why the erudite allusions, the foreign languages, the indirectness? What is his attitude toward women? What of the evidence of racial prejudice? What of his aloofness from and condescension to the concerns of ordinary human existence?

Major Themes, Historical Perspectives, Personal Issues

The symbolism of the waste land, garden, water, city, stairs, and so on, as Eliot expresses the themes of time, death-rebirth, levels of love (and attitude toward women), and the quest motif on psychological, metaphysical, and aesthetic levels. Dante's four levels—the literal (Eliot's use of geographic place is more basic than has been given sufficient attention), allegorical, moral, and anagogic—are interesting to trace throughout Eliot's developing canon. The relations between geographic place and vision; between the personal, individual talent and the strong sense of tradition, are also significant.

Significant Form, Style, or Artistic Conventions

Eliot's relation to romanticism, his significance in the development (with Ezra Pound) of modernism, and his role as an expatriate effecting a "reconciliation with America" in "The Dry Salvages" are all important considerations. His techniques of juxtaposition, aggregation of images, symbolism, the use of multiple literary allusions, and the influence of Dante are all worth attention, as is his use of "free verse" and many various poetic forms. Note also the musicality of his verse and his use of verbal repetition as well as clusters of images and symbols.

Original Audience

When Eliot's works first appeared, they seemed outrageously impenetrable to many, although he quickly became recognized as the "Pope of Russell Square." This recognition was partly through Pound's efforts as well as through Eliot's magisterial pronouncements in his criticism. Even as he challenged the literary establishment, he was in effect a literary "dictator" during much of his life, despite the shock felt by his followers when he announced in 1927 that he was "catholic, royalist and a classicist." With the religious emphasis of *Ash Wednesday* (1930) and *Four Quartets* (1943), as well as in his plays of the 1930s and 1940s, it seemed to many that he had become a different writer. More than forty years after his death, it is possible to see the continuing figure in the carpet, Eliot as a major figure in modernism, a movement superseded by subsequent developments. His eventual importance has been severely questioned by some critics (e.g., Harold Bloom).

Comparisons, Contrasts, Connections

Compare Eliot with Ezra Pound, Robert Frost, William Carlos Williams, and Wallace Stevens. Pound for his influence as "the better craftsman" and for his early recognition of and plumping for Eliot; all of these poets for their combined (but differing) contribution to modernism and the search for reality as a way out of "the heart of darkness." Williams and Stevens (Adamic poets) make interesting contrasts with their different goals and techniques: Williams criticizing Eliot's lack of immediacy, Stevens commenting that Eliot did not make the "visible a little difficult to see."

Questions for Reading, Discussion, and Writing

1. What are the similarities and differences in Eliot's protagonists?
    What is the continuing fundamental theme in his work?
    Is "The Dry Salvages" essentially different from his early poems? How
        so? Are there any continuities?
    Consider the thrust of a particular poem on literal, allegorical, moral,
        and anagogic levels.
    What is Eliot's attitude toward women?
    What are the techniques by which Eliot's poems achieve intensity?
2. Compare and contrast the protagonists of two poems.
    Trace the quest motif through Eliot's poems.
    How do the late poems ("DS") differ from "Prufrock"? *The Waste Land*?
    Discuss Eliot's attitude toward death as expressed in the poems.
    Discuss Eliot's symbolism; discuss the use of water as a symbol.

Bibliography

Baskett, Sam S. "Eliot's London." *Critical Essays on The Waste Land*. London: Longman Literature Guides, 1988. 73–89.

———. "Fronting the Atlantic: *Cape Cod* and 'The Dry Salvages.'" *New England Quarterly* 56.2 (June 1983): 200–19.

Drew, Elizabeth. *T. S. Eliot: The Design of His Poetry*. New York: Scribner's, 1949. See especially pages 1–30.

Gordon, Lyndall. *Eliot's Early Years*. Athens: Ohio UP, 1977.

———. *Eliot's New Life*. Athens: Ohio UP, 1988.

Julius, Anthony. *T. S. Eliot: Anti-Semitism and Literary Form*. Cambridge, UK: Cambridge UP, 1995.

Kermode, Frank. "A Babylonish Dialect." *T. S. Eliot*. Ed. Allen Tate. New York: Delacorte, 1966. 231–43.

Litz, A. Walton, ed. *Eliot in His Time*. Princeton: Princeton UP, 1973. Several useful, illuminating essays.

Martin, Jay, ed. *A Collection of Critical Essays on The Waste Land*. Twentieth Century Interpretations. Englewood Cliffs, NJ: Prentice, 1968. Several useful, illuminating essays.

Miller, J. Hillis. *Poets of Reality*. Cambridge, MA: Belknap P of Harvard U, 1965. 1–12.

Moody, A. D. *T. S. Eliot*. Cambridge, UK: Cambridge UP, 1979.

Ricks, Christopher. *T. S. Eliot and Prejudice*. London: Faber, 1994.

Williamson, George. *A Reader's Guide to T. S. Eliot*. New York: Farrar, 1967.

F. Scott Fitzgerald (1896–1940)

Contributing Editors: John F. Callahan and John Alberti

Classroom Issues and Strategies

Students often tend to view Fitzgerald as a participant in the excesses of the Jazz Age rather than as a writer who cast a critical eye on his generation's experience.

Fitzgerald's essays serve as important companions to his fiction. I fall back on the trick of photocopying one or more of the following essays: "Echoes of the Jazz Age," "My Lost City," "The Crack Up," "Sleeping and Waking," or "Pasting It Together."

Students are very interested in the relationship between Fitzgerald's life and his work and in his sense that the best possibilities of American history are in the past. Their questions include why relationships between men and women seem often bound up with money and social status, and whether or not Fitzgerald maintains a critical detachment from his characters' views of reality.

Major Themes, Historical Perspectives, Personal Issues

In "May Day," note how the story contrasts the smug complacency of Philip Dean with the disintegrating circumstances of his classmate, Gordon Sterret. Look for similar contrasts in the story, such as the juxtapositions of celebration and suicide, frivolity and despair, hope and bitterness. How do these conflicting attitudes darken the sense of postwar jubilation the narrator ironically refers to at the beginning of the story?

Significant Form, Style, or Artistic Conventions

In "May Day," how does the episodic structure of the story reinforce feelings of alienation and impending disaster both among the characters and in the readers? How does the ironic, almost sarcastic tone of the narrator color our view of events in the story in particular and in post–World War I America in general?

Original Audience

We call attention to Fitzgerald's self-conscious awareness of a double identity as a popular writer of stories for the *Saturday Evening Post* and as a serious novelist aspiring to the company of Conrad, Joyce, and James. We consider the relationship, the compatibility between popular and serious fiction in a democratic and vernacular culture.

The issues of freedom and responsibility and the cost of self-indulgent personal behavior seem particularly appropriate to our time.

Comparisons, Contrasts, Connections

The following stories in *The Heath Anthology* might provide a useful frame of reference: Hemingway's "Hills Like White Elephants"; Porter's "Flowering Judas"; Toomer's "Blood-Burning Moon," "Seventh Street," and "Box Seat." All involve landscape, social milieu, memory, and transitional moments of experience.

Bibliography

The best sources are Fitzgerald's essays listed above; a piece called "Ring," written after the death of Ring Lardner; and also Fitzgerald's letters.

Katherine Anne Porter (1890–1980)

Contributing Editor: Jane Krause DeMouy

Classroom Issues and Strategies

Porter's stories are powerful, but understanding their true content requires thought and sensitivity. They should be read for the psychological as well as the representational reality. In addition, her style is highly complex; even the best critics are not very specific in describing exactly what it is Porter does to achieve her impact. She may be difficult for undergraduates to understand but I think some fruitful discussion can come from focusing on issues of identity. This is an issue that all students know about instinctively; it can lead to interesting discussion to note that Granny Weatherall has had the same problems with identity that many adolescents have. One question becomes whether she has ever shaken them.

Students of Porter would do well to remember the Jamesian principle that art is selection. When Porter, like other artists, chooses certain subjects, she is not only shaping an entity but also saying what she considers important, so it is essential to know what she is writing about. Porter does utilize personal experience in her work, but more often than not it is her internal experience that is true while the factual events have been heightened, dramatized, and symbolized into fiction. In her most complex stories, symbols carry multiple meanings, and the writer's memories are transformed into mythopoeic structures based on the alogical associations common to dreams rather than precise logical sequences. Since art exists not in facts, but in myth, it is also important to note what she does to change personal knowledge into meaningful, universalized fiction.

Students respond strongly to Porter's theme of rebellion—the wish for independence and personhood.

Major Themes, Historical Perspectives, Personal Issues

Themes include the conflict between personal freedom and belonging to conventional society; Porter's Miranda/Laura as a female American Adam; the human confusion experienced when one has to confront the passing of the traditions/myths/structures of old Southern society into the chaos of a technologically speeded-up, wartorn, and jaded society; biological, cultural, and traditional constraints on women.

Miranda, for instance, has grown up seeing that women are valued for their beauty and ability to bear children; that women who want identity or power can get it only by marrying and bearing children; that land, money, and political voice (real power) belong to men; that women who want these are outcasts.

Miranda's problem is that while she has come to recognize that these practices and beliefs are inherently unjust, they are also part of her cultural imperative. She internalizes the moral "rightness" of these things even as she rejects them. This results in enormous conflict for her. Choosing her culture's values, she is biologically trapped; choosing her self, she must reject everything she has been without knowing what she might be. Being unable—or refusing—to choose results in the emotional paralysis of characters like Laura in "Flowering Judas."

Perhaps most important in approaching a study of Porter are several caveats. Readers must, first of all, be wary of false biographical accounts and the tendency of reviewers and critics to confuse Porter's fiction with those false accounts. For specific facts, one can consult Joan Givner's *Katherine Anne Porter: A Life.* Rev. ed. (New York: n.p., 1991), which carefully tracks a monumental amount of detail to clarify names, dates, and events. It is a diligent compilation of research, but a book that fails to find the personality that charmed lovers, friends, and audiences to the last days of Porter's life. Thomas F. Walsh's *Katherine Anne Porter and Mexico: The Illusion of Eden* (U of Texas P, 1992) is a thoroughly re-searched and insightful discussion that sheds light on both Porter's biography and work.

Significant Form, Style, or Artistic Conventions

"I shall try to tell the truth," she said in "My First Speech," (*Collected Essays*, p. 433), "but the result will be fiction." Porter felt that we really understand very little of what happens to us in the present moment, but by remembering, comparing, and waiting for the consequences, we can begin to understand the meaning of certain events. For her, that process of remembering and comparing takes place as she writes. It is a process clearly recorded in "The Jilting of Granny Weatherall," "The Grave," and "Old Mortality."

Fiction is made, she said, first of legend: those things told to her or read when she was a child. It is also made of memory: her childhood emotional experiences of certain events, as well as present memory; the adult's memory of what happened and explanation to herself of what that meant to the child. This confusion of experiences that took place in and over time is difficult to understand, but humanly true. Each person is a mesh of his or her "child" and what the person understands himself or herself to be in the present, which may be illusory, deluded, or "true" by someone else's objective observation.

It is out of this understanding that Porter creates richly layered characters, events, and conflicts. Characters are who they *were*, who they *are*, who they *think* they were and are, as well as who they are *going to be*—given what happens to them in the story and their capacity to deal with that conflict. It is no wonder that Porter's stories have tremendous impact while being incredibly hard to decipher.

Porter is a master of the twentieth-century short story; it was her métier—so much so that she found it all but impossible to write *Ship of Fools.*

Original Audience

These stories are universal and timeless; however, the diversity of Katherine Anne Porter's experience and stories offers a wealth of teaching approaches. Her stories range from the regional focus of nineteenth-century Texas ("The Grave," "Old Mortality," and others) to the urban sophistication of twentieth-century New York and Mexico ("Theft," "That Tree," "Hacienda") and even to horrible visions of an inverted brave new world, where every man is for himself, moral standards do not exist, and the waste land is realized in loveless sex and human isolation.

Comparisons, Contrasts, Connections

Thematically, the bildungsroman experiences and the loss of innocence recorded in "The Grave" and other stories in "The Old Order" invite comparison with Hemingway's Nick Adams stories, just as do "Pale Horse, Pale Rider" and *A Farewell to Arms.* Like William Faulkner, Porter has the historic memory of the Southern temper, but it is a more feminine and particular vision, arising from a heightened social awareness that makes her sensitive to social mores, moral values, and the individual strengths that allow a person to survive.

Bibliography

To best understand Porter, one can do no better than to thoroughly read her essays, particularly "Portrait: Old South," "Noon Wine: The Sources," the "Introduction to *Flowering Judas,*" and "Three Statements About Writing."

The most comprehensive bibliography is Kathryn Hilt and Ruth M. Alvarez, *Katherine Anne Porter: An Annotated Bibliography* (New York: Garland, 1990).

One of the best secondary sources, Lodwick Hartley and George Core's *Katherine Anne Porter: A Critical Collection,* is out of print but is available in library collections.

Robert Penn Warren's *Katherine Anne Porter* for the Twentieth Century Views series (Englewood Cliffs, NJ: Prentice, 1979) and Harold Bloom's *Modern*

Critical Views: Katherine Anne Porter (New Haven: Yale UP, 1987) also contain some of the seminal critical essays on Porter and essays that represent the critical controversy over *Ship of Fools*.

Thomas F. Walsh's *Katherine Anne Porter and Mexico: An Illusion of Eden*, already mentioned, provides interesting perspective on how Porter's experience with her "familiar country" reflected her psychology and informed her art. Janis P. Stout's *Katherine Anne Porter: A Sense of the Times* (U of Virginia P, 1995) is a thoughtful, intellectual biography that views Porter's "interests and contradictions" as a model of modernism itself, a "window on the pivotal social and intellectual movements within her century." Good articles may also be found in Virginia Spencer Carr, ed., *"Flowering Judas": A Casebook* (Rutgers UP, 1993).

Expanded comment on the idea in this article are in Jane DeMouy's *Katherine Anne Porter's Women: The Eye of Her Fiction* (Austin: Texas UP, 1983); and those interested in the role of Southern women will want to look at Anne Firor Scott's *The Southern Lady: From Pedestal to Politics, 1830–1930* (1970).

In addition, a fine overview of Porter, including interviews with her contemporaries Robert Penn Warren and Eudora Welty, as well as dramatization of parts of "The Grave" and "The Circus," is available in the one-hour PBS program *Katherine Anne Porter: The Eye of Memory*, American Masterworks Series, produced by Lumiere Productions (New York, 1986).

Marianne Moore (1887–1972)

Contributing Editor: Bernard F. Engel

Classroom Issues and Strategies

The general student block against poetry often causes difficulties. With Moore, it is useful to observe that she seeks accuracy of statement, that the alleged difficulty of her work does not arise from abstruse symbolism or reference to obscure autobiographical matters but rather from precision: seeking exact presentation, she does not fall back on expected phrasings. The attentive who will slow down and read thoughtfully can understand and enjoy.

Advise students to read through once quickly to get perspective. Then they should read slowly, and aloud. I also advise them that after this first reading they should let the poem sit two or three days, then repeat the process. In class, I read through short poems a few lines at a time, pausing to ask questions; I also ask students to read passages aloud. With undergraduates, I prefer not to spend hours on any one poem. It is better that they read carefully, but without the extended analysis that is appropriate in some graduate classes.

Students need help with the rhetoric and syntax; they need to be shown how to read with care. They rarely raise the abstruse questions of aesthetics or moral philosophy that fascinate the literary critic. Advanced students, however, may be asked to compare Moore's effort to achieve precision with the argument of some deconstructionists and postmodernists that it is not possible for verbal art to reach that goal.

Major Themes, Historical Perspectives, Personal Issues

Point out

1. The fact that though there is usually a "moral" point in a Moore poem, the overall aim is aesthetic: the moral is to contribute to the delight, not to dominate it.
2. The way the poems relate to the modernism of Wallace Stevens and others.

Significant Form, Style, or Artistic Conventions

In a freshman class, I focus on the poem itself; with juniors and seniors, I bring out relationships to modernism. The rhetorical form of a poem is usually worth pointing out; metrics should be mentioned, but only in passing.

Original Audience

I mention the fact that until the 1960s Moore's work was considered too difficult for any but the most elevated critics. I also point out that her early admirers were generally male, that only in the last few years have women come to appreciate her. She does not fit the stereotype of woman as emotional (in contrast to supposedly rational man). Moore, indeed, once remarked that only two or three American women have "even tried" to write poetry—meaning, one may be sure, Emily Dickinson and herself. (In her last years, she might have added Elizabeth Bishop to her list.)

Early strong objections to her work came from Margaret Anderson of the *Little Review,* who in 1918 asserted that she wrote too intellectually; Anderson reprinted her remarks in 1953. Babette Deutsch in 1935, and again in 1952, voiced similar objections. Some recent feminist critics have also had doubts.

Emily Stipes Watts in *The Poetry of American Women from 1632 to 1945* (1977) found Moore practicing a "feminine realism" that "will ultimately be unacceptable"; Watts saw male appreciation of Moore's poetry as condescension. Today, however, old stereotypes about male and female roles have broken down. Most women critics now praise Moore, and they are often the best interpreters of her work.

Comparisons, Contrasts, Connections

Moore knew and corresponded with William Carlos Williams, Ezra Pound, T. S. Eliot, and Wallace Stevens. All of them published comments on her, and she in turn wrote of them. There are obvious comparisons and contrasts in the work of these, the chief American modernists.

Questions for Reading, Discussion, and Writing

1. I sometimes use study questions. They usually focus on the "mere rhetoric"—what the poem "says": its argument or moral, the way it expresses feeling (with Moore, often the feeling of delight).
2. "Poetry": In both versions of the poem (located in the "Cluster: Modernism, Lyric Poetry, Facts"), Moore's speaker says, "I, too, dislike it." Why would a lifelong poet say this? What does the speaker like?

   "The Pangolin": The poem starts in a seemingly casual manner— "Another armored animal"—but moves quickly into exact, patient observation of the animal's structure and behavior. Is the speaker coolly rational? Delighted? Or . . . ? What kind of grace is the ultimate subject of this poem?

   "England": The poem is about America (an example of Moore's waggish wit). Compare it to the essay by Randolph Bourne, "Transnational America."

   "Nevertheless": How can a strawberry resemble "a hedgehog or a star-/fish"? How do apple seeds, the rubber plant, and the prickly pear illustrate the point that "Victory won't come/to me unless I go/to it"?

   "The Mind Is an Enchanting Thing": What is the difference between "enchanted" and "enchanting"? Explain the paradox in "conscientious inconsistency" (stanza 4).

Bibliography

For students and the hurried instructor, the most convenient assistance may be found by looking up the pages on individual poems in the indexes to the books by Engel (revised edition), Nitchie, and Hall. These books deal with all or most of Moore's poetry.

Excellent critical studies by Costello and others give an overall perspective but usually deal with fewer individual poems. There is a full-length biography by Charles Molesworth: *Marianne Moore: A Literary Life* (1990).

Louise Bogan (1897–1970)

Contributing Editor: Theodora R. Graham

Classroom Issues and Strategies

The instructor needs to explain Bogan's often distancing herself from the poem's ideas, creating what Adrienne Rich has called a "mask" or "code." Her use of the more traditional lyric form (though not in most of the poems selected for the anthology) raises questions about her relationship to the experimental verse that poets of the prior generation and those of her own were writing. Bogan seems quite accessible—except in poems like "The Sleeping Fury" and "After the Persian," which require calling students' attention to language, imagery, contrasts.

Introducing Bogan's more general literary career—and perhaps ideas from her essays, reviews, and Ruth Limmer's edited autobiography—will enrich students' understanding of the difficulties women faced as writers and the extraordinary success some achieved as editors (cf. Harriet Monroe, Marianne Moore) and reviewers.

Major Themes, Historical Perspectives, Personal Issues

A number of Bogan's poems concern love and the woman's need to maintain her identity. She also writes, indirectly, of the poet's demons, the "sleeping fury" that must be addressed in its violence and appeased. Bogan also turns her attention to skillful observation, both of crafted objects (and indirectly to the crafted poem) and of natural things (such as the dragonfly). In "Women" she offers a critique of some women's choice of a restricted, passionless, and dull existence.

Significant Form, Style, or Artistic Conventions

A poem entitled "Rhyme" ends "But once heart's feast/You were to me." A love poem about the rhyme between a man and a woman, the poem could also be read as Bogan's tribute to rhyme itself. In "Women" and "Roman Fountain" she demonstrates a distinct ability and interest in what might have seemed in 1922 and 1935 an old-fashioned technique. (The former consists of five stanzas rhyming abcb; the latter, more ingenious, like the fountain it describes, rhymes aabc / aabb / abcabca.) However, other poems selected are dramatically different in formal organization and are unrhymed. Bogan's line breaks, unlike (e.g.) William Carlos Williams's, generally follow syntactic units. But in "The Sleeping Fury" and "After the Persian" she writes in long lines, form following thought. Both poems contain a kind of elegance, issuing even from the fear and violence of the former.

Bogan's scope is not grand, but her talent in crafting verse and summoning images is noteworthy.

Original Audience

Bogan—like Marianne Moore—was writing for a man's world. Neither made concessions to the popular audience to gain a greater readership. Yet their natural reserve and privacy turned them in a direction away from the more soul-baring tendencies of some of their contemporaries. "The Sleeping Fury" could be about the poet's demon-muse; but it could equally concern her break-downs, the warring sides of her own personality. That she was poetry editor for the *New Yorker* for many years indicates that she understood a broader public's taste and chose to write a taut, lyric verse.

Comparisons, Contrasts, Connections

It is useful to compare her treatment of natural objects and personal, cloaked subjects with that of Emily Dickinson and with later poets such as Adrienne Rich and Denise Levertov, who use the personal "I" in more self-revealing ways.

Questions for Reading, Discussion, and Writing

1. I prefer to give students several pages of extracts from Bogan's prose, including reviews and Limmer's biographical collection.
2. Those interested in women writers might want to explore the kinds of verse other women of Bogan's generation—particularly those who

reached out to a larger audience—chose to write. What were women reading from *Ladies Home Companion* and other popular magazines? How does Bogan's writing compare?

Bibliography

See Bogan's prose and Ruth Limmer's *A Journey Around My Room,* extracted as autobiography from Bogan's diaries and other prose.

Ernest Hemingway (1899–1961)

Contributing Editors: Margaret Anne O'Connor and John Alberti

Classroom Issues and Strategies

Most students have already read something by Hemingway, and they come into class with preconceptions. They usually love him or hate him and try to pin labels rather than give his work a new reading. Also, they want to concentrate on biography and biographical readings of his works since most find his well-publicized life even more interesting than his work.

As the headnote to this story suggests, biography is important to understanding Hemingway's approach to writing, but I try to turn students' attention biographically from Hemingway the Adventurer-Philosopher to Hemingway the Writer. Since "Hills Like White Elephants" is much less often anthologized than other Hemingway stories, its newness to students might tempt them to read and reread in order to see how the story fits with other works they've read by him. I approach teaching this taut story as if it were a poem. Word choice and phraseology are keys to its success.

One possible strategy might be to ask two students, a male and a female, to read the dialogue from "Hills Like White Elephants" aloud to the class as if it were a drama. Then class discussion would move toward tone of voice. Questions of the man's sincerity and the girl's sarcasm would naturally emerge. The less preparation for this exercise, the better since a "flat" delivery would remind listeners that Hemingway expects his readers to "interpret."

Students are interested in the philosophy of life they discern from Hemingway's works, the code of behavior his characters follow that gives their lives dignity in the author's eyes. This story seems a self-critique of that code. Careful readers don't believe the girl at the end of the story when she says she's "fine." She's composed herself; she won't make a scene, but she's not "fine." Students want to know how Hemingway has succeeded in making us know that the man is lying to the girl—and perhaps to himself—throughout the story. There's no easy answer to this question, but a close reading of key phrases such as "the only thing that bothers us," "it's perfectly simple," or "I feel fine" will help them see how carefully constructed the story is.

Major Themes, Historical Perspectives, Personal Issues

"Hills" is a good story to shatter the false impression that Hemingway was insensitive to women. This carefully constructed vignette has a nameless man and woman discussing their relationship against the backdrop of the mountain landscape. As in the very best of Hemingway's novels and stories, the authorial stance is ambiguous; readers must pay close attention to small details to understand the progress of the narrative. Students should be encouraged to focus on the dialogue between the man and girl in order to discern their relationship. The issue of abortion and how each speaker feels about it is central to the story. Yet abortion itself is not the main issue; it is the not-too-subtle pressure "the man" is placing on "the girl" to have the abortion that is the key issue.

Significant Form, Style, or Artistic Conventions

Hemingway's minimalist style deserves consideration. If Faulkner confuses readers because he offers so many details for readers to sift through in order to understand what's going on, Hemingway confuses by offering so few.

Original Audience

The central issue in "Hills" is the abortion the girl is being pressured to have by her male companion. The author's stance on the issue of abortion is ambiguous, but the story clearly comes out against the male pressuring the female into an abortion that she doesn't seem to want. Pro-choice and pro-life students might want to concentrate class discussion not on abortion alone, but on the issue of subtle pressure at the heart of the story.

Comparisons, Contrasts, Connections

Of many possible works of comparison, one of the most fruitful would be T. S. Eliot's *The Waste Land*. Compare this rootless couple escaping the commitment of parenthood with Eliot's set of lovers in Book II of his poem. The song of the nightingale "so rudely forced" is "Jug, Jug," which is echoed in the man's choice of a nickname for the girl.

Questions for Reading, Discussion, and Writing

1. What's the purpose of the trip the two travelers are taking?
2. Why are the speakers only identified as "a man" and "girl"? How do these designations affect your reading of the story? What nickname does the man use for the girl?
3. How do the descriptions of the landscape relate to the conversation between the two travelers? What about the discussion of drink orders?
4. Note each sentence or paragraph that is not enclosed in quotation marks and explain how each brief commentary affects your understanding of the characters and the lives they lead.
5. Why does the girl repeat the word *please* seven times? Anger? Hysteria? Fear? Frustration? Why does the man leave her at the table?
6. The railroad station setting is important to the progress—the plot—of the story. How does this physical setting parallel the thematic concerns of the story as well?
7. How does the title relate to the story?

Bibliography

Jeffrey Meyers offers an excellent brief reading of this story in his biography (pp. 196–97).

Wallace Stevens (1879–1955)

Contributing Editor: Linda W. Wagner-Martin

Classroom Issues and Strategies

The sheer difficulty of apprehending meaning from some of Stevens's poems turns many students away. Yet Stevens is one of the most apt voices to speak about the perfection, and the perfectibility, of the poem—the supreme fiction in the writer's, and the reader's, lives. If students can read Stevens's poems well, they will probably be able to read anything in the anthology.

The elusiveness of meaning is one key difficulty: Stevens's valiant attempts to avoid paraphrase, to lose himself in brilliant language, to slide into repetition and assonantal patterns without warning. His work demands complete concentration, and complete sympathy, from his readers. Most students cannot give poetry either of these tributes without some preparation.

Close reading, usually aloud, helps. The well-known Stevens language magic has to be experienced, and since poems are difficult, asking students to work on them alone, in isolation, is not the best tactic. Beginning with the poems by Stevens might make reading T. S. Eliot, Robert Frost, and William Carlos Williams much easier, so I would make this selection central to the study of modern American poetry.

Major Themes, Historical Perspectives, Personal Issues

The value of poetry (and all art); the accessibility of great moral, and mortal, themes through language; the impenetrability of most human relationships; the evanescence of formalized belief systems, including religion; the frustration of imperfection; and others. Stevens often builds from historical and/or philosophical knowledge, expecting "fact" to serve as counterpoint for his readers' more imaginative exploits. But this technique is not meant to lead to easy or facile explication. It is a way of contrasting the predictable and the truly valuable, the imaginary.

Significant Form, Style, or Artistic Conventions

Stevens's intricate stanza and rhyme patterns are a school of poetry in themselves, and each of his poems should be studied as a crafted object. His work fits well with that of T. S. Eliot, as does some of his aesthetic rationale: "Poetry is not personal." "The real is only the base. But it is the base." "In poetry, you must love the words, the ideas and the images and rhythms with all your capacity to love anything at all." "Poetry must be irrational." "The purpose of poetry is to make life complete in itself." "Poetry increases the feeling for reality." "In the absence of a belief in God, the mind turns to its own creations and examines them, not alone from the aesthetic point of view, but for what they reveal, for what they validate and invalidate."

Original Audience

Modernism was so specific a mood and time that students must understand the modernists' rage for control of craft, the emphasis on the formalism of the way an art object was formed, and the importance craft held for all parts of the artist's life. Once those conventions are described, and Stevens placed in this period, his own distinctions from the group of modernists will be clearer. ("Not all objects are equal. The vice of imagism was that it did not recognize this." "A change of style is a change of subject." "In the long run the truth does not matter.") Conscious of all the elements of form, Stevens yet overlays his work with a heavily philosophical intention, and the shelves of commentary on his poetry have been occasioned because that commentary is, in many cases, useful.

Comparisons, Contrasts, Connections

The T. S. Eliot of the *Four Quartets* (likenesses) or the William Carlos Williams of the short poems (differences).

William Faulkner (1897–1962)

Contributing Editor: John Lowe

Students are resistant to texts that withhold key information, to narrative that is obscure and/or convoluted, and to characters who don't seem to have "common sense." All of these "sins" appear in Faulkner's work. He also requires a knowledge of Southern and American history that many students don't possess.

Begin by emphasizing the pleasures to be gained from unraveling Faulkner's mysteries. Especially focus on his parallels to and differences from the popular myths of Southern culture, as found in *Gone With the Wind, North and South,* and popular television series set in the South. Approach his works as though they were detective stories (some of them, in fact, are). Do brief presentations of relevant historical materials. Locate the text's place in Faulkner's career, drawing parallels between the character's concerns and the way those issues touched Faulkner as well. Explain how Faulkner explored and exploded stereotypes, of Southerners, African Americans, and women.

Teachers should be prepared to answer typical questions: students want to know if he "really thought of all those things when he was writing," referring to the hidden references we uncover in symbolism, imagery, and so on. They ask if his family owned slaves and how Faulkner felt about it if they did. Some students want to know if I think Faulkner was a racist and/or sexist.

Major Themes, Historical Perspectives, Personal Issues

Highlight Faulkner's tremendous importance as an interpreter of history—and not just Southern or American history—at a critical moment when modernism emerged as a questioning, probing tool used to redefine human nature and our relationship to nature. Issues of sex, class, and, above all, race should be explored using a battery of interdisciplinary techniques, including historical, social, anthropological, economic, political, and feminist perspectives. "Barn Burning," for example, has been profitably analyzed by Marxist critics as a class struggle.

Gender formation operates centrally in Faulkner's stories. Interestingly, each of these processes intersects with issues of class and community. These conjunctions could and should be profitably explored and linked to the way Faulkner struggled with them in his own life. All three stories employ mythic/biblical structures in the service of these various thematics; students should be asked to identify them and demonstrate why they are effective.

Significant Form, Style, or Artistic Conventions

Faulkner needs to be understood in both the context of Southern literary traditions and modernism. "Barn Burning," for example, in its employment of Jamesian point of view as confined to Sarty's consciousness, requires detailed analysis of its narrative structure, its language, and the consequent effects on the reader. Both stories attempt to present complicated psychological conditions and situations while adhering to the firm realities of dramatic plotting.

Comparisons, Contrasts, Connections

Faulkner needs to be related to the other great modernists who so influenced him, especially Joyce and Eliot, and his work should and could be profitably compared and contrasted with the similar but sometimes very different literary experiments of Hemingway, Stein, Fitzgerald, Wright, and so on. "Barn Burning" can easily be contrasted with *Huckleberry Finn*, where a young boy must abandon his father's standards in favor of more humane, just ones, or with a female *bildungsroman* such as Wharton's *Summer*. The injustices of sharecropping discussed by Faulkner could be examined alongside other treatments of rural life such as Hamlin Garland's "Under the Lion's Paw" or Richard Wright's "Long Black Song" and "The Man Who Was Almost a Man"; the latter similarly focuses on a young boy's coming of age against a rural backdrop. Twain, Morrison, and Oates could be helpful in explaining the interconnections between the *bildungsroman* and psychological fiction.

Questions for Reading, Discussion, and Writing

1. How does one establish individual independence as a teenager? Do you remember any crucial moment in your own life when you realized that you had to make a choice between what your parent(s) and/or family believed and your own values?
2. Is the destruction of another person's property ever something we can justify? Explain.
3. Does it matter that this story is rendered through Sarty's consciousness? What were Faulkner's options, and how would the story be different if he had exercised them?
4. What are the key symbols in the story, and how do they serve the thematic purposes Faulkner had in mind?
5. Do the class issues the story raises have any parallels today?
6. What is the tone of the story, and how is it established?

Paper Topics

I never arbitrarily assign students a particular story to write on; instead, I urge them to choose one they particularly like. They are then to ask themselves exactly *why* they like it, which will lead them to a topic (the humor employed, a certain character or method of characterization, a fascination with the depiction of the historical period on display, and so on).

Bibliography

Bradford, M. E. "Family and Community in Faulkner's 'Barn Burning.'" *Southern Review* 17 (1981): 332–39.

Fowler, Virginia C. "Faulkner's 'Barn Burning': Sarty's Conflict Reconsidered." *College Language Association Journal* 24 (1981): 513–21.

Franklin, Phyllis. "Sarty Snopes and 'Barn Burning.'" *Mississippi Quarterly* 21 (1968): 189–93.

Hiles, Jane. "Kinship and Heredity in Faulkner's 'Barn Burning.'" *Mississippi Quarterly* 38.3 (1985): 329–37.

Volpe, Edmond L. "'Barn Burning': A Definition of Evil." *Faulkner: The Unappeased Imagination: A Collection of Critical Essays*. Ed. O. Carey. Troy, NY: Whitson, 1980. 75–82.

These stories are treated in Hans Skei's *William Faulkner: The Short Story Career: An Outline of Faulkner's Short Story Writing from 1919 to 1962*. Oslo: U Forl, 1981; and James Ferguson's *Faulkner's Short Fiction*. Knoxville: U of Tennessee P, 1991. See also *Faulkner and the Short Story: Faulkner and Yoknapatawpha, 1990*. Ed. Ann Abadie and Doreen Fowler. Jackson: UP of Mississippi, 1992.

Hart Crane (1899–1932)

Contributing Editor: Margaret Dickie

Classroom Issues and Strategies

I set Crane in the context of Pound and Eliot, where students can see the ambitions he shared with his fellow modernists to "make it new," to write a poem including history, even to define the role of the poet as a cultural spokesman. And, in that context, I try to distinguish the larger concerns of his career that set him apart from his fellow poets: his interest in the "logic of metaphor" as making it new, his focus on American rather than world history, and his search to find his identity in his role as a poet. All indicate how he reinterpreted the modernist program to suit his own purposes. I urge students, who may have been reading Ezra Pound and T. S. Eliot through the footnotes to their poems, to abandon that approach to Crane and to concentrate instead on those elements they find most perplexing in his work: the language, the experience, and the dislocated references.

Central to any discussion of Crane is his role as a homosexual poet. Quite apart from the task of placing him in the modernist movement, students will need to understand Crane's sense of himself as a figure marginalized both by his chosen profession as a poet in a capitalist economy and by his sexual identity as a homosexual in the ideology of literary and cultural authority that made, as Thomas Yingling has suggested, "homosexuality an inadmissible center from which to write about American life" (27). I introduce Crane with "Black Tambourine" and "Chaplinesque," in which he identifies the poet with the "black man" and the tramp in order to show how he felt himself marginalized. As part of the discussion, I try to indicate also how he was willing to appropriate such marginal figures for his own use without much regard to their own status.

Major Themes, Historical Perspectives, Personal Issues

Major themes developed in the early lyric poems and carried through *The Bridge* and to the last poem he wrote, "The Broken Tower," include the artist as an outcast in the modern industrialized and urbanized world; Crane's need nonetheless to find ways to celebrate the modern world and to articulate an affirmative myth of America; the search to discover in the present the positive values of the American past; Crane's deepening despair over the possibilities of accomplishing such a bold program; and finally, the lifelong effort to find a means of expressing his homosexuality, of masking it, of making it viable and meaningful both for himself and for his audience.

Historically, Crane is a modernist who departs widely from the movement. His effort to write a long poem belongs to the early stages of modernism when Pound was starting *The Cantos*, Eliot completing *The Waste Land*, and William Carlos Williams was producing *Spring & All* and *In the American Grain*. Although Crane's effort, *The Bridge*, is too long to be included in full in the anthology, the selected sections—"To Brooklyn Bridge" and "The River"— should serve to indicate both his Native American subjects and the range of his style from formal quatrains through Whitmanian catalogs to collage and narrative. His place in the canon has seldom been challenged even by his earlier critics, who found his long poem intellectually and structurally flawed, his lifestyle reprehensible, and his suicide inevitable; but his achievement is of another order from Eliot's or Pound's, and it must be read on its own terms.

Personally, the central question in Crane's life was how to be a homosexual poet, a writer able to express his own identity in culturally meaningful ways. The central issue of his career was the composition of *The Bridge*, which he worked on during most of his writing life, even when the inspiration of the long poem failed him, and his belief in its purpose faltered.

Significant Form, Style, or Artistic Conventions

The modernist long poem was the form Crane hoped to invent. He offered various explanations of his program chiefly to Otto Kahn, a philanthropist from whom he sought financial aid, claiming, "What I am really handling, you see, is the myth of America. Thousands of strands have had to be searched for, sorted and interwoven. . . . For each section of the entire poem has presented its own unique problem of form, not alone in relation to the materials embodied within its separate confines, but also in relation to the other parts, *in series*, of the major design of the entire poem" (*Letters* 305). The two sections in the anthology should suggest something of Crane's method of interweaving different strands as well as the variety of forms that he employed. The design of the whole poem eluded him.

To Harriet Monroe, he described his theory of the logic of metaphor as distinct from pure logic, arguing that he was "more interested in the so-called illegal impingements of the connotations of words on the consciousness (and their combinations and interplay in metaphor on this basis) than I am interested in the preservation of their logically rigid significations at the cost of limiting my subject matter and perceptions involved in the poem." I encourage students to consider this statement, puzzling out its significance, and to examine the short poems in light of it in order to see how words interact and develop in a chain of free associations.

Original Audience

Crane's original audience included editors and readers of the little magazines of the 1920s, fellow poets, and literary friends such as Malcolm Cowley, Harry and Caresse Crosby, Waldo Frank, Gorham Munson, Katherine Anne Porter, and Allen Tate. He has always been a poet's poet, and his reputation has been nourished by the tributes of poets as different as Allen Ginsberg and Robert Lowell. The rise of gay and lesbian studies has inspired renewed interest in his career. For an extremely informative reading of his homosexual themes and style, see Yingling.

Comparisons, Contrasts, Connections

Crane pitted himself against the formidable reputation of Eliot and *The Waste Land*. *The Bridge* would, he hoped, be an answer to what he imagined as Eliot's negative view of modern life. He allied himself with William Carlos Williams, whose *In the American Grain* influenced him as he worked on his long poem, although the selections for Williams in the anthology are not ideal for drawing a comparison here. Perhaps Williams's "Spring and All" or "To Elsie" might serve as treatments of the American landscape and people that Crane would have shared.

Questions for Reading, Discussion, and Writing

1. If Crane identified with the "black man" and Charlie Chaplin or with the hoboes in "The River," did he have any sympathy for their plight, or was he simply appropriating them as suitable images of his own difficulties?
2. Consider why Melville would have been important to Crane. In what sense is a "scattered chapter, livid hieroglyph" an apt description of Crane's own verse?

3. Discuss the image of the Brooklyn Bridge as a technological achievement and as a significant poetic symbol for Crane.
4. In what sense is breaking an important imaginative act for Crane? Look at "The Broken Tower" as Crane's final acceptance of brokenness in himself and in his world.

The New Negro Renaissance

Alain Locke (1885–1954)

Contributing Editor: Beth Helen Stickney

Classroom Issues and Strategies

While students often have difficulty knowing how to approach nonfiction prose, particularly the kind that tends toward abstraction as Locke's essay does, once we have historically contextualized "The New Negro," students are quick both to sympathize with Locke and to become involved in a number of salient debates. One particular point of interest is Locke's own educational background; students want to know what it was like for an African American at Oxford, and they are also generally interested in learning about the milieu at Harvard in the early 1900s. Most will begin to sense the precariousness of Locke's position as a black intellectual struggling both to make a place for himself in an Anglo-American environment and to pave the way for other African Americans.

The centrality of art and culture in Locke's thought and political philosophy always touches off controversy. Students divide on issues of artistic freedom versus responsibility to one's race (and/or class/gender); the racial/cultural specificity of a given art form (e.g., is jazz, or rap/hip-hop, as students think today, a "black" form?); and finally, the broader concern of the role that art and culture can play in any political or social agenda (again, a point that usually prompts students to draw on their own experience).

When students do draw on contemporary culture, their references are usually to popular music, and I encourage this. Because *The New Negro* anthology itself (indeed the New Negro *movement*) was so deliberately an interdisciplinary project, I try to represent as many art forms as possible. (This is where student presentations can be profitably used.) Cary Nelson's *Repression and Recovery*, in addition to giving a history of much of the "noncanonical" literature of the period, includes reproductions (some in color) of artwork from *The*

New Negro and several other small African-American periodicals. Included in my bibliography are two fine art books, both with informative essays on individual artists and on African-American culture in general. Any number of musical recordings (Duke Ellington, Louis Armstrong, Bessie Smith, the spirituals) would give the opportunity to discuss Locke's distaste for the commercialized "Tin Pan Alley" jazz and his preference for the more "authentic" spirituals (though the latter were already being Westernized for the concert halls). As students begin to see that Locke's concerns are neither merely academic nor dead issues, they will sometimes bring me newspaper clippings or mention interviews in which they detect Lockean themes being raised. These, of course, I make a point of sharing with the class.

Major Themes, Historical Perspectives, Personal Issues

Major themes that Locke develops include the entrance onto the world scene of a new social type and a new psychology in the figure of the "new Negro"; the dialectical relationship between an outer reality (social, political, and cultural conditions) and inner consciousness; the centrality of Harlem as a "race capital" and the importance of the urban experience generally in promoting the cosmopolitan ideal; pan-Africanism and the importance of uniting African Americans with oppressed and politically awakening peoples worldwide; the significance of cultural renewal in bringing about social and political progress; the "enlarging of personal experience" as inseparable from a commitment to "a common vision of the social tasks ahead"; the authenticity of "folk" culture and the dangers inherent in empty imitation of "high" culture forms; the need for a reinvigoration of democratic ideals and institutions, and the unique ability of African Americans to address that need; the role that the "enlightened minorities" of each race must play in bringing the races together; the urgency of seeing racial interests in a "new and enlarged way" that would ultimately transcend a narrowly racialist vision.

As the only child of educated, middle-class parents, Locke was both a product and a proponent of an elite high-culture tradition. Though known for his devotion to cultural pluralism and what he came to call "critical relativism," Locke's early education would have instilled in him Victorian, specifically Arnoldian, notions of taste and cultural value; indeed, even as he supported young artists and emerging African-American cultural forms, he was often accused of elitism and Eurocentrism (charges that had also been leveled against W. E. B. Du Bois). But while he was educated in and became a vital part of the country's elite intellectual circles, he also knew racial prejudice (note his ostracism at Oxford even as a Rhodes scholar), and he actively fought racism and worked for full social, cultural, and political recognition of all African Americans. Thus, both privileged and oppressed, he found himself in much the same vexed position as many of his black contemporaries, most notably Du Bois and James Weldon Johnson (both of whom had also spent time in Europe, traveling and studying).

As the advance guard (in Du Bois's case one might already say, in 1925, the "older" guard) of an emerging black intelligentsia, these men, and women such as Jessie Fausset (literary editor of *The Crisis*, the NAACP's journal), Angelina Grimké, and Zora Neale Hurston, initiated and helped sustain public debate on issues of assimilation, nationalism, higher education, artistic freedom, economic independence, cultural self-determination, women's rights, and race leadership. (Here, the extensively researched and well-documented *Propaganda and Aesthetics* is extremely helpful in delineating the way these debates became public through a nexus of journals and small magazines.) Historically, these writers, artists, and activists were uniquely poised so as to inherit a set of social conditions shaped by Reconstruction, the black migration northward, economic fluctuation, and U.S. participation in World War I; *and* to set the terms for addressing and representing those conditions, terms that would in turn be inherited by future generations.

Personally, Locke seems to have been able to balance an active, even extravagant, social life among Manhattan's upper crust with his commitment to education, and even serious philosophical writing. Well respected by prominent philosophers like John Dewey and Sidney Hook, Locke was called upon both to speak at professional gatherings and to contribute to volumes on contemporary philosophy. One can only speculate on what his stature as a philosopher might have been had he exerted more sustained efforts in that area. And yet, the poet Claude McKay referred to him simply as a "charming, harmless fellow" (and at least on one occasion as the embodiment of the "Aframerican rococco," an even less flattering picture). Perhaps not without irony, Locke humbly referred to himself as the "midwife" of a generation of writers and artists who would be responsible for Harlem's renaissance.

Significant Form, Style, or Artistic Conventions

While the primary historical and cultural importance of Locke's essay certainly lies in its content rather than in its form or style, I do stress Locke's ability to appeal to an educated, and perhaps dispassionate, reader through careful control of tone and language. I also spend some time on the essay form itself as part of an American tradition of cultural criticism. This latter approach works especially well in writing-intensive courses; student-writers are likely to take their work more seriously if they are able to see their own essays as fitting into that tradition.

Original Audience

"The New Negro" makes a nice case study in audience because of its publication history. Originally written as the lead essay for a special issue of the magazine *Survey Graphic* that Locke had been called upon to edit, it later served as the introduction to a much expanded anthology based on that issue, published as *The New Negro: An Interpretation*. As the popular version of *Survey*, a professional journal devoted to social work, *Survey Graphic* was an extensively illustrated magazine designed to acquaint a general readership with social problems of the day. The anthology, published by the well-respected Albert and Charles Boni and illustrated with fine color portraits, drawings, decorative designs, and reproductions of African artwork, is clearly designed to avoid racial polemics and to reach an educated, enlightened audience composed of both black and white readers. (One might even say that Locke is aiming for a primarily white audience, presenting a well-reasoned defense of his cultural agenda to potential supporters.)

Comparisons, Contrasts, Connections

Locke's essay works well alongside Du Bois's "Of Our Spiritual Strivings" (chapter I of *The Souls of Black Folk*), Langston Hughes's "When the Negro Was in Vogue," and James Weldon Johnson's *The Autobiography of an Ex-Colored Man*. However, it is also important to remember that Locke was a vital member of an *American* intellectual community—be it "Anglo" or "Afro"—and therefore can be seen as addressing issues of *national* concern. An instructive connection to make in this light is with Randolph Bourne's "Transnational America." (See also Locke's 1911 essay, "The American Temperament.") Bourne's cosmopolitanism, his notion of a "trans-nationality" and a "federation of cultures," is compatible with Locke's own vision of an American democracy based on a rigorous sense of cultural pluralism. Further, on the dialectic between artistic innovation and cultural conservation, also an issue for Locke, see T. S. Eliot's "Tradition and the Individual Talent."

Questions for Reading, Discussion, and Writing

Students should be able to answer questions along the lines of the following:

1. What does Locke mean by the "new" negro? How does this figure differ from the "old" negro? To what extent does this figure correspond to an actual social type, and to what extent might it be an idealization? What might Locke's purpose be in idealizing the new negro?
2. What does Locke hope to achieve with his essay?

3. What concerns does Locke share with other writers of his day?
4. What influence do you think Locke had on the artists of the New Negro Movement? Can this influence be seen today? What issues of importance to Locke and the New Negro Movement generally are still of concern today?

Writing assignments might range from a work of original cultural criticism (that is, attack a contemporary issue/cultural problem related to those Locke dealt with, addressing a particular audience from the student's own viewpoint) to an analysis of Locke's vision of culture and democracy vis-à-vis that of another writer, say, Du Bois or Bourne (this, of course, might involve research and further reading in each author's body of work).

Bibliography

Baker, Houston A., Jr. *Modernism and the Harlem Renaissance.* Chicago: U of Chicago P, 1987.

Dallas Museum of Art. *Black Art, Ancestral Legacy: The African Impulse in African-American Art.* New York: Abrams, 1989.

Huggins, Nathan I. *Harlem Renaissance.* New York: Oxford UP, 1971.

Johnson, Abby A. and Ronald M. Johnson. *Propaganda and Aesthetics: The Literary Politics of African-American Magazines in the Twentieth Century.* 2nd ed. Amherst: U of Massachusetts P, 1991.

Lewis, David L. *When Harlem Was in Vogue.* New York: Knopf, 1981.

Nelson, Cary. *Repression and Recovery: Modern American Poetry and the Politics of Cultural Memory, 1910–1945.* Madison: U of Wisconsin P, 1989.

Studio Museum in Harlem. *Harlem Renaissance: Art of Black America.* New York: Abrams, 1987.

Jean Toomer (1894–1967)

Contributing Editor: Nellie Y. McKay

Classroom Issues and Strategies

Toomer's style is difficult, especially in view of earlier African-American literature. To a large extent, Toomer abandoned the predominant naturalistic and realistic representation of the black experience to experiment with newer modernistic techniques. When they first approach these texts, students usually feel that it is well beyond their understanding—that Toomer is engaged in abstractions that are too difficult to comprehend.

Have the students explore all the possibilities for a literal meaning of the metaphors and symbols. "Blood-Burning Moon" is less difficult for them because it has a traditional story line. In "Karintha," for instance, try to get them to see that Toomer is concerned with the sexual and economic oppression of women within their own communities, where they should be safe from the former at least.

These selections lend themselves to the visual imagination. Students may find it helpful to think of the "pictures" Toomer's images present as they read and try to understand, also, the written meanings these images present.

Students respond positively to the poetic qualities of the writing, and they enjoy its visual aspects. They have difficulty interpreting the underlying themes and meanings, mainly because the language is seductive and leaves them ambivalent regarding the positive and negative qualities the writer intends to portray. It is best to lead them through one section by reading aloud in class and permitting them to use a number of methods (listening to the words, visualizing the images, and so on) to try to fathom what is going on.

Major Themes, Historical Perspectives, Personal Issues

1. The significance of black women as representatives of African-American culture. What qualities do women have that are similar to those of the entire group of African Americans—at least as Toomer saw them?
2. The nature of the richness as well as the pain in African-American culture.
3. The symbolistic aspects of the Northern and Southern black experience.
4. The role of the black artist—for example, in "Song of the Son," in which the absent son returns to preserve the almost now-lost culture of his ancestors.

Significant Form, Style, or Artistic Conventions

Toomer is writing at a crucial time in American and African-American literary history. His friends are members of the Lost Generation of writers intent on reforming American literature. His effort is to make a different kind of presentation of African-America through the art of literature. He sees the loss of some of the strongest elements of the culture in the move toward modernization and technology. For example, he captures the beauty and pathos of the experience in "Karintha," the brutality in "Blood-Burning Moon," and the imitation of the white culture in "Box Seat."

Original Audience

Cane was written for an intellectual audience who could grasp the nuances the author was interested in promoting. The book sold fewer than 500 copies in its first year, but had enthusiastic reviews from the most avant-garde literary critics. It continues to appeal to intellectuals, especially those who are interested in the ways in which language can be manipulated to express particular life situations.

Comparisons, Contrasts, Connections

Toomer's work can be compared with some of Sherwood Anderson's stories and with Hart Crane's poetry. The three men knew each other and were friends during the 1920s. They read each other's work and advised each other. Their general thrust was that human beings were alienated from the basic "natural" qualities in themselves and needed to get back to more of the spiritual values that could be found in closer unity with nature.

Questions for Reading, Discussion, and Writing

Cane was a work to celebrate the African-American experience without denying the awful pain and oppression that made the strength of the group so apparent. Paper topics that focus on the history of black America between Reconstruction and the 1920s are useful in showing what a student can learn about Jean Toomer's reasons for the perceptions he revealed in these selections.

Bibliography

The best source on these is the discussion (in chronological order in the book) in the McKay biography of Toomer's literary life and work. The attempt here is to explicate the individual selections in the total book.

Langston Hughes (1902–1967)

Contributing Editor: Charles H. Nichols

Classroom Issues and Strategies

The primary problems encountered in teaching Langston Hughes grow out of his air of improvisation and familiarity. Vital to an understanding of Hughes's poetry and prose is the idiom, the quality of black colloquial speech and the rhythms of jazz and the blues.

The best strategies for teaching the writer involve the reading aloud of the poetry and prose, the use of recordings and films, and the use of the history of the "New Negro" and the Harlem Renaissance.

Major Themes, Historical Perspectives, Personal Issues

The major themes in Langston Hughes's work grow out of his personal life, his travels, his involvement in radical and protest movements, and his interest in Africa and South America as well as the Caribbean.

Significant Form, Style, or Artistic Conventions

In regard to questions of form, style, or artistic convention, the following considerations are relevant to Langston Hughes:

1. His debt to Walt Whitman, Carl Sandburg, and Paul Laurence Dunbar.
2. His enthusiasm for the language and songs of the rural folk and lower-class urban, "street" Negro. As Arna Bontemps once wrote, "No one loved Negroes as Langston Hughes did."
3. His capacity for improvisation and original rhythms. His use of jazz, blues, be-bop, gospel, and Harlem slang.

The poetry: Point out the occasion that inspired the poem "The Negro Speaks of Rivers" (cf. *The Big Sea*, pp. 54–56). "The Weary Blues," "Drum," and "Freedom Train" use the idioms of black speech with poetic effect.

Prose: Among Hughes's finest achievements are the Simple stories. Here we have the speech and idiom presented with irony, malapropisms, and humor.

Original Audience

Hughes's audience consisted of his literary friends (Countee Cullen, Carl Van Vechten, Wallace Thurman, and others) as well as the general public.

Comparisons, Contrasts, Connections

Comparisons or contrasts might be made with Carl Sandburg, Walt Whitman, and Claude McKay. The bases of such comparisons might be the language and metaphor, the degree of militancy, and so on.

Bibliography

Berry, Faith. "Saunders Redding as Literary Critic of Langston Hughes." *The Langston Hughes Review* 5.2 (Fall 1986).

Emanuel, James A. and Theodore L. Gross. *Dark Symphony: Negro Literature in America.* New York: Free, 1968. 191–221, 447–80.

Henderson, Stephen. *Understanding the New Black Poetry: Black Speech and Black Music as Poetic References.* New York: Morrow, 1973.

Hughes, L. *The First Book of Rhythms.* London: Franklin Watts, 1954.

———. "Ten Ways to Use Poetry in Teaching." *College Language Association Bulletin.* 1951.

Miller, R. Baxter, ed. *The Art and Imagination of Langston Hughes.* Lexington: UP Kentucky, 1990.

———. *Black American Poets Between Worlds, 1940–1960.* Knoxville: U of Tennessee P, 1986.

O'Daniel, Therman B. *Langston Hughes, Black Genius: A Critical Evaluation.* College Language Association. New York: Morrow, 1971. 65 ff., 171, 180.

Countee Cullen (1903–1946)

Contributing Editor: Walter C. Daniel

Classroom Issues and Strategies

Students who read Cullen need to develop a clear understanding of the temper of the Harlem Renaissance period in U.S. literary development. In addition, they may need help with the classical allusions in "Yet Do I Marvel" and in "Simon the Cyrenian Speaks." Also, students should come to understand the reference to Scottsboro as the poet's criticism of his fellow poets' neglect of what he considers a significant matter (obviously, this requires knowing about the Scottsboro incident in 1931 and following).

Significant Form, Style, or Artistic Conventions

Countee Cullen is an important figure of the African-American arts movement known as the Harlem Renaissance. Born in Louisville, Kentucky, Cullen was reared in New York City by his paternal grandmother until 1918, when he was adopted by the Reverend Frederick Asbury Cullen. This was a turning point in his life, for he was now introduced into the very center of black activism and achievement. Cullen displayed his talent early; already in high school he was writing poetry, and in his sophomore year at NYU he was awarded second prize in the nationwide Witter Bynner Poetry Contest for "The Ballad of the Brown Girl." Encompassing themes that would remain salient for the remainder of his career, Cullen's first major poem also revealed his unabashed reverence for the works of John Keats. Cullen was firmly convinced that traditional verse forms could not be bettered by more modern paradigms. It was, therefore, the task of any aspiring writer, he felt, to become conversant with and part of a received literary tradition simply because such a tradition has the virtue of longevity and universal sanction.

Cullen's first volume, *Color,* established him as a writer with an acute spiritual vision. Especially noteworthy in this respect is "Simon the Cyrenian Speaks," a work that eloquently makes use of Matthew 27:32 in order to suggest an analogue between blacks and Simon, the man who was compelled to bear the cross of Christ on his back. Sublimity was not Cullen's only strong point. In "Incident," the reader is brusquely catapulted into the all-too-realistic world of an impressionable eight-year-old as he experiences overt racism for the first time on a memorable ride through the history-filled streets of Baltimore.

In 1927, Cullen edited a significant anthology of black poetry, *Caroling Dusk,* and published two collections of his own, *The Ballad of the Brown Girl* and *Copper Sun.* Representative of Cullen's philosophical development in this period is the multifaceted "Heritage," a poem that summarizes his ambivalent relationship with Christian and pagan cultural constructs.

The 1930s and 1940s saw a change of direction in Cullen's work. His poetry output almost totally ceased as he turned his attention to the novel, theater, translation, teaching, and children's literature. The 1932 novel *One Way to Heaven* was Cullen's response to Carl Van Vechten's 1926 *Nigger Heaven,* a controversial and notorious work exploring the seamy underbelly of Harlem.

Cullen's best work was his poetry; he apparently knew this when he compiled his anthology, with the self-explanatory title *On These I Stand,* shortly before his death.

Original Audience

The Harlem Renaissance period between the two world wars saw the rise and definition of the "New Negro" in social, political, and literature activities of the nation.

Cullen, along with other formally educated black poets, established a new aesthetic for racial statement.

Comparisons, Contrasts, Connections

Cullen's contemporaries (the best-known ones among the writers) were Gwendolyn Bennett, Langston Hughes, and Claude McKay; contrast the poetic method of social protest by studying poems written by each of these poets.

Cullen has been criticized for taking an elitist attitude toward racial matters and of ignoring social protest. Is this criticism fair to Cullen in light of your reading of some poems written by him and, for instance, Claude McKay?

His first volume of poetry, *Color* (1925), revealed an indebtedness to traditional verse forms and an abiding interest in the tenets of romanticism, characteristics markedly absent from the blues-based folk rhythms of the poetry of Langston Hughes. Cullen looked beyond his own rich heritage for authorial models and chose John Keats, firmly convinced that "To make a poet black, and bid him sing" was a "curious thing" that God had done. So curious, indeed, that the voice of the black poet had to be assimilated to and harmonized with the bearers of an alien literary tradition. In "To John Keats, Poet, At Springtime," Cullen's adulation of the nineteenth-century lyricist is most pronounced: "I know, in spite of all men say/Of Beauty, you have felt her most."

Questions for Reading, Discussion, and Writing

1. Identify nonblack authors of the 1920s and determine their common themes in contrast with those of black writers.
2. Cullen grew up in a Methodist parsonage as the adopted son of a prominent Harlem pastor. Might the use of paradox about Christian religion and its practices in some of his poetry reflect his home experience? Which works and in which references?
3. Indications of Cullen's fascination with and influence by the English Romantic poets, especially John Keats.
4. Effectiveness of the metaphor of Simon the Cyrenian to black American life at the time; whether the allusion suggests some theological implications, such as nonredemptive suffering.
5. In the poem "Yet Do I Marvel," Cullen makes an implicit comparison between black poets and the mythical figures of Tantalus and Sisyphus. Explain how this comparison functions within the world of the poem.
6. Lying behind Cullen's title choice for "From the Dark Tower" is the phrase "ivory tower." How does this fact help explain the poem as well as its dedication to Charles S. Johnson?
7. As background to discussion of "Scottsboro, Too, Is Worth Its Song," comment on the historical importance of the Scottsboro Nine case and the trial of Sacco and Vanzetti. Why are these two events paired in Cullen's poem? What was the prevailing poetic current that prevented contemporary concerns from being broached in verse? In answering this last question, compare, for instance, some of the poems written by Wallace Stevens and William Carlos Williams during this period with the poetry of Cullen. Why did Cullen not follow the modernist precepts announced by writers such as T. S. Eliot, Ezra Pound, and Amy Lowell? How does Cullen's allusion to Walt Whitman's lines "I . . . sing myself" and "I sing the body electric" function in the context of this poem?
8. Cullen chooses to set his poem "Incident" in Old Baltimore. Why?
9. With reference to "Pagan Prayer," comment on the manner in which African Americans have used Christian religion as a repository for radical egalitarian hopes. How is Cullen's conception of the religion of the white man different from that of a contemporary Nigerian writer, such as Chinua Achebe in his novels *Things Fall Apart* and *Arrow of God*?
10. How does Cullen accommodate traditions of English poetry to themes of problems of living black in the United States?
11. How active is the poet (Cullen) in taking the position of racial spokesman in the poems? Effective?

Bibliography

Baker, Houston. *Black Literature in America.* New York: McGraw, 1971. 114–58.

Bontemps, Arna. *The Harlem Renaissance Remembered.* New York: Dodd, 1972.

Daniel, Walter C. "Countee Cullen as Literary Critic." *College Language Association Journal* 14 (March 1972): 281–90.

Davis, Arthur. *From the Dark Tower: African-American Writers 1900–1960.* Howard UP, 1974.

Wagner, Jean. *Black Poets of the United States.* Urbana-Champaign: U of Illinois P, 1973. Part II.

Critical discussion of Cullen's poetry was inaugurated by J. Saunders Redding in *To Make a Poet Black* (1939). More detailed attention was given to his oeuvre in a sympathetic and forthright monograph by Houston A. Baker Jr., *A Many-Colored Coat of Dreams: The Poetry of Countee Cullen* (1974). Alan R. Shucard in *Countee Cullen* (1984) provides a complete overview and assessment of Cullen's life and literary endeavors.

Perceptive comments about his novel are contained in Bernard W. Bell's *The African-American Novel and Its Tradition* (1987).

An invaluable general background of the Harlem Renaissance that also includes comments about Cullen is Nathan Irvin Huggins's *Harlem Renaissance* (1971). Equally indispensable is Margaret Perry's *A Bio-Bibliography of Countee P. Cullen 1903–1946* (1971).

The following are noteworthy articles touching upon particular aspects of Cullen's poetry:

Davis, Arthur P. "The Alien-and-Exile Theme in Countee Cullen's Racial Poems." *Phylon* 14 (1953): 390–400.

Dorsey, David F. "Countee Cullen's Use of Greek Mythology." *College Language Association Journal* 13 (1970): 68–77.

Webster, Harvey Curtis. "A Difficult Career." *Poetry* 70 (1947): 224–25.

Gwendolyn B. Bennett (1902–1981)

Contributing Editor: Walter C. Daniel

Classroom Issues and Strategies

Almost always overlooked in discussion about the Harlem Renaissance, Gwendolyn Bennett was, nevertheless, a significant part of the most important artistic movement in African-American history. Chiefly remembered for "The Ebony Flute," a regular column appearing in *Opportunity* that chronicled the creative efforts of the writers, painters, sculptors, actors, and musicians who made Harlem the center of a profound cultural flowering, Bennett was also a poet and short story writer of considerable skill. "To Usward," for instance, a poem dedicated to Jessie Fauset in honor of the publication of her novel *There Is Confusion*, celebrates the newly discovered sense of empowerment permeating the Harlem community—a community envisioned as a chorus of individual voices at once aware of a rich African cultural heritage and prepared to sing "Before the urgency of youth's behest!" because of its belief that it "claim[s] no part of racial dearth."

Although her work was never collected into a single volume, Bennett's poetry and prose were, nonetheless, included in major anthologies of the period such as Countee Cullen's *Caroling Dusk* (1924), Alain Locke's *The New Negro* (1925), and William Stanley Braithwaite's *Yearbook of American Poetry* (1927). Admired for her artistic work on five covers of *Opportunity* and two covers of *Crisis*, praised for her "depth and understanding" of character nuances in her short stories by the playwright Theodore Ward, she was, in the words of James Weldon Johnson, a "dynamic figure" whose keenest talent lay in composing "delicate poignant lyrics."

Questions for Reading, Discussion, and Writing

1. Why did the author coin the neologism *usward* as part of the title of the poem "To Usward"?
2. In Chinese culture, what is the significance of ginger jars?
3. In the poem "Advice," Bennett's choice of the word *sophist* is significant. Comment on the etymology and historical circumstances surrounding the first usage of this word.
4. Discuss the importance of Alexander Dumas as a literary figure.
5. The poem "Heritage" centers on a distinct yearning for Africa. Why did the poets of this period stress such a theme?

Sterling A. Brown (1901–1989)

Contributing Editor: John Edgar Tidwell

Classroom Issues and Strategies

The challenge of teaching Sterling A. Brown's poetry is to move students beyond the rather narrow perception of him as *African-American* poet to that of Brown the *poet*. While Brown himself was never troubled by the dilemma of being a black poet or a poet who happens to be black, the racial signifier often causes students to get stuck on racial identity, not on poetic ability. For many students, being African American is synonymous with a life of deprivation caused by "Jim Crow" laws or its modern permutation of "ghetto" life. As a consequence, they need guidance in viewing Brown as conscientiously crafting and representing experience in poetic form. Also, Brown saw himself as part of a modernist tradition established by Robert Frost, E. A. Robinson, Carl Sandburg, and Edgar Lee Masters, on the one hand; and by the many nameless vernacular figures who provided aesthetic forms via the blues, folktales, and work songs that he adapted for poetic purpose, on the other hand. Brown, then, must be taught as an Americanist, whose precepts and examples sought to argue his liberation from, as he considered it, the burden imposed by the more narrow designation *black writer*.

Redirecting students from identity politics to poetic ability can be accomplished in a number of ways. I begin by placing him within a thematic and structural context of black and white writers who sought the "extraordinary in ordinary life." In part, this means illustrating Brown's comment that when Sandburg said yes to his Chicago hog butchers and stackers of wheat, he was moved to celebrate the lives, lore, and language of black folk.

It also means locating him in a context of writers using black folk traditions during his era, such as Langston Hughes, Zora Neale Hurston, James Weldon Johnson, and Waring Cuney, among others. I discuss very generally the differing ways they made use of black folk experiences to establish texts and aesthetic contexts. What this permits is a comparative approach; it asks for ways Brown's blues poems, for example, conform and depart from those of Hughes and Cuney.

Many students pose questions related to the subtle way in which Brown calls into question the panoply of Jim Crow laws. In Brown's "Old Lem," for example, they ask for clarification about the nonverbal communication suggested by Old Lem's standing with bowed head, averted eyes, and open hands, in contrast to the whites with hands balled in fists and eyes in direct, confrontational stares. The history of these gestures dating from the formalization of Jim Crow laws during the early nineteenth century helps broaden the focus of Brown's poetry into discussions of relevant social and cultural issues.

Major Themes, Historical Perspectives, Personal Issues

How does Brown's work simultaneously refute racial stereotypes *and* affirm the humanity of black life? What is distinctive about Brown's humor? In what ways does it borrow from the vernacular tradition brought to prominence by Twain? How does the theme of the pursuit of democracy figure into Brown's aesthetic vision? How do sociological concerns coalesce with aesthetic pursuits without one overshadowing the other? What innovations in technique and craft can be discerned in Brown's poetry?

Significant Form, Style, or Artistic Conventions

I find the issues of period and school to be particularly interesting. Brown has been vociferous in refuting the term *Harlem* Renaissance. His opposition takes on two points: First, Harlem was *a*, not *the*, center of Negro creative activity during this era. Second, he often puns, if this era was the *Renaissance*, where is the *naissance*? Critics generally include him in the group of writers who came of age during the twenties. Brown questioned his inclusion in the group, by preferring to be considered a "lone wolf." And he further questioned the neat periodization of the New Negro Movement into the years 1922–1929. A renaissance, he contended, was much longer. One could use Brown's denials, then, as bases for defining problems of period, school, and even aesthetic convention. For example, how does Brown's use of black idiom differ from the styles of his immediate predecessors and of writers as early as Paul Laurence Dunbar and his imitators? Or how does his adaptation of vernacular speech—along with that of Langston Hughes and Zora Neale Hurston—restore a vitality and aesthetic possibility that James Weldon Johnson claimed was no longer possible?

Original Audience

Brown himself is his own best spokesman on the question of audience. In terms of an external audience, he confronted "the dilemma of a divided audience." On one hand, a white readership, thoroughly conditioned by racial stereotyping to expect superficial depictions of blacks, sought confirmation of their beliefs in black poetry. Bristling at any hint of a racially demeaning representation of blacks, the audience of black readers sought glorified portraits of blacks, which became stereotypes in another direction. Brown rejected both audiences and instead hypostatized one. The oral or speakerly quality of his poetry depends in part on the audience he creates within his poetry. The dynamics of speaker-listener are central to understanding the performative nature of his work. In Brown's description, poetry should communicate something. (The explanation of "communication" can be inferred from his letter to Langston

Hughes, in which he said poets should not follow the elitist path of Ezra Pound and T. S. Eliot, two poets he considers no longer talking to each other, only to themselves.) Communication is accomplished by using forms and structures and the language of black folk. Such use articulates a vision of the world that celebrates the dignity, humanism, and worth of a people largely misunderstood and misrepresented.

Readers of Brown's poetry today come away with a similar sense of the performative dimensions of his poetry, I think, because much of Brown's poetry continues to hold up. Even though today's audience may not know the character of racial discrimination in the way Brown experienced it, his poetry has a quality that transcends particular time and place. "She jes' gits hold of us dataway" the speaker in Brown's "Ma Rainey" tells us. Readers of the poem today, like those of an earlier generation, come away with the same feeling.

Working with Cultural Objects

Of the various presentational techniques I've used, one has been especially useful: listening to Brown reading his own poetry, which is available on several Folkways records and CDs. Brown is an exceptional reader, in part because of his background in drama and his reputation for being a raconteur. Some recordings of Brown are available online at the Academy of American Poets website at <http://www.poets.org/poems/poems.cfm?prmID=207>.

Questions for Reading, Discussion, and Writing

1. The questions I assign are determined by the approach and the poems I use. My approach to the Slim Greer poems, for example, centers on the poem as tall tale. I generally ask students to consult a literary handbook for features of the tall tale and to read the poems in light of their findings. In this same vein, I often assign actual tall tales (such as Roger Welsch's *Shingling the Fog and Other Plain Lies*) or other examples of poetry written in this tradition (such as *Fireside Tales* by Joe Allen) as a way of suggesting Brown's distinctiveness.

2. My paper topics are assigned to extend students' understanding of works we read and discuss in class by encouraging them to build upon the assigned reading a comparative critical analysis. The issues raised in the first part of this question give students a chance to range beyond class discussion.

Bibliography

"Brown, Sterling A." and "Slim Greer." *Oxford Companion to African American Literature.* Ed. William L. Andrews et al. New York: Oxford UP, 1996.

Stepto, Robert B. "Sterling A. Brown: Outsider in the Harlem Renaissance?" *The Harlem Renaissance: Revaluations.* Ed. Amritjit Singh et al. New York: Garland, 1989. 73–81.

Sterling A. Brown. Spec. issue of *African American Review* 31.3 (Fall 1997).

Tidwell, John E. "'The Summer of '46': Sterling A. Brown Among the Minnesotans." *Black Heartland* 1.1 (Spring 1996): 27–41.

Tidwell, John E., ed. "Oh, Didn't He Ramble: Sterling A. Brown (1901–1989)." Spec. sec. of *Black American Literature Forum* 23.1 (1989): 89–112.

Wagner, Jean. *Black Poets of the United States.* Urbana-Champaign: U of Illinois P, 1973. Chapter 11, "Sterling Brown."

Zora Neale Hurston (1891–1960)

Contributing Editor: Robert Hemenway

Classroom Issues and Strategies

While there are no particular difficulties in teaching Hurston, some students find the dialect hard to understand. To address this problem, I usually read several passages aloud to help students get a "feel" for the voices. Once they've heard Hurston read aloud, they can create her characters' speech in their minds so that it is understandable.

Major Themes, Historical Perspectives, Personal Issues

Women's issues
Race issues
Interface between oral and written literature

Significant Form, Style, or Artistic Conventions

Short story structure
Representations of an oral culture

Comparisons, Contrasts, Connections

Langston Hughes
Alice Walker

Claude McKay (1889–1948)

Contributing Editor: Elvin Holt

Classroom Issues and Strategies

I suggest that teachers begin with McKay's love poems. This approach allows students to relate to McKay on a purely human level and prepares them for the discomforting racial themes that dominate some of the other poems.

Students respond to the persistent racism in American society. Some nonblack students want to know why they have to read such poems. Many of them believe the poems are "for black people." Some students object to the eroticism of the love poems.

"Flame-Heart" evokes the romantic tradition of Wordsworth and Shelley, poets whose work McKay admired greatly. This finely wrought poem, which expresses the poet's deep longing for Jamaica, his beloved homeland, highlights McKay's interest in nonracial themes.

"A Red Flower," one of McKay's most striking love poems, features brilliant conceits similar to those found in the poetry of John Donne and other metaphysical poets. Identify the metaphor in the first and last stanzas of the poem.

In "Flower of Love," McKay presents another example of his passionate, yet controlled, love poetry. Like "A Red Flower," "Flower of Love" turns on an elaborate conceit, recalling the best work of Andrew Marvell. Describe the poem's central metaphor and explain the reference to the South.

"America" is one of McKay's best protest poems. Explain the poem's central theme and describe the prophecy the speaker relates in the final quatrain.

"The Lynching," a moving expression of McKay's outrage against the senseless killings of blacks that marked the early decades of this century, depicts Christ as the victim of the lynching. Is the Christ figure an effective image, considering the context?

McKay's best-known poem, "If We Must Die," urges blacks to wage war against their oppressors. Winston Churchill used McKay's poem to revive the spirit of his countrymen during World War II.

"The Harlem Dancer" focuses on a beautiful black woman performing in a nightclub. What is the central theme of the poem? Does the poet articulate a point of view with which black feminists might concur?

"Harlem Shadows" is the title poem from McKay's 1922 collection of poetry. Who or what are the "shadows" mentioned in the poem's title? What does the poem say about the plight of black Americans in general?

Major Themes, Historical Perspectives, Personal Issues

It is essential that students get a sense of what it was like to be black in America during the early decades of this century. Students must also realize that McKay's Jamaican background made him particularly sensitive to the plight of black Americans.

Significant Form, Style, or Artistic Conventions

It is important to give students a good introduction to the Harlem Renaissance. Students need to know what the writers (blacks) were trying to accomplish. Students should note McKay's dependence upon traditional British forms such as the sonnet.

Original Audience

I help students to understand the social history that shaped McKay's work and determined his first audience. Then I try to help students see why the poems remain fresh and vital to our own time.

Comparisons, Contrasts, Connections

Since McKay was influenced by important British poets such as Wordsworth, Shelley, and Donne, it is useful to compare and contrast his work with that of English romantic and metaphysical poets. Stylistic similarities are often evident.

Bibliography

James R. Giles's *Claude McKay* is a good book for teachers. The text is well organized, and the index makes it easy to locate specific information.

Anne Spencer (1882–1975)

Contributing Editors: Evelyn H. Roberts and J. Lee Greene

Classroom Issues and Strategies

Aside from black literature anthologies and general reference sources, limited critical material is available. The poet Anne Spencer can best be made accessible to students in various ways.

1. Relating Spencer's fascination with reading and studying at the Virginia Seminary (note, for example, her selection as the commencement speaker).
2. Presenting an overhead transparency of one of her longer poems, "At the Carnival." Most students enjoy this poem and can relate to such an experience—comparing or contrasting with their own carnival and/or county fair experiences.
3. Showing the photographs that appear in J. Lee Greene's *Time's Unfading Garden*.
4. Using selected black literature anthologies placed on library reserve for students who wish to prepare brief oral reports or short papers.

Many of Spencer's poems show dramatic compression and sharpness of image and phrase. She is no pleader of causes, rarely choosing to comment on the race issue in her published poetry. Yet her biography reveals a wide acquaintance with civil rights leaders, literary dignitaries, lecturers, and other prominent citizens, black and white, who would appear as public speakers and/or artists in Lynchburg, Virginia.

Students admire Spencer's commitment to maintaining a free, independent spirit, not being hampered or restrained by husband or offspring. They also admire her determination and concentration to create despite the reality that "art is long and time is fleeting." In addition, students applaud both Spencer's assertiveness as demonstrated by her work for women's suffrage and her determination to create options that allowed her to pursue her art by diverse routes (as demonstrated by her work as the first black librarian in Lynchburg).

Students are curious about Spencer's statement, published by Countee Cullen (*Caroling Dusk*, p. 47):

> But I have no civilized articulation for the things I hate. I proudly love being a Negro woman; [it's] so involved and interesting. *We* are the PROBLEM—the great national game of TABOO.

Major Themes, Historical Perspectives, Personal Issues

Like Ralph Waldo Emerson, Henry David Thoreau, Emily Dickinson, Amy Lowell, and Angelina Grimké, Anne Spencer maintained a strong belief in individual freedom and liberty to convey ideas and uphold ideals vital for personal expression. Further, Spencer possessed strong individual preferences and exhibited objections to various standards or beliefs that may have compromised her personal ideals. See poems not included in this anthology such as "Wife-Woman" and "Neighbors."

Further, Anne Spencer sustained a lifelong admiration for poets and the art of poetry. In her poem "Dunbar," she pays tribute to Chatterton, Shelley, and Keats.

Some additional similarities can be cited showing an interrelatedness in the art of the above-mentioned poets. As Emily Dickinson advanced in years, the circle of her world grew ever smaller. Dickinson became a hermit by deliberate and conscious choice. Similarly, Anne Spencer withdrew from the community as the years passed. For Dickinson, her isolation allowed her to become prey to the then-current Emersonian doctrine of "mystical individualism." As a flower of New England transcendentalism, she became a Puritan and free thinker obsessed with the problems of good and evil, of life and death, and of the nature and destiny of the human soul. Toward God, Emily Dickinson exhibited an Emersonian self-possession.

Moreover, Emerson's gnomic style became for Emily Dickinson epigrammatic to the point of being cryptic; a quality that Anne Spencer, Amy Lowell, and Angelina Grimké likewise display.

Finally, Anne Spencer in some of her poems—"Requiem," "Substitution," "Wife-Woman"—appears to embrace a pantheistic view that can be compared with Emerson's view in "Hamatreya" of recognizing God in nature.

Significant Form, Style, or Artistic Conventions

Though sometimes coupled with the Harlem Renaissance period, Anne Spencer follows the tradition of neo-romantic poetry, having composed some poems before the Harlem Renaissance era was clearly identified, or designated. Her poetry communicates a highly personal experience, revealing an arresting image. Her assessment of an experience may be occasionally ironic but discloses her profundity.

Anne Spencer's style reveals her individuality, an affinity for nature imagery, and the conventions of British and American romantics, as her sensibility to form and color, a rich and varied vocabulary, and a pantheistic philosophy disclose.

An admirer of Robert Browning, one of her favorite poets, who, despite his use of the idiom of conversation, achieved remarkable cogent compressed lines, Anne Spencer likewise achieved a similar style. Economy of phrase and compression of thought result from numerous revisions of the same poem. Compare with Emily Dickinson's extensive and/or intensive revision strategy.

Comparisons, Contrasts, Connections

Both Emily Dickinson and Spencer were philosophical in their observations and perspectives. Dickinson's simple yet passionate style was marked by economy and concentration. She developed sharp, intense images and recognized the utility of the ellipsis of thought and verbal ambiguity. Like Anne Spencer, Dickinson read extensively and intensively.

Compare Dickinson's "Because I Could Not Stop for Death" with Spencer's "Substitution."

Ralph Waldo Emerson created his own philosophy, believing that all forces are united by energetic truth. Though he lectured and composed many extended prose works, his poems, like those of Emily Dickinson and Anne Spencer, contain the core of his philosophy. He directed considerable thought to social reform and the growing issue of slavery.

Spencer, like Emerson, composed her poems in her garden. She has voiced high ethical, aesthetic, and independent positions on the topics she addresses in her poetry.

Although Anne Spencer did not vividly express her concern for social issues as did Henry David Thoreau and R. W. Emerson, her adult civic and professional life as librarian, and occasionally her poetry, addressed her concern for social and racial progress. Thoreau conveyed a genuine feeling for the unity of man and nature in *Walden*. His deep-rooted love for one place, Walden, characterized the epitome of his universe. Similarly, Anne Spencer's garden was central to her symbolic, historic, literary, and religious imagery and meaning.

Countee Cullen's "Foreword" to his work *Caroling Dusk* asserts that "Anne Spencer [writes] with a cool precision that evokes comparison with Amy Lowell and the influence of a rockbound seacoast" (p. x1).

Note: Examine Amy Lowell's "Patterns." Compare techniques and concepts as noted in Spencer's poems, for example, "Substitution," "Lines to a Nasturtium," and "For Jim, Easter Eve."

Both Angelina Grimké and Spencer studied well their neo-romantic models. Both writers reveal great sensitivity and emotional acuity. Neither is writing for a group or class, or a race, nor do they use the language of complex reasoning and emotional compression. Rather, there is the direct attempt to present and define an emotional experience.

Bibliography

"Anne Spencer." *Negro Poetry and Drama and The Negro in American Fiction.* Ed. Sterling Brown. New York: Atheneum, 1978, 65–66. With a new preface by Robert Bone.

Cullen, Countee, ed. *Caroling Dusk.* New York: Harper, 1927. 47–52.

Greene, J. Lee. *Time's Unfading Garden: Anne Spencer's Life and Poetry.* Baton Rouge: Louisiana State UP, 1977. 204. Since Anne Spencer's poems were published in nearly every major black anthology, it is essential to include Greene's work, for the appendix contains the largest collection of her published poems. Spencer never arranged for a collected publication, though she constantly composed poems and revised many of her earlier pieces through 1974, the year prior to her death. See also chapter 7, "The Poetry: Aestheticism" and chapter 8, "The Poetry: Controversy."

Hughes, Langston. "The Negro Artist and the Racial Mountain." *Nation* 23 June 1926: 692–94.

Locke, Alain. "The New Negro: An Interpretation." In *The American Negro: His History and Literature.* Ed. Alain Locke. New York: Ayer, 1968.

Primeau, Ronald. "Frank Horne and the Second Echelon Poets of the Harlem Renaissance." *The Harlem Renaissance Remembered.* Ed. with a memoir by Arna Bontemps. New York: Dodd, 1972. 247–67.

Stetson, Erlene. "Anne Spencer." *College Language Association Journal* 21 (March 1978): 400–09.

Nella Larsen (1891–1964)

Contributing Editor: Deborah E. McDowell

Classroom Issues and Strategies

As students become rightly more attuned to representations of gender, race, and class in literary and cultural texts, the subtleties of Nella Larsen's *Passing* create interesting problems. Such problems derive from the general tendency of readers to elevate one social category of analysis over all others, often ignoring the interactive working of each on the other: race on gender, gender on class, and so on. Readers attentive to class will find the narrow class spectrum of this novel offputting, for it can seem on the surface to be a mere apology for the black middle class, showing little awareness of and bearing on the poverty that the masses of blacks suffered in 1920s Harlem.

While attention to irony, point of view, and rhetorical strategy is essential to reading any text, with Nella Larsen it is especially so. In *Passing*, for example, understanding that Irene Redfield, from whose perspective much of the novel is told, is an unreliable narrator is key to understanding the novel. Equally important is the function of Clare and Irene as doubles, a strategy that undermines Irene's authority as the center of racial consciousness, clarifies the points in the narrative's critique of the black middle class, and uncovers the issues of sexuality and class that an exclusive focus on race conceals.

It is useful to read Fannie Hurst's *Imitation of Life* and to show the two film adaptations of the novel.

Students respond to the heightened attention to color and clothing and atmosphere in *Passing* and wonder if Larsen's concentration on mulatto characters indicates an unmistakable "privileging" of whiteness.

Major Themes, Historical Perspectives, Personal Issues

It is important to provide information about 1920s Harlem and the literary and cultural confluences that shaped the Harlem Renaissance. It is critical that the movement be defined not by its "unities" but rather by its "contraries" and that it be seen as the site of a class-based contestation over the terms and production of black art. The aesthetic theories produced by such writers and intellectuals as James Weldon Johnson (Introduction to the *Book of American Negro Poetry*), Alain Locke ("The New Negro"), Langston Hughes ("The Negro Artist and the Racial Mountain"), W. E. B. Du Bois ("Criteria of Negro Art" and "The Negro in Art: How Shall He Be Portrayed?"), Jessie Fauset (reviews in *The Crisis*), and Zora Neale Hurston ("What White Publishers Won't Print") are all essential readings. None of these attempts to articulate the terms of an emerging "black art" can be divorced from a discussion of the production and consumption of the texts, especially the system of white patronage during the period, which necessarily affected and at times constrained artistic freedom.

Significant Form, Style, or Artistic Conventions

The most obvious tradition in which to situate Larsen's novel must be the novel-of-passing, which problematized questions of race. Deemphasizing "biology," the novel-of-passing provided convenient ways to explore race as a construct of history, culture, and white supremacist ideology. Equally important is the tradition of the novel of manners, as well as the romance.

Original Audience

I note the fact that the audience for Nella Larsen's writings, as for the works of all black writers during the Harlem Renaissance, was primarily white, though a small group of black middle-class intellectuals read them as well.

Comparisons, Contrasts, Connections

Jessie Fauset's "Plum Bun & Comedy, American Style"
James Weldon Johnson's *The Autobiography of an Ex-Colored Man*
Charles Chesnutt's *The House Behind the Cedars*
Edith Wharton's *The House of Mirth*

Questions for Reading, Discussion, and Writing

1. The metaphor of *passing* accrues several layers of meaning. What are they? How do they relate to each other?
2. Whose story is this? Clare's or Irene's?
3. What does this passage mean: "[Irene] was caught between two allegiances, different, yet the same. Herself. Her race. Race: The thing that bound and suffocated her. Whatever steps she took, or if she took none at all, something would be crushed. A person or the race. Clare, herself, or the race. Or, it might be all three."
4. It has been suggested that *Passing* uses race more as a device to sustain suspense than as a compelling social issue. What is the relation of race to subjective experience in the text?
5. What is the significance of narrative endings in Larsen? Why does *Passing* refuse to specify how Clare is killed and who is responsible?

Bibliography

Carby, Hazel. "The Quicksands of Representation." *Reconstructing Woman-hood*. New York: Oxford UP, n.d.

Christian, Barbara. *Black Women Novelists*. Westport, CT: Greenwood, 1980.

Huggins, Nathan. *Harlem Renaissance*. New York: Oxford UP, n.d.

———. *Voices of the Harlem Renaissance*. N.p.: n.p., n.d.

Lewis, David Levering. *When Harlem Was in Vogue*. N.p.: n.p., n.d.

McDowell, Deborah E. "The 'Nameless, Shameful Impulse': Sexuality in Nella Larsen's *Quicksand* and *Passing*." *Studies in Black American Literature*. Vol. 3. Ed. Joe Weixlmann and Houston A. Baker, Jr. Greenwood, FL: Penkeville, 1988.

Tate, Claudia. "Nella Larsen's *Passing*: A Problem of Interpretation." *Black American Literature Forum* 14 (Winter 1980).

Wall, Cheryl. "Passing for What? Aspects of Identity in Nella Larsen's Novels." *Black American Literature Forum* 20 (Spring/Summer 1986).

Washington, Mary H. "The Mulatta Trap: Nella Larsen's Women of the 1920s." *Invented Lives*. New York: Anchor/Doubleday, 1987.

Youman, Mary M. "Nella Larsen's *Passing*: A Study in Irony." *College Language Association Journal* 18 (1974).

George Samuel Schuyler (1895–1977)

Contributing Editor: Michael W. Peplow

Classroom Issues and Strategies

Satire, especially the harsher Juvenalian mode, upsets students, who see it as too negative. And when satire deals with an emotional issue such as racial prejudice, it becomes even more controversial. Some students find Schuyler's satire offensive. In addition—though it has universal overtones—"Our Greatest Gift to America" is still a 1920s period piece. Some of the issues and language pose problems for modern students.

I make sure my students have a working definition of *satire* and, as we read the essay, I discuss the satiric devices Schuyler employs. Once we have finished reading the essay, I ask students to discuss *why* Schuyler chose satire and whether his approach was effective. The more background the students have in Juvenal, Swift, Twain, Ambrose Bierce, and H. L. Mencken (Schuyler's mentor and friend), the better the essay works in class.

I also make sure my students read some "straight" essays that address the racial situation in the 1920s. Articles from the NAACP's *Crisis* are helpful, especially those by its editor, W. E. B. Du Bois (see Daniel Walden, ed., *W. E. B. Du Bois: The Crisis Writings* [Greenwich: Fawcett, 1972]). The more exposure students have had to African-American and other minority literatures, the more they will appreciate Schuyler. I give students notes on the Harlem (or New Negro) Renaissance and read passages from Alan Locke's "The New Negro." I tell students about KKK activities and lynchings in the 1920s. I show them copies of *The Pittsburgh Courier,* a leading black newspaper for which Schuyler worked, that featured essays on race pride but included advertisements for skin lighteners and hair straighteners. For the teacher who does not have access to these materials, a valuable resource tool is *The Chronological History of the Negro in America.*

Students sometimes say the essay is too depressing, that Schuyler exaggerates and distorts the way things really were. They feel Schuyler so denigrates blacks that he must have been disgusted with his own people and secretly desired to be white himself. Finally, students say the essay is not relevant because people just aren't prejudiced any longer. Prejudice is not a comfortable thing to admit or discuss in class. It's easier to laugh a bit nervously and go on to the next essay. But questions about present-day prejudices lead to often dramatic discussions: fraternities or athletes on campus, a racial or religious or national group, AIDS victims and welfare recipients and street people—the list goes on.

Major Themes, Historical Perspectives, Personal Issues

The historical issues include American racism, the Harlem Renaissance vogue, the tendency of some black publications to preach race pride and at the same time publish skin-lightening and hair-straightening advertisements, the tendency of some black leaders to profit from American racism, and the all too prevalent belief among whites—and blacks—that "white is right." (You might remind students of an old black saying: "If you're white, you're all right. If you're brown, stick around. If you're black, get back.")

The personal issues include Schuyler's own encounters with racism in the army and during his journalistic tours, his courtship of and eventual marriage to a white woman, and his lifelong belief that America's "colorphobia" was so absurd it merited scathing ridicule.

Significant Form, Style, or Artistic Conventions

1. What literary conventions does Schuyler employ in his satire?

    The purpose of satire is to mock or ridicule human follies or vices. Horatian satire tends to be light, often comic, the assumption being that humans are more foolish than sinful and that they are capable of reformation. Juvenalian satire—Schuyler's mode—is harsh and slashing, the assumption being that humans are so corrupted that they are beyond reformation. In an early newspaper column Schuyler wrote that his dominant motive was malice and that his intent was "to slur, lampoon, damn, and occasionally praise anybody or anything in the known universe, not excepting the President of the Immortals." In his long career he rarely praised but did much damning, so much so that he was accused in a *Crisis* editorial in 1965 of being the incurable iconoclast who "dips his pen in his ever-handy [well] of acid."

    In "Our Greatest Gift," Schuyler creates a satiric persona much as his role model Swift did in "A Modest Proposal" and *Gulliver's Travels* (note the reference to "Brobdingnagian"). Schuyler's persona seems to be an intelligent but "plain folks" black man, literate and unafraid to speak the truth. He despises the inner circle of black intellectuals for their willingness to capitalize on racial tension and their secret belief that "white is right." He also despises redneck whites who believe a white skin makes them special. Both groups he sets out to shock; he even uses a number of current racial slurs. By the end of the essay, the persona seems to have become so disgusted with America's "colorphobia" that he sounds like the compleat misanthrope who despairs of ever converting America to rational behavior.

    Another technique Schuyler the satirist employs is irony—saying or implying the opposite of what one really believes. Throughout the essay—from the words "greatest gift" in the title, through references to "this enlightened nation" and "our incomparable civilization," to the devastating final paragraph—Schuyler is savagely ironic.

    A third technique Schuyler employs is exaggeration. Whether describing black poets, race leaders, or whites, Schuyler's portraits deliberately overstate. His character sketches of three "noble rednecks"—Isadore Shankersoff, Cyrus Leviticus Dumbbell, and Dorothy Dunce—are vintage Schuyler and anticipate his much more extended character sketches in *Black No More*.

2. What literary school does Schuyler belong to?

    Schuyler, noted the 1965 *Crisis* editorial, was "a veteran dissenter and incurable iconoclast," one of that "select breed of moral crusaders and apparent social misfits who, as journalists, delighted in breaking the idols of the tribe." He is a direct descendant of Ambrose Bierce, the "caustic columnist" from San Francisco and author of "The Devil's Dictionary" and *The Satanic Reader*; of Brann the Iconoclast; and of H. L. Mencken, the founder and editor of *The American Mercury*. He also worked side by side with important 1920s black iconoclasts Chandler Owen and A. Philip Randolph, Theophilus Lewis and Wallace Thurman, W. E. B. Du Bois and Rudolph Fisher—each of whom was capable of idol-smashing but not on the sustained level that Schuyler was. On an even larger scale, Schuyler, as noted before, was a satirist in the tradition of Juvenal, Swift, and Twain, all of whom he studied and admired.

Original Audience

1. Schuyler's audience was primarily black—the essay appeared in a black publication that was read by the very racial leaders Schuyler lampoons in the first part of his essay. If any whites read it at the time, they would have been those who, in typical Harlem Renaissance fashion, became obsessed with exotic and primitive blacks (see Rudolph Fisher, "The Caucasian Storms Harlem," in Huggins's *Voices from the Harlem Renaissance*; for a good example of white fascination with blacks, see Carl Van Vechten's melodramatic *Nigger Heaven*).

2. As suggested earlier, today's audience will have difficulty relating to "Our Greatest Gift." White students usually insist that the essay is dated because there are no more lynchings or overt acts of prejudice. Black students are sometimes offended by the racial epithets and the glancing attacks on black leaders. The teacher who wishes to challenge contemporary smugness can have a field day: Is white racism really dead? Do black or other leaders ever capitalize on racial tension? Is there still a "white is right" mentality in America?

Comparisons, Contrasts, Connections

There is no one author to whom Schuyler compares well, though he uses the same satiric devices that Juvenal, Swift, and Twain employ and the same iconoclastic manner that characterized Bierce, Brann, Mencken, Fisher, Lewis, and Thurman.

Questions for Reading, Discussion, and Writing

1. (a) Schuyler attacks two groups of people in his essay. Who are they? Is he even-handed in his double attack?

    (b) What is the satire? Distinguish between Juvenalian and Horatian
        satire and decide which mode Schuyler preferred.
    (c) What was the Harlem Renaissance?
2. (a) Have half the class (include the more creative writers) write a satire
        attacking a controversial issue à la Schuyler. Use a persona, employ
        irony, and develop two or three exaggerated character sketches.
        Have the rest of the class write reasoned essays from both groups and
        determine which type of approach—satire or reasoned essay—is
        more effective, and why.
    (b) Write a response to Schuyler's article assuming the persona of a
        white racist or a black nationalist in Schuyler's own time.
    (c) First discuss in class and then write an essay on the following topic: A
        Modern Response to Schuyler's "Our Greatest Gift to America."

Blues Lyrics

Contributing Editor: Steven C. Tracy

Classroom Issues and Strategies

Many students will be totally unfamiliar with the blues tradition and will
therefore benefit greatly from the playing of blues recordings in class in conjunction with the selections from blues lyrics printed in the text. In fact, playing
these blues selections in class will help introduce the important point that the
blues is an oral, not a written, tradition. Asking the students to write down
what they hear on the recordings played brings up not only the problems that
scholars have deciphering texts but also the issue of how one should render an
oral production on the printed page.

Students should be encouraged to respond to the voices of the lyrics. Are
they voices of resignation and defeat, or hope and transcendence, of strength
and pride, or of some mixture of all of these? What is it that has given the
blues their staying power? And what is it that writers like Langston Hughes,
Sterling Brown, Al Young, Alice Walker, Shirley Anne Williams, and Allen
Ginsberg see in them that makes these writers draw on them from their own
writing? Certainly comparing these blues lyrics to various blues poems will
help clarify authors' differing attitudes about the blues.

Religious and sexual themes are generally the most controversial. Students question the image of women in the blues and wonder whether the blues
singer is weak and self-pitying or strong and self-sufficient. The Furry Lewis
lyric is often seen as being bizarre and sick: a good starting point for a discussion
of the place of humor in the blues.

Major Themes, Historical Perspectives, Personal Issues

A number of important subjects are covered in these selections, including love, hate, sex, violence, hope, superstition, religion, and protest, indicating that the blues in fact deals with a range of subjects in a variety of ways. When blues songs are performed, they often provoke laughter from an audience that identifies with the experience being described or that appreciates the novel way in which the experience is described. There are a number of humorous verses here that could be compared for the way they achieve their effects—from Bracey's hyperbole to Carter's prurience to Cox's unexpected assertiveness to the startling images of Wheatstraw and Lewis. Such a discussion would emphasize the idea that the blues, though often discussing sadness and hardships, contains a pretty fair amount of humor. Ellison includes a good discussion of this subject in *Shadow and Act,* as does Garon in *Blues and the Poetic Spirit* (pp. 77–87).

Significant Form, Style, or Artistic Conventions

An advantage to playing the songs for the students is that it allows them to hear how the various stanza structures are fit into the music. For instance, the lyrics of Childers and Wheatstraw are both sung to eight-bar musical stanzas, but the lyric patterns are different. Students can discuss the advantages of one stanza over the other. The selection from "John Henry" is a ten-bar blues ballad, presenting in narrative form the story of the folk hero whose strength and perseverance in the face of incredible odds is a paradigm for the African-American experience (see Sterling Brown's "Strange Legacies"). The selection from Margaret Carter is from a sixteen-bar vaudeville blues especially, but present in other kinds of blues as well. The rest of the examples included come from twelve-bar blues, but certainly the examples from Jefferson, Bracey, Cox, Robert Johnson, and Holmes are sufficiently different to indicate the possibility of diverse phrasing in the blues, even within what is sometimes considered to be a rather restrictive form.

We can also see in "Got the Blues" the presence of several stock phrases—lines or parts of lines that turn up regularly in blues that are similar to but not the same as the formulaic lines discussed by Parry and Lord. Students might be encouraged to take the first line of stanza two or six and generate an individual rhyme line that completes the thought in some kind of personal manner as a way of helping them understand how tradition has an effect on the individual blues singer.

Comparisons, Contrasts, Connections

The only blues lyric quoted in its entirety here is Blind Lemon Jefferson's "Got the Blues," interesting because rather than developing a single theme, it progresses through associative linkages and contrasts. While some early commentary argued that blues lyrics were often incoherent, more recently texts have been discussed as nonthematic, partially thematic, or thematic; and the presence of such associative linkages and contrasts is important to see and recognize as a textual strategy rather than an example of textual incoherence. Again, students can be encouraged to discern the associations among lines and stanzas the way they might be asked to do for poetry by Ezra Pound, T. S. Eliot, or Amy Lowell.

Working with Cultural Objects

People have responded to the blues in a variety of ways: as a mode of entertainment; an exposition of African-American life in post-Reconstruction America; a repository of cultural wisdom; a protest against a racist America; and a call for social, political, and spiritual unity. They have also made use of the blues in a variety of genres ranging from poetry, the short story, the novel, and plays in printed form to painting, sculpture, and other visual arts, including filmmaking. Critics are beginning to examine how this musical medium is translated into other genres and how it has been utilized to communicate the variety of messages that it contains in settings that are sometimes different from its origins and the settings in which it was nurtured.

The blues must be understood in its historical and continuing cultural context, and in its complexity as it attempted to fit into or reject the world in which it grew, in order to appreciate it as both a time-bound and a timeless form and to approach the expressions of the blues in other genres with a broad-visioned notion of the varied expressions of the evolving tradition. Looking at the artifacts associated with blues recordings is a good way to discern how the blues was seen and marketed by those who were, for the most part, not members of the group from which the tradition sprang. Such a focus opens up issues of distribution, advertising, and the projection of images associated with the blues industry, and can lead to useful considerations of differences between folk and commercial settings as well as between personal and mass-media experiences and intentions.

John Tefteller's website at <http://www.bluesimages.com > reproduces photographs, record advertisements, and photos connected with the Paramount label, an important record company of the 1920s that recorded some of the giants of the blues. The site connects to links for contemporary auctions of 78 rpm recordings as well as for products that reproduce some of the images he has collected in his years as a researcher and blues aficionado. As for the visual arts, a reproduction of Archibald Motley's painting *Blues* is provided at <http://www.iniva.org/harlem/home.html>. Biographies, discographies, and topics for discussion and classroom activities keyed to the Martin Scorsese PBS series dealing with the blues can be located at <http://www.pbs.org/theblues>.

Questions for Reading, Discussion, and Writing

1. Have students listen to recordings by Langston Hughes, Sterling Brown, Zora Neale Hurston, Ishmael Reed, Michael Harper, Allen Ginsberg, or Jack Kerouac that have musical accompaniment (or are sung performances, in Hurston and Ginsberg) and discuss how the music affects our response to the words.
2. Have students write a blues song and discuss their rationale for choice of stanza form, themes, images, diction, and voice, establishing clearly the relation of their song to the tradition.
3. Have students survey the various methods of transcribing blues lyrics and defend one method as superior to the others.
4. Have students pick a theme developed in a blues-influenced poem by an author like Langston Hughes and search out blues lyrics that deal with a similar theme to see how the literary artist revises the traditional treatment of the theme.

Bibliography

Interviews with blues performers are included in the following:

Oliver, Paul. *Conversation with the Blues.* New York: Horizon, 1965.

Pearson, Barry L. *Sounds So Good to Me.* Philadelphia: U of Pennsylvania P, 1984.

For explanations of unfamiliar words, phrases, and places in blues lyrics see the following:

Gold, Robert. *Jazz Talk.* New York: Da Capo, 1982.

Major, Clarence. *From Juba to Jive.* New York: Viking, 1994.

Townley, Eric. *Tell Your Story.* Chigwell, Essex: Storyville, 1976.

Other valuable discussions of blues include the following:

Ellison, Ralph. *Shadow and Act*. New York: Random, 1964.

Evans, David. *Big Road Blues*. Berkeley: U of California P, 1982.

Garon, Paul. *Blues and the Poetic Spirit*. London: Eddison, 1975.

Harris, Sheldon. *Blues Who's Who*. New Rochelle, NY: Arlington, 1975.

Jahn, Janheinz. *A History of Neo-African Literature*. New York: Grove, 1968.

———. *Muntu: An Outline of the New African Culture*. London: Faber, 1961.

Jones, Leroi. *Blues People*. New York: Morrow, 1963.

Oliver, Paul. *The Blues Tradition*. New York: Oak, 1970.

———. *The Meaning of the Blues*. 1960. New York: Collier, 1972.

———. *Savannah Syncopators: African Retentions in the Blues*. N.p.: Kibsibm Studio Vista, 1970.

———. *The Story of the Blues*. Philadelphia: Chilton, 1973.

Titon, Jeff T. *Early Downhome Blues*. Urbana: U of Illinois P, 1978.

For discussions of the importance of the blues to African-American literature see the following:

Baker, Houston A., Jr. *Blues, Ideology, and Afro-American Literature*. Chicago: U of Chicago P, 1984.

Tracy, Steven C. *Langston Hughes and the Blues*. Urbana: U of Illinois P, 1988.

Williams, Sherley A. "The Blues Roots of Contemporary Afro-American Poetry." *Chant of Saints*. Ed. Michael Harper and Robert Stepto. Chicago: U of Chicago P, 1979.

Discography

Bogan, Lucille. *Lucille Bogan Vol. 3*. Document BDCD 6038, n.d.

Bracey, Ishmon. *Complete Recordings (1928–30)*. Wolf WSE 105, n.d.

Carter, Margaret. *Female Blues Singers Vol. 4.* Document 5508, 1997.

Childers, Virgil. *Carolina Blues Guitar.* Old Tramp OTCD 03, n.d.

Cox, Ida. *Ida Cox Vol. 2.* Document DOCD 5323, n.d.

Davis, Walter. *Walter Davis (1930–32).* JSP CD 605, n.d.

Dickson, Tom. *Memphis Blues.* Document DOCD 5014, n.d.

Henderson, Rosa. *Rosa Henderson Vol. 2.* Document DOCD 5402, 1995.

Holmes, Wright. *Country Blues Classics Vol. 3.* Blues Classics 7, n.d.

Jefferson, Blind Lemon. *Complete Recorded Works Vol. 1.* Document DOCD 5017, n.d.

Johnson, Robert. *The Complete Recordings.* Columbia C2K 46222, 1990.

Johnson, Tommy. *Complete Recorded Works (1928–29).* Document DOCD 5001, 1990.

Lewis, Furry. *Furry Lewis 1927–29.* Document DOCD 5004, n.d.

McClennan, Tommy. *Travelin' Highway Man.* Travelin' Man CD 06, 1990.

McCoy, Charlie. *Charlie McCoy.* Document BDCD 6018, n.d.

Rainey, Ma. *Ma Rainey.* Milestone M 47021, 1974.

Tucker, Bessie. *Bessie Tucker 1928–29.* Document DOCD 5070, n.d.

Wheatstraw, Peetie. *Peetie Wheatstraw Vol. 2.* Document DOCD 5242, 1994.

Issues and Visions in Modern America

Randolph Bourne (1886–1918)

Contributing Editor: Charles Molesworth

Classroom Issues and Strategies

Students should be asked to discuss how America might have looked to a social critic before World War I. While some of Bourne's ideas may seem "timely" to today's students, this is due in part to the rather prophetic aspects of this essay. Bourne was of course conscious of the immigration that was reshaping American society (especially in its large cities), and he was very aware of the social and political changes being brought about by modernization (such as the routinization of work, the development of the "culture industry" and mass media, urbanization, and so on). But his idealism about America was unaffected by the large-scale tragedies associated with the world wars, the rise of fascism, the atom bomb, and so forth. Also, Bourne would not have been familiar with the later developments in academic forms of social science. Thus, the "theoretical" nature of Bourne's formulations may strike some as implausible. Some of the main classroom issues might be put this way: How thoroughgoing can a criticism of American society be, and does a social critic have to be "practical" in his or her suggestions? To what extent must a social critic rely on surveys or statistical studies to justify his or her conclusions?

Major Themes, Historical Perspectives, Personal Issues

The call for a social identity that surpasses or transcends nationalistic feeling would be (paradoxically) both implausible and yet "logical" at the end of the nineteenth century, when nationalism was perhaps the main political sentiment shaping world events. Bourne's essay challenges and responds to, even at a distance, the same moods and arguments that animated romantic nationalism of the sort that had recently shaped Italy and Germany, among others, into nation-states. The American nexus for this nationalism involved many issues, but perhaps chiefly the fervent arguments about immigrants and whether or not they could be successfully assimilated into a modern nation. Could such assimilation proceed through cultural and social means, assuming a single, "uniform," biological basis for national identity was not available to all the various immigrant groups? The issue of nativism, which claimed that only people who descended from specific racial or ethnic groups could form harmonious social and political identities, was a form of racism. In response to nativism, which he thoroughly rejected, Bourne developed his cultural criticism so that, among other things, the very idea of identity could be redefined. This means that his focus on culture as a defining sociopolitical force was very distinctive. The German tradition of *kulturkampf* (or cultural struggle) had not been taken up in America on a large scale, but Bourne and many of his contemporaries were aware of it, having studied on the continent after their college years. Other writers at this time who shared some of Bourne's concerns were Van Wyck Brooks, Waldo Frank, and Lewis Mumford.

Significant Form, Style, or Artistic Conventions

Bourne used the essay as his main form of artistic expression. In this form, which had grown very popular through the spread of magazines such as *The New Republic* that were devoted to developing large readerships and influencing popular opinion and political policy, Bourne tried to advance his ideas in ways that were both oppositional and hortatory. This meant that he had to combine a certain amount of social observation (with the keen eye of a journalist), a matrix of reasoned argument (while avoiding any "dry" sense of logic), and a call to ethical values (without incurring the charge of sheer moralizing). All the while he kept in mind the general reader, an educated layperson who was assumed to have an abiding and interested stake in political issues. This meant that his vocabulary could not be a technical one, yet he had to make his argument convey more than the sense of an editorial in a daily newspaper.

Comparisons, Contrasts, Connections

Other essays in the anthology can be compared with Bourne's and studied for their stylistic approach and the contents of their arguments. For example, the selections from W. E. B. Du Bois are especially instructive in this context. T. S. Eliot's "Tradition and the Individual Talent" contains a sense of personal identity and group allegiance that can also be contrasted with Bourne's. And the place of culture and cultural politics in the New Negro Renaissance is germane to these issues: see, for example, Langston Hughes's "The Negro Artist and the Racial Mountain" and George Schuyler's "The Negro-Art Hokum." Perhaps the closest parallel is with Alain Locke's "The New Negro," in which the issue of social transformation through cultural renewal is paramount.

Questions for Reading, Discussion, and Writing

1. How are national identities usually understood, and how are they formed? Is there more than one way to "make a nation"? Does Bourne discuss these ways?
2. What other writers in the American tradition are explicitly occupied with the "national character"? Selections in *The Heath Anthology* from Franklin, Jefferson, and Whitman ("Democratic Vistas") could be assembled on this topic.
3. What are the specifically modern ways that Bourne defines national and personal identity?

Anzia Yezierska (1881?–1970)

Contributing Editor: Sally Ann Drucker

Classroom Issues and Strategies

Because Yezierska often uses a first-person narrator who speaks with a great deal of emotional intensity, readers sometimes assume that her stories are strictly autobiographical. In addition, her use of Yiddish-English dialect can obscure the fact that she crafted these stories deliberately and carefully. Readers unfamiliar with Yezierska may focus on how these stories relate to episodes in her life rather than on her vivid characters, rich imagery, and adept use of dialect.

It can be helpful to discuss one of Yezierska's purposes in writing—to immerse the reader in the ghetto experience. (She also wished to explore her own feelings and to earn a living in the process.) In addition, although most readers come from backgrounds totally different from that of her characters, her stories can be discussed in terms of contemporary problems encountered by new immigrants, ghetto youth, working-class employees, and women.

Photos of Lower East Side tenement scenes or films such as *Hester Street* (based on *Yekl*) are useful to set up a visual context for Yezierska's writing.

Yezierska's most-taught novel is *Bread Givers*. In that book, the patriarchal father represents traditional Jewish ways. Because of the negative aspects of the father-daughter relationship, students who are not familiar with Jewish culture come away with a skewed view of it. Even in Yezierska's other works, what the heroine is giving up in order to become Americanized—family and culture—may not be readily apparent, given the heroine's economic and status gains from the process. These issues can be clarified in class discussion.

Major Themes, Historical Perspectives, Personal Issues

The processes of acculturation and assimilation, and the positive and negative effects of these processes, are ongoing themes in Yezierska's writing. Her work is particularly interesting for its presentation of immigrant women's pursuit of the American Dream. "America and I" was originally published in 1922, right before immigration laws changed (1924), restricting access to everyone not from northern or western Europe. This may have affected the way Yezierska ended the story (see last paragraph).

Significant Form, Style, or Artistic Conventions

Yezierska's work has been called sentimental and melodramatic. It is important to understand that in the Yiddish language tradition that she came out of, emotionality was expected, particularly for women. Her work fuses aspects of realism (attention to detail) and romanticism (characters' idealism), ultimately making it difficult to categorize.

Original Audience

Yezierska's stories were first published in magazines that had a general readership. She wrote primarily for mainstream Anglo-American audiences of the 1920s, although her work was certainly seen by Jewish Americans and other ethnic readers as well. Contemporary audiences, particularly female readers, respond especially to the immigrant waif characters as women who forged cultural and economic identities by their own strength, energy, and perseverance.

Comparisons, Contrasts, Connections

Works on immigrant Jewish life in this volume include the following:

The Promised Land, by Mary Antin
Yekl, by Abraham Cahan
Jews Without Money, by Michael Gold
"Tell Me a Riddle," by Tillie Olsen

Yezierska's story can also be compared with stories and poems written about/by other immigrant/ethnic groups. There are many in this volume.

Questions for Reading, Discussion, and Writing

1. It can be useful to ask about conflicts described in her writing: in this story, old versus new, expectations versus reality; in other stories, Jewish tradition versus American opportunity, parent versus child.
2. General: Oral histories—students interview members of their families, focusing on questions of cultural transitions such as rural to urban, one decade to another, immigrant conflicts, and so on. Papers—on working-class women in early twentieth-century literature, on the Americanization process in literature.
3. Specific: Papers comparing this story with some of Yezierska's others in *Hungry Hearts* or *Children of Loneliness*.

Bibliography

Shorter Works:

Baum, Charlotte, et al. *The Jewish Woman in America*. New York: Dial, 1976. Chapters 3, 4, 5; 91–162.

Drucker, Sally A. "Yiddish, Yidgin & Yezierska." *Modern Jewish Studies Annual* 6 (1987): 99–113.

Henriksen, Louise L. "Afterword About Anzia Yezierska." *The Open Cage: An Anzia Yezierska Collection*. New York: Persea, 1979. 253–62.

Kessler-Harris, Alice. Introduction. *The Open Cage: An Anzia Yezierska Collection*. New York: Persea, 1979. v–xiii.

Pratt, Norma F. "Culture and Radical Politics: Yiddish Women Writers, 1890–1940." *American Jewish History* 70.1 (Sept. 1980): 68–90.

Yezierska, Anzia. "Mostly About Myself." *Children of Loneliness*. New York: Funk, 1923. 9–31.

Longer Works:

Dearborn, Mary V. *Love in the Promised Land: The Story of Anzia Yezierska and John Dewey*. NY: Free, 1988.

Henriksen, Louise. *Anzia Yezierska: A Writer's Life*. New Brunswick: Rutgers UP, 1988.

Schoen, Carol B. *Anzia Yezierska*. Boston: Twayne, 1982.

Michael Gold (1893–1967)

Contributing Editor: Barry Gross

Classroom Issues and Strategies

Because Gold's intentions are didactic, he says what he has to say very directly and his language is very plain. Since he does not deal with any complex or difficult concepts or ideas, his work is immediately accessible to students.

It's useful to provide some statistics for background—for instance, the population density on the Lower East Side, the mortality rate for infants, incidence of tuberculosis and other infectious diseases, and so on. It would also be helpful to show pictures, tapes, or movies depicting life on the Lower East Side, although there has been a tendency to sentimentalize that life, to make it something to feel nostalgia for, and, hence, it's gotten prettified.

Major Themes, Historical Perspectives, Personal Issues

The warpings of poverty. The malign effects of unmediated capitalism. The peculiarly American mix and juxtaposition of races, groups, minorities. The nature of a slum (a slum seems to be a slum regardless of who inhabits it). The threats to the traditional patriarchal structure of family and culture that American ghetto life posed. The role of the mother. The threats to traditional Jewish culture that America posed.

Significant Form, Style, or Artistic Conventions

Note the combination of a journalistic style characterized by short sentences, monosyllabic words, a kind of reportage we think of as Hemingwayesque, and the occasional sketches of sentimentality, exhortation, and lament.

Original Audience

To the extent that *Jews Without Money* is written by a member of the Communist party who called for the overthrow of capitalism, it is very important to locate it in 1930. To the extent that it is a sentimental and intellectual and artistic autobiography, it is not so important to locate it. To the extent that it's a book about being Jewish, some historical placement is necessary. (There will be students, even Jewish students, who will think that "Jews without money" is an oxymoron.)

Comparisons, Contrasts, Connections

The Bread Givers by Anzia Yezierska, *Call It Sleep* by Henry Roth, *Yekl* by Abraham Cahan, *The World of Our Fathers* by Irving Howe, *The Rise of David Levinsky* by Abraham Cahan, and *What Makes Sammy Run?* by Budd Schulberg are the most famous of many works that deal with Jewish immigrant life on the Lower East Side. It would also be useful/interesting to compare and contrast with works by and about other immigrant groups, other minorities, other slum dwellers.

Bibliography

There is much available on the Lower East Side (*World of Our Fathers, The Golden Door* et al.); the Anti-Defamation League of B'nai B'rith (chapters in all large cities) will usually provide bibliographies, secondary materials, source materials, and study guides for educational purposes.

H. L. Mencken (1880–1956)

Contributing Editor: John Alberti

Classroom Issues and Strategies

The work of H. L. Mencken, as represented by "The Sahara of the Bozarts," will strike many students as both historically distant and yet oddly familiar. In addition to the unfamiliar historical references (e.g., Anthony Comstock and the "Comstock laws" that equated and criminalized both erotic art and birth control), Mencken's attacks on what is referred to as the "genteel" tradition will seem foreign, as evidenced by how few in class will get Mencken's sarcastic rendering of the term *beaux arts* in his title. In addition, Mencken's unapologetic endorsement of genetic theories of racial, class, and ethnic superiority may lead contemporary readers to view him as being as ignorant as the Southerners he condemns.

It is this very iconoclasm on Mencken's part, however, that can provide a point of recognition and entry for students encountering his writing for the first time. Mencken built his public reputation and literary celebrity on his willingness not only to challenge but also to ridicule popular opinion and "respectable" society, and it is Mencken's protoversion of political incorrectness that may seem most familiar to a contemporary audience. As the headnote to Mencken suggests, his fearless willingness to shock and condemn the status quo inspired writers as different in outlook and philosophy as Richard Wright, who while not sharing Mencken's preference for the reign of a cultural and intellectual aristocracy, nevertheless admired Mencken's courage in writing the truth as he saw it without apology.

Mencken's desire to deliberately outrage and offend what he saw as the small-minded provincialism dominating the American culture of his day will inevitably prompt discussion of twenty-first-century examples of this rhetorical strategy. The fact that Mencken combined his shock tactics with an endorsement of cultural and intellectual elitism provides useful points of comparison and contrast with modern-day examples of political incorrectness across the political spectrum.

"The Sahara of the Bozarts" also obviously takes part in a debate over powerful cultural and political symbolic descriptions of America that resonate to this day, such as the moral, ethical, and cultural distinctions between the rural and the urban, the "heartland" and the cities. Mencken's essay further locates this argument in the enduring regional constructions of the North and South, and by consistently preferring the urban and intellectual over the rural and traditional, Mencken goes against a dominant strain in American culture and raises interesting questions about what is meant by the terms *populist* and *elitist*, questions that recur with pointed emphasis every election year.

Original Audience

Mencken was one of the most well-known figures in the dominant popular medium of his day: print journalism. His reading audiences would have ranged from the broad-based circulation of the *Baltimore Sun*, an urban daily newspaper, to the more self-selecting readership interested in arts, culture, and criticism that would have read the *American Mercury*. In approaching "The Sahara of the Bozarts," students can approach the question of audience by first identifying those statements that they believe would have been most shocking or challenging to his readers. In making this list, students are inevitably making assumptions about Mencken's audience, and investigating these assumptions can be as useful as considering Mencken's actual opinions. In what ways, for example, might Mencken's readers see themselves as coconspirators with Mencken, laughing with him at the absurdity of the South? In what ways might they also harbor a nagging fear that they themselves might also be the targets of Mencken's satire?

Comparisons, Contrast, Connections

As the headnote suggests, probably the writer who most obviously compares with Mencken is Mark Twain, whose work Mencken championed. Twain's "War Prayer" provides a clear example of a similar use of blunt, forceful satire. In his role as American iconoclast, however, Mencken can also be linked in rhetorical spirit, if not philosophy, with writers as varied as Benjamin Franklin, Frederick Douglass, Henry David Thoreau, Elizabeth Cady Stanton, and later Richard Wright and even Malcolm X.

Working with Cultural Objects

A website devoted to H. L. Mencken located at <http://www.io.com/gibbonsb/Mencken> provides images and information about Mencken that can allow students to explore his position as a public figure. With his trademark cigar, Mencken was a product of the emerging visual cultural of celebrity in the earlier part of the twentieth century, and students can analyze the visual rhetoric of photographs such as the one at <http://www.io.com/gibbonsb/mencken/menckencigar.gif> as a part of the public persona Mencken constructs in "The Sahara of the Bozarts." In addition, the site also includes "Mencken's Creed," a statement of his basic philosophical principles that provides an interesting context for reading "The Sahara of the Bozarts" and that also prevents the easy political classification of Mencken:

- I believe that religion, generally speaking, has been a curse to mankind—that its modest and greatly overestimated services on the ethical side have been more than overcome by the damage it has done to clear and honest thinking.
- I believe that no discovery of fact, however trivial, can be wholly useless to the race, and that no trumpeting of falsehood, however virtuous in intent, can be anything but vicious.
- I believe that all government is evil, in that all government must necessarily make war upon liberty.
- I believe that the evidence for immortality is no better than the evidence of witches, and deserves no more respect.
- I believe in the complete freedom of thought and speech.
- I believe in the capacity of man to conquer his world, and to find out what it is made of, and how it is run.
- I believe in the reality of progress.
- I—But the whole thing, after all, may be put very simply. I believe that it is better to tell the truth than to lie. I believe that it is better to be free than to be a slave. And I believe that it is better to know than be ignorant.

Questions for Reading and Discussions/Approaches to Writing

1. How do you understand what Mencken is trying to accomplish by writing and publishing "The Sahara of the Bozarts"? Can you think of any personal or political actions that might be prompted by this essay?
2. Try writing a Mencken-style piece on a contemporary issue, imitating the sarcastic, rhetorical style of "The Sahara of the Bozarts" but also keeping in mind the precepts of "Mencken's Creed."

John Dos Passos (1896–1970)

Contributing Editor: Robert C. Rosen

Classroom Issues and Strategies

The biographies of *U.S.A.* are slices of history; their broader contexts are alluded to but not spelled out. To appreciate fully the nuances of Dos Passos's language, the significance of his descriptive details, and the force of his sarcasm, a reader needs to know a lot of history.

The teacher probably needs to do some explaining, though he or she should avoid explaining the biographies to death. To appreciate "The Body of an American," students should know something about World War I, which Dos Passos saw and many of his original readers remembered. They should understand such things as the unprecedented carnage of that war (10 million killed and 20 million wounded); the particular brutality of trench warfare; the deeper causes of the war (and of U.S. entry into the war) that lay behind the noble rhetoric; and the irony of racism at home (alluded to in "The Body of an American") and repression of domestic dissent during and after a war fought, Wilson told Congress, because "the world must be made safe for democracy." "The Bitter Drink" is more difficult than "The Body of an American" because its historical sweep is greater. Perhaps assigning (or even reading aloud) a brief sample of Veblen's writing would help; it would at least give students a sense of his approach and style. (See, for example, the title excerpt "The Captain of Industry" in *The Portable Veblen*, edited by Max Lerner; the last paragraph alone might suffice.)

Major Themes, Historical Perspectives, Personal Issues

"The Body of an American" is about the waste of war and the public and official cant that surrounds it. These issues should be of interest to students who have friends or relatives in the military or who are themselves of draft or enlistment age. "The Bitter Drink" is about what it means to be a serious critic of society, to tell the truth and refuse to say "the essential yes." Students soon to begin careers in which they may have to compromise their values should find much to discuss.

Significant Form, Style, or Artistic Conventions

Since the excerpts included in the anthology represent only about 1 percent of the *U.S.A.* trilogy and one of its four narrative devices (biographies, newsreels, conventional narratives, and the camera eye), teaching these excerpts is very different from teaching *U.S.A.* Should you find time in the course to read *The 42nd Parallel* or *Nineteen Nineteen* or *The Big Money,* you might discuss with students the relationships among the four narrative devices as well as questions about the nature of fiction and the nature of written history raised by Dos Passos's mixing of real historical figures and fictional characters. If students are reading only "The Body of an American" and/or "The Bitter Drink," you might ask them what role they think such "nonfiction" biography might play in a novel. With "The Body of an American," you might also ask about the effect of Dos Passos's running the opening words together, of his juxtapositions of different kinds of language, and of his Whitmanesque list-making. With "The Bitter Drink," you might discuss how Dos Passos goes about communicating his own attitudes while narrating the life of Veblen.

Original Audience

Though the two excerpts in the text are brief, they should suffice to suggest the radicalism of *U.S.A.* To students surprised by it, you might explain that such views were not so uncommon during the 1930s (though, for Dos Passos, they came even earlier). At the height of the Depression, with no unemployment insurance and meager public relief, more than one in four U.S. citizens had no job, and millions more suffered wage cuts and underemployment. People lost all their money in bank failures; families were forced out of their homes and apartments; many went hungry while milk was dumped into rivers and crops were burned to keep up prices. The economic system seemed irrational, and millions marched in protest, fought evictions, joined unions. This was the context of *U.S.A.* for its original readers.

Comparisons, Contrasts, Connections

Almost any other work of fiction from the 1930s might usefully be compared with the excerpts from *U.S.A.* Alongside "The Body of an American" you might read Dalton Trumbo's *Johnny Got His Gun* (1939) or, for contrast, the tight-lipped antiwar fiction in Hemingway's *In Our Time* (1925). For a powerful contemporary comparison, you might look at Vietnam veteran Ron Kovic's *Born on the Fourth of July* (1976).

Questions for Reading, Discussion, and Writing

1. With "The Body of an American," you might ask students what kinds of contrasts Dos Passos sets up between the news coverage and political declarations (in smaller print) and the story of John Doe. They'll probably point to such contrasts as the nobility of the rhetoric versus the ugly actuality of war, the superficiality of the reporting versus the depth of human suffering, and the impersonality and abstractness of the public language versus the personal detail in those lists of possible facts about John Doe and in the many biographical particulars that suggest all that went into making the adult human being whose unidentifiable remains are being buried.

2. With "The Bitter Drink," you might ask what Dos Passos means by Veblen's "constitutional inability to say yes" and why Dos Passos makes this "essential yes" a refrain. Veblen's ideas are as much implied as spelled out, and you might ask students to summarize as much of them as they can infer from the biography. You might also ask them to draw connections between those ideas and Veblen's life. Dos Passos sets this life very firmly in its historical context, and students might discuss the whole sweep of history brought to life in the biography and what patterns and recurring themes they see. Students might also speculate on whether there is too much of the apology in Dos Passos's description of his hero's "woman trouble."

Albert Maltz (1908–1985)

Contributing Editor: Gabriel Miller

Classroom Issues and Strategies

It is useful for the students to have some historical/social background, particularly concerning the Depression, the rise of radicalism, and its various configurations (why so many writers and intellectuals were attracted to Marxism, socialism, and so on). Many of Maltz's novels are also grounded in historical events (*The Underground Stream, The Cross and the Arrow,* and *A Tale of One January*). You might provide background lectures and readings on the history of the thirties ("The Happiest Man on Earth"). For other Maltz pieces, a knowledge of radicalism, the radical literary wars, HUAC, and the blacklist would be very helpful. Concerning HUAC (House Un-American Activities Committee), many students will be interested in the blacklist, fronts, and the Hollywood Ten (Maltz was part of this group).

Major Themes, Historical Perspectives, Personal Issues

1. The Depression and the displacement and disenfranchisement of the individual
2. The totalitarian environment and the individual
3. The ideal of the democratic individual
4. The individual alone in nature and with the self

Significant Form, Style, or Artistic Conventions

Discuss the "proletarian novel," the relationship of art and politics, and the conventions of realism. Questions of what constitutes a political or radical novel would also be stimulating and useful.

Original Audience

The audience, at least in the beginning, was the "initiated": radicals who were sympathetic to Maltz's ideas. However, Maltz was always reaching out to a wider audience and would come to reject the restraints of didactic art.

Comparisons, Contrasts, Connections

More well-known writers whose work can be read along with Maltz are Richard Wright, *Native Son* (emphasis on the emerging radical consciousness, questions of class); John Steinbeck, *Grapes of Wrath* (Americans on the road, communal versus individual) and *In Dubious Battle* (political novel); James Farrell, the Studs Lonigan trilogy (realism, environment, politics); also Jack London and some of Whitman's poems, particularly those emphasizing the ideal of the democratic man.

Questions for Reading, Discussion, and Writing

1. I think questions regarding the effectiveness of presenting character and the character's relationship to the overriding issues of the story would be productive.
2. Discuss how successfully Maltz integrates didactic aims with "art." Is Maltz's best work at odds with its didactic intent? How does Maltz's work effectively convey the central issues of his time?

Bibliography

Maltz's essays in *The Citizen Writer*; his *New Masses* essay "What Shall We Ask of Writers?" (1946), in which he takes the notion of didactic art to task and for which he was harshly criticized.

Lillian Hellman (1905–1984)

Contributing Editor: Vivian Patraka

Major Themes, Historical Perspectives, Personal Issues

What is Hellman's idea of history? Who makes history, and how are events in history related? Why does she connect the events of the McCarthy Era to the Vietnam War? What is her conception of the average American's understanding of history? How is this related to the "deep contempt for public intelligence" Hellman ascribes to Nixon? Why does Hellman reserve her strongest sense of betrayal for the intellectuals who did not protest the events of the McCarthy Era? What assumptions about intellectuals did Hellman have to abandon? What qualities does she ascribe to the McCarthyites and their proceedings that should have made them the "hereditary enemies" of intellectuals?

Significant Form, Style, or Artistic Conventions

What kind of credibility does an autobiographical memoir have as compared to a history or a political science book? How convincing is Hellman in establishing her point of view about the McCarthy Era? Is she less convincing because the work identifies itself as someone's opinion? Because she is angry? How does a question like "Since when do you have to agree with people to defend them from injustice?" or a statement like "Truth made you a traitor as it often does in a time of scoundrels" make Hellman's work both persuasive and memorable? Why does Hellman use the word *scoundrel*, and what does she mean by it?

Elsewhere, Hellman has said that in a time of scoundrels, "The pious words come out because you know the pious words are good salesmanship." The idea that the language of morality, of patriotism, and of religion can be manipulated in an entrepreneurial way to capitalize on people's fears applies to more than just the fifties. Are there any examples from contemporary times of this sort of manipulation? Who benefits from it, and why? Who is harmed?

Why would Hellman use the phrase "black comedy" to describe activities she considered to be harmful and evil? Why doesn't she call them a tragedy, given that many people's lives were ruined? Elsewhere she says, "One is torn between laughter and tears. It's so truly comic. People were confessing to sins they'd never done; making up lies of meetings they'd been in when they'd been in no such meeting; asking God and the Committee's pardon for nothing but just going into a room and listening to some rather dull talk. . . . And that, to me was the saddest and most disgusting, as well as most comic. The effect was of a certain section of the country going crazy." What would motivate people to "confess" and "name names" in this manner?

Comparisons, Contrasts, Connections

Hellman has spoken of "the right of each man to his own convictions." Where is the line between having a conviction and being subversive or dangerous, and who is allowed to interpret that for us? In what direction is that line currently moving? Playwright Arthur Miller, writing about the McCarthy Era, said, "With the tiniest Communist Party in the world, the United States was behaving as though on the verge of a bloody revolution." Who would profit from creating this impression? What kinds of acts can be justified once this impression is created?

Mary McCarthy (1912–1989)

Contributing Editor: Wendy Martin

Classroom Issues and Strategies

Students will be interested in discussing McCarthy's depiction of social roles and norms and will want to relate her questioning of traditional beliefs to the social changes of the twentieth century. However, while this is a fruitful course of discussion for McCarthy's work, it is important not to lose sight of the literary artistry of her work. Students should learn to be attentive to the nuances of language, the symbolism and carefully controlled diction that characterize McCarthy's prose and make her a superb literary stylist as well as a chronicler of her times.

Major Themes, Historical Perspectives, Personal Issues

Mary McCarthy's life extended across most of the twentieth century, and her writing is as multifaceted as the rapidly changing American society in which she lived. She was concerned with issues of social justice and responsibility, and this concern manifests itself in her work in the form of repeated examinations of assumptions about gender, race, and class. For example, her novel *The Group* (1963) explores the irony, and sometimes the ugliness, in the lives of two decades of American women, dealing openly with adultery, misogyny, divorce, and insanity. The novel ridicules traditional notions of femininity and suggests new ways of conceptualizing marriage, work, and love.

Although McCarthy's work seems to be informed by a feminist sensibility, she asserted that she was not a feminist. While it is important to establish the political and social background of the leftist intellectual circles in which she moved, it is also important to recognize that McCarthy was always an independent thinker who resisted easy categorization.

Significant Form, Style, or Artistic Conventions

McCarthy's writing took a variety of forms, from early theater columns for the *Partisan Review* to incisive political essays on Vietnam and Watergate. Her best-known works are her novels and her collection of short autobiographical narratives, *Memories of a Catholic Girlhood*, from which the selection "Names" is taken. This collection is both a product of and a deviation from previous American autobiographical narratives. In revisiting her own life, McCarthy exposes the silences and boundaries in the lives of the traditional women who inhabited her childhood. McCarthy undertakes two projects simultaneously: she demystifies cultural assumptions of silent and passive femininity while simultaneously building up her own autobiographical persona. *Memories of a Catholic Girlhood* stands as an important model for American women's autobiography in a century of dramatic social change for women.

Original Audience

McCarthy wrote for a wide audience. She was, at one point, a staff writer for the *New Yorker*. *The Group,* her best-selling novel, has sold over five million copies worldwide. In general, both her fiction and her essays are meant to appeal to progressive and open-minded women and men, and to encourage these readers to question social traditions and assumptions that arbitrarily limit their lives.

Comparisons, Contrasts, Connections

McCarthy's intellectual background could be provided through the works of her close friend, Hannah Arendt, whose book *The Life of the Mind* McCarthy spent two years editing. Another interesting source of background material would be the literary criticism of her second husband, Edmund Wilson.

McCarthy said herself that John Dos Passos's *The 42nd Parallel,* which she read while at Vassar, was one of her most important influences. She met Dos Passos when she joined a group of radical writers living in Greenwich Village during the late thirties; other writers she met living in the Village were Sherwood Anderson, Erskine Caldwell, and Upton Sinclair. The political and intellectual debates that she participated in during this period were important formative influences for the ideas that would later appear in her writing. It would be useful to compare and contrast the work of these male radicals with McCarthy's vision.

McCarthy also stated that she had read Louisa May Alcott's *Little Women* and *Jo's Boys.* These works and the fiction of other earlier women writers, such as Edith Wharton and Willa Cather, could be used to establish the tradition of white women's literature in which she wrote, and which she transformed to fit her individual needs. In addition, a comparison and contrast could be developed between *Memories of a Catholic Girlhood* and, for example, *Report from Part One*, the autobiographical narrative of McCarthy's contemporary, Gwendolyn Brooks.

Questions for Reading, Discussion, and Writing

1. Many of the major issues of McCarthy's writing can be touched on in a discussion of "Names." Questions for discussion could include: What is the significance of the "frontier" setting of the narrative? How does the ethnic mix of names in the convent relate to the narrator's self-perception? How does the institutional structure of the convent force the narrator to be deceptive about "becoming a woman"? Why is she renamed at the same time that the incident with the blood occurs, and why does she say that the name "Cye" becomes her "new patron saint"? Discussion of these questions should bring out McCarthy's concern with exposing the reality beneath social surfaces and with the ways that social pressures affect the construction of the self. Another topic for discussion would be McCarthy's treatment of the women in the female society of the convent. How does she portray the various girls? The nuns?

2. McCarthy's prose at first seems light and readable, but on closer inspection it turns out to be quite dense and laden with interconnected levels of meaning. Having students write on brief passages gives them an opportunity to explore this richness of meaning. Ask students to make connections between seemingly disparate passages. For example, what does the passage at the beginning of "Names," in which she describes the society of Puget Sound, have to do with the passage at the end, in which she says, "What I wanted was a fresh start"? Students should be able to discover how the theme of re-created identity, treated both seriously and with irony, runs throughout "Names."

Bibliography

For a concise overview of McCarthy's life and work, see Wendy Martin, "Mary McCarthy," in *Modern American Women Writers*, edited by Elaine Showalter et al. (1991). For biographical information, see Carol W. Gelder-man, *Mary McCarthy: A Life* (1988), and Doris Grumbach, *The Company She Kept* (1967). For a study of her autobiographical writings, such as "Names," see Gordon O. Taylor, "The Word for Mirror: Mary McCarthy," in *Chapters of Experience: Studies in Twentieth-Century American Autobiography* (1983). For a more general treatment of McCarthy's artistry, see Wendy Martin, "The Satire and Moral Vision of Mary McCarthy," in *Comic Relief: Humor in Contemporary American Literature*, edited by Sarah Blacher Cohen (1978).

Clifford Odets (1906–1963)

Contributing Editor: Michael J. Mendelsohn

Classroom Issues and Strategies

If Odets occasionally seems dated, he is less so for those who put this play into its 1930s milieu. Consider having student reports or general class discussion on major concerns in the United States in the mid-1930s. With some understanding of the Depression decade, it may be less difficult for students to believe that this militant young dramatist was able to present such a play to sympathetic, even enthusiastic audiences.

Major Themes, Historical Perspectives, Personal Issues

Playwright Odets clearly believed in 1935 that through union solidarity the little man might find a way out of the despair of America's economic and social ills. For many, American society was not fulfilling its true promise; in the big novel of the thirties, *The Grapes of Wrath*, Steinbeck asserted much the same theme. With only a touch of hyperbole, Harold Clurman called *Waiting for Lefty* "the birth of the thirties."

Significant Form, Style, or Artistic Conventions

Techniques of speaking across the proscenium, a scenery-less stage, and planting actors in the audience give instructors plenty to work with. For instructors interested in theatrical links and analogues, Pirandello or Wilder would be appropriate points of departure.

Original Audience

Audience for this work is especially important. It was intended for presentation in union halls before small, typically preconvinced audiences. It is obviously strident, intended to make a militant emotional appeal. Unlike much of our theater today, it was not intended merely to entertain or inform. Politically, Odets was going through the same sort of youthful flirtation with communism that marked the careers of many of his 1930s contemporaries. Without this sort of context, the play comes off as merely a strident little piece of propaganda.

Comparisons, Contrasts, Connections

Compare with Steinbeck's *The Grapes of Wrath* (1939).

Examine Pirandello or Wilder for some comparison of theatrical techniques of crossing the proscenium and merging actors with audiences.

Questions for Reading, Discussion, and Writing

1. What is the unifying plot for all these episodes?
2. Is this play universal, or is it too tied to place (New York) and to time (the Great Depression of the 1930s)?
3. Is the message too blatant? Is the language too strident? Is Odets more a "revolutionary" or a "reformer" if you compare, for example, his work with Steinbeck's *The Grapes of Wrath*, a product of the same decade?
4. Which scenes have the greatest impact, and why?
5. Odets has often been praised for his use of vivid, colorful language. Which speeches work well for you? Which are less successful?
6. How successful is the playwright in crossing the proscenium and breaking down the traditional separation between audience and action? Why does he use this technique?

Bibliography

Brenman-Gibson, Margaret. *Clifford Odets*. Boston: Atheneum, 1981. 299–306.

Clurman, Harold. *The Fervent Years*. New York: Hill, 1957. 138–42.

Mendelsohn, Michael. *Clifford Odets*. New York: Everett, 1969. 21–26.

Murray, Edward. *Clifford Odets*. New York: Ungar, 1968. Chapter 1.

Weales, Gerald. *Clifford Odets*. Indianapolis: Pegasus, 1971. Chapter 3.

Meridel LeSueur (1900–1996)

Contributing Editor: Elaine Hedges

Classroom Issues and Strategies

Some knowledge of the Great Depression of the 1930s is helpful—the extent of unemployment, the fears about the future of American society, the disillusionment of many writers and intellectuals with the capitalist system, and especially the impact of the Depression on women. Our popular images of the period are of men standing in breadlines and selling apples. LeSueur was one of the few writers to focus on women, who also lost jobs, faced starvation, and were abandoned by husbands who were forced to seek work elsewhere.

Major Themes, Historical Perspectives, Personal Issues

As indicated above, the Depression of the 1930s is the historical context for "Women on the Breadlines." Instructors might want to ask why women have tended to be ignored in accounts of the Depression.

"Women" emerged from LeSueur's personal experience. She herself experienced unemployment and poverty during the Depression. She knew, and for a time lived with, the kinds of women she describes in "Women on the Breadlines."

Significant Form, Style, or Artistic Conventions

"Women on the Breadlines" is a piece of journalism. Though the emphasis is on factual observation, with details conveyed through short, simple declarative sentences, it is not "objective" reporting. (Students might be asked what "objective" writing is and whether in fact there is such a thing.) The reportorial voice doesn't keep itself distinct from the material it describes but, rather, identifies with the women and their suffering. Is this kind of journalism—called "reportage" in LeSueur's time—similar to the personal or "new" journalism written today?

Does the style, in its directness and simplicity, effectively capture the lives and feelings of the women described? Is it, despite being journalism, in any ways a "literary" style? Note LeSueur's use of imagery: for example, a scrubwoman with hands "like watersoaked branches." Can students find other examples of figurative language?

Also examine the structure of "Women on the Breadlines." It develops through a series of vignettes or portraits. Are these arranged in any particular order? Does the piece develop, as a short story might, toward a climax? What might be the difference between this kind of journalistic feature story and a literary short story?

Comparisons, Contrasts, Connections

Other writings in the anthology that describe the Depression can be compared and contrasted in content and style with "Women on the Breadlines."

Mourning Dove (Okanogan) (1888–1936)

Contributing Editor: Kristin Herzog

Classroom Issues and Strategies

Students tend to see these stories as folklore, not realizing their complexity and philosophical background. They cannot measure the difficulty of translating a corporate tradition into the narrative voice of an individual writer. They will wonder for what audience the stories were written.

Consider approaching Mourning Dove from the world of American Indian spirituality, especially since the sweat-house tradition is still alive in some tribes.

In order to teach the excerpts from *Coyote Stories,* a basic understanding of the trickster figure in the legends of various tribes is necessary. Though the trickster's shape can be Raven, Blue Jay, Raccoon, Crow, or Spider, and though his function differs in detail, he is most frequently Coyote, the creature of playful disguises and clever self-seeking, the breaker of taboos, teller of lies, and creator of possibilities. He is the restlessly moving, ever-changing, indomitable spirit of survival. Coyote is always at the mercy of his passions and appetites; he holds no moral or social values, yet through his actions all values come into being. Trickster tales give humorous vent to those impulses that the tribes had to repress in order to maintain social order.

Major Themes, Historical Perspectives, Personal Issues

Mourning Dove had to surmount almost incredible obstacles to become an author, and she personifies the ambivalent position of many ethnic women writers. Besides the lack of education and the ordeal of daily life in migrant labor camps, she had to contend with suspicious members of her tribe who did not see any purpose in giving away their sacred stories or who expected payment for telling them since some ethnologists had established that custom.

She also had to deal with the two men who made her publications possible: Lucullus McWhorter and Heister Dean Guie, the former an eminent scholar and faithful friend, the latter a journalist who wanted to establish a reputation as illustrator and editor. Both badgered her continually with questions of verification for certain customs' names or spellings. Both considered themselves authorities on the selection of stories "proper" for a white audience and on the addition of notes. Guie decided to eliminate at least ten tales from the final manuscript because they dealt with subjects like incest, transvestism, and infanticide. Donald Hines has retrieved these stories from Mourning Dove's manuscripts and has restored all the tales as closely as possible to her original version.

Significant Form, Style, or Artistic Conventions

Most difficult to grasp for the white reader is probably the concept of power. Usually an individual's power derived from or was related to an animal to which he or she felt kinship. Power for the Okanogans is not identical with what we call the mind or the soul, but instead is more like the Christian concept of a guardian angel—a force that protects and leads. When a young girl or boy received power, she or he also received a "power song" that was her or his very own. Thus power is immediately related to words.

Original Audience

When the oral tradition entered the literary mainstream, it first had to take on the conventions and proprieties of white literature. Only decades later was the mainstream audience able to understand orality "in the raw." In Mourning Dove's time, the often bizarre or obscene behavior of Coyote could easily be understood as reflection on Okanogan morals. Besides, *Coyote Stories* was written first of all for children.

Comparisons, Contrasts, Connections

Compare with Zitkala-Sa in terms of "translating" tribal traditions into white western narrative form.

On the surface, of course, the story of "The Spirit Chief Names the Animal People" is simply entertaining and educational. But, like any creation myth, it expresses a complex "philosophy." The animal people's need for "names" points to the coming of humans with a new kind of speech. But there were "tribes" already inhabiting the earth together with the animal people, and they were threatened by "people-devouring monsters." In a type of "Fortunate Fall" parable, it is the Coyote, the bragging, bungling fool, who by divine mercy is given the task of conquering these monsters. His special power may at times falter, but if he dies, his life can be restored by his twin brother, Fox, or by "others of the people."

The reader trained in the Judeo-Christian tradition may want to compare this story with biblical images and concepts. The Spirit Chief is "an all-powerful Man Above"—as McWhorter's note phrases it—but he has a wife who could be compared with the Sophia of the Hebrews: she participates in the creation and is the human, commonsensical aspect of the divinity who knows what the people need.

Questions for Reading, Discussion, and Writing

1. Compare the creation myths of various world religions or of various American Indian tribes. What do they have in common?
2. In what sense did Mourning Dove herself become a "trickster"? How do these stories compare with fairy tales and fables?

Bibliography

Allen, Paula G. *The Sacred Hoop: Recovering the Feminine in American Indian Traditions*. Boston: Beacon, 1986. 81–84, 151.

Astrov, Margot. *American Indian Prose and Poetry*. Qtd. in *Pocahontas's Daughters: Gender and Ethnicity in American Culture*. Ed. Mary V. Dearborn. New York: Oxford UP, 1986. 28.

Fisher, Alice P. "The Transformation of Tradition: A Study of Zitkala-Sa and Mourning Dove, Two Transitional Writers." Diss. City U of New York, 1979. 36. On the quality of the passage on hair cutting.

Fisher, Dexter. Introduction. *Cogewea, the Half-Blood: A Depiction of the Great Montana Cattle Range.* By Hum-ishu-ma. Lincoln: U of Nebraska P, 1981. v–xxix.

Hines, Donald M., ed. *Tales of the Okanogans, Collected by Mourning Dove.* Fairfield, WA: Ye Galleon, 1976. 14.

Radin, Paul. *The Trickster: A Study in American Indian Mythology.* New York: Philosophical Library, 1956. Rpt. New York: Greenwood, 1969.

Schöler, Bo. Introduction. *Coyote Was Here: Essays on Contemporary Native American Literary and Political Mobilization.* Aarhus, Den.: Dept. of English, U of Aarhus, 1984. 9.

Yanan, Eileen. *Coyote and the Colville.* Omak, WA: St. Mary's Mission, 1971. 29.

John Joseph Mathews (Osage) (1894–1979)

Contributing Editor: Andrew O. Wiget

Classroom Issues and Strategies

The principal issue in *Sundown* is the notion of progress. Students frequently identify progress with material improvements in lifestyle or increasingly complex technology. This selection questions whether those are the true marks of civilization. To see this, however, students must realize that this selection comprises two parts, each of which portrays a different moment, widely separated in time in the life of the principal character, Chal Windzer. Chal (short for "Challenge," so named because his father wanted him to be a challenge to the new generation) is a teenager in the first section, still closely identified with some element of his traditional Osage lifestyle. Note, however, that he is moving rapidly toward accepting the values of Anglos, as is suggested by his distance from the group of Indians he encounters during the storm.

The second section of the story occurs over a decade later. Chal has gone off to the University of Oklahoma, where he has been exposed to prejudice, bigotry, and romance. Falling in love with a white girl, he comes to despise his Indian appearance and later tries to pass himself off as a Spanish (not Mexican) gentleman. During World War I, he serves in the Army Air Force as an aviator and develops a passion for flying, which fulfills his need for a career. He loves the excitement, the danger, the thrill of flying. After serving in the Army Air Force, he returns home, where he falls back into an indolent lifestyle, marked by long periods of drunkenness. He is just coming out of one of these periods, referred to in the last section of this selection, when he attends the hearings at which Roan Horse speaks.

In addition to providing background plot information, I also certainly call attention to certain literary devices. For example the oil derricks symbolize both the march and retreat of "progress." I'd also remind students a little bit of the history of this period of time. Osages were exempted from the provisions of the Dawes General Allotment Act, along with the Five Civilized Tribes, because they held their land under patented title, not by treaty. The surface of their reservation land had been allotted and much of it alienated through sale, but the mineral rights were retained by the Osage tribe in common and leases were given out. In the 1920s, royalties from these leases brought the tribe up to 20 million dollars per year, divided equally, amounting to around 25 thousand dollars per capita. A county court in Oklahoma had declared the Osages incompetent to manage their estates and had appointed guardians who charged a fee to manage these estates. Between exorbitant fees and the malfeasance of these guardians, the Osages lost much money and land.

In 1925, Congress transferred supervision of these mineral rights from the county court alone to the county court working in conjunction with the Osage agency. The federal investigators referred to in the last section are not only members of Congress but also agents of the Federal Bureau of Investigation. The so-called "Osage Oil Murders" are a historical event of great notoriety and served to establish the credibility of the FBI as a law enforcement agency. As Mathews indicates, a conspiracy evolved to murder people who owned rights to oil land so that their inheritors would receive those rights. By murdering the inheritors, the conspirators planned to channel those rights into the hands of one person, an Anglo man who had married an Osage woman. She was the last person on the hit list, which today still leaves a trail of twenty-four unsolved murders and bombings.

The Osage oil boom needs to be understood in the context of the free-for-all capitalist economy of the 1890s and the first two decades of this century, during which the excesses of the robber barons were finally curbed by the creation of federal regulatory agencies. From the point of view of Indians in Oklahoma, however, the real question that needs to be asked is this: What happens to a community of people who go from a subsistence economy based on communal land, barter, and credit to an excess of cash, in the neighborhood of 25 thousand dollars per person per year (at the value of the 1920s dollar), all within the space of one generation? How does such a change affect people's values, beliefs, and behaviors?

Students seem concerned about the ambivalence of the ending, especially about whether or not Chal is really capable of being a challenge to his generation, as his father had hoped. After reading about Chal's life of indolence, it is difficult for students to believe that he will make such a bold move, requiring such a commitment of effort, especially if that move is motivated only by observing the very brief appearance of Roan Horse. On the other hand, Chal has shown the desire to be a warrior, and he has great ambitions. Does the ending mark a real turning point in his life?

Major Themes, Historical Perspectives, Personal Issues

I would highlight the structure of the boom-town society that appears in the beginning of the selection. I would indicate the characters' attitudes toward the upcoming storm (bad for business, dangerous) and contrast that with the attitudes of some of the older Indians, such as Black Elk. In between we have younger Indians, such as Sun-On-His-Wings and Chal.

The various attitudes that each of these people takes toward the onset of the storm and toward the damage that the storm does provide a keen insight into the different sets of values that are coming together under the pressure of "progress" and assimilation in this reservation community.

Significant Form, Style, or Artistic Conventions

I would point to the oil derricks as a symbol of "progress"; I would also look at the change in Chal's character between the first section and the second section. It's especially important that students try to understand Chal's apparent indifference and his drunkenness as a response to an excess of easy money in the absence of compelling community values. The recognition of this, on Chal's part, is what moves him to respond so affirmatively to Roan Horse's brief speech.

Original Audience

This book was published in the 1930s, when it met a receptive audience of people in the middle of the Depression who understood the tremendous personal cost and human devastation that was brought about by the unchecked exploitation of natural resources and poor people. In this context, especially, American Indians were highlighted as an oppressed minority within the United States. In 1928, the Meriam Report, commissioned by the U.S. government, found that Indians had a mortality rate twice as high as the white population, an infant mortality rate three times as high as the white population, and that in spite of all this, the government had been spending only fifty cents per year on the health care of each Indian. Statistics like this shocked the nation, and Indians became the object of renewed federal attention. Under the Roosevelt administration, the U.S. government took a number of important steps to redress these failures of its trust relationship, though many of them, such as the Indian Reorganization Act (1934), which allowed tribes to form their own governments with written constitutions, were controversial. Nevertheless, Mathews's work needs to be seen as speaking to the notion that the major difficulties on Indian reservations come from what today we would call a "culture of poverty." And that these can be remedied by government treatment.

Comparisons, Contrasts, Connections

Insofar as Mathews gives us a good picture of the transition on Indian reservations, he can be compared usefully with Oskison and Bonnin. Lynn Riggs's play *The Cherokee Night* also gives a good picture of the deculturation that has been visited upon American Indians as a result of the abuses in the trust relationship that they had with the U.S. government.

Questions for Reading, Discussion, and Writing

1. How do the oil derricks mark the changes in the life of the Osages and also in the personal history of Chal? Why is Chal impressed by Roan Horse's speech?
2. In the first section of the story, a young Indian comments about Black Elk: "His body is here but his mind is back in a place where we lived many years ago." How does this observation reflect the forces that are creating the conflict in this story?
3. At the very end of the story, Chal says that he is going to go off to Harvard Law School and become an orator. What do you think is the likelihood of Chal fulfilling this stated goal? How would you support your judgment?

Bibliography

Wiget, Andrew. "Modern Fiction." *Native American Literature.* Boston: Twayne, 1985.

Wilson, Terry. "John Joseph Mathews." *Dictionary of Native American Literature.* Ed. Andrew Wiget. New York: Garland, 1994. 245–50.

———. "Osage Oxonian: The Heritage of John Joseph Mathews." *Chronicles of Oklahoma* 59 (1981): 264–93.

Thomas S. Whitecloud (Chippewa) (1914–1972)

Contributing Editor: Daniel F. Littlefield Jr.

Classroom Issues and Strategies

Present "Blue Winds Dancing" as you would any well-written essay.

The social implication of being Indian in an Anglo-dominated society gets lost for students in the larger issue of simply feeling "at odds" as a result of "gaps"—social, political, generational, and so on.

Major Themes, Historical Perspectives, Personal Issues

1. Self-identify, self-realization
2. Individual caught between two cultures, one not fully lost and the other not fully gained
3. Culture loss and acculturation

Significant Form, Style, or Artistic Conventions

Stress the essay structure (this one is neatly divided; how do the three parts interlock, structurally and thematically?).

Stress the use of rich visual imagery. Which images *seem* to be drawn from Indian heritage; which not? Is there any difference in the effects of each?

Original Audience

It fits into the context of the whole scene of social disruption in the Great Depression, heightened in this case by the sense of being kicked loose, out of touch with two cultures.

For contemporary readers, it speaks to the large themes of searching out roots and self-realization.

Comparisons, Contrasts, Connections

For earlier generations of Indian writers who deal with the theme of being caught between cultures, see Copway and Apess, Eastman and Bonnin. For later writers, see Welch and Erdrich.

D'Arcy McNickle (1904–1977)

Contributing Editor: John Lloyd Purdy

Classroom Issues and Strategies

Like so much of McNickle's fiction, "Hard Riding" is a deceptively simple story. As in the verbal arts (such as storytelling), it implies and suggests more than it states. Students often accept the "joke" played upon the Agent and then dismiss it as clever but relatively insignificant. However, McNickle will work on them even after they have done so.

In his first novel, McNickle shows the effect of an evening of storytelling on his young protagonist, Archilde, who considers himself a "modern man" (an assimilated Indian who no longer believes as his mother and her people believe) and who easily dismisses "the old stories" they tell. On the night of a feast, however, he is captured by those same stories and taken to a new level of awareness in which he becomes an "insider" and sees his people's lives in new ways. They are no longer the residue of the old bowing under the new, but the bearers of a dynamic and important culture. In short, McNickle consistently attempted a similar end for non-Native readers, using a written medium.

Since the story "Hard Riding" is presented from Mather's point of view, one can examine what his thoughts and reactions reveal about his character at the outset. For instance, does the opening simply establish "setting," or does it enlighten an important aspect of Mather's nature as he spurs his horse on to the meeting? Also, he is, literally, a mediator: he represents the modern, the progressive, and therefore he possesses many of the same feelings and beliefs as McNickle's intended audience. Moreover, he is privy to knowledge of "Indian ways" that he shares with us, revealing what his years of experience have taught him about the people he has been sent to manage. He becomes, at least initially and momentarily, the expert, the authority.

The story obviously hinges on the thwarted efforts of that authority, so the conclusion needs careful examination, not only as it pertains to what precedes it, but also in how we, as readers, respond to Mather's failure to have his way, that is, to spur the men "below" him to accept a new way of "justice."

We are never involved in the debate that takes place among the Native American characters; instead, the action is filtered through an interpreter and the Agent himself, yet we become "insiders" when we reflect upon the implications of the maneuvering: that the orders of the "dominant society" have been followed, in form but certainly not in principle. Do we applaud, condemn, or dismiss the actions of the tribe?

Major Themes, Historical Perspectives, Personal Issues

In 1934, McNickle took a job on the staff of the Commissioner of Indian Affairs, John Collier, who reflected the New Deal ideals of the Roosevelt administration. It was Collier's belief that, as much as possible, tribes should be allowed to direct their own affairs using traditional, rather than Euro-American, governmental frameworks. McNickle subscribed wholeheartedly to this idea, which in turn directed his work for the remainder of his life. We can see that concept in this story. When a federal functionary attempts to impose a new way, a way he and the readers may consider wholly logical and in the best economic interests of his charges, he is not only frustrated but also humiliated. However, the significance of this dramatic crisis lies not in its overt political statements, but in its demonstration of the efficacy of traditional Native economic systems and governments in contemporary times.

As McNickle well knew, the survival and renewal of Native cultures rest in the communal aspects of tribal life perpetuated through ceremonialism and literature. Community, rather than alienation and individuality, is a major thematic concern in both, and in the writings of McNickle and those who followed him. This communalism calls for sharing hardships as well as bounty (that is, the cattle), and it is maintained through the ability to reach consensus through group reasoning and discussion, a governmental form McNickle's audience may uphold as an ideal of democracy but fail to recognize in practice in the story. The Indians whom Mather addresses work in concert and exert control over their own affairs. In a word, they are empowered by their communal presence, their group identity as "insiders." This, again, is a recurring theme in McNickle's fiction and his scholarly writings. (See also the "Original Audience" section below.)

Significant Form, Style, or Artistic Conventions

McNickle was fond of the juxtaposition of very divergent points of view. For instance, in his last novel, *Wind from an Enemy Sky* (1978), he often uses chapter breaks to move from his Native American to his Anglo characters. Given his subject—American Indian perspectives—and his non-tribal audience, this is an understandable technique. He forces readers to assess what they believe about American Indians by consistently undermining those beliefs with culture "shifting" and therefore ethnographic revelation. His humane handling of cross-cultural explorations creates moments of crisis.

In "Hard Riding," this can be seen in the final passages, where the primary point of view, that of the Indian Agent, is somehow inverted, or shifted, as readers move from "listening" to Mather's narrative to trying to understand what has happened beyond it, and how he has been duped.

McNickle also makes suggestive use of descriptions as a means of shaping an audience's preparation for events. More than simply foreshadowing, this technique often works as a symbolic subtext. For instance, in the opening ride he describes the time of day, noting the "crimson flame thwarting the prismatic heavens." This may be dismissed by students bred on stark realism as merely flowery prose; however, in discussion it could also be considered as a preface to what follows. Mather is thwarted at the story's end. Considering the idea of a prismatic effect, and McNickle's perspective on the religions that had subjugated Native America, one might be able to go further with the discussion. In fact, it may not be too difficult to question the use of the name *Mather* for the main character. McNickle was an avid reader in all disciplines, including colonial history, in which the Mather family and their ethnocentric beliefs figure prominently. McNickle played with language and its allusive qualities in some interesting ways.

Original Audience

McNickle's audience changed dramatically over his lifetime, which makes him, once again, a significant figure for study. Today, his books have been continuously reprinted since the midseventies and remain popular because they reflect what many have come to understand as a revised and therefore acceptable image of contemporary Natives and tribal issues. When this story was first written, however, history books and novels by non-Native writers still proffered as fact the popular stereotypes we have come to recognize and reject: Native Americans as either Noble Savages or savages; as the remnants of a dying race, on the brink of extinction; as the dull and sullen subhuman at a loss to deal with civilization; and so on. They also devalued Native cultural achievements, pre-Columbian populations, and the ill effects (and the morality) of European colonization. Moreover, the ideal of assimilation—the "melting pot" of America—was equally prominent. It is little wonder that McNickle's early works, although well-received by critics, were not widely popular; he presents Indians who exert a degree of control over their lives and who take pride in their tribal identities. He presents a very different American dream than his popular contemporaries, Ernest Hemingway and F. Scott Fitzgerald, do.

Comparisons, Contrasts, Connections

The anthology provides ample points of comparison and contrast. McNickle's work can be placed, in some ways, in the context of other writings from the 1930s, writings by non-Native writers; it can also be compared or contrasted with writings by Native Americans produced before 1935. For instance, White-cloud's "Blue Winds Dancing" (published in the same year as McNickle's first novel, *The Surrounded*) possesses some of the same issues of community and commercial America. Most profitably, however, one can compare the ways that his work anticipates later works by Native writers. There is a great deal of "resonance " to be found here.

Questions for Reading, Discussion, and Writing

1. Is Mather's proposal a logical one? Why or why not? On what basis is that logic built?
2. Is the group's alteration of Mather's plan a logical one? Why or why not? On what basis is its logic built? (McNickle offers another "logic," the logic of communal needs and obligations over financial expediency, and the latter is proffered as a distinct and viable alternative to that of "modern, commercial America.")
3. What is the significance of the title? How does McNickle's description of Mather's riding style reflect or imply the author's evaluation of governmental policy-making?

Bibliography

The four books on McNickle and his writings are John Purdy, *The Legacy of D'Arcy McNickle: Writer, Historian, Activist* (1996); Dorothy Parker, *Singing an Indian Song: A Biography of D'Arcy McNickle* (1992); John Purdy, *Word Ways: The Novels of D'Arcy McNickle* (1990); and James Ruppert, *D'Arcy McNickle* (1988). General criticism about McNickle's works can be found in several journals, including *Studies in American Indian Literatures* and *Western American Literature.*

Robert Penn Warren (1905–1989)

Contributing Editor: Robert H. Brinkmeyer Jr.

Classroom Issues and Strategies

Warren is a very accessible poet, with a strong sense of narrative and a nonintimidating diction, both of which students generally enjoy.

Warren's great concern with the historical vision and the meanings found in memory and the past are distinctly Southern. For students with no background in Southern literature, these interests may seem forced, even bizarre in their intensity. A general overview of some of the major themes of twentieth-century Southern literature would help put Warren into perspective.

The poetry speaks for itself, but discussing Warren's "Southernness" is an effective way to begin a discussion of him. One might go from there into a discussion of which poems clearly evoke a Southern perspective and which don't—and then, why and why not, which are more effective, and so on.

Students generally respond well to Warren's poetry, particularly to that in which the persona struggles with problems of identity and meaning. The poetry selected here is quite varied, so questions arise about continuities/discontinuities in terms of subject matter and poetic vision between the poems, and about the different stanza forms and the lines employed by the poet. Warren's depiction of the natural world—the hawk, for instance—is quite striking, and students like to discuss this aspect of his work.

Major Themes, Historical Perspectives, Personal Issues

1. The self in the world, particularly one's relationship with nature
2. The meaning and significance of history
3. The limits of the creative imagination and human knowledge
4. The quest for meaning in continuities and in the assimilation of the self with the world outside it

Significant Form, Style, or Artistic Conventions

Topics for questions might include the significance of narrative and the dramatic in Warren's verse; the effectiveness of a diction that frequently tends toward the colloquial; the contrast between Warren's narrative verse ("Amazing Grace in the Back Country") and his poetry of statement ("Fear and Trembling"); the role of the persona; and the form of Warren's verse, including stanza and line.

Original Audience

In "Infant Boy at Midcentury," one might discuss what was happening (and had just happened) in the world at midcentury, particularly in light of and in contrast to Warren's traditional upbringing and sympathies.

Comparisons, Contrasts, Connections

Three Southern poets with similar interests come to mind: John Crowe Ransom, whose verse is more formal and controlled than Warren's; Allen Tate, who explores in his poetry the tensions arising from problems of history, time, and identity; and James Dickey, whose verse is strongly narrative. In addition, look at any of the confessional poets, but particularly Robert Lowell; a comparison with them is fruitful in trying to establish whether Warren's poetry should be read as confessional.

Bibliography

Bedient, Calvin. *In The Heart's Last Kingdom: Robert Penn Warren's Major Poetry.* Chapter 2, "His Mature Manner."

Bloom, Harold. "Sunset Hawk: Warren's Poetry and Tradition." *A Southern Renascence Man: Views of Robert Penn Warren.* Ed. Walter B. Edgar.

Justus, James. *The Achievement of Robert Penn Warren.* Sec. 1, "Warren the Poet."

Strandberg, Victor. "Introduction: The Critical Reckoning." *The Poetic Vision of Robert Penn Warren.*

John Crowe Ransom (1888–1974)

Contributing Editor: Martha E. Cook

Classroom Issues and Strategies

Focusing on Ransom's use of language, his wit and irony, seems to be the best route to exploring his themes on a level that students will respond to. Moving from the particular to the universal works even for the poems that seem to be fairly abstract; certainly the theme of "The Equilibrists" is one that students can react to once they have discovered or uncovered it. Using the kind of close analysis practiced by the New Critics is invaluable in studying Ransom's poetry.

Reading Ransom's poetry aloud is a very good strategy since reading aloud reveals of lot of the liveliness that students sometimes miss on the printed page and also illuminates the ironic tone.

Students seem to be interested in the themes of transience and mutability and in the dichotomy of the body and the soul. They also sometimes get involved with Ransom's work by following up allusions to myths and legends.

Major Themes, Historical Perspectives, Personal Issues

Themes: tradition, ritual, myth; mutability; the transience of life and love; death; the dichotomy of body and soul.

Historical issues: Ransom's relationship to the Fugitive group and the little magazine, *The Fugitive*; Ransom as a New Critic; the relationship of a classical education to modernism in poetry; the 1920s and reaction to the great war.

Personal issues: Ransom's life as a teacher and editor, his experience as a Rhodes scholar and as a soldier in the war, his strong classical education.

Significant Form, Style, or Artistic Conventions

Ransom is so closely related to the metaphysical poets whom he knew so thoroughly that exploring this aspect of his style and form is particularly useful, as is any consideration of his juxtaposition of different levels of diction and his use of surprising words or word forms. Strong emphasis on diction can occur particularly when students have access to the *OED* online. He can be seen in the context of the Southern Renaissance of the 1920s or specifically as part of the Fugitive movement, primarily in his concern with tradition and traditional values, though not in his use of Southern objects. As one of the New Critics, his critical theories are important both for their own value and as they provide an avenue into the poetry. Howard's 1988 *Yale Review* essay gives a fascinating description of Ransom's teaching methods in a prosody course.

Original Audience

A different approach to Ransom that I have found invaluable is to place him in the context of the outpouring of literature in the 1920s and to relate his views of the world after the war to those of Ernest Hemingway, William Faulkner, John

Dos Passos, and others. The Fugitives are often seen as a group unrelated to other writers in the 1920s, but especially Ransom's European experiences can be compared with those of his contemporaries.

Comparisons, Contrasts, Connections

Ransom can be productively compared with other Fugitive poets, especially with Allen Tate in his wit and irony; with metaphysical poets, both early and modern; with the tradition of the elegy; and with other writers who explore the same subject matter, for example, "Philomela" with *The Waste Land*.

Questions for Reading, Discussion, and Writing

1. I tell students to be sure to look up the definitions of any unfamiliar words, and I also mention particular works we have already read that might be relevant, such as other poems on death, war, love, and so on. Usually Eliot would precede Ransom or immediately follow, so I might warn students to watch for parallels and contrasts.
2. Specifically, students usually do best with Ransom when they focus on his use of language. In general, I find it useful to have students draft their own ideas, using support from the particular work, before they go to outside sources for a historical context or other critics' views.

Bibliography

Howard, Maureen, "There Are Many Wonderful Owls in Gambier." *Yale Review* 77 (Summer 1988): 521–27.

Morton, Claire C. "Ransom's 'The Equilibrists.'" *Explicator* 41 (Summer 1983): 37–38.

Pratt, William. "In Pursuit of the Fugitives." *The Fugitive Poets*. New York: Dutton, 1965. 13–46.

Quinlan, Kieran. *John Crowe Ransom's Secular Faith*. Baton Rouge: Louisiana State UP, 1989.

Rubin, Louis D., Jr. "John Crowe Ransom: The Wary Fugitive." *The Wary Fugitives: Four Poets and the South*. Baton Rouge: Louisiana State UP, 1978. 1–68.

Tate, Allen. "Gentleman in a Dustcoat." *Sewanee Review* 76 (Summer 1968): 375–81.

Tillinghast, Richard. "John Crowe Ransom: Tennessee's Major Minor Poet." *New Criterion* 15.6 (Feb. 1997): 24–30.

Young, Thomas D. "The Fugitives: Ransom, Davidson, Tate." *The History of Southern Literature*. Ed. Louis D. Rubin Jr. et al. Baton Rouge: Louisiana State UP, 1985. 319–32.

Allen Tate (1899–1979)

Contributing Editor: Anne Jones

Classroom Issues and Strategies

It may be difficult to get students without some personal investment in/against the Confederacy or at least the American South to respond initially at all to a poem that presumes the identification of classical heroism with Confederate soldiery. Watching a segment from Ken Burns's popular PBS series *The Civil War*, which made much of the lives of ordinary soldiers from both sides, might help to get past initial alienation; so might a discussion of the place of the American South in contemporary ideology, especially in popular culture.

Major Themes, Historical Perspectives, Personal Issues

Tate described in his essay "Narcissus as Narcissus" what he conceived to be the major themes of "Ode to the Confederate Dead": the conflict between a vanished heroic community of "active faith" and the anomie of contemporary reductionism and isolation. These themes will be familiar to students, especially those who have read T. S. Eliot and other conservative modernists. Tate represents the conflict as taking place within the consciousness of a man standing alone at a Confederate graveyard; the conflict thus is reshaped as a problem for the imagination. What can this man's (the poet's?) imagination take hold of and how? How, in fact, does the imagination work? Tate looked first to Southern history and later to the Catholic church for answers. One might ask students, with Gertrude Stein, what is the question? This might encourage looking beyond Tate's own representations to other ways of framing the issues he is engaged in.

Significant Form, Style, or Artistic Conventions

Tate has compared (albeit self-disparagingly) the poem's structure to that of a Greek ode; he pays particular attention to questions of rhyme and rhythm. In short, he emphasizes poetic traditions. Yet he claims that the absence of these traditions is what shapes the "modern" side of the conflict in the protagonist's mind. Is Tate's understanding of his own formal and stylistic effects, his use and rejection of convention, adequate?

Original Audience

Tate worked on the first version of "Ode" during the winter of 1925, living in New York with his wife Caroline Gordon and, for a time, in a cramped apartment, with Hart Crane. That draft (the 1937 revision is not very severe) was published in the last collaboration of the Fugitives as a group, *Fugitives, an Anthology of Verse* (1928). It won him considerable national fame, which (in the words of Radcliffe Squires) he "took with him to Europe" on a Guggenheim fellowship in 1928. The "Ode" has remained his best-known poem, though he is no longer thought of as the national figure he once was. Why not?

Comparisons, Contrasts, Connections

T. S. Eliot's themes and images, especially in "The Waste Land" and "The Love Song of J. Alfred Prufrock," are rather clear influences on Tate's perhaps even more somber poem. Both Hart Crane and Wallace Stevens might well be read with Tate. And, of course, Tate's historical connections with the Fugitives, Agrarians, and New Critics—among them John Crowe Ransom, Robert Penn Warren, and Cleanth Brooks—provide a more regional and ideological context.

Charles Reznikoff (1894–1976)

Contributing Editor: Randy Chilton

Classroom Issues and Strategies

Reznikoff's verse offers many points of departure for study and class discussion. His images of contemporary urban scenes and characters remind us of the way William Carlos Williams transformed the "local" into poetry; his use of legal testimony and primary historical documents points to questions about the way poetry and history can intersect and interact. Moreover, Reznikoff (as well as Louis Zukofsky) emerged from the immigrant Jewish culture of New York City—both, like Williams, were first-generation Americans—and so questions of cultural identity, assimilation and resistance to it, and the attendant questions of identity politics are appropriate in approaching these poems, too. But if your students are interested in and ready for a discussion of the formal elements Zukofsky found in Reznikoff, you might have them look at Zukofsky's original essay, "Sincerity and Objectification: With Special Reference to the Poetry of Charles Reznikoff," reprinted in *Charles Reznikoff: Man and Poet*, or the edited version in Zukofsky's collected essays, *Prepositions*.

Major Themes, Historical Perspectives, Personal Issues

In the context of literary history, objectivist poetry, collected for and published in *Poetry* magazine at the encouragement of Ezra Pound, was a direct descendent of imagist verse (imagist verse before 1915, that is—the kind that Pound, not Amy Lowell, promoted). Zukofsky's reservations about objectivism as an *"ism"* grew out of the development of modern art forms and the movements associated with them such as futurism, dadaism, surrealism, cubism, and so on, over the previous twenty years or so. (In New York City, there was also the Yiddish-language "Inzikhist" ["Introspectivist"] group.) By 1931, literary avant-gardism had declined, in part because of the Depression, in part because of the diversity of literary modernism (or modernisms), among other reasons. Zukofsky was not interested in trying to break from the past so much as he was trying to find what was of genuine value within the broad spectrum of contemporary literary production. In Reznikoff's work, readers will see many short, imagist-like poems that make use of direct, unornamented language as well as somewhat experimental forms. But Zukofsky's idea that a poem could be a kind of "object" was not quite the same as Pound's call for "direct treatment of the thing, whether subjective or objective" or Williams's call for "No ideas but in things." Students might consider how by contrasting, say, "In a Station of the Metro" and "The Red Wheelbarrow" with "Aphrodite Urania" and "Hellenist."

Moreover, for both Zukofsky and Reznikoff, the place of the poem in history was an important concern. On a very rudimentary level, Reznikoff's imagistic observations of New York City street scenes can be considered "historical," but a class discussion of legal testimony and primary historical documents as material for poetry might lead to more serious questions about the ways in which history can be poetry and vice versa, and ways in which history and poetry involve the act of seeing. The vignette of the shoemaker is also quite typical of Reznikoff's early work and might be contextualized with a study of the complex diasporic Jewish communities in New York City at the beginning of the twentieth century.

Significant Form, Style, or Artistic Conventions

Issues of poetic form were very important to Zukofsky. First, regarding "sincerity," he said not only that it involved "thinking with the things as they exist" but also that it was a quality of language in which "shapes appear concomitants of word combinations." He remained convinced as late as the sixties that the sounds of words were connected in some way to their referents ("something must have led the Greeks to say *hudor* and . . . us to say *water*," he said in the 1968 interview). "Aphrodite Urania," as his best example of "sincere" language, is worth reading out loud with this in mind, and worth having your students read out loud. Have them look as well for words in other selections that are evocative in their sounds. As part of your discussion of "sincerity," you might also have your students notice the way in which Reznikoff can at times use repetition as a gesture that underscores a visual or aural image: "semicircles of spray, semicircles of spray."

Zukofsky's idea of "objectification" concerned the unity of form: it involved a "completed structure of relations," a "rested totality," in Zukofsky's phrases. If you want to explore the objectivist poetic with your students, Zukofsky's example of Reznikoff's "Hellenist" as an example of "objectification" is probably the best place to start. Ask your students what kinds of "relations" Zukofsky might have been looking at in the poem (in terms of rhythm and line length as well as "content," or the speaker's evolving understanding of Athena). In what sense do these relations form a "completed structure"?

Original Audience

By the late twenties, Ezra Pound and T. S. Eliot as well as sympathizers such as Sylvia Beach had been hard at work for some years cultivating an audience for experimental modernist literary expressions. However, Zukofsky was never very successful at appealing to that audience and received relatively little attention even from the academic world until the sixties. Reznikoff in the twenties turned to self-publishing. But the objectivists were interested as a group in getting one another into print. After the objectivists issue of *Poetry*, TO Publishers was formed with the support of George Oppen (a contributor to the issue) and his wife Mary, and then its successor, the Objectivist Press, put out a few books, including Williams's *Collected Poems, 1921–31*, and Reznikoff's original prose version of *Testimony*. Have your students consider the question of the relation between poetry and its readers—of the way poetry (especially new or previously unread poetry) both presumes and shapes an audience. Does writing poetry in a democracy necessarily mean writing poetry that can be understood by everyone? Is there a place for poetry at all in times like the Depression? (George Oppen thought not and put down his pen for almost thirty years.)

Comparisons, Contrasts, Connections

Pound, Williams, and H.D. are obvious predecessors. Have students compare short verse that is provided in the anthology or that you provide. Reznikoff's own poetic was relatively inexplicit, but in some of the few statements we do have, he cites Eliot's objective correlative as a useful concept. Students may find a helpful comparison here. Eliot's urban imagery can also be compared and contrasted with Reznikoff's.

For an idea of the cultural milieu from which Zukofsky and Reznikoff emerged, see the section from Michael Gold's *Jews Without Money* in the anthology. Students might also read in Henry Roth's *Call It Sleep*.

Working With Cultural Objects

Photos of Reznikoff, reproductions of original dust jackets, and information about the historical context for Reznikoff's poetry can be found at the *Modern American Poetry* website devoted to Reznikoff at <http://www.english.uiuc.edu/maps/poets/m_r/reznikoff/reznikoff.htm>.

Questions for Reading and Discussion/Approaches to Writing

In addition to the suggestions for discussion previously mentioned, instructors might find the following questions useful.

1. Does "Aphrodite Urania" *really* sound like the image it describes?
2. In what sense has Reznikoff made accounts by Holocaust survivors, legal testimony, and/or John Smith's description of his experience in Virginia "poetic," if he has? In what sense does this poetry constitute "history"? If students can locate any primary documents (for example, in the *State Reporter* series in a law library), a comparison with Reznikoff's poetic versions could be instructive.
3. If you are courageous, you might help students interrogate the notion of what it meant to be Jewish and American and a poet in the 1920s, a potentially frightful time for almost anyone in America who was not a white Anglo-Saxon Protestant male.

Bibliography

Students will find many useful articles in the journal *Sagetrieb*, which publishes work on poets in the "Pound–H.D.–Williams tradition." See also the following:

On Objectivists:

Contemporary Literature 10 (1969). Interviews with Zukofsky, Reznikoff, George Oppen, and Carl Rakosi.

du Plessis, Rachel B., and Peter Quartermain, eds. *The Objectivist Nexus: Essays in Cultural Poetics*. Tuscaloosa: U of Alabama P, 1999.

Giorcelli, Cristina, ed. "'The Idea' and 'The Thing' in Modernist American Poetry, 2001." Spec. issue of *Shofar* 21.1 (2002).

Heller, Michael. *Conviction's Net of Branches: Essays on the Objectivist Poets and Poetry*. Carbondale: Southern Illinois UP, 1985.

Perloff, Marjorie. "'Barbed-Wire Entanglements': The 'New American Poetry,' 1930–32." *Modernism/Modernity* 2.1 (1995).

Sharp, Tom. "Objectivists" 1927–1934: A Critical History of the Work and Association of Louis Zukofsky, William Carlos Williams, Charles Reznikoff, Carl Rakosi, Ezra Pound, George Oppen. Diss., 1982.

On Charles Reznikoff

Finklestein, Norman. *Not One of Them in Place: Modern Poetry and Jewish American Identity*. Albany: State U of New York P, 2001.

Fredman, Stephen. *A Menorah for Athena: Charles Reznikoff and the Jewish Dilemmas of Objectivist Poetry*. Chicago: U of Chicago P, 2001.

Hindus, Milton, ed. *Charles Reznikoff: Man and Poet*. National Poetry Foundation. Dartmouth: UP of New England, 1984.

Kenner, Hugh. *A Homemade World: the American Modernist Writers*. New York: Knopf, 1974.

Quartermain, Peter. *Disjunctive Poetics: From Gertrude Stein and Louis Zukofsky to Susan Howe*. Cambridge, UK, and New York: Cambridge UP, 1992.

Scroggins, Mark. *Louis Zukofsky and the Poetry of Knowledge*. Tuscaloosa: U of Alabama P, 1998.

Scroggins, Mark, ed. *Upper Limit Music: The Writing of Louis Zukofsky*. Tuscaloosa: U of Alabama P, 1997.

John Steinbeck (1902–1968)

Contributing Editor: Cliff Lewis

Classroom Issues and Strategies

Students read Steinbeck as a social critic and as a storyteller. The task is to define Steinbeck as a writer in the mode of the twenties who carried these tendencies into his works of social conflict. One must define such terms as *illusion, myth, archetype, depth psychology,* and *symbol* in establishing his link with those writing of individualism. It should be easy to show that Elisa in "The Chrysanthemums" reflects Steinbeck's interest in the power of illusion, the unconscious, and its conflict with masculine authority. You may comment that changed conditions allow Ma Joad to succeed where Elisa failed. To understand Steinbeck better, it might be useful to have students list such detail as setting, weather, and clothing, all of which reflect the inner lives of his characters.

To have students understand the opening of the novel, I recommend that you show them Pare Lorentz's documentary film *The Plow That Broke the Plains.* It, like the novel, champions the intervention of FDR in the Dust Bowl disaster. See Steinbeck's letters to Joseph Henry Jackson written around 1938 that describe the archetypal nature of the Joads' quest. Also, you might want to cite relevant passages to chapters 1 and 5 from the daily journal Steinbeck kept (DeMott's *Working Days*) writing *Grapes.*

In teaching chapter 5 one can compare the "downsizing" of today with circumstances then. Observe the causes for collapse: bad farming, quick profits. And point out that the economic system is one man created, one that man can change. To that end the Joads question and pursue their trek.

Try to show Steinbeck's pattern as the artist who first uses writing to dramatize the various drives—first of the individual and then of the group; sexual and religious drives; drives for acceptance and security; and then drives for land, cultural identity, and democratic rights.

Major Themes, Historical Perspectives, Personal Issues

Change underlies all of Steinbeck's writing: individual or group efforts to make it happen or individual and group efforts to resist changes. The question scholars debate is to what extent Steinbeck's characters are influenced by the biological and psychological memories and by cultural training. Often these provide the conflict for the individual will. To alter the world is essentially human, and Americans for Steinbeck are best at it. Certainly, the Joads must first overcome their own psychological and cultural resistance. Often a mythic Eden brings war. Making his audience aware of these hidden drives is one of Steinbeck's missions. *Grapes,* for instance, retains its power because Steinbeck made it clear that mankind will not accept poverty or repression but will fight or migrate to escape both. Certainly, this is true psychologically. His historical perspective is holistic—ecological today—with humans connected biologically and culturally to the past and using human will to blend past and present. (See my essay on Steinbeck's political commitments in *After the Grapes of Wrath.*)

Significant Form, Style, or Artistic Conventions

Steinbeck tried to find an organic means of expression for each book that he wrote. He considered his work to be experimental. He intentionally used a documentary style for *The Grapes of Wrath,* the fabular for *The Pearl,* the picaresque for *Tortilla Flat,* and so on. Generally, he belongs to the myth-symbol school of the twenties. Dreams, the unconscious, recurring myths, symbolic characters—these qualities are characteristic of what Jung called the "visionary" style. Realism, Steinbeck once noted, is the surface form for his interest in psychology and philosophy. To this *The Grapes of Wrath* is no exception. Finally, point out that Steinbeck's work included film scripts, plays, political speeches, and war propaganda.

Original Audience

Steinbeck's earliest writings, whose subject was the individual psyche, sold poorly. With his fifth book, the picaresque *Tortilla Flat,* Steinbeck became a popular writer, and with *In Dubious Battle* and *The Grapes of Wrath,* novels rooted in the issues of the Depression, Steinbeck achieved international fame. Before those publications, his West Coast audience did not comprehend his direction. For most he was a "mystic" writer, and for Edmund Wilson, Steinbeck was writing "biological" stories. It may be this lack of comprehension that led him to insert characters into his novels who commented on the significance of the action. The one reviewer who saw Steinbeck's literary subject as the "unconscious" received a note from Steinbeck thanking him for the insightful review.

Comparisons, Contrasts, Connections

The personal influence of Ed Ricketts and his biological and psychological ideas influenced and somewhat paralleled Steinbeck's own, and one can see a great deal of Darwin's influence in Steinbeck. That Eliot's *The Waste Land* and Dos Passos's *U.S.A.* influenced *Grapes* is evident. It is probable that Silko's *Ceremony* owes a debt to Steinbeck. Very likely, however, Steinbeck's connections have been felt outside of literature to a greater degree. From the 1940s to his death, he was an icon to the Democratic Party and a world symbol of human rights.

Questions for Reading, Discussion, and Writing

"The Chrysanthemums":

1. What are the boundaries of air and land limiting Elisa?
2. What is she capable of?
3. What about the stranger attracts her?
4. What does he want from her?
5. Is he happy?
6. What is she trying to scrub away?
7. What does she settle for?
8. Has she any illusions left?
9. Connect her relationship to the land with chapter 5.
10. Are there any archetypal, biological, or mythic allusions?

Chapter 1:

1. Contrast women and men.
2. Why are women stronger here?
3. What cultural pattern is the male losing?
4. What is the implication that the men will eventually overcome the cultural shock? Note: It continues to the end of the novel.

Chapter 5:

1. Is the chapter denouncing laissez-faire capitalism?
2. Is the farmer also at fault?
3. How does the farmer defend his ownership of the land?
4. What is the significance of moving from "hands-on" farming to factories in the field?
5. Did a book by that name influence Steinbeck?
6. What became of the Joads? See Gregory's *American Exodus* (New York: Oxford, 1989) to find out who went, who stayed, and what happened.
7. Can any link be made to the size and number of farms in America today to the novel? to plant downsizing?

8. Is the loss of individual enterprises today so different from what happened to the Joads?

Bibliography

Two *Steinbeck Study Guides,* edited by T. Hayashi, have good general information on Steinbeck's writings. P. Lisca's updated *Wide World of John Steinbeck* remains a valuable study. For short story analysis, see J. Hughes, *John Steinbeck, A Study of the Short Fiction,* 1989; J. Timmerman, *The Dramatic Landscape of Steinbeck's Short Stories,* 1990; and Jay Parini's 1994 study. For the novel, Robert DeMott's edition of *Working Days,* 1989, is essential. Critical essays include R. Davis, ed., 1982; J. Ditsky, ed., 1989; D. Wyatt, ed., 1990; H. Bloom, ed., 1996; and D. Coers et al., eds., *After the Grapes of Wrath,* 1995, for my essay on Steinbeck's relationship with the New Deal.

Richard Wright (1908–1960)

Contributing Editor: John M. Reilly

Classroom Issues and Strategies

Among sympathetic readers, there is an assumption that Wright is documentary, that his works can be read as elementary sociology. If these readers are familiar with literary movements, they also assume he can be classed as a naturalistic author displaying the experience of victims. Readers of a negative disposition are inclined to class Wright as an exponent of hate, an unreasonable writer who is not sensitive to the complexities of moral experience.

As with all of his writings, understanding of Richard Wright's "Bright and Morning Star" will be enhanced if students know something about his revisions. In this case, revisions amounted to the addition of this short story to a highly successful collection of narratives about Southern life informed by Wright's political outlook.

The first edition of *Uncle Tom's Children: Four Novellas* won first prize in a national contest sponsored by *Story* magazine in 1938 for writers employed in the Federal Writers Project who had not previously published a book. The well-known judges for the contest, which garnered more than five hundred entries, were Lewis Gannett, who conducted a regular book column at the time in the *New York Herald Tribune;* Harry Scherman of the Book-of-the-Month Club; and novelist Sinclair Lewis, winner of the Nobel Prize for Literature in

1930. Contest victory included both a cash prize and publication of the winning volume by Harper's. Reviews praised the judges' choice and heightened its significance by comparing Wright's newly discovered talent to that of canonical American authors such as Stephen Crane (the opinion of the anonymous reviewer in *Time*) and Ernest Hemingway (the view of Robert Van Gelder in the *New York Times Book Review*).

Some reviewers recognized that the stories in the original volume were arranged to argue for collective political action, but one notable review, that of Alan Calmer in the *Daily Worker*, larded its approval with the observation that the book lacked sufficient social perspective. As though in response to this comment in the Communist Party newspaper, Wright prepared a second edition to the volume, which now carried a new subtitle: *Five Long Short Stories*. Leading off the new book was the sketch entitled "The Ethics of Living Jim Crow," which had earlier appeared in *American Stuff: An Anthology of Prose and Verse by Members of the Federal Writers' Project* (1937); and to conclude it, Wright added the short story "Bright and Morning Star," originally published in May 1938 in the left-wing journal *New Masses*. Where the protagonists of the original stories in *Uncle Tom's Children* struggled to choose ways to confront caste oppression, Sue, the hero of "Bright and Morning Star" has gone beyond that because she and her children have committed themselves to working for social revolution. Wright's new edition of his first book thus became a unified work progressing from the autobiographical episodes in "The Ethics of Living Jim Crow" through four narratives relating the oppression of male protagonists and concluding with the triumphant rendering of a woman who revolutionizes the traditional role of matriarch.

Major Themes, Historical Perspectives, Personal Issues

Focus on point of view is helpful for drawing attention to the interest Wright has in social psychology, which dramatizes in narrative the consciousness of a character at the crossroads of social forces (race, class) and personal impulses and self-creation. Wright is dedicated to study of the production of personality and the arousal of a self-directive being. This, after all, is the substance of African-American history: how oppressed people create a world, a culture, and remake personalities the dominant group seeks to eradicate.

Significant Form, Style, or Artistic Conventions

The challenge is to describe "protest" literature as a repudiation of the dominant discourse on race without allowing readers to believe that rejection of the dominant literary styles is to become nonliterary. Wright should be seen as a major voice of African-American modernism (see the emphasis on the black self, the effort in his work to found a subjectivity). That's his literary period. His school may well be called protest. But the selection in the anthology requires attention to the language of symbolism—the charged objects and language of racial discourse.

Original Audience

Richard Wright tried to address a dual audience, but the responses by white and black readers were distinct. Writing in the daily *New York Times,* Charles Poore tempered his praise of *Uncle Tom's Children* by declaring that Wright "has merely shifted a bad process by making nearly all the white characters villains. That heightens the drama and the melodrama. But it plays havoc with plausibility" (2 April 1938). On the other hand, Sterling A. Brown, the distinguished African-American poet, wrote in *The Nation,* "[T]he South that Mr. Wright renders so vividly is recognizable and true, and it has not often been within the covers of a book." What made Brown's the most informed review the book received was the assertion that characters are seen from the inside and are, therefore, truer than the stereotypes populating the farces and pastorals of fiction influenced by unacknowledged Confederate sympathies. Despite these evident differences of perception among reviewers, "Bright and Morning Star" secured an appreciative audience for its craft. It was an O'Henry prize–winning story in 1938, and in 1939, Edward J. O'Brien included it along with stories by Ernest Hemingway, Theodore Dreiser, William Faulkner, Sherwood Anderson, F. Scott Fitzgerald, and Thomas Wolfe in *50 Best American Short Stories, 1915–1939.*

Comparisons, Contrasts, Connections

In its depiction of the self-realization of Sue, Wright's story provides a strong contrast to the treatment of "primitive" characters in European American Modernism. Her ethical reasoning and action presents a complexity undreamed of by those who saw the Negro as precivilized. Sue also allows for contrast with the figures in naturalism, including Theodore Dreiser's female victims. Connections might be explored by linking the political epiphany in "Bright and Morning Star" to that in Clifford Odet's "Waiting for Lefty." As a contribution to understanding the variety within African-American literature, Wright's short story can be juxtaposed with the selections by Booker T. Washington, Langston Hughes, and Zora Neale Hurston. It can be pointed out to students that Hurston interpreted *Uncle Tom's Children* as Communist propaganda: "state responsibility for everything, and individual responsibility for nothing."

Questions for Reading, Discussion, and Writing

1. Consider the place of violence in the story, its use as social control by exponents of the caste system, and its apparently inevitable necessity for liberation. On one level, that of relating the system of racial segregation, the appearance of violence is historically authentic. As an instrument for freedom, however, violence is at odds with the tactics of the civil rights movement. Is this simply a matter of different historical times, different politics, or could violence be inherent in Wright's worldview?
2. What is Wright's view of African-American culture in this story, its efficacy, and its value in delineating character? In this regard consider the imagery of resurrection and the "conversion" of Sue.
3. In what sense might Sue's death relate her story to the genre of tragedy?
4. What does the term *race* denominate in this story? Is it a fixed, biological category signifying essential qualities of a person, or is "race" a social construction?

Bibliography

Davis, Charles T., and Michel Fabre. *Richard Wright: A Primary Bibliography*. Boston: Hall, 1982. Information on editions and first publications.

Fabre, Michel. *The Unfinished Quest of Richard Wright*. New York: Morrow, 1973. Standard biography.

Joyce, Joyce A. *Richard Wright's Art of Tragedy*. Iowa City: U of Iowa P, 1986.

Reilly, John M., ed. *Richard Wright: The Critical Reception*. New York: Franklin, 1978.

Margaret Walker (1915–1998)

Contributing Editor: Maryemma Graham

Classroom Issues and Strategies

When she won a major award (the Yale Younger Poets Award), Walker was put in the public eye, but her writing always had a public dimension to it. Students might want to explore the pressures a writer would face if he or she were called upon to speak from more than a singular perspective. Can general experience form an urgent literary message? Can the students detect any change in Walker's style from that of the earlier poems and those published in the 1980s?

In the language of her novel, *Jubilee,* the rhetoric is shaped in part by a need to be informative about a subject that many people had never explored or even considered. In her poems, the use of "public" forms of expression—chants, litanies, and sermons—to generate structure as well as feeling should be explored and compared/ contrasted with the novel.

Major Themes, Historical Perspectives, Personal Issues

Freedom—in all its simplicity and complexity—is clearly the main subject of Walker's work. Much of her writing is informed by the experience of the Great Depression (she was fourteen years old when the stock market collapsed), and so racial freedom and economic freedom are intermingled in her consciousness. In some ways, the promise of post–Reconstruction political freedom for African Americans (and equally important, the nonfulfillment of that promise) stands behind her "call" to both the future and the past. The concern with hope and tradition—neither being ultimately satisfying by itself, but both being indispensable for a full consciousness of the story of her people—is a personal focus as well as a subject matter she must engage.

Significant Form, Style, or Artistic Conventions

Clearly, the poetry uses forms drawn from sermons and chants, the so-called "folk" tradition. Yet Walker was an educated, trained writer who spent years perfecting her craft. Students should be encouraged to examine precisely how the poetic structures are adapted and where they are altered in the expression of a more "modern" consciousness.

The novel should be compared to the various slave narratives, some of which are available in *The Heath Anthology*, providing a useful contrast between "first-person" and "third-person" narrative frameworks. Also, the poems and the novel both can be read in the context of Booker T. Washington and W. E. B. Du Bois. Here especially the theme of balancing the acknowledgment of past oppression and future hope can be fruitfully unfolded.

Questions for Reading, Discussion, and Writing

1. Does the passage from the novel read exactly like a newspaper account, or what is sometimes called "feature journalism"? If not, where does it most differ?

2. What effect is created by using specific names in the poems when the "general" context of the poem's language is so dominant?
3. Look at Langston Hughes's poetry and compare his use of rhythms and idioms with that of Walker.

Saunders Redding (1906–1988)

Contributing Editor: Eleanor Q. Tignor

Classroom Issues and Strategies

Since for about fifty years as a prolific author on the African-American experience Redding brought to his writings a personal voice, a learned racial and cultural perspective, and an analytical critique of American history in relationship to the Negro/black/African-American experience, he is easily teachable. *No Day of Triumph*, an autobiographical text, combines all of these elements, as can be observed in chapter 1.

One might also make linkages between him and a long range of other black writers and then move from that approach to teach Redding as an African-American literary critic.

Major Themes, Historical Perspectives, Personal Issues

1. The black American's double consciousness—being black and being American; its effect on self-development and on relations with others, black and white.
2. The role of the family (family philosophy and patterns, goals and values) in shaping offspring—the nurturing but also sometimes the hindrances.
3. Slavery and its effects on blacks—on personal development and behavior, on family life in the next generation and generations to come.
4. Slavery and its effects on whites, especially the master/slave "relationship."
5. The tragic mulatto—caught between being black and (not) being white.
6. Intraracial skin color consciousness and conflict.
7. The educated Negro and the "Negro burden": extraordinary responsibility "to uphold the race"; related theme—having to be better than whites in order to succeed.
8. The hold of religion on blacks, especially poorer blacks.

9. The black American folk past and its vestiges, especially its effects on blacks of little education.
10. The author as family member and individualist; as man of reason and humanist.

Significant Form, Style, or Artistic Conventions

1. The effects of a text that merges personal social history.
2. Objectivity versus subjectivity in this highly personal text.
3. Passionate tone and satirical humor.
4. Precise language.
5. Influence of the thinking of W. E. B. Du Bois (see especially *The Souls of Black Folk*); anti–Booker T. Washington philosophy (see Du Bois's *The Souls of Black Folk* and Washington's *Up from Slavery*).
6. Writing as catharsis (see the rest of *No Day of Triumph* and especially *On Being Negro in America*).
7. Skill in blending exposition, dialogue, and anecdote in the creation of a highly readable text.
8. Incorporation of black folk materials (songs, tales, prayers).

Original Audience

In 1942, most black Americans and other Americans who knew and were sensitive to the conditions of slavery and the post-slavery years would have had no difficulty with Redding's thesis and tone. The history may need to be sketched in for present-day students; skin color consciousness and the history of the slave and the free black must be understood to get the impact of each of the grandmothers on Redding, the boy.

Comparisons, Contrasts, Connections

1. Du Bois's *Souls of Black Folk* (1903) should be a major comparison. See Du Bois's chapter on Booker T. Washington (III: "Of Mr. Booker T. Washington and Others," in *Souls of Black Folk*) and Washington's *Up from Slavery*.
2. For the theme of being black in America, also highly personal as well as social responses, see for comparison: Richard Wright's "The Ethics of Living Jim Crow" (in Richard Wright's *Uncle Tom's Children*); James Baldwin's "The Discovery of What It Means to Be an American" and "Nobody Knows My Name: A Letter from the South" (both essays in

Baldwin's *Nobody Knows My Name*); Maya Angelou's *I Know Why the Caged Bird Sings*.

3. For facts and commentary on slavery, see Redding's *They Came in Chains*, as well as any slave narratives taught in the course.

4. For an understanding of the stereotyping of the mulatto and other black stereotypes in American literature, see Sterling A. Brown's "Negro Character as Seen by White Authors," *Journal of Negro Education* 2 (1933), reprinted in *Dark Symphony*, ed. James A. Emanuel and Theodore Gross (New York: Free, 1968).

5. For autobiographical comparison/contrast with other black boys who became famous men, see Richard Wright's *Black Boy* and Langston Hughes's *The Big Sea* (Part I, chapters 2–16).

Questions for Reading, Discussion, and Writing

1. State your impressions of the Redding daily household. Support your impressions, explaining how you arrived at them.

2. State and explain the tone of Redding's opening to the chapter, prior to his introduction of Grandma Redding.

3. Contrast Grandma Redding and Grandma Conway as they appeared to Saunders Redding, the boy.

4. Does Redding, the man, in retrospect, admire either grandmother, neither, or one more than the other? Explain.

5. Through their different manners of death and Redding's description of each death, what is implied about each of the grandmothers?

6. Who in the chapter is "troubled in mind"? Give your analysis.

7. Using Redding's style of writing as a model, write an analysis of your own "roots."

Bibliography

Baraka, Imamu A. "A Reply to Saunders Redding's 'The Black Revolution in American Studies.'" *Sources for American Studies*. Ed. Jefferson B. Kellogg and Robert H. Walker. Westport: Greenwood, 1983.

Berry, Faith, ed. Introduction. *A Scholar's Conscience: Selected Writings of J. Saunders Redding, 1942–1977*. Lexington: UP of Kentucky, 1992. 1–14.

Berry, Faith. "Saunders Redding as Literary Critic of Langston Hughes." *Langston Hughes Review* 5 (1986): 24–28.

Kellogg, Jefferson B. "Redding and Baraka: Two Contrasting Views on Afro-American Studies." *Sources for American Studies.* Ed. Jefferson B. Kellogg and Robert H. Walker. Westport: Greenwood, 1983.

Thompson, Thelma B. "Romantic Idealists and Conforming Materialists: Expressions of the American National Character." *MAWA Review* 3 (June 1988): 6–9.

Vassilowitch, John, Jr. "Ellison's Dr. Bledsoe: Two Literary Sources." *Essays in Literature* 8 (Spring 1981): 109–13.

Pietro Di Donato (1911–1992)

Contributing Editor: Helen Barolini

Classroom Issues and Strategies

The lack of perception of Italian-American authors as literary and the general lack of knowledge concerning the body of Italian-American writing is an obstacle to be overcome. In particular with Di Donato's classic work, *Christ in Concrete,* there is the question of linguistic uniqueness—a result of transposing Italian thought forms into English. This lends richness and texture to the work, but must be explained.

The Italian-American author and his or her work can be examined in terms of the general theme of the outsider and can be related to authors of other groups, bridging the narrow ethnic theme to the more general one. Students are interested in issues of workers' exploitation, what impels immigrants toward the American dream, and what the country was like seventy-five years ago as compared with today.

The language can be dealt with by showing how language forms thought patterns, and so viewpoints. However, beneath the uniqueness lies the same human feelings and their expression.

There is a film version of *Christ in Concrete* that could be useful to promote classroom discussion.

Major Themes, Historical Perspectives, Personal Issues

Di Donato's *Christ in Concrete* is an achievement in giving literary form to the oral culture of the immigrant peasant transformed into urban worker. His is a prime example of the proletarian novel of the 1930s.

Significant Form, Style, or Artistic Conventions

Di Donato created an American language that accommodated the oral culture of his protagonists, a language that reflects the texture of the peasant-worker discourse. It is important to note that dignity and intelligence are not the social prerogatives of the more articulate social group.

Original Audience

Di Donato's work was written in the 1930s period of the Depression, social protest, and growing interest in socialist solutions for the ills of the world and its workers. It was hailed, at its appearance, as "the epithet of the twentieth century." In some ways it continues to be extraordinarily actual, as witness the collapse of the building in Bridgeport during the summer of 1987 that duplicated the tragedy of *Christ in Concrete* with the loss of workers' lives.

Comparisons, Contrasts, Connections

Di Donato can be related to Clifford Odets, another writer of social protest, who had some influence on him. Also, compare his work with the lyric proletarianism of Steinbeck's *The Grapes of Wrath* and with John Fante's evocation of his mason father in *The Brotherhood of the Grape*.

It could be useful, also, to link Di Donato with the passionate outcry of James Baldwin in *Go Tell It on the Mountain* or with the working-class women of Tillie Olsen's *Yonnondio*.

Questions for Reading, Discussion, and Writing

1. I think it is useful to have some perspective on the social conditions of the times in this country as reflected in *Christ in Concrete*.
2. Study the techniques of characterization. What makes a character live, or, on the other hand, fade? What makes a successful character?

    How do Di Donato's Italian-American working-class characters relate to all people everywhere?

Bibliography

Diomede, Matthew. *Pietro Di Donato, the Master Builder.* Lewisburg, PA: Bucknell UP, 1995.

Esposito, Michael P. "The Evolution of Di Donato's Perceptions of Italian Americans." *The Italian Americans Through the Generations.* Proceedings of the 15th Annual Conference of the American Italian Historical Association. Staten Island: AIHA, 1986.

————. "The Travail of Pietro Di Donato." MELUS 7.2 (Summer 1980): 47–60.

Napolitano, Louise. *An American Story: Pietro Di Donato's* Christ in Concrete. New York: Lang, 1995.

Sinicropi, Giovannni. "Christ in Concrete." *Italian Americana* 3 (1977): 175–83.

Viscusi, Robert. "De Vulgari Eloquentia: An Approach to the Language of Italian American Fiction." *Yale Italian Studies,* 1.3 (Winter 1981): 21–38. An interesting commentary on language usage.

————. "The Semiology of Semen: Questioning the Father." *The Italian Americans Through the Generations.* Proceedings of the 15th Annual Conference of the American Italian Historical Association. Staten Island: AIHA, 1986.

Younghill Kang (1903–1972)

Contributing Editor: Elaine H. Kim

Classroom Issues and Strategies

East Goes West was finally reprinted by New York's Kaya Press. This edition provides an excellent chronology of Kang's life, a comprehensive bibliography of his publications and of publications about him and his work, and a very useful interpretive essay titled "The Unmaking of an Oriental Yankee" by Sunyoung Lee.

Students may be unfamiliar with Korean and Korean-American history. Teachers might read the sections about Korean Americans in Takaki's *Strangers from a Different Shore: A History of Asian Americans* (Boston: Little, 1989) and the chapters on Korean-American history in Nancy Abelmann and John Lie's *Blue Dreams: Korean Americans and the Los Angeles Riots* (Cambridge, MA: Harvard UP, 1995). They can also refer to various excellent chronologies, such as the one in *Quiet Odyssey: A Pioneer Korean Woman in America* (Sucheng Chan, ed., Seattle: U of Washington P, 1990) or the one in *East to America: Korean American Life Stories* (Elaine H. Kim and Eui-Young Yu, eds., New York: New, 1996). Students could conduct research on the Japanese colonization of Korea and the overseas Korean independence movement in which some of Kang's characters actively participate. If students have learned about the racist laws and policies against Asian immigrants during the period in which Kang's novel is set, they might discuss the different ways characters in *East Goes West* like Han, Kim, Park, and Jum respond to race discrimination.

Major Themes, Historical Perspectives, Personal Issues

Consider asking your students some of the following questions:

1. What is the relationship between the author and the narrator, particularly with respect to attitudes toward America?
2. How effective do you find the quite different strategies of survival deployed by the narrator's friends Kim, the educated aristocrat who falls in love with an upper-class American woman; Park, the ultra-nationalist who can think of nothing but his Korean homeland; and Jum, who tries to become a "hip" American? If you were to immigrate to a country where you faced a great deal of discrimination because of your origins, what strategies would you try?

Original Audience

East Goes West was written for a mainstream American readership at a time of intense anti-Asian activity in the United States.

Comparisons, Contrasts, Connections

East Goes West could be profitably taught in tandem with books set on the West Coast in the same period by Korean-American women writers, such as *Quiet Odyssey* and Ronyoung Kim's *Clay Walls* (Seattle: U of Washington P, 1987). Also, Kang's novel could be compared with other novels about immigrant life. Some interesting novels about Asian immigrants with which it could be contrasted are Carlos Bulosan's *America Is in the Heart* (Seattle: U of Washington P, 1946, 1973), which portrays Filipino migrant farm workers' lives on the

Pacific Coast in the 1930s; Louis Chu's novel, *Eat a Bowl of Tea* (New York: Stuart, 1961; Seattle: U of Washington P, 1979) set in Chinatown in the 1940s; and Wendy Law-Yone's *The Coffin Tree* (New York: Knopf, 1983; Boston: Beacon, 1987), which is about a Burmese refugee's experiences, mostly on the East Coast, in relatively recent times. Another fruitful approach might be to ask students to read Kang's *East Goes West* together with a very recent Korean-American novel, such as Chang-rae Lee's *Native Speaker* (New York: Putnam, 1995), Leonard Chang's *The Fruit 'N Food* (Seattle: Black Heron, 1996), or Nora Okja Keller's *Comfort Woman* (New York: Viking, 1997).

Carved on the Walls: Poetry by Early Chinese Immigrants

Contributing Editors: Him Mark Lai, Genny Lim, Judy Yung

Classroom Issues and Strategies

Because of the exclusion of racial minorities such as Chinese Americans from our American education and their continuous stereotyping in the popular media, most people do not have the historical or literary background to understand and appreciate Chinese poetry as written by the early immigrants at the Angel Island Immigration Station.

The headnote includes background information on the history of Chinese Americans and their detention experience at Angel Island as well as explanations of the literary style and content of the Chinese poems. We have also included footnotes to explain the literary and historical allusions used in the poems. It is important that students be aware of this background material in their reading of the poems as well as their significance as part of the earliest record of Chinese-American literature and history written from the perspective of Chinese immigrants in America.

As you teach these selections, consider a simulation exercise in which students can experience how Chinese immigrants must have felt as unwelcome aliens arriving at Angel Island. As students read these poems, they are made aware of the impact of discriminatory laws. They also learn to appreciate a different poetic style of writing. On the other hand, most students are puzzled by the historical context of the poems and by the larger moral issues of racism.

Major Themes, Historical Perspectives, Personal Issues

The poems express strong feelings of anger, frustration, uncertainty, hope, despair, self-pity, homesickness, and loneliness written by Chinese immigrants who were singled out for exclusion by American immigration laws on the basis of race. As such, they are important fragments of American history and literature long missing from the public record as well as strong evidence that dispels the stereotype of Chinese Americans as passive, complacent, and illiterate.

Significant Form, Style, or Artistic Conventions

Most of the poems were written in the 1910s and 1920s, when the classical style of Chinese poetry was still popular and when feelings of Chinese nationalism ran strong. Of the 135 poems that have been recovered, about half are written with four lines per poem and seven characters per line. The remainder consist of verses with six or eight lines and five or seven characters per line. The literary quality of the poems varies greatly, which is understandable considering that most immigrants at this time did not have formal schooling beyond the primary grades. Many poems violate rules of rhyme and tone required in Chinese poetry, and incorrect characters and usages often appear. However, these flaws do not appear in the translation, in which we chose to sacrifice form for content.

Original Audience

The Angel Island poems were written as a means to vent and record the response of Chinese immigrants to the humiliating treatment they suffered at the Angel Island Immigration Station. They were intended for other Chinese immigrants who would follow in the footsteps of the poets. But as read now, they are an important literary record of the experience and feelings of one group of immigrants who, because of their race and a weak motherland, were unwelcome and singled out for discriminatory treatment.

Comparisons, Contrasts, Connections

The only other work published so far that would serve as a useful tool of comparison in terms of form and content is Marion Hom's *Songs of Gold Mountain: Cantonese Rhymes from San Francisco Chinatown* (Berkeley: U of California P, 1987)—a collection of Chinese folk rhymes first published in 1911 and 1915. It would also be useful for students to read about the European immigrant experience at Ellis Island in order for them to see the different treatments of immigrants to America due to race and ethnicity.

Questions for Reading, Discussion, and Writing

1. (a) What are the themes of the Angel Island poems, and how do they reflect the historical circumstances for Chinese immigrants coming to the United States between 1910 and 1940?
   (b) How would you describe the nameless poets based on your reading of the Angel Island poems?
2. (a) Compare and contrast the Angel Island poems with those written by another American poet in the early twentieth century.
   (b) Show how the image of Chinese immigrants as reflected in the Angel Island poems confirms or contradicts prevailing stereotypes of Chinese Americans in the popular media.

Bibliography

Chan, Sucheng, ed. *Entry Denied: Exclusion and the Chinese Community in America, 1882–1943.* Philadelphia: Temple UP, 1991.

Lai, Him Mark, Genny Lim, and Judy Yung. *Island: Poetry and History of Chinese Immigrants on Angel Island, 1910–1940.* Seattle: U of Washington P, 1980, 1991.

Lim, Genny. *Paper Angels and Bitter Cane: Two Plays.* Honolulu: Kalamaku, 1991.

Lowe, Felicia. *Carved in Silence.* 1988. A film about the Chinese immigration experience at Angel Island. Available from National Asian American Telecommunications Assn. 346 9th Street, 2nd Floor, San Francisco, CA 94103.

Mark, Diane M. L., and Ginger Chih. *A Place Called Chinese America.* Dubuque, IA: Kendall/Hunt, 1993.

Takaki, Ronald. *Strangers from a Different Shore: A History of Asian Americans.* Boston: Little, 1989.

Pedagogical Introduction:

Contemporary Period
1945 to the Present

Earlier Generations
A Sheaf of Poetry and Prose from the Beat Movement
New Generations
A Sheaf of Vietnam Conflict Poetry and Prose
Cluster: Prison Literature

In Ralph Ellison's *Invisible Man*, the unnamed narrator explains the method behind his circular narrative by declaring that "the end is in the beginning," and in a way the section on contemporary literature bring us back to the texts about the origins of America that open *The Heath Anthology*. The introduction to the section on "Native American Oral Literatures" suggests that students consider the "creation stories" they bring with them in order to come to some sense of that cultural construct we call "America." Such a discussion questions how such stories are produced, by what groups of people, and for what purposes. Throughout the section introductions, this approach is described as an analysis of "cultural rhetoric"—the consideration of texts not as static artifacts with self-contained meanings but as strategic examples of what Jane Tompkins calls "cultural work"—the products of dynamic processes of cultural confrontation, negotiation, assimilation, and transformation. These processes include the printing and dispersal of these texts in *The Heath Anthology*, the revision of this anthology from edition to edition, the assignment of these texts in college classes, and the particular reading experiences of the students in the class taken as both individuals and as members of various communities. Such an approach demonstrates as well that since the study of the past involves the active creation of knowledge on the part of students and teachers, history becomes an active part of the present.

The study of recent culture reverses this equation as a part of the same pedagogical approach by regarding the present as part of history. The historical debates over the so-called "canon" of American literature can be illustrated for students by having them define a contemporary canon for themselves, an especially appropriate activity at the start of a new century. To do this, students will have to consider what is meant by contemporary culture, how we define what is central, what is marginal, why we might want to undertake such definitions, and what the consequences of different definitions might be. The anthology itself (as well as the class syllabus) can then be regarded as just one example of canon-building, complete with explanations and justifications of the choices made.

Such an analysis naturally invites the class to construct its own textbook—its own canons—and to engage in the same operation of historicizing the present and near-present past by examining the associations students have in conjunction with terms like *the fifties, the sixties, the seventies, the eighties,* and *the*

725

nineties. Where do these associations come from? How are they perpetuated through the mass media and popular culture, and for what ends? political? commercial? What other categories and groupings could we use to organize, read, and interpret the texts in this section? "Women Writers"? "The African-American Tradition"? "Poetic Experimentation"? This kind of pedagogical approach emphasizes multiculturalism as an activity, not an inert state of being, an activity that reads texts—all texts, not just texts by "ethnic" writers (as if it were possible for there to be "nonethnic" writers)—as complex, hybrid forms of discourse.

In a similar way, Gloria Anzaldúa developed the concept of "mestiza consciousness" primarily as a way of describing how her own complex identity as a multilingual, multinational lesbian Chicana writer taught her to "cope by developing a tolerance for contradictions, a tolerance for ambiguity" by learning how to "juggle cultures." She also implies, however, that such an experience is typical rather than exceptional, and that we are all to a greater or lesser extent juggling cultures as well, the difference being not between the pure and the mixed in terms of cultural identity, but between the conscious recognition of the complicated interrelationship of diverse cultural backgrounds and a kind of willful innocence/ignorance of this diversity:

> The struggle is inner: Chicano, *indo,* American Indian, *Mojado, mexicano,* immigrant Latino, Anglo in power, working class Anglo, Black, Asian—our psyches resemble the borderlands and are populated by the same people. The struggle has always been inner, and is played out in the outer terrains. Awareness of our situation must come before inner changes, which in turn come before changes in society. Nothing happens in the "real" world unless it first happens in the images in our heads. (87)

Anzaldúa's reference to the outer terrains—the rhetorical space where these internal issues of cultural definition, resistance, and transformation are played out—serves well as a pedagogical coda to this instructor's guide, reminding us that the point of cultural contestation or consensus, the site of struggle and mastery, doesn't lie between the covers of any particular anthology but takes place in what Louise Rosenblatt called the transaction between reader and text, a transaction that includes both the immediate historical context of the reader as well as that of the text. Whatever the particular selections made for any given class syllabus, the real focus of the class is that transaction—the "images in our heads" that constitute the internal terrain of American literature.

Bibliography

Anzaldúa, Gloria. *Borderlands/La Frontera: The New Mestiza.* San Francisco: Aunt Lute, 1987.

Ellison, Ralph. *Invisible Man.* New York: Vintage, 1989.

Earlier Generations

Ann Petry (1908–1997)

Contributing Editor: Hilary Holladay

Classroom Issues and Strategies

So much is going on in Petry's novels and short stories that you may wonder where to begin a classroom discussion. For a discussion of "The Witness," racial conflicts, power plays between men and women, and problems within the community of Wheeling are all equally valid starting points. Petry rarely dwells on one social problem, though students particularly sensitive to one or another issue (racism, for instance) may not recognize the range of her concerns on a first reading. Therefore, asking students to discuss the connections between matters of race and gender in "The Witness" may help them grasp this story. Once they see how entwined the social issues are in "The Witness," they will be well on their way to understanding the scope of Petry's vision.

Major Themes, Historical Perspectives, Personal Issues

Prejudice is a central concern in Petry's writing. In almost all of her works, complex relationships develop among individuals prejudiced against each other for reasons of race or gender. But her fiction contains few characters who are solely victim or solely oppressors. Never one to make snap judgments, she imbues even her most objectionable characters with humanity. The would-be rapist Boots Smith in *The Street*, for example, has been a victim of racial prejudice. While Petry does not excuse his behavior, she does acknowledge the pathos of his life. Likewise, in "The Witness," she provides the delinquent boys with a social context: they are intelligent young men, stifled by both church and school, who have no positive outlet for their myriad frustrations.

In addition to exploring the intersections of racism and sexism, Petry chronicles the ways in which people chase after the American dream, only to find that it is illusory. Petry's characters typically experience a profound disillusionment in their quests for success and/or peace of mind. This disillusionment drives them toward a drastic act that has significant implications for the whole community as well as the individual protagonist. This is true of "The Witness" as well as of Petry's novels.

In their emphasis on troubled communities and individual journeys toward freedom, Petry's works contain echoes of nineteenth-century slave narratives. *The Street*'s Lutie Johnson is a prime example of an oppressed character whose life devolves into a series of desperate escapes. The endings of Petry's works, however, depart from those of prototypical slave narratives: neither Lutie Johnson nor Charles Woodruff achieves a meaningful victory merely by escaping an intolerable situation.

Significant Form, Style, or Artistic Conventions

Although Petry's writing is clear and simply stated (reflecting her journalistic background), her frequently discursive style finds its full power in novels and long stories. Since her fiction focuses on relationships and communities, she often uses multiple points of view, flashbacks, and other devices that enable her to portray whole towns as well as individuals. Throughout her career, she has skillfully employed realism and naturalism (in her novels), stream-of-consciousness (notably in *The Narrows*), and indirect discourse (in her novels and many of her stories).

Her experiments with varied techniques and voices (male and female, black and white) underscore Petry's fascination with multiple perspectives. In "Has Anybody Seen Miss Dora Dean?" and *Country Place*, she explores the complementary roles that narrators and listeners play in a story's creation. "The Witness" contains a related theme: as readers, we "witness" Woodruff's tale, just as he witnesses a crime. At the end of "The Witness," we are in a position quite similar to Woodruff's. Our personal perspective influences our understanding of his tale. Given our individual circumstances, will we repeat his tale? Or will we try to keep the story, and all of its difficulties, as a troubling secret?

Comparisons, Contrasts, Connections

Petry defies easy categorization, partly because she is contemporary with writers as far removed from each other in time and aesthetics as Richard Wright and Toni Morrison. But Petry can be productively compared and contrasted with authors representing several different strands of American literature.

As an African-American woman, she fits in a historical continuum including Harriet Wilson and Harriet Jacobs in the nineteenth century; Nella Larsen, Zora Neale Hurston, and Gwendolyn Brooks in the first half of the twentieth century; and Toni Morrison, Alice Walker, Gloria Naylor, and Terry McMillan (among others) today. The beginning of her career in the mid-1940s also suggests a natural grouping with Wright as well as with Ralph Ellison and Chester Himes. As a writer preoccupied with communities and the social problems they harbor, Petry invites comparison with William Faulkner and Eudora Welty. And her fictional explorations of New England put her in the company of writers as diverse as Henry David Thoreau, Nathaniel Hawthorne, and Sarah Orne Jewett.

Questions for Reading, Discussion, and Writing

1. Students reading "The Witness" will have several natural points of identification: their experience as teenagers, their contact with teachers/authority figures, and their perceptions of race relations and sexual politics. But because "The Witness" invites us to transcend individual perspectives, I use study questions that probe the story's intriguing ambiguities: How does this story complicate conventional perceptions of protagonist versus adversary? Identify the characteristics that prevent Charles Woodruff and Dr. Shipley, the Congregational minister, from being wholly "good" characters. Are the boys who attack Nellie entirely "evil"? Explain your opinion. How are these boys different from the students Woodruff describes as the "Willing Workers of America"? How do the boys' violent acts reflect on the town of Wheeling? How might Woodruff's relationship with his wife (encapsulated in his memories) affect his decision to leave Wheeling? How might we as readers, and potential critics, identify with Woodruff's plight at the end of the story?
2. Critical essays might address the following topics: the theme of "witnessing" in both its religious and secular senses, the double standard Woodruff endures as a black male authority figure, and the story's connections between racism and sexism (a recurring theme in Petry's work). For longer papers, students might compare "The Witness" with one of the other Wheeling stories in *Miss Muriel and Other Stories*, or compare Woodruff with *The Street*'s Lutie Johnson.

Bibliography

See Hazel Arnett Ervin, *Ann Petry: A Bio-Bibliography* (Boston: Hall, 1993); Gates and Appiah, eds., *Ann Petry: Critical Perspectives Past and Present* (Amistad, 1994); Hilary Holladay, *Ann Petry* (Twayne, 1996); and Lindon Barrett, *Blackness and Value: Seeing Double* (Cambridge, UK: Cambridge UP, 1999).

Theodore Roethke (1908–1963)

Contributing Editor: Janis Stout

Major Themes, Historical Perspectives, Personal Issues

Personal Background: Roethke had extremely ambivalent feelings about his father, who was managing partner in a large greenhouse operation in Saginaw, Michigan. He also had problems relating to alcohol addiction and bipolar disorder, which resulted in periods of hospitalization. All of these personal tensions are confronted in his poetry.

Significant Form, Style, or Artistic Conventions

"Frau Bauman, Frau Schmidt, and Frau Schwartze"

The three "ancient ladies" preside over processes of growth (both vegetable and the poet's own) almost as personifications of natural forces, or even the three Fates. Their presence, like Mother Nature's, is somewhat ambiguous; there is a note of threat in their tickling of the child and in their night presence. The three women's vigor and authority should be noted, as well as their avoidance of limitation by sex-role stereotypes: clearly female (they wear skirts; they have a special association with the child), they also climb ladders and stand astride the steam-pipes providing heat in the greenhouse.

"Root Cellar"

"Root Cellar" and "Big Wind" represent the celebrated "greenhouse poems," a group characterized by close attention to details evident only to one who knows this particular world very well—as Roethke did. They are distinguished from, say, Wordsworth's nature poems in that they celebrate equally the natural processes themselves and the human effort and control involved. They share

Wordsworth's ability to appreciate the humble or homely elements of nature. Here, in particular, we see Roethke's wonder at the sheer life process even when manifested in forms that would ordinarily seem ugly or repellent.

"Big Wind"

We might say "Big Wind" celebrates the tenacity of human effort in the face of hostile natural forces, an effort that wrests out of chaos the beauty of the roses. However, that idea should not be pressed so far as to exclude the creative force of natural vitality. Nature and human effort join together in producing roses. The greenhouse itself, shown as a ship running before the storm, seems almost a living thing.

"The Lost Son"

"The Lost Son" illustrates three major elements in Roethke's work: surrealistic style; reflection of his own psychological disorders; and mysticism, his vision of spiritual wholeness as a merging of the individual consciousness with natural processes and life forms.

1. "The Flight" is a poem of anxiety about death and loss of identity.
2. "The Return" associates wellness with the greenhouse world of child-hood. The return spoken of is the return of light and heat—of full heat since the greenhouses would scarcely have been left unheated on winter nights. The plants are both an object of the poet's close observation and a representation of his life.

"Meditations of an Old Woman"

Probably the most far-reaching question that can be asked of students, but also the most difficult, is What difference does it make that the speaker is an old woman? Old, we can understand; we think of wisdom, experience, release from the distractions of youth. But why not an old man? One tempting answer is that our society has typically seen passivity and the passive virtues (patience, for instance) as feminine.

"Elegy"

Not often anthologized, this funerary tribute approaches a fusion of comedy with high seriousness. Aunty Tilly is a wonderfully strong, assertive, independent-minded woman who both fulfills traditional roles (housewife, cook, nurse, tender of the dead) and transcends them. The comedy emerges in the last stanza when Aunt Tilly comes "bearing down" on the butcher who, knowing he has met his match, quails before her indomitability and her clarity of vision.

Bibliography

Balakian Peter. *Theodore Roethke's Far Fields: The Evolution of His Poetry.* 1989.

Kalaidjian, Walter B. *Understanding Theodore Roethke.* 1987.

Seager, Allen. *The Glass House.* 1968.

Stout, Janis P. "Theodore Roethke and the Journey of the Solitary Self." *Interpretations* 16 (1985): 86–93.

Sullivan, Rosemary. *Theodore Roethke: The Garden-Master.* 1975.

Eudora Welty (1909–2001)

Contributing Editor: Jennifer L. Randisi

Classroom Issues and Strategies

Like many lyric novelists, Welty is easy to read. She therefore seems (to many students) very simple. They like her work, generally, and don't want to ruin their enjoyment by having to analyze it.

I like to begin by looking at what makes Welty seem simple (her lovely sentences, the homey metaphors, her "impulse to praise"). The difficulty here is not a lack of accessibility but rather that Welty seems too accessible, too superficial. The challenge is to get students to read Welty seriously, critically, analytically.

Welty has said that except what's personal there's so little to tell. I'd start where she did: with the hearts of the characters she's writing about— the universal emotions they share with us. Why do we feel a certain way about the story? the situation? the character? What is evoked? How is Welty able to evoke a certain response from us? What values emerge? A strong sense of values is something Welty shares with writers like William Faulkner, Flannery O'Connor, Katherine Anne Porter, Walker Percy, and Alice Walker. These novelists believe in certain things, and the communities created in their fiction share both a value system and a sense of what words like *love* and *compassion* mean.

As with most of the Southern writers, Welty's humor, her use of the grotesque, and her dialogue are often initial difficulties for students, who tend to take her too literally and thus miss the fun she's having. Welty's books often work the way folk or fairy tales do; students aren't used to this.

Major Themes, Historical Perspectives, Personal Issues

Major themes include the problem of balancing love and separateness (the community and one's sense of self), the role and influence of family and the land ("place"), and the possibilities of art (storytelling) to inform life. Welty is also very concerned with resonances of classical mythology, legend, and folktale, and with the intersection of history and romance.

Significant Form, Style, or Artistic Conventions

Welty clearly owes something to fellow Mississippian William Faulkner, and to the oral tradition of the South. She has a terrific ear, reproducing cadences of dialect and giving much insight into her characters by allowing her readers to hear them talk. Welty's work also owes something to the grotesque as developed in the American South.

Original Audience

Since Welty hasn't been grouped with writers critical of the South (her issues are neither political nor social in a broad sense), her work hasn't been read much differently over the years. She's been criticized for not attacking the South; that has never been her interest or her aim.

Comparisons, Contrasts, Connections

Any of the Southerners writing in the twentieth century could be compared with Welty in terms of voice, violence, attitude toward the land, feelings about community, and ways of telling a story. William Faulkner, Flannery O'Connor, Katherine Anne Porter, Walker Percy—even Alice Walker— would be good to start with.

Questions for Reading, Discussion, and Writing

1. I like to start with what students see. I think study questions (except for general questions relating to the elements of the story—point of view, character, theme) direct their reading toward what they think I want them to see rather than allowing them to see what they see.

2. I am fond of the short paper (2–3 pages) and of the directed journal. The former allows students to focus on a very specific problem or concern; the latter allows students to carry issues from one author to the next, or from one book to the next. I like assigning a formal paper from one of the journal entries.

Bibliography

Welty's essay "Place in Fiction" is very good. Welty's book of photographs, *One Time, One Place,* is a nice companion piece, as is her collection of essays, *The Eye of the Story.* Peggy Prenshaw's *Conversations with Eudora Welty* has some helpful information, and I think her collection of essays (*Eudora Welty: Critical Essays*) and John F. Desmond's (*A Still Moment: Essays on the Art of Eudora Welty*) are both worthwhile reading.

My chapter on *Losing Battles* (in *A Tissue of Lies*) is also worth reading.

Charles Olson (1910–1970)

Contributing Editor: Thomas R. Whitaker

Classroom Issues and Strategies

It will be most practical to approach Olson after some detailed work with poems by T. S. Eliot, Ezra Pound, and William Carlos Williams. Despite many stylistic similarities, Olson's poetic "enactment" dictates a different kind of progression and a different use of literary and other allusions. The teacher might suggest that the formalist concept of a "speaker" or "protagonist" (a character in a poetic drama outside of which the poem's maker is imagined to stand) might be replaced by the poet himself in the act of writing (a self-reflexive Charles Olson in the drama of making this poem). Although Pound's *Pisan Cantos*, Eliot's *Four Quartets*, and Williams's *Paterson* are partially amenable to this approach, Olson commits himself to it more fully in both shorter and longer forms.

His abstract style, his refusal to commit himself to the modernist "image," may also be a difficulty. The student can be reminded that all speech, all thought, even an "image," is the result of an abstractive process. Olson characteristically works with syntax and conceptual reference that are "in process"—often fragmentary, self-revising, incremental—as he struggles to "say" what is adequate to his present (and always changing) moment. Comparisons with Robert Creeley's often abstract and stammering forward motion may be illuminating.

Those interested in Olson as a teacher and as a collaborator with other poets and artists should consult *Letters for Origin* and *Mayan Letters*, and also Martin Duberman, *Black Mountain: An Exploration in Community* (1972), and Mary Emma Harris, *The Arts at Black Mountain College* (1987), which are richly informative. Duberman also quotes a comment by Merce Cunningham on Olson as a dancer, which may suggest one way of approaching Olson's poetic style: "I *enjoyed* him; . . . he was something like a light walrus" (p. 359). For Olson's own appreciation of Cunningham as a dancer, see the poem "Merce of Egypt," which is a meditation on man-the-maker that might be compared with "For Sappho, Back." For the extraordinary intensity and range of Olson's reading, see Ralph Maud, *Charles Olson's Reading: A Biography* (1996).

Questions for Reading, Discussion, and Writing

"The Kingfishers"

It may be useful for the instructor to have worked through this poem with the help of a commentator such as Sherman Paul, Thomas Merrill or Ralph Maud. Students can then be encouraged to approach the poem as a meditation on the need for change, and the will to change—as of 1949 but with contemporary applications. The poet sees the need to move beyond Eliot and Pound, beyond the irony and despair of *The Waste Land* and the modern inferno of *The Cantos*, without overlooking the cultural crisis to which they allude. What sources of vitality does he find amid the decay? What suggestions for personal and cultural renewal? And for a new poetic practice? Can we understand this poem on the model of elliptical diary notations by someone who is working toward a statement of position? What are the stages of its progress?

Students with an interest in the poem's philosophical implications may wish to explore Plutarch's "The E at Delphi" or G. S. Kirk, *Heraclitus: The Cosmic Fragments*. Students wondering how "feedback" may relate to social and poetic processes should turn to Norbert Wiener's *Cybernetics* or *The Human Use of Human Beings*. Of great interest in that direction is also the work of Gregory Bateson: see *Steps to an Ecology of Mind* (the chapter on "Cybernetic Explanation") and *Mind and Nature: A Necessary Unity*.

"For Sappho, Back"

In some respects more traditional in form and subject than the other Olson poems included here, "For Sappho, Back" might be a useful introduction to Olson's style for students not at ease with allusive modernism. How does the poem expand the tribute to a specific woman-poet so that it becomes a meditation on woman, nature, and poetry? What specific qualities of Sappho's style does it allude to? Does Sappho become here a Muse figure or Nature Herself? D. H. Lawrence has said in *Etruscan Places* (which Olson admired) that the Etruscan priest sought an "act of pure attention" directed inward. "To him the blood was the red stream of consciousness itself." As Olson wrote to the anthropologist Ruth Benedict, "I am alone again working down to the word where it lies in the blood. I continually find myself reaching back and down in order to make sense out of now and to lead ahead." (See Clark, *Charles Olson,* p. 95.) Does this help us with "Back" in the title and the use of "blood" later? Clark suggests that, on one level, this is a personal love poem, taken by its recipient, Frances Boldereff, to be a "very accurate portrait" of herself (p. 171). Olson often chose to incorporate in such love poems allusions to his wife Constance; can we find such clues here? How, finally, do we relate the historical, personal, and archetypal concerns of this poem?

Robert von Hallberg (*Charles Olson: The Scholar's Art,* pp. 34–38) offers suggestions for stylistic analysis of the use of fragmentary and self-revising syntax in this poem.

"I, Maximus of Gloucester, to You"

Students might usefully compare this poem to Hart Crane's "To Brooklyn Bridge"; both are invocations and statements of subject at the outset of modern "personal epics." One might also consult the preface to Williams's *Paterson*. What are the social issues in each case? What dominant images are established? What relations does Olson suggest between love and form? How do images gradually accrue additional meanings as the meditation proceeds? Does it help to know that this was happening in the process of composition—and that in an earlier draft "next second," was "next/second"? (See Clark, *Charles Olson,* p. 166.)

"Maximus, to himself"

As a self-assessment, this poem might usefully be compared with Creeley's "For Love." Both have the air of spontaneous meditation; both deal largely in abstractions; both are sharply self-critical. To what degree is the form of each an "extension of content"? How, in each, does a seemingly unplanned meditation assume the form of a coherent monologue, moving through a problem toward its momentary resolution?

Elizabeth Bishop (1911–1979)

Contributing Editor: C. K. Doreski

Classroom Issues and Strategies

Bishop's poems are highly accessible and do not present problems for most mature readers. I have found that more students come to hear the poetry of Bishop when they commit some of her work to memory. I often challenge students to find the poetry first and then discuss the theme. This encourages them to begin to find relationships among form, language, and topic.

Significant Form, Style, or Artistic Conventions

Bishop's voice communicates rather directly to beginning readers of poetry. What is difficult to convey is the depth of expression and learning evidenced in these poems. Her work shows not merely experience but also wisdom, the ability to reflect upon one's life, and that makes some poems difficult for younger readers.

For younger women readers, Bishop often seems old-fashioned, fussy, or detached. This perplexed the poet in that she felt that she had lived her life as an independent woman. This "generation gap" often provides an interesting class opportunity to talk about historical, cultural, and class assumptions in literature—and how those issues affect us as readers.

Students are often quite taken by Bishop's regard for animals. With the spirit of a Darwinian naturalist, the poet is willing to accord the natural world intrinsic rights and purposes. The dream-fusion world of the Man-Moth provides many students with an opportunity to discover this avenue into Bishop's world.

Original Audience

Bishop presents a curious "generational" case in that the circumstances of her childhood (raised by her maternal grandparents and an aunt) skew some of her references in favor of an earlier time. The kitchen setting in "Sestina" (not in this anthology), for example, seems more old-fashioned than Robert Lowell's interior scenes in "91 Revere Street." Otherwise, her poems may be seen as timely—or timeless.

Comparisons, Contrasts, Connections

In the British lyric tradition, Bishop, by admission and allusion, draws heavily from Herbert, Hopkins, Wordsworth, Tennyson, Keats, and Blake.

Most pertinent American contrasts are with her mentor Marianne Moore (large correspondence at the Rosenbach Museum, Philadelphia), her friends Robert Lowell (correspondence at Houghton Library, Harvard University; Vassar College Library, Poughkeepsie), and May Swenson (correspondence at Washington University Library, St. Louis).

Questions for Reading, Discussion, and Writing

1. "The Man-Moth"
   (a) This is but one of Bishop's many dream poems. In what ways does Bishop demonstrate her interest in and reliance upon surrealism?
   (b) How does Bishop attempt to humanize her exile through a multitude of sensory impressions? Are they effective?
   (c) The final stanza addresses the reader. How does Bishop intensify her creature's humanity through his ultimate vulnerability? Are we made to feel like the man-moth?
2. "Filling Station"
   (a) As Bishop describes setting and inhabitants of this "family filling station," she deliberately builds upon the initial observation, "Oh, but it is dirty!" Why dwell upon and develop this commentary? Does it suggest a missing family member? Is this station without a feminine presence?
   (b) The scale of the poem seems deliberately diminutive. Does this intensify the feminine quality of the poem? Is this intentional?
   (c) The closing stanza returns a sense of order or at least purpose to this scene. The symmetry of the cans lulls the "high-strung automobiles" into calmness. With the final line, "Somebody loves us all," does Bishop suggest a religious or maternal caretaker for this family?
3. Describe the voice and tone in a single poem. The casual humor of Bishop's world is often missed by casual readers (obsessed with travel and loss as themes).
4. Bishop owes much to her surrealist heritage. Sleep and dream states animate the worlds of the "Man-Moth" and "Crusoe in England." Such an essay would allow students to discover a new topical frame for discussion of experience, language, and poetic form.
5. A useful technical assignment would be to discuss Bishop's reliance upon simile rather than metaphor as her chief poetic device to link her world with the reader's. It says something critical about Bishop's belief in the limits of shared knowledge, experience.

Bibliography

Primary Works

North & South, 1946 (Houghton Mifflin Poetry Award); *Poems: North & South—A Cold Spring* (Pulitzer Prize, 1956); *Questions of Travel,* 1965; *The Complete Poems,* 1969 (National Book Award); *Geography III,* 1976; *The Complete Poems, 1927–1979,* 1983; *The Collected Prose,* 1984.

Secondary Works

Candace MacMahon, *Elizabeth Bishop: A Bibliography, 1927–1979,* 1980; Lloyd Schwartz and Sybil Estess, *Elizabeth Bishop and Her Art,* 1983; Harold Bloom, *Modern Critical Views: Elizabeth Bishop,* 1985; Robert Dale Parker, *The Unbeliever: The Poetry of Elizabeth Bishop,* 1988; Thomas J. Travisano, *Elizabeth Bishop: Her Artistic Development,* 1988; Bonnie Costello, *Elizabeth Bishop: Questions of Mastery,* 1991; Lorrie Goldensohn, *Elizabeth Bishop: The Biography of a Poetry,* 1992; C. K. Doreski, *Elizabeth Bishop: The Restraints of Language,* 1993; Brett Millier, *Elizabeth Bishop: Life and the Memory of It,* 1993.

Tennessee Williams (1911–1983)

Contributing Editor: Thomas P. Adler

Classroom Issues and Strategies

Students may tend to respond to the heroines, especially in Williams's earlier plays up through the end of the 1940s, differently from what he intended because their value system is not the same. His sensitive, poetic misfits who escape from reality into a world of illusion/art are likely to seem too remote, too soft. The very things that Williams values about them—their grace, their gentility—nowadays may appear dispensable adjuncts of life in an age when competition and aggressiveness are valorized among both sexes. So students need to be sensitized to Williams's romantic ideals and to what he sees as the civilizing, humanizing virtues.

It helps to place Williams in context as a Southern dramatist, and also as one who propounds the feminizing of American culture as a counter to a society built on masculine ideals of strength and power. Students also need to understand that Williams is a "poetic" realist, not simply in his use of a lyrical rhetoric but also in his handling of imagery, both verbal and visual. If they attend carefully to his command of visual stage symbolism, they can oftentimes discover the necessary clues about Williams's attitude toward his characters.

Any discussion of "Portrait of a Madonna" will necessarily focus upon Williams's characterization of his sexually frustrated and neurotic heroine, whose upbringing in a succession of Southern rectories, under the nay-saying and guilt-inducing "shadow" of the church and of the cross, has left her totally unprepared for life and prey to crazed delusions. Miss Collins becomes almost the archetypal unmarried daughter, restricted by the responsibility of caring for an aged mother, sensing the social pressure to be sexual and yet denied any morally sanctioned expression of these feelings, finally forced into madness as a result of unrealistic expectations. The image of the Madonna and Child becomes central to an understanding of the play: the Virgin and Mother whom Lucretia costumed for the Sunday School Christmas pageant; the children she visits twice a year on religious holidays with her scrapbooks of Campbell soup kids; Richard's many children; the fabricated "child" to be born of a woman virginal in body and heart, defiled only in her dreams.

Brief though it is, Williams's play is amenable to many critical approaches other than the psychological and feminist. A formalist approach might examine the way in which Williams structures his play—as he later will *Streetcar*—around a series of dichotomies: past/present; memory/fact; gentility/brutality; shadow/light; sanity/insanity; freedom/repression; virginal/defiled; harmless illusion/harmful delusion. A literary-historical approach could place the work within the tradition of Southern gothicism while a sociocultural framework could explore the way in which the myth of Southern chivalry curtails Lucretia's independence, as well as the way in which utilitarian technology threatens the artistic sensibility (elevator cage as machine played off against the music on the gramophone). A generic approach might consider the possibilities for seeing the play as a tragedy while a biographical approach might trace the relationship between Lucretia and Williams's own schizophrenic sister Rose. For some considerations of various new theoretical approaches in literary criticism together with examples of their application to a dramatic text by Williams, you might consult *Confronting Tennessee Williams's "A Streetcar Named Desire": Essays in Cultural Pluralism*, edited by Philip C. Kolin (Westport: Greenwood, 1993).

Major Themes, Historical Perspectives, Personal Issues

Central thematic issues include the question of illusion and reality, the relationship between madness and art, and the role of the artist in society, as well as the necessity to respond compassionately and nonjudgmentally to the needs of God's sensitive yet weak creatures who are battered and misunderstood. Historically, Williams's relation to the myth of the cavalier South should be explored. Finally, Williams's close identification with his heroines needs to be seen in light of his relationship with his schizophrenic sister Rose, as he admits in his *Memoirs,* the most intensely emotional attachment in his personal life.

Significant Form, Style, or Artistic Conventions

Although "Portrait" itself is essentially a realistic, albeit somewhat poetic, play, Williams himself should be approached as an innovator of a new "plastic" theater, a practitioner, along with Arthur Miller, of what some have termed "a theatre of gauze." To handle this aspect of Williams's aesthetic, the instructor might either read or reproduce as a handout the dramatist's Production Notes to *Glass Menagerie,* along with Tom's opening narration in that play, which really differentiates Williams's practice—"truth in the pleasant disguise of illusion"—from the strict realism—"illusion that has the appearance of truth"—of others.

Original Audience

The choice of the one-act play form itself tells something about Williams's intended audience. Rather than aim at a commercial production, "Portrait" seems more appropriate for an amateur (academic or civic) theater presentation, where the interest will be largely on character and dialogue rather than production values. Thus, it appears intended for a limited audience of intense theatergoers. From the perspective of the dramatist, it serves partly as a "study" for larger work(s), in the same way a painter might do a series of studies before attempting a full canvas. And so, in a sense, the artist too is his own audience.

Comparisons, Contrasts, Connections

Lucretia Collins bears comparison with other Williams heroines in "The Lady of Larkspur Lotion," *The Glass Menagerie, A Streetcar Named Desire,* and *Summer and Smoke.* Students might also contrast the way Miss Collins escapes from the sociocultural milieu that constricts her freedom with the heroines' responses in Susan Glaspell's short play "Trifles" and William Faulkner's short story "A Rose for Emily."

Questions for Reading, Discussion, and Writing

1. (a) Consider the dramatic function(s) of the minor characters, the Porter and the Elevator Boy, in the play.

   (b) Could "Portrait of a Madonna" have been expanded to a full-length work? To accomplish that, what else might Williams have dramatized? Would anything have been lost in the transformation?

2. (a) The director of the original production of "Portrait" had Lucretia exit clutching a doll. What, if anything, would justify such an interpolation in Williams's text, and what might be the impact on the audience?

   (b) Discuss the theater metaphor in "Portrait": the minor characters as onstage audience; the bedroom, scene of illusions, as stage; Mr. Abrams as stage manager/director, and so on.

   (c) In what way does Williams's characterization of Lucretia Collins lead the audience to conclude that he considered her story "tragic"?

Bibliography

Leverich, Lyle. *Tom: The Unknown Tennessee Williams.* New York: Crown, 1995.

Pagan, Nicholas. *Rethinking Literary Biography: A Postmodern Approach to Tennessee Williams.* Rutherford, NJ: Fairleigh Dickinson UP, 1993.

Rolin, Philip C., ed. *Tennessee Williams: A Guide to Research and Performance.* Westport, CT: Greenwood, 1998.

Spoto, Donald. *The Kindness of Strangers: The Life of Tennessee Williams.* Boston: Little, 1985.

Tillie Lerner Olsen (b. 1912 or 1913)

Contributing Editor: Deborah S. Rosenfelt

Classroom Issues and Strategies

Olsen's work is relatively easy to teach since it addresses themes of concern to contemporary students and since its experiments with language remain within the bounds of realism. *Tell Me a Riddle* is among the most difficult of Olsen's works, and some students have trouble for two reasons: they are unfamiliar with the social and political history embedded in the novella, and they are confused by the allusive, stream-of-consciousness techniques Olsen employs for the revelation of that history's centrality in the consciousness of the protagonist.

Since the knee-jerk negative reaction to "communists" is often a problem, I make sure I discuss thoroughly the historical soil out of which *Tell Me a Riddle* grows. Sometimes I show the film *Seeing Reds*. I always read students a useful passage from *A Long View from the Left: Memoirs of an American Revolutionary* (Delta, 1972, p. 8) by Al Richmond.

Showing the film version of *Tell Me a Riddle* can be a good strategy for provoking discussion. The film itself is one of the rare representations of older people's lives and one of the few in which an older woman figures as the protagonist. Reading passages from Olsen's *Silences*, especially the autobiographical ones, also proves helpful and interesting to students.

Students respond most immediately and deeply to Eva's rage and anger about the sacrifices her life has involved. They also get into painful discussions about aging and dying, and about the limited options for the elderly in American society. The questions they ask include the following: Why won't the grandmother (Eva) hold her grandchild? Can you please help us figure out the configuration of family relationships in the story (here it helps if students have also read the other stories in the *Tell Me a Riddle* volume)? Why doesn't Eva want to see the rabbi in the hospital? Where do they go when they go to the city on the beach (the answer to that one is Venice, California, an area near Los Angeles that houses an old Jewish community lovingly documented in the book and film *Number Our Days*). Why won't David let her go home again?

Major Themes, Historical Perspectives, Personal Issues

Tell Me a Riddle is very rich thematically, historically, and personally. Its central themes include the confrontation with aging, illness, and death; the deprivations and struggles of poverty; the conflicts, full of love and rage, in marital relations; the family, especially motherhood, as a site of both love and nurturance and of repression; the buying of women's sense of self and the silencing of their capacities for expression over years of tending to the needs and listening to the rhythms of others; the quest for meaning in one's personal life; and the affirmation of hope for and engagement on behalf of a freer, more peaceful, more just and humane world.

The themes of *Tell Me a Riddle* are in many ways the themes of Olsen's life. Olsen's parents took part in the 1905 revolution and became Socialist party activists in the United States. Olsen herself became a communist in the years when communism as a philosophy and as a movement seemed to offer the best hope for an egalitarian society. Eva is modeled partly on Olsen's mother, who died of cancer, as does Eva.

I see Olsen as belonging to a tradition of women writers in this country associated with the American left, who unite a class consciousness and a feminist consciousness in their lives and creative work.

Significant Form, Style, or Artistic Conventions

In *Tell Me a Riddle,* Olsen is deliberately experimental, fracturing chronological sequence, using stream-of-consciousness techniques to represent the processes of human consciousness, insisting on the evocative power of each individual word. Though remaining within the bounds of realism, she draws fully on the techniques of modernist fiction to render a humanistic and socially impassioned vision rare in modernist and postmodernist writing.

Original Audience

The question of audience is, I think, less relevant to contemporary writers than to those of earlier centuries. I do speak about Olsen's political back-ground and about her special importance for contemporary women writers and readers. It is also important that the stories of the *Tell Me a Riddle* volume were written during the McCarthy era. All of them, especially "Tell Me a Riddle," subtly bear witness to the disappointment and despair of progressives during that era, when the radical dreams and visions of the thirties and forties were deliberately eradicated. Olsen's family was one of many to endure harassment by the FBI. *Riddle's* topical allusions to Nazi concentration camps and the dropping of the atomic bomb at Hiroshima, and David's yearning for a time of belief and belonging, contribute to the subtext of anguish and betrayal so characteristic of the literature of the period.

Comparisons, Contrasts, Connections

I find it useful to compare *Tell Me a Riddle* with other works by women authors that record the tensions of "dual life," especially those which, like *Riddle,* deploy an imagery of speech and silencing not only to delineate the protagonist's quest for personal expression but also to develop her relationship to processes of social change. Among the many works that contain some configuration of these themes and images are Agnes Smedley's novel *Daughter of Earth,* Harriet Arnow's *The Dollmaker,* Maxine Hong Kingston's *The Woman Warrior: Memoirs of a Girlhood among Ghosts,* much of the poetry of Audre Lorde and Adrienne Rich, Alice Walker's *The Color Purple*, and Joy Kogawa's *Obasan*.

As stories of "secular humanist" Jewish family life, the work might be compared with Grace Paley's fiction or Meridel LeSueur's *The Girl*.

As part of the tradition of working-class writers, she could be compared with Rebecca Harding Davis's *Life in the Iron-Mills*, Agnes Smedley's *Daughter of Earth*, Mike Gold's *Jews Without Money*, Henry Roth's *Call It Sleep*, and Fielding Burke's *Call Home the Heart*.

As a story exploring the consciousness of one who is dying, students might want to compare *Riddle* with Tolstoi's *The Death of Ivan Ilych*.

Questions for Reading, Discussion, and Writing

1. What is the immediate cause of the conflict in this story? Does the author take sides in this conflict? Does this conflict have a resolution? What underlying causes does it suggest?
2. Try to explain or account for the story's title. What about the subtitle?
3. Who is the "hero" of this story? Why?
4. This is a story about a woman dying of cancer. Did you find it "depressing" or "inspiring"? Why?
5. Why is Eva so angry about the appearance of the rabbi in the hospital? What does she mean by "Race, human; religion, none"?
6. What do we learn about Eva's girlhood? Why do we learn it so late in the story?
7. Discuss Jeanne's role in the story.
8. Is David the same man at the end of the story as he was at the beginning? Explain your answer.

Bibliography

Olsen's personal/critical essays, those in *Silences* and that in *Mother to Daughter, Daughter to Mother*, are very important sources of insight and information. Especially recommended: pp. 5–46 in *Silences*, "Silences in Literature" (1962), and "One Out of Twelve: Writers Who Are Women in Our Century" (1971).

Other recommended reading:

Coiner, Constance. "Literature of Resistance: The Intersection of Feminism and the Political Left in Tillie Olsen and Meridel LeSueur." *Politics of Literature: Toward the 1990's*. Ed. Lennard Davis and Bella Mirabella. New York: Columbia UP, n.d.

Orr, Elaine N. *Tillie Olsen and a Feminist Spiritual Vision*. Jackson: UP of Mississippi, 1987. Especially chapters II and IV.

Rosenfelt, Deborah. "From the Thirties: Tillie Olsen and the Radical Tradition." *Feminist Studies* 7:3 (Fall 1981): 371–406.

Muriel Rukeyser (1913–1980)

Contributing Editors: Cary Nelson and Janet Kaufman

Classroom Issues and Strategies

The earliest poem here, taken from Rukeyser's second book, dates from 1938; the most recent poems, taken from her last book, date from 1976. These poems thus range across forty years of a career and forty years of American culture and American history. Though there are very strong continuities in Rukeyser's work, it would be a mistake to imagine that all these poems were written by a single consciousness in a single historical moment. Their diverse forms and rhetorical styles represent the work of a poet who sustained her core beliefs and commitments while responding to changing historical, aesthetic, and cultural opportunities and pressures. She wrote long sequence poems, documentary poems, short lyrics, and elegies. Of all the responses one might make to this selection, the simplest one—and the one most to be hoped for—is the decision to read more widely in her work. That is, in a way, almost necessitated by this particular selection, since one of the poems, "Absalom," is taken from a longer poem sequence. Certainly the instructor should read that sequence in its entirety and give the class some sense of the poem's context. The sequence, "The Book of the Dead," is available in both her *Collected Poems* (1979) and the *Selected Poems* (1992). Readers should be warned that her earlier *Selected Poems* is not a very successful representation of her work.

Since a number of these poems combine states of consciousness and physical sensation, it is important for students not only to analyze them rhetorically but also to place themselves empathetically inside the poems and read them phenomenologically. What does it feel like to be the mother in "Absalom" who has lost her family to industrial exploitation? What does it feel like to speak in the two very different voices Rukeyser gives her? How can one elaborate on the closing lines of "Martin Luther King, Malcolm X": "bleeding of my right hand/my black voice bleeding." These poems are at once gifts to the reader and demands made of us. In "Then," a poem published shortly before her death, Rukeyser wrote, "When I am dead, even then,/I will still love you, I will wait in these poems."

Major Themes, Historical Perspectives, Personal Issues

Some of Rukeyser's major concerns are summarized in the headnote to the poems themselves. Her biography, however, is not, so we sketch it briefly here: Rukeyser was the elder child of upwardly mobile, Jewish, American- born parents. In 1944, at the very moment when the outlines of the Holocaust were becoming known, she opened the seventh poem in her sequence "Letter to the Front" with the startling lines, "To be a Jew in the twentieth century/Is to be offered a gift." Her father was a partner in a sand-and-gravel company in New York. Seeing the concrete poured for sidewalks and skyscrapers made her feel part of the city; later, somewhat like Hart Crane, she would celebrate technology. From the Ethical Cultural and Fieldston Schools in New York, she went on to study at Vassar and Columbia until her father's supposed bankruptcy prevented her from continuing. Her mother had expected her to marry and write poetry only as an avocation. Instead, Rukeyser made poetry the focus of her life, traveled, lived in New York and California, and bore and raised a son as a single mother.

Her career as an activist began when she traveled to Alabama to cover the trial of the Scottsboro boys and was arrested. In 1972, she went to Vietnam with Denise Levertov on an unofficial writers' peace mission. She taught at the California Labor School in the mid-forties and from the mid-fifties through the sixties at Sarah Lawrence. She taught children in Harlem and led writing classes for women in the seventies. Especially in her later years, Rukeyser broke taboos about female sexuality. In poems like "Waiting for Icarus" and "Myth" she rewrote classical myths from a woman's perspective. Here in "Rite" she dramatizes the culture's investments in gender and in "The Poem as Mask" overturns gender dichotomy by treating it as a constructed myth. In a culture that does not recognize the sexuality of old age, Rukeyser celebrated it. She never labeled her sexuality, but in poetry and letters she celebrated her intimate relations with both women and men.

Significant Form, Style, or Artistic Conventions

"Absalom" is the ninth of twenty poems in Rukeyser's "The Book of the Dead" in her 1938 book *U.S. 1.* A number of the poems are given over to the perspective of individual figures in the Gauley Tunnel tragedy. Stylistically, the poem is unusual for shifting from journalistic reportage to interior monologue to lyrical description. It mixes public rhetoric and private speech, judges America's history and its contemporary institutions, and interrogates natural and industrial power. It is one of the most important modern poems in mixed forms and one of the major achievements of her career.

Questions for Reading, Discussion, and Writing

As with all socially conscious and progressive poetry read within a discipline that has doubts about its viability, it is important to raise both general intellectual issues and questions that lead students to read closely. Here are a few examples:

1. Compare and contrast how several white poets and several black poets deal with issues of race—perhaps Rukeyser, Genevieve Taggard, Kay Boyle, Jean Toomer, Gwendolyn Bennett, Claude McKay, and Langston Hughes.
2. Rukeyser's "Absalom" is a 1930s poem that would have been read at the time as part of the proletarian literature movement. Compare this with the 1930s poems in "Cluster: Political Poetry in the Modern Period."
3. Read about the classical myths behind "The Minotaur" and "The Poem as Mask: Orpheus" and discuss how Rukeyser adapts and transforms them.
4. What model of political action is put forward in "How We Did It"? What does the poem say about means and ends?
5. "Rite" manages with its economical phrasing to both describe a rite and enact one. Are they different?

Carlos Bulosan (1913–1956)

Contributing Editors: Amy Ling, Oscar Campomanes, and King-Kok Cheung

Classroom Issues and Strategies

Some readers may be repulsed by what they consider an overly negative portrayal of American society. Their reactions range from incredulity to discomfort to rejection of what they consider to be exaggeration. Other readers are quick to dismiss Bulosan on aesthetic criteria, believing *America Is in the Heart* to be autobiographical and sociological rather than "literary." The issue of genre is another problem area: his fiction seems autobiographical, his poetry prosy, his short stories read like essays and his essays like short stories.

Providing students with biographical background on Bulosan and giving them historical information on Philippine immigration will set this text into its proper context. This text is primarily a novel and at the same time, as Carey McWilliams has pointed out, "it reflects the collective life experience of thousands of Filipino immigrants who were attracted to this country by its legendary promises of a better life."

If a slide show or video on Philippine immigration is obtaïnable, it would provide useful information. The film *Manongs* from Visual Communications in California is an excellent introduction. NAATA/Cross Current Media at 346 Ninth Street, San Francisco, is an excellent source of Asian- American videos.

As students read Bulosan, they ask, "Who is this man? What group does he belong to? What are his concerns? Is the plight of the immigrant today different than it was in the 1930s and 1940s?"

Major Themes, Historical Perspectives, Personal Issues

Bulosan's major theme is exile and return—the effect of departure from home and the necessity to return to the Philippines in order to make sense of the exile's experience in the United States because of the colonial status of the Philippines.

His second purpose is to record his own, his family's, and his friends' experiences and lives, their loneliness and alienation.

Significant Form, Style, or Artistic Conventions

Bulosan wrote with an eye to violating literary conventions, as mentioned above. As a political activist and labor organizer, he also believed that creative literary activity and social purpose cannot be separated. Students should be made aware of the gulf between the ideals of America as the land of equality and opportunity and the painful, violent reality Bulosan delineates in this representative selection of *America Is in the Heart*.

Original Audience

Bulosan, at the beginning of his career, wrote for a mainstream American audience and was placed in the position of cultural mediator, a bridge between the Philippines (which America wanted to know better during World War II) and the United States. Late in life, he consciously cultivated a Filipino audience, sending stories back to the Philippines, most of which were rejected. In the 1970s, he was "rediscovered" by Asian-Americans delighted to have found a spokesperson as prolific and multifaceted as he.

Comparisons, Contrasts, Connections

In his unadorned, deceptively simple prose style, he resembles Ernest Hemingway; in his social concerns, John Steinbeck's *The Grapes of Wrath*. Bulosan may be compared with Maxine Hong Kingston in that both were critically acclaimed by a wide audience but denounced by certain portions of their own community who accused them of having "sold out." With Kingston he also shares a reliance on peasant forms of storytelling as well as the seeming incoherence of their works and the question of genre.

Questions for Reading, Discussion, and Writing

1. The students may be directed to think about whether there are distinguishing characteristics to Filipino immigrant experience setting it apart from that of the Chinese, Japanese, Korean, or any European group.
2. Ask students to keep a journal of their random reactions to the text. On a sheet of paper, have them record quotations, phrases, or words from the text that were particularly significant to them; on the right-hand side of the sheet, they are to record their reactions. Later, they write a one page statement of their responses, setting up a dialogue between themselves and their instructor. The instructor then makes a response and dittoes up the dialogue so that the entire class can enter into the dialogue. Finally, the class writes papers on the entire classroomwide dialogue.

Bibliography

Gier, Jean Vengua. "'. . . . to Have Come from Someplace': *October Light, America Is in the Heart,* and 'Flip' Writing after the Third World Strikes." *Hitting Critical Mass: A Journal of Asian American Cultural Criticism* 2.2 (1995): 1–33.

Gonzalez, N. V. M., and Oscar V. Campomanes. "Filipono American Literature. *An Interethnic Companion to Asian American Literature.* Ed. King-Kok Cheung. New York: Cambridge UP, 1996. 62–124.

Gotera, Vince. "Carlos Bulosan: Passion, Poetry, Politics." *Connecticut Review* 15.2 (1993): 11–23.

Jaskoski, Helen. "Carlos Bulosan's Literary Debt to Richard Wright." *Literary Influence and African-American Writers.* Ed. Tracy Mishkin. New York: Garland, 1996. 231–43.

Lee, Rachel C. *The Americas of Asian American Literature: Gendered Fictions of Nation and Transnation.* Princeton: Princeton UP, 1999.

Mostern, Kenneth. "Why Is America in the Heart?" *Hitting Critical Mass: A Journal of Asian American Cultural Criticism* 2.2 (1995): 35–65.

San Juan, E., Jr. "Beyond Identity Politics: The Predicament of the Asian Writer in Late Capitalism." *American Literary History* 3.3 (1991): 542–65.

———. "In Search of Filipino Writing: Reclaiming Whose 'America'?" *The Ethnic Canon: Histories, Institutions, and Interventions.* Ed. David Palumbo-Liu. Minneapolis: U of Minnesota P, 1995. 213–40.

———. "Searching for the Heart of 'America' (Carlos Bulosan)." *Teaching American Ethnic Literatures: Nineteen Essays.* Ed. John R. Maitino and David R. Peck. Albuquerque: U of New Mexico P, 1996. 259–72.

Robert Hayden (1913–1980)

Contributing Editor: Robert M. Greenberg

Classroom Issues and Strategies

It's important to get students to fully appreciate Hayden's effects of sound, image, and atmosphere. For better appreciation of the poems' aural qualities, have students read such selections as "Summertime and the Living" and "Mourning Poem for the Queen of Sunday" out loud.

Discuss a condensed narrative poem such as "Tour 5" as a short story. This should permit a discussion of the evolving point of view of the travelers and the evolving psychological quality of the imagery.

Point out also Hayden's control of voice. "Mourning Poem," for example, is spoken in the idiom of the black church, as if by a chorus of mourners; and if one reads the final lines to mean that the congregation *did* suspect her of misbehaving, then the poem becomes a masterpiece of wryness and irony.

Students are interested in questions like the following:

1. Is it possible to be both an ethnic and a universal (or liberal humanist) writer? What constitutes universality? What constitutes successful treatment of ethnic material?
2. Can a writer from a minority group write for a general educated audience without giving up in resonance what is gained in breadth of audience and reference?

Major Themes, Historical Perspectives, Personal Issues

Major themes are tension between the imagination and the tragic nature of life, the past in the present, and the nurturing power of early life and ethnically colored memories.

Significant Form, Style, or Artistic Conventions

Precede discussion of form and style with a discussion of the function of a particular type of poem. For example, Hayden wrote spirit-of-place poems such as "Tour 5," which depend heavily on imagery; folk character poems such as "Mourning Poem for the Queen of Sunday," which depend on economy of characterization and humor; and early neighborhood poems such as "Summertime and the Living," which depend on realism mixed with nostalgia, fancy, or psychological symbolism.

Original Audience

It is important to realize Hayden always wrote for a general literate audience, not exclusively or even primarily for a black audience. The issue of audience for him relates to the issue of the role of a poet.

Comparisons, Contrasts, Connections

Compare Yeats as an ethnic-universal poet with Hayden.

Questions for Reading, Discussion, and Writing

1. "Tour 5"
   (a) Discuss the human situation the poem describes. Consider its treatment of both the external and internal aspects of the experience for the travelers.
   (b) Discuss the allusive quality of the adjectives used in the first stanza to convey a festive mood and in the last three lines to convey the violence of the Civil War and the cruelty of slavery.
   (c) Discuss what makes this a poem of the first order. Conciseness, controlled intensity, human drama, eloquence, and powerful symbols are some of the qualities you might touch on.

2. "Summertime and the Living"
   (a) Discuss Hayden's use of a third-person retrospective point of view to write about childhood. (It gives him the ability to be both inside and outside the child's perspective.)
   (b) Discuss the sound of words and their connection with sense. Hayden is highly conscious of the aural dimension of language.
   (c) What is the function of the title, which is taken from a song in George and Ira Gershwin's opera *Porgie and Bess*?
3. "Mourning Poem for the Queen of Sunday"
   (a) Discuss the viewpoint of the speakers about the murdered diva. Discuss the final two lines. Are they at all ironic? Are the speakers totally surprised?
   (b) Discuss the importance of tone throughout the poem.
   (c) Discuss the poem's atmosphere and how elements other than tone contribute to the black church feeling.

Bibliography

Greenberg, Robert M. "Robert Hayden." *American Writers: A Collection of Literary Biographies*, Supplement II, Part I. Ed. A. Walton Litz. New York: Scribner's, 1981. 361–83. Has biographical, critical, and bibliographical material.

Hayden, Robert. *Collected Prose: Robert Hayden*. Ed. Frederick Glaysher. Ann Arbor: U of Michigan P, 1984. Has excellent interview material with Hayden about particular poems.

Bernard Malamud (1914–1986)

Contributing Editor: Evelyn Avery

Classroom Issues and Strategies

Jewish in style and character types, Bernard Malamud's fiction appeals to a broad range of students who appreciate the author's warmth, ironic humor, and memorable characters. Above all, they find his blend of the universal and the particular appealing and unique.

A writer who uses fantasy and history, who creates tragic and comic characters, who can write realistically and metaphorically, Malamud will challenge and delight students of varied backgrounds. Occasionally, "Yiddish" expressions or Jewish ritual will have to be explained, but, for the most part, meaning will be derived from context.

Since the effects of suffering are central to Malamud's fiction, students should learn that his Jews symbolize all victims and that his characters cannot be easily categorized as heroes or villains.

Major Themes, Historical Perspectives, Personal Issues

Writing in the last third of the twentieth century, Malamud was aware of social problems: rootlessness, infidelity, abuse, divorce, and more, but he believes in love as redemptive and sacrifice as uplifting. Often, success depends on cooperation between antagonists. In "The Magic Barrel," the matchmaker worries about his "fallen" daughter while the daughter and the rabbinic student are drawn together by their need for love and salvation.

If Malamud's readers are sometimes disappointed by ambiguous or unhappy endings, they are often reassured about the existence of decency in a corrupt world. Malamud's guarded optimism reflects several influences. He cites American authors Nathaniel Hawthorne and Henry James as guides to moral and spiritual struggles. Like them, Malamud holds individuals responsible for their behavior. He also admires the Russian writers Fyodor Dostoyevski and Anton Chekhov for their vibrant portrayal of the self versus society. Although he does not mention other Jewish writers as influences, he concedes "a common fund of Jewish experience and possibly an interest in the ethical approach."

In interviews, Malamud credits his hardworking "Yiddish" parents and their Eastern-European immigrant generation with providing models of morality, but he emphasizes that humanity is his subject and that he uses Jews to communicate the universal just as William Faulkner created a universe from a corner of the American South.

Despite his universality or perhaps because of it, Malamud resembles a number of American Jewish authors, including earlier twentieth-century writers such as Abraham Cahan, Anzia Yezierska, and Henry Roth as well as post–World War II authors such as Isaac Bashevis Singer, Saul Bellow, and Philip Roth. Because Jewish fiction can reflect life's uncertainties and absurdities, it has broad appeal to contemporary readers, who applaud the attempt of ordinary people to determine their fate. Such themes, however, are evident in the non-Jewish literature that Malamud recognized when he described himself, in a 1975 interview, as "an American . . . a Jew, and . . . a writer for all men."

His universality, however, is rooted in distinctive character types, settings, and details. Thus, the "schlemiel," a common type in Eastern European Yiddish literature, appears in some American Jewish fiction. Although at times a victim of back luck, the "schlemiel" compounds his problems by choosing wrongly. Yakov Bok (in *The Fixer*), fleeing his Jewish identity, Morris Bober (in *The Assistant*), attempting to burn his store down, and Leo Finkle (in "The Magic Barrel"), insisting that his future wife be young and beautiful, learn to revise their values, reject assimilation, materialism, and conformity, and embrace sacrifice and spirituality. Trapped in depressing, even dangerous settings; in cramped, deteriorating stores, suffocating apartments; condemned buildings; in a nation, Russia, where Jews are at risk everywhere, Malamud's characters are both archetypal Jews and suffering humanity. Malamud's awareness of Jewish pain is best portrayed in *The Fixer*, a novel of extreme anti-Semitism in Tzarist Russia, which for many critics evokes the Holocaust.

Although a serious writer, Malamud uses humor to underscore the preposterous, to highlight grief, and to instruct readers. Thus Frank Alpine (in *The Assistant*) tumbles into the grocer's grave, Seymour Levin (in *A New Life*) lectures with his pants unzipped, and Yakov Bok (in *The Fixer*) rescues an anti-Semite whose gratitude will later lead to Bok's persecution. If Malamud's fiction produces sorrow, it also provokes laughter, albeit nervous laughter.

Original Audience

A best-selling, critically acclaimed author, Bernard Malamud, like Isaac Bashevis Singer and Philip Roth, earned success with the publication of his early Jewish works, *The Magic Barrel* (a collection of short stories) and *The Assistant* in the late 1950s. Although the American Jewish literary renaissance peaked in the 1960s and 1970s, writers like Malamud continue to be read and enjoyed. In fact his reputation is steadily growing as students are introduced to his works. Moreover, the general interest in ethnicity draws readers to Jewish literature, where they discover that Bellow, Malamud, Ozick, and Singer, to name a few, speak to all sensitive, intelligent readers.

Comparisons, Contrasts, Connections

As indicated earlier, Malamud's fiction may be compared and contrasted with works by certain European, American, and Jewish authors. Like Fyodor Dostoyevski's characters, Malamud's protagonists are tormented, guilt-ridden, and paranoiac. Their suffering recalls *Crime and Punishment* and *Notes from the Underground* as well as Nathaniel Hawthorne's and Henry James's psychological tales. While Malamud has been identified as an American Jewish writer, his work can be differentiated from Saul Bellow's (considered more cerebral) and from Philip Roth's (judged more satiric). Perhaps the best of his Old World stories resemble those of Isaac Bashevis Singer, whose work attempts to reconcile the Old World and the New.

Questions for Reading, Discussion, and Writing

1. A variety of questions can be posed about Malamud's fiction. Is Malamud, for example, a Jewish writer or a writer who happens to be Jewish? Since "The Magic Barrel" includes a rabbinic student and a matchmaker, how universal is the story? Does the story have a happy ending? What happens? Is this tale representative of the author's works?

2. More ambitious assignments can analyze literary influences on Malamud, his style in comparison with that of other Jewish writers; or male-female relationships; or possibly an imaginative option such as rewriting the story's conclusion.

Bibliography

Since Malamud's death in 1986, his reputation continues to grow. With the establishment of the Bernard Malamud Society and the publication of a newsletter, Malamudian scholars are kept apprised of research and conferences. For further information contact Dr. Evelyn Avery at Towson State University, Towson, MD, 21204; or Dr. Lawrence Lasher, English Department, University of Maryland, Baltimore, Maryland, 21228.

Ralph Waldo Ellison (1914–1994)

Contributing Editor: John Alberti

Classroom Issues and Strategies

"Brave Words for a Startling Occasion," Ellison's acceptance speech on being presented the National Book Award in 1953 for *Invisible Man,* can provide some starting points for class discussion of the two short stories included in *The Heath Anthology.* In the speech, Ellison defines what he sees as the moral responsibilities of the American writer, in terms of both theme and style. Recalling "our classical nineteenth-century novelists" (presumably writers like Melville, Hawthorne, and Stowe), Ellison calls on contemporary writers to return to the "much greater responsibility for the condition of democracy" demonstrated in their novels, which he describes as "imaginative projections of the conflicts within the human heart when the sacred principles of the Constitution and the Bill of Rights clashed with the practical exigencies of human greed and fear, hate and love." As an African-American writer, Ellison says he is especially drawn to the way that in these novels "the Negro was the gauge of the human condition as it waxed and waned in our democracy." "Our task," Ellison concludes, "is always to challenge the apparent forms of reality" and to do so with a prose that is as "flexible, and swift as American change is swift." Operating as both goal and article of faith for Ellison is the idea that, ultimately, "American experience" (and by extension the American people) "is of a whole."

One way into Ellison's stories, then, is to consider how well they exemplify these ideals, both in their graphic, unsparing depictions of the brutality of racism and their invocation of flight as an image of freedom and possibility. In keeping with Ellison's insistence on expressing the multiplicity of experience, he tells these stories of racial oppression through two very different narrators: a young white boy facing initiation into a legacy of hatred and violence and a young black aviator struggling against internalizing social assumptions of black inferiority. Some overarching questions to consider might be whether and to what extent these different perspectives finally tell one story and what possibilities these stories hold out for challenging and transforming the realities they describe. What are the prospects for communication, empathy, and reconciliation between the narrators of these two stories?

In approaching these stories as rhetorical performances, it is important to consider the question of audience, both the original reading public Ellison may have had in mind when writing these stories (and in this light the fact that "A Party down at the Square" remained unpublished in Ellison's lifetime could be significant) and the demographic context of the classroom where the stories are being discussed: how students in the class identify themselves or find themselves identified racially, geographically, and historically will condition their identification with and interpretation of these two narrators, not necessarily in easily or stereotypically predictable ways, but in significant ways that can be foregrounded as part of class discussion.

This is especially true for "A Party Down at the Square," in which readers are asked to measure their reactions to the horrific events described against their understanding of and sympathy with the young white narrator of the story. The story shares with "Flying Home" the use of the airplane as a complex symbol of modernity, freedom, power, and affluence; in this case, however, the symbol becomes literally entangled in power lines, perhaps suggesting a similar contrast between the ideas of modernity and progress and the legacy of racial oppression embodied in the lynching and the statue of the Confederate Army general overseeing the spectacle. The narrator, significantly a child on the verge of adolescence, acts as a symbolic locus for this conflict, and the moral drama of the story centers on his reactions to the lynching and the ways we as readers think his outlook and actions will be affected. Of particular interest in this story is the way Ellison focuses on the ways white Americans destroy themselves spiritually and even physically through the maintenance of racism (both a white woman and a black man are burned alive during the story, achieving a grisly communion in the blackness of their ashes and the whiteness of bone) as the boy confronts the idea that his "racial" inheritance consists not only of social status and power but also unthinking hatred and violence.

"Flying Home" evokes both the Icarus myth from Greek mythology, with its focus on the heroism and tragedy of ambition, and the "flying African" story from African-American culture, with its invocation of freedom and escape. For Todd in the story, flight represents a way to soar above the limitations imposed by racism on the Earth below, but in his hopes that success as a military aviator will finally "prove" the legitimacy of his and other African Americans' claims to full and equal status in American society, the story suggests he carries those limitations with him as he flies. The story also points to a very specific historical context, as the experience of African-American soldiers in the Second World War, a war fought against a racist German government, in many ways brought to a head frustrations over segregation and racism in the United States and was a key contributing factor to the rise of the modern civil rights movement in the 1950s. One question for class discussion, then, can center on the strategies and difficulties of "proving" one's humanity according to the criteria of a racist society built on the systematic denial of any such claims.

Todd's own ambivalence about his chances for success are embodied in the tension between himself and Jefferson, the poor sharecropper who helps him after the plane crashes. Todd wants to distance himself from a man he sees as a symbol of rural ignorance and passive acceptance of racist oppression, yet he experiences feelings of guilt about these feelings and about how his accident will be interpreted both by white authority figures and other African Americans. At the center of this conflict, Jefferson tells Todd his folktale about his time in heaven, itself another use of the flying African myth. The result is a story within a story, and students can consider how Jefferson's story relates to Todd's, particularly in relation to Todd's fear and anger that Jefferson may be making fun of him.

These questions of insecurity again raise the issue of the psychological damage done by racism that we encounter in "A Party down at the Square," and they can also bring us back to the ironic title of Ellison's National Book Award acceptance essay. How does the self-mocking tone of "Brave Words for a Startling Occasion" lead us to think about Ellison's own rhetorical position in accepting the award? While he seizes the opportunity to make some very specific demands of American writers, there is also a note of suspicion in regards to what the motives of the (largely white) critics who present him this award might be. In the end, we are left thinking about in what ways Todd's ambitions and fears might relate to Ellison's own (successful) attempt to claim a position in American literary history.

Bibliography

Awkward, Michael. *Inspiriting Influences*. New York: Columbia UP, 1991.

Busby, Mark. *Ralph Ellison*. New York: Twayne, 1991.

Kostelanetz, Richard. *Politics in the African-American Novel*. Westport: Greenwood, 1991.

Arthur Miller (b. 1915)

Contributing Editor: Robert A. Martin

Classroom Issues and Strategies

Written and first produced for the 1953 drama season in New York, *The Crucible* continues to interest students for its witchcraft theme and setting in Salem, and for its more recent political association as a historical parable against the dangers of McCarthyism. While the latter issue has generally faded in the public mind, it was very much *the* issue when the play opened. The several layers of meaning—historical (witchcraft), political (McCarthy-ism and the activities of the House Un-American Activities Committee), and the ever-present approach to the play as stagecraft and theater—allow an instructor to open the play to a class probably not knowledgeable about any of the layers. I have found that such a class is quickly taken up to the level of the play. Miller has added a running commentary on the issues and personalities of Salem. It is important to point out that there is no character in the play "who did not play a similar—and in some cases exactly the same—role in history" (Arthur Miller in his "Note" on the historical accuracy of *The Crucible*).

The witch-hunt that occurred in Salem in 1692 resulted from a complex society at a turning point when the power of the Massachusetts theocracy was weakening. Reverend Parris was more representative of absolute church authority than Miller makes him out. Once the issues came into the open, he found that the whole "devilish" conspiracy needed wiser and more learned minds to uncover it, even if he was absolutely convinced of the reality of witchcraft. I usually begin a class by stating that at Salem on Gallows Hill in the spring of 1692, nineteen men and women were hanged; one man, Giles Corey, was pressed to death for standing mute; and two dogs were also hanged for witchcraft. The classroom then becomes a different place; the question of witchcraft, or how could those people have believed in it, brings out some interesting and fruitful ideas, discussions, viewpoints. Discussion of the play, however, should identify the McCarthyism parallels in a way that students can understand. Miller has said that the theme of the play is "the handing over of conscience to the state." The question is not entirely a remote one, as almost any major newspaper or television exposé can make the issue clear to today's students.

Major Themes, Historical Perspectives, Personal Issues

Central to this play, in addition to Miller's theme stated above, is one of illusion versus reality. In a society that held a doctrinal belief in the power and reality of the devil to "overthrow God's kingdom," the powers of persuasion to see "specters" where there were none resulted in mass hysteria. When John Proctor, a born skeptic, challenges the illusion, he is subsequently brought down by the reality of his adultery. As the witch-hunt spread to eventually cause the arrest of prominent citizens, some form of common sense prevailed and the girls were silenced. The Salem hysteria has been investigated and researched widely, and many excellent sources are available. One recent theory proposed that the whole business was the result of ergot poisoning, a bacteria that produces hallucinations if wheat is stored for too long and is allowed to ferment. This, of course, was the theory of a modern-day scientist who also happened to be a graduate student. It was a neat and "scientific" solution to a very old question. Unfortunately, the whole theory collapsed when expert senior biologists looked at the idea closer and declared it bad science. Miller, possibly as a result of the play, was called before the House Un-American Activities Committee in 1956 on the pretense of issuing him a passport. He was convicted of contempt of Congress for refusing to answer questions about the communistic connections of others. The decision was later reversed. Miller had in effect been convicted on the same principle as John Proctor—guilt by association—and like Proctor, he refused to name others.

Original Audience

In the early 1950s, there was something resembling a cohesive audience for serious plays. That audience was both shocked and fearful that the theme and subject of the play would unleash still further inquiries by the forces of McCarthyism. Reviewers, reflecting the mood of the audience, had several reactions. Some praised the acting, some thought it was a play without contemporary parallels, and others avoided the play's obvious point altogether. The best way to understand the response by critics is to read their reviews in the 1953 volume of *New York Theatre Critics' Reviews*.

Bibliography

Miller has written at length on the play and on the context of the time. The following are easily available sources I have my students use in their research. The first and probably most important are Miller's comments in volume one of *Arthur Miller's Collected Plays* (New York: Viking, 1957), pp. 38–48. All of Miller's essays are reprinted in my *The Theater Essays of Arthur Miller* (New York: Viking, 1978), including several comments made over the next several decades. An early work on *The Crucible* was (at the time) nicely complete and informative for its comprehensive critical collection of essays on the play, the history behind it, and the context: *The Crucible: Text and Criticism*, ed. Gerald Weales (Penguin, 1977, first published by Viking in 1971). John H. Ferres edited a useful collection of essays on the play titled *Twentieth Century Interpretations of The Crucible: A Collection of Critical Essays* (Prentice, 1972). Also of interest for its judicious selection of essays and an interview with Miller in 1979 in which many references and comments on *The Crucible* occur is *Critical Essays on Arthur Miller*, ed. James J. Martine (Boston: Hall, 1979). Somewhat of broader scope, but nevertheless useful for its international Miller bibliography by Charles A. Carpenter and a fine essay by Walter Meserve on *The Crucible* is *Arthur Miller: New Perspectives*, ed. Robert A. Martin (Prentice, 1982). My essay, "Arthur Miller's *The Crucible*: Background and Sources," has proven of use to many students and scholars who seek to learn some of the connections between the play and Salem in 1692, and has been reprinted numerous times, most recently in *Essays on Modern American Drama*, ed. Dorothy Parker (U of Toronto P, 1987), and in Martine's *Critical Essays* noted above. I recommend that my students read selectively in *Conversations with Arthur Miller*, ed. Matthew C. Roudane (U of Mississippi P, 1987). There are fifty-two page references listed in the index for *The Crucible*. Miller's comments in conversations and interviews are frequently more enlightening than any other playwright in our history because he is articulate as well as theoretically sophisticated. Finally, a more recent account is *The Crucible: Politics, Property, and Pretense* (New York: Twayne Masterworks Series, 1993), by James J. Martine, which is one of the most complete and comprehensive studies of *The Crucible* to date. Martine is a well-known Miller scholar, and his critical judgment is astute.

Saul Bellow (b. 1915)

Contributing Editor: Allan Chavkin

Classroom Issues and Strategies

I think the best strategy is to focus on specific parts of the story by asking a series of specific questions. This particular story can be approached on two different levels, for it is both a realistic depiction of a relief worker's dedicated attempt to search for an unemployed, crippled black man in the slums of Depression Chicago in order to deliver a welfare check and a symbolic quest to discover the relationship between reality and appearances.

My approach to the story is generally conventional—asking questions and prompting class discussion on key issues. Another possible approach would be to play all or part of an excellent unabridged audio-recording of the story by Books on Tape, P.O. Box 7900, Newport Beach, CA 92658-7900, and discuss the interpretation that the Books-on-Tape reader gives to the story.

Another classroom strategy might be to encourage students to explore some of the websites listed at the end of this article in order to better understand the bygone era of the Depression, the culture of African-American Chicago, and Plato's ideas on reality and appearance (e.g., the allegory of the cave), to which the story alludes. These topics might be good starting points for class discussion.

Students often respond actively to the following issues raised by "Looking for Mr. Green":

1. Money as a formative influence on the creation of identity
2. The problem of the noncompetitive in a highly competitive society
3. The clash between idealism and cynical "realism," between the noble idealist and the cynic
4. The quest of a stubborn idealist in an irrational world
5. Racism and stereotyping
6. Plato's world of appearances versus the world of reality

Major Themes, Historical Perspectives, Personal Issues

Historical Issues and Themes: How does society help the downtrodden (in this story an unemployed crippled black man) in bad economic times (e.g., the Depression)? The story also examines the problems of race, class, and gender. Other issues that the class might focus upon are the plight of the noncompetitive in a capitalistic, highly competitive society; how money influences character; and the alienation of the urban black man.

Personal Issues and Themes: How does an idealistic humanist (i.e., the typical Bellow hero) reconcile noble ideas with the harsh facts of the human condition? Is man essentially a victim of his situation, or is he the master of his fate? What is Bellow suggesting about the problem of human suffering and evil? The relationship of the individual to his society? The relationship of appearance to reality? The clash between the human need to order and make sense of life according to moral principles and life's amoral disorder, discontinuity, irrationality, and mystery?

Significant Form, Style, or Artistic Conventions

The story can be discussed as a bildungsroman, as a parable, as a symbolic quest, and as a realistic depiction of the Depression and of the alienation of the urban black man.

Comparisons, Contrasts, Connections

The story might be compared with some works by such black writers as James Baldwin, Richard Wright, and Ralph Ellison, or any other writers who have written about the Depression (e.g., John Steinbeck). The story could be compared with some stories by such naturalistic writers as Theodore Dreiser and Jack London who are also concerned with the free will versus determinism theme. An interesting comparison would be with F. Scott Fitzgerald, who wrote on the formative influence of money on the self. The idea that illusion is necessary for the survival of self in a harsh, predatory world is a central theme of modern American drama (Eugene O'Neill, Tennessee Williams, and Arthur Miller), and this story might be compared with the most important modern American plays. Bellow's depiction of women might be compared with that of other writers.

Questions for Reading, Discussion, and Writing

1. (a) What is the purpose in the story of Grebe's supervisor Raynor? What is Bellow's attitude toward Raynor's cynical "wisdom"? Is concern for the individual anachronistic? For philosophical studies?
   (b) What is the purpose of the encounter with the Italian grocer who presents a hellish vision of the city with its chaotic masses of suffering humanity?
   (c) The old man Field offers this view of money—"Nothing is black where it shines and the only place you see black is where it ain't

shining." Discuss. What do you think of the scheme for creating black millionaires? Why does Bellow include this scheme in the story?

(d) What is the purpose of the Staika incident in the story? Raynor sees her as embodying "the destructive force" that will "submerge everybody in time," including "nations and governments." In contrast, Grebe sees her as "the life force." Who is closer to the truth?

(e) The word *sun* and sun imagery are repeated throughout the story. Discuss.

2. (a) Discuss the theme of appearance versus reality.

(b) Bellow ends the story with Grebe's encounter with the drunken, naked black woman, who may be another embodiment of the spirit of Staika. Why does Bellow conclude the story this way? Has Grebe failed or succeeded? Is he deceiving himself?

(c) David Demarest comments: "Grebe's stubborn idealism is nothing less than the basic human need to construct the world according to intelligent, moral principles." Discuss.

(d) Believing that "Looking for Mr. Green" needs to be seen "as one of the great short stories of our time," Eusebio Rodrigues argues that the Old Testament flavors it. This story is "a modern dramatization of Ecclesiastes." Discuss.

Working with Cultural Objects

The *Modern American Poetry* website at <http://www.english.uiuc.edu/maps/depression/photoessay.htm> contains interesting photos of the Depression era. It is organized as a photo essay and will help students understand the historical context of the story.

The New Deal Network, at <http//www.feri.org>, an educational guide to the Great Depression of the 1930s, is sponsored by the Franklin and Eleanor Roosevelt Institute. Development of the NDN was funded in part through a grant from the National Endowment for the Humanities.

Archival resources on the Great Depression at the Carl Albert Center Congressional Archives can be found at <http//www.ou.edu/special/albertctr/archives/gd web.htm>. Broad subject areas on the Great Depression (1929–1941) are listed with entries describing specific materials contained in individual collections.

A site containing newspaper articles about the Great Depression can be found at <http//www.ramona.k12.ca.us/rhs/rhslmc/langarts/1930s_new.htm>.

The *Saul Bellow Journal* and the *Saul Bellow Annotated Bibliography and Research Guide* website at <http//www.saulbellow.org/index.html> is the definitive bibliographic resource for Bellow scholars. It combines the content of all previously printed bibliographies and has been updated to 2001, including the most recent materials that are available according to the current databases. It will be updated annually. This website also offers information about Saul Bellow events through the *SBS Newsletter,* as well as through the encyclopedia entry that Gloria Cronin, president of the Saul Bellow Society, has compiled concerning his life and works. The Library offers critical overviews for each of Bellow's novels.

Links to many websites about Chicago history can be found at <http://www .ukans.edu/history/VL/USA/urban/chicago.html>.

Understanding Plato's allegory of the cave might be useful in interpreting "Looking for Mr. Green." Students unfamiliar with Plato's thought will find the following websites informative:

<http//www.en.wikipedia.org/wiki/Plato's_allegory_of_the_cave>

<http//www.wsu.edu:8080/~wldciv/world_civ_reader/world_civ_reader_1/ plato.html>

<http//www.faculty.washington.edu/smcohen/320/cave.htm>

<http//www.wsu.edu/~dee/GREECE/ALLEGORY.HTM>

<http//www.plotinus.com/plato_allegory_of_the_cave.htm>

Bibliography

Atlas, James. *Bellow: A Biography.* New York: Random, 2000.

Chavkin, Allan. "The Problem of Suffering in the Fiction of Saul Bellow." *Comparative Literature Studies* 21 (Summer 1984): 161–74. Provides an overview of Bellow's work and analyzes key influences on the fiction.

Demarest, David. "The Theme of Discontinuity in Saul Bellow's Fiction: 'Looking for Mr. Green' and 'A Father-to-be.'" *Studies in Short Fiction* 6 (Winter 1969): 175–86. Reprinted in *Small Planets.*

Friedrich, Marianne M. *Character and Narration in the Short Fiction of Saul Bellow.* New York: Lang, 1995. 47–57.

Fuchs, Daniel. *Saul Bellow: Vision and Revision.* Durham: Duke UP, 1984. 287–89.

Kiernan, Robert F. *Saul Bellow.* New York: Continuum, 1988. 121–24.

Kindilien, Glenn A. "The Meaning of the Name 'Green' in Saul Bellow's 'Looking for Mr. Green.'" *Studies in Short Fiction* 15 (1978): 104–07.

Nakajima, Renji. "A Study of S. Bellow's 'Looking for Mr. Green.'" *Kyushu American Literature* 18 (1977): 5–18.

Opdahl, Keith M. *The Novels of Saul Bellow.* University Park: Pennsylvania State UP, 1967. 100–03.

Rodrigues, Eusebio L. "Koheleth in Chicago: The Quest for the Real in 'Looking for Mr. Green.'" *Studies in Short Fiction* 11 (Fall 1974): 387–93.

Gwendolyn Brooks (1917–2001)

Contributing Editor: D. H. Melhem

Classroom Issues and Strategies

Brooks's work is generally accessible. Occasionally, however, and more likely in some earlier works, like *Annie Allen* and individual poems like "Riders to the Blood-red Wrath," intense linguistic and semantic compression present minor difficulties.

My *Gwendolyn Brooks: Poetry and the Heroic Voice* can be used as a guide to her published works. As holds true for most poetry, Brooks's should be read aloud. In the process, its power (boosted by alliteration), the musicality, and the narrative are vivified.

Students seem taken with Brooks's identity poems like "The Life of Lincoln West" and the didactic "Ballad of Pearl May Lee," which was Hughes's favorite. The narrative aspect seems to be especially appealing. As these are not in this anthology, you may wish to recommend them as extra reading.

Major Themes, Historical Perspectives, Personal Issues

Themes include black pride, black identity and solidarity, black humanism, and caritas, a maternal vision. Historically, racial discrimination; the civil rights movement of the fifties; black rebellion of the sixties; a concern with complacency in the seventies; black leadership.

Significant Form, Style, or Artistic Conventions

Brooks was influenced at first by the Harlem Renaissance. Her early work featured the sonnet and the ballad, and she experimented with adaptations of conventional meter. Later, development of the black arts movement in the sixties, along with conceptions of a black aesthetic, turned her toward free verse and an abandonment of the sonnet as inappropriate to the times. She retained, however, her interest in the ballad—its musicality and accessibility—and in what she called "verse journalism."

Comparisons, Contrasts, Connections

In the early works: Langston Hughes, Emily Dickinson, Paul Laurence Dunbar, Merrill Moore, Edna St. Vincent Millay, Claude McKay, Anne Spencer.

In the later works: Amiri Baraka, Haki R. Madhubuti, and again, Hughes.

Bibliography

The most useful books on Brooks are the following:

Melhem, D. H. *Gwendolyn Brooks: Poetry and the Heroic Voice.* Lexington: UP of Kentucky, 1987. Chronologically discusses each major work in a separate chapter; biographical introduction; biocritical, prosodic, and historical approach; discusses correspondence with first publisher.

———. *Heroism in the New Black Poetry: Introductions and Interviews.* UP of Kentucky, 1990. The first of six chapters that offer introductions to and interviews with six outstanding black poets who bear some relation to or affinity with Brooks presents a summary of her life and art. Includes a discussion of new work (*The Near-Johannesburg Boy*, "Winnie" in *Gottschalk and the Grande Tarantelle*), an essay, "The Black Family," a new poem, and an interview arranged for the book. This American Book Award–winning work also features Dudley Randall, Haki R. Madhubuti, Sonia Sanchez, Jayne Cortez, and Amiri Baraka.

Other books include the following:

Bloom, Harold, ed. *Gwendolyn Brooks.* Broomall, PA: Chelsea, 2001. Essays.

Bolden, B. J. *Urban Rage in Bronzeville: Social Commentary in the Poetry of Gwendolyn Brooks, 1945–1960.* Third World, 1999.

Kent, George E. *A Life of Gwendolyn Brooks*. Foreword and Afterword by D. H. Melhem. Lexington: UP of Kentucky, 1990. Biography.

Mootry, M. K., and G. Smith, eds. *A Life Distilled*. Champaign/Urbana: U of Illinois P, 1987. Essays.

Shaw, Harry. *Gwendolyn Brooks*. New York: Twayne, 1980. Presents a thematic approach.

Wright, Stephen G., ed. *On Gwendolyn Brooks*. Ann Arbor: U of Michigan P, 1996. Essays.

Robert Lowell Jr. (1917–1977)

Contributing Editor: Linda Wagner-Martin

Classroom Issues and Strategies

Lowell's poetry is more difficult than readers expect, deceptively difficult. Since many students come to him expecting an accessible poet (after all, he's one of those "confessionals"), they sometimes resent having to mine his poems for the background and the allusive sources they contain. Attention to an explicative preparation usually helps. "New Critical" methods are very appropriate.

Major Themes, Historical Perspectives, Personal Issues

The combination of the historical with the personal is one of Lowell's most pervasive themes. His illustrious and prominent family (the Lowells) created a burden for both his psyche and his art. The reader must know history to read Lowell. The human mind in search, moving with intuitive understanding (as opposed to a reliance on fact), sometimes succeeding, sometimes not, is Lowell's continuing theme.

Significant Form, Style, or Artistic Conventions

A range of forms must be studied—Lowell is the most formal of poets, even toward the end, with the so-called "notebooks." Studying his intense revision (hardly a word left unchanged from the original version to the final) and examining his effort to skew natural language into his highly concentrated form are both good approaches.

Original Audience

Consider the whole business of the confessional, as Lowell moved from the historical into his unique blend of the personal and the historical.

Address the issue of location. Boston, the New England area, held not only Lowell's history but also the country's.

Comparisons, Contrasts, Connections

Compare Lowell's poetry to that of Randall Jarrell, Anne Sexton, Theodore Roethke, Elizabeth Bishop, and Sylvia Plath.

Hisaye Yamamoto (b. 1921)

Contributing Editor: King-Kok Cheung

Classroom Issues and Strategies

It is useful to spend some time introducing Japanese-American history and culture, especially the practice of "picture bride" (which sheds light on the marriage of Mr. and Mrs. Hayashi) and the style of communication among Issei and Nisei.

It would be helpful to analyze "Seventeen Syllables" in terms of a double plot: the overt one concerning Rosie and the covert one concerning Mrs. Hayashi. Students often relate to the interaction between mother and daughter and are appalled by Mr. Hayashi's callousness.

Instructors may also consider showing *Hot Summer Winds*, a film written and directed by Emiko Omori, and based on Yamamoto's "Seventeen Syllables" and "Yoneko's Earthquake." It was first broadcast in May 1991 as part of PBS's *American Playhouse* series.

Major Themes, Historical Perspectives, Personal Issues

1. The relatively restrained interaction between Issei (first generation) and Nisei (second generation) as a result of both cultural prescription and language barrier
2. The historical practice of "picture bride," according to which the bride and the groom had only seen each other's photos before marriage
3. The theme of aborted creativity
4. The sexual and racial barriers faced by the author herself, who came of age in an internment camp during World War II

Significant Form, Style, or Artistic Conventions

Stress the narrative strategies of the author, especially her use of naïve narrator. While Yamamoto may have been influenced by the modernist experimentation with limited point of view, she also capitalizes on the scant verbal interchange between her Japanese-American characters to build suspense and tension.

Original Audience

The work has always been intended for a multicultural audience, but the reader's appreciation will undoubtedly be enhanced by knowledge of Japanese-American history and culture.

Comparisons, Contrasts, Connections

1. James Joyce (*Dubliners*) for the use of naive narrator
2. Grace Paley for the interaction between husbands and wives, and between immigrant parents and their children
3. Wakako Yamauchi for the relationship between mothers and daughters

Questions for Reading, Discussion, and Writing

1. (a) How do cultural differences complicate intergenerational communication in "Seventeen Syllables"?
   (b) Are there any connections between the episodes about Rosie and those about her mother?
   (c) What effects does the author achieve by using a limited point of view?

2. (a) How does Yamamoto connect the two plots concerning Rosie and her mother in "Seventeen Syllables"?
   (b) Analyze the theme of deception in "Seventeen Syllables."
   (c) Compare the use of the daughter's point of view in Hisaye Yamamoto's "Seventeen Syllables" and Grace Paley's "The Loudest Voice."

Bibliography

Cheng, Ming L. "The Unrepentant Fire: Tragic Limitations in Hisaye Yamamoto's 'Seventeen Syllables.'" *MELUS* 19.4 (1994): 91–108.

Cheung, King-Kok. *Articulate Silences: Hisaye Yamamoto, Maxine Hong Kingston, Joy Kogawa.* Ithaca: Cornell UP, 1993.

——. "Double-Telling: Intertextual Silence in Hisaye Yamamoto's Fiction." *American Literary History* 3.2 (1991): 277–93. Rpt. in *Seventeen Syllables.* Ed. King-Kok Cheung. 161–80.

——. "Hisaye Yamamoto and Wakako Yamauchi: Interview by King-Kok Cheung." *Words Matter: Conversations with Asian American Writers.* Ed. King-Kok Cheung. Honolulu: U of Hawaii P, 2000. 243–82.

——. "Reading between the Syllables: Hisaye Yamamoto's *'Seventeen Syllables' and Other Stories."* *Teaching American Ethnic Literatures.* Ed. John R. Maitino and David R. Peck. Albuquerque: U of New Mexico P, 1996. 313–25.

Cheung, King-Kok, ed. *Seventeen Syllables* [A Casebook]. New Brunswick: Rutgers UP, 1994.

Crow, Charles L. "Home and Transcendence in Los Angeles Fiction." *Los Angeles in Fiction: A Collection of Original Essays.* Ed. David Fine. Albuquerque: U of New Mexico P, 1984. 189–205.

——. "The Issei Father in the Fiction of Hisaye Yamamoto." *Opening up Literary Criticism: Essays on American Prose and Poetry.* Ed. Leo Truchlar. Salzburg: Verlag Wolfgang Neugebauer, 1986. 34–40. Rpt. in *Seventeen Syllables.* Ed. King-Kok Cheung. New Brunswick: Rutgers UP, 1994. 119–28.

Goellnicht, Don C. "Transplanted Discourse in Yamamoto's 'Seventeen Syllables.'" *Seventeen Syllables.* Ed. King-Kok Cheung. New Brunswick: Rutgers UP, 1994. 181–93.

Kim, Elaine H. *Asian American Literature: An Introduction to the Writings and Their Social Context.* Philadelphia: Temple UP, 1982.

McDonald, Dorothy R., and Katharine Newman. "Relocation and Dislocation: The Writings of Hisaye Yamamoto and Wakako Yamauchi." *MELUS* 7.3 (1980): 21–38. Rpt. in *Seventeen Syllables.* Ed. King-Kok Cheung. New Brunswick: Rutgers UP, 1994. 129–42.

Matsumoto, Valerie. "Desperately Seeking 'Deirdre': Gender Roles, Multicultural Relations, and Nisei Woman Writers of the 1930s." *Frontiers* 12.1 (1991): 19–32.

Mistri, Zenobia B. "'Seventeen Syllables': A Symbolic Haiku." *Studies in Short Fiction* 27.2 (1990): 197–202. Rpt. in *Seventeen Syllables.* Ed. King-Kok Cheung. New Brunswick: Rutgers UP, 1994. 195–202.

Nakamura, Cayleen. *"Seventeen Syllables": A Curriculum Guide for High School Classroom Use in Conjunction with "Hot Summer Winds."* Los Angeles: Community Television of Southern California, 1991.

Payne, Robert M. "Adapting (to) the Margins: *Hot Summer Winds* and the Stories of Hisaye Yamamoto." *East-West Film Journal* 7.2 (1993): 39–53. Rpt. in *Seventeen Syllables.* Ed. King-Kok Cheung. New Brunswick: Rutgers UP, 1994. 203–18.

Rolf, Robert T. "The Short Stories of Hisaye Yamamoto, Japanese American Writer." *Bulletin of Fukuoka University of Education* 31.1 (1982): 71–86. Rpt. in *Seventeen Syllables.* Ed. King-Kok Cheung. New Brunswick: Rutgers UP, 1994. 89–108.

Schweik, Susan. *A Gulf So Deeply Cut: American Women Poets and the Second World War.* Madison: U of Wisconsin P, 1991.

Wong, Sau-ling C. *Reading Asian American Literature: From Necessity to Extravagance.* Princeton: Princeton UP, 1993.

Yogi, Stan. "Legacies Revealed: Uncovering Buried Plots in the Stories of Hisaye Yamamoto." *Studies in American Fiction* 17.2 (1989): 169–81. Rpt. in *Seventeen Syllables.* Ed. King-Kok Cheung. New Brunswick: Rutgers UP, 1994. 143–160.

——. "Rebels and Heroines: Subversive Narratives in the Stories of Wakako Yamauchi and Hisaye Yamamoto." *Reading the Literatures of Asian*

America. Ed. Shirley Geok-lin Lim and Amy Ling. Philadelphia: Temple UP, 1992. 131–50.

Grace Paley (b. 1922)

Contributing Editor: Rose Yalow Kamel

Classroom Issues and Strategies

The challenge in teaching "The Expensive Moment" lies in the fact that many conservative students define *family values* in direct contrast with the middle-aged Faith Asbury. Her character is a redefinition of that term; she is a secular humanist who is unabashedly sexual, and who has a relationship with her children that encourages them to argue, confront, and engage with her, a single parent, as an equal. Furthermore, younger students not only unfamiliar with this story's context—the aftermath of the Chinese Cultural Revolution—but also ignorant about *our* government's confrontations with its youth in the 1960s and 1970s, may find it difficult to understand why Faith mourns Rachel, her friend's daughter who went underground as a result of an "expensive moment" of choice to bomb military plants and prisons housing radical activists like Rachel herself.

I would therefore (1) encourage discussion and journal writing about the delicate balance that single mothers face maintaining their own personhood amidst political and personal biases that marginalize them; (2) expose students to other Paley stories told from Faith Asbury's first-person point of view (for example, "A Conversation With My Father," "Friends," "Ruthie and Edie") that depict this eponymous maternal narrator in her youth and middle age as receptive to change, yet consistent in advocating a green and sane world where children can live out their lives; (3) invite guest speakers familiar with the cultural context of the 1960s and 1970s; and (4) show political documentaries questioning establishment values, for example, "Letters from Vietnam," footage about the Kent State disaster juxtaposed with the Tiananmen Square massacre. As sophisticated media users, students will be better able to see the interrelatedness of national/international generational conflict.

Major Themes, Historical Perspectives, Personal Issues

Paley's is a multicultural perspective, historically aware of the great waves of immigration that peopled the vibrant New York neighborhoods she evokes so well. Woven into the texture of her fiction are the problems of grassroots working-class mothers who as urban, leftist Jews link playground politics with global conflict. Moreover, Paley is always aware that female sexuality is a source of literary creativity but never separates the craft of literature from the personal and political contexts in which gender conflicts arise.

Overarching is Paley's womanism, maternal and comradely rather than self-reflexive. It is that womanism that, despite the difference in their cultural backgrounds, links Faith with Xie Feng, newly arrived from mainland China to visit New York's teeming Vesey Street. Of an age, both women understand patriarchy, history, and the need to fight for a future to endure their loss of lovers, husbands, and especially, beloved children.

Significant Form, Style, or Artistic Conventions

Paley uses a stylistic collage—fragments and ellipses, a merging of past and present tense—that conveys a sense of wholeness in which setting, character, and point of view coalesce and render with absolute fidelity a small urban world. Tonal irony as well as a near-perfect ear for dialogue makes Paley a writer's writer.

Structurally, Paley's stories resemble women's diary writing—fragmented, fact-focused, immersed in the transitory, seemingly disconnected aspects of daily life that define women's lives.

Original Audience

Paley's reading audience for her earlier stories about growing up as a second-generation immigrant child ("The Loudest Voice," for example) was cosmopolitan, college-educated, and attuned to literary experimentation. Because the audience was not as responsive to political feminism as today's readers, Paley was considered a seamless stylist.

Comparisons, Contrasts, Connections

Some thematic comparison and contrast can be made with Tillie Olsen, whose ethnic and politically activist background is similar to Paley's. Olsen's "I Stand Here Ironing" and *Tell Me a Riddle* involve class and intergenerational conflicts; in fact, in Olsen's novella, feisty, elderly Jews, like Paley's parents, hold on to the secular humanism that they brought with them to America. But Olsen uses women's sexuality more sparingly, making it a problem of gender rather than one of physical urgency for women. Furthermore, Olsen's lush, elegiac style differs from Paley's deft use of irony, humor, economy, and earthiness. Another writer reminiscent of Paley in her depiction of the parent-child conflict and women-bonding in a fluid and changing world is Amy Tan, whose novel *The Joy Luck Club* has bits of dialogue and irony similar to Paley's, though Tan's humor is more life-affirming.

Questions for Reading, Discussion, and Writing

1. (a) Keep a journal focusing on the importance of place in your life. To what extent does place influence identity?
   (b) Write a first-person narrative focusing on your memory of exploring an experience or discovering an idea markedly different from those of your parents.
2. Compare the neighborhood settings in two other Grace Paley stories, "An Interest in Life" and "The Long-Distance Runner." Discuss the way settings in these stories make the first-person narrator feel integrated or marginal in her community.
3. Keep a collection of tapes or photograph albums focusing on intergenerational ties as well as conflicts.

Bibliography

Taylor, Jacqueline. *Grace Paley: Illuminating the Dark Lives.* Austin: U of Texas P, 1990.

Isaacs, Neil D. *Grace Paley: A Study of the Short Fiction.* Boston: Twayne, 1990.

John Okada (1923–1971)

Contributing Editor: King-Kok Cheung

Classroom Issues and Strategies

Students need historical background concerning World War II and the internment of Japanese Americans. Explain how people often internalize the attitudes of the dominant society even though the attitudes may seem unreasonable today. The documentary *Rabbits in the Moon* (1999), directed by Emiko Omori, provides an excellent background for the Japanese-American internment.

Major Themes, Historical Perspectives, Personal Issues

Historical context is crucial to the understanding of *No-No Boy* since the novel explores unflinchingly the issues of Japanese-American identity. Is it half Japanese and half American, or is it neither? After the bombing of Pearl Harbor, Japanese Americans in various coastal states—Washington, Oregon, California—were interned on account of their ethnicity alone. Camp authorities then administered a loyalty questionnaire that contained two disconcerting questions: "Are you willing to serve in the armed forces of the United States in combat duty wherever ordered?" and "Will you swear unqualified allegiance to the United States of America and faithfully defend the United States from any or all attacks of foreign or domestic forces, and forswear any form of allegiance or obedience to the Japanese Emperor, to any other foreign government, power, or organization?"

These questions divided the Japanese-American community and aggravated generational conflict. In some cases the parents still felt attached to their country of origin, while their American-born children—*nisei*— strived for an American identity. In other cases, the parents wanted to be loyal to America, but their children were too bitter against the American government to answer yes and yes.

Significant Form, Style, or Artistic Conventions

Okada commands a style that is at once effusive and spontaneous, quiet and deep. He has a keen eye for subtle details and psychological nuances that enables him to capture the reserved yet affectionate interaction of Kenji's family.

Yet Okada seldom lingers on one key. He can change his note rapidly from subdued pathos to withering irony, as when he moves from depicting the silent grief in Kenji's household to exposing racism at the Club Oriental, where Kenji feels totally comfortable because his being Japanese there does not call attention to itself. At that very moment, there is a commotion at the entrance: the Chinese owner reports that he has to prevent two "niggers" from entering the club with a Japanese. The one place where Kenji does not feel the sting of racial prejudice turns out to be just as racist as others.

Comparisons, Contrasts, Connections

Compare *No-No Boy* with Joy Kogawa's *Obasan* and Jeanne Wakatsuki Houston and James Houston's *Farewell to Manzanar*. All three describe the adverse impact of the internment of Japanese-American families. The novel can also be compared with Chester Himes's *If He Hollers Let Him Go* and Leslie

Silko's *Ceremony;* all three evoke the racial attitudes in the United States during and after World War II.

Questions for Reading, Discussion, and Writing

1. (a) Why does Ichiro feel alienated?
   (b) Why is Ichiro rejected by the people in his own ethnic community? Who are the exceptions?
   (c) How would you characterize the interaction in Kenji's family?
2. (a) Compare the dilemmas of Ichiro and Kenji.
   (b) Who is responsible for Ichiro's suffering? Ichiro himself? His family? The Japanese-American community? America at large?
   (c) Who is responsible for Kenji's suffering?

Bibliography

Book-length literary works that dwell on the Japanese internment include the following:

Houston, Jeanne W. *Beyond Manzanar: Views of Asian American Womanhood.* Santa Barbara: Capra, 1985.

Inada, Lawson F. *Legends from Camp.* St. Paul: Coffee House, 1993.

Kogawa, Joy. *Obasan.* New York: Doubleday, 1994.

Sone, Monica. *Nisei Daughter.* Seattle: U of Washington P, 1979.

Uchida, Yoshiko. 1982. *Desert Exile: The Uprooting of a Japanese American Family.* Seattle: U of Washington P, 1982.

Yamada, Mitsuye. *Camp Notes and Other Writings.* New Brunswick: Rutgers UP, 1998.

For a detailed study of the relation between historical circumstances and literature, see the following:

Kim, Elaine H. *Asian American Literature: An Introduction to the Writings and Their Social Context.* Philadelphia: Temple UP, 1982.

Ling, Jinqi. "Race, Power, and Cultural Politics in John Okada's *No-No Boy.*" *American Literature* 67.2 (1995): 359–81.

A brief survey of Japanese-American literature can be found in:

Baker, Houston A., Jr., ed. *Three American Literatures: Essays in Chicano, Native American, and Asian American Literature for Teachers of American Literature.* New York: MLA, 1982.

Cheung, King-Kok, ed. *An Interethnic Companion to Asian American Literature.* New York: Cambridge UP, 1996.

See also:

Palumbo-Liu, David. "Discourse and Dislocation: Rhetorical Strategies of Asian-American Exclusion and Confinement." *Lit: Literature Interpretation Theory* 2.1 (1990): 1–7.

Sato, Gayle K. F. "Momotaro's Exile: John Okada's *No-No Boy.*" *Reading the Literatures of Asian America.* Ed. Shirley Geok-lin Lim and Amy Ling. Philadelphia: Temple UP, 1992. 239–58.

James Baldwin (1924–1987)

Contributing Editors: Trudier Harris and John Reilly

Classroom Issues and Strategies

Problems surround Baldwin's voicing the subjectivity of characters, the great sympathy he awards to the outlook of the marginalized. Students normally meet the underclass as victims perhaps objectified by statistics and case studies. For that matter, students who are not African American have difficulty with the black orientation arising from Baldwin's middle-class characters: the artists and other, more conventionally successful people.

The strategies flow from the principle that people do not experience their lives as victims, even if Baldwin's popular social autobiographical essay *Notes of a Native Son*—the portion where he recounts contracting the "dread, chronic disease" of anger and fury when denied service in a diner—might be useful in raising the issue of why Baldwin says every African American has a Bigger Thomas in his head. The anger may become creative, as might the pain. A companion discussion explores the importance of blues aesthetic to Baldwin: the artful treatment of common experience by a singular singer whose call evokes a responsive confirmation from those who listen to it. In addition, an exploration of the aesthetic of popular black music would also enhance the students' understanding.

Within a literary context, the strategies should establish that fictional narrative is the only way we know the interior experience of other people. The imagination creating the narrative presents an elusive subjectivity. If a writer is self-defined as African American, that writer will aim to inscribe the collective subjectivity under the aspect of a particular character. Of course, the point is valid for women writers and other groups also, as long as the writers have chosen deliberately to identify themselves as part of the collective body.

Major Themes, Historical Perspectives, Personal Issues

Themes of personal importance include the significance of community identification, the communion achieved in "Sonny's Blues," for example; the conflicted feelings following success when that requires departure from the home community; the power of love to bridge difference. The chief historical issue centers on the experience of urbanization following migration from an agricultural society. The philosophical issue concerns Baldwin's use of religious imagery and outlook, his interest in redemption and the freeing of spirit. Interestingly, this philosophical/religious issue is often conveyed in the secular terms of blues, but transcendence remains the point.

Significant Form, Style, or Artistic Conventions

Baldwin's frequent use of the first-person narration and the personal essay naturally associates his writing with autobiography. His fiction should be discussed in relation to the traditions of African-American autobiography which, since the fugitive slave narratives, has presented a theme of liberation from external bondage and a freeing of subjectivity to express itself in writing. As for period, his writing should be looked at as a successor to polemical protest; thus, it is temporally founded in the 1950s and 1960s.

Original Audience

In class I ask students to search out signs that the narrative was written for one audience or the other: What knowledge is expected of the reader? What past experiences are shared by assumption? Incidentally, this makes an interesting way to overcome the resistance to the material. Without being much aware that they are experiencing African-American culture, most Americans like the style and sound of blues and jazz, share some of the ways of dress associated with those arts and their audiences, and know the speech patterns.

Comparisons, Contrasts, Connections

One can make a comparison with Herman Melville's *Benito Cereno* and Richard Wright's *Native Son.* The basis is the degree of identification with African Americans accomplished in each. How closely does the writer approach the consciousness of the black slave and street kids? Measure and discuss the gap between the shock felt by Delano and the communion of the brothers in Baldwin's story.

Questions for Reading, Discussion, and Writing

Keeping in mind that James Baldwin's first experiences with "the word" occurred in evangelical churches, see if that influences his use of the "literary word."

What does Baldwin's short story tell you about the so-called ghetto that you could not learn as well from an article in a sociology journal?

College students are responsive to questions of the ethics of success. They may raise it with this story of "Sonny's Blues" by wondering why the narrator should feel guilty and even by speculating about what will happen to the characters next.

Bibliography

"'Sonny's Blues': James Baldwin's Image of Black Community." *Negro American Literature Forum* 4.2 (1970): 56–60. Rpt. in *James Baldwin: A Collection of Critical Essays*. Ed. Keneth Kinnamon. Englewood Cliffs, NJ: Prentice, 1974. 139–46. Also rpt. in *James Baldwin: A Critical Evaluation*. Ed. Theman B. O'Daniel. Washington, DC: Howard UP, 1977. 163–69.

Flannery O'Connor (1925–1964)

*Contributing Editor: Beverly Lyon Clark**

Classroom Issues and Strategies

My students have trouble dealing with the horror that O'Connor evokes— often they want to dismiss the story out of hand while I want to use it to raise questions. Another problem pertains to religious belief: either students lack any such belief (which might make a kind of sense of O'Connor's violence) or else, possessing it, they latch onto O'Connor's religious explications at the expense of any other approach.

I like to start with students' gut responses—to start with where they already are and to make sure I address the affective as well as the cognitive. In particular, I break the class into groups of five and ask students to try to build consensus in answering study questions.

In general, the elusiveness of O'Connor's best stories makes them eminently teachable—pushing students to sustain ambiguity, to withhold final judgments. It also pushes me to teach better—to empower students more effectively since I don't have all the answers at my fingertips. My responses to O'Connor are always tentative, exploratory. I start, as do most of my students, with a gut response that is negative. For O'Connor defies my humanistic values—she distances the characters and thwarts compassion. Above all, O'Connor's work raises tantalizing questions. Is she, as John Hawkes suggests, "happily on the side of the devil"? Or, on the contrary, does the diabolical Misfit function, paradoxically, as an agent of grace? We know what O'Connor wants us to believe. But should we?

Major Themes, Historical Perspectives, Personal Issues

One important context that I need to provide for my students is background on O'Connor's Christianity. The most useful source here is O'Connor's own essays and lectures, which often explain how to read her works as she would have them read. Certainly O'Connor's pronouncements have guided much of the criticism of her work. I'll summarize some of her main points.

She states that the subject of her work is "the action of grace in territory held largely by the devil" (*Mystery and Manners* 118). She tries to portray in each story "an action that is totally unexpected, yet totally believable" (118),

---

* With thanks to LynAnn Mastaj and her classmates for comments on these questions.

often an act of violence, violence being "the extreme situation that best reveals what we are essentially" (113). Through violence she wants to evoke Christian mystery, though she doesn't exclude other approaches to her fiction: she states that she could not have written "A Good Man Is Hard to Find" in any other way but "there are perhaps other ways than my own in which this story could be read" (109).

In general O'Connor explains that she is not so much a realist of the social fabric as a "realist of distances" (44), portraying both concrete everyday manners and something more, something beyond the ordinary: "It is the business of fiction to embody mystery through manners" (124). She admits too that her fiction might be called grotesque, though she cautions that "anything that comes out of the South is going to be called grotesque by the northern reader, unless it is grotesque, in which case it is going to be called realistic" (40). And she connects her religious concerns with being Southern, for, she says, "while the South is hardly Christ-centered, it is most certainly Christ-haunted" (44).

I also find it important to address the question of racism in the story. Is the story racist? I ask. Is the grandmother racist, in her comments on cute little pickaninnies and her use of "nigger"? Does the narrator endorse the grandmother's attitude? And what do we make of her naming a cat *Pitty Sing*—a pseudo-Japanese name that sounds less like Japanese than like a babytalk version of "pretty thing"? Is O'Connor simply presenting characteristically racist attitudes of not particularly admirable characters? I find Alice Walker's comments helpful here, on O'Connor's respectful reluctance to enter the minds of black characters and pretend to know what they're thinking.

Comparisons, Contrasts, Connections

O'Connor is usually compared to writers who are Southern or gothic or Catholic or some combination thereof: for example, William Faulkner, Nathanael West, Graham Greene. Louise Westling (in *Sacred Groves and Ravaged Gardens: The Fiction of Eudora Welty, Carson McCullers, and Flannery O'Connor* [U of Georgia P, 1985]) has made fruitful comparisons with Eudora Welty and Carson McCullers, though most critics seem to find it difficult to discover points of comparison with other women writers.

Questions for Reading, Discussion, and Writing

The following questions can be given to students in advance or used to guide discussion during class:

1. What qualities of the grandmother do you like? What qualities do you dislike? How did you feel when The Misfit killed her? Why?
2. How would you characterize the other members of the family? What is the function of images like the following: the mother's "face was as broad and innocent as a cabbage and was tied around with a green head-kerchief that had two points on the top like a rabbit's ears" and the grandmother's "big black valise looked like the head of a hippopotamus"?
3. How does O'Connor foreshadow the encounter with The Misfit?
4. What does the grandmother mean by a "good man"? Whom does she consider good people? What are other possible meanings of "good"? Why does she tell The Misfit that he's a good man? Is there any sense in which he is?
5. What is the significance of the discussion of Jesus? Was he a good man?
6. What is the significance of the grandmother's saying, "Why you're one of my babies. You're one of my own children"?
7. What is the significance of The Misfit's saying, "She would of been a good woman if it had been somebody there to shoot her every minute of her life"?

There are, of course, no absolute answers to these questions; the story resists easy solutions, violates the reader's expectations.

Bibliography

Other O'Connor stories well worth reading and teaching include "The Displaced Person," "The Artificial Nigger," "Good Country People," "Everything That Rises Must Converge," "Revelation," and "Parker's Back" (all in *The Complete Stories* [Farrar, 1971]). O'Connor's essays have been collected in *Mystery and Manners* (Farrar, 1969). The fullest collection of works by O'Connor is the *Collected Works* (Library of America, 1988).

As for secondary sources, the fullest biography so far, at least until O'Connor's long-time friend Sally Fitzgerald completes hers, is Lorine M. Getz's *Flannery O'Connor: Her Life, Library and Book Reviews* (Mellen, 1980).

For discussion of O'Connor's social, religious, and intellectual milieux, see Robert Coles's *Flannery O'Connor's South* (Louisiana State UP, 1980). A fine companion piece is Barbara McKenzie's photographic essay, *Flannery O'Connor's Georgia* (U of Georgia P, 1980).

Four collections of essays provide a good range of criticism on O'Connor:

1. *The Added Dimension: The Art and Mind of Flannery O'Connor*. 1966. Ed. Melvin J. Friedman and Lewis A. Lawson. New York: Fordham UP, 1977.

2. *Critical Essays on Flannery O'Connor*. Ed. Melvin J. Friedman and Beverly Lyon Clark. Hall, 1985.
3. *Flannery O'Connor*. Ed. Harold Bloom. Chelsea, 1986.
4. *Realist of Distances: Flannery O'Connor Revisited*. Ed. Karl-Heinz Westarp and Jan Nordby Gretlund. Den.: Aarhus, 1987.

The Friedman and Clark collection, for instance, includes the Walker and Hawkes essays alluded to above: John Hawkes, "Flannery O'Connor's Devil," *Sewanee Review* 70 (1962): 395–407; Alice Walker, "Beyond the Peacock: The Reconstruction of Flannery O'Connor," *In Search of Our Mothers' Gardens*. Harcourt, 1983.

Overall, criticism of O'Connor has appeared in more than forty book-length studies and hundreds of articles (including those published annually in the *Flannery O'Connor Bulletin*). Most criticism continues to be either religious or formalist. But for a discussion that situates O'Connor's work historically, in the postwar era, addressing its intersections with liberal discourse, see Thomas Hill Schaub's chapter on O'Connor in *American Fiction in the Cold War* Madison: U of Wisconsin P, 1991.

A Sheaf of Poetry and Prose from the Beat Movement

Allen Ginsberg (1926–1997)

Contributing Editor: Linda Wagner-Martin

Classroom Issues and Strategies

Teaching Ginsberg requires addressing rampant stereotypes about the Beats and the kind of art they created; that is, the drug culture, homosexuality, Eastern belief systems, and, most important, the effects of such practices on the poem.

By showing the students what a standard formalist 1950s poem was, I have usually been able to keep them focused on the work itself. Ginsberg's long-lined, chantlike poems are so responsive to his speech rhythms that once students hear tapes, they begin to see his rationale for form. Connections with Walt Whitman's work are also useful.

Major Themes, Historical Perspectives, Personal Issues

Ginsberg's dissatisfaction with America during the 1950s prompted his jeremiads, laments, "Howls." When his macabre humor could surface, as it does in "A Supermarket in California," he shows the balance that clear vision can create. His idealism about his country marks much of his work, which is in many ways much less "personal" than it at first seems.

Significant Form, Style, or Artistic Conventions

Consider the tradition of American poetry as voice dependent (Whitman and William Carlos Williams) rather than a text for reading. The highly allusive, ornate, "learned" poems of T. S. Eliot or Wallace Stevens have much less influence on Ginsberg's work, although he certainly knows a great deal about poetry. His poems are what he chose to write, and he makes this choice from a plethora of models. The highly religious influence shapes much of his work (he once described himself as a Buddhist Jew with connections to Krishna, Siva, Allah, Coyote, and the Sacred Heart). Ginsberg was a personal friend of the Jewish philosopher Martin Buber. It was largely through Buber's influence that he gave up drugs.

"Howl," the first part of which appears here, is one of the most famous artifacts of the 1950s. Struggling to recover from the McCarthy trials that spelled doom for anyone charged with difference, the late 1950s was the edge of both promise and fear. The 1960s, with their recognition of the value of change and difference, were about to strike every American citizen, but "Howl" when it was first published in 1956 was still a threatening work. (A decade later, when a recording of the poet reading the work was played on radio, people responsible could have lost their jobs.) In alluding to the experiences of the Beats, especially Carl Solomon, whom Ginsberg met when both were patients at the Columbia Psychiatric Institute in 1949, the poem brings into focus a quantity of events unknown to the (polite) literary world, a more advantaged world.

It also alludes to the travels of William S. Burroughs, whose first book, *Junkie* (1953), was published through Solomon's efforts; Herbert E. Huncke, a con artist and junkie from New York; and Neal Cassady, a Denver hipster whose travels with Jack Kerouac were re-created in the latter's *On the Road* (1957). As a collective chronicle, the work draws on a number of people's experiences—all united in being marginal, offensive, and generally threatening to most academics and students.

Original Audience

Ginsberg's work can usefully be approached as protest as well as lament. Connections with the writings of racial minorities can help define his own Jewish rhythms.

Comparisons, Contrasts, Connections

Walt Whitman
William Carlos Williams
Theodore Roethke
Gary Snyder
Denise Levertov

Robert Creeley
Langston Hughes
Lawrence Ferlinghetti
Etheridge Knight
Pedro Pietri

Jack Kerouac (1922–1969)

Contributing Editor: John Alberti

Classroom Issues and Strategies

Even more so than the other "Beat" writers, Jack Kerouac simultaneously expresses his nonconformism and claims his membership in a long American tradition of nonconformism. Indeed, the title of this 1960 essay, "The Vanishing American Hobo," with its allusion to the elegaic cliché of the Indian as the Vanishing American, suggests an essential, primordial (or "primitive," as he puts it) American identity that transcends the political entity known as the United States and connects the American wanderer to worldwide traditions of spiritual visionaries and questers. One place to start, then, is with the title and with just how Kerouac defines *American* in this essay. Such a question both places Kerouac in the context of the long struggles over the meaning of the term *American* and provides an entry to discussion of the particular manifestations of this struggle in the 1950s cultural rebellion of the Beats.

The bohemian outsider remains a powerful American subject position to this day, and some students in class will identify strongly with both the tenor and form of his essay and may even be fans of Kerouac. Yet as the most visible of the Beat writers during the late fifties and early sixties, Kerouac also played the role of translator of the Beats' spiritual and aesthetic experiments for a larger, more conventional audience. Whether reading from *On the Road* on *The Tonight Show* or publishing this piece in *Holiday* magazine, an upscale magazine that featured serious travel writing, Kerouac seemed always aware of which ideas, propositions, and formal innovations might appear most unfamiliar and even shocking to some of his readers. In championing the hobo, Kerouac defends a lifestyle almost totally at odds with the success-driven, status-conscious culture of 1960 and of today. Even the term *hobo* seems quaint and out-of-place. Students can be asked to identify which values and ideas they think would have been most shocking in Kerouac's time—and which seem so today.

Early on, Kerouac sets the terms of his essay in the opposition between "absolute freedom" and "social protection," and these two concepts offer a good starting place for a discussion of what Kerouac sees as valuable in the life of the hobo, both for the hobo himself (and significantly, all of Kerouac's examples of hobos, both current and historical, are male) and for the larger society in which hobos are allowed to exist. This second part of the question suggests that Kerouac believes America will be damaged by the disappearance of the hobo, another focal point for class discussion.

Rhetorically, Kerouac moves back and forth between frank descriptions of what many readers would see as pathological behavior, such as chronic alcoholism, and references to "hobos" who have achieved cultural centrality and importance, such as Johnny Appleseed to Jesus Christ and Buddha. Students can be asked how successful they find this strategy to be by having them reconsider their preconceived ideas about the life of the hobo. When he finally offers an anecdote from his own history as a hobo, however, Kerouac refuses to offer a neat summary or thesis about the worth of the hobo, complaining that he was unable to communicate effectively with the Arizona police officers who stopped him in the desert in the middle of the night because "They wanted an *explanation* for my hoboing" (emphasis his). Instead, he says, "I have no ax to grind: I'm simply going to another world."

Major Themes, Historical Perspectives, Personal Issues

"The Vanishing American Hobo" appears at a key transitional moment in both Kerouac's career and the social history of the United States. Although he was only thirty-eight years old, most of his major writing was behind him. The publication of *On the Road* had made Kerouac a celebrity, but the genuine appreciation for his innovative writing style and philosophical nonconformity among serious readers became entangled in the mainstream media with a more voyeuristic fascination with the supposedly exotic and even immoral subculture of the Beats. The emergence of countercultural texts like *On the Road* into the mainstream was an early signal of the more widespread social and cultural upheavals of the 1960s, but at the very beginning of that decade Kerouac found himself caught in the middle between those seeking to expand the possibilities of American art and culture and those trying to maintain the status quo, an ambiguous fate he refers to in "The Vanishing American Hobo": "I knew some-day my literary efforts would be rewarded by social protection."

Significant Form, Style, or Artistic Conventions

It has become a commonplace to note the profound influence of jazz, especially the improvisatory styles of bebop, on Kerouac's writing style, but many students will be unfamiliar with this music and can benefit from hearing it in class. Also, there are many recordings of Kerouac reading from his own work that can help give students a sense of how he heard the rhythm of his prose. His writing offers an excellent opportunity for class performance as well, since students can prepare interpretive readings and presentations of excerpts from "The Vanishing American Hobo."

Original Audience

"The Vanishing American Hobo" originally appeared in *Holiday*, a magazine that featured travel writing by well-known contemporary authors. It appealed to a well-educated, affluent, middle-class readership, an audience that would take Kerouac's work seriously but that at the same time represented in part the conventional America that Kerouac's work in general and "The Vanishing American Hobo" called into question. In some sense, the essay is an act of translation as Kerouac attempts to convey the spiritual significance of the "hobo" to a more conservative (in terms of lifestyle more than politically) audience.

Comparisons, Contrasts, Connections

The other writers included in the section on the Beats are an obvious source of comparison, especially for the purpose of raising questions of what it means to describe a writer or other artist as part of a "movement." It's a question the Beat writers were especially concerned with, especially given how their close relationships with one another and their sense of themselves as a bohemian avant garde came into conflict with their intense sense of individualism and nonconformity.

Historically, many of the Beats saw themselves as the heirs of the tradition of American nonconformity (itself an intriguingly paradoxical idea) going back to Whitman and Thoreau, a tradition Alan Ginsberg directly names in "A Supermarket in California" and that Kerouac more generally evokes in "The Vanishing American Hobo." This tradition has tended to be seen as specifically male as well, and questions about how assumptions about gender inform Kerouac's romantic vision of the American hobo can lead to interesting comparisons with the women, such as Denise Levertov, included in the Beats section but also with American avant garde women writers from Emily Dickinson through Gertrude Stein.

The Beats have also had a tremendous influence on popular culture, both participating in it (Kerouac's appearances on *The Tonight Show* and other talk shows; Ginsberg's work with various rock groups) and inspiring popular artists and musicians, including Jim Morrison in the 1960s, Patti Smith from the 1970s to the present, and contemporary musicians such as Nine Inch Nails. In some ways, the Beats remain the dominant model for many young countercultural poets, musicians, and artists. Students can be encouraged to bring in examples of what they see as the Beat influence in contemporary culture as a way of discussing the various meanings and incarnations of Beat attitude and thought.

Working with Cultural Objects

Kerouac's prose can seem mannered or confusing to contemporary readers who lack the contextual and historical background to which Kerouac was responding. One powerful influence on his writing style, for example, was the contemporary jazz of the 1950s, particularly the rhythmically complex, technically difficult, and harmonically sophisticated genre practiced by such musicians as John Coltrane and Charlie Parker and known as *bebop.* Kerouac modeled his writing, both in structure and in his adherence to an improvisational composing process, on these jazz rhythms, and its influence can be heard in his own readings of his works.

The official Charlie Parker website at <http://www.cmgww.com/music/parker/home.html> includes a sample from his composition "Be-Bop" (<http://www.cmgww.com/music/parker/audioclips/bebop.ram>) that will give students a good initial idea of the musical style that Kerouac is imitating. Comparing the excerpt from Parker with the same of Kerouac reading from his work on *The Tonight Show* (accompanied by Steve Allen on the piano) at <http://www.factoryschool.org/content/sounds/poetry/kerouac/kerouac1.ram> allows students to begin considering the thematic and philosophical implications of Kerouac's stylistic imitation, a comparison that can be extended into student reports investigating the theoretical connections between the Bebop and Beat movements.

Questions for Reading, Discussion, and Writing

1. What associations, both positive and negative, do you have with the term *hobo*? What contemporary synonyms can you think of?
2. Kerouac refers to "absolute freedom," a powerful combination of words in American culture. How does he use the hobo to evoke a sense of what he means by "absolute freedom"?
3. Kerouac includes samples of interviews with "bums" he met in the Bowery in New York City. Why does Kerouac use the term *bums*, and how do their descriptions of their lives challenge the desire for "social protection" that his readers may have?

Websites

The Charlie Parker website: <http://www.cmgww.com/music/parker/home.html>

"Be-Bop" by Charlie Parker: <http://www.cmgww.com/music/parker/audio clips/bebop.ram>

Jack Kerouac reading from his work on *The Tonight Show:* <http://www.fac toryschool.org/content/sounds/poetry/kerouac/kerouac1.ram>

Lawrence Ferlinghetti (b. 1919)

Contributing Editor: Helen Barolini

Classroom Issues and Strategies

Ferlinghetti's work is immediately accessible and appealing, and these qualities should be emphasized. He uses everyday language to articulate his themes. A problem could be his critique of social problems in America; conservative students may find him too sharply satiric about their image of this country. You might note that although Ferlinghetti articulates the "outsider" view of society, he also espouses hope for the future; for instance, poems like "Popular Manifest" (not in this anthology) give a sense of vision and expectation.

Tape recordings of Ferlinghetti reading can be effective.

Major Themes, Historical Perspectives, Personal Issues

Ferlinghetti is a political activist, and his poetical career spans and reflects thirty years of U.S. political history.

His personal voice brings poetry back to the people. He has done this not only as a poet but also as a publisher, editor, translator, and discoverer of new talent.

Significant Form, Style, and Artistic Conventions

Ferlinghetti has been prominently identified with the Beat movement of the 1950s. It is important to consider the Beat movement as an ongoing part of American bohemianism, and to contrast it, for example, with the expatriate movement of post–World War I.

The hip vocabulary can well be examined, and the Beat experience of alienation can be connected with other marginals in the society.

Original Audience

The work of Ferlinghetti can be placed in the specific social context of the Beat movement in the fifties—Beats were the anarchists in a time of general postwar conformism.

Comparisons, Contrasts, Connections

Ferlinghetti can certainly be compared with his fellow Beats, like Allen Ginsberg and Gregory Corso, and contrasted with other poets of the time— for instance, the more mannered Wallace Stevens. There is also much to compare, stylistically, with e. e. cummings.

Questions for Reading, Discussion, and Writing

1. With this particular poet, the most effective approach is to plunge right into the work. He elicits the questions.
2. Discuss the San Francisco Renaissance, which centered around Ferlinghetti's City Lights Bookstore.
3. What is the counterculture in America?

Bibliography

General

Charters, Samuel. *Some Poems/Poets: Studies in American Underground Poetry Since 1945.* Oyez, 1971.

The Postmoderns: The New American Poetry Revised. New York: Grove, 1982.

Particular

Cherkovski, Neeli. *Ferlinghetti: A Biography.* New York: Doubleday, 1979.

Hopkins, Crale D. "The Poetry of Lawrence Ferlinghetti: A Reconsideration." *Italian Americana* 1.1 (Autumn 1974): 59–76.

Kherdian, David. *Six Poets of the San Francisco Renaissance.* Fresno: Giligia, 1967.

Silesky, Barry. *Ferlinghetti, the Artist in His Time.* New York: Warner, 1990.

Skau, Michael. *"Constantly Risking Absurdity": Essays on the Writings of Lawrence Ferlinghetti.* Troy, NY: Whitston, 1989.

Smith, Larry. *Lawrence Ferlinghetti, Poet-at-Large.* Carbondale: Southern Illinois UP, 1983.

Vestere, Richard. "Ferlinghetti: Rebirth of a Beat Poet." *Identity Magazine* (March 1977): 42–44.

Brenda Frazer (b. 1939)

Contributing Editor: Ronna C. Johnson

Classroom Issues and Strategies

The Beat generation writers have long been identified primarily by the best known of them—Jack Kerouac, Allen Ginsberg, and William S. Burroughs— that is, through a canonized triumvirate of famous white male writers. This exclusive focus is both inaccurate and misleading. Women wrote Beat litera- ture, too, and at least in part because of the sexist prejudices of the principal male Beat writers, their work has been ignored and elided from considerations of the movement. The recovery of Brenda Frazer's *Troia* permits a reconsideration of Beat movement aesthetics and cultural influences since as the expression of a female author, Frazer's Beat iconoclasm and bohemian nonconformity raise considerably different issues than those raised by the work of the men. To wit, what does it mean to be a woman on the road? Can women go on the road? What does free sexual expression mean for young women in an age of inadequate birth control and illegal abortion? How can a woman both be Beat and partake of the feminine?

Major Themes, Historical Perspectives, Personal Issues

This excerpt from *Troia* exemplifies Beat generation writing both aesthetically and in terms of content: it is a breath-based spontaneous prose narrative that depicts the author's experience on the road in Mexico. Although originally Frazer was writing the account to her husband, Ray Bremser, and although he was with her through much of the journey she recounts, she makes him a character in her narrative. This strategy, which fuses the actual with the fictive, the documentary with the invented, is emblematic of Beat writing.

Frazer's status as a woman on the road is dramatically underscored by her representation of traveling with her baby daughter Rachel on her lap—a domestic image quite at odds with familiar, even stereotyped, Beat generation images of footloose, freewheeling men liberated from women and families. Frazer merges the road ethos of improvised itinerary and unmoored self-sufficiency with women's reality of children and responsibility for their survival. Her story confronts the gendered aspect of the sexual freedom touted by Beat generation radicals since babies and childcare are obviously direct results of free sex for women. Frazer's writing remakes Beat movement values by foregrounding women in the narrative, depicting what the road looks like from a woman's perspective. Her tale anticipates the way second-wave feminism will demand that women be admitted as full subjects and accorded freedoms enjoyed by men. Her narrative refits the vaunted road tale for female participants and strikes a blow for women's equality in a radical bohemian circle which was itself no more sensitive to women's equality than the mainstream establishment culture it scorned and sought to reform.

Significant Form, Style, or Artistic Conventions

Troia originated as a series of letters from Frazer to her then-husband, the Beat poet Ray Bremser, who was at the time in prison in New Jersey; the letters were strung together by Bremser and the small press editor Michael Perkins to form the extended narrative that recounts Frazer's experience on the road in Mexico.

Thus, *Troia* is an exemplary Beat text since it emerges from an actual countercultural experience of life grubbing for survival on the road and is based on actual personal confessions the author made in her letters to her husband.

Students might be asked to consider the feeling and impact of *Troia* in light of the fact that it was first a private confession and only second a narrative launched into Beat-generation communities meant to be considered literary art of the movement. How can the personal, the private, be transformed into the public, the shared? Is this an essence of artistic creation? Is this example of Beat generation writing one that merely does what all writing essentially does but with less reliance on conventions of suspension of disbelief? Or is there some special quality to Frazer's alchemical transformation of life to art that we may call Beat?

Original Audience

Troia was published by Croton Press, a small art house press, in a run of 1500 copies; it has never been reprinted. Before it came out as a full-length book, an unedited excerpt was published in 1967 in a small press magazine devoted to experimental writing. As these venues suggest, the original audience for *Troia* was comprised of bohemian insiders, hipsters who appreciated outlaw writing and were likely familiar with the well-regarded poetry of Frazer's then-husband, Ray Bremser. Although Frazer's work appeals to postwar considerations of gender and women's status, and its publication in 1969 coincided with the emergence of second-wave feminism, its small, original bohemian audience would have been primarily concerned with its artistic innovation and effects—its character as a Beat movement text.

Comparisons, Contrasts, Connections

Frazer admits to emulating *On the Road* in her composition techniques for *Troia*, so comparison with the Kerouac selection in this volume would be relevant and illuminating: can a debt to Kerouac's style be discerned? Frazer also reveres Mexico, as Kerouac did, and has a special empathy for the world's poor and disenfranchised. In *Troia* she depicts herself as belonging in this marginalized caste of struggling and downtrodden folks. How is her membership in this community complicated by the fact that she has a young child and works as a prostitute? How is her status affected by the fact that, while in Mexico with her husband Ray, she is ultimately obliged to give up her daughter Rachel for adoption in order for both mother and daughter to survive?

Frazer's *Troia* may be profitably read against Joyce Johnson's memoir *Minor Characters*, as well as against her letter to Kerouac printed in the anthology, since *Troia* is a narrative based in memoir and actual experience that originated as letters to Ray Bremser. Also, Frazer and Johnson are both second-generation female Beat writers who had powerful relationships with first-generation Beat writers (Bremser and Kerouac, respectively). In spite of these overlapping similarities, the works of these writers are radically unlike each other, at least to a superficial consideration. In what ways are Frazer and Johnson demarcating two directions of Beat writing? Characterize those styles. In what ways do their experiences as women demarcate a common discourse of Beat writing determined by gender?

Working with Cultural Objects

See the audiotape compilation of *Women of the Beat Generation*, edited by Brenda Knight, 1996. In this audio version of the book, the Beat poet ruth weiss (weiss spells both her names with lowercase letters), who helped to invent the Beat generation fashion of reading poetry to jazz accompaniment, reads the work of fellow women Beat writers who are collected in the Knight volume, including that of Brenda Frazer.

The original dust cover for *Troia* has some interesting graphics and pictures of the author Bonnie Bremser, as Frazer then signed the book. There is also a photograph on that dust cover of Bremser with the baby Rachel she writes about and must give up for adoption while she is on the road in Mexico.

Questions for Reading, Discussion, and Writing

1. Frazer's depiction of the road life as she travels across Mexico with her husband and baby rivals the Mexican sequence in *On the Road*. How does she write about the road? How is a road experience delineated by Frazer's sentence structure and selection of detail?
2. Frazer writes about her baby as a travel companion and also suggests having an experience of sexual exploration and satisfaction. How are these often segregated female experiences (experiences dichotomized by the Madonna/whore binary) integrated into a coherent narrative movement? How do these disparate experiences redefine Beat-generation living?
3. Drawing on Frazer's account of life on the road, discuss ways in which gender determines her Beat bohemian experience.

Bibliography

See also *Women of the Beat Generation*, ed. Brenda Knight (1996); and *A Different Beat: Writings by Women of the Beat Generation*, ed. Richard

Peabody (1997). Both provide further selections from *Troia* and some biographical material as well as sketching out the milieu of women Beats in which Frazer lived and wrote. In *Girls Who Wore Black: Women Writing the Beat Generation*, ed. Ronna C. Johnson and Nancy M. Grace (2002), see Ronna C. Johnson and Nancy M. Grace, "Visions and Revisions of the Beat Generation," and Nancy M. Grace, "Snapshots, Sand Paintings, and Celluloid: Formal Considerations in the Life Writing of Women Writers from the Beat Generation." In *Breaking the Rule of Cool: Interviewing and Reading Women Beat Writers*, Nancy M. Grace and Ronna C. Johnson (2004), see Ronna C. Johnson, "Mapping Women Writers of the Beat Generation," and "Artista: Interview with Brenda (Bonnie) Frazer."

Joyce Johnson (b. 1934)

Contributing Editor: Ronna C. Johnson

Classroom Issues and Strategies

The Beat generation writers have long been identified primarily by the best known of them—Jack Kerouac, Allen Ginsberg, and William S. Burroughs— that is, through a canonized triumvirate of famous white male writers. This exclusive focus is both inaccurate and misleading. Women wrote Beat literature, too, and at least in part because of the sexist prejudices of the principal male Beat writers, their work has been ignored and elided from considerations of the movement. The recovery of Joyce Johnson as a Beat writer—particularly with regard to her first novel, *Come and Join the Dance* (1962)—permits a reconsideration of Beat movement aesthetics and cultural influences since as a female author, her work's Beat generation iconoclasm and bohemian nonconformity raise considerably different issues than those raised by the work of the men. To wit, what does it mean to be a woman who wants a free life of her own design? Can women be writers and also be self-reliant? What does free sexual expression mean for young women in an age of inadequate birth control and illegal abortion? How can a woman both be Beat and partake of the feminine? What are the costs of Beat-generation radicalism for white, middle-class women in the postwar era who are just being granted access to secondary education, white-collar employment, and the potential for greater social and economic self-sufficiency?

Major Themes, Historical Perspectives, Personal Issues

Johnson's writing as represented in the anthology's selections opens out to a larger historical movement, the Beat generation of cultural and social icono-clasm, and also anticipates later movements for women's equality. The selections can profitably be discussed both in terms of the Beat generation—what is the "Beat generation," according to Johnson's representations?—and in terms of women's struggles in the postwar era to enjoy the same freedoms and ambitions as those accorded by birthright to men. Can the seeds of women's liberation be discerned in Johnson's account of her experience as an undergraduate writing student at Barnard, her determined move to an apartment of her own against social expectations for "marriageable" middle-class women of her era, and her entry into the world of publishing and literary promise?

Significant Form, Style, or Artistic Conventions

Joyce Johnson has been a published author since 1962 and has been well known in New York literary and publishing circles since the late sixties. Although she was marginalized in Beat-generation writing scenes—largely because she is female—she has not been invisible in the mainstream writing world, which is an anomalous circumstance for a Beat writer. Moreover, her Beat writing is not very much like that of the familiar male exemplars. Rather, Johnson's style is emotionally restrained and concise; her work is intellectual and psychological, centering on rationally delineated states of mind and feeling. Nevertheless, it is still recognizably Beat.

Students might be asked to consider how Johnson's interaction with Kerouac, as represented by the letter included in the selection, positioned her in the Beat generation. How is her writing, as exemplified by the selection from her memoir, evocative of or representative of the Beat generation? What difference does it make that she is a woman writing about the Beat generation? How are her distinctive writing style and subject matter Beat?

Original Audience

In August 1982, Johnson premiered her forthcoming memoir *Minor Characters* with a reading at the Naropa Institute's Jack Kerouac Conference in Boulder, Colorado. Although the book was published in 1983 by a major trade house—and has been kept in print and most recently reissued by Viking Press, which has a considerable Beat list now—its first audience was comprised of bohemian insiders and Beat generation aficionados like those congregating at the 1982 Naropa conference commemorating the twenty-fifth anniversary of the publication of *On the Road*. This audience was avid for information about Kerouac and the Beat scene, which the memoir surely provides. Yet, *Minor Characters* is compelling not only for readers in Beat studies but also for those interested in understanding the postwar years just before the emergence of second-wave feminism in the late 1960s and the status of women who wanted more in their lives than was offered by gender conventions in the Eisenhower America of the 1950s. Johnson's account of her years at Barnard and her struggle to be economically self-sufficient and viable as a writer after the Second World War but before the emergence of the women's movement is provocative and enlightening.

Johnson's collection of letters to and from Jack Kerouac, *Door Wide Open* (2000)—one of which is printed in this anthology—has had wide appeal, encompassing issues of interest to readers in Beat studies as well as those in women's and cultural studies. The epistolary artifacts provide unmodified documentary evidence of the writers' concerns and interests as well as a picture of the era's obstacles and opportunities for women.

Comparisons, Contrasts, Connections

Although Johnson was writing her first novel, *Come and Join the Dance*, during the time she was involved with Jack Kerouac in the late 1950s at the apex of the Beat generation, she writes in a distinctly original Beat style that is restrained, understated, and ironic as opposed to the style exemplified by Kerouac and Ginsberg, which is emotionally extravagant, based on a long-breath line, and contentiously devoid of subtleties. That is, Johnson is "cool" whereas Kerouac and Ginsberg are "hot" Beat stylists. And, indeed, Johnson's style is diametrically opposed to that of her Beat peer Brenda Frazer, whose work also appears in this anthology and who developed a feminized version of the men's "hot" hipster style. Johnson's writing is modeled on the psychological acuity of Henry James and the existentialism of Andre Gide, according to statements she has made. How, then, is Johnson "Beat"? What does her style bring to our understanding of Beat literature? How does her style expand and augment received notions of Beat writing?

Working with Cultural Objects

See the audiotape version of *Women of the Beat Generation*, edited by Brenda Knight (1996). In this audio version of the book, the Beat poet ruth weiss (weiss spells both her names with lowercase letters), who helped to invent the Beat-generation fashion of reading poetry to jazz accompaniment, reads the work of fellow women Beat writers who are collected in the Knight volume, including that of Joyce Johnson.

Questions for Reading, Discussion, and Writing

1. Johnson depicts a postwar world in which "marriageable" middle-class, white women are not free to live on their own or to take to the road to garner "experience" for writing. Why, does she imply, are both those conditions desirable and/or relevant to becoming a writer?
2. Johnson refers to the "boy gang" of male camaraderie and mutual support enjoyed by the male writers of the Beat generation. What is suggested when she ironically scoffs at the idea of a similar "girl gang"? Does a double standard based on sex compromise notions of Beat-generation radicalism?
3. Johnson's "cool," ironic Beat style contradicts expectations of spontaneous "hot" Beat expression. How can her writing style be seen as Beat? What does her style bring to the spectrum of Beat writing?

Bibliography

See also *Women of the Beat Generation*, ed. Brenda Knight (1996); and *A Different Beat: Writings by Women of the Beat Generation*, ed. Richard Peabody (1997). Both provide further selections from *Minor Characters* and some biographical material as well as sketching out the milieu of women Beats in which Johnson lived and wrote. In *Girls Who Wore Black: Women Writing the Beat* Generation, ed. Ronna C. Johnson and Nancy M. Grace (2002), see Ronna C. Johnson and Nancy M. Grace, "Visions and Revisions of the Beat Generation," and Ronna C. Johnson, "'And then she went': Beat Departures and Feminine Transgressions in Joyce Johnson's *Come and Join the Dance.*" In *Breaking the Rule of Cool: Interviewing and Reading Women Beat Writers*, Nancy M. Grace and Ronna C. Johnson (2004), see Ronna C. Johnson, "Mapping Women Writers of the Beat Generation," and "In the Night Café: Interview with Joyce Johnson."

Gary Snyder (b. 1930)

Contributing Editor: Thomas R. Whitaker

Questions for Reading, Discussion, and Writing

"Riprap"

As Snyder tells us in his first volume, *riprap* is "a cobble of stone laid on steep, slick rock to make a trail for horses in the mountains." In *Myths & Texts* (p. 43), he calls poetry "a riprap on the slick rock of metaphysics." This poem may suggest the "objectivism" of William Carlos Williams—"No ideas but in things"—and yet it finally evokes an infinite, ever-changing system of worlds and thoughts. Such idealism, of course, also enters Williams's *Paterson.* Central to the poetics of both Williams and Snyder are strategies that enable particulars to evoke a pattern and so provide a link with the universal. What strategies can the class find here? Some poems for comparison: "Mid-August at Sourdough Mountain Lookout" and "Piute Creek" in *Riprap,* and "For Nothing" in *Turtle Island*—all concerned to relate "thing" and "mind" or "form" and "emptiness."

"Vapor Trails"

How does this poem relate aesthetic patterns, natural patterns, and the patterns of human violence? Is the poem finally a lament over such violence? Or a discovery of its beauty? Or a resignation to its naturalness? Or all or none of these? Can the class trace the shifting tone of the meditation from beginning to end?

This poem, too, has affinities with Williams's work. See, for example, such studies of symmetry and craft as "On Gay Wallpaper" and "Fine Work with Pitch and Copper." Does the ironic use of "design" at the end of "Vapor Trails" obliquely recall the concerns of Robert Frost's "Design"?

"Wave"

This poem, like others in *Regarding Wave,* links various manifestations of energy—inorganic, organic, sexual, linguistic, mental—through images and etymologies that evoke a cosmic wave, motion, or dance. Snyder's riprap, a human construction that enables a mental ascent, seems now to have yielded more fully to the perception of patterns inherent in natural process, patterns in which we dancingly participate.

Wave: wife. As that analogy develops, does the poem suggest that nature is our muse and that the energy of all sentience and all cosmic process is fundamentally sexual?

Would the class enjoy some visual analogies to "the dancing grain of things/of my mind"? If so, you might look at the photographs and calligraphy in Lao Tsu, *Tao Te Ching,* translated by Gia-Fu Feng and Jane English (New York: Random, 1972).

"It Was When"

This reverie over moments when Snyder's son Kai might have been conceived is both a love poem to his wife Masa and a celebration of the "grace" manifest in their coming together. Its imagery, cadences, and reverence for vital processes strongly recall the poetry of D. H. Lawrence. The class might like to make comparisons with Lawrence's "Gloire de Dijon" and perhaps other poems in *Look! We Have Come Through!*

"It Was When" is a densely woven pattern of alliteration and assonance. How do those sound effects cooperate with the poem's cadences and its meanings?

You may want to consult other poems in *Regarding Wave* that continue Snyder's meditation on his marriage and Kai's birth: "The Bed in the Sky," "Kai, Today," and "Not Leaving the House."

Comparisons, Contrasts, Connections

Snyder often plays variations on the imagist mode in which Ezra Pound and William Carlos Williams did much of their earlier work. D. H. Lawrence's love poems and animal poems are also important antecedents, as are Kenneth Rexroth's meditations amid Western landscapes and his translations from Japanese poetry.

Central to the poetics of both Williams and Snyder are strategies that enable particulars to evoke a pattern and so provide a link with the universal.

Bibliography

For Snyder's later career, including his essays and his ecological activism, see John Halper, ed., *Gary Snyder: Dimensions of a Life* (1991); and Patrick D. Murphy, *A Place for Wayfaring: The Poetry and Prose of Gary Snyder* (2000).

Malcolm X (1925–1965)

Contributing Editors: John Alberti and Keith D. Miller

Classroom Issues and Strategies

Forty years after his assassination, Malcolm X remains a galvanizing figure in American culture. As with Martin Luther King Jr., with whom Malcolm X is often (and often oversimplistically) contrasted, there can exist a wide gap between the received ideas and attitudes that students of diverse backgrounds have inherited about Malcolm X from the popular culture and the actual details of his life and thought. As often happens with important political figures, the tendency is to associate him with a single, fixed idea or position, such as black nationalism or anti-white rhetoric, whether that position accurately reflects any aspect of his thought or whether it is seen as positive or negative. One important teaching goal, then, is to help enrich students' understanding of the dynamic and evolving nature of Malcolm X's political strategy and world-view. A brief biographical timeline along with the material in the introductory headnote in the anthology can be used to stress the dramatic changes that marked Malcolm X's life, changes he frankly acknowledges in the haunting final chapter to his *Autobiography*. Throughout this excerpt, he affirms the need to remain open throughout one's life to new ways of thinking and perceiving.

Students can also be encouraged to confront the issue of Malcolm X's enduring reputation and legacy by writing about their preconceptions about him and the various sources of these preconceptions, and then using that work to discuss how this chapter reinforces and challenges their preconceptions. Similarly, students can select the passages they most agree and disagree with, as a way both to further examine their relationships to the legacy of Malcolm X and to enter into a discussion of his complex rhetoric. Throughout the chapter, he uses the strategy of openly confronting what he criticizes as misrepresentations of his ideas in the media in order to clarify his positions and to turn the tables on his critics by speculating about why he has been so misrepresented. Students can then look for how Malcolm X repeatedly uses this "turning the tables" approach throughout the chapter, most centrally in switching the focus from criticisms of various forms of black resistance to the issues of white racism and the violence committed against people of color. Instructors can point out how, in so doing, he participates in a long rhetorical tradition in African-American culture that stretches back to Frederick Douglass and includes his supposed rival Martin Luther King Jr., whose "Letter from a Birmingham Jail" similarly turns accusations of radicalism and rashness by white clergy into an indictment of their own complacency and the refusal of white America to address the continued oppression of African Americans.

Students may similarly be unaware of or be surprised by the depth and importance of religious belief and spirituality to Malcolm X, especially his moving testimony to the power of Islam in helping him achieve a vision of universal humanity. This aspect of "1965" has become especially relevant and provocative again in the wake of September 11 and the war on Iraq. Students may want to pursue the question of how Malcolm X might have extended his growing internationalist perspective to an analysis of contemporary relations between the United States and the Islamic nations of the world. In what ways does Malcolm X seem prescient?

Bibliography

Millions continue to read the *Autobiography of Malcolm X* (1965), co-authored by Alex Haley. I strongly recommend *Remembering Malcolm* (1992) by Malcolm X's assistant minister Benjamin Karim, who shows a sensitive leader inside the Muslim mosque and reveals information available nowhere else.

No thoroughly reliable, full-scale biography of Malcolm X exists. Many details about his life (especially before his public career) remain unknown. In *Malcolm* (1991), a detailed, provocative biography, Bruce Perry claims that the *Autobiography* features blatant exaggerations and outright falsehoods. But some of Perry's own claims seem unsupportable. Joe Wood compiled *Malcolm X: In Our Own Image* (1992), which contains helpful essays by Cornel West, Arnold Rampersad, John Edgar Wideman, Patricia Hill Collins, and others. In *Martin and Malcolm and America* (1991), James Cone usefully compares and contrasts King and Malcolm X, as do John Lucaites and Celeste Condit in "Reconstructing Equality: Culturetypal and Counter-Cultural Rhetorics in the Martyred Black Vision," *Communication Monographs* 57 (1990): 5–24. See also Rodnell Collins, *Seventh Child: A Family Memoir of Malcolm X.* (Secaucus, NJ: Birch Lane, 1998).

Robert Creeley (b. 1926)

Contributing Editor: Thomas R. Whitaker

Classroom Issues and Strategies

"Hart Crane"

Dedicated to a friend of Crane who became a friend of Creeley, this is the opening poem in *For Love.* Is it a negative portrait or a sympathetic study of difficulties central to Creeley's own career? Certainly it contains many leitmotifs of Creeley's poetry: stuttering, isolations, incompletion, self-conscious ineptness, the difficulty of utterance, the need for friends, the confrontations of a broken world.

"I Know a Man"

The colloquial anecdote as parable? How does the stammering lineation complicate the swift utterance? Why should the shift in speakers occur with such ambiguous punctuation—a comma splice? According to Creeley, "drive" is said not by the friend but by the speaker.

"For Love"

The closing poem in *For Love*, this is informed by the qualities attributed to Crane in the volume's opening poem. "For Love" is one of many poems to Bobbie—wife, companion, muse, and mother of children—that wrestle with the nature of love, the difficulty of utterance, and a mass of conflicting feelings: doubt, faith, despair, surprise, self-criticism, gratitude, relief. The poem is a remarkable enactment of a complex and moment-by-moment honesty.

"Words"

This poem drives yet further inward to the ambiguous point where an inarticulate self engages an imperfectly grasped language. Not the wife or muse but "words" seem now the objects of direct address, the poem's "you." Nevertheless, the poem's detailed phrases and its movement through anxious blockage toward an ambiguously blessed release strongly suggest a love poem.

"America"

Though seldom an explicitly political poet, Creeley here brings his sardonic tone and his belief in utterance as our most intimate identity to bear on the question: What has happened to the America that Walt Whitman celebrated? "The United States themselves are essentially the greatest poem," Whitman had said in his Preface to the 1855 *Leaves of Grass*. And he had often spoken of the "words" belonging to that poem, as in "One's-Self I Sing" and in the reflections on "the People" in *Democratic Vistas*.

"America" modulates those concerns into Creeley's own more quizzical language. We may read it as a dark response, a century later, to Whitman's "Long, Too Long America" in *Drum-Taps*. For Creeley's more extended response to Whitman, see his *Whitman: Selected Poems*.

Significant Form, Style, or Artistic Conventions

In "Projective Verse" Charles Olson quotes Creeley's remark that "Form is never more than an extension of content." Creeley liked, as an implicit definition of form, a Blakean aphorism that he learned from Slater Brown: "Fire delights in its form." His central statement of open poetics, involving "a content which cannot be anticipated," is "I'm Given to Write Poems" (*A Quick Graph*, pp. 61–72).

It is useful to know that, when reading his poetry aloud, Creeley always indicates line-ends by means of very brief pauses. The resultant stammer—quite unlike the effect of Williams's reading—is integral to Creeley's style, which involves a pervasive sense of wryly humorous or painful groping for the next line.

Comparisons, Contrasts, Connections

William Carlos Williams told Robert Creeley, "You have the subtlest feeling for the measure I have encountered anywhere except in the verses of Ezra Pound." For Creeley's relation to Williams, see his essays in *A Quick Graph*, and Paul Mariani, "Robert Creeley," in *A Usable Past* (Amherst: U of Massachusetts P, 1984). For his relation to Pound, see "A Note on Ezra Pound" (*A Quick Graph*), and for his sustained and mutually valuable relation to Charles Olson, see again *A Quick Graph*.

Perhaps the class would like to compare "Hart Crane" with Robert Lowell's "Words for Hart Crane" in *Life Studies*. Two views of Crane, two modes of portraiture, and two historically important styles of mid-twentieth-century American verse, these plus "The Broken Tower" itself would make a fascinating unit of study.

Frank O'Hara (1926–1966)

Contributing Editor: David Bergman

Classroom Issues and Strategies

Frank O'Hara's works look so effortless, so spontaneous, so stitched from his daily life that students may forget just how hard it is to make things look easy. It is important to stress the ways the poems are drawn from his life; they are more than a laundry list of "I do this, I do that." For example, in "The Day Lady Died," the precise and banal details of his train schedule and the presents he is bringing set the stage for the memory of Billie Holiday, a memory that seems to exist out of time. It is Holiday who breaks through the hustle and bustle of his life and has captured through her art—her voice—something nearly eternal. Although she had "stopped breathing" in reality, in his memory of her it is the audience who is dead, and she is the one most alive.

O'Hara studied music, and for quite a time he believed he would become a composer. He worked with Ned Rorem and was a friend of Virgil Thomson. (The Rorem/O'Hara collaboration is available on CD [PHCD 116].) Invite students to read the poems aloud. One discovers a subtle music in them. O'Hara diverges from modernist poets because of his emphasis on voice rather than on image. For all of his interest in painting, it is the immediacy of O'Hara's voice that is the most striking part of his poetry.

Some teachers are afraid to address the homosexual content of his poems. I have discovered that addressing the issue as just one more subject reduces the students' discomfort. If students remain uncomfortable, the best position to state is "We are all grown-ups here. We must be ready to confront attitudes and positions we both share and do not share."

Major Themes, Historical Perspectives, Personal Issues

Like John Ashbery, O'Hara's friend and fellow Harvard alumnus, O'Hara is always concerned with time and mutability. These questions of time spawn several subthemes: (1) the relationship of art to time (can art take us out of time?); (2) the weakness of the body, its susceptibility to disease, death, and pain; (3) the fleetingness of emotions, particularly love; (4) the pressure of friends and the difficulties of maintaining the bonds of friendship.

Openness is a key word for O'Hara. He wants his poems and his love to be open. We can discuss open poetic forms, open relationships, openness to experience, a willingness to court vulgarity and sentimentality. But openness makes one vulnerable. O'Hara is haunted by this sense of vulnerability to outside enemies and forces. In some ways this mirrors the American psyche of the Cold War—its sense of strength, its desire to be an open society, and its fears—frequently irrational—of enemy attack.

Significant Form, Style, or Artistic Conventions

O'Hara's work is free verse, but as the footnote suggests, "Poem" echoes Shakespeare's sonnet "When in disgrace to fortune and men's eyes." It might be useful to look at how the form of the sonnet, although not copied, haunts the structure of this poem. O'Hara's line breaks look arbitrary, but they often are extremely effective.

Comparisons, Contrasts, Connections

O'Hara's work is often compared with John Ashbery's. One can see their wit, humor, and desire to incorporate things from daily life into their work. But whereas these poems are open to the reader, Ashbery's poems often are hermetic. Allen Ginsberg was also one of O'Hara's friends. The homoerotic world of "A Supermarket in California" compares with O'Hara's "Poem." O'Hara disliked Robert Lowell's poetry. Lowell's formalism and highly wrought poetic surface contrasts strongly with O'Hara's work of the same period.

Working with Cultural Objects

O'Hara's connection to abstract expressionism is well established. It might be helpful to show the work of Mike Goldberg, Willem de Kooning, or Grace Hartigan. You might want to discuss the relationship between action painting and O'Hara's aesthetic, especially as developed in "Why I Am Not a Painter." Examples of all three painters can be found at Artnet.com at <http://www.artnet.com/artist/7124/Michael_Goldberg.html>; <http://www.artnet.com/artist/662752/Willem_de_Kooning.html>; and <http://www.artnet.com/artist/7888/Grace_Hartigan.html>.

Questions for Reading, Discussion, and Writing

Students may be encouraged to try their own I-do-this-I-do-that poems and see why the details in O'Hara's add up to something much more than a list of appointments. What are the similarities and differences between poetry and the other arts? How autobiographical should a poem be? How distanced from the poet's life does a poem have to be to affect a reader? Do the names of so many of O'Hara's personal friends keep the poem from communicating to you as a reader, or does this specificity—even if you don't know who these people are exactly—make the experience seem more immediate? When does gossip become art? How does O'Hara's expression of homosexual love differ from heterosexual love? Or does it?

John Ashbery (b. 1927)

Contributing Editor: David Bergman

Classroom Issues and Strategies

Students should be encouraged to explore the connections between seemingly unrelated passages. These connections are probably best found if the student is encouraged to move freely through the poem at first, finding whatever connection he or she can spot. Richard Howard convincingly argues that each Ashbery poem contains an emblem for its entire meaning. If allowed time, students usually find such emblems. Second, drawing connections between Ashbery's method and such graphic methods as collage and assemblage often helps. Students, of course, should be reminded to read the notes.

I have found it useful to present Ashbery in relation to the visual arts, in particular the shifting perspective of comic strips, the surprising juxtapositions of collage and assemblage, the vitality of abstract impressionism, and the metaphysical imagery of de Chirico.

Major Themes, Historical Perspectives, Personal Issues

The selection highlights three major themes or questions running through Ashbery's work: (1) the problem of subjective identity—Whose consciousness informs the poem? (2) the relationship between language and subjectivity—Whose language do I speak, or does the language have a mind of its own? (3) the connections among subjectivity, language, and place—What does it mean to be an American poet?

Significant Form, Style, or Artistic Conventions

Ashbery has long been interested in French art, especially dada and surrealism. Such interests have merged with an equally strong concern for poetic form and structure, as evinced by the sestina of "Farm Implements" and the 4 x 4 structure (four stanzas each of four lines) of "Paradoxes and Oxymorons," a structure he uses through *Shadow Train*, the volume from which the poem was taken. Ashbery's combination of surrealism and formalism typifies a certain strain of postmodernism.

Original Audience

Obviously Ashbery is writing for a highly sophisticated contemporary audience. The decade he spent in France provided him with an international perspective.

Comparisons, Contrasts, Connections

Frank O'Hara, Kenneth Koch, and James Schuyler are or were close friends of Ashbery; together they formed the nucleus of what is sometimes dubbed the New York School of Poetry. The dreamlike imagery bears some resemblance to the work of John Berryman and Allen Ginsberg. Walt Whitman provides a particularly vital touchstone to an American tradition.

Questions for Reading, Discussion, and Writing

How do comic strips (and other forms of popular art) inform both the content and style of Ashbery's poems? Who is speaking in an Ashbery poem? What is American about John Ashbery?

Bibliography

Altieri, Charles. "John Ashbery." *Self and Sensibility in Contemporary American Poetry.* New York: Cambridge UP, n.d.

Berger, Charles. "Vision in the Form of a Task." Lehman, 163–208.

Bergman, David. "Choosing Our Fathers: Gender and Identity in Whitman, Ashbery and Richard Howard." *American Literary History* 1 (1989): 383–403.

———. "Introduction: John Ashbery." *Reported Sightings: Art Chronicles* 1957–87. New York: Knopf, 1989. xi–xxiii.

Lehman, David, ed. *Beyond Amazement: New Essays on John Ashbery.* Ithaca: Cornell UP, 1980.

Cynthia Ozick (b. 1928)

Contributing Editor: Tresa Grauer

Classroom Issues and Strategies

This is a hard story to read, and some students may be reluctant to "analyze" it if their first response is emotional. At the same time, others may not have the background to understand the story's events. Students need to understand that the historical context of "The Shawl" is the systematic destruction of European Jewry during the Second World War. They may ask: What do we mean when we talk about the Holocaust? When was it? What happened? Those students with some historical knowledge may find sharing the knowledge with the others to be one way to begin talking about "The Shawl." You might also ask them to point out the clues within the story that helped them to know where they were. Consider, for example, "the march," or "the roll-call arena," or the "ash-stippled wind."

You may find that some students will want to universalize the experience of Jews during the Holocaust—to see it as one among many different kinds of human tragedies—in order to discuss it in terms that they are familiar with and can better understand. And/or they may want to argue that the experience was completely unique and thus cannot happen again. You might consider talking about what's at stake for them in these arguments. For example, is it less frightening if we say that the Holocaust was unique? If we can contain it

within our imagination, does it make it less horrible or horrifying? It's difficult to talk about why or how the Holocaust "happened," and students will
realize that the issues that come up around trying to make sense of it are those
that historians and fiction writers are confronting as well.

Students often want to judge Stella for taking Magda's shawl. While it's
important to talk about why she might have done this, it's also important to
realize that the story points insistently—thematically and stylistically—to
the fact that we cannot make moral judgments about behavior in the camps. The
standards of the outside world simply do not apply.

Major Themes, Historical Perspectives, Personal Issues

One of the most important things to keep in mind about "The Shawl" is Ozick's
fear of making art out of the Holocaust—of using aesthetics to make something
beautiful, or pleasurable, out of something that should only be viewed with
horror. In other words, she believes that there are limitations to what can
inspire art and to what can become art. These concerns are central to any discussion of Holocaust fiction, as artists and critics try to balance the potential
dangers of artistic expression with the valuable insights that they can also
provide. Ozick says that she accepts Theodor Adorno's famous dictum, "To
write poetry after Auschwitz is barbaric," in theory; nevertheless, she "cannot
not write about it." In Berel Lang's collection, *Writing and the Holocaust*, she
explains, "It rises up and claims my furies. All the same, I believe that the
duty of our generation, so close to the events themselves, is to absorb the data,
to learn what happened. I am not in favor of making fiction of the data, or of
mythologizing or poeticizing it. If we each had a hundred lifetimes, there
would not be enough time to assimilate the documents. I constantly violate this
tenet; my brother's blood cries out from the ground, and I am drawn, and driven"
(284).

"The Shawl" also makes clear that speech itself is dangerous: despite
Rosa's desire to hear her child's voice, Magda is safe only as long as she is
mute. The consequence of her cry—the only dialogue in the story—is death. In
discussion, you might also consider other situations in which it is dangerous (but
necessary? inevitable?) to speak out.

Historical texts and fiction about the Holocaust tend not to focus on the
specific experiences of women, despite the fact that men and women were
generally separated in the camps. As Carol Rittner and John Roth make clear in
Different Voices, the experiences of men and women—and their interpretations
of those experiences—were often much the same; however, they also faced
dangers that were particular to their gender. By raising the question of
Magda's paternity, "The Shawl" introduces the issue of rape—and subsequent
pregnancy—as a particular danger that women faced. (It also forces us to ask
whether "blood" makes any difference in determining who is a Jew.) The fact

that the protagonists in "The Shawl" are female makes this story unusual among stories about the Holocaust; however, Ozick has always refused to see her work as particularizing. Does gender affect your students' reading of "The Shawl"?

Significant Form, Style, or Artistic Conventions

Ozick's use of language demonstrates that all expectations must be subverted in writing and thinking about the unnatural world of a death camp. For example, she uses a series of paradoxical images that combine the fantastical and the realistic: here, a baby's first tooth is an "elfin tombstone"; a breast is a "dead volcano"; a starved belly is "fat, full and round"; and a shawl can be "magic," sheltering and nourishing a child as an extension of the mother's body. Ozick's prose is also extraordinarily compressed, giving the impression that there is much that is left unsaid, and the narrative voice is simultaneously appalled and oddly dispassionate. Her minimalism manages to convey her ambivalence about using metaphoric language to represent an experience that is nearly unimaginable.

Original Audience

"The Shawl" was originally published in *The New Yorker* in 1980. Since then, it has been reprinted together with the novella "Rosa" (in *The Shawl*, 1988) and anthologized many times.

Comparisons, Contrasts, Connections

Ozick wrote this story together with a longer novella, "Rosa," although "Rosa" was not published until three years later in *The New Yorker*. They are now published together in a single volume, and it may be useful to consider these two stories as part of a whole. Together, they provide different but complimentary ways to write about the Holocaust, considering the subject both directly and indirectly.

Students may be familiar with Art Spiegelman's *Maus*, which uses graphic art to approach the subject of the Holocaust. How does form function in depicting the Holocaust?

Questions for Reading, Discussion, and Writing

Although there are many questions incorporated into the previous discussion, you might also consider the following:

1. What does it mean for speech to be dangerous?
2. Discuss the image of the shawl (e.g., shawl as child, shawl as source of nourishment, shawl as that which mutes).

Bibliography

Texts listed in the headnote are the best places to begin reading about Ozick.

General History of the Holocaust

Bauer, Yehuda. *A History of the Holocaust*. New York: Watts, 1982.

Hilberg, Raul. *The Destruction of the European Jews*. 3 vols. Rev. and definitive ed. New York: Holmes, 1985.

Holocaust Literature and Representation

Ezrahi, Sidra. *By Words Alone: The Holocaust in Literature*. Chicago: U of Chicago P, 1980.

Lang, Berel, ed. *Writing and the Holocaust*. New York and London: Holmes, 1988.

Young, James. *Writing and Rewriting the Holocaust: Narrative and the Consequences of Interpretation*. Bloomington and Indianapolis: Indiana UP, 1988.

Women and the Holocaust

Koonz, Claudia. *Mothers in the Fatherland: Women, the Family, and Nazi Politics*. New York: St. Martin's, 1987.

Rittner, Carol, and John K. Roth, eds., *Different Voices: Women and the Holocaust*. New York: Paragon, 1993.

Edward Albee (b. 1928)

Contributing Editor: John Alberti

Classroom Issues and Strategies

One-act plays like *The Sandbox* work well in the classroom. Their brevity not only allows for detailed analysis of the text, but as dramatic works they invite the use of performance as a pedagogical strategy. Asking groups of students to prepare and put on their own productions of *The Sandbox,* whether live in the classroom or on videotape, transforms literary interpretation from an academic exercise to a pragmatic consideration of how to stage the play, as student actor/directors must make discussion about how lines are read, what body language is to be used, and even how to construct a set given the constraints of both Albee's script directions and the limitations of the classroom. If several student groups put together their own versions of the play, the class can then discuss and write on the different approaches taken and what these approaches say about the way theater works and the variability of the interpretive act.

A performative approach can help students deal with the difficulties of *The Sandbox.* While the diction of the characters in the play is accessible, almost clichéd, the very poverty of their powers of expression can provoke questions about how we are supposed to understand the motivations and feelings of the characters. This contrast between the banality of the language of Mommy and Daddy and the extremity of their plans (murder) is, of course, one of the themes of the play itself, and in deciding how to portray the characters students will have to make decisions about just how to deliver their lines, decisions they can then describe and reflect on in written assignments. Similarly the metatheatrical nature of the play, with Grandma's and Mommy's frequent references to the staging of the play itself and the identification of the Young Man as an actor ("playing" the Angel of Death), extends the theme of the poverty of interpersonal communication to the ritual of theater itself in modern, media-driven society (the Young Man is identified not just as an actor but as an actor from Southern California, with implications of the film industry).

Anne Sexton (1928–1974)

Contributing Editor: Diana Hume George

Classroom Issues and Strategies

Anne Sexton's poetry teaches superbly. It is accessible, challenging, richly textured, and culturally resonant. Her work is equally appropriate for use in American literature, women's studies, and poetry courses. The selections in this text represent many of the diverse subjects and directions of her work.

Three problems tend to recur in teaching Sexton; all are interrelated. First, the "confessional school" context is troublesome because that subgenre in American poetry is both misnamed and easily misunderstood; Sexton has been the subject of inordinately negative commentary as the first prominent woman poet writing in this mode. Second, contemporary readers, despite the feminist movement, often have difficulty dealing with Sexton's explicitly bodily and female subject matter and imagery. Finally, readers often find her poetry depressing, especially the poems that deal with suicide, death, and mental illness.

If the course emphasizes historical context, a sympathetic and knowledgeable explanation of resistance to the confessional mode is helpful. (Ironically, if historical context is not important to presentation of the material, I suggest not mentioning it at all.) Academic and public reactions to the women's movement, even though Sexton did not deliberately style herself as a feminist poet, will help to make students understand the depth and extent of her cultural and poetic transgressions. The third problem is most troubling for teaching Sexton; teachers might emphasize the necessity for literature to confront and deal with controversial and uncomfortable themes such as suicide, mortality, and madness. A discussion of the dangers of equating creativity and emotional illness might be helpful, even necessary, for some students. It's also important to demonstrate that Sexton wrote many poems of celebration, as well as of mourning.

Students often want to know how and why Sexton killed herself. They want to disapprove, yet they are often fascinated. I recommend one of two approaches. Either avoid the whole thing by not mentioning her suicide and by directing students toward the poems and away from Sexton's life; or engage the issue directly, in which case you need to allow some time to make thoughtful responses and guide a useful discussion that will illuminate more than one life and death.

Major Themes, Historical Perspectives, Personal Issues

A balanced presentation of Sexton would include mention of her major themes, most of which are touched upon in the selection of poems here: religious quest, transformation and dismantling of myth, the meanings of gender, inheritance and legacy, the search for fathers, mother-daughter relationships, sexual anxiety, madness and suicide, issues of female identity.

Significant Form, Style, or Artistic Conventions

The problem of placement in the confessional school can be turned into an advantage by emphasizing Sexton's groundbreaking innovations in style and subject matter. Sexton's early poetry was preoccupied with form and technique; she could write in tightly constrained metrical forms, as demonstrated in *To Bedlam and Part Way Back* and *All My Pretty Ones*. She wrote in free verse during the middle and late phases of her poetic career. Most important is her gift for unique imagery, often centering on the body or the household.

Original Audience

Many of Sexton's readers have been women, and she has perhaps a special appeal for female readers because of her domestic imagery. She also found a wide readership among people who have experienced emotional illness or depression. But Sexton's appeal is wider than a specialist audience. She is exceptionally accessible and writes in deliberately colloquial style, and her diversity and range are such that she appeals to students from different backgrounds.

Comparisons, Contrasts, Connections

Among other confessionals, she can be discussed in context with Robert Lowell, Sylvia Plath, John Berryman, and W. D. Snodgrass. Among women poets, she shares concerns of subject and style with Adrienne Rich, Denise Levertov, Sylvia Plath, Alicia Ostriker, and, in a different way, Maxine Kumin. It's also appropriate to mention her similarities to Emily Dickinson, another female New England poet who wrote in unconventional ways about personal subjects, religion, and mortality. Because she was a religious poet whose work is part of the questing tradition, she might be usefully compared with John Donne and George Herbert. Since many of her poems are spoken from the perspective of a child speaker, the standard literary tradition for comparative purposes can include Blake and Wordsworth, Vaughan and Traherne. Extraliterary texts that illuminate her work include sections of psychoanalytic theory, especially Freudian.

Questions for Reading, Discussion, and Writing

1. I try to avoid giving students a predisposition to Sexton and instead discuss difficulties and questions as they arise in discussion.
2. (a) Examine the range of Sexton's subject matter and poetic style.
   (b) Pick a theme in a Sexton poem and trace it in other poems she wrote.
   (c) In what sense is Sexton a religious poet? A heretic?
   (d) Examine several surprising, unconventional images from several Sexton poems. What makes them surprising? Successful?
   (e) If Sexton is confessional, what is it that she is confessing?
   (f) Select another poet with whom Sexton can be compared, such as a confessional poet, a feminist poet, or a religious poet, and discuss similarities and differences in their perspectives.
   (g) What are some of the possible uses for poetry that speaks from the perspective of madness or of suicide?

Bibliography

Excellent articles on Sexton are most readily available in recent and forthcoming anthologies of criticism. Instructors can select articles that bear most directly on their concerns.

Sexton: Selected Criticism, ed. Diana Hume George (Champaign-Urbana: U of Illinois P, 1988) includes many previously published articles from diverse sources in addition to new criticism, as does *Ann Sexton: Telling the Tale,* ed. Steven E. Colburn (Ann Arbor: U of Michigan P, 1988).

Original Essays on Anne Sexton, ed. Frances Bixler (U of Central Arkansas P, 1988) contains many new and previously unpublished selections.

Critical Essays on Anne Sexton, ed. Linda Wagner-Martin (Boston: Hall, 1989) includes a number of reviews as well as essays and reminiscences.

J. D. McClatchy's *Anne Sexton: The Poet and Her Critics* (Indianapolis: Indiana UP, 1978) is the original critical collection.

Diane W. Middlebrook's *Anne Sexton: A Biography* was published by Houghton Mifflin in 1991.

Critics who specialize in Sexton or who have written major essays on her, whose works will be found in most or all of the above anthologies, include Alicia S. Ostriker, Diane W. Middlebrook, Diana H. George, Estella Lauter, Suzanne Juhasz, and Linda Wagner-Martin.

Paule Marshall (b. 1929)

Contributing Editor: Dorothy L. Denniston

Classroom Issues and Strategies

One strategy for approaching Marshall's fiction is to explain the "Middle Passage" to illustrate the placement of blacks all over the world (African diaspora). It might also be helpful to discuss the notion of traditional African cyclical time, which involves recurrence and duration, as opposed to Western linear time, which suggests change and progress. The cyclic approach applies thematically (Da-duh's symbolic immortality) and structurally (the story comes full circle). Also important is the traditional African view of the world as being composed of dualities/opposites that work together to constitute a harmonious moral order. (For a more complete explanation, see Marshall's "From the Poets in the Kitchen" in *Reena and Other Short Stories*.)

Consider also discussing the African oral tradition as a recorder of history and preserver of folk tradition. Since it is centered on the same ideas as written literatures (the ideas, beliefs, hopes, and fears of a people), its purpose is to create and maintain a group identity, to guide social action, to encourage social interaction, and simply to entertain. The oral arts are equally concerned with preserving the past to honor traditional values and to reveal their relevance to the modern world. Marshall's craftsmanship is executed in such a dynamic fashion as to elicit responses usually reserved for oral performance or theater.

Students readily respond to similarities/differences between black cultures represented throughout the diaspora. Once they recognize African cultural components as positive, they reevaluate old attitudes and beliefs and begin to appreciate differences in cultural perspectives as they celebrate the human spirit.

Major Themes, Historical Perspectives, Personal Issues

A major theme is the search for identity (personal and cultural). Marshall insists upon the necessity for a "journey back" through history in order to come to terms with one's past as an explanation of the present and as a guiding post for the future. For the author, in particular, the story becomes a means to begin unraveling her multicultural background (American, African American, African Caribbean). To be considered foremost is the theme embodied in the epigram: the quality of life itself is threatened by giving priority to materialistic values over those that nourish the human spirit.

Significant Form, Style, or Artistic Conventions

Questions for form and style include Marshall's manipulation of time and her juxtaposition of images to create opposites (landscape, physical description, culture). This suggests an artistic convention that is, at base, African as it imitates or revives in another form the African oral narrative tradition. In fact, Marshall merges Western literary tradition with that of the African to create a new, distinctive expression.

Original Audience

All audiences find Marshall accessible. It might be interesting to contrast her idyllic view of Barbados in "To Da-duh" with her later view in the story "Barbados." The audience may wish to share contemporary views of third world countries and attitudes toward Western powers.

Comparisons, Contrasts, Connections

Both Toni Morrison and Paule Marshall deal with ancestral figures (connections to the past) to underscore cyclical patterns or deviations from them. Morrison's *Song of Solomon* (1977), *Tar Baby* (1981), or *Beloved* (1988) might be effectively compared with Marshall's *Praisesong for the Widow* (1983); *Brown Girl, Brownstones* (1959); *The Chosen Place, The Timeless People* (1969); or *Daughters* (1991).

Questions for Reading, Discussion, and Writing

Discuss the use of African and Caribbean imagery and explain why it is essential to Marshall's aesthetic.

Bibliography

Barthold, Bonnie. *Black Time: Fiction in Africa, the Caribbean and the United States.* New Haven: Yale UP, 1981.

Christian, Barbara. *Black Women Novelists: The Development of a Tradition, 1892–1976.* Westport, CT: Greenwood, 1980.

Denniston, Dorothy. "Early Short Fiction by Paule Marshall." *Callaloo* 6.2 (Spring/Summer, 1983). Rpt. in *Short Story Criticism.* Detroit: Gale, 1990.

————. *The Fiction of Paule Marshall: Reconstructions of History, Culture and Gender*. Knoxville: U of Tennessee P, 1995.

Evans, Mari, ed. Sec. on Paule Marshall in *Black Women Writers (1950–1980): A Critical Evaluation*. Garden City, NY: Anchor, 1983.

Marshall, Paule. "Shaping the World of My Art." New Letters (Autumn 1973).

Pettis, Joyce. *Toward Wholeness in Paule Marshall's Fiction*. Charlottesville: U of Virginia P, 1995.

Review especially the following:

Marshall, Paule. "From the Poets in the Kitchen." *Reena and Other Short Stories*. Old Westbury, NY: Feminist, 1983. 3–12.

Mbiti, John S. *African Religions and Philosophies*. New York: Doubleday, 1970.

Adrienne Rich (b. 1929)

Contributing Editor: Wendy Martin

Classroom Issues and Strategies

Rich's poetry is extremely accessible and readable. However, there are a few allusions that cannot be understood, and, from time to time, there will be references to events or literary works that will not be immediately recognized by students. This material or these references are glossed in the text so that the student can understand the historical or literary context.

Other problems occur when there is fundamental hostility to the poet over feminism. The instructor will have to explain that feminism simply means a belief in the social, political, and economic equality of women and men. Explain, also, that Rich is not a man-hater or in any way unwilling to consider men as human beings. Rather, her priority is to establish the fundamental concerns of her women readers.

Major Themes, Historical Perspectives, Personal Issues

It is important to read these poems out loud, to understand that Rich is simultaneously a political, polemical, and lyric poet. It is important also to establish for the poems of the 1960s, the Vietnam War protests as background as well as the feminist movement of the 1960s and 1970s.

It is also important to emphasize that in many respects the 1960s and 1970s were reaction to the confinement of the 1950s and the feminine mystique of that period. In addition, stress that the political background of the poems by Adrienne Rich connects the personal and the political.

Significant Form, Style, or Artistic Conventions

Rich employs free verse, dialogue, and the interweaving of several voices. She evolves from a more tightly constructed traditional rhymed poetry to a more open, loose, and flexible poetic line. The instructor must stress again that poetic subjects are chosen often for their political value and importance. It is important once again to stress that politics and art are intertwined, that they cannot be separated. Aesthetic matters affect the conditions of everyday life.

Original Audience

Adrienne Rich has written her poetry for all time. While it grows out of the political conflicts and tensions of the feminist movement and the antiwar protests of the sixties and seventies, it speaks of universal issues of relationships between men and women and between women and women that will endure for generations to come.

Comparisons, Contrasts, Connections

The feminist activist poets like Audre Lorde, June Jordan, and Carolyn Forché would be very useful to read along with Rich. Also, it might be useful to teach poets like Allen Ginsberg and Gary Snyder, who were, after all, poets of the Beat movement of the late 1950s and early 1960s. They were poets with a vision, as is Rich.

Questions for Reading, Discussion, and Writing

1. It might be useful to discuss the evolution of the more free and more flexible line that begins with Walt Whitman and the greater flexibility of subject matter that also begins with Whitman and Emily Dickinson and to carry this discussion on through William Carlos Williams and Allen Ginsberg to discuss the evolution of the free verse that Rich uses.

2. Any writing topic that would discuss either the evolution of flexible poetics or aesthetics—that is, a concern with people's actual lived experiences, for the way they actually talk and think.

In addition, in the case of Rich, any paper that would link her to other women writers of the twentieth century (and the nineteenth, for that matter) would be useful. Rich is often quoted as an important cultural critic who provides the context for feminist thought in general in the twentieth century. It might also be useful to assign parts of her prose, either in collected essays or in *Of Woman Born.*

Bibliography

I would highly recommend my own book: *An American Triptych: The Lives and Work of Anne Bradstreet, Emily Dickinson, and Adrienne Rich.* I am recommending this book because it provides both a historical and an aesthetic context for the poetry of Rich. It links her to earlier traditions that have shaped her work and demonstrates effectively how American Puritanism and American feminism are intertwined. It gives a lot of biographical material as well as historical background and literary analysis.

Sylvia Plath (1932–1963)

Contributing Editor: Linda Wagner-Martin

Classroom Issues and Strategies

Students usually begin with the fact that Plath committed suicide and then read her death as some kind of "warning" to talented, ambitious women writers. (The biography by Stevenson only supports this view, unfortunately.) What must be done is to get to the text, in each case, and read for nuance of meaning—humor, anger, poignance, intellectual tour de force. Running parallel with this sense of Plath as some inhuman persona is a fearful acknowledgment that women who have ambition are not quite normal. Plath receives a very gender-based reading. A good corrective is to talk about people who have tendencies toward depression, a situation that affects men as well as women.

Focus on the text and ready information about the possible biographical influence on that text. Often, however, the influences are largely literary— Medea is as close a persona for some of the late poems as Plath herself—T. S. Eliot, Wallace Stevens, W. S. Merwin, W. B. Yeats, and so on. Criticism is just now starting to mine these rich areas. Some attention to the late 1950s and early 1960s is also helpful: seeing the poetry and *The Bell Jar* as the same kind of breakthrough into the expression of women's anger as Betty Friedan's or Simone de Beauvoir's is useful.

As mentioned above, the fact of Plath's suicide seems primary in many students' minds. Partly because many of them have read, or know of, *The Bell Jar*, it is hard to erase the image of the tormented woman, ill at ease in her world. But once that issue is cleared, and her writing is seen as a means of keeping her alive, perhaps the study of that writing becomes more important to students: it seems to have a less than esoteric "meaning."

Major Themes, Historical Perspectives, Personal Issues

Themes include women's place in American culture (even though Plath lived the last three years in England, thinking wrongly that she had more freedom in England to be a writer); what women can attempt; how coerced they were by social norms (i.e., to date, marry, have children, be a helpmate, support charities); the weight society places on women—to be the only support of children, to earn livings (Plath's life, echoing her mother's very difficult one, with little money and two children for whom she wanted the best of opportunities); the need for superhuman talent, endurance, and resourcefulness in every woman's life.

Significant Form, Style, or Artistic Conventions

Versatility of form (tercet, villanelle, many shapes of organic form, syllabics); use of rhyme (and its variations, near rhyme, slant rhyme, assonance); word choice (mixed vocabularies)—Plath must be studied as an expert, compelling poet, whose influence on the contemporary poetry scene—poems written by men as well as women—has been inestimable. Without prejudicing readers, the teacher must consider what "confessional" poetry is: the use of seemingly "real" experience, experience that often is a supreme fiction rather than personal biography; a means of making art less remote from life by using what might be life experience as its text. Unfortunately, as long as only women poets or poets with abnormal psychiatric histories are considered "confessional," the term is going to be ineffective for a meaningful study of contemporary poetry.

Original Audience

Although most of Plath's best poems were written in the early 1960s, the important point to be made is that today's readers find her work immediate. Her expression of distrust of society, her anger at the positions talented women were asked to take in that society, were healthful (and rare) during the early 1960s, so she became a kind of voice of the times in the same way Ernest Hemingway expressed the mood of the 1920s. But while much of Hemingway's work seems dated to today's students (at least his ethical and moral stances toward life), Plath's writing has gained currency.

Comparisons, Contrasts, Connections

The most striking comparison can be made between the early work of Anne Sexton and Plath (Plath learned a lot from Sexton), and to a lesser extent, the poems of Theodore Roethke. W. D. Snodgrass's long poem "Heart's Needle" was an important catalyst for both Sexton and Plath, as was some of Robert Lowell's work. If earlier Plath poems are used, Wallace Stevens and T. S. Eliot are key. And, in moderation, Ted Hughes's early work can be useful—especially the animal and archaic tones and images.

Working with Cultural Objects

Hearing Plath read from her own late work is effective: She has an unusual, almost strident voice, and the humor and gutsiness of the 1962 poems come across well. Caedmon has one recording that has many of the late poems backed with Plath's interview with Peter Orr for the BBC, taped on October 30, 1962 (many of the poems she reads were written just that week, or shortly before). The PBS *Voices and Visions* Plath segment is also fairly accurate and effective. Websites featuring recordings of Plath include HarperCollins.com at <http://www.harpercollins.com/hc/features/poetry/voices.asp>, Learner.org at <http://www.learner.org/catalog/extras/vvspot/Plath.html/>, and Salon. com at <http://www.salon.com/audio/poetry/2001/03/19/plath/index>.

Bibliography

Susan Van Dyne's essays on the manuscripts are invaluable (see *Centennial Review*, Summer 1988). See also the *Massachusetts Review* essay, collected in Wagner's *Sylvia Plath: Critical Essays* (Boston: Hall, 1984) and Van Dyne's 1993 book from the U of North Carolina P.

Wagner's Routledge collection, *Sylvia Plath: The Critical Heritage* (1988) includes a number of helpful reviews.

Linda Bundtzen's *Plath's Incarnations* (U of Michigan P, 1983), Steven Axelrod's 1990 *Sylvia Plath, The Wound and the Cure of Wounds*, along with the Wagner-Martin biography of Plath, are useful. See also Linda Wagner-Martin's *Plath's The Bell Jar, A Novel of the Fifties* (1992).

Martin Luther King Jr. (1929–1968)

Contributing Editor: Keith D. Miller

Major Themes, Historical Perspectives, Personal Issues

Unfortunately, many students remain blissfully unaware of the horrific racial inequities that King decried in "I Have a Dream." In 1963, Southern states featured not only separate black and white schools, churches, and neighborhoods, but also separate black and white restrooms, drinking fountains, hotels, motels, restaurants, cafes, golf courses, libraries, elevators, and cemeteries. African Americans were also systematically denied the right to vote. In addition, Southern whites could commit crimes against blacks— including murder—with little or no fear of punishment. The system of racial division was enshrined in Southern custom and law. Racism also conditioned life in the North. Although segregationist practices directly violated the Fourteenth and Fifteenth Amendments of the Constitution, the federal government exerted little or no effort to enforce these amendments. Leading politicians—including John Kennedy, Robert Kennedy, and Lyndon Johnson—advocated racial equality only when pressured by King, James Farmer, John Lewis, Ella Baker, Fannie Lou Hamer, and other nonviolent activists who fostered social disruption in the pursuit of equal rights. Fortunately, black students are often knowledgeable about the civil rights era.

"I Have a Dream" has been misconstrued and sentimentalized by some who focus only on the dream. The first half of the speech does not portray an American dream but rather catalogs an American nightmare. In the manner of Old Testament prophets and Frederick Douglass, King excoriated a nation that espoused equality while forcing blacks onto "a lonely island of poverty in the midst of a vast ocean of material prosperity."

Significant Form, Style, or Artistic Conventions

Important in reaching King's enormous and diverse audience were the resources of black folk preaching, including biblical quotations; call-and-response interaction with listeners; a calm-to-storm delivery that begins in a professorial manner before swinging gradually and rhythmically to a dramatic climax; schemes of parallelism, especially anaphora (e.g., "I have a dream that . . ."); and clusters of light and dark metaphors. African-American students can frequently inform their classmates about these time-honored characteristics of the African-American folk pulpit that animate King's address.

Original Audience

King spoke "I Have a Dream" to an immediate crowd of 250,000 followers who had rallied from around the nation in a march on Washington held in front of the Lincoln Memorial. His audience also consisted of millions across the nation and the world via radio and television.

Comparisons, Contrasts, Connections

Old Testament prophets, Frederick Douglass's "The Fourth of July" oration, John Lewis's speech preceding "I Have a Dream," and speeches by Malcolm X.

"I Have a Dream" harnesses the voices of Lincoln, Jefferson, Shakespeare, Amos, Isaiah, Jesus, Handel's *Messiah*, "America the Beautiful," a slave spiritual, and African-American preachers.

King never fully acknowledged the importance of female civil rights leaders. See JoAnn Robinson, *The Montgomery Bus Boycott and the Women Who Started It*, ed. David Garrow (Knoxville: U of Tennessee P, 1987).

Working with Cultural Objects

Playing records or audio/video tapes of King's speeches substantially facilitates discussion of the oral dynamics of the black pulpit that nurtured King and shaped his discourse. The PBS series "Eyes on the Prize" is especially useful. King's "I Have a Dream" is available on the Internet, in particular at History and Politics Out Loud at <http://www.hpol.org/record.php?id=72>.

Bibliography

For a valuable analysis of King's 1963 address, see Alexandra Alvarez, "Martin Luther King's 'I Have a Dream': The Speech Event as Metaphor," *Journal of Black Studies* 18 (1988): 337–57.

For background on King, see James Cone, "Martin Luther King, Jr.: Black Theology—Black Church," *Theology Today* 40 (1984): 409–20; James Cone, *Martin and Malcolm and America*, Maryknoll, NY: Orbis, 1991; David Garrow, *Bearing the Cross*, New York: Morrow, 1986; Keith D. Miller, *Voice of Deliverance: The Language of Martin Luther King, Jr., and Its Sources*, New York: Free, 1992.

See also the following:

Hansen, Drew. *The Dream: Martin Luther King, Jr., and the Speech that Inspired a Nation*. New York: Ecco, 2003.

Olson, Lynne. *Freedom's Daughters: The Unsung Heroines of the Civil Rights Movement from 1830–1970.* New York: Scribner's, 2001.

New Generations

Rolando Hinojosa-Smith (b. 1929)

Contributing Editor: Juan Bruce-Novoa

Classroom Issues and Strategies

Most students know nothing about the author or the context of this selection. Useful information can be found in Hinojosa's interview included in *Chicano Authors, Inquiry by Interview* (Juan Bruce-Novoa).

I find it useful to ask students to write an accurate version of something they have experienced as a group: a short reading, a brief video, or even a planned interruption in class by an outsider. They then must consider the differences in the accounts of the same event. Sometimes I ask them to write an accurate description of an object I place in their midst; then we compare versions.

They respond to the element of different versions and observe how justice, represented in the newspaper reports, is not necessarily served. They ask if the person is guilty, raising the question of what is guilt.

Major Themes, Historical Perspectives, Personal Issues

The major themes are the search for an accurate version of any event in the midst of the proliferation of information, the conflict between oral and written texts, the historical disregard for the Chicano community in South Texas and elsewhere, and the placement of the author in the role of cultural detective. The selection can be read as an allegory of Chicano culture within U.S. history in which Mexicans have been criminalized without a fair hearing.

Significant Form, Style, or Artistic Conventions

The basic form is that of a criminal investigation, related to the detective story. Yet it breaks with the genre in that it does not resolve the case by discovery of the culprit; instead, the frame of the story maintains its position, and—

if anything—gets worse, the degradation of process reflected in the errata contained in the final segment.

Fragmentation does not bother students much now. The small units emphasize the postmodern experience of life as short sound bites.

The style is marked by shifts in voices, an attempt to capture the community in its speech patterns.

Original Audience

In the period of Chicano renewal (1965–1975) there was a need expressed then in literature to search for communal history. It was aimed at an audience that would sympathize with the victim, considering itself an abused and ignored group in a society controlled by the forces represented in the newspaper clippings that frame the story. This has changed. Now audiences are much less sympathetic to marginal peoples, and even Chicanos are not as willing to accept the old version of oppression of minority groups.

Comparisons, Contrasts, Connections

Faulkner's creation of a fictional county in several works coincides well with Hinojosa's project. The use of multiple voices to give different perspectives is quite similar.

Questions for Reading, Discussion, and Writing

1. I ask students to consider what history is. What is news reporting? What is a fact? I often ask them to look up the etymology of *fact* and consider its relation to *manufacture*.
2. Assign the reporting of an imaginary event; give them the basic facts and characters and even an official summary statement. Then have them reconstruct the fragments as seen from one perspective. Compare the papers.

John Barth (b. 1930)

Contributing Editor: Julius Rowan Raper

Classroom Issues and Strategies

To call an author "a writers' writer" is often the kiss of death. Yet Barth in "Lost in the Funhouse" and in other works goes out of his way to draw to himself this label that sets him apart from more popular "men's writers" (or "businessmen's writers") like Ernest Hemingway or "women's writers" like Willa Cather. By foregrounding the writerly nature of his work, Barth, perhaps more than any American author before him, prevents his readers from ignoring the style and form of his work while they pursue the content. Rather than focus on the relatively accessible content about Ambrose, Peter, Magda, and the three adults, as a teacher I want students to speculate about Barth's reasons for so intrusively and self-consciously focusing on the writing process.

Major Themes, Historical Perspectives, Personal Issues

At least three large explanations for the self-consciousness of Barth's works come to mind. In *Chimera* he will have the Genie report that in the United States in our time "the only readers of artful fiction [are] critics, other writers, and unwilling students who, left to themselves, [prefer] music and pictures to words." In short, a serious writer has to recognize that his only willing readers *are* other writers; that he or she is, in fact, a writers' writer.

A second explanation is that, for postmodern writers, especially for Barth, the traditional modes of fiction have been used up—in Barth's favorite term, exhausted. This is especially true of the *bildungsroman*, the story of the development of an individual, and even more so if that individual happens to be an artist. In our century, James Joyce had his Stephen Dedalus, D. H. Lawrence his Paul Morel, Sherwood Anderson his George Willard, Thomas Wolfe his Eugene Gant, Ernest Hemingway his Nick Adams, William Faulkner his Quentin Compson, and so on. "'Is anything more tiresome, in fiction, than the problems of sensitive adolescents?'" Indeed! Even this self-negating idea has to appear in quotation marks because it has been uttered before. Rather than ignore this remark, which could easily alienate already unwilling students (one of the three groups remaining among readers of artful fictions), I would note the curious detail that Barth has his own seemingly autobiographical portrait of an artist in the character named Ambrose Mensch (meaning roughly "Immortal Man"), who appears here and in other stories of the collection and figures as well as a major figure in the later megafiction, *LETTERS: a*

Novel. Why would Barth devote such energy to an apparently exhausted fictional form? He obviously believes that problems of adolescents are important and that such stories can be told in a new way that "replenishes" (another key term for Barth) an entire mode of fiction. That new way must include "metafiction," an important postmodern device that allows novelists to write the criticism of their own fiction while creating the fiction itself. The reasons metafiction has become important in our time are another large topic that could lead the class to fruitful discussions.

These could include the fact that at the critical moment in the fiction, both the boy and the writer, out of whom the reader may wish to construct a single subject, realize that the self-reflexiveness that plagues each of them "makes perfect observation impossible," a Sartrean truth vital to many contemporary postrealist fictions.

A third explanation for the self-consciousness here is at once more personal and more cultural. The narrator of Ambrose's story is a writer trapped inside his story, unable to come to its end. He is a blocked writer. In a number of works, Barth fictionalizes the writer's block he apparently suffered after the two gigantic novels of the early 1960s. Self-consciousness and writer's block may belong to a single vicious circle; each may lead to the other. Barth takes writer's block as his theme so often that one suspects it represents more than a personal event—no matter how engrossing such "autobiographic" episodes may be to readers primarily interested in "real life." At this other level, writer's block appears to be Barth's metaphor for Western Civilization at present. In the recurring conflicts between women and men, East and West, Marxists and capitalists, liberals and conservatives, and blacks and whites, our culture finds itself so lacking in true invention that it can do little except, like the fated characters in *Chimera*, repeat a pattern passed down through centuries, the swing of the pendulum between extremes. If the blocked writer belongs to the Waste Land, Eliot's metaphor that haunted the twentieth century, the writer Barth imagines into being would feel more at home in the Funhouse (as opposed to the funny farm), where values and options would be far different. At the same time, the blocked writer provides an appropriate motive for producing the metafictional passages with which Barth frames his fictions, the seeming digressions that allow him to create an audience for his generally nonrealistic stories.

Significant Form, Style, or Artistic Conventions

In giving up the conventional mimesis of realism, Barth, however, elects the contrary powers of what, in *Chimera*, he terms the Principle of Metaphoric Means, "the investiture by the writer of as many of the elements and aspects of his fiction as possible with emblematic as well as dramatic value" (*Chimera* 203). This device leads to an additional motive for Barth's frequent dramatizations of the blocked writer. Such writers, as noted above, may be metaphors for something important in our culture. Students in class discussion may want to explore possible referents for the metaphor by asking themselves what aspects of American or Western culture appeared especially "blocked" in 1968, a year that, it turns out, may stand roughly as the midpoint of the Cold War. What is there about contemporary culture that it has lost its ability to move forward in the progressive fashion that the Enlightenment, Positivism, and modern scientific thinking once promised?

Students may then move to the possibility that every individual is a potential writer, that each of us lives out a script that someone else will write for us if we do not write it ourselves, that many women and men seem caught, like the narrator of this story, in scripts they do not want and whose end they cannot find. The next step would be to explore the degree to which the devices Barth employs, including metafiction, parody, Metaphoric Means, and (elsewhere) myth and fantasy, could be used to frame the stories of blocked lives, to liberate one from such narratives, and to write more promising life scripts. In short, can Barth's postmodern approach free up blocked lives or replenish a stymied, possibly exhausted culture? If not, might the attempt to do so still comprise a tragic gesture with a touch of the heroic in it? Students could then weight the elements of parody, satire, and muted tragedy in Barth's story.

Consideration of Metaphoric Means as a global device leads to a careful reconsideration of every aspect of the story, including seeming authorial mistakes. If in the postexistential world we are all writers, then not only must we watch how we dot our i's and cross our t's but also how we drop our apostrophes. For example, the narrator mentions "Peter and Ambrose's father" but speaks of "Ambrose's and Peter's mother." Is this a simple slip, or a telling one? Students may want to pay special attention to parallel usages in the story or explore the later adventures of Ambrose, Peter, Magda, their parents, and/or Uncle Carl in *LETTERS*.

Original Audience

It may appear that Barth's audience is made up of other writers, critics, and writing teachers. If we are, however, to write our way out of the (doomed?) scripts we inherited from our culture, then every thinking person may have something to learn from Barth. The risks Barth takes indicate he arrived on the literary scene when the success of T. S. Eliot and James Joyce in having critics prepare an audience for their difficult texts inspired him to trust that time would provide readers for his works. By 1968, however, like other metafictionists to come, he was covering himself by providing guidelines, sometimes ironic ones, for critics still working within the modernist aesthetic.

Comparisons, Contrasts, Connections

The most useful comparisons for Barth are with the international fictionists whom he cites as inspirations: Jorge Luis Borges, Vladimir Nabokov, and Italo Calvino; and to the experimental writers who are his fellow postmodernists: Robert Coover, Thomas Pynchon, Raymond Federman, Cynthia Ozick, John Hawkes, Donald Barthelme, Lawrence Durrell, John Fowles, Ishmael Reed, David Foster Wallace, Richard Powers, John Wideman, and others. The most obvious contrasts are with traditional flat realists like Cather and Hemingway, naturalists like Theodore Dreiser, engaged novelists like John Dos Passos and John Steinbeck, and representative modernists like Faulkner and Joyce, especially as the latter two use the mythic method that Barth in *Chimera* and elsewhere stands on its head. Less obvious contrasts would be to the three contemporary trends that retreat from the more audacious experiments of the postmodernists: the minimalists like Raymond Carver, Bobbie Ann Mason, and Ann Beattie; other contemporary Southern authors such as Walker Percy, William Styron, Reynolds Price, and Lee Smith; and the Magical Realists, who make minimal use of the fantasy devices that Barth, like Coover, Fowles, Durrell, and Pynchon, employs with such relish. Another sort of contrast can be made—in an age that commodifies not only space and time but also gender, class, and race—with Toni Morrison, Adrienne Rich, Alice Walker, James Baldwin, E. L. Doctorow, and Allen Ginsberg, among others. While for many of his contemporaries the message has become the *merchandise,* Barth persists in focusing on the challenges and powers of the fictional medium itself.

Questions for Reading, Discussion, and Writing

"Lost in the Funhouse" cries out for student papers of two types. First, one might want students to try a reader-response approach, to let them work out their anger against intrusive metafictional commentary, to identify the causes of their anger, and perhaps to discover reasons for Barth's choosing this device. Next, students could employ a traditional close-reading approach to take up the following questions.

1. What are the indications in the story that Barth has taught creative writing courses? Is this story good pedagogy, or a parody thereof?
2. Why doesn't the narrator complete many of his sentences? How does this fit with Barth's interest in the literature of exhaustion? How does Barth attempt here to replenish the exhausted story of sensitive adolescents?
3. What is the temporal setting of the paragraph in which the narrator says, "I'll never be an author"? What is the author's problem here, and how does Ambrose's problem mirror it?

4. What happened to Ambrose in the toolshed when he was ten? How did it influence his later life? Is the lyre important?

5. What does Ambrose see under the boardwalk? How does it affect him?

6. What is odd about Ambrose's invitation to Magda to accompany him through the funhouse? How can you explain it?

7. What metaphors for a life, or the world of fiction, can you develop as effectively as Barth does in the funhouse?

8. How do the "head" and "eye" getting in the way affect the self-consciousness theme dramatized in the technique of the story? Is there a "human tragedy" in this problem?

9. Is Barth in danger here of turning the medium into the merchandise as well as into his message? What subject other than fiction itself would writers be in so expert a position to offer their readers? On what topics did Homer, Dante, Petrarch, Shakespeare, Milton, Goethe, Lawrence, and others purport to be experts? On what authority did they write of these subjects? Why might writers of Barth's period lack the confidence of earlier ones in exploring parallel realms of knowledge?

10. If the "Funhouse" were to replace Eliot's "Waste Land" as the reigning metaphor for contemporary culture, would it make a difference?

A Sheaf of Vietnam Conflict Poetry and Prose

Michael Herr (b. 1940)

Contributing Editor: Raymund Paredes

Classroom Issues and Strategies

It's probably necessary and certainly a good idea to provide some sort of historical context for the consideration of Herr's work. This can be done by assigning supplementary reading or lecturing on the history of the Vietnam War. As a Vietnam War veteran myself, I relate my own personal experiences of the war to students to compare with Herr's. If you, or any older students, have direct experience with the Vietnam era, this is a useful approach. There are many good films about Vietnam (both feature and documentary) that could complement Herr's book.

Students respond very strongly to the graphic depiction of the inhumanity and insanity of the war. They want to know more about the causes of the Vietnam War and the political climate of the United States at the time.

Major Themes, Historical Perspectives, Personal Issues

The major themes in the excerpted passage are the dehumanizing and brutalizing influences of war, particularly the way war renders soldiers incapable of functioning in "normal" social circumstances; the relationship between the writer's style and presentation of the war and the drug culture of the 1960s and 1970s; and the author's view that the war was fundamentally immoral, even more so than other wars. Key here is Herr's use of the Spanish phrase "la vida loca" (the crazy life). On a personal level, Herr emphasizes his troubling, even macabre, attraction to the war, its combination of bloodshed, madness, camaraderie, and heroism.

Significant Form, Style, or Artistic Conventions

Dispatches is an extraordinary work stylistically, a brilliant execution of the speaking styles of young American soldiers: fast paced, full of slang, very much shaped by popular culture (films, television, rock and roll music) and the drug culture. Herr is also adept at capturing the officialese of the U.S. military establishment. Many of the formal and stylistic qualities of *Dispatches* connect Herr to postmodernism.

Original Audience

Dispatches is a very contemporary book in terms of its values and its points of view. It is a book about young men written by a young man.

Comparisons, Contrasts, Connections

Herr's work can be compared with that of other writers about the Vietnam War and with the so-called "new journalists" such as Tom Wolfe. The second connection is especially interesting. Students might note how Herr uses literary/fictional techniques—figurative language, characterization, narrative development—in what is ostensibly, as indicated by the title, a work of journalism. Students might look at other treatments of the Vietnam War— both fictional and journalistic—to compare points of view about the war, its impact on the humanity of the soldiers, and so on.

Questions for Reading, Discussion, and Writing

1. What is the author's attitude toward the war? What are the effects of the war on human behavior? From your knowledge, is Herr's position on the war widely shared?
2. How would you describe Herr's style? In what ways is Herr's style compatible (or not) with its subject? From what sources does Herr draw his images, his metaphors? How does this compare with the practices of other writers? In what sense is the notion of "la vida loca" symbolic of both the literary situation and the temper of the times?

Bibliography

Other books on Vietnam are very useful. I recommend Stanley Karnow's *Vietnam*, Neil Sheehan's *A Bright Shining Lie*, Wallace Terry's *Bloods*, and Philip Caputo's *A Rumor of War*.

Tim O'Brien (b. 1946)

Contributing Editor: Alex Vernon

Classroom Issues and Strategies

With each passing year, the American war in Vietnam recedes further from our collective memory. Our current undergraduates were born roughly ten years after the United States pulled its troops out of Southeast Asia in 1975. Their images of that conflict largely come from such movies as *Apocalypse Now* (1979), *Full Metal Jacket* (1987), and *Platoon* (1986). Providing some historical context seems a necessity, especially as Tim O'Brien himself rejects the popular image of the Vietnam War promoted by these movies. Michael Bibby has recently argued that the Vietnam War is constitutive of the postmodern condition, and while I disagree, finding the origins of postmodernism predating the war and not restricted to the American scene, Bibby rightly reminds us of the deep and lasting influence of that divisive war in U.S. culture (*The Vietnam War and Postmodernity*, 1999).

One strategy then is to first discuss the historical context, and then address O'Brien's artistic response as illustrated by "In the Field"—perhaps alongside the artistic response of other veterans included in this anthology. Several resources on teaching the war are listed in the bibliography below.

Some concise historical introductions to the war include George C. Herring, *America's Longest War: The United States and Vietnam, 1950–1975* (2nd ed., 1986); Anthony Edmonds, *The War In Vietnam* (1998); Thomas D. Boettcher, *Vietnam: The Valor and the Sorrow* (1985); Phillip B. Davidson, *Vietnam at War: The History, 1946–1975* (1988); William S. Turley, *The Second Indochina War: A Short Political and Military History, 1954–1975* (1986, 1987); James Joes, *The War for South Vietnam: 1954–1975* (1989); George Donelson Moss, *Vietnam: An American Ordeal* (1990). Less work for you and perhaps more interesting for the students might be to show a short film, such as the CBS production *Vietnam: Chronicle of a War* (1981; 88 minutes). To help students appreciate O'Brien's attitude toward the war, consider reviewing with them one of his early essays on the subject, "The Violent Vet" (*Esquire*, Dec. 1979). Among other things, that essay criticizes Hollywood's depiction of the war's madness as being inaccurate and too simple an explanation, one that relieves us of the duty of serious retrospection. It also argues for the universality of the soldier's war experience to counter the myth of the Vietnam War as somehow aberrant.

You might provide to students the other stories in *The Things They Carried* related to Kiowa's death ("Speaking of Courage" and "Notes"; less directly, "Field Trip") and ask students to reflect on how these stories either challenge or reinforce the themes and style of "In the Field." O'Brien's most anthologized pieces, "The Things They Carried" and "How to Tell a True War Story" (both in *Things*) are easily accessible and afford other points of comparison and insight. The other significant reading that can lead to fruitful discussion is the chapter "July" in O'Brien's war memoir *If I Die in a Combat Zone*. O'Brien has described his artistic method as a mixing of memory and imagination, and clearly he transformed the real event described in this chapter to create the fictional situation of Kiowa's death. In "How to Tell a True War Story," he asserts that factual occurrence may be less true than a story that never happened. Do students agree that "In the Field," despite its status as fiction, strikes more deeply at the war's truth than does the nonfiction account in "July"?

Finally, studying literature from Vietnam offers an excellent opportunity for personal interaction between students and veterans. Finding veterans to bring into class should not be difficult. I have had students for whom reading O'Brien enabled them, for the first time in their lives, to talk with veterans close to them, like fathers and uncles, about the war. Colleagues of mine have arranged for students to interview veterans through the local Department of Veterans Affairs and to turn those interviews into meaningful essays.

Major Themes, Historical Perspectives, Personal Issues

1. The two major themes of "In the Field" are interrelated and involve every American's moral responsibility for waging the war. First, the story makes quite explicit that both everybody and nobody bears the blame for Kiowa's death: the headquarters for assigning the platoon to set up in the shit field, the lieutenant for failing to disobey a bad order, the North Vietnamese for firing the mortars, the anonymous young soldier for shining his flashlight on a picture of a girl (perhaps the girl herself for inspiring the picture, inspiring the soldier to carry it and share it, and perhaps whoever took the photograph), Azar for making jokes, the weather and the river and the villagers for creating the shit field, even "an old man in Omaha" for forgetting to vote. Second, Kiowa's getting sucked into the shit field becomes a metaphor for the United States' getting sucked into the quagmire that was the Vietnam War. By extension, everybody and nobody bears the blame for the war. The anonymous soldier, in this context, might be read as a kind of Everyman.

2. O'Brien's writing career circles around the personal issue of his own moral accountability. He did not agree with the war and modestly protested it during college. Yet he allowed himself to be drafted—he neither found a legal way to dodge the draft, nor did he take the illegal and bolder option of fleeing to Canada. Partially, he allowed himself to be drafted because he felt he "owed" his small Minnesota town. "For twenty-one years I'd lived under its laws, accepted its education, eaten its food, wasted and guzzled its water, slept well at night, driven across its highways, dirtied and breathed its air, wallowed in its luxuries" (*If I Die*). In other words, he felt the obligation of a social contract. Perhaps "In the Field" can be read against O'Brien's persistent moral struggle. On one level, by acknowledging the soldier's function as agent of the state and society, O'Brien shifts some of the blame and guilt off himself. On another level, by shifting blame away from soldiers, he admits that he could never have completely avoided some responsibility for the war even if he had managed to evade combat duty. As he writes in "How to Tell a True Story," in a slightly different context, "the only certainty is overwhelming ambiguity."

3. In interview after interview, O'Brien has insisted that his war stories aren't only about the war, sometimes not about the war at all, but he uses the immediacy, drama, and ambiguity of his war experience to explore issues more universal to the human condition. "In the Field" is not the best example of this, though we can somewhat broaden the story's themes and achieve wider applicability. The web of contributing causes to Kiowa's death suggest the complex and ultimately indeterminate causality of any event. It proposes the degree to which we are all responsible to one an-

other. Finally, by shifting its perspective among the soldiers, the story dramatizes the subjective nature of all experience, not just war.

Significant Form, Style, or Artistic Conventions

1. "In the Field" constantly shifts the storytelling perspective among the soldiers. This structural decision reinforces the story's meaning or moral, specifically how Kiowa's death—and the war itself and everything about it—are both nobody's and everybody's fault. "Speaking of Courage" and "Notes" extend this technique by adding the voices of Norman Bowker and the book's narrator (named "Tim O'Brien"). Bringing these two voices into class discussion might help students better understand Norman's role in this story, and the final line in "Notes" adds another dimension to the ambiguity of complicity. In discussing Norman Bowker's story and the actions Bowker took that might have contributed to Kiowa's death, "Tim O'Brien" states that "that part of the story is my own." Does he mean that he, the narrator, took the actions the other story attributes to Bowker, or does he mean that he, the narrator, the author of Bowker's tale, invented the entire thing?

2. This shifting of perspectives also enhances the story's realism by providing a kind of *fog of war* reading experience—a technique employed in other twentieth-century war fiction, like Shelby Foote's *Shiloh* (1952) and Michael Shaara's *Killer Angels* (1974). The very bare, direct language reinforces the story's realism; indeed, since Hemingway and the other major post–Great War prose authors, such stark, "realistic" language seems almost a requisite for war fiction. Even with O'Brien's more fantastic war novel, *Going After Cacciato,* he insists upon a realistic rendering of a soldier's flight of fancy while passing the time on guard duty.

3. The story begins in the middle of the search for Kiowa (*in medias res*) and refuses to proceed chronologically. This places the reader into the story instantly and pulls the reader along by unfolding the facts piecemeal. The story in fact has no climax; the most climactic event of this story (and "Speaking of Courage" and "Notes"), Kiowa's death, occurs beforehand. By refusing to include a climax as the turning point of the plot, O'Brien further reconstructs any sense of simple causality. The nonlinear, even recursive nature of the narrative reflects the nonlinear, even recursive experience of the Vietnam War and war in general. In this story, three soldiers discover Kiowa's rucksack and begin "circling out" from there to look for his body, perhaps serving as a metaphor for this narrative method.

4. "In the Field"'s realism makes it challenging to discuss O'Brien in the context of stylistic postmodernism. If postmodernism constitutes an important part of your course, I would strongly recommend having your students read "Speaking of Courage" and "Notes." These stories have a metafictional element through the "Tim O'Brien" narrator, a character who is distinct from the author even though both have apparently authored some of the same stories and have nearly identical biographies.

5. *The Things They Carried* had a peculiar composition process. Many of the pieces were written and published individually over the course of several years. When O'Brien decided to make a collection, he wrote new pieces, modified a number of the original ones, and ordered them in a very deliberate sequence. The result is a book that falls somewhere between a novel and a story collection. If it fits your pedagogical goals, invite your students to compare the original versions of these stories with the book's versions (e.g., "Speaking of Courage," *Massachusetts Review* 17 [1976]).

Original Audience

O'Brien's moral and his direct language suggest that he wants to appeal to as wide an audience as possible. He has expressed some dissatisfaction that war fiction does not tend to attract women readers. The most meaningful feedback on his work comes from women who tell him that he communicated the war experience to them better than anyone and helped them understand the veterans in their lives. "The joy is not the joy of touching veterans or touching people who have lived what you have lived," O'Brien has said in an interview. "The joy is just the opposite . . . because the purpose of art is to touch the human heart in its solidarity and solidity." This is not to say that O'Brien writes specifically for women but rather that he tries to make his fiction accessible, enjoyable, and meaningful for all readers.

Comparisons, Contrasts, Connections

1. Compare and contrast the O'Brien selection with those by other Vietnam veterans included in this anthology, especially Robert Bly's war poems. The significant exercise here is in contrasting the messages and the styles of the authors, for by distinguishing them we can begin to reconstruct the clichéd images, popular conceptions, and common stereotypes about that war. In contrasting O'Brien and Herr, it might help to inform students that the latter contributed to the screenplays of both *Apocalypse Now* and *Full Metal Jacket* (for O'Brien's feelings about the Hollywood image of the Vietnam Veteran, see "The Violent Vet" [*Esquire*, Dec. 1979]).

2. Compare the O'Brien story with pieces (especially stories) by veterans from other wars, like Hemingway. Does the modern war experience tend to generate a "realist" style?

3. You might also compare this story's style with that of contemporary stories in this anthology, specifically the more postmodern stories like John Barth's. I would recommend reading additional works by O'Brien (intelligent selections from *The Things They Carried*, such as "Speaking of Courage" and "Notes") if you want a solid inquiry of O'Brien in a postmodern context. O'Brien's status as a postmodern stylist is, I believe, very debatable and may help to focus more general definitional discussions.

4. Students interested in film might want to compare *Apocalypse Now* with *A Soldier's Sweetheart* (1998), a fairly faithful screen adaptation of O'Brien's "Sweetheart of the Song Tra Bong" (in *Things*), with Kiefer Sutherland as Rat Kiley and Georgina Cates as Mary Anne, and the only film of any O'Brien work. Both movies are in dialogue with Conrad's *Heart of Darkness*.

5. A few of the canonized Vietnam novels to which you might direct interested students (or add to your syllabus) are O'Brien's *Going After Cacciato* (1978), Robert Stone's *Dog Soldiers* (1974), Stephen Wright's *Meditations in Green* (1983), John M. Del Vecchio's *The Thirteenth Valley* (1982), Larry Heinemann's *Paco's Story* (1986), and William Eastlake's *The Bamboo Bed* (1969). Poets include John Balaban, W. D. Ehrhart, Walter McDonald, Bruce Weigl, and Yusef Komunyakaa. David Rabe is the most prominent dramatist.

Questions for Reading and Discussion

1. What kills Kiowa? Is it any one event or exact sequence of events?

2. Elsewhere in *The Things They Carried*, O'Brien writes that a "true war story is never moral. It does not instruct, nor encourage virtue, nor suggest models of proper human behavior, nor restrain men from doing the things men have always done. If a story seems moral, do not believe it" ("How to Tell a True War Story"). Does this story support that assertion? If not, what moral or morals does it propose? Is the assertion that "a true war story is never moral" itself a kind of moral, a declaration of value?

3. How does the story serve as a metaphor for something bigger? In other words, might we equate the shit field that sucks in Kiowa with the war?

4. This story is an imaginative reinvention of an actual episode that occurred during O'Brien's tour of duty in Vietnam. For O'Brien, *happening-truth* (what actually happened) can be less true than *story-truth* (what only happened in fiction). The fictional status of this story (and the book)

bothers some readers—it diminishes its power. Do these readers have a higher expectation of actuality for works about the Vietnam War, and if that is the case, why? Do any students agree with O'Brien's artistic philosophy?

5. In other writings O'Brien has observed that when the enemy is so thoroughly mixed in with the local civilian population, and when the enemy lives in the villages, hides in the jungle, and tunnels underground, it seems that the land itself becomes "the true enemy—the physical place, the soil and the paddies" ("The Vietnam in Me"). How does this help explain the lieutenant's choice to set his escapist fantasies on a golf course?

6. Lieutenant Jimmy Cross calls the anonymous young soldier "not a man, really," but "a boy." The average age for soldiers in Vietnam was about the same age as traditional undergraduates. Do any of your students have siblings or friends who enlisted in the military instead of going to college? Who have fought in Iraq or Afghanistan? Would any of your students consider joining the service? Would any of them refuse to serve? Would it depend upon the war? How have Vietnam, the Gulf War, the Iraq War, and recent war movies (e.g., *Saving Private Ryan*) affected your students' feelings about war and military duty? Such questions get at the heart of O'Brien's concerns, and do it in a very personal way.

7. Kiowa is a Native American. What might O'Brien be suggesting by this fact?

Approaches to Writing

1. Students often have very immediate and strong responses to O'Brien's short stories. Ask students to record their responses, and use their writing to explore those responses.

2. Encourage students to talk with a veteran, either a family member, a family friend, or a stranger. A personal encounter can lead to a third-person retelling of the veteran's story or a first-person reflection on the encounter. Alternatively, ask students to research and write about a soldier who did not return from Vietnam, either as a result of being killed or missing in action.

3. Have students write a formal essay comparing any two (or more) of the texts mentioned in this guide (two stories, different versions of the same story, story with essay, different writers, etc.). Similarly, have students write a formal essay exploring any of the discussion prompts in this guide.

4. Images from the Vietnam War—still photos or motion films—are readily available. Ask students to compare how different artistic forms (fiction, creative nonfiction, visual arts) work to generate different responses. Hollywood's response to the war also gives an excellent opportunity for student reflection in writing.

Bibliography

Dunn, Joe P. *Teaching the Vietnam War: Resources and Assessments.* Ed. Udo Heyn. Occasional Paper Series No. 18. Los Angeles: California State U, Center for the Study of Armament and Disarmament, 1990.

Gilbert, Marc J. Ed. *The Vietnam War: Teaching Approaches and Resources.* New York: Greenwood, 1991.

Johannessen, Larry R. *Illumination Rounds: Teaching the Literature of the Vietnam War.* Urbana, IL: NCTE, 1992.

Kelsey, Ann L., ed., with Anthony O. Edmonds. *Resources for Teaching the Vietnam War: An Annotated Guide.* Rev. ed. Pittsburgh: Center for Social Studies Education, 1996.

McNerney, Brian C. "Responsibly Inventing History: An Interview with Tim O'Brien." *War, Literature & the Arts* 6.2 (Fall/Winter 1994): 1–26.

O'Brien, Tim. *If I Die in a Combat Zone, Box Me Up and Ship Me Home.* New York: Delacorte, 1973; New York, Broadway, 1999.

———. "The Vietnam in Me." *New York Times Magazine.* Cover Story. 2 Oct. 1994: 48–57.

Norman Mailer (b. 1923)

Contributing Editor: Barry H. Leeds

Classroom Issues and Strategies

To begin with, any approach to teaching Norman Mailer's work must take into consideration his flamboyant and controversial public image, which often obscures critical responses to the works. Many college students will not recognize Mailer's name at first; but those who do will very probably be armored in negative preconceptions, often based on incomplete or erroneous information.

The selections from *The Armies of the Night* presented in the anthology provide an opportunity to deal effectively with this issue: Mailer is ultimately shown not as an unconscionable egotist presenting himself as his own hero, but as a rather self-deprecating narrator/ protagonist. For example, crossing the line of MPs in his act of civil disobedience, he describes himself as a somewhat ridiculous figure: "It was his dark pinstripe suit, his vest . . . the barrel chest, the early paunch—he must have looked like a banker himself, a banker, gone ape!" (pp. 150–151, Signet edition).

Again, before being arrested, Mailer feels, almost unwillingly, that "a deep modesty was on its way to him . . . as well as fear, yes now he saw it, fear of the consequences of this weekend in Washington" (Signet, p. 93).

This emerging new sense of self leads to a crucial realization: "No, the only revolutionary truth was a gun in the hills, and that would not be his, he would be too old by then, and too incompetent, yes, too incompetent said the new modesty, and too showboat, too lacking in essential judgment" (Signet, p. 94).

Yet despite the constant interplay here (as in his life and work as a whole) between the performer and the thoughtful commentator, what looms far larger is Mailer's evocative capacity to strike to the heart of an issue of national significance in his prose. Consider the forceful and moving conclusion to *The Armies of the Night*, entitled "The Metaphor Delivered" (Signet, p. 320).

The unusual point of view used in this book, which was to become a hallmark of Mailer's nonfiction of the 1970s, provides interesting possibilities for a discussion of point of view and genre.

Major Themes, Historical Perspectives, Personal Issues

The historical themes are obvious from the nature of *The Armies of the Night* and its relationship to the Vietnam War. Mailer's preoccupation with existential choice, personal courage, and integrity are evident in the passages selected.

Significant Form, Style, or Artistic Conventions

As I have explained in my headnote, Mailer's development from a derivative and naturalistic vision in *The Naked and the Dead* (1948) to a unique and highly existential one in later works such as *An American Dream* (1965) is evident in *The Armies of the Night*. The concept of the "nonfiction novel" and the unusual third-person participant/narrator point of view are important in any discussion of *Armies* and Mailer's subsequent work.

Original Audience

It is interesting and important to discuss the significance (or perceived insignificance) of those events recounted in *The Armies of the Night* to today's students. Further, my footnotes will to some degree ameliorate unfamiliarity with particular people or events.

Comparisons, Contrasts, Connections

Parallels can be drawn to Ernest Hemingway's *Green Hills of Africa* (1935), Tom Wolfe's *The Electric Kool-Aid Acid Test* (1968) and even *The Education of Henry Adams* (1907). Further, Mailer's early work, notably *The Naked and the Dead* (1948), was influenced profoundly by James T. Farrell, John Dos Passos, and John Steinbeck.

Questions for Reading, Discussion, and Writing

1. Do you find Mailer's use of himself as a third-person participant effective or confusing? This book, which won both a Pulitzer Prize and the National Book Award, has often been cited, along with Tom Wolfe's *The Electric Kool-Aid Acid Test* (1968), as an example of the "new journalism." But a similar point of view was used by Henry Adams in *The Education of Henry Adams* as early as 1907, and the concept of a "nonfiction novel" dates back at least as far as Ernest Hemingway's *Green Hills of Africa* (1935). Does this relatively unusual form attract or repel you?
2. Mailer writes (Signet, p. 63): "The American corporation executive . . . was perfectly capable of burning unseen women and children in the Vietnamese jungles, yet felt a large displeasure and fairly final disapproval at the generous use of obscenity in literature and public." Do you agree with Mailer that depersonalized governmental violence is more obscene that the use of four-letter words?
3. Consider Mailer's final statements in "The Metaphor Delivered." Do you feel that Mailer, despite his antiwar civil disobedience, is a patriot? Do the U.S. Marshals who think him a traitor love their country more? Were you emotionally moved by this conclusion?
4. These events took place more than thirty years ago. Do they seem to have any bearing on your life, and on the America you live in today, or do they seem like ancient history? Are the participants (e.g., Robert Lowell, Dwight MacDonald) familiar or alien to you?
5. Can you envision any future national situation in which similar demonstrations might occur? Are there any that you might find justifiable?

Bibliography

"The Armies of the Night," in *The Structured Vision of Norman Mailer* by Barry H. Leeds (New York UP, 1969), seems to help render the book more accessible to my students. Chapter 8. See also:

Lennon, J. Michael, ed. *Critical Essays on Norman Mailer*. Boston: Hall, 1986.

Manso, Peter. *Mailer: His Life and Times*. New York: Simon, 1985.

Robert Bly (b. 1926)

Contributing Editor: John Alberti

Classroom Issues and Strategies

Bly's two haunting poems on the Vietnam War, "Counting Small-Boned Bodies" and "The Teeth Mother Naked at Last," have a acquired a dual resonance that forms the context for student reception and classroom discussion: as cultural and historical artifacts providing contemporary students access to that war and the 1960s, and as commentaries on the U.S. wars of their own lifetimes, most powerfully the Gulf wars against Iraq. In a way, these two kinds of cultural work represent Bly's poetic approach in protesting a specific military invasion using language and metaphors that invoke transhistorical mythic and archetypal meanings, as in the Jungian symbol of the "teeth mother" or the references to the death wish.

The poems challenge students with stark images of the horrors of war, including the physical details of the violence done to human bodies as well as the complex psychological reactions of soldiers, ranging from fear and confusion to, in "Counting Small-Boned Bodies," the attractions of power and mastery that can accompany mass slaughter. These issues are difficult for any reader, but classroom reactions will also be strongly affected by the students' differing experiences of combat and war: whether they are veterans of the Vietnam War that ended thirty years ago or the contemporary wars of the Middle East, whether they have friends or relatives in the military, or whether the war remains mainly a disturbing event on television. One approach that works well with any poetry but especially with these poems is to begin by asking students to choose passages that affected them strongly and then to do some brief writing about their reactions. If done anonymously, these reactions can then be shared in the classroom either through the instructor reading them aloud or by distributing them to the class.

The dual resonance of the poems also reflects how the Vietnam War can seem both past and present to students. While the events of the war took place long before traditional college-age students were born, the legacies of Vietnam, from the formation of contemporary U.S. foreign policy to modern reactions to the Gulf wars, still haunt America today. Accurate historical information about Vietnam can be essential for classroom discussion, especially since many students will have inherited various myths and stereotypes about the Vietnam War period. Students are sometimes surprised to learn, for example, that the antiwar movement included members of the military serving in Vietnam. Bly's poems also provide the opportunity for students to do oral history involving family members' experiences during the Vietnam War.

Yusef Komunyakaa (b. 1947)

Contributing Editor: Linda Wagner-Martin

Classroom Issues and Strategies

Born in Bogalusa, Louisiana, the oldest of five children, Komunyakaa was the son of a carpenter and of a mother who bought a set of encyclopedias for her children. When he was sixteen, he discovered James Baldwin's essays and decided to become a writer himself.

From 1965 to 1968, Komunyakaa served a tour of duty in Vietnam as an information specialist, editing a military newspaper called the *Southern Cross*. There he won the bronze star. After military service, he enrolled as a double major in English and sociology at the University of Colorado, where he began writing poetry. Upon graduation in 1980, he studied further at both Colorado State University (where he received an MA in Creative Writing) and the University of California, Irvine, where he received an MFA. He then taught at various universities before moving to New Orleans. While teaching at the University of New Orleans, in 1985, he married Australian novelist Mandy Sayer.

Only then, nearly twenty years after his Vietnam experiences, did Komunyakaa write his important war poems, published in 1988 as *Dien Cai Dau*. The violence of war, the pain of identifying with the Vietnamese, and the anguish of returning to the States had seldom been so eloquently and hauntingly expressed. By 1994, when these poems were included in *Neon Vernacular: New and Selected Poems, 1977–1989*, Komunyakaa had already won two creative writing fellowships from the National Endowment for the Arts and the San Francisco Poetry Center Award, and had held the Lilly Professorship of Poetry at Indiana University. *Neon Vernacular* received the Pulitzer Prize for Poetry, as well as the Kingsley-Tufts Poetry Award from the Claremont Graduate School, and as a result his earlier eight collections of work have been reevaluated.

In 1998 his poetry collection *Thieves of Paradise* was a finalist for the 1999 National Book Critics Circle Award, and that same year saw the publication of his recording, *Love Notes from the Madhouse*. In 2000, Radicloni Clytus edited a book of Komunyakaa's prose, *Blue Notes: Essays, Interviews, and Commentaries,* for the University of Michigan Press series. In an essay from that collection, "Control Is the Mainspring," the poet writes:

I learned that the body and the mind are indeed connected: good writing is physical and mental. I welcomed the knowledge of this because I am from a working-class people who believe that physical labor is sacred and spiritual.

This combination of the realistic and the spiritual runs throughout Komunyakaa's poems, whether they are about his childhood, the father-son relationship, the spiritual journey each of us takes—alone, and in whatever circumstances life hands us—or the various conflicts of war. He has become an important poet for our times.

Bibliography

Dedications and Other Darkhorses, 1977; *Lost in the Bonewheel Factory,* 1979; *Copacetic,* 1984; *I Apologize for the Eyes in My Head,* 1986; *Toys in the Field,* 1987; *Dien Cai Dau,* 1988; *February in Sydney,* 1989; *Magic City,* 1992; *Neon Vernacular,* 1994; *Thieves of Paradise,* 1998; *Blue Notes: Essays, Interviews, and Commentaries,* ed. Radicloni Clytus, 2000.

Denise Levertov (1923–1997)

Contributing Editor: Joan F. Hallisey

Classroom Issues and Strategies

With an adequate introduction to her life and works, Denise Levertov is not a difficult author. Levertov can best be made accessible to students when they are familiar with the poet's own prose reflections on poetry, the role of the poet, and "notes" on organic form. You might prepare an introduction to her work by making reference to her quite precise discussion of these themes in *The Poet in the World* (1973), *Light Up the Cave* (1982), and *New and Selected Essays* (1992).

Consider using tapes of Levertov reading her own poetry. The most recent cassette, "The Acolyte" (Watershed), contains a fine sampling from her earlier poetry through *Oblique Prayers*. Encourage students to listen to both her poetry readings and interviews and to incorporate information from them in class or seminar discussions and presentations or as material for research papers. When students are doing a class presentation, strongly urge them to be certain that their classmates have copies of the poems they will be discussing.

Students respond favorably to Levertov's conviction that the poet writes more than "[she] knows." They also respond positively to the fact that an American woman "engaged" poet has spoken out strongly on women's rights, peace and justice issues, race, and other questions on human rights.

Students may ask you if Levertov is discouraged in the face of so much darkness and disaster evident in the late twentieth century. This presents a good opportunity to have the students examine "Writing in the Dark" and "The May Mornings" (*Candles in Babylon*, 1982) and her essay "Poetry, Prophecy, Survival" (*New and Selected Essays*, 1992).

Major Themes, Historical Perspectives, Personal Issues

Levertov's work is concerned with several dimensions of the human experience: love, motherhood, nature, war, the nuclear arms race, mysticism, poetry, and the role of the poet. If you are teaching a women's literature course or an upper-level course focusing on a few writers, several of these themes might be examined. In a survey course, you might concentrate on three themes that include both historical and personal issues: poetry, the role of the poet, and her interest in humanitarian politics.

Significant Form, Style, or Artistic Conventions

Levertov in "Some Notes on Organic Form" tells the reader that during the writing of a poem the various elements of the poet's being are in communion with one another and heightened. She believes that ear and eye, intellect and passion, interrelate more subtly than at other times, and she regards the poet's "checking for accuracy," for precision of language that must take place throughout the writing, not as a "matter of one element supervising the others but of intuitive interaction between all the elements involved" (*The Poet in the World*, p. 9).

Like Wordsworth and Emerson, Levertov sees content and form as being in a state of dynamic interaction. She sees rhyme, echo, and reiteration as serving not only to knit the elements of an experience "but also as being the means, the sole means, by which the density of texture and the returning or circling of perception can be transmuted into language, apperceived" (Ibid., p. 9).

You might point out that as an artist who is "obstinately precise" about her craft, Levertov pays close attention to etymologies as she searches for the right words, the right image, the right arrangement of the lines on the page. It will be helpful for students to be able to recognize other poetic techniques that Levertov uses in her poetry: enjambment, color, contrast, and even the pun to sustain conflict and ambiguity. Levertov will sometimes make use of the juxtaposition of key words and line breaks.

Levertov does not consider herself a member of any particular school.

Original Audience

Levertov has said, on several occasions, that she never has readers in mind when she is writing a poem. She believes that a poem has to be not merely addressed to a person or a problem *out there* but must come from *in here*, the inner being of the poet, and it must also address something *in here*.

It is important to share Levertov's ideas with the students when you discuss audience. One might stress the universality of some themes: familial and cultural heritage, poetry, and the role of the poet/prophet in a "time of terror." There is a "timeless" kind of relevance for these themes, and they need not be confined to any one age.

Comparisons, Contrasts, Connections

There is enough evidence to suggest that a fruitful comparison might be made between several of Muriel Rukeyser's finest poems ("Akiba," "Kathe Kollwitz" [*Speed of Darkness*, 1968], "Searching/Not Searching" [*Breaking Open*, 1973]) and some of Levertov's poems on comparable themes.

Questions for Reading, Discussion, and Writing

1. (a) What kinds of feelings do you have about the Holocaust? About nuclear war?
   (b) What do you think the role of the poet should be today? Do you think she or he should speak out about political or social issues? Why? Why not?

2. (a) Several of Levertov's poems can be used for a writing sample and subsequent discussion at the beginning of the course. Brief poems that students respond strongly to are "The Broken Sandal" (*Relearning the Alphabet*), "Variation on a Theme from Rilke" (*Breathing the Water*), and "The Batterers" and "Eye Mask" (*Evening Train*, 1992).

    (b) One might give a short assignment to compare the themes, tone, and imagery of Levertov's "The Broken Sandal" with Adrienne Rich's "Prospective Immigrants—Please Note."

    (c) Examine several of Levertov's poems on poetry and the role of the poet in light of Ralph Waldo Emerson's call for the "true" poet in several of his essays, most notably in "The Poet," "Poetry and the Imagination," and "The American Scholar."

Bibliography

Denise Levertov's *The Poet in the World* (1973), *Light Up the Cave* (1982), and *New and Selected Essays* (1992) are essential primary source materials for a deeper understanding of the poems included in the text.

"The Sense of Pilgrimage" essay in *The Poet in the World* and "Beatrice Levertoff" in *Light Up the Cave* offer valuable background material for teaching "Illustrious Ancestors."

Levertov has acknowledged the significant influence of Rilke on her poetry and poetics throughout her career, and several of her recent "Variation on a Theme from Rilke" poems will be enriched by Edward Zlotkowski's insightful essay "Levertov and Rilke: A Sense of Aesthetics" in *Twentieth Century Literature* (Fall 1992).

Audrey Rodger's *Denise Levertov's Poetry of Engagement* will be helpful in discussing Levertov's understanding of the role of the poet and her poetry of engagement.

Donald Barthelme (1931–1989)

Contributing Editors: Linda Wagner-Martin and Charles Molesworth

Classroom Issues and Strategies

The brevity and irony of Barthelme's work are sometimes surprising to students. Again, the high modernist quality—every word crafted for its purpose, but caught in a web of style and form that makes the whole seem artlessly natural—must be explained. Students may have read less contemporary fiction than modern, and what contemporary fiction they have read may well be limited to the genres of romance, science fiction, and mystery. As with any period of art, the determining craft and language practices need explication.

In the case of such a short selection, ask students to write about the work at the beginning of the class—and again at the end, once discussion has finished—something simple like "What were your reactions to this work?" Then ask them to compare their two answers with the hope of showing them that reading must be an active process, that they must form opinions. And in this author's case, getting his readers to respond is his first priority.

Major Themes, Historical Perspectives, Personal Issues

People's inability to learn to live in their culture, and the omnipresent romantic attitudes that society continues to inscribe, whatever the subject being considered, are the main subjects of Barthelme's fiction. At base is the belief that people will endure, will eventually figure it out. Barthelme's fiction is, finally, positive—even optimistic—but first readings may not give that impression.

Significant Form, Style, or Artistic Conventions

Discuss the way humor is achieved, the interplay between irony and humor, the effects of terse and unsentimental language—students must be given ways of understanding why this story has the effect it does.

Contemporary fiction—whether minimalist or highly contrived parodic or allusive and truly postmodern—needs much more attention in the classroom. Connections must be made between writing students already understand, such as Ernest Hemingway's, and more recent work so that they see the continuum of artistry that grows from one generation to the next.

Original Audience

Anticonservative in many ways, Barthelme's fiction taunts the current society and its attitudes at every turn. The teacher will have to be subtle in not claiming that "we all" think the way Barthelme does, or the legions of all-American conservatives will be on his or her doorsteps; but the fiction itself can do a great deal to start students examining their own social attitudes.

Comparisons, Contrasts, Connections

Barthelme is given as a kind of example of metafiction, which flourished in the 1970s and 1980s. Interesting approaches can be created by contrasting this fiction with much of that by writers of minority cultural groups—James Welch, Alice Walker—to see how such fiction differs.

Bibliography

See *The Teachings of Don B.*, ed. Kim Herzinger (1993). Also, see *The Ironist Saved from Drowning: The Fiction of Donald Barthelme*, by Charles Molesworth (U of Missouri P, 1983) in which this story is discussed in detail.

Toni Morrison (b. 1931)

Contributing Editor: Kristine Yohe

Classroom Issues and Strategies

In her novels, Toni Morrison's narrative approach sometimes poses special challenges to her readers since she asks a great deal of them and requires them, as she has said in several venues, to "participate" in the texts. Therefore, she demands active readers; it is not possible to sit passively when engaging her work. "Recitatif," her one published short story, is no different. This work focuses on two girls, Twyla and Roberta, as they briefly share a room in an orphanage and then grow into maturity, with chance encounters along the way. In this story, Morrison overtly states that one of the characters is black and one white, but she prevents her readers from figuring out, with any certainty, which is which. Told from Twyla's first-person perspective, "Recitatif" invites scrutiny about racial identity, simultaneous to its deliberate attempt to deny absolutes and invert stereotypes.

While reading a story that at once emphasizes and obscures racial categorization, students will inevitably find themselves distracted by the racial ambiguity of the two protagonists. When early in the story Twyla regards Roberta as "a girl from a whole other race," it is irresistible to try and discern which girl is black and which one white. Nevertheless, the scholarship and Morrison herself confirm that attempting to figure this question out is futile. Yet readers regularly respond to this story with absolute certainty that it must be Twyla who is black or that it must be Twyla who is white. The story's "clues" may yield temporary certitude, but such decisions are fleeting. Engaging in this debate can be enlightening, however, as it requires readers to question assumptions about racial stereotypes.

One of Morrison's points here is quite similar to her approach to the ambiguity of racial identity in her seventh novel, *Paradise* (1998): when you know someone's race, what exactly do you know?

Major Themes, Historical Perspectives, and Personal Issues

Like many works of American, and particularly African-American, literature, "Recitatif" examines issues of identity. When Roberta and Twyla end up rooming together at a shelter, St. Bonaventure, otherwise known as St. Bonny's, they necessarily deal with the difficulties of family relationships and questions of whom one can trust. Because Roberta's mother is sick, and Twyla's mother "likes to dance all night," the eight-year-old girls end up in this state-sanctioned safety net. And, although they are referred to as "salt and pepper," they come to depend upon one another—perhaps even more than on their mothers. Therefore, in addition to family issues overall, the themes of motherhood and connections to abandonment are dominant here (much as they are in most of Morrison's other works).

Gender roles are also important in this story as Roberta and Twyla experience genuine bonding in part because of their fear of the older girls—referred to as "gar girls," a misunderstanding of the term *gargoyles*. The occasional strife among the shelter's girls contributes to Twyla and Roberta's confusion about their own roles as women.

Class membership and mobility are other prominent themes in the story since both girls start out poor—although Roberta seems to come from a more stable home environment, or at least a place of regular meals—and the story ends with Twyla in a working-class life and Roberta ascended into the upper class, complete with servants and chauffeured limousines. These class markers complicate readers' temptations to ascribe racial categories to the girls.

Perhaps the most interesting theme in the story is that of "passing." Often now regarded as a relic of a bygone era, passing evokes a time of rigid racial stratification when appearance meant everything, and the ability to "cross over" from black to white culture often had benefits in financial and personal safety. Earlier African-American writers such as Nella Larsen and James Weldon Johnson engage this issue directly in their literary works. Yet, as critic Juda Bennett explains, although passing is less prominent in contemporary writing, Morrison's treatment of the theme is noteworthy. Bennett asserts that, for Morrison, instead of passing appearing between characters, it occurs in "Recitatif" between the reader and the text. That is, although the characters within the story know who is black and who is white, the reader cannot figure this out, so the characters can "pass" for either. Through their conversations over the racial ambiguity of the character Maggie, Roberta and Twyla explore further questions of what racial categories really mean.

In the preface to her 1992 work of literary criticism, *Playing in the Dark: Whiteness and the Literary Imagination*, Morrison makes a rare direct reference to this story: "The only short story I have ever written, 'Recitatif,' was an experiment in the removal of all racial codes from a narrative about two characters of different races for whom racial identity is crucial" (xi). Clearly, much as in the tradition of passing literature, Morrison sees this story as engaging "racial codes" while it seeks to erase them. On many levels, the story invites an investigation of the power of stereotyping—not only via race but also in terms of dis/ability and class.

Finally, "Recitatif" echoes interesting elements of Toni Morrison's own childhood, involving the sometimes positive and often negative interactions between racial groups. In biographical material, she is frequently described as being the only African-American child—and the only reader—in her first-grade class. Already, she was breaking boundaries of race and accomplishment, all the while debunking negative stereotypes. The girls in her story, however, are less equipped for such success.

Significant Forms, Style, or Artistic Conventions

"Recitatif" often is considered to be a particularly postmodern story, in part because of its metatextual approach, whereby it seems to comment upon itself. Through the story's open-endedness, and the impossibility of deciphering its purported racial markers, Morrison deconstructs the very question of racial stratification—as well as interpretive certainty.

Like many of Morrison's other works—notably *Beloved* (1987), *Jazz* (1992), and *Paradise*—"Recitatif" involves elements of stream-of-consciousness writing. Twyla's thoughts flow into the story's action, with associated thematic links. More linear and chronological than most of her novels, and without overt flashbacks, the story nevertheless maintains its emphasis on the power of the past, which, Morrison has said in interviews, she regards as "infinite."

The story's title, the French spelling of the musical term *recitative*, refers to an operatic style wherein singing is done in a manner akin to natural speech and as a sort of bridge between other action; it is used in order to advance the plot and to develop a progression of states of mind. This connection is perhaps related to how Roberta and Twyla try to understand the emotional meaning of their shared past through conversation. While we do not know for sure what Morrison intends by her use of this title, it is interesting to consider it against the backdrop of the historical events referred to in the story. Perhaps she is suggesting that the turbulent times in U.S. history evident from the 1950s to the 1970s (the story's setting) inform the reactions of the two characters. As the story is mainly comprised of their five encounters—at the orphanage, at Howard Johnson's, at the gourmet grocery store, on a busing-oriented picket line, and in a diner on Christmas Eve—perhaps we are to consider what the bridges, or recitatives, are in between these meetings.

Original Audience

This story was first published in 1983 in *Confirmation: An Anthology of African American Women*, edited by Amiri Baraka and Amina Baraka. Since then, it has been anthologized elsewhere and is now often taught in college classes.

It seems apparent that Morrison intended a multiethnic reading audience since the story's racial ambiguity seems designed to evoke different reactions in readers from varying backgrounds.

Comparison, Contrasts, Connections

If included in a class with time to read longer works, "Recitatif" would be fascinating taught alongside Morrison's novel *Paradise* since the two works share uncertainty about racial categorization. The story's racial identity themes would also compare well with selections from Jean Toomer's *Cane* (1923), such as "Blood-Burning Moon," as well as with such works by William Faulkner as *Light in August* (1932). Fruitful connections also exist between "Recitatif" and Paul Laurence Dunbar's poem, "We Wear the Mask" (1895).

Questions for Reading and Discussion / Approaches to Writing

1. How do you respond to the story's simultaneous highlighting and subverting of racial categorization? Did you find yourself seeking evidence to support theories of the racial identification of each woman? Why or why not?
2. What role do you perceive the character Maggie serving in the story? How does their memory of her affect Twyla and Roberta? Of what relevance is her racial identity? How is class connected?
3. What comparisons and contrasts do you see between the two girls' mothers?
4. What seems important about Roberta and Twyla's interaction with the older girls at St. Bonny's?
5. Why do you think Morrison presents the two women as having four more chance encounters, many years after their time together at the shelter? Why is each of these meetings different?

Bibliography

Bennett, Juda. "Toni Morrison and the Burden of the Passing Narrative." *African American Review* 35.2 (Summer 2001): 205–17.

Morrison, Toni. Preface. *Playing in the Dark: Whiteness and the Literary Imagination*. Cambridge, MA: Harvard UP, 1992. v–xiii.

John Updike (b. 1932)

Contributing Editors: George J. Searles and John Alberti

Classroom Issues and Strategies

It is sometimes said that Updike is too narrowly an interpreter of the WASP/ yuppie environment, a realm of somewhat limited interest; another is that his work proceeds from a too exclusively male perspective. The former concern will, of course, be more or less problematic depending on the nature of the college (more problematic at an urban community college, less so at a "prestige" school). The latter charge, however, provides the basis for fruitful discussion in any academic environment.

First, it's important to point out what Henry James once said, to the effect that we must grant an author's donnée and evaluate only in terms of what is made of it. But in Updike's case, it's also necessary to stress that his real concerns transcend his surface preoccupations. Although he is often described as a chronicler of social ills, really he's after larger game—the sheer intractability of the human predicament. Students must be shown that in Updike the particular is simply an avenue to the universal.

In "Trust Me," John Updike uses precise description to examine a series of profound metaphysical problems centered on the issue of trust: the limits of intimacy and the ability and inability of love and compassion to bridge the fundamental isolation of individuals. Although these are large and abstract themes, Updike renders them accessible through the careful telling of a series of more or less traumatic violations of trust in the life of the story's protagonist, Harold. By including incidents from Harold's childhood through middle age, the story also allows access to both traditional age and returning students.

One simple way into classroom discussion of the story is to have students choose and write briefly about the incidents of trust and mistrust in Harold's life that they responded to most strongly. As an extension of the story, students could also write and tell about similar incidents from their own lives that they feel are relevant to Updike's purposes. Encourage them to try and provide the same level of sensory detail that Updike does. The focused recollection of sense memory can help students explore the significance of the personal stories they are telling as well as gain insight into Updike's artistic strategy.

Rather than drawing deliberate conclusions about the meanings of each of these cases of trust gone awry, Updike instead asks his readers to consider a series of paradoxes: "Unaccountably, all through his growing up he continued to trust his father; it was his mother he distrusted, her swift sure-handed anger"; "The gaiety of his voice revealed a crucial space, a gap between their situations. . . . Another's pain is not our own. . . . Without it [this gap] compassion would crush us." The story itself ends with Harold pondering the slogan "In God We Trust" (interestingly, not explicitly stated in the story) above the "ONE" on the back of a dollar bill, raising the stakes involved in the inability to trust one another to the level of religion and nationhood. The spiritual dimensions of human isolation and their relationship to the Protestant tradition in American culture is a recurring interest of Updike's, and the conclusion of "Trust Me" allows students to consider how Updike's story fits into the long, Puritan-based tradition of religious self-examination and uncertainty. Finally, the title of the story, "Trust Me," connects to the main theme of the story but also raises questions about the relationship between writer and reader, and to the nature of the compact formed between an author and his or her audience.

Original Audience

As this is a contemporary story, the "when/now" issue is not relevant. As for audience, I think that Updike sees himself writing for people more or less like himself: WASP, affluent, and so on. But again, it's important when teaching Updike's work to show that the problems his characters confront are in a broad sense everyone's problems: responsibility, guilt, mortality, and so on.

Comparisons, Contrasts, Connections

While Updike can be fruitfully compared with other contemporary writers who depict the social condition of the American white middle class, he also sees himself as part of the Puritan tradition leading back through Nathaniel Hawthorne to Jonathan Edwards, Anne Bradstreet, and William Bradford. Hawthorne's "Young Goodman Brown," for example, presents an earlier instance of the treatment of similar themes linked specifically to an exploration of how the religious anxieties of the seventeenth century persisted into the nineteenth.

Bibliography

Atlas, James. "John Updike Breaks Out of Suburbia." *New York Times Magazine* 10 December 1978: 60–64, 68–76.

Kakutani, Michiko. "Turning Sex and Guilt into an American Epic." *Saturday Review* October 1981: 14–22.

———. "Updike's Struggle to Portray Women." *The New York Times* 5 May 1988.

Luscher, Robert M. *John Updike: A Study of the Short Fiction.* New York: Twayne, 1993.

Plath, James, ed. *Conversations with John Updike.* Jackson: UP of Mississippi, 1994.

Ernest J. Gaines (b. 1933)

Contributing Editor: John F. Callahan

Classroom Issues and Strategies

The simplicity and tautness of Gaines's "The Sky Is Gray" sometimes lulls students to sleep and leads them, at first, not to look for some of the abiding, archetypal patterns in this story. Partly, this is due to the young boy's voice. Given the changes in race relations between the time in which the story was set, then written, and now, students need to read very carefully to pick up the nuances of this 1940s social milieu.

Instructor and students should read large chunks of the story out loud. Secondly, background on this milieu is very helpful; for this reason I urge that Gaines's essay "Miss Jane and I" (*Callaloo* 1.3 [May 1974]) be offered as a companion to the story.

Students often ask about the actuality of segregation—they wonder whether Gaines's details are accurate. In addition, they ask whether the story's voice is consistently that of the young boy James.

Major Themes, Historical Perspectives, Personal Issues

The story is about a young boy having to grow up earlier than he might have wished or than the adults in his family might have wished because his father is serving in World War II. The boy's mother must be father as well as mother to James. He learns about courage and dignity, about pain, and about the love and will that make pain bearable. The story also shows breaks in the color line enforced by Jim Crow laws and customs.

Significant Form, Style, or Artistic Conventions

How authentic are young James's voice and point of view? How (and why) does Gaines rely on the oral tradition of storytelling in his fiction?

Original Audience

Gaines has said over and over again that he writes especially for young people, with particular reference to the young whites and, preeminently, the young blacks of the South. That is worth exploring along with three different layers of time: (1) the story's time of the 1940s, (2) the writer's time of the mid-1960s, and (3) the reader's changing moment.

Comparisons, Contrasts, Connections

Other relevant stories in *The Heath Anthology* include Faulkner's "Barn Burning" and McPherson's "A Solo Song: For Doc."

Questions for Reading, Discussion, and Writing

1. When does James become a man?
2. How does James come into his own voice?

Bibliography

See the special issue of *Callaloo* 1.3 (May 1978) devoted to Gaines and his work.

Callahan, John F. "The Landscape of Voice in Ernest J. Gaines's *Bloodline*." *Callaloo* 7.1 (Winter 1984): 86–112. See especially pp. 86–90, 96–99.

N. Scott Momaday (Kiowa) (b. 1934)

Contributing Editor: Kenneth M. Roemer

Classroom Issues and Strategies

In several areas, teachers of *Rainy Mountain* are in agreement. For example, whether an instructor uses excerpts or the entire book (the University of New Mexico paperback is the best classroom edition), acquainting students with a few of Momaday's other works can help them to establish important thematic, generic, and cultural contexts for reading *Rainy Mountain*. Especially relevant are the two sermons delivered by the Kiowa Priest of the Sun in Momaday's novel *House Made of Dawn* (1968), the intense Oklahoma landscape descriptions (for example, Book 3, Section 4) in *Ancient Child* (1989), and Momaday's essay "The Man Made of Words" (available in John Purdy and James Ruppert's anthology *Nothing But the Truth* [2001]), which outlines the major phases of composition of *Rainy Mountain* and sets forth Momaday's theory of language. The excellent interviews in Charles Woodard's *Ancestral Voice* (1989) and Matthias Schubnell's *Conversations with N. Scott Momaday* (1997) and two videos—*N. Scott Momaday* (available from Films for the Humanities) and *Momaday: Voice of the West* (available from PBS Home Videos)—also offer insights into Momaday's concepts of identity and language.

Beyond recommending an acquaintance with *House Made of Dawn* and "Man Made of Words," there is little agreement among teachers of *Rainy Mountain* about how much "background" information students "need to know" in order to "understand" Momaday's book. This apparent confusion can become the focus for classroom discussions of an important question. How can works frequently omitted from literary canons and characterized by unfamiliar subject matter and unusual forms of expression be made accessible and meaningful to "typical" college students? One approach to this question is to ask students to complete their first readings and initial discussions of the excerpts from *Rainy Mountain* before they have received any background information; students should even be discouraged from reading the headnote in *The Heath Anthology*. The initial discussion can center on questions about what type of writing the excerpts represent (e.g., should they be in a poetry section?) and about what types of information (if any) they think they need to understand the excerpts.

Major Themes, Historical Perspectives, Personal Issues

The forms and themes of *Rainy Mountain* suggest numerous other classroom strategies, many of which are described in detail in Part Two of *Approaches to*

Teaching Momaday's The Way to Rainy Mountain, and in my *College English* essay on teaching survey courses (37 [1976]: 619–24).

The importance of landscape in Momaday's book also suggests a way to bridge discussions of nineteenth-century classic American literature and *Rainy Mountain.* As J. Frank Papovich has argued in "Landscape, Tradition and Identity" in *Perspectives on Contemporary Literature* (12 [1986]: 13–19), students should be made aware that there are alternatives to the concept of the American landscape articulated in the myth of the isolated male hero escaping from domesticity and society to confront the challenges of the wilderness. By contrast, Momaday's nature is a place teeming with intricate networks of animal, human, and cosmic life connected by mutual survival relationships, storytelling traditions that embrace social gatherings at his grandmother's house as well as the growth of a babe into the Sun's wife, and an imagination that can transform an Oklahoma cricket into a being worthy of kinship with the moon.

Significant Form, Style, or Artistic Conventions

Autobiography, epic, sonnet, prose-poem, history, folk tale, vision, creation hymn, lyrical prose, a collection of quintessential novels—these are a few of the labels critics, scholars, and N. Scott Momaday have used to describe *The Way to Rainy Mountain.* The four essays in the "Critical Contexts: Forms" section of *Approaches to Teaching Momaday's The Way to Rainy Mountain* (47–77) invite students to discuss the appropriateness of these terms.

Comparisons, Contrasts, Connections

I recommend comparisons between Momaday's written excerpts and parallel Kiowa oral narratives or pictorial histories (e.g., comparing the buffalo story in XVI to the narrative in Maurice Boyd's *Kiowa Voices,* Vol. 2 [1983, 70–73] or comparing the descriptions in XVII of how women were treated to James Mooney's accounts drawn from Kiowa calendar histories in *Calendar History of the Kiowa Indians* [1898, 1979. 280, 281, 294]). For other possible comparisons, see Appendix B of my *Approaches to Teaching Momaday's The Way to Rainy Mountain.*

Within the context of American literature courses, various comparative studies can be made between *Rainy Mountain* and other more familiar works. Instructors interested in narrative structure can compare Momaday's discontinuous and multivoiced text to poetic works by Edgar Lee Masters, T. S. Eliot, and Ezra Pound and to prose works by Sherwood Anderson and William Faulkner.

Momaday's treatment of identity formation can be compared with other authors' attempts to define personae who—because of their ethnic heritage, gender, or class status—had to integrate creatively the apparently unrelated elements of their mainstream and nonmainstream backgrounds and experiences.

Questions for Reading, Discussion, and Writing

One participatory approach to the identity issue is to require students to select a significant landscape in their own backgrounds and to use this selection as the basis for composing three-voice sections modeled on the structure of *Rainy Mountain*. See my "Inventive Modeling" article in *College English* 46 (1984): 767–82, and Jean Molesky-Poz and Lauren Muller's "Native American Literatures: Pedagogies for Engaging Student Writing" in *American Quarterly* 45 (1993): 596–630.

Bibliography

Allen, Chadwick. "N. Scott Momaday: Becoming the Bear." *The Cambridge Companion to Native American Literature.* Ed. Kenneth M. Roemer and Joy Porter. New York: Cambridge UP, 2005, forthcoming.

Isernhagen, Hartwig, ed. *Momaday, Vizenor, Armstrong: Conversations on American Indian Writing.* Norman: U of Oklahoma P, 1999.

Lincoln, Kenneth. "Tai-me to Rainy Mountain: The Makings of American Indian Literature." *American Indian Quarterly* 10 (1986): 101–17.

Roemer, Kenneth M. *Approaches to Teaching Momaday's The Way to Rainy Mountain.* New York: MLA, 1989.

Scarberry-Garcia, Susan. *Landmarks of Healing: A Study of House Made of Dawn.* Albuquerque: U of New Mexico P, 1990.

Schubnell, Matthias, ed. *Conversations with N. Scott Momaday.* Jackson: UP of Mississippi, 1997.

———. "N. Scott Momaday." *Native American Writers of the United States.* Ed. Kenneth M. Roemer. *DLB*, vol. 175. Detroit: Bruccoli/Gale, 1997. 174–86.

———. *N. Scott Momaday: The Cultural and Literary Background.* Norman: U of Oklahoma P, 1985.

Schweninger, Lee. *N. Scott Momaday.* Vol. 12. Gale Study Guides to Great
    Literature. Detroit: Gale, 2001.

Woodward, Charles L., ed. *Ancestral Voice: Conversations with N. Scott
    Momaday.* Lincoln: U of Nebraska P, 1989.

Audre Lorde (1934–1992)

Contributing Editor: Claudia Tate

Classroom Issues and Strategies

Students need to be taught to empathize with the racial, sexual, and class
characteristics of the persona inscribed in Lorde's works. Such empathy will
enable them to understand the basis of Lorde's value formation.

Students immediately respond to Lorde's courage to confront a problem, no
matter what its difficulty, and to her deliberate inscription of the anguish
that problem has caused her. Both the confrontation and the acknowledged
pain serve as her vehicle for resolving the problem.

It is difficult to secure the entire corpus of her published work. Most
libraries have only those works published after 1982. Many of those published
prior to this date are out of print.

To address this issue, I have made special orders for texts that are still in
print and asked the library to place them on reserve. In other cases, I have
selected specific works from these early texts and photocopied them for class
use.

Major Themes, Historical Perspectives, Personal Issues

Lorde's work focuses on lyricizing large historical and social issues in the voice
of a black woman. This vantage point provides stringent social commentary on
white male, middle-class, heterosexual privilege inherent in the dominant
culture, on the one hand, and on the disadvantage accorded to those who
diverge from this so-called standard. In addition, students should be aware
that there have historically been racial and class biases between white and
black feminists concerning issues that centralize racial equality, like enfranchisement, work, and sexuality.

Significant Form, Style, or Artistic Conventions

Students studying Lorde's poetry should familiarize themselves with the aesthetic and rhetorical demands of the lyrical mode. In addition, they should be prepared for the high degree of intimacy inscribed in Lorde's work.

Comparisons, Contrasts, Connections

Although Lorde is known primarily as a poet, she also wrote a substantial amount of prose. Her most prominent prose includes *The Cancer Journals* (1980), the record of her struggle with breast cancer; *Zami: A New Spelling of My Name* (1982), an autobiography; and *Sister Outsider* (1984), a collection of essays and speeches. Students should be encouraged to explore Lorde's prose in order to see how genre mediates the expression of her most salient themes. Comparisons can also be drawn with the work of Adrienne Rich, June Jordan, and Ntozake Shange in order to stress the intimacy of the woman-centered problematic that informs and structures Lorde's work.

Bibliography

Over the last decade Lorde has attracted considerable scholarly interest. See the headnote for a listing of recent criticism. Also see the selections in *Home-making: Women Writers and the Politics and Poetics of Home*, eds. Catherine Wiley and Fiona R. Barnes; *Critical Essays: Gay and Lesbian Writers of Color*, ed. Emmanuel S. Nelson; *New Lesbian Criticism: Literary and Cultural Readings*, ed. Sally Munt; *Some of Us Are Brave*, eds. Barbara Smith et al.; *Sturdy Black Bridges*, eds. Gloria Hull et al.; *Color, Sex, and Poetry*, ed. Gloria Hull; and *Wild Women in the Whirlwind*, ed. Joanne M. Braxton.

Amiri Baraka (LeRoi Jones) (b. 1934)

Contributing Editor: Marcellette Williams

Classroom Issues and Strategies

The typical problems in teaching Baraka's poetry have to do with what has been called his "unevenness"—perhaps more accurately attributable to the tension inherent in balancing Baraka's role as poet and his role as activist—

and the strident tone of some of his poems—also related to his political activism.

Both problems are probably best addressed directly by inviting the students to describe or characterize their impressions of the impetus for the poems as they read them (stressing "their reading" is critical and complements what current reading theory regards as the essential role of the reader in any reading paradigm), then asking them to substantiate textually those impressions. Such a strategy finesses the temptation to engage in a definitive debate of the politics of the time as the genesis and raison d'être of Baraka's poetry. Further, such a strategy allows students to explore the aesthetics as well as the politics of his poetry and understand better the inter/inner-(con)textuality of the two.

Because the "sound" of Baraka's poetry is essential to texturing or fleshing out its meaning, readings aloud should contribute to discussions as well as to the introduction to his work.

Students respond almost always to the intimacy of Baraka's poems; sometimes they are offended by that intimacy, and this posture often leads to discussions of poetic necessity. Students also raise the question of the paradox of Baraka's clear aesthetic debts and his vehemence in trying to tear down that very Western ideal.

Major Themes, Historical Perspectives, Personal Issues

It is important to emphasize the themes of death and despair in the early poems, moral and social corruption with its concomitant decrying of Western values and ethics, the struggle against self-hatred, a growing ethnic awareness, and the beneficent view of and creative energy occasioned by "black magic."

The issues to focus on historically involve the racial tenor of the decades represented by his poetic output as well as the poetic aesthetics of imagism, projectivism, and Dadaism—all of which influenced Baraka to some extent.

From the perspective of personal issues, his bohemian acquaintances of the fifties (Charles Olson and Allen Ginsberg, for example), his marriage to Hettie Cohen, his visit to Cuba, his name change, the death of Malcolm X, and his Obie for *The Dutchman* are all important considerations.

Significant Form, Style, or Artistic Conventions

It is appropriate to refer to the question of "school," here again in the context of the poet's use of sound and images as the articulation of form and meaning. I would further encourage the students to pay careful attention to Baraka's use of repetition—at the lexical, syntactic, semantic, and phonological levels. What is its effect? Does it inform? If so, how? Are there aspects of the poems one might regard as transformations? If so, what might they be? What effect might they have? How might they function in the poem?

Baraka's consideration of the significance of "roots" appears to evolve in his poetry. How might you characterize it?

Original Audience

A consideration of progenitors and progeny provides a convenient point of departure for a discussion of audience for Baraka's work. Students interested in imagism and projectivism, for example, will certainly value Baraka's efforts as an effective use of those aesthetic doctrines toward the shaping of poetry of revolution appropriate for the time.

Baraka's influence is apparent in the poetry of Sonia Sanchez and Ntozake Shange. What aspects of this influence, if any, might contribute to considerations of audience with regard to time and poetry?

Comparisons, Contrasts, Connections

In considering Baraka's conscious use of language for poetic effect, com-parisons with William Carlos Williams (for the use of the vernacular and the idiom) and with Ezra Pound (for its communicative focus) are appropriate. Sometimes in discussions of Baraka's early poems, the criticism compares them in tone and theme—moral decay and social disillusionment—with T. S. Eliot's *The Waste Land*.

Questions for Reading, Discussion, and Writing

1. Frank Smith discusses the "behind the eyeball" information a reader brings to text. Louise Rosenblatt discusses the expectations and experiences a reader brings to "transact" or negotiate meaning with text. Given those considerations of the reader, prediscussion questions might be designed to elicit from the reader whatever information or preconceptions he or she has about the author and/or his work. If the students are totally unfamil-iar with Baraka, then questions eliciting experiential responses to the broad issues of theme or technique would be appropriate—"What, if anything, do the terms *social fragmentation* and/or *moral decay* mean to you?" "What would you imagine as a poetic attack on society? Or a poetic ethnic response to a dead or dying society?"
2. Writing assignments and topics for the students are derived from the assumption that as readers their participation is essential to meaning. Topics are not generally prescribed but, rather, derived from the questions

about and interest in the author and his (Baraka's) work. These assignments sometimes take the form of poetic responses, critical essays, or
"dialogues" with Baraka.

Bibliography

Brown, Lloyd W. "Baraka as Poet." *Amiri Baraka.* Boston: Twayne, 1980.
Chapter 5, 104–35.

Harris, William J. "The Transformed Poem." *The Poetry and Poetics of Amiri
Baraka: The Jazz Aesthetic.* Columbia: U of Missouri P, 1985. 91–121.

Lacey, Henry. "Die Schwartze Bohemien: 'The Terrible Disorder of a Young
Man'" and "Imamu." *To Raise, Destroy, and Create.* Troy, NY: Whitstone,
1981. 1–42, 93–162.

Sollors, Werner. "Who Substitutes for the Dead Lecturer?: Poetry of the Early
1960s." *Amiri Baraka/LeRoi Jones: The Quest for a Populist Modernism.*
New York: Columbia UP, 1978, 83–95.

Sonia Sanchez (b. 1934)

Contributing Editors: Joyce A. Joyce and John Reilly

Classroom Issues and Strategies

There is a widespread feeling that protest and politics are either inappropriate to literature or, if acceptable at certain times, the time for it has now
passed.

The whole course should be founded upon an acceptance of the fact that
there are no *a priori* definitions for literature. Poetry is what the poet writes or
the audience claims as poetry. The real issues are whether or not the poet sets
out a plausible poetics (one neither too solipsistic nor so undiscriminating as to
dissolve meaning) and whether or not the practice of the poet has the local
excitement and disciplined language to make it aesthetically satisfying. Upon
these premises, the study of Sonia Sanchez can proceed with attention to her
idea of revolutionary poetry associated with nation building, as it was discussed into the 1960s and 1970s.

Operating on the assumption that there is some common tradition underlying work of poets who declare ethnicity (African American) as their common

identity, useful discussion is possible about ways Sanchez differs from Michael Harper and Jay Wright. What differences in aesthetic and practice account for the relative complexity of Harper and Wright when contrasted with Sanchez? But, then, what allows us to consider them all black poets? Surely not merely the selection of subject matter?

Major Themes, Historical Perspectives, Personal Issues

The historical and political are boldly set out in Sanchez's poetry. The personal may be overlooked by the hasty reader, but the poetry develops a persona with a highly subjective voice conveying the impression of a real human being feeling her way to positions, struggling to make her expressive declarative writing conform to her intuitions and interior self. This tension once observed makes all the themes arranged around the black aesthetic and black politics also accessible.

Significant Form, Style, or Artistic Conventions

The "eye" devices (lowercase letters, speed writing, fluid lines) along with the free form of verse and vernacular word choice are avant-garde devices seen in the work of many other poets. The point here is to see them associated with an aesthetic that privileges the oral and musical. For Sanchez it would be valuable to point to the frequency with which African-American poets allude to jazz performers, even making their lines sound like a musical instrument, just as, historically, musical instruments imitated the sounds of voice in early jazz and blues. This would make the vigor of the poem on the Righteous Brothers understandable, for music is a talisman of African-American culture. It would also set up a useful contrast between poetry written for print and poetry written to simulate the ephemerality of performed music or song.

Original Audience

For Sanchez these questions have great importance, for she has undergone important changes that have brought the spiritual and personal more forward in her verse. Dating her poems in connection with political events is very important. One might, for example, talk about an avowedly nationalist poetry written for a struggle to assert values believed to be a source of community solidarity. There are many parallels to suggest, including the writing of Irish authors in English, Jewish-American writers adapting the sounds of Yiddish to an exploration of traditional values in English, and so on. Following the nationalist period of her work we see a shift of focus. One must ask students if the elements centered in the newer poems were not already present before. The appropriate answer (yes) will permit assertion of the developing nature of a writer's corpus, something worth presenting in all courses.

Comparisons, Contrasts, Connections

"Just Don't Never Give Up on Love" could be contrasted with confessional verse such as Plath's "Daddy" to distinguish the ways feeling can be distanced. Similarly the feminist voices of Adrienne Rich and Marge Piercy can introduce subtle distinctions when contrasted with the same Sanchez narrative/poem. What, we might ask, is the basis of distinction: formal or attitudinal?

Questions for Reading, Discussion, and Writing

1. Recalling the use of the mask by Paul Laurence Dunbar, consider what differences have occurred to change the meaning of that image in the eighty-eight years until Sanchez published "Masks."
2. A society may be culturally diverse, yet that does not mean that cultures are similarly powerful or influential. Discuss the way that Sonia Sanchez and other revolutionary black poets see the relationship between their culture and that of the dominant white society.

Bibliography

Joyce, Joyce A. "The Development of Sonia Sanchez: A Continuing Journey." *Indian Journal of American Studies* 13 (July 1983): 37–71.

———. *Ijala: Sonia Sanchez and the African Poetic Tradition*. Chicago: Third World, 1996.

Harris, Trudier, and Thadious Davis, eds. *Dictionary of Literary Biography: Afro-American Poets Since 1955*. Farmington Hills: Gale, 1985. 295–306.

Tate, Claudia. *Black Woman Writers at Work*. New York: Continuum, 1983. 132–48.

Tomás Rivera (1935–1984)

Contributing Editor: Ramón Saldívar

Classroom Issues and Strategies

Rivera's novel is written in nonsequential chronology, with a multiplicity of characters, without an easily identifiable continuous narrator, and without a strictly casual narrative logic. While each of the selections is coherent within itself, students will need to be prepared for the apparent lack of continuity from one section of work to the next.

I begin with a careful discussion of the first selection, "The Lost Year," to show that there is, at least in sketchy form, the beginnings of a narrative identity present. As in other modernist and postmodernist writings, in William Faulkner's *As I Lay Dying* and *Go Down, Moses,* for example, or in Juan Rulfo's *Pedro Páramo,* the narrative is not expository, attempting to give us historical depiction. It offers instead complex subjective impressions and psychological portraiture. Students should be asked to read the first selection looking for ways in which the narrative does cohere. Ask: Who speaks? Where is the speaker? What does the speaker learn about him- or herself here, even if only minimally? As students proceed to the following selections, it is appropriate to ask what this unconventional narrative form has to do with the themes of the work.

Rivera's work is openly critical of and in opposition to mainstream American culture. What does it accomplish by being oppositional? What does it share with other "marginal" literatures, such as African-American, feminist, gay and lesbian, or third world writings? Instead of attempting to locate Rivera within American or modernist writings, it might be useful to think of Rivera's place within the group of other noncanonic, antitraditional, engaged writings.

Students are sometimes misled by the apparent simplicity of the first selection: they might need to be carefully alerted to the question of identity being posed there. Also, the historical context of racial violence and political struggle may need to be constructed for students: they may want to see these stories as exclusively about the plight of *individuals* when in reality Rivera is using individual characters as *types* for a whole community

Major Themes, Historical Perspectives, Personal Issues

General Themes: The coming to maturity of a young child as he begins to get a glimmer of the profound mystery of the adult world. The child, apparently a boy, raises in the second selection the traditional *lehresjahre* themes, having to do with the disillusionment of childhood dreams.

Specific Themes: This coming to maturity and the posing of universal existential questions (Who am I? Where do I belong?) take place within the specific historical and social context of the working-class life and political struggle of the Mexican-American migrant farmworker of the late 1940s and 1950s in Texas.

Universal themes are thus localized to a very high degree. What does this localizing of universal themes accomplish in the novel? Also, the question of personal identity is in each of the three selections increasingly tied to the identity of the community (*la raza*). The stories thus also thematize the relationship between private history and public history.

Significant Form, Style, or Artistic Conventions

Questions of style are intimately involved with questions of substance in these selections. Rivera claims to have been influenced by his reading in James Joyce, Marcel Proust, William Faulkner, and the great Latin American novelists. Rivera also acknowledged that he had been profoundly influenced by the work of the great Mexican-American anthropologist and folklorist Américo Paredes, whose ethnographic work realistically pictured turn-of-the-century life in the Southwest. Why does this work about the "local" theme of life in the American Southwest offer itself in the form of high modernism? Would not a more straightforward social realism have been more appropriate for the themes it presents?

Original Audience

The work was originally written in Spanish, using the colloquial, everyday cadences of working-class Spanish-speaking people. Bilingual instructors should review the original text and try to point out to students that the English translations are but approximations of a decidedly *oral* rhythm. Written at the height of the Chicano political movement and in the midst of an often bitter labor struggle, at times Rivera's work bristles with anger and outrage. The turmoil of the late 1960s and early 1970s plays a large role in the tone of the work.

Comparisons, Contrasts, Connections

Rivera claimed to have been influenced by many modern authors, Faulkner chief among them. A useful discussion of the relationships between form and theme might arise by comparing Rivera's work with Faulkner's *As I Lay Dying* or *Absalom, Absalom!* What does narrative experimentation have to do with social realism? Why does an author choose nontraditional narrative techniques? What does one gain by setting aside casually motivated character action?

Questions for Reading, Discussion, and Writing

1. Many of the questions posed by this study guide might be fruitfully addressed to students before they read Rivera's work. Especially useful are those questions that ask students to think about the relationship between form/content and that take into account the historical/political circumstances of the period during which these stories were written.
2. Students might consider in the piece entitled "And the Earth Did Not Devour Him": Why does the earth not devour him? What does the narrator learn, and why does this knowledge seem so momentous? Concerning the last selection, "When We Arrive," students might discuss the journey motif: Where are these migrant workers going? What will they find at the end of the road?

Bibliography

Ramón Saldívar, *Chicano Narrative* (Madison: U of Wisconsin P, 1990), 74–90, includes a discussion of the selections. *International Studies in Honor of Tomás Rivera*, ed. Julian Olivares (Houston: Arte Público, 1985) is an excellent collection of essays on *And the Earth Did Not Devour Him*.

Lucille Clifton (b. 1936)

Contributing Editor: James A. Miller

Classroom Issues and Strategies

Clifton's poetry is generally very accessible, so accessible that careless readers may overlook the way she often achieves her poetic effects. Her poetry is best read aloud, and students should be encouraged to read and hear her poems first, then to explore issues of language, form, and theme.

Major Themes, Historical Perspectives, Personal Issues

Clifton is deeply concerned with the ways in which the weight of racial memory and history extends into the present, with family and community history, and with the possibilities of transcendence and reconciliation. A deeply spiritual vein shapes much of her poetry, which conveys a sense of wonder and mystery as well as optimism and resilience.

Significant Form, Style, or Artistic Conventions

Clifton's poems seem guided by the dictates of her own experience and consciousness rather than by any *a priori* sense of form or poetic conventions. Her primary commitment is to economical, everyday language, and to the rhythmic and musical qualities of the language that shapes her poems.

Original Audience

Clifton's first collection of poems, *Good Times*, was published during the heyday of the Black Arts Movement, and her early work in particular owes important debts to the mood and outlook of that period, particularly in her celebration of the ordinary life of African Americans.

Comparisons, Contrasts, Connections

Clifton can fruitfully be compared with other African-American women poets who emerged out of the same historical moment—Mari Evans, June Jordan, and Sonia Sanchez, for example—but she can also be read in conjunction with Amiri Baraka and Etheridge Knight. Her poems can also be compared with those of her predecessors like Langston Hughes, Sterling A. Brown, Margaret Walker, Robert Hayden, and Gwendolyn Brooks. And intriguing relationships can also be established between her works and the poems of Emily Dickinson and Walt Whitman.

Working with Cultural Objects

The American Academy of Poets Poetry Exhibits: Lucille Clifton at <www.poets.org/exh/lclif> includes a brief biography, recordings of Clifton reading "Cutting Greens" and "Homage to My Hips," and three poems: "blessing the boats," "miss rosie," and "wishes for sons."

Modern American Poetry: Lucille Clifton, prepared and compiled by Cary Nelson, at <www.english.uiuc.edu/maps/poets/a_f/clifton/about> includes commentary on Lucille Clifton by Jocelyn K. Moody, James Miller, and Jane Todd Cooper; analyses of "poem to my uterus" and "to my last period" by Hilary Holladay; an excerpt from an interview with Bill Moyers about "at the cemetery, walnut grove plantation, 1989"; a discussion of "brothers" by Andrew Moss; reproductions of Lucille Clifton book jackets; and an online poem, "the Mississippi river empties into the gulf."

Questions for Reading, Discussion, and Writing

1. Discuss the domestic images in "The Thirty Eighth Year" and "I Am Accused of Tending to the Past." How do images of nurturing function in these poems? What is the relationship of these images to the consciousness which shapes the poems?
2. Discuss the function of history in Clifton's poems. What, for example, is the poet seeking "at the cemetery, walnut grove plantation, south carolina, 1989"? Is there any relationship between this poem and "Reply"?
3. Discuss the relationship between "I" and "Them" in "in white america." Trace the development of the poem through the final stanza and comment upon the resolution the poem achieves.
4. Listen to Lucille Clifton read "Cutting Greens" and "Homage to My Hips." Discuss the ways in which she uses sound to achieve her effects. Consider the ways in which she translates sound into the written word.
5. Read the excerpt from Clifton's interview with Bill Moyers. How do her comments help to illuminate "at the cemetery, walnut grove plantation, 1989"? What do they suggest about her beliefs in the power of poetry?
6. Carefully study the Lucille Clifton book jackets. What relationships do you see between them and the themes of her poetry?

Bibliography

Evans, Mari, ed., *Black Women Writers 1950–1980: A Critical Evaluation*. New York: Anchor: 1984. 137–61.

Golladay, Hilary. "'I Am Not Grown Away from You': Lucille Clifton's Elegies for Her Mother." *CLA Journal* 42 (June 1999): 430–44.

Harris, Trudier, and Thadious Davis, eds. *Dictionary of Literary Biography: Afro-American Poets Since 1955*. Farmington Hills: Gale, 1985. 55–60.

Ostriker, Alice. "Kin and Kin: The Poetry of Lucille Clifton." *American Poetry Review* 22 (Nov./Dec. 1993): 41–48.

Wall, Cheryl A. "Sifting Legacies in Lucille Clifton's Generations." *Contemporary Literature* 40.4 (Winter 1999): 552–74.

White, Mark B. "Sharing the Living Light: Rhetorical, Poetic, and Social Identity in Lucille Clifton." *CLA Journal* 40 (Mar. 1997): 288–304.

June Jordan (b. 1936)

Contributing Editor: Agnes Moreland Jackson

Classroom Issues and Strategies

Students of the 1960s and early 1970s (as well as today's college-age youth) thought about and acted on nonfamilial kinships, that is, relationships between individuals *having agency*; groups, personhood in the community, space or turf—local/national/global; responsibility—private and corporate; power/powerlessness; most of the "-isms" and phobias of historical and contemporary societies worldwide. These are some of the recurring subjects in Jordan's three poems included in *The Heath Anthology* and throughout her volumes of poetry and essays. She belongs to the world (though it despises and rejects her), and her voice of discovery, pain, rage, and resolution penetrates our minds and emotions. College students, therefore, recognize her concerns while also wondering sometimes whether Jordan's societal and world portrait is "as bad" as her texts declare. Even those as wounded as she describes herself have to think deeply to make the connections, see the intricate patterns, and analyze situations to determine Jordan's accuracy or error about social and human conditions. Because the issues in her poetry reflect our everyday experiences, we can comprehend Jordan's poetry and note correspondences between and among the following: Jordan's observations and protestations; daily news about victims of violence whose lives are affected by political and economic decisions. An invitation to discuss the poems here could prompt students' own sharing of their personal experiences (of physical or emotional assault, acceptance or rejection of opportunity, and reaction to media images, health, and health services).

Moreover, *hearing* Jordan is crucial to appreciating and understanding the power of her poetry. Beyond urging my students to read all poetry aloud (and we read aloud in class), I stress the rich *orality* of poetic expression by many African Americans (from Dunbar to Hughes and Brown, from Hayden and Walker and Brooks to Evans and Sanchez and Cortez, as well as Lorde, Knight,

Reed, Clifton, and Harper), among whom Jordan is outstanding for the "being-spoken-now" qualities of her poems. Two of the "talking passages" (describing aptly the entire 114 lines) in "Poem about My Rights" are its opening and lines 45 to 49. Reading this poem aloud in a class need not be difficult in any college for at least two reasons: its personal, intimate, talking-directly-to-you quality and the generally acknowledged present-day awareness of the 25 percent probability that rape might become real to any woman in the United States. Single voices (including those of male students) reading the poem in sequence diminish possible embarrassment over the sustained and repeated use of the words *rape, penetrate,* and *ejaculate* as reality and as metaphor. The poem's insistence upon the *equal status* of *all* oppressions stimulates serious discussion that includes not only homo- and bisexuality; instead, interest remains for persistent philosophical quests to engage and understand freedom and responsibility, law and justice, power and respect, and so on. Students usually agree with the linking of all oppressions, not withstanding the risk of having to reveal their own characteristics and/or prejudices. Anglo males, especially, need time and much reassurance that female peers understand the socially constructed bases of male behavior deemed to be oppressive, for Jordan denounces hurtful action, not its causes—including females complicit in maintaining patriarchal privilege to oppress.

"To Free Nelson Mandela" has the oral qualities of a ritual chant. Its repetitions enhance (1) recognition of the many years of Mandela's imprisonment and—hence—(2) the near miracle of his survival which invokes urgent and continually growing *cosmic* demands that he be freed, and (3) the power and rightness of a wife's loyalty *and work*—instead of withdrawal into seclusion (hence, no Penelope is she but a warrior who has taken up the battle). However protracted, however gross, atrocities do not dehumanize their victims, nor can horror outlast living "waters of the world" as they "turn to the softly burning/light of the moon." Ironically, almost mystically, atrocities eventually cause oppressed people, however despised, to come together in reaffirmation and in ritual, including the ceremonies of life to be lived fully before dying. (Cf. African slaves in the Western world, their understanding of self-worth, i.e., somebodiness conferred by a *believed-in* God—despite the ineffable horrors of bondage.)

Major Themes, Historical Perspectives, Personal Issues

These three poems reveal the speakers' firm understanding that their respective experiences (or those witnessed and reported on in "To Free Nelson Mandela") validate the deduction by the speaker in "Poem about My Rights" that she and all other oppressed persons, nations, and peoples are victims because they are *viewed by their torturers* to be *wrong*. Therefore, *wrong* are the victims enumerated in lines 7 through 12 in "To Free Nelson Mandela": the "twelve-year-old girl," "the poet," "the students," "the children." "[M]urdered Victoria Mxenge" (1.17) was *wrong* to have been a lawyer who "defended [B]lacks charged with political crimes" (*Hollywood Reporter* 19 July 1991), writes the reviewer of the hit musical *Sarafina*, based on the horrors of and spiritual triumphs over South African apartheid. Martyred in 1985 in the midst of her daring and skillful work, "Durban human rights lawyer" (*Agence France Presse* 22 June 1993) Mxenge was killed (by the official police, think most in the world) "the day before she was scheduled to defend 17 . . . [black activists] on charges of treason" (Los Angeles *Times* 29 August 1991). Her ANC-supporter spouse, Griffiths Mxenge, also a lawyer, had been murdered in 1981.

These data, only the tip of the iceberg, demonstrate again Jordan's total immersion in the lives of oppressed people of color wherever they suffer in the world. Revelations in the 1990s—most carried in newspapers around the globe—about allegedly police-perpetrated murders in South Africa during the mid-1980s were not news to Jordan, who in 1989 had published the Mandela poem among other "new" poems composed between 1985 and 1989. From line 36 through line 57 of "To Free Nelson Mandela," Jordan commemorates the beginning-to-heal black township community of Lingelihle (outside Cradock), where in 1985 (as reported in *The Guardian* of August 11, 1992, "[f]rom all over South Africa, tens of thousands of mourners converged on . . . [the township] . . . for the funeral of . . . [four black activists]" including Matthew Goniwe, an "immensely popular leader" in a "'backveld revolution' [that had swept] South Africa" in 1983. Less poetic than Jordan's rendering of Goniwe's transformational impact on his comrades in suffering is the following very helpful newspaper explanation of why his death was felt so deeply by so many:

> Son of a domestic servant and a seller of firewood, he had inspired the community to form a residents' association which demanded urgent reforms in the dusty, poverty-stricken township. Studious, quiet, small and bespectacled, Goniwe had raised educational standards, given self-respect to unemployed young [b]lacks and stopped much of the drinking and pot smoking. Repeatedly detained and accused of agitating, he remarked, "[Agitation] is not required when you have apartheid—the greatest agitator of all."

> (*The Guardian* 11 August 1992)

The journalistic furor in 1992 about events in 1985 was sparked by the publication in June 1992 of an official, top-secret message "dated June 7, 1985" that revealed senior officers in South Africa's security forces to have plotted the murders of Goniwe and three others. On March 9, 1991, the Chicago *Tribune* had carried a report of Amnesty International's having cited the death of Victoria Mxenge among other crimes against human rights.

In her 1976 essay "Declaration of an Independence I Would Just as Soon Not Have" (in the 1981 collection of essays, *Civil Wars*, published by Beacon Press), in which she remarks on the practical necessity of folks' uniting and working together to effect changes toward justice, Jordan writes of the "hunger and . . . famine afflicting some 800 million lives on earth" as "a fact that leaves . . . [one] nauseous, jumpy, and chronically enraged." She says also that "with all . . . [her] heart and mind . . . [she] would strive in any way . . . to eradicate the origins of . . . [the] colossal exploitation and abuse" experienced by "[t]he multimillion-fold majority of the peoples on earth [who] are neither white, nor powerful, nor exempt from terrifying syndromes of disease, hunger, poverty that defies description, and prospects for worse privation or demeaning subsistence" (115–16; 117). Jordan's rage at injustices and violations of personhood, as well as her compassion and empathy, are large and constant, as can be recognized by even a quick reading of her poetry and essays.

Although not among her most recent poems, "Moving Towards Home" is as significant as any to be related to Jordan's personal life, a life informed by her love of black people, a love that anchors her love for, and work and yearning for, freedom and justice for all oppressed people. She can relate to, can feel as, can *be* a Palestinian because the space, the room for living has become smaller and smaller geographically and in all other ways that destruction, death, bigotry, and hatred have crowded out life. "[T]o make our way home" would be to reclaim life, to reclaim "room" for "living" for ourselves and oppressed others.

Significant Form, Style, or Artistic Conventions

Like many contemporary black and other poets of the United States, Jordan uses language boldly and fully, not shying away from stereotypically or conventionally "ugly" words or ideas. Thus, she writes about what is real and what should not be: all manner of injustice, repression, oppression; diverse kinds of self- and personhood. "Poem about My Rights" captures most completely the unbounded range of Jordan's subjects, as well as the rich juxtaposing and combining of free verse, linearly arranged sentences, parallelism, unpunctuated parenthetical remarks, repetition, freely (but *not* randomly) used virgules or slashes to hold or pull ideas together. Opening the poem *in medias res* gives form to Jordan's repeated thesis that self-determination is precluded by *all* oppressions and *any* oppression— occurring in any order at any age anywhere on the earth, and perpetrated by nominal friends (e.g., parents; members of one's own racial, sexual, occupational, and gender group) or recognized enemies. Jordan makes situational analogies and projections that meld all aspects of her being into one seamless *personal*: family; politics—local, national, worldwide, as well as racial and sexual; geography—general space, particular places, personified places, urban and rural spaces; history; esthetics; economics; her body and the bodies of others; sexism, racism, classism, ageism.

Comparisons, Contrasts, Connections

As is true for her contemporaries Adrienne Rich and Audre Lorde, sexuality is a crucial attribute of June Jordan's identity and her premise for self-expression and interaction with others. These distinguished, radically iconoclastic writers demand full recognition of the "difference/s." Lorde emphasizes her blackness, femaleness, lesbianism—in "butch" and "fem" roles (as I read her essays, particularly), her relatedness to all other women needing/seeking autonomy of personhood, and the ultimately fatal possession of her life by cancer. Progressively through her poetry and essays, Lorde becomes a winner, psychologically triumphant over all of these popularly acknowledged detractors from fullness of living. Rich defines herself as female, lesbian, white, Southern, and a Jew. Together with emphatically engaging myriad and worldwide economic, cultural, educational, and political oppressions (as Jordan does), both Rich and Lorde, respectively as applicable, recognize and experience (as Jordan does) abuses of power—shaped usually as sexism, heterosexism, homophobia, racism, anti-Semitism, classism, and ageism—and "triggered," presumably, by the women's "differences"—however ageless and normal, immutable, and real. For Jordan add bisexuality, that is, difference with a difference, and she stands out from the others in the triad. Possessing sexualities, Jordan experiences discrimination among the less complex or more "normal" lesbians. This experience is what seems to have clarified her view that any oppression equals all other oppressions without hierarchical or invidious distinctions. Jordan also refuses to privilege oppressors who are more "like" her than some other oppressors might be. Thus, African Americans and lesbians who would presume to judge her bisexuality or any attribute or freely chosen nonthreatening behavior toward others must be called what they are: tyrants ("A New Politics of Sexuality," *Technical Difficulties* 90; the entire essay is *must* reading for any who would try to comprehend Jordan fully).

Questions for Reading, Discussion, and Writing

The following are suggestions for class enjoyment of reading/thinking aloud about Jordan's "Moving Towards Home": (1) Do students detect any slowing down, possibly an emphasis at lines 35 and 37 and in lines in which the persona quotes other people's voices? (2) Does it matter that readers might not/probably do not know the actual speakers? That the quoted passages might be/might not be historical? (3) Ask students to consider structure, meaning, and context by noting differences between the quoted passages and lines 47, 48, 49.

(4) The importance of reading aloud and carefully can be stressed by discussing the difference between "those who dare" in lines 35, 39, and 41 and "those who dare" in line 46. (5) Visual interest enhances that of sound as readers notice that "speak about" in the poem's first thirty-one lines all line up/stack up, one above the next succeeding instance, that "about unspeakable events" breaks this pattern spatially as well as linguistically in the reversed order of the main words, and in the negativizing of "speak" by use of the prefix *un*. All events that the persona does "not wish to speak about" *are* spoken with chilling effect; *about* from line 53 to the end precedes *home* & *living room; home* envelopes *living room*.

Bibliography

Arnold Adoff's 1973 anthology *The Poetry of Black America* includes four outstanding Jordan poems while Erlene Stetson in *Black Sister* (1981) contains only one by Jordan (a must, however, about Native Americans) but six by Lorde, seven by Jayne Cortez, and three by Sanchez.

Rudolfo A. Anaya (b. 1937)

Contributing Editor: Raymund Paredes

Classroom Issues and Strategies

Bless Me, Ultima is a bildungsroman and can be compared usefully to other works of this type, notably James Joyce's *A Portrait of the Artist as a Young Man*. Another important quality of *Bless Me, Ultima* is its heavy reliance on Mexican folklore, particularly such well-known legends as "La Llorona." There are many collections of Mexican and Mexican-American folklore that would give students a sense of the traditions that influence Anaya's novel. I recommend, for example, Americo Paredes's *Folktales of Mexico* (which has a very useful introduction) and *Mexican-American Folklore* by James O. West. Another important issue to consider is how Anaya tries to impart a flavor of Mexican-American culture to his work. In the excerpt from *Bless Me, Ultima*, Anaya uses Mexican names and Spanish words and phrases and focuses on one of the strongest institutions of Mexican-American life, the Catholic church. If it is true that much of American culture and literature grow out of Protestantism, it would be worth examining how those parts of American culture that are based in Catholicism are distinctive.

Major Themes, Historical Perspectives, Personal Issues

The protagonist of *Bless Me, Ultima* is Antonio, who is coming of age at the conclusion of World War II. Participation in the war has clearly had a dramatic impact on Antonio's older brothers, who now regard the rather isolated life of central New Mexico as dull and confining. Clearly, Antonio's community is in a state of transition, and its citizens must face the inevitability of greater interaction with the world beyond their valley. Not far from Antonio's community, at White Sands, the atomic bomb is being tested. Anaya uses the bomb not only to represent the unprecedented capacity of the human race to annihilate itself but also to symbolize the irresistible encroachment of modern technology not only in rural New Mexico but everywhere.

Perhaps the major question that Anaya confronts is how Mexican Americans can retain certain key traditional values while accepting the inevitability—and desirability—of change. In dealing with this issue, Anaya places the boy Antonio under the tutelage of the wise *curandera* (folkhealer), Ultima, who prepares her charge for the future by grounding him in the rich Spanish and Indian cultures of his past. For Ultima, tradition is not confining but liberating.

One of the striking characteristics of *Bless Me, Ultima* is its critical stance toward Catholicism, which is presented here as rigid, intimidating, and, at least to Antonio and his friends, largely unintelligible. The Catholic God is punishing while Antonio and his friends long for a nurturing deity. In attacking certain aspects of Catholicism, Anaya follows a long line of Latin American, Mexican, and Chicano writers including José Antonio Villarreal and Tomás Rivera.

Significant Form, Style, or Artistic Conventions

Bless Me, Ultima is a fairly conventional novel structurally, although Anaya does use such devices as stream of consciousness, flashbacks, and shifting narrators. As noted above, the key formal and stylistic question is how Anaya attempts to present his novel as a distinctly *Chicano* work of fiction. Again, Anaya employs Spanish words and names (a boy called *Florence*, for example, from the Spanish "Florencio") and focuses on important cultural events in Chicano experience. But for the most part, in terms of formal qualities and structure, *Bless Me, Ultima* is very much a contemporary American novel.

Original Audience

Bless Me, Ultima is a work that intends to explain and depict Mexican-American culture in New Mexico for a general American audience. Nevertheless,

Anaya's presentation of Mexican-American culture is relatively "thick" so as to appeal to Chicano readers as well.

Comparisons, Contrasts, Connections

Bless Me, Ultima has clearly been influenced by Joyce's *A Portrait of the Artist as a Young Man.* Another interesting juxtaposition is with *Native Son*, Richard Wright's account of a young man—older than Antonio—who comes of age without much of a sense of his past and with few prospects in the harsh, urban environment of Chicago. Anaya's presentation of the Catholic Church can be fruitfully compared with that of José Antonio Villarreal in *Pocho*; Anaya's focus on Mexican-American childhood is complemented nicely by Tomás Rivera's *. . . y no sé lo tragó la tierra* and Sandra Cisneros's *The House on Mango Street.*

Questions for Reading, Discussion, and Writing

1. The excerpt from *Bless Me, Ultima* focuses on events surrounding Lent. Students can be asked to write about their experiences of this occasion or other important religious events. Comparing different sorts of religious experiences could be very useful.
2. As Anaya presents Catholicism, the Church emphasizes punishment and damnation rather than forgiveness and salvation. What is the effect on Antonio and his friends? How do they respond to church practices and rituals? Do students have any ideas about how religion might be presented to children more positively and successfully?
3. Have the students consider the bildungsroman as a literary form. Why is it so enduring? How would the students write one of their own lives? What would be the central experiences they would focus on?

Thomas Pynchon (b. 1937)

Contributing Editor: Derek C. Maus

Classroom Issues and Strategies

Reading Pynchon's work is never an easy task, but it can be especially daunting for a student approaching his work for the first time. Even in this relatively early story, Pynchon's broad range of knowledge is on display, and students will need to understand references to everything from the Laws of thermodynamics to the music theory behind jazz to the progressive historical model of Henry Adams's *Education*. As several critics have noted (and Pynchon himself freely admits), one need not be a physicist to understand entropy at the level in which Pynchon is using it as a guiding metaphor in this story. A very basic discussion of entropy in the context of thermodynamics and information theory will greatly enhance the comprehension of the story. Critic David Seed claims that a simple explanation of the dictionary definitions of *entropy* suffices in this regard, but additional reference to theorists like Marshall McLuhan or Norbert Wiener (both of whom Pynchon cites as influences upon his writing) could be useful in a course beyond an introductory level.

In addition to the difficult subject matter, the language of the characters, especially those in Meatball Mulligan's apartment, may be difficult for the students to understand since much of it is specific to the story's 1957 setting. Instructors may have to "translate" phrases like "tea time" or the jazzy slang used by the Duke di Angelis quartet. Furthermore, Pynchon includes a number of untranslated foreign words or phrases in the story, thus creating a further difficulty for most readers. In sum, the language of the story presents a number of obstacles for readers, even those fairly accustomed to complex material.

A good point of entry for discussion of the story is Pynchon's satire, which ranges from an indictment of the falsity of "American expatriates around Washington" to the absurdity of music played without instruments. Having the students discern which characters Pynchon seems to be holding up for ridicule and which he seems to treat with more sympathy can shed some light on the ways in which the various forms of entropy are used as metaphors. For example, ask the students whether or not they find themselves siding more with Meatball, Saul, or Callisto and then have them discuss whether or not they think this is consistent with Pynchon's intention. What are the differences in their respective reactions to the force of entropy in their lives? Correspondingly, what are the differences that underlie their perceptions of entropy in the first place? Are all three characters' attitudes satirized, or does Pynchon favor one of them?

Aubade's role in the story also serves as a good discussion starter. Her breaking the window (thus disrupting the hermetically sealed environment of Callisto's apartment) is the final action in the story and to some extent unifies the two separate narrative strands. Have the students discuss the way Pynchon describes her actions in musical terms and compare this with the satirical portrayal of the jazz musicians in Meatball's apartment.

Major Themes, Historical Perspectives, Personal Issues

In addition to entropy, the story contains a pointed critique of attitudes associated with the so-called "Lost Generation" of American literary history. A number of the characters, especially Callisto, embody attitudes that can be read as parodies of Fitzgerald, Hemingway, and others. Also, note the satirical reference to the shallow culture of the "American expatriates" in 1957 and the ways in which the party at Meatball's is a parody of modernist depictions of intellectual profligacy (cf. *The Sun Also Rises, The Great Gatsby,* or *The Autobiography of Alice B. Toklas*). Such a discussion can be used as a gateway for exploring the differences between modernist and postmodernist literature.

Significant Form, Style, or Artistic Conventions

Have the students discuss Pynchon's lack of transitions between the two narratives (Meatball's apartment vs. Callisto's apartment) and how this potentially disorienting technique both supports the central themes of the story (i.e., order, even in the elements of a story, is illusory) and also serves to accentuate the ambiguity of the ending.

Original Audience

It may be useful to contextualize the story both in terms of its original 1960 publication in *Kenyon Review* and as part of the 1984 book *Slow Learner.* Since the initial audience was minuscule (both because of the small circulation of the journal and Pynchon's relative lack of notoriety), a discussion of the different cultural milieu into which the story emerged upon its larger-scale publication twenty-four years later can bear significant fruit. Also, reading from Pynchon's self-deprecating comments in the introduction to *Slow Learner* may help students see how this story is in many ways an emergent, but unpolished, expression of ideas that Pynchon would return to in much greater detail later in his work.

Nicholasa Mohr (b. 1938)

Contributing Editor: Frances R. Aparicio

Classroom Issues and Strategies

Mohr's writings are quite accessible for the college-age student population. There is no bilingualism, her English is quite simple and direct, and her stories in general do not create difficulties in reading or comprehension.

Major Themes, Historical Perspectives, Personal Issues

1. The universal theme of "growing up" (bildungsroman), and in her case in particular, growing up female in El Barrio.
2. The theme of the family; views of the Hispanic family and the expectations it holds of its members, in contrast to its Anglo-American counterpart.
3. Sexual roles in Latino culture; traditional versus free vocations (for men).
4. Mother/daughter relationships; tensions, generational differences.
5. Women's issues such as career versus family, the economic survival of welfare mothers, dependency and independence issues.
6. Outside views of the barrio "ghetto" in relation to the voices of those who have lived in the inner cities.

Significant Form, Style, or Artistic Conventions

The autobiographical form is quite predominant in Mohr's writings, as is James Clifford's concept of "ethnobiography," in which the self is seen in conjunction with his or her ethnic community. And Mohr employs traditional storytelling; simple, direct, accessible, chronological use of time; and a logical structure.

   Very dynamic discussions emerge when students are asked to evaluate Mohr's transparent, realist style as good literature or not. This discussion should include observations of how many U.S. Latino and Latina writers have opted for a less academic and so-called "sophisticated" style that would allow for wider audiences outside the academic world.

Original Audience

It is important to read many of Mohr's works as literature for young adolescents. This explains and justifies the simplicity and directness of her style.

Comparisons, Contrasts, Connections

Fruitful comparisons could be made if we look at other Latina women who also write on "growing up female and Hispanic in the United States": Sandra Cisneros's *The House on Mango Street* (Houston: Arte Público, 1983); *Cuentos by Latinas*, eds. Alma Gómez, Cherríe Moraga, and Mariana Romo-Carmona (New York: Kitchen Table Women of Color, 1983); and Helena Maria Viramontes's *The Moths and Other Stories* (Houston: Arte Público, 1985). Viramontes's stories promise fruitful comparisons with Mohr's *Ritual of Survival*.

In addition, Mohr has been contrasted with Piri Thomas's *Down These Mean Streets*, another autobiographical book in which El Barrio is presented in terms of drugs, gangs, and violence. I would propose a comparison with Eduard Rivera's *Family Installments* as yet another example of ethnobiography.

Finally, interesting contrasts and parallelisms may be drawn from looking at North American women writers such as Ann Beattie and the Canadian Margaret Atwood; while class and race perspectives might differ, female and feminist issues could be explored as common themes.

Questions for Reading, Discussion, and Writing

1. Study questions: Specific questions on text, characters, plot, endings, issued raised. More major themes could also be explored such as How do we define epic characters, history, and great literature? Where would Mohr's characters fit within the traditional paradigms?
2. Writing assignment: Students may write their own autobiography, experiment with first- and third-person narratives, contrast female students' writings with male students'.

Paper topics: (a) Discuss the role of women within family and society in Mohr's stories, (b) discuss Mohr as a feminine or feminist writer, (c) analyze the Hispanic cultural background to her stories vis-à-vis the universal themes.

Bibliography

Not much has been written on Nicholasa Mohr's work per se. The following are good introductory articles, and the Rivero article is particularly good for the study of bildungsroman in Latina women's writings:

Acosta-Belén, Edna. "The Literature of Puerto Rican National Minority in the United States." *Bilingual Review* 5.1–2 (Jan.–Aug. 1978): 107–16.

Cruz, Arnaldo. "Teaching Puerto Rican Authors: Modernization and Identity in Nuyorican Literature." *ADE Journal* (Dec. 1988).

Mohr, Nicholasa. "On Being Authentic." *The Americas Review* 14.3–4 (Fall-Winter 1986): 106–09.

———. "Puerto Rican Writers in the United States, Puerto Rican Writers in Puerto Rico: A Separation Beyond Language." *The Americas Review* 15.2 (Summer 1987): 87–92.

Rivero, Eliana. *"The House on Mango Street*: Tales of Growing Up Female and Hispanic." Working Paper 22. Tucson: Southwest Institute for Research on Women, U of Arizona, 1986.

Raymond Carver (1938–1988)

Contributing Editor: Paul Jones

Classroom Issues and Strategies

Carver has been quoted as saying that his stories could happen anywhere. That is pretty much true. Additionally, they are so contemporary that they require almost no background material or preparation for reading and understanding by an American audience. Even the issues of class (most of Carver's characters, if they have jobs, are marginally employed), although they do exist in Carver stories, are not too heavily at play in "A Small, Good Thing." However, this lack of location, class, and even time can be used to start a classroom discussion. You might ask: Where is this story set and in what year? How old are the characters? How does this affect your reading of the story? Does this lack diminish the story? Would it have been a better story if we knew it had been set in, say, Cleveland in May 1978? How would this story be read by readers outside of Carver's culture? Would it be understood differently in France or in Cameroon? The questions can draw the class toward a discussion of style in literature and to one of the major issues for Carver: What constitutes a good story?

To bring Carver himself into the classroom, I recommend the Larry McCaffery and Sinda Gregory interview found in *Raymond Carver: A Study of the Short Fiction* or in *Alive and Writing: Interviews with American Authors of the 1980s* as sources for rich Carver quotations and his own insights into the stories and the writing process. For example, Carver cites Isaac Babel's dictum,

"No iron can pierce the heart with such force as a period put in just the right place," as one of his own guiding principles.

Major Themes, Historical Perspectives, Personal Issues

In many of Carver's stories, the issues of loss and of alcoholism are a part of the larger issue, which is the isolation and terror of people when a total breakdown of survival systems is at hand. The near-inarticulateness of his characters in the face of this terror and loss is significant and has been a major point of contention among his critics. Some say that Carver's characters are too ordinary, underperceptive, and despairing to experience the philosophical questions of meaning into which they have been thrust. His defenders say that Carver characters demonstrate that people living marginal, routine lives can come close to experiencing insight and epiphany under pressure of intruding mysteries, such as the death of a loved one.

Significant Form, Style, or Artistic Conventions

You would definitely want to talk about "minimalism" in fiction. The style has become so pervasive that students may just assume that this pared-down method of storytelling is simply how one writes fiction. Frederick Barthelme writes that as a minimalist "you're leaving room for the readers, at least for the ones who like to use their imaginations." John Barth counters with this definition of a minimalist aesthetic: "[its] cardinal principle is that artistic effect may be enhanced by a radical economy of artistic means, even where such parsimony compromises other values: completeness, for example, or richness or precision of statement." Carver was at first the most influential practitioner of minimalism, and then, through the rewriting of his earlier stories, a writer who repudiated the style.

Luckily, Carver's stories can be used to show both the power of the so-called minimalist approach and its limits. Have the students first read the brief (ten-page) story "The Bath," which was the earlier version of "A Small, Good Thing." "The Bath" is an excellent example of what minimalism does well and can be more terrifying and unsettling than anything by Stephen King. Contrasting and comparing "The Bath" and "A Small, Good Thing" from Carver's later, more expansive period will allow the students to participate in the intense debate about style. Carver preferred the second version, but he didn't pass judgment on those who like "The Bath" best.

Another useful approach for showing the nuances of revision at work in Carver's writing is to look at a few other versions of his stories. A particularly illustrative case is a short-short-story of under five hundred words that has been known as "Mine" (*Furious Seasons*), "Popular Mechanics" (*What We Talk*

About When We Talk About Love), and "Little Things" (*Where I'm Calling From*). The last two differ only in title, but there are significant differences in "Mine." Students need not be textual critics to talk about the choices that Carver has made in the various versions of his stories.

Finally, students can be asked to consider the effect of translating Carver's story into film narrative by watching the relevant portion of Robert Altman's *Short Cuts*.

Original Audience

Carver's stories were published in most of the important slick magazines of the seventies and eighties, including *Esquire* and *The New Yorker*. All along the way his work also appeared in small literary magazines. David Bellamy called Carver "the most influential stylist since Donald Barthelme." He was writing for writers, for those who appreciated experimental literature as well as for a general, though sophisticated, reading audience.

Comparisons, Contrasts, Connections

Anton Chekhov, Franz Kafka, and Ernest Hemingway are the obvious influences on Carver's work. The seemingly simple pared-down style of writing follows straight through to Carver. You might consider teaching Carver and Hemingway and perhaps Donald Barthelme together, then entering into a discussion of the bare bones style of each.

Another way to consider Carver's style is to remember that he began writing poetry before he tried fiction and continued writing and publishing poetry throughout his career. He said (in a *Paris Review* interview with Mona Simpson), "In magazines, I always turned to poems first before I read the stories. Finally, I had to make a choice, and I came down on the side of fiction. It was the right choice for me." Carver's poetry has been compared with that of William Carlos Williams, although I see many obvious differences in their approach, sense of the line, and sense of narrative. His poetry can also be compared with that of James Wright, particularly with respect to the class of people from which the poems and stories are drawn.

Bibliography

The following collections by Carver include stories mentioned above:

"Little Things." *Where I'm Calling from: New and Selected Stories*. New York: Atlantic Monthly, 1988.

"Mine." *Furious Seasons and Other Stories*. Santa Barbara: Capra, 1977.

"Popular Mechanics" and "The Bath." *What We Talk About When We Talk About Love*. New York: Vintage, 1982.

Critical books on Carver are as follows:

Campbell, Ewing. *Raymond Carver: A Study of the Short Fiction*. New York: Twayne, 1992.

Runyon, Randolph. *Reading Raymond Carver*. Syracuse: Syracuse UP, 1992.

Saltzman, Arthur M. *Understanding Raymond Carver*. Columbia: U of South Carolina P, 1988.

Carver talks about his writing and the writing of others in the following books:

Carver, Raymond. *Fires: Essays, Poems, Stories*. New York: Vintage, 1984.

Gentry, Marshall B. and William L. Stull. *Conversations with Raymond Carver*. Jackson: UP of Mississippi, 1990.

The following book of photographs helps show the locations for several of Carver's stories:

Adelman, Bob. *Carver Country: The World of Raymond Carver*. Introduction by Tess Gallagher. New York: Scribner's, 1990.

I find it always helpful to hear the author read his stories, which is especially true in the case of Carver, although only the following early tape is available:

Ray Carver Reads Three Short Stories. Columbia: American Audio Prose Library, 1983.

"A Small, Good Thing" can be found on audiotape (but not read by Carver) in the following:

Where I'm Calling From. Read by Peter Riegert. New York: Random House Audio, 1989.

Lawson Fusao Inada (b. 1938)

Teaching material for Lawson Inada is available on *The Heath Anthology* website. To access the site, please go to the Houghton Mifflin college homepage at <http://www.college.hmco.com>. Select *English;* then select *The Heath Anthology* textbook site.

Michael S. Harper (b. 1938)

Contributing Editor: Herman Beavers

Classroom Issues and Strategies

Harper's poems often prove difficult because he is so deft at merging personal and national history within the space of one metaphor. One must be aware, then, of Harper's propensity toward veiled references to historical events. One can think here of a series of poems like "History as Apple Tree." The result, in a series like this, is that the reader cannot follow the large number of historical references Harper makes—in this case, to the history of Rhode Island and its founder, Roger Williams. The poems can be seen as obscure or enigmatic when, in fact, they are designed to highlight a mode of African-American performance. In the same manner that one finds jazz musicians "quoting" another song within the space of a solo, Harper's use of history is often designed to suggest the simultaneity of events, the fact that one cannot escape the presence of the past.

Harper's interviews are often helpful, particularly those interviews in which he discusses his poetic technique. Harper is a storyteller, a performer. He is adept at the conveyance of nuance in the poems. A valuable strategy is teaching Harper's poems in conjunction with a brief introduction to modern jazz. Team teaching with a jazz historian or an ethnomusicologist while focusing on Harper's strategies of composition is a way to ground the student in Harper's use of jazz as a structuring technique in his poems. Moreover, it allows for dialogue between literary and musical worlds. Since Harper's poems are often about both music and the context out of which the music springs, such a dialogue is important for students to see. As far as history is concerned, pointing the student toward, for example, a history of the Civil War or a biography of John Brown will often illuminate Harper's propensity to "name drop" in his poems. What becomes clear is that Harper is not being dense, but rather he sees his poetic project as one of "putting the reader to work."

You might introduce Harper by showing the film *Birth of a Nation* in order to flesh out Harper's revisionary stance toward myth. Using the film as a kind of countermilieu, one can point out that Harper's poetry is designed to create a renewed, more vital American mythos. Also, listening to John Coltrane's *A Love Supreme* album will prove invaluable to understanding Harper's jazz poems.

Students often protest the inaccessibility of the poems: for example, "I don't understand this poem at all!" There are often questions regarding Harper's use of the word *modality*. Also, they do not understand Harper's use of repetition, which is designed to evoke the chant, or the poem as song.

Major Themes, Historical Perspectives, Personal Issues

Harper is very concerned in his poems with the "American tradition of forgetfulness." In his poetry, one finds him creating situations in which the contradictions between oral and written versions of history are brought into focus. Because Harper thinks of poetry as a discourse of song, the poems utilize improvisation to convey their themes. The intent of this is to highlight the complexity of American identity.

Harper's personal issues are, further, not necessarily distinguishable from the historical in his poems. If one were to point to a set of events that spur Harper's poetic voice, it would be the deaths of two of his children shortly after birth. Harper's poems on the subject express not only the personal grief of his wife and himself, but also the loss of cultural possibility the children represent. As a black man in a country so hostile to those who are black, Harper's grief is conflated into rage at the waste of human potential, a result of American forms of amnesia.

In short, the historical and the personal often function in layered fashion. Thus, Harper may use his personal grief as the springboard for illuminating a history of atrocities; the source of grief is different, but the grief is no less real.

Significant Form, Style, or Artistic Conventions

While Harper does not write in "forms" (at least of the classical sort), his work is informed by jazz composition and also several examples of African-American modernism. Clearly, Sterling Brown, Ralph Ellison, and Robert Hayden have each had an impact on Harper's poetry, not only formally but also in terms of the questions Harper takes up in his poems. I would also cite W. H. Auden and W. B. Yeats as influences.

Formally and stylistically, Harper's poetry derives from jazz improvisation. For example, in one of his poems on the jazz saxophonist John Coltrane, Harper works out a poem that doubles as a prayer-chant in Coltrane's memory.

What this suggests is that Harper does not favor symmetricality for the mere sake of symmetricality; thus, he eschews forms like the sonnet or the villanelle. One does find Harper, however, using prosody to usher the reader into a rhythmic mode that captures the nature of poetry as song as opposed to written discourse.

Original Audience

Harper's poems have indeed been widely read. However, his work has undergone a shift in audience. When he came on the scene in the late sixties, the black arts movement produced a large amount of poetry, largely because of poetry's supposed immediacy of impact. For that reason, I believe Harper's work was read by a number of people who expected militancy, anger, and a very narrow subject matter. However, one can see that his work has a different stylistic quality than that of many of his contemporaries who claimed to be writing for a narrower audience. Harper's poetry is more oriented toward inclusiveness; thus his poems utilize American history as a poetic site rather than just relying on a reified notion of racial identity that is crystallized into myth. Thus, after the sixties, Harper's audience became more clearly located in the poetry establishment. Though he still writes about musicians and artists, his readership is more specialized, more focused on poetry than twenty years ago.

Comparisons, Contrasts, Connections

Compare Harper with Brown, Ellison, Auden, and Yeats, as well as James Wright, Philip Levine, and Seamus Heaney. Hayden, Wright, and Yeats can, in their respective fashions, be considered remembrancers. That is, their work (to paraphrase Yeats) suggests that "memories are old identities." Hence, they often explore the vagaries of the past. A fruitful comparison might, for example, be made between Harper's and Hayden's poems on Vietnam. Brown and Harper are both interested in acts of heroism in African-American culture and lore. Ellison and Harper share an inclusive vision of America that eschews racial separatism in favor of a more dualistic sense of American identity.

Joyce Carol Oates (b. 1938)

Contributing Editor: Eileen T. Bender

Classroom Issues and Strategies

In a time of instant fare—both literal and intellectual—Joyce Carol Oates is most demanding. A master of short fiction, she has also published a large number of novels and novellas, both under her own name and under a pseudonym, "Rosamond Smith." Indeed, Oates has produced an amazing variety of work in virtually all literary genres: novels, short stories, drama, critical essays, screenplays, opera libretti, poetry, reviews of contemporary writing and ideas. She reads, edits, and teaches, currently holding a chair professorship at Princeton University. She defeats those readers who want artists to fit certain categories. Extremely well read and at home in the classroom, Oates is often deliberately allusive.

While she calls her writing "experimental," Oates's works are highly accessible—at least at first glance. Often, as in "Where Are You Going, Where Have You Been?" they begin in familiar territory. The central characters and the scenes are vivid and recognizable. Details (in this case, the drive-in teen culture, the sibling rivalry, the snatches of popular songs) enhance the sense of *déjà vu*. Yet by the end, dark and violent forces surface to baffle conventional expectations of both character and plot. Once again, the so-called "Dark Lady of American Letters" creates a disturbance, challenging the reader to think of both fiction and reality with new and deeper understanding.

Because of the variety of her work, Oates can be viewed as a "woman of letters." Students will be interested in a writer who is constantly engaged in public discussion (in print most frequently) of the arts: they should watch for her letters to the editor, interviews, essays, and reviews in the *New York Times*, and frequent articles in the popular press.

Oates's work itself can be approached at different levels of sophistication. It is always interesting to explore the many allusive patterns in her fiction. Several of her short stories are meant as explicit imitations of famous forebears (e.g., "The Dead," "Metamorphosis," "The Lady With the Pet Dog"), and those can be read in tandem to see the complexity of Oates's relationship to literary tradition.

In "Where Are You Going, Where Have You Been?" Oates makes an ordinary tale extraordinary by juxtaposing two powerful legends: the modern rock hero (the story is dedicated to activist-songwriter Bob Dylan) and the ancient demon lover. Drawing together these threads, Oates is able to tell a chilling tale of a young adolescent, tantalized by glamorous surfaces, unable to resist more satanic designs. In this case, the "accessible" story needs to be peeled back in order for Oates's intentions and the full sense of the work to be understood.

In responding to this story, students are disturbed by the violence that erupts from ordinary reality, and question its function or purpose—especially if they view literature as a kind of moral lesson or as an escape into a world elsewhere (the romantic paradigm). They will ask questions about the author herself, surprised that so academic and soft-spoken a person is capable of describing such violence in her stories. These responses provide an ideal occasion to discuss the creative process and the difference between author and character, biography and literature, reality imagined and imaginative reality.

Major Themes, Historical Perspectives, Personal Issues

At the center of much of Oates's work is concern about the singular power of the self and the high cost of the struggle for autonomy. In this, she is like those contemporary "third force" psychologists she has studied and admired (chiefly Maslow) who posit a different human ideal: communion rather than mastery. Readers might focus on the patterns of selfhood and the possibilities for relationship in her work.

Oates also calls herself a "feminist" although she does not like the restrictive title of "woman writer"; rather, she prefers being described as a woman who writes. In her exploration of character and relationships, the nature of love and sexual power are frequently at issue. Again, this would be a fruitful topic for further reading and discussion, using Oates's own essays on androgyny, feminism, and the special circumstances of the "woman who writes" as a starting point.

Oates is not only an avid student of literature and reader of history, psychology, and philosophy; she is also a keen interpreter of the contemporary scene, concerned in her work with issues relevant to most modern readers. Besides feminist questions, her work has dealt with politics, migrant workers, racial conflict, academic life, girl gangs, medical and legal ethics, urban riots, and, perhaps most surprisingly, boxing. Such work is immediately accessible to students. It also allows Oates to expose her own sense of the wonder and mystery of human character and personality.

Significant Form, Style, or Artistic Conventions

Since her first novel was published in 1964, Oates has tested almost every major literary school or set of conventions: naturalism, existentialism, social realism, detective stories, epic chronicle, romance. Presenting excerpts from

Oates's novels would not only show her versatility but would also convey the way literature has an important and imposing influence on the modern writer.

While the story in this anthology unfolds chronologically and appears conventional, the more surrealistic subtext imposes itself and frustrates the fairy-tale or "happy ending" quest. The subversion of one convention by another here is not only interesting in its own right but also enforces Oates's thematic design.

Original Audience

"Where Are You Going, Where Have You Been?" is of course a contemporary story, yet it also rests on a diminishing sense of recent history. It was written for an audience who had themselves lived through the tumultuous American 1960s, with its antiwar activism, folk and rock music, and emergent "youth culture." If indeed the hippies of that time are the middle-aged establishment of today, it would be important for students to acquaint themselves with the work of Bob Dylan (the story's dedicatee) and others represented, as well as with the perilous uncertainty of those times, which would have heightened the risks of adolescent passage.

Comparisons, Contrasts, Connections

While Oates has been variously compared and contrasted with Eudora Welty, William Faulkner, John Steinbeck, and even Theodore Dreiser, one of the more interesting writers with whom she might be compared is Flannery O'Connor. (Oates even wrote a moving poem about her, following O'Connor's death.) "Where Are You Going, Where Have You Been?" can best be compared with O'Connor's "A Good Man Is Hard to Find," in which gratuitous and even mindless violence bursts through and destroys the pious confidence of O'Connor's ordinary country people. Both Oates and O'Connor emphasize the reality and presence of evil. But in O'Connor's case, the imminence of evil transforms visible reality into mere illusion. For Oates, naivete (not innocence) is dangerous in a perennially fallen but vividly real world.

Questions for Reading, Discussion, and Writing

Questions useful *before* reading the selection would concern the two "legends" that are important to the story: Dylan and Demon.

1. Why is this story dedicated to Bob Dylan?

2. Who is Arnold Friend? Do you think he is appropriately named? What is the significance of his car? His clothing? His language?
3. When and why does Connie begin to question his identity? What impact does her confusion have on her own personality? How are "personality" and "identity" displayed and defined in this story?
4. Note the complex interactions among the female characters in the story: girlfriends, siblings, and the mother-daughter relationship. In what sense is the story about a woman's "coming of age"?

Additionally, students may need more background on Dylan and the 1960s to understand Oates's view of the demonic aspect of those times in America.

In dealing with this story, students might be asked to put themselves in the place of Connie's sister or one of Connie's "real" friends, describing Friend or their perception of what has happened. The title should be discussed. Students can be asked to find the Dylan lyric that gives the story its title, play it for the class, and lead a discussion of the culture and politics of the 1960s; photographs of that time could be especially useful in picturing the look and style Friend tries to emulate. Students might write about the danger of "codes": their power to distort perception.

Another approach could be aesthetic: specifically, viewing the story not as realistic but surrealistic. Here, paintings of modern masters such as Magritte or Dali could illustrate the hauntingly familiar contours of the surrealistic imagination—another possible written assignment. Oates herself refers to an earlier surrealist, Bosch, in the title of an early novel, *A Garden of Earthly Delights*. That painting might generate a lively discussion of Oates's vision of evil.

Finally, Joyce Chopra's excellent 1985 film adaptation of the story, *Smooth Talk*, can spark an interesting discussion of how Oates's narrative is transformed cinematically.

Bibliography

Bender, Eileen T. *Joyce Carol Oates, Artist in Residence*. Bloomington: Indiana UP, 1987.

Clemons, Walter. "Joyce Carol Oates: Love and Violence." *Newsweek* 11 Dec. 1972: 72–77.

Creighton, Joanne. *Joyce Carol Oates*. Boston: Hall, 1979.

Daly, Brenda. *Lavish Self-Divisions; The Novels of Joyce Carol Oates*. Jackson: UP of Mississippi, 1996.

Friedman, Ellen. *Joyce Carol Oates.* New York: Ungar, 1970.

Johnson, Greg. *Understanding Joyce Carol Oates.* Columbia: U of South Carolina P, 1987.

Norman, Torburg. *Isolation and Contact: A Study of Character Relationships in Joyce Carol Oates's Short Stories.* Gothenburg Studies in English 57. Goteburg, Swe. 1984.

Showalter, Elaine, ed. *"Where Are You Going, Where Have You Been"/Joyce Carol Oates.* New Brunswick, NJ: Rutgers UP, 1994. Story with critical essays, introduction.

Wagner, Linda. *Critical Essays on Joyce Carol Oates.* Boston: Hall, 1979.

Ishmael Reed (b. 1938)

Contributing Editor: Michael Boccia

Classroom Issues and Strategies

Ishmael Reed frequently offends readers who feel that they and the institutions they hold sacred (the church, American history, schools, and so on) are attacked and ridiculed by him. His humorous exaggerations and sharp barbs are misunderstood partly because satire and irony are so often misunderstood. In addition, most students are ignorant of the many contributions to American culture made by blacks and other minorities. Black and minority contributions in every field are highlighted in Reed's work. Reed often lists his historical, mythical, or literary sources in the text itself and has his own version of history, politics, literature, and culture.

Pointing out that Reed is a jokester and a humorous writer often makes his work more palatable to students. Once they begin to laugh at Reed's humor, they can take a more objective look at his condemnations of society. Of course, students refuse to accept his version of history, politics, and religion. Most commonly, students want to know if Reed's version of the "truth" is really true. They challenge his veracity whenever he challenges their beliefs. This permits me to send them off to check on Reed's statements, which proves rewarding and enlightening for them.

Of course, Reed does not want readers to accept a single viewpoint; he wishes our view of reality to be multifaceted. In Reed's Neo-HooDoo Church, many "truths" are accepted. In fact, one source that is extremely helpful in understanding Reed's viewpoint is the "Neo-HooDoo Manifesto" (*Los Angeles Free Press* [18–24 Sept. 1969]: 42).

Major Themes, Historical Perspectives, Personal Issues

Reed covers the gamut of issues, writing about politics, social issues, racism, history, and just about everything else. Most of his satire is aimed at the status quo, and thus he often offends readers. It is important to remind students that he is writing satire but that there is truth to his comic attacks on the establishment. Closely related to his allusions to black artists and history are his themes. He views the counterculture as the vital force in life and hopefully predicts that the joyous side of life will triumph over the repressive side.

His radical beliefs appear as themes in his work. Knowledge of the cultures (popular, American, African, etc.) Reed draws upon is very helpful. Knowing about black history and literature is very valuable and can best be seen through Reed's eyes by reading his own commentary. *Shrovetide in Old New Orleans* is especially helpful in this area.

Reed's vision of history cries out for the recognition of minority contribution to Western civilization. Estaban (the black slave who led Cortez to the Grand Canyon), Squanto (the Native American who fed the Pilgrims), Sacajawea (the Native American woman who helped Lewis and Clark), and many other minority contributors are referred to in Reed's work, and because students are often ignorant of these contributions, some small survey of minority history is very useful.

Significant Form, Style, or Artistic Conventions

Reed's originality is rooted in his experimental forms, so introducing the traditional art forms that Reed distorts often helps readers understand his experiments. A survey of the forms of novels, journalism, television and radio programs, movies, newsreels, popular dances, and music will help students understand the fractured forms Reed offers.

The symbols Reed selects also reflect the eclectic nature of his art, in that the symbols and their meanings include but transcend traditional significance. Reed will blend symbols from ancient Egypt with rock and roll or offer the flip side of history by revealing what went on behind the veil of history as popularly reported. In all cases one will find much stimulation in the juxtaposition of Reed's symbols and contexts.

Original Audience

The students are often angry at Reed's satire of their culture. The provocation that they feel is precisely the point of Reed's slashing wit. He wants to provoke them into thinking about their culture in new ways. Pointing this out to students often alleviates their anger.

Comparisons, Contrasts, Connections

Introducing students to Swift's "A Modest Proposal" is an effective way to clarify how Reed's satire functions. Few readers think that eating babies is a serious proposal by Swift, and once satire is perceived as an exaggeration meant to stir controversy and thought, students are willing to listen to Reed's propositions.

Placing Reed in literary context is difficult because he writes in numerous genres and borrows from many nonliterary art forms. No doubt his innovations place him with writers like James Joyce and William Blake, and his satire places him among the most controversial writers of any literary period.

Certainly his use of allusion and motif is reminiscent of T. S. Eliot or James Joyce, but Reed likes to cite black writers as his models. Reed feels that the minorities have been slighted, and a review of some of the black writers he cites as inspiration is often helpful to students.

Questions for Reading, Discussion, and Writing

Students respond well to hunting down the literary, historical, and topical references in the poetry. I often ask them to select a single motif, such as Egyptian myth, and track it through a poem after researching the area.

Bibliography

I strongly recommend reading Reed on Reed: *Shrovetide in Old New Orleans*, especially "The Old Music," "Self Interview," "Remembering Josephine Baker," and "Harlem Renaissance."

For a detailed discussion of his literary and critical stances, see John O'Brien, "Ishmael Reed Interview," *The New Fiction, Interviews with Innovative American Writers,* ed. David Bellamy (Urbana: U of Illinois P, 1974), 130–41.

For a view of the Dionysian/Appollonian struggle as portrayed by Reed, see Sam Keen, "Manifesto for a Dionysian Theology," *Transcendence,* ed. Herbert W. Richardson (Boston: Beacon, 1969), 31–52.

Toni Cade Bambara (1939–1995)

Contributing Editor: Tiffany N. Hinton

Classroom Issues and Strategies

"The Lesson" is a first-person narrative containing serious social commentary, which is balanced by the humorous viewpoint of its young narrator. Although the story begins with an adult narrator recalling her youth, this adult perspective is quickly replaced by the point of view of the narrator as a young girl. Young Sylvia is a naïve narrator—one who lacks the maturity necessary for a thorough assessment of Miss Moore and the lesson she attempts to impart.

Major Themes, Historical Perspectives, and Personal Issues

"The Lesson" was written during a highly political time in American history. The civil rights sit-in movement, the black power movement, and the black arts movement are just a few examples of many organized, collective efforts to bring about fundamental social reform that shook the United States during the 1960s. During this time and the years following, one of the most striking expressions of political consciousness among many African Americans—particularly young people in urban areas—was the Afro and other natural hairstyles.

Significant Form, Style, or Artistic Conventions

Perhaps the stylistic device that will most readily draw students' attention is diction. Students should be encouraged to understand the nonstandard diction spoken by Sylvia not as "broken" or "bad" English but as a black vernacular dialect of the English language. Attention might be paid to the masterful way in which Bambara captures the rhythms and idioms of the children's speech as well as to the way in which she contrasts this language use with Miss Moore's "proper" speech.

Bambara intends this story to be as instructive for readers as for the children in Miss Moore's charge. Students could be guided to consider how Bambara's skillful use of point of view and characterization allows her to take such a strong position about social inequality without sounding preachy, overbearing, or boring.

Comparisons, Contrasts, Connections

The Bluest Eye, a novel by Toni Morrison, is also told from the narrative point of view of a young and outspoken African-American female.

Questions for Reading, Discussion, and Writing

1. How does Sylvia's use of language serve to characterize her?
2. Explain what makes Miss Moore so different from others in the neighborhood. Why do the adults put their children in Miss Moore's charge?
3. Compare your impression of Miss Moore at the end of the story with your impression of her at the story's beginning? How and or why does your impression change?
4. How would this story change if it were told from Miss Moore's point of view? From the adult Sylvia's point of view?
5. What is the lesson Miss Moore tries to teach Sylvia and her peers? Is she successful?
6. Why is Sylvia annoyed when Sugar answers Miss Moore's question correctly?
7. What might the story's last line mean? Who else might the "nobody" in this line refer to besides Sugar?

Frank Chin (b. 1940)

Contributing Editor: John Alberti

Classroom Issues and Strategies

Students may be puzzled initially by the plot structure of Chin's story. Rather than a linear, chronological narrative, the story consists of a series of reflective meditations occurring at various times in the narrator's life, often prompted by either the deaths of parents and grandparents or his own conflicted encounters with U.S. popular culture. His grandfather's railroad watch thus functions as a focal point for the story, a master symbol for the cultural conflicts explored in "Railroad Standard Time." One way into the story is for students to discuss how the symbol of the watch draws together different issues and tangents in the story.

Chin's story especially foregrounds questions of audience. Like Chin, the narrator is also an author of books about the Chinese-American experience, and the ambivalence the narrator feels toward his work relates to Chin's own critical interest in the nature and function of Chinese-American and Asian-American literature. "I hate my novel about a Chinatown mother like mine dying, now that Ma's dead," the narrator writes, "but I'll keep it." Clearly, the story invites the reader to consider why the narrator has such mixed feelings about his work, but at the same time it challenges its readers to consider their own relationships to Chinese-American experience(s) in particular and to the question, central to the enterprise of *The Heath Anthology,* of writing for/about/against a marked racial and/or ethnic identity.

Obviously, whether a reader identifies or is identified by others as Chinese or Chinese American will make for a different relationship to the issues and experiences discussed in "Railroad Standard Time," and the question of what Chin wants to communicate to readers both inside and outside the Chinese-American community can provide another entry point for class discussion of both the story and student responses to it. Chin's story also problematizes, however, the stability of "inside" and "outside" through its depiction of the complicated relationship that characters in the story have to the dominant U.S. culture, represented through their reactions to movies, cartoons, popular music, and perhaps most significantly, the English language itself.

The narrator in the story remains torn between assimilation and resistance, between embracing American culture and despising himself and others for what he sees as subservience and submission to that culture. Some students may struggle with the lack of resolution provided for this conflict, as well as what may be perceived as the narrator's negativity. The fact that Chin has turned these contradictory feelings and desires into a compelling work of art can provide one avenue for students to escape the need for a definitive answer. Students can also be encouraged to explore the implications of the narrator's often expressing his frustration and anger in terms of gender identity, sexuality, and his relationships with women. The link between a strong cultural identity and manhood has a long tradition in American multicultural history and can provide a means of critique and connection with other texts in the anthology.

Cluster: Prison Literature

Etheridge Knight (1931–1991)

Contributing Editor: Patricia Liggins-Hill

Classroom Issues and Strategies

Students often lack the knowledge of the new black aesthetic, the black oral tradition, and contemporary black poetry, in general. I lecture on major twentieth-century black poets and literary movements. In addition, I provide supplementary research articles, primarily from *BALF* (*Black American Literature Forum*) and *CLA* (*College Language Association*).

Since Knight has read his poems on various college campuses throughout the country, I use tapes of his poetry readings. I also read his poetry aloud and invite students to do likewise since his punctuation guides the reader easily through the oral poems.

Students, black and white, identify with the intense pain, loneliness, frustration, and deep sense of isolation Knight expresses in his prison poetry. They often compare their own sense of isolation, frustration, and depression as college students with his institutional experience.

Students often ask the following questions:

1. Why haven't they been previously exposed to this significant poet and to the new black aesthetic?
2. How did Knight learn to write poetry so well in prison with only an eighth-grade education?
3. What is the difference between written and transcribed oral poetry?

Major Themes, Historical Perspectives, Personal Issues

Knight's major themes are (1) liberation and (2) the black heritage. Since slavery has been a crucial reality in black history, much of Knight's poetry focuses on a modern kind of enslavement, imprisonment; his work searches for and discovers ways in which a person can be free while incarcerated. His poems are both personal and communal. As he searches for his own identity and meaning in life, he explores the past black American life experience from both its Southern and its African heritage.

Knight's poetry should be taught within the historical context of the civil rights and black revolutionary movements of the 1960s and 1970s. The social backdrop of his and other new black poets' cries against racism were the assassinations of Malcolm X, Martin Luther King Jr., and John and Robert Kennedy and also the burning of ghettos, the bombings of black schools in the South, the violent confrontations between white police and black people, and the strong sense of awareness of poverty in black communities.

What the teacher should emphasize is that—while Knight shares with Baraka, Madhubuti, Major, and the other new black poets the bond of black cultural identity (the bond of the oppressed, the bond formed by black art, etc.)—he, unlike them, emerged after serving an eight-year prison term for robbery from a second consciousness of community. This community of criminals is what Franz Fanon calls "the lumpenproletariat," "the wretched of the earth." Ironically, Knight's major contribution to the new aesthetic is derived from this second sense of consciousness which favorably reinforces his strong collective mentality and identification as a black artist. He brings his prison consciousness, in which the individual is institutionally destroyed and the self becomes merely one number among many, to the verbal structure of his transcribed oral verse.

Significant Form, Style, or Artistic Conventions

Consider the following questions:

1. What is the new black aesthetic, and what are Knight's major contributions to the arts movement?
2. What are the black oral devices in Knight's poetry, and what are his major contributions to the black oral tradition?
3. What are the universal elements in Knight's poetry?
4. In the "Idea of Ancestry" and "The Violent Space," how does Knight fuse various elements of "time and space" not only to denote his own imprisonment but also to connote the present social conditions of black people in general?
5. How does Knight develop his black communal art forms in his later poems "Blues for a Mississippi Black Boy" and "Ilu, the Talking Drum"?
6. What are the major influences on Knight's poetry? (Discuss the influences of Walt Whitman, Langston Hughes, and Sterling Brown.)
7. How does Knight's earlier poetry differ from his later poems? (Discuss in terms of the poet's voice, tone, and techniques, e.g., oral devices, imagery.)

Original Audience

Knight addresses black people in particular, and a mixed audience in general. He uses a variety of communal art forms and techniques such as blues idioms and jazz and African pulse structures as well as clusters of communal images that link the poet and his experience directly to his reader/audience. For the latter, the teacher should use examples of images from "The Idea of Ancestry" and "The Bones of My Father" (if this poem is available).

Comparisons, Contrasts, Connections

Langston Hughes, Sterling Brown, and Walt Whitman are the major influences on Knight's poetry. Knight's "The Idea of Ancestry" flows in a Whitmanesque style, and his "Blues for a Mississippi Black Boy" stems from the transcribed oral blues poetic tradition of Hughes and Brown. He has indicated these influences in "An Interview with Etheridge Knight" by Patricia L. Hill (*San Francisco Review of Books* 3.9 [1978]: 10).

Questions for Reading, Discussion, and Writing

1. (a) How does Knight's poetry differ in content, form, and style from that of the earlier oral poets Hughes and Brown? How is his poetry similar to theirs?
   (b) How does Knight's poetry differ in content, form, and style from that of Baraka, Madhubuti, and the other major new black aesthetic poets? How is his poetry similar to theirs?
2. (a) The Western "Art for Art's Sake" aesthetic principle versus the new black aesthetic
   (b) The importance of Knight's prison "lumpenproletariat" consciousness to the new black aesthetic
   (c) The major poetic influences on Knight's poetry
   (d) The written and oral poetry elements in Knight's poetry
   (e) Whitman's versus Knight's vision of America
   (f) Knight's open and closed forms of poetry

Bibliography

Nketia, J. H. Kwalena. *The Music of Africa*. New York: Norton, 1974.

Jimmy Santiago Baca (b. 1952)

Contributing Editor: Bell Gale Chevigny

Classroom Issues and Strategies

For students unfamiliar with prison writing, the work of Jimmy Santiago Baca is doubly important; there is his own outstanding work and his commitment to the prison population, which is at least seven times larger nationwide than it was when he was incarcerated. As Baca notes, more writers are held incommunicado in U.S. prisons than ever before, and Baca is committed to speaking for them. It is helpful to read his work in connection with other prison writers in this anthology and in the anthologies edited by Chevigny and Franklin listed later. For further information on the use of poetry in healing circles and men's support groups in prison, contact the Inside Circle Foundation at <http://www.insidecircle.org>. The program is directed by Rob Allbee, "that guy in Sacramento" in "Ghost Reading in Sacramento."

Students unfamiliar with Chicano culture should be offered some background. Baca describes his first encounter with a book about Chicanos, which affirmed his life's and his people's validity as nothing else had done. "Coming into Language" from *Working in the Dark* (and excerpted in *Doing Time: 25 Years of Prison Writing*), provides a superb point of departure for understanding his passion for language, for his people, and for human growth and love.

Baca's wide-ranging work is integrated by what Denise Levertov identified as "an intense lyricism and that transformative vision which perceives the mythic and archetypal significance of life-events." His moods are many and volatile. Hence the more examples of his work students can experience, the better they will understand its profound unity. All these selections are from *Set This Book on Fire,* a limited edition (and many of these have reappeared in the more available *Healing Earthquakes*), but for Baca's more humorous work; his love poems; his celebrations of the barrio, of Chicano lives, and of nature, one should go beyond this collection.

Recordings of Baca's readings are an unusually powerful resource. A champion in poetry slams, Baca is an extraordinary performer of his own work, which ranges from tender and meditative to volcanic and euphoric. His 1993 film, *Bound by Honor* (a.k.a. *Blood In, Blood Out*), provides a good introduction to Baca's complex sensibility and to the prison experience.

Major Themes, Historical Perspectives, Personal Issues

The power of literacy for freeing the spirits of oppressed people has a deep and wide tradition in the United States. Think of Frederick Douglass overhearing his master reproving his wife for teaching Douglass to read, inadvertently showing Douglass that reading was the path to freedom. Consider how Malcolm X's vision and mission were transformed by his taking up books in prison.

In a recent interview with Elizabeth Farnsworth, Baca said he finds God's blessings in what is broken, crumbling, decomposing: "Blessings in the rot, in the dark matter that is breaking apart like a fractured wall, bricks falling to the ground because life wants opened fields, not separation—everything integrating into one black mass of decreation and creation—birthing and dying. In the wound is freedom . . . walls that fall are where life feasts on miracles or where God lives." Many of his themes are implicit here: the coexistence of beauty and loss, pain and joy, death and recreation; the healing capacity of earthquakes.

Drawing on his own experience as a Chicano, Baca contrasts the raw loveliness of barrio life with the experience of degradation and invisibility when Chicanos enter the Anglo world. Chicano life is shrouded in many kinds of darkness, but in darkness strength too may be found. "Working in the dark" is a rich and bottomless theme for Baca. It refers chiefly to his own intuitive process; he pays "very close attention to the intuitive voice that travels through the canyons of the bone." But it also signifies the ways that those dispossessed by society function outside its boundaries, when night falls and they enter "the culture of night where our daily selves are transformed."

Significant Form, Style, or Artistic Conventions

Baca favors a direct, spontaneous, and personal style in prose and verse. But he is also irrepressibly, volcanically metaphoric—he gravitates toward paired oppositions: "lightning crackles of elation and thunderhead storms of grief." His best work is energetic; his images are breathtaking, surprising; and the most brutal realism is shot through with his signature sweetness and compassion. He knows everything about being tough, including toughness' secret vulnerability and hunger for love.

Original Audience

Baca writes in "Coming into Language" that he first heard Pablo Neruda and Octavio Paz read aloud by inmates in a holding facility. And his first audience for his own work was in prison.

Comparisons, Contrasts, Connections

Like Etheridge Knight, who wrote, "I died in 1960 from a prison sentence and poetry brought me back to life," Baca found himself and the value of life through writing in prison. Knight learned in prison his bond with the wretched of the earth. Baca writes in *A Place to Stand*, "Feeling inferior in a white world, alien and ashamed, I longed for another place to [live], outside of society. By the time I arrived at Florence [Prison], a part of me felt I belonged there." As Knight explored his black heritage, so is the Chicano cultural heritage central to Baca's work.

Compare Jimmy Santiago Baca's collecting of miraculous memories in "Ghost Reading in Sacramento" with Kathy Boudin's collection of memories in her three poems and compare his mental travel in "I Put on My Jacket" with hers in her poems. Consider how the habit of linking disparate events may deepen in prison.

Baca may be seen as a Southwestern indigenous Whitman (minus Whitman's imperialist strain) with his exuberant hyperboles, his deep empathies for lives lived unseen, his capacities for cosmic elation, and his ability to lose himself in something as humble and grand as a blade of grass. In his laments and protests, he evokes Allen Ginsberg, if Ginsberg were barrio-bred.

Questions for Reading, Discussion, and Writing

1. In "I've Taken Risks," how does Baca's portrayal of himself striding in six layers of choir robes set the tone for the poem? What does the imagery of the ace and the joker say about the role of chance in the life of these young boys? What does the poet find beautiful in the arrested boys? Why don't the boys want second chances?

2. In the short poem "I Put on My Jacket," three different settings are invoked: mesa, the remote Half-Moon Bay, and isolation cells. What ties them together? How do the words *softer and meaner* control the poem's feeling? What do they suggest about the poet's history? Why do fugitives, prisoners, gypsies, and outlaws have a privileged understanding of "indecipherable messages"? What is it?

3. "Commitment" describes two laborious projects: what is this commitment for? The poet tells us he learns a lesson from the second project; does he also learn one from the first? What do these apprenticeships have to do with making poems?

4. In "Ghost Reading in Sacramento" what does the comparison to a rosebud "on the verge of breaking free" tell you about the ghost? What is the poet trying to say about miracles? Is the sailor who feels "that the world is too

large for him to see it all" a failure, or has he new wisdom? In the introductory note to this section, "that guy in Sacramento" is explained: what kind of thinking is drawn out of our eyes? How does the final line define the ghost?

Bibliography

Chevigny, Bell Gale. *Doing Time: 25 Years of Prison Writing: A PEN American Center Prize Anthology.* New York: Arcade, 2000.

Farnsworth, Elizabeth. Interview with Jimmy Santiago Baca. *Online Newshour* 9 Aug. 2001 <http://www.pbs.org/newshour/conversation/july-dec 01/baca_8-09.html>.

Franklin, H. Bruce. *Prison Writing in 20th-Century America.* New York: Penguin, 1998.

Keene, John. "Poetry is what we speak to each other." Interview with Jimmy Santiago Baca. *Callaloo* 17.1 (Winter 1994).

Kathy Boudin (b. 1943)

Contributing Editor: Bell Gale Chevigny

Classroom Issues and Strategies

It may be useful to discuss the fact that, with more than two million prisoners, the United States is now the world's largest jailer, confining one-quarter of the prisoners in the world (the general population of the United States is only one twenty-fifth of the world's population.) Because the prison population constitutes a significant minority group—a nation hidden in our midst—students should take an interest in writing about this significant experience from which most of us are locked out.

Women's experiences behind bars are even less known than men's; the female population in prison stands at around 7 percent. As Boudin and Smith write in "Alive Behind the Labels" about Bedford Hills: "There are no big-time gangsters here, no serial killers, no Godmothers running drug empires, no Enron or WorldCom executives. A typical woman entering prison has at least two kids, most likely a drug-abuse problem, and is herself probably a product of welfare or workfare." (This essay in *Sisterhood is Forever* is the best introduction I know to women in prison.) Women now constitute the fastest-growing segment of the inmate population as a consequence of the mandatory minimum drug laws. A vast majority of women prisoners are mothers, and most were their children's primary caregivers. The number of children who have one or more parents in prison was estimated recently at 2 million.

As the vast majority of prisoners are eventually released, it can be argued that to be "tough on crime" is to break the cycle of recidivism by helping them become whole emotionally and to educate them to be useful, tax-paying citizens. In her desire to make reparations to society, Kathy Boudin participated in programs that would help her and her fellow prisoners develop resources to take responsibility for their pasts and their futures. The three poems selected here all concern mother-child relations. It is interesting to know that the two about her son were written while she was developing programs for Parenting from a Distance and Parenting Adolescents.

A few students may question the value of reading work by people who have committed crimes. This question is central to the self-examination by women prisoners in the poem, "What I Want My Words To Do To You." It may also help to quote Sister Helen Prejean (*Dead Man Walking*), who argued that every human being is more than the worse thing he or she ever did. Literature students might profitably consider how in Hawthorne's *Scarlet Letter* Hester Prynne was no more to the Puritans than the letter *A* for "Adulteress" that she was made to wear on her breast until her good deeds made some come to believe that the *A* stood for "Able." However, Hawthorne always presented her as a full and complex human being.

Other poems by Boudin and by other women in prison are worth teaching; both can be found in anthologies edited by Jones, Chevigny, and Franklin. At the end of the discussion of writing from prison, students may ask why they have not been required to read more of this powerful literature, and why, given its worth and the large subculture it represents, it is not considered an essential element in multicultural studies.

Major Themes, Historical Perspectives, Personal Issues

Students in the twenty-first century need help understanding what the 1960s were like for a dedicated radical. Going to college in 1960, Boudin was influenced by the student movement, the civil rights movement, the black power movement, the antiwar movement, and the women's movement (more or less in that order) within her first decade after high school. Anti-imperialism and the struggle for prisoners' rights also drew her. The ferment, cross-fertilization, and sheer excitement of that period are difficult for some to imagine today. The recent documentary film about the Weathermen gives a reasonably fair taste of the temper of the times as Boudin experienced them. Jane Lazarre's "Conversations with Kathy Boudin" gives a searching and nuanced account of Boudin in 1984.

Significant Form, Style, or Artistic Conventions

In her Bedford Hills workshop, Hettie Jones encouraged an open form and a direct, conversational style. Boudin often uses narrative in her poems.

Original Audience

Boudin's writing was born first of her need, as she once put it, to hang on to the self, "to keep it from being shattered, to keep it from being ground under." Hettie Jones and the several women in her Bedford Hills creative writing workshop then helped her shape her craft. For a firsthand experience of those women reading, students should see the videocassette *Aliens at the Border*, which features the Bedford Hills poets reading from their book, *Aliens at the Border*. Later, working with Eve Ensler and another group of inmates, Boudin wrote materials that were read by actresses at benefits for the Bedford Hills college project. Those workshops can be experienced in the film, *What I Want My Words To Do To You*.

Comparisons, Contrasts, Connections

Compare Etheridge Knight's preoccupation with family in "The Idea of Ancestry" with Boudin's in these three poems.

Compare Boudin's poems about her tenuous but precious connections with her son with Judee Norton's story, "Norton 59900," about her son's visit. Note the many subtle ways in which both women must suppress the fullness of their feelings. Consider the multiple worlds, inner and outer, that these mothers must negotiate to parent from a distance.

Compare Jimmy Santiago Baca's collecting of miraculous memories in "Ghost Reading in Sacramento" with Boudin's collection of memories in her three poems.

Questions for Reading, Discussion, and Writing

1. "Our Skirt": How much of the mother-child relation is·encapsulated in the garment? How is the skirt made to transcend time and space?

2. "The Call": The conversation on the mother's side is minimal. The poet says, "My son has taken my voice." What are the many things this may mean? How does the statement relate to the two settings, prison and the boy's room? What is the actual space of "The Call"—and what has it to do with the space that each mother must grant a child. What do the boy's "treasures" reveal?
3. "Trilogy of Journeys": three (or four) different journeys are described. What are they?

Bibliography

Chevigny, Bell Gale. *Doing Time: 25 Years of Prison Writing: A PEN American Center Prize Anthology.* New York: Arcade, 2000.

Franklin, H. Bruce. *Prison Writing in 20th-Century America.* New York: Penguin, 1998.

Lazarre, Jane. "A Conversation with Kathy Boudin." *Village Voice* 14 Feb. 1984.

Leonard Peltier (b. 1944)

Teaching material for Leonard Peltier is available on *The Heath Anthology of American Literature* website. To access the site, please go to the Houghton Mifflin college homepage at <http://www.college.hmco.com>. Select *English;* then select *The Heath Anthology* textbook site.

Judee Norton (b. 1949)

Contributing Editor: Judith Scheffler

Classroom Issues and Strategies

Reading prison literature is likely to be an eye-opening and possibly unsettling experience for many students, especially when they read works by authors from the general prison population who were not imprisoned for reasons of conscience or political views. Most students are accustomed to reading about authors' unconventional and nonconformist lifestyles, but literature dealing with imprisonment has the potential to raise questions of values, justice, and social responsibility, questions which students may not have considered. Modern selections in particular may be disturbing since readers cannot dismiss raw details of prison life as relics from a less-enlightened past.

Students may need to confront stereotypes and assumptions that they bring to the reading of prison literature and reevaluate their expectations about the writer's literacy and decency and the value of reading what she has to say. It may help to prepare students by confronting those expectations. Instructors may acquaint students with current statistics about the increasing rates of incarceration in the United States and the fact that women, although still a minority of the prison population, are being imprisoned at a rate that is growing faster than the rate for men.

Students may find it uncomfortable to read a story about the thoughts and feelings of a woman prisoner, especially those of an imprisoned mother, because it may shatter preconceptions about appropriate female and maternal behavior. They may find Norton's story particularly affecting because the prisoner's son is a "rebellious" teenager with whose feelings they may identify on some level. It may, in fact, help to begin with their responses to the son's behavior and then discuss in what ways he is like his imprisoned mother in his response to authority. Discussion could then proceed to consideration of the purpose of prison rules and the extent to which those rules are necessary means to maintain discipline or are potential instruments of sadistic punishment.

Major Themes, Historical Perspectives, Personal Issues

The following are some major themes found in Norton's stories:

- The strength of the mother-child connection and its ability to overcome the stresses of imprisonment.
- The steadfast assertion of personal identity despite authority's attempt to reduce the prisoner to a number. The prisoner's moral triumph over the tyranny of rule books and prison codes when they are used to demean and dehumanize.
- The pain caused to the prisoner by the necessity to protect herself and hide her feelings from other inmates.
- The absurdity of the prison's institutional environment.
- Ethical questions of how to identify truth and goodness in prison. Who inflicts more harm—prisoners or those who guard them?

Significant Form, Style, or Artistic Conventions

Norton chooses to write about her prison experiences by using autobiographical fiction. "Norton #59900" is one story in a larger work in progress entitled "Slick," which Norton describes as "an account of my experiences in prison, along with some often stark revelations about why and how I came to be there."

Fiction is not, however, the primary genre chosen by most women who write about their imprisonment. Historically, women prisoners have chosen forms of life-writing to describe their experience of imprisonment. Since the 1970s, women prisoners have increasingly chosen to write poetry—and fiction, to a lesser extent. Many of these women have been encouraged in their creative writing by participation in prison writing workshops, which are often sponsored by universities, sometimes for academic credit. Norton, however, has done much of her writing on the outside since her release from prison in 1992.

Original Audience

"Norton #59900" received the PEN American Center Prison Writing Award in short fiction for 1991. This is a prestigious annual competition sponsored by the PEN American Center to showcase and recognize the best writing done by men and women incarcerated in prisons in the United States. Norton has received this award for this story as well as for her poem "Arrival"(1990) (see Bibliography below). "Norton #59900" was selected by Bell Gale Chevigny for inclusion in *Doing Time: 25 Years of Prison Writing: A PEN American Center Prize Anthology* (1999), which honors the best of the best prison writing. Norton's work is therefore among the works read by the increasingly large audience interested in prison literature.

"Norton #59900" was also included in the 2000 Feminist Press anthology *Bearing Life: Women's Writings on Childlessness*, edited by Rochelle Ratner. In this context, it caught the attention of readers from an angle totally unrelated to prison issues because of its inclusion in a collection of works focusing on maternal issues.

Comparisons, Contrasts, Connections

Judee Norton's stories may be read on their own, apart from works written by other prisoners, but students will appreciate her creativity more by reading her story in the context of other prison writing, both contemporary and historical. Her work bears one of the distinguishing marks of writing by women prisoners in its focus upon family and children. While male prisoners, too, write of their concerns about separation from family, this theme is a hallmark of works across the centuries of women's prison writing. It is, moreover, a theme found internationally, uniting writing by imprisoned women throughout the world.

Students may be introduced to the concept that prison literature constitutes a literary tradition in its own right, deserving of respect and attention by serious readers.

Questions for Reading, Discussion, and Writing

1. What are the similarities and differences between prison writing by men and that written by women, as suggested by "Norton #59900"?
2. In what ways were you surprised by the responses, thoughts, or actions of the narrator of the story?
3. What strategies does Norton use to draw her reader into the story and help the reader identify with her situation?
4. Why do you think the narrator does not seek comfort and support from the other women prisoners?
5. Why do you think Norton uses her prison number for the title of this story?

Bibliography

Primary works

Norton, Judee. "Arrival." *Doing Time: 25 Years of Prison Writing: A PEN American Center Prize Anthology.* Ed. Bell Gale Chevigny. New York: Arcade, 1999. 22–23. Poem.

———. "Gerta's Story." *Wall Tappings: An International Anthology of Women's Prison Writings 200 to the Present.* Ed. Judith Scheffler. 2nd ed. New York: Feminist, 2002. 163–69. Short story.

———. "Slick and the Beanstalk." *Wall Tappings: An International Anthology of Women's Prison Writings 200 to the Present.* Ed. Judith Scheffler. 2nd ed. New York: Feminist, 2002. 169–74. Short story.

James Welch (Blackfeet-Gros Ventre) (b. 1940)

Contributing Editor: Linda Wagner-Martin

Classroom Issues and Strategies

Welch's fiction is immediately accessible. Students find it powerful. They shirk from its relentlessly depressing impact, but Welch has written *Winter in the Blood, The Death of Jim Loney,* and much of his poetry to create that impact. His writing is protest literature, so skillfully achieved that it seems apolitical.

Sometimes hostile to the completely new, students today seem to be willing to rely on canon choices. Once Welch is placed for them, they respond with empathy to his fiction.

The general setting of the culture, the hardships generations of Native Americans have learned to live with, and the socioeconomic issues make deciphering characters' attitudes easier. The strengths of the Indian culture need to be described as well because students in many parts of the country are unfamiliar with customs, imagery, and attitudes that are necessary in reading this excerpt.

Welch's precision and control must be discussed. Students must see how they are in his power throughout this excerpt. Further, they must want to read not only this novel but the others as well.

Major Themes, Historical Perspectives, Personal Issues

It is also good to emphasize the choice of art as profession. For Welch, giving voice to frustration has created memorable fiction and poetry. His most recent novels, *Fools Crow* and *Indian Lawyer,* do much more than depict the alienation of the contemporary Native American man—but to do so, he draws on nineteenth-century history as the basis of his plot in *Fools* and a different stratum of culture for *Lawyer.*

Significant Form, Style, or Artistic Conventions

Questions of realism and how realistic writing is achieved: characterization, language, situation, emphasis on dialogue rather than interior monologue.

Questions of appropriateness: What is believable about the fiction, and how has Welch created that intensity that is so believable? Why is a plot like this more germane to the lives Welch describes than an adventurous, action-filled narrative would have been?

Original Audience

The issue of political literature (which will occur often in selections from the contemporary section) will need attention. How can Welch create a sympathetic hero without portraying the poverty and disillusion of a culture? How can he achieve this accuracy without maligning Native Americans?

Comparisons, Contrasts, Connections

Ernest Hemingway and Richard Wright are obvious choices for comparison, but the differences are important as well. Wright relied in many cases on dialect, with language spelled as words might have been pronounced, and Hemingway used carefully stylized language in his quantities of dialogue so that identifying characters by place or education was sometimes difficult. Welch creates a dialect that is carefully mannered, as if the insecure speaker had modeled his language, like his life, on the middle-class TV image of a person and a family.

Bharati Mukherjee (b. 1940)

Contributing Editor: Roshni Rustomji-Kerns

Classroom Issues and Strategies

It is important to read and discuss Mukherjee's "A Wife's Story" as an integral part of twentieth-century American literature and not as an "exotic" short story by a foreign writer. As the essay accompanying "A Wife's Story" points out, Mukherjee identifies herself very strongly as an American writer writing about twentieth-century Americans. Although most of her stories are about South Asian Americans (South Asia in the contemporary geopolitical arena usually consists of Bangladesh, India, Pakistan, Sri Lanka, and the Maldive Islands), she sees herself as being primarily influenced by, as well as being part of, the tradition of Euro-American writers. In a brief interview published in the November 1993 issue of *San Francisco Focus* in which she discusses her novel *The Holder of the World*, she says, "I think of myself as an American writer . . . I want to focus on the making of the American mind." But instead of an exploration of the making of the American mind, *The Holder of the World* is a reflection and an echoing of the existing dominant American attitudes and concepts about the American colonial period and the "exotic" India of the past with self-indulgent emperors and rajas, wealthy merchants, and self-sacrificing women.

In order to avoid the trap of reading "A Wife's Story" as being from a "marginal" group, I have found it best to first discuss the crafting of the story as a literary work in the tradition of English/American literature, and then move on to the aspects of the story that deal with specific concepts and cultures.

Keeping in mind Mukherjee's own comments on racism, multiculturalism, and literary influences, it is interesting to discuss how she uses, or does not use, her ideas on these subjects in "A Wife's Story." A classroom discussion on the students' views regarding these concepts helps them understand the importance of these concepts in American literature.

Questions for Reading, Discussion, and Writing

I have found the following assignments/approaches helpful:

1. Discuss the story as a literary work.
2. Read stories and poems by other American writers who deal with the American expatriate/immigrant experience and compare/contrast "A Wife's Story" with the other readings. The bibliography that follows includes some collections of immigrant/expatriate writings.
3. Gain some knowledge of the history of Asian Americans, especially within the context of the different patterns of immigration in the United States.
4. I have sometimes asked students to interview expatriates or immigrants from South Asia on the campus or in their community and see how Mukherjee's story and her distinctive literary style differ from, expand upon, imitate, or use the style and subject matter of the oral history/interviews conducted by the students. This is often a suitable time to discuss, compare, and contrast the styles and techniques of oral and written literature.
5. I have sometimes invited South Asian women from the community to speak to us of their experiences in the United States with an emphasis on how they would communicate their experiences to a larger audience. For example, we ask the guest speakers about the kinds of stories they would like to write for a book or for a TV show that deals with South Asian Americans.
6. Interestingly, after having read the works of South Asian–American writers, many students have explored the immigrant histories of their own families and have then written stories, poems, essays, and screen/TV scripts based on their projects.

Further discussions of the story, especially on specific issues related to Mukherjee's major themes and the literary influences that emerge out of her root culture, may be based on the statements made in the following parts of this Instructor's Guide essay.

Major Themes, Historical Perspectives, Personal Issues

Mukherjee's earlier works dealt mainly with encounters between cultures that take place when her South Asian–American protagonists who live in Canada or the United States return as visitors to their home in India (*Tiger's Daughter* and *Days and Nights in Calcutta*). Her later, and maybe more important works, deal with these encounters as they take place in America. The protagonists in her later works are not all from South Asia, but nearly all of them are people who have arrived in America during this century.

Her 1993 novel, *The Holder of the World*, takes place in the United States as well as in India. It also takes place across historical time. The framework of the novel takes place in contemporary United States and India. The central story takes place in seventeenth-century America and India. The Euro-American woman protagonists of this work have lovers who are from other cultures or countries.

Her 1997 novel, *Leave It to Me*, takes the reader from Asia to the United States, from the San Francisco of the 1960s to the San Francisco of the 1990s. It is a fiercely independent novel which shows Mukherjee's grasp of the landscapes and cultures of the late-twentieth-century "globalization" of California and Asia.

A significant number of her stories and novels present the encounters between cultures in the context of encounters between women and men either of different root cultures or from the same root culture. Some of these very personal encounters have the poignancy of underlying affection, some of them range from gentle humor to an attempt at broad satire, and some are marred by stereotypical characters and events while others reveal the dangerous, violent side of such encounters.

"A Wife's Story" is an excellent example of encounters between cultures presented in a narrative of encounters between women and men. It is a fascinating story because it presents the surprise of role reversal and because of the sense of a dramatic presentation that permeates the story. It is the wife, not the husband, who has come to America and who is knowledgeable about this new home. Panna is the guide and often the protector for her husband, who is visiting her. And her story is constantly dramatic. It begins with her in a theatre, and every episode that follows is carefully situated in a stage-like setting with set actors.

The story also contains echoes of the memory and nostalgia for the past that plays a significant role in the writings of many South Asian Americans. This memory and nostalgia for the landscape of places and people of the writers' childhood is often juxtaposed with the excitement and challenges of their new life and the unfamiliar landscape of the people and places of the United States. It is interesting to explore how Mukherjee uses these two strands in this story, bringing one or the other—memory or the excitement of novelty—into the foreground to present her characters and to build the circular, winding pattern of her story.

Significant Form, Style, or Artistic Conventions

Much as Mukherjee seems to insist that she belongs to the Euro-American traditions of American literature and as easily as she is able to be fit into that tradition, there are aspects of her work that are derived mainly from her cultural roots in India. She has spoken of the important influences in her life of the images and ideas of her childhood in India and the sounds and sights of the great traditions of Indian mythology and literature. Her awareness of these influences enriches her stories and novels. For example, she can give the impression of a larger work even in a short story such as "A Wife's Story," which carefully meanders from one place to another and in which stories live within other stories. This technique of winding stories and embedding stories within stories dominates the Sanskrit epics, the *Mahabharata* and the *Ramayana,* and much of Indian literature.

Her ability to let us hear her characters speak to us not only about themselves but as narrators of others' experiences is a reflection of the oral traditions of Indian literature. In "A Wife's Story," we can hear Panna telling us not only the many stories of her life in India and in New York but also the stories of the people she introduces to us.

Bharati Mukherjee is an enthusiastic and extremely knowledgeable collector of Indian miniatures. Keeping in mind this interest in miniatures, we see that Mukherjee can also paint small-scale yet detailed episodes and characters.

Mukherjee's careful manipulation of moods and emotional tones in her stories may be influenced by classical Indian literature, art, and music. In Indian classical art, the universally recognizable essence of an emotion or a mood often dominates the work of art. In "A Wife's Story," Mukherjee portrays Panna through her emotions and moods that move from anger and outrage to perplexity and frustration, to humor and affection, and in the end to the joy of self-discovery of her body and her sense of freedom. Even the memory of old customs and the excitement of new discoveries for both Panna and her husband are presented in terms of emotions and moods.

Bibliography

Collections that contain South Asian–American writings

Asian Women United of California, eds. *Making Waves: An Anthology of Writings by and about Asian American Women.* 1989.

Aziz, Nurjehan, ed. *Her Mother's Ashes and Other Stories.* Toronto: Tsar, 1994, 1999.

Gillan, M. M., and J. Gillan, eds. *Growing Up Ethnic in America.* New York: Penguin, 1999.

Katrak, Ketu H., and R. Radhakrishna, eds. *Desh-Videsh: South Asian Expatriate Writing and Art.* Special issue of *The Massachusetts Review* 29.4 (Winter 1988–1989).

Maira, Sunaina, and Rajini Srikant, eds. *Contours of the Heart: South Asians Map North America.* New Jersey: Rutgers UP, 1997.

A Meeting of Streams: South Asian Canadian Literature. Toronto: South Asia Review, 1985.

Mukherjee, Bharati, and Ranu Vanikar, eds. *The Literary Review: Writers of the Indian Commonwealth* 29.4 (Summer 1986).

Rustomji, Roshni, ed. *The Immigrant Experience.* Special issue of *Journal of South Asian Literature: South Asian Women Writers.* 21.2 (Winter–Spring 1986).

Rustomji-Kerns, ed. *Living in America: Poetry and Fiction by South Asian American Writers.* Boulder: Westview, 1995.

Women of South Asian Descent Collective. *Our Feet Walk the Sky: Women of the South Asian Diaspora.* San Francisco: Aunt Lute, 1993.

South Asians in America

Agarwal, Priya. *Passage from India: Post-1965 Immigrants and Their Children.* Palo Verdes: Yutavi, 1991.

Bahri, Deepika, and Mary Vasudeva, eds. *Between the Lines: South Asians and Postcoloniality.* Philadelphia: Temple UP, 1996.

Fisher, Maxine P. *Indians of New York City.* Asia Book Corp of America, 1980.

Jensen, Joan M. *Passage from India: Asian Indian Immigrants in North America.* New Haven: Yale UP, 1988.

Saran, Parmatma. *The Asian Indian Experience in the United States.* Cambridge: Schenkman, 1985.

Singh, Jane. *South Asians in America: An Annotated and Selected Biography.* 1988.

Takaki, Ronald. *A Different Mirror: A History of Multicultural America.* Boston: Back Bay, 1994.

———. *Strangers from a Different Shore: A History of Asian Americans.* Boston: Back Bay, 1998.

Anthologies of cross-cultural and multicultural writings

Brown, Wesley, and Amy Ling, eds. *Imagining America: Stories from the Promised Land.* New York: Persea, 1991.

Divakaruni, Chitra B. *Multitude: Cross-Cultural Readings for Writers.* New York: McGraw-Hill, 1993.

Hongo, Garrett. *The Open Boat: Poems from Asian America.* New York: Anchor, 1993.

Rustomji-Kerns, Rashni, with Rajini Srikanth and Lenny Strobel. *Encounters: People of Asian Descent in the Americas.* Chicago: Rowman & Littlefield, 1999.

Shankar, Lavina D., and Rajini Srikanth, eds. *A Part, Yet Apart: South Asians in Asian America.* Philadelphia: Temple UP, 1998.

Verburg, Carol J. *Ourselves among Others: Cross-Cultural Readings for Writers.* New York: Bedford, 1991.

Watanabe, Sylvia, and Carol Bruchac. *Home to Stay: Asian American Women's Fiction.* Greenfield Center: Greenfield Rev. P., 1990.

Maxine Hong Kingston (b. 1940)

Contributing Editors: Amy Ling and King-Kok Cheung

Classroom Issues and Strategies

The primary question for any initial reading of Kingston's *The Woman Warrior* has to do with genre or form. Is this text nonfiction? (It won the National Book Critics Circle Award for the best book of nonfiction published in 1976.) Since the word *memoirs* is in the title, is it autobiography, or is it a piece of imaginative fiction. *The Woman Warrior*, of course, is all of the above, sequentially and simultaneously.

Major Themes, Historical Perspectives, Personal Issues

Since her mother's talking-story was one of the major forces of her childhood and since she herself is now talking-story in writing this book, stories, factual and fictional, are an inherent part of Kingston's autobiography. Finding one's voice in order to talk-story, a metaphor for knowing oneself in order to attain the fullness of one's power, becomes one of the book's major themes.

"No Name Woman" tells the story of the paternal aunt who bears a child out of wedlock and is harried by the villagers and by her family into drowning herself; the family now punishes this taboo-breaker by never speaking of her, by denying her her name. The author, however, breaks the family silence by writing about this rebel whom she calls "my forebear."

Significant Form, Style, or Artistic Conventions

One of the distinctive accomplishments of *The Woman Warrior* is that it crosses boundaries among genres, dictions, styles, between fact and fiction, as it crosses the boundaries between cultures, Chinese and American. In the collage of style and form, in the amalgam of language and content, in the combination of Chinese myth, family history, and American individualism and rebelliousness, Kingston defines herself as a Chinese-American woman.

Original Audience

The Woman Warrior is decidedly a product of the sixties, of the civil rights and women's liberation movements. It directly addresses Chinese Americans, whom it seeks to bring into its exploration of identity, but, as an immigrant story for a nation of immigrants, it is obviously intended as well for a mainstream audience.

Questions for Reading, Discussion, and Writing

Which aspects of Kingston's childhood experience is true of all immigrants in the United States? What is particular to Chinese Americans?

Bibliography

Cheung, King-Kok. *Articulate Silences: Hisaye Yamamoto, Maxine Hong Kingston, Joy Kogawa.* Ithaca, NY: Cornell UP, 1993.

———. "'Don't Tell': Imposed Silences in *The Color Purple* and *The Woman Warrior.*" *PMLA* (Mar. 1988): 162–74.

———. "The Woman Warrior versus The Chinaman Pacific: Must a Chinese American Critic Choose between Feminism and Heroism?" *Conflicts in Feminism.* Ed. Marianne Hirsch and Evelyn Fox Keller. New York: Routledge, 1990. 234–51.

Hunt, Linda. "'I Could Not Figure Out What Was My Village': Gender vs. Ethnicity in Maxine Hong Kingston's *The Woman Warrior.*" *MELUS* 12.3 (1985): 5–12.

Kingston, Maxine Hong. "Cultural Mis-readings by American Reviewers." *Asian and Western Writers in Dialogue: New Cultural Identities.* Ed. Guy Amirthanayagam. London: Macmillan, 1982. 55–65.

Lee, Rachel C. "Claiming Land, Claiming Voice, Claiming Canon: Institutionalized Challenges in Kingston's *China Men* and *The Woman Warrior.*" *ReViewing Asian America: Locating Diversity.* Ed. Wendy Ng et al. Pullman: Washington State UP, 1995. 147–59.

Li, David L. "The Naming of a Chinese American 'I': Cross-Cultural Sign/ification in *The Woman Warrior.*" *Criticism* 30.4 (1988): 497–515.

Lim, Shirley G., ed. *Approaches to Teaching Kingston's* The Woman Warrior. New York: MLA, 1991.

Ling, Amy. "Maxine Hong Kingston and the Dialogic Dilemma of Asian American Writers." *Having Our Way: Women Rewriting Tradition in Twentieth-Century America.* Ed. Harriet Pollack. Lewisburg, PA: Bucknell UP, 1995.

Rabine, Leslie W. "No Lost Paradise: Social Gender and Symbolic Gender in the Writings of Maxine Hong Kingston." *Signs* 12 (1987): 471–92.

Schueller, Malini. "Questioning Race and Gender Definitions: Dialogic Subversions in *The Woman Warrior.*" *Criticism* 31.4 (1989): 421–37.

Wong, Sau-ling C. "Ethnic Dimensions of Postmodern Indeterminacy: Maxine Hong Kingston's *The Woman Warrior* as Avant-garde Autobiography." *Autobiographie and Avant-garde.* Ed. Alfred Hornung and Ernstpeter Ruhe. Tübingen: Gunter Narr Verlag, 1992. 273–84.

——. "Necessity and Extravagance in Maxine Hong Kingston's *The Woman Warrior:* Art and the Ethnic Experience." *MELUS* 15.1 (1988): 3–26.

——. *Reading Asian American Literature: From Necessity to Extravagance.* Princeton, NJ: Princeton UP, 1993.

Bobbie Ann Mason (b. 1940)

Contributing Editor: D. Quentin Miller

Classroom Issues and Strategies

Mason's critics have used pejorative terms like "Diet Pepsi minimalism" and "K-Mart realism" to describe her work. Class prejudice might reveal itself in students' responses to this story, too, partially because the story is relatively contemporary: some students want to believe that rural poverty is a thing of the past. You might do well to ask students where they have encountered characters like those in this story before; then ask them to explore issues of how the author presents her characters. Clipping coupons, redeeming Green Stamps, and working at Wal-Mart might not be a part of some students' experience, but the characters in this story are profoundly affected by the work they do and how it shapes their identity. The story is largely about the connection between work and identity: the only reading Jane does during the story is Studs Terkel's book *Working*, and her superficial conclusion about it is that "It takes all kinds."

She clearly has more on her mind, but she is unable or unwilling to express it. Students might benefit from weighing the different types of work available to all of the characters to decide if there are any "American Dream" possibilities here or if the only options for escape are to join the army or to purvey a sham religion as Jane's brother does.

A related issue is the debate over men's and women's roles, a subject hashed out on a television talk show. The irony is multilayered here: men and women seem to communicate only on television, or through television, or imperfectly on the phone. The title of the story puts forth its theme of communication and its shortcomings in the contemporary world: with all of this noise floating around, surprisingly little gets said.

Major Themes, Historical Perspectives, Personal Issues

The theme of female empowerment and independence is initiated right away as Jane listens to female rock stars on the radio. Yet there is a good deal of confusion in her mind about how men and women should behave in relation to each other. She wants a man who isn't entirely fragile, as Coy seems to be, yet she appreciates Coy's sensitivity and is sure that other women would, too. She is similarly ambivalent about her own role in the army, not wanting to go to war but believing that "if there is [a war], women should go."

The authenticity of experience, a major theme in Mason's work, is evident in this story. If everything we see is so deeply affected by popular culture, how do we know what to believe? Her brother and her nearly rapturous revelation about the nature of radio airwaves help to define that theme in this story.

One would think that little historical knowledge is necessary to contextualize this story, which was published in the late 1980s, yet it is possible that students might not know a few of the classic television sitcoms alluded to here (*Hogan's Heroes*, *M*A*S*H*, and *The Mary Tyler Moore Show*), nor the talk show hosted by Phil Donahue (as popular in its time as *The Oprah Winfrey Show* is now), and especially the allusion to Alexander Haig, secretary of state under Ronald Reagan until 1982.

Original Audience

"Airwaves" was originally published in *The Atlantic*; its readership is largely of a wealthier class than that of the characters in the story.

Comparisons, Contrasts, Connections

Hamlin Garland's story "Up the Coulé," though of an earlier time period, also deals with the politics of leaving one's rural, agricultural hometown to pursue "a better life." Mason could also be productively compared with Flannery O'Connor or Raymond Carver.

Questions for Reading, Discussion, and Writing

1. What is the place of Mrs. Bush, Jane's neighbor, within the story? Is she a neutral presence in Jane's life, a cautionary tale, or a kindred spirit?
2. Jane's last name (only mentioned once, as her father's last name) is *Motherall*. Is this name ironic? Is she in any way maternal?
3. The story is partially about radio communication, as the first and last paragraphs and the title suggest. Jane briefly makes the connection between radio waves and "the magic of love," but she also wonders if her brother's speaking in tongues is a kind of magic. What is the status of mystery in this story, and has Jane made progress toward figuring anything out by the story's end?

Bibliography

"Shiloh" is probably Mason's most famous story: it also centers on a breakup precipitated when a man loses his job. It would make an interesting companion piece to this story because it is told from the man's point of view. As indicated in the headnote, Mason's novel *In Country* shares a number of themes with this story. There is a film adaptation of the novel. The only book-length study of Mason is Joanna Price's *Understanding Bobbie Ann Mason* (U of South Carolina P, 2000).

Simon Ortiz (Acoma Pueblo) (b. 1941)

Contributing Editor: Andrew O. Wiget

Classroom Issues and Strategies

The principal problem with Ortiz's poetry from a student perspective is that it is so intensely political and that it takes a political view of past events. Students can be reactionary and feel that what is past is past and that there has been too much of a tendency to cast aspersions upon America's reputation in recent years. This jingoism is often accompanied by a belief that poetry should not be political but rather should concern itself with eternal truths. These are not problems that are associated with Ortiz's poetry exclusively, of course, but are part of the naive vision of poetry that teachers of literature struggle to overcome.

I think it's very important to begin this poem with a reflection upon the historical experiences of Native Americans. Begin with the historical epigraph describing the Sand Creek Massacre of Black Kettle's band which gives this poem sequence its name. That particular massacre is very well documented, and students should spend some time trying to understand the forces that came together to create that massacre: Colonel Chivington's own political ambitions, his ability to mobilize the fears and anxieties of the frontier Colorado communities, his success at taking advantage of the militarization of the frontier during the Civil War, the remoteness of Chivington's forces from federal supervision, and the nonresistance of the Indians.

A second important issue to be discussed is how well we all use key events in the past to give us a sense of what our history is, emphasizing that the historical memory of people is selective and formed for very contemporary reasons.

I think that there are certain key lines in the poetry that are worth looking at in some detail. In addition, I ask students to look at the relationships between the epigraphs and the poems, how each speaks to the other. Finally, I ask students how these poems as a group, framed as they are by the boldfaced short poems about America and prefaced by the historical statement concerning the Sand Creek Massacre, all work together to create a unified statement.

The poems move between some very concrete historical references (on the one hand) such as those to Cotton Mather, Kit Carson, and Saigon, and (on the other hand) to some highly surrealistic imagery and abstract language. Students frequently have difficulty bringing the two together, and it's helpful to explore some of Ortiz's more provocative statements as a way of creating the matrix of values from which the poetry emerges.

Major Themes, Historical Perspectives, Personal Issues

The major theme of Ortiz's poem sequence is that Euro-Americans were as much victims of their own ambitions and blindness as were Native Americans, and the recognition by Euro-Americans that they have victimized themselves is the first step toward the beginning of a healing of America that will be based on a common appreciation of our shared responsibility for her future.

Significant Form, Style, or Artistic Conventions

Certainly the principal formal question will be the juxtaposition of the epigraphs, with their blunt ideological focus, and the poems, with their convoluted syntax and high rhetoric. It would be important to remind students, I think, that Ortiz's cycle of poems about the American historical experience is only one example in a long history of poetry about the American historical experience that stretches back through Hart Crane's *The Bridge* and Walt Whitman's *Leaves of Grass* to early national poems such as Joel Barlow's *The Columbiad*.

Original Audience

I don't think the original audience for this poetry is significantly different from the student audience, except perhaps in their political orientation (the students may be more conservative). These poems were written at the end of the seventies and represent in some sense a considered reflection upon the traumatization of the American psyche by the domestic turmoil of the 1960s, the loss of confidence evoked by Watergate, and crisis of conscience provoked by the Vietnam War. Many of the younger students who will be reading these poems for the first time remember none of those events.

Comparisons, Contrasts, Connections

Certainly I think Whitman, whom Ortiz does admire greatly, can be invoked. Ortiz tries to cultivate a prophetic voice and a historical vision similar to Whitman's. I think he may also be effectively contrasted with many writers for whom a historical criticism of America's past terminates in an attitude of despair. Ortiz has transformed anger into hope through compassion.

Questions for Reading, Discussion, and Writing

I would look at the first poem and ask students what is meant by the juxtaposition of the lines "No waste land,/No forgiveness." Or have students look at the third poem, which may be an even more provocative example, and ask them why Ortiz believes he should have stolen the sweater from the Salvation Army store, and why, in the end, he didn't.

Bibliography

Ortiz, Simon. "Sending a Voice: The Emergence of Contemporary Native American Poetry." *College English* 46 (1984): 598–609.

————. "The Story Never Ends: An Interview with Simon Ortiz." *Survival This Way: Interviews with American Indian Poets.* Ed. Joseph Bruchoc. Tucson: U of Arizona P, 1987. 211–30.

Wiget, Andrew. "Contemporary Poetry." *Native American Literature.* Boston: Twayne, 1985.

————. *Simon Ortiz.* Boise State University Western Writers Ser. 74. Boise: Boise State UP, 1986.

John Edgar Wideman (b. 1941)

Contributing Editor: James W. Coleman

Classroom Issues and Strategies

I usually start by discussing the students' typical responses to Wideman with them. Students, like most readers generally, want to read linear narratives that purport to relate directly to their lives or that they can visualize in a clear real-world context, and the aspects of Wideman's works that challenge their notions about narratives and their approaches to reading put them off. I ask them to examine their very traditional assumptions about narratives, about how narratives should relate to them, and about how they should read and judge fiction. Another question that I eventually ask is whether Wideman might have a purpose (beyond the desire to be a difficult writer) for writing as he does. And what is one of the first things about Wideman's fiction that they should see before they try to determine his meaning and relate to his work in their usual fashion?

They should see that Wideman disrupts their normal narrative approach because as he questions and tests the process in which he engages as the writer, he wants readers to question what they do, too. If students will think about it, they will see that words written on a page cannot replicate the concreteness, complexity, and convolution of their experience. The language of a narrative may pretend to appear to do so, but it cannot. This is one of the first things that Wideman reminds them of and that they must accept when they approach

Wideman's work. This does not mean that they should no longer read narratives that give them what they expect. But might there be a place for Wideman's kind of writing, too?

Wideman shows students this not to abdicate a social, political, and real-life responsibility in his fiction but to indicate the difficulty of the writer's task and the truth of what narratives are and what they do. Some students, perhaps many, however, will not be convinced by this. But some will appreciate Wideman, and one can also generate a pretty good discussion based on the students' pure emotional response to fiction such as Wideman's that requires them to work so hard.

Major Themes, Historical Perspectives, Personal Issues

Wideman indeed portrays clear historical perspectives and intense personal issues; however, in the context of his postmodern approach, he also questions the ability of writing to do fully and successfully what he wants it to do. In the selection in *The Heath Anthology*, "Valaida," the Jewish experience of the Holocaust and the African-American historical experience of racism intersect, and Wideman also foregrounds the life and history of a black entertainer, Valaida Snow, whom few of us know. In a historical perspective, racism and oppression are pervasive themes in Wideman's work.

If we move beyond "Valaida" to examine Wideman's work since 1981, we see him focusing very directly on himself personally, on his family, and especially on the tragedies and tribulations of specific family members. Wideman's fiction often takes as a theme the very thing that he struggles with as a writer—the quest to be a black writer who writes about the black community and its experience and makes a difference through his writing. Wideman sometimes makes himself (or a surrogate writer figure) a character in his fiction and shows himself as a character undergoing the struggle that he undergoes as a writer in real life. He writes intimately about people in his family and about a community of black people in the process.

The tragic stories of Wideman's brother and son have also become major aspects of his work since 1981. Starting in *Hiding Place* (1981) and *Damballah* (1981) and reaching a focus in the semifictional *Brothers and Keepers* (1984), Wideman deals with his relationship to his younger brother Robby; jailed for life for robbery and murder. And in *Philadelphia Fire* (1990), some of the stories in *All Stories Are True* (1993); and *Fatheralong: A Meditation on Fathers and Sons, Race and Society* (1994), he talks to his incarcerated son.

Significant Form, Style, or Artistic Conventions

As I have been saying, Wideman will seem very unconventional to many student readers. He uses modernist techniques and creates dense modernist fictional forms in his early work, but the majority of his work since 1981 utilizes post-modernist approaches and techniques. However, this later work also draws increasingly on black cultural forms, religious rituals and practices, black folk stories, and black street ways, for example. "Valaida" is a story that combines a postmodernist approach with the traditional African-American themes of racism and oppression.

Original Audience

Wideman has always enjoyed high praise from critics, intellectuals, and some academics, but he has never had a wide general audience. Few undergraduates have heard of Wideman, and fewer have read anything by him. Yet Wideman's books continue to win awards, and critics continue to praise him. Perhaps Wideman's work draws acclaim from critics, intellectuals, and academics for the same reason (its complexity and ingenuity) that it denies access to more general readers.

Comparisons, Contrasts, Connections

On the one hand, Wideman provides a contrast to other black writers who do not make the writing itself an explicit theme, and this is the large majority of them, I think. This would include so difficult and complex a writer as Toni Morrison, who manages to keep her focus on the theme of black struggle without foregrounding the problems and difficulties of writing the narrative itself. But on the other hand, there are black writers such as Charles Johnson who share concerns about writing similar to Wideman's, and Wideman's thematic concern with racism and the black cultural tradition connects him strongly to the black literary tradition generally. I would also point out that Wideman's work separates itself from the radical textuality, the complete focus on language and the workings of the narrative, of such white writers as Raymond Federman and Ronald Sukenick. And the reality of Wideman's narratives is not the same detached reality of a writer such as Thomas Pynchon.

Questions for Reading, Discussion, and Writing

The following study questions may be helpful for "Valaida": How do the story's style and form force you to approach it? What is the connection of the italicized section at the beginning to the rest of the story? What is the relationship between the story Mr. Cohen tells Mrs. Clara and the beginning section? What is Mr. Cohen trying to do by telling Mrs. Clara the story? How do style, form, and theme coalesce in the story? Students might start to approach writing about "Valaida" by looking at this convergence of style, form, and theme and the resulting tension between postmodernist treatment and social and political intention.

Bibliography

Although Wideman published his first book in 1967 and has published thirteen books since then, one still finds a relative dearth of work about him. The most comprehensive source is James W. Coleman's *Blackness and Modernism: The Literary Career of John Edgar Wideman* (1989), which has an interview with Wideman as an appendix. Other helpful interviews are John O'Brien's in *Interviews with Black Writers* (1973) and Wilfred Samuel's "Going Home: A Conversation with John Edgar Wideman," *Callaloo* 6 (Feb. 1983): 40–59. Good analyses of Wideman's works also appear in Bernard W. Bell's *The Afro-American Novel and Its Tradition* (1987); Michael G. Cooke's *Afro-American Literature in the Twentieth Century: The Achievement of Intimacy* (1981); and Trudier Harris's *Exorcising Blackness: Historical and Literary Lynching and Burning Rituals* (1984). Kermit Frazier's "The Novels of John Wideman," *Black World* 24.8 (1975): 18–35 is one of the very first pieces on Wideman and is still useful. The special issue on Wideman, *Callaloo* 22.3 (Summer 1999), is a very important addition to the scholarly work on the writer.

Gloria Anzaldúa (1942–2004)

Contributing Editor: Kristin Dietsche

Classroom Issues and Strategies

Students may be challenged or even put off by Anzaldúa's tone, the non-linear form of her argument, her explicit feminism, and her use of Spanish, Nahuatl, and Chicano languages along with English. Students' reactions to the work may be the best place to begin a discussion of the text's challenges to linguistic, literary, and cultural boundaries, and an instructor might begin to work on student resistance by asking whether they considered themselves part of the intended audience of *Borderlands/La Frontera*. A class might work toward isolating those features that they found persuasive or made them feel invited to enter the argument of the text and those that may have made them feel excluded. This exercise will position students on the borderlands of Anzaldúa's text and open a way to implement her own strategy of transforming resistance into a consciousness that is able to hold contradictory positions simultaneously.

Significant Form, Style, or Artistic Conventions

The form of *Borderlands* resists traditional literary classification, and its intentionally antiliterary qualities might provide an entry into a discussion of the roles of both form and intention in an ongoing discussion of canon. The text does not fall easily into traditionally "privileged" genres like epic, novel, lyric, short fiction, or even essay and autobiography. She combines personal narrative, folklore, history, personal revelation, and poetry and uses a wide range of seemingly contradictory features from conversational slang to footnote citations of academic authorities.

Students who keep reading journals might be asked to stop and record their expectations for the text after reading the first page of "Entering into the Serpent." They might identify features of narrative here and expect to read a first-person short story, an expectation that is fully frustrated by the third page. Experiences of confusion, uncertainty, and ambiguity along with frustration at the failure of the text to follow a clear narrative course can be legitimized in discussion as the class works to understand why the author may want to provoke these kinds of responses.

Anzaldúa has created a work that cannot be judged using traditional critical tools. She speaks of her text instead as an "Aztec-like" mosaic—"a weaving pattern, thin here, thick there" (66) and, later, "a flawed thing, a clumsy, complex groping thing" but alive (67). The text actively challenges both what literature and feminist argument are supposed to be while creating a new hybrid all its own. You might use a close reading of the first paragraph of "A Tolerance for Ambiguity" in *La conciencia de la mestiza* as a way to explore ways that the form of the larger work reflects its thesis.

Original Audience

The potential audience for this work is a crucial question, and since it is a fairly contemporary text, students might be brought into a discussion of whether they think they are a part of it. Is she writing to speakers of all these languages, perhaps *tejanas* or *mestizas* like herself, or is her audience broader? What is the effect of writing in languages that the audience may not understand? You may consider asking students who know Spanish to talk about and translate some of the Spanish passages. Do native speakers make different observations from students studying Spanish as a second language? Are there students who are able to identify different kinds of Spanish used in the text or students who are familiar with the various dialects she has chosen? You might also discuss the whole issue of "translation"—and suggest Spanish speakers supply missed nuance. Students can bring different linguistic authority to an analysis of this text, illustrating that while this work may be difficult, the traditional literary academy (English professors) may not be the best place to look for the right answers or the best interpretation. Instead, the reader must consult a *mestiza* for answers and interpretation.

Questions for Reading, Discussion, and Writing

For Anzaldúa, the choice of language itself becomes a significant personal and political decision, one as significant as her challenge to political authority and patriarchal culture. Language is a significant part of Anzaldúa's cultural identity, and she chooses border language to express her border self, a self speaking from the languages of multiple cultures.

Connections might be made between Anzaldúa's argument and the experiences of students through an analysis of the languages that define their own cultures. In chapter 5 of *Borderlands*, she lists some of the languages that Chicanos speak:

1. Standard English
2. Working-class and slang English
3. Standard Spanish
4. Standard Mexican Spanish
5. North Mexican Spanish dialect
6. Chicano Spanish (Texas, New Mexico, Arizona, and California have regional variations)
7. Tex-Mex
8. *Pachuco* (called *caló*)

Using this list as a starting point, students might be encouraged to list the languages that they and their family members speak. What kind of authority do these languages hold? Are there social consequences for their use? Are these languages complicit in structures of political power? Which of these languages come from the borderlands? Do any have the potential to express a "new mestiza consciousness"? While Anzaldúa says that Spanish-speaking people accuse her of either "speaking the oppressor's language by speaking English" or "ruining the Spanish language" by writing in substandard dialect, she defends her choice of English and Chicano Spanish. For people who are neither Spanish nor English, she argues "what recourse is there left but to create their own language" (55), and she maintains "Chicano Spanish is not incorrect, it is a living language" (55).

From the borders of language and dialect a class might list other borders that this work challenges—cultural, historical, geographical, sexual, metaphysical, for instance. This listing exercise might then be followed by a discussion of which borders are "real" and which are "imaginary." Here you might examine "The Presences" in *Entering into the Serpent*.

Students might be encouraged to try to write in Anzaldúa's multivoiced form in order to write about *la fronteras* of their own cultural experiences. To do this, some care should be taken to identify "borders" in your own community: Where are they located? Who do they divide? Is language an issue? Is there a potential for *mestiza* consciousness?

Janice Mirikitani (b. 1942)

Contributing Editor: Shirley Lim

Classroom Issues and Strategies

Students need to learn about the internment of Japanese-American citizens during World War II. You might consider reading historical extracts of laws passed against Japanese Americans during internment or passages from books describing camp life. If possible, show students paintings and photographs of internment experience. Students tend to resist issues of racism in mainstream white American culture; counter this tendency by discussing the long history of persecution of Asians on the West Coast.

Deal with the strong aural/oral quality of Mirikitani's writing—the strong protest voice.

Students often raise questions about the poet's anger: How personally does the reader take this? How successfully has the poet expressed her anger and transformed it into memorable poetry? What kinds of historical materials does the poet mine? Why are these materials useful and significant?

Major Themes, Historical Perspectives, Personal Issues

Themes are the historical documentation of legislation against Asians in the United States, internment during World War II, Mirikitani's father's experience in Tule Lake during World War II, economic and psychological experiences of Japanese Americans during that period, and stereotypes of Asian-American women in U.S. popular culture.

Significant Form, Style, or Artistic Conventions

Consider the issue of protest and oral poetry, traditions of such poetry in black literature in the 1960s and 1970s, and the influence of the "black is beautiful" movement on Mirikitani.

Original Audience

Consider the didactic and sociopolitical nature of the writing: a divided audience, her own people and an audience to be persuaded and accused of past prejudices. Much of her poetry was written in the 1970s at the peak of social protests against white hegemony.

Comparisons, Contrasts, Connections

Compare her poems with those of Sonia Sanchez and Don L. Lee, for example, on sociopolitical and minority concerns.

Questions for Reading, Discussion, and Writing

1. Personal accounts or observations of racism at work in their own society
2. How they themselves perceive Asian Americans, their stereotypes of Asian-American women

Bibliography

Refer to Mini Okubo's books on camp life, the movie of the Houstons' book on Manzanar, and newspaper accounts of the recent debate and settlement of repayments to Japanese Americans for injustice done to them by the U.S. government during their internment period. See also Deirdre Lashgari's "Disrupting the Deadly Stillness: Janice Mirikitani's Poetics of Violence" in *Violence, Silence, and Anger: Women's Writing as Transgression* (Charlottesville: UP of Virginia, 1995); and Stan Yogi's "Yearning for the Past: The Dynamics of Memory in Sansei Internment Poetry" in *Approaches to American Ethnic Literatures* (Boston: Northeastern UP, 1996).

Pat Mora (b. 1942)

Contributing Editor: Juan Bruce-Novoa

Classroom Issues and Strategies

The ethnic background of the students will greatly determine the nature of class discussion. How sympathetic they are to Mora's position will vary. Students may be first-generation immigrants who themselves are adapting to English and U.S. culture, or second- or third-generation residents whose relatives are the living reminders of the process. Others may see it as an experience their ancestors went through years ago while some will never have asked themselves if their ancestors ever spoke anything but English. You may find yourself in the middle of a heated discussion of English as the official national language or the threat to American culture that the use of other languages represents for many people. I prefer to guide the discussion toward the universal quality of the experience of acculturation that the poems express.

Major Themes, Historical Perspectives, Personal Issues

The Mora selections feature the theme of English language acquisition as a painful experience of conflict and suffering for native Spanish speakers. In each poem, school is at least partially the setting for the conflict. Her perspective characterizes the experience as one of gain and loss, emphasizing the latter as the loss of cultural authenticity while the value of the gain is left in doubt. This position is common among proponents of bilingual education and ethnic pluralism and can be found among the majority of writers from the Chicano communities. It reflects a turn away from the historical paradigm of U.S. culture as English-based that in turn made the learning of English a necessary rite of passage. However, it should be noted that each poem includes a touch of ambivalence: the characters are attracted to English-based culture, producing a desire whose satisfaction they seek.

Significant Form, Style, or Artistic Conventions

Mora's form and style are direct and should present few problems for students. The most notable feature is the use of Spanish words, but she does so on the most basic level that requires only dictionary translating for understanding. One should note, however, that the girl's name, *Esperanza*, in "Border Town," means hope—an obvious pun.

Original Audience

Mora tends to publish in small presses specializing in distribution to a Latino readership. Hence, her poetry can count on a mostly sympathetic audience, one that probably will not find the smattering of Spanish hinders comprehension.

Comparisons, Contrasts, Connections

Mora can be placed in the context of Bernice Zamora and Lorna Dee Cervantes, among Chicana writers included here, as well as Judith Ortiz Cofer. For a similar depiction of the situation faced by Chicanos in Texas schools, see Tomás Rivera's *And the Earth Did Not Part*; for the ambivalent attitude of desire and fear, see Richard Rodriguez's *Hunger of Memory*; for a contrasting view on the question of English language acquisition, see Linda Chavez's *Out of the Barrio*.

Questions for Reading, Discussion, and Writing

1. Students can be asked to locate the verses in each poem in which the dilemma of attraction and repulsion are conveyed. Ask them to consider the pros and cons of acculturation, especially as it relates to education.
2. Have students write about their own experience and, specifically, about whether education has demanded of them anything similar to what Mora describes. They could consider the question of private versus public codes of discourse and if education can serve both.

James Alan McPherson (b. 1943)

Contributing Editor: John F. Callahan

Classroom Issues and Strategies

Students are unfamiliar with the railroads and the extent to which black men were a fraternity in the service jobs on the trains. There is some need to explain the argot of railroading, to familiarize students with the vocabulary and syncopated accents of the black vernacular.

Involve students with the rich variations of the oral tradition. Get them telling stories, in particular stories of how they met and came to know people of very different backgrounds because of summer jobs. It helps to read chunks of the story out loud.

Students are often interested in Youngblood's attitude toward the story-teller and the storyteller's attitude toward Doc Craft.

Major Themes, Historical Perspectives, Personal Issues

Themes include the complexity and richness as well as the hardships of the lives lived by black traveling men, the initiative and kinship developed by the black workers, the qualities of the trickster, and also the ways racism surcharges the attempts by blacks and whites to master situations and each other. Once again, the fact that the story is told by an old-timer about to quit (in 1964 or so) to Youngblood—the college student in a temporary job—about working on the road for the last twenty years or more sets up important con-trasts between the past and the present, particularly the impact of technology on older ways of work and life.

Significant Form, Style, or Artistic Conventions

The relationship of oral storytelling as an initiation ritual to McPherson's craft of fiction writing, particularly his resolve to initiate readers of all races into a facet of their culture passing quickly out of sight.

Comparisons, Contrasts, Connections

See Baldwin's "Sonny's Blues" and Silko's "Lullaby."

Questions for Reading, Discussion, and Writing

What is the significance of the name *Doc Craft*?

Bibliography

Ellison, Ralph, and James McPherson. "Indivisible Man." *Atlantic* (Dec. 1970): 45–60.

McPherson, James. "On Becoming an American Writer." *Atlantic* 242.6 (Dec. 1978): 53–57.

Lee Smith (b. 1944)

Teaching material for Lee Smith is available on *The Heath Anthology* web-site. To access the site, please go to the Houghton Mifflin college homepage at <http://www.college.hmco.com>. Select *English;* then select *The Heath An-thology* textbook site.

Pedro Pietri (1944–2004)

Contributing Editor: Frances R. Aparicio

Classroom Issues and Strategies

As with other Nuyorican poets, the language switching and references to either Spanish or Puerto Rican culture need to be explained. Preparing a handout with a glossary and giving a small introduction to life in El Barrio (perhaps with photos, pictures, or videos) might also be helpful.

Pedro Pietri has produced two records, *Loose Joints* and *One is a Crowd* (Folkway Records). If available, they would be good for classroom use.

Some students might have a difficult time understanding the anger and the bitterness of Pietri's voice against "the system," an issue for disagreement and discussion.

Major Themes, Historical Perspectives, Personal Issues

Pietri's poetry is political poetry in its most direct sense: a poetry of denuncia-tion, directed to create a cultural consciousness among the members of the Puerto Rican community. Other themes are the demythification of authority figures and social institutions (government, schools, church, "the system"), alienation in contemporary urban life, and a surrealistic search for the truth in the irra-tional and the absurd. In addition, the political status and the poverty levels for Puerto Ricans in New York can be discussed in light of Pietri's denunciation of "the system." How do students feel about the welfare system and about the Hispanic poor in this country? About the first world/third world dichotomies within the United States?

Significant Form, Style, or Artistic Conventions

"Puerto Rican Obituary" can be read as a parody of an epic poem (the dream and the search and the epic deeds of a nation inverted), and within an anti-aesthetic attitude. Again, as in Laviera, this is oral poetry to be recited and *screamed*. In *Traffic Violations*, Pietri's poetry falls within the surrealistic mode—fragmented images; search for the absurd in everyday life; irrational, surprising metaphors; and imagery, humor, and sarcasm.

Original Audience

Though quite contemporary, Pietri's poetry has to be understood in terms of its original objective of addressing the masses as oral poetry. This is important in order to achieve a true understanding of his use of popular language, anger, and antiaesthetic style.

Comparisons, Contrasts, Connections

I believe that fruitful comparisons may be drawn if one looks into Allen Ginsberg and other poets of the Beat generation and of the 1960s (as poetry of social denouncement, protest, and harsh antiacademic language). Also compare with contemporary African-American poets who deal with urban themes, alienation, and social injustice.

Questions for Reading, Discussion, and Writing

1. For "Puerto Rican Obituary," questions dealing with theme: What is it denouncing? How are the "puertorriqueños" portrayed? Analyze image of *death*. Would you define it as an "epic" poem? What is the use of Spanish in the poem? Consider the poem as an example of urban literature; define the utopian space that Pietri proposes.
2. Paper topics might deal with Puerto Rican migration, use of Spanish and English (for aesthetic effect), or functions of humor and irony. Analyze the poems as "outlaw" literature.

Bibliography

Two general articles on Puerto Rican writers discuss Pietri's work:

Acosta-Belén, Edna. "The Literature of the Puerto Rican National Minority in the United States." *Bilingual Review* 5.1–2 (Jan.–Aug. 1978): 107–16.

Cruz, Arnaldo. "Teaching Puerto Rican Authors: Modernization and Identity in Nuyorican Literature." *ADE Journal* (Dec. 1988).

Richard Rodriguez (b. 1944)

Teaching material for Richard Rodriguez is available on *The Heath Anthology* website. To access the site, please go to the Houghton Mifflin college homepage at <http://www.college.hmco.com>. Select *English;* then select *The Heath Anthology* textbook site.

Alice Walker (b. 1944)

Contributing Editor: John Alberti

Classroom Issues and Strategies

"Laurel" challenges its readers to engage the story on many dimensions. On one level, it is a story of erotic attraction, a testimony to the power and mystery of the bond that forms between Annie and Laurel, a bond that even survives severe physical and mental injury as well as the passage of time. It is also the story of an interracial relationship set in the civil rights struggles of the 1960s, but politics and society are more than "background" in "Laurel"; they are intricately woven into the economy of desire and are in fact as constitutive of that desire as nature and biology. It is also a story told in retrospect, filtered and interpreted through layers of experience. And Laurel's androgynous qualities—the "charming lilt" to his voice, his sensitive breasts—suggest in themselves an expansive understanding of the erotic that can be connected with Walker's major contribution to feminist theory: her conception of womanism.

One strategy, then, might be to have the class divide the story into different levels such as these (and the ones listed above are only suggestions) and then have smaller groups of students discuss them individually according to interest. As they work, each group should note where their discussions begin to connect to other levels of the story. When the class meets again as a single group, the discussion of the interrelationship of these different levels can take place with a richness of detail that avoids the need to reduce the story to any one dimension. In a way, this method follows that of Annie in "Laurel" as she reassesses her relationship with the title character from the perspective of several years.

A remarkable quality of the narrative voice in the story has to do with how open and nonjudgmental Annie remains to different perspectives and interpretations of experience, even while never losing sight of her core values and beliefs, as when she resists her husband's efforts to characterize Laurel's post-coma desire for her as unequivocally misguided and destructive. Similarly, the story resists setting up romantic rivalries among the women in the story: the letter from Laurel's wife turns out to be generous rather than accusatory, and Laurel's sister hugs Annie when they meet for the first time. As a result, readers are left with an open-ended sense of Annie's relationship with Laurel. Students can discuss to what extent she regrets never consummating their relationship or not later running off with him for the "adventure." Returning to the multidimensional quality of the story, both Annie's relationship with Laurel and with her husband also function as case studies in race relations, as Laurel's post-coma letters openly refer to racism, anti-Semitism, and the attraction of the exotic. Given his brain damage, these letters can be read as messages from the subconscious unfiltered by the screens of decorum or social restraint, and they add to the rich complexity of the relationships described in the story.

Leslie Marmon Silko (Laguna) (b. 1948)

Contributing Editor: Norma C. Wilson

Classroom Issues and Strategies

When I first began to read Silko's poetry and fiction, I attempted to use the critical methods I had used in my prior study of European and American literature. I sought primary sources of the traditional stories that appeared in her work. But I soon found that very little of the traditional literature of the Lagunas had been recorded in writing. I realized that I needed to know more of the background—cultural and historical—of Silko's writing.

In the spring of 1977, I arranged to meet with Silko at the University of New Mexico. She explained to me that her writing had evolved from an outlook she had developed as a result of hearing the old stories and songs all her life. She also led me to a number of helpful written sources, including Bertha P. Dutton and Miriam A. Marmon's *The Laguna Calendar* (Albuquerque: U of New Mexico P, 1936) and the transcript of an interview with Mrs. Walter

K. Marmon in the Special Collections Department of the Zimmerman Library, U.N.M. Another source I've found helpful is Leslie A. White, "The Acoma Indians" (*Forty-seventh Annual Report of the Bureau of American Ethnology* [Washington, DC: U.S. Gov. Printing Office, 1932]). Leslie Silko's *Yellow Woman and a Body of the Spirit: Essays on Native American Life Today* (New York: Simon, 1996) provides invaluable insights about the beliefs, oral traditions, and history of the Laguna pueblo and details Silko's own life experiences.

One can use the videotape *Running on the Edge of the Rainbow* produced by Larry Evers at the University of Arizona, Tucson. A more recent video, *Leslie Marmon Silko* (produced by Matteo Bellinelli and published by Films for the Humanities in Princeton, NJ, 1995), can also be useful. I often begin looking at Silko's writing by using a transparency of her poem "Prayer to the Pacific." Students frequently come to think in new ways about their relationships to nature and about the exploitation of Native American people and the natural earth. They ask such questions as "Did the government really do that to the Navajos?"

Major Themes, Historical Perspectives, Personal Issues

In teaching "Lullaby," the idea of harmony is essential—the Navajo woman is balanced because she is aware of her relation to the natural world, that she is a part of it and that is the most important relationship. This allows her to nurture as the earth nurtures. One should emphasize forced changes in the Navajo way of life that have resulted from the encroachment of industry and the government on Navajo land. Today the struggle centering on Big Mountain would be a good focus. Of course, alcoholism and the splitting up of Indian families would be other important issues to focus on.

Significant Form, Style, or Artistic Conventions

It is important to note that Silko's fiction is a blending of traditional with modern elements. And just as "Lullaby" ends with a song, many of Silko's other works are also a blend of prose and poetry.

Original Audience

"Lullaby" seems to be a story from out of the 1950s. We talk about the U.S. government's relocation policy during that decade. Relocation was an attempt to remove Indians from reservations and relocate them in urban environments. We also discuss the long history of the U.S. government's removing Indian children from their families and culture. Recently this kind of removal has been somewhat reversed by the Indian Child Welfare Act, which gives the tribes authority over the placement of the children enrolled in these tribes.

Comparisons, Contrasts, Connections

One might compare and contrast Silko's work with that of Simon J. Ortiz. One might also consider comparing and contrasting it with the work of James Wright, Gary Snyder, and Louise Erdrich.

Questions for Reading, Discussion, and Writing

One might ask the students to look up specific places mentioned in the story on a map—Cebolleta Creek, Long Mesa, Cañoncito, and so on.

1. Discuss the importance of the oral tradition in Silko's writing.
2. Discuss the structure of Silko's fiction. Is it linear or cyclic?
3. What is the image of woman in Silko's fiction? Compare or contrast this with the images of women in the broader context of American society and culture.
4. What criticisms of American society are implicit in Silko's fiction?
5. What Navajo cultural values are evident in the story "Lullaby"?

Bibliography

Allen, Paula G. "Special Problems in Teaching Leslie Marmon Silko's *Cere-mony*." *American Indian Quarterly* (Fall 1990): 379–86.

Fisher, Dexter. "Stories and Their Tellers—A Conversation with Leslie Marmon Silko." *The Third Woman: Minority Women Writers of the United States*. Boston: Houghton, 1990.

Wilson, Norma C. "*Ceremony:* from Alienation to Reciprocity." *Teaching American Ethnic Literatures*. Ed. David Peck and John Maitino. Albuquer-que: U of New Mexico P, 1996. 69–82.

Wendy Rose (Hopi) (b. 1948)

Contributing Editor: C. B. Clark

Classroom Issues and Strategies

Background knowledge about Indian culture and history will help students pick up on comments about imperialism, removals, atrocities, resentments, and so on.

Major Themes, Historical Perspectives, Personal Issues

Themes are colonialism, imperialism, dependency, nostalgia for the old ways, reverence for grandparents, resentment for conditions of the present, plight of reservation and urban Indians, sense of hopelessness, the power of the trickster, feminism as synonymous with heritage, deadly compromise, symbolism of all that has been lost (such as land), tension between the desire to retrieve the past and the inevitability of change, arrogance of white people, and problems of half-breeds (or mixed-bloods).

Significant Form, Style, or Artistic Conventions

Rose uses free verse. She is aware of classical European form but chooses not to use it. In addition, she is less an oral poet using chants and more of a lyric poet. She is not in any school, except American Indian.

Original Audience

I ask this question: Is there an audience outside American Indians? A second audience, of course, would be the students in class. A third audience would be the general reader.

Questions for Reading, Discussion, and Writing

1. What are the major themes of Hopi religion? Who are the Hopi? Where do they live? Why do they lie atop mesas? Where do the Hopi claim to come from? What contemporary problems do they face? Who are some Hopi leaders today? How do the Hopi view the world?
2. Hand out a reading list on the Hopi containing ethnographic, historical, and contemporary works. Hand out a theme list containing topics like

manifest destiny or acculturation. Hand out a subject list with subjects like alcoholism, jails, and kachinas. Then, ask students to write an essay using Rose's works in reference to any of these topics.

Bibliography

No single biographical or critical work exists on Rose. Information must be gleaned from critical pieces, collections, and book reviews. Additionally, information can come from autobiographical statements preceding selections printed in anthologies of American Indian works.

Rose is included in Joseph Bruchac's *Survival This Way;* Swann and Krupat's *I Tell You Now;* Andrew Wiget's *Native American Literature;* and *Winged Words: American Indian Writers Speak,* ed. Laura Coltelli.

Wilson, David Babe. "Review of *Bone Dance.*" *American Indian Culture and Research Journal* 18 (1994): 274–78.

Sandra María Esteves (b. 1948) and Luz María Umpierre (b. 1947)

Contributing Editor: Lawrence La Fountain-Stokes

Major Themes, Historical Perspectives, Personal Issues

The poetic dialogue presented in *The Heath Anthology* represents a very limited sample of the literary production of both of these women, although Esteves's "A La Mujer Borrinqueña [To The Puerto Rican Woman]" is one of her most widely anthologized poems, and issues of the decolonization of Puerto Rico, Puerto Rican migration to the United States, the social problems of the migrant community, people-of-color struggles for civil rights, feminism, women's liberation, and women's role in society are central to the aesthetic and political projects of both authors. It might be useful to consult Esteves's and Umpierre's numerous published works (or the selection in Turner's anthology) to get a more complete sense of the topics they address and how their views have evolved over the years. It should be stressed that these four poems do share the general commitment to grassroots Latino/Latina and people-of-color politics, to community building, and to fighting racial, ethnic, sexual, and class oppression expressed throughout their work, as well as the general militant and/or lyrical tone and first-person poetic voice that appears elsewhere.

Providing a general overview of feminism and of Puerto Rican culture and history can help to ground this debate, particularly as the general register of the poems might lead students to favor an individual or personal interpretation (something that undoubtedly forms part of the verses) and to ignore the broader social context that determined their production. Students should understand that although an individual voice is speaking, this voice really proposes a wider collective viewpoint and that there is a tension between the unitary and the multiple. A discussion of Puerto Rico's pre-Hispanic Taíno past and its Spanish colonial period (1493–1898), of the particular nature of Puerto Rico as a colony of the United States, of the history of twentieth-century Puerto Rican migration as well as of the history of Puerto Rican and Latin American feminism (which dates back to the nineteenth century), and of the differences between general international migration and migration that results from colonialism can serve to locate both of these poets' work. Students (and some instructors) might not be familiar with terms such as *Borinquen* (the indigenous name for the island) or *Boricua* (Puerto Rican), and might not know that *La Borinqueña* is also the name of the national anthem, whose revolutionary lyrics were penned by a woman poet, Lola Rodríguez de Tió (1843–1924). Key dates in Puerto Rican history that might be of use for students are

- 1898 (the year of the Spanish-Cuban-American War, during which Puerto Rico was invaded and annexed by the United States)
- 1917 (the year of the Jones Act, under which all Puerto Ricans were classified as U.S. citizens)
- 1945–1965 (the period of the "Great Migration" to the United States)
- 1952 (the establishment of the Estado Libre Asociado, or Commonwealth of Puerto Rico)

Both of these poets' lives were profoundly marked by the effect of these historical events. A review of the history of migration can help to explain the centrality of the "barrio" as ethnic enclave or immigrant community, particularly in New York (see Sánchez Korrol). A discussion of Hispanic Caribbean notions of race and different forms of racism will help students understand the use of the term *negra* (feminine declension of *black*) as a term of affection used regardless of the individual's skin color (see Duany).

Although there have been Puerto Ricans in the United States since the late nineteenth century, it is not until the mid-1960s and 1970s that a distinct literary voice surfaces in English and receives widespread recognition, with such authors as Piri Thomas and Nicholasa Mohr, as well as the Nuyorican poets (see Flores and Cruz Malavé). These voices also formed part of the broader social and civil rights struggles carried out by individuals and groups such as the Young Lords Party. Students will benefit from understanding the similarity among these and other social struggles effected by groups such as the

Black Panthers, the Brown Berets, and the American Indian Movement (AIM), particularly in terms of the positions women held or were expected to hold. Students should also be reminded that both Esteves and Umpierre are engaged in projects of creating literary kinships and genealogies, particularly among female Puerto Rican poets, and that as such, the mention of Julia de Burgos is very important.

The most direct and obvious subject of the poems included in this anthology is social expectations for women's behavior, particularly the issue of how women can form a meaningful part of a community and contribute to social struggles while maintaining dignified positions as individuals. Esteves's first poem stresses traditional conceptions of femininity as tools of resistance to social oppression while Umpierre's response indicates how women are oppressed within their social group (the Puerto Rican diasporic community) by complying with or participating in these expectations. Both poems locate a strong, empowered first-person speaking subject as the agent of these actions: one a "race woman" who defends her ethnic community while the other positions herself as a feminist who defends women's rights to be independent and assertive subjects. The third and fourth poems work as extensions of this dialogue, emphasizing notions of women's friendship and community, and try to reconcile their viewpoints and to overcome or transform the initial anger expressed in the first two poems (something William Luis completely missed in his analysis of this debate; Yamila Azize Vargas's reading is more nuanced).

Students generally enjoy reading the poetic exchange, and very fruitful classroom conversations can be had, with students defending and criticizing both positions. Students can be asked to discuss issues of gender and sexuality (and particularly of women's role in society) in the context of their own families and communities in relation to historical change; they can also be invited to discuss their knowledge of Puerto Rico and Puerto Rican/Nuyorican literature and the literature's relation to broader American literature and culture. In addition, students can be asked to discuss orality and the current poetry-slam scene in the context of hip-hop and of the Nuyorican Poets Café and see how it has evolved from these more militant origins.

Significant Form, Style, or Artistic Conventions

The work of both of these women can be located in relation to *Nuyorican aesthetics* as defined by Miguel Algarín and Miguel Piñero in *Nuyorican Poetry* (1975), in which Algarín highlights the streets as compositional theme and location of performance, the poet as troubadour or oral bard, and the centrality of Afro-Diasporic music and culture. Esteves's and Umpierre's work differs radically in its emphasis on gender and its move toward domestic spaces of the house. The poems demonstrate an introspective voice (that of the poet in the world) but are moored in broader social movements and communities. Students should be encouraged to discuss this relationship or tension as well as the links between these poems and feminist work.

Original Audience

Esteves's first poem, "A La Mujer Borrinqueña," comes out of the same literary and cultural environment as Pedro Pietri's "Puerto Rican Obituary" and Tato Laviera's work. It comes from an oral tradition and was primarily meant to be recited out loud by the poet at community events and political gatherings usually dominated by male artists. Umpierre's "In Response" first appeared in *Third Woman*, a feminist, woman-of-color literary and scholarly journal. Umpierre is also an impassioned performer of her poetry.

Comparisons, Contrasts, Connections

These poems can be read in relation to those of other women-of-color poets (African-American, Native American, Asian American, Latina) as well as to those of white women poets who deal with social issues, the role of women in society, women's politics, and related topics. It is very useful to place these poems in the context of civil rights struggles and 1970s and 1980s feminism. The poems can also be fruitfully compared with those of other Nuyorican poets such as Tato Laviera and Pedro Pietri or even with those of Chicano male writers, such as Tomás Rivera and Rudolfo Anaya, who are also representative of communities engaged in social struggles. Their works can also be compared with the works of gay authors, such as James Baldwin and Rane Arroyo, who also question their own communities' notions of gender and sexuality. Another possibility is to use this poetic debate as an entryway into discussions about the differences between heterosexual women's and lesbian women's experiences and literature; Umpierre's work can be compared with that of Audre Lorde, Gloria Anzaldúa, and others.

Working with Cultural Objects

Esteves (like Nicholasa Mohr) is a visual artist and her first book, *Yerba Buena: Dibujos y Poemas*, which is out of print and somewhat difficult to obtain, includes numerous drawings and prints by the poet. Photocopies can be made of some of these drawings, which tend to emphasize indigenous iconography. The work of the Nuyorican artist Juan Sanchez shares this visual imagery and is more accessible on the Web. Many of his images focus on his mother, his wife, and his daughter Liora and incorporate photographs of them. See his website at <http://www.ps1.org/official>.

Students can be invited to compare the portrayal of Puerto Rican women that appears in these poems with other portrayals, such as that of Esmeralda Santiago (*When I Was Puerto Rican*) or even the portrayal of Maria and Anita in *West Side Story*, a play and film written by non-Puerto Rican white men that present stereotypical views but were made famous by Puerto Rican and non-Puerto Rican actresses such as Rita Moreno, Chita Rivera, and Natalie Wood. PBS offers a complex, detailed, and very valuable website for the film version of Esmeralda Santiago's *Almost a Woman*, with many useful links at <http://www.pbs.org/wgbh/masterpiece/americancollection/woman>.

Questions for Reading, Discussion, and Writing

1. Consult Sandra María Esteves's poems "Here" and "Not Neither" and discuss her debate with Luz María Umpierre in relation to the views on cultural identity that she expresses in those two poems. The poems are available at <http://www.pbs.org/wgbh/masterpiece/americancollecti on/woman/ei_poetry_esteves.html>.

Bibliography

Azize Vargas, Yamila. "A Commentary on the Works of Three Puerto Rican Women Poets in New York." *Breaking Boundaries: Latina Writing and Critical Readings*. Ed. Asunción Horno-Delgado et al. Amherst: U of Massachusetts P, 1989. 146–65.

Cruz Malavé, Arnaldo. "Teaching Puerto Rican Authors: Identity and Modernization in Nuyorican Texts." *ADE Bulletin* 91 (Winter 1988): 45–51. <http://www.mla.org/ade/bulletin/N091/091045.htm>.

Duany, Jorge. "Neither White Nor Black: The Representation of Racial Identity among Puerto Ricans on the Island and in the U.S. Mainland." *The Puerto Rican Nation on the Move: Identities on the Island and in the United States*. Chapel Hill: U of North Carolina P, 2002. 236–60.

Flores, Juan. "Puerto Rican Literature in the United States: Stages and Perspectives." *ADE Bulletin* 91 (Winter 1988): 39–44. <http://www.mla.org/ade/bulletin/N091/091039.htm>.

Hernández, Carmen D. *Puerto Rican Voices in English: Interviews with Writers*. Westport, CT: Praeger, 1997.

Horno-Delgado, Asunción. *"Señores, don't leibolmi, please!*: ya *soy* Luz María Umpierre." *Breaking Boundaries: Latina Writing and Critical Readings.* Ed. Asunción Horno-Delgado et al. Amherst: U of Massachusetts P, 1989. 136–45.

Luis, William. "Puerto Rican American Poetry." *Dancing Between Two Cultures: Latino Caribbean Literature in the United States.* Nashville: Vanderbilt UP, 1997. 37–98.

Rodríguez de Laguna, Asela, ed. *Images and Identities: The Puerto Rican in Two World Contexts.* New Brunswick: Transaction, 1985.

Sánchez Korrol, Virginia. *From Colonia to Community: The History of Puerto Ricans in New York City.* Berkeley: U of California P, 1994.

Turner, Faythe, ed. *Puerto Rican Writers at Home in the USA: An Anthology.* Seattle: Open Hand, 1991.

Umpierre, Luz María. "Manifiesto: Whose Taboos? Theirs, Yours, or Ours?" *Letras Femeninas* 22.1–2 (1996): 263–68.

Jessica Hagedorn (b. 1949)

Contributing Editor: John Alberti

Classroom Issues and Strategies

Concise enough to be read aloud in class but rich with playful allusion and cross-referencing, Jessica Hagedorn's poems can form the basis of a mini-seminar on the politics, cultures, and legacies of colonialism. Hagedorn's work functions as both a critique of colonialism and as a form of resistance to it. These two kinds of cultural work can provide a template for student discussion of these two poems: the damage, confusion, and uncertainty about identity brought about by colonialism, and the ways an artist can draw on the multicultural context of colonialism to cope and even transcend the injuries caused by colonialism. Both intensely personal and deeply embedded in history and popular culture, Hagedorn's poems can help students explore the connections between the personal and the political in art and poetry.

Students may struggle with Hagedorn's frames of reference in these poems, especially given the changes in popular culture since 1971. As an instructor, you can provide the relevant historical context in relation to the history of U.S. occupation of the Philippines and the stereotyped representations of Asian Americans in popular culture. Time permitting, Hagedorn's poems also provide excellent opportunities for student research and reports, perhaps especially in relation to the popular culture references since they seem to suffer the most when translated into a lecture format. For example, students can first identify the references that seem most unfamiliar to them and then do research aimed at understanding why Hagedorn might be using them in her poems. Anna May Wong, Alice Coltrane, Dorothy Lamour, *Bonanza*, Dale Evans—all may be initially and equally obscure to modern students, yet the Internet offers the opportunity not just to read about these and other figures alluded to in the poems but to see and hear them as well. Students can be encouraged to bring in film clips, sound files, and images to share with the class.

As students explore how Hagedorn uses these images to evoke a sense of identity fractured between past and present, between East and West, between the very idea of dividing the world into "East" and "West," they can also be asked to gather references to contemporary popular culture that they feel speak to these same issues or that represent how these issues have evolved over the last thirty years.

Dorothy Allison (b. 1949)

Contributing Editor: John Alberti

Classroom Issues and Strategies

Allison's powerful story of survival and reconciliation among the women of a working-class Southern family may seem exotic to some students or hit very close to home for others. The stereotyping that surrounds the portrayal of poor Southern whites in cultural texts of many kinds may emerge as a classroom issue and definitely operates as part of Allison's artistic consciousness, especially in a story that includes sexual abuse and domestic violence. Students can be encouraged to examine how her story confronts, complicates, and in some cases refutes those stereotypes.

It is important to keep in mind when assigning this story that the narrator's climactic revelation of the sexual abuse she suffered along with her description of the shame, betrayal, and anger she feels as a result can evoke strong and painful responses in students who have been victims of sexual abuse, particularly if that abuse has also been kept secret. While care is called for when asking for students to speak or write about their reactions to the story, an important part of Allison's purpose in "Don't Tell Me You Don't Know" and the other stories in *Trash*, as well as her novel *Bastard Out of Carolina*, is to challenge the silence that surrounds and thus enables sexual abuse and domestic violence. In this sense, the title of the story can refer to society as a whole and not just the characters in the story, and the need for sensitivity in teaching the story should not stand in the way of assigning it.

Allison slowly provides details and information about the relationship and history between the narrator and Aunt Alma, and a reader response approach can help make students more aware of her technique. Students can be asked to trace their evolving sense of and attitude toward the characters, especially Aunt Alma, by registering their understanding of the story at key points in their progress through it. A formal version of this assignment can ask students to stop at the end of every page to jot notes about how their reactions to the story are changing as they move through it. After completing the story, students can then analyze which details and narrative techniques they feel were most effective and significant in influencing these periodic reactions.

Major Themes, Historical Perspectives, Personal Issues

The idea of strength emerges as a central theme in the story and the focus of Allison's feminist critique of the women's culture in the narrator's family. Throughout the story, the narrator contrasts images and descriptions of the physical and psychological strength of Alma and her sisters (the narrator remembers them as "mountains, mountains") with what she initially sees as their fatalism and inability (or refusal) to fight back against male violence or to protect their children adequately. Many students will share the narrator's frustration with her mother and Aunt Alma, especially immediately after the shocking revelation of her rape and the sterility caused by an untreated sexually transmitted infection.

As a result, the narrator's realization that "strength was not enough" and her question "Who can say where that strength ended, where the world took over and rolled us all around like balls on a pool table?" become critical points in discussing the larger analysis of class and gender oppression Allison invites us to consider. Students can be asked to consider what might constitute "enough" as part of a discussion of the final scene of reconciliation and female solidarity. The conclusion points to the enduring power and strength of love, but in neither a simplistic nor a clichéd way.

Questions for Reading, Discussion, and Writing

1. Compile a list of the physical descriptions the narrator gives us of her Aunt Alma. What complex portrait of Alma emerges as the result of these descriptions?
2. What is the significance of the pool game in the story? How does it function as a sign of Alma's strength and power? Of her fatalism? Of the complicated relationships among the women in their family?
3. What are the mixed ideas and attitudes about "family" that emerge from this story? What kind of value do you think "family" holds for Allison?
4. As a reader, what were your expectations for "the most special night"? Did the story surprise you? Why do you think the narrator describes the night as "special"?
5. Explore the implications of the title, "Don't Tell Me You Don't Know." Who could say it to whom, and what kinds of knowledge are being referred to?

Víctor Hernández Cruz (b. 1949)

Contributing Editor: Frances R. Aparicio

Classroom Issues and Strategies

Cruz's poetry may seem hermetic at times, and partly this is due to the use of imagery, words, and references that originate in Hispanic culture or mythology. Also, his poetry demands a reader who is familiar with both English and Spanish since he frequently plays with both languages.

I would advise students to read carefully and aid them by preparing a glossary or handout that would clarify the difficult references. (The problem is that not all English teachers have access to the meaning of local references to Puerto Rican towns, Indian gods, or mythological figures.)

I would emphasize the importance of the concrete poetry movement in relation to Cruz's work. The importance of the collage text, the use of space, the page, the graphics, and the significance of *play* as integral elements in the reading of a poem could be clearly explained by a visual presentation of concrete poems from Brazil, Europe, and the United States.

Major Themes, Historical Perspectives, Personal Issues

Urban life; meaning of language as an identity construct; importance of the cultural and historical past and how it flows into the present; importance of music and drugs as a basis for the poet's images; Hispanic culture and identity: How is it reaffirmed through literary creation?

Significant Form, Style, or Artistic Conventions

Focus on the importance of collage or hybrid texts; influence of concrete poetry; linguistic mixtures and lucid bilingualism; concept of metaliterary texts; contemporary American poetry: free verse, fragmentation, minimalism, surrealism.

Comparisons, Contrasts, Connections

Compare and contrast with Allen Ginsberg and other poets of the Beat generation (use of imagery based on drugs, music of the 1960s, influence of surrealism and irreverent language); an additional comparison with e. e. cummings, as well as with the concrete poets, would be helpful in terms of use of space, punctuation, and the page as signifiers. Contrast with poets like Pedro Pietri and Tato Laviera, in which the elements of popular culture are central to the understanding of their works (Cruz is much more introspective and abstract, and does not fit totally into the paradigm of Nuyorican aesthetics).

Questions for Reading, Discussion, and Writing

Study questions will focus mostly on the assigned text and would require students to identify major theme, use of language and imagery, and aesthetic effect of each poem.

Paper topics would focus on major themes. For example:

1. Discuss how "Speech changing within space," the epigraph to *By Lingual Wholes*, encapsulates Víctor Hernández Cruz's poetics.
2. Would you agree that English is transformed or affected by Spanish in Cruz's works? If so, how is this achieved?
3. Discuss the presence of Hispanic culture within contemporary urban life in the United States as it is reflected in Cruz's literature; that is, how he tropicalizes the U.S. cultural identity.

4. Analyze Cruz's texts as an example of urban literature: How do his point of view, attitudes, imagery, and rhythms create a sense of life in American cities?
5. Write on Cruz's use of music and drugs as basis for his poetic imagery.

Bibliography

Acosta-Belén, Edna. "The Literature of the Puerto Rican National Minority in the United States." *Bilingual Review* 5.1–2. Jan.-Aug. 1978: 107–16.

Aparicio, Frances. "Salsa, Maracas and Baile: Latin Popular Music in the Poetry of Víctor Hernández Cruz." *MELUS* 16.1 (Spring 1989–1990): 43–58.

Cruz, Arnaldo. "Teaching Puerto Rican Authors: Modernization and Identity in Nuyorican Literature." *ADE Bulletin* (1988): 45–51.

Cruz, Víctor Hernández . "Mountains in the North: Hispanic Writing in the USA." *The Americas Review*. 14.3–4 (Fall/Winter 1986): 110–14.

Carolyn Forché (b. 1950)

Contributing Editor: Constance Coiner

Classroom Issues and Strategies

Because two of the five poems included in this anthology appear in the section *The Country Between Us* (*TCBU*) titled "In Salvador, 1978–80," students will need some introduction to the situation in El Salvador at the time when Forché went there as a journalist/poet/human rights investigator. My students have been curious about the U.S. role in El Salvador's twelve-year civil war that ended with a United Nations (U.N.)–brokered peace accord on January 1, 1992. In "A Lesson in Commitment" (*TriQuarterly* [Winter 1986]: 30–38) Forché recounts the events that led to her going to El Salvador—an interesting, even amusing story that students will welcome. Forché's "El Salvador: An Aide Mémoire" (*The American Poetry Review* [July/August 1981]: 3–7), which both prefaces and theoretically frames the "El Salvador" poems, is essential to students' understanding "The Colonel" and "Because One Is Always Forgotten."

Findings of the U.N.-sponsored "truth commission," which investigated some of the worst human rights abuses of the twelve-year civil war, appear, for example, in the *New York Times*—"U.N. Report Urges Sweeping Changes in Salvador Army" (16 March 1993, A1 and A12) and "How U.S. Actions Helped Hide Salvador Human Rights Abuses" (21 March 1993, sec. 1: 1 and 10). Consider also "The Military Web of Corruption," *The Nation* (23 October 1982: 391–03), by Forché and Leonel Gomez. Students could also profit from renting on their own or your showing clips from *Romero,* a 1989 film directed by John Duigan and featuring Raul Julia as Monsignor Oscar Romero, the Archbishop of San Salvador, to whom Forché dedicated the eight "El Salvador poems." (Romero was murdered by a death squad in 1980 while saying mass at a hospital for the terminally ill.)

Students and teachers who want more background on El Salvador's history and the country's political and economic conditions can consult the following: *El Salvador: Another Vietnam* (1981), a fifty-minute documentary produced and directed by Glenn Silber and Tete Vasconcellos; Robert Armstrong and Janet Shenk's *El Salvador: The Face of Revolution* (Boston: South End, 1982); *A Decade of War: El Salvador Confronts the Future,* ed. Anjli Sundaram and George Gelber (New York: Monthly Review, 1991); and the North American Congress on Latin America (NACLA), an independent organization founded to analyze and report on Latin America and U.S. foreign policy toward Latin America. NACLA (475 Riverside Drive, Room 454, New York, NY 10115; 212-870-3146) publishes a journal and has a library open to the public.

I strongly recommend addressing the controversy in the United States concerning "political poetry," perhaps at the beginning and then at the end of your discussion of Forché's poems. Forché herself addresses this controversy briefly in "El Salvador: An Aide Mémoire." Forché's poetry and her views point to differences between formalist and "cultural studies" approaches to literature, differences that can also be usefully discussed in relation to other writers assigned in your course.

An audiocassette of Forché reading from *TCBU* is available from Watershed Tapes, P.O. Box 50145, Washington, DC 20004. Students respond favorably to hearing Forché read the poems. I also ask for volunteers to read the poems aloud. They have done so effectively, especially if given a few days to prepare.

"The Colonel"

Forché invented the term *documentary poem* for "The Colonel." This alternative form works partly because she sparingly employs traditional poetic forms as touchstones within it and partly because its seeming "artlessness" elicits belief from her readers.

In the journalistic way that it sets the scene, "The Colonel" takes little poetic license, inviting readers to trust that it has not caricatured the truth. Its simple, declarative sentences do not resemble poetic lines. Even visually, with its justified right-hand margin, the piece resembles a newspaper report more than a poem. In the twentieth century, the lyric has become by far the dominant poetic form, but because Forché wants her readers to experience what she witnessed in El Salvador from 1978 to 1980, she consciously resists lyricizing the experience. Before turning to Forché's poems, I define and provide examples of well-known lyrical poems so students can better understand how she subverts traditional lyrical poetry.

Forché first draws us into "The Colonel" by conversing with us about the rumors that have crept north of brutal Latin American military dictatorships: "WHAT YOU HAVE HEARD is true." Forché extends that sense of familiarity for her reader by creating in the first lines a scene that, except for the pistol on the cushion, could occur in any North American home: the wife serves coffee, the daughter files her nails, the son goes out for the evening; there are daily papers, pet dogs, a TV turned on even at meal time. The minutiae of ordinary domestic life draw us into the scene, as if we're entering the room with Forché; we feel as if *we're* having dinner with the colonel.

"The moon swung bare on its black cord over the house" is one of two figures foregrounded in the poem, and Forché deliberately draws attention to its artfulness. Although the image is ominous, suggestive generally of the gothic and particularly of a swinging interrogation lamp or of someone hanging naked from a rope, it is too decorative for its place between a pistol and a cop show, thus announcing itself as art.

The following lines portray the colonel's house as a fortress: "Broken bottles were embedded in the walls around the house to scoop the kneecaps from a man's legs or cut his hands to lace. On the windows there were gratings like those in liquor stores." The outside of this fortress, constructed to mutilate anyone who tries to get inside, stands in stark contrast to the several images of "civilization" and affluence inside, such as "dinner, rack of lamb, good wine, a gold bell [that] was on the table for calling the maid."

Until the parrot says hello from the terrace, triggering the colonel's anger and the action of the poem—that is, his spilling human ears on the table—the poem is a string of the verbs *to be*. As passive as her verbs, the poet can only catalog nouns, unable to exercise control or take action. In fact, her friend warns her with his eyes: "say nothing." And so, many readers identify with the poet rather than feel manipulated by her; like us, she is frightened, wary. (Students may be surprised to learn that Forché did not invent the Colonel's displaying severed ears as a startling, violent metaphor. The incident actually occurred, she has reported.)

Note the contrast between the single stylized line, "the moon swung bare on its black cord over the house," and the numerous declarative, weak-verb sentences

There were daily papers . . .
On the television was a cop show. It was in English.
Broken bottles were embedded in the walls . . .
On the windows there were gratings like those in liquor stores.

This contrast between the stylized line and the weak-verb sentences suggests the range of possible responses to situations such as dinner with the colonel as well as the range of possible responses to *reading* about dinner with the colonel: Will the poet remain impotent, unable to invent strong verbs—in other words, be unable to take action? Do more appropriate responses exist? Forché thus puts her readers in her place, in that room with the colonel, in a state of nascent political and moral awareness. The form itself suggests that we must make choices and take positions, not only as we read "The Colonel" but also as we respond to military dictatorships and to our government's support of them.

With the poem's second foregrounded figure, a simile describing the ears as "dried peach halves," the poet at once manipulates the mundane and is confined by it. She knows we have all seen dried fruit, and so she could not more vividly describe those severed ears, but she apologizes for the limits of her inherited poetic and for the limits of language itself, acknowledging simply: "There is no other way to say this." However, she also defends poetic language here. Because "there is no other way to say this," she must rely on a poetic device, a simile, to communicate with us.

The colonel shakes one of the ears in the faces of his guests. A human ear is an unusual—an even extraordinary—metonymy, as Forché well knows. It stands for the Salvadoran people, for those who have been mutilated and murdered as well as for those who continue to resist the military dictatorship. It might be helpful to students to think of the colonel's actions as a perverse magic show. He is able to make a severed ear come "alive" by dropping it into a glass of water, just as the death squads are able to make Salvadorans disappear. The sweeping gesture ("He swept the ears to the floor with his arm and held the last of his wine in the air") is theatrical and sends the ears down to the floor while the colonel elevates his glass of wine. The glass of wine carries us back to the "good wine" at dinner and the other markers of the affluent life maintained within the colonel's fortress at the expense of the extreme poverty outside. The glass of wine, then, is a metonymy for all the trappings of "civilization" we have seen in the colonel's fortress and for the power of the military over ordinary Salvadorans. And as the ears of ordinary Salvadorans go down to the floor, that wineglass, that metonymy for the affluence of the few, is hoisted triumphantly above them.

With this theatrical action come the colonel's climactic words: "Something for your poetry, no?" Most immediately, "Something" refers to the grand theatrical show the colonel has put on for his guests' "entertainment." But the colonel's ironic sneer also mocks Forché's position as a North American poet, drawing attention to the belief held by many North Americans that poetry has certain "proper" subjects, and that mutilation—and by extension politics—are not among them. Since the eighteenth century, mainstream North America has lost touch with the sense of literature as political catalyst. Nineteenth-century romanticism and some twentieth-century poetry promoted by New Criticism have been especially individualized, introspective, and self-referential. In "A Lesson in Commitment" Forché recalls how Leonel Gomez Vides tried to persuade her to come to El Salvador, asking her, "Do you want to write poetry about yourself for the rest of your life?" Forché, who came to understand Gomez Vides's point, believes that the "twentieth century human condition demands a poetry of witness" ("El Salvador: An Aide Mémoire").

Now look at the poem's final lines: "Some of the ears on the floor caught this scarp of his voice. Some of the / ears on the floor were pressed to the ground." Some of the ears seem to be alive, even though the colonel didn't believe for a minute during his mock magic show that he was actually bringing a dead ear back to life. Some of the ears seem to be listening and feeling for vibrations, for sounds and motion of resistance to the colonel's fortress. This poem, especially these concluding lines, implicitly questions the reader: Is *your* ear pressed to the ground? Are *you* listening? Have *you* "HEARD" (to return to the poem's opening words, written for emphasis in uppercase)? Are you responding to and involving yourself in resistance to the brutality of this colonel and others like him?

"Because One Is Always Forgotten"

This poem makes an excellent pedagogical companion piece to "The Colonel." As in her documentary poem, Forché writes in calculated relation to bourgeois forms, calling attention to the limits of inherited poetic forms and at the same time insisting that poetry can be used for political as well as aesthetic purposes. The obverse of "The Colonel," which appears artless, this elegy is the most highly structured piece in *TCBU*. Before turning to "Because One Is Always Forgotten," I define the elegy and provide examples of well-known elegies.

Forché wrote "Because One Is Always Forgotten" in memory of José Rudolfo Viera, who was Salvador's Deputy of Agrarian Reform under President Napoleon Duarte. (If teachers have read aloud excerpts from "A Lesson in Commitment" or made copies available, students will recall that Leonel Gomez Vides visited Forché in San Diego, urging her to come to El Salvador; Gomez Vides was Viera's assistant Deputy for Agrarian Reform.) Viera discovered that money that had been designated for agrarian reform (that is, an attempt to divide some of the largest landholdings so that most of the country's wealth would no longer reside in the hands of a few families) was being pocketed by members of Duarte's administration and men high up in the military. Some of that money was coming from the Carter administration in the United States, from U.S. taxpayers, and going not toward agrarian reform but instead to support the expensive tastes of a few. Think for a moment of words from "The Colonel"—rack of lamb, good wine, a gold bell for calling the maid. Think for a moment, too, of Forché's words in "El Salvador: An Aide Mémoire": "I was taken to the homes of landowners, with their pools set like aquamarines in the clipped grass, to the afternoon games of canasta over quaint local pupusas and tea, where parrots hung by their feet among the bougainvillea and nearly everything was imported, if only from Miami or New Orleans."

Viera, who reported the corruption on news televised in San Salvador, was murdered by "the White Glove," a right-wing death squad. Viera was shot along with two North Americans, Michael Hammer and Mark Pearlman, who were in El Salvador as consultants for agrarian reform. At the time of the murders, the three men were having a meal in the Sheraton Hotel dining room in San Salvador. No one was arrested, much less brought to trial, for the murder of the three men. Some North American newspapers reported the deaths of Michael Hammer and Mark Pearlman, but because Viera's death was not included in those reports, Forché felt the need to memorialize Viera.

"Because One Is Always Forgotten" tightly compresses rhythm and images, suggesting that traditional forms necessarily strain or snap under the weight of political imprisonment, murder, mutilation. After the second line, the lines start "losing" beats, as if atrocities in Salvador defy even one more word or beat. Forché undercuts the stylization that would comfort us, that would provide the consolation and closure that elegies have traditionally provided.

She also uses *heart*, a word common in poetry, in a way that is the opposite of what we expect.

> I could take my heart, he said, and give it to a *campesino*
> and he would cut it up and give it back:
>
> you can't eat heart in those four dark
> chambers where a man can be kept years.

"You can't eat heart" is a spondee—all unaccented syllables have been removed. A spondee represents language at its most compressed, its most structured, because English is more naturally a combination of accented and unaccented syllables. "You can't eat heart" also announces the limitations of poetic language. You can't *eat* it. It cannot, literally, sustain human life. In other words, an elegy, however necessary, is not a sufficient response to events such as those in El Salvador.

Students may volunteer that "those four dark chambers" refer to the left and right ventricles and the left and right auricles of the heart. But unless they have read "The Visitor," one of Forché's "El Salvador" poems not included in *The Heath Anthology*, they won't know that "dark chambers" also refers to "la oscura" (the dark place), a prison within a prison that inspired "The Visitor." Forché describes "la oscura"—where men were kept in boxes, one meter by one meter, with barred openings the size of a book—in her introduction to "The Visitor" on the Watershed audiocassette; she also describes "la oscura" in "El Salvador: An Aide Mémoire."

Now look at the following lines from the fourth stanza:

> A boy soldier in the bone-hot sun works his knife
> to peel the face from a dead man

The second line of this stanza stops abruptly; again, it is as if the atrocities in Salvador defy even one more word or beat. "To peel the face from a dead man" is no more an invented metaphor than "The Colonel"'s severed ears; in Salvador Forché actually saw human faces hanging from tree branches. Too often we have been taught to expect hearts and flowers from poetry, sometimes used sentimentally, but such sentimentality is turned on its head here. "Flowering with such faces" uses conventional poetic language in an extraordinary way.

Ask students what they make of the last, paradoxical stanza: "The heart is the toughest part of the body / Tenderness is in the hands." This stanza asks readers to examine something we have long accepted, the cliché of the tender heart, implying that we should probe some of our other assumptions as well.

Hands can *do* something; they can take action. *TCBU* includes many other references to hands, suggesting a wide range of possibilities for their use. Hands can "peel the face from a dead man / and hang it from the branch of a tree." The colonel uses his hands to spill human ears on the table and to shake one of the ears mockingly at his guests. Hands can be the White Glove (the name for a notorious Salvadoran death squad). But hands can also be tender; hands can connect people (the poet and Victoria in "As Children Together" hold "each other's coat sleeves"); hands can communicate (Forché tells Victoria to write to her). Rather than provide consolation and closure, as would a traditional elegy, "Because One Is Always Forgotten," like "The Colonel" and other poems in *TCBU*, asks readers to consider choices about their hands, their actions, their lives.

"As Children Together"

This poem is included in the section of *TCBU* titled "Reunion." Addressed to Forché's girlhood friend, Victoria, this poem gives us a sense of the poet's working-class roots. Although Forché continues to identify strongly with the class of her origin and with other oppressed groups, even as a youngster she "always believed . . . that there might be a way to get out" of Detroit. Victoria, ashamed of the "tins of surplus flour," the "relief checks," and other trappings of poverty, was also eager to escape: "I am going to have it," Victoria asserted, while believing that granting sexual favors to men was her only conduit.

The first stanza represents the girls' lives and futures as boxed in, closed off: the snow is "pinned"; the lights are "cubed"; they wait for Victoria's father to "whittle his soap cakes away, finish the whiskey," and for Victoria's mother to turn off the lights. Confined by "tight black dresses"—which, in this context, arguably represent a class marker—they nevertheless attempt to move away from the limitations of class, "holding each other's coat sleeves" for support. They slide "down the roads . . . *past* / crystal swamps and the death / face of each dark house, / *over* the golden ice / of tobacco spit" (my emphasis). They try to move away from their diminished options—the "*quiet* of ponds," "the *blind* white hills," "a *scant* snow" (my emphasis). But, sliding on ice, their movement is literally as well as metaphorically precarious.

Like "The Colonel" and "Because One Is Always Forgotten," this is a documentary poem, if less apparently so. The poet reports to Victoria and to us the poet's memory of their life together as children, the little she has heard about Victoria since their childhood, and one major event in the poet's life since her childhood ("I have been to Paris / since we parted"). In this stanza we hear the voice of the reporter, as we do in the other two poems. Although the poet doesn't know Victoria's current state, she reports what "They say."

If what "they say" is true, and if Victoria reads this poem, the poet has two simple messages for her childhood friend: "write to me" and "I have been to Paris / since we parted." On first reading, many students may think that the poet is bragging about the contrast between her own adult life and what she believes that of Victoria to be (the poet has been to Paris while Victoria did not even get as far as Montreal, the city of her childhood dreams). However, by taking the last line in the context of the entire poem, we see the implications, not of going to Paris, but how the poet got there: *not* by relying on the men of this poem as her vehicle. "Write to me" suggests that the poet wants to share with Victoria her experiences of—and perhaps her strategies for—getting out.

Victoria has not escaped the cycle of poverty and battered men. In the second-to-last stanza the poet reports a rumor that Victoria lives in a trailer near Detroit with her children and with her husband, who "returned from the Far East broken / cursing holy blood at the table" and whose whittling of soap cakes associates him with Victoria's whiskey-drinking father, who appears in the first stanza.

At first glance, "As Children Together" seems far removed from Salvador's civil war. In the context of *TCBU*, however, "As Children Together" links "the Far East" (Vietnam) to El Salvador. Young men from Forché's working-class neighborhood were drafted by or enlisted in the military when many of the more privileged of their generation managed student deferments or, after the draft lottery was established, other alternatives to military service. In "A

Lesson in Commitment," Forché reports that her interest in Vietnam was fueled partly by her first husband's fighting in Vietnam and his suffering "from what they now call Post-Vietnam Syndrome." The Vietnam War, as well as her opposition to it, schooled Forché for "another Vietnam" in El Salvador.

"As Children Together" provides a good opportunity to discuss the range of meanings for the deliberately ambiguous title of *The Country Between Us*. "Between" can mean something that separates and distances people, but "between" can also mean that which we share, that which connects us. The "country" is El Salvador, but it is also the United States. "Us" can be people on opposing sides of a civil war, people polarized by their opinions about political issues, or people sharing a common opposition to oppression. "Us" can be people inhabiting two nations (Salvador and the United States). "Us" can also refer to two individuals, such as the poet and Victoria, who may be at once separated by geography and recent experience but connected by common roots and class origin. The poet's saying to Victoria "write to me" suggests a desire for "between" as separation to become the "between" of reunion and connection.

From "The Recording Angel" and "Elegy"

Both the excerpt from "The Recording Angel" and "Elegy" are from Forché's recent collection of poems, *The Angel of History*. As the title of the collection suggests, the work is not so much based on personal experience in the ways of poems of witness and remembrance such as "Because One Is Always Forgotten" and "As Children Together," but is instead a meditation on history, specifically, the nightmare history of the twentieth century, from the Holocaust and Hiroshima to the tragedy of El Salvador. In her Notes at the end of *The Angel of History*, Forché says that "these utterances issue from my own encounter with the events of this century but do not represent 'it.' The first-person, free-verse, lyric-narrative of my earlier years has given way to a work which has desired its own bodying forth: polyphonic, broken, haunted, and in ruins, with no possibility of restoration." These comments speak to the potential difficulty of these later poems to students, but by explaining some of the rationale behind the composition of these poems, they also can help students make their own sense of Forché's style. Writing in response to the horror of the Second World War in these two poems, Forché resists the aesthetic impulse to make whole that which has been shattered by war and genocide. Instead, the class can take Forché's description of this history as "polyphonic, broken" and "haunted" as a way of reading Forché's poems not as attempts to obscure history but as parts of her commitment to honesty and even realism. Rather than "explaining" the war or the Holocaust, and thereby running the risk of substituting her voice for the voice of the victims and those who resisted, or even of explaining away the past, Forché instead remains true to the ethic of witnessing by presenting us with shards from a past "in ruins," both in terms of descriptions and physical places and quotations from various sources. (The Notes at the end of *The Angel of History* provide some helpful references for these quotations.) As a result, we retain as readers the moral responsibility to confront the horror of twentieth-century history and craft our own response, without the safety net of received opinion or the comfort of conventional aesthetic unity.

Major Themes, Historical Perspectives, Personal Issues

1. U.S. imperialism.
2. The difference between poetry that calls attention chiefly to form and poetry like Forché's that is formally interesting as well as socially and politically engaged.
3. The difference between poetry that is individualized and self-referential and poetry like Forché's that addresses social and political issues and engenders human empathy.
4. *TCBU* has renewed the controversy about the relation of art to politics, about "suitable" subjects for poetry. This peculiarly American debate assumes that only certain poems are political, stigmatizing "political" poems and failing to acknowledge the ideological constitution of all literary texts. The opposition to "political" poetry, as Forché herself has observed, extends beyond explicitly polemical work to any "impassioned voices of witness," to any who leave the "safety of self-contemplation to imagine and address the larger world" ("A Lesson in Commitment").
5. Forché's poetry resonates with a sense of international kinship. "For us to comprehend El Salvador," Forché has written, "for there to be moral revulsion, we must be convinced that Salvadorans—and indeed the whole population of Latin America—are people like ourselves, contemporary with ourselves, and occupying the same reality" ("Grasping the Gruesome," *Esquire* [Sept. 1983]). Forché's poetry moves us with a forceful sense of "the other" rare in contemporary American verse.
6. The merging of personal and political.

Significant Form, Style, or Artistic Conventions

In the twentieth century, the lyric became the preponderant poetic form, but in *TCBU* Forché is a storyteller, her poetry predominantly narrative. Because she wants her readers to experience what she witnessed in El Salvador from 1978 to 1980, she consciously resists lyricizing experiences. Forché has said that "the twentieth-century human condition demands a poetry of witness" ("El Salvador: An Aide Mémoire").

To show how Forché departs from the lyric, teachers should define the *lyric* and provide well-known examples. To show how Forché departs from the elegy in "Because One Is Always Forgotten," teachers should define the *elegy* and provide known examples. For "The Colonel" teachers should define and provide other examples of *metonymy*.

Original Audience

The particular audience for Forché's poetry is the American people. Monsignor Romero (again, the Archbishop of San Salvador who was assassinated by a right-wing death squad while praying at mass) urged Forché to return to the United States and "tell the American people what is happening" ("El Salvador: An Aide Mémoire"). Poets do not often so purposefully address such a wide audience.

Students should discuss whether—and, if so, in what ways—Forché's poems effectively address the wide popular audience she seeks, one that would include more people than the "already converted." Do the three poems under consideration avoid or fall into off-putting didacticism? Students, of course, will have their own responses, but I would argue that Forché has consciously adopted strategies throughout *TCBU* that invite the reader into the poems. One of those strategies is to acknowledge her own ignorance rather than point to the reader's; another is to place herself or someone else in the poem as an object of ridicule or admonition rather than the reader. For example, the colonel sneers at the poet; the poet does not upbraid her reader. And in "Because One Is Always Forgotten," a hungry *campesino* would reject Viera's heart, admonishing: "you can't eat heart."

Comparisons, Contrasts, Connections

Denise Levertov, Muriel Rukeyser, Adrienne Rich, Pablo Neruda—these are anti-imperialist, politically engaged writers whose lives and literary texts promote a global as well as a private kinship.

The private anguish of Sylvia Plath's, Anne Sexton's, and Robert Lowell's confessional poetry provides a provocative contrast to the public issues of human rights violations, U.S. foreign policy, war, and class oppression addressed in "The Colonel," "Because One Is Always Forgotten," and "As Children Together."

Questions for Reading, Discussion, and Writing

"The Colonel":

1. How does the capitalization of the first four words function in the poem?
2. Can anyone identify the traditional poetic forms that Forché sparingly employs as "aesthetic centerpieces" in this "artless," "journalistic," documentary poem? (I'm thinking here of "the moon swung bare on its black cord over the house" and the simile describing the ears as "dried peach halves").
3. Why is the television "cop show" in English, the commercial in Spanish?
4. Why the proliferation of *to-be* verbs (*is*, *was*, *were*)?
5. What are the women in this poem doing?
6. What might the colonel have in mind when he says, "Something for your poetry, no?"
7. What are the implied and explicit cultural and political relationships between Salvador and the United States?

"Because One Is Always Forgotten":

1. In the first line, what does "it" refer to?
2. What are the relationships between "heart" and other body parts?
3. Who is "you" in the third stanza?
4. Identify similarities/differences (including formal ones) between this poem and "The Colonel."
5. This poem concludes the section of *TCBU* titled "In Salvador, 1978–80." Why might have Forché chosen *hands* as the last word of this section?

"As Children Together":

1. What are some of the similarities/differences between Victoria and the poet as children? What might be some similarities/differences between them as adults?
2. What is the significance of "Paris" in the last line?
3. What are some of the difficulties of remaining in touch with one's community, cultural group, or class of origin after being separated from them by emigration, formal education, or class mobility?
4. What's the difference between the poet's saying, "I always believed this,/Victoria, that there might / be a way to get out" and Victoria's asserting, "I am going to have it"?
5. Identify similarities/differences (including formal ones) between this poem and "The Colonel" and "Because One Is Always Forgotten."

"The Recording Angel":

1. How does Forché's description of these poems as "polyphonic, broken, haunted, and in ruins, with no possibility of restoration" affect our understanding of their structure?
2. What is the effect of the juxtaposition of images of both peace and terror, such as the wings of doves with "a comic wedding in which corpses exchange vows"? What other such contrasts can be found, and what is their effect?
3. In Section I, the city seems deserted in the aftermath of some great calamity. Which images do you seize on to make sense of what has happened?
4. As we move into sections II and III, we encounter a child (referred to only as "it") and a woman in a photograph. What clues (such as the ominous image of "the fresh claw of a swastika on Rue Boulard") does the poem provide as to who these people are (or even if they are the same person) and what happened to them?

"Elegy":

1. The quoted material in the poem is from descriptions of concentration camps in Claude Lanzmann's 1985 film about the Holocaust, *Shoah*. What is the affect of such prosaic, almost matter-of-fact descriptions of the brutality of the Holocaust?
2. "And so we revolt against silence with a bit of speaking" can suggest the difficulty, almost impossibility, of finding adequate expression for the horror of the Holocaust. How would you describe the strategy that "Elegy" uses and its effectiveness?
3. Who is the ghost figure in the poem? What kind of witness does he provide?
4. Notice the simultaneously beautiful and ominous image of the "tattoo of stars," both suggesting the delicacy of the night sky but also reminding us of the ID numbers tattooed on the arms of concentration camp inmates. How does such imagery work as part of the "bit of speaking" against the silence of the aftermath of the Holocaust? What other examples of such imagery can you find?

Approaches to Writing

Students in my undergraduate courses write one-page (double-spaced, typed) "response" essays to each assigned text, which they turn in before I have said anything about the writer of text(s). In these essays, students reflect on why they have responded to the text(s) as they have, including some identification of their own subject position (gender, race, national origin, class origin, political views, and so on), but they must also refer specifically to the text. In the case of these five poems, students could choose to focus the response essay on just one poem, or they could write about a recurring theme, image, and strategy, briefly citing all five poems.

A few students have elected to write creative responses, trying their hand at imitating the form of one of the assigned poems.

Bibliography

Forché, Carolyn. "El Salvador: An Aide Mémoire." *American Poetry Review* (July/Aug. 1981): 3–7.

———. "A Lesson in Commitment." *TriQuarterly* (Winter 1986): 30–38.

Greer, Michael. "Politicizing the Modern: Carolyn Forché in El Salvador and America." *Centennial Review* (Spring 1986): 160–80.

Kufeld, Adam. *El Salvador: Photographs by Adam Kufeld.* Introduction by Arnoldo Ramos and poetry by Manlio Argueta.

Mann, John. "Carolyn Forché: Poetry and Survival." *American Poetry* 3.3 (Spring 1986): 51–69.

Mattison, Harry, et al., ed. *El Salvador: Work of Thirty Photographers.* Text by Carolyn Forché. New York: Writers and Readers Publishing Cooperative, 1983.

Useful interviews include David Montenegro's in *American Poetry Review* 17.6 (Nov./Dec. 1988): 35–40; Constance Coiner's in *The Jacaranda Review* (Winter 1988): 47–68; and Kim Addonizio and John High's in *Five Fingers Review* 3 (1985): 116–31.

Paula Vogel (b. 1951)

Contributing Editor: Susan C. W. Abbotson

Classroom Issues and Strategies

It helps if students realize that Paula Vogel is a dramatist whose mission is to expose the ways in which women are entrapped and oppressed, yet also to reveal that those same women have the capability and strength to break free if they could only see themselves from a different perspective. As a feminist, Vogel sees American women living in a culture of victimization in which people are encouraged to remain victims and so remain disempowered. Her plays try to show that there are other alternatives. Taking a creative approach to sensitive issues, her sexual and social criticism is at times nuanced and subtle and at other times blunt and intentionally shocking. The plays should be read as acts of retaliation against the accepted norms, but they are speculative rather than polemical: Vogel prefers that her audience think up new questions rather than settle for easy answers. The daring content of many of her plays is designed to bait an audience, often revealing things they had subconsciously preferred to keep hidden, so expect some lively classroom discussion.

By and large, students will enjoy this play as it has a contemporary feel, and they will be comfortable with its language and setting. Although a few may not fully understand the complex nature of the relationship between Li'l Bit and her Uncle, most will, even to the point of recognizing that Li'l Bit is not entirely a victim and is complicit in the relationship. Some may need you to underline the oblique reference to Uncle Peck's own possible history of abuse as a child and to explain the sexual innuendo of what was actually happening on the fishing outing with Cousin Bobby.

A good starting point could be a discussion of the possible meanings behind the opening phrase: "Safety First—You and Driver Education." Whose safety? Safety from what? Who is the "driver," and who is the "you"? Who is being educated (and about what)? This could connect to a discussion of the idea to which Li'l Bit frequently refers of a line being drawn: what line, who draws it, and who moves it? It may also be useful to ask the students what they believe Li'l Bit's "secret" to be and what they see as the lesson of the play. Although the issue of sexual molestation may dominate, they should be drawn toward the wider issues of family relationships, growing up and surviving in our contemporary culture, and becoming independent. Vogel has said that the play "dramatizes the gifts we receive from people who hurt us" and that the gift Li'l Bit received was "how to survive." This truthfulness of this statement is a good springboard for a discussion of the play as a whole.

Major Themes, Historical Perspectives, Personal Issues

Vogel makes jokes about pedophilia in the play, but in interviews she insists that this is not what the play is about. For her, the play is about survival and the complicated ways in which we "come of age" in a complex and often hostile contemporary culture. She resists portraying Li'l Bit as mere victim, and by depicting Uncle Peck as an attractive, kindly, and well-loved person, she emphasizes the ambiguities of the situation. Peck is not necessarily the villain despite his predatory nature, and Vogel allows us to see both his own sad, mitigating background and elements of complicity in Li'l Bit's behavior. As the *New York Times* suggests: "It is hard to say who is the more accomplished seducer in *How I Learned to Drive*," none the least when Li'l Bit tries her own hand at the pleasures of seducing a schoolboy.

Next to the girls and boys at school who tease her because of her breasts, and her own family circle, with its crude, lecherous grandfather; and grandmother and mother who offer ugly, negative assessments of men, even while they themselves treat Li'l Bit as a sex object, Uncle Peck, with his sensitivity to her feelings, evident care, and greater refinement, appears much the better company for an insecure young girl looking for love and guidance. Li'l Bit is drawn to Peck "like a plant to the sun" (61). We are made aware that Peck loves Li'l Bit, and her rejection of him leads to his descent into alcoholism and death. That he is not a blood relative is frequently stressed, usually by Peck himself, and he does not actually have intercourse with her, which may ameliorate his crime. However, the fact that at her tender age of eleven he openly masturbated while she sat on his lap, unable to object, was wrong. It has scarred Li'l Bit for life, and the play expresses her coming to terms with this damage. Her forgiveness, of both herself and Uncle Peck at the close, should be seen as a positive move forward.

Vogel's decision to title the volume in which she printed this play *The Mammary Plays* speaks to another central issue of the play: the way in which society and women themselves tend to view a woman's body and how that view can both restrict and reduce an individual. Vogel has explained that the image of a large-breasted woman was a central image she had in mind when writing the play. As a feminist, Vogel is interested in the way society that tends to fetishize women's bodies in particular, and people's reactions toward and comments about Li'l Bit's breasts tell us a lot about our socially conditioned subconscious reactions to the female body.

Another issue that dominates the play and the interaction of the characters is that of control: in a sense, this is at the heart of the relationship between Li'l Bit and Uncle Peck as each strives for the upper hand. When he literally holds her in his hand, when he manages her pose and attire while taking photographs, when he holds her on his knee as he masturbates, Peck is in control and seems the sleazy predator. However, at other times, though in a position of potential power, he holds himself back, such as when he gets her drunk but chooses not to take advantage of her. There are other times when it is clear that Li'l Bit is in control of their relationship, such as when she suggests they meet for regular talks and when she goes off to college and finally rejects him. The "driving" metaphor of the play is clearly related to this issue of control and helps students to realize that Li'l Bit does emerge the survivor in this play as she ends up in the position of control, driving her car down the highway to future possibilities. It is, ironically, a skill taught to her by that same uncle who initially abused her. The characters' abuse of alcohol—Peck, Li'l Bit, and her mother are all shown to be potential alcoholics—is also something of which many students will be aware, and this too can be related to the issue of control (or lack of it).

Significant Form, Style, or Artistic Conventions

Vogel's earliest efforts at playwriting were met with general rejection: she was turned down by both Yale School of Drama and the O'Neill National Playwright's Conference. Yet she feels that these disappointments helped nurture her skills outside the influence of mainstream theater. "A crucial influence on my future writing career," she has said, "was my dismissal from the theatre arts faculty of Cornell University." Vogel's work is marked by its ability to break the rules in terms of accepted taste, form, and convention; her plays rebel against both theatrical and social assumptions and stereotypes. She is partly indebted to the work of the German playwright Bertolt Brecht, who similarly strove to disconcert and unsettle audiences, often by making the familiar appear suddenly strange in order to provoke a reevaluation. Both try to show audiences that what they accept as real is only a subjective construct and that alternative realities are possible when you observe from a different perspective. Due to the controversial nature of much of her work, Vogel has been mostly produced in Off-Off Broadway and Off-Broadway theaters rather than on Broadway, but she finds this liberating rather then restrictive.

Typical of the way in which many contemporary writers work, Vogel's plays tend to gestate over a period of years, as they undergo a series of readings, workshops, and revisions. In the late 1970s, Vogel wrote "Heirlooms," a short play that contained the seeds of *How I Learned to Drive*. This was set aside and not developed until twenty years later, when the first draft of *How I Learned to Drive* was written in two weeks. She wrote the play with what she terms a "reverse syllogistic plot," an idea that she got from British playwright Harold Pinter's *Betrayal* (1978). Essentially, the play starts with the end result, and then the action takes us backwards through the events which led up to that point, therefore ending with the event that started the action. It is a kind of circular structure in terms of cause and effect, but played out in reverse order. The first image that came to her was that of "a woman driving someplace in the Arizona desert. She adjusts her rearview mirror, and a dead man materializes in the back seat." In a sense, the play then proceeds to explain this image and explore its possible meanings.

When producing a play, Vogel works with both the director and the actors to hone the production, and often major changes are made during rehearsal. Not all directors, for example, use the slides that Vogel in the text requests be used. With her agreement, they were left out of the original New York production. But her use of music, slides, and headlines to underline the play's thematic points is part of its innovative approach. It recalls Tennessee Williams's *The Glass Menagerie* (1945) and its attempt to create what Williams termed "plastic theater," a theater that invokes a more poetic view of events through spectacle as well as words. Like *Menagerie*, *How I Learned to Drive* can also be viewed as a memory play, and it is related to us by a potentially unreliable narrator in that the person telling the story is a central player in the events that are being related. But whereas the events of *Menagerie* unfold in a fairly linear fashion, *How I Learned to Drive* moves back and forth as it gradually creeps up on the defining moment of Li'l Bit's life, with which she has been endeavoring to come to terms. Vogel assists us with her jokey references to driving made through the use of Driver's Education titles; thus, "Driving in First Gear" leads to memories being reenacted before us, "Reverse Gear" sends us looping back in time, and "Idling in Neutral Gear" pulls us away from memory into the present time.

Other interesting techniques are the drama's use of a three-person Greek chorus that plays the roles of family and passersby and the way in which the actors mostly mime their interactions while facing front (so that Peck fondles imaginary breasts rather than those of the actress). Later in the play, Vogel has the younger chorus figure substitute for Li'l Bit as she sits on Peck's lap while he masturbates when she is supposedly eleven years old; this is a means of distancing the audience from the event in a way that makes it seem more clinical and therefore all the more shocking.

Original Audience

How I Learned to Drive was first produced in February 1997 by the Vineyard Theater in New York City. Mary-Louise Parker played Li'l Bit, and David Morse played Uncle Peck. The play was an instant sensation, receiving warm reviews and winning an array of awards, including an Obie and the Drama Desk and New York Drama Critics Circle awards as well as the Pulitzer Prize that year. *USA Today* called it one of the "best plays of the decade," and the *Village Voice* described it as "genuine and genuinely disturbing." Given its dark themes, it is not an easy play, but the surface comedy makes it more palatable, and its inventiveness has won critical admiration. Partly, perhaps, because it is a relatively inexpensive play to produce, with little in the way of necessary staging, but also because of its timely topic and clever blending of the serious and the comic, in 1998, *How I Learned to Drive* was the most produced play in America, with twenty-six regional productions and more than thirty additional productions scheduled for abroad.

Comparisons, Contrasts, Connections

Vogel has said that her biggest influence in writing this play was Vladimir Nabokov's *Lolita* (1955), to which she sees the play as both an homage and a response. While Nabokov tells his story from the point of view of the man, Humbert Humbert, she tries to tell her version from the viewpoint of the girl to see how that narrative strategy affects our sympathies and reactions. It may be useful to look at some extracts from *Lolita* or scenes from one of the movie versions and to compare and contrast the relationship of Lolita and Humbert Humbert to that of Li'l Bit and Uncle Peck. The ambivalent treatment of the sexes in David Mamet's *Oleanna* (1992), which problematizes gender relationships so that it is hard to see either side as entirely innocent or guilty, was another admitted influence, although Vogel hopes that *How I Learned to Drive* offers a finer balance than she sees in *Oleanna*. In terms of form, Vogel has mentioned the connection to Harold Pinter's *Betrayal*.

It may be useful to study this play alongside other works in the anthology that look at the way women are (or have been) treated and to make comparisons and connections. Obvious examples are the short stories of Kate Chopin and Charlotte Perkins Gilman, Susan Glaspell's play *Trifles,* or a poem like Louise Bogan's "Women," against which it would be interesting to read the character of Li'l Bit. Although it involves a very different character, a psychological comparison of Li'l Bit against Miss Collins from Tennessee Williams's *Portrait of a Madonna* might also be interesting, especially in an exploration of the ways in which family and surrounding culture affect the development of an individual female. The oblique way in which Li'l Bit and Uncle Peck converse, more through inference and metaphor than direct meaning, could be usefully compared with the exchanges between the man and woman in Ernest Hemingway's "Hills Like White Elephants," as could the relationship between the two "couples." In terms of form, the play could be compared with either Eugene O'Neill's *The Hairy Ape* or Edward Albee's *The Sandbox*, both of which are similarly experimental and expressionistic (as well as dealing, in part, with the same underlying themes regarding gender stereotypes).

Working with Cultural Objects

Vogel is very concerned with social constructs of women and how these images impact upon the unwary: both male and female. There are several slide shows during the play, including those typical garage-calendar images of erotic women draped over cars, bending over hoods, and squirting hoses; images from *Playboy*; Calvin Klein advertisements; and those sexualized portraits of young girls that were so popular in Victorian times, such as the photographs Lewis Carroll took of Alice Liddell. Some of these images could be displayed in the classroom and their strategies and effects discussed. Students should be encouraged to bring in their own images of girls and women from magazines and advertisements for class discussion.

The website at <http://www.saintmarys.edu/%7Emedi0639/femalestereotypes.html> offers some brief graphics and clear categorization to start you off, or extracts from a book like Carole Moog's *Are They Selling Her Lips? Advertising and Identity* (1990) may be useful in generating further discussion.

Vogel also discusses the music (mostly from the 1960s) that she felt was inspirational and that she played while writing *How I Learned to Drive*: "Dream Baby" and "Sweet Dreams" by Roy Orbison, "Dedicated to the One I Love" by the Mamas and the Papas, "Surfer Girl" by the Beach Boys, "This Girl is a Woman Now" by Gary Puckett and the Union Gap, "You're Sixteen" by Johnny Burnett, "Come Back When You Grow Up" by Bobby Vee, and the sounds of the Tijuana Brass. Just one of the LP covers of the latter may be worth bringing in for discussion—especially the ever-popular *Whipped Cream and Other Delights* album, which has on its front cover a woman dressed in nothing but whipped cream!

Most of these songs support the sexualization of young girls, and a number of them could be played for the class and/or the lyrics distributed. The class could then discuss what it is that these songs teach and what gender stereotypes they support. What do they make their teen listeners want and expect from life? Do songs of the twenty-first century offer any more positive images of femininity? The sample assignment in the Pedagogy section on the *The Heath Anthology* website is based upon an exploration of these media aspects of the play.

Vogel also discusses the ways in which traffic signs could be used to underline and expand the central driving metaphor of the play. It would be worth displaying several to the class to read in the new sexualized context Vogel uses in the play: *No Passing, Slow Children, Dangerous Curves,* and *One Way,* as well as the visual symbols for children, deer crossing, hills, and school buses.

Questions for Reading, Discussion, and Writing

Group Discussion

1. At what point do you realize that a) it is Li'l Bit's uncle who molests her, and b) the age at which he started to do this?

2. Why do you think Vogel chooses initially to withhold this information? Why not tell us straight out at the start? Could it be for the same reason that she never shows Peck directly molesting Li'l Bit?
3. Why does Vogel not tell the story in a strict chronology but instead jump back and forth in time throughout the play? How does the Greek chorus add to the play?
4. How does Vogel build up the character of Uncle Peck? In what ways can he be seen as a positive or a negative character? Why does Vogel include the fishing episode with Cousin Bobby?
5. In what ways is Li'l Bit shown to be an active participant in the relationship with Peck? Where does she draw her line, and what does her ability to do this suggest?
6. Why do you think Li'l Bit is attracted to Peck, and why is he attracted to her? What is it that Li'l Bit needs—first as a child, and then as an adult?
7. What do the slides, music, and Driver's Education titles contribute to the play? What might be lost if they were omitted?
8. What does Peck teach Li'l Bit that helps her to finally survive?

Formal Paper Topics

1. If Paula Vogel's *How I Learned to Drive* is a play about survival, what exactly is Li'l Bit surviving from, and how does she achieve this survival?
2. To what extent are the troubles of Li'l Bit based on gender?
3. In what ways does Paula Vogel use the metaphor of driving?

See also the sample assignment in the Pedagogy section on *The Heath Anthology* website, which focuses on the issue of the female body image and how that issue informs and influences the play.

Bibliography

There is little critical material currently in print on the work of Paula Vogel since her rise to fame has been relatively recent. Interviews and reviews of *How I Learned to Drive* are about the most useful resources available to date, and these are some of the better ones.

Guare, John. ed. *Conjunctions 25: The New American Theatre*. Annandale-on-Hudson: Bard College, 1995.

Mead, Rebecca. "Drive-by Shooting." *New York* 30 (7 April 1997): 46–47.

Parker, Mary-Louise. "Paula Vogel." *Bomb* 61 (1997): 44–49.

Savran, David. *The Playwright's Voice: American Dramatists on Memory, Writing and the Politics of Culture.* New York: Theatre Communications Group, 1999.

Sova, Kathy. "Time to Laugh." *American Theater* 14.2 (1997): 24.

Karen Tei Yamashita (b. 1951)

Contributing Editor: John Alberti

Classroom Issues and Strategies

Just as the rich cultural diversity fueled by waves of immigration made New York City a focal point for U.S. artists for much of the twentieth century, Los Angeles has emerged over the last twenty-five years as a symbol of contemporary multicultural America. Representing at the same time the western edge of U.S. continental expansion, the eastern border of the Asian Pacific rim, and the northern region of Latin America, Los Angeles is both a patchwork and a synthesis of ethnic and cultural identities that resists easy definition. Again, as with New York City, however, Los Angeles stands as both a physical geographic space and a potent symbolic terrain for artists, writers, and the culture industry in general. Karen Tei Yamashita's novel *Tropic of Orange* functions as both a unique artistic vision of contemporary Los Angeles and as part of an ongoing artistic and cultural conversation about the reality and meaning of Los Angeles and, by extension, multicultural America.

Students might begin by first writing about and discussing their previous encounters with images and constructions of Los Angeles, ranging from television shows to films to political ads. Obviously, this initial exercise will have different resonance for students living and studying in Los Angeles than for students for whom Los Angeles mainly exists as an imaginary construct. Even among Angelinos, though, as Yamashita's novel suggests, you will find multiple visions and experiences of Los Angeles.

Given this necessary context and understanding that there is no single "correct" representation of Los Angeles, students will be prepared to consider what issues—political, cultural, personal—are at stake in the various images of Los Angeles they have encountered—from the familiar obsession with the wealth of Beverly Hills and the glamour of the movie industry to art that works to be more inclusive of the diversity of Los Angeles while also destabilizing familiar stereotypes about the major ethnic communities within the city. It is from this perspective that the narrator's description of Bobby Ngu as a "Chinese from Singapore with a Vietnam name speaking like a Mexican living in Koreatown" takes on resonance. Yamashita is clearly engaged in the process of challenging the reductive stereotypes signaled by the narrator's sarcastic reference to readers who might think they "know their Asians," but she is also concerned with exploring the survival strategies and cultural syntheses that are creating new cultural realities in Los Angeles.

Thus, a seemingly simple question for class discussion such as "What is Bobby's ethnic identity?" opens the way for a complex consideration of the performative aspects of ethnicity, race, and class. Similarly, Yamashita's multivocal narrative strategy raises similar interesting questions about where to locate the author in the text. A female Asian-American writer comfortable with being identified as such, Yamashita here writes in a persona linguistically marked as Latino to describe an "Asian" character who might be "Chinamex." Within this discussion, Yamashita's work studying immigrant Japanese communities in Brazil as well as her interest in Latin American fiction can take on special relevance.

Finally, Bobby's story can also be read and discussed as yet another take, at once ironic and sincere, on the Benjamin Franklin/Horatio Alger American dream story. Students can consider the ways in which Yamashita signifies on the specifically immigrant variation of this story, particularly in the ways in which Bobby's history is intertwined with that of the Vietnam War and economic globalization.

Comparisons, Contrasts, Connections

Tropic of Orange can be compared with other examples in *The Heath Anthology* of writers self-consciously creating a sense of place and even a mythology about a specific geographic location, from those discussed in the "Cluster: America in the European Imagination" to the various writers involved in the construction of New York City, perhaps most significantly those such as Abraham Cahan and Mary Antin from the early twentieth century who helped foster powerful symbolic fictions about the immigrant experience. Writers of more contemporary depictions of the Asian immigrant experience, from Carlos Bulosan to Gish Jen, are of obvious relevance as well.

More theoretically, the selection from *Borderlands*/La Frontera by Gloria Anzaldúa (a writer Yamashita admires) provides speculations on the multiplicity of identity and the multivocality of contemporary American culture that can inform a discussion of Yamashita's narrative and stylistic strategies in this excerpt from *Tropic of Orange*.

Working With Cultural Objects

As the name of this chapter from *Tropic of Orange* suggests, Los Angeles is a collection of neighborhoods with rich and dynamic ethnic histories, from Koreatown to South Central to the Fairfax district to East Los Angeles. Yamashita, however, is careful not to reify or stereotype the ethnic mix of any of these communities, and she does this through the specific artistic depiction of a complex fictional character.

Both students who live in Los Angeles and those who don't can enrich their understanding and conversation about what cultural diversity means in Los Angeles by sampling another rich multicultural Los Angeles tradition, the public mural, at the University of Southern California's *Los Angeles Murals* website at <http://www.usc.edu/isd/archives/la/pubart/LA_murals>. As students view the wide variety of murals on display, they can discuss the multiple images of "Los Angeles" they find there and think about and even create a mural reflective of their understanding of this chapter from *Tropic of Orange*.

Questions for Reading, Discussion, and Writing

1. What dominant impressions of Los Angeles have you received from other cultural texts? How does this chapter from *Tropic of Orange* play off these existing images of Los Angeles?
2. What kind of a narrator does Yamashita construct in this chapter? How does his perspective influence our understanding of Bobby Ngu? Do you think we are meant to see his story as heroic, tragic, or some combination of the two?
3. Compare Yamashita's story of Bobby Ngu's immigrant experience with others you have encountered in *The Heath Anthology*. How does *Tropic of Orange* both extend and modify dominant constructions of the immigrant experience?

Garrett Kaoru Hongo (b. 1951)

Contributing Editors: Amy Ling and King-Kok Cheung

Classroom Issues and Strategies

Explain that Hongo's themes and craft are evident even in the small selection we have in this text. The title poem of his first book, *Yellow Light*, emphasizes the centrality of the Asian perspective by ascribing a positive, fertile quality to the color commonly designating Asian skin and formerly meaning "cowardly." By focusing his sights on ordinary people in the midst of their daily rounds, as in "Yellow Light," "Off from Swing Shift," and "And Your Soul Shall Dance"; by describing their surroundings in precise detail; by suggesting their dreams, Hongo depicts both the specificities of the Japanese-American experience and its universality. "And Your Soul Shall Dance" is a tribute to playwright and fiction writer Wakako Yamauchi.

Major Themes, Historical Perspectives, Personal Issues

The work of any Asian-American writer is best understood in the context of the black civil rights and the women's liberation movements of the 1960s and 1970s. These movements by African Americans and women led Asian Americans to join in the push for change. Asian Americans as a group had endured racial discrimination in the United States for over a century, from the harassment of Chinese in the California gold mines to the internment of thousands of Japanese Americans during World War II. Furthermore, the last three wars the United States has engaged in have been fought in Asia, a fact that further consolidated a sense of community among the hitherto disparate Asian groups in this country.

Significant Form, Style, or Artistic Conventions

In Hongo's volume *Yellow Light*, we no longer find a dependence on language and rhythm borrowed from African-American culture nor strident screams of bitterness and anger characteristic of polemic Asian-American poetry, the dominant mode and tone of the 1970s. Hongo is at home in his skin, positive about his background and the people around him, confident in his own voice, concerned as much with his craft as with his message.

Hongo's poems paint portraits of the people around him, and he invests his people with dignity and bathes them in love. Pride in an Asian-American heritage shines through in the catalog of foods in "Who Among You Knows the Essence of Garlic?" Hongo's eye has the precision of seventeenth-century Flemish still-life painters, but his art is dynamic and evokes the sounds, smells, and tastes of the foods he describes.

He has combined the consciousness of the late-twentieth-century ethnic nationalist with the early-twentieth-century imagist's concern for the most precise, the most resonant image and added to this combination his own largeness of spirit.

Comparisons, Contrasts, Connections

The examples of Lawson Inada and Frank Chin excited Garrett Hongo, who was encouraged by their work to do his own.

Frank Chin displayed his artistic and verbal talent, making his claim for a place in American history and expressing his deep ambivalence about Chinese Americans in his plays. "Chickencoop Chinaman" was a dazzling display of verbal pyrotechnics but underlying the surface razzle-dazzle is a passionate throbbing of anger and pain for the emasculation of Chinese men in the United States.

Lawson Fusao Inada was another visible and vocal model for younger Asian-American writers. His book of poetry *Before the War* provided a range of models and styles from lyrical musings, to sublimated anger from a Japanese-American perspective, to colloquial outbursts inspired by black jazz and rhythms.

Hongo acknowledges other models and mentors as well: Bert Meyers, Donald Hall, C. K. Williams, Charles Wright, and Philip Levine.

Bibliography

Filipelli, Laurie. *Garrett Hongo.* Boise: Boise State UP, 1997.

Jarman, Mark. "The Volanco Inside." *Southern Review* 32.2 (1996): 337–43.

Kodama-Nishimoto, Michi, and Warren Nishimoto. "Interview with Writer Garrett Hongo: Oral History and Literature." *Oral History Recorder* (1986): 2–4.

Joy Harjo (Creek) (b. 1951)

Contributing Editor: C. B. Clark

Classroom Issues and Strategies

It's important to make certain that the students read the biographical notes and footnotes provided in the text. Consider also using audiotapes of Harjo reading and discussing her own work.

Major Themes, Historical Perspectives, Personal Issues

Imperialism, colonialism, dependency, nostalgia for the old ways, reverence for grandparents and elders, resentment of conditions of the present, the plight of reservation and urban Indians, the natural world, a sense of hopelessness, the power of the trickster, the idea that the feminine is synonymous with heritage, deadly compromise, a symbol of all that has been lost (such as the land), tension between the desire to retrieve the past and the inevitability of change, the arrogance of white people, problems of half-breeds (or mixed-bloods).

Significant Form, Style, or Artistic Conventions

Harjo uses free verse. She is aware of classic European form but chooses not to use it. She does try oral chant. She is not in any school, except American Indian.

Original Audience

Ask the question: Is there any audience besides American Indians? The second audience is the student, and the third is the general reader.

Questions for Reading, Discussion, and Writing

1. Who are the Creeks? What is their origin? What impact did removal have on the Five Civilized Tribes? Where are the Creeks today? How are they organized? What was the role of the Christian missionary? What is traditional Creek religion? What is an urban Indian? Does Harjo travel much, and is that reflected in her poetry?
2. Hand out a reading list containing ethnographic, historical, and contemporary works on the Creeks. Hand out a theme list containing such items as removal, acculturation, and identity. Hand out a subject list containing topics such as removal, alcoholism, and jails. Ask the students to write an essay on each of the lists. Require some library research for the essays, which will provide background for the poetry.

Bibliography

There are no separate works on Harjo. Bits on her can be found in critical pieces on her work, in collections, in autobiographical pieces, and through interviews.

Published works that deal in part with her include Joseph Bruchac's *Survival This Way* and Andrew O. Wiget's *Native American Literature*, part of the Twayne series, as well as Laura Coltelli, ed., *Winged Words: American Indian Writers Speak,* and *World Literature Today* (Spring 1992).

Tato Laviera (b. 1951)

Contributing Editor: Frances R. Aparicio

Classroom Issues and Strategies

Give handouts or glossaries that explain local references and Spanish words; also, it might be helpful to try to translate Spanish phrases and words in order to show the unique value of bilingualism within Laviera's poetry and the fact that most of it is untranslatable.

It would be wonderful to recite Laviera's poems aloud and to intro-duce them to the students as such, as oral poetry. One might also relate his poetry to the tradition of rapping in New York City. Again, students need to clarify references to Puerto Rico and El Barrio with which they might be unfamiliar. They respond to issues of bilingual education, social criticism, and language (Spanish in the United States). Discussions on how Anglo monolingual students feel when reading Hispanic bilingual poetry such as Tato Laviera's and Hernández Cruz's texts can lead to fruitful observations on patterns of exclusion and marginalization in the United States via language and linguistic policies.

Major Themes, Historical Perspectives, Personal Issues

Major themes are tension between Puerto Rican and Nuyorican societies and identity; language and bilingualism as ethnic identity markers; life in El Barrio; music and popular culture; denouncement of social institutions such as schools, Puerto Rican and U.S. governments, the Catholic church, and others; major context of the history of Puerto Rican immigration to the United States and Operation Bootstrap in the 1940s and 1950s; presence of African-Caribbean and African-American cultures.

Significant Form, Style, or Artistic Conventions

Laviera's poetry best exemplifies the new genre of bilingual poetry in the United States. Discuss historical context of bilingual literature in other coun-tries, aesthetic innovation within contemporary literature, political stance, and use of oral speech and traditions versus written, academic, and intellectual poetry; relate to Mexican-American poets, and to African-American poets of the 1960s and discuss the common space between the black poets and Laviera's work regarding the reaffirmation of the African heritage for both communities. How do they differ, and what do they have in common?

Original Audience

This is poetry meant to be sung and recited. Originally addressed to the Puerto Rican community in New York and presented in the Nuyorican Café, it is poetry for the masses.

Questions for Reading, Discussion, and Writing

Study questions for Laviera would try to help students contextualize his poetry both historically and aesthetically. For example:

1. How would you describe El Barrio in New York? How does Laviera present it in his poems?
2. After reading Laviera's poems, how would you define *poetry*? What kind of language is appropriate for poetry? Would Laviera's work fit into your definition?

A good and challenging writing assignment is to ask students to write their own bilingual poem (using any other language they may know). Discuss problems and effects.

Paper topics would include textual analysis of one poem; a discussion of the functions of language and bilingualism, and its problems; language and ethnic identity; and the functions of humor and irony.

Bibliography

Juan Flores, John Attinasi, and Pedro Pedraza Jr., "La Carreta Made a U-Turn: Puerto Rican Language and Culture in the United States," *Daedalus* 110.2 (Spring 1981): 193–217; Wolfgang Binder, "Celebrating Life: The AmeRícan Poet Tato Laviera," Introduction to *AmeRícan*, by Tato Laviera (1985) 5–10; Juan Flores, "Keys to Tato Laviera," Introduction to *Enclave*, by Tato Laviera (1985) 5–7; Frances Aparicio, "La vida es un spanglish disparatero: Bilingualism in Nuyorican Poetry," *European Perspectives on Hispanic Literature of the United States*, ed. Genvieve Fabre (1988) 147–60.

Judith Ortiz Cofer (b. 1952)

Contributing Editor: Juan Bruce-Novoa

Classroom Issues and Strategies

Ortiz Cofer is quite clear and accessible, although students have questions about who she is and why she uses Spanish.

I present the students something from my own cultural background, with allusions to Mexican history and culture. Then I ask them to jot down what has been said. We compare the results, finding that those who do not share the background will choose different elements out of the material than those who come from a background similar to my own. We discuss the function of ethnic identification through shared allusions about the drawing of the ethnic circle around some readers while excluding others, even when the latter can understand the words.

Students respond to the theme of the abandoned female, which often results in discussions of the single-parent family.

Major Themes, Historical Perspectives, Personal Issues

The theme of male absence and women who wait is perhaps the major one touched on here. Also, there is the historical theme of Puerto Ricans and other minorities in the military as a way of life that gives them mobility yet divides their families.

The colonization of Puerto Rico by the United States and the division of its population into island and mainland groups are reflected in the division of the family. The bilingual child is another result of the confluence of these two nations, reflected in the preoccupation with which of the languages authority will accept from would-be participants.

Significant Form, Style, or Artistic Conventions

This is confessional poetry, but with a twist. The author walks a fine line between writing for her own group and writing for the general audience. Thus she introduces Spanish and some culture items from the island but recontextualizes them into English and U.S. culture. The style becomes an intercultural hybrid.

Original Audience

There is the Puerto Rican audience that will bring to the poems a specific knowledge of cultural elements that they share with the poet. This audience will place the poem in a wider catalog of cultural references. The non–Puerto Rican audience must draw only from the information given, and will perhaps apply the situations to universal myths or archetypes.

Comparisons, Contrasts, Connections

You can compare her well with many other women writers, especially in the sense of women alone in a male world. For example, "Claims" can be read with Lorna Dee Cervantes's "Beneath the Shadow of the Freeway."

Questions for Reading, Discussion, and Writing

1. I ask them to consider what is the function of ethnic writing. How does it work for insiders as compared to outsiders? They should try to determine at what point ethnic writing becomes incomprehensible to outsiders and what it means to open it to readers beyond the ethnic circle.
2. Write on the theme of the distant patriarch in U.S. contemporary life.
3. Write on the pros and cons of foreign language in literature. The "God" of "Latin Women Pray" can be taken as a metaphor for the U.S. reading public.

Bibliography

Acosta-Belen, Edna. "The Literature of the Puerto Rican National Minority in the United States." *Bilingual Review* 5.1–2 (Jan.–Aug. 1978): 107–16.

Rita Dove (b. 1952)

Contributing Editor: Hilary Holladay

Classroom Issues and Strategies

In my experience, students like Dove's poems, even though they don't fully understand them. I found that dividing the class into small groups (and providing them with several discussion questions) works well with her poems. This gives students a chance to raise issues they might not air otherwise—and accommodates poems that seem to be more about asking questions than answering them. Walking from group to group, I am able to address specific concerns without usurping control of a free-flowing discussion.

Major Themes, Historical Perspectives, Personal Issues

In her poems, Dove often distills the experiences of oppressed groups: women, blacks, and working-class Americans, among others. She does not strike a victim's pose, however. Whether she is dealing with contemporary scenes or historical events, she speaks with the calm confidence of one who knows she will be listened to.

As an African-American woman who has spent virtually her entire adult life affiliated with one university or another, she represents an intriguing mix of "outsider" and "insider" perspectives. The academic life seems to have provided her with a forum quite compatible with her interest in the intersections of the personal, the political, and the intellectual. As an American who believes strongly in the value of traveling to other countries and learning other languages, Dove brings an international perspective to many of her poems as well.

Significant Form, Style, or Artistic Conventions

Dove has published several prose books and a verse drama, but she seems most at home in lyric poetry. Although the prose poem published here is a departure from her usual style, it is characteristic of Dove's interest in obliquely stated narratives. *Thomas and Beulah,* a narrative sequence, is hardly straightforward in its development; in that Pulitzer Prize–winning collection, Dove provides the pieces with which we can envision (and continually reenvision) the evolving puzzle of two interwoven lives. Something similar occurs in her sonnet sequence based on the Persephone myth, *Mother Love* (1995).

Comparisons, Contrasts, Connections

Dove can be grouped with other African-American poets, women poets, and poets exemplary for their use of imagery. Because of her German and Scandinavian influences, her poems would also work well in a comparative literature course.

Questions for Reading, Discussion, and Writing

1. Study questions for the Dove poems selected here might focus on voice and perspective, characterization, and rhetorical strategies. For example, how would you describe the speaker in each of these poems? What is the speaker's perspective on the events described in each poem? How does the mood differ from poem to poem? How does "Kentucky, 1833" blend the historical with the personal? What are the paradoxes at work in this poem? How is the poem's form significant? How would you paraphrase "Ö"? Can you think of other words, in English or other languages, that change "the whole neighborhood"? Explain your selections. What do you think the speaker in "Arrow" means by "the language of fathers"? What is the significance of the enjambment and the three-line stanzas in "The Oriental Ballerina"?

2. Students writing about Dove's poems should read all (or at least a couple) of her poetry collections so they will have a sense of the breadth of her concerns. Their papers could address family relationships, narrative perspective, or her enigmatic image patterns. They could also explore her international themes or compare one or more of her poems about family life with those of another woman poet—such as Sylvia Plath, Adrienne Rich, or Lucille Clifton. An alternative assignment: Write a letter to Dove and present her with a possible interpretation of one of her poems. Then pose several questions that would help you develop your interpretation and perhaps help you better understand her other poems as well. This latter assignment worked well in an advanced composition class because it enabled students to develop their skills in writing query letters as well as analyzing poetry.

Bibliography

Numerous interviews with Dove have been published since her tenure as poet laureate. See, for example, Malin Pereira's interview with her in *Contemporary Literature* 40.2 (Summer 1999): 182–213. Here, Dove discusses her verse drama, *The Darker Face of the Earth*, and comments on the Black Arts Movement as well as the relation between "national" history and her personal experience as a black woman. Another good resource is the journal *Callaloo*, which has published a number of essays on Dove; the Winter 1996 issue, for instance, contains several articles on her sonnet sequence, *Mother Love*. In addition to a recent surge of journal essays and book chapters on Dove's writing, a new study looks at the whole of Dove's work: Therese Steffen's *Crossing Color: Transcultural Space and Place in Rita Dove's Poetry, Fiction, and Drama* (2000).

Naomi Shihab Nye (b. 1952)

Contributing Editor: Marcy Jane Knopf-Newman

Classroom Issues and Strategies

Arab-American literature arrived with the onset of the first wave of Arab-American immigration in the early twentieth century. Most of the region from which writers emigrated was then known as Syria, but these writers today come from what we would identify now as Palestine, Lebanon, and Syria. Arab Americans were one of the first groups of immigrants to organize a literary and writing society called Al Rabital al Qalamiyah, or the New York Pen League, which lasted until the 1940s. Ameen Rihani and Gibran Khalil Gibran are the best known of these writers. Elmaz Abinader's online essay "Children of Al-Mahjar: Arab American Literature Spans a Century" is a helpful overview for students and instructors alike to situate Nye in the context of more than a century of Arab-American literature; see <http://usinfo.state.gov/journals/itsv/0200/ijse/abinader.htm>.

It is essential for instructors to spend some time familiarizing themselves with this body of literature as well as with the history and geography of the region since for many American students reading literature by and about Arab Americans will be a new experience. Also, since Nye is the only Arab writer in *The Heath Anthology*, it may seem to students that the category of Arab-American literature is a relatively recent phenomenon. This perception must be debunked from the outset by sharing with them some writing by other Arab-American writers from earlier periods of American history, like Rihani and Gibran; these and other writers are included in Orfalea's anthology. If your library does not contain works by Rihani, you can order his works for your library at <http://www.ameenrihani.org>.

Another useful website is the Arab American Cultural Institute, which contains resources on Arab-American literature and culture that may be helpful for teaching Nye's work; see <http://www.aaci-us.org/literature.html>.

Finally, *Al-Jadid* magazine is a wonderful resource in which you can find interviews with Arab-American contemporary writers and artists. It can be accessed at <http://www.aljadid.com/about.html>. Lisa Suhair Mujaj's interview with Nye is particularly good; see <http://www.aljadid.com/interviews/0213majaj.html>.

Major Themes, Historical Perspectives, Personal Issues

In addition to lacking sufficient knowledge of the history of Arab-American literature, students will likely not have a strong grasp of Middle East history and its relationship to American history. It is vital to provide some sort of background, at least on Palestinian history, because if students know anything at all about the region, they may likely come to class with only a working knowledge that is deeply influenced by Israeli versions of that history. Because it is difficult for teachers of American literature to compile information for a comprehensive lecture about conflicts in the region, I encourage professors to ask their university libraries to purchase films from Arab Film Distribution at <http://www.arabfilm.com>; there are many films, which I list in the Bibliography, that would provide a broad overview and a new perspective on Palestine.

One other subject that it is helpful to discuss is the religious imagery in Nye's poems. This is most evident in her poem "Different Ways to Pray." John Esposito's book offers a nice overview of Islam for beginners, and I recommend Leila Ahmed's book as well because it provides readers with a feminist perspective on the subject. Islamic religion and cultures may also come up for instructors teaching June Jordan's poem "Intifada" or Malcolm X's work, so I find it helpful to provide students with some background on the religion in ways that dispel some of the myths and stereotypes prevalent in the United States.

Islam is one theme that appears in Nye's writing. Others that you will find in this selection include family, dispossession, occupation, in/visibility, alienation, home, and the refugee and the settler, all of which are set against a backdrop of people's daily lives—the ordinary, storytelling, and traveling. Like many of the writers in *The Heath Anthology*, Nye explores the theme of displacement while simultaneously imagining attachment to land, to Bedouin folk roots. All of these themes are a means of thinking about identity in a new context.

Significant Form, Style, or Artistic Conventions

Nye's poems may be thought of as a type of lyrical protest poetry. She grounds this style in the context of daily family life, storytelling, and oral traditions in Arab folktales. Her poems vary from long, rhythmic, prosaic lines—influenced by Walt Whitman, Carl Sandburg, and Allen Ginsberg—to spare, chiseled lines, with a reportorial voice and eye reminiscent of Carolyn Forché's style of documentary poetry.

Like Forché's work, Nye's writing is infused with an empathic form of humanism that is devoted to humanizing Arab and Mexican Americans. Her work experiments with the power of language as a means for helping people see humanity in those who are often invisible and othered. Nye's use of images is one way she conveys this in her work: the omnipresent elements of Palestinian life expressed through food, plants, and folktales, all of which translate across cultural borders.

Original Audience

Perhaps the most important theme in her work is a precept that Nye lives by: if grandmothers and children had more of a voice in the world, the world would be a more peaceful place. Although Nye writes for a wide-ranging audience, much of her work is specifically directed toward children. The following books are wonderful resources to use in your classroom as you share Nye's breadth of work with your students. For instance, her edited collections, *The Space Between Our Footsteps* and *The Tree Is Older Than You Are*, are two volumes of collected art and poetry from the Middle East and Mexico, respectively. By looking at these two volumes, students can glean a sense of the relationship between these two borderland areas and Nye's attempt to draw children into poetry and painting by helping them to humanize themselves and others.

Some of Nye's poetry that is not included here demonstrates her powerful attempt to intercede in the headlines. For example, in "For the 500th Dead Palestinian, Ibtisam Bozieh," Nye constructs a poem that intervenes in the world in ways that newspapers cannot. The poem was banned in Israel, in its translated form, by the Israeli censors after a group of journalists translated it with the hope of publishing it in a newspaper. The poem centers on the young girl Ibtisam who dreamed of becoming a doctor and on Nye's image of this girl as a doctor healing alongside Jewish doctors treating "tumors of pain." Also like Forché, Nye bears witness to the suffering of the people in her poems. In this way, Nye intervenes in the headlines by using poetry to portray people who are other than human beings. Poetry for Nye is healing and can help to ease tensions in the world by helping people recognize one another's humanity.

Her poems and those she edits exemplify one of the most important qualities of her work—her investment and interest in children. She has written children's books, and many of her poems can be enjoyed and understood by children and teenagers alike. Both *Sitti's Secrets* and *Habibi* carry on that project in important ways and have been demonized in some American-Jewish newspapers as a result. *Habibi*, in particular, depicts fourteen-year-old Liyana Abboud, who is spending the year living in Palestine with her Palestinian father and American mother when she finds herself befriending an Israeli boy. *Sitti's Secrets* was reviewed in a Jewish periodical and called anti-Semitic because it detailed the life of a Palestinian-American girl who misses her Palestinian grandmother. There have been other similar incidents involving Jewish schools and periodicals, most notably in 2003, when a Jewish teacher at a Los Angeles Orthodox Jewish school taught Nye's novel *Habibi* and was fired for doing so. The story reported in the *Los Angeles Times* is worth reading and sharing with students, especially to illustrate some of the resistance to Nye's work; it can be found at <http://www.latimes.com/news/specials/shalhevet/la-me-shalhavet3aug03.htmlstory>.

Finally, shortly after September 11, 2001, Naomi Shihab Nye composed "Letter from Naomi Shihab Nye, Arab American Poet: To Any Would-Be Terrorists," which now is posted widely on the Internet and may be a useful addition to your classroom texts; it can be found at <http://www.arches.uga.edu/~godlas/shihabnye.html>.

Comparisons, Contrasts, Connections

The entries in *The Heath Anthology* that feature orature can be useful starting points of comparison for a number of reasons. Drawing comparisons between Palestinian Americans and Native Americans or Mexican Americans, for instance, may help students to comprehend the issues at stake for Nye in her work. Using Jamal Salim Nuwayhid's anthology of Arab folktales can help instructors make connections between Nye's use of the Joha trickster figure in "My Father and the Figtree" and "The Words Under the Words" and Native-American and African-American uses of trickster figures. Also, in "Different Ways to Pray," she incorporates Fowzi the fool, another character from Arab folklore. Using some of the *Corrido* selections can also be helpful in establishing links between orature and the resistance to enforced borders.

Nye's own essay collection, *Never in a Hurry*, will provide instructors with some insight into the role of immigration in Nye's family history and the way in which it permeates her poetry. Nye's reflections on her childhood experience of learning about Thanksgiving and identifying more with Native Americans than with Pilgrims or missionaries sheds some interesting light on the works of Zitkala-Sa and Joy Harjo, for instance. She perceptively describes how as a young girl, she became conscious of the ways in which Pilgrims altered the original culture of Native Americans. Nye traces her family's history as well as that of her husband in this collection in ways that reflect the breadth of immigrant writing from Sui-Sin Far to Bharati Mukherjee.

If you teach Mark Twain in the same section in which you teach Nye, it makes for an interesting frame if you begin your course with his *Innocents Abroad*. Themes of travel and migration in the Middle East may also help you show how the Middle East gets characterized differently over time. Twain, too, is one of many writers who have influenced Nye's work. Indeed, much of Nye's prose and poetry consists of her own travel writing about Pakistan, Bangladesh, and the American West.

Some of the connections that can be made with Nye's work also have to do with the literary and cultural influences that are found in her poetry. For example, in her poem "Where the Soft Air Lives," she begins with an epigraph from Jack Kerouac's *On the Road*, a book that informed much of her literary sensibility during her college years. At other points in her life, Langston Hughes, Lucille Clifton, and Allen Ginsberg have been important models for Nye's poetic sensibility. "Where the Soft Air Lives," in particular, highlights not only the influence of Beat writing on her work but also the influence of the borderland region of the American Southwest. In order to sufficiently frame this aspect of her poetry, I think it is useful to have students read writers such as Gloria Anzaldúa, Pat Mora, María Amparo Ruiz de Burton, and Tomás Rivera to get a sense of what Nye observes and responds to. Anzaldúa's theories about the borderland will be especially helpful for students trying to gain a sense of Palestinians' parallel struggles in the diaspora. I also recommend Ruiz de Burton's excerpt because it offers students a vision of the U.S. annexation of Mexican and Native American lands that can help them see what Nye expresses in her writing about the Palestinian and Iraqi people.

Finally, I would include a discussion of Nye's work in the larger context of the feminist writing in *The Heath Anthology*. I think that instructors can see visible ties between Nye and poets like Muriel Rukeyser, Carolyn Forché, Audre Lorde, Lucille Clifton, and June Jordan, all of whom make a commitment to empathic expressions with people who are rendered invisible. Jordan's poem "Intifada" would make a wonderful pairing with one of Nye's poems, such as "Blood."

Working with Cultural Objects

In addition to being a writer, Nye is also a musician; there is one recording that I recommend using when teaching her poetry *Texas Poets in Concert*. Nye also reads her poem "Blood" in the PBS documentary *The United States of Poetry*, which many libraries own; it can be found at <http://www.worldofpoetry. org/usop>.

One topic of discussion that might emerge amidst the conversations about the Middle East and Nye's poetry will likely concern specifics about the layout of the region. Looking at present-day maps can be limiting, so I encourage instructors to photocopy maps from books like Hourani and Cleveland's historical texts because they offer a sense of how the region has changed since the end of World War I. Also, for people using computer classrooms, there is a wonderful website at the University of Texas at Austin that contains maps from around the world and demonstrates how lines in the sand have been altered over time; see <http://www.lib.utexas.edu/maps/middle_east.html>.

Questions for Reading, Discussion, Writing

Some of Nye's poems encourage people to question categories, as does the little girl in "Blood" who contemplates what "a true Arab" does now. Likewise, examining maps and learning about the history of the region may trigger questions about what makes a person Lebanese, Palestinian, or even Middle Eastern. It may be useful to question these terms as your students consider that Palestine is located in West Asia and that much of the "Middle East" is in North Africa. Naming places and people can be a useful exercise, especially if you use postcolonial theory in your course. Have students unpack these regional words and consider what they connote: Who named these places and people? How do shifting borders and names affect the way that history gets represented in poems by Nye as compared with how it is in the work of earlier Arab-American poets?

Since it is likely that issues surrounding borderland areas, whether the U.S./Mexican border or the Palestinian/Israeli border, will be in the news when you teach Nye, it often makes for vital classroom discussion and writing assignments if you have students explore themes from the literature and connect them with what Nye expresses in her poetry, especially since her work is actively engaged with challenging the stereotypes that pervade the media. There are a number of excellent news sources on the Internet that offer students an alternative perspective on the Middle East, such as *Al Ahram* at <http://www.weekly.ahram.org.eg/index.htm>, *Al Jazeera* at <http://www.english.aljazeera.net/HomePage>, or the *Jerusalem Post* at <http://www.jerusalem-times.net>.

There are also an increasing number of websites dedicated to posting narratives, poetry, and art in the form of a website or weblog (or blog). Although many universities support Blackboard, I find it exciting for students to create a Web-based discourse community by constructing a blog to document their responses to the literature we read. For an example of one Iraqi-based Palestinian blogger, see <http://www.afamilyinbaghdad.blogspot.com>, which is composed by a woman named Faiza who also has sons with blogs linked to hers. If you choose to set up a blog, you can assign students to write responses to various readings at certain intervals during the semester in addition to writing comments on their peers' work. Creative students can provide links to other blogs, news stories, and poems posted on the Internet.

When I teach, I often encourage students to get involved in a particular issue that emerges from the literature if they feel the passion to do so. Sometimes this takes the form of a service learning project; at other times, it can involve participating in campus or community protests. I often create class websites with links for various media and activist organizations directly related to the classes I teach. Should you wish to offer your students such material, here are some websites for students wanting to join various activist organizations related to this issue:

- Stop the Wall at <http://www.stopthewall.org>
- International Solidarity Movement at <http://www.palsolidarity.org>
- Electronic Intifada at <http://www.electronicintifada.net/new.shtml>
- Palestine Media Watch at <http://www.pmwatch.org/pmw/index.asp>
- Arab American Anti-Discrimination Committee at <http://www.adc. org>

Any of the activities previously discussed can easily be woven into a longer writing assignment or research project by having students draw connections among the various genres of writing about events in the Middle East.

For instructors interested in a more conventional approach to teaching Nye, I recommend exploring a lesson plan for teaching her posted on Bill Moyers's website: <http://www.pbs.org/now/classroom/poet.html>.

Bibliography

Abraham, Sameer Y., and Nabeel Abraham. *Arabs in the New World: Studies on Arab American Communities.* Detroit: Wayne State UP, 1983.

Ahmed, Leila. *Women and Gender in Islam: Historical Roots of a Modern Debate.* New York: Yale UP, 1992.

Akash, Munir, and Khaled Mattawa, eds. *Post-Gibran Anthology of New Arab American Writing.* Syracuse: Syracuse UP, 1999.

Aruri, Naseer H. *Dishonest Broker: The U.S. Role in Israel and Palestine.* Cambridge: South End, 2003.

Chomsky, Noam. *Fateful Triangle: The United States, Israel and the Palestinians.* Boston: South End, 1983.

Cleveland, William. *A History of the Modern Middle East.* 2nd ed. Colorado: Westview, 1999.

Esposito, John L. *Islam: The Straight Path.* New York: Oxford UP, 1988.

Handal, Nathalie. *The Poetry of Arab Women.* Northampton, MA: Interlink, 2000.

Hourani, Albert H. *A History of the Arab Peoples.* Cambridge: Belknap-Harvard UP, 2002.

Little, Douglas. *American Orientalism: The United States and the Middle East Since 1945.* Chapel Hill: U of North Carolina P, 2003.

McAlister, Melani. *Epic Encounters: Culture, Media, and U.S. Interests in the Middle East, 1945–2000.* Berkeley: U of California P, 2001.

Nuwayhid, Jamal S., et al., ed. *Abu Jmeel's Daughter and Other Stories: Arab Folk Tales From Palestine and Lebanon.* Northampton, MA: Interlink, 2002.

Nye, Naomi Shihab, ed. *The Same Sky: A Collection of Poems from Around the World.* New York: Aladdin, 1996.

———. ed. *The Space Between Our Footsteps: Poems and Paintings from the Middle East.* New York: Simon, 1998. Children's book.

———. ed. *The Tree Is Older Than You Are: A Bilingual Gathering of Poems and Stories from Mexico with Paintings by Mexican Artists.* New York: Simon, 1995. Children's book.

Orfalea, Gregory. *Before the Flames: A Quest for the History of Arab Americans.* Austin: U of Texas P, 1988.

Orfalea, Gregory, and Sharif Elmusa, eds. *Grape Leaves: A Century of Arab-American Poetry.* Salt Lake City: U of Utah P, 1988.

Said, Edward. *The Question of Palestine.* New York: Times, 1979.

Shakir, Evelyn. *Bint Arab: Arab and Arab American Women in the United States.* Westport, CT: Praeger, 1997.

Films

Bing-Canar, Jennifer. *Collecting Stories from Exile: Chicago Palestinians Remember 1948.* Seattle: Arab Film Distribution, 1999. [Film]

Byrd, Nikki, and Jennifer Jajeh. *In My Own Skin: The Complexity of Living as an Arab in America.* Seattle: Arab Film Distribution, 2001. [Film]

Jhally, Sut. *Edward Said: On Orientalism*. Seattle: Arab Film Distribution, 1998. [Film]

Longley, James. *Gaza Strip*. Seattle: Arab Film Distribution, 2002. [Film]

Masri, Mai. *Children of Fire*. Seattle: Arab Film Distribution, 1990. [Film]

Pellington, Mark. *The United States of Poetry*. New York: Bay Books Video, 1995. [Videocassette]

Salloum, Jayce, and Elia Suleiman. *Introduction to the End of an Argument*. Seattle: Arab Film Distribution, 1990. [Film]

Wright, Tom, and Therese Saliba. *Checkpoint*. Seattle: Arab Film Distribution, 1997. [Film]

Recording

Texas Poets in Concert: A Quartet—R. S. Gwynn, Jan Epton Seale, Naomi Shihab Nye, William Virgil Davis. Denton: U of North Texas P, 1990. [Record album]

Gary Soto (b. 1952)

Contributing Editor: Raymund Paredes

Classroom Issues and Strategies

As a Chicano working-class poet, Soto sometimes uses figurative language that might be unfamiliar to and difficult for some readers. Occasionally, he uses a Spanish word or phrase. As a poet with a strong sense of kinship with people who are poor, neglected, and oppressed, Soto tries to create poetry out of ordinary working-class experience and images. All this is very different from typically bourgeois American poetry.

It is useful to connect Soto's work to contemporary events in Mexican-American experience. Reading a bit about Cesar Chavez and the California farmworker struggle places some of Soto's sympathies in context. General reading in Chicano (or Mexican-American) history would also be useful. It is also useful to consider Soto among other contemporary poets whose sensibilities were shaped by the post-1960s struggles to improve the circumstances of minority groups and the poor.

Urge students to try to see the world from the point of view of one of Soto's working-class Chicanos, perhaps a farmworker. From this perspective, one sees things very differently than from the point of view generally presented in American writing. For the tired, underpaid farmworker, nature is neither kind nor beautiful, as, for example, Thoreau would have us believe. Soto writes about the choking dust in the fields, the danger to the workers' very existence that the sun represents. Imagine a life without many creature comforts; imagine feelings of hunger; imagine the pain of knowing that for the affluent and comfortable, your life counts for very little.

Students are generally moved by Soto's vivid and honest presentation of personal experiences, his sympathy for the poor, and the accessibility of his work. They generally wish to know more about Mexican-American and Mexican cultures, more about the plight of farmworkers and the urban poor.

Major Themes, Historical Perspectives, Personal Issues

Despite Soto's distinctiveness, he is very much a contemporary American poet. Like many of his peers, he writes largely in an autobiographical or confessional mode. As an intensively introspective poet, he seeks to maintain his connection to his Mexican heritage as it exists on both sides of the border. His work often focuses on the loss of a father at an early age, on the difficulties of adolescence (especially romantic feelings), and on the urgency of family intimacy. On a broader level, Soto speaks passionately on behalf of tolerance and mutual respect while he denounces middle- and upper-class complacency and indifference to the poor.

Significant Form, Style, or Artistic Conventions

Again, Soto is very much a contemporary American poet, writing autobiographically in free verse and using images that are drawn from ordinary experience and popular culture. His sympathies for the poor are very typical of contemporary writers from ethnic or underprivileged backgrounds. It is also important to note that some of Soto's poetry has been influenced by the "magical realism" of modern Latin American writing, especially that of Gabriel Garciá-Márquez.

Original Audience

Although Soto is a Chicano poet in that his Mexican-American heritage is a key aspect of his literary sensibility, he nevertheless aims for a wider audience. He clearly wants a broad American audience to feel sympathies for his poetic characters and their circumstances. The product of a contemporary sensibility, Soto's poetry is topical and vital.

Comparisons, Contrasts, Connections

Again, as an autobiographical poet, Soto can be compared with such figures as Robert Lowell, John Berryman, and Sylvia Plath. His working-class sensibility is reminiscent of James Wright and Philip Levine (who was Soto's teacher at California State University, Fresno). His celebration of certain Chicano values and denunciation of bigotry are comparable to those of other Chicano poets such as Lorna Dee Cervantes.

Questions for Reading, Discussion, and Writing

1. Students might be asked to look for clues in his work as to ethnic background, economic status, and geographical setting.

   Furthermore, they might be asked to consider certain formal qualities of his work: Where do Soto's images and symbols come from? Does Soto attempt to make his work accessible to ordinary readers?

2. Soto's work is fruitfully compared with that of other autobiographical poets (Lowell, Berryman, Plath) and with that of working-class poets such as Wright and Levine.

   Soto's book *The Tale of Sunlight* (particularly in its final section) might be studied for its elements of "magical realism."

   Soto, of course, can be studied in connection with other Chicano poets such as Lorna Dee Cervantes and Umar Salinas.

Bibliography

Probably the most useful general source of information on Soto (complete with various references) is the article on Soto in "Chicano Writers," *The Dictionary of Literary Biography*, Vol. 82 (1989).

Rane Arroyo (b. 1954)

Contributing Editor: Lawrence La Fountain-Stokes

Major Themes, Historical Perspectives, Personal Issues

Some of the major themes in Arroyo's work are Puerto Rican migration to the Midwest, the persistence and transformation of Puerto Rican cultural traditions in the diaspora, the meaning of gender and sexuality (traditional heterosexual masculinity and femininity as well as the transgression of these social codes), and the role of the poet in society and of poetry in the life of an artist (both as chronicle of daily life and register of cultural translation). Students will benefit from understanding the general context of Puerto Rican experience in the United States (see the Instructor's Guide notes for Sandra María Esteves and Luz María Umpierre) as well as the specific case of Chicago as a city with a large Puerto Rican and Mexican-American population (see the pioneering work of Padilla and the more recent findings of Ramos Zayas and De Genova, as well as the special issue on Puerto Ricans in Chicago of *Centro Journal* (13.2 [Fall 2001]) available online at <http://www.centropr.org/journal/jrnal24.html>).

Arroyo is an openly gay poet who addresses his affective life directly in many of his poems. A discussion of "My Transvestite Uncle Is Missing" will allow students to differentiate between gender presentation (in this case, a man dressing as a woman) and sexual attraction (the poem does not indicate the uncle's sexuality). The uncle and his nephew's relationship is marked by a deep bond of love and by a shared sense of difference. "Caribbean Braille" is a very tender poem about the relationship between a father and a son, specifically how the father's work-related blindness (the result of oppressive work conditions in the United States) brings the two closer together through their common link to a (nonutopian) Puerto Rico represented by mosquito bites. The centrality of the body is apparent in this poem. "Write What You Know" and "That Flag" highlight both the poet's social experience as a Puerto Rican and his sexuality as well as how poetry can be used to address social issues. Students can easily relate to the poems' popular culture references.

Arroyo's poetry stands out due to the clarity of the images he presents and of the emotions he conveys.

Significant Form, Style, or Artistic Conventions

The selection of poems includes a variety of approaches to metrics and versification, ranging from controlled stanza forms to prose poetry. Students can be invited to discuss the effect of these choices on the poems as they appear on the written page and in terms of their content. Instructors might want to contextualize these forms in the tradition of broader American poetry. The use of colloquial language is also notable.

Original Audience

Arroyo publishes and has been published extensively in anthologies and poetry journals across the nation. His four books have been published by a range of small and university publishing houses, including some largely focused on a Latino/Latina readership, such as the Bilingual Press. Although he was a very active member of the Chicago arts scene in the 1980s, he has been more focused on his publications and professional obligations since the 1990s.

Comparisons, Contrasts, Connections

It is useful to think of Arroyo within the tradition of U.S. Puerto Rican poets (William Carlos Williams, Sandra María Esteves, Victor Hernández Cruz, Tato Laviera, Judith Ortiz Cofer, Pedro Pietri, Luz María Umpierre) because of both his similarities to and his differences from those writers. Points of contact include his concern about issues of social oppression and cultural persistence (including use of or reference to the Spanish language). Differences include his interest in establishing poetic links with English and American poets from the nineteenth and twentieth centuries (something more visible in other poems not included in this anthology), the poet's homosexuality, and the fact that he focuses on the Midwest. Arroyo can also be located within a genealogy of gay writers (Walt Whitman, James Baldwin, Allen Ginsberg). Very interesting comparisons can be made with the work of the Cuban-American lesbian writer Achy Obejas, who also foregrounds issues of Latinos and Latinas in Chicago in her published works, or with Sandra Cisneros, who is also from Chicago.

Working with Cultural Objects

The articles and photo-essays in the *Centro Journal* special issue on Puerto Ricans in Chicago provide a variety of opportunities for fascinating comparisons. See <http://www.centropr.org/journal/jrnal24.html>.

Questions for Reading, Discussion, and Writing

1. What is the poetic speaker's relationship to his family? How does his sexual orientation affect this relationship? What does it mean for him to be gay?
2. Discuss the poet's views on racism in the United States as it manifests itself at a personal, community, and institutional level. Compare his views with those of other poets you have read in this anthology.
3. What makes these texts poems?

Bibliography

De Genova, Nicholas and Ana Y. Ramos-Zayas. *Latino Crossings: Mexicans, Puerto Ricans, and the Politics of Race and Citizenship.* New York: Routledge, 2003.

Padilla, Félix M. *Latino Ethnic Consciousness: The Case of Mexican-Americans and Puerto Ricans in Chicago.* Notre Dame: U of Notre Dame P, 1985.

————. *Puerto Rican Chicago.* Notre Dame: U of Notre Dame P, 1987.

Ramos Zayas, Ana Y. *National Performances: The Politics of Class, Race, and Space in Puerto Rican Chicago.* Chicago: U of Chicago P, 2003.

Sheldon, Glenn. "Arroyo, Rane." *Latin American Writers on Gay and Lesbian Themes.* Ed. David W. Foster. Westport, CT: Greenwood, 1994. 43–46.

Louise Erdrich (Chippewa) (b. 1954)

Contributing Editor: Andrew O. Wiget

Classroom Issues and Strategies

One problem in teaching *Love Medicine* is the intensity of religious experience, which many students in today's secular society may have difficulty relating to. Another is the surrealistic imagery that Marie Lazarre uses in describing her relationship with Sister Leopolda. And yet a third is understanding the historical and cultural context of reservation life at this period of time in the 1930s.

In terms of the historical and cultural context, I would point out to students that Indian reservations in the 1930s were notorious for their poverty, their high mortality rate, their chronic unemployment, and the destruction of the fabric of Native American social and cultural forms. One of the principal policies of the United States government was to transform Native Americans into carbon copies of Anglo-Americans, and one of the principal ways that they hoped to accomplish this, ever since the Grant administration in the 1870s, was through religion.

During the 1870s, the Native American communities were allocated among the various major Christian sects, and missionary activity was understood to be an agent of social and cultural transformation. The objective was to get rid of the Indian while saving the man. Culture was imagined as a number of practices and behaviors and customs, which—if they could be changed—would eliminate all the historic obstacles to the Indians' participation in Anglo-American culture. Of course, if they were eliminated, so would the Indian nest be eliminated. Religion then is hardly a simple spiritual force but rather an agent of the interests of the Euro-American majority. Such an understanding, I think, should help students appreciate the intensity with which Marie and Sister Leopolda enter their confrontation.

A fine introduction to this story would be to spend a good deal of time focusing on the first paragraph, trying to understand the tone of the narrator and also the structure of her vision of herself, which she repeats later in the story. I would use the imagery and the tone as a way of developing the narrator's sense of herself, and I would try to account for her intense antagonism to the "black robe women on the hill."

Most students are puzzled by the intensity of the antagonism, and they have real questions as to whether or not Marie or Leopolda or both are crazy. Students tend to think that they're crazy because of the surrealistic imagery and because of the intensity of the emotion, which strikes most of them as excessive. Students need to realize that religion, especially when it is the lens through which other issues are magnified, can become the focus of such intense feelings and that when one's feelings are so intense, they frequently compel the creation of surrealistic imagery as the only means to adequately shape what one sees.

Major Themes, Historical Perspectives, Personal Issues

I think that there are two major themes that could be addressed in this story. The first is to understand religion, as described in the previous question, as a field upon which two different sets of interests contest their right to define the terms by which people will understand themselves and others. For all the black comedy in this story, the battle that Leopolda fights with the Dark One over the soul of Marie Lazarre is understood by both Leopolda and Marie as a very real battle. Leopolda represents a set of values, and so does the Dark One. Marie is understood as struggling to choose between the values of the Dark One and the values of Sister Leopolda, and these values are cultural as well as spiritual, for it is precisely the Indian character of Marie—her pride, her resistance to change, her imagination—that Leopolda identifies with the Dark One.

A second theme is to view the formation of identity in bicultural environments as an enriching, rather than an impoverishing, experience. Too often in bicultural situations, Indian protagonists are represented as being helpless, suspended in their inability to make a decision between two sets of values offered to them. The John Joseph Mathews novel *Sundown* is an example. In this story, however, Marie Lazarre chooses, and she chooses to identify herself as an Indian over and against the black robe sisters precisely by turning their own naiveté against them. The "veils of faith" that she refers to early in this story not only prevent the sisters from seeing the truth, but they also obscure their faith from shining forth, like the Reverend Mr. Hooper's veil in Hawthorne's story "The Minister's Black Veil."

Significant Form, Style, or Artistic Conventions

This story succeeds principally as a study of characterization. I would ask students to pay special attention to matters of tone and point of view. Since this story is told in the first person, I would ask them, on the basis of what they have read, to form an opinion of Marie Lazarre and, secondly, to develop some sense of her judgment of Sister Leopolda. I would ask them to look especially at the imagery and the language that Marie uses to describe her encounters with Leopolda and to describe herself, as the basis for their opinions.

Original Audience

The audience for whom this story is written is contemporary, but differs from the students we meet in university settings by perhaps being older and therefore more familiar with a traditional religiosity. Students who are not Catholic may need to know something about Catholicism, especially the role of nuns, and this historic role of missionaries in relationship to Indian communities. Other explicitly Catholic references, such as to the stigmata, are explained by their context in the story.

Comparisons, Contrasts, Connections

This story can be usefully contrasted with some of Flannery O'Connor's stories, which focus on the discovery of real faith, especially from a Catholic perspective. The emphasis on surrealistic imagery provides interesting connections with poems like those of Adrienne Rich; since this is a retrospective narrative, one might usefully compare this probing of a formative event from the narrator's past with Rich's poem "Diving into the Wreck." Insofar as this offers us a sensitive and imaginative teenage minority narrator, the story invites comparisons with the work of Toni Morrison and Alice Walker. In Native American terms, useful comparisons would be with Gertrude Bonnin's "Why I Am a Pagan," as well as John Oskison's "The Problem of Old Harjo."

Questions for Reading, Discussion, and Writing

1. I've never used questions ahead of time for this particular story, though if I did, I think they would be addressed to issues of characterization and tone.
2. An interesting assignment, because this story is told from Marie's point of view, is to retell the encounter between Marie and Sister Leopolda from Sister Leopolda's perspective. This would require students to formulate characterizations of Leopolda and of Marie, which would be useful touchstones for evaluating their comprehension of the issues on which the conflict in this story rests.

Bibliography

Erdrich, Louise. "Whatever Is Really Yours: An Interview with Louise Erdrich." *Survival This Way: An Interview with American Indian Poets.* Tucson: U of Arizona P, 1987, 73–86.

Lorna Dee Cervantes (b. 1954)

Contributing Editor: Juan Bruce-Novoa

Classroom Issues and Strategies

Students may object to the strident tone of "Poem for the Young White Man." Even Chicanos can get turned off by it. The feminism has the same effect on the men. Why is she so hostile toward males, they ask. Some now say that she is passé, radicalism being a thing of the sixties. I prepare the students with information on feminist issues, especially the single-parent families, wife abuse, and child abuse. I also prepare them by talking about racial and ethnic strife as a form of warfare, seen as genocide by minority groups.

I use Bernice Zamora's poetry as an introduction. Her alienation from the male rituals in "Penitents" produces the all-female family in "Beneath. . . ." The sense of living in one's own land, but under other's rules (Zamora's "On Living in Aztlán"), explains the bitterness of "Poem for the Young White Man." And both of the poets eventually find a solution in their relation to nature through animal imagery; yet just like Zamora in "Pico Blanco," Cervantes maintains an uneasy relationship with the macho world with which women still contend.

Major Themes, Historical Perspectives, Personal Issues

The historical theme of the disappearance of the nuclear family in the United States is primary here. There is also the effect of urban renewal on ethnic and poor communities whose neighborhoods were often the targets for projects that dislodged people from an area.

On the personal level, Cervantes's family history is reflected auto-biographically in "Beneath. . . ."

Significant Form, Style, or Artistic Conventions

Cervantes uses the form of the narrative poem, with a few key metaphors. Her confessional mode is reminiscent of Robert Lowell's. Her style is conversational, direct, unpretentious, but there is a constant sharp edge to her verses, a menacing warning against overstepping one's welcome.

Original Audience

Although her audience was and is generally "third worldist" and Chicano, these poems show a range of different target audiences. "Beneath . . ." is a feminist poem, appealing greatly to women. When it was first published, there was little discussion of the issue of female heads of households in Chicano circles because few wanted to admit to the problem in the Chicano community. Now the discussion is much more common.

"Poem for . . ." had great appeal in the closing days of the radical movement but has since faded to a smaller audience of older Chicanos who have heard the radical poetry to the point of exhaustion. However, mainstream liberals like "Poem for . . ." because it speaks as they assume all minorities should speak, harshly, bitterly, and violently. Young Chicanos are once again picking up the strident tone, faced as they are with the economic decline that has exacerbated social problems, especially in urban schools.

Comparisons, Contrasts, Connections

I compare her with Margaret Atwood in their sense of women being submerged and needing to surface by finding their own traditions. They both have a capacity for stringent statement when pushed by violent circumstances. Both have strong links to nature, in which their ancestors cultivated not only food, but their culture. Comparisons with Bernice Zamora are suggested above.

Carlos Castaneda's theory of the enemy is significant for Cervantes. It explains how the "Young White Man" is tempting the author into violence.

Questions for Reading, Discussion, and Writing

1. Students are asked to consider the significance of mainstream con-struction projects on local communities; from here they are asked to ponder the cycle of change and its victims.
2. Write on the links between "Beneath . . ." and "Poem for. . . ."
3. Write on Cervantes's view of the world as a threat to existence and what she offers as a response.

Bibliography

The best article is my "Bernice Zamora and Lorna Dee Cervantes," *Revista Iberoamericana* 51 (July–Dec. 1985): 132–33, 565–73. See also Cordelia Candelaria's *Chicano Poetry* and Martin Sonchez's *Contemporary Chicana Poetry*.

Helena María Viramontes (b. 1954)

Contributing Editor: Juan Bruce-Novoa

Classroom Issues and Strategies

The story touches on so many social issues that class discussion is almost assured. Some students, however, may express a sense of overkill: too many social and political ills too rapidly referenced to produce a profound impression. The class may also divide over the issues, some finding that they are so often covered by the media that they hardly need repetition while others like the story because it seems like a familiar exposé on subjects they consider everyday reality.

You may find yourself in a discussion more of the headnote and its advocacy of the rights of undocumented aliens than of the story itself. I would try to focus on close textual reading to prevent the discussion from drifting away from the text and into arguments over social and political policies. Yet some explanation of U.S. immigration policies and the political issues in Central America may be necessary (see "Historical Perspectives").

Major Themes, Historical Perspectives, Personal Issues

Viramontes has published few stories, and the headnote provides ample information on her themes and the personal connection with them. Historically, however, students may need more help. The Latino characters are undocumented aliens, and as such they can be detained by Immigration and Naturalization agents. After a hearing, they can be repatriated to their country of origin. However, in the recent past the process for Central Americans has more often than not tended to allow delay of their return, especially for those who claim political asylum. For Mexican aliens, the process is usually more automatic, although their return to the United States is also quite usual. The headnote suggests that the female refugee comes from El Salvador, which may provoke some confusion since in the story her son is accused of collaborations with "Contras," a right-wing terrorist group supported by the United States in the 1980s to undermine the Sandinista regime in Nicaragua. This could lead to ambiguous interpretations (just who has killed the woman's son, the Nicaraguan left or the Salvadorean right?) that can be used to lend the story interesting ambiguity to undermine simplistic political positions of right and wrong.

Significant Form, Style, or Artistic Conventions

Narrative perspective varies, moving from one character to another. While the technique may disorient some students, most will have encountered it in previous studies. It is important for them to note how Viramontes changes diction levels to achieve characterization. The use of interior monologue, especially in Section II, is noteworthy but not difficult to comprehend. The dashes of the "Rashamon" technique—the viewing of the same event from different perspectives at different times—adds to the text's fragmented feel.

Original Audience

Viramontes addresses a contemporary U.S. audience with topics relatively well known to most readers.

Comparisons, Contrasts, Connections

Comparisons can be made with Rolando Hinojosa's selection, which also utilizes the fragmented narrative while the subtlety of Hinojosa's social commentary can be contrasted with Viramontes's blatant approach. One might also place Viramontes in the tradition of such writers as Harriet Beecher Stowe, Frances Ellen Watkins Harper, or Upton Sinclair, writers who did not shy away from explicit advocacy of political positions, even at the risk of melodramatic excess. While the headnote refers to García Márquez and Isabel Allende, there is little of the Latin American Magical Realism associated with those authors; the connection would be to their political positions, not to their style.

Questions for Reading, Discussion, and Writing

1. The basic assignment here is to establish how the story is being narrated: from whose perspective is something seen? Then I ask students to characterize the different perspectives by picking specific words, turns of phrases, motifs, and so on.
2. I ask students to identify the specific Latino content of the story. Then I ask them to consider if the experiences apply to other immigrant groups or to the human condition in general.
3. This story lends itself to creative writing assignments. Have students pick a recent news event and narrate it from the objective perspective of a reporter and then from at least two others; for example, a witness of and a participant in the event.

Aurora Levins Morales (b. 1954)

Contributing Editor: Frances R. Aparicio

Classroom Issues and Strategies

Since Levins Morales's major book is authored in collaboration with her mother, Rosario Morales, it would be appropriate to present her work in this context. Instructors could familiarize themselves with *Getting Home Alive* and make a selection of texts in which the dialogue—as well as the differences—between mother and daughter is exemplified.

Major Themes, Historical Perspectives, Personal Issues

Major themes in Aurora Levins Morales's work: identity as a female minority in the United States; feminism; multiple identity (Puerto Rican, Jewish, North American), also inherited versus self-defined identities; concept of *immigrant*; Jewish culture and traditions; mother/daughter relationships; importance of language, reading, words, and writing; remembering and memory as a vehicle to surpass sense of fragmentation and exile/displacement; images of spaces and cities; "internationalist" politics.

Significant Form, Style, or Artistic Conventions

Heterogeneous forms and texts constitute Levins Morales's writings. *Getting Home Alive* is a collage of poems, short stories, lyrical prose pieces, essays, and dialogues. Note the importance of eclectic style: she is lyrical, subdued at times, sensorial, and quite visual in her imagery. She does not belong to any major literary movement; her writings cannot be easily categorized into one style or another, though they definitely respond to the preoccupations of other U.S. women of color.

Comparisons, Contrasts, Connections

Fruitful comparisons can be drawn with the works of other women of color, such as Cherríe Moraga, *Loving in the War Years* in *Cuentos: Stories by Latinas*, ed. Gómez, Moraga, Romo-Carmona (New York: Kitchen Table, 1983). Levins Morales has been particularly influenced by Alice Walker. In addition, I believe comparisons and contrasts with mainstream U.S. feminist writers would also prove valuable.

Questions for Reading, Discussion, and Writing

1. Study questions would deal with textural analysis and with clarifying references to Spanish words, places in Puerto Rico or El Barrio, and other allusions that might not be clear to students.
2. (a) Have students do their own version of "Child of the Americas" in order to look into their own inheritance and cross-cultural identities.

   (b) Paper topics might include the importance of multiple identity and "internationalist" politics; comparison and contrast of mother's and daughter's experiences, points of view, language, and style; meaning of language, reading, and writing for Levins Morales; an analysis of images of space, borders, urban centers, mobility, exile, displacement; contrast to Nuyorican writers from El Barrio: how would Levins Morales diverge from this movement, and why should she still be considered as representative of Puerto Rican writers in the United States?

Bibliography

Benmayor, Rina. "Crossing Borders: The Politics of Multiple Identity." *Centro de Estudios Puertorriqueños Bulletin* 2.3 (Spring 1988): 71–77.

Rojas, Lourdes. "Latinas at the Crossroads: An Affirmation of Life in Rosario Morales and Aurora Levins Morales's *Getting Home Alive.*" In *Breaking Boundaries: Latina Writing and Critical Reading.* Ed. A. Horno-Delgado, E. Ortega, N. Scott, and N. Saporta-Sternbach. Amherst: U of Massachusetts P, 1989. 166–77.

Sandra Cisneros (b. 1954)

Contributing Editor: Lora Romero

Classroom Issues and Strategies

Students generally find reading Cisneros a delightful experience. The brevity and humor of her stories help make them accessible even to those unfamiliar with the Mexican-American culture in which much of her writing is set. In fact, one of my colleagues taught Cisneros very successfully to students in Galway, Ireland.

One potential source of discomfort for students is Cisneros's manifestly feminist sensibility. Some students may accuse her (as they would accuse virtually any other feminist writer) of "man-bashing." When this issue comes up, I point out that, ironically, defining *feminism* in that way makes men the center of attention. Then I encourage students to talk about what they think *feminism* means and/or should mean. Sometimes students with more sophisticated definitions of *feminism* can convince their peers that *feminism* does not reduce to *man-hating*; in any case, giving students a forum for talking through the issue is usually productive since it is one about which they will probably have strong (if unexamined and unarticulated) opinions.

The feminism of women of color, however, is complicated by ethnic identification. Some students will be assuming that ethnic authors should offer only "positive" images of minorities—which means, in effect, talking about sexism in minority communities is off-limits. I encourage students to interrogate their assumptions about ethnic authors' "duties." At the same time, I acknowledge that being both a woman of color and a feminist can be a difficult task since one of the stereotypes of Latino men (and nonwhite men generally) is that "they treat their women badly." Then I try to turn students' attention back to the text to see if they can find evidence that some tension between ethnic and gender identity is shaping the narrative.

Major Themes, Historical Perspectives, Personal Issues

Students may bring to Cisneros's work a conception of immigrant culture that is based on the model of European immigration to the United States. That model is not entirely appropriate; in fact, Chicanos have a saying: "We didn't come to the United States. It came to us." Before the Mexican-American War (1846–1848), most of what is now the southwestern United States (including Texas and California) was part of Mexico. After the war, many erstwhile Mexicans automatically became U.S. citizens when the United States annexed the land where Mexicans had lived since the sixteenth century. Reminding students that national boundaries are often arbitrarily imposed should help deepen their understanding of national culture. In addition, most students will have only linear and unidirectional models of "assimilation" for understanding ethnic cultures, but the culture of Latinos living in the United States has been shaped by a very different historical experience. Anthropologists and historians have argued that the southwestern United States is really part of a much older, regional culture that includes Northern Mexico and that this regional culture is constantly being reinvigorated by a continuous flow of population back and forth over the border.

One important theme in Cisneros's work is the heterogeneity of the Mexican-American community (as it is expressed through differences of class, gender, education, language use, politics, and so on). Cisneros is, typically, more interested in detailing the dynamics of her own community rather than representing conflicts between Anglo Americans and Mexican Americans. Conflicts between Anglo and Latino cultures are, of course, present in Cisneros's writing, but they often take the form of encounters between relatively assimilated Latinos and relatively unassimilated ones.

The shape of such encounters undoubtedly reflects personal issues in the sense that Cisneros, as an educated, middle-class intellectual, seems simultaneously committed to identifying with her Mexican-American characters and to never losing sight of her difference from them. Often in her stories, there is a narrator or character who seems to represent Cisneros herself: a Chicana artist who has done something to scandalize her community, who exists (as it were) on the border between Mexican-American and Anglo-American cultures, and who has an uneasy relation to both.

Significant Form, Style, or Artistic Conventions

Cisneros's stories typically move in the direction of reconciliation of the Chicana intellectual with the Mexican-American community, but not all of her stories achieve that resolution. Cisneros's work thus provides fertile grounds for discussion of the politics of narrative closure. For this reason, it would be helpful if, before reading Cisneros, students had some sense of the conventions of the short story. Cisneros writes in a modernist narrative mode with both North American and Latin American precursors. Her stories do not typically center on a single consciousness or point of view; they are often populated by voices rather that characters; if there is an identifiable narrator, she is usually ironized.

In a more advanced class where you can assume some familiarity with a modernist narrative, you could use Cisneros as a test case for differentiating between modernism and postmodernism. In addition to formal considerations, some topics crucial to such discussion would include Cisneros's feminism, her ethnic identification, and her attitude toward mass culture.

Comparisons, Contrasts, Connections

To encourage students to think about how ethnic feminist writers negotiate between their gender and their ethnic identifications, it would be worthwhile to compare Cisneros with writers like Toni Morrison, Maxine Hong Kingston, Louise Erdrich, and Helena María Viramontes. On the other hand, reading Cisneros in the context of contemporary Latin American women writers (for example, Claire Lipesector, Isabel Allende, Carolina María de Jesus) would put pressure on received categories of national/cultural identity. Including even one

Latin American writer at the end of a course on what is called "*American* Literature" can be a useful way of getting students to think about the ethnocentrism of the term and the politics of cultural study more generally.

For contrast as much as comparison, Cisneros might also be placed in the context of nonfiction writings by lesbian Chicana writers like Gloria Anzaldúa and Cherríe Moraga. The comparison/contrast helps bring attention to the specifically heterosexual nature of Cisneros's feminism: how does the fact that Cisneros is heterosexual (and hence unable to declare herself simply "independent" of men) shape her articulation of feminism and illuminate the particular erotic dilemmas faced by her female characters? In order to highlight the question of class, pairing Cisneros with Tomás Rivera works well because—although Cisneros has certain stylistic affinities with Rivera—his work is more obviously compatible with the version of Chicano identity constructed by the Chicano movement.

Bibliography

Cisneros's *House on Mango Street* has already generated a number of critical responses, including Ellen McCracken, "Sandra Cisneros' *The House on Mango Street:* Community-Oriented Introspection and the Demystification of Patriarchal Violence" in *Breaking Boundaries: Latina Writings and Critical Readings,* ed. Asunción Horno-Delgado et al. (1989); Julián Olivares, "Sandra Cisneros' 'The House on Mango Street' and the Poetics of Space" in *Chicana Creativity and Criticism: Charting New Frontiers in American Literature,* ed. María Hererra-Sobek and Helena María Viramontes (1988); Ramón Saldívar, *Chicano Narrative: The Dialectics of Difference* (1990); and Alvina E. Quintana, *Home Girls: Chicano Literary Voices* (1996). There is also a growing body of work on *Woman Hollering Creek.* Particularly interesting studies of language, identity, and authenticity can be found in Katherine Rios, "'And you know what I have to say isn't always pleasant': Translating the Unspoken Word in Cisneros' *Woman Hollering Creek*" in *Chicana (W)rites on Word and Film,* ed. María Hererra-Sobek and Helena María Viramontes (1995); Jean Wyatt, "On Not Being *La Malinche:* Border Negotiations of Gender in Sandra Cisneros's 'Never Marry a Mexican' and 'Woman Hollering Creek,'" *Tulsa Studies in Women's Literature* 14 (Fall 1995); and Harryette Mullen, "'A Silence between Us Like a Language': The Untranslatability of Experience in Sandra Cisneros's *Woman Hollering Creek,*" *MELUS* 21 (Summer 1996). One study of *Woman Hollering Creek* in the context of inter-American feminism is Sonia Saldívar-Hulls "Feminism on the Border: From Gender Politics to Geopolitics" in *Criticism in the Borderlands: Studies in Chicano Literature, Culture, and Ideology,* ed. Héctor Calderón and José David Saldívar (1991).

Gish Jen (b. 1955)

Contributing Editor: Bonnie TuSmith

Classroom Issues and Strategies

The father's patriarchal and feudal attitudes can easily arouse feminist ire. While such attitudes need to be acknowledged and discussed, it is important to point out the narrator's viewpoint toward her father. The narrator pulls no punches in pointing out Ralph Chang's sexist and domineering ways. Such information does not, however, trigger brooding resentment or a desire for vengeance. In addressing this issue in the classroom, the instructor might combine feminist and cultural theories to promote a richer understanding of difference.

Major Themes, Historical Perspectives, Personal Issues

A key theme found in Jen's work is the Asian immigrant's coming to terms with American society. For people who come from cultures that are significantly different from the hegemonic European one, the process of acculturation can be awkward and even destructive. Like the father's Western suit, Asians who take on what they consider typically American culture often find that this does not fit well. The mother's statement "But this here is the U—S—of—A!" reveals the disease with which nonwhite, non-Europeans attempt to assimilate into European-American society. Historically excluded from the "good life," Americans of Asian descent necessarily exhibit ambivalence toward symbols of American success such as the town country club that is about to be sued by a waiting black family.

Significant Form, Style, or Artistic Conventions

The two-part structure of the story offers us a view of the father's feudal lord behavior in two different settings. In the first, treating his employees like servants—even if done magnanimously—simply does not work. In the second, the same arrogant impulse stands him in good stead when confronting racism. The structure gives us a clear picture of Ralph Chang's background and personality and enables us to consider the appropriateness of social behavior based on class and cultural differences.

The use of an observer/child narrator who is older and more reserved than the talkative younger sister Mona lends credibility to the narration and situates the story in a comfortable, firsthand point of view. The narrator's

English fluency and assumption of her American birthright render her voice easily accessible to a white audience. In this story, at least, there are no barriers based on language.

Original Audience

"In the American Society" was first published in *Southern Review* in 1986. It was subsequently anthologized in various collections of contemporary literature and, in 1999, it was included in Jen's own short story collection, *Who's Irish?* As one of the author's first published works and the prototype for the Chang family in *Typical American*, the story has garnered an academic audience of students, teachers, and scholars. Its special blend of disarming humor and social commentary has also rendered this and other works by Jen consistently appealing to the general reader.

Comparisons, Contrasts, Connections

Jen's stories are easily anthologized and can be compared with numerous American short stories—immigrant, classic, and ethnic—that explore issues of Americanization and the tensions that exist among various American cultures.

Questions for Reading, Discussion, and Writing

In teaching ethnic literature I use the approach of moving from the familiar—what European-American students already know about and have in common with all human beings as well as what they know about literature—to the unfamiliar. This strategy helps students and instructors get past their fear of what seems foreign: namely the "exotic other." Questions such as the following might be helpful:

1. Describe the dynamics of this nuclear family. What is the relationship of each family member to the others, and how does this reflect or challenge your notions of family?
2. Identify the source of humor in this story. How does humor contribute to the tone, mood, and overall message of the work?
3. How does the two-part narrative structure of the story enable meaningful comparison/contrast between the father's own society and the rest of American society? Is there ironic contrast between the two sections?
4. Does the dialogue seem realistic? How does the writer use dialogue to convey the racist, sexist, and classist attitudes of the characters?

Kimiko Hahn (b. 1955)

Contributing Editor: John Alberti

Classroom Issues and Strategies

Woven together from different cultural strands, intermixing the personal and political, Kimiko Hahn's work similarly invites readers to stitch together their own responses and reactions to her poetry. In so doing, her work challenges readers to consider how issues of cultural, gender, and racial identity are parts of a composite process of synthesis and, as the title of one of her poems indicates, resistance. Students can be drawn into her work by suggesting that instead of trying to pin down a single meaning for each work, they should consider each poem itself as part of a search for meaning, a search that remains necessarily open, experimental, and both serious and playful.

Students might be most comfortable approaching Hahn's work by reading "Cuttings" first, both because Hahn's writing is more expository here than in the other works and because the occasion of the piece—the death of Hahn's mother—is clearly defined. Hahn identifies the form of "Cuttings" as a *zuihitsu*, a type of writing developed in medieval Japan and historically associated with women's writing that can also feel very contemporary in its emphasis on informal, occasional, almost stream-of-consciousness writing. One commentator has even compared the form to blogging, at least in spirit, and this comparison does capture Hahn's practice of combining cultural forms and practices across historical periods.

"Cuttings" is also representative of the other texts by Hahn included in *The Heath Anthology* in that it contains an implicit narrative underlying the thoughts and feelings captured in each observation. One useful strategy in approaching "Strands" and "Resistance" is to ask students to construct what they see as the "story" behind each poem based on the fragmentary details of the poems themselves. This forensic approach to the works further foregrounds the extent to which the works resist simplification or reduction. Rather than a single story, students can consider multiple possibilities for the dramatic situations inspiring each poem. Students can likewise be encouraged to consider how permeable the boundaries of any story are, as, for example, the context of "Cuttings" ranges from minute details of the week of the funeral to the Second World War to the centuries-old literary tradition in which Hahn situates her work. Similarly, the story in "Strands" stretches from intimate memories of a love affair to the global politics of empire.

The secondary title of "Resistance"—"A Poem on Ikat Cloth"—can also be used as a metaphor for Hahn's compositional practice. An intricate form of textile production involving the painstaking process of tying individual "strands" of thread on a weaving loom and using resistance dyeing techniques to produce an overall pattern, the production of Ikat cloth serves as an apt description of the poetic process for a consciously multicultural poet like Hahn. The added sense in which "resistance" is figured as a form of creativity, beauty, and expression can also help students struggling with overly binary distinctions between cultural assimilation and preservation.

Working with Cultural Objects

As suggested above, the process of Ikat cloth production works as a helpful metaphor for Hahn's poetics, but simple verbal descriptions of that process and the resulting Ikat cloth can fail to give students a concrete sense of this tradition. Several websites provide visual examples both of Ikat cloth and the production process, such as the ArtXchange site at <http://www.artxchange. org/news2003sept/page2.asp>.

Questions for Reading, Discussion, and Writing

1. What did you imagine the story to be behind each poem? Write out a narrative version of the poem referencing what for you are the key details that Hahn provides. When you have finished, share your story with others in the class. In what ways did you agree and disagree? Where did others in the class see the details of the poem differently?
2. "Cuttings" is a *zuihitsu*, a word that roughly translates as "flowing writing" or "occasional writing." Based on Hahn's example of the form, try writing your own *zuihitsu* based on a specific important occasion in your own life (keeping in mind that what is "important" is for you to decide).

Li-Young Lee (b. 1957)

Contributing Editor: Zhou Xiaojing

Classroom Issues and Strategies

In discussing Li-Young Lee's poems it is important to avoid tendencies toward ethnocentric and Eurocentric readings. Some readers tend to overemphasize the "Chinese sensibility" in Lee's poems without acknowledging the influence of biblical writings and Western literature on Lee's work; others tend to judge

Lee's poems as "sentimental," without placing them within the context of his family history and personal experience as a refugee and immigrant. Students will better understand the importance of family, especially of Lee's father, in his poems when provided with some specific biographical information.

In her discussion of Li-Young Lee's poems, Judith Kitchen says that though "the story is personal and unique, the poems are declamatory, public even in their intimacy" ("Auditory Imagination" 161). Such a stance of the "lyric I" in Lee's poetry would be a good starting point for classroom discussions. Some critics argue that the authoritative and transcendental "lyric I" is inaccessible to Asian-American poets. Others regard the utterances of the "lyric I" as an outdated mode of Romantic lyric poetry. Indeed, many contemporary poets such as the New York School poets, Language poets, and some Asian-American poets, are resisting the Romantic "lyric I." It might be interesting to compare Lee's speaking "I" with that in poems of Wordsworth, of the American "confessional" poets, of John Ashbery, Charles Olson, Gary Snyder, and other Asian-American poets such as Garrett Hongo and Cathy Song, as well as African, Latino, and Native American poets. This comparison would yield more insights when it is situated in the poets' respective historical and social contexts. Students may also be asked to consider the relationship between the individual and the collective identities for European Americans and minority Americans, and to investigate the connections between identities and the status of the "lyric I."

Major Themes, Historical Perspectives, Personal Issues

The major themes in Lee's poems, such as love, loss, exile, the evanescence of life, human mortality, displacement and disconnection, the necessity and violence of change, and cultural and racial identity, are in one way or another related to Lee's unique experience and to his bicultural heritage. Lee's distinctive style and voice are also markedly established in "The Cleaving," which can be read in connection with the poems carved on the walls of barracks by Chinese immigrants detained on Angel Island and in the context of racism and racial stereotypes in American history and culture. Bret Harte's poem "Plain Language from Truthful James," better known as "The Heathen Chinee" (1870), can be used to contrast Lee's representation of the Chinese in "The Cleaving." Discussions of Lee's poem in connection with Harte's representational tactics in con-structing the "Otherness" of the Chinese can yield some insights into the notions and constructions of the American identity in nineteenth- and twenti-eth-century American literature.

Lee's prose-poem autobiography, *The Winged Seed: A Remembrance*, is very informative of his family history, his difficulty with the English language as a child, his search for the possibilities of language as a poet, the connection of his life to his father's, and his understanding of "death in life," all of which underlie the subject matter of his poems.

Significant Form, Style, or Artistic Conventions

Lee has developed a flexible strategy in employing imagery for multiple functions. He often uses a central image to organize and develop his ideas and feelings through free association. His representations of images sometimes reflect and enhance emotions ("I Ask My Mother to Sing") and sometimes visualize the felt quality of a particular reality. While Lee's use of imagery to express feelings and perceptions may be influenced by classical Chinese poetry, his strategy of employing the anecdotal descriptive-narrative as a springboard to launch into the emotional and abstract is characteristic of contemporary American poetry.

But the down-to-earth, sometimes violent sensualness of Lee's images, and their unlikely metaphorical connections and surprising transformations within a single poem, are unmistakably the results of Lee's innovative style. The surrealistic quality in Lee's style partly derives from French surrealism, in which Lee discerns "a new interiority," and partly from Lao Zi and Chuang Zi, in whose writings Lee finds freedom and sanity in the seemingly irrational.

Original Audience

Lee does not like to be confined by the label of "an Asian-American poet." One of his goals as a poet is to "birth a new and genuine . . . interiority into the world" (Li-Young Lee's letter to the author, May 1995). His poems, written in plain speech and accessible style, appeal to a general audience. As Lee writes in "With Ruins," his poems offer a space "for those who own no place/to correspond to ruins in the soul" (*The City in Which I Love You* 45).

Comparisons, Contrasts, Connections

In his foreword to *Rose*, Gerald Stern has singled out one of Lee's differences from other contemporary American poets. "The 'father' in contemporary poetry," Stern notes, "tends to be either a pathetic soul or a bungler or a sweet loser, overwhelmed by the demands of family and culture and workplace. . . . The father in Lee's poems is nothing like that" (9). It would be mutually illuminating to compare the father figure in Lee's poems with those in poems by Robert Lowell ("Commander Lowell"), Anne Sexton ("All My Pretty Ones"), Sylvia Plath ("Daddy"), and Cathy Song ("The Tower of Pisa") in relation to their cultural and historical contexts and in terms of their specific personal situations.

A similar comparative approach can also be used in discussing Lee's treatment of love, death, and the body. Use, for example, "The Song of Songs," poems by John Donne, Emily Dickinson, Walt Whitman, and Dylan Thomas, particularly his "The Force That through the Green Fuse Drives the Flower" and "Fern Hill."

Bibliography

Primary Sources

Lee, James Kyung-Jin. "Li-Young Lee: Interview by James Kyung-Jin Lee." *Words Matter: Conversations with Asian American Writers.* Ed. King-Kok Cheung. Honolulu: U of Hawaii P, 2000.

Lee, Li-Young. *The City in Which I Love You.* New York: BOA, 1990.

———. "The Father's House." *Transforming Vision: Writers on Art.* Selected and intro. Edward Hirsch. New York: Bulfinch/Little, 1994. 119–20.

———. *Rose.* New York: BOA, 1986.

———. *The Winged Seed: A Remembrance.* New York: Simon, 1996.

Moyers, Bill. "Li-Young Lee." Interview with Li-Young Lee. *The Language of Life: A Festival of Poets.* Ed. James Haba. New York: Doubleday, 1995. 257–69.

Tabios, Eileen. "Li-Young Lee's Universal Mind—A Search for the Soul." Interview with Li-Young Lee including Tabios's comments and Lee's draft of a new poem, "The Father's House." *Black Lightning: Poetry-In-Progress.* Intro. Arthur Sze. New York: Asian American Writers Workshop. 1998, 110–32.

Secondary Sources

Engles, Tim. "Lee's 'Persimmons.'" *Explicator* 54.3 (Spring 1996): 191–92.

Hesford, Walter A. "*The City in Which I Love You:* Li-Young Lee's Excellent Song." *Christianity and Literature* 46.1 (Autumn 1996): 37–60.

Kitchen, Judith. Essay review of *Rose* by Li-Young Lee. "Speaking Passions." *Georgia Review* 42.2 (Summer 1988): 419–22.

————. Essay review of *The City in Which I Love You* by Li-Young Lee. "Auditory Imagination: The Sense of Sound." *Georgia Review* 45.1 (Spring 1991): 160–63.

Stern, Gerald. Foreword. *Rose*. By Li-Young Lee. New York: BOA, 1986. 8–10.

Zhou, Xiaojing. "Inheritance and Invention in Li-Young Lee's Poetry." *MELUS* 21.1 (Spring 1996): 113–32.

David Foster Wallace (b. 1962)

Contributing Editor: Joseph Dewey

Classroom Issues and Strategies

Wisely, the editors elected not to excerpt from Wallace's massive *Infinite Jest* or reprint any one of Wallace's familiar hip pop-culture essays; rather, the editors have drawn attention to Wallace's short fiction that, despite its considerable achievement as a most original hybrid of postmodernism and minimalism, has been overlooked. Most students initially react from preconceived notions of what a short story should do, and this narrative, of course, violates those expectations. The story is strikingly brief and nothing much happens; the only character, the speaker, actively resists definition (nameless, featureless, genderless, context-less), and Wallace refuses to intrude with any authorial direction. The monologue does not resolve itself with any certainty and points to a closing observation that is unsettling and provocative. In addition, the presumed first-person intimacy is roundly violated—the speaker appears at times hostile, only grudgingly reveals any information, withholds much of the critical context for the act of generosity, and appears genuinely uncomfortable with any level of sharing.

And yet the achievement of the narrative is to move us toward sympathy. The best place to start is with the notion of a voice and the concept of indirect revelation—how when given a chance to talk, we all end up revealing much about ourselves that we may or may not want to reveal. Specifically, how does the story deploy tension between what the speaker says and what the speaker reveals? The reader is given no help—no adverbs to script the monologue, no context to create an understanding, no physical description to create a reassuring picture. We are not told why the monetary gift has been offered, we are not told the background of this friendship, and we are not even given the particulars of the gift. Students may resist; authors, they say, should provide a clearer compass for character definition. That Wallace creates this voice and then allows it to be suspended among easy definitions is not done to frustrate but rather to encourage reader involvement and to allow the narrative to reflect the difficult and ambiguous nature of real-world motivations and psychology.

Of course, discussion can ultimately address the moral universe that Wallace conjures through this voice: here is a character who has done some nonspecific (but apparently significant) act of charity, given a gift of money to an apparently needy couple with the responsibility of a new baby and a crippling (but nonspecified) financial debt. That kind of generosity classified under traditional moral rubrics would be an unalloyed good—indeed, the fundamental gesture of a Judeo-Christian ethos that encourages us to care for each other selflessly. However, here the character must confront the uncertain motivation for the act, and the more the character reasons, the more the character thinks, the more we begin to see that such moral certainty is not workable. (In a companion story in the same volume, in fact one with the same name, Wallace explores the reason that junk—castoff furniture and damaged appliances—is more attractive if someone pays for it rather than if it is given free.) The pivotal sentence for such a discussion in this story occurs when the character unexpectedly concedes, "I was almost dying with temptation," to reveal his involvement with the act of generosity, to accept thanks and the consequent inevitable debt of gratitude. The vehemence of that observation, the intensity of its self-serving emotion, signals a complex character and an uneasy motivation.

The students could be asked to define the *Good Samaritan Syndrome*, the impulsive act of intrusive charity, as a model for exemplary behavior. The brief narrative here deconstructs that act until Wallace compels us to accept that absolute good and absolute evil are actually the very same act. This should raise significant and probing speculations about morality and ethics and whether the Judeo-Christian code is actually operable. Given Wallace's much-documented discontent with over-intellectualizing (despite his own considerable academic background), students might be directed to consider whether the problem here is an overactive mind, the character relentlessly probing a simple act of generosity. Perhaps this could lead to a discussion of the head versus heart tension that has centered American moral fictions since Hawthorne. Caution should be taken: Wallace is not cynically dismissing such ethics; he is not suggesting some simplistic pessimistic worldview in which virtue and vice are the same impulse, so why bother. He has repeatedly and eloquently argued against just such dead-ends. Rather, he is taking an unblinking look at the heart of morality and examining the complex dilemma generosity inevitably involves. Do not let the students slide into simplicities—this character struggles with the responsibility of others.

Major Themes, Historical Perspectives, Personal Issues

Brief Interviews with Hideous Men (1999), the collection from which this story is taken, appeared at a crucial moment not only in Wallace's career but in American cultural history as well.

Coming after the massive intricacies of *Infinite Jest*, this story reflects Wallace's turn toward conciseness, how less is more in character revelation. It might help to reproduce a small portion of *Infinite Jest*, perhaps Section 17's description of a teleputer or Section 22's bizarre instructions for the fantasy game Eschaton or the self-indulgent extensive footnotes on pharmaceuticals, to give students some idea of how sharply Wallace has shifted his narrative focus. Taking his cue from the sculptured precision of minimalists such as Raymond Carver (the anthology selection "Cathedral" is particularly helpful), Wallace here defies the labels his own work had been given to display a nuanced irony, a careful and subtle use of language to reveal a character that, in rereading and upon reflection, is more a part of us than perhaps we want to acknowledge.

As the title of the collection indicates, Wallace (like Carver) is particularly drawn to initially unlikable characters. It is the reader's job not to judge or to advise this character but rather to engage the moral dilemma through Wallace's manipulations of language. Instructors might use Wallace's comments from a *Review of Contemporary Fiction* interview (1993) to begin this discussion: "[P]art of what we humans come to art for is an experience of suffering, true empathy's impossible. But if a piece of fiction can allow us imaginatively to identify with a character's pain, we might then also more easily conceive of others identifying with our own. This is nourishing, redemptive; we become less alone inside."

Culturally, the story can be used to signal how the unearned pessimism and dead-end irony of the grunge generation had run its course. After *Infinite Jest*, Wallace was positioned as the chief voice of Generation X, the Grunge Novelist—a reference to the massive text as a sort of extended joke by a massively intelligent writer cynically amused by the idea of any reader finally getting the joke, the writer as a sort of cross between the smirking irony of David Letterman and the cool despair of Kurt Cobain—both cultural references that could be introduced profitably to show, in one case, laugh-at-everything cynicism and, on the other, an impossible distance from hope. Wallace himself rejected both positions for the writer as dead-ends, and this story indicates his emerging sense that narrative is a redemptive act as it allows the violation of loneliness in the generous act of a reader identifying with the character. Wallace has argued passionately that the function of lasting literature—and he invokes Tolstoy, Flannery O'Connor, Don DeLillo, and Carver—is to touch the reader.

Significant Form, Style, or Artistic Convention

It is the voice that students need to hear, a heart-in-dilemma, struggling to understand that impulse we feel to help and to handle the awesome burden of self-consciousness, the problems we will encounter if we examine too closely what our heart does. Of course, the instructor must make clear that despite the first-person narrative, this is not fiction used to reveal the author. This is an experiment in creating a voice—comparisons to Henry James's centering consciousnesses would help remind them: "Daisy Miller" or "The Aspern Papers," for example. This character's anxiety of introspection can best be approached by understanding that he is not particularly interested in intimacy, that here is a hesitant confidence, a character who views confession itself with vague uneasiness. Thus, the deliberate attempts to conceal the details—including the deliberately heavy-handed extended blanks—create a feeling in the reader of being unwanted, of eavesdropping. Appropriate ties can be made to Carver's shallow, mean-spirited narrator in "Cathedral." But students should be shown how Wallace (and Carver) refuses tidiness—we must overcome such initial resistance and move to a position of sympathy from which we cannot entirely condemn nor easily embrace this character.

As a voice without context, the character here can be read in a variety of moods. Challenge the students to cast the voice—whom do they hear? Certainly the tenor of the story changes if you hear, for instance, Jack Nicholson or, say, Woody Allen; Jennifer Aniston or Larry King; Johnny Depp or Robert DeNiro—or to decide on some of the larger details of the character that Wallace does not give: Is this character rich or poor? Male or female? Old or young? Religious or not? What profession, what circumstances forged the friendship that is here so threatened by the act of charity? Experimenting with context can lead to a discussion of why Wallace refuses such reassuring context and allows this voice to become a sort of Every-Voice. It is detective-style guesswork that can never reach resolution but will compel the students to become creatively involved in the text, to see how every element of the monologue can help shape a sense of the character. List a variety of modes available for this character's definition—overly intellectual, earnestly introspective, hopelessly self-involved, fiercely paranoid, angry, sociopathic, crudely mercenary, well intentioned, self-important, fussy, hypocritical, desperately lonely, morally confused, cartoonishly pompous—and have different students read a passage with one of those tempers in mind. Of course, that it could be any of those is the value of Wallace's experiment, the narrative as a kind of an inkblot perception test.

Clearly, as the character works through the monologue, as the act of charity comes under closer scrutiny (particularly when the receiver of the money enquires about the gift), as the character starts to panic as the layers of the apparently simple gesture are exposed, the prose shifts appropriately.

Instructors might compare the prose line at the beginning against the prose line at the end. We move from tidy sentences and compact paragraphs to increasingly overburdened sentences that stretch for lines within unwieldy paragraphs that reveal the narrator's growing uneasiness, the disturbing implications of introspection.

The central issue clearly is whether we should share with others or stay apart. Instructors can show how Wallace deploys the simple comma to suggest this dilemma—by the closing paragraph the sentences are chopped with often unnecessary and intrusive commas that reflect stylistically the character's dilemma over being a part or being apart, isolation or community. An effective way to reveal this is simply to have students read the last paragraph aloud; it is a most difficult and abrasive read.

Original Audience

Ironically, Wallace's considerable audience, a sort of cultish band of enthusiastic readers, mostly university types, generated in large part from Wallace's considerable presence among websites, would have expected something far different. A Wallace reader comes to his work through the defining avantgarde works of the postmodernists and appreciates the revolution in form. Given the shock tactics and exaggerated emphasis on language and the ambitious form of *Infinite Jest*, here is an apparently conservative form intricately deployed but not foregrounded. Only in the rereading do the story's focus, intricacies, and moral dilemmas emerge.

A career academic (he currently holds an endowed chair in creative writing at Pomona College in California), Wallace has always addressed a university-educated, sophisticated reader willing to sustain the stamina of multiple-readings (a standard university literature class) rather than those who turn to literature for entertainment and diversion. Indeed, Wallace has frequently pointed out that narrative can engage readers and create a fragile but viable community with the writer, unlike entertainment media that merely exploit such isolation by surrounding the viewer with depthless images and simulated experiences. Such readers would approach this as an experimental narrative and not expect author revelation and/or autobiographical content despite the first-person intimacy.

Comparisons, Contrasts, Connections

The confessional monologue has been a fixture in American narrative literature since Poe's tormented characters who so articulately confess to hideous barbarities. Students need to be reminded of how authors in such experimental texts use irony and depth psychology—how we can never assume reliability in a character given to us as fallible and imperfect.

Wallace as well reflects the Jamesian strategy of allowing a story to be slanted from a character's perspective, a character (rather than the author) who is struggling with difficult moral dilemmas. That sense of dramatic revelation is fundamental to Wallace's enterprise. John Updike is an obvious, more contemporary model, although Wallace's moral universe is bleaker. Of course, Carver's "Cathedral" would be an optimum context with that sensibility of stripping narrative act to its minimal expression and allowing every aspect of the narrative—diction, syntax, even punctuation—to reveal character, largely because Wallace has publicly acknowledged that debt. The clear difference, however, is in the ending: Carver, a recovered alcoholic whose fictions had begun to define those critical moments when strangers heal strangers, offers a luminous resolution full of promise. Wallace, who was rumored to have gone through alcoholic recovery after the success of his first novel, instead leaves the reader (and the character) suspended amid questions.

Contrast would best be introduced by drawing on midcentury postmodern metafiction. Because of Donald Barthleme's enormous influence on Wallace's decision to pursue writing (particularly the influential metafiction "The Balloon" that Wallace has often said convinced him to abandon a promising career in philosophy and mathematical logic for fiction) and because of the postmodern avant-garde experimental texts that clearly inform Wallace's willingness to test formal conventions, students can be asked to compare such texts to this story. Have them consider how form is positioned so prominently in any of the short fiction experiments of Robert Coover or John Barth, how self-reflexive irony plays such a defining role in those audacious narratives, how the writer tends to assume that the reader will not be entirely comfortable within the game-text, and how ultimately the larger questions of moral dilemmas or character behavior are marginalized as writers reveal a cunning inventiveness and an exuberant playfulness.

For context, the most prominent example of a writer who has also moved beyond the irony and self-conscious play of postmodernism to explore how to balance form and character is Don DeLillo, another influence Wallace has acknowledged. And, of course, context can be provided by drawing on any of Wallace's contemporaries—Richard Powers, Rick Moody, William Vollmann, Jonathan Franzen—who have formed something of an unofficial group: each entirely a product of the television and computer era and all white, upper-middle-class, university-educated, self-described nerds; voracious readers; and interdisciplinary auto-didacts whose fictions bring together the inherited traditions of postmodernism's exuberant, liberating play-with-form and minimalism's generous sympathy for characters in dilemmas.

Working with Cultural Objects

Two clear cultural influences could be introduced, both of which have figured in Wallace's career and evolution: television and rap music.

Himself the product of a childhood spent in unexamined absorption of television, Wallace, a sharp critic of the media age, has long argued that television exploits emotions by simplifying them and exploits the loneliness of the viewer by providing the illusion of connection while offering only a collection of distancing images. What he offers here is a talking head, a familiar fixture on television. Instructors might draw on two models of confessional television programming that students would readily identify: the talk show and the reality show. In both cases, the complicated and distressing emotional traumas of centering characters are simplified, often packaged, and dismissed in tidy segments. Those centering characters deal in platitudes and clichés and create a moral universe that is easily defined and clearly lit. Television, as Wallace has argued, cannot handle complexity or depth. Have the students reimagine Wallace's character on one of those forums—how out of place the considerable angst and hesitant confidences would be, how the voice talks its way into mystery and ambiguity, how unsettling this monologue/segment would be, how difficult it would be to segue neatly into a commercial.

Rap is another interesting influence. Wallace cowrote a fascinating exploration of the early years of rap music: *Signifying Rappers: Rap and Race in the Urban Present* (with Mark Costello, 1990). The work was short-listed for that year's Pulitzer Prize for nonfiction. Although most of the discussion centered on larger issues of race and politics and the persistent problem of African-American disenfranchisement, Wallace and Costello reflected on the sheer energy of the language and how rap artists deftly use that language to create characters rather than frame autobiography (one problem was addressing all those who sought to censor the artists for use of inflammatory words that the artists tirelessly pointed out were actually being spoken by their created characters). Students could be encouraged to revisit this groundbreaking era of street rappers (among them Ice Cube, Run D.M.C., Cypress Hill, and A Tribe Called Quest) to see where the contemporary hip hop movement originated and then to explore ways in which dramatic monologues and rap intersect, how character and language cooperate, how writers/rappers rework a sentence to make its syllables crisp and sonically sound.

In addition, students might be interested in accessing either of the main Wallace websites to see how fans of the writer lovingly and enthusiastically dissect his work and communicate with each other via the websites' bulletin boards. The sites both provide extensive commentary on the works and access to a variety of interviews and reviews.

Questions for Reading, Discussion, and Writing

1. What associations do you make with being a Good Samaritan? List the kinds of acts that might come under such a heading. What motivates such random acts of kindness? How does Wallace test those assumptions?
2. Consider the implications of the title. Given the growing moral dilemma the character reveals, what sort of moral/ethical universe does the title create?
3. How does Wallace manipulate language to create the dilemma with which the character tangles? How does the story manipulate the expectations of intimacy? What adjectives would you use to describe this character?
4. Wallace himself has a long-standing interest in television and rap music. Do you see any connections between those cultural expressions and the first-person monologue he presents here?

Bibliography

Boswell, Matthew. *Understanding David Foster Wallace*. Columbia: U of South Carolina P, 2003.

Burn, Stephen. *David Foster Wallace's* Infinite Jest: *A Reader's Guide*. New York: Continuum Contemporaries, 2003.

LeClair, Tom. "The Prodigious Fiction of Richard Powers, William Vollmann, and David Foster Wallace." *Critique* 38.1 (1996): 12–37.

McCaffery, Larry. "An Interview with David Foster Wallace." *Review of Contemporary Fiction* 13.2 (1993): 127–50. Available at <http://www.centerforbookculture.org/interviews/interview_wallace.html>.

Miller, Laura. The Salon Interview with David Foster Wallace. 1996. Available at <http://www.archive.salon.com/09/features/wallace1.html>.

Star, Alexander. Review of Wallace's *A Supposedly Fun Thing I'll Never Do Again*. *New Republic* 30 June 1997: 27–34.

Websites

Official website devoted to David Foster Wallace: <http://www.thehowling fantods.com>.

Unofficial website: <http://www.davidfosterwallace.com>.

Chang-rae Lee (b. 1965)

Contributing Editor: Grace H. Park

Classroom Issues and Strategies

Students will probably relate easily to the issues raised by Lee's departure from home to attend boarding school since they too are negotiating the distance between home environments and collegiate culture as well as their changing relationships with their parents. The patriarchal values in Lee's family, however, may present more difficulties for students. In order to counteract the tendency to think of Lee's family in terms of Korean cultural difference, it might be useful to point out ways in which patriarchy influences practices in other American families, such as the expectation that working mothers will shoulder the brunt of the domestic chores and childcare. The self-effacement of Lee's mother, while extreme, should be considered in relation to current assumptions about maternal self-sacrifice.

The many descriptions of food that may be unfamiliar to some students may reinforce stereotypes of Asian exoticism. The essay intercepts such a response in the second section by suggesting that ideas of what constitutes the exotic depend on one's point of view. To Lee's family, Mrs. Churchill's recipes and ingredients are exotic and intriguing.

Although these cultural issues are crucial, it is also important not to lose sight of the artistry of Lee's work. Students should be encouraged to attend to the nuances of language and the use of symbolism in the essay.

Major Themes, Historical Perspectives, Personal Issues

The preparation and consumption of food is the theme that ties the three sections of "Coming Home Again" together. For classroom discussion, the students should explore the different ways in which food signifies in the essay as a symbol of domestic life and a marker of the shifting of care-giving responsibilities from parent to adult child. In addition, food takes on added significance within the context of Lee's immigrant family. Because of the value of indirection and subtlety of speech in Korean culture, the mother and son's shared interest in food allows them to talk about more emotionally charged topics under the cover of culinary matters.

Additional themes found in Lee's work are family life, immigration, assimilation, and alienation.

Significant Form, Style, or Artistic Conventions

Flashbacks and the juxtaposition of events separated in time but united by common themes are stylistic devices that Lee often uses in his work. "Coming Home Again" balances the rupture to the family's domestic life occasioned by his mother's death against the rift caused by his departure for Phillips Exeter Academy ten years previous to his mother's bout with cancer.

Original Audience

"Coming Home Again" was originally published in the 16 October 1995 issue of *The New Yorker*. The essay's appearance in this magazine is an early indication of Lee's growing crossover appeal to a well-educated, affluent mainstream audience.

Comparisons, Contrasts, Connections

Lee's work departs from Asian-American literary traditions through its emphasis on upper-middle-class characters. Asian-American literature tends to focus on working-class experiences since Asian immigrants either previously came from working-class backgrounds or experienced downward social mobility in the United States because their educational attainments or professional credentials were not recognized. In terms of class orientation, Lee's work can be compared with Jhumpa Lahiri's collection of short stories, *Interpreter of Maladies*, as well as with her novel *The Namesake*. Stylistically, Lee's elliptical, gently nuanced prose resembles Kazuo Ishiguro's writing.

Bibliography

Biographical information:

McGrath, Charles. "Deep in Suburbia." *New York Times Magazine* 29 Feb. 2004: 44.

Literary criticism on Lee's novels:

Chuh, Kandice. *Imagine Otherwise: On Asian Americanist Critique.* Durham: Duke UP, 2003.

Palumbo-Liu, David. *Asian/American: Historical Crossings of a Racial Frontier.* Palo Alto: Stanford UP, 1999.

Website:

A comprehensive list of Internet resources can be found at <http://www.
princeton.lib.nj.us/ptonreads/ptonreads-web.html>.

Sherman Alexie (Spokane—Coeur d'Alene) (b. 1966)

Contributing Editor: Martha Viehmann

Classroom Issues and Strategies

The title of Alexie's work "Because My Father Always Said He Was the Only
Indian Who Saw Jimi Hendrix Play 'The Star Spangled Banner' at Woodstock"
is at once intriguing and enigmatic. Because it is long enough to be a story in
itself (which it is, a story told within the story), it seems an appropriate place
to begin discussion. The title raises key issues in Alexie's writing: familiar
relationships; the role of oral communication and stories; majority culture
perceptions of Native Americans; and the relationships, cultural and political,
among Native Americans, the broader U.S. culture, and other American ethnic
groups. In addition, the title appears on the surface to have a simple, self-
explanatory meaning, yet on consideration, its meaning may remain elusive.
The story operates in a similar fashion. Narrated in deadpan style, loaded
with explicit and mundane detail yet recounting little action in which almost
nothing happens. Upon reflection, one finds that the story is grounded in deep
emotions, especially longing and anger, and touches on a wide array of issues,
many central themes in contemporary Native American literature and thought.
While a strong grounding in the history and contemporary culture of Native
North American is helpful for understanding the story, such knowledge is not
necessary. The story can also be read and discussed for its cross-cultural themes,
especially family and the power of music.

Family relationships are at the center of "Because My Father Always
Said." Victor, the first-person narrator, reconstructs the family life of his
childhood through vignettes about his father and his mother, both of whom
also speak in the story. The stories they tell and their conversations with
Victor present contrasting pictures of the father and the marriage. The father
is a "reservation philosopher" yet also a motorcycle-riding drunk pulled by
unexplained forces off the reservation. The mother dances at powwows and
continually brings Victor and his father back to concrete realities. Between the
two characters, Alexie soundly defeats any notions of non–Native American
readers finding transcendence through Native American characters. The major-

ity culture has routinely imagined Native Americans as more deeply spiritual than the rest of America, despite the extreme poverty of reservation life and the history of oppression of tribal cultures. In place of transcendence, Alexie offers only temporary satisfaction. Victor's longing for his father is never resolved; instead, the story concludes with the words "and we ate until we were full."

Students may need background information on Woodstock, Jimi Hendrix, and Robert Johnson. While in this particular story the references aren't specific, its context in Alexie's collection *The Lone Ranger and Tonto Fistfight in Heaven* makes it apparent that Victor and his mother live on the Spokane Indian reservation, located in arid central Washington state.

Alexie's dry humor may be difficult for students to understand. The humor comes through better when the story is heard rather than read. Assigning students specific sections to read aloud can help them read more attentively and understand the humor.

Major Themes, Historical Perspectives, Personal Issues

One of the subtly potent ways that Alexie comments on the relationship between Native Americans and the larger American culture is his use of exceptional and superlative imagery. Using descriptive terms like the "only Indian" at Woodstock, the only real cowboys in a cowboy bar, or the best traditional dancer, Victor's father makes linguistic connections to the American dream of fame and to images of vanishing Native Americans such as the "Last of the Mohicans." That such achievements prove hollow undercuts American values, "assimilationist" goals (alluded to in the wry comment about the father being assimilated because he abandons his wife and child), and the idea that Native people might value the celebrity status of the exceptional position of being the "only" (or "first") Indian.

The interplay between broader cultural assumptions and stereotypes of Native Americans and between the contemporary and historical realities that Alexie presents is related to his exploration of reality and imagery. A conversation between Victor and his father directly questions the relationship between reality and the imagination: Victor says, "Sometimes you sound like you ain't even real." And his father replies: "What's real? I ain't interested in what's real. I'm interested in how things should be." Talking like a "bad movie" and sounding like he isn't even real, the father continually says things that we must question, as Victor does when he muses that his father probably wasn't the only Indian at Woodstock, but he thought he was. Victor's understanding of his father's need to create the lie adds poignancy to the story, for like Victor and his mother, the reader cannot despise the father even though he leaves.

Other major themes are the relationship between African-American and Native American experience, music, and popular culture.

Significant Form, Style, or Artistic Conventions

The tug between longing and fullness is part of the essential dualism of the story. Throughout, opposing elements come together but never fully combine, from the parents' marriage, to Hendrix and the national anthem, to the conflation of hippies with Native Americans and a Native American's undermining of the hippies' peaceful protest. When Jimi Hendrix played the national anthem at Woodstock, he was literally playing "The Star Spangled Banner," and he was signifying on it, re-creating and changing the familiar tune (which was originally a drinking song). Discussion of signifying and humor as strategies that unsettle cultural assumptions can help reveal meaning in the story. On a simpler level, students can see how Alexie repeatedly creates situations in which disconnection prevails. Here, the musical metaphors of harmony and dissonance may be helpful in guiding discussion.

The style and structure of "Because My Father Always Said" closely correlates with its meaning. Narrated by Victor in the past tense, the story weaves specific events with examples of recurring elements that together create patchwork or scrapbook images of his family and especially his father. The combination of memories, recollected conversations, dreams, and flights of fancy results in a confusing chronology that remains indeterminate because Victor, who should be a young man in the 1990s, comes across always as a needy child, longing for the father who is lost to alcohol, caught up in his own past, or simply not there. This structure represents the improvisational nature of thought processes and conversations, which are in turn made concrete in the orality of Alexie's style. Likewise, the images I have used to describe the story also have concrete representations: the father's scrapbook of photographs and news clippings and the mother's quilt, in which she wraps Victor on the night he misses his father the most.

The process of constructing a story or a person through scraps produces something that is at once incomplete and fragmentary (like the scrapbook, an unsatisfying replacement for the father) and serviceable and comforting (like the mother's quilt). Alexie's fragmentary style and improvisational structure thus acknowledge that the stories we tell and the images we have of others are always partial and that this must be enough, which is also a way of explaining the final image of fullness in the story. Again, the construction of the story and the concrete images within it work together, creating a whole that is greater than the sum of its parts.

Questions for Reading, Discussion, and Writing

1. Have students write down and then discuss their preconceptions about Native Americans. What do we expect to find in a piece of contemporary Native American literature? How does the story confirm or confound those preconceptions and expectations?
2. Why is it important for Victor's father to believe that he was the only Indian at Woodstock to see Jimi Hendrix play "The Star-Spangled Banner"?
3. Compare and contrast the conversations between Victor and each of his parents. How do their actions and words characterize the father and the mother? What actions of the mother and father best illustrate their relationships with their son?
4. Victor comments, "Music had powerful medicine." Does music prove to have power in the story?
5. Victor reflects: "Plus and minus. Add and subtract. It comes out just about even." Does coming out even match your initial impression of the story? Take time to identify the pluses and minuses in the story and discuss what Victor might hope to have come out even and if you think it does.
6. The story ends with a reference to being full, leading to an irresistible metaphor: do you find the ending of the story satisfying?

Edwidge Danticat (b. 1969)

Contributing Editor: Katharine Capshaw Smith

Classroom Issues and Strategies

Students enjoy piecing together the narrator's motivations for tracking her mother across midtown Manhattan. An instructor might ask the class to define what Suzette thinks of her mother and explain why Suzette wants to spy on her mother. This topic often leads to a discussion about the form of the story. Why does it use two voices? When Suzette imagines her mother's voice, what do we learn about Suzette's impressions of her mother? What does she know about her mother, and what information is missing? A discussion of Suzette's needs might move into an analysis of her character. What do we discover about Suzette's cultural alliances from her imagined responses to her mother?

Major Themes, Historical Perspectives, Personal Issues

Complicated relationships between mothers and daughters are at the heart of Danticat's work. But students also recognize that the story depicts a larger cultural divide between generations and are often intrigued by the context of Haitian migration. Many students will be, at best, ignorant about Haitian history and culture and the Haitian-American experience. At worst, some may carry prejudicial assumptions about Haiti into the classroom. An instructor might bring Haiti into relief by noting that Haiti became the first independent black republic in the Americas, liberating itself from French colonizers in 1804. For Danticat, this long legacy of independence, dignity, and self-sufficiency takes shape in the character of the mother.

An instructor might also note that there are several cultural allusions offered through the mother's voice, the most powerful of which is the image of salt that surfaces midway through the story and at its conclusion. Since we do not get a gloss on this allusion from Suzette, we might assume that she (like students, in some cases) does not fully understand the mother's statement that "Salt is heavier than a hundred bags of shame" (especially since Suzette associates the comment with her mother's high blood pressure). Students might like to know about the comment's connection to a Caribbean folktale: the tale explains that whites offered enslaved Africans salt in order to counteract the sweat of physical labor. According to the tale, those Africans who refused to eat the salt, who refused to participate in the system of labor, were able to fly back to Africa. Those who accepted the salt were too heavy to fly. An instructor might ask the students how this context explains the mother's assertion that she "cannot just swallow salt. Salt is heavier than a hundred bags of shame."

Significant Form, Style, or Artistic Conventions

Students might like to know that many stories in *Krik? Krak!* experiment with form. The fragmentation and dual voices in "New York Day Women" allow students to appreciate not just the intricacies of characterization but also the process of memory. The fragmentation also allows students to recognize that there is much Suzette does not know about her mother. Suzette's journey down the streets of New York becomes a quest to understand her mother's character, and in so doing to understand her own cultural legacy. As the sample assignment on *The Heath Anthology* website suggests, students grow in their appreciation of the form by reading the story out loud.

Original Audience

"New York Day Women" comes from Danticat's second book, *Krik? Krak!* Her first text, the novel *Breath, Eyes, Memory*, brought Danticat a wide-ranging national audience when it was selected for Oprah Winfrey's monthly book discussion. From the beginning of her career, then, Danticat has received acclaim from academics and popular audiences alike. All of her books have been well reviewed in major national newspapers and magazines. In colleges and universities, her work is taught in courses in American literature, women's literature, Caribbean literature, and ethnic studies.

Comparisons, Contrasts, Connections

This story would connect with others in *The Heath Anthology* that explore the diversity of African-American experiences. One could also discuss cultural displacement, Americanization, and generational divides in Danticat alongside Maxine Hong Kingston, Gish Jen, Tato Laviera, and others.

Working with Cultural Objects

Bob Corbett of Webster University describes the history of Haiti at <http://www.webster.edu/~corbetre/haiti/history/course/unitone/short.htm > and <http://www.webster.edu/~corbetre/haiti/history/history.htm>.

An advocacy group for Haitians and Haitian Americans, the National Coalition for Haitian Rights, posts a website with information on politics and migration at <http://www.nchr.org>.

Questions for Reading, Discussion, and Writing

1. Why does Suzette follow her mother down the street?
2. Why is it so surprising for Suzette to see her mother in the setting of midtown Manhattan?
3. What does Suzette learn about her mother by watching her? What amazes Suzette, and why?
4. What does Suzette know about her Haitian heritage? What does she want to understand? Does she feel alienated from Haiti? How does she define her difference from her mother and from Haiti?
5. What does Suzette think about her mother's job as a "day woman"? Does Suzette consider herself a New Yorker, in contrast to her mother?
6. Why does Suzette say that the nannies and babysitters "look like a Third World Parent-Teacher Association meeting"? Does this comment reveal

anything about her attitude toward her mother? Does Suzette feel displaced since her mother is a surrogate parent for "other people's children"?

7. What does Suzette mean when she says that someday she might mistakenly follow another woman, "somebody else's mother," down the street?

8. What do you make of the mother's last comment? How does it connect with the earlier image of salt?

Bibliography

Alexandre, Sandy, and Ravi Y. Howard. "My Turn in the Fire: A Conversation with Edwidge Danticat." *Transition* 93 (2002): 110–28.

Lyons, Bonnie. "An Interview with Edwidge Danticat." *Contemporary Literature* 44.2 (Summer 2003): 183–98.

N'Zengou-Tayo, Marie-José. "Rewriting Folklore: Traditional Beliefs and Popular Culture in Edwidge Danticat's *Breath, Eyes, Memory* and *Krik? Krak!*" *MaComère* 3 (2000): 123–40.

Minh Duc Nguyen (b. 1972)

Contributing Editor: Christine Cao

Classroom Issues and Strategies

Since Vietnamese-American literature is a relatively new field, "Tale of Apricot" offers an opportunity to both contextualize this work within the existing body of writings on Vietnam, which has been dominated by the Vietnam War, and examine contemporary issues such as transnationalism, diaspora, and interculturality.

Major Themes, Historical Perspectives, Personal Issues

Students should know about the Vietnam War, particularly the fall of Saigon (now Ho Chi Minh City) in 1975 and the subsequent fifteen years marked by the mass exodus of Vietnamese refugees. The trauma of war and separation from the homeland is a common theme in early Vietnamese-American literature, and younger generations of Vietnamese Americans often address the difficulty of negotiating their own or their parents' memories of Vietnam and experiences of exile with American sentiments and representations of the war—a war generally regarded as best forgotten. A challenge for many of the writers in this younger generation raised in the United States is expressing the balance between insisting upon recognition of their memories and perspectives while at the same time seeking to move beyond the conflation of their ethnicity with the trauma of war and "boat people."

Significant Form, Style, or Artistic Conventions

Early Asian-American texts, including Vietnamese-American literature, were largely comprised of autobiographical accounts and memoirs. "Tale of Apricot" makes brief references to the larger historical events of the Vietnam War (the fall of Saigon, the boat refugees, resettlement in the United States) and focuses on the unique relationship between a homeless man and the orphan child he raises. The fantastic elements in the story, most notably the use of a ghost as the narrator, function to challenge the convention of realism and authenticity that dominate most narratives by or about Vietnamese Americans.

Original Audience

Minh Duc Nguyen has stated that he did not have an intended audience in mind when he wrote "Tale of Apricot," though the use of Vietnamese words makes his references more accessible to readers of Vietnamese heritage. Most of these references can be inferred from context, but the presence of Vietnamese language and cultural references creates a sense of familiarity and ambiguity, two strains that are suggested by the narrator of the story when she desires "recognition" by others while also acknowledging that "[s]ometimes it is better to leave something unknown."

Comparisons, Contrasts, Connections

It is useful to compare Minh Duc Nguyen with other Asian-American writers, noting how Vietnamese-American refugee experiences inform his work in ways that differ from the immigrant experiences of other Asian-American writers. Whereas the earlier immigrant literature addressed questions of assimilation into American culture, early Vietnamese-American writers were concerned with the trauma of war and exile and the possibility of returning to their homeland. As Asian-American literature expands and diversifies, reflecting new populations of South and Southeast Asians in the United States, colonial histories, transnational migrations, and multicultural communities, "Tale of Apricot" can be used to discuss the changing currents of Asian-American studies and draw broader, interethnic comparisons and questions of diaspora.

Working with Cultural Objects

Students interested in contemporary Vietnamese-American writers and artists can visit the Association for Viet Arts at <http://www.vietarts.org/htdocs/homepage.html>. The "Projects" link contains examples of specific exhibitions and art pieces that explore similar themes in "Tale of Apricot."

Questions for Reading, Discussion, and Writing

1. What kinds of parallels can be drawn among images of water, apricot seeds, and scars in relation to themes of origins, the past, and memory?
2. What is the significance of Little Trang's encounter with the ghost's body and her inability to recognize the woman as having passed away?
3. The story juxtaposes fantastic and/or spiritual elements such as having a ghost as the narrator with the material reality of war, poverty, and migration. What effects do these juxtapositions create?

Bibliography

There are no secondary works specifically on Minh Duc Nguyen, but instructors and students may find the following surveys of Vietnamese-American literature useful.

Janette, Michele. "Vietnamese American Literature in English, 1963–1994." *Amerasia Journal*. 29:1 (2003): 267–86.

Renny, Christopher. "A Cross-Cultural Context for Vietnamese and Vietnamese American Writing." *Of Vietnam: Identities in Dialogue*. Ed. Jane B. Winston and Leakthina C. Ollier. New York: Palgrave, 2001. 69–83.

Tran, Qui-Phiet. "From Isolation to Integration: Vietnamese Americans in Tran Dieu Hang's Fiction." *Reading the Literatures of Asian America*. Philadelphia: Temple UP, 1992.

Truong, Monique T. D. "Vietnamese American Literature." *An Interethnic Companion to Asian American Literature*. Ed. King-Kok Cheung. Cambridge, UK: Cambridge UP, 1997. 219–46.

Index of Authors and Entries